June 13–15, 2010
Thira, Santorini, Greece

I0011371

**Association for
Computing Machinery**

Advancing Computing as a Science & Profession

SPAA'10

Proceedings of the Twenty-Second Annual Symposium on
Parallelism in Algorithms and Architectures

Sponsored by:
ACM SIGACT & ACM SIGARCH

and supported by:
**Sun Microsystems, Akamai, Intel, IBM Research,
Sandia National Laboratories, & RA CTI**

**Association for
Computing Machinery**

Advancing Computing as a Science & Profession

The Association for Computing Machinery
2 Penn Plaza, Suite 701
New York, New York 10121-0701

Notice to Past Authors of ACM-Published Articles
ACM intends to create a complete electronic archive of all articles and/or other material previously published by ACM. If you have written a work that has been previously published by ACM in any journal or conference proceedings prior to 1978, or any SIG Newsletter at any time, and you do NOT want this work to appear in the ACM Digital Library, please inform permissions@acm.org, stating the title of the work, the author(s), and where and when published.

ISBN: 978-1-4503-0079-7

Additional copies may be ordered prepaid from:

ACM Order Department
PO Box 11405
New York, NY 10286-1405

Phone: 1-800-342-6626 (USA and Canada)
   +1-212-626-0500 (all other countries)
Fax: +1-212-944-1318
E-mail: acmhelp@acm.org

ACM Order Number 417100

Printed in the USA

Foreword

This volume consists the 35 regular papers and 10 brief announcements selected for presentation at the *22nd ACM Symposium on Parallelism in Algorithms and Architectures (SPAA'10)*, held June 13-15, 2010, in Santorini, Greece. It contains abstracts of the two keynote talks given by Anastasia ("Natassa") Ailamaki and Geoffrey Fox. At the end, there is a corrigendum by Srikanth Sastry, Scott Pike, and Jennifer Welch for their paper "Weakest Failure Detector for Wait-Free Dining under Eventual Weak Exclusion," which appeared last year in SPAA'09.

The program committee selected the 35 regular and 10 brief presentations after an initial electronic discussion, a nearly all-day telephone conference on March 11, 2010, and a final round of electronic discussion on March 11 and 12, 2010. There were 110 submissions, of which 108 survived the first day after the submission deadline. Of these, 104 were long submissions and 4 were short submissions. The paper "Basic Network Creation Games" by Noga Alon, Erik Demaine, MohammadTaghi Hajiaghayi, and Tom Leighton was selected the best paper.

The mix of selected papers reflects SPAA's intention to bring together the theory and practice of parallel computing. Thus this year's papers include strong theory papers, as well as papers containing strong experimental analysis. SPAA defines parallelism broadly to encompass any computational device or scheme that can perform multiple operations or tasks simultaneously or concurrently. Thus papers in this volume consider multithreading, multicore platforms, streaming, network algorithms, energy-aware computing, software tools, and more.

The technical papers in this volume are to be considered preliminary versions, and authors are generally expected to publish polished and complete versions in archival scientific journals. The committee selected the 10 brief announcements based on perceived interest to the SPAA attendees and their potential to seed new research in parallel algorithms and architectures. Extended versions of the SPAA brief announcements may be published later in other conferences or journals.

The program committee would like to thank all who submitted papers and all the external reviewers who helped us evaluate the submissions. The names of these external reviewers appear later in the proceedings. As the program chair of SPAA 2010, I would like to express my deep gratitude to the program committee for all of their hard work during the paper selection process, especially the willingness of the seven non-US PC members to teleconference at difficult hours. The committee was amazingly productive and collegial during that long day of teleconferencing. I thank Christos Kaklamanis for all his work on local arrangements. I thank the SPAA officers Friedhelm Meyer auf der Heide, Andrea Richa, David Bunde, and especially Christian Scheideler for their help. Finally, I thank previous program chair Michael Bender for his advice and support.

SPAA 2010 was sponsored by the ACM Special Interest Groups on Algorithms and Computation Theory (SIGACT) and Computer Architecture (SIGARCH) and organized in cooperation with the European Association for Theoretical Computer Science (EATCS). Akamai, Intel, Sun Microsystems, IBM Research, Sandia National Laboratories, and Research Academic Computer Technology Institute (RA CTI) provided financial or in-kind support.

Cynthia Phillips
Sandia National Laboratories
SPAA 2010 Program Chair

Table of Contents

Session 1: Scheduling
Session Chair: David Bunde *(Knox College)*

Session 2: Keynote Talk
Session Chair: Nectarios Koziris *(National Technical University of Athens)*

Session 3: Computing Despite an Adversary
Session Chair: Paul Spirakis *(CTI)*

Session 4: Brief Announcements I
Session Chair: David Bunde *(Knox College)*

Session 5: Resource Management

Session 6: Network Algorithms

Session 7: Keynote Talk

Session 8: Tools and Methods for Performance Analysis

Session 9: Brief Announcement II

Session 10: Matrix Algorithms

Session 11: Local and Distributed Algorithms

Session 12: Transactional Memory

Session 13: Graph Algorithms

Session Chair: Paul Spirakis *(CTI)*

Session 14: Concurrent Data Structures

Session Chair: Christos Kaklamanis *(University of Patras)*

Corrigendum to SPAA 2009

SPAA 2010 Symposium Organization

General Chair: Friedhelm Meyer auf der Heide (*University of Paderborn, Germany*)

Program Chair: Cynthia Phillips (*Sandia National Laboratories, USA*)

Program Committee: Kunal Agrawal (*Washington University in St. Louis, USA*)
Hagit Attiya (*Technion, Israel*)
Jon Berry (*Sandia National Laboratories, USA*)
David Bunde (*Knox College, USA*)
Sándor Fekete (*Braunschweig University of Technology, Germany*)
James Goodman (*University of Auckland, New Zealand*)
Dan Grossman (*University of Washington, USA*)
Torben Hagerup (*University of Augsburg, Germany*)
Nectarios Koziris (*National Technical University of Athens, Greece*)
Madhav Marathe (*Virginia Polytechnic Institute & State University, USA*)
Sotiris Nikoletseas (*University of Patras and CTI, Greece*)
Alex Pothen (*Purdue University, USA*)
Yves Robert (*Ecole Normale Superieure de Lyon, France*)
Jared Saia (*University of New Mexico, USA*)
Mike Spear (*Lehigh University, USA*)
Torsten Suel (*Polytechnic Institute of NYU, USA*)
Joel Wein (*NYU-POLY and Akamai, USA*)
Adam Welc (*Intel Labs, USA*)
Jennifer Welch (*Texas A&M, USA*)

Publicity Chair: Andrea W. Richa (*Arizona State University, USA*)

Treasurer: David Bunde (*Knox College, USA*)

Secretary: Christian Scheideler (*University of Paderborn, Germany*)

Local Arrangements Chair: Christos Kaklamanis (*University of Patras & RA CTI, Greece*)

Steering Committee: Guy Blelloch *(Carnegie Mellon University, USA)*
David Culler *(University of California at Berkeley, USA)*
Frank Dehne *(Carleton University, Canada)*
Pierre Fraigniaud *(University of Paris-Sud, France)*
Phillip B. Gibbons *(Intel Research, USA)*
Maurice Herlihy *(Brown University, USA)*
Tom Leighton *(MIT and Akamai Technologies, USA)*
Charles Leiserson *(Massachusetts Institute of Technology, USA)*
Fabrizio Luccio *(University of Pisa, Italy)*
Friedhelm Meyer auf der Heide *(University of Paderborn, Germany)*
Gary Miller *(CMU and Akamai Technologies, USA)*
Burkhard Monien *(University of Paderborn, Germany)*
Franco Preparata *(Brown University, USA)*
Vijaya Ramachandran *(University of Texas at Austin, USA)*
Arnold Rosenberg *(University of Massachusetts at Amherst
   and Colorado State University, USA)*
Paul Spirakis *(Computer Technology Institute, Greece)*
Uzi Vishkin *(UMIACS, University of Maryland, USA)*

Additional reviewers:

Susanne Albers	Michael Elkin
Nikos Anastopoulos	Robert Elsaesser
Zakia Asad	Thomas Erlebach
James Aspnes	Phil Gibbons
Haim Avron	Seth Gilbert
Ariful Azad	Eric Goodman
Shankha Banerjee	Georgios Goumas
Nikhil Bansal	Vincent Gramoli
Leonid Barenboim	MohammadTaghi Hajiaghayi
Luca Becchetti	Mourad Hakem
Petra Berenbrink	William Hart
Tom Bergan	Andrew Hay
Shuvra Bhattacharyya	Eshcar Hillel
Slim Bouguerra	Bill Howe
Nevil Brownlee	Richard Hudson
Alfredo Buttari	John Iacono
Louis-Claude Canon	Klaus Jansen
Ioannis Caragiannis	Colette Johnen
Keren Censor	Tom Kamphans
Ioannis Chatzigiannakis	Michal Kapalka
Yun-Chul Chung	Shiva Kasivishwanathan
Jaewoong Chung	Maleq Khan
Karen Devine	Kornilios Kourtis
Stéphane Devismes	Dariusz Kowalski
Michael J. Dinneen	Alexander Kroeller
Aleksandar Dragojevic	Chris Kuhlman
Pierre-François Dutot	Fabian Kuhn

Additional reviewers:

Jean-Yves L'Excellent	Elad Michael Schiller
Edya Ladan Mozes	Christiane Schmidt
Hyunyoung Lee	Ulrich M. Schwarz
ITing Lee	Nils Schweer
Vitus Leung	Maria Serna
Brandon Lucia	Tatiana Shpeisman
Kevin McCurley	Aleksandrs Slivkins
Rami Melhem	Paul Spirakis
Alessia Milani	Aravind Srinivasan
Shahin Mohammadi	Jim Sukha
John Morris	Jukka Suomela
Duc Nguyen	Fuad Tabba
Jelani Nelson	Sadaf Tariq
Yang Ni	Clark Thomborson
Konstantinos Nikas	Corentin Travers
Dimitrios Nikolopoulos	Denis Trystram
Rotem Oshman	Moran Tzafrir
Ojas Parekh	Alexandros Tzannes
Fanny Pascuel	Marc Uetz
Guanhong Pei	Bora Uçar
Ali Pinar	Saira Viqar
William Plishker	Frédéric Vivien
Gilles Pokam	Anil Vullikanti
Kirk Pruhs	Frédéric Wagner
Bruno Raffin	Cong Wang
Mohan Rajagopalan	Jiaqi Wang
Paul Renaud-Goud	Emmett Witchel
Giovanni Resta	Philipp Woelfel
Navin Rustagi	Maxwell Young
Srikanth Sastry	Norbert Zeh
Christian Scheideler	Zhao Zhao

SPAA 2010 Sponsors & Supporters

Sponsors:

Supporters:

Buffer-space Efficient and Deadlock-free Scheduling of Stream Applications on Multi-core Architectures

Jongsoo Park
Computer Systems Laboratory
Stanford University, California, USA
jongsoo@cva.stanford.edu

William J. Dally
Computer Systems Laboratory
Stanford University, California, USA
dally@cva.stanford.edu

ABSTRACT

We present a scheduling algorithm of stream programs for multi-core architectures called *team scheduling*. Compared to previous multi-core stream scheduling algorithms, team scheduling achieves 1) similar synchronization overhead, 2) coverage of a larger class of applications, 3) better control over buffer space, 4) deadlock-free feedback loops, and 5) lower latency. We compare team scheduling to the latest stream scheduling algorithm, SGMS, by evaluating 14 applications on a multi-core architecture with 16 cores. Team scheduling successfully targets applications that cannot be validly scheduled by SGMS due to excessive buffer requirement or deadlocks in feedback loops (e.g., GSM and W-CDMA). For applications that can be validly scheduled by SGMS, team scheduling shows on average 37% higher throughput within the same buffer space constraints.

Categories and Subject Descriptors

D.3.4 [**Programming Languages**]: Processors—*Compilers*

General Terms

Algorithms, Languages, Performance

Keywords

Compiler and Tools for Concurrent Programming, Stream Programming, Green Computing and Power-Efficient Architectures, Multi-core Architectures

1. INTRODUCTION

In order to support the ever-increasing computation requirements of mobile devices with a high level of energy efficiency, there has been growing interest in stream architectures [18, 14] and programming systems [35, 28, 9]. In a

stream programming language, an application is abstracted as a *stream graph* [20] whose nodes are actors and edges are streams. Computation is described by actors that are fired when enough input stream tokens arrive (e.g., in Figure 1(a), actor b represents a computation that consumes 30 tokens and produces 20 tokens per firing). Unidirectional data flow between actors are described as streams, providing two benefits to the compiler. First, the compiler can easily detect parallelism by analyzing data dependences exposed as streams. Second, the compiler can efficiently orchestrate data movement by explicitly managing local memories and keep data coherent by maintaining queues, without relying on expensive hardware cache coherency protocols. By exploiting these benefits, stream compilers have shown a consistent speedup even for applications with low computation-to-communication ratios. For example, a StreamIt compiler shows an average of $14.8\times$ speedup on a 16-core Cell [14] platform [20].

Static parts of stream programs, in which the number of tokens consumed and produced per actor firing are compile-time constants, follow the model of computation called *synchronous data flow* (SDF). SDF provides a theoretical background by which we can dramatically reduce synchronization overhead and buffer requirements. Lee and Messerschmitt [25] present an algorithm that constructs single-core static schedules with bounded buffer requirement and no synchronization overhead. Bhattacharyya et al. [4] present an algorithm that significantly reduces the buffer requirement of single-core static schedules. For multi-core architectures, [25, 24, 5, 31] present scheduling algorithms based on *homogeneous SDF graph* (HSDFG), a graph in which every actor consumes and produces only one token from each of its inputs and outputs [24]. However, constructing an HSDFG from an equivalent SDF graph can take an exponential amount of time [31], and their algorithms do not fully exploit pipeline parallelism [34]. These issues are resolved by Stream Graph Modulo Scheduling (SGMS) that is implemented in a StreamIt compiler [20].

SGMS applies software pipelining [22, 32] to the entire stream graph and synchronizes steady states of the pipeline with barriers. Consider a part of a stream graph shown in Figure 1(a). The partitioning phase that precedes scheduling has assigned actor a to core 0 and actors b and c to core 1. Numbers at each edge denote the number of stream tokens that are consumed or produced per actor firing. SGMS first finds the *minimum steady state* [16] in which the number of

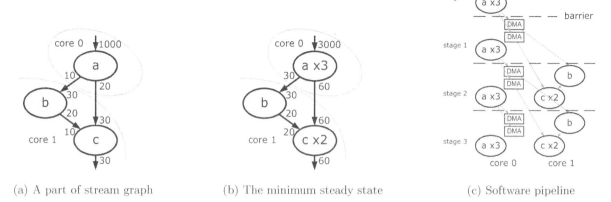

(a) A part of stream graph   (b) The minimum steady state   (c) Software pipeline

Figure 1:   An example of Stream Graph Modulo Scheduling (SGMS). We assume that actor a is assigned to core 0 and actors b and c are assigned to core 1 in the partitioning phase that precedes scheduling. Numbers at each edge denote the number of stream tokens that are consumed or produced per actor firing. For example, actor b consumes 30 tokens and produces 20 tokens per firing. DMA denotes direct memory access.

produced tokens and consumed tokens are balanced at each edge with the minimum number of actor firings. For example, a must be fired three times per b's firing to produce 30 tokens required by b as shown in Figure 1(b). An efficient algorithm to find such a minimum steady state is described in [25]. After finding the steady state, SGMS constructs a software pipeline as shown in Figure 1(c). By starting execution of a producer actor and its consumer actor[1] at different *stages* [32] (a starts at stage 0 while its consumer, b, starts at stage 2), SGMS eliminates intra-stage dependencies so that processor cores do not need to synchronize with each other within a steady state. An actor periodically writes tokens to its output buffer whose data is DMA-transferred at the next stage. Barriers between each stage guarantee that, whenever an actor fires, the input tokens required by the actor are already in place.

SGMS has the advantage of low synchronization overhead (one barrier per steady state), but has the following three drawbacks. First, SGMS requires information that may not be available at compile time. For example, the number of tokens to be produced can vary at run-time for certain streams. We call these *variable-rate streams* (e.g., the output of the Huffman encoder in JPEG). Second, SGMS has little control over buffer space; the minimum buffer space for each stream[2] is imposed by the minimum steady state. For example, in the steady state shown in Figure 1(b), we require buffer space that accommodates at least 3000 tokens at the incoming stream of actor a. We cannot reduce this buffer requirement because the minimum number of a firings between barriers is set to 3 by the steady state. If each core has a 2K-word local memory and the unit token size of a's incoming stream is 1 word, a remote memory must be accessed to further buffer the tokens. This leads to higher energy consumption and less predictable execution time which makes guaranteeing load balance and real-time constraints at compile-time a challenge. Our evaluation and [27] show

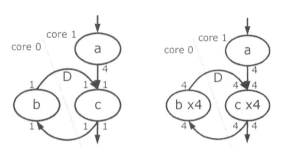

(a) A stream graph with feedback   (b) Minimum steady state with a deadlock

Figure 2:   A deadlock in a feedback path caused by SGMS. (a) An example stream graph. "D" at edge (b, c) denotes a single initial token that makes the stream graph deadlock-free. (b) The minimum steady state used by SGMS in which c never fires.

that buffer space requirements can grow exponentially in the minimum steady state of real-life applications such as W-CDMA. Third, SGMS does not handle feedback loops satisfactorily. In [20], the authors mention that a feedback loop is naïvely handled by fusing the entire loop into a single actor, which results in complete serialization of the loop. If we do not fuse feedback loops into single actors to avoid serialization, SGMS is prone to deadlock. Consider a feedback path $c \rightarrow b \rightarrow c$ shown in Figure 2(a). This feedback path is deadlock-free due to an initial token at edge (b, c) denoted as D. The value of the initial token is specified by the programmer and adds a unit delay at (b, c), thus the use of symbol 'D' commonly used in signal processing [29]. However, in the steady state shown in Figure 2(b), actor c cannot be fired because it never receives enough input tokens. The compiler cannot create additional initial tokens because doing so changes the semantic of the application. Our evaluation (Section 3) shows that a similar deadlock occurs in a real-life application, GSM.

In this paper, we present an alternative algorithm called *team scheduling* that addresses the drawbacks of SGMS, while maintaining a similar synchronization overhead. Team schedul-

---

[1] More specifically, its consumer actor at a different core since SGMS starts producer and consumer actors at the same stage if they are assigned to the same core.

[2] More specifically inter-core stream: the buffer requirement for intra-core streams depends on how to schedule actors assigned to a single-core, which is described in [4, 16].

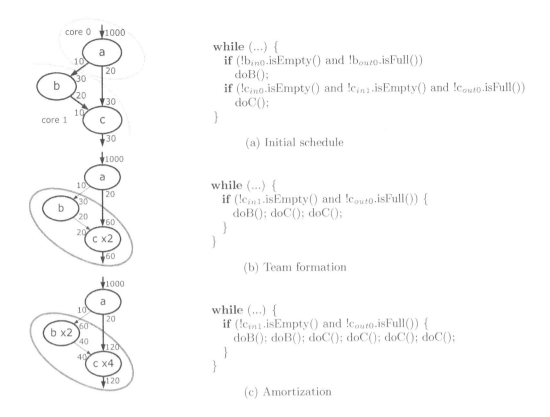

```
while (...) {
    if (!b_in0.isEmpty() and !b_out0.isFull())
        doB();
    if (!c_in0.isEmpty() and !c_in1.isEmpty() and !c_out0.isFull())
        doC();
}
```

(a) Initial schedule

```
while (...) {
    if (!c_in1.isEmpty() and !c_out0.isFull()) {
        doB(); doC(); doC();
    }
}
```

(b) Team formation

```
while (...) {
    if (!c_in1.isEmpty() and !c_out0.isFull()) {
        doB(); doB(); doC(); doC(); doC(); doC();
    }
}
```

(c) Amortization

Figure 3: An example of team scheduling and its generated code for core 1. (a) An initial schedule (b) Form team $\{b, c\}$ and construct a static schedule of it, which eliminates synchronization between b and c. Section 2.1 describes why synchronization between a and b can also be eliminated. (c) Amortize the team $\{b, c\}$ by a factor of 2.

ing starts with a simple initial schedule as shown in Figure 3(a). Actor firings are pair-wise synchronized through queue empty and full checks. This initial schedule involves high synchronization overhead (i.e., frequent queue empty and full checks). Nevertheless, this is a correct schedule for a wide range of applications including the ones that cannot be validly scheduled by SGMS. Moreover, the synchronization overhead can be minimized with aggregation and amortization of actors as follows. We assume that the partitioning phase precedes scheduling similar to SGMS, where actor-to-core mapping is predetermined when reaching the scheduling phase.

First, we selectively aggregate actors that are assigned to the same core, and form a *team* in which actors are statically scheduled. By statically scheduling actors in a team, we eliminate intra-team synchronizations. For example, in Figure 3(b), we form a team by aggregating actors b and c, and eliminate synchronization between them (b_{out0}.isFull() and c_{in0}.isEmpty() checks are removed). We can also eliminate inter-team synchronization such as the one between a and b (explained in Section 2.1). In order to construct a static schedule of team $\{b, c\}$, we find its steady state — fire b once and c twice. This is in contrast to SGMS that must use a steady state of the *entire stream graph*; in team scheduling, the unit of steady state construction is a team whose formation is under the compiler's control. We continue team formation as long as it does not violate constraints such as maximum buffer space per core.

Second, we selectively amortize communication overhead of teams by increasing the number of actor firings per synchronization. Each amortized actor accumulates its output tokens in its local buffer and transfers the accumulated tokens in bulk to consumer's local memory. For example, in Figure 3(c), we amortize team $\{b, c\}$ so that its actors fire twice as many times than they do in the minimum steady state of the team. Actor c accumulates 120 tokens in its local buffer and transfers them at once. Amortizing communication overhead is an important optimization scheme, especially for actors with a low computation-to-communication ratio; the locality of memory access is improved, and the fixed cost associated with each data transfer initiation is amortized. In Section 3, we show up to 2.1× speedup from amortization. The same optimization can be done in SGMS but with limited flexibility: minimum amortization factors are predetermined by the minimum steady state; and if we want to amortize an actor by 2, we must amortize all the other actors by 2 as well. Note that the flexibility in choosing amortization factor is crucial for finding the right trade-off between synchronization overhead and buffer requirement. For example, in Figure 3(c), team scheduling is able to selectively amortize b and c without excessively increasing the buffer requirement. On the other hand, SGMS incurs a large buffer requirement increase in order to amortize b and c because it must amortize a as well. Similar to team formation, we continue amortization as long as it does not violate constraints such as maximum buffer space per core.

The contributions of this paper are as follows: 1) We present an algorithm for scheduling stream programs on multi-core architectures that has better control over buffer space, lower latency, and better support for variable-rate streams than SGMS. 2) We present a method to compute minimum queue lengths to avoid deadlock or serialization that can be introduced by team scheduling. 3) We evaluate team scheduling with 14 stream applications on ELM [1], a multi-core architecture for energy-efficient embedded computing. Our evaluation shows that team scheduling achieves a similar throughput to that of SGMS with lower latency and smaller buffer requirement. Our evaluation also shows that team scheduling has better control over buffer space: when we set maximum buffer space per core as a constraint, team scheduling consistently satisfies the constraint while SGMS does not.

The remainder of this paper is organized as follows: Section 2 describes the details of team scheduling. Section 3 presents simulation results comparing team scheduling with SGMS. Section 4 reviews related work and Section 5 summarizes our work.

2. TEAM SCHEDULING

This section describes details of the team scheduling algorithm. Pseudo-code for the algorithm is presented in Appendix E.

2.1 Team Formation

We start from an initial schedule in which each actor forms a separate team. For example, in Figure 3(a), actors a, b, and c each form teams on their own. In a pair-wise manner, we merge teams in the same core starting with the pair that leads to the highest gain. We compute the gain as synchronization reduction divided by additional buffer requirement resulting from team merge. This is a greedy heuristic to maximize synchronization overhead reduction (i.e., the reduction of queue empty or full checks) per additional buffer space requirement. We maintain a *team graph* that represents the connectivity of teams. The team graph is initially identical to the stream graph, and then we contract the corresponding nodes for each team merge.

We adhere to the following four constraints when merging. First, we do not merge across variable-rate streams. Second, we do not merge teams if doing so exceeds the buffer limit per core. Suppose that actors a, b, and c are all assigned to the same core in Figure 3. If each core has a 2K-word local memory and the unit token size of a's incoming stream is 1 word, we avoid merging a with any other actor. A detailed method of computing buffer sizes is described in Section 2.3. Third, we must not introduce a cycle to the team graph since it may result in deadlocks. Suppose again that actors a, b, and c are all assigned to the same core in Figure 3. We avoid merging a with c because it forms a cycle $b \rightarrow \{a, c\} \rightarrow b$. Fourth, a merge must not introduce any deadlock in an existing cycle (i.e., feedback path). We can check for such deadlocks by inspecting *precedence expansion graphs* (PEG) [25] of each cycle containing the merged team in the team graph. If every PEG is acyclic, it is guaranteed that the team merge does not introduce any deadlock. This is because a PEG has a cycle if and only if the corresponding stream subgraph has a deadlock [25]. Suppose that we are about to merge a and c in Figure 2(a). If we construct a PEG of the cycle $b \rightarrow c \rightarrow b$ after the merge, we will see a

cycle in the PEG since merging a and c introduces a deadlock. For the details of PEG construction, please refer to [25, 24, 31]. A PEG can grow exponentially when the number of actor firings in the minimum steady state of a team or the number of cycles in the stream graph is exponential. In this case, we use a heuristic described in [31] that conservatively but quickly checks for deadlocks.

After merging a team, we construct a static schedule of the actors within the team. There are several ways of constructing such a single-core schedule [4, 16], but we find that *loose interdependence scheduling framework* (LISF) [3] works well in our evaluation (Section 3). For most of applications, LISF finds a *single appearance schedule* in which each actor lexically appears only once, resulting in a minimal code size [3]. For example, b $2c$ (fire b once, then fire c twice) is a single appearance schedule of team $\{b, c\}$ shown in Figure 3(b). Other single-core scheduling methods such as *push schedule* or *phased schedule* save significant buffer space at the expense of marginal increase in code size when applied to the entire stream graph [16]. However, when we target multi-cores, applications are partitioned into small pieces, and applying either scheduling method to each piece shows little buffer space saving (on average 8% for 16 cores).

By constructing a static schedule of a team, we eliminate intra-team synchronizations such as the one at edge (b, c) in Figure 3(b). We can also eliminate certain inter-team synchronizations such as the one at edge (a, b). This is possible because production-to-consumption ratios of streams between a given team pair (with no variable-rate streams) are constant (proof shown in Appendix A). For example, at $(a, \{b, c\})$ in Figure 3(b), production-to-consumption ratios are $\frac{10}{30} = \frac{20}{60}$. To generalize, consider the streams from team T to team U denoted as S_{TU} (in Figure 3(b), $S_{TU} = \{(a, b), (a, c)\}$ when $T = \{a\}$ and $U = \{b, c\}$). Let s_1 be the stream in S_{TU} that is enqueued last in T's static schedule (in Figure 3(b), s_1 is (a, c) if T enqueues tokens to (a, b) before (a, c)). Let s_2 be the stream in S_{TU} that is dequeued last in U's static schedule (in Figure 3(b), s_2 is (a, c)). Then among the conditions with respect to S_{TU} that we need to check before firing U, we can eliminate everything except the check for if s_1 is not empty (in Figure 3(b), checking if the queue at (a, b) is not empty is redundant when s_1 is (a, c)). Similarly, among the conditions with respect to S_{TU} that we need to check before firing T, we can eliminate everything except the check for if s_2 is not full. More details of inter-team synchronization elimination are described in Appendix B.

2.2 Amortization

After team formation, we amortize communication cost of teams starting from the one that leads to the highest synchronization reduction per additional buffer requirement. Similar to the team formation procedure, we do not amortize a team if doing so exceeds buffer space limit or introduces deadlock in a feedback path.

We define amortization as follows. The *minimum repetition vector* [25] $\vec{q_G}$ of stream subgraph G is a vector such that $\vec{q_G}(a)$ is the number of a firings in the minimum steady state of G. For example, the minimum repetition vector of the stream graph shown in Figure 1(a) is $(3, 1, 2)$ where we index the vector in the order of a, b, and c; the minimum repetition vector of team $\{b, c\}$ in Figure 3(b) is $(1, 2)$. For each stream subgraph G that is statically scheduled (the entire stream graph in SGMS or a team in team scheduling), we define the *repetition vector* $\overrightarrow{r_G}$ such that $\overrightarrow{r_G}(a)$ is the number of a firings in the current static schedule of G. We call $\overrightarrow{r_G}(a)$ the *repetition* of actor a. For example, the repetition vector of team $\{b, c\}$ in Figure 3(b) is the same as its minimum repetition vector, $(1, 2)$, because the team has not been amortized. In Figure 3(c), the repetition vector of team $\{b, c\}$ is $(2, 4)$. In this paper, *amortization* of stream subgraph G by a factor of k means multiplying G's repetition vector by k. For example, in Figure 3(c), amortization of team $\{b, c\}$ by a factor of 2 has updated its repetition vector from $(1, 2)$ to $(2, 4)$.

In SGMS, note that the repetition vector is identical to the minimum repetition vector of the stream graph before any amortization. If we amortize a schedule by a factor of 2, we multiply the repetition of *every* actor by 2. In team scheduling, each team has its own repetition vector, and each team is amortized separately.

We use the following method of selecting amortization factors. Suppose that we are about to amortize team T in stream graph G. If $\exists$ an integer $k > 1$ such that $\forall a \in T$, $\overrightarrow{q_G}(a) = k \cdot \overrightarrow{r_T}(a)$, we amortize T by the smallest integer bigger than 1 that divides k. For example, for team $\{a\}$ in Figure 3(b), $\overrightarrow{q_G}(a) = 3$ and $\overrightarrow{r_{\{a\}}}(a) = 1$, thus $k = 3$. Otherwise, we amortize T by a factor of 2. We use this method in order to first amortize T up to the minimum steady state of the entire graph and additionally amortize T by a factor of 2 thereafter.

2.3 Sizing Queues to Avoid Deadlocks

When each team is amortized separately, deadlock or serialization due to insufficient queue capacity can occur as shown in Figure 4. In Figure 4(a), after firing a 6 times, the queue at (a, c) is full and "$b \times 3$" does not have enough input tokens to be fired, resulting in a deadlock (assume that each actor is assigned to different cores). Note that this is a different kind of deadlock from the ones that occur in feedback loops shown in Figure 2(b). In Figure 2(b), deadlock is inherent in the stream graph: we cannot avoid deadlock no matter how large a queue we use for each stream. To avoid the deadlock shown in Figure 4(a), we need to increase the length of queue at (a, c) to 180. However, this still is not large enough to support serialization-free execution during the latency along path $a \rightarrow b \rightarrow c$ as shown in Figure 4(b). To avoid such serialization, the queue length must be at least 400. This section presents a method that computes the minimum queue length to avoid deadlock and serialization.

Before team merge and amortization, we first determine the queue lengths of streams along feedback loops. We can bound the queue length of a feedback stream s as (see [5])

$$\min_{\text{cycle } C \text{ containing } s} (\text{sum of delays along } C).$$

When we compute queue lengths of other streams, we use the *acyclic team graph* which is constructed by removing a stream with non-zero delay from each cycle in the team graph.

After merging or amortizing a team, for each stream s that is adjacent to the team, we set the queue length of s to

$$2(prod(s) + cons(s) - gcd(prod(s), cons(s))),$$

where $prod(s)$ is the number of tokens produced per s's producer firing and $cons(s)$ is the number of tokens consumed

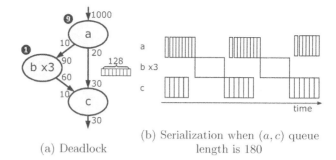

(a) Deadlock

(b) Serialization when (a, c) queue length is 180

Figure 4: **An example of deadlock and serialization from insufficient queue capacity. In (a), b is amortized by a factor of 3. ⑨ denotes that actor a must be fired at least 9 times to provide enough input tokens for c firing. Assume that the queue at (a, c) can buffer 128 tokens. A deadlock occurs after firing a 6 times. (b) shows a steady state execution when the queue length of (a, c) is 180.**

per s's consumer firing. Appendix C shows that this prevents serialization between a producer and consumer pair.

After sizing queues only based on the information associated with its producer and consumer, we consider global information. First, we find split-join patterns that contain a team that has been merged or amortized. A team is a *splitter* if it has multiple successors, while a team is a *joiner* if it has multiple predecessors. We define the *split-join pattern* of S and J, G_{SJ}, as the teams that are reachable from S and reachable to J. In Figure 4(a), assume that a, b, and c each form teams of their own, then $\{b\}$ belongs to $G_{\{a\}\{c\}}$. Second, we compute $x_J(U)$ for each $U \in G_{SJ}$, the minimum number of U firings to fire J. In Figure 4(a), $x_{\{c\}}(\{a\}) = 9$. This can be computed by an algorithm similar to backward data-flow analysis [15] whose details are shown in Appendix D. Third, we find the longest latency path from S to J with the latency defined as follows. Let $q(T)$ be the minimum repetition of T that can be computed by $\frac{\overrightarrow{q}(d)}{\overrightarrow{r_T}(d)}$ for any $d \in T$. In Figure 4(a), $q(\{b\}) = \frac{1}{3}$. Let $l(T, U) = \frac{x_J(T)}{q(T)}$ be the latency of edge (T, U), which represents the latency introduced at (T, U), normalized to the period of repeating the minimum steady state of the application. In Figure 4(a), $l(\{a\}, \{b\}) = \frac{9}{3}$, $l(\{b\}, \{c\}) = \frac{1}{1/3}$, and $l(\{a\}, \{c\}) = \frac{9}{3}$. Therefore, the longest latency path is $\{a\} \rightarrow \{b\} \rightarrow \{c\}$ with normalized latency 6, which means that buffers along each path from $\{a\}$ to $\{c\}$ should support serialization-free execution during the latency equivalent to the time for repeating the minimum steady state 6 times. Denote the number of S firings during the longest latency as $y_{SU} = \lceil q(S) \cdot (\text{longest latency from } S \text{ to } J) \rceil$. In Figure 4(a), $y_{\{a\}\{c\}} = 3 \cdot 6 = 18$. Fourth, we simulate firing actors in the split-join pattern until S is fired y_{SU} times. This can be done by an algorithm similar to forward data-flow analysis. In the simulation, we do not fire J and we set queue lengths of J's incoming streams to infinity. Let $z_{SJ}(s)$ be the number of tokens in J's incoming stream s after the simulation, which is the minimum number of tokens to start a steady state with respect to s's producer and J, while supporting serialization-free execution during the longest latency from S to J. During the steady state, the buffer at s requires $prod(s) + cons(s) - gcd(prod(s), cons(d))$ additional space

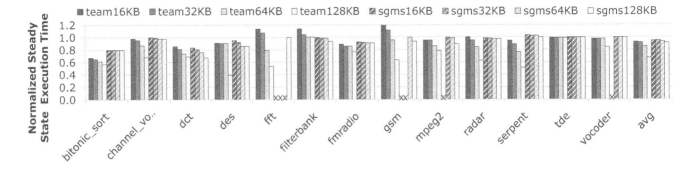

Figure 5: Steady state execution time when team scheduling and SGMS amortize actors within different buffer space constraints. Execution times are normalized to those of SGMS without any amortization (same as the numbers of SGMS in Figure 6(a)).

(Appendix C). Therefore, we increase the queue length of s to $z_{SJ}(s) + prod(s) + cons(s) - gcd(prod(s), cons(d))$. In Figure 4(a), $\{a\}$ is fired 18 times during the simulation and leaves 360 tokens at (a, c) $(z_{\{a\}\{c\}}((a, c)) = 360)$. We increase the queue length of (a, c) to $360 + 20 + 30 - 10 = 400$.

3. RESULTS

This section describes the experimental setup for our algorithm evaluation and the analysis of results.

3.1 Experimental Setup

We use the same set of StreamIt benchmark applications that were used for SGMS evaluation [20] plus GSM encoder and W-CDMA searcher [36]. We have ported the StreamIt applications into a language called Elk [8] that extends StreamIt. Elk supports multiple input/output streams and variable-rate streams, though language difference is not essential in our evaluation. W-CDMA searcher is ported from a proprietary benchmark from Qualcomm™. GSM encoder is ported from MiBench [12] and contains a feedback path.

We use ELM [1], a multi-core architecture for energy-efficient embedded computing. ELM has tiled multi-cores connected through an on-chip interconnection network [7]. Each core executes instructions with MIPS-like ISA in 4-stage in-order dual-issue pipeline. ELM supports DMA-like stream memory instructions that transfer a block of data to other cores' local memory in the background, and these stream memory instructions are used to implement queue operations. ELM has an ensemble organization in which four cores share their local memory. We made each core have its own separate local memory, changed the local memory size to 256KB, and used 16 cores to make the evaluation setup similar to that of the SGMS paper [20] which uses Cell processors.

The Elk compiler generates C++ code from Elk code, and an LLVM-based [23] C++ compiler [30] generates ELM assembly code. The assembly code is executed in a cycle-accurate ELM simulator. We model interconnection as a mesh network with word-wide channels and canonical 4-stage pipeline routers [7]. Therefore, the latency of a message is $4(d + 1)$ cycles if the Manhattan distance to the destination is d. For SGMS, we idealistically assume that every core can access a dedicated memory in 1 Manhattan distance latency (8 cycles) and implement sense-reversing barrier [13] using fetch-and-add instructions on the dedicated memory. This

results in 75 cycles per barrier while each barrier takes 1600 cycles in the SGMS paper [20].

Similar to previous work [11, 10, 20], partitioning is done before scheduling. We first fission stateless actors with high computation requirement so that every stateless actor has at most 1/16 of the total computation requirement. Then we assign actors to cores using METIS, a graph partitioning package [17].

In the first experiment, we compare throughput of team scheduling and SGMS as we change the buffer space limit per core from 16KB to 128KB. This experiment measures efficiency of using limited local memory space, which is critical for multi-core embedded processors. In the second experiment, we intentionally avoid exploiting the amortization flexibility of team scheduling by limiting the maximum repetitions to the ones in the minimum steady state of the entire stream graph, and compare throughput, latency, and buffer usage of the two algorithms. This experiment compares performance of the two scheduling algorithms independent of amortization effects.

3.2 Buffer Space Limited Experiment

Figure 5 compares throughput of both algorithms as we change the buffer space limit per core from 16KB to 128KB. Steady state execution time is measured as the time between the generation of the first and the last output of the furthest downstream actor, and is inversely proportional to throughput. Steady state execution times are normalized to those of SGMS without any amortization. The average spee-up from single-core executions is 11×. The results for WCDMA are not shown here because SGMS requires an excessive buffer space even without amortization, which will be shown in Section 3.3. We fuse feedback loops in GSM to single actors for SGMS since SGMS results in a deadlock similar to Figure 2(b) without fusion. For the particular case of GSM, SGMS does not show its disadvantage with respect to complete serialization of feedback loops since the feedback loops in GSM do not have parallelism that only can be exploited by team scheduling.

SGMS does not satisfy the buffer space constraint for fft, gsm, mpeg2, and vocoder when the space constraint is as small as 16KB. In contrast, team scheduling satisfies buffer space constraints across all configurations. The averages are computed only on the applications that satisfy the buffer space constraint with both scheduling algorithms (e.g., the averages for `team16KB` and `sgms16KB` are computed excluding `fft`, `gsm`, `mpeg2`, and `vocoder`). When the buffer space limit is as large as 128KB, team scheduling achieves an average of 37% higher throughput than that of SGMS, which is especially apparent in `fft`, `fmradio`, and `serpent`. We can see the importance of amortization from its up to 2.1× speedup (`serpent` at `team128KB`).

As mentioned in Section 2.1, there are several ways of scheduling actors that belong to a team (in team scheduling) or that are assigned to the same core and the same software pipeline stage (in SGMS). However, push schedule — the most buffer space efficient single-core schedule [16] — saves buffer space only an average of 8% from single appearance schedule. In addition, push schedule does not make SGMS meet buffer space constraints of any application which already does not satisfy the constraint in single appearance schedule. If we apply push schedule to the entire stream graph, it makes a significant difference from single appearance schedule in buffer space requirement as shown in [16]. However, when we target 16 cores, the application is already partitioned into 16 pieces; and it does not make a big difference using either scheduling method on each small piece.

In this experiment, we show that team scheduling has better control over buffer space: given buffer space constraint, team scheduling has a better chance of satisfying the constraint and achieves higher throughput by efficiently utilizing the limited buffer space for amortization (i.e., team scheduling achieves balanced trade-off between synchronization overhead and buffer space requirement).

3.3 Amortization Factor Limited Experiment

Figure 6 shows throughput, latency, and buffer requirement of both algorithms while we limit repetition factors to those in the minimum steady state of the entire stream graph. In this experiment, we set the buffer space limit per core to 64KB for team scheduling which achieves a similar (0.4% higher) throughput to that of SGMS as shown in Figure 6(a) — a larger buffer space limit improves throughput at the expense of longer latency. In Figure 6(b), latency is measured as the time until the first output of the furthest downstream actor is generated. Team scheduling shows 65% lower latency and 46% smaller buffer requirement when its throughput is similar to that of SGMS. SGMS has high latency because of poor load balancing in its software pipeline prologue, resulting in idle cycles while waiting for barriers. Team scheduling does not suffer from this problem since actors are pair-wise synchronized and can be fired whenever input tokens are ready.

Since we set the buffer space limit to 64KB for team scheduling, team scheduling uses less than 64KB for every application as shown in Figure 6(c). SGMS requires 2MB buffer space for `wcdma`, which is well over the local memory size of each core, 256KB. Hence, we omit `wcdma` in Figure 6(a) and (b). In `wcdma`, there is a series of reduction actors that produce fewer tokens than it consumes, thus actors upstream must be executed hundreds of times consuming hundreds of KB of data in steady state. Team scheduling avoids excessive buffer requirement from the upstream actors by decoupling the scheduling of upstream and downstream actors.

4. RELATED WORK

Lee and Messerschmitt [25] lay the foundation of SDF including a necessary and sufficient condition to the exis-

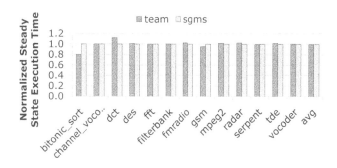

(a) Steady state execution time normalized to SGMS

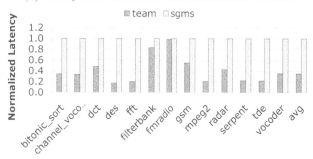

(b) Latency normalized to SGMS

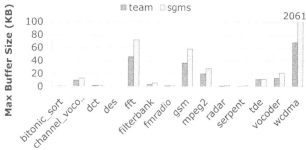

(c) Buffer requirement

Figure 6: Results of amortization factor limited experiment with team scheduling and SGMS for 16 cores.

tence of a valid static schedule which does not deadlock and requires bounded buffer space. Bhattacharyya et al. [4] present an SDF scheduling algorithm for single-core architectures that reduces buffer size of single appearance schedules. They use *pairwise grouping of adjacent nodes* (PGAN) heuristic, in which some aspects are similar to our team formation procedure, but in the context of single-core scheduling. In [5], Bhattacharyya et al. present a post-pass optimization scheme that eliminates redundant synchronization in an existing multi-core SDF schedule. Their method eliminates the same set of redundant inter-team synchronizations (e.g., synchronization at (a, b) in Figure 3(b)) as team scheduling, but team scheduling does so without running a sophisticated analysis by exploiting a property of team scheduling that production-to-consumption ratios of streams between a team pair are constant. They also present a method of reducing synchronization overhead by introducing a few feedback paths that make full checks of other queues unnecessary. However, this method requires additional buffer space and, it will be interesting to evaluate whether using the buffer space for eliminating queue full checks as in [5] is more beneficial than using the same buffer space for amortization as in team scheduling.

The body of SDF work [25, 24, 4, 5, 34, 31] provides a solid theoretical background for optimizing static parts of stream programs. However, their multi-core scheduling algorithms [25, 24, 5, 31] are based on *homogeneous* SDF *graph* (HSDFG) whose construction from an equivalent SDF graph can take an exponential amount of time [31]. In addition, their algorithms do not overlap the execution of different HSDFG iterations, resulting in a smaller degree of parallelism.

[33, 21, 19] present SDF *vectorization* that amortizes the cost associated with actor interactions. For example, Ko et al. [19] develop a vectorization algorithm that reduces context switch overhead and increases memory locality within memory constraints, which is similar to amortization described in this paper in some aspects but is done in the context of single-core scheduling. Amortization, or vectorization, plays a more important role in multi-core scheduling because it not only improves the locality of memory access but also minimizes fixed costs associated with each DMA initiation.

Lin et al. [27] point out exponential buffer space growth in their W-CDMA evaluation and present an algorithm that applies software pipelining in a hierarchical manner. However, in their algorithm, the programmer must define the hierarchy, and the authors fail to keep the scheduling algorithm free from exponential buffer space growth when they design their later work, SGMS [20].

Gordon et al. [11] point out deadlocks in split-join patterns. However, their deadlock resolving method targets a subset of what is described in this paper and does not handle the case shown in Figure 4(a).

5. CONCLUSION

Previous scheduling algorithms such as SGMS make several assumptions on target applications; e.g., the entire application should follow synchronous data flow (SDF) model. On the contrary, team scheduling starts from an initial schedule that makes minimal assumptions, thus targeting a larger class of applications. Team scheduling successively refines the initial schedule by aggregation and amortization of actors, achieving low synchronization overhead similar to that of SGMS. In addition, team scheduling realizes key performance features such as deadlock-free feedback loops, low latency, and flexible buffer space control since it is less constrained from the minimum steady state of the entire application. Due to its flexibility in buffer space control, team scheduling efficiently utilizes limited local memory space of each core. This is clearly shown when team scheduling consistently satisfies the buffer space constraint while SGMS fails to do so when the space limit per core is as small as 16KB. In the case where the space limit is as large as 128KB, team scheduling achieves on average 37% higher throughput than that of SGMS. These results demonstrate team scheduling as a critical optimization scheme in stream compilers for a large class of applications targeting embedded multi-core processors that commonly have limited local memory space.

6. ACKNOWLEDGEMENTS

We thank Aaron Lamb and his colleagues at Qualcomm™ for providing their W-CDMA searcher implementation. We thank James Balfour for the ELM architecture simulator implementation, Ji Young Park for fruitful discussions on our algorithm, and Jooseong Kim for the Elk frontend implementation. We thank the anonymous reviewers who provided valuable feedback. This work is supported in part by the Semiconductor Research Corporation under Grant 2007-HJ-1591 and in part by the National Science Foundation under Grant CNS-0719844. Jongsoo Park is supported by a Samsung Scholarship.

7. REFERENCES

[1] J. Balfour, W. J. Dally, D. Black-Schaffer, V. Parikh, and J. Park. An Energy-Efficient Processor Architecture for Embedded Systems. *Computer Architecture Letters*, 7(1):29–32, 2008.

[2] R. Bellman. On a Routing Problem. *Quarterly of Applied Mathematics*, 16(1):87–90, 1958.

[3] S. S. Bhattacharyya, J. T. Buck, S. Ha, and E. A. Lee. Generating Compact Code from Dataflow Specifications of Multirate Signal Processing Algorithms. *IEEE Transactions on Circuits and Systems*, 42(3):138–150, 1995.

[4] S. S. Bhattacharyya, P. K. Murthy, and E. A. Lee. APGAN and RPMC: Complementary Heuristics for Translating DSP Block Diagrams into Efficient Software Implementations. *Design Automation for Embedded Systems*, 2(1):33–60, 1997.

[5] S. S. Bhattacharyya, S. Sriram, and E. A. Lee. Optimizing Synchronization in Multiprocessor DSP Systems. *IEEE Transactions on Signal Processing*, 45(6):1605–1618, 1997.

[6] R. Cytron, J. Ferrante, B. K. Rosen, M. N. Wegman, and F. K. Zadeck. Efficiently Computing Static Single Assignment Form and the Control Dependence Graph. *ACM Transactions on Programming Language and Systems (TOPLAS)*, 13(4):451–490, 1991.

[7] W. J. Dally and B. Towles. *Principles and Practices of Interconnection Networks*. Morgan Kaufmann, 2004.

[8] ELM Webpage. Concurrent VLSI Architecture Group, Stanford University. http://cva.stanford.edu/projects/elm/software.htm.

[9] K. Fatahalian, T. J. Knight, M. Houston, M. Erez, D. R. Horn, L. Leem, J. Y. Park, M. Ren, A. Aiken, W. J. Dally, and P. Hanrahan. Sequoia: Programming the Memory Hierarchy. In *Conference on Supercomputing (SC)*, 2006.

[10] M. I. Gordon, W. Thies, and S. P. Amarasinghe. Exploiting Coarse-grained Task, Data, and Pipeline Parallelism in Stream Programs. In *International Conference on Architecture Support for Programming Language and Operating Systems (ASPLOS)*, pages 151–162, 2006.

[11] M. I. Gordon, W. Thies, M. Karczmarek, J. Lin, A. S. Meli, A. A. Lamb, C. Leger, J. Wong, J. Hoffman, D. Maze, and S. P. Amarasinghe. A Stream Compiler for Communication-Exposed Architectures. In *International Conference on Architecture Support for Programming Language and Operating Systems (ASPLOS)*, pages 291–303, 2002.

[12] M. R. Guthaus, J. S. Ringenberg, D. Ernst, T. M. Austin, T. Mudge, and R. B. Brown. MiBench: A Free, Commercially Representative Embedded Benchmark Suite. In *IEEE Annual Workshop on Workload Characterization*, pages 83–94, 2001.

[13] M. Herlihy and N. Shavit. *The Art of Multiprocessor Programming*. Morgan Kaufmann, 2008.

[14] H. P. Hofstee. Power Efficient Processor Architecture and the CELL Processor. In *International Symposium on High-Performance Computer Architectures (HPCA)*, pages 258–262, 2005.

[15] J. B. Kam and J. D. Ullman. Monotone Data Flow Analysis Frameworks. *Acta Informatica*, 7(3):305–317, 1977.

[16] M. Karczmarek, W. Thies, and S. P. Amarasinghe. Phased Scheduling of Stream Programs. In *Conference on Language, Compiler, and Tool Support for Embedded Systems (LCTES)*, pages 103–112, 2003.

[17] G. Karypis and V. Kumar. METIS: Unstructured Graph Partitioning and Sparse Matrix Ordering System. Technical report, Department of Computer Science, University of Minnesota, 1995.

[18] B. Khailany, W. J. Dally, U. J. Kapasi, P. Mattson, J. Namkoong, J. D. Owens, B. Towles, A. Chang, and S. Rixner. Imagine: Media Processing with Streams. *IEEE Micro*, 21(2):35–46, 2001.

[19] M.-Y. Ko, C.-C. Shen, and S. S. Bhattacharyya. Memory-constrained Block Processing for DSP Software Optimization. *Journal of Signal Processing Systems*, 50(2):163–177, 2008.

[20] M. Kudlur and S. Mahlke. Orchestrating the Execution of Stream Programs on Multicore Platforms. In *Conference on Programming Language Design and Implementation (PLDI)*, pages 114–124, 2008.

[21] K. N. Lalgudi, M. C. Papaefthymiou, and M. Potkonjak. Optimizing Computations for Effective Block-Processing. *ACM Transactions on Design Automation of Electronic Systems*, 5(3):604–630, 2000.

[22] M. Lam. Software Pipelining: An Effective Scheduling Technique on VLIW Machines. In *Conference on Programming Language Design and Implementation (PLDI)*, pages 318–328, 1988.

[23] C. Lattner and V. Adve. LLVM: A Compilation Framework for Lifelong Program Analysis & Transformation. In *International Symposium on Code Generation and Optimization (CGO)*, pages 75–86, 2004.

[24] E. A. Lee. *A Coupled Hardware and Software Architecture for Programmable Digital Signal Processors*. PhD thesis, University of California, Berkeley, 1986.

[25] E. A. Lee and D. G. Messerschmitt. Static Scheduling of Synchronous Data Flow Programs for Digital Signal Processing. *IEEE Transactions on Computers*, 36(1):24–35, 1987.

[26] T. Lengauer and R. E. Tarjan. A Fast Algorithm for Finding Dominators in Flowgraph. *ACM Transactions on Programming Language and Systems (TOPLAS)*, 1(1):121–141, 1979.

[27] Y. Lin, M. Kudlur, S. Mahlke, and T. Mudge. Hierarchical Coarse-grained Stream Compilation for

Software Defined Radio. In *International Conference on Compilers, Architecture, and Synthesis for Embedded Systems (CASES)*, pages 115–124, 2007.

[28] P. Mattson. *A Programming System for the Imagine Media Processor*. PhD thesis, Stanford University, 2002.

[29] A. V. Oppenheim, A. S. Willsky, and S. H. Nawab. *Signals & Systems*. Prentice Hall, 1997.

[30] J. Park, J. Balfour, and W. J. Dally. Maximizing the Filter Rate of L0 Compiler-Managed Instruction Stores by Pinning. Technical Report 126, Concurrent VLSI Architecture Group, Stanford University, 2009.

[31] J. L. Pino, S. S. Bhattacharyya, and E. A. Lee. A Hierarchical Multiprocessor Scheduling Systems for DSP Applications. Technical Report UCB/ERL M95/36, University of California, Berkeley, 1995.

[32] B. R. Rau. Iterative Modulo Scheduling: An Algorithm for Software Pipelining Loops. In *International Symposium on Microarchitecture (MICRO)*, pages 63–74, 1994.

[33] S. Ritz, M. Pankert, V. Živojnović, and H. Meyr. Optimum Vectorization of Scalable Synchronous Dataflow Graphs. In *International Conference on Application-Specific Array Processors (ASAP)*, pages 285–296, 1993.

[34] S. Sriram and S. S. Bhattacharyya. *Embedded Mutiprocesors: Scheduling and Synchronization*. CRC, 2009.

[35] W. Thies, M. Karczmarek, and S. P. Amarasinghe. StreamIt: A Language for Streaming Applications. In *International Conference on Compiler Construction (CC)*, pages 179–196, 2002.

[36] Y.-P. E. Wang and T. Ottosson. Cell Search in W-CDMA. *IEEE Journal on Selected Areas in Communications*, 18(8):1470–1482, 2000.

APPENDIX

A. Constant Production-to-Consumption Ratios between a Team Pair

Let $\vec{q_G}$ be the minimum repetition vector of stream subgraph G. For teams T and U in stream graph G, according to [4]:

$$\exists \text{ an integer } m \text{ such that } \forall a \in T, \ \vec{q_G}(a) = m \cdot \vec{q_T}(a) \quad (1)$$

$$\exists \text{ an integer } n \text{ such that } \forall a \in U, \ \vec{q_G}(a) = n \cdot \vec{q_U}(a) \quad (2)$$

For stream s, let $src(s)$ be s's producer and $dst(s)$ be s's consumer. Since the number of tokens produced and consumed at a stream are equal in the minimum steady state of G, $\vec{q_G}(src(s)) \cdot prod(s) = \vec{q_G}(dst(s)) \cdot cons(s)$, which is called the *balanced equation* [4]. Substituting Equation (1) and (2) into the balanced equation shows that, for each stream s from T to U, $m \cdot \vec{q_T}(src(s)) \cdot prod(s) = n \cdot \vec{q_U}(src(s)) \cdot cons(s)$. This means that the ratio of the number of tokens produced at s by each T firing ($\vec{q_T}(src(s)) \cdot prod(s)$) to the number of tokens consumed from s by each U firing ($\vec{q_U}(dst(s)) \cdot cons(s)$) is a constant, $\frac{n}{m}$.

B. Inter-team Synchronization Elimination

Let S_{TU} be the streams from team T to team U. Let s_1 be the stream in S_{TU} that is enqueued last in T's static sched-

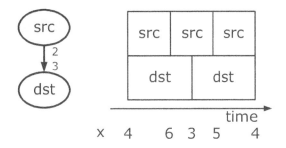

x   4   6   3   5   4

Figure 7: A steady state execution when $p = 2$, $c = 3$, and $x(0) = 4$.

ule. Consider the situation when we check conditions to fire U. Assume that we have checked that s_1 is not empty. This implies that all the other streams in S_{TU} are also not empty, which makes checking if any of those streams is empty unnecessary. This can be shown through contradiction as follows. Suppose that the queue at $s_3 \in S_{TU} - \{s_1\}$ is empty. Then due to the constant production-to-consumption ratios of S_{TU}, the queue at s_1 must be empty which contradicts our assumption.

Let s_2 be the stream in S_{TU} that is dequeued last in U's static schedule. Suppose that the queue lengths of S_{TU} are proportional to their respective number of tokens produced by each T firing. Consider the situation when we check conditions to fire T. Similarly, we can show that, if s_2 is not full, all the other streams in S_{TU} must not be full as well.

C. Serialization-free Queue Length for Producer-consumer Pairs

Consider a stream s. Let p be the number of tokens produced per $src(s)$ firing. Let c be the number of tokens consumed per $dst(s)$ firing. Assume that $src(s)$ is fired every p time steps and $dst(s)$ is fired every c time steps (perfect load balance). Suppose that s has $x(0)$ tokens at time step 0, when a steady state with respect to $src(s)$ and $dst(s)$ begins. At time step t, the number of tokens at s is

$$x(t) = x(0) + \left\lfloor \frac{t}{p} \right\rfloor \cdot p - \left\lfloor \frac{t}{c} \right\rfloor \cdot c$$
$$= x(0) + (t \bmod c) - (t \bmod p)$$
$$(\because t = \left\lfloor \frac{t}{p} \right\rfloor \cdot p + (t \bmod p) = \left\lfloor \frac{t}{c} \right\rfloor \cdot c + (t \bmod c))$$

Let l be the queue length. When $src(s)$ finishes, $t \bmod p = 0$, thus $x(t) = x(0) + (t \bmod c) \leq x(0) + c - gcd(p, c)$. Since we need p space to fire $src(s)$ immediately to avoid stalls, $l \geq x(0) + p + c - gcd(p, c)$. When $dst(s)$ finishes, $t \bmod c = 0$, thus $x(t) = x(0) - (t \bmod p) \geq x(0) - p + gcd(p, c)$. Since we need c remaining tokens to fire $dst(s)$ immediately to avoid stalls, $x(0) - p + gcd(p, c) \geq c$. Therefore, the minimum l that avoids stalls is $2(p + c - gcd(p, c))$, which is achieved by $x(0) = p + c - gcd(p, c)$. Figure 7 shows an example where $p = 2$ and $c = 3$.

D. Minimum Splitter Firings to Fire a Corresponding Joiner

We initialize $x_J(J) = 1$. We traverse G_{SJ} in a reverse topological order (recall that we traverse an acyclic team

graph). For each team T we visit, we compute $x_J(T)$ as follows.

$$x_J(T)$$
$$= \max_{\text{successor } U \text{ of } T} (\text{number of } T \text{ firings to fire } U \ x_J(U) \text{ times})$$
$$= \max_{\text{successor } U \text{ of } T} (\lceil \frac{x_J(U) \cdot cons(s)}{prod(s)} \rceil)$$

E. Team Scheduling Pseudo Code

```
01   construct an initial schedule;
02   initial queue sizing; // Feedback queues are sized here.
03
04   // merge teams
05   q = a priority queue with pairs of teams
            that do not introduce a cycle;
06   while (!q.isEmpty()) {
07     ⟨a, b⟩ = q.remove();
08     if (merging a and b does not exceed buffer limit
            and does not deadlock) {
09       m = merge(a, b);
10       remove all team pairs containing a or b from q;
11       for each (neighbor c of a or b) {
12         if (merging m and c does not introduce a cycle)
13           add ⟨m, c⟩ to q;
14       }
15     }
16   }
17
18   // amortize teams
19   q = construct a priority queue with teams;
20   while (!q.isEmpty()) {
21     a = q.remove();
22     if (amortizing a does not exceed buffer limit
            and does not deadlock) {
23       amortize a;
24       add a to q;
25     }
26   }
```

The time complexity of team scheduling is dominated by the longest path algorithm for buffer requirement computation. Let $|V|$ be the number of actors and $|E|$ be the number of streams. We compute buffer requirement $O(|V| log(b))$ times (lines 8 and 22), when b is the buffer space limit per core and we amortize each team at least by a factor of 2. We use the Bellman-Ford algorithm [2] to compute the longest distance, whose time complexity is $O(|V| \cdot |E|)$. Bellman-Ford is invoked $O(|V|)$ times per each buffer requirement computation; thus the time complexity of team scheduling is $O(|V|^3 |E| log(b))$.

The time complexity for cyclicity check is $O(|V|^3)$: cyclicity check is done $O(|V|^2)$ times (line 12) and each check takes $O(|V|)$ by using reachability matrix [4]. The time complexity of finding split-join patterns is $O((|E| log(|E|) + |V|^2)|V| log(b))$: we apply the concept of *dominance frontier* used for constructing *static single assignment* form in the compiler [6], which takes $O(|E| log(|E|) + |V|^2)$ [6, 26].

If the time complexity is unacceptable (e.g., in just-in-time compilation), we can stop during algorithm execution since we maintain a valid schedule throughout the algorithm execution.

Scheduling Jobs with Varying Parallelizability to Reduce Variance

Anupam Gupta[*]
Computer Science Dept.
Carnegie Mellon University
Pittsburgh PA 15213
anupamg@cs.cmu.edu

Sungjin Im[†]
Dept. of Computer Science.
University of Illinois
Urbana, IL 61801.
im3@illinois.edu

Ravishankar Krishnaswamy[*]
Computer Science Dept.
Carnegie Mellon University
Pittsburgh PA 15213
ravishan@cs.cmu.edu

Benjamin Moseley[‡]
Dept. of Computer Science.
University of Illinois
Urbana, IL 61801.
bmosele2@illinois.edu

Kirk Pruhs[§]
Computer Science Dept.
University of Pittsburgh
Pittsburgh PA 15260
kirk@cs.pitt.edu

ABSTRACT

We give a $(2+\epsilon)$-speed $O(1)$-competitive algorithm for scheduling jobs with arbitrary speed-up curves for the ℓ_2 norm of flow. We give a similar result for the broadcast setting with varying page sizes.

Categories and Subject Descriptors

F.2.2 [**Analysis of Algorithms and Problem Complexity**]: Nonnumerical Algorithms and Problems

General Terms

Algorithms, Theory

Keywords

Online Algorithms, Scheduling Algorithms

1. INTRODUCTION

We consider scheduling dynamically arriving jobs that have varying degrees of parallelizability (that is, some jobs may be sped up considerably when simultaneously run on multiple processors, while other jobs may speed up by very

[*]Supported in part by NSF awards CCF-0448095 and CCF-0729022, and an Alfred P. Sloan Fellowship.
[†]Partially supported by NSF grants CCF-0728782, CNS-0721899, and Samsung Fellowship.
[‡]Partially supported by NSF grant CNS-0721899.
[§]Supported in part by NSF grants CNS-0325353, IIS-0534531, and CCF-0830558, and an IBM Faculty Award.

little) on a multiprocessor system. The most obvious settings where this problem arises is scheduling multi-threaded processes on a chip with multiple cores/processors, and scheduling multi-process applications in a server farm. We adopt the following general model of parallelizability, which was apparently first introduced in [6] and later used in [5, 7, 8, 16, 15, 4]: we have m identical fixed speed processors. Each job i arrives at time a_i, and consists of a sequence of phases. Each phase needs to finish some amount of work, and has a speedup function that specifies the rate at which work is processed in that particular phase (as a function of the number of processors assigned to the job). The speedup functions have to be nondecreasing (a job doesn't run slower if it is given more processors), and sublinear (a job satisfies Brent's Theorem: increasing the number of processors doesn't increase the efficiency of computation), but the functions are unconstrained otherwise.

The scheduler needs an *assignment policy* to determine how many processors are allocated to each job at each point in time. In order to be implementable in a real system, we require that this policy be *online*, since the scheduler will not in general know about jobs arriving in the future. This policy also ideally should be *nonclairvoyant*, since a scheduler usually does not know the size/work of a job when the job is released, nor the degree to which that job is parallelizable. So a nonclairvoyant algorithm only knows when jobs have been released and which have finished in the past, and how many processors have been allocated to each job at each point of time in the past.

Given a schedule, the most natural quality of service measure for a job is its response time (also called the flow or waiting time) $F_i := C_i - a_i$, which is the length of time between when the job i is released at time a_i and when it completes at time C_i. To get a quality of service measure for the entire schedule, one must combine the quality of service measures of the individual jobs. The most commonly used way to do this is to take the average, or the sum (the ℓ_1 norm), of the flow times of the individual jobs. But to quote from Silberschatz and Galvin's classic text *Operating Systems Concepts* [17], "A system with reasonable and predictable response time may be considered more desirable than a system that is faster on the average, but is highly variable." and " … for interactive systems, it is more important to minimize the variance in the response time than it is to minimize the average response time." Hence, in many settings, the ℓ_2 norm (the square root of the sum of the squares) of job flow times may be a better quality of service measure of schedules than the ℓ_1 norm of job flow times.

A Simple Instance: *As a well known concrete example of difference between the ℓ_1 and ℓ_2 norms, consider a single-machine instance where two jobs are released at time 0, and one job is released at each integer time $1, 2, \ldots, n$. All jobs are identical, and the system takes one unit of time to finish each job. When the objective is to minimize the ℓ_1 norm of the flow time, one can see that every non-idling schedule is optimal. In particular, the schedule that has flow time 1 for all jobs except for one of the jobs released at time 0 (which will have flow time n) is also optimal. This however is not optimal for the ℓ_2 norm. Scheduling jobs in order of their release time results in the optimal schedule where all jobs have flow time at most 2. Thus a schedule that is good under the ℓ_2 norm reduces the variance of the job flow times relative to an optimal schedule for the ℓ_1 norm.*

Our Results: To recap, we address the problem of designing an online nonclairvoyant assignment policy that is competitive for the objective of the ℓ_2 norm of the flow time for jobs with arbitrary speed-up curves. Our main result is the following:

Theorem 1.1 *We give a nonclairvoyant assignment policy that is $(2 + \epsilon)$-speed $O(1)$-competitive for minimizing the ℓ_2 norm of the flow time for jobs with arbitrary speedup curves.*

Note that all our results use *resource augmentation*: An algorithm A is s-speed c-competitive if, for every instance, the algorithm A with processors running at speed s guarantees a schedule whose objective is within a factor of c of the value of the optimal objective with unit speed processors. Intuitively, an s-speed $O(1)$-competitive algorithm guarantees that the schedule can handle a load up to a $\frac{1}{s}$ fraction of the load that an optimal offline scheduler can handle. Thus an $(1 + \epsilon)$-speed $O(1)$-competitive algorithm is said to be *scalable* since it can handle almost the same load as optimal. For further elaboration, see [14, 13]. It is well known that no online algorithm can be $O(1)$-competitive for ℓ_k norms of flow time without resource augmentation [2].

1.1 Context, Intuition, and Our Techniques

To get a feel for the problem, let us consider two special cases: Consider first the case that all jobs are *fully parallelizable* (i.e., increasing the number of processors assigned to a job by a factor f reduces the time required by a factor of f), which is essentially equivalent to having a single processor. In the initial paper popularizing resource augmentation analysis [10], the algorithm Shortest Elapsed Time First (SETF) which shares the processors evenly among all jobs that have been processed the least (which necessarily are the later arriving jobs) was shown to be scalable for the ℓ_1 norm of flow. This was generalized by [2] to show that SETF is scalable for all ℓ_k norms of flow for $1 \le k < \infty$. So intuitively, in the case of parallel work, the "right" algorithm is independent of the norm, equivalently the "right" algorithm for the ℓ_1 norm extends to all ℓ_k norms!

Now consider the more general case of jobs with arbitrary speed-up curves, but only for the ℓ_1 norm. [5] showed

that the assignment policy EQUI that shares the processors evenly among all active jobs is $(2 + \epsilon)$-speed $O(1)$-competitive for average flow time. Subsequently, [8] introduced the algorithm Late Arrival Processor Sharing (LAPS), which shares the processors evenly among the latest arriving constant fraction of the jobs, and showed that LAPS is scalable for average flow time. The intuition behind LAPS was to mimic SETF, by giving more processors to later arriving jobs, but to spread the processing power more evenly in case that the latest arriving jobs are sequential (their processing rate does not increase even if they are assigned more processors). In this special case, the "right" strategy for arbitrary speed-curves is basically the same as the "right" strategy for parallel work.

Given these two special cases, everyone's (that we are aware of) initial reaction to the question of the design of a policy for the ℓ_2 norm of flow for jobs with arbitrary speed-up curves, was that LAPS should be scalable. The intuition is understandable: [10] showed that for parallel work, favoring the most recent jobs is the right strategy to minimize the ℓ_1 norm of flow. Then [2] showed that considering general ℓ_k norms didn't change the "right" strategy, and [8] showed that allowing jobs with arbitrary speed-up curves didn't drastically change the right strategy. Intuitively it seems that considering arbitrary ℓ_k norms and arbitrary speed-up curves *together* shouldn't drastically change the right strategy. However, this intuition is misleading: we show in Section 3 that LAPS is not $O(1)$-speed $O(1)$-competitive for the ℓ_k norm of flow when $k \ge 2$.

1.1.1 The Mistake in the Intuition, and Our Algorithm

Considering why LAPS fails to be $O(1)$-competitive for the ℓ_2 norm, even with faster processors, offers insight into how to design such an algorithm. Just as the total flow time $\sum_i F_i$ is the integral over time of the number of jobs unfinished at that time, the sum of the squares of the flow times $\sum_i F_i^2$ is proportional to the integral over time, of the *ages* of the jobs at that time. The key observation in [2] was that if SETF, with a $(1 + \epsilon)$-speed processor, has unfinished jobs of a particular age, then any schedule on a unit speed processor must have a comparable number of unfinished jobs that are at least as old: this observation implies the competitiveness of SETF for all ℓ_k norms rather directly. The lower bound instance in Section 3 shows that for jobs with arbitrary speed-up curves, LAPS may have devoted too much processing to sequential jobs in the past, and hence it may have many more old jobs than is necessary. And as LAPS focuses on new jobs, these old jobs will remain unfinished, driving up the ℓ_2 norm of flow for LAPS relative to optimal. This lower bound instance, and the simple instance of the stream of unit work jobs, suggests that the online algorithm must give a greater share of the processing power to older jobs for ℓ_2 norm of flow time for jobs with arbitrary speed-up curves.

Our algorithm addresses this by distributing the processors proportional to the age of the jobs, which is the rate at which that job is currently driving up the ℓ_2 norm of flow. Combining this intuition with an idea used in [8] to focus only on a fraction of the recent jobs, we design an algorithm WLAPS that is $(2 + \epsilon)$-speed $O(1)$-competitive for the ℓ_2 norm of flow. Essentially, WLAPS distributes the processors to the latest arriving constant fraction of jobs. However, the proportion of resources a job gets is related to the age of the job.

1.1.2 Other Results: Broadcast Scheduling, and Other Norms

To explain broadcast scheduling, consider a web server serving static content on a broadcast channel. If the web server has multiple unsatisfied requests for the same file, broadcasting that file only once simultaneously satisfies all the users who issued these requests. [7] observed that broadcast scheduling in the ℓ_1 norm can be viewed as a special case of scheduling jobs with arbitrary speed-up curves in the ℓ_1 norm, in which all jobs consist of a sequential phase followed by a parallel phase. Indeed, the results of [7, 1] showed how to convert any s-speed c-competitive nonclairvoyant algorithm for scheduling jobs with arbitrary speedup curves into a $(1+\epsilon)s$-speed c-competitive nonclairvoyant algorithm for broadcast scheduling. Combining this reduction with the analysis of LAPS in [8], one obtains a scalable algorithm for broadcast scheduling for the ℓ_1 norm of flows. Unfortunately, this reduction from broadcast scheduling given in [7, 1] does not seem to work for the ℓ_2 norm of flow. However, in Section 4, we directly show that the broadcast version of WLAPS is indeed $(2+\epsilon)$-speed $O(1)$-competitive for the ℓ_2 norm of flow for broadcast scheduling.

Our techniques give algorithms for other ℓ_k norms as well. In particular, we can give nonclairvoyant algorithms that are $(k+\epsilon)$-speed $O(k^2)$-competitive for the objective of minimizing the ℓ_k norm of the flow times. We should remark that improving our results for larger values of k would be interesting, though mostly of academic interest, since as a practical matter, the interesting values of k are those in $[1,3] \cup \{\infty\}$.

1.2 Related Results

Consider first the case that all the work is fully parallelizable and and the ℓ_1 norm. It is well known that the online clairvoyant algorithm Shortest Remaining Processing Time is optimal. The competitive ratio of any deterministic nonclairvoyant algorithm is $\Omega(n^{1/3})$, and the competitive ratio of every randomized algorithm against an oblivious adversary is $\Omega(\log n)$ [12]. A randomized version of the Multi-Level Feedback Queue algorithm is $O(\log n)$-competitive [11, 3].

As for broadcast scheduling, a recent result of Im and Moseley [9] gives a scalable algorithm for the problem of minimizing the ℓ_1 norm of the requests, when all pages are of unit size. Subsequently [1] shows a scalable algorithm, inspired by LAPS, for the general problem with arbitrary page sizes.

Chan et al. [4] consider the problem of nonclairvoyant scheduling of jobs with varying degrees of parallelizability on a multiprocessor, where each machine can be scaled at a different speed. They give a $O(\log m)$-competitive algorithm for the problem of minimizing the sum of average flow time and energy, where the power function varies as s^α for constant α, under some assumptions about the jobs.

1.3 Formal Problem Statement and Notation

We now formally define the problem and introduce notation required for our algorithm and analysis. An arbitrary problem instance consists of a collection of jobs $\mathcal{J} = \{J_1, \ldots, J_n\}$ where job J_i has a release/arrival time of a_i and a sequence of phases $\langle J_i^1, J_i^2, \ldots, J_i^{q_i} \rangle$. Each phase is

an ordered pair $\langle w_i^q, \Gamma_i^q \rangle$, where w_i^q is a positive real number that denotes the amount of work in the phase and Γ_i^q is a function, called the speedup function, that maps a nonnegative real number to a nonnegative real number. The function $\Gamma_i^q(p)$ represents the rate at which work is processed for phase q of job i when the job is run on p processors running at speed 1. Henceforth, we may interchangeably use job i and job J_i when the context is clear.

A feasible schedule $\mathcal{S}_s$ for the job set $\mathcal{J}$ with n jobs with sm available processors (one may think of s as a parameter) specifies for each time, and for each job, a nonnegative real number specifying the number of processors assigned to the job. Notice that we allow a job to be scheduled on a non-integral number of machines, and this can be translated to an actual scheduling on machines by having schedules which are preemptive and migratory. Such an assignment would be feasible as long as $\sum_{i=1}^{n} \mathcal{S}_s(i,t) \leq sm$ for all time instants t, where $\mathcal{S}_s(i,t)$ is the number of processors schedule $\mathcal{S}_s$ allocates to job i at time t. In words, at any time, the total number of processors allocated to the jobs must not exceed sm.

For such a schedule $\mathcal{S}_s$, suppose a job i begins its qth phase at time t_q. Then, the completion time of this stage (which is also when the subsequent stage begins) is the unique time t_{q+1} such that $\int_{t_q}^{t_{q+1}} \Gamma_i^q(\mathcal{S}_s(i,t))dt = w_i^q$. The completion time C_i of the job is then the completion time of its final phase q_i.

In the ℓ_k norm objective, the total cost incurred by this solution can then be expressed as

$$\text{cost}(\mathcal{S}_s) = \left(\sum_{i \in [n]} (C_i - a_i)^k \right)^{1/k}$$

Recall that a nonclairvoyant algorithm only knows when jobs have been released and finished in the past, and which jobs have been run on each processor each time in the past. In particular, for any phase q, the algorithm does not know the values of w_i^q, and the speedup function Γ_i^q. In fact, it is not even aware of the progression of a job from one phase to the next.

Notice that, by having a parameter s to alter the number of available processors, the notion of resource augmentation we have (implicitly) assumed here is that of machine augmentation and not speed augmentation. However, since an s speed processor is as powerful as s unit speed processors when preemption is allowed, our results would translate to the speed augmentation model as well. This enables us to make the following simplification: for ease of analysis, we scale the number of processors by a factor of m, and assume that the optimal solution has a single unit speed processor and the online algorithm has s unit speed processors.

2. NON-CLAIRVOYANT SCHEDULING WITH ARBITRARY SPEEDUP CURVES

2.1 Restricted Instances are Sufficient

As by now is standard, we can show that we only need to focus on restricted instances where every job is composed of either fully parallelizable phases or completely sequential phases. A phase is said to be completely parallelizable if $\Gamma_i^q(p) = p$ for all p, and completely sequential if $\Gamma_i^q(p) = 1$

for all values of p. That is, sequential phases progress at the same rate regardless of the number of processors allocated.

To show this, we perform the following reduction from an arbitrary instance $\mathcal{I}$ of the problem to such a restricted instance $\mathcal{I}'$ with the following properties holding true: (i) the schedule produced by the non-clairvoyant algorithm *remains the same* for both instances $\mathcal{I}$ and $\mathcal{I}'$, and (ii) the cost of the optimal offline solution for the instance $\mathcal{I}'$ is at most the cost of an optimal offline solution for the first instance $\mathcal{I}$. This would ensure that if our algorithm is α-competitive on instance $\mathcal{I}'$, then it has a competitive ratio of at most α on instance $\mathcal{I}$ as well.

Let `NCAlg` denote any non-clairvoyant algorithm. Our reduction works in the following fashion: For each job i that is released in $\mathcal{I}$, we release the job i' in $\mathcal{I}'$ at the same time a_i. Now consider an infinitesimally small interval $[t, t + dt]$, and let `NCAlg` devote p_i^a processors towards j in this time interval. Also, let the job be in some phase with parallelizability Γ in this time interval. Therefore, the online algorithm effectively does a work of $w = \Gamma(p_i^a)dt$ for job i in time interval $[t, t+dt]$. Now, let us focus on the time interval $[t^*, t^* + dt^*]$ when the optimal solution works on this exact w amount of the job i (note that it could occur before or after t). Let the optimal solution devote p_i^o processors towards doing this work w. Notice that the definition of $[t^*, t^* + dt^*]$ and p_i^o imply that $\Gamma(p_i^o)dt^* = w = \Gamma(p_i^a)dt$, which in turn implies that

$$\frac{\Gamma(p_i^o)}{\Gamma(p_i^a)} = \frac{dt}{dt^*} \tag{1}$$

If $p_i^o \geq p_i^a$, then in the new instance $\mathcal{I}'$, we replace this w amount of work for job i with $w' = p_i^a dt$ amount of *fully parallelizable* work. Notice that by this change, when w amount of work was finished by the online algorithm in $\mathcal{I}$, an equivalent w' amount of work is done in $\mathcal{I}'$, and so the job progresses at the same rate for the online algorithm in either instance. Furthermore, since $p_i^o \geq p_i^a$, we have that

$$\frac{p_i^o}{p_i^a} \geq \frac{\Gamma(p_i^o)}{\Gamma(p_i^a)} = \frac{dt}{dt^*} \tag{2}$$

and therefore an optimal solution for $\mathcal{I}'$ can fit in the w' amount of fully parallelizable work at same time interval $[t^*, t^* + dt^*]$ when the optimal solution for $\mathcal{I}$ worked on the corresponding w amount of i. Here, the equation (2) follows from the sublinear nature of the speed-up function.

On the other hand, if $p_i^o < p_i^a$, then in our instance $\mathcal{I}'$, we replace this w amount of work for job i with $w' = dt$ amount of *fully sequential* work. Notice that by this change, when w amount of work was finished by the online algorithm in $\mathcal{I}$, an equivalent w' amount of work is done in $\mathcal{I}'$, and again the job progresses at the same rate for the online algorithm in either instance. Furthermore, since in this case $p_i^o < p_i^a$, we have that

$$1 \geq \frac{\Gamma(p_i^o)}{\Gamma(p_i^a)} = \frac{dt}{dt^*} \tag{3}$$

and therefore $dt^* \geq dt$. Therefore, an optimal solution for $\mathcal{I}'$ can fit in the $w' = dt$ amount of fully sequential work in same time interval $[t^*, t^* + dt^*]$ when the optimal solution for $\mathcal{I}$ worked on the corresponding w amount of i.

Hence, in either case, we see that the flow time of every job in the non-clairvoyant online algorithm is same for both instances, and the flow time in the optimal solution for $\mathcal{I}'$ is

at most that for $\mathcal{I}$. Therefore, it is sufficient to design non-clairvoyant algorithms which are competitive against such extremal instances. Furthermore, since any phase of a job is either completely sequential or completely parallelizable, an algorithm working on s machines is equivalent to one working on a single machine with speed s. Hence, in the following section, we shall refer to s as the speed advantage the online algorithm has over the optimal offline adversary.

2.2 Non-clairvoyant Algorithm WLAPS

We first describe our non-clairvoyant preemptive algorithm WLAPS for Weighted Latest Arrival Processor Sharing. As can be deduced from its name, WLAPS is inspired by LAPS [8], a scalable algorithm for minimizing the total flow time of the jobs (i.e. when $k = 1$). Before we describe our algorithm, let us introduce some notation. First and foremost, we will assume that the algorithm WLAPS is given a speed-up of a factor of s. In other words, we can assume that WLAPS is given a s-speed processor while the optimal adversary is given only a unit-speed processor. Let β be a scaling parameter that determines the fraction of weight we consider at any instant of time. The speed-up s will depend on β, and we will fix this parameter later.

For each job $i \in [n]$, let us define its *weight* at time t to be $w_i(t) = k(t - a_i)^{k-1}$. Informally, $w_i(t)$ denotes the rate of increase of the kth power of the flow time of job i at time t (which is also the incremental cost incurred by the algorithm due to job i being alive at time t). At any time t, let $N_a(t)$ denote the set of jobs that are alive in the queue of our algorithm, i.e. $N_a(t) := \{i \in [n] \mid a_i \leq t < C_i\}$, where C_i is the completion time of job i. Among the set of jobs $N_a(t)$, let $N_a'(t)$ denote the set of those jobs with the *latest arrival times* whose weights sum up to $\beta w(t)$, where $w(t) = \sum_{i \in N_a(t)} w_i(t)$.

It would be useful to observe that the objective function we are interested in is equivalent to (after raising the ℓ_k objective by a power of k) minimizing

$$\sum_{i \in [n]} (C_i - a_i)^k = \int_0^\infty \sum_{i \in N_a(t)} w_i(t)\mathsf{dt}$$

We are now ready to describe our algorithm: At any time t, the algorithm WLAPS simply distributes its processing power among the jobs in $N_a'(t)$, in proportion to their weights at time t. Let $x_i(t)$ denote the fraction of processing power job i receives at time t under the schedule of WLAPS. Then,

$$x_i(t) := s \cdot \frac{w_i(t)}{\beta w(t)}, \quad \forall i \in N_a'(t)$$

Notice that the total processing power used at any time is exactly s. We remark that when $k = 1$ our algorithm WLAPS is exactly the same as LAPS, since the weights of all jobs are identically equal to 1.

A Simplifying Assumption: We assume that there exists a set of latest arriving jobs whose weights sum up to exactly $\beta w(t)$. Otherwise, a slight modification should be made to the algorithm. The set $N_a'(t)$ which WLAPS works on is now defined to be the minimal set of latest arriving jobs whose weights exceed $\beta w(t)$. Let j be the earliest arriving job in $N_a'(t)$. The amount of processing power that every job gets in $N_a'(t)$ except j stays the same. The job j receives a processing power of $x_j(t) := s \cdot \frac{\beta w(t) - (\sum_{i \in N'_a(t) \setminus \{j\}} w_i(t))}{\beta w(t)}$. In words, roughly speaking, the processing power the job j gets is proportional to its weight which "overlaps" the β fraction of weights. With this small elaboration, we can remove the assumption and the analysis easily follows. We however stick to the simplifying assumption to make our analysis more readable.

2.3 Analysis

Our analysis is based on a potential function argument, inspired by [8]. To formally describe the potential function, we need to introduce some more notation.

For any job i, let σ_i denote the total sequential work for job i and ρ_i denotes the total parallel work for job i. Recall (from Section 2.2) that for any job i and time t, $x_i(t)$ denotes the fraction of processing the algorithm WLAPS dedicates towards job i. Similarly, let $x_i^*(t)$ denote the fraction of processing the optimal offline schedule OPT allocates for i at time t. Without loss of generality, we can assume that $x_i^*(t) > 0$ only if job i is in parallel phase under the schedule by the adversary. Since we assumed that the total processing power for WLAPS is s and that for OPT is 1, it follows that $\sum_{i \in N'_a(t)} x_i(t) \le s$ and that $\sum_{i \in N_o(t)} x_i^*(t) \le 1$.

For any job $i \in [n]$, let $\mathrm{On}(i, t_1, t_2)$ denote the *total amount of parallel work* for job i done by WLAPS during the time interval $[t_1, t_2]$. To quantify this formally, we need to define a variable $\mathbb{I}_i(t)$ which indicates whether job i is in a parallel phase for WLAPS at time t, (in which case $\mathbb{I}_i(t) = 1$) or in a sequential phase ($\mathbb{I}_i(t) = 0$). Then,

$$\mathrm{On}(i, t_1, t_2) := \int_{t_1}^{t_2} x_i(t) \mathbb{I}_i(t) dt$$

Note that $\mathrm{On}(i, t_1, t_2) \le \rho_i$ for any job i and any time interval $[t_1, t_2]$.

Similarly, for each job $i \in [n]$, let $\mathrm{Opt}(i, t_1, t_2)$ denote the total amount of parallel work for job i done by OPT during $[t_1, t_2]$. Since we had assumed that OPT works on a job only if it is in a parallel phase, we have that

$$\mathrm{Opt}(i, t_1, t_2) := \int_{t_1}^{t_2} x_i^*(t) dt$$

We will then introduce the following variable that will be used in our potential function to keep track of parallel work for job i:

$$z_i(t) = \frac{\mathrm{On}(i, t, \infty) \cdot \mathrm{Opt}(i, a_i, t)}{\rho_i}$$

As for sequential work, let $y_i(t)$ denote how much the adversary OPT is ahead of WLAPS in the sequential work of job i at time t. If WLAPS is ahead of the adversary in the sequential work, $y_i(t)$ is set to zero.

Once again, recall that $N_a(t)$ denotes the set of jobs that are yet unfinished at time t by the algorithm WLAPS. Similarly, define $N_o(t)$ to denote the jobs alive under OPT's schedule.

Our potential function $\Phi(t)$ is defined as follows

$$\Phi(t) := \frac{1}{\beta} \sum_{i \in N_a(t)} z_i(t) \sum_{a_j \le a_i, j \in N_a(t)} w_j(t) + \frac{8k}{\beta^3} \sum_{i \in N_a(t)} w_i(t) y_i(t)$$

For the remainder of this section, our goal is to show the following bound

$$\frac{d}{dt} A(t) + \frac{d}{dt} \Phi(t) \le \frac{16k^3}{\beta^3} \frac{d}{dt} \mathrm{OPT}(t) \qquad (4)$$

Here $\frac{d}{dt} A(t) = \sum_{i \in N_a(t)} w_i(t)$ denotes the rate of increase of the objective function for WLAPS, and $\frac{d}{dt} \mathrm{OPT}(t)$ denotes the analogous quantity for the optimal schedule OPT. (some exceptional details should be taken care of). Since $\Phi(0) = \Phi(\infty) = 0$, this would suffice to analyze competitive ratio of WLAPS, by a simple amortized analysis (by integrating both sides of the above inequality from 0 to ∞).

In order to show equation (4), let $\Phi_1(t)$ and $\Phi_2(t)$ denote the first and the second term in $\Phi(t)$ respectively. For ease of analysis, we will separately investigate the change of $\Phi(t)$ for the following events, and then put the pieces together.

Change of the Potential Function: We will first consider time instants that induce discontinuities in Φ and show that it does not jump abruptly. It is easy to see that the only sources of discontinuity is when new jobs arrive, and when jobs are completed by WLAPS (in which case they leave the set $N_a(t)$). We consider these two situations now.

Job Arrival: We show that $\Delta\Phi = 0$. When a job i arrives at time t, $z_i(t) = y_i(t) = 0$ because the optimal solution has not had a chance to work on job i yet. It is easy to see that any new terms which appear are zero, since the jobs are indexed according to their arrival time. Thus, $\Delta\Phi = 0$.

Job Completion for WLAPS: When a job i is completed by the online algorithm, some terms may disappear from $\Phi(t)$. Since all terms are always non-negative, $\Delta\Phi(t) \le 0$.

We now consider an infinitesimally small time interval $[t, t + dt)$ and show that the equation (4) holds. To show this, we individually consider the various changes that occur to Φ, and collect them all at the end.

Processing by OPT: The amount of parallel work for job $i \in N_a(t)$ done by the adversary in $[t, t + dt)$ is at most $x_i^*(t) dt$. Thus,

$$
\begin{aligned}
\Delta\Phi_1(t) &\le \frac{1}{\beta} \sum_{i \in N_a(t)} \frac{\mathrm{On}(i, t, \infty) \cdot x_i^*(t) dt}{\rho_i} \sum_{a_j \le a_i, j \in N_a(t)} w_j(t) \\
&\le \frac{1}{\beta} dt \sum_{i \in N_a(t)} x_i^*(t) \sum_{a_j \le a_i, j \in N_a(t)} w_j(t) \\
&\le \frac{1}{\beta} dt \sum_{i \in N_a(t)} x_i^*(t) \frac{d}{dt} A(t) \\
&\le \frac{1}{\beta} \frac{d}{dt} A(t) \, dt \quad [\text{since } \textstyle\sum_i x_i^*(t) \le 1]
\end{aligned}
$$

We now consider $\Delta\Phi_2(t)$. The maximum increase occurs when all jobs in $N_o(t)$ are in sequential phase. Since $y_i(t)$ could increase by dt for each job $i \in N_o(t) \cap N_a(t)$, we have $\Delta\Phi_2(t) \le \frac{8k}{\beta^3} \sum_{i \in N_o(t)} w_i(t) dt \le \frac{8k}{\beta^3} \Delta\mathrm{OPT}(t)$. Hence,

$$\frac{d}{dt} \Phi(t) \le \frac{1}{\beta} \frac{d}{dt} A(t) + \frac{8k}{\beta^3} \frac{d}{dt} \mathrm{OPT}(t)$$

Processing by WLAPS: We partition $N_a(t)$ into $\mathcal{S}(t)$ and $\mathcal{P}(t)$ depending on whether a job in $N_a(t)$ is in sequential phase or parallel phase at time t under the schedule by WLAPS. Also, let $\mathcal{P}'(t) := N'_a(t) \cap \mathcal{P}(t)$ denote the set of jobs that WLAPS is working on at time t, which are in their parallel phases.

Consider any job $i \in \mathcal{P}'(t) \setminus N_o(t)$. Since OPT has already finished job i, we have that $z_i(t) = \mathrm{On}(i, t, \infty)$. Furthermore,

$z_i(t)$ decreases at a rate of $-s\frac{w_i(t)}{\beta w(t)}$ by definition of our algorithm. Also we have that $\sum_{j\in N_a, a_j\leq a_i} w_j(t) \geq (1-\beta)w(t)$ from the fact that $i \in N_a'(t)$. Hence,

$$\frac{d}{dt}\Phi_1(t) \leq -\frac{s}{\beta}\sum_{i\in\mathcal{P}'(t)\setminus N_o(t)} \frac{w_i(t)}{\beta w(t)}\sum_{j\in N_a(t),a_j\leq a_i} w_j(t)$$

$$\leq -\frac{s(1-\beta)}{\beta^2}\sum_{i\in\mathcal{P}'(t)\setminus N_o(t)} w_i(t)$$

For any job $i \in \mathcal{S}(t)\setminus N_o(t)$, whether WLAPS works on i or not, the rate of change of $y_i(t)$ is -1, since i is in a sequential phase and OPT has completed the job. Thus $\frac{d}{dt}\Phi_2(t) \leq -\frac{8k}{\beta^3}\sum_{i\in\mathcal{S}(t)\setminus N_o(t)} w_i(t)$. In sum, we have that

$$\frac{d}{dt}\Phi(t) \leq -\frac{s(1-\beta)}{\beta^2}\sum_{i\in\mathcal{P}'(t)\setminus N_o(t)} w_i(t) - \frac{8k}{\beta^3}\sum_{i\in\mathcal{S}(t)\setminus N_o(t)} w_i(t)$$

In the remaining case, the following lemma will be used.

Lemma 2.1 *For any job* $j \in [n]$, $\sum_{i\in[n],a_i\geq a_j} \mathtt{Opt}(i,a_i,t) \leq t-a_j$.

Proof: Consider any job i such that $a_i \geq a_j$. Note that OPT did $\mathtt{Opt}(i,a_i,t)$ amount of parallel work for job i during $[a_i,t]$, therefore during $[a_j,t]$. The lemma immediately follows from the fact that the adversary is given only speed 1. ∎

Time Elapse: We investigate the increase rate of the potential function only due to time elapsing.

$$\frac{d}{dt}\Phi_1(t) = \frac{1}{\beta}\sum_{i\in N_a(t)} z_i(t)\sum_{j\in N_a(t),a_j\leq a_i} k(k-1)(t-a_j)^{k-2}$$

$$= \frac{1}{\beta}k(k-1)\sum_{j\in N_a(t)}(t-a_j)^{k-2}\sum_{i\in N_a(t),a_i\geq a_j} z_i(t)$$

But notice that $z_i(t) = \frac{\mathtt{On}(i,t,\infty)\cdot \mathtt{Opt}(i,a_i,t)}{\rho_i} \leq \mathtt{Opt}(i,a_i,t)$, since $\mathtt{On}(i,t,\infty) \leq \rho_i$. Therefore, we get that $\frac{d}{dt}\Phi_1(t)$ is at most

$$\frac{1}{\beta}k(k-1)\sum_{j\in N_a(t)}(t-a_j)^{k-2}\sum_{i\in N_a(t),a_i\geq a_j}\mathtt{Opt}(i,a_i,t)$$

$$\leq \frac{1}{\beta}k(k-1)\sum_{j\in N_a(t)}(t-a_j)^{k-2}(t-a_j) \quad\text{[By Lemma 2.1]}$$

$$= \frac{1}{\beta}k(k-1)\sum_{j\in N_a(t)}(t-a_j)^{k-1} = \frac{1}{\beta}(k-1)\frac{d}{dt}A(t)$$

Before addressing $\frac{d}{dt}\Phi_2(t)$ due to time, notice that for any job i, it holds that $(t-a_i) \geq y_i(t)$ because $y_i(t)$ amount of time is required to complete $y_i(t)$ amount of sequential work of job i.

$$\frac{d}{dt}\Phi_2(t) = \frac{8k}{\beta^3}\sum_{i\in N_a(t)} k(k-1)(t-a_i)^{k-2}y_i(t)$$

$$\leq \frac{8k^2}{\beta^3}(k-1)\sum_{i\in N_a(t)}(t-a_i)^{k-2}y_i(t)$$

In sum we obtain

$$\frac{d}{dt}\Phi(t) \leq \frac{1}{\beta}(k-1)\frac{d}{dt}A(t) +$$

$$\frac{8k^2}{\beta^3}(k-1)\sum_{i\in N_a(t)}(t-a_i)^{k-2}y_i(t) \quad (5)$$

We now want to bound $\sum_{i\in N_a(t)}(t-a_i)^{k-2}y_i(t)$ by $\frac{d}{dt}A(t)$. Now, since we know that $y_i(t) \leq (t-a_i)$, it is easy to see that $k\sum_{i\in N_a(t)}(t-a_i)^{k-2}y_i(t) \leq \frac{d}{dt}A(t)$. However, this bound does not suffice for the rest of the analysis, because of the magnitude of the constant sitting in front of this term (which is $\frac{8k^2}{\beta^3}(k-1)$). To handle this issue, we only consider the jobs which are "*old*" when compared to $\frac{8k^2}{\beta^3}\sigma_i$, for this sum, and terms due to all other "*young*" jobs will be accounted for, separately. The trick to do this is simple. For all $i \in N_a(t)$, we charge $(t-a_i)^{k-2}y_i(t)$ *directly* to the optimal solution as long as $t-a_i \leq \frac{8k^2}{\beta^3}\sigma_i$; this can be done since OPT requires at least σ_i amount of time to get job i done.

Lemma 2.2 *The total contribution of all the young jobs, integrated over time is at most* $(\frac{8k^2}{\beta^3})^k \text{OPT}$

Proof: Consider any job i. We now show that that the *total* contribution of the term $(t-a_i)^{k-2}y_i(t)$ over all times at which i remains young (i.e. $(t-a_i) \leq \frac{8k^2}{\beta^3}\sigma_i$) can be bounded by the cost it incurs in OPT's schedule. This can then be charged to the optimal solution by adding an extra factor to the competitive ratio. More specifically, the total increase (summed over all jobs) can be at most

$$\sum_{i\in[n]}\int_{a_i}^{a_i+\frac{8k^2}{\beta^3}\sigma_i}\frac{8k^2}{\beta^3}(k-1)(t-a_i)^{k-2}y_i(t)\,dt$$

$$\leq \sum_{i\in[n]}(\frac{8k^2}{\beta^3}\sigma_i)^k$$

$$\leq (\frac{8k^2}{\beta^3})^k\text{OPT}.$$

The last inequality holds knowing that $\text{OPT} \geq \sum_{i\in[n]}(\sigma_i)^k$ because each job i takes at least σ_i time units to complete in the optimal solution's schedule. ∎

Since we can handle all young jobs in the above fashion, let us only consider old jobs, such that $t-a_i \geq \frac{8k^2}{\beta^3}\sigma_i \geq \frac{8k^2}{\beta^3}y_i$. In the worst case, all the jobs are old. In this case, equation (5) can be simplified to,

$$\frac{d}{dt}\Phi(t) \leq (\frac{1}{\beta}+1)(k-1)\frac{d}{dt}A(t).$$

Final Step of the Analysis:

Recall that throughout the analysis, our main goal has been to show that

$$\frac{d}{dt}A(t) + \frac{d}{dt}\Phi(t) \leq \frac{16k^3}{\beta^3}\frac{d}{dt}\text{OPT}(t) \quad (6)$$

We first complete this proof, and then show how this leads us to the desired guarantees. By summing up the change (rate) of $\Phi(t)$ for all the cases, it is easy to see that showing the following inequality, is sufficient for showing that in equation (6) holds.

$$\frac{8k^3}{\beta^3}\frac{d}{dt}\mathrm{OPT}(t) \geq (\frac{1}{\beta}+1)k\frac{d}{dt}A(t) - \frac{s(1-\beta)}{\beta^2}\sum_{i\in\mathcal{P}'(t)\setminus N_o(t)}w_i(t) - \frac{8k}{\beta^3}\sum_{i\in\mathcal{S}(t)\setminus N_o(t)}w_i(t)$$

To this end, we consider the following three cases.

(a) $\frac{d}{dt}\mathrm{OPT}(t) \geq \frac{\beta^2}{4}\frac{d}{dt}A(t)$: This is the simplest case. Since the adversary has unfinished jobs whose total weight is significant, we can charge the positive term involving $\frac{d}{dt}A(t)$ to $\frac{d}{dt}\mathrm{OPT}(t)$. Formally, $(\frac{1}{\beta}+1)k\frac{d}{dt}A(t) \leq \frac{2k}{\beta}\frac{4}{\beta^2}\frac{d}{dt}\mathrm{OPT}(t) \leq \frac{8k^2}{\beta^3}\frac{d}{dt}\mathrm{OPT}(t)$.

(b) $\sum_{i\in\mathcal{S}(t)\setminus N_o(t)}w_i(t) \geq \frac{\beta^2}{4}\frac{d}{dt}A(t)$: In this case, the second negative term for jobs in $\mathcal{S}(t)$ will be used to offset the positive term. Indeed, we have $(\frac{1}{\beta}+1)k\frac{d}{dt}A(t) - \frac{8k}{\beta^3}\sum_{i\in\mathcal{S}(t)\setminus N_o(t)}w_i(t) \leq \frac{2k}{\beta}\frac{d}{dt}A(t) - \frac{2k}{\beta}\frac{d}{dt}A(t) \leq 0$

(c) $\frac{d}{dt}\mathrm{OPT}(t) < \frac{\beta^2}{4}\frac{d}{dt}A(t)$ and $\sum_{i\in\mathcal{S}(t)\setminus N_o(t)}w_i(t) < \frac{\beta^2}{4}\frac{d}{dt}A(t)$: This is the final case, where the first negative term involving parallel-phase jobs will override the positive term. Since $\mathcal{P}'(t)\setminus N_o(t) = (N_a'(t)\cap\mathcal{P}(t))\setminus N_o(t) = N_a'(t)\setminus\mathcal{S}(t)\setminus N_o(t)$, it follows that $\sum_{i\in\mathcal{P}'(t)\setminus N_o(t)}w_i(t) \geq \sum_{i\in N_a'(t)}w_i(t) - \sum_{i\in\mathcal{S}(t)}w_i(t) - \sum_{i\in N_o(t)}w_i(t) \geq \beta(1-\frac{1}{2}\beta)\frac{d}{dt}A(t)$. Substituting $s = k(1+16\beta)$ we obtain,

$$(\frac{1}{\beta}+1)k\frac{d}{dt}A(t) - \frac{s(1-\beta)}{\beta^2}\sum_{i\in\mathcal{P}'(t)\setminus N_o(t)}w_i(t)$$
$$\leq \left((\frac{1}{\beta}+1)k - \frac{k(1+16\beta)(1-\beta)(1-\frac{1}{2}\beta)}{\beta}\right)\frac{d}{dt}A(t)$$
$$\leq \frac{k}{\beta}\left((1+\beta) - (1+16\beta)(1-\frac{3}{2}\beta)\right)\frac{d}{dt}A(t)$$
$$\leq 12k(-1+2\beta)\frac{d}{dt}A(t) \leq 0 \quad [\text{By } 0 < \beta \leq \frac{1}{2}]$$

And this completes the proof that equation (6) holds at all times. To complete the analysis, let WLAPS_s denote the total cost incurred by WLAPS (when given a speed of s), and OPT_1 denote the cost of the optimal schedule (operating at unit speed). We have that the cost incurred by WLAPS_s is

$$\int_0^\infty \frac{d}{dt}A(t)dt = \int_0^\infty(\frac{d}{dt}A(t) + \frac{d}{dt}\Phi(t))dt$$
$$\leq \int_0^\infty\left(\frac{16k^3}{\beta^3}\frac{d}{dt}\mathrm{OPT}(t)dt\right) + (\frac{8k^2}{\beta^3})^k\mathrm{OPT}_1$$
$$= (\frac{16k^3}{\beta^3} + (\frac{8k^2}{\beta^3})^k)\mathrm{OPT}_1 \leq 2(\frac{8k^2}{\beta^3})^k\mathrm{OPT}_1$$

Here, the second equality easily follows from the fact that $\Phi(0) = \Phi(\infty) = 0$. The third inequality follows from in-

equality (6). The additional term is due to the fact that we had not accounted for the contribution of "young" jobs towards $\frac{d}{dt}\Phi(t)$ in (6), but showed (in Lemma 2.2) that the total cost integrated over time is at most $(\frac{8k^2}{\beta^3})^k\mathrm{OPT}_1$. As a result, by scaling the speed WLAPS is given, we obtain the following theorem.

Theorem 2.3 *Let $0 < \beta \leq \frac{1}{2}$ be a constant. Then WLAPS is $k(1+16\beta)$-speed $\frac{16k^2}{\beta^3}$-competitive for the problem of minimizing ℓ_k norm flow time with arbitrary speed up curves.*

Remark 2.4 *The assumption $0 < \beta \leq \frac{1}{2}$ that is used in Theorem 2.3 is not essential in the analysis. Rather, it is to make our analysis relatively simpler.*

3. LIMITATION OF LAPS FOR ℓ_K-NORM SCHEDULING

In this section, we show that for minimizing ℓ_k-norm flow time LAPS performs poor in the non-work-preserving setting. More specifically, we will test LAPS in the scheduling setting with arbitrary speedup curves and broadcast scheduling setting.

We first show that LAPS can be arbitrarily bad even with any constant speed given for jobs with arbitrarily speedup curves. The main idea of constructing the adversarial example is to repeatedly request fully sequential jobs to prevent LAPS from working on parallel jobs. Consequently, LAPS wastes its processing power procrastinating parallel jobs substantially; unlike in L_1-norm flow time, these delayed jobs will cause a huge penalty.

Theorem 3.1 *Let $k \geq 2$ be an integer. For any $0 < \beta \leq 1$, the algorithm LAPS_β is not $O(1)$-competitive even with any constant speed given for the problem of minimizing ℓ_k norm flow time where jobs have arbitrarily speed up curves.*

Proof: Recall that LAPS works on only β fraction of alive jobs which arrived most recently. Let σ denote the adversarial instance. For simplicity of our argument, suppose that LAPS is given an integer speed $s > 1$. Let $\mathrm{LAPS}_s(\sigma)$ and $\mathrm{OPT}_1(\sigma)$ denote the kth power of flow time for the given instance σ; the subscript s and 1 are used to denote the speed LAPS and OPT are given, respectively. Let $M > 0$ be a sufficiently large integer which will be defined later. The instance σ is constructed as follows.

- At time 0, one fully parallelizable job j_0 having size M arrives.

- At each integer time $t \in [0, M^2 - 1]$, sM sequential unit-sized jobs arrive. Let $\mathcal{J}_t$ denote the set of sequential jobs that arrive at time t.

Note that all sM jobs in $\mathcal{J}_t$ are unsatisfied by LAPS during $[t, t + 1)$, since they are unit-sized sequential jobs. Therefore during $[0, M^2]$, as long as j_0 is alive, it is processed at a rate of at most $\frac{1}{M}$, since even in the best case $\beta = 1$, it equally shares the processors with other sM sequential jobs. Thus job j_0 is not finished until time M^2, which implies that $\mathrm{LAPS}_s(\sigma) \geq (M^2)^k$. To the contrary, let OPT work on only job j_0. Then job j_0 is finished at time M, and all sequential jobs are finished in one time step. Hence, $\mathrm{OPT}_1(\sigma) \leq M^k + sM^3$. It is easy to check that $\mathrm{LAPS}_s(\sigma)/\mathrm{OPT}_1(\sigma) \to \infty$ as $M \to \infty$. ∎

Using a similar idea, we can show a negative result for broadcast scheduling.

Theorem 3.2 *Let $k \geq 2$ be an integer. For any $0 < \beta \leq 1$, the algorithm* LAPS *is not $O(1)$-competitive even with any constant speed for the problem of minimizing ℓ_k norm flow time in broadcast scheduling where pages are varying sized.*

Proof: Let σ denote the adversarial instance. For simplicity, suppose that LAPS is given an integer speed $s > 1$. Let $\mathrm{LAPS}_s(\sigma)$ and $\mathrm{OPT}_1(\sigma)$ denote the kth power of flow time for the given instance σ; the subscript s and 1 are used to denote the speedup LAPS and OPT are given respectively. Let M be a sufficiently large integer which will be defined later. The instance σ is defined as follows.

- At time 0, a request r_0 for page p having size M, arrives.
- At each integer time $t \in [0, M^2 - 1]$, sM requests for page q having size s, arrive.

We first investigate the schedule by LAPS. We observe that during the interval $[0, M^2]$ there are at least sM alive requests. This is because the new requests which are released at each integer time $t \in [0, M^2 - 1]$ cannot be satisfied within unit time, since they are asking for pages having size s. As a result, the request r_0 is processed at a rate of at most $\frac{1}{M}$ for each unit time slot. Hence request is not satisfied until time M^2 and we obtain $\mathrm{LAPS}(\sigma)_s \geq M^{2k}$.

We now shift our attention to the schedule by OPT. We let OPT work on r_0 during $[t, t+1)$ for every odd integer t until request r_0 is finished. Thus, r_0 will be satisfied at time $2M$. For other empty time slots, we let OPT broadcast page q sequentially in a round robin fashion. Notice that this implies that a request for page q is satisfied in at most $4s$ time steps. Hence we have that $\mathrm{OPT}_1(\sigma) \leq (2M)^k + sM^3(4s)^k$. It is easy to see that $\mathrm{LAPS}_s(\sigma)/\mathrm{OPT}_1(\sigma)$ goes to infinity as $M \to \infty$. ∎

4. BROADCAST SCHEDULING FOR VARYING SIZED PAGES

In this section, we address the problem of minimizing ℓ_k-norm flow time in broadcast scheduling where pages have non-uniform sizes. Recently, Bansal et al. [1] gave a very clean solution for the same problem when $k = 1$, which is the inspiration of our algorithm and analysis. The problem is formally defined as follows: There are n pages stored at the server and each page p has an integer size σ_p; it is composed of σ_p unit-sized parts, $\{(p, i) \mid i \in [\sigma_p]\}$. For each integer time t, the server can transmit one part of a specific page p during $[t - 1, t)$. Each request $r \in [m]$ asking for a page p_r arrives at the server at time a_r in online fashion. Request r is satisfied when it receives all points $\{(p, i) \mid i \in [\sigma_p]\}$ *in the order of* $(p, 1), (p, 2), ..., (p, \sigma_p)$, but not necessarily contiguously. Let C_r denote the time when the request r is satisfied. The goal is to give a scheduling of the server which minimize the ℓ_k-norm of the flow times, i.e. $(\sum_r (C_r - a_r)^k)^{1/k}$. Again, like in the previous sections, this is equivalent to minimizing $(\sum_r (C_r - a_r)^k)$, and this is the objective function which we will focus on optimizing.

4.1 The Fractional Algorithm WLAPS for Broadcast Scheduling

We use the same algorithm WLAPS with some small modifications. However, our algorithm is a *fractional* algorithm in the sense that it is allowed to transmit an infinitesimal amount of data for more than one pages during any arbitrarily short interval. Furthermore, the notion of when a request is *fractionally completed* is different from our original requirement: suppose that our algorithm WLAPS broadcasts each page $p \in [n]$ at rate of $y_p(t)$. Then, in the fractional setting, we say that a request r is completed at time

$$C_r := \inf\{t : \int_{a_r}^t y_p(t)dt \geq \sigma_p\}.$$

In words, C_r is the earliest time when σ_p units of page p are broadcast after a_r. Notice that we require nothing about the order of the unit-sized components in this definition of fractional completion. To fix this issue, we can then apply the rounding technique of Bansal et al. [1] (Section 5.3) to convert such a fractional solution to one which is integral with an additional loss in the competitive ratio.

4.2 Notation

Our notation is similar to that used in earlier sections. Let $N_a(t)$ denote the set of unsatisfied requests at time t, i.e. all those requests r such that $t < C_r$. For each request $r \in N_a(t)$, let us define its *weight* at time t to be $w_r(t) = k(t - a_r)^{k-1}$. Among the set of requests $N_a(t)$, let $N'_a(t)$ denote those requests with the *latest arrival times* whose weights sum up to $\beta w(t)$, where $w(t) = \sum_{r \in N_a(t)} w_r(t)$; here we, as did in Section 2.2, rely on the same simplifying assumption that there exists a set of latest arriving requests whose total weight is exactly $\beta w(t)$.

4.3 Algorithm

The algorithm is similar to WLAPS, except that it shares its processing power based on the requests which are yet unsatisfied. At any time t, the algorithm WLAPS distributes its processing power among the requests in $N'_a(t)$, in proportion to their weights at time t. Let $x_r(t)$ denote the fraction of processing power request r receives at time t under the schedule of WLAPS. Then,

$$x_r(t) := s \cdot \frac{w_r(t)}{\beta w(t)}, \quad \forall r \in N'_a(t)$$

What this means is the following: whenever the algorithm devotes processing towards a request r, it broadcasts the page p_r at a rate of $x_r(t)$ at time t. Note that if there are several unsatisfied requests for the same page p, the total rate at which p is broadcast at time t is then $y_p(t) = \sum_{r \in N'_a(t), p_r = p} x_r(t)$. It is important to note that although request r is processed at a rate of $y_{p_r}(t)$ due to other requests for the same page p_r, the fraction of processing power dedicated to request r is only $x_r(t)$. For this reason, sometimes we will say that $x_r(t)$ is the *share* of request r at time t.

4.4 Analysis

The analysis again employs a potential function based argument. Let $y_p^*(t)$ denote the transmission rate of page p by OPT at time t. For each request $p \in [n]$, let $\mathrm{Opt}(p, t_1, t_2)$

denote the total amount for page p transmitted by OPT during $[t_1, t_2]$, i.e.

$$\texttt{Opt}(p, t_1, t_2) := \int_{t_1}^{t_2} y_p^*(t) dt$$

For any request $r \in [m]$, define the *total share* for request r during $[t_1, t_2]$, denoted by $\texttt{On}(r, t_1, t_2)$. Formally,

$$\texttt{On}(r, t_1, t_2) := \int_{t_1}^{t_2} x_r(t) dt$$

Again, notice that $\texttt{On}(r, a_r, C_r)$ could be much smaller than σ_p if there are multiple pending requests for the same page p_r. We now define a variable z_r for each request r which will be used to define the potential function $\Phi(t)$.

$$z_r(t) = \frac{\texttt{On}(r, t, \infty) \cdot \texttt{Opt}(p_r, a_r, t)}{\sigma_{p_r}}$$

The potential function $\Phi(t)$ is then defined as follows.

$$\Phi(t) := \frac{2}{\epsilon} \sum_{r \in N_a(t)} z_r(t) \sum_{a_{r'} \leq a_r, r' \in N_a(t)} w_{r'}(t)$$

We start by investigating the change of the potential function for all possible events.

Change of the Potential Function

Request Arrival: When a request r arrives at time t, $z_r(t) = 0$ because the optimal solution has not had a chance to work on request r yet. It is easy to see that any new terms which appear are zero, since the requests are indexed according to their arrival time. Thus $\Delta\Phi = 0$.

Request Completion by WLAPS: When a request r is completed, r is removed from $N_a(t)$. As a result, some terms may disappear from $\Phi(t)$. This can only decrease Φ, since all terms are non-negative in $\Phi(t)$. Thus $\Delta\Phi(t) \leq 0$.

Processing by OPT: Fix a sufficiently small interval $[t, t+dt]$. Consider any page $p \in [n]$. The amount that OPT broadcasts for page p is $y_p^*(t) dt$. Let $\mathcal{R}(t, p)$ denote all requests for page p which are not satisfied yet under the schedule by WLAPS at time t. Formally,

$$\mathcal{R}(t, p) := \{r \in [m] \mid p_r = p, a_r \leq t < C_r\}$$

The total increase of the potential function is at most

$$\frac{2}{\epsilon} \sum_p \sum_{r \in \mathcal{R}(t,p)} \frac{\texttt{On}(r, t, \infty) \cdot y_p^*(t) dt}{\sigma_p} \sum_{a_{r'} \leq a_r, r' \in N_a(t)} w_{r'}(t)$$

Following the argument of [1] (Section 5.2), we can show that $\sum_{r \in \mathcal{R}(t,p)} \texttt{On}(r, t, \infty) \leq \sigma_p$ as in [1]. The idea is the following: all the requests in $\mathcal{R}(t, p)$ are yet unsatisfied at time t, but none of them will be unsatisfied, once a collective total of σ_p units of this page are transmitted *in the future*. Hence, it must be that total share of processing devoted to these requests in the future cannot exceed σ_p.

Now, by combining this observation with the fact that $\sum_p y_p^*(t) \leq 1$ (since the optimal offline solution is only given unit speed), we obtain

$$\Delta\Phi(t) \leq \frac{2}{\epsilon} dt \sum_p y_p^*(t) \sum_{r \in \mathcal{R}(t,p)} \frac{\texttt{On}(r, t, \infty)}{\sigma_p} \sum_{a_{r'} \leq a_r, r' \in N_a(t)} w_{r'}(t)$$

$$\leq \frac{2}{\epsilon} dt \sum_p y_p^*(t) \sum_{r \in \mathcal{R}(t,p)} \frac{\texttt{On}(r, t, \infty)}{\sigma_p} \sum_{r' \in N_a(t)} w_{r'}(t)$$

$$\leq \frac{2}{\epsilon} \Delta A(t)$$

Processing by WLAPS: Consider any request $r \in N_a'(t) \backslash N_o(t)$. Since OPT has already finished the request r, we have that $\frac{\texttt{Opt}(p_r, a_r, t)}{\sigma_{p_r}} \geq 1$. Thus, $z_r(t) \geq \texttt{On}(r, t, \infty)$. Moreover, since $r \in N_a'(t)$, $\texttt{On}(r, t, \infty)$ *decreases* at a rate of $x_r(t) = s \frac{w_r(t)}{\beta w(t)}$. Therefore, $z_r(t)$ also decreases at at least the same rate. Additionally we also have that $\sum_{r' \in N_a, a_{r'} \leq a_r} w_{r'}(t) \geq (1 - \beta) w(t)$, again because $r \in N_a'(t)$. As a consequence, we have

$$\frac{d}{dt}\Phi(t) \leq -\frac{2}{\epsilon} \sum_{r \in N_a'(t) \backslash N_o(t)} \frac{s\, w_r(t)}{\beta w(t)} \sum_{r' \in N_a(t), a_{r'} \leq a_r} w_{r'}(t)$$

$$\leq -\frac{2}{\epsilon} \sum_{r \in N_a'(t) \backslash N_o(t)} \frac{s\, w_r(t)}{\beta w(t)} (1 - \beta) w(t)$$

$$= -\frac{2s(1 - \beta)}{\beta \epsilon} \sum_{r \in N_a'(t) \backslash N_o(t)} w_r(t)$$

$$\leq -\frac{2s(1 - \beta)}{\beta \epsilon} \left(\sum_{r \in N_a'(t)} w_r(t) - \sum_{r \in N_o(t)} w_r(t) \right)$$

$$= -\frac{2s(1 - \beta)}{\epsilon} \frac{d}{dt} A(t) + \frac{2s(1 - \beta)}{\beta \epsilon} \frac{d}{dt} \text{OPT}(t)$$

Time Elapse: Recall that $\mathcal{R}(t, p)$ denotes the set of all requests that are yet unsatisfied for page p under the schedule of WLAPS at time t.

$$\frac{d}{dt}\Phi(t) = \frac{2}{\epsilon} \sum_{r \in N_a(t)} z_r(t) \sum_{r' \in N_a(t), a_{r'} \leq a_r} k(k-1)(t - a_{r'})^{k-2}$$

$$= \frac{2}{\epsilon} k(k-1) \sum_{r' \in N_a(t)} (t - a_{r'})^{k-2} \sum_{r \in N_a(t), a_r \geq a_{r'}} z_r(t)$$

But again, notice that in the inner summation, we have $z_r(t) = \frac{\texttt{On}(r,t,\infty) \cdot \texttt{Opt}(p, a_r, t)}{\sigma_p} \leq \frac{\texttt{On}(r,t,\infty) \cdot \texttt{Opt}(p, a_{r'}, t)}{\sigma_p}$, since $a_{r'} \leq a_r$. Thus, we can obtain the following set of inequalities

$$\sum_{r \in N_a(t), a_r \geq a_{r'}} z_r(t) = \sum_p \sum_{r \in \mathcal{R}(p,t), a_r \geq a_{r'}} z_r(t)$$

$$\leq \sum_{r \in cR(p,t), a_r \geq a_{r'}} \frac{\texttt{On}(r, t, \infty) \cdot \texttt{Opt}(p, a_{r'}, t)}{\sigma_p}$$

$$\leq \texttt{Opt}(p, a_{r'}, t)$$

The last inequality is because $\sum_{r \in \mathcal{R}(p,t)} \texttt{On}(r, t, \infty) \leq \sigma_p$, following the arguments in [1] (Section 5.2). Moreover, recall that $\texttt{Opt}(p, a_{r'}, t)$ is the amount of processing OPT spent on page p during $[a_{r'}, t]$. Since the optimal solution has one speed, the total amount of all pages transmitted in the interval $[a_{r'}, t]$ can be at most $(t - a_{r'})$. Therefore, we get

19

$$\frac{d}{dt}\Phi(t) \leq \frac{2}{\epsilon}k(k-1)\sum_{r'\in N_a(t)}(t-a_{r'})^{k-2}(t-a_{r'})$$
$$= \frac{2}{\epsilon}(k-1)\frac{d}{dt}A(t)$$

Final Step of Analysis

We show that $\frac{d}{dt}A(t) + \frac{d}{dt}\Phi(t) \leq \frac{8k}{\epsilon^2}\frac{d}{dt}\mathrm{OPT}(t)$. Let $\beta = \frac{\epsilon}{4k}$. Recall that $s = k + \epsilon$. By summing up all the change (rate) of $\Phi(t)$ for all the events, we obtain

$$\frac{d}{dt}A(t) + \frac{d}{dt}\Phi(t) \leq \left(1 + \frac{2k}{\epsilon} - \frac{2s(1-\beta)}{\epsilon}\right)\frac{d}{dt}A(t) +$$
$$\frac{2s(1-\beta)}{\beta\epsilon}\frac{d}{dt}\mathrm{OPT}(t)$$
$$= (-\frac{1}{2} + \frac{\epsilon}{2k})\frac{d}{dt}A(t) + \frac{16k^2}{\epsilon^2}\frac{d}{dt}\mathrm{OPT}(t)$$
$$\leq \frac{16k^2}{\epsilon^2}\frac{d}{dt}\mathrm{OPT}(t)$$

With the fact that $\Phi(0) = \Phi(\infty) = 0$, the following theorem easily follows.

Theorem 4.1 *For any $0 < \epsilon \leq 1$, there exists a $(k + \epsilon)$-speed $(\frac{4k}{\epsilon})^{2/k}$-competitive deterministic online algorithm which gives a fractional broadcast schedule for minimizing ℓ_k norm flow time.*

4.5 Rounding to Integer Broadcast Schedule

Bansal et al. [1] (Section 5.3) show a very elegant deterministic rounding algorithm which takes a 1-speed fractional broadcast schedule and yields $(1+\delta)$-speed integer broadcast schedule satisfying the following property: for any request r, $C_r^I - a_r \leq \frac{3}{\delta}(C_r - a_r) + \frac{5}{\delta}$, where C_r^I denotes the finish time of r under the integer broadcast schedule. By applying this rounding technique to Theorem 4.1, we obtain an integer broadcast schedule, which completes our analysis.

Theorem 4.2 *Let $k \geq 1$ be a constant. For any $0 < \epsilon \leq 1$, there exists a $(k + \epsilon)$-speed $O((\frac{1}{\epsilon})^{1+2/k})$-competitive deterministic online algorithm in broadcast scheduling for minimizing ℓ_k norm flow time.*

5. CONCLUSION

In this paper we showed how to obtain a $(2 + \epsilon)$-speed $O(1)$-competitive algorithm for scheduling jobs with arbitrary speed-up curves for the ℓ_2 norm of flow. Currently we do not know whether WLAPS is scalable or not. To find an scalable algorithm, either showing that WLAPS is scalable or finding another algorithm, would be a good problem worthy of attention.

Acknowledgments: The authors thank Nikhil Bansal for his helpful discussion about this problem. Sungjin Im and Benjamin Moseley thank Chandra Chekuri for his support and encouragement.

6. REFERENCES

[1] Nikhil Bansal, Ravishankar Krishnaswamy, and Viswanath Nagarajan. Better scalable algorithms for broadcast scheduling. Technical report, Carnegie Mellon University, 2009.

[2] Nikhil Bansal and Kirk Pruhs. Server scheduling in the lp norm: a rising tide lifts all boat. In *ACM Symposium on Theory of Computing*, pages 242–250, 2003.

[3] Luca Becchetti and Stefano Leonardi. Nonclairvoyant scheduling to minimize the total flow time on single and parallel machines. *J. ACM*, 51(4):517–539, 2004.

[4] Ho-Leung Chan, Jeff Edmonds, and Kirk Pruhs. Speed scaling of processes with arbitrary speedup curves on a multiprocessor. In *SPAA*, pages 1–10, 2009.

[5] Jeff Edmonds. Scheduling in the dark. *Theor. Comput. Sci.*, 235(1):109–141, 2000.

[6] Jeff Edmonds, Donald D. Chinn, Tim Brecht, and Xiaotie Deng. Non-clairvoyant multiprocessor scheduling of jobs with changing execution characteristics. *J. Scheduling*, 6(3):231–250, 2003.

[7] Jeff Edmonds and Kirk Pruhs. Multicast pull scheduling: When fairness is fine. *Algorithmica*, 36(3):315–330, 2003.

[8] Jeff Edmonds and Kirk Pruhs. Scalably scheduling processes with arbitrary speedup curves. In *SODA*, pages 685–692, 2009.

[9] Sungjin Im and Benjamin Moseley. An online scalable algorithm for average flow time in broadcast scheduling. In *ACM-SIAM Symposium on Discrete Algorithms*, page To Appear, 2010.

[10] Bala Kalyanasundaram and Kirk Pruhs. Speed is as powerful as clairvoyance. *J. ACM*, 47(4):617–643, 2000.

[11] Bala Kalyanasundaram and Kirk Pruhs. Minimizing flow time nonclairvoyantly. *J. ACM*, 50(4):551–567, 2003.

[12] Rajeev Motwani, Steven Phillips, and Eric Torng. Nonclairvoyant scheduling. *Theorertical Computer Science*, 130(1):17–47, 1994.

[13] Kirk Pruhs. Competitive online scheduling for server systems. *SIGMETRICS Performance Evaluation Review*, 34(4):52–58, 2007.

[14] Kirk Pruhs, Jiri Sgall, and Eric Torng. Online scheduling. In *Handbook on Scheduling*. CRC Press, 2004.

[15] Julien Robert and Nicolas Schabanel. Non-clairvoyant batch sets scheduling: Fairness is fair enough. In *European Symposium on Algorithms*, pages 741–753, 2007.

[16] Julien Robert and Nicolas Schabanel. Non-clairvoyant scheduling with precedence constraints. In *ACM-SIAM Symposium on Discrete Algorithms*, pages 491–500, 2008.

[17] Abraham Silberschatz and Peter Galvin. *Operating System Concepts, 4th edition*. Addison-Wesley, 1994.

Scheduling to Minimize Power Consumption using Submodular Functions

Erik D. Demaine
MIT
edemaine@mit.edu

Morteza Zadimoghaddam
MIT
morteza@mit.edu

ABSTRACT

We develop logarithmic approximation algorithms for extremely general formulations of multiprocessor multi-interval offline task scheduling to minimize power usage. Here each processor has an arbitrary specified power consumption to be turned on for each possible time interval, and each job has a specified list of time interval/processor pairs during which it could be scheduled. (A processor need not be in use for an entire interval it is turned on.) If there is a feasible schedule, our algorithm finds a feasible schedule with total power usage within an $O(\log n)$ factor of optimal, where n is the number of jobs. (Even in a simple setting with one processor, the problem is Set-Cover hard.) If not all jobs can be scheduled and each job has a specified value, then our algorithm finds a schedule of value at least $(1-\varepsilon)Z$ and power usage within an $O(\log(1/\varepsilon))$ factor of the optimal schedule of value at least Z, for any specified Z and $\varepsilon > 0$. At the foundation of our work is a general framework for logarithmic approximation to maximizing any submodular function subject to budget constraints.

Categories and Subject Descriptors

F.2.2 [**Analysis of Algorithms and Problem Complexity**]: Nonnumerical Algorithms and Problems; G.2.2 [**Discrete Mathematics**]: Graph Theory

General Terms

Algorithms, Theory

Keywords

sleep state, pre-emptive scheduling, multiprocessor scheduling, approximation algorithms

1. INTRODUCTION

Power management systems aim to reduce energy consumption while keeping the performance high. The motiva-

tions include battery conservation (as battery capacities continue to grow much slower than computational power) and reducing operating cost and environmental impact (both direct from energy consumption and indirect from cooling).

Processor energy usage. A common approach in practice is to allow processors to enter a *sleep state*, which consumes less energy, when they are idle. All previous work assumes a simple model in which we pay zero energy during the sleep state (which makes approximation only harder), a unit energy rate during the awake state (by scaling), and a fixed restart cost α to exit the sleep state. Thus the total energy consumed is the sum over all awake intervals of α plus the length of the interval.

There are many settings where this simple model may not reflect reality, which we address in this paper:

1. When the processors are not identical: different processors do not necessarily consume energy at the same rate, so we cannot scale to have all processors use a unit rate.

2. When the energy consumption varies over the time: keeping a processor active for two intervals of the same length may not consume the same energy. One example is if we optimize energy *cost* instead of actual energy, which varies substantially in energy markets over the course of a day. Another use for this generalization is if a processor is not available for some time slots, which we can represent by setting the cost of the processor to be infinity for these time slots.

3. When the energy consumption is an arbitrary function of its length: the growth in energy use might not be an affine function of the duration a processor is awake. For example, if a processor stays awake for a short time, it might not need to cool with a fan, saving energy, but the longer it stays awake, the faster the fan may need to run and the more energy consumed.

We allow the energy consumption of an awake interval to be an arbitrary function of the interval and the processor. We also allow the processor to be idle (but still consume energy) during such an interval. As a result, our algorithms automatically choose to combine multiple awake intervals (and the intervening sleep intervals) together into one awake interval if this change causes a net decrease in energy consumption.

Multi-interval task scheduling. Most previous work assumes that each task has an arrival time, deadline, and processing time. The goal is then to find a schedule that executes all tasks by their deadlines and consumes the minimum energy (according to the notion above). This setup implicitly assumes identical processors.

We consider a generalization of this problem, called *multi-interval scheduling*, in which each task has a list of one or more time intervals during which it can execute, and the goal is to schedule each job into one of its time intervals. The list of time intervals can be different for each processor, for example, if the job needs specific resources held by different processors at different times.

Prize-collecting version. All previous work assumes that all jobs can be scheduled using the current processors and available resources. This assumption is not necessarily satisfied in many practical situations, when jobs outweigh resources. In these cases, we must pick a subset of jobs to schedule.

We consider a general weighted *prize-collecting* version in which each job has a specified *value*. The bicriterion problem is then to find a schedule of value at least Z and minimum energy consumption subject to achieving this value.

Our results. We obtain in Section 3 an $O(\log n)$-approximation algorithm for scheduling n jobs to minimize power consumption. For the prize-collecting version, we obtain in Section 4 an $O(\log(1/\varepsilon))$-approximation for scheduling jobs of total value at least $(1 - \varepsilon)Z$, comparing to an adversary required to schedule jobs of total value at least Z (assuming such a schedule exists), for any specified Z and $\varepsilon > 0$. Both of our algorithms allow specifying an arbitrary processor energy usage for each possible interval on each processor, specifying an arbitrary set of candidate intervals on each processor for each job, and specifying an arbitrary value for each job.

These results are all best possible assuming P $\neq$ NP: we prove in Appendix A that even simple one-processor versions of these problems are Set-Cover hard.

Our approximation algorithms are based on a technique of independent interest. In Section 2, we introduce a general optimization problem, called *submodular maximization with budget constraints*. Many interesting optimization problems are special cases of this general problem, for example, Set Cover and Max Cover [7, 11] and the submodular maximization problems studied in [9, 10]. We obtain bicriteria $((1 - \varepsilon), O(\log 1/\varepsilon))$-approximation factor for this general problem.

In Section 3, we show how our schedule-all-jobs problem can be formulated by a bipartite graph and its matchings. We define a matching function in bipartite graphs, and show that this function is submodular. Then the general technique of Section 2 solves the problem.

In Section 4, we show how the prize-collecting version of our scheduling problem can be formulated with a bipartite graph with weights on its nodes. Again we define a matching function in these weighted bipartite graphs, and with a more complicated proof, show that this function is also submodular. Again the general technique of Section 2 applies.

The general algorithm in Section 2 has many different and independent applications because submodular functions arise in a variety of applications. They can be seen as utility and cost functions of bidding auctions in game theory application [5]. These functions can be seen as covering functions

which have many applications in different optimization problems: Set Cover functions, Edge Cut functions in graphs, etc.

Previous work. The one-interval one-processor case of our problem with simple energy consumption function (α plus the interval length) remained an important and challenging open problem for several years: it was not even clear whether it was NP-hard.

The first main results for this problem considered the power-saving setting, which is easier with respect to approximation algorithms. Augustine, Irani, and Swamy [1] gave an online algorithm, which schedules jobs as they arrive without knowledge of future jobs, that achieves a competitive ratio of $3 + 2\sqrt{2}$. (The best lower bound for this problem is 2 [2, 6].)

For the offline version, Irani, Shukla, and Gupta [6] obtained a 3-approximation algorithm. Finally, Baptiste [2] solved the open problem: he developed a polynomial-time optimal algorithm based on an sophisticated dynamic programming approach. Demaine et al. [4] later generalized this result to also handle multiple processors.

The multi-interval case was considered only by Demaine et al. [4], after Baptiste mentioned the generalization during his talk at SODA 2006. They show that this problem is Set-Cover hard, so it does not have an $o(\log n)$-approximation. They also obtain a $1 + \frac{2}{3}\alpha$-approximation for the multi-interval multi-processor case, where α is the fixed restart cost. Note that α can be as large as n, so there is no general algorithm with approximation factor better than $\Theta(n)$ in the worst case (when α is around n).

However, both the Baptiste result [2] and Demaine et al. results [4] assume that processors enter the sleep state whenever they go idle, immediately incurring an α cost. For this reason, the problem can also be called *minimum-gap scheduling*. But this assumption seems unreasonable in practice: we can easily leave the processor awake during sufficiently short intervals in order to save energy. As mentioned above, the problem formulations considered in this paper fix this issue.

2. SUBMODULAR MAXIMIZATION WITH BUDGET CONSTRAINTS

Submodular functions arise in a variety of applications. They can represent different forms of functions in optimization problems. As a game theoretic example, both profit and budget functions in bid optimization problems are Set-Cover type functions (including the weighted version) which are special cases of submodular functions. As another application of these functions in online algorithms, we can mention the secretary problem in different models, the bipartite graph setting in [8], and the submodular functions setting in [3].

The authors of [10] studied the problem of submodular maximization under matroid and knapsack constraints (which can be seen as some kind of budget constraints), and they give the first constant factor approximation when the number of constraints is constant. We try to find solutions with more utility by relaxing the budget constraints. We give the first $(1 - \varepsilon)$-approximation for utility maximization with relaxing the budget constraint by $\log(1/\varepsilon)$. In our model, we allow the cost of a subset of items be less than their sum. This way we can cover more general cases (non-linear or submodular cost functions). All previous works on submodular functions assume that the cost function is linear. Therefore they can not cover many interesting optimization problems including the scheduling problems we are studying in this paper. Later we combine this result with other techniques to give optimal scheduling strategies for energy minimization problem with parallel machines.

Now we formulate the problem of submodular maximization with budget constraints.

DEFINITION 1. *Let* $U = \{a_1, a_2, \ldots, a_n\}$ *be a set of* n *items. We are given a set* $S = \{S_1, S_2, \ldots, S_m\} \subseteq 2^U$ *specifying* m *allowable subsets of* U *that we can add to our solution. We are also given costs* $C_1, C_2, \ldots, C_m$ *for the subsets, where* S_i *costs* C_i. *Finally, we are given a* utility function $F : 2^U \to \mathbb{R}$ *defined on subsets of* U. *We require that* F *is* submodular *meaning that, for any two subsets* A, B *of* U, *we have*

$$F(A) + F(B) \geq F(A \cap B) + F(A \cup B).$$

We also require that F *is* monotone *(being a utility function) meaning that, for any subsets* $A \subseteq B \subseteq U$, *we have* $F(A) \leq F(B)$.

The problem is to choose a collection of the input subsets with reasonable cost and utility. The cost of a collection of subsets is the sum of their costs. The utility of these subsets is equal to the utility of their union. In particular, if we pick k *subsets* $S_1, S_2, \ldots, S_k$, *their cost is* $\Sigma_{i=1}^{k} C_i$ *and their utility is equal to* $F(\cup_{i=1}^{k} S_i)$. *We are given a utility threshold* x, *and the problem is to find a collection with utility at least* x *having minimum possible cost.*

Note that all previous work assumes that the set S of allowable subsets consists only of single-item subsets, namely $\{a_1\}, \{a_2\}, \ldots, \{a_n\}$. Equivalently, they assume that the cost of picking a subset of items is equal to the sum of the costs of the picked items (a linear cost function). By contrast, we allow that there be other subsets that we can pick with different costs, but that all such subsets are explicitly given in the input. The cost of a subset might be different from the sum of the costs of the items in that subset; in practice, we expect the cost to be less than the sum of the item costs.

We need the following result in the proof of the main algorithm of this section. Similar lemmas like this are proved in the literature of submodular functions. But we need to prove this more general lemma.

LEMMA 2.1. *Let* T *be the union of* k *subsets* $S_1, S_2, \ldots, S_k$, *and* S' *be another arbitrary subset. For a monotone submodular function* F *defined on these subsets, we have that*

$$\sum_{j=1}^{k} [F(S' \cup S_j) - F(S')] \geq F(T) - F(S').$$

PROOF. Let T' be the union of T and S'. We prove that $\sum_{j=1}^{k} [F(S' \cup S_j) - F(S')] \geq F(T') - F(S')$ which also implies the claim. Define subset S'_i be $(\cup_{j=1}^{i} S_j) \cup S'$ for any $0 \leq i \leq k$. We prove that

$$F(S' \cup S_i) - F(S') \geq F(S'_i) - F(S'_{i-1}).$$

Because F is submodular, we know that $F(A) + F(B) \geq F(A \cup B) + F(A \cap B)$ for any pair of subsets A and B. Let

A be the set $S' \cup S_i$, and B be the set S'_{i-1}. Their union is S'_i, and their intersection is a superset of S'. So we have that

$$\begin{aligned} F(S' \cup S_i) + F(S'_{i-1}) &\geq F(S'_i) + F([S' \cup S_i] \cap [S'_{i-1}]) \\ &\geq F(S'_i) + F(S'). \end{aligned}$$

This completes the proof of the inequality, $F(S' \cup S_i) - F(S') \geq F(S'_i) - F(S'_{i-1})$.

If we sum this inequality over all values of $1 \leq i \leq k$, we can conclude the claim:

$$\begin{aligned} \sum_{i=1}^{k} F(S' \cup S_i) - F(S') &\geq \sum_{i=1}^{k} F(S'_i) - F(S'_{i-1}) \\ &= F(T') - F(S') \\ &\geq F(T) - F(S'). \end{aligned}$$

□

Now we show how to find a collection with utility $(1-\varepsilon)x$ and cost $O(\log{(1/\varepsilon)})$ times the optimum cost. Later we show how to find a subset with utility x in our particular application, scheduling with minimum energy consumption. It is also interesting that the following algorithm generalizes the well-known greedy algorithm for Set Cover in the sense that the Set-Cover type functions are special cases of monotone submodular functions. In order to use the following algorithm to solve the Set Cover problem with a logarithmic approximation factor (which is the best possible result for Set Cover), one just needs to set ε to some value less than 1 over the number of items in the Set-Cover instance.

LEMMA 2.2. *If there exists a collection of subsets (optimal solution) with cost at most* B *and utility at least* x, *there is a polynomial time algorithm that can find a collection of subsets of cost at most* $O(B \log{(1/\varepsilon)})$, *and utility at least* $(1 - \varepsilon)x$ *for any* $0 < \varepsilon < 1$.

PROOF. The algorithm is as follows. Start with set $S = \emptyset$. Iteratively, find the set S_i with maximum ratio of $\min\{x, F(S \cup S_i)\} - F(S)/C_i$ for $1 \leq i \leq m$ where $\min\{a, b\}$ is the minimum of a and b. In fact we are choosing the subset that maximizes the ratio of the increase in the utility function over the increase in the cost function, and we just care about the increments in our utility up to value x. If a subset increases our utility to some value more than x, we just take into account the difference between previous value of our utility and x, not the new value of our utility. We do this iteratively till our utility is at least $(1 - \varepsilon)x$.

We prove that the cost of our solution is $O(B \log{(1/\varepsilon)})$. Assume that we pick some subsets like $S'_1, S'_2, \ldots, S'_{k'}$ respectively. We define the subsets of our solution into $\log{(1/\varepsilon)}$ phases. Phase $1 \leq i \leq \log{(1/\varepsilon)}$. ends when the utility of our solution reaches $(1 - 1/2^i)x$, and starts when the previous phase ends. In each phase, we pick a sequence of the k' subsets $S'_1, S'_2, \ldots, S'_{k'}$. We prove that the cost of each phase is $O(B)$, and therefore the total cost is $O(B \log{(1/\varepsilon)})$ because there are $\log{(1/\varepsilon)}$ phases.

Let S'_{a_i} be the last subset we pick in phase i. So $F(\cup_{j=1}^{a_i} S'_j)$ is our utility at the end of phase i, and is at least $(1 - 1/2^i)x$, and $F(\cup_{j=1}^{a_i-1} S'_j)$ is less than $(1 - 1/2^i)x$. So we pick subsets $S'_{a_{i-1}+1}, S'_{a_{i-1}+2}, \ldots, S'_{a_i}$ in phase i. We prove that the ratio of utility per cost of all subsets inserted in phase i is at least $\frac{x/2^i}{B}$. Assume that we are in phase i,

23

and we want to pick another set (phase i is not finished yet). Let S' be our current set (the union of all subsets we picked up to now). $F(S')$ is less than $(1 - 1/2^i)x$. We also know that there exists a solution (optimal solution) with cost B and utility x. Without loss of generality, we assume that this solution consists of k subsets $S_1, S_2, \ldots, S_k$. Let T be the union of these k subsets. Using lemma 2.1, we have that

$$\sum_{j=1}^{k} [F(S' \cup S_j) - F(S')] \geq F(T) - F(S') > x/2^i.$$

If $F(S' \cup S_j)$ is at most x for any $1 \leq j \leq k$, we can say that

$$\sum_{j=1}^{k} [\min\{x, F(S' \cup S_j)\} - F(S')] =$$

$$\sum_{j=1}^{k} [F(S' \cup S_j) - F(S')] \geq F(T) - F(S') > x/2^i.$$

Otherwise there is some j for which $F(S' \cup S_j)$ is more than x. So $\min\{x, F(S' \cup S_j)\} - F(S')$ is at least $x/2^i$ because $F(S')$ is less than $(1 - 1/2^i)x$. So in both cases we can claim the above inequality. We also know that

$$\sum_{j=1}^{k} C_j \leq B,$$

where C_j is the cost of set S_j. In every iteration, we find the subset with the maximum ratio of utility per cost (the increase in utility per the cost of the subset). Note that we also consider these k subsets $S_1, S_2, \ldots, S_k$ as candidates. So the ratio of the subset we find in each iteration is not less than the ratio of each of these k subsets. The ratio of subset S_j is $[\min\{x, F(S' \cup S_j)\} - F(S')]/C_j$. The maximum ratio of these k subsets is at least the sum of the nominators of the k ratios of these sets over the sum of their denominators which is

$$\frac{\sum_{j=1}^{k} [\min\{x, F(S' \cup S_j)\} - F(S')]}{\sum_{j=1}^{k} C_j} > \frac{x}{2^i B}.$$

So in phase i, the utility per cost ratio of each subset we add is at least $\frac{x}{2^i B}$. Now we can bound the cost of this phase. We pick subsets $S'_{a_{i-1}+1}, S'_{a_{i-1}+2}, \ldots, S'_{a_i}$ in phase i. Let u_0 be our utility at the beginning of phase i. In other words, u_0 is $F(\cup_{j=1}^{a_{i-1}} S'_j)$. Assume we pick l subsets in this phase, i.e., l is $a_i - a_{i-1}$. Let u_j be our utility after inserting jth subset in this phase where $1 \leq j \leq l$. Note that we stop the algorithm when our utility reaches $(1 - \varepsilon)x$. So our utility after adding the first $l - 1$ subsets is less than x. Our utility at the end of this phase, u_l might be more than x. For any $1 \leq j \leq l-1$, the utility per cost ratio is $u_j - u_{j-1}$ divided by the cost of the jth subset. For the last subset, the ratio is $\min\{x, u_l\} - u_{l-1}$ divided by the cost of the last subset of this phase. According to the definition of the phases, our utility at the beginning of this phase, u_0 is at least $(1 - 1/2^{i-1})x$. So we have that

$$\min\{x, u_l\} - u_{l-1} + \sum_{j=1}^{l-1} u_j - u_{j-1} =$$

$$\min\{x, u_l\} - u_0 \leq x - (1 - 1/2^{i-1})x = x/2^{i-1}.$$

On the other hand, we know that the utility per cost ratio of all these subsets is at least $\frac{x}{2^i B}$. Therefore the total cost of this phase is at most

$$\frac{[\min\{x, u_l\} - u_{l-1} + \sum_{j=1}^{l-1} u_j - u_{j-1}]}{x/2^i B} \leq \frac{x/2^{i-1}}{x/2^i B},$$

which is at most $2B$. So the total cost in all phases is not more than $\log(1/\varepsilon) \cdot 2B$. $\square$

3. SCHEDULING TO MINIMIZE POWER IN PARALLEL MACHINES

We proved how to find almost optimal solutions with reasonable cost when the utility functions are submodular. Here we show how the scheduling problem can be formulated as an optimization problem with submodular utility functions.

First we explain the power minimization scheduling problem in more detail.

DEFINITION 2. *There are p processors $P_1, P_2, \ldots, P_p$ and n jobs $j_1, j_2, \ldots, j_n$. Each processor has an energy cost $c(I)$ for every possible awake interval I. Each job j_i has a unit processing time (which is equivalent to allowing preemption), and set T_i of valid time slot/processor pairs. (Unlike previous work, T_i does not necessarily form a single interval, and it can have different valid time slots for different processors.) A feasible schedule consists of a set of awake time intervals for each processor, and an assignment of each job to an integer time and one of the processors, such that jobs are scheduled only during awake time slots (and during valid choices according to T_i) and no two jobs are scheduled at the same time on the same processor. The cost of such a schedule is the sum of the energy costs of the awake intervals of all processors.*

In the simple case which has been studied in [2, 4], it is assumed that the cost of an interval is a fixed amount of energy (restart cost α) plus the size of the interval. We assume a very general case in which the cost of keeping a machine active during an interval is a function of that machine, and the interval. For instance, it might take more energy to keep some machines active comparing to other machines, or some time intervals might have more cost. So there is a cost associated with every pair of a time interval and a machine. These costs might be explicitly given in the input, or can be accessed through a query oracle, i.e., when the number of possible intervals are not polynomial.

If we pick a collection of active intervals for each machine at first, we can then find and schedule the maximum number of possible jobs that can be all together scheduled in the active time slots without collision using the maximum bipartite matching algorithms. So the problem is to find a set of active intervals with low cost such that all jobs can be done during them.

Let U be the set of all time slots in different machines. In fact for every unit of time, we put p copies in U, because at each unit of time, we can schedule p jobs in different machines, so each of these p units is associated with one of the machines. We can define a function F over all subsets of U as follows. For every subset of time slot/processor pairs like $S \subset U$, $F(S)$ is the maximum number of jobs that can be scheduled in time slot/processor pairs of S. Our scheduling problem can be formulated as follows. We want to find a collection of time intervals $I_1, I_2, \ldots, I_k$ with minimum cost and $F(\cup_{i=1}^k I_i) = n$ (this means that all n jobs can be scheduled in these time intervals). Note that each I_i is a pair of a machine and a time interval, i.e., I_1 might be $(P_2, [3, 6])$ which represents the time interval $[3, 6]$ in machine P_2. The cost of each I_i can be accessed from the input or a query oracle. The cost of this collection of intervals is the sum of the costs of the intervals. We just need to prove that function F is monotone and submodular. The monotonicity comes from its definition. The submodularity proof is involved, and needs some graph theoretic Lemmas. Now we can present our main result for this broad class of scheduling problems.

THEOREM 3.1. *If there is a schedule with cost B which schedules all jobs, there is a polynomial time algorithm which schedules all jobs with cost $O(B \log n)$.*

PROOF. We are looking for a collection of intervals with utility at least n, and cost $O(B \log n)$. Lemma 3.2 below states that F (defined above) is submodular. Using the algorithm of Lemma 2.2, we can find a collection of time intervals with utility at least $(1 - \varepsilon)n$ and cost at most $O(B \log(1/\varepsilon))$ because there exists a collection of time intervals (schedule) with utility n (schedules all n jobs) and cost B. Let ε be $1/(n + 1)$. The cost of the result of our algorithm is $O(B \log(n + 1))$, and its utility is at least $(1 - 1/(n + 1))n > n - 1$. Because the utility function F always take integer values, the utility of our result is also n. So we can find a collection of time intervals that all jobs can be scheduled in them. We just need to run the maximum bipartite matching algorithm to find the appropriate schedule. This means that our algorithm also schedules all jobs, and has cost $O(B \log(n + 1))$. $\square$

There is another definition of submodular functions that is equivalent to the one we presented in the previous section. We will use this new definition in the following lemma.

DEFINITION 3. *A function F is submodular if for every pair of subsets $A \subset B$, and an element z, we have:*

$$F(A \cup \{z\}) - F(A) \geq F(B \cup \{z\}) - F(B)$$

Now we just need to show that F is submodular. We can look at this function as the maximum matching function of subgraphs of a bipartite graph. Construct graph G as follows. Consider time slots of U as the vertices of one part of G named X. Put n vertices representing the jobs in the other side of G named Y. Note that the time slots of U are actually pairs of a time unit and a processor. Put an edge between one vertex of X and a vertex of Y if the associated job can be scheduled in that time slot (which is a pair of a time unit and a processor), i.e., if the job can be done in that processor and in that time unit. Now every subset of $S \subset X$ is a subset of time slots, and $F(S)$ is the maximum number of jobs that can be executed in S. So $F(S)$ is in fact the maximum cardinality matching that saturates only vertices of S in part X (it can saturate any subset of vertices in Y). A vertex is saturated by a matching if one of its incident edges participates in the matching. Now we can present this submodularity Lemma in this graph model.

LEMMA 3.2. *Given a bipartite graph G with parts X and Y. For every subset $S \subset X$, define $F(S)$ to be the maximum*

cardinality matching that saturates only vertices of S in part X. The function F is submodular.

PROOF. We just need to prove that, for two subsets $A \subset B \subset X$ and a vertex v in X, the following inequality holds:

$$F(A \cup \{v\}) - F(A) \geq F(B \cup \{v\}) - F(B).$$

Let M_1 and M_2 be two maximum matchings that saturate only vertices of A and B respectively. Note that there might be more than just one maximum matching in each case (for sets A and B). We first prove that there are two such maximum matchings that M_1 is a subset of M_2, i.e., all edges in matching M_1 also are in matching M_2. This can be proved using the fact that $A \subset B$ as follows.

Consider two maximum matchings M_1 and M_2 with the maximum number of edges in common. The edges of $M_1 \Delta M_2$ form a bipartite graph H where $A_1 \Delta A_2$ is $A_1 \cup A_2 - A_1 \cap A_2$ for every pair of sets A_1 and A_2. Because it is a disjoint union of two matchings, every vertex in H has degree 0, 1 or 2. So H is a union of some paths and cycles. We first prove that there is no cycle in H. We prove this by contradiction. Let C be a cycle in H. The edges of C are alternatively in M_1 and M_2. All vertices of this cycle are either in part Y of the graph or in $A \subset X$. Now consider matching $M_1' = M_1 \Delta C$ instead of M_1. It also saturates only some vertices of A in part X, and has the same size of M_1. Therefore M_1' is also a maximum matching with the desired property, and has more edges in common with M_2. This contradiction implies that there is no cycle in H.

Now we study the paths in H. At first we prove that there is no path in H with even number of edges. Again we prove this by contradiction. The edges of a path in H alternate between matchings M_1 and M_2. Let P be a path in H with even number of edges. This path has equal number of edges from M_1 and M_2. Now if we take $M_2' = M_2 \Delta P$ instead of M_2, we have a new matching with the same number of edges, and it has more edges in common with M_1. This contradiction shows that there is no even path in H.

Finally we prove that all other paths in H are just some single edges from M_2, and therefore there is no edge from M_1 in H. This completes the proof of the claim that M_1 is a subset of M_2. Again assume that there is a path P' with odd and more than one number of edges. Let $e_1, e_2, \ldots, e_{2l+1}$ are the edges of P'. The edges with even index are in M_1, the rest of the edges are in M_2 otherwise $M_2'' = M_2 \Delta P'$ would be a matching for set B which has more edges than M_2 (this is a contradiction). Because P' is an odd path, we can assume that it starts from part Y, and ends in part X without loss of generality. Now if we delete edges $e_2, e_4, \ldots, e_{2l}$ from M_1, and insert edges $e_1, e_3, \ldots, e_{2l-1}$ instead, we reach a new matching M_1'. This matching uses a new vertex from Y, but the set of saturated vertices of X in matching M_1' is the same as the ones in M_1. These two matchings also have the same size. But M_1' has more edges in common with M_2. This is also contradiction, and implies that there is no such a path in H. So M_1 is a subset of M_2.

We are ready to prove the main claim of this theorem. Note that we have to prove this inequality:

$$F(A \cup \{v\}) - F(A) \geq F(B \cup \{v\}) - F(B).$$

We should prove that if adding v to B increases its maximum matching, it also increases the maximum matching of A. Let M_3 be the maximum matching of $B \cup \{v\}$. Let H' be the subgraph of G that contains the edges of $M_2 \Delta M_3$.

Because M_3 has more edges than M_2, there exists a path Q in H' that has more edges from M_3 than M_2 (cycles have the same number of edges from both matchings). The vertex v should be in path Q, otherwise we could have used the path Q to find a matching in B greater than M_2, i.e., matchings $M_2 \Delta Q$ could be a greater matching for set B in that case which is a contradiction.

The degree of v in H is 1, because it does not participate in matching M_2, does participate in M_3. So v can be seen as the starting vertex of path Q. Let $e_1, e_2, \ldots, e_{2l'+1}$ be the edges of Q. The edges $e_2, e_4, \ldots, e_{2l'}$ are in M_2, and some of them might be in M_1. Let $0 \leq i \leq l'$ be the maximum integer number for which all edges $e_2, e_4, \ldots, e_{2i}$ are in M_1. If e_2 is not in M_1, we set i to be 0. If we remove edges $e_2, e_4, \ldots, e_{2i}$ from M_1, and insert edges $e_1, e_3, \ldots, e_{2i+1}$ instead, we reach a matching for set $A \cup \{v\}$ with more edges than M_1. So adding v to A increases the size of its maximum matching.

Now the only thing we should check is that edges $e_1, e_3, \ldots, e_{2i+1}$ does not intersect with other edges of M_1. Let $v = v_0, v_1, v_2, \ldots, v_{2l'+1}$ be the vertices of Q. Because we remove edges $e_2, e_4, \ldots, e_{2i}$ from M_1, we do not have to be worried about inserting the first i edges $e_1, e_3, \ldots, e_{2i-1}$. The last edge we add is $e_{2i+1} = (v_{2i}, v_{2i+1})$. If v_{2i+1} is not saturated in M_1, there will be no intersection. So we just need to prove that v_{2i+1} is not saturated in M_1.

If i is equal to l', the vertex $v_{2i+1} = v_{2l'+1}$ is not saturated in M_2. Because M_1 is a subset of M_2, the vertex v_{2i+1} is also not saturated in M_1.

If i is less than l', the vertex v_{2i+1} is saturated in M_2 by edge e_{2i+2}. Assume v_{2i+1} is saturated in M_1 by an edge e'. The edge e' should be also in M_2 because all edges of M_1 are in M_2. The edge e' intersects with e_{2i+2}, so e' has to be equal to e_{2i+2}. The definition of value i implies that e_{2i+2} should not be in M_1 (we pick the maximum i with the above property). This contradiction shows that the vertex v_{2i+1} is not saturated in M_1, and therefore we get a greater matching in $A \cup \{v\}$ using the changes in M_1. $\square$

4. PRIZE-COLLECTING SCHEDULING PROBLEM

We introduce the prize-collecting version of the scheduling problems. All previous work assumes that we can schedule all jobs using the existing processors. There are many cases that we can not execute all jobs, and we have to find a subset of jobs to schedule using low energy. There might be priorities among the jobs, i.e., there might be more important jobs to do. We formalize this problem as follows.

As before, there are P processors and n jobs. Each job j_i has a set T_i of time slot/processor pairs during which it can execute. Each job j_i also has a value z_i. We want to schedule a subset of jobs S with value at least a given threshold Z, and with minimum possible cost. The *value* of set S is the sum of its members' values, and it should be at least Z. Following we prove that there is a polynomial-time algorithm which finds a schedule with value at least $(1-\varepsilon)Z$ and cost at most $O(\log{(1/\varepsilon)})$ times the optimum solution. Note that the optimum solution has value at least Z.

Later in this section, we show how to find a solution with utility at least Z, and logarithmic approximation on the energy consumption (cost).

THEOREM 4.1. *If there is an schedule for the prize-collecting scheduling problem with value at least Z and cost B, there is an algorithm which finds a schedule with value at least $(1-\varepsilon)Z$ and cost at most $O(B \log{(1/\varepsilon)})$.*

PROOF. Like the simple version of the scheduling problem, we construct a bipartite graph, and relate it to our algorithm in Lemma 2.2. The difference is that the bipartite graph here has some weights (job values) on the vertices of one of its parts. And it makes it more complicated to prove that the corresponding utility function is submodular. At first we explain the construction of the bipartite graph, and show how to reduce our problem to it. Then we use Lemma 4.2 to prove that the utility function is submodular.

We make graph G with parts X and Y. The vertices of part X represent the time slot/processor pairs. So for each pair of a time unit in a processor, we have a vertex in X. On the other part, Y, we have the n jobs. The edges connect jobs to their sets of time slot/processor pairs, i.e., job j_i has edges only to time slot/processors pairs in T_i, so a job might have edges to different time units in different processors. The only difference is that each edge has a weight in this graph. Each edge connects a job to a time slot/processor pair, the weight of an edge is the value of its job. Every schedule is actually a matching in this bipartite graph, and the value of a matching is the sum of the values of the jobs that are scheduled in it. This is why we set the weight of an edge to the value of its job.

The problem again is to find a collection of time intervals for each processor, and schedule a subset of jobs in those intervals such that the value of this subset is close to Z, and the cost of the schedule is low. If we have a subset of intervals, we can find the best subset of jobs to schedule in it. This can be done using the maximum weighted bipartite matching. The only thing we have to prove is that the utility function associated with this weighted bipartite graph is submodular. This is also proved in Lemma 4.2. $\square$

LEMMA 4.2. *Given a bipartite graph G with parts X and Y. Every vertex in Y has a value. For every subset $S \subset X$, define $F(S)$ be the maximum weighted matching that saturates only vertices of S in part X. The weight of a matching is the sum of the values of the vertices saturated by this matching in Y. The function F is submodular.*

PROOF. Let A and B be two subsets of X such that $A \subseteq B$. Let v be a vertex in X. We have to prove that:

$$F(A \cup \{v\}) - F(A) \geq F(B \cup \{v\}) - F(B)$$

Let M_1 and M_2 be two maximum weighted matchings that saturate only vertices of A and B in X respectively. Among all options we have, we choose two matchings M_1 and M_2 that have the maximum number of edges in common. We prove that every saturated vertex in M_1 is also saturated in M_2 (note that we can not prove that every edge in M_1 is also in M_2). We prove this by contradiction.

The saturated vertices in M_1 are either in set A or in set Y. At first, let v' be a vertex in A that is saturated in M_1, and not saturated in M_2. Let u' be its match in part Y (v' is a time slot/processor pair, and u' is a job). The vertex u' is saturated in M_2 otherwise we could add edge (v', u') to matching M_2, and get a matching with greater value instead of M_2. So u' is matched with a vertex of B like v'' in matching M_2. If we delete the edge (v'', u')

from matching M_2, and use edge (v', u') instead, the value of our matching remains unchanged, but we get a maximum matching instead of M_2 that has more edges in common with M_1 which is contradiction. So any vertex in X that is saturated in M_1 is also saturated in M_2.

The other case is when there is vertex in Y like u' that is saturated in M_1, and not saturated in M_2. The vertex u' is matched with vertex $w \in A$ in matching M_1. Again if w is not saturated in M_2, we can insert edge (w, u') to M_2, and get a matching with greater value. So w should be saturated in M_2. Let u'' be the vertex matched with w in M_2. For now assume that u'' is not saturated in M_1. Note that u' and u'' are some jobs with some values, and w is a time slot/processor pair. If the values of jobs u' and u'' are different, we can switch the edges in one of the matchings M_1 or M_2, and get a better matching. For example, if the value of u' is greater than u'', we can use edge (w, u') instead of (w, u'') in matching M_2, and increase the value of M_2. If the value of u'' is greater than u', we can use edge (w, u'') instead of (w, u') in matching M_1, and increase the value of M_1. So the value of u' and u'' are the same, we again can use (w, u'') instead of (w, u') in matching M_1, and get a matching with the same value but more edges in common with M_2. This is a contradiction. So u'' should be saturated in M_1 as well, but if we continue this process we find a path P starting with vertex u'. The edges of this path alternate between M_1 and M_2. Path P starts with an edge in M_1, so it can not end with another edge in M_1 otherwise we can take $M_2 \Delta P$ instead of M_2 to increase the size of our matching for set B which is a contradiction. So path P starts with vertex u' and an edge in M_1, and ends with an edge in M_2. We have the same situation as above, and we can reach the contradiction similarly (just take the last vertex of the path as u''). So we can say that all saturated vertices in M_1 are also saturated in M_2.

Despite the unweighted graphs, $F(A \cup \{v\}) - F(A)$ and $F(B \cup \{v\}) - F(B)$ might take values other than zero or one.

If M_2 is also a maximum matching for set $B \cup \{v\}$, we do not need to prove anything. Because $F(B \cup \{v\})$ would be equal to $F(B)$ in that case, and we know that $F(A \cup \{v\})$ is always at least $F(A)$. So assume that M_2' is a maximum matching for set $B \cup \{v\}$ that has the maximum number of edges in common with M_2, and its value is more than the value of M_2. Consider the graph H that consists of edges $M_2' \Delta M_2$. We know that H is union of some paths and cycles. We can prove that H is only a path that starts with vertex v. In fact, if there exists a connected component like C in H that does not include vertex v, we can take matching $M_2' \Delta C$ which is a matching for set $B \cup \{v\}$ with more edges in common with M_2. Note that the value of matching $M_2' \Delta C$ can not be less than the value of M_2' otherwise we can use the matching $M_2 \Delta C$ for set B instead of matching M_2, and get a greater value which is a contradiction (M_2 is a maximum value matching for set B).

So graph H has only one connected component that includes vertex v. Because vertex v does not participate in matching M_2, its degree in graph H should be at most 1. We also know that v is saturated in M_2', so its degree is one in H. Therefore, graph H is only a path P. This path starts with vertex v, and one of the edges in M_2'. The edges of P are alternatively in M_2' and M_2. If P ends with an edge in M_2, the set of jobs that these two matchings, M_2 and M_2', schedule are the same. So their values would be also the same, and

$F(B \cup \{v\})$ would be equal to $F(B)$ which is a contradiction. So path P has odd number of edges. Let $e_1, e_2, \ldots, e_{2l+1}$ be the edges of P, and $v = v_0, v_1, v_2, \ldots, v_{2l+1}$ be its vertices. Note that $v_0, v_2, \ldots, v_{2l}$ are some time slot/processor pairs, and the other vertices are some jobs with some values. Edges $e_2, e_4, \ldots, e_{2l}$ are in M_2, and the rest are in M_2'.

The only job that is scheduled in M_2', and not scheduled in M_2 is the job associated with vertex v_{2l+1}. Let x_i be the value of the vertex v_{2i+1} for any $0 \leq i \leq l$. So $F(B \cup \{v\}) - F(B)$ is equal to x_l. We prove that x_l is not greater than any x_i for $0 \leq i < l$ by contradiction. Assume x_i is less than x_l for some $i < l$. We could change the matching M_2 in the following way, and get a matching with greater value for set B. We could delete edges $e_{2i+2}, e_{2i+4}, \ldots, e_{2l}$, and insert edges $e_{2i+3}, e_{2i+5}, \ldots, 2_{2l+1}$ instead. This way we schedule job v_{2l+1} instead of job v_{2i+1}, and increase our value by $x_l - x_i$. Because M_2 is a maximum matching for set B, this is a contradiction so x_l should be the minimum of all x_is.

If all edges $e_2, e_4, \ldots, e_{2l}$ are also in matching M_1, we can use path P to find a matching for set $A \cup \{v\}$ with value x_l more than the value of M_1. We can take matching $M_1 \Delta P$ for set $A \cup \{v\}$. Because vertex v_{2l+1} is not saturated in M_2, it is also not saturated in M_1. So $M_1 \Delta P$ is a matching for set $A \cup \{v\}$. We conclude that $F(A \cup \{v\}) - F(A)$ is at least x_l which is equal to $F(B \cup \{v\}) - F(B)$. This completes the proof for this case.

In the other case, there are some edges among $e_2, e_4, \ldots, e_{2l}$ that are not in M_1. Let e_{2j} be the first edge among these edges that is not in M_1. So all edges $e_2, e_4, \ldots, e_{2j-2}$ are in both M_1 and M_2. Note that e_{2j} matches job v_{2j-1} with the time slot/processor pair v_{2j} in matching M_2. If job v_{2j-1} is not used (saturated) in matching M_1, we can find a matching as follows for set $A \cup \{v\}$. We can delete edges $e_2, e_4, \ldots, e_{2j-2}$ from M_1, and insert edges $e_1, e_3, \ldots, e_{2j-1}$ instead. This way we schedule job x_{2j-1} in addition to all other jobs that are scheduled in M_1. So the value of $F(A \cup \{v\})$ is at least x_{j-1} (the value of job x_{2j-1}) more than $F(A)$. We conclude that $F(A \cup \{v\}) - F(A) = x_{j-1}$ is at least $F(B \cup \{v\}) - F(B) = x_l$.

Finally we consider the case that v_{2j-1} is also saturated in M_1 using some edge e other than e_{2j}. Edges e and e_{2j} are in M_1 and M_2 respectively, and vertex v_{2j-1} is their common endpoint. So these two edges should come in the same connected component in the graph $M_1 \Delta M_2$. We proved that all connected components of $M_1 \Delta M_2$ are paths with odd number of edges that start and end with edges in M_2. Let Q be the path that contains edges e and e_{2j}. This path contains edges $e_1', e_2', \ldots, e_i' = e_{2j}, e_{i+1}' = e, e_{i+2}', \ldots, e_{2l'+1}'$. The last edge of this path, $e_{2l'+1}'$ matches a job v' with a time slot/processor pair. Let x' be the value of v'. Vertex v' is not scheduled in matching M_1. At first we prove that x' is at least x_l (the value of job v_{2l+1}). Then we show how to find a matching for set $A \cup \{v\}$ with value at least x' more than the value of M_1.

If x' is less than x_l, we can find a matching with greater value for set B instead of M_2. Delete edges $e_i' = e_{2j}$, $e_{i+2}', e_{i+4}', \ldots, e_{2l'+1}'$, and also edges $e_{2j+2}, e_{2j+4}, \ldots, e_{2l}$ from M_2, and insert edges $e_{i+1}' = e, e_{i+3}', \ldots, e_{2l'}'$, and edges $e_{2j+1}, e_{2j+3}, \ldots, e_{2l+1}$ to M_2 instead of the deleted edges. In the new matching, job v' with value x' is not saturated any more, but the vertex v_{2l+1} with value x_l is saturated. So the value of the new matching is $x_l - x' > 0$ more than the value of M_2 which is a contradiction. So x' is at least x_l.

Now we prove that there is a matching for set $A \cup \{v\}$ with value x' more than the value of M_1. We can find this matching as follows. Delete edges $e'_{i+1} = e$, e'_{i+3}, ..., $e'_{2l'}$, and edges $e_2, e_4, \ldots, e_{2j-2}$, and insert edges $e'_{i+2}, e'_{i+4}, \ldots, e'_{2l'+1}$, and edges $e_1, e_3, \ldots, e_{2j-1}$. This way we schedule job v' with value x' in addition to all other jobs that are scheduled in M_1. So we find a matching for set $A \cup \{v\}$ with value x' more than the value of M_1.

So $F(A \cup \{v\}) - F(A)$ is at least x'. We also know that $F(B \cup \{v\}) - F(B)$ is equal to x_l. Because x' is at least x_l, the proof is complete. $\square$

Now we are ready to represent our algorithm which finds an optimal solution (with respect to values).

THEOREM 4.3. *If there is an schedule for the prize-collecting scheduling problem with value at least Z and cost B, there is an algorithm which finds a schedule with value at least Z and cost at most $O([\log n + \log \Delta]B)$ where δ is the ratio of the maximum value over the minimum value of all n jobs.*

PROOF. Let v_{max} and v_{min} be the maximum and minimum value among all n jobs respectively. We know that Z can not be more than $n \cdot v_{max}$. Define ε to be $\frac{v_{min}}{n \cdot v_{max}} = \frac{1}{n\Delta}$. Using Theorem 4.1, we can find a solution with value at least $(1 - \varepsilon)Z$ and cost at most $O(B \log(n\Delta)) = O([\log n + \log \Delta]B)$. Let S' be this solution. If the value of S' is at least Z, we exit and return this set as our solution. Otherwise we do the following. Note that we just need εZ more value to reach the threshold Z, and εZ is at most v_{min}. So we just need to insert another interval which increases our value by at least v_{min}. In the proof of Lemma 4.2, we proved that the value of $F(B \cup \{v\}) - F(B)$ is either zero or equal to the value of some jobs (in the proof it was x_l the value of vertex v_{2l+1}). So if we add an interval the value of set is either unchanged or increased by at least v_{min}. So among all intervals with cost at most B, we choose one of them that increase our value by at least v_{min}. At first note that this insertion reaches our value to Z, and our cost would be still $O([\log n + \log \Delta]B)$.

We now prove that there exists such an interval. Note that the optimum solution consists of some intervals $S_1, S_2, \ldots, S_k$. The union of these intervals, T has value $F(T)$ which is at least Z. So $F(T)$ is greater than the value of our solution $F(S')$. Using Lemma 2.1, $F(S' \cup S_i) - F(S')$ should be positive for some $1 \leq i \leq k$. We also know that the cost of this set is not more than B because the cost of the optimum solution is not more than B. So there exists a time interval (a set like S_i) that solves our problem with additional cost at most B. We also can find it by a simple search among all time intervals. $\square$

Note that in the simple case studied in the literature, the values are all identical, and Δ is equal to 1.

5. REFERENCES

[1] J. Augustine, S. Irani, and C. Swamy. *Optimal power-down strategies.* In Proceedings of the 45th Symposium on Foundations of Computer Science, pages 530–539, Rome, Italy, October 2004.

[2] P. Baptiste. *Scheduling unit tasks to minimize the number of idle periods: a polynomial time algorithm for offline dynamic power management.* In Proceedings of the 17th Annual ACM-SIAM Symposium on Discrete Algorithm, pages 364–367, Miami, Florida, 2006.

[3] MohammadHossein Bateni, MohammadTaghi Hajiaghayi, Morteza Zadimoghaddam. *The submodular secretary problem and its extensions* Manuscript.

[4] Erik D. Demaine, Mohammad Ghodsi, MohammadTaghi Hajiaghayi, Amin S. Sayedi-Roshkhar and Morteza Zadimoghaddam. *Scheduling to Minimize Gaps and Power Consumption.* In Proceedings of the 19th ACM Symposium on Parallelism in Algorithms and Architectures (SPAA), Pages 46-54, San Diego, California, June 2007.

[5] E. Even-dar, Y. Mansour, V. S. Mirrokni, M. Muthukrishnan, U. Nadav. *Bid Optimization for Broad-Match Ad Auctions.* In Proceedings of the 18th International World Wide Web Conference, Pages 231-240, Madrid, Spain, 2009.

[6] S. Irani, S. Shukla, and R. Gupta. *Algorithms for power savings.* In Proceedings of the 14th Annual ACM-SIAM Symposium on Discrete Algorithms, pages 37–46, Baltimore, Maryland, 2003.

[7] Johnson, D. S. *Approximation Algorithms for Combinatorial Problems.* In Proceedings of the fifth annual ACM Symposium on Theory of Computing, Pages 38-49, Austin, Texas, 1973.

[8] Nitish Korula and Martin Pal. *Algorithms for Secretary Problems on Graphs and Hypergraphs.* In Proceedings of the 36th International Colloquium on Automata, Languages and Programming, Pages 508-520, Rhodes, Greece, July, 2009.

[9] Ariel Kulik, Hadas Shachnai, and Tami Tamir. *Maximizing submodular set functions subject to multiple linear constraints.* In Proceedings of the Nineteenth Annual ACM -SIAM Symposium on Discrete Algorithms, Pages 545-554, New York, 2009.

[10] Jon Lee, Vahab S. Mirrokni, Viswanath Nagarajan, Maxim Sviridenko. *Non-monotone submodular maximization under matroid and knapsack constraints.* In Proceedings of the 41th annual ACM Symposium on Theory of Computing, Pages 323-332, Bethesda, Maryland, 2009.

[11] Raz, R., and Safra, S. *A sub-constant error-probability low-degree test, and sub-constant error-probability PCP characterization of NP.* In Proceedings of the 29th annual ACM Symposium on Theory of Computing, Pages 475-484, El Paso, Texas, 1997.

APPENDIX

A. HARDNESS RESULTS

Here we show some matching hardness results to show that our algorithms are optimal unless $P = NP$. Surprisingly the problem we studied does not have better than $\log n$ approximation even in very simple cases, namely, one interval scheduling with nonuniform parallel machines, or multi-interval scheduling with only one processor.

It is proved in [4] that the multi-interval scheduling problem with only one processor and simple cost function is Set-Cover hard, and therefore the best possible approximation factor for this problem is $\log n$. We note that in the simple cost function the cost of an interval is equal to its length plus a fixed amount of energy (the restart cost). All previous work studies the problem with this cost function. In fact, Theorem 7 of [4] shows that the problem does not have a $o(\log N)$-approximation even when the number of time intervals of each job is at most 2 (each job has a set of time intervals in which it can execute).

THEOREM A.1. *It is NP-hard to approximate 2-interval gap scheduling within a $o(\log N)$ factor, where N is the size of input.*

Now we show that the one-interval scheduling problem, for which there exists a polynomial-time algorithm in [4], does not have any $o(\log N)$-approximation when only a subset of processors are capable of executing a job. Assume that each job has one time interval in which it can execute, and for each job, we have a subset of processors that can execute this job in its time interval, i.e., the other processors do not have necessary resources to execute the job. We also consider the generalized cost function in which the cost of an interval is not necessarily equal to its length plus a fixed amount. We call this problem *one-interval scheduling with nonuniform processors*.

THEOREM A.2. *It is NP-hard to approximate one-interval scheduling with nonuniform processors problem within a $o(\log N)$ factor, where N is the size of input.*

PROOF. Like previous hardness results for these scheduling problems, we give an approximation-preserving reduction from Set Cover, which is not $o(\log n)$-approximable unless P = NP [11]. Let $E = \{e_1, e_2, \ldots, e_n\}$ be the set of all elements in the Set-Cover instance. There are also m subsets of E, $S_1, S_2, \ldots, S_m$ in the instance. We construct our scheduling problem instance as follows. For each set S_j, we put a processor P_j in our instance. For each element e_i, we put a job j_i. Only jobs in set S_j can be done in processor P_j. The time interval of all jobs is $[1, n]$. The cost of keeping each processor alive during a time interval is 1. Note that the cost a time interval is not a function of its length in this

case, i.e., the cost of an interval is almost equal to a fixed cost which might be the restart cost. So the optimum solution to our scheduling problem is a minimum size subset of processors in which we can schedule all jobs because we can assume that when a processor is alive in some time units, we can keep that processor alive in the whole interval $[1, n]$ (it does not increase our cost). In fact we want to find the minimum number of subsets among the input subset such that their union is E. This is exactly the Set Cover problem. $\square$

B. POLYNOMIAL-TIME ALGORITHM FOR PRIZE-COLLECTING ONE-INTERVAL GAP MINIMIZATION PROBLEM

The simple cost function version of our problem is studied in [2, 4] as the gap-minimization problem. Each job has a time interval, and we want to schedule all jobs on P machines with the minimum number of gaps. (A gap is a maximal period of time in which a processor is idle, which can be associated with a restart for one of the machines.) There are many cases in which we can not schedule all jobs according to our limitation in resources: number of machines, deadlines, etc. So we define the prize-collecting version of this simple problem. Assume that each job has some value for us, and we get its value if we schedule it. We want to get the maximum possible value according to some cost limits. Formally, we want to schedule a subset of jobs with maximum total value and at most g gaps. The variable g is given in the input. Now we show how to adapt the sophisticated dynamic program in [4] to solve this problem.

THEOREM B.1. *There is a $(n^7 p^5 g)$-time algorithm for prize-collecting p-processor gap scheduling of n jobs with budget g, the number of gaps should not exceed g.*

PROOF. In the proof of Theorem 1 of [4], C_{t_1,t_2,k,q,l_1,l_2} is defined to be the number of gaps in the optimal solution for a subproblem defined there. If we define $C'_{t_1,t_2,k,q,l_1,l_2,g'}$ to be the maximum value we can get in the same subproblem using at most $g' \leq g$ gaps, we can update this new dynamic program array in the same way. The rest of the proof is similar; we just get an extra g in the running time. $\square$

Assigning Tasks for Efficiency in Hadoop

[Extended Abstract]

Michael J. Fischer
Computer Science
Yale University
P.O. Box 208285
New Haven, CT, USA
michael.fischer@yale.edu

Xueyuan Su[*]
Computer Science
Yale University
P.O. Box 208285
New Haven, CT, USA
xueyuan.su@yale.edu

Yitong Yin[†]
State Key Laboratory for Novel
Software Technology
Nanjing University, China
yinyt@nju.edu.cn

ABSTRACT

In recent years Google's MapReduce has emerged as a leading large-scale data processing architecture. Adopted by companies such as Amazon, Facebook, Google, IBM and Yahoo! in daily use, and more recently put in use by several universities, it allows parallel processing of huge volumes of data over cluster of machines. Hadoop is a free Java implementation of MapReduce. In Hadoop, files are split into blocks and replicated and spread over all servers in a network. Each job is also split into many small pieces called tasks. Several tasks are processed on a single server, and a job is not completed until all the assigned tasks are finished. A crucial factor that affects the completion time of a job is the particular assignment of tasks to servers. Given a placement of the input data over servers, one wishes to find the assignment that minimizes the completion time. In this paper, an idealized Hadoop model is proposed to investigate the Hadoop task assignment problem. It is shown that there is no feasible algorithm to find the optimal Hadoop task assignment unless $\mathcal{P} = \mathcal{NP}$. Assignments that are computed by the round robin algorithm inspired by the current Hadoop scheduler are shown to deviate from optimum by a multiplicative factor in the worst case. A flow-based algorithm is presented that computes assignments that are optimal to within an additive constant.

Categories and Subject Descriptors

D.3.2 [**Programming Languages**]: Language Classifications—*concurrent, distributed, and parallel languages*; F.1.2 [**Computation by Abstract Devices**]: Modes of Computation—*parallelism and concurrency*; F.1.3 [**Computation**

[*]Supported by the Kempner Fellowship from the Department of Computer Science at Yale University.

[†]Supported by the National Science Foundation of China under Grant No. 60721002. This work was done when Yitong Yin was at Yale University.

by Abstract Devices]: Complexity Measures and Classes—*reducibility and completeness*; F.2.2 [**Analysis of Algorithms and Problem Complexity**]: Nonnumerical Algorithms and Problems—*sequencing and scheduling*

General Terms

Algorithms, Performance, Theory

Keywords

task assignment, load balancing, NP-completeness, approximation algorithm, MapReduce, Hadoop

1. INTRODUCTION

1.1 Background

The cloud computing paradigm has recently received significant attention in the media. The cloud is a metaphor for the Internet, which is an abstraction for the complex infrastructure it conceals. Cloud computing refers to both the applications delivered as services over the Internet and the hardware and software that provide such services. It envisions shifting data storage and computing power away from local servers, across the network cloud, and into large clusters of machines hosted by companies such as Amazon, Google, IBM, Microsoft, Yahoo! and so on.

Google's MapReduce [8, 9, 16] parallel computing architecture, for example, splits workload over large clusters of commodity PCs and enables automatic parallelization. By exploiting parallel processing, it provides a software platform that lets one easily write and run applications that process vast amounts of data.

Apache Hadoop [4] is a free Java implementation of MapReduce in the open source software community. It is originally designed to efficiently process large volumes of data by parallel processing over commodity computers in local networks. In academia, researchers have adapted Hadoop to several different architectures. For example, Ranger et al. [18] evaluate MapReduce in multi-core and multi-processor systems, Kruijf et al. [7] implement MapReduce on the Cell B.E. processor architecture, and He et al. [14] propose a MapReduce framework on graphics processors. Many related applications using Hadoop have also been developed to solve various practical problems.

1.2 The MapReduce Framework

A Hadoop system runs on top of a distributed file system, called the Hadoop Distributed File System (HDFS). HDFS usually runs on networked commodity PCs, where data are replicated and locally stored on hard disks of each machine. To store and process huge volume of data sets, HDFS typically uses a block size of 64MB. Therefore, moving computation close to the data is a design goal in the MapReduce framework.

In the MapReduce framework, any application is specified by jobs. A MapReduce job splits the input data into independent blocks, which are processed by the *map* tasks in parallel. Each map task processes a single block[1] consisting of some number of records. Each record in turn consists of a key/value pair. A map task applies the user defined map function to each input key/value pair and produces intermediate key/value pairs. The framework then sorts the intermediate data, and forwards them to the *reduce* tasks via interconnected networks. After receiving all intermediate key/value pairs with the same key, a reduce task executes the user defined reduce function and produces the output data. Finally, these output data are written back to the HDFS.

In such a framework, there is a single server, called the *master*, that keeps track of all jobs in the whole distributed system. The master runs a special process, called the *job-tracker*, that is responsible for task assignment and scheduling for the whole system. For the rest of servers that are called the *slaves*, each of them runs a process called the *task-tracker*. The tasktracker schedules the several tasks assigned to the single server in a way similar to a normal operating system.

The map task assignment is a vital part that affects the completion time of the whole job. First, each reduce task cannot begin until it receives the required intermediate data from all finished map tasks. Second, the assignment determines the location of intermediate data and the pattern of the communication traffic. Therefore, some algorithms should be in place to optimize the task assignment.

1.3 Related Work

Since Kuhn [15] proposed the first method for the classic assignment problem in 1955, variations of the assignment problem have been under extensive study in many areas [5]. In the classic assignment problem, there are identical number of jobs and persons. An assignment is a one-to-one mapping from tasks to persons. Each job introduces a cost when it is assigned to a person. Therefore, an optimal assignment minimizes the total cost over all persons.

In the area of parallel and distributed computing, when jobs are processed in parallel over several machines, one is interested in minimizing the maximum processing time of any machines. This problem is sometimes called the minimum makespan scheduling problem. This problem in general is known to be $\mathcal{NP}$-complete [11]. Under the

identical-machine model, there are some well-known approximation algorithms. For example, Graham [12] proposed a $(2 - 1/n)$-approximation algorithm in 1966, where n is the total number of machines. Graham [13] proposed another 4/3-approximation algorithm in 1969. However, under the unrelated-machine model, this problem is known to be APX-hard, both in terms of its offline [17] and online [1, 2] approximability.

As some researchers [3, 4] pointed out, the scheduling mechanisms and polices that assign tasks to servers within the MapReduce framework can have a profound effect on efficiency. An early version of Hadoop uses a simple heuristic algorithm that greedily exploits data locality. Zaharia, Konwinski and Joseph [19] proposed some heuristic refinements based on experimental results.

1.4 Our Contributions

We investigate task assignment in Hadoop. In Section 2, we propose an idealized Hadoop model to evaluate the cost of task assignments. Based on this model, we show in Section 3 that there is no feasible algorithm to find the optimal assignment unless $\mathcal{P} = \mathcal{NP}$. In Section 4, we show that task assignments computed by a simple greedy round-robin algorithm might deviate from the optimum by a multiplicative factor. In Section 5, we present an algorithm that employs maximum flow and increasing threshold techniques to compute task assignments that are optimal to within an additive constant.

2. PROBLEM FORMALIZATION

Definition 1. A *Map-Reduce schema (MR-schema)* is a pair (T, S), where T is a set of *tasks* and S is a set of *servers*. Let $m = |T|$ and $n = |S|$. A *task assignment* is a function $A \colon T \to S$ that assigns each task t to a server $A(t)$.[2] Let $\mathcal{A} = \{T \to S\}$ be the set of all possible task assignments. An *MR-system* is a triple (T, S, w), where (T, S) is an MR-schema and $w \colon T \times \mathcal{A} \to \mathbb{Q}^+$ is a *cost function*.

Intuitively, $w(t, A)$ is the time to perform task t on server $A(t)$ in the context of the complete assignment A. The motivation for this level of generality is that the time to execute a task t in Hadoop depends not only on the task and the server speed, but also on possible network congestion, which in turn is influenced by the other tasks running on the cluster.

Definition 2. The *load* of server s under assignment A is defined as $L_s^A = \sum_{t:A(t)=s} w(t, A)$. The *maximum load* under assignment A is defined as $L^A = \max_s L_s^A$. The *total load* under assignment A is defined as $H^A = \sum_s L_s^A$.

An MR-system models a cloud computer where all servers work in parallel. Tasks assigned to the same server are processed sequentially, whereas tasks assigned to different servers run in parallel. Thus, the total completion time of the cloud under task assignment A is given by the maximum load L^A.

---

[1] Strictly speaking, a map task in Hadoop sometimes processes data that comes from two successive file blocks. This occurs because file blocks do not respect logical record boundaries, so the last logical record processed by a map task might lie partly in the current data block and partly in the succeeding block, requiring the map task to access the succeeding block in order to fetch the tail end of its last logical record.

[2] In an MR-schema, it is common that $|T| \geq |S|$. Therefore in this paper, unlike the classic assignment problem where an assignment refers to a *one-to-one* mapping or a *permutation* [5, 15], we instead use the notion of *many-to-one* mapping.

Our notion of an MR-system is very general and admits arbitrary cost functions. To usefully model Hadoop as an MR-system, we need a realistic but simplified cost model.

In Hadoop, the cost of a map task depends frequently on the location of its data. If the data is on the server's local disk, then the cost (execution time) is considerably lower than if the data is located remotely and must be fetched across the network before being processed.

We make several simplifying assumptions. We assume that all tasks and all servers are identical, so that for any particular assignment of tasks to servers, all tasks whose data is locally available take the same amount of time w_{loc}, and all tasks whose data is remote take the same amount of time w_{rem}. However, we do not assume that w_{rem} is constant over all assignments. Rather, we let it grow with the total number of tasks whose data is remote. This reflects the increased data fetch time due to overall network congestion. Thus, $w_{rem}(r)$ is the cost of each remote task in every assignment with exactly r remote tasks. We assume that $w_{rem}(r) \geq w_{loc}$ for all r and that $w_{rem}(r)$ is (weakly) monotone increasing in r.

We formalize these concepts below. In each of the following, (T, S) is an MR-schema.

Definition 3. A *data placement* is a relation $\rho \subseteq T \times S$ such that for every task $t \in T$, there exists at least one server $s \in S$ such that $\rho(t, s)$ holds.

The placement relation describes where the input data blocks are placed. If $\rho(t, s)$ holds, then server s locally stores a replica of the data block that task t needs.

Definition 4. We represent the placement relation ρ by an unweighted bipartite graph, called the *placement graph*. In the placement graph $G_\rho = ((T, S), E)$, T consists of m task nodes and S consists of n server nodes. There is an edge $(t, s) \in E$ iff $\rho(t, s)$ holds.

Definition 5. A *partial assignment* α is a partial function from T to S. We regard a partial assignment as a set of ordered pairs with pairwise distinct first elements, so for partial assignments β and α, $\beta \supseteq \alpha$ means β *extends* α. If $s \in S$, the *restriction of* α *to* s is the partial assignment $\alpha|_s = \alpha \cap (T \times \{s\})$. Thus, $\alpha|_s$ agrees with α for those tasks that α assigns to s, but all other tasks are unassigned in $\alpha|_s$.

Definition 6. Let ρ be a data placement and β be a partial assignment. A task $t \in T$ is *local in* β if $\beta(t)$ is defined and $\rho(t, \beta(t))$. A task $t \in T$ is *remote in* α if $\beta(t)$ is defined and $\neg\rho(t, \beta(t))$. Otherwise t is *unassigned in* β. Let ℓ^β, r^β and u^β be the number of local tasks, remote tasks, and unassigned tasks in β, respectively. For any $s \in S$, let ℓ_s^β be the number of local tasks assigned to s by β. Let $k^\beta = \max_{s \in S} \ell_s^\beta$.

Definition 7. Let ρ be a data placement, β be a partial assignment, $w_{loc} \in \mathbb{Q}^+$, and $w_{rem} : \mathbb{N} \to \mathbb{Q}^+$ such that $w_{loc} \leq w_{rem}(0) \leq w_{rem}(1) \leq w_{rem}(2) \ldots$. Let $w_{rem}^\beta = w_{rem}(r^\beta + u^\beta)$. The *Hadoop cost function* with parameters ρ, w_{loc}, and $w_{rem}(\cdot)$ is the function w defined by

$$w(t, \beta) = \begin{cases} w_{loc} & \text{if } t \text{ is local in } \beta, \\ w_{rem}^\beta & \text{otherwise.} \end{cases}$$

We call ρ the *placement* of w, and w_{loc} and $w_{rem}(\cdot)$ the *local* and *remote* costs of w, respectively. Let $K^\beta = k^\beta \cdot w_{loc}$.

The definition of remote cost under a partial assignment β is pessimistic. It assumes that tasks not assigned by β will eventually become remote, and each remote task will eventually have cost $w_{rem}(r^\beta + u^\beta)$. This definition agrees with the definition of remote cost under a complete assignment A, because $u^A = 0$ and thus $w_{rem}^A = w_{rem}(r^A + u^A) = w_{rem}(r^A)$.

Since ρ is encoded by mn bits, w_{loc} is encoded by one rational number, and $w_{rem}(\cdot)$ is encoded by $m + 1$ rational numbers, the Hadoop cost function $w(\rho, w_{loc}, w_{rem}(\cdot))$ is encoded by mn bits plus $m + 2$ rational numbers.

Definition 8. A *Hadoop MR-system (HMR-system)* is the MR-system (T, S, w), where w is the Hadoop cost function with parameters ρ, w_{loc}, and $w_{rem}(\cdot)$. A HMR-system is defined by $(T, S, \rho, w_{loc}, w_{rem}(\cdot))$.

Problem 1 Hadoop Task Assignment Problem (HTA)

1. **Instance:** An HMR-system $(T, S, \rho, w_{loc}, w_{rem}(\cdot))$.

2. **Objective:** Find an assignment A that minimizes L^A.

Sometimes the cost of running a task on a server only depends on the placement relation and its data locality, but not on the assignment of other tasks.

Definition 9. A Hadoop cost function w is called *uniform* if $w_{rem}(r) = c$ for some constant c and all $r \in \mathbb{N}$. A *uniform HMR-system (UHMR-system)* is an HMR-system $(T, S, \rho, w_{loc}, w_{rem}(\cdot))$, where w is uniform.

Problem 2 Uniform Hadoop Task Assignment Problem (UHTA)

1. **Instance:** A UHMR-system $(T, S, \rho, w_{loc}, w_{rem}(\cdot))$.

2. **Objective:** Find an assignment A that minimizes L^A.

The number of replicas of each data block may be bounded, often by a small number such as 2 or 3.

Definition 10. Call a placement graph $G = ((T, S), E)$ *j-replica-bounded* if the degree of t is at most j for all $t \in T$. A *j-replica-bounded-UHMR-system (j-UHMR-system)* is a UHMR-system $(T, S, \rho, w_{loc}, w_{rem}(\cdot))$, where G_ρ is j-replica-bounded.

Problem 3 j-Uniform Hadoop Task Assignment Problem (j-UHTA)

1. **Instance:** A j-UHMR-system $(T, S, \rho, w_{loc}, w_{rem}(\cdot))$.

2. **Objective:** Find an assignment A that minimizes L^A.

---

3. HARDNESS OF TASK ASSIGNMENT

In this section, we analyze the hardness of the various HTA optimization problems by showing the corresponding decision problems to be $\mathcal{NP}$-complete.

3.1 Task Assignment Decision Problems

Definition 11. Given a server *capacity* k, a task assignment A is *k-feasible* if $L^A \leq k$. An HMR-system is *k-admissible* if there exists a k-feasible task assignment.

The decision problem corresponding to a class of HMR-systems and capacity k asks whether a given HMR-system in the class is k-admissible. Thus, the k-HTA problem asks about arbitrary HMR-systems, the k-UHTA problem asks about arbitrary UHMR-systems, and the k-j-UHTA problem (which we write (j,k)-UHTA) asks about arbitrary j-UHMR-systems.

3.2 $\mathcal{NP}$-completeness of (2,3)-UHTA

The (2,3)-UHTA problem is a very restricted subclass of the general k-admissibility problem for HMR-systems. In this section, we restrict even further by taking $w_{\text{loc}} = 1$ and $w_{\text{rem}} = 3$. This problem represents a simple scenario where the cost function assumes only the two possible values 1 and 3, each data block has at most 2 replicas, and each server has capacity 3. Despite its obvious simplicity, we show that (2,3)-UHTA is $\mathcal{NP}$-complete. It follows that all of the less restritive decision problems are also $\mathcal{NP}$-complete, and the correponding optimization problems do not have feasible solutions unless $\mathcal{P} = \mathcal{NP}$.

THEOREM 3.1. *(2,3)-UHTA with costs $w_{\text{loc}} = 1$ and $w_{\text{rem}} = 3$ is $\mathcal{NP}$-complete.*

The proof method is to construct a polynomial-time reduction from 3SAT to (2,3)-UHTA. Let $\mathcal{G}$ be the set of all 2-replica-bounded placement graphs. Given $G_\rho \in \mathcal{G}$, we define the HMR-system $\mathcal{M}_G = (T, S, \rho, w_{\text{loc}}, w_{\text{rem}}(\cdot))$, where $w_{\text{loc}} = 1$ and $w_{\text{rem}}(r) = 3$ for all r. We say that G is *3-admissible* if $\mathcal{M}_G$ is 3-admissible. We construct a polynomial-time computable mapping $f : 3\text{CNF} \rightarrow \mathcal{G}$, and show that a 3CNF formula ϕ is satisfiable iff $f(\phi)$ is 3-admissible. We shorten "3-admissible" to "admissible" in the following discussion.

We first describe the construction of f. Let $\phi = C_1 \wedge C_2 \cdots \wedge C_\alpha$ be a 3CNF formula, where each $C_u = (l_{u1} \vee l_{u2} \vee l_{u3})$ is a clause and each l_{uv} is a literal. Let $x_1, \cdots, x_\beta$ be the variables that appear in ϕ. Therefore, ϕ contains exactly 3α instances of literals, each of which is either x_i or $\neg x_i$, where $i \in [1, \beta]$.[3] Let ω be the maximum number of occurrences of any literal in ϕ. Table 1 summarizes the parameters of ϕ.

Table 1: Parameters of the 3CNF ϕ

clauses (C_u)	α	variables (v_i)	β
literals (l_{uv})	3α	max-occur of any literal	ω

For example, in $\phi = (x_1 \vee x_2 \vee x_3) \wedge (x_1 \vee \neg x_4 \vee x_5) \wedge (\neg x_1 \vee x_4 \vee \neg x_6)$, we have $\alpha = 3$, $\beta = 6$, and $\omega = 2$ since x_1 occurs twice.

Given ϕ, we construct the corresponding placement graph G which comprises several disjoint copies of the three types of gadget described below, connected together with additional edges.

The first type of gadget is called a *clause gadget*. Each clause gadget u contains a *clause server* C_u, three *literal*

tasks l_{u1}, l_{u2}, l_{u3} and an *auxiliary task* a_u. There is an edge between each of these tasks and the clause server. Since ϕ contains α clauses, G contains α clause gadgets. Thus, G contains α clause servers, 3α literal tasks and α auxiliary tasks. Figure 1 describes the structure of the u-th clause gadget. We use circles and boxes to represent tasks and servers, respectively.

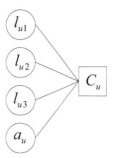

Figure 1: The structure of the u-th clause gadget.

The second type of gadget is called a *variable gadget*. Each variable gadget contains 2ω *ring servers* placed around a circle. Let $R_j^{(i)}$ denote the server at position $j \in [1, 2\omega]$ in ring i. Define the set $\mathcal{T}_i$ to be the servers in odd-numbered positions. Similarly, define the set $\mathcal{F}_i$ to be the servers in even-numbered positions. Between each pair of ring servers $R_j^{(i)}$ and $R_{j+1}^{(i)}$, we place a *ring task* $r_j^{(i)}$ connected to its two neighboring servers. To complete the circle, $r_{2\omega}^{(i)}$ is connected to $R_{2\omega}^{(i)}$ and $R_1^{(i)}$. There are also ω *variable tasks* $v_j^{(i)} : j \in [1, \omega]$ in ring i, but they do not connect to any ring server. Since ϕ contains β variables, G contains β variable gadgets. Thus, G contains $2\beta\omega$ ring servers, $2\beta\omega$ ring tasks and $\beta\omega$ variable tasks. Figure 2 describes the structure of the i-th variable gadget.

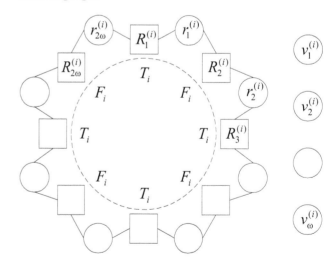

Figure 2: The structure of the i-th variable gadget.

The third type of gadget is called a *sink gadget*. The sink gadget contains a *sink server* P and three *sink tasks* p_1, p_2, p_3. Each sink task is connected to the sink server. G only contains one sink gadget. Figure 3 describes the structure of the sink gadget.

There are also some inter-gadget edges in G. We connect

[3] The notation [a,b] in our discussion represents the set of integers $\{a, a + 1, \cdots, b - 1, b\}$.

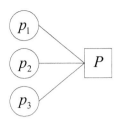

Figure 3: The structure of the sink gadget.

each variable task $v_j^{(i)}$ to the sink server P. We also connect each literal task l_{uv} to a unique ring server $R_j^{(i)}$. To be more precise, if literal l_{uv} is the j-th occurrence of x_i in ϕ, connect the literal task l_{uv} to ring server $R_{2j-1}^{(i)} \in \mathcal{T}_i$; if literal l_{uv} is the j-th occurrence of $\neg x_i$ in ϕ, connect the literal task l_{uv} to ring server $R_{2j}^{(i)} \in \mathcal{F}_i$. These inter-gadget edges complete the graph G. Table 2 summarizes the parameters of G.

Table 2: Parameters of the HMR-graph G

clause server C_u	α	literal task l_{uv}	3α
auxiliary task a_u	α	ring server $R_j^{(i)}$	$2\beta\omega$
ring task $r_j^{(i)}$	$2\beta\omega$	variable task $v_j^{(i)}$	$\beta\omega$
sink server P	1	sink task p_j	3

LEMMA 3.2. *For any $\phi \in$ 3CNF, the graph $f(\phi)$ is 2-replica-bounded.*

PROOF. We count the number of edges from each task node in $f(\phi)$. Each clause task has 2 edges, each auxiliary task has 1 edge, each ring task has 2 edges, each variable task has 1 edge, and each sink task has 1 edge. Therefore, $f(\phi)$ is 2-replica-bounded. □

The following lemma is immediate.

LEMMA 3.3. *The mapping $f :$ 3CNF $\to \mathcal{G}$ is polynomial-time computable.*

LEMMA 3.4. *If ϕ is satisfiable, then $G = f(\phi)$ is admissible.*

PROOF. Let σ be a satisfying truth assignment for ϕ, and we construct a feasible assignment A in $G = f(\phi)$. First of all, assign each sink task to the sink server, i.e., let $A(p_i) = P$ for all $i \in [1, 3]$. Then assign each auxiliary task a_u to the clause server C_u, i.e., let $A(a_u) = C_u$ for all $u \in [1, \alpha]$. If $\sigma(x_i) = true$, then assign ring tasks $r_j^{(i)} : j \in [1, 2\omega]$ to ring servers in $\mathcal{T}_i$, variable tasks $v_j^{(i)} : j \in [1, \omega]$ to ring servers in $\mathcal{F}_i$. If $\sigma(x_i) = false$, then assign ring tasks $r_j^{(i)} : j \in [1, 2\omega]$ to ring servers in $\mathcal{F}_i$, variable tasks $v_j^{(i)} : j \in [1, \omega]$ to ring servers in $\mathcal{T}_i$. If literal $l_{uv} = x_i$ and $\sigma(x_i) = true$, then assign task l_{uv} to its local ring server in $\mathcal{T}_i$. If literal $l_{uv} = \neg x_i$ and $\sigma(x_i) = false$, then assign task l_{uv} to its local ring server in $\mathcal{F}_i$. Otherwise, assign task l_{uv} to its local clause server C_u.

We then check this task assignment is feasible. Each ring server is assigned either at most three local tasks (two ring tasks and one literal task), or one remote variable task. In either case, the load does not exceed the capacity 3. The number of tasks assigned to each clause server C_u is exactly the number of false literals in C_u under σ plus one (the auxiliary task), and each task is local to C_u. Thus, the load is at most 3. The sink server is assigned three local sink tasks and the load is exactly 3. Therefore, all constraints are satisfied and A is feasible. This completes the proof of Lemma 3.4. □

The proof of the converse of Lemma 3.4 is more involved. The method is given a feasible assignment A in $G = f(\phi)$, we first construct a feasible assignment B in G such that $B(t) \neq P$ for all $t \in T - \{p_1, p_2, p_3\}$. Then we remove the sink tasks and the sink server from further consideration and consider the resulting graph G'. After that, we partition G' into two subgraphs, and construct a feasible assignment B' such that no tasks from one partition are remotely assigned to servers in the other partition. This step involves a case analysis. Finally, a natural way of constructing the satisfying truth assignment for ϕ follows.

LEMMA 3.5. *Let A be a feasible task assignment. Then there exists a feasible task assignment B such that $B(t) \neq P$ for all $t \in T - \{p_1, p_2, p_3\}$.*

PROOF. When A satisfies that $A(t) \neq P$ for all $t \in T - \{p_1, p_2, p_3\}$, let $B = A$. Otherwise, assume there exists a task t' such that $A(t') = P$ and $t' \in T - \{p_1, p_2, p_3\}$. Since the capacity of P is 3, there is at least one sink task, say p_1, is not assigned to P. Let $A(p_1) = Q$. Since $\rho(p_1, Q)$ does not hold, Q has only been assigned p_1 and $L_Q^A = 3$. Let $B(p_1) = P$ and $B(t') = Q$. Repeat the same process for all tasks other than p_1, p_2, p_3 that are assigned to P in A. Then let $B(t) = A(t)$ for the remaining tasks $t \in T$. To see B is feasible, note that $L_s^B \leq L_s^A \leq 3$ for all servers $s \in S$. □

Let G' be the subgraph induced by $(T - \{p_1, p_2, p_3\}, S - \{P\}) = (T', S')$. We have the following lemma.

LEMMA 3.6. *Let A be a feasible task assignment in G. Then there exists a feasible task assignment A' in G'.*

PROOF. Given A, Lemma 3.5 tells us that there exists another feasible assignment B in G such that $B(t) \neq P$ for all $t \in T'$. Let $A'(t) = B(t)$ for all $t \in T'$. Then A' is an assignment in G' since $A'(t) \in S - \{P\}$ for all $t \in T'$. To see A' is feasible, note that $L_s^{A'} \leq L_s^B \leq 3$ for all servers $s \in S'$. □

We further partition G' into two subgraphs G_C and G_R. G_C is induced by nodes $\{C_u : u \in [1, \alpha]\} \cup \{a_u : u \in [1, \alpha]\} \cup \{l_{uv} : u \in [1, \alpha], v \in [1, 3]\}$ and G_R is induced by nodes $\{R_j^{(i)} : i \in [1, \beta], j \in [1, 2\omega]\} \cup \{r_j^{(i)} : i \in [1, \beta], j \in [1, 2\omega]\} \cup \{v_j^{(i)} : i \in [1, \beta], j \in [1, \omega]\}$. In other words, G_C consists of all clause gadgets while G_R consists of all variable gadgets.

If a task in one partition is remotely assigned to a server in the other partition, we call this task a *cross-boundary* task. Let n_c^A be the number of cross-boundary tasks that are in G_C and assigned to servers in G_R by A, n_r^A be the number of cross-boundary tasks that are in G_R and assigned to servers in G_C by A. We have the following lemmas.

LEMMA 3.7. *Let A be a feasible assignment in G' such that $n_c^A > 0$ and $n_r^A > 0$. Then there exist a feasible assignment B in G' such that one of n_c^B and n_r^B equals $|n_c^A - n_r^A|$ and the other one equals 0.*

PROOF. Assume $t_i \in G_C$, $s_i \in G_R$ and $A(t_i) = s_i$; $t'_i \in G_R$, $s'_i \in G_C$ and $A(t'_i) = s'_i$. Then each of s_i and s'_i is assigned one remote task. Let $B(t_i) = s'_i$ and $B(t'_i) = s_i$, and then $L^B_{s_i} \leq L^A_{s_i} = 3$ and $L^B_{s'_i} \leq L^A_{s'_i} = 3$. This process decreases n_c and n_r each by one, and the resulting assignment is also feasible. Repeat the same process until the smaller one of n_c and n_r becomes 0. Then let $B(t) = A(t)$ for all the remaining tasks $t \in T'$. It is obvious that B is feasible, and one of n^B_c and n^B_r equals $|n^A_c - n^A_r|$ and the other one equals 0. □

LEMMA 3.8. *Let A be a feasible assignment in G' such that $n^A_c = 0$. Then $n^A_r = 0$.*

PROOF. For the sake of contradiction, assume $t_i \in G_R$, $s_i \in G_C$ and $A(t_i) = s_i$. For each server $s_j \in G_C$, there is one auxiliary task $a_u : u \in [1, \alpha]$ such that $\rho(a_u, s_j)$ holds. Since $w_{\mathrm{loc}} = 1$ and $w_{\mathrm{rem}} = 3$, if A is feasible then $A(a_u) \neq A(a_v)$ for $u \neq v$. Since there are α auxiliary tasks and α servers in G_C, one server is assigned exactly one auxiliary task. Since $A(t_i) = s_i$, $L^A_{s_i} \geq 1 + 3 > 3$, contradicting the fact that A is feasible. Therefore, there is no $t_i \in G_R$ and $s_i \in G_C$ such that $A(t_i) = s_i$. Thus, $n^A_r = 0$. □

LEMMA 3.9. *Let A be a feasible assignment in G' such that $n^A_r = 0$. Then $n^A_c = 0$.*

PROOF. For the sake of contradiction, assume $t_i \in G_C$, $s_i \in G_R$ and $A(t_i) = s_i$. Let k_0, k_1, k_2, k_3 denote the number of ring servers filled to load $0, 1, 2, 3$, respectively. From the total number of servers in G_R, we have

$$k_0 + k_1 + k_2 + k_3 = 2\beta\omega \qquad (1)$$

Similarly, from the total number of tasks in G_R, we have

$$0 \cdot k_0 + 1 \cdot k_1 + 2 \cdot k_2 + 1 \cdot k_3 = 3\beta\omega \qquad (2)$$

Subtracting (1) from (2) gives $k_2 = \beta\omega + k_0$. Assigning both neighboring ring tasks to the same ring server fills it to load 2. Since there are only $2\beta\omega$ ring servers, we have $k_2 \leq \beta\omega$. Hence, $k_0 = 0$ and $k_2 = \beta\omega$. This implies that all ring tasks are assigned to ring servers in alternating positions in each ring.

There are $\beta\omega$ remaining ring servers and $\beta\omega$ variable tasks. Therefore, a variable task is remotely assigned to one of the remaining ring servers by A.

Now consider the server s_i that has been remotely assigned $t_i \in G_C$. If it is assigned two ring tasks, its load is $L^A_{s_i} = 2 + 3 > 3$. If it is assigned one variable task, its load is $L^A_{s_i} = 3 + 3 > 3$. A is not feasible in either case. Therefore, there is no $t_i \in G_C$ and $s_i \in G_R$ such that $A(t_i) = s_i$. Thus, $n^A_c = 0$. □

Now we prove the following Lemma.

LEMMA 3.10. *If $G = f(\phi)$ is admissible, then ϕ is satisfiable.*

PROOF. Given feasible task assignment A in $G = f(\phi)$, we construct the satisfying truth assignment σ for ϕ. From Lemmas 3.6, 3.7, 3.8 and 3.9, we construct a feasible assignment B in G', such that $n^B_c = n^B_r = 0$, and in each variable gadget i, either servers in $\mathcal{T}_i$ or servers in $\mathcal{F}_i$ are saturated by variable tasks. If ring servers in $\mathcal{F}_i$ are saturated by variable tasks, let $\sigma(x_i) = true$. If ring servers in $\mathcal{T}_i$ are saturated by variable tasks, let $\sigma(x_i) = false$.

To check that this truth assignment is a satisfying assignment, note that for the three literal tasks l_{u1}, l_{u2}, l_{u3}, at most two of them are assigned to the clause server C_u. There must be one literal task, say l_{uv}, that is locally assigned to a ring server. In this case, $\sigma(l_{uv}) = true$ and thus the clause $\sigma(C_u) = true$. This fact holds for all clauses and thus indicates that $\sigma(\phi) = \sigma(\bigwedge C_u) = true$. This completes the proof of Lemma 3.10. □

Finally we prove the main theorem.

PROOF OF THEOREM 3.1. Lemmas 3.3, 3.4 and 3.10 establish that 3SAT $\leq_p$ (2,3)-UHTA via f. Therefore, (2,3)-UHTA is $\mathcal{NP}$-hard. It is easy to see that (2,3)-UHTA $\in \mathcal{NP}$ because in time $O(mn)$ a nondeterministic Turing machine could guess the assignment and accept iff the maximum load under the assignment does not exceed 3. Therefore, (2,3)-UHTA is $\mathcal{NP}$-complete. □

4. A ROUND ROBIN ALGORITHM

In this section, we analyze a simple round robin algorithm for the UHTA problem. Algorithm 1 is inspired by the Hadoop scheduler algorithm. It scans over each server in a round robin fashion. When assigning a new task to a server, Algorithm 1 tries heuristically to exploit data locality. Since we have not specified the order of assigned tasks, Algorithm 1 may produce many possible outputs (assignments).

Algorithm 1 The round robin algorithm exploring locality.

1: **input:** a set of unassigned tasks T, a list of servers $\{s_1, s_2, \cdots, s_n\}$, a placement relation ρ
2: **define** $i \leftarrow 1$ as an index variable
3: **define** A as an assignment
4: $A(t) = \perp$ (task t is unassigned) for all t
5: **while** exists unassigned task **do**
6:     **if** exists unassigned task t such that $\rho(t, s_i)$ holds **then**
7:         update A by assigning $A(t) = s_i$
8:     **else**
9:         pick any unassigned task t', update A by assigning $A(t') = s_i$
10:     **end if**
11:     $i \leftarrow (i \bmod n) + 1$
12: **end while**
13: **output:** assignment A

Algorithm 1 is analogous to the Hadoop scheduler algorithm up to core version 0.19. There are three differences, though. First, the Hadoop algorithm assumes three kinds of placement: data-local, rack-local and rack-remote, whereas Algorithm 1 assumes only two: local and remote. Second, the Hadoop scheduler works incrementally rather than assigning all tasks initially. Last, the Hadoop algorithm is deterministic, whereas Algorithm 1 is nondeterministic.

THEOREM 4.1. *If $w_{\mathrm{rem}} > w_{\mathrm{loc}}$, increasing the number of data block replicas may increase the maximum load of the assignment computed by Algorithm 1.*

PROOF. The number of edges in the placement graph is equal to the number of data block replicas, and thus adding a new edge in the placement graph is equivalent to adding a new replica in the system. Consider the simple placement graph G where $m = n$, and there is an edge between task t_i and s_i for all $1 \leq i \leq n$. Running Algorithm 1 gives an assignment A in which task t_i is assigned to s_i for all

35

$1 \leq i \leq n$, and thus $L^A = w_{\text{loc}}$. Now we add one edge between task t_n and server s_1. We run Algorithm 1 on this new placement graph G' to get assignment A'. It might assign task t_n to server s_1 in the first step. Following that, it assigns t_i to s_i for $2 \leq i \leq n-1$, and it finally assigns t_1 to s_n. Since t_1 is remote to s_n, this gives $L^{A'} = w_{\text{rem}}$. Therefore $L^{A'} > L^A$. $\square$

Theorem 4.1 indicates that increasing the number of data block replicas is not always beneficial for Algorithm 1. In the remaining part of this section, we show that the assignments computed by Algorithm 1 might deviate from the optimum by a multiplicative factor. In the following, let O be an assignment that minimizes L^O.

THEOREM 4.2. *Let A be an assignment computed by Algorithm 1. Then $L^A \leq (w_{\text{rem}}/w_{\text{loc}}) \cdot L^O$.*

PROOF. On the one hand, pigeonhole principle says there is a server assigned at least $\lceil m/n \rceil$ tasks. Since the cost of each task is at least w_{loc}, the load of this server is at least $\lceil m/n \rceil \cdot w_{\text{loc}}$. Thus, $L^O \geq \lceil m/n \rceil \cdot w_{\text{loc}}$. On the other hand, Algorithm 1 runs in a round robin fashion where one task is assigned at a time. Therefore, the number of tasks assigned to each server is at most $\lceil m/n \rceil$. Since the cost of each task is at most w_{rem}, the load of a server is at most $\lceil m/n \rceil \cdot w_{\text{rem}}$. Thus, $L^A \leq \lceil m/n \rceil \cdot w_{\text{rem}}$. Combining the two, we have $L^A \leq (w_{\text{rem}}/w_{\text{loc}}) \cdot L^O$. $\square$

THEOREM 4.3. *Let T and S be such that $m \leq n(n-2)$. There exist a placement ρ and an assignment A such that A is a possible output of Algorithm 1, $L^A \geq \lfloor m/n \rfloor \cdot w_{\text{rem}}$, and $L^O = \lceil m/n \rceil \cdot w_{\text{loc}}$.*

PROOF. We prove the theorem by constructing a placement graph G_ρ. Partition the set T of tasks into n disjoint subsets $T_i : 1 \leq i \leq n$, such that $\lceil m/n \rceil \geq |T_i| \geq |T_j| \geq \lfloor m/n \rfloor$ for all $1 \leq i \leq j \leq n$. Now in the placement graph G_ρ, connect tasks in T_i to server s_i, for all $1 \leq i \leq n$. These set of edges guarantee that $L^O = \lceil m/n \rceil \cdot w_{\text{loc}}$. We then connect each task in T_n to a different server in the subset $S' = \{s_1, s_2, \cdots, s_{n-1}\}$. Since $m \leq n(n-2)$, we have $\lceil m/n \rceil \leq m/n + 1 \leq n-1$, which guarantees $|S'| \geq |T_n|$. This completes the placement graph G_ρ. Now run Algorithm 1 on G_ρ. There is a possible output A where tasks in T_n are assigned to servers in S'. In that case, all tasks that are local to server s_n are assigned elsewhere, and thus s_n is assigned remote tasks. Since s_n is assigned at least $\lfloor m/n \rfloor$ tasks, this gives $L^A \geq \lfloor m/n \rfloor \cdot w_{\text{rem}}$. $\square$

When $n \mid m$, the lower bound in Theorem 4.3 matches the upper bound in Theorem 4.2.

5. A FLOW-BASED ALGORITHM

Theorem 3.1 shows that the problem of computing an optimal task assignment for the HTA problem is $\mathcal{NP}$-complete. Nevertheless, it is feasible to find task assignments whose load is at most an additive constant greater than the optimal load. We present such an algorithm in this section.

For two partial assignments α and β such that $\beta \supseteq \alpha$, we define a new notation called *virtual load from α* below.

Definition 12. For any task t and partial assignment β that extends α, let

$$v^\alpha(t, \beta) = \begin{cases} w_{\text{loc}} & \text{if } t \text{ is local in } \beta, \\ w_{\text{rem}}^\alpha & \text{otherwise.} \end{cases}$$

The *virtual load of server s under β from α* is $V_s^{\beta,\alpha} = \sum_{t:\beta(t)=s} v^\alpha(t,\beta)$. The *maximum virtual load under β from α* is $V^{\beta,\alpha} = \max_{s \in S} V_s^{\beta,\alpha}$.

Thus, v assumes pessimistically that tasks not assigned by β will eventually become remote, and each remote task will eventually have cost w_{rem}^α. When α is clear from context, we omit α and write $v(t,\beta)$, V_s^β and V^β, respectively. Note that $v^\alpha(t,\alpha) = w(t,\alpha)$ as in Definition 7.

Algorithm 2 works iteratively to produce a sequence of assignments and then outputs the best one, i.e., the one of least maximum server load. The iteration is controlled by an integer variable τ which is initialized to 1 and incremented on each iteration. Each iteration consists of two phases, *max-cover* and *bal-assign*:

- *Max-cover*: Given as input a placement graph G_ρ, an integer value τ, and a partial assignment α, max-cover returns a partial assignment α' of a subset T' of tasks, such that α' assigns no server more than τ tasks, every task in T' is local in α', and $|T'|$ is maximized over all such assignments. Thus, α' makes as many tasks local as is possible without assigning more than τ tasks to any one server. The name "max-cover" follows the intuition that we are actually trying to "cover" as many tasks as possible by their local servers, subject to the constraint that no server is assigned more than τ tasks.

- *Bal-assign*: Given as input a set of tasks T, a set of servers S, a partial assignment α computed by max-cover, and a cost function w, bal-assign uses a simple greedy algorithm to extend α to a complete assignment B by repeatedly choosing a server with minimal virtual load and assigning some unassigned task to it. This continues until all tasks are assigned. It thus generates a sequence of partial assignments $\alpha = \alpha_0 \subseteq \alpha_1 \subseteq \cdots \subseteq \alpha_u = B$, where $u = u^\alpha$. Every task t assigned in bal-assign contributes $v^\alpha(t, B) \leq w_{\text{rem}}^\alpha$ to the virtual load of the server that it is assigned to. At the end, $w_{\text{rem}}^B \leq w_{\text{rem}}^\alpha$, and equality holds only when $r^B = r^\alpha + u^\alpha$.

The astute reader might feel that it is intellectually attractive to use real server load as the criterion to choose servers in bal-assign because it embeds more accurate information. We do not know if this change ever results in a better assignment. We do know that it may require more computation. Whenever a local task is assigned, $r + u$ decreases by 1, so the remote cost $w_{\text{rem}}(r + u)$ may also decrease. If it does, the loads of all servers that have been assigned remote tasks must be recomputed. In the current version of the algorithm, we do not need to update virtual load when a local task is assigned because the virtual cost of remote tasks never changes in the course of bal-assign.

5.1 Algorithm Description

We describe Algorithm 2 in greater detail here.

5.1.1 Max-cover

Max-cover (line 6 of Algorithm 2) augments the partial assignment $\alpha^{\tau-1}$ computed by the previous iteration to produce α^τ. (We define α^0 to be the empty partial assignment.) Thus, $\alpha^\tau \supseteq \alpha^{\tau-1}$, and α^τ maximizes the total number of local tasks assigned subject to the constraint that no server is assigned more than τ tasks in all.

Algorithm 2 A flow-based algorithm for HTA.

1: **input:** an HMR-system $(T, S, \rho, w_{\text{loc}}, w_{\text{rem}}(\cdot))$
2: **define** A, B as assignments
3: **define** α as a partial assignment
4: $\alpha(t) = \bot$ (task t is unassigned) for all t
5: **for** $\tau = 1$ to m **do**
6:     $\alpha \leftarrow \text{max-cover}(G_\rho, \tau, \alpha)$
7:     $B \leftarrow \text{bal-assign}(T, S, \alpha, w_{\text{loc}}, w_{\text{rem}}(\cdot))$
8: **end for**
9: **set** A equal to a B with least maximum load
10: **output:** assignment A

The core of the max-cover phase is an augmenting path algorithm by Ford and Fulkerson [10]. The Ford-Fulkerson algorithm takes as input a network with edge capacities and an existing network flow, and outputs a maximum flow that respects the capacity constraints. A fact about this algorithm is well-known [6, 10].

FACT 5.1. *Given a flow network with integral capacities and an initial integral s-t flow f, the Ford-Fulkerson algorithm computes an integral maximum s-t flow f' in time $O(|E| \cdot (|f'| - |f|))$, where $|E|$ is the number of edges in the network and $|f|$ is the value of the flow f, i.e., the amount of flow passing from the source to the sink.*

During the max-cover phase at iteration τ, the input placement graph G_ρ is first converted to a corresponding flow network G'_ρ. G'_ρ includes all nodes in G_ρ and an extra source u and an extra sink v. In G'_ρ, there is an edge (u, t) for all $t \in T$ and an edge (s, v) for all $s \in S$. All of the original edges (t, s) in G_ρ remain in G'_ρ. The edge capacity is defined as follows: edge (s, v) has capacity τ for all $s \in S$, while all the other edges have capacity 1. Therefore, for any pair of (t, s), if there is a flow through the path $u \to t \to s \to v$, the value of this flow is no greater than 1. Then the input partial assignment α is converted into a network flow f_α as follows: if task t is assigned to server s in the partial assignment α, assign one unit of flow through the path $u \to t \to s \to v$.

The Ford-Fulkerson algorithm is then run on graph G'_ρ with flow f_α to find a maximum flow f'_α. From Fact 5.1, we know that the Ford-Fulkerson algorithm takes time $O(|E| \cdot (|f'_\alpha| - |f_\alpha|))$ in this iteration. This output flow f'_α at iteration τ will act as the input flow to the Ford-Fulkerson algorithm at iteration $\tau + 1$. The flow network at iteration $\tau + 1$ is the same as the one at iteration τ except that each edge (s, v) has capacity $\tau + 1$ for all $s \in S$. This incremental use of Ford-Fulkerson algorithm in successive iterations helps reduce the time complexity of the whole algorithm.

At the end of the max-cover phase, the augmented flow f'_α is converted back into a partial assignment α'. If there is one unit of flow through the path $u \to t \to s \to v$ in f'_α, we assign task t is to server s in α'. This conversion from a network flow to a partial assignment can always be done, because the flow is integral and all edges between tasks and servers have capacity 1. Therefore, there is a one-to-one correspondence between a unit flow through the path $u \to t \to s \to v$ and the assignment of task t to its local server s. It follows that $|f'_\alpha| = \ell^{\alpha'}$. By Fact 5.1, the Ford-Fulkerson algorithm computes a maximum flow that respects the capacity constraint τ. Thus, the following lemma is immediate.

LEMMA 5.2. *Let α^τ be the partial assignment computed by max-cover at iteration τ, and β be any partial assignment such that $k^\beta \leq \tau$. Then $\ell^{\alpha^\tau} \geq \ell^\beta$.*

5.1.2 Bal-assign

Definition 13. Let β and β' be partial assignments, t a task and s a server. We say that $\beta \xrightarrow{t:s} \beta'$ is a step that assigns t to s if t is unassigned in β and $\beta' = \beta \cup \{(t, s)\}$. We say $\beta \to \beta'$ is a step, if $\beta \xrightarrow{t:s} \beta'$ for some t and s.

A sequence of steps $\alpha = \alpha_0 \to \alpha_1 \to \ldots \to \alpha_u$ is a *trace* if for each $i \in [1, u]$, if $\alpha_{i-1} \xrightarrow{t:s} \alpha_i$ is a step, then $V_s^{\alpha_i, \alpha} \leq V_{s'}^{\alpha_i, \alpha}$ for all $s' \neq s$.

Given two partial assignments α_{i-1} and α_i in a trace such that $\alpha_{i-1} \xrightarrow{t:s} \alpha_i$, it follows that

$$V_s^{\alpha_i, \alpha} \leq V_s^{\alpha_{i-1}, \alpha} + w_{\text{rem}}^\alpha$$
$$V_{s'}^{\alpha_i, \alpha} = V_{s'}^{\alpha_{i-1}, \alpha} \text{ for all } s' \neq s$$

The following lemma is immediate.

LEMMA 5.3. *Let $u = u^{\alpha^\tau}$ and $\alpha^\tau = \alpha_0^\tau \subseteq \alpha_1^\tau \subseteq \cdots \subseteq \alpha_u^\tau$ be a sequence of partial assignments generated by bal-assign at iteration τ. This sequence is a trace that ends in a complete assignment $B^\tau = \alpha_u^\tau$.*

5.2 Main Result

It is obvious that Algorithm 2 is optimal for $n = 1$ since only one assignment is possible. Now we show that for $n \geq 2$, Algorithm 2 computes, in polynomial time, assignments that are optimal to within an additive constant. The result is formally stated as Theorem 5.4.

THEOREM 5.4. *Let $n \geq 2$. Given an HMR-system with m tasks and n servers, Algorithm 2 computes an assignment A in time $O(m^2 n)$ such that $L^A \leq L^O + \left(1 - \frac{1}{n-1}\right) \cdot w_{\text{rem}}^O$.*

LEMMA 5.5. *Algorithm 2 runs in time $O(m^2 n)$.*

PROOF. By Fact 5.1, we know that the Ford-Fulkerson algorithm takes time $O(|E| \cdot |\Delta_f|)$ to augment the network flow by $|\Delta_f|$. At iteration $\tau = 1$, max-cover takes time $O(|E| \cdot |f_1|)$, where $|f_1| \leq n$. Then at iteration $\tau = 2$, max-cover takes time $O(|E| \cdot (|f_2| - |f_1|))$, where $|f_2| \leq 2n$. The same process is repeated until $|f_m| = m$. The total running time of max-cover for all iterations thus adds up to $O(|E| \cdot (|f_1| + |f_2| - |f_1| + |f_3| - |f_2| + \cdots + |f_m|)) = O(|E| \cdot |f_m|) = O(|E| \cdot m) = O(m^2 n)$.

We implement the greedy algorithm in the bal-assign phase with a priority queue. Since there are n servers, each operation of the priority queue takes $O(\log n)$ time. During the bal-assign phase at each iteration, at most m tasks need to be assigned. This takes time $O(m \log n)$. The total running time of bal-assign for all iterations is thus $O(m^2 \log n)$.

Combining the running time of the two phases for all iterations gives time complexity $O(m^2 n)$. □

Lemma 5.5 suggests the max-cover phase is the main contributor to the time complexity of Algorithm 2. However, in a typical Hadoop system, the number of replicas for each data block is a small constant, say 2 or 3. Then the degree of each $t \in G$ is bounded by this constant. In this case, the placement graph G is sparse and $|E| = O(m + n)$. As a result, max-cover runs in time $O(m(m + n))$. Therefore the bal-assign phase might become the main contributor to the time complexity.

5.2.1 Properties of optimal assignments

In order to prove the approximation bound, we first establish some properties of optimal assignments.

Definition 14. Given an HMR-system, let $\mathcal{O}$ be the set of all optimal assignments, i.e., those that minimize the maximum load. Let $r_{\min} = \min\{r^A \mid A \in \mathcal{O}\}$ and let $\mathcal{O}_1 = \{O \in \mathcal{O} \mid r^O = r_{\min}\}$.

LEMMA 5.6. *Let $O \in \mathcal{O}_1$. If $\ell_s^O = k^O$, then $r_s^O = 0$ and $L_s^O = K^O$.*

PROOF. Let $\ell_s^O = k^O$ for some server s. Assume to the contrary that $r_s^O \geq 1$. Then $L_s^O \geq K^O + w_{\mathrm{rem}}$. Let t be a remote task assigned to s by O. By definition 3, $\rho(t, s')$ holds for at least one server $s' \neq s$.

Case 1: s' has at least one remote task t'. Then move t' to s and t to s'. This results in another assignment B. B is still optimal because $L_s^B \leq L_s^O$, $L_{s'}^B \leq L_{s'}^O$, and $L_{s''}^B = L_{s''}^O$ for any other server $s'' \in S - \{s, s'\}$.

Case 2: s' has only local tasks. By the definition of k^O, s' has at most k^O local tasks assigned by O. Then move t to s'. This results in another assignment B. B is still optimal because $L_s^B < L_s^O$, $L_{s'}^B = K^O + w_{\mathrm{loc}} \leq K^O + w_{\mathrm{rem}} \leq L_s^O$, and $L_{s''}^B = L_{s''}^O$ for any other server $s'' \in S - \{s, s'\}$.

In either case, we have shown the new assignment is in $\mathcal{O}$. However, since t becomes local in the new assignment, fewer remote tasks are assigned than in O. This contradicts that $O \in \mathcal{O}_1$. Thus, s is assigned no remote tasks, so $L_s^O = k^O w_{\mathrm{loc}} = K^O$. $\square$

Definition 15. Let $O \in \mathcal{O}_1$. Define $M^O = \frac{H^O - K^O}{n-1}$.

LEMMA 5.7. $L^O \geq M^O$.

PROOF. Let s_1 be a server of maximal local load in O, so $k_{s_1}^O = k^O$. Let $S_2 = S - \{s_1\}$. By Lemma 5.6, $L_{s_1}^O = K^O$. The total load on S_2 is $\sum_{s \in S_2} L_s^O = H^O - K^O$, so the average load on S_2 is M^O. Hence, $L^O \geq \max_{s \in S_2} L_s^O \geq \mathrm{avg}_{s \in S_2} L_s^O = M^O$. $\square$

5.2.2 Analyzing the algorithm

Assume throughout this section that $O \in \mathcal{O}_1$ and $\alpha = \alpha_0 \to \alpha_1 \to \ldots \to \alpha_u = B$ is a trace generated by iteration $\tau = k^O$ of the algorithm. Virtual loads are all based on α, so we generally omit explicit mention of α in the superscripts of v and V.

LEMMA 5.8. $w_{\mathrm{loc}} \leq w_{\mathrm{rem}}^B \leq w_{\mathrm{rem}}^\alpha \leq w_{\mathrm{rem}}^O$.

PROOF. $w_{\mathrm{loc}} \leq w_{\mathrm{rem}}^B$ follows from the definition of a Hadoop cost function. Because $B \supseteq \alpha$, $r^B \leq r^\alpha + u^\alpha$. By Lemma 5.2, $\ell^\alpha \geq \ell^O$, so $r^\alpha + u^\alpha = m - \ell^\alpha \leq m - \ell^O = r^O$. Hence, $w_{\mathrm{rem}}(r^B) \leq w_{\mathrm{rem}}(r^\alpha + u^\alpha) \leq w_{\mathrm{rem}}(r^O)$ by monotonicity of $w_{\mathrm{rem}}(\cdot)$. It follows by definition of the w_{rem}^β notation that $w_{\mathrm{rem}}^B \leq w_{\mathrm{rem}}^\alpha \leq w_{\mathrm{rem}}^O$. $\square$

LEMMA 5.9. $k^\alpha = k^O$.

PROOF. $k^\alpha \leq k^O$ because no server is assigned more than τ local tasks by max-cover at iteration $\tau = k^O$. For sake of contradiction, assume $k^\alpha < k^O$. Then $u^\alpha > 0$, because otherwise $\alpha = B$ and $L^B = k^\alpha \cdot w_{\mathrm{loc}} < K^O \leq L^O$, violating the optimality of O. Let t be an unassigned task in α. By definition, $\rho(t, s)$ holds for some server s. Assign t to s in α to obtain a new partial assignment β. We have $k^\beta \leq k^\alpha + 1 \leq k^O = \tau$. By Lemma 5.2, $\ell^\alpha \geq \ell^\beta$, contradicting the fact that $\ell^\beta = \ell^\alpha + 1$. We conclude that $k^\alpha = k^O$. $\square$

LEMMA 5.10. $L^B \leq V^B$.

PROOF. By definition, $L_s^B = \sum_{t:B(t)=s} w(t, B)$ and $V_s^B = \sum_{t:B(t)=s} v(t, B)$. By Lemma 5.8, $w_{\mathrm{rem}}^B \leq w_{\mathrm{rem}}^\alpha$, and thus $w(t, B) \leq v(t, B)$. It follows that $\forall s \in S$, $L_s^B \leq V_s^B$. Therefore $L^B \leq V^B$, because $L^B = \max_s L_s^B$ and $V^B = V^B = \max_s V_s^B$. $\square$

For the remainder of this section, let s_1 be a server such that $\ell_{s_1}^\alpha = k^O$. Such a server exists by Lemma 5.9. Let $S_2 = S - \{s_1\}$ be the set of remaining servers. For a partial assignment $\beta \supseteq \alpha$, define N^β to be the average virtual load under β of the servers in S_2. Formally,

$$N^\beta = \frac{\sum_{s \in S_2} V_s^\beta}{|S_2|} = \frac{\ell^\beta w_{\mathrm{loc}} + r^\beta w_{\mathrm{rem}}^\alpha - V_{s_1}^\beta}{n-1}$$

To obtain the approximation bound, we compare N^β with the similar quantity M^O for the optimal assignment. For convenience, we let $\delta = w_{\mathrm{rem}}^O/(n-1)$.

LEMMA 5.11. *Let $\beta = \alpha_i \xrightarrow{t:s} \alpha_{i+1} = \beta'$. Then*
$$V_s^\beta \leq N^\beta \leq M^O - \delta.$$

PROOF. Proof is by a counting argument. By Lemma 5.9, we have $k^\alpha = k^O$, so $\ell_{s_1}^\beta \geq \ell_{s_1}^\alpha = k^O$. Hence, $V_{s_1}^\beta \geq K^O$. By Lemma 5.2, we have $\ell^\alpha \geq \ell^O$. Let $d = \ell^\beta - \ell^O$. $d \geq 0$ because $\ell^\beta \geq \ell^\alpha \geq \ell^O$. Because $\ell^\beta + r^\beta + u^\beta = m = \ell^O + r^O$, we have $r^\beta + u^\beta + d = r^O$. Also, $u^\beta \geq 1$ since t is unassigned in β. Then by Lemma 5.8,

$$
\begin{aligned}
(n-1)N^\beta &= \ell^\beta w_{\mathrm{loc}} + r^\beta w_{\mathrm{rem}}^\alpha - V_{s_1}^\beta \\
&= (\ell^O + d) w_{\mathrm{loc}} + (r^O - u^\beta - d) w_{\mathrm{rem}}^\alpha - V_{s_1}^\beta \\
&\leq \ell^O w_{\mathrm{loc}} + (r^O - u^\beta) w_{\mathrm{rem}}^O - K^O \\
&\leq (n-1)M^O - w_{\mathrm{rem}}^O.
\end{aligned}
$$

Hence, $N^\beta \leq M^O - \delta$.

Now, since β is part of a trace, we have $V_s^\beta \leq V_{s'}^\beta$ for all $s' \in S$. In particular, $V_s^\beta \leq N^\beta$, since N^β is the average virtual load of all servers in S_2. We conclude that $V_s^\beta \leq N^\beta \leq M^O - \delta$. $\square$

PROOF OF THEOREM 5.4. Lemma 5.5 shows that the time complexity of Algorithm 2 is $O(m^2 n)$. Now we finish the proof for the approximation bound.

Let s be a server of maximum virtual load in B, so $V_s^B = V^B$. Let i be the smallest integer such that $\alpha_i|_s = B|_s$, that is, no more tasks are assigned to s in the subtrace beginning with α_i.

Case 1: $i = 0$: Then $\ell_s^{\alpha_0} \leq k^{\alpha_0} = k^O$ by Lemma 5.9, and $r^{\alpha_0} = 0$, so $V^B = V_s^{\alpha_0} \leq K^O$. Hence, $V^B \leq K^O \leq L^O$.

Case 2: $i > 0$: Then $\beta = \alpha_{i-1} \xrightarrow{t:s} \alpha_i = \beta'$ for some task t. By lemma 5.11, $V_s^\beta \leq M^O - \delta$, so using Lemma 5.8,

$$V_s^{\beta'} \leq V_s^\beta + w_{\mathrm{rem}}^\alpha \leq M^O - \delta + w_{\mathrm{rem}}^O.$$

Then by Lemma 5.7,

$$V^B = V_s^B = V_s^{\beta'} \leq M^O + w_{\mathrm{rem}}^O - \delta \leq L^O + w_{\mathrm{rem}}^O - \delta.$$

Both cases imply that $V^B \leq L^O + w_{\mathrm{rem}}^O - \delta$. By Lemma 5.10, we have $L^B \leq V^B$. Because the algorithm chooses an assignment with least maximum load as the output A, we have $L^A \leq L^B$. Hence,

$$L^A \leq L^O + w_{\mathrm{rem}}^O - \delta = L^O + \left(1 - \frac{1}{n-1}\right) \cdot w_{\mathrm{rem}}^O$$

$\square$

6. CONCLUSION

In this paper, we present an algorithmic study of the task assignment problem in the Hadoop MapReduce framework and propose a mathematical model to evaluate the cost of task assignments. Based on this model, we show that it is infeasible to find the optimal assignment unless $\mathcal{P} = \mathcal{NP}$. Theorem 3.1 shows that the task assignment problem in Hadoop remains hard even if all servers have equal capacity of 3, the cost function only has 2 values in its range, and each data block has at most 2 replicas.

Second, we analyze the simple round robin algorithm for the UHTA problem. Theorem 4.1 reveals that the intuition is wrong that increasing the number of replicas always helps load balancing. Using round robin task assignment, adding more replicas into the system can sometimes result in worse maximum load. Theorems 4.2 and 4.3 show there could be a multiplicative gap in maximum load between the optimal assignment and the assignment computed by Algorithm 1.

Third, we present Algorithm 2 for the general HTA problem. This algorithm employs maximum flow and increasing threshold techniques. Theorem 5.4 shows that the assignments computed by Algorithm 2 are optimal to within an additive constant that depends only on the number of servers and the remote cost function.

There are many interesting directions for future work. We have sketched a proof of a matching lower bound to Theorem 5.4 for a class of Hadoop cost functions. We plan to present this result in followup work. Sharing a MapReduce cluster between multiple users is becoming popular and has led to recent development of multi-user multi-job schedulers such as fair scheduler and capacity scheduler. We plan to analyze the performance of such schedulers and see if the optimization techniques from this paper can be applied to improve them.

7. ACKNOWLEDGMENTS

We would like to thank Avi Silberschatz, Daniel Abadi, Kamil Bajda-Pawlikowski, and Azza Abouzeid for their inspiring discussions. We are also grateful to the anonymous referees for providing many useful suggestions that significantly improved the quality of our presentation.

8. REFERENCES

[1] J. Aspnes, Y. Azar, A. Fiat, S. Plotkin, and O. Waarts. On-line routing of virtual circuits with applications to load balancing and machine scheduling. *Journal of the ACM*, 44(3):486–504, 1997.

[2] Y. Azar, J. S. Naor, and R. Rom. The competitiveness of on-line assignments. In *Proceedings of the 3rd Annual ACM-SIAM symposium on Discrete algorithms*, pages 203–210. SIAM Philadelphia, PA, USA, 1992.

[3] K. Birman, G. Chockler, and R. van Renesse. Towards a cloud computing research agenda. *SIGACT News*, 40(2):68–80, 2009.

[4] E. Bortnikov. Open-source grid technologies for web-scale computing. *SIGACT News*, 40(2):87–93, 2009.

[5] R. E. Burkard. Assignment problems: Recent solution methods and applications. In *System Modelling and Optimization: Proceedings of the 12th IFIP Conference, Budapest, Hungary, September 2-6, 1985*, pages 153–169. Springer, 1986.

[6] T. Cormen, C. Leiserson, R. Rivest, and C. Stein. *Introduction to algorithms, 2nd ed.* MIT press Cambridge, MA, 2001.

[7] M. de Kruijf and K. Sankaralingam. MapReduce for the Cell B. E. architecture. *University of Wisconsin Computer Sciences Technical Report CS-TR-2007*, 1625, 2007.

[8] J. Dean. Experiences with MapReduce, an abstraction for large-scale computation. In *Proceedings of the 15th International Conference on Parallel Architectures and Compilation Techniques*. ACM New York, NY, USA, 2006.

[9] J. Dean and S. Ghemawat. MapReduce: Simplified data processing on large clusters. *Proceedings of the 6th Symposium on Operating Systems Design and Implementation, San Francisco, CA*, pages 137–150, 2004.

[10] L. R. Ford and D. R. Fulkerson. Maximal flow through a network. *Canadian Journal of Mathematics*, 8(3):399–404, 1956.

[11] M. R. Garey, D. S. Johnson, et al. *Computers and Intractability: A Guide to the Theory of NP-completeness*. Freeman San Francisco, 1979.

[12] R. L. Graham. Bounds for certain multiprocessing anomalies. *Bell System Technical Journal*, 45(9):1563–1581, 1966.

[13] R. L. Graham. Bounds on multiprocessing timing anomalies. *SIAM Journal on Applied Mathematics*, pages 416–429, 1969.

[14] B. He, W. Fang, Q. Luo, N. K. Govindaraju, and T. Wang. Mars: A MapReduce framework on graphics processors. In *Proceedings of the 17th International Conference on Parallel Architectures and Compilation Techniques*, pages 260–269. ACM New York, NY, USA, 2008.

[15] H. W. Kuhn. The Hungarian method for the assignment problem. *Naval Research Logistics*, 52(1), 2005. Originally appeared in *Naval Research Logistics Quarterly, 2, 1955, 83–97*.

[16] R. Lämmel. Google's MapReduce programming model—Revisited. *Science of Computer Programming*, 68(3):208–237, 2007.

[17] J. K. Lenstra, D. B. Shmoys, and E. Tardos. Approximation algorithms for scheduling unrelated parallel machines. *Mathematical Programming*, 46(1):259–271, 1990.

[18] C. Ranger, R. Raghuraman, A. Penmetsa, G. Bradski, and C. Kozyrakis. Evaluating MapReduce for multi-core and multiprocessor systems. In *Proceedings of the 2007 IEEE 13th International Symposium on High Performance Computer Architecture*, pages 13–24. IEEE Computer Society Washington, DC, USA, 2007.

[19] M. Zaharia, A. Konwinski, A. D. Joseph, R. Katz, and I. Stoica. Improving MapReduce performance in heterogeneous environments. In *Proceedings of the 8th Symposium on Operating Systems Design and Implementation, San Diego, CA*, 2008.

Keynote Talk

Database Systems in the Multicore Era

Anastasia Ailamaki

School of Computer and Communication Sciences, EPFL

Lausanne, Switzerland

natassa@epfl.ch

Abstract

Database systems have long optimized for parallel execution; the research community has pursued parallel database machines since the early `80s, and several the key ideas from that era underlie the design and success of commercial database engines today. Computer architectures have shifted drastically during the intervening decades, however, and today the constraints of semiconductor technology combine with Moore's Law to double the number of processors per chip every 18 months. Converting this available raw parallelism into scalable performance is increasingly difficult with conventional servers, for both business intelligence and transaction processing workloads.

This talk analyzes database performance scaling results on future chip multiprocessors and demonstrates that current parallelism methods are insufficient and of bounded utility as the number of processors per chip exponentially increase. Common sense is often contradicted; for instance, the effect of using larger and slower on-chip caches may be detrimental to the absolute database performance. To achieve scalability for database applications on chip multiprocessors, major rethinking of the database storage manager is necessary. First, concurrency needs to be converted into parallelism – a challenging task, even for database systems. Then, parallelism needs to be extracted from seemingly serial operations; extensive research in distributed systems proves to be very useful in this context. At the query processing level, service-oriented architectures provide an excellent framework to exploit available parallelism. I will use the StagedDB/CMP and ShoreMT projects at EPFL as examples to outline the above research directions.

Categories & Subject Descriptors: H.2.4 [Database Management]: Systems—Concurrency, Query Processing, Parallel Databases, Transaction Processing.

General Terms: Performance, Design, Experimentation.

Bio

Anastasia (Natassa) Ailamaki is a Professor of Computer Sciences at the Ecole Polytechnique Federale de Lausanne (EPFL) in Switzerland. Her research interests are in database systems and applications, and in particular (a) in strengthening the interaction between the database software and the underlying hardware and I/O devices, including flash technology, and (b) in automating database design and computational database support for scientific applications. She has received a Finmeccanica endowed chair from the Computer Science Department at Carnegie Mellon (2007), a European Young Investigator Award from the European Science Foundation (2007), an Alfred P. Sloan Research Fellowship (2005), six best-paper awards at top conferences (2001-2006), and an NSF CAREER award (2002). She earned her Ph.D. in Computer Science from the University of Wisconsin-Madison in 2000.

Collaborative Scoring with Dishonest Participants

Seth Gilbert
EPFL
Lausanne, Switzerland
seth.gilbert@epfl.ch

Rachid Guerraoui
EPFL
Lausanne, Switzerland
rachid.guerraoui@epfl.ch

Faezeh Malakouti Rad
Boston University
Boston MA, USA
faezeh@bu.edu

Morteza
Zadimoghaddam
MIT
Cambridge MA, USA
morteza@mit.edu

ABSTRACT

Consider a set of players that are interested in collectively evaluating a set of objects. We develop a *collaborative scoring* protocol in which each player evaluates a subset of the objects, after which we can accurately predict each players' individual opinion of the remaining objects. The accuracy of the predictions is near optimal, depending on the number of objects evaluated by each player and the correlation among the players' preferences.

A key novelty is the ability to tolerate malicious players. Surprisingly, the malicious players cause no (asymptotic) loss of accuracy in the predictions. In fact, our algorithm improves in both performance and accuracy over prior state-of-the-art collaborative scoring protocols that provided no robustness to malicious disruption.

Categories and Subject Descriptors

C.2.4 [**Computer Communication Networks**]: Distributed Systems; F.2.2 [**Analysis of Algorithms and Problem Complexity**]: Nonnumerical Algorithms and Problems

General Terms

Algorithms, Theory

Keywords

fault tolerance, randomized algorithms, collaborative filtering, recommendation systems

1. INTRODUCTION

Imagine a group of researchers (say, a program committee) that is attempting to evaluate a set of papers (say, SPAA

submissions). Each researcher wants to know whether or not she/he likes each paper. However, none of the busy researchers have enough time to read all of the papers. Therefore, each researcher is assigned some subset of the papers to evaluate, and their scores are then used to determine, for each researcher, his/her (supposed) opinion on the remaining (unread) papers. (Notice that this differs from standard program committees in that, in the end, every researcher develops an opinion on every paper.) In fact, it is possible to accurately guess each committee member's opinion on his/her unread paper as long as there is sufficient correlation among the opinions of the researchers.

This process of collecting and correlating information is an example of *collaborative scoring*, which has been extensively studied (e.g., [2–5, 9]). Our goal in this paper is to design a collaborative scoring algorithm that minimizes the number of items each player must evaluate (i.e., the number of papers that each researcher has to read), while at the same time maximizing the accuracy of the predictions. Intuitively, there is an inherent trade-off between the number of items evaluated and the accuracy of the predictions.

Dishonest players.

One of the problems with collaborative solutions is that some of the players may violate the protocol or act dishonestly. For example, some researchers may be too busy and, instead of reading their assigned papers, they may simply choose scores at random (or based on the reputation of the authors). Alternatively, researchers might attempt to bias the algorithm toward their colleagues' papers[1]. In either case, some researchers may be tricked into liking a paper that they would otherwise dislike, if they had read it (or *vice versa*).

An important goal of this paper is to develop a collaborative scoring protocol that is robust to malicious interference[2]. Even if a reasonable fraction of the players collude in an attempt to subvert the system, the honest players are still

---

[1]While such practices are of course rare, perhaps nonexistent, in the honest community of computer science researchers, these problems remain worthy of consideration in a broader context.
[2]For historical reasons, such malicious parties are often referred to as "Byzantine."

guaranteed near-optimal predictions as to their scores[3]. To the best of our knowledge, this is the first collaborative scoring algorithm that can tolerate dishonest players[4]. Interestingly, our algorithm also improves even over state-of-the-art algorithms that do not allow for dishonest behavior.

Correlation of preferences, accuracy of predictions.

The basic idea behind collaborative scoring is to leverage the correlation in preferences among players. For example, imagine that there are two researchers Alice and Bob with very similar opinions regarding the papers to be evaluated; in that case if Alice evaluates some paper, then Bob can reliably predict that, for that paper, he will have the same opinion as Alice. Thus if we have significant correlation among the researchers, and if we can determine efficiently which researchers share the same opinions, then we can develop very accurate predictions, even if the number of papers evaluated by each researcher is relatively small.

In fact, the accuracy of the predictions depends on the correlation of the players' preferences. For example, if the preferences are entirely independent, then collaboration provides no benefit: each researcher has to read every paper themselves. On the other hand, if there are large subsets of the players that share the same preferences, then collaboration can be quite effective. The question we address in this paper is how to discover such correlations, and how to leverage these correlations to provide good predictions.

Our results.

Assume we have n players and n objects. (Generalizing to more objects is straightforward.) Each player has some unknown opinion of each object. Our goal is to determine for each player whether she likes or dislikes each object. We present a collaborative scoring protocol with the following attributes:

- *Optimality:* Our protocol predicts each player's preferences with near-optimal levels of precision in the following sense. Given a bound B on the number of objects that can be evaluated by each player, and given a particular (though unknown) level of correlation among preferences, there is some minimum rate of error that can be achieved. Our algorithm achieves a *constant-factor approximation* of this minimum rate of error, in the worst-case, while requiring each player to evaluate $O(B \log^{O(1)} n)$ objects. Thus, by slightly augmenting the budget of each player, we achieve an asymptotically optimal rate of error, despite knowing nothing about the level of correlation among the preferences.

- *Fault-tolerance:* We achieve this (almost) optimal rate of error, despite up to $n/(3B)$ of the users behaving in a dishonest fashion.

Prior to this paper, the best known algorithm [2,3]—which does not tolerate dishonest players—requires each player to examine $O(B^2 \log^{O(1)} n)$ objects, and yet achieves only a B-

approximation (instead of a constant-factor approximation) of the optimal rate of error[5].

Our basic strategy is to discover clusters of players that can cooperatively evaluate the objects. If we can identify, for each player, a sufficiently large set of other players that have similar preferences, then these players can share the work of evaluating the objects. For instance, if there are n objects and each player is part of a cluster containing at least n/B other players with similar preferences, then no player needs to evaluate more than B objects. Thus one of the main goals of the protocol is to find such clusters of players with similar preferences. In general, standard sampling techniques can be used to find such clusters. A key problem, however, is that the dishonest players may attempt to disrupt the process by "hijacking" some of the clusters. In order to compensate for this the samples would have to be too large; thus we augment the sampling with collaborative scoring techniques to reduce the cost.

More specifically, in order to find clusters of players with similar preferences, we want to examine the players' preferences on a smaller subset of the objects, specifically, a randomly chosen sample of size $\Theta(n \log n/D)$, where D represents the maximum divergence of preferences. It is too expensive, however, for each player to evaluate each of the objects even in this smaller sample, as each player can only evaluate $B \log^{O(1)} n$ objects. Since the sample is chosen at random, players that have similar preferences over the larger set have very similar preferences on the smaller set. Thus we can use a collaborative scoring algorithm optimized for players with very similar preferences, first described in [2,3]. This provides a good estimate of the preferences on the small sample, which can then be used to produce a clustering of the players. In order to ensure that no cluster is "hijacked" by dishonest players, we show that there are enough honest players in each cluster to dominate. Finally, the work of probing objects is divided among players in each cluster, with sufficient redundancy to overcome the dishonest players.

Roadmap.

In Section 2, we describe the basic model and define the problem of collaborative scoring and what it means for an algorithm to be optimal. In Section 4, we discuss some of the related work. In Section 5, we review some existing algorithms that we will use as sub-components of our protocol. In Section 6, we present and analyze our new algorithm in the absence of dishonest players, and in Section 7, we show how to cope with dishonest players. Finally, we conclude in Section 8.

2. BASIC MODEL

We consider a world consisting of a set Π of n *players* and a set Λ of n *objects*. (Generalizing for more objects than players is straightforward, and omitted for clarity.) Let P be the set of players and O the set of objects. Associated with each player $p \in P$ is a binary (0/1) vector $v(p)$ of size n that indicates whether player p likes or dislikes each object. We refer to $v(p)$ as player p's *preference* vector, and it is initially unknown. (In Section 8 we discuss some generalizations of this model.)

---

[3]See Section 2 for more intuition on what is meant here by *optimal.*

[4]There do exist collaborative *recommendation* systems that tolerate malicious users, e.g., [5,16], but these are solving a somewhat different problem, as discussed in Section 4.

[5]In [2,3], B is assumed to be constant, and hence it also claims to achieve a constant-factor approximation.

Notice that there may be some hidden structure on the distribution of preferences, for example, certain sets of players may have correlated preferences on certain subsets of the objects. However, we do not make any *a priori* assumptions on such structure. If such structure does exist, it is unknown to the players and must be discovered. (It is, in fact, just such correlations between players that makes collaborative scoring effective.)

We assume that some of the players are honest and some of the players are dishonest. A dishonest player may ignore the protocol, lying about its preferences and attempting to improperly influence the output of the protocol.

The game proceeds in synchronous rounds. In each round, each player can choose one object to probe. Every time a player probes an object, it learns its preference for that object. For example, when player p probes object k, it learns whether $v(p)_k$ is equal to 0 or 1.

Players have access to a public "bulletin board" (e.g., a distributed shared memory). In each round, the players can update and read the bulletin board after each probe. Without loss of generality, we assume that each honest player writes the result of each probe to the bulletin board. A dishonest player cannot modify the data written by honest players on the bulletin board.

Throughout the paper, when we say that an event occurs with high probability, we mean with probability $1 - 1/n$. By increasing the probe complexity by a constant factor, we can achieve a probability of error of $1/n^c$ for any constant c.

3. COLLABORATIVE SCORING

The problem of *B-budget collaborative scoring* is defined as follows. Each player may make up to $O(B)$ probes. The goal is to generate for each player p a vector $w(p)$ that minimizes $|w(p) - v(p)|$, i.e., the Hamming distance between the real preference vector $v(p)$ and the output vector $w(p)$. The *rate of error* is the maximum such difference for any player, for any set of initial preference vectors.

Initially, in Section 6, we assume that all the players behave correctly, obeying the protocol. In Section 7, we show that our protocol can tolerate up to $n/(3B)$ of the players behaving dishonestly.

Our goal is to devise an algorithm that, while using only $O(B \log^{O(1)} n)$ probes, performs asymptotically as well as any algorithm using only B probes. (One might think of this as a form of *resource augmentation*: by using somewhat more probes, the algorithm presented here can perform almost as well as an optimal B-budget collaborative scoring algorithm.) We now state more precisely what this claim means.

We begin by providing some intuition as to why Definition 1 in fact describes the best performance that a B-budget collaborative scoring protocol can achieve, in the worst case. While this may seem a somewhat non-intuitive definition of optimality, it does define a lower bound on what is achievable and hence a benchmark to which we can later compare the algorithm developed in this paper.

Given a subset of the players P, we define $D(P)$ to be the diameter of P: $D(P) = \max_{p,q \in P} (|v(p) - v(q)|)$. Assume we have some B-budget algorithm $\mathcal{ALG}$.

Consider some particular player p. Since each player can only probe B objects, it is easy to see that, in a sense, p must "collaborate" with at least $(n/B) - 1$ other players in order to ensure that p has information on every object. (If

p collaborates with any fewer players, then it has access to data on less than n objects. In this case, there is some object for which p has no information, i.e., it can only guess at random its preference.) Notice that p may certainly examine information from more than $(n/B) - 1$ other players, and we in no way restrict $\mathcal{ALG}$ from collecting information in any way it chooses. However, in order to do better than random guessing, p must use information from probes performed by at least $(n/B) - 1$ other players.

Ideally, player p would collaborate with the $(n/B) - 1$ players that have preferences *most similar* to p. That is, player p would collaborate with a set of players P with minimum diameter. (Again, player p may also use information from farther away players.)

In fact, in the worst case, player p can do no better than to collaborate with the $(n/B) - 1$ closest players. That is, if P is the set containing p with minimum diameter $D(P)$, then no algorithm can have a rate of error less than $D(P)/4$. Thus we define *optimality* in terms of the diameter of the set of players closest to p.

Formally, we define the notion of optimality (much as in [2, 3]) as follows:

DEFINITION 1. *A collaborative scoring algorithm is said to be* asymptotically optimal with respect to some budget B *if there exists some constant c such that for every input set of preferences vectors, for every player p, with high probability:*

$$|w(p) - v(p)| \leq \min_{P \subseteq \Pi, \ p \in P, \ |P| \geq n/B} cD(P) \ .$$

In the worst-case, every B-budget collaborative scoring algorithm may perform only as well as specified in Definition 1. We give here a simple proof of this claim, demonstrating a particular distribution of preferences that yields the specified rate of error.

CLAIM 2. *For every B-budget collaborative scoring algorithm $\mathcal{ALG}$, there is some distribution of preferences and some player p such that, with constant probability:*

$$|w(p) - v(p)| \geq \min_{P \subseteq \Pi, \ p \in P, \ |P| \geq n/B} D(P)/4 \ .$$

PROOF. Given a constant D such that $n/4 > D > 2B$, we define an input distribution of preference vectors as follows. Let P be a set of players of size n/B and let p be some arbitrary player in P. For every player $q \notin P$, assign its preference vector $v(q)$ at random. In addition, for player p, assign its preference vector $v(p)$ at random. Choose an arbitrary special set S of D objects, and for every player $q \in P \setminus \{p\}$, define $v(q) = v(p)$ on every object *except* those in the set S; for the objects in S, choose $v(q)$ at random.

Since the preference vectors of every player not in P are chosen at random (with respect to p), obviously the probes performed by players outside of P provide no information to p. Similarly, the probes performed by players in P provide no information to p on objects in S. Since p probes at most B objects, and since S contains at least $D > 2B$ objects, there are at least $D/2$ objects on which p has no information. Thus, no algorithm can do better for p than guessing its preferences on objects in S, and hence $\mathcal{ALG}$ has a rate of error of at least $D/4$, in expectation. At the same time, the diameter of $P \leq D$ (and every other set of size n/B is of distance at least $n/4 > D$, whp), concluding the proof. $\square$

While the above proof uses a very specific distribution to demonstrate the worst-case notion of optimality, in fact, for a broad set of preference distributions, this notion of optimality really does capture the best that any B-budget collaborate scoring protocol can achieve[6].

In this paper, we give a new algorithm for solving the $B \log^{O(1)} n$-budget collaborative scoring problem; and this new algorithm is asymptotically optimal with respect to B.

4. RELATED WORK

The problem of determining preferences via collaborative scoring (or "collaborative filtering") has been widely studied. We focus here on the on-line solutions; other research focuses on off-line solutions that examine historical data to reconstruct preferences.

Early work in this area [1, 6–9, 12] defined the problem as one of reconstructing a matrix of preferences, and brought a series of linear algebraic techniques to bear on the problem. In [9], for example, they rely on singular-value decomposition, which requires some strong assumptions: users are partitioned into types that have orthogonal preferences; and users of the "dominant" type outnumber users of "subdominant" types.

Awerbuch et al. [4] and Alon et al. [2,3] relax these different assumptions, introducing a combinatorial approach to the problem of collaborative scoring. They define the model that we use in this paper, and formulate precisely the problem of collaborative scoring. In [4], they introduce the algorithm that we here refer to as ZeroRadius (and the associated Select protocol), optimally solving the problem of collaborative scoring under the assumption that there are large clusters of users with *exactly* identical preferences. In [2,3], they address the more general problem, which attempts to leverage correlation among users where preferences are similar, even when not identical. They develop an algorithm in which each user makes $O(B^2 \log^{O(1)} n)$ probes, and the resulting output is a B-approximation of optimal with respect to a budget of B. (As they assume that B is a constant, they refer to this as a constant-factor approximation of optimal.)

Another area of research has focused on the problem of *recommendation systems*, a problem closely related to collaborative scoring. The goal of a *recommendation system* is to provide each user with a small number of recommendations (e.g., one per day), with the goal of maximizing the number of "good" objects recommended. By contrast, a *collaborative scoring* system attempts to determine a user's score for every item. As one example of this line of research, Kleinberg and Sandler [11] develop a near optimal recommendation algorithm (based on mixture models).

While there has been no prior work (to our knowledge) on collaborative scoring robust to malicious players, there has been research on robust recommendation systems. In [5], Awerbuch et al. develop such a recommendation system; their algorithm runs in $O(n \log n)$ time, and is within a $\log n$ factor of optimal in the size of the recommendation set. In [16], Yu et al. presents a protocol that provides a continuous stream of recommendations (e.g., one per day), while maximizing the percentage of good recommendations. It too can tolerate dishonest players (known as "Sybils"), and relies on careful reputation management to choose rec-

ommendations. There is other work on robust recommendation systems that relies on pre-existing social networks (e.g., [14, 15]).

Finally, Nisgav and Patt-Shamir [13] have recently developed algorithms for partitioning users based on their preferences. Their goal is not to determine preferences, but instead to group users into sets with similar preferences. It is possible that such a partitioning could be used as the basis for a collaborative scoring protocol (though it is unclear how the performance would compare), and their sampling techniques bear some similarity to the techniques used in this paper. However they do not consider the possibility of malicious failures.

5. BACKGROUND

In developing our algorithm, we use as building blocks three existing algorithms from [2–4]. To be self-contained, we briefly repeat them here. (They need little modification to tolerate dishonest players; see Section 7.)

5.1 Choose Closest Candidate

The first building block is a protocol for selecting among a set of candidate preference vectors. Assume a set of candidate vectors $w_1, w_2, \ldots, w_k$. Player p wants to determine which vector is closest to $v(p)$. The goal of the RSelect protocol, found in Figure 1, is to identify, with high probability, the best candidate.

THEOREM 3 (THEOREM 6.1 [2]). *Let w^* be the vector in $w_1, \ldots, w_k$ that is closest to $v(p)$. Then, with high probability, RSelect outputs a vector w such that $|v(p) - w| \leq O(|v(p) - w^*|)$, using only $O(k^2 \log n)$ probes.*

5.2 Special Case: Zero Radius Sets

A second building block, originally from [4], implements collaborative scoring under the assumption that for each $p \in P$, there exists a subset $S(p) \subseteq \Pi$ of size n/B with the *exact same* preferences as p. That is, the subset $S(p)$ has diameter of size 0. See Figure 1 for the pseudocode.

THEOREM 4 (THEOREM 3.1 [2]). *Assume that at least n/B' players have identical preferences to player p. Then, with high probability, ZeroRadius$(\cdot, \cdot, B')$ outputs preference vector $v(p)$ with $O(B' \log n)$ probes.*

5.3 Special Case: Small Radius Sets

A third algorithm from [2,3] solves the collaborative scoring problem under the assumption that for each $p \in P$, there exists some subset $S(p)$ of size n/B where the diameter $D(S(p))$ is no greater than $\log n$. In this case, the diameter D is a parameter to the algorithm. The pseudocode can be found in Figure 1. The Select protocol is a deterministic version of RSelect with slightly difference performance guarantees.

THEOREM 5 (THEOREM 4.4 [2]). *Assume that at least n/B players have preferences within distance D of player p. Then, with high probability, SmallRadius outputs a preference vector $w(p)$ such that $|w(p) - v(p)| \leq 5D$, making $O(B \log n D^{3/2}(D + \log n))$ probes.*

---

[6]Notice this same notion of optimality can be found in [2,3], where the *stretch* is divided by the diameter.

algorithm RSELECT$(w_1, \ldots, w_k)_p$;

For every pair of vectors $w, w' \in \{w_1, \ldots, w_k\}$ do:

1. Let X be the set of objects on which w and w' differ.
2. Randomly probe $\Theta(\log n)$ objects from X.
3. Eliminate w' if at least 2/3 of the probed objects agree with w, and eliminate w if at least 2/3 of the probed objects agree with w'. Otherwise, keep both w and w'.

Output any vector that remains.

---

algorithm ZERORADIUS$(P, O, B')_p$ // players P, objects O, bound B'

1. If $min(|P|, |O|) < O(B' \log(n))$, player p probes all objects in O and outputs their values.
2. Otherwise, partition P and O randomly into two sets: place each player from P in P' or P'' with probability 1/2; place each object from O in O' or O'' with probability 1/2. The same partition is chosen by all players in P.
3. Assume wlog that $p \in P'$. Player p recursively executes ZERORADIUS(P', O', B') to determine the preferences for players in P' on objects in O'.
4. Let V be a set of vectors for O'' such that each vector in V is output by at least $|P''|/(2B')$ players in P''. Let C be the set of objects for which there are different votes in V.
5. While $C \neq \emptyset$ do: Choose an arbitrary object in C and probe it. Remove from V all objects that disagree with the probe, and update C.

---

algorithm SMALLRADIUS$(P, O, D)_p$ // players P, objects O, diameter D

Repeat $\Theta(\log n)$ times:

1. Partition the objects O randomly into $s = \Theta(D^{3/2})$ disjoint subsets: $O = O_1 \cup O_2 \cup \cdots \cup O_s$.
2. For each $i \in \{1, \ldots, s\}$: all players execute ZERORADIUS$(\cdot, \cdot, 5B)$ for the objects of O_i, allowing for $5B$ probes; let U_i be the set of vectors output by at least $n/(5B)$ players.
3. Each player p executes SELECT$(U_i, D)_p$, obtaining vector $u^i(p)$ for each $i \in \{1, \cdots, s\}$. Concatenate the vectors $u^i(p)$ over all i, and add the result to the set V.

Each player p applies procedure SELECT$(V, D)_p$ and outputs the result.

Figure 1: Building Block Protocols (see [2, 3]). The pseudocode is given for player p. The procedure Select, not included here, is a deterministic version of RSelect that takes two parameters: a set of vectors V, and a diameter bound D such that for a least one vector $v' \in V$, $|v(p) - v'| \leq D$.

6. BASIC PROTOCOL

We now present and analyze the protocol for calculating each players' preferences, which we refer to as CALCULATEPREFERENCES. The analysis in this section assumes that all the players are honest; in Section 7, we examine the problem of dishonest behavior.

6.1 Preliminaries

Initially, players have no knowledge about the correlation among their preferences. Thus, we begin by "guessing" a diameter D such that for every player p there is a set of a least n/B other players, including p, with diameter no greater than than D. Specifically, we execute our protocol $\lceil \log n \rceil + 1$ times, parameterized with $D = 1, 2, 4, \ldots, n$; the protocol works correctly when D is guessed correctly. For each player p, this process produces $O(\log n)$ candidate vectors $w_1, w_2, \ldots, w_{\log n}$, at least one of which near-exactly represents p's preferences. (This is depicted in Step 1 of Figure 2.) We then execute the RSELECT$(w_1, \ldots, w_{\log n})_p$ protocol, for each p, to determine which of these candidate vectors is best.

We fix the target diameter D for the remainder of the paper. We assume throughout that for every player p, there exists a set of player $P' \subseteq P$ of size at least n/B, and containing p, such that $D(P') \leq D$. For at least one choice of D, this assumption will hold. (It should be noted that [2,3] follows this same strategy.)

We rapidly dispense with two easy cases. If the budget $B = \Omega(n/\log n)$, then every player probes every object, and the problem is trivially solved using $O(B \log^{O(1)} n)$ probes. On the other hand, if diameter $D < \log n$, then the SMALLRADIUS algorithm from [2,3] solves the collaborative scoring problem using only $O(B \log^{O(1)} n)$ probes. For the remainder of this paper, we focus on the case where $B = O(n/\ln n)$ and $D \geq \log(n)$.

6.2 Overview

The key idea in our algorithm is to discover clusters of players with similar preferences that can cooperatively probe the objects. Specifically, if we can identify, for each player, a set of at least n/B other players that have similar preferences, then these players can each sample just B objects.

A natural approach is to rely on sampling to determine which players have similar preferences. Consider a randomly chosen set of objects of size $\Theta(n \log n/D)$. Such a set is large enough that it provides a good indication of whether two players have similar preferences. Unfortunately, it is too expensive for each player to probe each element in the set. Fortunately, any two players that have preference distance at most D over all the objects will differ in at most $O(\log n)$ objects on the smaller sample. Thus clusters of diameter D in the entire object space reduce to clusters of diameter $O(\log n)$ on this smaller sample. We can then use the SMALLRADIUS algorithm to efficiently determine each player's preference on this smaller set.

Finally, we use this information to construct a *neighbor graph* in which players with similar preferences share an edge, and we use this to group the players into clusters. The work of probing all n objects is then divided among the players in each cluster. The protocol is described in Figure 2.

6.3 Step 1: Selecting a Sample Set

Each object is added to set S with probability $10 \ln(n)/D$. (For now: designate one player to make these random selection and publish them on the bulletin board; see Section 7 for the case of dishonest players.) We observe that the set S provides a good estimate of the similarity (or dissimilarity) of two players' preferences.

LEMMA 6. *For every pair of players p and q:*

1. *If $|v(p) - v(q)| < D$, then they differ in their preferences for at most $20 \ln n$ objects, whp.*

2. *if $|v(p) - v(q)| \geq cD$, for $c \geq 3$, then they differ in their preferences for at least $5c \ln n$ objects, whp.*

PROOF. Fix players p and q. Let $A = \{o_1, o_2, \cdots, o_k\}$ be the set of objects on which p and q have different preferences. Note that $k \leq D$. For part (1), the expected number of elements in $A \cap S$ is at most $10 \ln(n)$, and hence by a Chernoff bound, with high probability $|A \cap S| \leq 20 \ln(n)$. For part (2), the expected number of elements in $A \cap S$ is at least $10c \ln(n)$, and hence by a Chernoff bound, with high probability $|A \cap S| \geq 5c \ln(n)$. Taking a union bound over all pairs $p, q \in P \times P$ concludes the proof. □

6.4 Step 2: Probing the Sample Set

Next, we use the SMALLRADIUS algorithm to determine each player's preferences on the set S. By Lemma 6, we know that each set of players with diameter D differs in their preferences for at most $20 \ln n$ objects in the set S. Thus, the SMALLRADIUS algorithm ensures that each player correctly discovers his preferences on the set S, with high probability.

LEMMA 7. *For every player p, let $z(p)$ be the output of the SMALLRADIUS algorithm on set S with distance $20 \ln n$. Then for every pair of players p and q:*

1. *If $|v(p) - v(q)| \leq D$, then $|z(p) - z(q)| \leq 220 \ln(n)$, with high probability.*

2. *If $|v(p) - v(q)| \geq 84D$, then $|z(p) - z(q)| \geq 220 \ln(n)$, with high probability.*

PROOF. For part (1): According to Lemma 6, the number of differences between p and q for objects in S is at most $20 \ln(n)$. By Theorem 5, we know that, restricted to objects in S, $|v(p) - z(p)| \leq 100 \ln n$ and $|v(q) - z(q)| \leq 100 \ln n$. Thus, $|z(p) - z(q)| \leq (2 \cdot 100) \ln(n) + 20 \ln(n) = 220 \ln n$.

For part (2): According to Lemma 6, the number of differences between p and q for objects in S is at least $(5 \cdot 84) \ln(n)$.

By Theorem 5, we know that, restricted to objects in S, $|v(p) - z(p)| \leq 100 \ln n$ and $|v(q) - z(q)| \leq 100 \ln n$. Thus, $|z(p) - z(q)| \geq 420 \ln(n) - (2 \cdot 100) \ln(n) = 220 \ln n$. □

6.5 Step 3: Calculating Clusters

We now use the output of the SMALLRADIUS algorithm on the sample set S to cluster the players in sets of size at least n/B, where each cluster has diameter $O(D)$. (Recall that we have assumed that for every player p, there exists a set of size n/B, containing p, with diameter $\leq D$.) Assume that for every player p, vector $z(p)$ is the output from SMALLRADIUS. We construct a graph $G = (P, E)$, adding an edge between players p and q if $|z(p) - z(q)| \leq 220 \ln n$. We conclude as a corollary of Lemma 7:

LEMMA 8. *For all players p, q: (i) p has degree at least $n/B - 1$ in the neighbor graph; (ii) if (p, q) is an edge, then $|v(p) - v(w)| \leq 84D$.* □

To construct the clusters, we begin with graph $G = (P, E)$, empty sets $V_1, V_2, \ldots$, and a counter $j = 1$. Repeat the following until there is no p in G with degree $\geq n/B - 1$:

1. Choose a player p that has degree $n/B - 1$ in G.

2. Add p and the $(\geq n/B - 1)$ neighbors of p to V_j.

3. Remove p and the neighbors of p from G.

4. Increment j.

We have now constructed a sequence of sets $V_1, \ldots, V_\ell$ each of size at least n/B. Moreover, after this process, the graph G contains no player with $n/B - 1$ neighbors. Let q be one of the remaining vertices in the graph with degree less than $n/B - 1$. Since previously, by Lemma 8, q had $n/B - 1$ neighbors, there must be some $p \in V_j$ that was previously a neighbor of q; add q to V_j', and remove it from G. Once every player has been removed from G, then combine V_j and V_j' to create the final sequence of clusters $V_1, \ldots, V_\ell$.

LEMMA 9. *The clustering has the following properties:*

1. *Every player is contained in exactly one of the sets $V_1, \ldots, V_\ell$.*

2. *For every $j \in [1, \ldots, \ell]$, each set V_j contains at least n/B players.*

3. *For every $j \in [1, \ldots, \ell]$, the diameter $D(V_j) = O(D)$.*

PROOF. The first two properties are immediate by construction. The third follows from the fact that every pair of nodes $p, q \in V_j$ are within distance 4 in the initial neighbor graph. According to Lemma 7, the total number of differences between p and q is then at most $4 \times 84D = 336D$. □

6.6 Step 4: Sharing the Work

Finally, for each cluster and for each object, we choose $\Theta(\log n)$ of the players from the cluster uniformly random, and assign those players to probe the object. Each player p observes the $\Theta(\log n)$ values output for each object o by the assigned players in its cluster, and sets its output $w(p)_o$ to the value that is probed by a majority of the assigned players.

LEMMA 10. *In the final phase, no player probes more than $O(B \log n)$ objects, with high probability.*

46

---

algorithm CALCULATEPREFERENCES$_p$;

1. For $d = 0$ to $\lceil \log n \rceil$ do:

   (a) Let $D = 2^d$.

   (b) Add each object independently with probability $O(\log n / D)$ to the sample set S.

   (c) Execute SMALLRADIUS$(\Pi, S, 20 \ln n)_p$ on the sample set S.

   (d) Construct a *neighbor graph* and cluster the players into sets $V_1, V_2, \ldots, V_\ell$ of size at least n/B and diameter at most D.

   (e) For each cluster V_i and for each object o, repeat $\Theta(\log n)$ times: choose at random one of the players in V_i to probe object o. Each player $p \in V_i$ sets $w(p_i)_d$ to the value that is discovered by a majority of the players that probe o.

2. Each player p executes RSELECT$(w(p))_p$, and outputs the result.

Figure 2: High-Level Description of the CalculatePreferences Algorithm

PROOF. A player p probes each object with probability at most $O(B \log(n)/n)$, as every cluster is of size at least n/B. The expected number of probes per player is $O(B \log(n))$, and hence by a Chernoff bound, with high probability no player makes more than $O(B \log n)$ probes. □

6.7 Concluding Claims.

In the absence of malicious players, COMPUTEPREFERENCES is asymptotically optimal with respect to a budget of B, as it successfully identifies a cluster of size n/B with asymptotically minimum diameter (see Lemma 9), and uses this cluster to generate the output preference vector. We discuss this in more detail in Section 7, while considering the behavior of malicious players. We now examine the probe complexity of the entire protocol:

LEMMA 11. *In* COMPUTEPREFERENCES, *no player makes more than* $O(B \log^{O(1)} n)$ *probes, whp.*

PROOF. Each player repeats the protocol $O(\log n)$ times for varying choices of diameter D. In the SMALLRADIUS algorithm, the diameter is $20 \ln(n)$, and hence, by Theorem 5, in each iteration, the number of probes per player is $O(B \log^{3.5} n)$. In the final phase, by Lemma 10, each player makes $O(B \log n)$ probes. Finally, the RSELECT protocol requires each player to make $O(\log^3 n)$ additional probes. □

Lastly, we argue that the protocol outputs preference vectors that are near to the real preference vectors. This follows from the observation that every cluster has diameter $O(D)$:

LEMMA 12. *Let D be the minimum integer such that for every player p there exists a set of at least n/B players, including p, with diameter no greater than D. Then for every player p: $|w(p) - v(p)| = O(D)$.*

PROOF. Let d be the smallest integer such that $2^d \geq D$. We consider the iteration where $D' = 2^d$ is the target diameter. Fix a player p, and let V_j be the cluster produced by the protocol containing p. Let s be the number of players in V_j. For object o_i, let x_i be the number of players q where $v(q) \neq v(p)$. By Lemma 9, we know that V_j has diameter $O(D')$, and hence $\Sigma_{i=1}^n x_i = O(sD')$.

We now argue that if $x_i < s/3$, then, with high probability, v's output is correct, i.e., $v(p)_i = w(p)_i$. In particular, there are $\Theta(\log n)$ objects assigned to probe object o_i. If $x_i < s/2$, then in expectation, at least $2/3$ of these probes

return the correct value for p. Thus by a Chernoff bound, with high probability, at least a majority of the probes return the right value for p.

It remains to bound the number objects o_j for which $x_j \geq s/3$. Since we have $\Sigma_{i=1}^n x_i = O(sD')$, by a simple counting argument there cannot be more than $O(D')$ objects for which v outputs an incorrect preference, with high probability. Thus $|v(p) - w(p)_d| = O(D') = O(D)$. Finally, by Theorem 3, since one of the candidate vectors $w_1, \ldots, w_{\log n}$ is within distance $O(D)$ of $v(p)$, we know that the final output $w(p)$ is within distance $O(D)$ of $v(p)$. □

7. DISHONEST PLAYERS

We now address the problem of dishonest players. The algorithm presented in Section 6 has already been designed to mostly prevent dishonest disruption. There are two issues that must be resolved. First, the algorithm presented in Section 6 (along with the building block algorithms in Section 5) rely on random choices that are agreed upon by all honest players. In Section 7.1, we discuss how to generate such randomness in the presence of dishonest players. Second, the dishonest players may attempt to hijack the clusters formed by the CALCULATEPREFERENCES protocol. In Section 7.2, we show that the CALCULATEPREFERENCES protocol is still asymptotically (almost) optimal even if up to $n/(3B)$ of the players are dishonest.

7.1 Generating Shared Random Numbers

The CALCULATEPREFERENCES protocol depends on random choices that are known to all players. For example, in step (1.b), the protocol selects a sample set S uniformly at random; and in step (1.e), players are randomly assigned objects to evaluate. If the dishonest players can bias these random choices, then the predicted preferences output by the protocol may be inaccurate.

Basic idea.

Consider the following simple solution. Prior to executing the CALCULATEPREFERENCES protocol, the players collaboratively elect a leader at random via a protocol that guarantees an honest leader with constant probability (as discussed below). The leader then writes a set of randomly chosen bits to the public bulletin board, and these are used as a shared source of randomness throughout the protocol.

With constant probability, the leader is honest and these bits are truly random.

This entire process of choosing a leader and executing CALCULATEPREFERENCES is iterated $\Theta(\log n)$ times, generating $\Theta(\log n)$ candidate output vectors. With high probability, at least one of these candidate vectors is generated from an execution in which an honest participant was elected leader. The players then execute RSELECT to choose the best vector, ensuring that the final output is sufficiently accurate. (Note that RSELECT is run locally at each player and does not depend on shared randomness.)

Electing an honest leader.

There exist in the literature several *Byzantine-tolerant* leader election algorithms (for shared-memory) that guarantee an honest leader is elected with constant probability. Here, we focus on the leader election protocol proposed by Feige [10] as a particularly nice solution to the problem.

The leader election protocol assumes that $(1+\delta)n/2$ players are honest, which is the case for all $B \geq 1$ as there are at most $n/(3B)$ dishonest players. The protocol also assumes a *full information* model in which each player can broadcast her information to all other participant; this is easily implemented using the shared bulletin board. The guarantee is that with probability $\Omega(\delta^{1.65})$, an honest leader is elected.

The idea underlying the protocol is to model the situation as a balls-and-bins game. Each player has a ball that it throw at random into one of the bins. The players that choose the lightest bin proceed to the next round, while the other players are eliminated. After repeating a sufficient number of times, one leader remains. The key principle ensuring correctness is that the lightest bin will have approximately the same fraction of honest players as the original set of players; the dishonest players cannot bias the fraction of honest player too much, as if they disproportionately join the lightest bin, it will cease to be the lightest.

7.2 Analysis with Dishonest Players

In this section, we show that the CALCULATEPREFERENCES protocol achieves the same (asymptotic) rate of error, even when there up to $n/(3B)$ dishonest players, as long as the shared random bits are unbiased. We assume that the dishonest players may be colluding to bias the results.

Specifically we show that the dishonest players cannot bias the predicted preferences for too many objects, and thus they cannot increase the asymptotic rate of error. Recall that each cluster assigned $\Theta(\log n)$ players to probe each object (in step (2.e)), and these players vote on the predicted preference. If all the honest players in a cluster have the same preference for an object, it is easy for the honest players to "out-vote" the dishonest players since at most $1/3$ of the players in a cluster are dishonest. The hard case, however, is when there are roughly the same number of players in a cluster that like an objects as dislike it. In that case, the votes of the dishonest players can bias the prediction. The crux of the argument, then, is that within each cluster, there are only $O(D)$ objects in which the honest players have significant disagreement as to the predicted preference.

LEMMA 13. *For each cluster constructed in step (1.d), the dishonest players can influence the predicted preferences for at most $O(D)$ objects.*

PROOF. Consider cluster V_i. Let X be the set of dishonest players that are part of this cluster. We examine their impact on step (1.e), the probing phase, focusing on a particular object o. Let A_1 be the set of players in V_i that are honest and like object o; let A_0 be the set of players in V_i that are not malicious and dislike object o. Without loss of generality, assume that $|A_1| \geq |A_0|$.

We now show that if $|A_1| > 5|A_0|$, then the result of the probing phase for object o in cluster V_i is 1, with high probability. Since $|V_i| \geq n/B$, as per Lemma 9, and $|X| \leq n/(3B)$, we know that $|A_0 \cup A_1| \geq 2|V_i|/3$. Assuming $|A_1| > 5|A_0|$, we can say that $|A_1| \geq 5|V_i|/9$. In step (1.e), object o is assigned at random (as the shared random bits are unbiased) to $c \log n$ players (for some constant c). Hence in expectation at least $5c\log n/9$ players in A_1 are assigned to probe object o. Thus, with high probability, the majority of players probing o are in A_1, and hence the dishonest players have no impact on the prediction. The symmetric claim also holds: if $|A_0| > 5|A_1|$, then the result of the probing phase for object o in cluster V_i is 0, with high probability, again preventing the dishonest players from having any impact.

We say object o is zero-strange if $5|A_0| \geq |A_1| \geq |A_0|$, and one-strange if $5|A_1| \geq |A_0| \geq |A_1|$. We now show that there are at most $O(D)$ zero-strange objects, using the *double counting* method. (The symmetric claim about one-strange objects follows by the same argument.) We count the number of triples (p_1, p_2, o) where p_1 and p_2 are two honest players, and o is an object on which p_1 and p_2 disagree in their preferences. Since the number of differing preferences between any pair of players is $O(D)$ (by Lemma 9), the total number of such triples in a cluster is $O(|V_i|^2 D)$. On the other hand, for any strange object, we know that $|A_0| + |A_1| \geq 2|V_i|/3$, so we have that $|A_1| \geq |V_i|/3$, and $|A_0| \geq |A_1|/5 \geq |V_i|/15$. We conclude that the number of triples for a given object o is $|A_1||A_0| = \Omega(V_i^2)$, implying that there are at most $O(D)$ zero-strange objects. By the same logic, there are at most $O(D)$ one-strange objects. We conclude that the dishonest players can only impact a player's preferences with respect to $O(D)$ objects. □

As a final remark, it is relatively easy to see that the dishonest players cannot significantly impact the ZERORADIUS and SMALLRADIUS routines that are used as building blocks: in each case, all that matters is that there are sufficiently many honest players that participate to ensure a good outcome. We can now conclude with the main theorem of the paper:

THEOREM 14. *The CALCULATEPREFERENCES protocol is a $O(B\log^{O(1)} n)$-budget collaborative scoring algorithm that is asymptotically optimal with respect to a budget of B.*

8. CONCLUSION

In this paper, we have presented an algorithm for collaborative scoring that can tolerate some fraction of the players acting dishonestly. Moreover, the protocol is almost optimal in the sense that, given a budget of $O(B\log^{O(1)} n)$, it performs asymptotically as well as any algorithm with a budget of B, in the worst case.

There are several interesting open questions. One observation is that we have proposed a relatively restricted definition of collaborative scoring in order both to simplify the presentation and to make the analysis tractable. For example, players are restricted to binary preferences; in reality, players may rate items on a numerical scale. As a related example, we use the Hamming distance to measure the similarity of two players' preferences; in a real system (with non-binary preferences), other metrics may be more useful. We believe that many of the techniques developed in this paper generalize to these more realistic settings: the basic idea of using sampling to cluster players does not rely on these particular assumptions.

Another interesting scenario concerns the situation where different players have different budgets. For example, some players may be willing to probe a large number B_{big} of objects, while other players may be willing to probe only a small number B_{small} of objects. Again, the techniques in this paper should generalize to such a scenario: each cluster must be chosen to contain a sufficient total number of queries among all the members.

Another aspect to collaborative scoring is the communication complexity. Here, we assume a shared bulletin board which is, effectively, free to access. In reality, there are costs to sharing information, either via sending messages or accessing a shared memory. It remains an open question to minimize the underlying communication costs.

More technically, there are two obvious gaps. First, do we really need the augmented budgets to achieve asymptotic optimality? That is, can we develop an algorithm that uses only $O(B)$ queries, and yet is still asymptotically optimal with respect to a budget of B? Second, can we show, formally, a stronger lower bound on the worst-case performance? The notion of optimality in this paper is worst-case: there is a distribution of preferences for which it is impossible to do better. Yet we conjecture that there is a stronger notion of optimality: *for every* distribution of preferences, a player p can do no better than, say, the median distance to the closest n/B others.

Finally, there remains the question of tolerating a larger number of dishonest players. The key requirement, here, is that not too many malicious players are included in any one cluster. By preventing the malicious players from biasing the selection of clusters, it seems possible to adapt the techniques developed here to tolerate more dishonest players.

9. REFERENCES

[1] D. Achlioptas and F. McSherry. *Fast computation of low rank approximations*. In *Proceedings of the 33rd Annual Symposium on Theory of Computing*, pp, 611–618, 2001.

[2] N. Alon, B. Awerbuch, Y. Azar, and B. Patt-Shamir. *Tell me who I am: An interactive recommendation system*. In *Proceedings of the 18th Annual Symposium on Parallelism in Algorithms and Architectures*, pp. 1–10, 2006.

[3] N. Alon, B. Awerbuch, Y. Azar, and B. Patt-Shamir. *Tell me who I am: An interactive recommendation system*. Theory of Computing Systems, 45(2): 261–279, August, 2009.

[4] B. Awerbuch, Y. Azar, Z. Lotker, B. Patt-Shamir, and M. Tuttle. *Collaborate with strangers to find own preferences*. In *Proceedings of the 17th Annual Symposium on Parallelism in Algorithms and Architectures*, pp. 263–269, 2005.

[5] B. Awerbuch, B. Patt-Shamir, and D. Peleg. *Improved recommendation systems*. In *Proceedings of the 16th Annual Symposium on Discrete Algorithms*, pp. 1174–1183, 2005.

[6] Y. Azar, A. Fiat, A. Karlin, F. McSherry, and J. Saia. *Spectral analysis of data*. In *Proceedings of the 33rd Annual Symposium on Theory of Computing*, pp. 619–626, 2001.

[7] P. Drineas, A. Frieze, R. Kannan, S. Vempala, and V. Vinay. *Clustering in large graphs and matrices*. In *Proceedings of the 10th Annual Symposium on Discrete Algorithms*, pp. 291–299, 1999.

[8] P. Drineas and R. Kannan. *Fast monte-carlo algorithms for approximate matrix multiplication*. In *Proceedings of the 42nd Annual Symposium on Foundations of Computer Science*, p. 452, 2001.

[9] P. Drineas, I. Keredinis, and P. Raghavan. *Competitive recommendation systems*. In *Proceedings of the 34th Annual Symposium on Theory of Computing*, pp. 82–90, 2002.

[10] U. Feige. *Non-cryptographic selection protocols*. In *Proceedings of the 40th Annual Symposium on Foundations of Computer Science*, p. 142, 1999.

[11] J. Kleinberg and M. Sandler. *Using mixture models for collaborative filtering*. In *Proceedings of the 36th Annual Symposium on Theory of Computing*, pp. 569–578, 2004.

[12] R. Kumar, P. Raghavan, S. Rajagopalan, and A. Tomkins. *Recommender systems: A probablistic analysis*. In *Proceedings of the 39rd Annual Symposium on Foundations of Computer Science*, p. 664, 1998.

[13] A. Nisgav and B. Patt-Shamir. *Finding similar users in social networks*. In *Proceedings of the 21st Annual Symposium on Parallelism in Algorithms and Architectures*, pp. 169–177, 2009.

[14] H. Yu, P. B. Gibbons, M. Kaminsky, and F. Xiao. *SybilLimit: A near-optimal social network defense against sybil attacks*. In *Proceedings of the Symposium on Security and Privacy*, pp. 3–17, 2008.

[15] H. Yu, M. Kaminsky, P. B. Gibbons, and A. Flaxman. *SybilGuard: Defending against sybil attacks via social networks*. Transactions on Networking, 16(3):576–589, June 2008.

[16] H. Yu, C. Shi, M. Kaminsky, P. B. Gibbons, and F. Xiao. *DSybil: Optimal sybil-resistance for recommendation systems*. In *Proceedings of the 30th Annual Symposium on Security and Privacy*, pp. 283–298, 2009.

Securing Every Bit:
Authenticated Broadcast in Radio Networks

Dan Alistarh[*]
EPFL
dan.alistarh@epfl.ch

Seth Gilbert
EPFL
seth.gilbert@epfl.ch

Rachid Guerraoui
EPFL
rachid.guerraoui@epfl.ch

Zarko Milosevic
EPFL
zarko.milosevic@epfl.ch

Calvin Newport
MIT
cnewport@csail.mit.edu

ABSTRACT

This paper studies non-cryptographic authenticated broadcast in radio networks subject to malicious failures. We introduce two protocols that address this problem. The first, NeighborWatchRB, makes use of a novel strategy in which honest devices monitor their neighbors for malicious behavior. Second, we present a more robust variant, MultiPathRB, that tolerates the maximum possible density of malicious devices per region, using an elaborate voting strategy. We also introduce a new proof technique to show that both protocols ensure asymptotically optimal running time.

We demonstrate the fault tolerance of our protocols through extensive simulation. Simulations show the practical superiority of the NeighborWatchRB protocol (an advantage hidden in the constants of the asymptotic complexity). The NeighborWatchRB protocol even performs relatively well when compared to the simple, fast epidemic protocols commonly used in the radio setting, protocols that tolerate no malicious faults. We therefore believe that the overhead for ensuring authenticated broadcast is reasonable, especially in applications that use authenticated broadcast only when necessary, such as distributing an authenticated digest.

Categories and Subject Descriptors

C.2.4 [**Computer-Communication Networks**]: Distributed Systems; C.4 [**Performance of Systems**]: Fault Tolerance

General Terms

Algorithms, Security, Reliability

Keywords

Broadcast, Wireless networks, Byzantine faults

[*]This author's work was supported by the Swiss NCCR MICS project.

1. INTRODUCTION

We study the problem of non-cryptographic authenticated broadcast in a multi-hop radio network. Consider a single source attempting to disseminate an important message to every device in an ad hoc wireless network. This broadcast should be *reliable*—every device receives the message—and *authenticated*—a device should only accept the message actually sent by the source. These properties should still hold even if some of the network devices are corrupted and behaving in an unpredictable, perhaps adversarial manner.

When public-key cryptography is available, this problem is solved with relative ease: the message is signed by the base station, and flooded through the network. Each receiver can verify the signature. Public-key cryptography, however, can be quite expensive, and is often impractical in resource-constrained settings such as sensor networks. Even lightweight cryptographic techniques, such as message authentication codes, may prove too costly in terms of computation or deployment costs. With this in mind, in this paper we study *non-cryptographic* authenticated broadcast.

Contribution. We present and analyze two protocols for authenticated reliable broadcast in multi-hop wireless networks subject to malicious failures. The MultiPathRB protocol is the first protocol that is provably optimally resilient and achieves asymptotically optimal running time. The NeighborWatchRB protocol, by contrast, is less robust in theory, but performs much better in practice, as seen in our simulations.

System Overview. The key challenge we face is that some of the devices in the network may be corrupted. Formally, we capture this corruption with *Byzantine* failures. Devices suffering from Byzantine faults can disrupt a protocol in several ways: they may remain silent when required to broadcast; they may lie about their view of the system; they may spoof messages from other devices; they may overpower honest messages, replacing them with dishonest messages; or they may jam the airwaves with noise, preventing any communication. In placing no limitations on the behavior of Byzantine devices, we capture scenarios where devices are simply *malfunctioning*, as well as scenarios where devices have been compromised by a malicious hacker. An advantage of this approach is that the resulting protocols are resilient to *all possible* attacks, rather than focusing on a particular known attack. A protocol proved correct is this setting provides a strong measure of comfort to the practitioner deploying it in an unpredictable real world setting. As established by Koo [22], reliable broadcast is impossible if more than 1/4 of a device's neighbors are Byzantine. We thus assume that the density of malicious devices does not exceed this bound.

Wireless devices in the network have a few capabilities that help to overcome this challenging environment. First, they can perform *carrier sensing* in order to determine whether or not the channel is currently in use (this is also referred to as *collision detection* in the literature). That is, if there is some activity on the channel—be it a single message being sent, a collision of multiple messages, or a malicious device jamming the airwaves—the protocol can distinguish this case from the case of no activity. (Implementation details for such a carrier-sensing MAC layer are discussed in [12].) Second, we also assume that each device has access to a localization service that provides an (approximate) location. (Such a service might calculate location directly, as in GPS or Cricket [30], or indirectly via trilateration, as in [29, 13]).

Metrics. We focus on two metrics: fault tolerance and running time. Our protocols aim to tolerate the maximum possible density of Byzantine faults in the network, and achieve an optimal running time as expressed in terms of the adversary's power. In more detail, if corrupt devices jam the channel in every round, then no protocol will ever complete. Continual disruption, however, is not sustainable in practice: it drains the batteries of the malicious devices, and it makes them easier to detect and eliminate. Thus, we analyze executions in which there is some bound β on the total number of messages broadcast by Byzantine devices in each neighborhood. It is easy to see that no protocol can terminate in less than $\Omega(\beta D)$ time, where D is the diameter of the network, since the adversary may jam transmission at every hop. And in [19], it was shown that no protocol can terminate in less than $\Omega(\log |\Sigma|)$ time, where Σ is the set of all possible messages. Our protocols match this combined lower bound of $\Omega(\beta D + \log |\Sigma|)$ rounds.

For this analysis, we consider a specific topology where devices are deployed at unit intervals in the plane, forming a grid (or mesh). We assume that each device can communicate with every other device that is within R units on the vertical axis and R units on the horizontal axis. We call this set of nodes within broadcast range the device's *neighborhood*. Let t be the maximum number of Byzantine nodes in a neighborhood. (This model has been previously used in, e.g., [22, 4, 23].) Extension of the analytic bounds to arbitrary topologies is left as important future work.

The NeighborWatchRB Protocol. Our first main result in this paper is a protocol, NeighborWatchRB, which tolerates malicious interference while guaranteeing an asymptotically optimal running time of $O(\beta D + \log |\Sigma|)$. There are two key challenges in devising such a protocol. First, devices cannot necessarily determine which device sent a given message; that is, Byzantine devices may effectively spoof messages. Second, in order to reach the edge of the network, the message from the source is passed along a multi-hop path; the receiver must ensure that it has not been modified along the way by a malicious user. Our protocol is divided into two levels to cope with these different problems.

Single hop level: At the lower level, we develop a sub-protocol that can send a block of bits, i.e. a multi-bit message, over a single hop of a multi-hop network. The key idea is to use silent rounds of communication to confirm that the transmission has been successful. An additional challenge in the multi-hop setting is to synchronize the sender and the receiver, ensuring that they agree on the order of the transmitted bits. Some ideas are common to the one-hop protocol of [19, 20]; however, new insights are required for tolerating adversaries in the multi-hop setting.

Multi-hop level: Next, we implement a complete multi-hop broadcast protocol on top of the previous layer. The idea is that honest devices are clustered into regions, and they implement a "neighborhood watch" system by actively preventing devices in their region from disseminating corrupted information.

The protocol is successful as long as there is no region occupied solely by Byzantine devices; this requirement translates into the bound $t < \frac{1}{4}R^2$. We also introduce a "2-voting" variant that tolerates $t < \frac{1}{2}R^2$. The protocol is *adaptive*, in that the message is delivered as soon as Byzantine interference stops. Unlike the protocols of [23, 5], nodes do not need to know the bound β on the Byzantine budget; moreover, they do not even need to know the bound t on the number of Byzantine nodes in their area.

The MultiPathRB Variant. Second, we introduce a variant of the protocol that achieves optimal fault tolerance, i.e., it tolerates $t < \frac{1}{2}R(2R + 1)$, while maintaining asymptotically optimal running time. The protocol re-uses level one of NeighborWatchRB, and employs a voting strategy to ensure multi-hop authentication. A similar strategy is used by the protocol of [5]. However, note that this previous protocol assumed authenticated communication, and did not allow Byzantine nodes to jam the network or otherwise disrupt communication. Further, our variant improves on the protocol of [5] by adapting to the *actual* number of malicious broadcasts, by delivering the message as soon as interference stops.

Analysis. An important technical contribution of this paper is the upper bound on the running time of the two protocols. (Prior work or reliable broadcast, e.g. [22], focused on feasibility, omitting any analysis of performance.) First, note that combining the single-hop transmission layer and the multi-hop layer in the natural way results in protocols with sub-optimal running time of $\Omega(\beta \cdot D \cdot \log |\Sigma|)$, since the adversary may jam the message for $\Omega(\beta)$ rounds at each network hop. The protocols we introduce carefully integrate the sub-protocols to achieve a *pipelined* data flow, and hence the optimal running time of $O(\beta \cdot D + \log |\Sigma|)$. The main technical difficulty in the analysis is showing that the pipeline continues to flow, and cannot be (too) disrupted by interference (see Theorem 5).

Evaluation. We evaluate both protocols using the WSNet wireless network simulator (Section 6). Devices are deployed at random in a two-dimensional plane, using both uniform and clustered distributions. We focus on three different models of faulty behavior: crash failures, jamming devices that aim to delay the protocol, and malicious attacks (i.e., Byzantine devices that attempt to spread a fake message).

In all three cases, both protocols show good levels of fault tolerance. In general, we observe a close link between the density of deployment and the number of Byzantine devices that the protocol can tolerate. We also notice that, in practice, if the bad devices are distributed at random, then the supposedly less robust NeighborWatchRB protocol easily outperforms MultiPathRB, even for greater numbers of bad devices.

We also compare the performance of the NeighborWatchRB

protocol to a simple epidemic flooding protocol. The latter protocol has no built-in fault tolerance, and can be disrupted by any Byzantine interference. We found that the NeighborWatchRB protocol takes about seven times longer to complete. In many ways, this shows the success of our pipelining strategy, as much of the additional single-hop cost is defrayed by the inherent cost of propagating a message across multiple hops.

Interpretation. One conclusion from these experiments is that, while there is some inherent overhead in tolerating Byzantine failures, it may be possible to engineer protocols that are quite efficient. For example, consider the dual-mode protocol that operates as follows: (a) every message is broadcast via simple epidemic flooding, using no security; and (b) a small digest of each message is broadcast using a protocol such as NeighborWatchRB. Good security is ensured as long as the digest is chosen appropriately. And as long as the digest is no more than 1/7 the size of the original message, the induced overhead may be tolerable. We conjecture, in fact, that the overhead in such an implementation may compare well to systems the rely on cryptography, while at the same time avoiding the costs of a cryptographic solution.

Because of space limitations, some proofs and figures are deferred to the full version of the paper, available at [18], together with the source code for the simulations.

2. RELATED WORK

Jamming in wireless networks is a problem that has been extensively studied by the applied networking community. The literature analyzes efficient jamming attacks (e.g., [26]), as well as mechanisms to detect and circumvent such attacks (e.g., [15, 14]). Recent work [3] shows both in theory and experimentally that adaptive jammers can efficiently reduce the throughput of a wireless network. Most defense mechanisms focus on preventing a specific attack, and are based on physical layer methods (e.g., [24, 25]) and on MAC layer strategies [2, 31].

Koo [22] studied the problem of broadcast in *multi-hop* wireless networks, under the assumption that single-hop communication is reliable and authenticated (i.e., no jamming or spoofing). He proved that no algorithm can tolerate more than $\frac{1}{2}R(2R+1)$ malicious devices per neighborhood. Bhandari and Vaidya [4, 5] present a protocol that matches this lower bound. The problem of broadcast in the context of malicious interference and jamming was also considered in [23, 19, 20], under weaker adversarial models than the one of this paper.

Another approach can be found in [11], where they develop "Integrity Codes" that allow the transfer of information in a single-hop network based on collision detection (i.e., carrier sensing). This premise, together with the coding technique, originates from Unidirectional Error-Detecting Codes [7, 10], and is similar to the assumptions we make in this paper. In [19, 20] the authors develop a broadcast protocol for single-hop wireless networks in the presence of Byzantine nodes. In this paper, we generalize their protocol in the case of multi-hop networks. Although the algorithm in [19, 20] is similar to our 1Hop-Protocol, new insights are required in order to tolerate Byzantine nodes in the multi-hop case.

Other lines of research have considered the power of an adversary that is restricted to behave in a probabilistic manner (e.g., [27, 6]), or solutions to the problem when more than

one communication channel is available, via frequency hopping (e.g., [8], [16]) .

A parallel approach studies broadcast authentication using cryptographic techniques (e.g., [28, 1]). Boneh et al. [9] prove that authentication is impossible without relying on digital signatures or on synchronization. Perhaps the best known protocol in this line of research is μTESLA, by Perrig et al. [28], which relies on weak time synchronization between sender and receivers and on message authentication codes. A survey of recent work on lightweight cryptographic techniques is presented in [17].

3. MODEL

We now describe the two models of wireless networks that we rely on in this paper. The first is somewhat simplified, and is used for analysis; the second is more realistic, and is used for simulations.

Analytical model. For the purpose of analysis, we model a system consisting of devices, which we refer to as *nodes*, that communicate via wireless radio. Let R be the communication radius. We define a *neighborhood* of a node v to be the area within distance R of v. Additionally, each node knows its location.

Time is divided into slots, which we refer to as *rounds*, and we assume that slots are *small*; each round is large enough to transmit at most a few bits of data. Only one node in each neighborhood can send a message in each time slot without causing a collision. When two neighbors of a node v broadcast in the same round, v may receive either of the two messages, or no message at all. In the latter case v detects a *collision*.

Nodes are either *honest*, in which case they follow the protocol, or *Byzantine*, in which case they may deviate arbitrarily. Let t be the maximum number of Byzantine nodes in any neighborhood. Also, let β (the *budget*) be the maximum number of broadcasts for Byzantine nodes in a neighborhood.

While our algorithms remain correct for any network topology (as long as t is sufficiently low), we analyze performance in the context of a specific topology: a two-dimensional grid where nodes are placed at every grid point. We express our results in the L_∞ norm, meaning that, given two nodes $v = (x_1, y_1)$ and $w = (x_2, y_2)$, we say that v is in the neighborhood of w if $|x_2 - x_1| \leq R$ and $|y_2 - y_1| \leq R$. A similar model is used for analysis in [22, 23, 5].

Simulation model. Our simulations were performed using the WSNet Worldsens simulator [32]. The simulator uses the *Friis freespace* propagation model for radio wave propagation. Communication depends on the actual topology, as opposed to the analytical model. We modified the MAC layer to implement carrier sensing, i.e. to provide a notification of when the channel seems to be in use, but no message is delivered. The intent here was to emulate MAC layers that can detect when there are significant changes in the level of signal on the channel. The setup captures realistic behavior missed by our theoretical analysis (real topology, lost messages, capture effect). Simulated devices have access to a synchronized clock, and we use this clock to implement a fixed (TDMA-like) schedule. We discuss the implementation details in Section 6.

Relation between models. Although the theoretical analysis is performed in the L_∞ topology, the protocols remain provably correct in the actual geometry as well, as long as the assumptions on the density of malicious nodes still hold. However, our experiments do not specifically enforce these assumptions (nodes are randomly distributed, an arbitrary fraction becomes malicious, packets may be lost, etc.), since the intention is to investigate the behavior of the protocols in a more realistic setting.

4. AUTHENTICATED BROADCAST

In this section, we present our authenticated broadcast protocols, sketching some of the key properties.

Notice that it is difficult for a node to trust the contents of a message, as it cannot determine whether that message originated at the ostensible sender s, or at a malicious device spoofing messages that claim to be from s. However, if a receiver does *not* receive a message in a round, it can be certain that no message was sent; the malicious nodes cannot "forge" silence. Thus, we make frequent use of silence to authenticate data.

To minimize the damage caused by a malicious broadcast, the message is transmitted and authenticated one bit at a time. In this way, we ensure that any interference by a malicious device can cause only a small amount of damage. Otherwise, a single malicious broadcast might force the entire protocol to restart!

Schedule. To prevent contention among honest nodes, we allocate a simple (TDMA-like) broadcast schedule such that no two nodes within distance $3R$ of each other are scheduled in the same round (recall that, in the analytical model, nodes are placed on a two-dimensional grid of unit length 1). Since each node knows its location, we can easily construct such a schedule *locally*, i.e. without any communication between nodes, by assigning each grid point a schedule slot, and re-using schedule slots as long as no two (honest) neighbors of a node may collide. It is straightforward to build such a schedule of size $O(R^2)$. At the beginning of the protocol, each node locally computes its schedule slot, and the schedule slots of its neighbors. For simplicity, each schedule slot is 6 consecutive rounds long, which we also call the *broadcast interval* of the node. During its interval, the node broadcasts messages, and may receive acknowledgments from its neighbors.

In the following, we divide the protocol into two layers, a lower layer responsible for single-hop propagation, and a higher layer responsible for end-to-end delivery.

Level 1: Single Hop Transmission

We split the presentation of the lower communication layer into two protocols: the 2Bit-Protocol, which transmits two bits across a single communication hop, and the 1Hop-Protocol, which ensures the transmission of a stream of bits over one hop.

Assume that an honest sender s attempts to transmit two bits $\langle b_1, b_2 \rangle$ to a set of honest nodes P in the neighborhood of s. In the 2Bit-Protocol, the sender transmits the two bits via a pattern of broadcasts and silence: when it wants to send a '1', it broadcasts a message; when it wants to send a '0', it remains silent[1]. The receivers acknowledge

---

[1] Notice, of course, that a physical layer implementation will most likely encode both a "broadcast" and "silence" via some waveforms; the key property is that the Byzantine nodes cannot overwrite a broadcast with silence. We continue using the terminology of "broadcasts" and "silence," leaving physical layer implementations for future work.

the information, and two veto rounds are used to determine whether the protocol has succeeded. The protocol proceeds in six rounds (i.e., during one schedule slot):

R1) *Sender:* If $b_1 = 1$, then the sender s transmits a message '*bit1*'; otherwise, it remains silent.

R2) *Acknowledge:* Every receiver in P (the neighborhood of s) that receives a message or detects a collision in round R1, broadcasts a (non-empty) *bit1-response* message in round R2; otherwise, it remains silent. Notice that if $b_1 = 1$, then this acknowledgment is likely to cause a collision. If a node in P broadcasts a *bit1-response*, then it assumes that $b_1 = 1$; otherwise, it assumes that $b_1 = 0$.

R3) *Sender:* If $b_2 = 1$, then the sender transmits a *bit2* message; otherwise, it remains silent.

R4) *Acknowledge:* Every receiver in P that receives a message or detects a collision in round R3 broadcasts a *bit2-response* message in round R4; otherwise, it remains silent. If a node in P broadcasts a *bit2-response*, then it assumes that $b_2 = 1$; otherwise, it assumes that $b_2 = 0$.

R5) *Sender Veto:* The sender s transmits a veto message in any of the following cases:

- Bit $b_1 = 0$ and it receives a message or detects a collision in round R2.
- Bit $b_1 = 1$ and it does *not* receive a message or detect a collision in round R2.
- Bit $b_2 = 0$ and it receives a message or detect a collision in round R4.
- Bit $b_2 = 1$ and it does *not* receive a message or detects a collision in round R4.

R6) *Receiver veto:* Every node in P broadcasts a veto message if it receives a message or detects a collision in round R5.

If the sender s receives no messages and detects no collisions in round R6, then it returns success; otherwise, it returns failure. Similarly, if a receiver in P receives no messages and detects no collision in round R5, then it returns success along with its estimate of b_1 and b_2; otherwise, it returns failure. The following theorem captures the key properties of this sub-protocol:

THEOREM 1. *If honest sender v and honest receivers P in the neighborhood of v begin the 2Bit-Protocol in the same round. Then at the end of the sixth round:*
- Authenticity: *A receiver returns bits $\langle b_1, b_2 \rangle$ only if the sender s sent $\langle b_1, b_2 \rangle$.*
- Termination: *Sender v returns success only if every honest node in v's neighborhood returns success.*
- Energy: *If sender or receiver returns failure, then a Byzantine device in the neighborhood of s expended at least one broadcast.*

We continue with the 1Hop-Protocol, in which a sender s reliably sends a constant-sized message to a set of honest receivers P in its neighborhood. Unlike the 2Bit-Protocol, which can fail, the 1Hop-Protocol always delivers the message eventually. The 1Hop-Protocol divides the message into individual bits, and each bit, along with some control information, is sent using the 2Bit-Protocol. Whenever the 2Bit-Protocol returns failure, the failed bit is re-transmitted.

The key difficulty involves synchronizing the sender and the receivers. If the sender successfully completes the protocol, then we know that the receivers delivered the bits. The converse, however does not hold: some (or all) of the receivers may finish receiving a bit, while the sender continues to repeat the transmission. The receivers should not confuse this repeated transmission with the next bit in the sequence.

To remedy this problem, we use an alternating bit strategy. That is, prior to sending each bit of the message, we send an additional control bit; this control bit alternates between '1' and '0'. Thus, the two bits sent by the 2Bit-Protocol are this alternating "parity" bit, and the one bit of data. The receiver can determine when the sender has advanced to a new bit by examining the parity bit. Note that the parity bit mechanism also ensures that silence on the sender side is not misinterpreted as a $\langle 0, 0 \rangle$ transmission (the first value of the parity bit is '1'). The receiver delivers the entire message once it has received all the bits. The resulting protocol has the following properties:

THEOREM 2. *If honest sender v and honest receivers P in the neighborhood of v begin the* 1Hop-Protocol *in the same round:*
- *Authenticity: A receiver returns m only if v sent m.*
- *Termination: When the sender terminates, every node in P has received the message.*
- *Energy: If m consists of k bits, and v does not complete sending m for r rounds, then Byzantine nodes in the neighborhood of v expend at least $(r - 6k)/6$ broadcasts.*

Notice that the protocol requires $6k$ rounds to transmit the message in the absence of malicious interference. For the rest of $(r - 6k)$ rounds, the adversary needs to broadcast at least once every 6 rounds to prevent the delivery of the message. The claim regarding the energy usage by the Byzantine nodes follows because each bit is sent individually; otherwise, a single disruption by the adversary would force the entire message to be repeated.

Level 2: NeighborWatchRB

NeighborWatchRB implements authenticated broadcast across multiple hops on top of the 1Hop-Protocol. We partition the plane into squares of maximum size such that any two nodes located in neighboring squares are able to communicate. In the analytic model, the squares are of size $\lceil R/2 \rceil \times \lceil R/2 \rceil$, that is, each square contains $\lceil R/2 \rceil^2$ nodes.

All the nodes in the same square act identically: whenever one broadcasts, they all broadcast; whenever one is silent, they all are silent. The clustering into squares and the assignment of schedule slots are performed without any communication, since each node knows its location. For example, if the 1Hop-Protocol calls for a silent round (to confirm the authenticity of a message), all the honest nodes in the square are silent; if the 1Hop-Protocol calls for a broadcast during a veto round, all the honest nodes broadcast (ensuring that the message is vetoed, as long as there is at least one honest node in the square). Effectively, all the nodes in a square act like one "meta-node."

In this case, each square is assigned to a schedule slot; as before, the schedule is chosen to avoid collisions between neighboring squares. Whenever a square is scheduled, all the nodes in that square execute the next step of the 1Hop-Protocol. The source node is the only exception: it behaves independently of any square and it always is awarded the first broadcast interval in the schedule. The source begins the protocol by using the 1Hop-Protocol to disseminate the bits of the message to its neighbors.

Each node maintains a buffer of bits received through the 1Hop-Protocol for each of its neighboring squares (plus the source, for nodes that are in range of the source). We say that a node *commits* to bit number i if it has received bits number $1, 2, \ldots, i$ from one of its neighbors, through the 1Hop-Protocol.

Once a node has committed to a new bit, it executes rounds of the 1Hop-Protocol for that bit whenever its square is scheduled, until the 1Hop-Protocol returns success. Note that a node will not proceed to broadcasting bit number $i+1$ as long as bit number i has not been successfully broadcast.

Assume node n has no new bits to send. However, it notices that a node is trying to broadcast a new bit during n's broadcast interval. Then node n blocks the 1Hop-Protocol initiated by the other node, by broadcasting during veto rounds. Thus, we can be sure that data is propagated only when every node in a square has committed to it. Note that, in this way, the protocol will perform correctly if there is no Byzantine interference.

A Byzantine node may disrupt the protocol either by trying to disseminate corrupt information, or by broadcasting during veto rounds. However, in order to delay the broadcast, the Byzantine node must continue to expend its broadcast budget. On the other hand, notice that a Byzantine node cannot relay bad data, as it can only propagate a bit when every node in the square agrees on that bit. Thus, as long as there is at least one honest node in every square of size $\lceil R/2 \rceil \times \lceil R/2 \rceil$, that is $t < \lceil R/2 \rceil^2$, the protocol succeeds.

An alternate way of viewing the protocol is as creating a grid of *honest* meta-nodes located at the center of each $\lceil R/2 \rceil \times \lceil R/2 \rceil$ square, where any two neighboring meta-nodes can communicate. If a device tries to deviate from the behavior of its corresponding "meta-node," then it is vetoed by honest members of the cluster. The spreading of the message implements a simple epidemic protocol on top of this grid. To gain efficiency, one could use a more complex routing protocol on this overlay. The following theorem guarantees correctness of the protocol.

THEOREM 3. *If an honest source sends m and if $t < \lceil R/2 \rceil^2$, then: (1) If a node commits to bit b_i, then b_i is the ith bit of m. (2) Eventually every node commits to every bit of the message.*

We also consider a variant of NeighborWatchRB which we refer to as "2-voting" NeighborWatchRB: in this case, a node only commits to a bit if it receives it from two different neighboring squares. Thus, the protocol is able to tolerate roughly $t < R^2/2$ adversaries per neighborhood.

Level 2: MultiPathRB

We conclude by describing a variant of the top layer which implements the MultiPathRB protocol. MultiPathRB also uses the 1Hop-Protocol for single hop authentication. Instead of grouping devices into meta-nodes, it employs an elaborate voting strategy at the multi-hop level in order to tolerate the maximal number of adversaries. More precisely, in order to deliver a message, it must be transmitted along a sufficient number of node-disjoint paths located in the same neighborhood. This strategy was first introduced in [5].

Specifically, the protocol uses three types of messages: SOURCE messages, COMMIT messages, and HEARD messages. Initially, for each bit b_i of the message, the source s sends a message $\langle SOURCE, b_i \rangle$ using the 1Hop-Protocol. Every neighbor of s can commit to any bit that it receives directly from the source, as Theorem 2 guarantees the authenticity of the message.

When a node commits to a bit b_i, it sends a $\langle COMMIT, b_i \rangle$ message using the 1Hop-Protocol. When a node receives $\langle COMMIT, b_i \rangle$ from some node v, it sends a $\langle HEARD, v, b_i \rangle$ message. We say that v is the *cause* of the HEARD message.

A node can commit to a bit when it has received at least $t + 1$ COMMIT and HEARD messages, such that: there is some neighborhood N where (a) the source of every COMMIT message, (b) the source of every HEARD message, and (c) the cause of every HEARD message all lie in that neighborhood N. Recall that a node identifies the location of a message's sender based on the slot in the broadcast schedule in which the message has been sent. Since at most t of these nodes are dishonest, at least one version of the received message must be correct. This implies that the broadcast protocol never delivers a fake message (authentication). Following the analysis in [5], we can also show that the protocol always terminates.

THEOREM 4. *If an honest source sends m via* MultiPathRB, *and if $t < \frac{1}{2}R(2R+1)$, then (1) a node commits to b_i only if b_i is the ith bit of m and (2) eventually every node commits to every bit of m.*

5. RUNNING TIME ANALYSIS

In this section, we analyze the performance of MultiPathRB. The upper bound on the running time of NeighborWatchRB will follow as a special case.

There are two issues that arise. The first issue is related to bounding adversarial interference as the data traverses the network: at each hop, the Byzantine nodes can delay different parts of the protocol. The second issue is related to bounding queuing delays at the nodes themselves: a given node may have a long queue of protocol messages to send (e.g., COMMIT messages, HEARD messages, etc.). The adversary may cause more delay than expected by creating a backlog of messages, thus initiating a data "traffic jam." The argument is structured to show that such a jam does not affect the asymptotic running time.

Proof Preliminaries. Each SOURCE, COMMIT and HEARD message is of size $O(1)$, consisting of an identifier indicating its type, along with the value of the transmitted bit; the HEARD message also includes the identifier of the node that caused the HEARD message—the identifier can be encoded in $O(\log R)$ bits by its relative location from the sender. Treating R as constant (as we do throughout), each message consists of only $O(1)$ bits.

Recall that each node is scheduled at least once every $O(R^2)$ slots. As a corollary of Theorem 2, we conclude that if the adversary uses $\leq \beta_i$ broadcasts to delay a particular SOURCE, COMMIT, or HEARD message, then the message transmission completes in $O(\beta_i)$ scheduled slots, i.e., in $O(\beta_i)$ time.

For each node q, our goal is to bound the time it takes for q to receive the message from the source. We first isolate

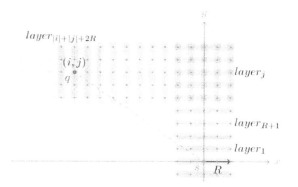

Figure 1: Rectilinear path of width $2R + 1$ from source to node q.

a rectilinear path from the source s to q that is of width $2R + 1$ and extends distance R beyond q (see Figure 1). For each bit i, we can trace the progression of messages along this path. We say that a node is in layer k if a path to the source takes no more than k_v vertical hops, k_h horizontal hops, and either ($k = k_v$ and $k_h = 0$) or ($k = k_h + k_v + 2R$ and $k_h \neq 0$). See Figure 1 for a layer numbering example.

For bit i, we introduce the following notation:

- Let S_i be the time interval during which the source transmits its $SOURCE$ message for bit number i.

- Let $C^*_{i,[1,R]}$ be the interval during which nodes in layers $[1, R]$ transmit $COMMIT$ messages associated with bit i.

- Let $C_{i,k}$ be the interval during which nodes in layer k transmit $COMMIT$ messages for bit i.

- Let H^*_i be the interval during which the nodes in layers $[k + 1, k + R]$ send $HEARD$ messages caused by COMMIT messages for bit i from nodes in layers $[1, R]$.

- Let $H_{i,[k+1,k+R]}$ be the interval during which the nodes in layers $[k + 1, k + R]$ send $HEARD$ messages caused by COMMIT messages for bit i from nodes in layer k.

A sender transmits a COMMIT message for bit i before transmitting a COMMIT message for bit $i+1$. Also, a sender transmits its HEARD messages for bit i before transmitting HEARD messages for bit number $i + 1$.

Thus we can split the execution into segments, as depicted in Figure 2. Each row in Figure 2 follows an individual bit as it progresses through the path, while the columns capture the events that may occur concurrently. Formally, a segment G_i is the smallest interval that contains all the intervals in column i.

Different segments may overlap. However, given two segments G_i and G_j, where $i > j$, the protocol ensures that G_i finishes *after* G_j finishes. Moreover, G_{i+1} begins, at the latest, as soon as G_i completes. Thus, the running time can be bounded by the sum of the segment lengths.

Also, notice that by construction, a given node is involved, for each segment, in transmitting in at most $R + 1$ different rows: one for a COMMIT message, and R for HEARD messages.

$S_1(bit_1)$ $C_{1,[1,R]}^*$ $H_{1,[R+1,2R]}^*$ $C_{1,R+1}$ $H_{1,[R+2,2R+1]}^*$ .... $H_{1,[D-1,D+R-1]}$

$S_2(bit_2)$ $C_{2,[1,R]}^*$ $H_{2,[R+1,2R]}^*$ $C_{2,R+1}$ $H_{2,[D-1,D+R-1]}$

$S_3(bit_3)$ $C_{3,[1,R]}^*$ $H_{3,[R+1,2R]}^*$ $H_{3,[D-1,D+R-1]}$

G_1 G_2 G_3 G_4 G_5 $G_{2(D-R)+3}$

Figure 2: Execution segmentation for analyzing performance. Each vertical segment $\langle G_1, G_2, \ldots \rangle$ captures a set of events that occur concurrently. Each horizontal row traces a single bit along the path from source to target.

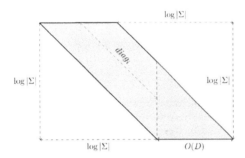

Figure 3: When $D \leq \log|\Sigma|$, we analyze the first $\log|\Sigma|$ segments separately from the remaining $O(D)$ segments. In the first $\log|\Sigma|$ segments, there are at most $O(D)$ diagonal stripes, each of which captures the behavior of a single layer, and hence can be delayed by at most $O(\beta)$ adversarial broadcasts.

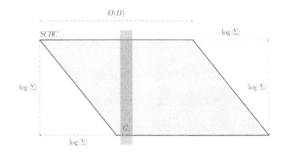

Figure 4: When $D > \log|\Sigma|$, there are $O(D)$ segments. Each node may have to broadcast at most $O(R^3)$ messages in a segment. It follows that a single node may be delayed for at most $O(R^3\beta)$ rounds within a segment. Since there are $O(D)$ segments in this case, we obtain that the total length of the execution is $O(\beta D)$.

Finally, observe that there are $\Theta(D) + \log|\Sigma|$ segments: $\Theta(D)$ segments for the first bit to travel across the path, and then $\log|\Sigma|$ segments while the remaining bits exit the pipelined path. The goal of the remainder of the section is to bound the number of rounds required to complete each of the segments.

Case 1: Large Diameter. Assume that the diameter of the network is large when compared to the message, specifically $D > \log|\Sigma|$ (see Figure 4).

As already indicated, a node p can appear in at most $R+1$ rows in a segment. For a given segment, for a given row, node p may have to broadcast $O(R^2)$ messages: if node p is at distance $> R$ from the source, it may have to broadcast $O(R^2)$ HEARD messages in a single segment. Thus, node p broadcasts at most $O(R^3)$ messages in a segment.

Notice that only Byzantine nodes situated at distance at most $2R$ from p can cause p's messages to be delayed. Thus, the total number of adversarial broadcasts that delay p is bounded by 4β. Since, as we observed above, β_i broadcasts can only delay a message for $O(\beta_i)$ time, we conclude that node p can broadcast all of its messages for a given segment in time $O(R^3\beta) = O(\beta)$. Finally, since $D > \log|\Sigma|$, there are $O(D)$ segments, and hence the total length of the execution is $O(\beta \cdot D)$.

Case 2: Small Diameter. Assume now that the diameter of the network is small, i.e., $D < \log|\Sigma|$, as is depicted in Figure 3. In this case, we focus on the first $\log|\Sigma|$ segments; there are at most $O(D)$ segments in the remainder, and, by the rationale above, their total length is bounded by $O(\beta \cdot D)$. Again, we are interested in determining the maximum delay for each segment. For segment

G_i, let r_i be the row with the longest interval. If we assume that the adversary delays r_i with β_i broadcasts, we can bound the total delay of the first $\log|\Sigma|$ segments by $\sum_{i=1}^{\log|\Sigma|} O(1 + \beta_i) = O\left(\log|\Sigma| + \sum_{i=1}^{\log|\Sigma|} \beta_i\right)$.

The segment tableau (see Figure 3) can be considered in terms of diagonal stripes from the top-left to the bottom-right. Notice that each such stripe involves nodes that are in the same layer along the path. Nodes in the same layer can be delayed by at most 9β broadcasts. Since there are at most $O(D)$ stripes, we can bound $\sum_{i=1}^{\log|\Sigma|} \beta_i$ by $O(\beta D)$.

We can obtain an asymptotic bound on the worst-case running time of NeighborWatchRB as a special case of the previous argument. Specifically, we transform MultiPathRB into NeighborWatchRB as follows: SOURCE and COMMIT messages are shortened to contain only the message bit;and HEARD messages are suppressed. Thus, we re-arrive at the same asymptotic bound of $O(\beta \cdot D + \log|\Sigma|)$ rounds. Thus we conclude:

THEOREM 5. *If an honest source sends a message m via* MultiPathRB *or via* NeighborWatchRB, *then every honest node delivers a message within time* $O(\beta \cdot D + \log|\Sigma|)$.

6. SIMULATION RESULTS

In this section, we simulate the two protocols presented in Section 4. Additional graphs and measurements can be found in the full version [18], together with the code required to run the simulations.

Methodology. Experiments were performed on maps of size varying from 20×20 to 60×60 length units with up to 4000 nodes distributed either uniformly at random (in most simulations), or in a clustered fashion (where noted). We define the density as the total number of nodes divided by the area of the map. For most experiments, each node had an average broadcast range R of approximate 4 length units, and thus the network was between 7 and 21 hops from corner to corner. For an overview of the simulation model, see Section 3.

We implemented the two algorithms following the descriptions in Section 4. For the NeighborWatchRB protocol, the implementation assumes a (reduced) square size of $R/3 \times R/3$, in order to ensure propagation of messages between any two adjacent squares. We tested two variants of MultiPathRB with $t = 3$ and $t = 5$. (Here, t refers to the number of faults per region that the algorithm is tuned to tolerate.)

In each of our simulations, a single honest source node, located at the center of the network, initiates a broadcast of a short message. (Most experiments simulated the broadcast of a 4-bit message; longer messages simply increase the simulation times while yielding little additional insight.) Each experiment was repeated between 6 and 12 times, with outliers being discarded. We measured four parameters: how long the broadcast took to terminate, the percentage of nodes that completed the protocol, the number of broadcasts needed for all nodes to complete the protocol, and the percentage of completed nodes that received the correct message.

6.1 Resilience

Resilience to Crash Failures. The first set of experiments, depicted in Figure 5, assumes that nodes fail by crashing, i.e., taking no steps. Effectively, this results in varying numbers of devices that remain active.

For the NeighborWatchRB protocol, broadcasts complete as long as the network remains connected. The 2-Vote version of NeighborWatchRB requires slightly stronger connectivity guarantees, as every bit has to be received from two neighbors. The MultiPathRB protocol requires even stronger connectivity guarantees, as message bits have to be received across $t + 1$ node-disjoint paths.

For each protocol, we varied the number of active nodes, i.e. the density of the network, and examined the percentage of devices that completed the protocol. As the density increases, we observe that almost every device completes the protocol. For MultiPathRB with $t = 5$, however, the devices in the corners of the network do not always receive the broadcast, as they do not always have enough active neighbors. As expected, NeighborWatchRB yields the best results for low densities.

Resilience to Jamming. The second set of experiments examines performance in the presence of jamming. These experiments were run with 800 devices on a 24×24 map (i.e., a density of ~ 1.5), where 10% were selected at random to jam. Each malicious device broadcasts a jamming message in each veto round with probability $1/5$. (We found this probability to be approximately optimal for the jammers, as it prevented too much redundant jamming.) During the experiment, we varied the budget of broadcasts allocated to each malicious device, and observed how long it took for the algorithm to complete. Despite the jamming, the protocols complete much as expected. There is a linear relationship between the amount of jamming and the delay, i.e., damage caused by the Byzantine devices is proportional to the

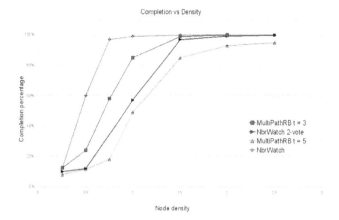

Figure 5: Tolerating crashed devices. Percentage of devices that complete the protocol versus the density of the deployment, for different versions of the protocols. Observe that with a density of 1.5, there are sufficiently many correct nodes for all but MultiPathRB with $t = 5$ to complete almost all the time. In the latter case, the nodes near the edges of the network do not have enough correct neighbors. The experiments were conducted on a 24×24 map.

amount of jamming. The graph is omitted due to space constraints.

Resilience to Lying. In the third set of experiments, we study the resilience to lying, that is, to Byzantine devices attempting to persuade honest devices to adopt an incorrect value. The experiments were performed on a 20×20 map with range $R = 4$ and 600 nodes (i.e., a density of ~ 1.5).

We simulate the Byzantine nodes by initializing the "corrupt" devices with a fake message to propagate, but have them run the *correct* protocol. These devices appear correct, hence their neighbors are likely to adopt the fake message. For MultiPathRB, the corrupt devices broadcast COMMIT messages for the fake value, and they never relay HEARD messages from correct nodes. For NeighborWatchRB, the malicious devices act as sources initialized with the fake message. Throughout these experiments, we do not limit the broadcast budget of the malicious devices.

Figure 6 presents the relation between the percentage of Byzantine devices and the percentage of nodes that receive the correct message. For MultiPathRB, observe that the ability to tolerate malicious devices increases with the tolerance threshold t, as expected: for $t = 3$, the theoretic analysis implies a tolerance of approximately 2.5%, and for $t = 5$, a tolerance of approximately 5% (Each device has approximately 80 neighbors, in expectation, and these numbers represent 3/80 and 5/80, respectively.). We can readily prevent devices from ever delivering a fake message by increasing the threshold t; however, in that case, some devices never deliver any message. For example, for $t = 9$ (not shown in Figure 6), even for 15% corrupt devices, almost no honest device delivers a fake message. However, only 15% of devices deliver any message at all!

The NeighborWatchRB protocol tolerates larger densities of Byzantine nodes in practice, despite the worst-case theoretical analysis. In fact, the probability of success depends only on the probability that in any square containing a cor-

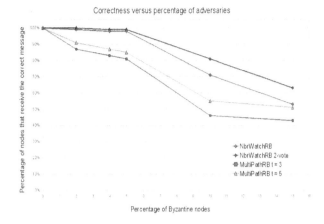

Figure 6: Tolerating lying devices. The percentage of delivered messages that are correct, versus the percentage of malicious devices for different variants of the protocols. NeighborWatchRB performs better than MultiPathRB, even though, in theory, it should be less resilient. The experiments were performed on a 20×20 map, with 600 nodes.

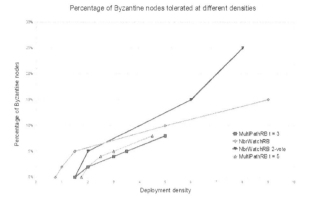

Figure 7: Tolerating lying devices. For a given deployment density, the graph shows the maximum percentage of Byzantine nodes tolerated in order for at least 90% of honest nodes to receive the correct message, for different versions of the protocols. NeighborWatchRB benefits most from the increase in density. Experiments are performed on a 20×20 map, with 300 to 3600 nodes.

rupt device, there is also an honest device. The two-voting variant is more robust, as a corrupt message is only propagated if two nearby squares are populated only by corrupt devices.

Notice that, for both protocols, there is a steep drop-off after the threshold of tolerated Byzantine devices is exceeded. This is because of a snowball effect: once honest devices start adopting the incorrect message, the process accelerates as they join in to convince their neighbors to adopt the incorrect message. This effect is accentuated for lower deployment densities.

A secondary goal is that robustness should scale well with density: as we deploy more devices, we should achieve a higher level of robustness. In Figure 7, we examine this relationship. (Our experiments involving MultiPathRB max out at a density of 5, as the simulation becomes prohibitively slow.) At high levels of density, NeighborWatchRB can tolerate up to 25% of the devices being corrupted. In this sense, the robustness of NeighborWatchRB scales well with density.

6.2 Additional Experiments

Non-uniform Node Distributions. We have also run a series of experiments for NeighborWatchRB where the devices are not distributed uniformly at random, but are deployed in clusters. More specifically, we choose at random a fixed set of *cluster centers*; each device is randomly assigned to a cluster, and within a cluster, devices are spread according to a normal distribution. (The algorithm used for generating the normal distribution of points is that of Marsaglia [21].) The experiments were performed for $R = 4$ and 1200 nodes on a 30×30 map.

We found that, as long as there is sufficient connectivity, the NeighborWatchRB algorithm continues to work well. The algorithm does not always attain 100% completion, since a small fraction of the nodes are disconnected from the source. In experiments where a fraction of the nodes are Byzantine, NeighborWatchRB benefits from the inherent clustering of

the nodes, which increases its correctness ratio by up to 10%, when compared to the uniform distribution.

Varying Map Size. We have also verified the performance of NeighborWatchRB on maps of varying sizes. We have found that both the running time and message complexity scale linearly with the diameter of the network, much as expected.

Comparison with simple Epidemic algorithm. As a point of comparison, we implemented a simple epidemic protocol that provides no resilience to faults or jamming. Unsurprisingly, such an algorithm is more efficient than any of our fault-tolerant protocols. The epidemic algorithm is orders of magnitude faster than MultiPathRB. This considerable gap in terms of performance can be explained by the complexity of the voting protocol that MultiPathRB employs, combined with the fact that messages are sent bit by bit. By contrast, NeighborWatchRB performs a lot better, taking on average about 7.7 times longer to complete. The experiments were performed on maps from 30×30 to 50×50, with a node density of 1.25, a range of 3, and message length of 5 bits. Each experiment was repeated 20 times. Much of the reason for the good performance comes from the fact that data propagation is pipelined, so that the additional cost incurred by NeighborWatchRB can be amortized against the inherent cost of sending data across a multi-hop network.

These experiments support our conjecture that a dual-mode protocol combining an epidemic broadcast of the entire message, along with a secure broadcast of short digest, may be sufficiently efficient. In particular, it seems plausible that a sufficient level of security can be achieved with a digest that is 1/10 the size of the original message, which would yield a slow down of less than a factor of 2 for providing Byzantine fault-tolerance.

7. CONCLUDING REMARKS

We have presented two authenticated broadcast protocols for multi-hop wireless networks subject to Byzantine failures. Together, these two protocols take a first step toward better understanding the problem of authenticated broadcast. In terms of future work, several improvements might be considered, such as improving message efficiency, weakening the synchronization requirements, and adapting the protocol to mobile nodes.

Acknowledgements. The authors would like to thank Prof. Guevara Noubir for his useful comments on earlier drafts of this paper.

8. REFERENCES

[1] R. Anderson, F. Bergadano, B. Crispo, J. Lee, C. Manifavas, and R. Needham. A new family of authentication protocols. *Operating Systems Review*, 32:9–20, 1998.

[2] B. Awerbuch, A. Richa, and C. Scheideler. A jamming-resistant mac protocol for single-hop wireless networks. In *PODC '08*.

[3] E. Bayraktaroglu, C. King, X. Liu, G. Noubir, R. Rajaraman, and B. Thapa. On the performance of ieee 802.11 under jamming. *INFOCOM 2008*.

[4] V. Bhandari and N. Vaidya. On reliable broadcast in a radio network. In *PODC '05*, pages 138–147.

[5] V. Bhandari and N. Vaidya. On reliable broadcast in a radio network: A simplified characterization. Technical report, University of Illinois at Urbana-Champaign, May 2005.

[6] V. Bhandari and N. Vaidya. Reliable broadcast in a wireless grid network with probabilistic failures. Technical report, University of Illinois at Urbana-Champaign, February 2006.

[7] M. Blaum and H. van Tilborg. On t-error correcting/all unidirectional error detecting codes. *IEEE Trans. Computers*, 38(11):1493–1501, 1989.

[8] Bluetooth Consortium. *Bluetooth Specification v. 2.1*, July 2007.

[9] D. Boneh, G. Durfee, and M. Franklin. Lower bounds for multicast message authentication. In *EUROCRYPT*, 2001.

[10] J. M. Borden. Optimal asymmetric error detecting codes. *Information and Control*, 53(1/2):66–73, 1982.

[11] M. Cagalj, S. Capkun, R. Rengaswamy, I. Tsigkogiannis, M. Srivastava, and J.-P. Hubaux. Integrity (i) codes: Message integrity protection and authentication over insecure channels. In *IEEE Security and Privacy*, 2006.

[12] S. Capkun, M. Cagalj, R. Rengaswamy, I. Tsigkogiannis, J.-P. Hubaux, and M. Srivastava. Integrity codes: Message integrity protection and authentication over insecure channels. *Dependable and Secure Computing, IEEE Transactions on*, 5(4):208–223, Oct.-Dec. 2008.

[13] S. Capkun and J.-P. Hubaux. Secure positioning of wireless devices with application to sensor networks. *INFOCOM '05*, pages 1917–1928.

[14] A. Chan, X. Liu, G. Noubir, and B. Thapa. Broadcast control channel jamming: Resilience and identification of traitors. *ISIT '07*.

[15] J. Chiang and Y.-C. Hu. Cross-layer jamming detection and mitigation in wireless broadcast networks. In *MobiCom '07*, pages 346–349. ACM, 2007.

[16] S. Dolev, S. Gilbert, R. Guerraoui, and C. Newport. Secure communication over radio channels. In *PODC '08*.

[17] T. Eisenbarth, S. Kumar, C. Paar, A. Poschmann, and L. Uhsadel. A survey of lightweight-cryptography implementations. *IEEE Des. Test*, 24(6):522–533, 2007.

[18] Full version of this paper. http://lpd.epfl.ch/alistarh/wireless-byzantine/.

[19] S. Gilbert, R. Guerraoui, and C. Newport. Of malicious motes and suspicious sensors: On the efficiency of malicious interference in wireless networks. In *OPODIS '06*.

[20] S. Gilbert, R. Guerraoui, and C. Newport. Of malicious motes and suspicious sensors: On the efficiency of malicious interference in wireless networks. *Theoretical Computer Science*, 2008.

[21] D. Knuth. *The Art of Computer Programming, Seminumerical Algorithms*. Addison-Wesley, 3rd edition, 1997.

[22] C-Y. Koo. Broadcast in radio networks tolerating byzantine adversarial behavior. In *PODC '04*.

[23] C-Y. Koo, V. Bhandari, J. Katz, and N. Vaidya. Reliable broadcast in radio networks: The bounded collision case. In *PODC '06*.

[24] Xin Liu, G. Noubir, R. Sundaram, and San Tan. Spread: Foiling smart jammers using multi-layer agility. *INFOCOM 2007*, May 2007.

[25] V. Navda, A. Bohra, S. Ganguly, and D. Rubenstein. Using channel hopping to increase 802.11 resilience to jamming attacks. *INFOCOM 2007*.

[26] G. Noubir and G. Lin. On link layer denial of service in data wireless lans. *Wiley Journal on Wireless Comm. and Mobile Computing*, August 2005.

[27] A. Pelc and D. Peleg. Feasibility and complexity of broadcasting with random transmission failures. In *PODC*, 2005.

[28] A. Perrig, J. D. Tygar, D. Song, and R. Canetti. Efficient authentication and signing of multicast streams over lossy channels. In *SP '00*, page 56, 2000.

[29] N. Priyantha, H. Balakrishnan, E. Demaine, and S. Teller. Mobile-assisted localization in wireless sensor networks. In *INFOCOM '05*, pages 172–183.

[30] N. Priyantha, A. Chakraborty, and H. Balakrishnan. The cricket location-support system. In *MOBICOM*, 2000.

[31] M. Strasser, C. Pöpper, S. Capkun, and M. Cagalj. Jamming-resistant key establishment using uncoordinated frequency hopping. In *IEEE SP '08*.

[32] WSNet / Worldsens simulator: an event-driven simulator for large-scale wireless networks. http://wsnet.gforge.inria.fr/.

Multi-Sided Shared Coins and Randomized Set-Agreement

Keren Censor Hillel[*]
Department of Computer Science
Technion
Haifa 32000, Israel
ckeren@cs.technion.ac.il

ABSTRACT

This paper presents wait-free randomized algorithms for solving *set-agreement* in asynchronous shared-memory systems under a *strong adversary*. First, the definition of a shared-coin algorithm is generalized to a *multi-sided shared-coin* algorithm, and it is shown how to use any multi-sided shared coin in order to obtain a randomized set-agreement algorithm for agreeing on k values out of $k + 1$. Then, an implementation is given for a $(k + 1)$-sided shared coin for n processes with a constant agreement parameter, $O(n^2/k)$ total step complexity, and $O(n/k)$ individual step complexity. This implementation yields a randomized set-agreement algorithm for agreeing on k values out of $k + 1$ with a total step complexity of $O(n^2/k + nk)$ and an individual step complexity of $O(n/k + k)$. Next, other set-agreement algorithms for agreeing on ℓ values out of $k + 1$, where ℓ is smaller than k, are presented. This includes the case of *multi-valued consensus* in which $\ell = 1, k > 1$. To the best of our knowledge, these are the first wait-free algorithms for set-agreement in the asynchronous shared-memory model under a strong adversary that are not for the specific case of binary consensus, where $\ell = k = 1$. Finally, an application of asynchronous wait-free multi-valued consensus is presented, in implementing *at-most-once* semantics with optimal effectiveness.

Categories and Subject Descriptors

D.1.3 [**Software**]: Programming Techniques—*Concurrent programming*; F.2 [**Theory of Computation**]: Analysis of Algorithms and Problem Complexity—*Nonnumerical Algorithms and Problems*; G.3 [**Mathematics of Computing**]: Probability and Statistics—*Probabilistic algorithms*

General Terms

Algorithms, Theory

[*]Supported in part by the Adams Fellowship Program of the Israel Academy of Sciences and Humanities and by the *Israel Science Foundation* (grant number 953/06).

Keywords

distributed computing, shared memory, randomized algorithms, set-agreement, multi-valued shared coins

1. INTRODUCTION

The problem of *set-agreement* was introduced by Chaudhuri [9] as a generalization of the consensus problem, in order to overcome the well-known impossibility of solving consensus deterministically in an asynchronous system which allows even one crash-failure [13]. In the set-agreement problem, n processes start with input values in $\{0, \ldots, k\}$ and should produce output values such that there are at most ℓ different outputs, for some $\ell < n$. The termination condition requires every non-faulty process to eventually decide, and to avoid trivial solutions, the validity condition requires each output value to be the input value of some process.

Chaudhuri showed that if the bound f on the number of faulty processes is smaller than ℓ, then set-agreement can be solved by a deterministic algorithm. Later, it was shown by Borowsky and Gafni [7], Herlihy and Shavit [14], and Saks and Zaharoglou [20], using topological arguments, that set-agreement cannot be solved deterministically in an asynchronous system if $f \geq \ell$, and in particular it does not have a wait-free solution (i.e., $f = n - 1$, implying that it may be that all but one process fail).

Another approach to overcome the FLP impossibility result for consensus, is to relax the termination condition to hold only with probability 1, and thus allow the use of randomization. Many randomized consensus algorithms were designed for different models of communication and timing assumptions. As in the case of consensus, randomization also allows to overcome the impossibility result for set-agreement.

In this paper, we present randomized wait-free algorithms for solving set-agreement in an asynchronous shared-memory system. First, in Section 3, we generalize the definition of a *shared-coin* algorithm, and define *multi-sided shared-coin* algorithms. In such an algorithm, each process outputs one of $k + 1$ values (instead of one of two values as in a regular shared-coin), such that each subset of k values has probability at least δ for containing the outputs of all the processes. In other words, each value has probability at least δ of *not* being the output of any process. We then extend the Aspnes-Herlihy framework for using a shared coin for obtaining a randomized consensus algorithm [4], and show how to use any multi-sided shared coin in order to obtain a randomized set-agreement algorithm, for agreeing on k values out of $k + 1$.

Next, in Section 4, we present an implementation of a $(k + 1)$-sided shared-coin algorithm which has a constant agreement parameter, $O(n^2/k)$ total step complexity, and $O(n/k)$ individual step complexity. We then derive a set-agreement algorithm from the $(k + 1)$-sided shared coin using the above framework.

Algorithm	Parameters	Method	Individual Step Complexity	Total Step Complexity
Section 3	$k, k+1$	multi-sided shared coin	$O(n/k + k)$	$O(n^2/k + nk)$
Section 5.1	$\ell, k+1$	space reduction	$O(n(\log k - \log \ell))$	$O(n^2(\log k - \log \ell))$
Section 5.2	$\ell, k+1$	iterative	$O((k - \ell + 1)k$ $+ n(\log k - \log \ell))$	$O((k - \ell + 1)nk$ $+ n^2(\log k - \log \ell))$
Section 5.3	$1, k+1$	bit-by-bit	$O(n \log k)$	$O(n^2 \log k)$

Figure 1: The agreement algorithms presented in this paper.

In Section 5, we present set-agreement algorithms that are designed for agreeing on ℓ values out of $k + 1$, for $\ell < k$. In particular, they can be used for the case $\ell = 1$, where the processes agree on the same value, i.e., for *multi-valued consensus*. By definition, solving multi-valued consensus is at least as hard as solving *binary consensus* (where the inputs are in the set $\{0, 1\}$, i.e., $k = 1$), and potentially harder. One algorithm uses multi-sided shared coins, while the other two embed binary consensus algorithms in various ways.

To the best of our knowledge, these are the first wait-free algorithms for set-agreement in the shared-memory model under a strong adversary, other than binary consensus. Figure 1 shows the properties of the different algorithms we present. For $\ell < k$ one of our algorithms is better than the others; however, intrigued by the question of whether multi-valued consensus is inherently harder than binary consensus, we find the different methods interesting in hope that one of them could lead to a lower bound.

Finally, we show in Section 6 an application of asynchronous wait-free multi-valued consensus in implementing *at-most-once* semantics with optimal effectiveness. At-most-once semantics [15] requires m jobs to be executed with the guarantee that no job is performed more than once. A trivial solution simply does not execute any job. However, the *effectiveness* of an algorithm for solving the at-most-once problem is the number of *completed* jobs, and it is desired to find algorithms with the maximal effectiveness possible. Section 6 shows how to use a randomized multi-valued consensus algorithm in order to solve the at-most-once problem while obtaining the optimal effectiveness, thus answering an open question raised in [15].

Related Work:. Previous randomized agreement algorithms for asynchronous shared-memory systems under a strong adversary are for the specific case of binary consensus (e.g., [1–5, 8, 19]). The optimal individual and total step complexities are $O(n)$ and $O(n^2)$, respectively [3, 5].

Unlike the shared-memory model, several set-agreement algorithms for asynchronous *message-passing* systems have been proposed. Mostefaoui et al. [17] use binary consensus to construct a multi-valued consensus algorithm for message-passing systems. This work assumes reliable broadcast. In the same model, Zhang and Chen [23] present improved algorithms, which reduce the number of binary consensus instances that are required. Under the above assumption, Ezhilchelvan et al. [12] also present a randomized multi-valued consensus algorithm, while Mostefaoui and Raynal [16], present a randomized set-agreement algorithm for agreeing on ℓ values out of n. The above algorithms require a bound on the number of failures $f < n/2$, a restriction that can be avoided in the shared-memory model. Moreover, there is an exponentially small agreement probability for the coins that are used, which causes the expected number of phases until agreement is reached to be large.

There is additional literature on set-agreement in *synchronous* systems. Chaudhuri et al. [10] show that $f/k + 1$ is the number of rounds needed for solving set-agreement in shared memory. Turpin and Coan [22] propose a set-agreement algorithm for message passing with Byzantine failures that embeds consensus to agree on the credibility of sent messages. Their algorithm satisfies a weaker validity condition, which requires that if all input values are the same, then every output value is that input value. Raynal and Travers [18] propose new algorithms in addition to a good survey on synchronous set-agreement algorithms.

2. MODEL AND DEFINITIONS

We consider a standard model of an asynchronous system in which n processes $\{p_0, \ldots, p_{n-1}\}$ communicate by reading and writing to shared multi-writer multi-reader registers. A *step* of a process consists of one access to the shared memory, followed by local computation and/or local coin-flips. Processes may fail by crashing, in which case they do not take any further steps. We require our algorithms to be *wait-free*, i.e., to be correct even if $n - 1$ processes may fail during an execution. The system is *asynchronous*, meaning that the steps of processes are scheduled according to an adversary. This implies that there are no timing assumptions, and specifically no bounds on the time between two steps of a process, or between steps of different processes.

For completeness, we formally define the problem of set-agreement as follows. In an algorithm for solving $(\ell, k + 1, n)$-*agreement* each process p_i starts with an input value in $\{0, \ldots, k\}$ and should produce an output value such that the following conditions hold:

- Set-Agreement: there are at most ℓ different outputs.
- Validity: every output is the input of some process.
- Termination: every non-faulty process eventually decides.

We sometimes use the term *set-agreement* without parameters for abbreviation. The particular case in which $\ell = 1, k > 1$ is the problem of *multi-valued consensus*, while in case $\ell = k = 1$ we have *binary consensus*.

A *randomized* algorithm for set-agreement is required to satisfy a relaxed termination condition: *with probability 1*, every non-faulty process eventually decides.

We measure the *individual step complexity* of a randomized set-agreement algorithm as the expected number of steps taken by any single process. Similarly, the *total step complexity* is the expected number of steps taken by all the processes.

In Section 3 we present a framework for randomized algorithms which solve $(k, k + 1, n)$-agreement using a *multi-sided shared-coin* algorithm. We now formally define such a procedure, which is a generalization of a shared coin (which in our terms is a 2-sided shared coin). A $(k + 1)$-*sided shared-coin* algorithm with *agreement parameter* δ is an algorithm in which every non-faulty process

p produces an output value in $\{0, \ldots, k\}$, such that for every subset of size k there is probability at least δ that all the outputs are within that subset. Alternatively, for every value v in $\{0, \ldots, k\}$ there is probability at least δ that v is *not* the output of any process. We emphasize that unlike the requirement of set-agreement, the probability of disagreement in a shared coin may be greater than 0. Notice that there are no inputs to this procedure.

Since our algorithms are randomized, different assumptions on the power of the adversary may yield different results. Throughout this work, we assume a *strong adversary*. Such an adversary can base its next scheduling decision on the local state of all the processes, including the results of local coin-flips. Notice, however, that the adversary does not know the results of local coins that were not yet flipped[1].

3. A $(k, k+1, n)$-AGREEMENT ALGORITHM USING A $(k+1)$-SIDED SHARED COIN

In this section we present a framework for randomized $(k, k+1, n)$-agreement algorithms. It is a generalization of the framework of Aspnes and Herlihy [4] for deriving a randomized binary consensus algorithm from a weak shared coin, and specifically follows the presentation given by Saks, Shavit, and Woll [19]. However, its complexity is improved by using multi-writer registers, based on the construction of Cheung [11].

We assume a $(k+1)$-sided shared-coin algorithm called shared-Coin$_{k+1}$, with an agreement parameter δ_{k+1}. The set-agreement algorithm is given in Algorithm 1. Throughout the paper, we assume that shared arrays are initialized to a special symbol $\perp$. Informally, the set-agreement algorithm proceeds by (asynchronous) phases, in which each process p writes its own preference to a shared array $Propose$, checks if the preferences agree on k values, and notes this in another shared array $Check$. If p indeed sees agreement, it also notes its preference in $Check$.

Process p then checks the agreement array $Check$. If p does not observe a note of disagreement, it decides on the value of its preference. Otherwise, if there is a note of disagreement, but also a note of agreement, p adopts the value associated with the agreement notification as preference for the next phase. Finally, if there is only a notification of disagreement, the process participates in a $(k+1)$-sided shared-coin algorithm and prefers the output of the shared coin.

LEMMA 1. *Consider a phase $r \geq 1$ and a non-faulty process p that finishes phase r. If all the processes that start phase r before p finishes it have at most k preferences in $\{v_1, \ldots, v_k\}$, then p decides $v \in \{v_1, \ldots, v_k\}$ in this phase r.*

PROOF. We claim that p reads $Check[r][disagree] == $ false in line 9 of phase r, and therefore decides in phase r. This will also imply that its decision value v is in $\{v_1, \ldots, v_k\}$, otherwise p is among the processes that start phase r before p finishes, but does not have a preference in $\{v_1, \ldots, v_k\}$, which contradicts our assumption. Assume towards a contradiction, that p reads $Check[r][disagree] == $ true in line 9 of phase r. This implies that there is a process q that writes $Check[r][disagree] = $ true in line 7 of phase r, and this happens before p finishes. Therefore, q reads more than k values in $Propose[r]$ in line 3 of phase r, which means that there are $k+1$ processes that write $k+1$ different values to $Propose[r]$ in line 2 of phase r, and all this happens before p finishes. But this contradicts our assumption that all the processes

[1]Thus, if we model local coin-flips as having a random tape for each process, then the adversary knows the content of the tape only in locations that were accessed by the process.

Algorithm 1 A $(k, k+1, n)$-agreement algorithm, code for p_i

Local variables: $r = 1$, $decide = $ false, $myValue = input$,
  $myPropose = [\ ]$, $myCheck = [\ ]$
Shared arrays: $Propose[\ ][0..k], Check[\ ][agree, disagree]$
1: while $decide == $ false
2:   $Propose[r][myValue] = $ true
3:   $myPropose = $ collect($Propose[r]$)
4:   if the number of values in $myPropose$ is at most k
5:     $Check[r][agree] = \langle$true, $myValue\rangle$
6:   else
7:     $Check[r][disagree] = $ true
8:   $myCheck = $ collect($Check[r]$)
9:   if $myCheck[disagree] == $ false
10:     $decide = $ true
11:   else if $myCheck[agree] == \langle$true, $v\rangle$
12:     $myValue = v$
13:   else if $myCheck[agree] == $ false
14:     $myValue = $ sharedCoin$_{k+1}[r]$
15:   $r = r + 1$
16: end while
17: return $myValue$

---

that start phase r before a non-faulty process p finishes it have at most k preferences. □

Lemma 1 implies validity, by applying it for phase $r = 1$. The next two lemmas are used to prove the agreement condition. Below, we use the notation $\langle$true, ?$\rangle$ for an entry in the array $Check$ which has *true* as its first element, and any value as its second element.

LEMMA 2. *For every phase $r \geq 1$, all the processes that read $Check[r][agree] == \langle true, ?\rangle$ and finish phase r have at most k different preferences at the end of phase r.*

PROOF. We first claim that all the processes that write to $Check[r][agree]$ wrote at most k different preferences to $Propose[r]$. Assume, towards a contradiction, that among the processes that write to $Check[r][agree]$ there are $k+1$ processes $\{p_{i_1}, \ldots, p_{i_{k+1}}\}$ that wrote $k+1$ different preferences to $Propose[r]$. Let p_{i_j} be the last process to write to $Propose[r]$. When p_{i_j} collects $Propose[r]$ in line 3, it reads $k+1$ values, and therefore does not write to $Check[r][agree]$, which is a contradiction.

The above claim implies that at most k different preferences may be written to $Check[r][agree]$. Since a process that reads $Check[r][agree] == \langle$true, $v\rangle$ adopts v as its preference, at most k values can be a preference of such processes at the end of phase r. □

LEMMA 3. *For every phase $r \geq 1$, if processes decide on values in $\{v_1, \ldots, v_k\}$ in phase r, then every non-faulty process decides on a value in $\{v_1, \ldots, v_k\}$ in phase r', where r' is either r or $r + 1$.*

PROOF. We first claim that if a process decides v in phase r, then every non-faulty process that finishes phase r reads $Check[r][agree] == \langle$true, ?$\rangle$. To prove the claim, let p be a process that decides v in phase r. Let q be a non-faulty process that finishes phase r, and assume towards a contradiction that q reads $Check[r][agree] == $ false. This implies that q collects $Check[r]$ in line 8 before p writes to $Check[r]$ in line 5, and therefore p collects $Check[r]$ after q writes to $Check[r][disagree]$, which implies that p does not decide in phase r, a contradiction.

Now, let p be a process that decides in phase r, and let q be a non-faulty process. By the above claim, q reads $Check[r][agree] == \langle true, ?\rangle$ in line 8. By Lemma 2, there are at most k different values that can become a preference of a process at the end of phase r. Therefore, if q decides at the end of phase r then it decides a value in $\{v_1, \ldots, v_k\}$. Otherwise, all the non-faulty processes write at most k preferences to $Propose[r+1]$, and by Lemma 1, they decide on one of these values at the end of phase $r + 1$. $\square$

Lemma 3 implies agreement. Notice that both validity and agreement are *always* satisfied, and not only with probability 1. For termination, we prove the following lemma. Below, we denote the agreement parameter of the $(k+1)$-sided shared coin by $\delta = \delta_{k+1}$.

LEMMA 4. *The expected number of phases until all non-faulty processes decide is at most $1 + 1/\delta$.*

PROOF. For every subset $\{v_1, \ldots, v_k\} \subseteq \{0, \ldots, k\}$ there is a probability of at least δ for all processes that run sharedCoin$_{k+1}$ to output values in $\{v_1, \ldots, v_k\}$. Therefore, for any value v in $\{0, \ldots, k\}$, there is a probability of at least δ that v is not the output of any process running sharedCoin$_{k+1}$. This is because $\{0, \ldots, k\} \setminus \{v\}$ has probability of at least δ for containing the outputs of all the processes.

Consider a phase $r \geq 2$. By Lemma 2, all the processes that finish phase $r - 1$ and in line 8 read $Check[r-1][agree] == \langle true, ?\rangle$ propose at most k values to $Propose[r]$. The other processes propose to $Propose[r]$ a value obtained from their shared coin. Therefore, there is a probability of at least δ that all processes write at most k different values to $Propose[r]$, and by Lemma 1, decide by the end of phase r.

Therefore, after phase $r = 1$, the expected number of phases until all non-faulty processes decide, is the expectation of a geometrically distributed random variable with success probability at least δ, which is at most $1/\delta$.

For the first phase $r = 1$, the values written to $Propose[1]$ are the inputs and are therefore controlled by the adversary. This implies that the expected number of phases until all non-faulty processes decide is at most $1 + 1/\delta$. $\square$

Consider a $(k+1)$-sided shared coin algorithm with an agreement parameter $\delta = \delta_{k+1}$, a total step complexity of $T = T_{k+1}$, and an individual step complexity of $I = I_{k+1}$. In each phase, a process takes $O(k)$ steps in addition to the I steps it takes in the sharedCoin$_{k+1}$ algorithm. Combining this with Lemma 4, which bounds the expected number of phases until all non-faulty processes decide, gives:

THEOREM 5. *Algorithm 1 solves $(k, k+1, n)$-agreement with $O(\frac{I+k}{\delta})$ individual step complexity and $O(\frac{T+nk}{\delta})$ total step complexity.*

4. A $(k+1)$-SIDED SHARED COIN

We present, in Algorithm 2, a $(k+1)$-sided shared-coin algorithm which is constructed by using k instances of a 2-sided shared coin. We statically partition the processes into k sets of at most $\frac{n}{k}$ processes each. That is, for every j, $0 \leq j \leq k - 1$, we have a set $P_j = \left\{p_{\frac{jn}{k}}, \ldots, p_{\frac{(j+1)n}{k} - 1}\right\}$ (for $j = k - 1$ the set may be smaller). The processes of each set P_j run a 2-sided shared-coin algorithm sharedCoin$[j]$ and output the result plus the value j. The idea is that in order to have a value j that is not the output of any process, it is enough that all processes running sharedCoin$[j - 1]$ agree on the value 0 and therefore output $j - 1$, and that all the processes running sharedCoin$[j]$ agree on the value 1 and therefore output $j + 1$.

Algorithm 2 A $(k+1)$-sided shared coin algorithm, code for process p_i

Local variables: $j = \lfloor \frac{ik}{n} \rfloor$
1:   return sharedCoin$[j] + j$

Let $\delta = \delta_2$ be the agreement parameter of the 2-sided shared coin. We bound the agreement parameter of the $k+1$-sided shared coin in the next lemma.

LEMMA 6. *Algorithm 2 is a $(k+1)$-sided shared coin with an agreement parameter δ^2.*

PROOF. There is a probability of at least δ for all processes who run sharedCoin$[j]$ to return the value j, and a probability of at least δ for all processes who run sharedCoin$[j]$ to return the value $j + 1$. Therefore, for any value in $\{0, \ldots, k\}$, there is a probability of at least δ^2 that this value is not the output of any process running sharedCoin$[j]$, for any $0 \leq j \leq k - 1$ (because $j = 0$ may be the output only of sharedCoin$[0]$, $j = k$ only of sharedCoin$[k-1]$, and $j \in \{1, \ldots, k-1\}$ only of sharedCoin$[j-1]$ and sharedCoin$[j]$). Therefore, Algorithm 2 is a $(k+1)$-sided shared coin with an agreement parameter δ^2. $\square$

The next lemma gives the complexity of the $k+1$-sided shared coin, and follows immediately from the fact that each process runs a 2-sided shared coin algorithm for $\frac{n}{k}$ processes. Since the complexities depend on the number of processes t that may run an algorithm, we now carefully consider this in the notation. Let $I(t) = I_2(t)$ and $T(t) = T_2(t)$ be the individual and total step complexities, respectively, of the 2-sided shared coin with t processes.

LEMMA 7. *Algorithm 2 has individual and total step complexities of $O(I(\frac{n}{k}))$ and $O(k \cdot T(\frac{n}{k}))$, respectively.*

Plugging Lemmas 6 and 7 into Theorem 5 gives:

THEOREM 8. *Algorithm 1 solves $(k, k+1, n)$-agreement with individual step complexity of $O((I(\frac{n}{k})+k)/\delta^2)$ and total step complexity of $O((k \cdot T(\frac{n}{k}) + nk)/\delta^2)$.*

By using an optimal 2-sided shared coin [3] with a constant agreement parameter, an individual step complexity of $O(t)$, and a total step complexity of $O(t^2)$, we get that Algorithm 2 is a $(k+1)$-sided shared coin with a constant agreement parameter, and individual and total step complexities of $O(\frac{n}{k})$ and $O(\frac{n^2}{k})$, respectively. Therefore, Algorithm 1 solves $(k, k+1, n)$-agreement with individual step complexity of $O(\frac{n}{k} + k)$ and total step complexity of $O(\frac{n^2}{k} + nk)$. Note that for $n \geq k^2$, Algorithm 1 has $O(\frac{n}{k})$ individual step complexity, and $O(\frac{n^2}{k})$ total step complexity, which are the same as the complexities of binary consensus divided by k.

5. $(\ell, k+1, n)$-AGREEMENT ALGORITHMS

In this section we construct several algorithms for the solving $(\ell, k+1, n)$-agreement, where $\ell < k$.

5.1 An $(\ell, k+1, n)$-Agreement Algorithm by Space Reduction

For agreeing on one value out of $\{0, \ldots, k\}$ we can get a total step complexity of $O(n^2 \log k)$ by reducing the possible values by half until we have one value. We later show how this construction can be used for agreeing on $\ell > 1$ values.

In Algorithm 3 we assume an array *Agree* of binary consensus instances, which a process can execute with a proposed value. Algorithm 3 can be modelled as a binary tree, where the processes begin at the leaves, which represent all of the values, and in every iteration j the processes agree on the value of the next node, going up to the root. This means that at most half of the suggested values are decided in each iteration. In addition, all decided values are valid because this is true for each node.

Algorithm 3 A $(1, k+1, n)$-agreement algorithm by space reduction, code for p_i

---

Local variables $myValue = input$, $myPair$, $mySide$
Shared arrays: $Agree[1..\lceil \log(k+1)\rceil][1..k/2^j]$,
$\quad Values[1..\lceil \log(k+1)\rceil][1..k/2^j][0..1]$
1: for $j = 1 \ldots \lceil \log(k+1)\rceil$
2: $\quad myPair = \lfloor \frac{myValue}{2^j} \rfloor$
3: $\quad$ if $myValue - myPair \cdot 2^j < 2^{j-1}$
4: $\quad\quad mySide = 0$
5: $\quad$ else $mySide = 1$
6: $\quad Values[j][myPair][mySide] = myValue$
7: $\quad side = Agree[j][myPair](mySide)$
8: $\quad myValue = Values[j][myPair][side]$
9: end for
10: return $myValue$

LEMMA 9. *(Validity) For every j, the variable myValue of a process p at the end of iteration j is an input of some process.*

PROOF. The proof is by induction on j. The base case $j = 1$ is clear since $myValue$ is initialized with the input of the process. For the induction step, assume the lemma holds up to $j - 1$, and notice that $myValue$ is updated only in line 8, to the value written in the $Values$ array in the location $side$ which is returned from the binary consensus protocol. Since the consensus protocol satisfies validity, $side$ has to be the input of some process to the consensus protocol, and this only happens if that process first writes to that location in the $Values$ array in line 6. By the induction hypothesis, that value is the input of some process. □

LEMMA 10. *(Agreement) Every two process executing Algorithm 3 output the same value.*

PROOF. We claim that there can be at most one value written to $Values[j][pair][side]$, and prove this by induction, where the base case is trivial since at the beginning a process writes to $Values[1][pair][side]$ only if its input value is $2 \cdot pair + side$. Assume this holds up to iteration $j - 1$. By the agreement property of the consensus protocol, all processes that execute $Agree[j-1][pair]$ output the same value. Therefore, in iteration j, only one value out of $\{2^j \cdot pair, \ldots, 2^j(pair + 1) - 1\}$ can be written to $Values[j][pair][side]$. The lemma follows by applying the claim to the root, which satisfies agreement. □

Termination follows from the termination property of the binary consensus instances. For each j, a process executes one consensus protocol, plus $O(1)$ additional accesses to shared variables. By using an optimal binary consensus protocol where a process completes within $O(n)$ steps, this implies:

THEOREM 11. *Algorithm 3 solves $(1, k+1, n)$-agreement with an individual step complexity of $O(n \log k)$ and a total step complexity of $O(n^2 \log k)$.*

Note that we can backstop this construction at any level j at the tree to get an agreement on $\ell = 2^{\log k - j}$ values. This means that instead of having j iterate from 1 to $\lceil \log(k+1)\rceil$, the algorithm changes so that j iterates from 1 to $\lceil \log(k+1)\rceil - \lceil \log \ell\rceil$. The individual step complexity is $O(n(\log k - \log \ell))$, and the total step complexity is $O(n^2(\log k - \log \ell))$.

5.2 An Iterative $(\ell, k+1, n)$-Agreement Algorithm

In Algorithm 5, we construct an $(\ell, k+1, n)$-agreement algorithm by iterating Algorithm 1 and reducing the number of possible values by one until all processes output no more than ℓ values. The idea is that the processes execute consecutive iterations of $(s, s+1, n)$-agreement algorithms for values of s decreasing from k to ℓ. In each iteration the number of possible values is reduced until it reaches the desired bound ℓ.

This procedure is less trivial than it may appear because, for example, after the first iteration outputs no more than k values out of $k + 1$, in order to decide on $k - 1$ out of the k values that are possible, the processes need to know *which* are the k possible values. However, careful inspection shows that they need to know these k values only if they disagree upon choosing the $k - 1$ values out of them. In this case, a process that sees k values indeed knows which are these values among the initial $k + 1$.

The pseudocode appears in Appendix A, as well as the proof of its correctness and complexity, as stated in the following theorem. When using the $(s + 1)$-sided shared coins of Section 4 we have:

THEOREM 12. *Algorithm 5 solves $(\ell, k+1, n)$-agreement with $O((k - \ell + 1)k + n(\log k - \log \ell))$ individual step complexity and $O((k - \ell + 1)nk + n^2(\log k - \log \ell))$ total step complexity.*

5.3 A Bit-By-Bit $(1, k+1, n)$-Agreement Algorithm

For agreeing on one value out of $\{0, \ldots, k\}$ we construct Algorithm 6, which agrees on each bit at a time while making sure that the final value is valid. A similar construction appears in [21, Chapter 9], but does not address the validity condition. In this algorithm, obtaining validity is a crucial point in the construction, since simply agreeing on enough bits does not guarantee an output that is the input of some process.

The idea of our algorithm is that in every iteration j, all the $myValue$ local variables share the same first $j - 1$ bits, and they are all valid (each is the input of at least one process).

The pseudocode appears in Appendix B, as well as the proof of its correctness and complexity, as stated in the following theorem. We denote by $\delta = \delta_2$ the agreement parameter of the 2-sided shared coin, and $T = T_2$ and $I = I_2$ are its total and individual step complexities, respectively.

THEOREM 13. *Algorithm 6 solves $(1, k+1, n)$-agreement with $O(\lceil \log(k+1)\rceil \cdot \frac{I}{\delta})$ individual step complexity and $O(\lceil \log(k+1)\rceil \frac{T}{\delta})$ total step complexity.*

Using an optimal shred coin with a constant agreement parameter, an individual step complexity of $O(n)$, and a total step complexity of $O(n^2)$, we get a $(1, k+1, n)$-agreement algorithm with an individual step complexity of $O(n \log k)$ and a total step complexity of $O(n^2 \log k)$. Notice that the step complexity could be improved if agreement on the bits could be run in parallel. However, this is not trivial because of the need to maintain validity.

6. APPLICATION: THE AT-MOST-ONCE PROBLEM

In addition to the importance of set-agreement as a basic problem in distributed computing, it can also be used to solve other practical problems. In this section, we show how to use a randomized multi-valued consensus algorithm in order to solve the *at-most-once* problem, while improving previous known guarantees for a measure of performance.

The at-most-once semantics ensures that operations in a distributed system occur no more than once. This requirement was studied in contexts of at-most-once message delivery, and of at-most-once remote procedure calls (RPC), and has been recently addressed in the context of asynchronous shared memory by Kentros et al. [15]. In this problem, n processes are required to perform m jobs. Any job may be performed by any process, but it is required that no job is executed more than once. While a trivial solution would be to simply not execute any job, we are interested in algorithms that can nevertheless guarantee some amount of completed jobs.

DEFINITION 1 ([15]). *The* effectiveness *of an algorithm for the at-most-once problem with m jobs, and n processes prone to f crash-failures, is the minimal number of completed jobs over all possible executions.*

Kentros et al. [15] present a deterministic solution for the at-most-once problem with effectiveness $(k - 1)^h$, where $m = k^h$ and $n = 2^h$, for wait-free solutions[2]. They also prove a lower bound of $m - f$ on the effectiveness of any such algorithm. While the proof is non-trivial, the intuition is rather simple: a process p may fail just before it is about to execute a certain job, but no other process q can take over that job, since it cannot distinguish this situation and the case where p is simply slow. If q executes the job and p was just slow and eventually also executes the job, the at-most-once semantics is violated. Following this intuition, and although we do not give a formal proof, it is clear that the lower bound of $m - f$ also holds for randomized solutions, which allow termination with probability 1, but require the at-most-once condition to always hold.

Using our randomized wait-free $(1, n, n)$-agreement algorithms (multi-valued consensus out of n values), we show a randomized algorithm for the at-most-once problem, that has optimal effectiveness of $m - f$. The idea is that for every job the processes execute $(1, n, n)$-agreement, and the process whose value was decided is the process that executes the job. A process participates in the multi-valued consensus algorithm for a job only after it finished participating in the multi-valued consensus algorithms for all the previous jobs. In the algorithm we assume m objects of $(1, n, n)$-agreement called $Agreement[1..m]$.

Algorithm 4 An at-most-once algorithm, code for p_i

Local variables j
Shared arrays: $Agreement[1..m]$
1: for $j = 1..m$
2:    if $Agreement[j](i) == i$ execute job j

Algorithm 4 solves the at-most-once problem because of the agreement property of the multi-valued consensus algorithm. Further, in Algorithm 4 a failed process p_i can only block one job j, if

---

[2]We note that in [15] the number of processes is noted by m and the number of jobs by n, as opposed to this work.

i was the value decided upon in $Agreement[j]$, and p_i fails before executing job j. This is because the value i can only be proposed to $Agreement[j]$ by p_i, and therefore by validity can only be decided if p_i invokes $Agreement[j](i)$. This can only happen for one value of j at any given time, by ensuring that a process participates only in one multi-valued consensus algorithm at a time. Therefore we have:

THEOREM 14. *Algorithm 4 solves the at-most-once problem and has effectiveness $m - f$.*

Notice that our algorithm can be easily adapted to the case where the number of jobs is unknown in advance, by simply having an array $jobs$ that indicates whether another job exists, and having the processes check this array before proceeding. Moreover, our solution also works in an online setting of this problem where the jobs arrive during the execution, at times that are controlled by the adversary. This is done by having the processes repeatedly read the first empty location in the $jobs$ array (or linked-list) until they see an indication for a new job.

Another algorithm for the at-most-once problem can use the tree construction of Kentros et al. [15], and add a binary consensus object for every node in the tree, in order to improve the effectiveness of their algorithm. This addition prevents having a location in the array of a node in the tree, which is not addressed by processes of either "side" because of a possibility for a conflict (we refer the reader to the above paper for more details on their algorithm). However, our implementation using multi-valued consensus is more powerful in the sense of being adaptive to the number of jobs that need to be executed.

7. DISCUSSION

This paper presents wait-free randomized algorithms for the set-agreement problem in asynchronous shared-memory systems. There are many open questions that arise and are interesting subjects for further research, as we elaborate next.

We extended the definition of shared-coin algorithms to multi-sided shared coins. It is an open question whether our $(k + 1)$-sided shared-coin algorithm can be improved while keeping the agreement parameter constant. In addition, the definition can be modified so that the agreement parameter holds for subsets of less than k values. It is interesting to find good implementations for multi-sided shared coins that satisfy this modified definition.

For randomized set-agreement algorithms, it is open whether better algorithms exist in this model. In addition, it would be intriguing to prove lower bounds on the complexities of such algorithms, as no such bounds are currently known.

We note that for $k \leq \sqrt{n}$ the total and individual step complexities of our $(k, k + 1, n)$-agreement algorithm are the same as for the optimal algorithm for randomized binary consensus, only divided by k (see [5] and [3] for the total and individual step complexities of randomized consensus, respectively). First, it is an open question whether the same complexities can be obtained for larger values of k. In addition, a similar relation between consensus and set-agreement occurs also for complexities in deterministic synchronous algorithms and lower bounds under f failures, since the optimal number of rounds for solving consensus is $f + 1$ [6], while the optimal number of rounds for solving set-agreement is $f/k + 1$ [10]. It is interesting whether this is a coincidence or an indication of an inherent connection between the two problems.

We presented a randomized algorithm for the at-most-once problem, which achieves optimal effectiveness. It is interesting to find algorithms that have a better step complexity, while retaining the optimal effectiveness. Our algorithm does not require knowledge of the number of jobs, and can even work for an online setting, but it still requires the number of processes to be known in advance, and it is an open question whether there is a solution which avoids this assumption.

We believe that similar algorithms to the ones presented in this paper can be constructed for weaker adversarial models. It is an open question whether there can be improved algorithms for weaker adversaries, and it is also important to find analogous algorithms for solving set-agreement in message-passing systems. Needless to say, obtaining lower bounds for these models is an important direction for further research.

Acknowledgements:. The author thanks Hagit Attiya for many valuable discussions, David Hay for a useful suggestion, and Noga Zewi for comments on an earlier version of this paper.

8. REFERENCES

[1] K. Abrahamson. On achieving consensus using a shared memory. In *Proceedings of the 7th Annual ACM Symposium on Principles of Distributed Computing (PODC)*, pages 291–302, 1988.

[2] J. Aspnes. Time- and space-efficient randomized consensus. *J. Algorithms*, 14(3):414–431, 1993.

[3] J. Aspnes and K. Censor. Approximate shared-memory counting despite a strong adversary. In *SODA '09: Proceedings of the Nineteenth Annual ACM -SIAM Symposium on Discrete Algorithms*, pages 441–450, Philadelphia, PA, USA, 2009. Society for Industrial and Applied Mathematics.

[4] J. Aspnes and M. Herlihy. Fast randomized consensus using shared memory. *Journal of Algorithms*, 11(3):441–461, 1990.

[5] H. Attiya and K. Censor. Tight bounds for asynchronous randomized consensus. *J. ACM*, 55(5):1–26, 2008.

[6] H. Attiya and J. L. Welch. *Distributed Computing: Fundamentals, Simulations and Advanced Topics*. John Wiley & Sons, 2nd edition, 2004.

[7] E. Borowsky and E. Gafni. Generalized FLP impossibility result for t-resilient asynchronous computations. In *STOC '93: Proceedings of the twenty-fifth annual ACM symposium on Theory of computing*, pages 91–100, New York, NY, USA, 1993. ACM Press.

[8] G. Bracha and O. Rachman. Randomized consensus in expected $O(n^2 \log n)$ operations. In *Proceedings of the 5th International Workshop on Distributed Algorithms (WDAG)*, pages 143–150, 1991.

[9] S. Chaudhuri. More choices allow more faults: Set consensus problems in totally asynchronous systems. *Information and Computation*, 105(1):132–158, 1993.

[10] S. Chaudhuri, M. Herlihy, N. A. Lynch, and M. R. Tuttle. Tight bounds for k-set agreement. *J. ACM*, 47(5):912–943, 2000.

[11] L. Cheung. Randomized wait-free consensus using an atomicity assumption. In *OPODIS*, pages 47–60, 2005.

[12] P. Ezhilchelvan, A. Mostefaoui, and M. Raynal. Randomized multivalued consensus. In *Proceedings of the 4th IEEE International Symposium on Object-Oriented Real-Time Computing*, pages 195–200, 2001.

[13] M. J. Fischer, N. A. Lynch, and M. S. Paterson. Impossibility of distributed consensus with one faulty process. *J. ACM*, 32(2):374–382, Apr. 1985.

[14] M. Herlihy and N. Shavit. The topological structure of asynchronous computability. *Journal of the ACM*, 46(6):858–923, 1999.

[15] S. Kentros, A. Kiayias, N. C. Nicolaou, and A. A. Shvartsman. At-most-once semantics in asynchronous shared memory. In *DISC*, pages 258–273, 2009.

[16] A. Mostefaoui and M. Raynal. Randomized k-set agreement. In *SPAA '01: Proceedings of the thirteenth annual ACM symposium on Parallel algorithms and architectures*, pages 291–297, New York, NY, USA, 2001. ACM Press.

[17] A. Mostefaoui, M. Raynal, and F. Tronel. From binary consensus to multivalued consensus in asynchronous message-passing systems. *Inf. Process. Lett.*, 73(5-6):207–212, 2000.

[18] M. Raynal and C. Travers. Synchronous set agreement: a concise guided tour (including a new algorithm and a list of open problems). In *PRDC '06: Proceedings of the 12th Pacific Rim International Symposium on Dependable Computing*, pages 267–274, Washington, DC, USA, 2006. IEEE Computer Society.

[19] M. Saks, N. Shavit, and H. Woll. Optimal time randomized consensus—making resilient algorithms fast in practice. In *Proceedings of the 2nd annual ACM-SIAM symposium on Discrete algorithms*, pages 351–362, 1991.

[20] M. Saks and F. Zaharoglou. Wait-free k-set agreement is impossible: The topology of public knowledge. *SIAM J. Comput.*, 29(5):1449–1483, 2000.

[21] G. Taubenfeld. *Synchronization Algorithms and Concurrent Programming*. Prentice-Hall, Inc., Upper Saddle River, NJ, USA, 2006.

[22] R. Turpin and B. A. Coan. Extending binary byzantine agreement to multivalued byzantine agreement. *Inf. Process. Lett.*, 18(2):73–76, 1984.

[23] J. Zhang and W. Chen. Bounded cost algorithms for multivalued consensus using binary consensus instances. *Inf. Process. Lett.*, 109(17):1005–1009, 2009.

APPENDIX

A. PROOF OF THE ITERATIVE $(\ell, k + 1, n)$-AGREEMENT ALGORITHM

We now present the pseudocode of Algorithm 5 which solves $(\ell, k+1, n)$-agreement by iteratively decreasing the number of possible values using Algorithm 1, as discussed in Section 5.2.

Notice that Algorithm 1 is correct for agreeing on k values out of $k + 1$ values, even if the $k + 1$ possible input values are not necessarily $\{0, \ldots, k\}$, as long as they are a fixed and known set $\{v_0, \ldots, v_k\}$. This is done by having a bijective mapping between the two sets.

The following lemma guarantees the correctness of the algorithm.

LEMMA 15. *For each iteration s, $\ell \leq s \leq k$, the number of different values that appear in the $myValue$ variables of the processes that finish iteration s is at most s, and each of these values is the input of some process.*

PROOF. The proof is by induction over the iterations, where the base case is for $s = k$ and its proof is identical to that of Algorithm 1. For the induction step, we assume the lemma holds up to $s + 1$ and prove it for s. A process finishes iteration s when it assigns $decide = $ true in line 13. This can only happen after it reads $myCheck[\text{disagree}] == $ false in line 10, which implies that the number of different entries in $myPropose$ that contain $true$ is at most s. Moreover, every value that is written to the $Propose[s]$ array is the $myValue$ variable of some process at the end of iteration $s+1$, and therefore is the input of some process, by the induction hypothesis. $\square$

Algorithm 5 An $(\ell, k+1, n)$-agreement algorithm, code for process p_i

---

local variables: $myValue$, $myPropose = [0..k]$,
   $myCheck = [\text{agree}, \text{disagree}]$,$s$,$m$,$r$,$decide$
shared arrays: $Propose[1..k][\,][0..k]$,
   $Check[1..k][\,][\text{agree}, \text{disagree}]$
1:   for $s = k$ down to ℓ
2:     $r = 1$
3:     $decide = \text{false}$
4:     while $decide == \text{false}$
5:       $Propose[s][r][myValue] = \text{true}$
6:       $myPropose = \text{collect}(Propose[s][r])$
7:       if the number of entries in $myPropose$ that contains true
         is at most s
8:         $Check[s][r][\text{agree}] = \langle \text{true}, myValue \rangle$
9:       else
10:       $Check[s][r][\text{disagree}] = \text{true}$
11:      $myCheck = \text{collect}(Check[s][r])$
12:      if $myCheck[\text{disagree}] == \text{false}$
13:       $decide = \text{true}$
14:      else if $myCheck[\text{agree}] == \langle \text{true}, v \rangle$
15:       $myValue = v$
16:      else if $myCheck[\text{agree}] == \text{false}$
17:       $m = \text{sharedCoin}_{s+1}[r]$
18:       $myValue = $ the m-th entry in $myPropose$ that
         contains true   // At most $s+1$ such values
19:     $r = r+1$
20:   end while
21: end for
22: return $myValue$

Applying Lemma 15 to $s = \ell$ gives the validity and agreement properties. This leads to the following theorem:

THEOREM 16. *Algorithm 5 solves $(\ell, k+1, n)$-agreement with $O(\sum_{s=k}^{\ell} \frac{I_{s+1}+k}{\delta_{s+1}})$ individual step complexity and $O(\sum_{s=k}^{\ell} \frac{T_{s+1}+nk}{\delta_{s+1}})$ total step complexity, where δ_{s+1}, I_{s+1}, and T_{s+1} are the agreement parameter, individual step complexity, and total step complexity, respectively, of the $(s+1)$-sided shared coins.*

PROOF. For each value of s, a process runs an iteration of the agreement algorithm for s out of $s+1$ values. By an analog of Theorem 1, this takes $O(\frac{I_{s+1}+k}{\delta_{s+1}})$ individual step complexity, and $O(\frac{T_{s+1}+nk}{\delta_{s+1}})$ individual step complexity. Notice that we add $O(k)$ steps for collecting the arrays and not $O(s)$ steps, since it may be that a process does not know which are the $s+1$ current possible values among the initial $k+1$ values.

Summing over all iterations gives the resulting complexities. $\square$

Using the multi-sided shared coins of Section 4 gives:

Theorem 12 [restated] *Algorithm 5 solves $(\ell, k+1, n)$-agreement with $O((k-\ell+1)k + n(\log k - \log \ell))$ individual step complexity and $O((k-\ell+1)nk + n^2(\log k - \log \ell))$ total step complexity.*

PROOF. For the individual step complexity we have:

$$
\begin{aligned}
\sum_{s=k}^{\ell} \frac{I_{s+1}+k}{\delta_{s+1}} &= O(\sum_{s=k}^{\ell} \frac{n}{s} + k) \\
&= O((k-\ell+1)k + n\sum_{s=k}^{\ell} \frac{1}{s}) \\
&= O((k-\ell+1)k + n(\log k - \log \ell)),
\end{aligned}
$$

where the last equality follows from the fact that the harmonic series $H_k = \sum_{s=1}^{k} \frac{1}{s}$ is in the order of $\log k$. Similarly, we have that the total step complexity is $O((k-\ell+1)nk + n^2(\log k - \log \ell))$. $\square$

Note that for $\ell = 1$, i.e., for agreeing on exactly one value out of the initial $k+1$ possible inputs, we get an individual step complexity of $O((k-\ell+1)k + n(\log k - \log \ell)) = O(k^2 + n\log k)$, and a total step complexity of $O((k-\ell+1)nk + n^2(\log k - \log \ell)) = O(nk^2 + n^2 \log k)$.

B. PROOF OF THE BIT-BY-BIT $(1, k+1, n)$-AGREEMENT ALGORITHM

We now present the pseudocode of Algorithm 6 which solves $(1, k+1, n)$-agreement by agreeing on every bit of the value, as discussed in Section 5.3.

Algorithm 6 A $(1, k+1, n)$-agreement algorithm by agreeing on $\log k$ bits, code for p_i

---

local variables: $myValue = input$, $myPropose = [0.. \log k]$,
   $myCheck = [\text{agree}, \text{disagree}]$,$r = 0$,$decide = \text{false}$
shared arrays: $Propose[1..k][\,][0.. \log k]$,
   $Check[1..k][\,][\text{agree}, \text{disagree}]$
1:   for $j = 1 \ldots \lceil \log(k+1) \rceil$
2:     while ($decide == \text{false}$)
3:       $r += 1$
4:       $Propose[j][r][myValue[j]] = myValue$
5:       $myPropose = \text{collect}(Propose[j][r])$
6:       if $myPropose[0] \neq \perp$ and $myPropose[1] \neq \perp$
7:         $Check[j][r][\text{disagree}] = myPropose$
8:       else $Check[j][r][\text{agree}] = myValue$
9:       $myCheck = \text{collect}(Check[j][r])$
10:      if $myCheck[\text{disagree}] \neq \perp$
11:       $coin = \text{sharedCoin}_2(j, r)$
12:       if $myCheck[\text{agree}] \neq \perp$
13:         $myValue = Propose[j][r][myCheck[\text{agree}]]$
14:       else $myValue = myCheck[\text{disagree}][coin]$
15:      else $decide = true$ and $r = 0$
16:     end while
17:   end for
18:   return $myValue$

LEMMA 17. *For every j, $1 \leq j \leq \lceil \log(k+1) \rceil$, at the beginning of iteration j every process has $myValue$ that is the input of some process, and all the processes have $myValue$ with the same first $j-1$ bits.*

PROOF. The proof is by induction on j. The base case for $j = 1$ clearly holds since at the beginning of the algorithm $myValue$ is initialized to the input of the process, and $j - 1 = 0$ so there is no requirement from the first bits of $myValue$.

Induction step: Assume that the lemma holds up to value $j - 1$. That is, the variable $myValue$ of all processes at the beginning of iteration $j - 1$ has the same $j - 2$ first bits, and they are all inputs of processes.

First, we notice that in iteration $j - 1$ the variable $myValue$ can only change to a value written in the *Propose* array in line 13, or to a value written in the *Check* array in line 14. This implies that $myValue$ is always an input of some process.

Next, assume that at the end of the iteration processes p and q have $myValue$ variables with different first $j - 1$ bits. By the induction hypothesis, this implies that their $j - 1$-th bit is different. Let r be the first phase in which such two processes exist and decide in that phase. Assume, without loss of generality, that p executes line 4 after q does. This implies that when p reads the array *Propose* in line 5, both entries are non-empty. But then p writes its value into the *disagree* location of the array *Check* and therefore cannot decide in that phase. □

Lemma 17, in an analog to Section 3, implies validity and agreement. The following theorem shows the correctness and complexity of the algorithm:

Theorem 13 [restated] *Algorithm 6 solves* $(1, k + 1, n)$-*agreement with* $O(\lceil \log (k + 1) \rceil \cdot \frac{I}{\delta})$ *individual step complexity and* $O(\lceil \log (k + 1) \rceil \frac{T}{\delta})$ *total step complexity.*

PROOF. In each iteration j, $1 \leq j \leq \lceil \log (k + 1) \rceil$, by an analog to Lemma 4, the expected number of phases until all non-faulty process decide is $1 + 1/\delta$ which is $O(\frac{1}{\delta})$. In each phase, a process takes $O(1)$ steps in addition to the I steps it takes in the shared-Coin$_2$ algorithm. Therefore, the individual step complexity of Algorithm 6 is $O(\lceil \log (k + 1) \rceil \cdot \frac{I}{\delta})$, and the total step complexity is $O(\lceil \log (k + 1) \rceil \frac{T}{\delta})$. □

Brief Announcement: On Speculative Replication of Transactional Systems*

Paolo Romano

INESC-ID
Lisbon, Portugal
romano@gsd.inesc-id.pt

Roberto Palmieri,
Francesco Quaglia
Sapienza Rome University
Rome Italy
palmieri@dis.uniroma1.it,
quaglia@dis.uniroma1.it

Nuno Carvalho,
Luís Rodrigues
INESC-ID/IST
Lisbon, Portugal
nonius@gsd.inesc-id.pt,
ler@ist.utl.pt

ABSTRACT

We define the problem of speculative processing in a replicated transactional system layered on top of an optimistic atomic broadcast service. A realistic model is considered in which transactions' read and write sets are not a priori known and transactions' data access patterns may vary depending on the observed snapshot. We formalize a set of correctness and optimality properties ensuring the minimality and completeness of the set of explored serialization orders within the replicated transactional system.

Categories and Subject Descriptors

D4.7 [**Organization and Design**]: Distributed Systems; D4.5 [**Fault Tolerance**]: Operating Systems

General Terms

Algorithms,Performance,Reliability

Keywords

Replication, Serialization Theory, Atomic Broadcast.

1. INTRODUCTION

Active Replication (AR) is a fundamental approach for achieving fault-tolerance and high availability. When applied to transactional systems, classic AR schemes, e.g. [5], require that, prior to start executing transactions, replicas agree on a common total order for transactions' serialization. This is typically achieved by executing some form of non-blocking distributed consensus protocol, such as Atomic Broadcast [3] (AB).

Since the latency of AB can significantly degrade the performance of a replicated system, recent approaches, e.g. [6], have pursued the idea of overlapping transaction processing and replica coordination by relying on a, so called, Optimistic Atomic Broadcast (OAB) service. OAB provides an "early" (though potentially erroneous) guessing of the final outcome of the coordination phase [11]. Exploiting optimistic message delivery, each site may immediately start the (optimistic) processing of the transactional request without waiting for the completion of the coordination phase. Clearly, this strategy pays off only if the final total order does not contradict the initial guess; otherwise optimistically activated transactions may access inconsistent snapshots and be forced to rollback.

Unfortunately, existing OAB-based replication solutions suffer from several limitations. First, they only permit the parallel activation of optimistically delivered transactions that are known not to conflict with each other [6]. Such a choice simplifies the management of local processing activities, sparing from the risks of propagating the results generated by optimistically delivered transactions. On the other hand, it requires a-priori knowledge of both read and write sets associated with incoming transactions in order to label transactions in distinct conflict classes. This requirement raises the non-trivial problem of systematically predicting transaction data access patterns and may, in practice, lead to significant over-estimation of the likelihood of transaction conflicts, especially in scenarios entailing forms of non-determinism in the data access pattern. As discussed in [8], this can yield to a strong reduction of the achievable parallelism, thus representing a major performance impairment for modern multi-core systems. Further, the effectiveness of existing OAB-based solutions is severely challenged in geographical scale replication, where the chances of accurately guessing the final order are often very small [7]. Finally, if the ratio between the coordination delay and the computation granularity is very large, as in the emerging scenario of Distributed Transactional Memories (DTMs) [2, 12], the actual performance gains achievable by existing OAB-based approaches can be extremely limited. As shown in [12], in fact, the local transaction processing time in a DTM environment is typically one or two orders of magnitude smaller than the replicas' coordination latency. In such contexts, the overlap between processing and communication achievable by existing OAB-based approaches provides negligible performance benefits [8], even in favorable scenarios where the optimistic guessing of the final delivery order happens to be correct with an extremely high probability.

In this paper, we address these limitations by investigating, from a theoretical perspective, the issues related to the adoption of a speculative approach to replication of transactional systems, which we call Speculative Transactional Replication (STR). The idea underlying STR is rather simple and consists of two main aspects: i) exploring multiple serialization orders for each optimistically delivered transac-

*This work was partially supported by the ARISTOS (PTDC/EIA-EIA/102496/2008) project.

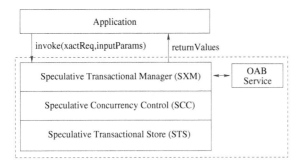

Figure 1: Software Architecture of Each Process.

tion, so to increase the probability of guessing a serialization order equivalent to the one finally determined by the OAB service; ii) allowing to observe the snapshots generated by optimistically executed transactions, rather than pessimistically blocking waiting for the outcome of the coordination phase, so to maximize the performance gains achievable by overlapping communication with local processing.

We frame the problem in a realistic model which does not assume the availability of any a-priori information on the set of data items to be accessed by the transactions (in either read or write mode), and in which transaction data access patterns can be influenced by the state observed during execution. Next, we formalize a set of correctness and optimality criteria for the speculative exploration of the permutations of the optimistically delivered transactions, demanding the *on-line* identification of all and only the transaction serialization orders that would cause the optimistically executed transactions to exhibit distinct outcomes.

2. SYSTEM MODEL

We consider a classical asynchronous distributed system model consisting of a set of processes $\Pi = \{p_1, \ldots, p_n\}$ that communicate via message passing and can fail according to the fail-stop (crash) model. We assume that the number of correct processes (i.e. the processes that do not fail) and the system's synchrony level are sufficient to permit implementing an OAB service.

OAB provides the following interface: *TO-broadcast(m)*, which allows broadcasting messages to all the processes in Π; *Opt-deliver(m)*, which delivers message m to a process in Π in a tentative, also called optimistic, order; *TO-deliver(m)*, which delivers a message m to a process in Π in a so called *final order* which is the same for all the processes in Π.

The diagram in Figure 1 shows the architecture of each process $p_i \in \Pi$. Applications generate transactions by calling the **invoke** method of the local Speculative Transaction Manager (SXM), specifying the business logic to be executed (e.g. a DBMS stored procedure, or a method in a transactional memory) and any associated input parameters. The SXM is responsible of (i) propagating (through the OAB service) the transactional request across the set of replicated processes, (ii) executing the transactional logic on the underlying Speculative Transactional Store (STS), and (iii) returning the corresponding result to the application.

The STS layer abstracts low level storage mechanisms, which may encompass RAM-only memory accesses (as in transactional memories) and logging on persistent storage to ensure durability (as in conventional DBMSs). The STS

maintains the state of a replica, modelled as a set of (multiversioned) data items, and provides classical facilities for making visible the new versions of the set of data items updated by transactions. We assume that each data item X maintained by STS is associated with a set of versions, of which, at any time, a single committed version exists. Uncommitted versions residing in STS are, on the other hand, reflections of speculative computations, used to propagate updates along chains of speculatively executed transactions.

The interactions between the SXM and the STS are mediated by the Speculative Concurrency Control (SCC) layer, which externalizes a classical interface to trigger read/write operations on the data items maintained by the STS, as well as to commit and abort transactions. SCC can additionally trigger the re-spawn (i.e. the restart) and the fork of a (not yet committed) transaction, so to speculatively explore different serialization orders for that transaction. In order to univocally identify multiple, speculatively executed, instances of a same transaction T_i, we use the notation T_i^j to refer to the j-th instance of transaction T_i. We say that two speculative instances of the same transaction, say T_i^j and T_i^k, are two sibling transactions.

Each transaction T_i^j is associated with a sequence of operations $\mathcal{O}(T_i^j) = \{o_1^{T_i^j}, \ldots, o_n^{T_i^j}\}$ where an operation $o_l \in \mathcal{O}(T_i^j)$ is either a read or a write on a data item X, denoted, resp., as $r_l(X)$ and $w_l(X)$. We say that a transaction T_i^j is *completed* when it has fully executed its sequence of operation $\mathcal{O}(T_i^j)$. We assume that neither the sequence of operations to be executed within a transaction, nor the data items to be accessed by each operation are a-priori known. Conversely, we assume that the transaction data access pattern can vary depending on the current state of the underlying transactional store. More precisely, we assume that the transactional business logic is *snapshot deterministic* in the sense that if the same transaction is activated multiple times, the sequence of read/write operations it executes does not change unless the return value of any of its reads changes. In other words, if whichever instance of a transaction T always sees a snapshot S, defined as the set of values returned by all its read operations, then it behaves deterministically by always executing the same set of read/write operations. On the other hand, instances of a transaction T activated on different snapshots may generate different sequences of operations. More formally, consider two sibling transactions T_i^a, T_i^b, producing, respectively, the two sequences of operations $\mathcal{O}(T_i^a) = \{o_1^{T_i^a}, \ldots, o_n^{T_i^a}\}$ and $\mathcal{O}(T_i^b) = \{o_1^{T_i^b}, \ldots, o_k^{T_i^b}\}$. Let us assume, with no loss of generality, that $k \leq n$ and that $j \in [1 \ldots k]$ is the index of the first operation in $\mathcal{O}(T_i^a), \mathcal{O}(T_i^b)$ for which $o_j^{T_i^a} \neq o_j^{T_i^b}$. This implies that before executing $o_j^{T_i^a}$, resp. $o_j^{T_i^b}$, a read on a data item X was previously executed by T_i^a, resp. T_i^b, and that the two reads returned two different values.

3. THE STR PROBLEM

Our target correctness criteria is 1-copy serializability [1], which ensures that a transaction execution history $\mathcal{H}$ across the whole set of replicated processes Π is equivalent to a serial transaction execution history in a non-replicated system. More specifically, we are interested in *view serializability* [1, 10] defined as a property of $\mathcal{H}$ such that, for any prefix $\mathcal{H}'$ of

$\mathcal{H}$, its committed projection $C(\mathcal{H}')$ (obtained by deleting all operations not belonging to transactions committed in $\mathcal{H}'$) is *view equivalent* to some serial history.

We now introduce the notion of optimality for an STR algorithm. This is done by formalizing a set of properties ensuring both the consistency (view serializability) of the snapshot observed by any speculative transaction, and that *all and only* the speculative serialization orders in which the transactions observe *distinct* snapshots are explored.

Let $\Sigma = \{T_1, \ldots, T_n\}$ be the set of Opt-delivered, but not yet TO-delivered, transactions, and denote with $\Sigma^* = \{T_1^1, \ldots, T_1^k, \ldots, T_n^1, \ldots, T_n^m\}$ the set of the corresponding speculative transactions that have run to completion. We say that an STR algorithm is optimal if it guarantees the following properties:

- **Consistency:** *the history of execution of every speculative transaction in Σ^* is view serializable.*
- **Non-redundancy:** *no two sibling transactions in Σ^* observe the same snapshot, i.e.:*
$$\forall T_i^a, T_i^b \in \Sigma^* \Rightarrow$$
$$\exists r_l^{T_i^a}(X) \in \mathcal{O}(T_i^a), \exists r_l^{T_i^b}(X) \in \mathcal{O}(T_i^b) \text{ s.t. } r_l^{T_i^a}(X) \neq r_l^{T_i^b}(X)$$
- **Completeness:** *if the system is quiescent, namely the OAB service stops Opt-delivering and TO-delivering transactions, then for every permutation of Σ, say $\pi(\Sigma)$, there eventually exists a speculative transaction $T_i^j \in \Sigma^*$ that observes the snapshot produced by sequentially executing all the transactions preceding T_i in $\pi(\Sigma)$.*

The optimality property of an STR algorithm filters out trivial solutions based on the exhaustive enumeration of every possible permutation of the Opt-delivered transactions for the construction of plausible serialization orders. In fact, while such an approach would certainly enumerate the permutation that will be eventually generated by the final TO-deliver (thus providing completeness), it would require the processing of $\sum_{i=1 \ldots n} \frac{n!}{(n-i)!} = \Theta(n!)$ speculative transactions (i.e. the number of nodes of a permutation tree [4] for a set of cardinality n), being n the number of Opt-delivered (but not yet TO-delivered) messages. More importantly, such a number of speculative transactions would be spawned independently of the actually developed conflict relations. This would likely cause the useless exploration of a (possibly very large) number of redundant serialization orders in which transactions execute along identical trajectories, thus producing the same snapshots and externalizing the same results to the application.

It is therefore desirable to design conflict-aware mechanisms able to identify all and only the serialization orders that would cause the Opt-delivered transactions to exhibit distinct execution trajectories and, ultimately, externalize different results to the application. The problem's complexity appears clearly manifest if one considers that the transactions' data access patterns, and consequently their mutual conflict relations, can be in practice significantly influenced by the observed state values. This raises the requirement for *on-line* solutions able to correctly deal with scenarios in which the activation of a same transaction according to different serialization orders causes the generation of different sequences of operations (as captured by the *snapshot deterministic* transaction execution model formalized in Section 2).

4. AN OPTIMAL STR ALGORITHM

An optimal solution to the STR problem can be found in our technical report in [9]. In order to determine the set of speculative serialization orders in which transactions need to be executed, this optimal STR algorithm relies on a novel graph-based construct, called Speculative Polygraph (SP). SPs are inspired by Papadimitirou's polygraphs, originally introduced in [10] to test the view-serializability of a non-speculative history. Conventional polygraphs are in fact unfeasible to reason on view serializability of a speculative transaction history since the simultaneous coexistence within a polygraph of two sibling transactions, representative of non-conciliable serialization orders, can corrupt the polygraph by introducing cycles that might render it useless.

Another interesting finding highlighted in [9] is that, when considering different realistic application workloads, an optimal STR algorithm requires on average the exploration of at most 5 serialization orders per transaction when the number of Opt-delivered, but not yet TO-delivered, messages is lower than 15. This result highlights, on one hand, the factual importance of the STR's non-redundancy property. On the other hand, it shows that the additional amount of hardware resources required by an optimal STR algorithm is, in realistic settings, expected to be relatively low and, we argue, likely satisfiable by modern multi-core processors.

5. REFERENCES

[1] P. A. Bernstein, V. Hadzilacos, and N. Goodman. *Concurrency Control and Recovery in Database Systems.* Addison-Wesley, 1987.

[2] M. Couceiro, P. Romano, N. Carvalho, and L. Rodrigues. D^{2}STM: Dependable Distributed Software Transactional Memory. In *Proc. Int. Symp. on Dependable Computing (PRDC).* IEEE Computer Society Press, 2009.

[3] D. Powell (ed.). *Special Issue on Group Communication*, volume 39. ACM, 1996.

[4] G. Hetyei and E. Reiner. Permutation trees and variation statistics. *Eur. J. Comb.*, 19(7):847–866, 1998.

[5] B. Kemme and G. Alonso. A suite of database replication protocols based on group communication primitives. In *Proc. Int. Conf. on Distributed Computing Systems (ICDCS)*, IEEE Computer Society, 1998.

[6] B. Kemme, F. Pedone, G. Alonso, and A. Schiper. Processing transactions over optimistic atomic broadcast protocols. In *Proc. Int. Conf. on Distributed Computing Systems (ICDCS)*, IEEE Computer Society, 1999.

[7] J. Mocito, A. Respicio, and L. Rodrigues. On statistically estimated optimistic delivery in large-scale total order protocols. *In Proc. Int. Symp. on Dependable Computing (PRDC)*, IEEE Computer Society Press, 2006.

[8] R. Palmieri, F. Quaglia, P. Romano, and N. Carvalho. Evaluating database-oriented replication schemes in software transactional memory systems. *In Proc. Workshop on Dependable Parallel, Distributed and Network-Centric Systems (DPDNS)*, IEEE Computer Society Press, 2010.

[9] P. Romano, R. Palmieri, F. Quaglia, N. Carvalho and L. Rodrigues. On Speculative Replication of Transactional Systems, INESC-ID Tec. Rep. 38/2009, 2009.

[10] C. H. Papadimitriou. The serializability of concurrent database updates. *J. ACM*, 26(4):631–653, 1979.

[11] F. Pedone and A. Schiper. Optimistic atomic broadcast: a pragmatic viewpoint. *Theor. Comput. Sci.*, 291(1):79–101, 2003.

[12] P. Romano, N. Carvalho, and L. Rodrigues. Towards distributed software transactional memory systems. In *Proc. of the Workshop on Large-Scale Distributed Systems and Middleware (LADIS)*, ACM press, 2008.

Brief Announcement: Combine—an Improved Directory-Based Consistency Protocol

Hagit Attiya*
Technion, Israel
EPFL, Switzerland
hagit@cs.technion.ac.il

Vincent Gramoli
EPFL, Switzerland
University of Neuchâtel
vincent.gramoli@epfl.ch

Alessia Milani†
LIP6, Université Pierre et
Marie Curie, France
alessia.milani@lip6.fr

Categories and Subject Descriptors

D.1.3 [**Programming Techniques**]: Concurrent Programming—*Distributed programming*

General Terms

Algorithms, Theory, Reliability

Keywords

Combining, overlay tree, stretch

1. MOTIVATION

Distributed applications in large-scale systems aim for good *scalability*, offering proportionally better performance as the number of processing nodes increases, by exploiting communication to access nearby data items. This paper presents a scalable *directory-based consistency protocol*: A node can introduce a new object by notifying the system (publish); to write an object, a node first acquires the object locally (move); to read an object, a node only has to get a read-only copy of the object (lookup).

Consistency protocols play a key role in *data-flow* distributed implementations of software transactional memory (DSTM) in large-scale distributed memory systems [2]. In these systems, remote accesses require expensive communication, and reducing the *cost of communication* with the objects and the number of remote operations is crucial for achieving good performance in transactional memory implementations. This stands in contrast with smaller-scale hardware shared-memory systems, providing faster access to local or remote addresses, where the critical factor seems to be the *single-processor* overhead induced by bookkeeping.

Several directory-based consistency protocols were presented in the context of DSTM implementation, e.g., [2, 5]. The general idea of a directory-based consistency protocol for a single object x, is to organize nodes in a tree and have nodes maintain a path towards a *sink* node. Initially, the sink is the node that creates the object. Then, the first request to modify x which reaches the sink will become the next to acquire the object after the current sink releases it,

and the corresponding node will become the new sink. This is done by redirecting the followed pointers towards itself. To retrieve the value of x, a node has simply to follow the pointers and obtain a read-only copy from the reached node.

The message complexity of prior protocols deteriorates in the presence of concurrent requests. RELAY [5] uses a spanning tree, whose stretch can be quite high in common networks like rings and grids. Moreover, concurrent moves may cause nodes to communicate through the root of the tree, despite being close. Thus, its communication cost is proportional to the diameter of the spanning tree. BALLISTIC [2] uses an overlay tree augmented with shortcuts. Without concurrent requests, the cost is proportional to the stretch of the overlay tree, however, a mutual exclusion protocol is necessary to probe shortcuts in presence of concurrent requests, which increases its cost significantly. (See [1].)

We present a new directory-based consistency protocol, COMBINE, tolerating non-fifo message delivery and concurrent requests for the same object. COMBINE is designed to work in large-scale systems, where the cost of communication is not uniform, namely, some nodes are "closer" than others. Scalability in COMBINE is achieved by communicating on an *overlay tree* and ensuring that the cost of performing a lookup or a move is proportional to the cost of the shortest path between the requesting node and the serving node, in the overlay tree. Specifically, the cost of a lookup request by node p that is served by node q is proportional to the shortest path between p and q; the cost of a move request by node p is similar, with q being the previous node holding the object.

2. OVERVIEW OF COMBINE

We briefly describe COMBINE; more details, as well as proof of correctness, can be found in [1]. We assume that the cost of communication over single links forms a *metric*, that is, there is a symmetric positive *distance* between nodes, denoted $d(.,.)$, which satisfies the triangle inequality.

A key idea in COMBINE is that requests are combined as they pass through the same node. Originally used to reduce contention in multistage interconnection networks [4], *combining* means piggybacking information of distinct requests in the same message.

In more detail, a leaf node i can add a new object, look for its current value, or acquire it exclusively, as follows:

- A node i adds a new object x that it owns locally using a publish(x) request. This request sets a new pointer at each node located between i and the root of the overlay tree so that it points towards i.

*Supported by the *Israel Science Foundation* (grant number 953/06).
†Supported in part by ANR SHAMAN.

– A node i looks for the value of x by executing a lookup(x) request. This request goes up in the overlay tree until it discovers a pointer towards the downwards path to the sink of x; the lookup(x) records its identifier at each visited node. When the request arrives at the node holding x, it sends a read-only copy directly to i. Each node stores the information associated to at most one request for any other node.

– A node i acquires an object by sending a move(x) request that goes up towards the root of the overlay tree upon it finds a pointer to the sink. When looking for the object the move request redirects the path for the sink of object x towards i. If the move(x) discovers a stored lookup(x) it simply embeds it rather than passing over it. When the move(x) and (possibly) its embedded lookup(x) reach the sink of x, this node will sends x to i and a read-only copy of x to the node that issued the lookup, as soon as it releases it.

Let $d_T(p, q)$ be the distance between p and q in the overlay tree. The proof of the next theorem appears in [1].

THEOREM 1. *The cost of a* lookup *or* move *request issued by node p and terminating at node q is $O(d_T(p, q))$.*

Clearly, the cost of serving a request in COMBINE depends on the *stretch* of the overlay tree, namely, the worst case ratio between the cost of direct communication between two nodes p and q in the network, that is, $d(p, q)$, and the cost of communicating along the shortest tree path between p and q (i.e., the sum of the distances from p and q to their lowest common ancestor), that is, $d_T(p, q)$.

An overlay tree with small stretch can be constructed by recursively computing maximal independent sets, one for each level of the tree, similarly to [2]. There is a distributed algorithm to compute maximal independent sets in *constant-doubling* metric networks in $O(\log \Delta \log^* n)$ time, where Δ is the diameter of the graph [3].

Handling Message Reordering. When a lookup traverses its path to the object, it stores its identifier in all the nodes it visited. This allows an overtaking move to embed the lookup and ensures termination of concurrent requests, even when messages are reordered. In contrast, BALLISTIC may get stuck when links are not FIFO, while RELAY may send an unbounded number of unnecessary messages. (See [1].)

Handling Concurrent Moves. A move(x) operation modifies the orientation of the tree links by setting pointers indicating the new location of object x, thus, it may impact the performance of concurrent operations targeting x. Since no move(x) can happen before the publish(x) terminates, it can only affect a concurrent lookup(x) or another concurrent move(x). In COMBINE, when two requests go up, one arrives at the common ancestor first. If this request is a move, the other request follows the freshly redirected path.

In contrast, the *shortcut* links in the overlay tree, used in BALLISTIC [2], may degrade the message complexity of lookup and move, when executed concurrently with another move(x): During the up-phase of an operation, each node at level ℓ probes multiple nodes at level $\ell + 1$, its *parent-set*,

using these shortcuts to locate a potential downward link. A node probes its father in the tree last, before the node issuing the move sets a downward pointer from its father to itself. There can be two nodes i and j at the same level ℓ, each of their fathers belonging to the *parent-set* of the other. If i is executing the up-phase of a move while j is executing the up-phase of its operation, j may miss the downward pointer to i that is being set. The same scenario may occur at higher levels between the father of i that sets the pointer to itself and the father of j. Consequently, even though i and j have one common ancestor among their respective ancestors at level $\ell + 1$, the operation of j may traverse higher levels before reaching i. Sun's thesis discusses this problem and suggests a variant that integrates a mutual exclusion protocol in each level; however, this version is blocking and introduces further delay.

RELAY [5] uses a simple spanning tree structure, without shortcuts, however, a similar scenario can occur since a move operation redirects the path to the object only on its way back. Consider two concurrent operations, one of them a move, issued by two nodes with a common ancestor in the tree. It may happen that the move operation m follows the path to the current position of the object and the other operation just follows m, since m does not redirect the links it traverses before reaching the object. Once m reaches the object, it follows the same path in the other direction to come back to its issuing node. In this second traversal m redirects each link it travels. The other operation will simply follows the links to the object, and then, once at the node where the object was expected to be, it will be redirected to the node where m was issued. Thus, the second operation traverses to the root of the tree, although it obtains the object from a nearby node. (This scenario does not happen in COMBINE or BALLISTIC, since m redirects the path as it is going up.)

The next table summarizes the above comparison.

Protocol	Cost	Assumes FIFO
COMBINE	O(distance in overlay tree)	No
RELAY	O(diameter of spanning) tree	Yes
BALLISTIC	O(diameter of overlay structure)	Yes

3. REFERENCES

[1] H. Attiya, V. Gramoli, and A. Milani. COMBINE: An improved directory-based consistency protocol. Technical Report LPD-2010-002, EPFL, 2010.

[2] M. Herlihy and Y. Sun. Distributed transactional memory for metric-space networks. *Distributed Computing*, 20(3):195–208, 2007.

[3] F. Kuhn, T. Moscibroda, T. Nieberg, and R. Wattenhofer. Fast deterministic distributed maximal independent set computation on growth-bounded graphs. In *DISC*, pages 273–287, 2005.

[4] G. F. Pfister and V. A. Norton. "hot spot" contention and combining in multistage interconnection networks. *IEEE Trans. Comp.*, 34(10):943–948, 1985.

[5] B. Zhang and B. Ravindran. Relay: A cache-coherence protocol for distributed transactional memory. In *OPODIS*, pages 48–53, 2009.

Brief Announcement: Byzantine Agreement with Homonyms

Carole Delporte-Gallet[*]
LIAFA, Université Paris
Diderot
cd@liafa.jussieu.fr

Hugues Fauconnier
LIAFA, Université Paris
Diderot
hf@liafa.jussieu.fr

Rachid Guerraoui
Ecole Polytechnique Fédérale
de Lausanne
Rachid.Guerraoui@epfl.ch

Anne-Marie Kermarrec
INRIA Rennes
Anne-Marie.Kermarrec@inria.fr

ABSTRACT

In this work, we address Byzantine agreement in a message passing system with homonyms, *i.e.* a system with a number l of authenticated identities that is independent of the total number of processes n, in the presence of $t < n$ Byzantine processes.

We prove the following results: (i) agreement is possible if (and only if) $l > 3t$ in a synchronous model; (ii) agreement is impossible, independently of the number of failures, in an eventually synchronous model; (iii) eventual agreement is possible, if (and only if) $l > 3t$, in an asynchronous model.

Categories and Subject Descriptors

C.2.1 [**Computer-Communication Networks**]: Network Architecture and Design—*distributed networks*; C.2.4 [**Computer-Communication Networks**]: Distributed Systems; C.4 [**Performance of Systems**]: [Fault tolerance]

General Terms

Algorithms, Theory, Reliability

Keywords

Consensus, Message-Passing, Byzantine Agreement, Authentication.

1. INTRODUCTION

We study Byzantine agreement in a message passing system with a limited number of *authenticated identities*, i.e., a system with *homonyms*. Basically, there is a set of l different identities used to identify processes. This set can be much smaller than the set of processes and hence several processes may have the same identity. Such processes can be considered as homonyms. Identities are authenticated in the sense that if a process p receives a message from a process q with

*Work of Carole Delporte-Gallet and Hugues Fauconnier was supported by grant ANR-08-VERSO-SHAMAN and the INRIA project GANG.

identity id, p knows that the message does not come from a process with name $id' \neq id$. The message could however come from a homonym process $q' \neq q$, also with identity id.

In this context, we ask whether Byzantine agreement can be solved if l is independent of the total number of processes n. Beyond intellectual curiosity, the motivation of addressing this question is twofold.

Firstly, the assumption, underlying many distributed systems, e.g. [12, 14], that all processes have unique (unforgeable) identities might, we believe, be considered too strong. More specifically, authenticated unique identities are typically achieved through collision-free hash functions. Yet, such functions are potentially breakable, e.g.[15], namely they may lead to the same output with different inputs. Even the ones that have not been broken yet, such as SHA-256, might be in a near future.

Secondly, in many cases, processes (users) do care about their privacy and would rather not reveal their identity. In a fully anonymous system where processes do not have identities [2], reaching agreement is simply impossible in the face of Byzantine players. With a limited number of identities, one can preserve some level of anonymity and hide, to some extent, the association between every user and every identity. A limited number of identities, may render some agreement possible, as we will show in the sequel.

2. RESULTS

Assuming a system of n processes, t potential Byzantine failures and l identities, we prove the three following main results:

1. In a synchronous model [9], Byzantine agreement is possible if (and only if) $l > 3t$. This result is to be contrasted with the classical impossibility of Byzantine agreement if $n \leq 3t$: in a sense, we show that what really matters is the ratio between the number of Byzantine processes and the number of authenticated identities rather than the one between the number of Byzantine processes and the total number of processes.

   We prove the existence of our algorithm by simulation: we show how to transform any synchronous Byzantine agreement protocol, where all processes have uniquely authenticated identities (i.e., $n = l$), into a Byzantine agreement protocol using only l ($n \geq l > 3t$) authenticated identities. In short, we do so by adding a communication round between any two communication rounds of the original agreement protocol. The added rounds are used by the processes with the same identities to agree on the same message to send in the next round of the original protocol.

2. In an eventually synchronous model [5] agreement is impossible. More specifically, we show, using a partitioning argument, that processes can decide on different values if $n \geq 2l$. The proof does not require any failure, which might be surprising at first glance.

   Interestingly, this highlights the very fact that, in a setting with limited identities, the demarcation line between the possibility and impossibility of agreement is different that in a model where all processes have identities [6].

3. In an asynchronous model, eventual agreement is possible, if (and only if) $l > 3t$. In *eventual agreement* (also called *stabilizing consensus* [1]), processes can decide several times, possibly on different values, but eventually converge to the same value.

   We first present a binary eventual agreement protocol and then show how to use a transformation close to [2, 10] to obtain a multi-valued agreement.

3. CONCLUDING REMARKS

To the best of our knowledge, this paper is the first to study a distributed system model with a limited number of identities, i.e., homonyms. In a sense, the model unifies both classical non-anonymous [3, 9] and anonymous models [1, 2, 4, 7, 8, 11, 13]. As we argued in the introduction, we believe this model to be interesting for both intellectual and practical considerations.

While studying the spectrum of possibilities for Byzantine agreement in a system with homonyms, we shed a different light on this problem. Whereas the traditional agreement impossibility result holds only in a fully asynchronous model only, we show than in a system with homonyms, the impossibility holds as soon as there is some (even partial) asynchrony. In addition, in a synchronous setting, the relevant crucial ratio turns out to be between the number of identities l and the number of Byzantine processes t, while the classical result considers a ratio between n and t.

It is important to note that we only scratched the surface of what can be computed with homonyms: many challenging issues are open. For instance, we considered a message passing model and it would be interesting to explore the impact of a shared memory. Also, we focused on agreement and many other problems should be considered. Finally, we focused on computability, complexity is yet to be explored.

Acknowledgments

We are grateful to Christian Cachin for his useful comments on our model with homonyms and to the reviewers for their helpful comments.

4. REFERENCES

[1] Dana Angluin, Michael J. Fischer, and Hong Jiang. Stabilizing consensus in mobile networks. In *DCOSS*, volume 4026 of *LNCS*, pages 37–50, 2006.

[2] Hagit Attiya, Alla Gorbach, and Shlomo Moran. Computing in totally anonymous asynchronous shared memory systems. *Inf. Comput.*, 173(2):162–183, 2002.

[3] Hagit Attiya and Jennifer Welch. *Distributed Computing: fundamentals, simulations and advanced topics, 2nd edition*. Wiley, 2004.

[4] Harry Buhrman, Alessandro Panconesi, Riccardo Silvestri, and Paul M. B. Vitányi. On the importance of having an identity or, is consensus really universal? *Distributed Computing*, 18(3):167–176, 2006.

[5] Cynthia Dwork, Nancy A. Lynch, and Larry Stockmeyer. Consensus in the presence of partial synchrony. *Journal of the ACM*, 35(2):288–323, April 1988.

[6] Michael J. Fischer, Nancy A. Lynch, and Michael S. Paterson. Impossibility of distributed consensus with one faulty process. *Journal of the ACM*, 32(2):374–382, April 1985.

[7] Rachid Guerraoui and Eric Ruppert. Anonymous and fault-tolerant shared-memory computing. *Distributed Computing*, 20(3):165–177, 2007.

[8] Rachid Guerraoui and Eric Ruppert. Names trump malice: Tiny mobile agents can tolerate byzantine failures. In *ICALP*, volume 5556 of *LNCS*, pages 484–495. Springer, 2009.

[9] Nancy A. Lynch. *Distributed Algorithms*. Morgan Kaufmann, 1996.

[10] Achour Mostéfaoui, Michel Raynal, and Frederic Tronel. From binary consensus to multivalued consensus in asynchronous message-passing systems. *Inf. Process. Lett.*, 73(5-6):207–212, 2000.

[11] Michael Okun and Amnon Barak. Efficient algorithms for anonymous byzantine agreement. *Theory Comput. Syst.*, 42(2):222–238, 2008.

[12] Antony I. T. Rowstron and Peter Druschel. Pastry: Scalable, decentralized object location, and routing for large-scale peer-to-peer systems. In *Middleware*, volume 2218 of *LNCS*, pages 329–350, 2001.

[13] Eric Ruppert. The anonymous consensus hierarchy and naming problems. In *OPODIS*, volume 4878 of *LNCS*, pages 386–400. Springer, 2007.

[14] Ion Stoica, Robert Morris, David R. Karger, M. Frans Kaashoek, and Hari Balakrishnan. Chord: A scalable peer-to-peer lookup service for internet applications. In *ACM SIGCOMM*, pages 149–160, 2001.

[15] Xiaoyun Wang and Hongbo Yu. How to break md5 and other hash functions. In *EUROCRYPT*, volume 3494 of *LNCS*, pages 19–35, 2005.

Brief Announcement: Fun In Numbers - A Platform for Sensor-based Multiplayer Pervasive Games

Ioannis Chatzigiannakis, Georgios Mylonas, Orestis Akribopoulos,
Marios Logaras, Panagiotis Kokkinos, Paul Spirakis
Research Academic Computer Technology Institute (RACTI) &
Computer Engineering and Informatics Department, University of Patras, Greece
{ ichatz, mylonasg, akribopo, logaras, kokkinop, spirakis}@cti.gr

ABSTRACT

We examine multi-player pervasive games that rely on the use of ad-hoc mobile sensor networks. The unique feature in such games is that players interact with each other and their surrounding environment by using movement and presence as a means of performing game-related actions, utilizing sensor devices. We briefly discuss the fundamental issues and challenges related to these type of games and the scenarios associated with them. We have also developed a framework, called Fun in Numbers (FinN) that handles a number of these issues, such as such as neighbors discovery, localization, synchronization and delay-tolerant communication. FinN is developed using Java and is based on a multilayer architecture, which provides developers with a set of templates and services for building and operating new games.

Categories and Subject Descriptors

H.4 [**Information Systems Applications**]: Miscellaneous;
K.8.0 [**Computing Milieux**]: Personal Computing—*Games*

General Terms

Algorithms, Design

Keywords

wireless sensor networks, pervasive games, protocols

1. SENSOR-BASED PERVASIVE GAMES

In this applied research work we first identify the main issues and research challenges that arise in multiplayer pervasive games based on distributed sensor networks. Such games can be categorized based on their features like *movement*, *presence*, and *sensors input*, or based on the diverse possibilities of the projected applications in terms of interaction between users, existence of an infrastructure and timewise operation.

We envisage *pervasive games that involve multiple players and rapid physical activity* and offer a *diversity of player strategies and combinations of actions* that can be performed in a simple game and we identify the following challenges:
Simultaneous participation of multiple users: groups of players participate, potentially in large numbers. The players will be in close proximity, in indoor or outdoor environments, and will have to engage in such applications by either interacting between themselves or with the infrastructure provided.
Multiple types of inputs: we envisage the utilization of a plethora of inputs, the most generic of which are presence, motion and sensory input.
Distributed network operation: the use of embedded sensors and the ad hoc networking capabilities lead to the execution of distributed lightweight mechanisms on the mobile devices.
Need for synchronization and coordination between players: in most games players are competing or cooperating in order to reach/fulfill their goals. Interaction between players and the system must be done in a synchronized way.
Need for reliability and dependability: since this type of games are to be played using even low-cost devices and in "harsh" settings, i.e., devices could be rebooted by mistake, etc., players need to be reassured that such characteristics will not interfere with the smooth operation of the games.
The world-as-a-gameboard: the games should be implemented in such a manner providing both the distributed nature and the context-awareness factors to the players.
Multiple platforms / Crossmedia applications: apart from using multiple, different inputs, this kind of applications might else be based on a variety of platforms, depending on the environment they are played at or even the logical level involved at separate time instances (e.g., playing the game with a mobile device and then playing other aspects of the game or watching statistics on a desktop computer).

2. FUN IN NUMBERS

We believe that the knowledge stemming from the recent WSN-related research can be applied in the gaming domain so as to produce efficient systems. We design and implement the *Fun in Numbers*[1] (FinN) platform for creating, deploying and administering multi-player games with pervasive and locative features that employ wireless sensor network nodes as the gaming devices. FinN currently utilizes Sun SPOT [4] nodes as a prototype implementation hardware platform and essentially provides developers with a set of templates and services for building and operating new games upon. These can be easily customized, so as to reduce the overall effort of implementing a new game from scratch to the minimum.

FinN's architecture is based on a hierarchy of layers for

---

[1]For additional information, you can visit http://finn.cti.gr or http://youtube.com/funinnumbers

scalability and easy customization to different scenarios (heterogeneity). A number of services are currently implemented, allowing location awareness of wireless devices in indoor environments, perform sensing tasks while on the move, coordinate basic distributed operations and offer delay-tolerant communication. FinN consists of several elements. Players carry one or more handheld device with wireless communication and sensing capabilities. A "backbone" infrastructure may also be available, possibly forming a wireless mesh network. Such an infrastructure consists of *Stations*, which are able to provide a number of services to the player devices (e.g., localization, context awareness) and may also control actuators that add certain gaming elements. Each game instance is assigned to and coordinated by a specific *Engine*, i.e., it is the local authority for each physical game site. The *World* is the topmost element that manages multiple physical game sites and allows interaction with social networking sites, e.g., Twitter or Facebook. Figure 1 illustrates these elements.

These *heterogeneous* elements (in terms of role, communication, computation and energy capabilities) form a loosely coupled, highly modular and customizable hierarchy. This allows FinN to support both *ad-hoc* and *infrastructure-based games* (or interactive installations). In the first case, a very limited backbone infrastructure is available, thus almost all communication and computation must be performed by the handheld devices in a fully distributed manner. In the second case, we wish to take advantage of the backbone by following a "2-tier principle", thus moving communication and computation to the fixed part of the network. Our approach allows services (e.g., discovery, proximity detection, gesture recognition) to be seamlessly reallocated from the player devices (where computation and communication is expensive) to the backbone infrastructure (where resources are practically unlimited) with minimum programming effort.

We have thus far placed our effort in two types of applications; multiplayer pervasive games and interactive installations. The "Hot Potato" game is a tag-based game, where players try to pass on to one another an "exploding" token; "Casanova" features a "follow-me and stop-when-I-stop" concept between a pair or a group of players (with one as the leader); "Moving Monk" resembles a hidden treasure game where a group of players must discover hidden sites and perform "rituals" (that is specific gestures) upon their visits. On the interactive installations side, "Tug-of-war" resembles a rhythm game where two groups of players try to outrace one another while following on-screen instructions, while on "Chromatize it!" players use the devices to colour certain on-screen objects.

2.1 Protocols and Services

In this section we describe the basic elements of FinN with specific reference to the issues and challenges described in Section 1. As we shall see, several design choices present themselves even in the context of the specific games that we implemented. We elaborate on these design choices while describing the design of our platform.

Neighbor Discovery: Echo Protocol offers local connectivity awareness, while it is designed to run on resource-limited devices. It is also robust, able to adjust quickly to frequent and significant topology changes and capable of distinguishing the different roles of the discovered neighboring nodes (i.e., Players, backbone Station, Mobile Station).

In addition, it allows customization of the propagated messages. In particular, FinN player devices and backbone stations are *characterized* by a list of attribute-value pairs that describe the status of the game. For example:

```
id = 131 // unique id of device
type = player // type of device
location = [10,2] // coordinates of node
```

These descriptions are constantly broadcasted by the devices. In this way, *Echo Protocol* is also used as the building block of other protocols and services, such as localization (Section 2.1) and leader election. In particular, in the leader election service the id of the device/player broadcasted, is used as key parameter for selecting the leader among a set of players.

Echo Protocol it is able to recognize whether the communication with the surrounding devices is bi-directional or not. In general, players interact in pairs or in groups by executing (simultaneously or not) *actions*. The coordination of player actions almost always requires symmetric communication. The majority of theoretical works consider wireless links to be symmetric, however in practice most of the times this is not true for a multitude of reasons. This fact significantly complicates game design; a unidirectional link cannot provide acknowledgments of receipt of messages. To overcome this problem, the Echo protocol attaches to each broadcasted packet the list of detected neighbors; that is the devices that has received a beacon from in the last $3 \times$ beacon_interval period. This attribute-value pair may look like: neighbors = [11,81,5,43].

Echo Protocol relies on the devices' IEEE 802.15.4 radio. In contrast to Bluetooth, data is exchanged without establishing a connection and concurrent transmission of messages to multiple devices is supported. Thus the *interval* between consecutive broadcasts can be set to less than 100ms time period while Bluetooth devices may take up to 10.24sec [1], *significantly improving discovery* among devices.

Clearly, by decreasing the value of the interval of broadcasts, a near real-time response to the topology changes can be achieved, in the expense of increased network load and energy consumption due to the beacon messages exchanged.

Localization: In some games player devices need to sense their relative location to each other and to specific landmarks. A simple approach for proximity detection is to use the attribute-value pairs of the Echo protocol. By properly adjusting the *transmission power* and assuming that the players hold the devices in a particular way (e.g., strapped on their knee), the distance to another device can be estimated by the player device. For example, in "moving monk" we attach *mobile stations* to the hidden treasures so that devices can detect if the players have discovered them.

In other games, more accurate location information is required on the absolute position of the players on the gameboard. Of course, the incorporation of location awareness in ad hoc mobile sensor networks is far from a trivial task. In this case, localization of the devices is performed using a fixed infrastructure consisting of at least three backbone stations (the so-called anchor nodes) and the periodic broadcasts of the Echo protocol. The modular architecture of FinN allows an orthogonal implementations of a centralized algorithm. In this approach, the presence of a fairly large number of backbone station provide accurate location information.For each Echo protocol message (beacon) received, by the stations, the Received Signal Strength In-

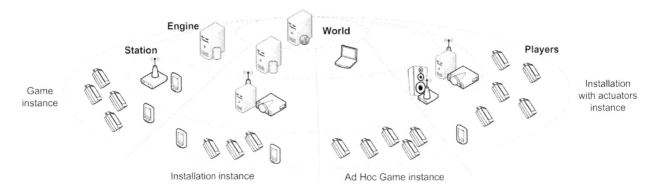

Figure 1: Overall multilayer architecture of FinN.

dicator (RSSI) and the Link Quality Indicator (LQI) are extracted to measure the power of the signal. These indicators are continuously forwarded to the Engine (unique in each game instance) that computes the position of the nodes and transports them back to all the Station nodes. Note that the communication cost of moving data between the Stations and Engine nodes is very low if not totally negligible. Finally the Station nodes attach the device location information to their Echo Protocol broarcast beacons:

```
neighbors = [11(9,3),81(7,2),5(7,3),43(10,3)]
```

This approach allows the implementation of a wide range of centralized localization algorithms (e.g., [3]).

Information Exchange: Given our choice of discovery and localization schemes, we now describe how game related information is exchanged between player devices and across FinN layers. The basic element of communication is the *Event*, which maintains a list of attribute-value pairs. E.g., in the "hot potato" game when a player is tagged the following event is exchanged:

```
initiator = 131 // device that performed the tag
responder = 81 // device that received the tag
type = tag // type of device
```

Notifications of events can be delivered in three different modes: *real time, multi-hop* or *delay-tolerant*. *Real-time mode* is available when both sender and receiver devices are within transmission range. In the "Tug-of-war" interactive installation, this mode is used to transmit continuous readings from the accelerometer, so that the backbone Station can perform gesture recognition. In this mode, failed transmissions are not repeated. *Multi-hop mode* is available when sender and receiver are not within communication range and the event needs to be delivered without any time constraint. The default routing protocol provided by Sun SPOT is AODV ([2]). Of course, different routing protocols can be used depending on the expected network conditions and desired performance.

Furthermore, due to various reasons (e.g., arbitrary movement of players, game strategies) communication with the "backbone" infrastructure (the Stations) may not be always possible. During this period, the evolution of the game should not be affected, as players interact with each others and create events. In this case, the *Delay-Tolerant mode* allows operation on both connected and disconnected modes. When communication with the infrastructure is available, events are transmitted, otherwise events are stored and sent when communication is established. Thus, players can enter

and leave from the range of the infrastructure, enjoying the games and keeping their statistics or history consistent.

User Interface: The provided *User Interface* takes advantage of the 8 Sun SPOTs LEDs, the 2 user buttons and the accelerometer found on the SPOT boards. Player devices provide a subsystem, which processes the samples of a 3-axis accelerometer and recognizes gestures that correspond to game-related actions. We currently aim at user-independent gesture recognition, with no training phase involved, supporting four basic gestures: i) clockwise, ii) counter-clockwise and iii) violent movement with direction to the right/left. If a more advanced gesture recognition system is required, this service can be transferred in upper architecture tiers in a similar way to the Localization module.

3. CONCLUSIONS - FUTURE WORK

In this paper, we have presented a framework, called Fun in Numbers, which provides a set of templates and services for building and operating pervasive games. Our implementation offers services for the completely distributed operation of the game and synchronization between players, enabling the instant setup of games at anyplace. Our experience so far with the implemented games strengthens our belief that the knowledge stemming from the WSN-related research can be applied in the gaming domain, in order to enhance the overall gaming experience and eventually produce exciting results. Our future work includes the refinement of our services and protocols, the implementation of additional games and their qualitative and guantitative evaluation conducting large scale game sessions. In addition, we consider to provide our framework as a libary and to port the games to other platforms.

4. REFERENCES

[1] S. Hay and R. Harle. Bluetooth tracking without discoverability. In *4th International Symposium of Location and Context Awareness (LoCA 2009)*, volume 5561 of *Lecture Notes in Computer Science*, pages 120–137. Springer, 2009.

[2] C. E. Perkins and E. M. Royer. Ad-hoc on demand distance vector (AODV) routing. In *2nd IEEE Annual Workshop on Mobile Computing Systems and Applications*, pages 90–100, 1999.

[3] A. Savvides, M. Srivastava, L. Girod, and D. Estrin. Localization in sensor networks. *Wireless sensor networks*, pages 327–349, 2004.

[4] Sun Spot website, http://www.sunspotworld.com/.

Brief Announcement: Lower Bounds on Communication for Sparse Cholesky Factorization of a Model Problem

Laura Grigori
INRIA Saclay - Ile de France
Université Paris-Sud 11
France
Laura.Grigori@inria.fr

Pierre-Yves David
INRIA Saclay - Ile de France
Pierre-yves.david@ens-lyon.org

James W. Demmel
Departments of Mathematics
and CS, University of
California Berkeley, USA
demmel@cs.berkeley.edu

Sylvain Peyronnet
LRI, Université Paris-Sud 11
France
syp@lri.fr

ABSTRACT

Previous work has shown that a lower bound on the number of words moved between large, slow memory and small, fast memory of size M by any conventional (non-Strassen like) direct linear algebra algorithm (matrix multiply, the LU, Cholesky, QR factorizations, ...) is $\Omega(\#flops/\sqrt{(M)})$. This holds for dense or sparse matrices. There are analogous lower bounds for the number of messages, and for parallel algorithms instead of sequential algorithms.

Our goal here is to find algorithms that attain these lower bounds on interesting classes of sparse matrices. We focus on matrices for which there is a lower bound on the number of flops of their Cholesky factorization. Our Cholesky lower bounds on communication hold for any possible ordering of the rows and columns of the matrix, and so are globally optimal in this sense. For matrices arising from discretization on two dimensional and three dimensional regular grids, we discuss sequential and parallel algorithms that are optimal in terms of communication. The algorithms turn out to require combining previously known sparse and dense Cholesky algorithms in simple ways.

Categories and Subject Descriptors: F.2.1 [Theory of Computation]: Analysis of Algorithms and Problem Complexity - Numerical Algorithms and Problems, Computations on matrices

General Terms: Algorithms

Keywords: communication bounds, sparse Cholesky

1. INTRODUCTION

Recent research has raised an increasing interest on identifying lower bounds on communication for operations in linear algebra and algorithms that attain them. This research started with results from [10, 11] that show that a lower bound on the volume of communication (bandwidth) for computing the product of two dense matrices is $\Omega(W/M^{1/2})$ and a lower bound on the number of messages transferred (latency) is $\Omega(W/M^{3/2})$, where W is the number of flops and M is the fast memory size in the case of a sequential algo-

rithm and the local memory size in the case of a parallel algorithm. Here communication refers to the data transferred between large, slow memory and fast, small memory for a sequential algorithm, and to the data transferred between processors for a parallel algorithm. It has been shown that the same bound applies to LU factorization [4], Cholesky factorization [2], and other operations in linear algebra and their sparse implementations in [3]. Some of the algorithms in the literature attain the bounds, as the block algorithm and Cannon algorithm for sequential and parallel matrix multiplication. For QR and LU factorizations, new optimal algorithms have been designed [4, 8] that show significant speedups in practice.

In this paper we derive bounds on communication for sparse Cholesky factorization $A = LL^T$. We focus our analysis on matrices whose graphs satisfy a property, from which a lower bound on the number of flops of the Cholesky factorization can be derived [12]. This includes matrices arising from the discretization of PDEs (in particular using a finite difference operator) on regular grids of dimension k^s. The graphs of these matrices have good separators, and in this case the Cholesky factors L are sparse and the Cholesky factorization can be performed efficiently. In contrast, the Cholesky factors of matrices whose graphs don't have good separators are almost dense, and so the Cholesky factorization costs almost as much as the dense case. Lipton et al. show that almost all graphs don't have good separators [12].

For two dimensional (2D) and three dimensional (3D) regular grids, we describe a sequential algorithm and we identify that the parallel algorithm implemented in PSPASES [9] (when using an optimal layout) attain the lower bounds on communication. Both algorithms use nested dissection to order the input matrix [6].

2. SPARSE CHOLESKY FACTORIZATION

In this section we derive lower bounds on communication for matrices whose graphs satisfy a property that we describe in the following. Let A be a symmetric matrix of size $n \times n$. Its undirected graph, denoted $G = (V, E)$, has a vertex $i \in V$ for each row and column of A, and an edge $(i, j) \in E$ for each nonzero symmetric off-diagonal element $A_{ij} = A_{ji}$. We consider in this paper a matrix whose graph has the following property for some l: every set of vertices

$W \subset V$ such that $n/3 \leq |W| \leq 2n/3$, is adjacent to at least l vertices in $V - W$. Here $|W|$ denotes the cardinality of W. Then Lemma 2 and Theorem 10 in [12] show that for any ordering of A, its Cholesky factor contains a dense lower triangular matrix of size $l \times l$. This property can be used to compute a lower bound on the number of flops performed in the Cholesky factorization, independent of any reordering of the input matrix. These results can be applied to matrices resulting from a finite difference operator on regular grids [12], that is matrices whose graphs are defined on a $k \times k \times \ldots \times k$ (s times) mesh of k^s points, where each point is connected to its nearest neighbours (points on the boundary have fewer neighbours). In this particular case, similar results are also derived in [5].

THEOREM 1. *Consider the Cholesky factorization LL^T of an $n \times n$ symmetric matrix A whose undirected graph $G = (V, E)$ has the following property for some l: every set of vertices $W \subset V$ with $n/3 \leq |W| \leq 2n/3$ is adjacent to at least l vertices in $V - W$. A lower bound on communication for computing the Cholesky factorization of A is*

$$\#words \geq \Omega\left(\frac{W}{\sqrt{M}}\right), \quad \#messages \geq \Omega\left(\frac{W}{M^{3/2}}\right)$$

For a sequential algorithm, $W = l^3$ and M is the fast memory size. For a parallel algorithm executed on P processors that is work-balanced, $W = \frac{l^3}{P}$. We assume that the matrix and the L factor are distributed evenly over all the processors and the local memory size used is estimated to be $M = \Theta(nnz(L)/P)$.

PROOF. Lemma 2 in [12] says that the graph of the Cholesky factor L contains a clique of at least l vertices. This means that L contains a dense lower triangular matrix L_s of size $l \times l$. Theorem 10 in [12] uses this result to derive a lower bound on the number of floating point operations of the Cholesky factorization of $l(l-1)(l-4)/6$.

The lower bounds on communication developed in [2, 3] provide a lower bound on communication for the computation of L_s, and hence a lower bound for the Cholesky factorization of the entire matrix A. This leads to the communication bounds in the theorem. $\square$

For a regular grid of dimension k^s, with $n = k^s$, $l = \Theta(n^{(s-1)/s})$. For 2D and 3D regular grids, the lower bounds derived from Theorem 1 are presented in Table 1 for the parallel case and Table 2 for the sequential case. We note that [3] presents also the lower bound for the 2D case. However our results apply to a larger class of graphs and in particular to regular grids of higher dimension. Nested dissection is an optimal ordering for the grid [6], and consists of partitioning the associated undirected graph of the sparse symmetric matrix using a divide-and-conquer paradigm. The nested dissection method is based on finding a small vertex separator, S, that partitions the graph into two disconnected subgraphs. The rows and columns associated with the vertices of the disconnected subgraphs are ordered first, followed by those corresponding to the vertices of the separator S. The permuted matrix PAP^T has the form

$$\begin{pmatrix} A_{11} & 0 & A_{13} \\ 0 & A_{22} & A_{23} \\ A_{13}^T & A_{23}^T & A_{33} \end{pmatrix}.$$

The partitioning can then be applied recursively on the subgraphs corresponding to the submatrices A_{11} and A_{22}. The

partitioning defines a binary tree structure, called the separator tree. Each node of this tree corresponds to a separator. The root of the tree corresponds to the separator from the first level partitioning.

In the following we briefly analyze sequential and parallel algorithms that attain the communication bounds. Detailed performance counts for these algorithms will be presented in an extended version of this paper. Our analysis considers that nested dissection uses $+$ separators. That is, in the case of 2D grids, a separator partitions a square grid into four square subgrids. In the case of 3D grids, a separator formed by three orthogonal planes partitions the grid into eight subgrids. We discuss multifrontal methods, that compute the Cholesky factorization by using the separator tree. We give a brief description here. Each node in the separator has associated a frontal matrix. This matrix is formed by the vertices of the separator and the vertices that correspond to columns modified by the vertices of the separator. The Cholesky factorization is performed during a bottom-up traversal of the separator tree. At each node of the tree, a number of steps equal to the size of the separator of Cholesky factorization is performed on the associated frontal matrix. Then, the update matrix is transmitted to the parent node. At the parent node, the update matrices are merged through extend-add operations to form a frontal matrix. And then the factorization continues on this new frontal matrix.

The parallel algorithm implemented in PSPASES is based on a multifrontal method and uses the separator tree to distribute the input matrix over the processors using a cyclic approach and a subtree to subcube mapping [7]. This algorithm maps nodes to processors during a top-down traversal of the separator tree. It starts by assigning all the P processors to the root. Then it assigns (recursively) $P/4$ processors to each of the four subtrees of the root. The frontal matrix is distributed among those processors using a 2D cyclic distribution. The communication complexity of the algorithm is analyzed in [9], and we display it in Table 1. With an appropriate layout as described in [9], the merge of the update matrices has a low communication cost. Hence the communication in the Cholesky factorization of the frontal matrices associated with nodes in the separator tree dominates the overall communication. PSPASES attains the lower bound

	PSPASES	PSPASES with optimal layout	Lower bound Thm. 1
2D grids			
# flops	$O\left(\frac{n^{3/2}}{P}\right)$	$O\left(\frac{n^{3/2}}{P}\right)$	$O\left(\frac{n^{3/2}}{P}\right)$
# words	$O\left(\frac{n}{\sqrt{P}}\right)$	$O\left(\frac{n}{\sqrt{P}}\log P\right)$	$\Omega\left(\frac{n}{\sqrt{P\log n}}\right)$
# messages	$O(\sqrt{n})$	$O\left(\sqrt{P}\log^3 P\right)$	$\Omega\left(\frac{\sqrt{P}}{(\log n)^{3/2}}\right)$
3D grids			
# flops	$O\left(\frac{n^2}{P}\right)$	$O\left(\frac{n^2}{P}\right)$	$O\left(\frac{n^2}{P}\right)$
# words	$O\left(\frac{n^{4/3}}{\sqrt{P}}\right)$	$O\left(\frac{n^{4/3}}{\sqrt{P}}\log P\right)$	$\Omega\left(\frac{n^{4/3}}{\sqrt{P}}\right)$
# messages	$O(n^{2/3})$	$O\left(\sqrt{P}\log^3 P\right)$	$\Omega\left(\sqrt{P}\right)$

Table 1: Performance of PSPASES, PSPASES with optimal layout and lower bounds on communication when factoring an $n \times n$ matrix resulting from 2D and 3D regular grids. Some lower order terms are omitted. The analysis assumes the local memory of each processor is $M = O(n\log n/P)$ in the 2D case and $M = O(n^{4/3}/P)$ in the 3D case.

on bandwidth, but not on latency, as displayed in Table 1.

This is due to the fact that the analysis of PSPASES uses a cyclic distribution, and this involves the exchange of a message for each step of Cholesky factorization. A block cyclic distribution will decrease the latency but will still not allow to attain the lower bound. To attain the lower bound on latency an optimal layout needs to be used. We use the same approach as in [4] in which the matrix is distributed in a two dimensional block cyclic layout using square blocks of size $b \times b$ and letting b be close to its maximal value. In other words, we consider that the factorization of each frontal matrix is performed using a ScaLAPACK-like algorithm with an optimal layout. This leads to performance results presented in Table 1, which show that with an optimal layout, PSPASES attains the latency and bandwidth lower bounds, modulo polylog factors. The number of floating point operations is optimal, modulo constant factors.

We discuss now an optimal algorithm for sequentially computing the Cholesky factorization of matrices arising from 2D and 3D regular grids. The analysis is performed in a big O sense. The algorithm considers that the input matrix has been ordered using nested dissection based on + separators and uses a multifrontal Cholesky factorization. The algorithm computes the factorization during a postorder traversal of the separator tree. At each node of the tree, the factorization consists of two main steps. The update matrices of its child nodes are read from slow memory and merged through an extend-add operation to form the frontal matrix of this node. The postorder traversal ensures that the update matrices can be stored on a stack. Then a number of steps of Cholesky factorization are performed on this frontal matrix. The update matrix is then stored on slow memory, such that the parent node can use it. For the partial

Problem		Optimal Cholesky	Lower bound
2D grids	# flops	$O\left(n^{3/2}\right)$	$O\left(n^{3/2}\right)$
	# words	$O\left(\frac{n^{3/2}}{\sqrt{M}} + n\log n\right)$	$\Omega\left(\frac{n^{3/2}}{\sqrt{M}}\right)$
	# messages	$O\left(\frac{n^{3/2}}{M^{3/2}} + \frac{n\log n}{M}\right)$	$\Omega\left(\frac{n^{3/2}}{M^{3/2}}\right)$
3D grids	# flops	$O\left(n^2\right)$	$O\left(n^2\right)$
	# words	$O\left(\frac{n^2}{\sqrt{M}} + n^{4/3}\right)$	$\Omega\left(\frac{n^2}{\sqrt{M}}\right)$
	# messages	$O\left(\frac{n^2}{M^{3/2}} + \frac{n^{4/3}}{M}\right)$	$\Omega\left(\frac{n^2}{M^{3/2}}\right)$

Table 2: Performance of optimal sequential multifrontal Cholesky factorization when factoring an $n \times n$ matrix resulting from 2D and 3D regular grids. The lower bounds on communication are also presented, and M is the fast memory size. The analysis assumes $M = O(\sqrt{n})$ in the 2D case and $M = O(n^{2/3})$ in the 3D case.

Cholesky factorization of each frontal matrix, the algorithm uses a recursive Cholesky factorization algorithm. This algorithm presented in [1] has been shown to be optimal through multiple levels of memory hierarchy with an appropriate recursive block storage [2], where each block fits in the fast memory of size M. The communication necessary to copy a dense matrix of size $n \times n$ stored in column major or row major order into a block format is asymptotically equal to the communication necessary to perform the Cholesky factorization of this matrix given $M = O(n)$ [2]. We assume this or a smaller bound in our analysis, depending on the size of the frontal matrix. The reads and writes between different levels of memory occur at two different phases of the algorithm, when the partial Cholesky factorization of a frontal matrix is computed, and when the update matrices

are merged to form a frontal matrix. The upper bounds on communication of this optimal Cholesky algorithm, presented in Table 2, attain the lower bounds of Theorem 1.

3. CONCLUSIONS

In this paper we have discussed bounds on communication for sparse Cholesky factorization of a certain class of matrices, that includes matrices resulting from regular grids. The approach used here to derive optimal algorithms can be used for other classes of graphs with good separators as well. Consider the case when the computation and communication to factor the submatrix formed by the vertices of the first separator dominates the overall communication and computation. Then an optimal algorithm can be derived by using an optimal dense algorithm to factor the submatrix formed by the vertices of the separator.

We do not discuss other approaches as right-looking or left-looking. It is possible that a right looking factorization with an appropriate optimal layout that takes into account the sparsity of the input matrix might be optimal. This remains as future work.

4. ACKNOWLEDGMENTS

The work of L. Grigori is supported in part by French National Research Agency (ANR) through COSINUS program (project PETAL no ANR-08-COSI-009). The research of J. W. Demmel is supported by Microsoft (Award #024263) and Intel (Award #024894) funding and by matching funding by U.C. Discovery (Award #DIG07-10227).

5. REFERENCES

[1] N. Ahmed and K. Pingali. Automatic generation of block-recursive codes. In Springer-Verlag, editor, *Euro-Par*, 2000, pages 368–378, 2000.

[2] G. Ballard, J. Demmel, O. Holtz, and O. Schwartz. Communication-optimal parallel and sequential Cholesky decomposition. *ACM SPAA*, 2009.

[3] G. Ballard, J. Demmel, O. Holtz, and O. Schwartz. Minimizing communication in linear algebra. Technical Report UCB/EECS-2009-62, UC Berkeley, 2009.

[4] J. Demmel, L. Grigori, M. Hoemmen, and J. Langou. Communication-optimal parallel and sequential QR and LU factorizations. Technical Report UCB/EECS-2008-89, UC Berkeley, 2008. LAPACK Working Note 204.

[5] S. C. Eisenstat, M. H. Schultz, and A. H. Sherman. Applications of an element model for Gaussian elimination. In J. Bunch and D. Rose, editors, *Sparse Matrix Computations*, pages 85–96. Academic Press, New York, 1976.

[6] A. George. Nested dissection of a regular finite element mesh. *SIAM Journal on Numerical Analysis*, 10:345–363, 1973.

[7] A. George, J. W.-H. Liu, and E. G. Ng. Communication results for parallel sparse Cholesky factorization on a hypercube. *Parallel Computing*, 10(3):287–298, 1989.

[8] L. Grigori, J. W. Demmel, and H. Xiang. Communication avoiding Gaussian elimination. *Proceedings of the ACM/IEEE SC08 Conference*, 2008.

[9] A. Gupta, G. Karypis, and V. Kumar. Highly scalable parallel algorithms for sparse matrix factorization. *IEEE Transactions on Parallel and Distributed Systems*, 8(5), 1995.

[10] J.-W. Hong and H. T. Kung. I/O complexity: The Red-Blue Pebble Game. In *STOC '81: Proceedings of the Thirteenth Annual ACM Symposium on Theory of Computing*, pages 326–333, New York, NY, USA, 1981. ACM.

[11] D. Irony, S. Toledo, and A. Tiskin. Communication lower bounds for distributed-memory matrix multiplication. *Journal of Parallel and Distribed Computing*, 64(9):1017–1026, 2004.

[12] R. J. Lipton, D. J. Rose, and R. E. Tarjan. Generalized nested dissection. *SIAM Journal on Numerical Analysis*, 16:346–358, 1979.

Data-Aware Scheduling of Legacy Kernels on Heterogeneous Platforms with Distributed Memory

Michela Becchi, Surendra Byna, Srihari Cadambi and Srimat Chakradhar
NEC Laboratories America, Inc.
4 Independence Way, Princeton NJ 08540
{mbecchi, sbyna, cadambi, chak}@nec-labs.com

ABSTRACT

In this paper, we describe a runtime to automatically enhance the performance of applications running on heterogeneous platforms consisting of a multi-core (CPU) and a throughput-oriented many-core (GPU). The CPU and GPU are connected by a non-coherent interconnect such as PCI-E, and as such do not have shared memory. Heterogeneous platforms available today such as [9] are of this type. Our goal is to enable the programmer to seamlessly use such a system without rewriting the application and with minimal knowledge of the underlying architectural details. Assuming that applications perform function calls to computational kernels with available CPU and GPU implementations, our runtime achieves this goal by automatically scheduling the kernels and managing data placement. In particular, it intercepts function calls to well-known computational kernels and schedules them on CPU or GPU based on their argument size and location. To improve performance, it defers all data transfers between the CPU and the GPU until necessary. By managing data placement transparently to the programmer, it provides a unified memory view despite the underlying separate memory sub-systems.

We experimentally evaluate our runtime on a heterogeneous platform consisting of a 2.5GHz quad-core Xeon CPU and an NVIDIA C870 GPU. Given array sorting, parallel reduction, dense and sparse matrix operations and ranking as computational kernels, we use our runtime to automatically retarget SSI [25], K-means [32] and two synthetic applications to the above platform with no code changes. We find that, in most cases, performance improves if the computation is moved to the data, and not vice-versa. For instance, even if a particular instance of a kernel is slower on the GPU than on the CPU, the overall application may be faster if the kernel is scheduled on the GPU anyway, especially if the kernel data is already located on the GPU memory due to prior decisions. Our results show that data-aware CPU/GPU scheduling improves performance by up to 25% over the best data-agnostic scheduling on the same platform.

Categories and Subject Descriptors

D.3.4 [**Programming Languages**]: Processors – *run-time environments*.

General Terms

Performance, Design, Experimentation.

Keywords

Heterogeneous platforms, multi-core processors, accelerators, distributed memory, runtime.

1. INTRODUCTION

Heterogeneous platforms consist of one or more multi-core general-purpose CPUs and one or more throughput-oriented many-core processors (for example, GPUs). Driven by many emerging data-parallel applications and by the need for higher performance, server vendors are beginning to rapidly commercialize these platforms [9], a trend that is expected to continue.

The most straightforward (and currently available) configuration that allows fast time-to-market is to have the many-core processor on an add-on card that is connected to the system via a non-coherent interconnect such as PCI Express. This has two implications. First, the CPU processing and its memory sub-system is completely separated from the many-core processor (GPU) and its memory sub-system, *i.e.*, the two memory sub-systems are not coherent and there is no shared memory. This makes programming difficult since the programmer has to manage the data that is manipulated by the CPU as well as the GPU. Second, with current PCI-E bandwidths, large data transfers between the two processing sub-systems can at times overwhelm any speedup achieved by the many-core when the processing alone is taken into consideration.

Such "loosely-coupled" distributed memory heterogeneous systems do not present the programmer with a unified view of the memory and compute elements. Today, applications that require acceleration from heterogeneous systems must be carefully profiled to discover data-parallel portions ("kernels") that could benefit from a many-core GPU. Once GPU custom implementations for those kernels are available, the application developer must explicitly schedule not only the kernel computations but also the required data transfers.

Ideally, a heterogeneous system should enable any legacy code written for homogeneous systems to run faster, in a way that is transparent to the programmer. GPU libraries for commonly available kernels (such as linear algebra for example) are necessary in order to enable this, but are not enough to allow complete transparency. A runtime that schedules computations as well as data transfers in order to maximize performance is required.

In this paper, we propose such a runtime. As a significant difference from past work [3], our runtime is cognizant of data transfer overheads and dynamically schedules operations taking into account not only the predicted processing performance, but also data transfers. For instance, suppose an application has three candidate kernels with both CPU and GPU implementations. Assume that during a certain execution path, the first kernel is estimated to be much faster, but the second and third much slower on the GPU (based, say on the sizes of their parameters). Given this information, a data-agnostic scheduler is likely to run the first kernel on the GPU, transfer data back and run the remaining two kernels on the CPU. However if the first kernel produces a large amount of data that is consumed by the second kernel, a better schedule may be to run the second kernel also on the GPU and avoid the intermediate data transfer. With legacy code, the system is unaware what will follow the first kernel. After running the first kernel on the GPU, our runtime postpones data transfers back to the CPU until necessary. This way, when the second kernel is encountered, it can make a more informed decision taking into account the data transfer overhead, as well as the estimated performance. Although the GPU is slower in processing the second kernel compared to the CPU, running the kernel on the GPU could still result in an overall speedup. Our runtime analyzes these situations using simple, history-based models to predict processing as well as data transfer time, and uses these to guide the scheduling policy. It intercepts calls to candidate kernels, examines their arguments, and uses historical information and prior decisions to devise a schedule on-the-fly. Once a decision is reached for a kernel, the runtime invokes its CPU or GPU implementation transparently to the user.

One basic objective of our runtime is to target legacy code. In other words, we do not require source code modifications, but assume that the application performs function calls to well known kernels for which implementations targeting both the CPU and GPU are available. Our runtime's invocation happens by function call interception. This mechanism alone would lead to data coherence problems when accesses performed outside function calls target data residing on the GPU. In [7], we discuss operating system modifications to avoid this problem. In particular, the proposed design adds synchronization points within the page fault handler; at each synchronization point our runtime's API is invoked. As an alternative, it is possible to add synchronization points in the application via minimal source-level annotation (we discuss this in Section 4). Note that our goal is to propose a runtime, therefore we do not force the user to code a new application (or recode an existing one) according to specific primitives or frameworks. Therefore, our work fundamentally differs from previous efforts that propose programming models [1][5].

In summary, our contribution could be viewed as a runtime for a heterogeneous platform that provides a unified memory and compute view to the programmer despite the underlying platform being composed of two separate CPU and GPU, each one having its own memory sub-system. Such a view is enabled by automatically scheduling kernels on the compute units while simultaneously optimizing data placement on the two memories. The goal of the runtime is to maximize the overall application performance without requiring application rewriting. In [7] we discuss how the design can be generalized to the case where multiple GPUs or accelerators are connected to the CPU, and to that where CPU and GPU share (pinned) memory regions residing on the CPU.

The rest of the document is organized as follows. In Section 2, we overview closely related work. In Section 3, we present a motivational example that illustrates the benefits of data-aware scheduling. In Section 4, we detail the design, implementation and operation of our proposed runtime. In Section 5, we present an experimental evaluation on some real and synthetic applications. We conclude in Section 6.

2. RELATED WORK

Various programming languages and libraries have been introduced by multi-core CPU and many-core GPU vendors to utilize their computing power. Nvidia's CUDA [8], AMD's Brook+ [10], Intel's TBB [11] and Ct [12] provide programming interfaces to better utilize the underlying hardware. These interfaces, while making programming easier, target specific GPUs or CPUs and not a heterogeneous platform containing both. Similarly, solutions such as Microsoft Accelerator [13], Rapidmind [14], and Google's Peakstream [15] only target GPUs. Programming models targeting heterogeneous and distributed memory systems are presented in [1] and [5]. However, programming models and languages can be used either to write new applications, or to rewrite existing ones. In contrast, this proposal aims to enable legacy applications on heterogeneous platforms without requiring source code modifications.

PGI Accelerator [16], CAPS HMPP workbench [17], and HPC Project's Par4All [18] developed compilers to generate CUDA code for data parallel portions, especially loops. These tools use compiler level information to decide whether to run a code segment on CPUs or GPUs, but do not take the cost of data transfers into account. Compiler solutions also cannot make scheduling decisions that are best made at runtime. Our runtime uses parameters such as data size and data locality and decides when to schedule computations as well as data transfers.

Multicore-CUDA (MCUDA) [19] and Ocelot [20] translate CUDA code to run on multi-core processors. Liao et al [21] propose a similar translation of Brook-like code into multithreaded CPU code. The goal of these approaches is to provide a way to develop code for both CPUs and GPUs, but scheduling them on the hardware is left to the programmers.

OpenCL [22] attempts to provide a common programming interface for multi-core and many-core platforms. However, the programmer must decide the mapping of the kernels to the processing elements. IBM's OpenMP for Cell [23] and Intel's Merge framework [24] are also capable of running code on both CPUs and GPUs, but the mapping is not automatic (and involves code modifications). Harmony [3] proposes a runtime to schedule kernels either on CPU or on GPU based on estimated kernel performance using an API. Qilin [4] proposes an API with automatic and adaptive mapping support, which reduces the decision burden on programmers. However, Qilin's mapping is based on a curve fitting model to split computation on CPU and GPU. Neither Harmony nor Qilin consider the data transfer overhead, especially for legacy code. StarPU's unified runtime system [34][35] proposes implementing CPU-GPU memory coherence using the MSI protocol. However, it requires programmers to use a new API proposed by the system.

Data-aware scheduling strategies exist in cluster and distributed computing [28][29][30]. However, these techniques are used in scheduling jobs to fit data in disks and to reduce data transfers among cluster and grid computing nodes. We focus on a node within a cluster.

Table 1: Processing and data transfer times for SSI classification. For each input data size, the schedule resulting in the best performance is highlighted.

Number of simultaneous queries (Q)	Kernel Location (Schedule)		Kernel Processing Time			Data Transfer Time	Overall Speed
	sgemm	*topk_rank*	*sgemm*	*topk_rank*	Total		
32	CPU	CPU	1.25s	0.06s	1.31s	-	41.12 ms/query
	GPU	CPU	0.08s	0.06s	0.14s	0.11s	7.91 ms/query
	GPU	GPU	0.08s	0.31s	0.39s	0.06 ms	12.14 ms/query
64	CPU	CPU	2.07s	0.12s	2.19s	-	34.20 ms/query
	GPU	CPU	0.15s	0.12s	0.27s	0.23s	7.85 ms/query
	GPU	GPU	0.15s	0.33s	0.48s	0.09 ms	7.51 ms/query
96	CPU	CPU	2.88s	0.18s	3.06s	-	31.84 ms/query
	GPU	CPU	0.23s	0.18s	0.41s	0.34s	7.83 ms/query
	GPU	GPU	0.23s	0.36s	0.59s	0.12 ms	6.13 ms/query

Finally, CUBA [6] proposes an architectural model where co-processors are encapsulated as function calls, as well as mechanisms to allow data physically residing on accelerator memory to be cached on CPU. CUBA assumes that the CPU has access to the co-processor memory mapped registers and to the co-processor local memory (which is not the case of the architecture we are considering). Moreover, the CUBA proposal discusses hardware changes (specifically, changes to the memory controller) whereas we operate at the runtime level.

3. MOTIVATIONAL EXAMPLE

In this section, we motivate the need for data-aware scheduling on heterogeneous platforms with a real application. The application we use is Supervised Semantic Indexing (SSI) classification [25].

SSI is an algorithm used to semantically search large document databases. It ranks the documents based on their semantic similarity to text-based queries. Each document and query is represented by a vector, with each vector element corresponding to a word. Since documents and queries only contain a small fraction of possible words, each vector is sparse and has as many elements as the dictionary's size. Each vector element is the product of Term Frequency (TF) and Inverse Document Frequency (IDF) of the word that it corresponds to. TF is the number of times a word occurs in the document and IDF is the reciprocal of the number of documents that contain the word (thus IDF reduces the importance of commonly occurring words). Before classification can take place, the system must be trained. During this training process, a weight matrix is generated. By multiplying a query or document vector with the weight matrix, we obtain a smaller dense vector which contains relevant information for document-query classification. Each dense document and query vector is C elements long, where C is the number of concepts [25]. The classification process multiplies the query vector with all document vectors and identifies documents whose vectors produced the top k results.

The SSI classification process has two compute-intensive kernels which are good candidates for the many-core GPU. The first *(sgemm)* is the multiplication of the query vectors with all document vectors, essentially a dense matrix-matrix multiplication. With D documents in the database and Q simultaneous queries, the document matrix size is DxC and the query matrix size is QxC. The second kernel *(topk_rank)* must

select, for each query vector, the top k best classification documents, that is, it selects the top k elements from the products of query vectors with document vectors. With millions of documents to search for each query, these two kernels take up 99% of the SSI execution time.

We motivate data-aware scheduling with three example runs of SSI classification. Our data set contains 1.6M documents and 128 conceptual categories. For each run, we vary the number of simultaneous queries performed (we consider 32, 64 and 96 queries). Each query requires the identification of 64 top classification documents from the document database. The document database contains documents selected from the Wikipedia [25]. For matrix multiplication, we use the Intel Math Kernel Library [26] on the CPU and the CUBLAS Library implementation of the *sgemm* function [27] on the GPU.

Table 1 shows the processing and data transfer times for three possible schedules of the two kernels used in SSI classification, as well as the overall throughput. The first schedule assumes both kernels are run on the CPU with no data transfer required. In the second schedule, the kernels are profiled and run on the computational element (either CPU or GPU) that has the smaller kernel processing time. In the third schedule, all kernels are run on GPU. However, data transfers are not performed before and after every kernel invocation, but only when required. In other words, the *topk_rank* kernel will be able to use the results of the previous call to *sgemm* without transferring them from the CPU.

As can be observed, dense matrix multiplication is much faster on GPU (by 12-15X), whereas *topk_rank* is slower on the GPU. However, as the number of queries increases, the speed of *topk_rank* on the GPU improves.

The poor performance of *sgemm* on the CPU affects the first schedule making it the worst for all the considered data sets. When the number of queries is small (32), the second schedule is preferable. As the number of queries increases, the third schedule tends to provide best performance. In particular, the throughputs achieved with the second and third schedules are comparable when 64 queries are processed in parallel. However, when the data set size increases to 96 queries, then the third schedule performs substantially better (the throughput achieved increases by 20%).

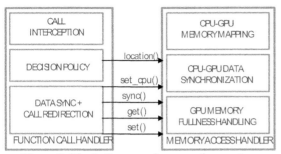

Figure 1: Block diagram of our runtime system.

Interestingly, what makes the third schedule preferable for large input sets is not the processing time, but the savings in terms of data transfer time. In fact, the *sgemm* call produces a matrix of size 1.6MxQ floats, which normally is transferred back to the CPU. If the runtime recognizes this and schedules the second kernel on the GPU even though the GPU is slower, the performance shown in the table is achieved. Note that the GPU-GPU schedule would never be preferable if data transfers were performed before and after each kernel invocation, such as would be the case if the runtime were handling legacy code, and was data-agnostic.

The key take-away is the following. First, the best schedule depends on data set size, determined at runtime for legacy kernels. Second, execution time alone is insufficient to achieve an optimal schedule. In particular, once a kernel executes on the GPU, the runtime should defer transferring back the data to the CPU until access to that data is performed. When subsequent kernels are invoked, the runtime should determine if it is worthwhile transferring back the data based on its predicted data transfer overhead, as well as the processing times of the kernel to run.

4. THE PROPOSED RUNTIME

In this section, we describe our runtime system design.

4.1 Overview of our Runtime

The primary goal of the runtime is to dynamically schedule computational kernels onto heterogeneous computing resources, namely the CPU and the GPU, in order to minimize the execution time of the overall application. To this end, the runtime aims to minimize kernel execution time as well as data transfer overheads. In effect, it hides the compute- and memory-heterogeneity from the programmer.

As mentioned above, the runtime operates at the granularity of a function call. The application runs by default on the CPU and may perform calls to well known kernels for which CPU or GPU implementations are provided. When one of these kernels is invoked, the runtime must determine the implementation to instantiate. This decision depends on two factors: kernel execution time and data transfer time. In turn, these factors depend on the size of the function call parameters and the location of the corresponding data. GPU kernel implementations assume that their parameters reside on the GPU memory: it is the responsibility of the runtime to hide this fact to the calling application, and to maintain a mapping between data structures residing on CPU and on GPU memories. As we will see, data is not transferred to the CPU memory at the end of each GPU kernel invocation, but only when required.

Note that each computational kernel – whether it targets the CPU or GPU – is essentially a "black box" to the runtime: *the only visible data transfers which can be optimized by the runtime pertain to the function arguments, and not to the data structures within the kernel itself.* In other words, the runtime aims at minimizing CPU-GPU data transfers; optimizing data transfers at different level of the GPU memory hierarchy is outside the scope of this work.

Figure 1 depicts our proposed runtime. It consists of two modules: *function call handler* and *memory access handler*. The function call handler intercepts kernel calls, determines which kernel implementations (CPU or GPU) to instantiate, and invokes them. The memory access handler maintains a mapping between CPU and GPU data structures, and handles data transfers and synchronizations. The services offered by the memory access handler are available to the function call handler through an API.

We now give more details on the two modules.

4.2 Function Call Handler

The function call handler intercepts predefined kernel calls and invokes proper library implementations depending on the call parameters and the data location. For each kernel `fn` having (read-only) input parameters `in_pars` and (write-only) output parameters `out_pars`, the module contains a function whose structure is exemplified in the pseudo-code below (`void` is used for illustration only).

The `mam` object (at lines 4, 7, 9, 11 and 13) represents the interface offered by the memory access module, that we will describe in more detail in the next section.

```
(1)    void fn(in_pars, *out_pars){
(2)      /* determine the best target for fn */
(3)      if(eval_loc(&fn,in_pars,out_pars)==CPU){
(4)        for (p in in_pars) mam->sync(p);
(5)        /* schedule on CPU */
(6)        cpu_fn(in_pars,out_pars);
(7)        for (p in out_pars) mam->set_cpu(p);
(8)      }else{
(9)        in_pars_d = out_pars_d = Ø;
(10)       for (p in in_pars)
(11)         in_pars_d ∪= mam->get(p,true);
(12)       for (p in out_pars)
(13)         out_pars_d ∪= mam->get(p,false);
(14)       /* schedule on GPU */
(15)       gpu_fn(in_pars_d, &out_pars_d);
(16)       for (p in out_pars) mam->set(p);
(17)     }
(18)   }
```

The `cpu_fn` and `gpu_fn` routines (at line 6 and 15, respectively) represent the CPU and GPU implementation of the intercepted kernel. Under GNU/Linux based operating systems, the function call handler can be dynamically linked to the application through the `LD_PRELOAD` directive. Pointers to `cpu_fn` and `gpu_fn` are obtained using the combination of `dlopen`/`dlsym` directives (the pointer to `cpu_fn` can also be obtained simply using `dlsym` and setting the handle to `RTLD_NEXT`).

The `eval_loc` routine (line 3) is also defined within the function call handler, and determines the best target for the intercepted function call. This decision is made by estimating the data transfer time of the input parameters and the kernel execution time on both CPU and GPU. We reiterate that the runtime transfers (input) data only when they do not reside on the memory of the executing processor. `eval_loc` queries the memory access module for the location of each input parameter, and estimates the data transfer time based on the parameter size. In case of GPU execution, `eval_loc` considers the size and the location of the output parameters to determine whether the GPU has enough free memory to allocate them. In order to estimate the kernel execution time on both CPU and GPU, `eval_loc` uses profiling information. In particular, for all considered kernels, we measured the CPU and GPU execution time for different input parameters and we obtained the input size/execution time characteristic. At runtime, the `eval_loc` routine uses the actual input parameters to locate the operation point.

If the `eval_loc` routine establishes that the execution must happen on the CPU (lines 3-7), then the `cpu_fn` kernel must be invoked. Before its invocation, all input parameters must be synchronized (line 4). As we will see, `mam->sync` will have no effect if the CPU has an up-to-date copy of the data. After kernel execution, the output parameters are marked as residing on the CPU (line 7). This operation does not imply any data transfer.

If the kernel execution must take place on the GPU (lines 9-16), then `gpu_fn` is invoked (line 15). However, this kernel implementation operates on GPU memory. Therefore, a local copy of all input and output parameters (`in_pars_d` and `out_pars_d`) must be created (lines 9-13). For each parameter, the `mam->get` function returns the pointer to that copy (and, if necessary, allocates the corresponding memory on GPU). The last parameter of the `mam->get` call specifies whether the GPU must have an up-to-date copy of the data, which is necessary only for the input parameters. After kernel execution, the output parameters are marked as residing on the GPU (line 16). Again, this operation does not imply any data transfer.

4.3 Memory Access Handler

The goal of the memory access handler module is to orchestrate data transfers and synchronizations between CPU and GPU memory. In order to do so, it maintains a mapping between CPU and GPU memory regions. In particular, GPU global memory is seen as a set of *non overlapping data blocks,* each of them corresponding to a CPU data block. The mapping is stored in the *data block list*, a linked list of `data_block_t` structures, as represented below.

```
typedef enum {SYNCED,ON_CPU,ON_GPU} sync_t;

typedef struct {
    void *cpu_addr;
    void *gpu_addr;
    size_t size;
    sync_t sync;
    time_t timestamp;
}data_block_t;
```

Each data block has a CPU address `cpu_addr`, a GPU address `gpu_addr`, a `size` expressed in bytes, a synchronization status (`sync`) and a `timestamp` indicating the last access to the block. The synchronization status indicates whether the content of CPU and GPU blocks is synchronized (SYNCED) or whether the up-to-date copy of the data resides in CPU memory/GPU memory (ON_CPU/ON_GPU). Note that, since the application runs on the CPU and the runtime operates at the granularity of the function call, the memory access module

allocates GPU memory (and updates the data block list) only when the runtime invokes the GPU implementation of an intercepted function.

The memory access handler offers primitives that are invoked by the runtime. The bulk of the CPU-GPU memory mapping's handling is performed within the `get` primitive, which is invoked by the runtime on all the parameters of a GPU kernel call.

```
void *get(void *cpu_addr, size_t size, bool update) throw Exception
```

Given a CPU memory block, `get` returns the pointer to the corresponding GPU memory block, and throws an exception if the block does not exist and cannot be allocated or transferred. If the parameter `update` is set to `true`, then the content of the GPU memory block must be up-to-date. This is typically valid when `get` is invoked on an input parameter of a function call, but is not required when this routine is called on an output parameter. For NVIDIA's GPUs, `get` uses cudaMalloc and cudaMemcopy [8] to perform memory allocations and data transfers.

When `get` is invoked, one of the following situations can occur (Figure 2). First, the required data block does not reside in GPU memory. In this case, a GPU memory allocation is performed, and a new entry is added to the data block list. The memory allocation is followed by a data transfer (from CPU to GPU) only if

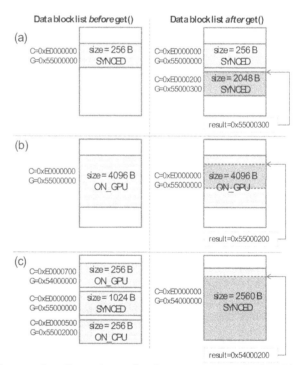

Figure 2: Examples of the outcome of invoking `get(0xE0000200, 2048B, true)` in different situations: (a) the requested data block is not yet allocated; (b) the requested data block is already present in GPU memory and its content is up-to-date; (c) the requested data block overlaps with several data blocks previously allocated. In all cases, we show the content of the data block list before (left hand side) and after (right hand side) the get's invocation, as well as the result of the operation (C=`cpu_addr`, G=`gpu_addr`) and the returned data block (highlighted in dark grey).

the `update` parameter of the `get` call is set to true. Second, the required data block already resides in GPU memory (possibly as part of a larger block). In this case, no memory allocation is required, and the content of the data block list is used to return the proper GPU address. A data transfer (from CPU to GPU) is performed only if the `update` parameter of the `get` call is set to true and the `sync` attribute of the block is equal to `ON_CPU`. In fact, no data transfer is needed if the GPU has already an up-to-date copy of the data. Finally, the requested data block – say B_{REQ} - spans multiple existing blocks B_i and possibly extends beyond them. In this case, it is necessary to allocate a new data block B_{NEW} which covers B_{REQ} and all the B_i. Each B_i can then be de-allocated and removed from the data block list. To understand why, consider that GPU kernels are a black box to the runtime, and that their parameters must point to contiguous memory regions. Again, the data transfer of block B_{NEW} from CPU to GPU is required only if the `update` parameter of the `get` call is set to true. However, if some B_i have attribute `sync` equal to `ON_GPU`, the portion of B_{NEW} overlapping them must be restored from GPU memory before their de-allocation. In Figure 2 (c) the following sequence of operations is assumed: first, block (`cpu_addr=0xE0000700, size=256`) is copied from GPU to CPU; second, all three blocks on the left hand side are de-allocated and removed from the data block list; finally, block (`cpu_addr=0xE0000000, size=2560`) is allocated and copied from CPU to GPU.

GPU kernel execution only affects GPU memory. The runtime does not enforce any GPU to CPU memory transfer after the invocation of a GPU kernel. Data consistency is ensured by invoking `set` on the output parameters of the GPU kernel call.

```
void set(void *cpu_addr) throw Exception
```

Given a CPU address, this routine sets the `sync` attribute of the corresponding data block to `ON_GPU`. An exception is thrown if such block cannot be found in the data block list.

When a kernel is invoked on CPU, the runtime must ensure that the CPU memory has an up-to-date copy of all input parameters. This is done with `sync`:

```
void sync(void *cpu_addr, size_t size) throw Exception
```

This function checks whether the data block list has one or more blocks B_i containing addresses in the range [`cpu_addr`, `cpu_addr+size`] and having attribute `sync` equal to `ON_GPU`. In this case, blocks B_i are copied to the CPU (and their attribute `sync` is set to `SYNCED`). Note that no action is required if the given address range is not mapped to GPU memory. An error during data transfer will cause an exception to be thrown.

After execution of a CPU kernel call, output parameters must be marked as residing on the CPU memory. This is accomplished by calling the `set_cpu` function.

```
void set_cpu(void *cpu_addr, size_t size)
```

This function sets the `sync` attribute of data blocks containing the given address range to `ON_CPU`. Again, no action is required if the data block list contains no such blocks.

As mentioned earlier, the `eval_loc` primitive in the function call handling module must obtain from the memory access module information about the location of the input parameters. This is achieved through the `location` function.

```
sync_t location(void *cpu_addr,size_t size)
```

`location` returns `ON_GPU` if the given address range belongs to a block B in the data block list, and the attribute `sync` of B is not equal to `ON_CPU`. In all other cases, `ON_CPU` is returned. Note that the goal of this function is to report whether invoking the `get` operation on the given address range would cause any GPU memory allocation and/or data transfer. This holds whenever `location` returns `ON_CPU`.

Finally, the memory access module provides a `free` primitive.

```
void free (void *cpu_addr, size_t size) throw Exception
```

`free` eliminates from the data block list all entries containing addresses from the given address range, and frees the corresponding GPU memory. This function is invoked in two circumstances: when the application de-allocates data, and when GPU memory runs full. In the latter case, the runtime uses the `timestamp` field in the `data_block_t` structure to determine the least recently used blocks. "Dirty" blocks are copied back to CPU before GPU de-allocation.

When running legacy applications, accesses performed *outside intercepted function calls* to address ranges mapped on GPU can originate data inconsistency problems. In the experiments presented in this work, we performed source code inspection and determined all accesses to variables which could potentially be modified by the intercepted function calls. We then modified the application by adding a call to `sync` before every memory read, and to `set_cpu` after every memory write to these variables. In [7] we describe operating system modifications to avoid this manual operation. The idea is to mark pages mapped to GPU as invalid, and to modify the page fault handler so that it will interact with our runtime and automatically call the proper function whenever a page fault is detected. In particular, handling will be performed within the runtime if the page fault involves a page mapped to GPU, whereas the page fault handler will resume its normal operation otherwise.

4.4 Additional Considerations
The runtime can be extended to support multiple GPUs or other devices connected to the CPU through the PCI-bus and having a local address space (e.g. FPGA-based accelerators). The extensions, which primarily involve the memory access module, depend on whether the design allows the same data to reside at the same time on multiple devices. The interested reader can find more discussion on this aspect in [7].

5. EXPERIMENTAL EVALUATION
In this section, we present some experimental results.

5.1 Methodology
We run our experiments on a heterogeneous workstation consisting of an Intel Xeon quad-core CPU and an NVIDIA Tesla C870 GPU. Table 2 shows the details of the architecture. As workloads, we used two real applications – K-means and SSI classification – as well as two synthetic applications consisting of various combinations of kernels, as summarized in Table 3.

The first application consists of two kernels, *Sort* (*quick sort* algorithm) and *Reduce*. *Sort* is implemented on the CPU using Intel TBB while *Reduce* is implemented using pthreads (in both cases, four threads are used). Both are implemented on the GPU

Table 2: Experimental setup.

Table 2: Experimental setup.

	CPU	GPU
Model	Intel Xeon E5420	Tesla C870
Cores	4	128
Frequency	2.5 GHz	1.35 GHz
Memory size	12 GB	1.5 GB
Threading API	Pthreads, TBB	CUDA 2.3
Compiler	gcc -O3	nvcc 2.3 –O3

Table 3: Benchmarks.

Apps	Description	Input Size
Sort + Reduce	Synthetic benchmark with parallel sorting and parallel reduction kernels	Data size from 4K elements to 1024K elements
K-means	Clustering algorithm used in image segmentation	1K to 1M pixels clustered into 32 regions
SpMV+ topk-rank	Synthetic benchmark with sparse matrix-dense vector multiplication and top k ranking	Sparse matrices with 100-700K rows/columns, up to 3.9M non-zeros
SSI	Supervised Semantic Indexing of documents based on text queries	1.8M documents with 32-96 simultaneous queries

using CUDA 2.3. The GPU version of *Reduce* is from CUDA SDK [31].

K-means is the well-known clustering algorithm used in image segmentation [32]. We use Lloyd's algorithm [33] to select k means given n points (e.g., pixels in an image). Starting with an initial value for the k means, the algorithm proceeds iteratively. Each iteration consists of three parallelizable kernels that we call *K1*, *K2* and *K3*. *K1* calculates the Euclidean distance between the n points and the current k means. *K2* picks the closest mean for each point, and *K3* updates the values of the k means by averaging all points closest to each mean. Since *K3* could only be parallelized into k threads, and k is small (under 64), it was always faster on the CPU. We implemented *K1* and *K2* on both the CPU and GPU using Intel's MKL [26] and CUDA 2.3 respectively.

The third application consists of two kernels, *SpMV* and *topk_rank*. *SpMV* [31] performs sparse matrix-vector multiplication. For *topk_rank*, the same kernel used in the example of Section 3, we use our own implementation on both CPU (using pthreads) and GPU (using CUDA).

Finally, SSI classification uses two kernels (dense matrix multiplication and topk_rank) and has been described in Section 3.

For all applications, we measure wall-clock processing as well as data transfer times. In the experiments that use our data-aware runtime system, we also accounted for the overhead due to call interception and runtime scheduling.

5.2 Results
In this section, we report our findings using our data-aware runtime for the above applications.

5.2.1 Sort and Reduce
Figure 3 shows the performance of running Sort and Reduce on CPU and GPU separately. The GPU performance bars show the split costs for real processing, memory allocation and data transfer. We see that Sort on GPU is slightly faster for small data

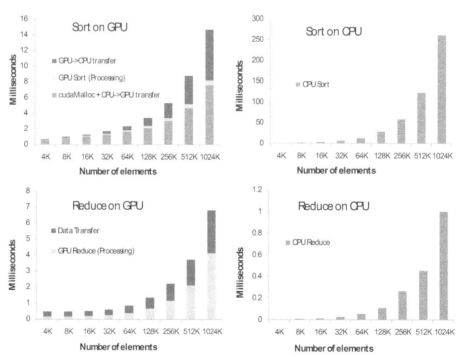

Figure 3: Processing and data transfer time for *Sort* and *Reduce* on GPU (left) and CPU (right). The GPU is faster for *Sort* while the CPU is faster for *Reduce*.

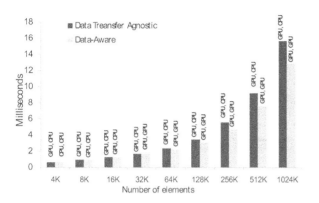

Figure 4: Execution time for *Sort* and *Reduce*. The labels on the bars indicate where the kernels were scheduled.

sizes (4K elements) and much faster as the data size increases. For Reduce, the CPU multithreaded version is faster than the GPU implementation.

When running an application consisting of multiple kernels, a data-agnostic scheduler assigns each kernel to the computational unit that offers the best performance, in this case the GPU for Sort and the CPU for Reduce. However, being unaware of data location, such a scheduler leads to data transfers before and after each GPU kernel invocation. The data-agnostic runtime must do this since it is unaware of which kernel may be invoked next, as is the case for legacy code. As can be observed, the transfer time is not trivial for large data sizes. Our runtime keeps track of data location, delays data transfers and takes the cost of data transfers into consideration when performing online scheduling decisions.

Figure 4 compares the performance of a data agnostic runtime with our data-aware runtime, where the data-agnostic runtime schedules kernels on the processor that is estimated to be faster, regardless of data location. In this case, a data-agnostic scheduler would always pick the GPU for Sort and CPU for Reduce. Our data-aware runtime schedules both kernels on the

CPU when data size is small (4K elements), but picks the GPU for Sort and CPU for Reduce for intermediate data sizes (8K-16K), and runs both kernels on GPU for larger data. While there is a small performance loss due to our runtime overhead (under 2%) for small data sizes, we achieve around 20% performance improvement when these kernels work with 256K or more elements.

5.2.2 K-means

We recall that K-means has two candidate kernels *K1* and *K2*. The third kernel *K3* is always faster on the CPU, and with negligible data transfer into and out of *K3*, it is always scheduled on the CPU. We segmented random images of sizes ranging from 1K pixels to 1M pixels into 32 clusters (i.e., $k = 32$). We found that for small images (specifically 1K and 4K pixels), the CPU was faster than the GPU for kernel *K1* (it used MKL sgemm for most of its Euclidean distance computation), but the GPU was faster (with its CUBLAS sgemm implementation [27]) for larger images. Our custom implementation of Kernel *K2* was faster on the GPU for images 4K or larger. Figure 5 shows the performance of K-means with data-agnostic and data-aware runtimes for small images and large images. Labels above the bars indicate the schedule for the two kernels. While the two runtimes schedule the kernels the same way for 16K and larger images, the performance improvement with the data-aware runtime is due to the optimization of data transfers. Specifically, after kernel *K1* runs on the GPU, the runtime postpones the data transfer back to the CPU until *K2* has been scheduled. From the figure, we see the data-aware runtime improves performance by up to 25% for both large and small data sets. Figure 6 shows the performance profile of the 3 different kernels in K-means. The data-aware runtime profile is shown on the left, and the data-agnostic on the right. We see that the data transfer portion of the profile is significantly reduced by the data-aware runtime resulting in the 25% performance improvement.

5.2.3 SpMV and topk_rank

Sparse matrix (*SpMV*) performance on the CPU and GPU depends on the number of non-zeros in the matrix. For our experiments,

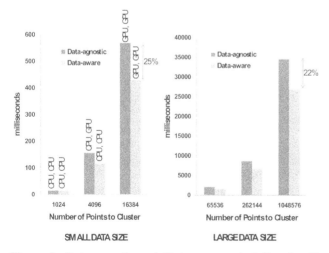

Figure 5: Data-agnostic and Data-aware scheduling for K-means with small (left) and large data sizes (right). Data-aware scheduling makes the application 25% faster than a data-agnostic runtime.

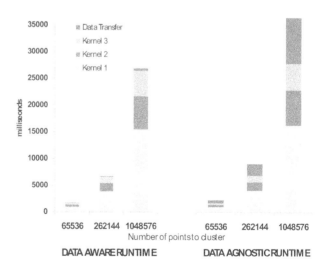

Figure 6: Performance profile of K-means, and data transfer time for data-agnostic and data-ware runtimes.

Table 4: Results for synthetic application with SpMV and topk_rank kernels.

Matrix	Rows/Cols	Non-zeros	# Vectors	Data-Agnostic Runtime		Data-aware Runtime	
				Schedule	Time (ms)	Schedule	Time (ms)
SparseM1	100	460	64	CPU, CPU	1.02	CPU, CPU	1.02
			128	CPU, GPU	1.75	CPU, GPU	1.75
SparseM2	36057	341088	64	GPU, GPU	94.51	GPU, GPU	74.46
			128	GPU, GPU	186.25	GPU, GPU	147.29
SparseM3	682862	3871773	64	CPU, GPU	1540.15	CPU, GPU	1540.15
			128	CPU, GPU	3091.81	CPU, GPU	3091.81

we use three matrices (ranging in size from 100 to nearly 700K rows/columns, and up to 3.9M non-zeros, obtained from [36]) each multiplied by 64 and 128 dense vectors, as shown in Table 4. For each case, we multiply a given sparse matrix with the vectors, and select the top 64 elements of each result vector. The data-agnostic runtime selects a schedule solely based on the estimated performance of the kernel, while our data-aware runtime selects the schedule based on estimated performance as well as the estimated data transfer overhead. For this benchmark, although our runtime chooses the same schedule as the data-agnostic runtime, it has better performance (for SparseM2) due to the fact that it defers data transfer and figures out it can avoid them. For SparseM2, once the SpMV has executed on the GPU, the data is not transferred back to the CPU until the next kernel is encountered a decision made regarding its schedule. We see improvements of up to 21% for SparseM2, but do not significantly affect the performance of the other matrices (our runtime overhead is under 2%).

5.2.4 Supervised Semantic Indexing (SSI)
We ran SSI with 32, 64 and 96 parallel queries, semantically searching the Wikipedia database consisting of 1.8M documents. SSI has two compute-intensive kernels: matrix multiplication *sgemm* and *topk_rank*. Table 5 shows the schedules and overall SSI performance in milliseconds per query for each case under a data-agnostic and our data-aware runtime. We see a performance improvement of 21.7% for 96 queries, of 4.4% for 64 queries and a negligible degradation for the small data set.

6. CONCLUSION, FUTURE DIRECTIONS
We presented a runtime for heterogeneous platforms consisting of one or more multi-core CPUs coupled with one or more many-core GPUs via a non-coherent interconnect. The CPU and GPU do not have shared memory. The runtime provides a unified memory view to the programmer, and aims at enabling legacy programs to run seamlessly on the heterogeneous platform with higher performance.

The key contribution is making the runtime data-aware. The proposed runtime schedules computations as well as data transfers taking into account the estimated performance and the time required to move data. In doing so, it may schedule a kernel on the slower processor simply because of data proximity. It also defers transferring data until necessary; thus, a kernel that runs on the GPU will not have its data transferred back to the CPU even though the runtime is unaware of when the data will be used in future. Rather, when another kernel requires those data, the runtime decides if they should be moved to a different processor, or the kernel should be scheduled on the processor hosting the data.

We implemented the data-aware runtime and evaluated it on a heterogeneous platform with a quad-core x86 CPU and an NVIDIA Tesla C870 (128-core) GPU. For synthetic as well as real applications, our runtime shows a performance improvement of up to 25% when compared to a runtime that schedules in a data-agnostic manner.

REFERENCES
[1] K. Fatahalian *et al*, "Sequoia: Programming the memory hierarchy," in Proc. of the 2006 ACM/IEEE Conference on Supercomputing, Tampa, FL.

[2] T. J. Knight *et al*, "Compilation for Explicitly Managed Memory Hierarchies," in Proc. of PPoPP 2007, San Jose, CA.G.

[3] Diamos and S. Yalamanchili, "Harmony: an execution model and runtime for heterogeneous many core systems," in Proc. of HPDC 2008, New York, NY.

[4] C. Luk, S. Hong and H. Kim, "Qilin: Exploiting Parallelism on Heterogeneous Multiprocessors with Adaptive Mapping," in Proc. of MICRO 2009, New York, NY.

[5] B. Saha *et al*, "Programming model for a heterogeneous x86 platform," in Proc. of PLDI 2009, Dublin, Ireland.

[6] I. Gelado *et al*, "CUBA: An Architecture for Efficient CPU/Co-processor Data Communication," in Proc. of ICS'08, Island of Kos, Greece.

[7] M. Becchi, S. Cadambi and S. T. Chakradhar, "Enabling Legacy Applications on Heterogeneous Platforms," in Proc. of HotPar 2010, Berkeley, CA, June 2010.

[8] CUDA documentation: http://www.nvidia.com/object/cuda_develop.html.

Table 5: Results for SSI with data-aware scheduling for 1.8M document database.

# Parallel Queries	Data-Agnostic Runtime		Data-aware Runtime	
	Schedule	Performance	Schedule	Performance
32	GPU, CPU	7.91 ms/query	GPU, CPU	7.91 ms/query
64	GPU, CPU	7.85 ms/query	GPU, GPU	7.51 ms/query
96	GPU, CPU	7.83 ms/query	GPU, GPU	6.13 ms/query

[9] http://www.supermicro.com/products/nfo/files/GPU/GPU_White_Paper.pdf: "Shattering the 1U Server Performance Record".

[10] AMD, AMD Stream SDK User Guide v 2.0, 2009.

[11] Intel, Intel Threading Building Blocks 2.2: http://www.threadingbuildingblocks.org.

[12] A. Ghuloum *et al*, "Future-Proof Data Parallel Algorithms and Software on Intel Multi-Core Architecture", Intel Technology Journal 11, 4, 333-348, Nov 2007.

[13] D. Tarditi, S. Puri and J. Oglesby, "Accelerator: Using Data Parallelism to Program GPUs for General-Purpose Uses," in Proc. of the 2006 ASPLOS, October 2006.

[14] Intel RapidMind, http://software.intel.com/en-us/articles/rapidmind.

[15] Peakstream, "Peakstream Stream Platform API C++ Programming Guide v 1.0", May 2007.

[16] PGI, PGI Accelerator Compilers, http://www.pgroup.com/resources/accel.htm.

[17] CAPS, HMPP Workbench, http://www.caps-entreprise.com/hmpp.html.

[18] HPC Project, Par4All, http://www.par4all.org.

[19] J. A. Stratton, S. S. Stone and W-m. W. Hwu, "MCUDA: An Efficient Implementation of CUDA Kernels from Multi-Core CPUs," in Proc. of the 2008 Workshop on Languages and Compilers for Parallel Computing, 2008.

[20] G. Diamos *et al*, "GPUocelot – A binary Translator Framework for GPGPU" http://code.google.com/p/gpuocelot.

[21] S.-W. Liao *et al*, "Data and Computation Transformations for Brook Streaming Applications on Multiprocessors," in Proc. of the 4th Conference on CGO, March 2006.

[22] A. Munshi, "OpenCL Parallel Computing on the GPU and CPU", in ACM SIGGRAPH 2008.

[23] K. O'Brien *et al*, "Supporting OpenMP on Cell," in International Journal on Parallel Programming, 36, 289—311, 2008.

[24] M. D. Linderman *et al*, "Merge: A Programming Model for Heterogeneous Multi-core Systems," in Proc. of the 2008 ASPLOS, March 2008.

[25] B. Bai *et al*, "Learning to Rank with (a lot of) word features," in Special Issue: Learning to Rank for Information Retrieval. Information Retrieval. 2009.

[26] Intel MKL: http://software.intel.com/en-us/intel-mkl.

[27] http://developer.download.nvidia.com/compute/cuda/1_0/CUBLAS_Library_1.0.pdf.

[28] T. Kosar, "A New Paradigm in Data Intensive Computing: Stork and the Data-Aware Schedulers," in Proc. of Challenges of Large Applications in Distributed Environments, 2006.

[29] J. Bent *et al*, "Coordination of Data Movement with Computation Scheduling on a Cluster," in Proceedings of Challenges of Large Applications in Distributed Environments, 2005.

[30] G. Khanna, "A Data-Locality Aware Mapping and Scheduling Framework for Data-Intensive Computing", MS Thesis, Dept. of Computer Science and Engineering, The Ohio State University, 2008.

[31] Nvidia, "CUDA SDK Code examples", http://www.nvidia.com/object/cuda_get.html.

[32] J. B. MacQueen, "Some methods for classification and analysis of multivariate observation," in Proc. of the Berkeley Symposium on Math. Stat. and Prob., pp 281–297.

[33] S.P. Lloyd, "Least squares quantization in PCM," IEEE Transactions on Information Theory 28 (2): pp 129–137.

[34] C. Augonnet and R. Namyst, "A unified runtime system for heterogeneous multicore architectures," in Proc. of HPPC'08, Las Palmas de Gran Canaria, Spain, August 2008.

[35] C. Augonnet *et al*, "StarPU: A Unified Platform for Task Scheduling on Heterogeneous Multicore Architectures," in Proc. of the 15th International Euro-Par Conference, Delft, The Netherlands, August 2009.

[36] http://www.cise.ufl.edu/research/sparse/matrices/

Online Capacity Maximization in Wireless Networks *

Alexander Fanghänel, Sascha Geulen, Martin Hoefer, Berthold Vöcking
RWTH Aachen University
Department of Computer Science
52056 Aachen, Germany
{fanghaenel,sgeulen,mhoefer,voecking}@cs.rwth-aachen.de

ABSTRACT

In this paper we study a dynamic version of capacity maximization in the physical model of wireless communication. In our model, requests for connections between pairs of points in Euclidean space of constant dimension d arrive iteratively over time. When a new request arrives, an online algorithm needs to decide whether or not to accept the request and to assign one out of k channels and a transmission power to the channel. Accepted requests must satisfy constraints on the signal-to-interference-plus-noise (SINR) ratio. The objective is to maximize the number of accepted requests.

Using competitive analysis we study algorithms using distance-based power assignments, for which the power of a request relies only on the distance between the points. Such assignments are inherently local and particularly useful in distributed settings. We first focus on the case of a single channel. For request sets with spatial lengths in $[1, \Delta]$ and duration in $[1, \Gamma]$ we derive a lower bound of $\Omega(\Gamma \cdot \Delta^{d/2})$ on the competitive ratio of any deterministic online algorithm using a distance-based power assignment. Our main result is a near-optimal deterministic algorithm that is $O\left(\Gamma \cdot \Delta^{(d/2)+\varepsilon}\right)$-competitive, for any constant $\varepsilon > 0$.

Our algorithm for a single channel can be generalized to k channels. It can be adjusted to yield a competitive ratio of $O\left(k \cdot \Gamma^{1/k'} \cdot \Delta^{(d/2k'')+\varepsilon}\right)$ for any factorization (k', k'') such that $k' \cdot k'' = k$. This illustrates the effectiveness of multiple channels when dealing with unknown request sequences. In particular, for $\Theta(\log \Gamma \cdot \log \Delta)$ channels this yields an $O(\log \Gamma \cdot \log \Delta)$-competitive algorithm. Additionally, we show how this approach can be turned into a randomized algorithm, which is $O(\log \Gamma \cdot \log \Delta)$-competitive even for a single channel.

*This work has been supported by DFG through UMIC Research Centre at RWTH Aachen University.

Categories and Subject Descriptors

C.2.1 [**Computer-Communication Networks**]: Network Architecture and Design—*Wireless communication, Distributed networks*; F.1.2 [**Computation by Abstract Devices**]: Modes of Computation—*Online computation*; F.2.2 [**Analysis of Algorithms and Problem Complexity**]: Nonnumerical Algorithms and Problems—*Sequencing and scheduling*

General Terms

Algorithms, Performance, Theory

Keywords

Physical Model, SINR, Online Algorithms, Competitive Analysis.

1. INTRODUCTION

Determining the capacity of wireless networks is a major challenge in networking. Most studies in this area rely on the *physical model* taking into account that the strength of a signal fades with the distance from the sender. A node can successfully receive a signal if the *signal to interference plus noise ratio (SINR)* is above some threshold, that is, if the signal's strength is sufficiently large in comparison to the sum of other signals received simultaneously plus ambient noise.

Only very recently, we have seen significant progress in understanding the algorithmic aspects of the scheduling problems arising in the physical model [2–4,7,8,10,13]. Previous work focusses on offline optimization problems of the following kind. Suppose one is given a set of n requests for connections between pairs of points in Euclidean space of constant dimension d. One has to specify a subset of requests and a power assignment to each pair such that the requests can be scheduled simultaneously, that is, the chosen requests with the power assignments satisfy the SINR constraint. The objective is to maximize the number of chosen requests. This variant is sometimes referred to the *throughput version of the capacity maximization problem*. A related problem is to minimize the number of batches such that the requests in each batch satisfy the SINR constraint. In this case batches can be mapped to orthogonal channels or time slots.

Most of the previous work focusses on power assignments that are *distance-based*, i. e., the power assignment is a function of the distance between the two nodes of a request. Prominent examples are the linear power assignment in which the power is chosen proportional to the loss in power between the nodes of a request (and, hence, depends polynomially on the distance) and the uniform power assignment in which all requests get assigned the same power. Such assignments are inherently local and, hence, particularly useful in distributed settings. The linear power assignment has the additional advantage of being energy-minimal.

The best known offline results for the uniform power assignment are achieved in [7] and [11]. In [7] an algorithm is presented that achieves an $O(1)$ approximation guarantee with respect to the number of requests that can be scheduled simultaneously when restricting to the uniform power assignment. In [11], it is shown how to extend this approach obtaining an $O(1)$ approximation ratio on the number of batches for the uniform power assignment. Similarly, in [6] an algorithm is presented that achieves an $O(\log n)$ approximation on the number of batches when restricting to linear power assignments.

Let us remark that offline approximation ratios restricted to uniform and linear power assignments can be translated into approximation ratios with respect to general power assignments by spending an additional factor of order $\log \Delta$, where Δ is the ratio between the largest and the smallest distance among all request pairs. In particular, the algorithms from [7] and [11] using uniform power assignments achieve $O(\log \Delta)$ approximation ratios in comparison to general power assignments. The same approximation ratio has been achieved independently in [1]. It follows from the analyses presented in [5, 12] that this approximation ratio is best possible for algorithms using uniform or linear power assignments.

A drawback of the previous work is that it neglects the dynamic nature of request scheduling in wireless network. The focus of our paper lies exactly on this aspect. We study request scheduling in wireless networks as an online problem, that is, requests arrive one by one. When a new request arrives, an online algorithm needs to decide whether or not to accept the request and to assign a power rate. In the multichannel version, accepted requests must also be assigned to one out of k available channels. Decisions about acceptance as well as power and channel assignments cannot be revoked later.

1.1 Online Request Scheduling

In our online model we receive an unknown number of n *communication requests* sequentially over time. Each request $1 \leq i \leq n$ consists of a point pair. For a *directed* request there is a *sender* s_i and a *receiver* r_i that strive to establish an uninterrupted connection. For *undirected* requests, both points are receiver and sender at the same time. In this paper we consider sets of directed and undirected requests, as well as mixed sets of requests. We assume that points come from a metric space with a distance function $d(x, y)$. We use short notation for $d_{ii} = d(s_i, r_i)$, the *distance* between sender s_i and receiver r_i. More generally, for two different directed requests we use $d_{ij} = d(s_i, r_j)$. We denote by $\Delta = (\max_i d_{ii})/(\min_i d_{ii})$ the so called *aspect ratio*. Further, each request pair i comes with a parameter t_i, which denotes the duration of the request. We denote by $\Gamma = (\max_i t_i)/(\min_i t_i)$, where w.l.o.g. we let $\min_i t_i = 1$ and $\max_i t_i = \Gamma$. We assume requests lie in $\mathbb{R}^d$ of constant dimension d, and the distance function is an l_p-norm or the l_{max}-norm.

Requests arrive sequentially over time and are assumed to be characterized by the physical model [9]. The goal is to accept the maximum number of requests that can successfully communicate simultaneously. For each request an online algorithm must make a decision whether to accept the request or not. For an accepted request i it needs to set a *power level* p_i and a *channel* $k_i \in \{1 \ldots, k\}$ for the sender s_i to emit a signal. For undirected requests we assume that both points emit signals with the same power and on the same channel. The algorithm iteratively expands the sets $S_1, \ldots, S_k$ of accepted requests on the corresponding channels. Decisions on acceptance, power levels, and channels of a request cannot be revoked later on. If a request is accepted, the algorithm must ensure that it remains successful throughout the time. The criterion of "successful" for an accepted directed request i is the following *SINR constraint*:

$$\frac{p_i}{d_{ii}^\alpha} \geq \beta \left(\sum_{j \in S_{k_i}, j \neq i} \frac{p_j}{d_{ji}^\alpha} + N_{k_i} \right) . \qquad (1)$$

This constraint is the central condition for successful communication in the physical model. It characterizes the strength at r_i of the signal emitted by s_i compared to *ambient noise* N_{k_i} and the *interference* from signals of all other senders *on the same channel* k_i. In this expression α is the *path loss exponent* that characterizes the decay of a signal over a distance. In this paper we consider a Euclidean *fading metric* [10], i.e., we require that $\alpha > d$, where we treat both α and d as constants. The constant β is called the *gain*.

For a successful undirected request the SINR constraint has to be satisfied at both points of the pair. Similarly, when considering another receiver i, both points of j are senders and create interference. For notational simplicity, however, we will treat them as two directed requests in the right-hand side of (1). An online algorithm has to ensure that (1) is satisfied for all $i \in S = S_1 \cup \ldots \cup S_k$ throughout.

For simplicity we assume that noise is absent, $N_1 = \ldots = N_k = 0$. Our algorithms will satisfy the SINR constraint with strict inequality. This allows to scale powers up sufficiently to satisfy the constraints also when there is noise. Clearly, such a scaling might be wasteful or infeasible in practice, but this aspect is beyond our analysis. When there is no noise, we can scale all distances such that $\min_i d_{ii} = 1$ and $\max_i d_{ii} = \Delta$.

In this paper we are particularly interested in distance-based power assignments because of their simplicity and locality, which is a striking conceptual advantage in distributed wireless systems. A *distance-based* power assignment p is given by $p_i = \phi(d_{ii})$ with a function $\phi : [1, \Delta] \to (0, \infty)$. For uniqueness we assume ϕ is always scaled such that $\phi(1) = 1$. Examples are *uniform* $\phi(d_{ii}) = 1$ or *linear* $\phi(d_{ii}) = d_{ii}^\alpha$ assignments. Recently, a *square-root* assignment $\phi(d_{ii}) = d_{ii}^{\alpha/2}$ has attracted some interest [5, 10] as it yields better approximation ratios for the offline version of request scheduling than uniform and linear power assignments. We generalize these three classes to *polynomial* assignments of the form $\phi(d_{ii}) = d_{ii}^{r\alpha}$ with parameter $r \in \mathbb{R}$.

For the analysis of our online algorithms we make use of the following definitions. Let $A(\omega)$ denote the number of request pairs an online algorithm A accepts, and let $\text{OPT}(\omega)$ denote the number of requests in an optimal offline solution on an input sequence ω. An online algorithm is c-*competitive* (or "yields competitive ratio c") if there exists a constant a, such that for every input ω we have $A(\omega) \geq (\text{OPT}(\omega)/c) + a$. We call algorithm A *strictly c-competitive* if it is c-competitive with $a = 0$. Note that all algorithms presented in this paper are strictly competitive. For the lower bounds we do not need to rely on strictness.

1.2 Our Results

Our first contribution are lower bounds for deterministic online algorithms choosing requests for a single channel. We show that any deterministic online algorithm using a polynomial power assignment with parameter r cannot yield a competitive ratio better than $\Omega\left(\Gamma \cdot \Delta^{d \cdot \max\{r, 1-r\}}\right)$. For uniform and linear power assignments, this results in a lower bound of $\Omega\left(\Gamma \cdot \Delta^d\right)$; for the square root power assignment, it yields a lower bound of $\Omega\left(\Gamma \cdot \Delta^{d/2}\right)$. In fact, we can show that the $\Omega\left(\Gamma \cdot \Delta^{d/2}\right)$ lower bound on the competitive ratio is not restricted to polynomial power assignments: In the case of directed requests, this bound holds for any distance-based power assignment and, in the case of undirected requests, the same bound holds even for general power assignments.

Our lower bounds reveal an exponential gap between the approximation guarantees achievable by deterministic online and offline algorithms. The main difficulty of the online scenario turns out to be that requests cannot be ordered by length. This has been a crucial ingredient to all existing deterministic offline algorithms with polylogarithmic approximation guarantee [1, 7, 10].

Our second contribution is a deterministic online algorithm for a single channel that almost matches the lower bounds. All following results hold for directed and undirected requests. Algorithm SAFE-DISTANCE works for polynomial power assignments with $r \in [0, 1]$. For uniform and linear power assignments, it achieves a competitive ratio of $O\left(\Gamma \cdot \Delta^d\right)$. For the square-root power assignment, we extend the basic idea and obtain algorithm MULTI-CLASS SAFE-DISTANCE. For any constant $\epsilon > 0$ it achieves a competitive ratio of $O\left(\Gamma \cdot \Delta^{d/2 + \epsilon}\right)$.

Let us explicitly point out that these competitive ratios compare the performance of online algorithms with polynomial power assignments to optimal offline algorithms with general power assignments. Combining the upper bound for the square root power assignment with the lower bounds above shows that this power assignment achieves nearly the best possible competitive ratio among all (distance-based) power assignments (in case of directed requests) and is superior to any other polynomial power assignment.

Our third contribution is an illustration of the power of multiple channels for deterministic online algorithms. We generalize algorithm MULTI-CLASS SAFE-DISTANCE and its analysis from 1 to k channels and achieve an exponential reduction in the competitive ratio. We prove that algorithm MULTI-CLASS SAFE-DISTANCE using $k = k' \cdot k''$ channels is only $O\left(k \cdot \Gamma^{1/k'} \cdot \Delta^{(d/2k'') + \varepsilon}\right)$-competitive. In particular, with just a logarithmic number of channels we obtain a deterministic algorithm with logarithmic competitive ratio. This algorithm is only constant-competitive against an optimum solution that uses only one channel. By randomly choosing a channel, we thus obtain a randomized algorithm

for a single channel that is $O(\log \Gamma \cdot \log \Delta)$-competitive with respect to the expected number of accepted requests.

Outline.

For technical reasons, we present our results in a different order than listed above. In Section 2 we first analyze algorithm SAFE-DISTANCE before stating the general lower bound in Theorem 2.5. In Section 3 we give the near-optimal algorithm MULTI-CLASS SAFE-DISTANCE (Section 3.1), the generalization to k channels (Section 3.2) and the randomized algorithm (Section 3.3). In Section 4 we reach the full level of generality by describing the adjustments to requests with duration.

2. A SIMPLE ALGORITHM AND A LOWER BOUND

In the following we first analyze the spatial aspect of the problem and assume that requests last forever, i.e., for all requests i, $t_i = \infty$. We begin by analyzing a simple online algorithm for the case of a single channel and any polynomial power assignment. Subsequently, we show a general lower bound. Our analysis of the online algorithm introduces a number of critical observations that we use in later sections.

The main idea of the algorithm is to accept a new request only if it keeps a *safe distance* σ from every other previously accepted request. In particular, we accept incoming request i only if $\min\{d_{ij}, d_{ji}\} \geq \sigma$ for every other previously accepted request $j \in S$. We call this algorithm SAFE-DISTANCE. For the choice of σ there is a conflict between correctness and competitive ratio. A larger σ blocks out a larger portion of the space, in which an optimal algorithm knowing the request sequence might be able to accept requests. If σ is too small, then at some point the interference at an accepted request can get too large and the SINR constraint becomes violated.

We strive to choose σ as small as possible to ensure correctness of SAFE-DISTANCE. To bound the interference at accepted requests we construct a worst-case scenario. We consider a receiver r_i from a single accepted request and bound the maximum number of senders that can be at a certain distance from r_i. In the following we show that for $r \in [0, 1]$ the choice of

$$\sigma = \max\left\{2\Delta, \Delta \cdot 18d \cdot \sqrt[\alpha]{2\beta/(\alpha - d)}\right\}$$

is sufficient to yield the following result.

THEOREM 2.1. SAFE-DISTANCE *is* $O(\Delta^d)$*-competitive for any polynomial power assignment with* $r \in [0, 1]$ *and a single channel.*

PROOF. We first show that SAFE-DISTANCE is correct, i.e., for an accepted request i the SINR constraint of i never becomes violated. In particular, we will underestimate the distances of accepted senders of other requests to overestimate the interference at receiver r_i. However, even under such pessimistic conditions the SINR constraint at r_i will remain valid.

Consider a receiver r_i of an accepted request i. To estimate the interference at r_i we have to count how many senders may be placed at which distance. Using $\sigma \geq 2\Delta$ and the choice rule of the algorithm it is straightforward to verify that senders of any two different accepted requests are at least a distance of $\sigma - \Delta \geq \sigma/2$ apart. We segment all of $\mathbb{R}^d$ into d-dimensional hypercubes with length $\sigma/3d$, which we call *sectors*. The greatest distance within a sector is $\sigma d/3d = \sigma/3 < \sigma/2$. Each sector can contain senders from at most one request, so there are at most 2 senders in every sector. Without loss of generality, we assume that sectors are created such that r_i lies in a corner point of 2^d sectors. We divide the set of sectors into *layers*. The first layer consists of the 2^d sectors incident to r_i. The second layer are all sectors that are not in the first layer but share at least a point with a sector from the first layer, and so on. In this construction there are exactly $(2\ell)^d$ sectors from layers 1 through ℓ, and their union is a hypercube of side length $2\ell\sigma/3d$ with r_i in the center. Therefore, there are exactly $2^d(\ell^d - (\ell-1)^d)$ sectors in layer ℓ.

Due to the algorithm there can be no sender at a distance smaller than σ from r_i. The sector of smallest layer that is at a distance at least σ from r_i can be reached along the volume diagonal of the layer hypercubes. There can be no sender in all sectors from layers 1 through ℓ', where ℓ' is bounded by $\sigma \leq \ell'(\sigma/3)$, which yields $\ell' \geq 3$. For bounding the interference assume that in all sectors of layer $\ell \geq 3$ there are 2 senders. Note that all senders in sectors from a layer ℓ have a distance at least $(\ell-1)\sigma/3d$ to r_i. To bound the interference that is created at r_i, we use the following technical lemma.

LEMMA 2.2. *For $\alpha > d \geq 1$ it holds that*

$$2^d \cdot \sum_{\ell=3}^{\infty} \frac{\ell^d - (\ell-1)^d}{(\ell-1)^\alpha} < \frac{6^d}{\alpha - d} .$$

PROOF. We observe

$$2^d \cdot \sum_{\ell=3}^{\infty} \frac{\ell^d - (\ell-1)^d}{(\ell-1)^\alpha}$$
$$\leq 2^d \cdot \sum_{\ell=3}^{\infty} \frac{2^d \ell^{d-1}}{(\ell-1)^\alpha}$$
$$= 2^{2d} \cdot \sum_{\ell=3}^{\infty} \frac{\ell^{d-1}}{(\ell-1)^\alpha} .$$

We now bound $\ell^{d-1}/(\ell-1)^\alpha$, where we assume that $\epsilon = \alpha - d > 0$. This yields

$$2^{2d} \cdot \sum_{\ell=3}^{\infty} \frac{\ell^{d-1}}{(\ell-1)^\alpha}$$
$$= 2^{2d} \cdot \sum_{\ell=3}^{\infty} \frac{\ell^{d-1}}{(\ell-1)^{d-1}} \cdot \frac{1}{(\ell-1)^{1+\epsilon}}$$
$$= 2^{2d} \cdot \sum_{\ell=3}^{\infty} \left(1 + \frac{1}{\ell-1}\right)^{d-1} \cdot \frac{1}{(\ell-1)^{1+\epsilon}}$$
$$< 6^d \cdot \sum_{\ell=3}^{\infty} \frac{1}{(\ell-1)^{1+\epsilon}}$$
$$= 6^d \cdot \sum_{\ell=2}^{\infty} \ell^{-1-\epsilon} .$$

The assumption $\epsilon > 0$ yields a constant value for the expression, which is $6^d \cdot (\zeta(1 + \epsilon) - 1)$. We estimate this value by $\sum_{\ell=2}^{\infty} \ell^{-1-\epsilon} < \int_{\ell=1}^{\infty} \ell^{-1-\epsilon} = 1/\epsilon$, which proves the lemma. $\square$

This yields

$$
\begin{aligned}
I &= \sum_{j \in S, j \neq i} \frac{d_{ii}^{r\alpha}}{d_{ji}^\alpha} \\
&\leq 2\Delta^{r\alpha} \sum_{\ell=3}^{\infty} 2^d(\ell^d - (\ell-1)^d) \cdot \frac{1}{((\ell-1)\sigma/3d)^\alpha} \\
&< 2\Delta^{r\alpha} \left(\frac{3d}{\sigma}\right)^\alpha \cdot \frac{6^d}{\alpha - d} .
\end{aligned}
$$

Note that the SINR constraint is satisfied if $p_i/d_{ii}^\alpha \geq \Delta^{r\alpha}/\Delta^\alpha \geq \beta I$, or

$$2\beta\Delta^{r\alpha} \cdot \left(\frac{3d}{\sigma}\right)^\alpha \cdot \frac{6^d}{\alpha - d} \leq \Delta^{(r-1)\alpha} .$$

This yields a lower bound for the distance of

$$\sigma \geq \Delta \cdot 3d \cdot \sqrt[\alpha]{\frac{2\beta 6^d}{\alpha - d}} , \qquad (2)$$

which can be verified to hold for our choice of σ.

To bound the competitive ratio we need the following *Density Lemma*, which is an extension of Lemma 3 in [1] to both senders and receivers, and to metric spaces of arbitrary dimension d.

LEMMA 2.3. (DENSITY LEMMA). *Consider a sector A with side-length $x \geq 1$ and any feasible solution with arbitrary power assignment. There can be only $(d + 1)^\alpha x^d/\beta$ requests with a receiver in A and only $(d+1)^\alpha x^d/\beta$ requests with a sender in A.*

PROOF. The proof requires some adjustments from [1]. We first assume $x = 1$ and consider the number of receivers and senders in A separately.

Receivers: We first prove the lemma for the receivers. Let us assume that the transmission powers in the solution are such that there is a constant $\overline{p}$ such that the signal strength received by a receiver $p_i/d_{ii}^\alpha = \overline{p}$ for any request with $r_i \in A$. Consider another request with $r_j \in A$. The interference of j at r_i is $p_j/d_{ji}^\alpha \geq p_j/(d(r_i, r_j) + d_{jj})^\alpha)$. Due to the size of the sector we have that $d(r_i, r_j) \leq d$. Also $d_{jj} \geq 1$, which implies

$$\frac{p_j}{(d(r_i, r_j) + d_{jj})^\alpha} \geq \frac{1}{(d+1)^\alpha} \cdot \frac{p_j}{d_{jj}^\alpha} \geq \frac{\overline{p}}{(d+1)^\alpha} .$$

Thus, if more than $(d + 1)^\alpha/\beta$ such connections are present, the SINR constraint *for all of them* is violated.

Now consider a solution with arbitrary powers. Here we artificially reduce powers such that all connections experience a minimal signal strength $\overline{p}$ and then increase powers to their original value. The increase deteriorates SINR ratios for the requests that continue to have a signal strength of $\overline{p}$. Hence, if more than $(d+1)^\alpha/\beta$ receivers are present in A, at least one SINR constraint is violated.

Senders: For bounding the number of senders in A we use a similar approach. This time, however, we first assume that all senders have the same power. For two requests i and j this yields $p_j/d_{ji}^\alpha \geq p_j/(d(s_i, s_j) + d_{ii})^\alpha$. We have that $d(s_i, s_j) \leq d$. Also $d_{jj} \geq 1$, so $p_j/(d(s_j, s_i) +$

95

$d_{ii})^\alpha \geq \frac{1}{(d+1)^\alpha} \cdot \frac{p_j}{d_{ij}^\alpha}$ as before. Thus, for the SINR constraint it is necessary that

$$\frac{p_i}{d_{ii}^\alpha} \geq \frac{\beta}{(d+1)^\alpha} \cdot \sum_{j \neq i} \frac{p_j}{d_{ii}^\alpha} \ .$$

Using $p_i = p_j$ for all requests i and j, there can be at most $(d+1)^\alpha/\beta$ senders in A, otherwise the SINR constraint *for all* requests is violated. A similar observation as before generalizes the argument to arbitrary powers.

This proves the lemma for $x = 1$. If $x > 1$ we can divide A into sectors of length 1, apply the above arguments, and the bound follows. $\square$

The density lemma allows a simple way to bound the number of connections the optimum solution can accept in the blocked area. First consider a sender s_i of a request accepted by SAFE-DISTANCE. The sender blocks a hypersphere of radius σ for receivers of other requests. We overestimate its size by a sector of side-length 2σ centered at s_i. By the density lemma, the optimum solution can accept at most $(d+1)^\alpha (2\sigma)^d/\beta$ requests, which is $O(\Delta^d)$ for fixed α, β, and d. For the receiver r_i there is a similar estimation. This time we bound the number of senders in a hypersphere around r_i, which is $O(\Delta^d)$ for fixed α, β, and d. Finally, note that σ is chosen to maximize conceptual simplicity and does not optimize the involved constants in the competitive ratio. $\square$

We can use similar arguments to show a result for any other polynomial power assignment. As safe distance we pick $\sigma^+ = \Delta^r \cdot \sigma$ if $r > 1$, and $\sigma^- = \Delta^{1-r} \cdot \sigma$ if $r < 0$.

COROLLARY 2.4. SAFE-DISTANCE *is* $O\left(\Delta^{d \cdot \max\{r, 1-r\}}\right)$-*competitive for a polynomial power assignment with* $r \notin (0, 1)$ *and a single channel.*

PROOF. In the case $r > 1$ we note for correctness of the algorithm that the interference at an accepted receiver r_i is again bounded by

$$\begin{aligned} I &= \sum_{j \in S, j \neq i} \frac{d_{jj}^{r\alpha}}{d_{ji}^\alpha} \leq \Delta^{r\alpha} \sum_{j \in S, j \neq i} \frac{1}{d_{ji}^\alpha} \\ &< 2\Delta^{r\alpha} \cdot \left(\frac{3d}{\sigma^+}\right)^\alpha \cdot \frac{6^d}{\alpha - d} \ . \end{aligned}$$

The SINR constraint now requires that $p_i/d_{ii}^\alpha = d_{ii}^{(r-1)\alpha} \geq 1 \geq \beta I$. This yields a lower bound of

$$\sigma^+ \geq \Delta^r \cdot 3d \cdot \sqrt[\alpha]{\frac{2\beta 6^d}{\alpha - d}} \ . \tag{3}$$

Bounding the competitive ratio can be done as before and proves the result for the case $r > 1$.

If $r < 0$, then the interference is maximized with requests of length 1 in each sector. The interference is thus bounded by

$$\begin{aligned} I &= \sum_{j \in S, j \neq i} \frac{d_{jj}^{r\alpha}}{d_{ji}^\alpha} \leq \sum_{j \in S, j \neq i} \frac{1}{d_{ji}^\alpha} \\ &< 2 \cdot \left(\frac{3d}{\sigma^-}\right)^\alpha \cdot \frac{6^d}{\alpha - d} \ . \end{aligned}$$

The SINR constraint now requires that $p_i/d_{ii}^\alpha = d_{ii}^{(r-1)\alpha} \geq \Delta^{(r-1)\alpha} \geq \beta I$. This yields a lower bound

$$\sigma^- \geq \Delta^{1-r} \cdot 3d \cdot \sqrt[\alpha]{\frac{2\beta 6^d}{\alpha - d}} \ . \tag{4}$$

The corollary follows. $\square$

As it turns out, the competitive ratio of SAFE-DISTANCE is asymptotically best possible for polynomial power assignments with $r \notin (0, 1)$. This includes both the uniform and linear power assignment. Next, we bound the competitive ratio for any deterministic online algorithm using polynomial power assignments. This can be generalized to a lower bound for any distance-based power assignment.

THEOREM 2.5. *Every deterministic online algorithm using polynomial power assignments has a competitive ratio of* $\Omega\left(\Delta^{d \cdot \max\{r, 1-r\}}\right)$. *Every deterministic online algorithm is* $\Omega\left(\Delta^{d/2}\right)$-*competitive (1) using arbitrary power assignments in the case of undirected requests and (2) using distance-based power assignments in the case of only directed requests.*

PROOF. The main observation in the proof is that every deterministic online algorithm has to accept the first request that arrives, otherwise it risks having an unbounded competitive ratio. While this is true only for strictly competitive algorithms, we can repeat the following instance sufficiently often and keep a sufficiently large distance between the instances. In this way we can neglect the constant a from the competitive ratio.

We first consider the case that all requests are directed and polynomial power assignment. Let the first request have length Δ. From the SINR constraint we bound the minimum distance every other successful request has to keep to sender s_1 or receiver r_1. This yields a blocked area in which the online algorithm is not able to accept any request. We then count the maximum number of requests that can be placed into this area, and which the optimum solution can accept simultaneously. The next Proposition yields a bound on the minimum distance between two requests with a polynomial power assignment.

PROPOSITION 2.6. *Consider two directed successful requests i and j with polynomial power assignment. The distance between s_i and r_j must be at least $d_{ij} \geq \sqrt[\alpha]{\beta} \cdot d_{ii}^r \cdot d_{jj}^{1-r}$.*

PROOF. Consider the SINR constraint for request j when only requests i and j are accepted. It reads

$$d_{jj}^{\alpha(r-1)} \geq \beta(d_{ii}^{r\alpha}/d_{ij}^\alpha) \ ,$$

and rearranging yields the result. $\square$

Now suppose the online algorithm has accepted the first request of length Δ. The adversary subsequently presents requests of length 1. If the sender of one such request is closer than $\sqrt[\alpha]{\beta} \cdot \Delta^{1-r}$ to r_1, the online algorithm cannot accept the request. The same holds if the receiver is closer than $\sqrt[\alpha]{\beta} \cdot \Delta^r$ to s_1. Thus, there are two hyperspherical areas blocked around sender and receiver of request 1. Let us consider the case $r \leq 0.5$ and the hypersphere around the receiver. All subsequent arguments follow similarly for $r > 0.5$ and the sender.

The adversary can place requests, all of equal length $d_{ii} = 1$, into the hypersphere of radius $\sqrt[d]{\beta} \cdot \Delta^{1-r}$ around r_1. Similar to the proof of Theorem 2.1 we divide the space into sectors of length $2\sigma_1$, where

$$\sigma_1 = 2\max\left\{2, 18d \cdot \sqrt[\alpha]{2\beta/(\alpha-d)}\right\} \; .$$

We again assume that r_1 is located on the boundary of d sectors. How many sectors are completely enclosed by the blocked hypersphere around r_1? The side-length of the maximum hypercube that is contained is $2\Delta^{1-r}\sqrt[d]{\beta}/d$. There are at least $\frac{2\Delta^{1-r}\sqrt[d]{\beta}}{d\sigma_1} - 1$ sectors along each dimension within the hypercube, a number in $\Theta(\Delta^{1-r})$. This obviously yields a total number of $\Omega(\Delta^{(1-r)d})$ sectors, in which the online algorithm must not accept any request. However, we observe that σ_1 is chosen using the formula for σ with ratio 1. It is possible to locate one request of length 1 in each sector such that receivers and senders of two different requests are at least a distance of σ_1 apart. By Theorem 2.1 it is possible to accept all these $\Omega(\Delta^{(1-r)d})$ small requests simultaneously, which proves the theorem for case $r \leq 0.5$. For $r > 0.5$ we can place requests in the hypersphere around s_1 to derive a similar result.

To extend the previous arguments to arbitrary distance-based power assignments, we observe that the previous lower bound uses only requests of length 1 and Δ. Let ϕ be the function of the distance-based power assignment, then $\phi(\Delta)$ is the power of the first request. The lower bound for this power assignment behaves exactly as for a polynomial assignment with $r = (\log\phi(\Delta))/(\alpha\log\Delta)$.

Note that when a power assignment is not distance-based, it might assign different powers to small requests based on whether they are near the sender or the receiver of the first request. This, however, does not help if the requests are undirected. In this case we create the same instance using only undirected requests. Then we get a blocked area of at least $\Omega\left(\Delta^{d/2}\right)$ for any polynomial power assignment around both points of the first request. Using the normalization of powers as before we observe that there is a blocked area of size $\Omega\left(\Delta^{d/2}\right)$ for any small request, *no matter which power we assign to it*. This proves the theorem. $\square$

3. IMPROVED COMPETITIVE RATIOS

3.1 A Near-Optimal Algorithm for the Square-Root Assignment

Algorithm 1 MULTI-CLASS SAFE-DISTANCE

1: Initialize accepted requests $S = \emptyset$.
2: **while** a new request i arrives **do**
3:    Set $p_i = \sqrt{d_{ii}^\alpha}$ and temporarily accept $S' \leftarrow S \cup i$
4:    **for** all $j \in S$ **do**
5:       Let $\mathcal{C}_x$ and $\mathcal{C}_y$ be the length classes of requests i and j, respectively
6:       **if** $\min\{d_{ij}, d_{ji}\} \leq \min\{\sigma(\mathcal{C}_x), \sigma(\mathcal{C}_y)\}$ **then**
7:          decline request: $S' \leftarrow S$.
8:       **end if**
9:    **end for**
10:   Update: $S \leftarrow S'$.
11: **end while**

In this section we extend algorithm SAFE-DISTANCE to achieve a competitive ratio, which is close to the best-possible ratio for any distance-based power assignment. The algorithm uses the square-root power assignment, and the main idea of the algorithm is to block areas based on the distances of the involved requests. In particular, we classify requests into m length classes, where class $\mathcal{C}_x$ contains requests i with $d_{ii} \in [\Delta^{a_x}, \Delta^{a_{x-1}}]$ with $a_x = 1/2^x$, for $x = 1, \ldots, m-1$ and $[1, \Delta^{a_{m-1}}]$ for class $\mathcal{C}_m$. With each class we associate a safe distance $\sigma(\mathcal{C}_x)$ chosen as

$$\sigma(\mathcal{C}_x) = \max\left\{2\Delta^{a_{x-1}}, \Delta^{0.5+a_x} \cdot 18d \right.$$
$$\left. \cdot \sqrt[\alpha]{2\beta m \cdot \left(2 + \frac{1}{\alpha-d}\right)}\right\} \; .$$

This yields the following result.

THEOREM 3.1. *For any constant* $\varepsilon > 0$, MULTI-CLASS SAFE-DISTANCE *is* $O\left(\Delta^{d/2+\varepsilon}\right)$-*competitive for a single channel.*

PROOF. We first show that the algorithm is correct. We again treat a single accepted request and bound the interference from other accepted requests. This time, however, we have to consider the class the request is contained in. Suppose a request i is from class $\mathcal{C}_x$. To show that it is successful we have to estimate the distances d_{ji} for other requests. We will bound the interference from requests of each class separately and apply the construction outlined in Theorem 2.1. For requests of class $\mathcal{C}_y$ we assume a worst-case placement and divide the space into sectors of side-length $\sigma(\mathcal{C}_y)/3d$. This again shows that no sector can contain more than two senders. The consideration of layers allows to bound the joint interference from all senders. For a class $y \geq x$, the minimum distance from r_i to each sender is at least $\sigma(\mathcal{C}_y)$. Thus, there is no sender in layers 1 and 2, and we can apply previous arguments to bound the interference. For classes with $y < x$ the minimum distance between r_i and any sender from this class is only $\sigma(\mathcal{C}_x) < \sigma(\mathcal{C}_y)$. Senders can be closer to r_i creating more interference. In particular, there can be senders in sectors of layers 1 and 2. For these senders we explicitly bound the distance using $\sigma(\mathcal{C}_x)$.

$$\begin{aligned}
I &\leq \sum_{y=1}^{m} \sum_{j\in\mathcal{C}_y, j\neq i} \frac{d_{jj}^{\alpha/2}}{d_{ji}^\alpha} \\
&\leq \sum_{y\geq x}\sum_{j\in\mathcal{C}_y, j\neq i} \frac{\Delta^{\alpha/2^y}}{d_{ji}^\alpha} + \sum_{y<x}\sum_{j\in\mathcal{C}_y} \frac{\Delta^{\alpha/2^y}}{d_{ji}^\alpha} \\
&< \sum_{y\geq x} 2\Delta^{\alpha/2^y}\cdot\left(\frac{3d}{\sigma(\mathcal{C}_y)}\right)^\alpha \cdot \frac{6^d}{\alpha-d} \\
&\quad + \underbrace{\sum_{y<x}\Delta^{\alpha/2^y}\sum_{j\in\mathcal{C}_y}\frac{1}{d_{ji}^\alpha}}_{I^{<x}} \; .
\end{aligned}$$

Using Lemma 2.2, the definition of $\sigma(\mathcal{C}_x)$, and $y \geq 1$ we see that

$$
\begin{aligned}
I^{<x} \;\leq\; & 2\sum_{y<x} \Delta^{\alpha/2^y} \cdot \frac{2^d}{\sigma(\mathcal{C}_x)^\alpha} \\
& +2\sum_{y<x} \Delta^{\alpha/2^y} \cdot \left(\frac{3d}{\sigma(\mathcal{C}_y)}\right)^\alpha \cdot 4^d \\
& +2\sum_{y<x} \Delta^{\alpha/2^y} \cdot \left(\frac{3d}{\sigma(\mathcal{C}_y)}\right)^\alpha \cdot \left(2^d \sum_{\ell=3}^\infty \frac{\ell^d-(\ell-1)^d}{(\ell-1)^\alpha}\right) \\
\;<\; & 2\sum_{y<x} \Delta^{\alpha/2^y} \cdot \frac{2^d}{\sigma(\mathcal{C}_x)^\alpha} \\
& +2\sum_{y<x} \Delta^{\alpha/2^y} \cdot \left(\frac{3d}{\sigma(\mathcal{C}_y)}\right)^\alpha \cdot 4^d \\
& +2\sum_{y<x} \Delta^{\alpha/2^y} \cdot \left(\frac{3d}{\sigma(\mathcal{C}_y)}\right)^\alpha \cdot \left(\frac{6^d}{\alpha-d}\right) \\
\;\leq\; & \sum_{y<x} 2\Delta^{\alpha/2^y} \cdot \left(\frac{3d}{\sigma(\mathcal{C}_x)}\right)^\alpha \cdot 6^d \cdot \left(2+\frac{1}{\alpha-d}\right) \\
\;<\; & \sum_{y<x} \frac{\Delta^{\alpha/2^y}}{\beta m \cdot \Delta^{\alpha/2+\alpha/2^x}} \\
\;\leq\; & \frac{x-1}{\beta m \cdot \Delta^{\alpha/2^x}} \;.
\end{aligned}
$$

For the total interference we use $x \geq 1$ and bound as follows

$$
\begin{aligned}
I \;<\; & \sum_{y\geq x} 2\Delta^{\alpha/2^y} \cdot \left(\frac{3d}{\sigma(\mathcal{C}_y)}\right)^\alpha \cdot \frac{6^d}{\alpha-d} + \frac{x-1}{\beta m \cdot \Delta^{\alpha/2^x}} \\
\;\leq\; & \frac{m-x+1}{\beta m \cdot \Delta^{\alpha/2}} + \frac{x-1}{\beta m \cdot \Delta^{\alpha/2^x}} \\
\;\leq\; & \frac{1}{\beta \cdot \Delta^{\alpha/2^x}} \;.
\end{aligned}
$$

As request i is in class $\mathcal{C}_x$, the minimum signal strength is $p_i/d_{ii}^\alpha \geq 1/\Delta^{\alpha/2^x} > \beta I$, which proves correctness of the algorithm.

For bounding the competitive ratio we consider the number of requests from the optimum solution that are blocked per accepted request. We consider blocked requests from each class separately. Obviously, the largest blocked areas are generated by a request from class 1. It blocks a hypersphere of radius $\sigma(\mathcal{C}_x)$ for requests from class $\mathcal{C}_x$, which we overestimate by the corresponding sector of side-length $2\sigma(\mathcal{C}_x)$. We must take into account that requests from class $\mathcal{C}_x$ are bounded from below in distance. The proof of the density lemma can be adjusted to show that there can be only $(d+1)^\alpha/\beta$ receivers and senders in a sector of side-length h when each request has distance at least $d_{ii} \geq h$. There are only $(d+1)^\alpha (x/h)^d/\beta$ requests of minimum length h in a sector of side-length x. In the blocked area of $\mathcal{C}_x$ we can schedule at most $(d+1)^\alpha (2\sigma(\mathcal{C}_x)/\Delta^{1/2^x})^d/\beta$ requests. Assuming that d, α, and β are constants, this number is in $O(m\Delta^{d/2})$ for each $x = 1, \ldots, m-1$. For class $\mathcal{C}_m$ it is in $O(m\Delta^{d/2+d/2^m})$. Hence, the total number of requests blocked per accepted request is $O(m^2\Delta^{d/2+d/2^m})$. In order to obtain a bound for a constant ε, we apply MULTI-CLASS SAFE-DISTANCE using $m = \log d/\varepsilon$ length classes. This proves the theorem. $\square$

3.2 Multiple Channels

In this section we show how to generalize the algorithms above to k channels and decrease their competitive ratio. We propose a k-channel adjustment, in which we separate the problem by using certain channels only for specific request lengths. All requests with length in $[\Delta^{(i-1)/k}, \Delta^{i/k}]$ are assigned to channel i, for $i = 1, \ldots, k$, where we assign requests of length $\Delta^{i/k}$ arbitrarily to channel i or $i+1$. For each channel i we apply an algorithm outlined above, which makes decisions about acceptance and power of requests assigned to channel i. Using this separation, we effectively reduce the aspect ratio to $\Delta^{1/k}$ on each channel. If the optimum solution has to adhere to the same length separation on the channels, this would yield a denominator k in the exponents of Δ of the competitive ratios. Obviously, the optimum solution is not tied to our separation, but the possible improvement due to this degree of freedom can easily be bounded by a factor k. This yields the following corollary.

COROLLARY 3.2. MULTI-CLASS SAFE-DISTANCE with k-channel adjustment is $O\left(k\Delta^{(d/2k)+\varepsilon}\right)$-competitive for the square-root power assignment. SAFE-DISTANCE with k-channel adjustment is $O\left(k\Delta^{d/k}\right)$-competitive for any polynomial power assignment with $r \in [0,1]$, and $O\left(k\Delta^{\max\{r,1-r\}\cdot d/k}\right)$-competitive for $r \notin [0,1]$.

3.3 A Randomized Algorithm

In the previous section for $k = \Theta(\log \Delta)$, the length differences on each channel reduce to a constant factor, e.g., for suitable k the requests on channel j are of length $[2^{j-1}, 2^j]$. This implies that we approximate the requests on each channel by a constant factor. Thus, we obtain an $O(\log \Delta)$-competitive algorithm against an optimum that can use $k = \Theta(\log \Delta)$ channels. Similarly, if the optimum was restricted to use only one channel, we would obtain a constant factor approximation algorithm. This is the main insight for designing our randomized algorithm RANDOM SAFE-DISTANCE. We virtually set up $\Theta(\log \Delta)$ channels, pick one channel uniformly at random, and then run our algorithm restricted to this channel. This yields a $O(\log \Delta)$-competitive randomized algorithm, even for the case of a single channel. Using an additional k-channel adjustment in this case shows a similar result for k channels. We have the following corollary.

COROLLARY 3.3. RANDOM SAFE-DISTANCE with k-channel adjustment is $O(\log \Delta)$-competitive for any polynomial power assignment and any number k of channels.

Note that for polynomial assignments with $r \notin (0,1)$ and one channel the logarithmic ratio is asymptotically optimal. This follows with a simple example from [5]. There are $n = \Theta(\log \Delta)$ nested request pairs on the line with exponentially increasing distance. The optimum power assignment can successfully schedule $\Omega(\log \Delta)$ requests. Using any polynomial assignment with $r \notin (0,1)$ there can be only $O(1)$ successful requests. Thus, using such a power assignment even an optimal offline algorithm knowing all requests is $\Omega(\log \Delta)$-competitive. A similar observation holds with results of [5] in the case of directed request sets and any distance-based power assignment. In this case, however, the lower bound is only $\Omega(\log \log \Delta)$. Closing this gap remains as an open problem.

4. REQUESTS WITH DURATION

In the previous sections we assumed that requests last forever, analyzing only the spatial aspect of the problem. We now show how our results extend when each request i has a duration t_i. After time t_i an accepted request stops sending and leaves (thus, no longer causing interference). For simplicity requests are assumed to arrive in ordered starting time. The extension to arbitrary starting and ending times is straightforward and changes the results by at most a constant factor.

We first show the modification for the algorithm SAFE-DISTANCE for $r \in [0,1]$. Whenever a request arrives, SAFE-DISTANCE accepts this request iff the safe distance σ to all previous accepted and still sending requests holds. Observe that the optimal solution accepts at most $O(\Delta^d)$ requests, when SAFE-DISTANCE accepts a request i with $t_i = 1$. Request i blocks only requests that start while i sends, and each blocked request has length at least t_i. This reduces the analysis to spatial aspects. Furthermore, a request i with $t_i = \Gamma$ can be split into Γ requests of length 1, thus blocking at most $O(\Gamma \cdot \Delta^d)$ requests. The argumentation is similar for other polynomial power assignments and results in an additional factor of Γ in all previously shown bounds (cf. Section 1.2).

In the case of multiple channels, for $k = k' \cdot k''$, clustering of requests w.r.t. similar length and duration values can be used to improve the ratio for MULTI-CLASS SAFE-DISTANCE to $O\left(k \cdot \Gamma^{1/k'} \Delta^{(d/2k'')+\varepsilon}\right)$. Choosing $k = \log \Gamma \cdot \log \Delta$, RANDOM SAFE-DISTANCE becomes $O(\log \Gamma \cdot \log \Delta)$-competitive.

5. REFERENCES

[1] M. Andrews and M. Dinitz. Maximizing capacity in arbitrary wireless networks in the SINR model: Complexity and game theory. In *Proc. 28th IEEE Conf. Computer Communications (INFOCOM)*, pages 1332–1340, 2009.

[2] C. Avin, Z. Lotker, and Y. A. Pignolet. On the power of uniform power: Capacity of wireless networks with bounded resources. In *Proc. 17th European Symposium on Algorithms (ESA)*, pages 373–384, 2009.

[3] H. Balakrishnan, C. L. Barrett, V. A. Kumar, M. V. Marathe, and S. Thite. The distance-2 matching problem and its relationship to the MAC-layer capacity of ad hoc wireless networks. *IEEE J. Selected Areas in Communications*, 22(6):1069–1079, 2004.

[4] D. Chafekar, V. S. A. Kumar, M. V. Marathe, S. Parthasarathy, and A. Srinivasan. Approximation algorithms for computing capacity of wireless networks with SINR constraints. In *Proc. 27th IEEE Conf. Computer Communications (INFOCOM)*, pages 1166–1174, 2008.

[5] A. Fanghänel, T. Kesselheim, H. Räcke, and B. Vöcking. Oblivious interference scheduling. In *Proc. 28th Symp. Principles of Distributed Computing (PODC)*, pages 220–229, 2009.

[6] A. Fanghänel, T. Kesselheim, and B. Vöcking. Improved algorithms for latency minimization in wireless networks. In *Proc. 36th Intl. Colloq. Automata, Languages and Programming (ICALP)*, volume 2, pages 208–219, 2009.

[7] O. Goussevskaia, M. M. Halldórsson, R. Wattenhofer, and E. Welzl. Capacity of arbitrary wireless networks. In *Proc. 28th IEEE Conf. Computer Communications (INFOCOM)*, pages 1872–1880, 2009.

[8] O. Goussevskaia, Y. A. Oswald, and R. Wattenhofer. Complexity in geometric SINR. In *Proc. 8th Intl. Symp. Mobile Ad-Hoc Networking and Computing (MOBIHOC)*, pages 100–109, 2007.

[9] P. Gupta and P. R. Kumar. The capacity of wireless networks. *IEEE Trans. Information Theory*, 46:388–404, 2000.

[10] M. M. Halldórsson. Wireless scheduling with power control. In *Proc. 17th European Symposium on Algorithms (ESA)*, pages 361–372, 2009.

[11] M. M. Halldórsson and R. Wattenhofer. Wireless Communication is in APX. In *Proc. 36th Intl. Colloq. Automata, Languages and Programming (ICALP)*, volume 1, pages 525–536, 2009.

[12] T. Moscibroda and R. Wattenhofer. The complexity of connectivity in wireless networks. In *Proc. 25th IEEE Conf. Computer Communications (INFOCOM)*, pages 1–13, 2006.

[13] T. Moscibroda, R. Wattenhofer, and A. Zollinger. Topology control meets SINR: The scheduling complexity of arbitrary topologies. In *Proc. 7th Intl. Symp. Mobile Ad-Hoc Networking and Computing (MOBIHOC)*, pages 310–321, 2006.

Balls into Bins with Related Random Choices

Petra Berenbrink
School of Computing Science
Simon Fraser University
Burnaby, B.C.,V5A 1S6
Canada
petra@cs.sfu.ca

André Brinkmann
Paderborn Center for Parallel
Computing
University of Paderborn
33102 Paderborn
Germany
brinkman@upb.de

Tom Friedetzky
School of Engineering and
Computing Sciences
Durham University
Durham DH1 3LE
United Kingdom
tom.friedetzky@dur.ac.uk

Lars Nagel
School of Engineering and
Computing Sciences
Durham University
Durham DH1 3LE
United Kingdom
lars.nagel@dur.ac.uk

ABSTRACT

We consider a variation of classical *balls-into-bins* games. We randomly allocate m balls into n bins. Following Godfrey's model [6], we assume that each ball i comes with a β-balanced set of clusters of bins $\mathcal{B}_i = \{B_1, \ldots, B_{s_i}\}$. The condition of β-balancedness essentially enforces a uniform-like selection of bins, where the parameter $\beta \geq 1$ governs the deviation from uniformity. We use a more relaxed notion of balancedness than [6], and also generalise the concept to *deterministic balancedness*.

Each ball $i = 1, \ldots, m$, in turn, runs the following protocol: (i) it *i.u.r.* (*independently and uniformly at random*) chooses a cluster of bins $B_i \in \mathcal{B}_i$, and (ii) it *i.u.r.* chooses one of the empty bins in B_i and allocates itself to it. Should the cluster not contain at least a single empty bin then the protocol fails.

If the protocol terminates successfully, that is, every ball has indeed been able to find at least one empty bin in its chosen cluster, then this will obviously result in a maximum load of one. The main goal is to find a tight bound on the maximum number of balls, m, so that the protocol terminates successfully (with high probability). We improve on Godfrey's result and show $m = \frac{n}{\Theta(\beta)}$. This upper bound holds for all mentioned types of balancedness. It even holds when we generalise the model by allowing *runs*. In this extended model, motivated by P2P networks, each ball i tosses a coin, and with constant probability p_i ($0 < p_i \leq 1$) it runs the protocol as described above, but with the remaining probability it copies the previous ball's choice B_{i-1}, that is, it re-uses the previous cluster of bins.

Categories and Subject Descriptors

G.3 [**Probability and Statistics**]: Stochastic Processes; C.2.4 [**Computer-communication Networks**]: Distributed Systems

General Terms

Algorithms, Theory

Keywords

balls into bins, peer-to-peer

1. INTRODUCTION

Balls-into-bins games (or urn games, or allocation games) have been studied for decades. In these games, m balls are randomly allocated into n bins. Due of the conceptual simplicity of *balls-into-bins* games, it has been possible to successfully use them to model load balancing schemes in networks as well as many other "real world" applications.

It is well known that if we allow each of m balls to choose exactly one of n bins at random, the maximum load in any bin is approximately $m/n + \sqrt{m/n \log n}$ [10]. Azar, Broder, Karlin, and Upfal's paper [1] (using ideas based on earlier work by Karp, Luby and Meyer auf der Heide [7]) has shown that the maximum load can be considerably decreased by allowing each ball just a small amount of random choices. The authors have shown that the maximum load can be bounded by $\ln \ln n / \ln d + \Theta(1)$ if $m = n$ balls are thrown and each ball has d bins as choices, among which it will choose a least loaded one. Vöcking's *always-go-left* protocol improves on these results and decreases the maximum load of any bin to $\ln \ln n / d + O(1)$ by introducing a degree of asymmetry [14]. This result implies that if we allow a ball $\Omega(\ln \ln n)$ many choices, then the maximum load will be constant.

In this paper we consider a variation of the *balls-into-bins* game, which has been introduced by Godfrey. In Godfrey's model $m < n$ balls have to be allocated into n bins with a maximum load of one [6]. In contrast to the simple case from [1] he assumes that the choices of the bins are *not* uniform and independent at random. Each ball comes with a set of "clusters", where each cluster is simply a set of bins. The ball will randomly pick a cluster, and then commit to one of the empty bins within that cluster (if any). In Godfrey's model for every ball the probability that a fixed bin is in the chosen cluster has to be roughly the same. Hence, the assignment of the bins to the clusters can be arbitrary or even regular as long as every bin is in roughly the same amount of clusters. We consider two main generalisations of Godfrey's model. Again, we assume that each ball comes with a set of "clusters" and the ball will randomly pick a cluster and then commit to one of the empty bins within that cluster. In contrast to Godfrey we only assume that on average (the average is taken over the choices of all balls) any bin will occur in not too many chosen clusters. This model is captured by what we will introduce in Definition 1 and Definition 2, as (one-sided) probabilistic balancedness and averaged balancedness, respectively, later on. In the second model, we assume that each ball comes with one fixed cluster, see Definition 3. Again, we have to assume that no bin occurs in too many clusters. For details, the reader is referred to the corresponding definitions. A further generalisation of the original model assumes that the same cluster can be chosen in multiple successive steps.

1.1 Applications

With regards to the dependencies as mentioned above, consider, for example, the case where the balls and the bins are distributed as points in $\mathbb{R}^2$. This is actually a relevant model, since when designing and analysing *e.g.* peer-to-peer or cloud-based systems, it is often assumed that the participants (peers in the former case, users and data servers in the latter) are somehow embedded into some geometric space. B_i will then consist of the bins "closest" to ball i *w.r.t.* the embedding and a given distance metric. In this case, the distribution of bins in the set B_i is not chosen *i.u.r.*, and the geographical distance between two bins might determine their probability to be in a joint set B_i.

As already hinted at, the model can be considered as being motivated by demands arising in cloud and grid computing. If a cloud or grid provider accepts to run a job, it has to place this job as near as possible to the data being accessed by this job. Otherwise, access latencies might significantly reduce the performance for this job. Nevertheless, the provider increases the number of choices by either replicating frequently accessed data to different computing centres, or by allowing to distribute the data over multiple data centres [9, 13]. Translating back to our scenario, none of these approaches will generally result in a perfectly uniform and independent choice of bins for our balls. This model will be analysed in Section 2.

The cloud scenario includes an additional extension to the standard *balls-into-bins* games, where the selection of bins may or may not depend on the choices of previous balls. It may be assumed that there is a given probability that the peer accessing the cloud in step i will also be the peer accessing the network in step $i + 1$, and therefore, in our setting, that $B_{i+1} = B_i$. The underlying process is that a new peer in a cloud environment typically moves multiple objects, like big data bases, into the cloud after entering it for the first time. After this initialisation step, the allocated storage capacity typically stays relatively invariant. These "runs" are analysed in Section 3.

1.2 Known results

There is a vast number of papers dealing with *balls-into-bins* games in their many different flavours. We shall restrict our attention to previous work that is relevant to the results presented in this paper. That is, we concentrate on protocols that achieve a fixed maximum bin load, usually one or some constant, in settings where the balls' choices of bins are not (necessarily) independent or uniform.

The model used in this paper may be viewed as a generalisation of the multiple-choice model – in that a cluster represents a ball's choices – but this is not the focus of this paper. In the case of the multiple-choice model every ball is allowed to choose d bins independently and uniformly at random. Usually, the ball is allocated to the least loaded bin among its choices, and typically one is interested in deriving tight bounds on the maximum load of any bin, given the numbers of balls and bins. For a discussion of this type of model the reader is referred to [8] and [14] and references therein. Note that the results of [1] yield constant load per bin for $d = \ln n$, and the always-go-left protocol of [14] achieves constant load for $d = \ln \ln n$.

Most recently several papers have examined the case when bins are not chosen *i.u.r.*. The motivation for these models comes from the properties of P2P networks like Chord, where one interval on a ring is randomly assigned to each bin, and the selection process leads to different arc lengths [12]. The deviation of the lengths of the resulting intervals on the ring, called the *smoothness* of the environment, becomes $\Omega(n \log n)$ with high probability if each bin is mapped only to a single point on the ring. This arc length determines the probability for each bin to be selected by a ball. The smoothness of a P2P environment can be decreased to a constant if each bin is represented by multiple "virtual bins", or, if each bin is responsible for only a single interval on the ring, if join or leave operations can trigger some redistribution of the intervals on the ring [2, 3].

Byers *et al.* have shown that this imbalance only leads to a small shift in the maximum load, even if the likelihood of some bins to be chosen is larger than the average by a factor of $O(\log n)$ [4]. Wieder aims to distribute the load as evenly as possible, if the smoothness of the environment is bounded by a constant $\alpha \cdot \beta$ [15]. It is shown that the *balls-into-bins* approach leads to a maximum load of $\frac{m}{n} + \frac{\ln \ln n}{\ln(1+\epsilon)} + O(1)$, if the randomisation process can choose between $d = f(\alpha, \beta)$ choices. The presented bounds are tight in a way that a smaller d leads to a deviation of the load linear in m.

Most relevant to our paper, Godfrey introduced the notion of β-balancedness [6]. The main contribution of his paper is a proof showing that if the number of balls can be bounded by $m = O(n/(\beta \log \beta))$ then *w.h.p.* Algorithm 1 succeeds in finding an allocation with maximum load equal to one. This bound on m is not explicitly stated in his paper; the $\beta \cdot \log \beta$-term is hidden in his parameters k and α, but can be easily verified. He also shows an upper bound (of greater than one) on the maximum load in the case $m = n$ by trivially running the original algorithm a constant number of times.

1.3 Our contributions

Our main contributions are the following:

1. We introduce relaxed definitions of balancedness (one-sided balancedness and averaged balancedness) as well

as a deterministic version of balancedness. Our results hold for all these models.

2. We improve Godfrey's upper bound on the number of balls m from $\frac{n}{\Theta(\beta \cdot \log \beta)}$ to $\frac{n}{\Theta(\beta)}$. This is asymptotically optimal (β need not be constant); see Observation 1. Note that we did not try to optimise the constants in this version of the paper.

3. We extend the original model so that we allow for the concept of *runs*. In this new model, each ball i tosses a coin, and with probability $1/2$ (or, indeed, any constant $0 < p_i < 1$) it runs the protocol as described above, but with the remaining probability it copies the previous ball's choice B_{i-1}, that is, it re-uses the previous cluster of bins. We prove the same asymptotic upper bound on m.

4. We considerably simplify Godfrey's original proof. Our proofs are essentially simply applications of Chernoff bounds, where [6] employed a somewhat diffuse coupling argument.

While the concept of balancedness allows one to investigate the *balls-into-bins* model in the presence of bounded dependencies, or may be viewed as a generalisation of the multiple-choice paradigm, the runs, in addition to the obvious effect of saving on randomness, are also of practical relevance (*e.g.* for cloud computing). The authors are not aware that this particular model introducing runs (with or without the concept of balancedness) has been studied previously.

1.4 Models and Definitions

In this section we introduce notation used in the remaining technical sections. Balls are numbered $1, \ldots, m$ and bins are denoted $b_1, \ldots, b_n$. Ball i comes with a set of s_i many clusters of bins $\mathcal{B}_i = \{B_1, \ldots, B_{s_i}\}$. Each such cluster contains $c \cdot \log n$ many bins for some positive constant c, which will be specified later. Each $\mathcal{B}_i$ contains arbitrarily many such clusters, subject to it being β-balanced (see Definitions 1, 2, and 3). However, notice that for deterministic balancedness (Def. 3) $s_i = 1$ for every i. In a model with *runs* we assume that every ball i has the choice between choosing the cluster that was used by ball $i - 1$, or choosing a random $B_i \in \mathcal{B}_i$. For details see Algorithm 2.

Notice that we fix the cluster size in order to make the proof more accessible; a *lower bound* of $c \cdot \log n$ would be quite sufficient. It is worth pointing out that "accessibility" simply refers to technicalities; a generalisation to the more general case is straightforward. Even in the general setting our proof is still conceptually much simpler than Godfrey's in [6]. Our definition of *one-sided β-balancedness* is based on the definition from [6]. Godfrey defines a random set of bins B to be β-balanced if it holds for all bins j that

$$\frac{1}{\beta n} \leq \mathbf{P}(j \in B) \cdot \mathbb{E}\left[\frac{1}{|B|} \mid j \in B\right] \leq \frac{\beta}{n}.$$

Our definition varies slightly in notation but, more importantly, we are able to drop the lower bound $1/(\beta n)$.

DEFINITION 1 (ONE-SIDED β-BALANCEDNESS). *For $\beta \geq 1$, a set of clusters $\mathcal{B}_i$ is β-balanced if for all bins j and*

i.u.r. *chosen $B_i \in \mathcal{B}_i$,*

$$\mathbf{P}(j \in B_i) \leq \frac{\beta \cdot c \cdot \log n}{n}.$$

It would also be sufficient if $\mathbf{P}(j \in B_i) \leq (\beta c \log n)/n$ *on average*, where the average is taken over all balls:

DEFINITION 2 (AVERAGED β-BALANCEDNESS). *For $\beta \geq 1$, a sequence of clusters $\mathcal{B}_1, \ldots, \mathcal{B}_m$ of sets is averaged β-balanced if for all bins j and i.u.r. chosen $B_1 \in \mathcal{B}_1, \ldots, B_m \in \mathcal{B}_m$,*

$$\sum_{i=1}^{m} \mathbf{P}(j \in B_i) \leq m \cdot \frac{\beta \cdot c \cdot \log n}{n}.$$

We also consider the following deterministic model.

DEFINITION 3 (DETERMINISTIC BALANCEDNESS). *Assume ball i can be allocated only to the bins of the fixed cluster B_i ($1 \leq i \leq m$) with $|B_i| = c \log n$. Let s_j be the number of sets containing bin j. A set of clusters $B_1, \ldots B_m$ is deterministically balanced if for all $1 \leq j \leq n$*

$$s_j \leq \frac{c \cdot \log n}{12}.$$

Similar to Godfrey's paper, in our simple model each ball $i = 1, \ldots, m$ runs the protocol presented in Algorithm 1. Actually, in his paper a ball commits to an *i.u.r.* chosen bin of *minimum load* from within its chosen cluster. Inside this paper, we are only interested in a final maximum load of one (as is Godfrey throughout the main part of his paper) and for the purpose we may as well assume that this is what his algorithm does.

In our extended model, allowing for runs, we consider the algorithm as described in Algorithm 2. Let p be a constant strictly between 0 and 1 (it is trivial to extend the algorithm and proof to individual p_i but we have chosen to fix one single p for reasons of presentation). We assume that there is a randomly pre-selected set of bins B_0.

Algorithm 1 The simple protocol for ball $i \in \{1, \ldots, m\}$

1: *i.u.r.* choose a cluster of bins $B_i \in \mathcal{B}_i$
2: **if** B_i contains at least one empty bin **then**
3:     *i.u.r.* choose an empty bin $b \in B_i$ and allocate to b
4: **else**
5:     Fail
6: **end if**

Algorithm 2 The extended protocol for ball $i \in \{1, \ldots, m\}$

1: With constant probability p, choose B_{i-1}. With the remaining probability $1-p$, choose a cluster of bins $B_i \in \mathcal{B}_i$. Either way, let B denote the chosen cluster.
2: **if** B contains at least one empty bin **then**
3:     *i.u.r.* choose an empty bin $b \in B$ and allocate to b
4: **else**
5:     Fail
6: **end if**

1.5 Chernoff Bounds

We will use the following standard Chernoff bounds in our proofs.

LEMMA 1. *Consider n independent random Bernoulli variables $X_1, \ldots, X_n$ with $\boldsymbol{P}[X_i = 1] = p_i$ and $\boldsymbol{P}[X_i = 0] = 1 - p_i$ for all $1 \leq i \leq n$. Let $X = \sum_{i=1}^{n} X_i$ and let $\mu := \mathbb{E}[X] = \sum_{i=1}^{n} p_i$. Then for $0 \leq \epsilon \leq 1$,*

$$\boldsymbol{P}[X \geq (1 + \epsilon)\mu] \leq \left(\frac{e^\epsilon}{(1 + \epsilon)^{1+\epsilon}} \right)^\mu \leq e^{-\epsilon^2 \mu / 3}.$$

We will also use the following well-known result (see e.g. [5]). Notice that it does not require the random variables to be independent but assumes "nice" correlation. It may easily be verified by reproving any proof of standard Chernoff bounds using the conditions as stated.

LEMMA 2. *Let $X_1, \ldots X_n$ be random variables bounded in $[0, 1]$ such that for each $i \in [n]$,*

$$E[X_i \mid X_0, \ldots, X_{i-1}] \leq p_i.$$

then

$$\boldsymbol{P}[X \geq (1 + \epsilon)\mu] \leq \left(\frac{e^\epsilon}{(1 + \epsilon)^{1+\epsilon}} \right)^\mu \leq e^{-\epsilon^2 \mu / 3}.$$

The following lemma states a fairly straight-forward variant of Chernoff-type bounds for geometrically distributed variables.

LEMMA 3 (LEMMA 1.7 IN [11], PAGE 51). *Given a collection of n independent geometrically distributed random variables $X_1, X_2, \ldots, X_n$ with parameters $p_1, \ldots p_n \in (0, 1)$ and $p = \min_i p_i$, then*

$$\boldsymbol{P}(X \geq (1 + \delta) \cdot \mathbb{E}[X]) \leq \left(1 + \frac{\delta \cdot \mathbb{E}[X] p}{n} \right)^n \cdot e^{-\delta \cdot \mathbb{E}[X] p}$$

where $\delta > 0$ and $X = X_1 + X_2 + \cdots + X_n$. $\square$

2. THE SIMPLE MODELS

For $n \in \mathbb{N}$ let $[n] = \{1, \ldots, n\}$. For any set B of bins let EMPTY(B) denote the number of empty bins in B. For $i = 1, \ldots, m$, we call the i-th ball *good* if it finds strictly more than half of its chosen cluster empty, that is, EMPTY$(B_i) > |B_i|/2 = \frac{c}{2} \log n$. Otherwise we call it *bad*. The factor of $1/2$ has been chosen for convenience. In principle any constant would do just as well – we do generally not attempt to optimise any constants. We will occasionally refer to the "goodness" of balls $1, \ldots, i$ as the induction hypothesis for ball $i + 1$ (note that the induction base is trivial).

THEOREM 1. *Let $m \leq \frac{n}{36\beta}$ and $c \geq 108(k + 1)$. The probability for Algorithm 1 to fail if the bin's choices are one-sided (averaged) β-balanced is at most n^{-k} for any positive constant k.*

PROOF. Here we present only the proof for a one-sided β-balanced system. The generalisation to the proof for averaged β-balanced is straightforward (by, in the notation as used below, essentially averaging "point-wise" probabilities that $X_q = 1$). For $i \in [m]$, let $\mathcal{E}_i$ denote the event that balls $1, \ldots, i$ are good. For $i \in [m]$, let $\mathcal{F}_i$ denote the event that ball i is the first bad ball, that is, $\boldsymbol{P}(\mathcal{F}_i) = \boldsymbol{P}(\text{ball } i \text{ bad}|\mathcal{E}_{i-1})$. Let $\mathcal{F}_0$ denote the event that no ball is

bad, *i.e.*, $\mathcal{F}_0 = \mathcal{E}_m$. If we consider the probability space of all possible combinations of good and bad balls then $\{\mathcal{F}_i\}_{i=0,\ldots,m}$ defines a partition. Therefore,

$$
\begin{aligned}
\boldsymbol{P}(\neg\mathcal{E}_m) &= \sum_{i=0}^{m} \boldsymbol{P}(\neg\mathcal{E}_m|\mathcal{F}_i) \cdot \boldsymbol{P}(\mathcal{F}_i) \\
&= \boldsymbol{P}(\neg\mathcal{E}_m|\mathcal{F}_0) \cdot \boldsymbol{P}(\mathcal{F}_0) + \sum_{i=1}^{m} \boldsymbol{P}(\neg\mathcal{E}_m|\mathcal{F}_i) \cdot \boldsymbol{P}(\mathcal{F}_i) \\
&= \sum_{i=1}^{m} \boldsymbol{P}(\neg\mathcal{E}_m|\mathcal{F}_i) \cdot \boldsymbol{P}(\mathcal{F}_i) \\
&= \sum_{i=1}^{m} \boldsymbol{P}(\mathcal{F}_i) = \sum_{i=1}^{m} \boldsymbol{P}(\text{ball } i \text{ bad}|\mathcal{E}_{i-1}).
\end{aligned}
$$

In the following we fix an arbitrary $i \in [m]$ and upper bound $\boldsymbol{P}(\mathcal{F}_i) = \boldsymbol{P}(\text{ball } i \text{ bad}|\mathcal{E}_{i-1})$. We can assume $i > (c \log n)/2$; otherwise the probability for ball i to be bad is zero. We consider the following variant of Algorithm 1. For all balls $j \in [i]$ we *i.u.r.* choose a cluster of bins $B_j \in \mathcal{B}_j$ and place a *token* with label j into *each* bin $b \in B_j$. Then, for all balls $j \in [i]$ we allocate the ball into an empty bin *i.u.r.* chosen from the bins containing a token with label j. We say a token with label j is *redeemed* if the corresponding bin receives ball j. Note that we redeem at most one token per bin.

We first upper-bound the number of tokens any bin receives. Fix any bin $b \in B_i$. Since the number of tokens received by a fixed bin is monotonic in the number of balls thrown and therefore in the number of tokens placed, it suffices to consider i to be as large as possible, that is $i = m$. Consider Bernoulli random variables $X_1, \ldots, X_m$ with $X_q = 1$ if the fixed bin b contains a token with label q, and $X_q = 0$ otherwise. Because of β-balancedness, $\boldsymbol{P}(X_q = 1) \leq \beta c \log(n)/n$. Let $X = \sum_{q=1}^{m} X_q$. Then

$$\mathbb{E}[X] \leq m \cdot \frac{\beta c \log n}{n}.$$

Define $\mu = \frac{m\beta c \log n}{n}$. Since $m \leq \frac{n}{36\beta}$ we have $\mu \leq \frac{c \log n}{36}$. Using Lemma 1 we obtain

$$\boldsymbol{P}\left[X \geq \frac{c \log n}{18} \right] \leq e^{-(c \log n/108)} \leq n^{-(k+1)}$$

for c large enough, *i.e.*, $c \geq 108 \cdot (k + 1)$. Hence, with sufficiently large probability every bin in B_i has at most $c \log(n)/18$ tokens and the total number of tokens in bins from B_i is at most $(c \log(n))^2/18$. This immediately gives us a bound on the number of times that bins from B_i can appear in previously selected bins B_j with $1 \leq j < i$:

$$\sum_{j=1}^{i-1} |B_i \cap B_j| \leq \frac{(c \log n)^2}{18}.$$

Now we define the set $T = \{T_{j_1}, T_{j_2}, \cdots, T_{j_\ell}\}$ as the set of steps in which $B_i \cap B_j \neq \emptyset$. Since every bin of B_i occurs in at most $c \log(n)/18$ sets B_j with $i \neq j$ we have $\ell \leq (c \log(n))^2/18$. For every set $T_j \in T$ we define a random variable Y_j with $Y_j = 1$ if a token in $B_i \cap B_j$ is redeemed in step j and $Y_j = 0$ otherwise. The probability that an empty bin in B_j receives the ball (meaning the token is redeemed) is at most $2/(c \log n)$ due to the induction hypothesis. Hence, the probability that a token in $B_i \cap B_j$ is redeemed is at most

$$\frac{|\mathrm{EMPTY}(B_i \cap B_j)| \cdot 2}{c \log n} \leq \frac{|B_i \cap B_j| \cdot 2}{c \log n}.$$

We now consider two cases.

Case1:$(|\mathbf{B_i} \cap \mathbf{B_j}| \cdot \mathbf{2})/(\mathbf{c \log n}) \geq \mathbf{1}.$.
Then we assume $\mathbf{P}[Y_j = 1] = 1$. Since the total number of tokens in all bins from B_i over all time steps is at most $(c \log(n))^2/18$ this can happen at most $c \log n / 9$ times.

Case 2:$(|\mathbf{B_i} \cap \mathbf{B_j}| \cdot \mathbf{2})/(\mathbf{c \log n}) < \mathbf{1}.$.
In this case we can assume that the probability that a token in $B_i \cap B_j$ is redeemed is smaller than one. We now define a new set of random variables $Y'_{j_1}, \ldots, Y'_{j_r}$ with $\mathbf{P}[Y'_{j_r} = 1] = \mathbf{P}[Y_{j_r} = 1]$ if $(|B_i \cap B_{j_r}| \cdot 2)/(c \log n) < 1$ and $\mathbf{P}[Y'_{j_r} = 1] = 0$ otherwise.
Y'_{j_r} describes the event that a token is redeemed from $B_i \cap B_{j_r}$ in case 2. With $Y' = \sum_{r=1}^{\ell} Y'_{j_r}$ we have

$$\mathbb{E}[Y'_{j_r}] \leq (|B_i \cap B_{j_r}| \cdot 2)/(c \log n)$$

and therefore

$$\mathbb{E}[Y'] \leq \frac{(c \log(n))^2}{18} \cdot \frac{2}{c \log n} \leq \frac{c \log(n)}{9}$$

Notice that the Y'_{j_r} are not independent but satisfy the conditions of Lemma 2. We apply said Lemma with $\mu = \frac{c \log(n)}{9}$ and obtain

$$\mathbf{P}\left[Y' \geq (1+2) \cdot \mu = \frac{c \log(n)}{3}\right] \leq e^{-(4c \log n)/27} \leq n^{-(k+1)}.$$

which holds for each $c \geq 8(k+1)$. Putting the two cases together we get that with a probability of $2n^{-(k+1)}$ there are at most $c \log n / 9 + c \log n / 3 < c \log n / 2$ many redeemed tokens in B_i and that the ith ball is good. $\square$

OBSERVATION 1. *The result of Theorem 1 is asymptotically tight in terms of the number of balls m.*

PROOF. Consider the case where the n bins are divided into $n/(c \log n)$ disjunct cluster of size $c \log n$ each. Now fix a cluster and assume that in every step the cluster is chosen with a probability of $(\beta c \log n)/n$. Obviously, after the allocation of n/β balls the expected number of balls allocated into that cluster will be larger than $c \log n$. $\square$

THEOREM 2. *Let $m \leq n/12$ and $c \geq 18(k+1)$. The probability for Algorithm 1 to fail if the bin choices are deterministically balanced is at most n^{-k} for any positive constant k.*

PROOF. This theorem can be shown similar to Theorem 1. This time we do not have to bound the number of tokens in bins of B_i using Chernoff bounds. In this model the number of tokens per bin is upper bounded by $(c \log n)/12$ due to the definition of deterministically balancedness. The rest of the proof is similar to that of Theorem 1. $\square$

3. THE MODEL WITH RUNS

In this section we show results for the model with runs for the case of one-sided β-balancedness. Note that a similar version of the result can also be shown using deterministic balancedness.

THEOREM 3. *For any constants $\ell > 0$ and $0 < p < 1$, let $d = 12(1 + \frac{2p}{1-p})$, $c \geq 24(\ell+1)\frac{p}{1+p}$ and $m \leq \frac{n}{3d\beta} = \frac{n}{\Theta(\beta)}$. The probability for Algorithm 2 to fail (that is, to not successfully allocate all m balls) is at most $n^{-\ell}$.*

PROOF. The proof of this result is similar to the proof of Theorem 1. Following a similar approach, we consider a variant of Algorithm 2. Fix $i \in [m]$ and each ball $j \in [i]$ *i.u.r.* chooses a cluster of bins B_j following Algorithm 2, and places a *token* with label j into *each* bin $b \in B_j$. In order to upper bound $\mathbf{P}(\text{ball } i \text{ bad}|\mathcal{E}_{i-1})$, all we have to do is to upper bound the number of tokens that a bin $b \in B_i$ receives.
In each step $\hat{i}$, Algorithm 2 tosses a coin whether to choose a fresh $B_{\hat{i}} \in \mathcal{B}_{\hat{i}}$ or to re-use B_{i-1}. In the following we denote by a *run* a maximal sequence of steps $k, k+1, \ldots, k'$ where the algorithm chooses a fresh $B_k \in \mathcal{B}_k$, and then uses B_k throughout steps $k, k+1, \ldots, k'$ but not $k' + 1$. We assume now that we have two different types of token. If the algorithm chooses a new set (first step of a run) a *blue* is used, otherwise (remaining steps of a run) a *red* token is used. Then, for all balls $j \in [i]$, we allocate the ball into an empty *i.u.r.* chosen bin containing a (red or blue) token labelled j. We say a token with label j is *redeemed* if it receives ball j.
Similar to the proof of Theorem 1 we can show that every bin $b \in B_i$ contains at most $(c \log n)/d$ blue tokens with a probability of $1 - n^{-(\ell+1)}$ (note, we allocate at most $n/(3d\beta)$ balls instead of $n/(36\beta)$ balls). It remains to bound the number of red tokens. To do so we fix a bin b_j first. W.h.p., b_j receives at most $(c \log n)/d$ many blue tokens. For $1 \leq k \leq (c \log n)/d$, let Y_k denote the number of red tokens after the allocation of the k-th blue token. Then the Y_k ($1 \leq k \leq (c \log n)/d$) are geometrically distributed random variables with $\mathbf{Pr}[Y_k = z] = p^z \cdot (1 - p)$ and $\mathbb{E}[Y_k] = \frac{p}{1-p}$. Let $Y = Y_1 + \cdots + Y_k$. Then $\mathbb{E}[Y] = \frac{cp \log(n)}{d(1-p)}$. Using the tail estimate for geometrically distributed random variables (see Lemma 3 with $\delta = 1$) we get for $c = c(\ell, p)$ large enough (as chosen in the statement of the Theorem)

$$\mathbf{P}\left(Y \geq \frac{2cp \log n}{d(1-p)}\right) \leq 2 \exp\left(-\frac{cp \log n}{d(1-p)}\right) \leq n^{-(\ell+1)}.$$

Hence, since $d = 12(1 + \frac{2p}{1-p})$, with a probability of $1 - n^{-\ell}$ no bin receives more than

$$\frac{c \log n}{d} + 2 \cdot \frac{cp \log n}{d(1-p)} = \frac{c \log n}{d}\left(1 + \frac{2p}{1-p}\right)$$
$$= \frac{c \log n}{12(1 + \frac{2p}{1-p})}\left(1 + \frac{2p}{1-p}\right) = \frac{c \log n}{12}$$

(red or blue) tokens. The rest of the proof is similar to that of Theorem 1. $\square$

4. CONCLUSIONS

In this paper we have considered a variation of classical *balls-into-bins* games where m balls are allocated into n bins. Each ball $i = 1, \ldots, m$, in turn, runs the following simple protocol: (i) it *i.u.r.* chooses a cluster of bins $B_i \in \mathcal{B}_i$, and (ii) it *i.u.r.* chooses one of the empty bins in B_i and allocates itself to it. Should the cluster not contain at least a single empty bin then the protocol fails.

We have introduced the notion of one-sided β-balancedness roughly saying that every bin should expectedly show up in no more that $\frac{\beta m (c \log n)}{n}$ many of the m many chosen clusters. For this protocol we have shown that with high probability the maximum load is at most one. We then have generalised our results to a model where the bin cluster choices between the balls are no longer independent from each other and show a maximum load of one for the new model.

5. REFERENCES

[1] Y. Azar, A. Broder, A. Karlin, and E. Upfal. Balanced allocations. In *Proceedings of the 26th ACM Symposium on Theory of Computing (STOC)*, pages 593–602, 1994.

[2] M. Bienkowski, M. Korzeniowski, and F. Meyer auf der Heide. Dynamic load balancing in distributed hash tables. In *Proceedings of the 4th International workshop on Peer-To-Peer Systems (IPTPS)*, pages 217–225, 2005.

[3] J. Byers, J. Considine, and M. Mitzenmacher. Simple load balancing for distributed hash tables. In *Proceedings of the 2nd International workshop on Peer-To-Peer Systems (IPTPS)*, pages 80–87, February 2003.

[4] J. Byers, J. Considine, and M. Mitzenmacher. Geometric generalizations of the power of two choices. In *Proceedings of the 16th ACM Symposium on Parallel Algorithms and Architectures (SPAA)*, pages 54–63, 2004.

[5] D. P. Dubhashi and A. Panconesi. *Concentration of Measure for the Analysis of Randomized Algorithms.* Springer, 2009.

[6] B. Godfrey. Balls and bins with structure: Balanced allocations on hypergraphs. In *Proceedings of the 19th ACM-SIAM Symposium on Discrete Algorithms (SODA)*, pages 511–517, 2008.

[7] R. Karp, M. Luby, and F. Meyer auf der Heide. Efficient PRAM simulation on a distributed memory machine. In *Proceedings of the 24th ACM Symposium on Theory of Computing (STOC)*, pages 318–326, 1992.

[8] M. Mitzenmacher, A. Richa, and R. Sitaramani. *Handbook of Randomized Computing, Volume 1*, chapter: The power of two random choices: A survey of techniques and results, pages 255–312. Springer, 2001.

[9] M. Palankar, A. Iamnitchi, M. Ripeanu, and S. Garfinkel. Amazon S3 for Science Grids: a Viable Solution? In *Proceedings of the 2008 International Workshop on Data-aware Distributed Computing (DADC)*, pages 55–64, 2008.

[10] M. Raab and A. Steger. Balls into Bins - A Simple and Tight Analysis. In *Proceedings of the 2nd International Workshop on Randomization and Approximation Techniques in Computer Science (RANDOM)*, pages 159–170, 1998.

[11] C. Scheideler. *Probabilistic methods for coordination problems.* Habilitation thesis, 2000.

[12] I. Stoica, R. Morris, D. Liben-Nowell, D. Karger, M. Kaashoek, F. Dabek, and H. Balakrishnan. Chord: a scalable peer-to-peer lookup protocol for internet applications. *IEEE/ACM Transactions on Networking*, 11(1):17–32, 2003.

[13] U. Čibej, B. Slivnik, and B. Robič. The complexity of static data replication in data grids. *Parallel Computing*, 31(8+9):900–912, 2005.

[14] B. Vöcking. How asymmetry helps load balancing. *Journal of the ACM*, 50(4):568–589, 2003.

[15] U. Wieder. Balanced allocations with heterogenous bins. In *Proceedings of the 19th ACM Symposium on Parallel Algorithms and Architectures (SPAA)*, pages 188–193, 2007.

Basic Network Creation Games

Noga Alon[*]
Schools of Mathematics &
Computer Science
Tel Aviv University
Tel Aviv, Israel
& IAS
Princeton, NJ, USA
nogaa@tau.ac.il

Erik D. Demaine
Computer Science & AI Lab
M.I.T.
Cambridge, MA, USA
edemaine@mit.edu

MohammadTaghi Hajiaghayi
AT&T Labs — Research
Florham Park, NJ, USA
& Dept. of Computer Science
University of Maryland
College Park, MD, USA
hajiagha@mit.edu

Tom Leighton
Department of Mathematics
M.I.T.
Cambridge, MA, USA
& Akamai Technologies
Cambridge, MA, USA
ftl@math.mit.edu

ABSTRACT

We study a natural network creation game, in which each node locally tries to minimize its local diameter or its local average distance to other nodes, by swapping one incident edge at a time. The central question is what structure the resulting equilibrium graphs have, in particular, how well they globally minimize diameter. For the local-average-distance version, we prove an upper bound of $2^{O(\sqrt{\lg n})}$, a lower bound of 3, a tight bound of exactly 2 for trees, and give evidence of a general polylogarithmic upper bound. For the local-diameter version, we prove a lower bound of $\Omega(\sqrt{n})$, and a tight upper bound of 3 for trees. All of our upper bounds apply equally well to previously extensively studied network creation games, both in terms of the diameter metric described above and the previously studied price of anarchy (which are related by constant factors). In surprising contrast, our model has no parameter α for the link creation cost, so our results automatically apply for all values of α without additional effort; furthermore, equilibrium can be checked in polynomial time in our model, unlike previous models. Our perspective enables simpler and more general proofs that get at the heart of network creation games.

[*]Research supported in part by a USA Israeli BSF grant, by a grant from the Israel Science Foundation, by an ERC Advanced Grant, and by the Hermann Minkowski Minerva Center for Geometry at Tel Aviv University.

Categories and Subject Descriptors

F.2.2 [**Theory of Computation**]: Analysis of Algorithms and Problem Complexity—*Nonnumerical Algorithms and Problems*; G.2.2 [**Mathematics of Computing**]: Discrete Mathematics—*graph theory, network problems*

General Terms

Performance, Design, Economics

Keywords

network design, routing, price of anarchy, Nash equilibrium

1. INTRODUCTION

In a *network creation game* (see, e.g., [9, 2, 5, 4, 11, 7, 1, 12, 8]), several players (the nodes) collectively attempt to build an efficient network that interconnects everyone. Each player has two (selfish) goals: to minimize the cost spent building links (*creation cost*) and to minimize the average or maximum distance to all other nodes (*usage cost*). Together, these goals capture the issues of both network design and network routing.

Many different network creation games have been proposed, for example, varying which players can participate in the building of a link. All of the games, however, mediate the two objectives (creation cost and usage cost) by defining the cost of each link to be a parameter α, and minimizing the sum of creation cost and usage cost. The resulting behavior of these games seems quite intricate, and heavily dependent on the choice of α, with most bounds and proofs applying only to specific ranges of α. Furthermore, despite much effort in this area, the behavior remains poorly understood for certain ranges of α, in particular when the cost of creating a link is equivalent within a logarithmic factor to decreasing the distance to all other nodes by 1.

We introduce a basic form of the game that is at the heart of essentially all network creation games, while avoiding parameterization by a parameter α. Namely, we suppose that creation cost cannot be transformed into usage cost or vice versa, but that the cost of every edge remains equal. Equivalently, we can suppose that the uniform edge cost α is unknown. Thus, given some existing network (undirected graph), the only improving transformations that agents consider performing is the replacement of one set of edges with an equal number of other edges. We focus on the simplest form, called *basic network creation*, where each agent performs *edge swaps*: replacing an existing (incident) edge with another (incident) edge, whenever that swap improves the agent's usage cost. As a special case, the agent can swap an edge with an already existing edge, which corresponds to deleting an (extraneous) edge.

Our hope is that by simplifying the model to have no parameters, we get at the essence of the problem and shed new light on it. One motivation for this approach comes from the cache-oblivious model of computation [10, 6], which has successfully transformed the study of external-memory algorithms by removing parameters from the model. Indeed, we show that results for our basic network creation game carry over directly to other network creation games for all values of the parameter α. Therefore our approach enables a new uniform treatment of all values of α by carefully removing the parameter from the model.

The study of network creation games in general, and in this paper, focuses on *equilibria*: locally stable networks in which no agent can greedily improve their situation by changing the network. In general, there are many types of equilibria depending on the types of moves allowed. The most famous is *Nash equilibria*, where each agent can change their entire strategy, while fixing all other agents' strategies. In the original network creation game [9], this notion corresponds to one node deleting and/or adding any number of incident edges, without changing any other edges. In our basic network creation game, we require a weaker condition, called *swap equilibrium*, that no edge swap decreases an agent's usage cost. Thus, swap equilibria is a much broader class of strategies than previous notions of equilibria, so any theorems about swap equilibria apply equally well to many previous structures as well.

The study of equilibria in network creation games focuses on the *price of anarchy*: the worst possible overall cost in an equilibrium network divided by the best possible overall cost in any network. This ratio gives a measure of how effectively greedy agents approximate an optimal, socially planned solution. In most existing network creation games, as well as ours, the price of anarchy turns out to be within a constant factor of the largest possible diameter of an equilibrium network, as proved in [7]. Thus we arrive at the central question: how effectively greedy agents trying to minimize cost arrive at a low-diameter network. This question is important in its own right, beyond the application to price of anarchy, as it offers a first step toward understanding the structure of equilibria, in particular suggesting the emergence of a small-world phenomenon.

Because swap equilibria are broader than previous notions of equilibria, all upper bounds we prove on their diameter, and thus on price of anarchy, apply equally well to previous network creation games. What is interesting about this relation is that swap equilibria are defined independent of α, while other notions of equilibria require knowledge of the parameter α. As a consequence, all upper bounds we transfer from swap equilibria to other equilibria automatically apply for all values of parameter α. This opens the exciting possibility of a uniform treatment of network creation games without parameterization by α.

Another motivation for our basic network creation game is that Nash equilibria in network creation games are actually unrealistic: computationally bounded agents cannot even tell if they are in a Nash equilibrium (the problem is NP-complete) [9], and thus cannot tell whether they want to change their local strategy while not changing all others. In a network creation game of computationally bounded agents, it is much more reasonable to assume that an agent can only weigh a constant or sublogarithmic number of edges against each other. Our approach is to focus on the most general extreme of these models, where agents can weigh only one edge against another edge. Questions of the form "would I rather have this edge instead of this edge?" seem natural local decisions for agents to make. In addition, the theoretical advantage of this approach is that any bounds we obtain apply equally well to all other computationally bounded models as well. When we find that diameters can actually be large in the most general model, namely in Section 4, we also consider the effect of a more powerful agent that can weigh more (up to $\Theta(\lg n/\lg\lg n)$) edges against each other, and how this improves the diameter.

Problem statement.

More formally, we define two *basic network creation games*. As in previous work, we consider two possible definitions of the usage cost of a node: sum and max. For the sum version, we define a graph to be in *sum equilibrium* if, for every edge vw and every node w', swapping edge vw with edge vw' does not decrease the total sum of distances from v to all other nodes.

For the max version, we define the *local diameter* of a vertex v to be the maximum distance between v and any other vertex. We define a graph to be in *max equilibrium* if, for every edge vw and every node w', swapping edge vw with edge vw' does not decrease the local diameter of v, and furthermore, deleting edge vw strictly increases the local diameter of v. The latter condition is equivalent to the following graph property: a graph is *deletion-critical* if deleting any edge strictly increases the local diameter of both of its endpoints. A closely related property is the following: a graph is *insertion-stable* if inserting any edge does not decrease the local diameter of either endpoint. If a graph is both insertion-stable and deletion-critical, then it is certainly in max equilibrium. In our lower-bound constructions for the max version, we design graphs that are both insertion-stable and deletion-critical, as these properties are even stronger than max equilibrium.

Note that both sum and max equilibria can be detected easily in polynomial time, even locally by each agent: simply try every possible edge swap and deletion. Thus these equilibria are more natural for computationally bounded agents.

Our results.

For the sum version, we prove in Section 3.2 an upper bound of $2^{O(\sqrt{\lg n})}$ on the diameter of sum-equilibrium graphs. This result is stronger than a previous result which depends on α [7]. Our result effectively gets to the essence of the previous result, using a simpler proof that is independent of α and generalizes to a broader class of equilibria.

We conjecture that the diameter of sum equilibrium graphs is polylogarithmic, and offer interesting evidence for this conjecture in Section 5. Specifically, call a graph *distance-uniform* if all vertices have almost all vertices at the same distance d. We prove that sum equilibrium graphs induce distance-uniform graphs whose diameter is smaller by at most a factor of $O(\lg^2 n)$. We conjecture that distance-uniform graphs have polylogarithmic diameter—even getting superconstant diameter seems difficult—and prove this conjecture for Cayley graphs of Abelian groups. A proof for the general case would clearly imply our conjecture about sum equilibrium graphs. This connection shows that the structure of equilibria is closely linked to a deeper, purely graph theoretic problem of independent interest.

Fabrikant et al. [9] conjectured that Nash equilibria in the sum version are trees. Later, their conjecture was disproved [2]. We prove in Section 2.1 that, in fact, all trees in sum equilibrium have diameter exactly 2. In other words, the only tree in sum equilibrium is the star. (This result immediately transfers to Nash equilibria as well.)

In fact, all previous examples of sum equilibrium graphs have diameter 2. The disproof of the tree conjecture [2] constructed a cyclic sum equilibrium graph arising from finite projective planes, but it too has diameter 2. Thus it seems reasonable to conjecture that all sum equilibrium graphs have diameter 2. We rule out this possibility in Section 3.1 by proving the first diameter lower bound of 3 for sum equilibria, which also serves as the first separation between trees and general graphs.

For the max version, we prove in Section 4 a strong lower bound of $\Omega(\sqrt{n})$ on the diameter of max equilibrium graphs (or more precisely, insertion-stable deletion-critical graphs). We also construct graphs that are both deletion-critical and stable under k insertions, meaning that the graph is stable when the agent is permitted to change any k (incident) edges. We prove a lower bound of $\Omega(n^{1/(k+1)})$ in this case, giving a smooth trade-off between diameter and computational power. In the extreme case of $k = \Theta(\lg n / \lg\lg n)$, the lower bound becomes $\Omega(\lg n)$.

For trees in the max version, we show in Section 2.2 that, in contrast to the sum version, the diameter can be as large as 3. Conversely, we prove that no diameter larger than 3 is possible.

Overall, we offer stronger results with simpler and more elegant proofs, leading to a clearer understanding of network creation problems. We propose that further attention to network creation games focus on the basic network creation game, as it captures the same essence while being easier to work with and enabling more powerful techniques.

2. TREES

We start by analyzing equilibrium trees for both the sum and max versions. In both cases, we tightly characterize the maximum possible diameter: 2 for sum and 3 for max.

2.1 Sum $\Rightarrow$ Diameter 2

For the sum version, we prove that there is essentially only one equilibrium tree:

THEOREM 1. *If a sum equilibrium graph in the basic network-creation game is a tree, then it has diameter at most 2, and thus is a star.*

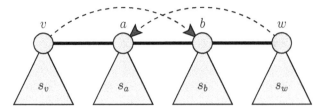

Figure 1: Illustration of Theorem 1.

PROOF. Suppose for contradiction that an equilibrium tree has diameter at least 3; refer to Figure 1. Thus it has two vertices v, w at distance exactly 3, inducing a length-3 shortest path $v \to a \to b \to w$. Let s_v, s_a, s_b, s_w denote the size of the subtrees rooted at v, a, b, w, respectively, counting the roots themselves. Consider two possible swaps: (1) v replaces its edge to a with an edge to b, and (2) w replaces its edge to b with an edge to a. The first swap improves v's distance to b's and w's subtrees by 1 (the unique shortest path in the tree no longer having to pass through a), and worsens v's distance to a's subtrees by 1; thus, the swap is a net win unless $s_b + s_w \le s_a$. Similarly, the second swap is a net win unless $s_v + s_a \le s_b$. For both swaps to not be net wins, we must have both inequalities. Summing these inequalities, we obtain that $s_v + s_a + s_b + s_w \le s_a + s_b$, i.e., $s_v + s_w \le 0$, contradicting that $s_v + s_w \ge 2$ (because in particular they count v and w). $\square$

Obviously, diameter 2 can also be achieved (and is optimal), as evidenced by the star.

2.2 Max $\Rightarrow$ Diameter 3

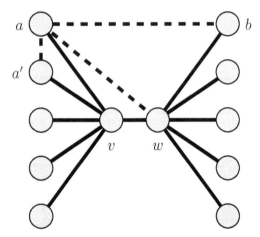

Figure 2: A tree of diameter 3 that is in max equilibrium. There are three types of edges we might try to add, shown dashed: from a leaf a to a cousin leaf a' or to a distinct leaf b or to the other root w. The only option that decreases the local diameter of either endpoint is adding aw which decreases the local diameter of a (but not w) by 1. In any swap around a, however, this addition must be combined with the deletion of edge av, which restores the original local diameter of a.

In contrast to the sum version, max-equilibrium trees can have diameter as high as 3; see Figure 2. However, this diameter is the maximum possible. To prove this, we first need a general lemma about balance in max equilibrium graphs:

LEMMA 2. *In any max-equilibrium graph, the local diameters of any two nodes differ by at most 1.*

PROOF. Suppose vertex v has local diameter d while vertex w has local diameter at least $d+2$. Let T be a breadth-first search tree from v. We claim that w prefers to swap its edge to its parent in T with an edge to v (the root of T). Observe that this swap only decreases the depths of nodes in T, so the local diameter of v remains at most d. Thus w's local diameter decreases to at most $d+1$, because w can take a unit step to reach v and then follow v's path to any other node. This swap contradicts being in max-equilibrium. □

LEMMA 3. *If a max equilibrium graph has a cut vertex v, then only one connected component of $G - v$ can have a vertex of distance more than 1 from v.*

PROOF. Let d be the local diameter of v. Let w be a vertex at distance d from v, and let W be the connected component of $G - v$ that contains w. Suppose for contradiction that there is a vertex x in $G - W$ of distance more than 1 from v. Then any path from x to W must pass through v, so is at least 2 longer than the corresponding path from v. Therefore the local diameter of w is at least $d+2$, contradicting Lemma 2. □

THEOREM 4. *If a max equilibrium graph in the basic network-creation game is a tree, then it has diameter at most 3.*

PROOF. Suppose for contradiction that an equilibrium tree has diameter at least 4. Thus it has two vertices v, w at distance exactly 4, inducing a length-4 shortest path $v \to a \to b \to c \to w$. But then b is a cut vertex and two connected components of $G - b$ have vertices v, w of distance more than 1 from b, contradicting Lemma 3. □

Therefore, there are two families of max equilibrium trees: stars (of diameter 2) and "double-stars" (of diameter 3, as in Figure 2). To be in max equilibrium, the latter type must have at least two leaves attached to each star root (v and w).

3. SUM VERSION

Next we analyze the case of general networks in the sum version. We start in Section 3.1 by giving the first lower bound of 3, and then turn to our sub-n^ε upper bound in Section 3.2.

3.1 Lower Bounds

Currently all examples of sum equilibrium graphs have diameter 2. Initially, Fabrikant et al. [9] conjectured that sum equilibrium graphs are trees, and we have shown in Section 2 that such graphs must have diameter 2. Albers et al. [2] disproved this conjecture with a cyclic sum equilibrium graph, arising from finite projective planes, but it too has diameter 2. Thus it seems reasonable to conjecture that all sum equilibrium graphs have diameter 2. Here we rule out this conjecture:

THEOREM 5. *There is a diameter-3 sum equilibrium graph.*

First we establish a few tools for proving equilibrium in graphs of small diameter/girth. The proofs are straightforward and hence omitted.

LEMMA 6. *For a vertex v of local diameter 2, swapping an incident edge does not improve the sum of distances from v.*

LEMMA 7. *Consider a vertex v of local diameter 3. Adding an edge from v to a vertex w of distance r decreases the sum of the distances from v by at most $r-1$ for w and by at most 1 for any neighbors of w whose distance to v was 3.*

LEMMA 8. *In any graph of girth 4, swapping an edge vw with edge vw' increases the distance from v to w by at least 2, unless w' is a neighbor of w, in which case it increases by at least 1.*

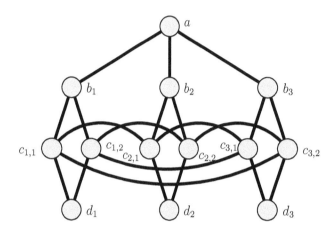

Figure 3: A diameter-3 sum equilibrium graph.

PROOF OF THEOREM 5. Figure 3 illustrates the graph. One vertex a has three neighbors: b_1, b_2, b_3. Each vertex b_i has two unique neighbors other than a: $C_i = \{c_{i,1}, c_{i,2}\}$. Furthermore, for each $i \in \{1, 2, 3\}$, we have an additional vertex d_i connected to all of C_i. Finally, for each $i, j \in \{1, 2, 3\}$, $i \neq j$, we add a particular perfect matching between C_i and C_j. Between C_1 and C_2 and between C_2 and C_3, we use the obvious matching: $c_{i,1}c_{j,1}$ and $c_{i,2}c_{j,2}$. Between C_1 and C_3, we use the other matching: $c_{i,1}c_{j,2}$ and $c_{i,2}c_{j,1}$.

We consider all possible edge swaps around each vertex, characterizing vertices by their local diameter. By inspection, vertices a, b_i, and d_i have local diameter 3, while vertices $c_{i,k}$ have local diameter 2. In particular, the graph has diameter 3. Also observe that the graph has girth 4 (by checking that the neighbor set of each vertex is an independent set), so Lemma 8 applies.

By Lemma 6, swapping edges incident to any $c_{i,k}$ does not help. For all other vertices, we apply Lemma 7.

For vertex a, swapping an edge ab_i with $ac_{j,k}$ or ad_j decreases the sum of distances from a by at most 2: in the former case, 1 for $c_{j,k}$ and 1 for d_j; and in the latter case, 2 for d_j. Now, if $i \neq j$ or if we add edge ad_j, then by Lemma 8, the distance from a to b_i increases by at least 2, absorbing any possible benefit to the swap. If $i = j$ and we add $ac_{j,k}$, then the distances from a to b_i and to $c_{i,3-k}$ increase by 1, again absorbing the benefit.

For a vertex b_i, swapping with an edge to b_j (for $i \neq j$) or to d_i is not useful by Lemma 7, because all neighbors of b_j are already at distance at most 2 from b_i. If we swap with an edge to d_j for $j \neq i$, then by Lemma 7 we gain at most 2, but by Lemma 8 we lose at least 2, so the swap is useless. If we swap the edge $b_i a$ with $b_i c_{j,k}$ for $i \neq j$, then by Lemma 7 we gain at most 1 for $c_{j,k}$ and 1 for d_j, but by Lemma 8 we lose at least 2, so the swap is useless. If we swap an edge $b_i c_{i,k}$ with $b_i c_{i,l}$ for $i \neq j$, then by Lemma 7 we gain at most 1 for $c_{j,l}$ and 1 for d_j, but we increase the distances from b_i to $c_{i,k}$ and to at least one of its c neighbors by at least 1, so again the swap is useless.

Finally, for a vertex d_i, if we swap edge $d_i c_{i,k}$ with $d_i b_i$, then by Lemma 7 we gain at most 1 for b_i and 1 for a, but we increase the distance from d_i to $c_{i,j}$ and to each of its c neighbors by at least 1, absorbing the benefit. If we swap edge $d_i c_{i,k}$ with $d_i a$, then by Lemma 7 we gain at most 2 for a and 2 total for b_j, $j \neq i$, but by Lemma 8 we increase the distance from d_i to $c_{i,j}$ by at least 2, and we increase the distances from d_i to each of $c_{i,j}$'s c neighbors by at least 1, absorbing the benefit. If we swap edge $d_i c_{i,k}$ with anything else, then by Lemma 8 we increase the distances from d_i to $c_{i,j}$ by at least 2, and we increase the distance from d_i to at least one of $c_{i,j}$'s c neighbors by at least 1. If we swap edge $d_i c_{i,k}$ with $d_i b_j$ or $d_i d_j$ for $j \neq i$, then by Lemma 7 we gain at most 2 for b_j, and in the former case, 1 for a. If we swap edge $d_i c_{i,k}$ with $d_i c_{j,l}$ for $j \neq i$, then by Lemma 7 we gain at most 1 for $c_{j,l}$ and 1 for each of b_j and d_j. In all cases, the gain is at most the loss, so the swap is useless. $\square$

3.2 $2^{O(\sqrt{\lg n})}$ Bound

Next we prove our upper bound, which generalizes the previous result of [7]:

THEOREM 9. *All sum equilibrium graphs have diameter $2^{O(\sqrt{\lg n})}$.*

First we need two basic results, which will find use in Section 5 as well.

LEMMA 10. *Any sum equilibrium graph either has diameter at most $2\lg n$ or, given any vertex u, there is an edge xy where $d(u,x) \leq \lg n$ and whose removal increases the sum of distances from x by at most $2n(1 + \lg n)$.*

PROOF. Consider a breadth-first search from any vertex u in a sum equilibrium graph G. Let T denote the top $2 + \lg n$ levels of the BFS tree, from level 0 (just u) to level $1 + \lg n$. If there are any nontree edges connecting two vertices in T, then there is a cycle C whose distance from u is at most $\lg n$ and whose length is at most $1 + 2(1 + \lg n)$. In this case, each edge xy of the cycle has the property that $d(x,u) \leq \lg n$ and removing xy decreases the sum of distances from x by at most $2n(1+\lg n)$ (replacing any use of xy with the alternate path around the cycle). Thus we can assume that the graph $G[V(T)]$ induced on these top vertices is exactly the tree T.

For a vertex v in T, let T_v denote the subtree of T rooted at v. Call v *grounded* if T_v includes a node at layer $1 + \lg n$ ("the ground"). Define the *ground distance* gd(v) of a grounded vertex v to be $1 + \lg n$ minus the level of vertex v, i.e., the difference in levels between v and the ground. If the root u is ungrounded, then every vertex has distance at most $\lg n$ from u, so the diameter of the graph is at most

$2\lg n$, proving the lemma. Thus we can assume that u is grounded.

We claim that every grounded vertex v other than u has $|T_v| \geq 2^{\text{gd}(v)}$. In particular, applying this claim to a grounded child v of u implies that $|T| > |T_v| \geq 2^{\lg n} = n$, contradicting that the whole graph has only n vertices, and thus proving the lemma. Now we prove the claim by induction on gd(v). In the base case, if v is in the ground (level $1 + \lg n$), i.e., gd$(v) = 0$, then $|T_v| \geq 1$ as desired because T_v includes v.

In the induction step, there are two cases. Because v is grounded, it must have at least one grounded child. If it has at least two grounded children, say a and b, then $|T_v| \geq 1 + |T_a| + |T_b| \geq 1 + 2 \cdot 2^{\text{gd}(a)} = 1 + 2^{\text{gd}(v)} > 2^{\text{gd}(v)}$, proving the claim. Otherwise, v has exactly one grounded child, say a. Let k denote the number of ungrounded descendants of v, plus 1 to count v itself. Consider the parent p of v in T (which exists because $v \neq u$) replacing its edge pv with the edge pa. This replacement increases the distance from p to all ungrounded descendants of v, as well as v itself, by 1, increasing the sum of distances from p by (at most) k. On the other hand, ignoring these ungrounded descendants and v, the replacement shortcuts a degree-2 vertex v, so it does not increase any other distances from p. Furthermore, the replacement strictly improves the distances to all vertices in T_a by 1. Because the graph is in equilibrium, the improvement $|T_a| - k$ cannot be positive, i.e., $k \geq |T_a|$. Therefore, $|T_v| = |T_a| + k \geq 2|T_a| \geq 2 \cdot 2^{\text{gd}(a)} = 2^{\text{gd}(v)}$, proving the claim. $\square$

COROLLARY 11. *In any sum equilibrium graph, the addition of any edge uv decreases the sum of distances from u by at most $5n \log n$.*

PROOF. Suppose for contradiction that the addition of edge uv decreases the sum of distances from u by more than $5n \log n$. If the graph has diameter at most $2\lg n$, then adding any edge can decrease each distance by at most $2\lg n$, for a total decrease of at most $2n \lg n$. Otherwise, we find the edge xy of Lemma 10 with $d(u, x) \leq \lg n$ and whose removal decreases the sum of distances from x by less than $2n(1 + \lg n)$. We claim that x prefers to replace edge xy with edge xv. The loss from deleting edge xy is at most $2n(1 + \lg n) \leq 4n \lg n$. The benefit from inserting edge xv is more than $5n \lg n - n \lg n$, because distances from u and from x differ by at most $\lg n$. The net improvement is therefore more than $5n \lg n - n \lg n - 4n \lg n = 0$, i.e., positive, contradicting that the graph is in sum equilibrium. $\square$

PROOF OF THEOREM 9. Consider a sum equilibrium graph G on n vertices. For any vertex u, let $S_k(u)$ denote the number of vertices at distance exactly k from u (the radius-k *sphere* centered at u). Let $B_k(u) = \sum_{i \leq k} S_k(u)$ denote the number of vertices within distance at most k from u (the radius-k *ball* centered at u). Let $B_k = \min_u B_k(u)$. We claim that

$$B_{4k} > n/2 \quad \text{or} \quad B_{4k} \geq \frac{k}{20 \lg n} B_k. \tag{1}$$

To prove (1), fix a vertex u, and assume that $B_{4k}(u) \leq n/2$. Then certainly $B_{3k}(u) \leq n/2$. Let T be a maximal set of vertices at distance exactly $3k$ from u subject to the distance between any pair of vertices in T being at least $2k + 1$. We claim that, for every vertex v of distance more than $3k$ from u, the distance of v from the set T is at most $d(u,v) - k$. Indeed, v is of distance $d(u,v) - 3k$ from some vertex at distance exactly $3k$ from u, and any such vertex is within distance $2k$ from some vertex of T, by the maximality of T. Because we assumed that at least $n/2$ vertices have distance more than $3k$ from u, by the pigeonhole principle, there are at least $n/(2|T|)$ such vertices v whose distance from the same vertex $t \in T$ is at most $d(u,v) - k$. Adding an edge from u to t improves the sum of distances from u by at least $(k-1)n/(2|T|) \geq kn/(4|T|)$. By Corollary 11, this improvement must be at most $5n \lg n$, so we conclude that $|T| \geq k/(20 \lg n)$. Now the balls of radius k centered at the vertices of T are all pairwise disjoint, all lie withing distance $4k$ of u, and each of them has at least B_k vertices (by the definition of B_k). Thus $B_{4k}(u) \geq B_k k/(20 \lg n)$, proving (1).

Now (1) easily implies that the diameter is at most $2^{O(\sqrt{\lg n})}$. First, $B_{2\sqrt{\lg n}} \geq 2^{\sqrt{\lg n}}$ simply because the graph is connected. Starting from this $k = 2^{\sqrt{\lg n}}$ and applying (1), whenever we multiply k by 4, B_k increases by a factor of at least $k/(20 \lg n) \geq 2^{\sqrt{\lg n} - \lg \lg n - \lg 20} = 2^{\Omega(\sqrt{\lg n})}$, unless B_k is already more than $n/2$. Taking logarithms, $O(\sqrt{\lg n})$ such iterations suffice to reach a k where $B_k > n/2$. The diameter of the graph is then at most twice such a k, because any two vertices u, v must have overlapping balls of radius k. $\square$

4. MAX VERSION

Next we consider the max version, where we can prove a strong lower bound:

THEOREM 12. *There is a max equilibrium graph of diameter* $\Theta(\sqrt{n})$.

PROOF. Our graph G can be described roughly as 2D torus rotated $45°$; refer to Figure 4. (Note, however, that a standard torus is not in max equilibrium, so the precise definition is critical.) Specifically, G has $n = 2k^2$ vertices, one for each pair (i,j) of integers where $0 \leq i, j < 2k$ and $i + j$ is even. We treat the integers as modulo $2k$; in particular, 0 and $2k$ are equivalent coordinates. Each vertex (i,j) has exactly four neighbors: $(i+1, j+1)$, $(i-1, j+1)$, $(i+1, j-1)$, and $(i-1, j-1)$. In particular, G is vertex-transitive.[1] The distance between two vertices (i,j) and (i',j') in G is exactly $\max\{d(i,i'), d(j,j')\}$, where the 1D distances are measured on the modulo-$2k$ circle: for $0 \leq i, i' \leq 2k$, $d(i,i') = \min\{|i - i'|, 2k - |i - i'|\}$. (To prove this distance formula, we simply need to observe that each coordinate can change by ± 1 in each step.)

First we show that the local diameter of every vertex is exactly k. By vertex-transitivity, it suffices to show that the local diameter of vertex (k,k) is exactly k. The distance between (k,k) and any vertex (i,j), where $0 \leq i, j \leq 2k$, is $\max\{|i - k|, |j - k|\}$, which is maximized when either i or j equals $0 \equiv 2k$.

Second we show that G is deletion-critical. By vertex-transitivity and rotational symmetry, it suffices to show that deleting the edge from (k,k) to $(k+1, k+1)$ strictly increases the local diameter of (k,k). Indeed, we claim that this deletion increases the distance from (k,k) to $(2k-1, 2k-1)$

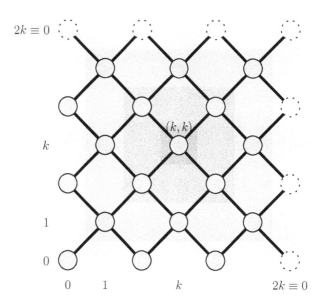

Figure 4: The $\Theta(\sqrt{n})$-diameter max equilibrium graph of Theorem 12. The rightmost and topmost columns ($x = 2k$ and $y = 2k$) are actually duplicates of the leftmost and bottommost columns ($x = 0$ and $y = 0$), respectively, and hence dotted. Shaded squares indicate distance contours from the central point (k,k).

to $k + 1$. Any such path must first proceed to a neighbor of (k,k), all of which have at least one coordinate of $k - 1$. Thus, even in the original graph G, the distance from that neighbor to $(2k-1, 2k-1)$ is k, implying that the path has length at least $k + 1$.

Third we show that G is insertion-stable (and thus in equilibrium). By vertex-transitivity and rotational symmetry, it suffices to show that inserting an edge from (k,k) to $(k+i, k+j)$ does not decrease the local diameter of (k,k) for all $0 \leq i, j \leq k$. Consider the vertex $(2k, j - j \bmod 2)$, which belongs to G because $2k + j - j \bmod 2$ is even. As we showed above, this vertex has distance k from (k,k) in the original graph G, so it remains to show that the additional edge does not make a shorter path. Such a path must first use the added edge, so it suffices to show that the distance from $(k+i, k+j)$ to $(2k, j - j \bmod 2)$ is at least $k-1$ in the original graph G. This claim follows because the second coordinates differ by $d(k + j, j - j \bmod 2) = k - j \bmod 2 \geq k - 1$. $\square$

In fact, we can also increase the dimension of the construction to d between 2 and $O(\lg n / \lg \lg n)$. Then we have a vertex for each point $(i_1, i_2, \ldots, i_d)$ where $i_1 \equiv i_2 \equiv \cdots \equiv i_d$ (mod 2), with edges to $(i_1 \pm 1, i_2 \pm 1, \ldots, i_d \pm 1)$ for all possible (independent) choices of signs for $\pm$. The resulting graph has diameter $\Theta(n^{1/d})$, which ranges from $\sqrt{n}$ to $\lg n$. This graph is deletion-critical and has the stronger property that it is stable (local diameter does not improve) under the insertion (or swapping) of up to $d - 1$ edges from one vertex. The proof is similar; for insertion-stability, we can find a point that is simultaneously far from all endpoints of the added edges by devoting one coordinate to each such endpoint. This generalization is interesting because it offers a computationally tractable alternative to Nash equilibrium defined in [9], where a vertex can insert/swap an arbitrary subset of edges.

[1] A graph is *vertex-transitive* if any vertex can be mapped to any other by a vertex automorphism, i.e., a relabeling of vertices that preserves edges.

5. CONNECTION TO DISTANCE UNIFORMITY

Call an n-vertex graph ε-*distance-uniform* if there is a value r such that, for every vertex v, the number of vertices w at distance exactly r from v is at least $(1 - \varepsilon)n$. Slightly weaker, call an n-vertex graph ε-*distance-almost-uniform* if there is a value r such that, for every vertex v, the number of vertices w at distance either r or $r + 1$ from v is at least $(1 - \varepsilon)n$. The following result connects high-diameter sum equilibrium graphs to high-diameter distance uniformity. We assume that the graph has more than a constant number of vertices; otherwise, the diameter is trivially constant and thus uninteresting.

THEOREM 13. *Any sum equilibrium graph G with $n \geq 24$ vertices and diameter $d > 2 \lg n$ induces an ε-distance-almost-uniform graph G' with n vertices and diameter $\Theta(\varepsilon d / \lg n)$ and an ε-distance-uniform graph G' with n vertices and diameter $\Theta(\varepsilon d / \lg^2 n)$.*

PROOF. We use one definitional tool to establish distance uniformity. Call an ordered triple (a, b, c) of vertices *skew* if $d(a, c) > p \lg n + d(a, b)$, for a constant p to be chosen later.

First we claim that, if $p \geq 4/\alpha$, then less than an α fraction of all $n(n - 1)(n - 2)$ possible triples (a, b, c) are skew. For if a constant fraction $\alpha n(n - 1)(n - 2)$ are skew, then by averaging, there is a choice of b and c such that an α fraction of the $n - 2$ choices for node a have (a, b, c) skew. Then adding edge bc improves the sum of distances from c by at least $(p \lg n - 1)\alpha(n - 2) = \Omega(n \lg n)$. By Lemma 10, and because $d > 2 \lg n$, there is an edge xy where $d(c, x) \leq \lg n$ and whose removal decreases the sum of distances from x by at most $2n(1 + \lg n)$. Because $d(c, x) \leq \lg n$, adding edge xb still improves the sum of distances from x by at least $((p - 1)\lg n - 1)\alpha(n - 2)$. Thus, swapping edge xy with edge xb improves the sum of distances from x by at least $((p - 1)\lg n - 1)\alpha(n - 2) - 2n(1 + \lg n)$. If $p \geq 4/\alpha$, this improvement is at least $(2 - \alpha)n \lg n + 2\alpha(1 + \lg n) - (2 + \alpha)n - 8 \lg n$. Because $\alpha \leq 1$, this improvement is at least $n \lg n - 3n - 8 \lg n$, which is positive for $n \geq 24$, contradicting equilibrium.

Second we claim that, for some vertex a, if we ignore the nearest βn and farthest βn nodes from a, then the remaining nodes b have distances $d(a, b)$ forming an interval of length at most $2p \lg n$. Let $[\ell_a, u_a]$ denote the interval of distances $d(a, b)$ for b among the middle $(1 - 2\beta)n$ nodes from a. If the claim is false, then the interval has length more than $p \lg n$ for all a. But then we claim that a constant fraction of (a, b, c) triples are skew, contradicting the first claim for sufficiently large p. We form two sets of triples as follows. For each a, take b to be any node whose distance from a is in the range $[\ell_a, \frac{1}{2}(\ell_a + u_a)]$, and take c to be any node among the βn farthest nodes from a. Also, for each a, take b to be any node among the nearest βn nodes from a, and take c to be any node whose distance from a is in the range $[\frac{1}{2}(\ell_a + u_a), u_a]$. All of these triples are skew because they span a distance of at least $\frac{1}{2}(u_a - \ell_a) > p \lg n$. The total number of these triples is at least $n(1 - 2\beta)n\beta n$: n choices for a, $(1 - 2\beta)n$ choices for either b or c from the middle range $[\ell_a, u_a]$, and βn choices for either c or b from the farthest or nearest βn nodes from a. Therefore $(1 - 2\beta)\beta n^3$ triples (a, b, c) are skew, which by the first claim is a contradiction provided $p \geq 4/((1 - 2\beta)\beta)$.

Third we claim that roughly the same property holds for all a'. More precisely, let a be the node from the previous claim, and suppose all nodes b among the middle $(1 - 2\beta)n$ have distances in an interval $D \pm p \lg n$. We claim that, for every vertex a', if we ignore the nearest $3\beta n$ and farthest $3\beta n$ nodes from a', then the remaining nodes b have distances $d(a, b)$ in the interval $D \pm 2p \lg n$. Otherwise, for some vertex a', either the nearest $3\beta n$ nodes have distances from a' less than $D - 2p \lg n$ or the farthest $3\beta n$ nodes have distances from a' more than $D + 2p \lg n$ (or both). Among these $3\beta n$ nodes, at most $2\beta n$ of them are among the nearest βn or farthest βn nodes from a. Thus, we obtain βn nodes whose distance from a is in the interval $D \pm p \lg n$ but whose distance from a' is outside the interval $D \pm 2p \lg n$. Thus adding the edge aa' decreases the sum of distances from a and a' by at least $\beta np \lg n$ total. By averaging, the sum of distances from either a or a' decreases by at least $\frac{1}{2}\beta np \lg n$. Relabel a and a' so that the sum of distances from a' so improves. By Lemma 10, and because $d > 2 \lg n$, there is an edge xy where $d(a', x) \leq \lg n$ and whose removal decreases the sum of distances from x by at most $2n(1 + \lg n)$. Because $d(a', x) \leq \lg n$, adding edge xa still improves the sum of distances from x by at least $\beta n(\frac{1}{2}p - 1) \lg n$. Thus, swapping edge xy with edge xa improves the sum of distances from x by at least $\beta n(\frac{1}{2}p - 1) \lg n - 2n(1 + \lg n)$. If $p \geq 8/\beta$, this improvement is at least $(2 - \beta)n \lg n - 2n$. Because $\beta \leq 1$, this improvement is at least $n \lg n - 2n$, which is positive for $n \geq 5$, contradicting equilibrium.

Finally we take the xth power of the graph for an integer x. If two vertices a and b have distance $d(a, b)$ in the original graph, then they have distance $\lceil d(a, b)/x \rceil$ in the power graph. In other words, the power-graph construction coalesces distances between consecutive integer multiples of x down to a common distance (the larger of the two multiples). Therefore, choosing $x = 2p \lg n + 1$ implies that all distances in the range $D \pm 2p \lg n$ convert to at most two distances r and $r + 1$. As argued by the previous claim, every vertex a has at least $(1 - 6\beta)n$ vertices b within this distance range, mapping to distances of either r or $r + 1$ in the power graph. The diameter of the power graph is $\lceil d/x \rceil = \Theta(d/(p \lg n)) = \Theta(\beta d / \lg n)$.

To obtain distances of just r, we need a power x with the property that no integer multiple of x falls in the interval $D \pm 2p \lg n$. We show that this is possible for $x = O(\lg^2 n)$: for any interval $I = [i, j]$ where $|j - i| = O(\lg n)$ and $0 < i, j < n$, there is a number $x = O(\lg^2 n)$ such that no integer multiple of x is in $[i, j]$. By a simple consequence of the prime number theorem, the product P of all primes in $[1, y]$ is $e^{(1 + o(1))y}$. On the other hand, the product P' of all members of the interval I is at most $n^{|I|} \leq e^{O(\lg^2 n)}$. For $y = c \lg^2 n$ with an appropriate constant c, P exceeds P', implying that there is a prime $x \leq c \lg^2 n$ that does not divide P' and hence does not divide any member of I, as needed. $\square$

CONJECTURE 14. *Distance-almost-uniform graphs have diameter $O(\lg n)$.*

If Conjecture 14 is true, Theorem 13 implies that sum equilibrium graphs have diameter $O(\lg^2 n)$. (The slightly weaker conjecture for distance-uniform graphs implies an upper bound of $O(\lg^3 n)$.) Note that for Conjecture 14 it is crucial that we require *every* vertex to have distance exactly r to almost every vertex, not just that almost all pairs of vertices have distance exactly r. Otherwise, a large-diameter example would be a node of degree $\Theta(1/\varepsilon)$ attached to paths of length $(d-2)/2$, with $\Theta(\varepsilon n)$ vertices attached to the end of each path. Provided $d = O(\varepsilon n)$, the number of vertices can be made $\Theta(n)$.

While we have not been able to prove or disprove Conjecture 14, we can prove it (in a strong form) for Cayley graphs of Abelian groups. Recall that the Cayley graph of an Abelian group A with respect to a set $S \subset A$ satisfying $S = -S$ is a graph in which the set of vertices is the set of all elements of the group A, where a, a' are adjacent if and only if there exists an $s \in S$ so that $a + s = a'$. Thus, for example, the graph described in Section 4 is the Cayley graph of the group of all elements of Z_{2k}^2 with an even sum of coordinates, with respect to the generating set $S = \{(1,1),(1,-1),(-1,1),(-1,-1)\}$.

THEOREM 15. *Let G be an ε-distance-uniform graph with n vertices, and suppose that G is a Cayley graph of an Abelian group and that $\varepsilon < 1/4$. Then the diameter of G is at most $O\left(\frac{\lg n}{\lg(1/\varepsilon)}\right)$.*

PROOF. Let G be the Cayley graph of the Abelian group A with respect to the set S. For each integer $i \geq 1$ put

$$iS = \{s_1 + s_2 + \cdots + s_i : s_j \in S \text{ for all } 1 \leq j \leq i\}.$$

Note that iS is the set of all vertices of G that can be reached from the element $0 \in A$ by a walk of length i. Since G is ε-distance-uniform, there is an integer r so that all vertices of G but at most εn are of distance r or $r+1$ from 0. Therefore $|(r-1)S| \leq \varepsilon n$, while $|(r+1)S| \geq (1-\varepsilon)n$.

A known consequence of the Plünnecke Inequalities (see, e.g., [13]), which can also be derived from the results in [3, Section 2], is that if S is a subset of an Abelian group then for every $q > p$, $|qS| \leq |pS|^{q/p}$. Applying it in our setting with $q = r+1$ and $p = r-1$ we conclude that

$$(1-\varepsilon)n \leq |(r+1)S| \leq |(r-1)S|^{1+\frac{2}{r-1}} \leq \varepsilon n \cdot n^{2/(r-1)}.$$

Therefore $\lg(\frac{1-\varepsilon}{\varepsilon}) \leq \frac{2}{r-1} \lg n$, implying that $r \leq O\left(\frac{\lg n}{\lg(1/\varepsilon)}\right)$. The desired result follows, as the diameter of G is clearly at most $2r+2$. $\square$

6. REFERENCES

[1] S. ALBERS, *On the value of coordination in network design*, in Proceedings of the 19th Annual ACM-SIAM Symposium on Discrete Algorithms, 2008. To appear.

[2] S. ALBERS, S. EILTS, E. EVEN-DAR, Y. MANSOUR, AND L. RODITTY, *On Nash equilibria for a network creation game*, in Proceedings of the 17th Annual ACM-SIAM Symposium on Discrete Algorithms, Miami, Florida, 2006, pp. 89–98.

[3] N. ALON, *Problems and results in extremal combinatorics. I*, Discrete Mathematics, 273 (2003), pp. 31–53.

[4] N. ANDELMAN, M. FELDMAN, AND Y. MANSOUR, *Strong price of anarchy*, in Proceedings of the 18th Annual ACM-SIAM Symposium on Discrete Algorithms, 2007, pp. 189–198.

[5] J. CORBO AND D. PARKES, *The price of selfish behavior in bilateral network formation*, in Proceedings of the 24th Annual ACM Symposium on Principles of Distributed Computing, Las Vegas, Nevada, 2005, pp. 99–107.

[6] E. D. DEMAINE, *Cache-oblivious algorithms and data structures*, in Lecture Notes from the EEF Summer School on Massive Data Sets, Lecture Notes in Computer Science. To appear.

[7] E. D. DEMAINE, M. HAJIAGHAYI, H. MAHINI, AND M. ZADIMOGHADDAM, *The price of anarchy in network creation games*, in Proceedings of the 26th Annual ACM SIGACT-SIGOPS Symposium on Principles of Distributed Computing, 2007, pp. 292–298.

[8] ———, *The price of anarchy in cooperative network creation games*, in Proceedings of the 26th International Symposium on Theoretical Aspects of Computer Science (STACS 2009), Freiburg, Germany, February 2009. To appear.

[9] A. FABRIKANT, A. LUTHRA, E. MANEVA, C. H. PAPADIMITRIOU, AND S. SHENKER, *On a network creation game*, in Proceedings of the 22nd Annual Symposium on Principles of Distributed Computing, Boston, Massachusetts, 2003, pp. 347–351.

[10] M. FRIGO, C. E. LEISERSON, H. PROKOP, AND S. RAMACHANDRAN, *Cache-oblivious algorithms*, in Proceedings of the 40th Annual IEEE Symposium on Foundations of Computer Science, New York, October 1999, pp. 285–297.

[11] Y. HALEVI AND Y. MANSOUR, *A network creation game with nonuniform interests*, in Proceedings of the 3rd International Workshop on Internet and Network Economics, vol. 4858 of Lecture Notes in Computer Science, San Diego, CA, December 2007, pp. 287–292.

[12] N. LAOUTARIS, L. J. POPLAWSKI, R. RAJARAMAN, R. SUNDARAM, AND S.-H. TENG, *Bounded budget connection (BBC) games or how to make friends and influence people, on a budget*, in Proceedings of the 27th ACM Symposium on Principles of Distributed Computing, 2008, pp. 165–174.

[13] T. TAO AND V. VU, *Additive combinatorics*, Cambridge University Press, Cambridge, 2006.

113

Tree Network Coding for Peer-to-Peer Networks

Arne Vater   Christian Schindelhauer*   Christian Ortolf

Department of Computer Science
University of Freiburg
Georges-Köhler-Allee 51
Freiburg im Breisgau, Germany
{vater, schindel, ortolf}@informatik.uni-freiburg.de

ABSTRACT

Partitioning is the dominant technique to transmit large files in peer-to-peer networks. A peer can redistribute each part immediately after its download. BitTorrent combines this approach with incentives for uploads and has thereby become the most successful peer-to-peer network. However, BitTorrent fails if files are unpopular and are distributed by irregularly participating peers. It is known that Network Coding always provides the optimal data distribution, referred as optimal performance. Yet, for encoding or decoding a single code block the whole file must be read and users are not willing to read $O(n^2)$ data blocks from hard disk for sending n message blocks. We call this the disk read/write complexity of an encoding.

It is an open question whether fast network coding schemes exist. In this paper we present a solution for simple communication patterns. Here, in a round model each peer can send a limited amount of messages to other peers. We define the depth of this directed acyclic communication graph as the maximum path length (not counting the rounds). In our online model each peer knows the bandwidth of its communication links for the current round, but neither the existence nor the weight of links in future rounds.

In this paper we analyze BitTorrent, Network Coding, Tree Coding, and Tree Network Coding. We show that the average encoding and decoding complexity of Tree Coding is bounded by $O(kn \log^2 n)$ disk read/write-operations where k is the number of trees and n the number of data blocks.

Tree Coding has perfect performance in communication networks of depth two with a disk read/write complexity of $O(pnt \log^3 n)$ where p is the number of peers, t is the number of rounds, and n is the number of data blocks. For arbitrary networks Tree Coding performs optimally using $2(\delta + 1)^{t-1} p \log^2 n$ trees which results in a read/write complexity of $O((\delta + 1)^{t-1} n \log^3 n)$ for t rounds and in-degree δ.

---

*Partly supported by DFG research fund Schi 372/5-1.

Categories and Subject Descriptors

C.2.4 [**Computer-Communication Networks**]: Distributed Systems — *Distributed applications*;
E.4 [**Data**]: Coding and Information Theory — *Nonsecret encoding schemes*;
F.2.2 [**Theory of Computation**]: Analysis of Algorithms and Problem Complexity — *Nonnumerical Algorithms and Problems*

General Terms

Algorithms, Performance

Keywords

Peer-to-Peer Networks, BitTorrent, Network Coding

1. INTRODUCTION

The exchange of data without centralized infrastructure is the main motivation for the wide-spread use of peer-to-peer networks. From a user's perspective the fast distribution of large files is the killer argument to choose peer-to-peer network software. For such a task the IP Multicast protocol seems to be the best solution, allowing routers to duplicate packets on their paths to their destination, thus relieving the bottleneck at the server [17, 6]. However, IP Multicast suffers from the absence of reliable delivery and the lack of support of most Internet service providers.

Peer-to-Peer Networks.

Peer-to-Peer Networks started in 1999 with Napster and Gnutella which swiftly became very successful although they were not very elaborated. In the following years, researcher focused on finding robust network structures and efficient lookup services, like CAN [13], Chord [16], Pastry [15], and Tapestry [8]. Later on, for some of these networks, efficient multicast extensions were proposed, e.g. Bayeux [19], CAN-Multicast [14], and Scribe [3], filling the gap of the unsupported multicast in the Internet network layer.

In a multicast tree the leaf position is the most favorable one, since they do not upload any data to others. Usually, the upload is the crucial bottleneck in peer-to-peer networks, since asymmetric connections designed for client-server networks provide larger download than upload capacities (not mentioning the legal distinction between uploaders and downloaders). A solution was presented with Splitstream [2], where files are partitioned into small blocks, such that a peer can start redistributing blocks immediately after downloading while continuing receiving further blocks of the same file. The resulting multiple distribution trees are overlaid to achieve fairness among peers by balancing both upload and download for each of them.

BitTorrent [5] incorporates the block-based approach of Splitstream and combines it with incentives for uploading blocks. So, BitTorrent has become traffic-wise the most successful peer-to-peer network.

Network Coding.

In their seminal paper Ahlswede et al. [1] showed that the encoding of data can improve the data throughput beyond the limits of standard packet delivery. Later work showed that linear combinations of data units achieve optimal network information flow. This idea has been adapted for use in peer-to-peer networks like Practical Network Coding [4]. Some peer-to-peer networks use this new method. Yet, BitTorrent without any coding technique remains unchallenged.

In our opinion the main obstacle for the wide-spread use of Network Coding is the high computational complexity of the coding and encoding process. For encoding (or decoding) a single code block the whole file must be read and users are not willing to read $O(n^2)$ data blocks from hard disk for sending n message blocks. The additional overhead after downloading the code blocks is simply not acceptable for most users: When a user downloads 4 GByte of data consisting of 1024 blocks, Network Coding requires disk operations reading 4096 GByte on each participating host while BitTorrent only reads 4 GByte of data.

Our goal is to find coding schemes which provide the same information flow as Network Coding with a disk access complexity comparable to BitTorrent.

Previous Work.

In our previous work we have presented new network codes with small read/write complexity. In [11] we have introduced Pair Coding. We have shown that it performs at least as good as BitTorrent with a constant factor increase in complexity. For some scenarios it outperforms BitTorrent, while Pair Coding fails for many scenarios like BitTorrent.

Furthermore, we have introduced Tree Coding [10]. It outperforms a special version of Pair Coding called Fixed Pair Coding, while its relationship to Pair Coding is unknown. Pair Coding and Fixed Pair Coding are as efficient as BitTorrent. Likewise the complexity of Tree Coding for $k > 1$ trees was stated as an open problem, which is solved in this paper.

Coding Model.

All coding schemes presented here are restricted versions of the Practical Network Coding introduced in [4]. A large file of length m over an alphabet Σ (e.g. binary alphabet, bytes, words) is partitioned into n equal units of size $s = \lceil \frac{m}{n} \rceil$. We denote the blocks of the file by $x = (x_1, \ldots, x_n)$. The last block may be filled up with zeros. We assume $n = 2^a, a \in \mathbb{N}^+$ since this supports the binary presentation of data. The linear network code schemes presented use scalar products in finite fields.

For efficiency the block x_i is interpreted as a vector over a finite field, i.e. $x_i = (x_{i,1}, \ldots, x_{i,\ell}) \in GF[2^h]^\ell$ such that 2^h is larger than the number of blocks, but the product nh is smaller than the block size $2^{h\ell}$. Then the additional infor-

mation of the encoding can be seen as a minor contribution to the packet size.

A **linear code block** is defined as

$$b(c) = \left(\sum_{i=1}^{n} c_i x_{i,\nu} \right)_{\nu \in \{1, \ldots, \ell\}} .$$

If n such linear code blocks $b(c) = b_1, \ldots, b_n$ with codes $c_1, \ldots, c_n$ have been collected the matrix $C_{ij} = (c_{i,j})$ gives the information for decoding since

$$x_{i,\nu} = \sum_{i=1}^{n} (C^{-1})_{i,j} b_{j,\nu} .$$

A random choice of the code variables produces an invertible matrix with probability of at least $1 - \frac{2}{2^h}$. Since the space requirements of the parameters (nh) grow linearly with h this allows exponential small failure probability. In practice such a failure would usually result in the transmission of an additional encoded block and presents a minor problem.

Communication Graph.

We model the communication of peers as a directed acyclic graph. For this we consider a round model where each participating peer P_i is multiply represented in the graph by nodes $P_{i,j}$ indicating the state of P_i in the j-th round. The directed edges are of form $(P_{i,j}, P_{k,j+1})$ and are weighted according to the number of blocks peer P_i can transmit to peer P_k in round j. We consider only the transmission of full blocks according to the linear encoding. By definition the edges $(P_{i,j}, P_{i,j+1})$ always exist and have weight n. In every round a peer may receive any number of blocks and send any number of blocks within the edge weight. The sum of all received blocks of a peer P is denoted as $n_r(P)$ and clearly we observe $n_r(P) \leq n$ if no unnecessary blocks are sent around. The number of outgoing blocks of a peer P is denoted by $n_s(P)$. Peers in round 1 have either all blocks or no blocks of the file. Peers of the first type are called seeds and the latter ones leeches. We define $n_r(P) = n$ if P is a seed.

In this paper we assume that there are no edges with zero weight and we consider only edges that lie on a directed path coming from a seed.

In the communication graph we define the in-degree of a node as the number of incoming edges of a node $P_{i,j}$ not counting the edge from the past round $P_{i,j-1}$. Since many nodes represent the same peer we redefine the depth of the graph as follows. All nodes corresponding to seeds have depth 0 in all rounds. The depth of nodes in the first round is also 0. In all other cases the depth is defined as

$$\text{depth}(P_{i,j+1}) =$$
$$\max \Big\{ \text{depth}(P_{i,j}),$$
$$1 + \max_{k \neq i, (P_{k,j}, P_{i,j+1}) \in E(G)} \{\text{depth}(P_{k,j})\} \Big\}.$$

The depth of the communication graph describes the maximum number of different peers a piece of information passes through. According to this definition the number of rounds can easily exceed the depth of a communication graph.

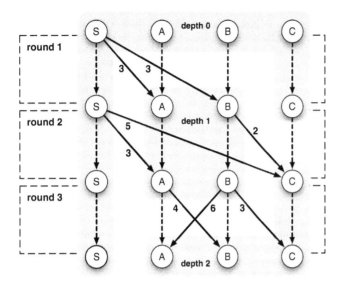

Figure 1: Communication graph.

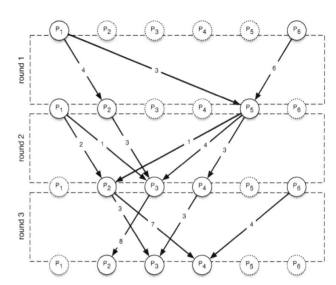

Figure 2: Example of a communication graph with 3 rounds. Inactive nodes are depicted dashed, the nodes P_1 and P_6 are seeds, and the depth of the communication graph is 3.

THEOREM 1. *[4] If there exists a flow from all seeds to a peer of size of at least n then linear network coding distributes the complete file to all these peers.*

In this paper we investigate variants of Network Coding which share this optimal performance.

Definition 1. A file sharing system S_1 **performs perfectly** if the complete file is received at all peers which have a flow of n from the set of seeding peers.

The fundamental disadvantage of Network Coding is the large computational complexity for encoding and decoding. To reflect the cost of coding we use the read/write complexity regarding disk access. We assume that any operation involving two blocks (coded or plain) can be performed in main memory, i.e. it requires only to read those two blocks and write the result. The number of blocks a peer can store in its main memory is constant (non-zero).

Definition 2. Consider a machine model where the main memory is restricted to a constant number of blocks and a mass storage device is available, which is an unbounded random access memory (hard disk). The **read/write complexity** of a peer is the number of accesses to the mass storage for an operation. It is measured with respect to the number n_r of blocks received by a peer and the number n_s of blocks sent by a peer.

We consider the worst-case given by the peer of maximum read/write complexity and the average read/write complexity which is the sum of read/write operations averaged over all peers.

Knowledge Model.

In the **offline model** the whole communication graph with all future rounds is known to all peers in advance, i.e. each node knows the activity and communication limits of all peers in all upcoming rounds. In the **online model** this knowledge is limited to the current round. Thus a plan can only be made for this round, while no information about future rounds is available. Basically, this is a guarantee that each peer remains active until the end of the current round and will be able to fulfill its transmission bounds published at the beginning of the round.

2. BITTORRENT

BitTorrent is at the moment the most popular file sharing system. Except for error detection via hash function it does not use coding. A file is divided into n blocks, that are distributed to the downloading peers. When a copy of each original block is present, the download is finished. The crucial advantage of BitTorrent compared to prior peer-to-peer systems is the capability of downloading from multiple other peers in parallel, and start uploading completed blocks before the download of the whole file is finished. The so-called policy describes the decision which block should be uploaded to whom. It is based on the current status of the whole network, including for example the progress of the receiving peer, the amount of copies of a certain block in the network, etc. BitTorrent uses incentives that encourage uploading by delivering more blocks in return. Thereby, so-called leeching, i.e. peers (leeches) download more blocks than they are willing to upload to others, is discouraged.

This game-theoretic approach of using incentives helps to increase network throughput, and together with the file partitioning this explains the success and popularity of BitTorrent. The game-theoretic aspects have been subject to a lot of research, e.g. [9, 12], and they still are. However, we focus on shortcomings of block-based file distribution systems, that are unsovable with incentives: In case a block is completely missing in the whole network, i.e. no active peer has a copy, BitTorrent is incapable of compensating this loss and no peer is able to finish the download.

Performance Analysis of BitTorrent.

In the following, we describe the communication graphs that can be handled perfectly by BitTorrent and also give the read/write complexity. We will show that BitTorrent fails for more complex communication graphs.

THEOREM 2. *BitTorrent performs perfectly for communication graphs with depth 1 for the online model and has worst case read/write complexity $n_r + n_s$ and average complexity $2n$.*

PROOF. A simple policy downloading one missing block at a time suffices. The downloading peer can explicitly request a desired block from each seed. So with each received block the information available at the downloading peer increases. Thus, the total information flow to that peer is optimal in the online model, and each block has to be sent and received exactly once, yielding the given read/write complexity in average. In worst case, a peer (in particular a seed) has to upload more than n blocks for several downloading peers, $n_s > n$, resulting in the above worst case complexity.

For the average complexity note that

$$\sum_{peer\ P} n_r(p) = \sum_{peer\ P} n_s(p) \le np$$

where p is the number of peers. □

The following theorem shows the unsolvable shortcomings of BitTorrent. If the communication graph has a depth larger than one, even in the offline model with complete knowledge, BitTorrent cannot provide the optimal performance.

THEOREM 3. *There is a communication graph of depth 2 where BitTorrent fails in the offline model.*

PROOF. The communication graph in Figure 3 depicts an example. In round one, the seed S may transmit $n/2$ blocks to each of the peers P_1, P_2, P_3. Since there exist only n different blocks, at least two peers have an identical block after the first round. Due to the duplicate blocks at two peers, in round two (without any transmission limits), at least one of the peers P_4, P_5, P_6 cannot download all original blocks. No distribution strategy can solve this, not even for the offline model with full knowledge.

However, there exists an optimal straight-forward solution using Network Coding: In round one all transmitted blocks are linearly independent code blocks. Then in round two the nodes P_4, P_5, P_6 each can collect n of those code blocks and decode the original file, maximizing the network flow. □

3. NETWORK CODING

The problem of missing blocks can be optimally solved by using Network Coding [1] with its efficient implementation given as the Practical Network Coding scheme [4]. Instead of transmitting the original blocks of the file, linear combinations of all n blocks are distributed. Those code blocks are generated by interpreting each original block as a vector over a Galois field. If all linear coefficients used in this encoding are linearly independent, then any n code blocks are sufficient to decode all n original blocks from the file. Linear independency of the coefficients can be achieved easily with high probability by a random choice, if the order of the Galois field is chosen large enough.

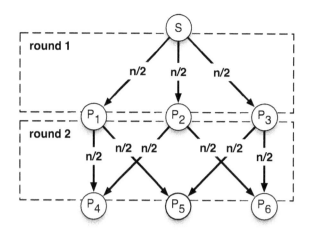

Figure 3: Scenario used in proof of Theorem 3.

THEOREM 4. *[1] Network Coding performs perfectly in any communication graph.*

However, encoding and decoding of blocks have a high computational complexity and a high read/write complexity. The computational overhead is basically the inversion of an $(n \times n)$-matrix C of the linear coefficients which has a complexity of $O(n^{2.376\cdots})$. While this is manageable with modern personal computers the read/write complexity displays the growing gap between the processing speed of the CPU and had disks.

THEOREM 5. *The read/write complexity of Network Coding of each peer is in the worst case at most $n_r \cdot n_s$ and $O(n^2)$ in the average.*

PROOF. Creating a code block requires to read n_r blocks, leading to $n_r n_s$ read operations to create n_s code blocks, which is the same for decoding like in Practical Network Coding. Since $n_r \le n$ the average performance is at most n^2 since

$$\sum_{peer\ P} n_s(P) n_r(P) \le \sum_{peer\ P} n_s(P) n$$
$$= \sum_{peer\ P} n_r(P) n$$
$$\le n^2 p\ ,$$

where p is the number of peers. □

We think that this read/write complexity is the reason that systems using Network Coding, like Avalanche [7], by far fall behind BitTorrent's success and there are empirical analyses backing up this opinion [18].

4. TREE CODING

Code blocks in Tree Coding, which was already introduced in [10], are defined by a complete binary tree. The leaves of this tree form the original file blocks multiplied by a coefficient. Starting from the second layer code blocks are generated by adding two children code blocks in the Galois field, i.e. computing the vector-wise Xor of the code blocks.

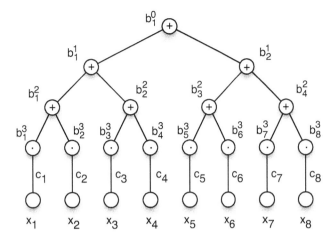

Figure 4: Coding tree with $n = 8$.

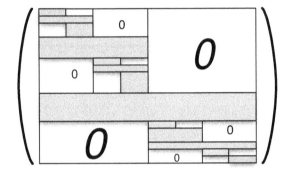

Figure 5: A typical matrix of the Tree Coding using several trees.

$$
\begin{aligned}
b_i^{\log n}(c) &= c_i x_i && \text{for } i \in \{1, \ldots, n\} \\
b_i^{j-1}(c) &= b_{2i-1}^j(c) + b_{2i}^j(c) && \text{for } j \in \{1, \ldots, \log n\}, \\
& && i \in \{1, \ldots, 2^{j-1}\}
\end{aligned}
$$

Such a tree imposes an implicit partitioning of the file, which may lead to the same problems we have seen for Bit-Torrent, see Figure 5. The solution is to use several coding trees with different coefficients.

Decoding from multiple coding trees is computationally more complex. In the extreme case n coding trees are given by their root nodes. Then, Treecoding is equivalent to Network Coding. However, for a small number of trees the decoding remains feasible.

Definition 3. A sub-tree in a coding tree $T(c)$ is defined by the position of its root node b_i^j and contains all successor nodes. It is denoted by $T_i^j(c)$, where c is the tree's coding vector.

Definition 4. The function

$$
\text{count}\left(b_i^j(c_1), \ldots, b_i^j(c_k)\right) \to \{0, \ldots, k\}
$$

denotes the amount of blocks that are present in the coding trees $T(c_1), \ldots, T(c_k)$ at the node position indicated by i

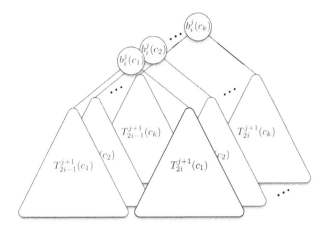

Figure 6: A set of trees $T_i^j(c_1), \ldots, T_i^j(c_k)$ and their left and right sub-trees.

and j. Furthermore, $\text{count}(T(c))$ denotes the number of code blocks from the tree $T(c)$.

The following lemma will allow to abstract from the matrix representation. It shows that the rank of the trees is described by the position of the code blocks within the trees. See Figure 6 for an illustration of the notation.

LEMMA 1. *There exists a set of coding vectors $c_1, \ldots, c_k$, such that for all trees $T(c_1), \ldots, T(c_k)$ with*

$$
\text{count}(T(c_\nu)) = \text{rank}(T(c_\nu))
$$

the rank of the set of trees equals

$$
\text{rank}\left(T_i^j(c_1), \ldots, T_i^j(c_k)\right) =
$$

$$
\min\left\{\frac{n}{2^j}, \text{rank}\left(T_{2i-1}^{j+1}(c_1), \ldots, T_{2i-1}^{j+1}(c_k)\right) \right.
$$
$$
+ \text{rank}\left(T_{2i}^{j+1}(c_1), \ldots, T_{2i}^{j+1}(c_k)\right)
$$
$$
\left. + \text{count}\left(b_i^j(c_1), \ldots, b_i^j(c_k)\right) \right\}.
$$

PROOF. This can be proved by an induction over the height of the sub-trees. For leaves the statement is true, since the rank of a leaf is 1 if at least one code block exists at the leaf's position in any of the trees $T(c_1), \ldots, T(c_k)$. If not, the rank is 0.

Assume that the lemma holds for depth of at least $j + 1$, i.e. height smaller or equal $\log n - j - 1$. Now, consider a matrix built by the coefficient vectors of the two sub-trees and the code blocks at the current root. The matrix has the form depicted in Figure 7.

Clearly, the coefficients of the left and right sub-tree are linearly independent. It remains to prove that the coefficients $b_i^j(c_1), \ldots, b_i^j(c_k)$ of the root are no linear combinations of the rest of the matrix, if the overall number of coefficients is bounded by $\frac{n}{2^j}$. If more coefficients are given, we reduce the number of root coefficients such that the overall number equals $\frac{n}{2^j}$.

First note, that within the same tree this holds since the number of block codes equals the rank of all coefficients. To ensure that it also holds for all trees we have to choose the coding vectors. These vectors are the entries of the matrix in Figure 7 at the non-zero positions. It is well known that a Vandermonde matrix fulfills this property. □

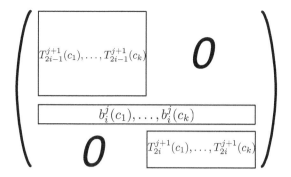

Figure 7: The resulting coefficient matrix of joining the left and right sub-trees of $T(c_1), \ldots, T(c_k)$.

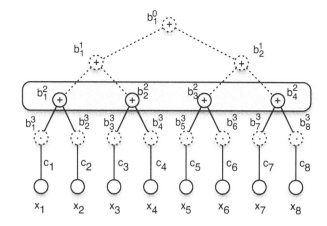

Figure 8: Complete tree level code of depth 2.

The following theorem solves the open problem stated in [10], where for the complexity of Tree Coding a bound of $O(n)$ for the case $k = 1$ has been shown. Here, we show that every strategy which relies on Tree Coding with small number of trees can be performed efficiently.

THEOREM 6. *In Tree Coding with k trees each peer has worst case read/write complexity of $O(kn \log^2 n + n_s)$ and average complexity $O(kn \log^2 n)$.*

PROOF. The seeds (peers in depth 0) calculate all k trees and store them. This takes $O(kn)$ read and write operations. Note that by definition $n_r = n$ and hence we face the complexity of $O(kn_r) + n_s$ for sending n_s code blocks in all rounds.

Each other peer follows the following strategy. The main goal is to construct all inner nodes of the k trees. The peers store code blocks in a complete binary tree T of height $\log n$. Here, in every node of depth d at most $k(d+1)$ code blocks are stored. These code blocks are linear combinations of all original blocks according to the presentation introduced for Tree Coding.

This tree T is initialized with all the received code blocks and will be updated after each round as follows: If a new code blocks has been received it will be added at the corresponding position of the tree. The other positions will be filled up with tree nodes of the same form, i.e. in sub-tree T_i^j the vectors have the form

$$(\underbrace{0, \ldots, 0}_{(i-1)n/2^j}, h_1, \ldots, h_{n/2^j}, \underbrace{0, \ldots, 0}_{n-in/2^j}).$$

After downloading the blocks of the current round the peer starts the following computation from the top of the tree to the leaves.

- Store all received code blocks into the tree at the corresponding positions.

- For $j = 1$ to $\log n$,
  for $i = 1$ to 2^j,
  for all unmarked blocks b of the parent node of T_i^j, i.e the root node $T_{\lfloor (i+1)/2 \rfloor}^{j-1}$

  - Find a vector v of form g_i^j which is linearly independent from all vectors in the sub-tree T_i^j such that it preserves the rank of the matrix of the parent tree $T_{\lfloor (i+1)/2 \rfloor}^{j-1}$ if it is replaced with b.

  - If such a vector v exists store v into the tree and mark b.

The number of disk read/write operations for computing v in depth j is bounded by $n/2^{j-1}$ because this is the maximum number of linearly independent vectors with $n/2^{j-1}$ non-zero entries. By the marking mechanism it is clear that the maximum number of $k(j+1)$ code blocks in depth d is an upper bound (in fact it is also upper-bounded by $n/2^j$). Furthermore, each entry is computed only once, which leads to the following complexity for constructing the tree:

$$\sum_{j=1}^{\log n} k(j+1) 2^j \frac{n}{2^{j-1}} = 2kn \sum_{j=1}^{\log n} (j+1)$$
$$= kn(3 + \log n) \log n$$

As an additional term we have to consider the number n_s of sent code blocks which are read from the data structure, resulting in the worst case read/write complexity of $O(n_s + kn \log^2 n)$ and the average read/write complexity of $O(kn \log^2 n)$. □

Note that for some policies smaller read/write complexity can be achieved. For some communication graphs it is advantageous to use only a special subset of all possible tree codes. A Tree Coding is called a **tree level coding** if for each of the k trees only codes b_i^j for one level j are used. We call a tree level coding **complete** if for each tree all or no block codes of a level are available at each peer, see Figure 8.

THEOREM 7. *Tree Coding performs perfectly for*

1. *communication graphs of depth 1 in the online model with one tree with a policy with worst case read/write complexity $n_r + n_s$.*

2. *communication graphs of depth 2 in the online model with $k = 2pt \log n$ trees where p is the number of peers in depth 1, t is the number of rounds and n the number of blocks with a policy with an average read/write complexity $O(ptn \log^3 n)$.*

PROOF. The first claim follows from the observation that BitTorrent is a degenerated version of Tree Coding and is thus implied by Theorem 2.

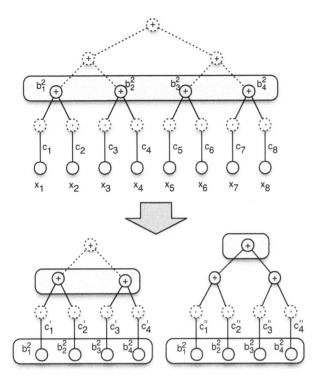

Figure 9: Recursive application of complete tree level coding generating for $w = 3$ new complete level tree codes of depth 0 and 1.

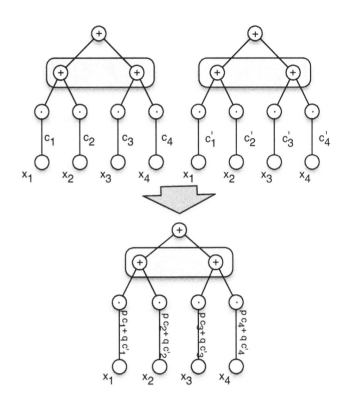

Figure 10: Tree Network Coding describes the generation of new tree codes from different existing tree codes.

For the second claim we consider the following strategy. Seeds use complete tree level codes by sending in each round at most $\log n$ new trees to each peer in depth 1. In particular, if w is the bandwidth between seed S and leech P and $w = \sum_{j=0}^{\log n} w_j 2^j$ is the binary representation, then the seed S sends a new tree with a complete level of 2^j code blocks to P for all $w_j = 1$ in this round.

After t rounds a node in communication depth 1 has collected only complete levels of various depths. We denote by $m_j(P)$ the number of complete tree level codes of coding tree level j of a peer P. On request of a peer Q with communication depth 2 peer P will only send complete levels. For this, P may construct new tree codes out of a received level code. Later on, P may construct further new tree codes out of the same level for Q. Therefore, Q has to remember the amount of codes received from P for each level code.

The construction of an encoding over the code blocks of a level is done by an recursive approach of complete tree level coding. If w' is the number of blocks requested by Q for this level in this round, then tree level codes at height w'_j are generated if $w'_j = 1$ ($w' = \sum_{j=0}^{\log n} w'_j 2^j$) using given code blocks, see Figure 9.

Furthermore, we want to restrict the generation of new code blocks to two levels per round and communication partner. For this, between P and Q there is only one tree level that currently serves as basis for the generation of new tree level codes in every round. Q greedily requests as many complete unsent levels of P as possible. For the residual bandwidth, it acquires as much independent new tree level codes from the currently used new tree level code. If this

level has been exhausted, then a new tree level code will be started. So, the number of new trees used in this round is bounded by $2 \log n$, since the complete level codes are just copies of existing trees built for P.

By Lemma 1 it follows that the rank of the coding matrix of Q equals the number of received block nodes if not more than n block nodes have been received. From this, the optimal performance follows.

The overall number of trees at any peer is bounded by $2pt \log n$ and the read/write complexity follows by Theorem 6. $\square$

Up to now different trees have not been used to produce new tree codes. If we allow peers to produce new tree codes we refer to it as **Tree Network Coding**.

As an example consider two tree codes $T(c)$ and $T(c')$ in Figure 10. An intermediate node has received the tree nodes $b_1^1(c), b_2^1(c)$ and $b_1^1(c'), b_2^1(c')$. Then the node can produce some blocks of the new tree code $T(pc + qc')$, since

$$b_i^j(pc + qc') = pb_i^j(c) + qb_i^j(c') \ .$$

Clearly, it is not always possible to produce all code blocks of the new code tree from this limited input. On the other hand, re-encoding helps in the case of deeper communication graphs.

We will now prove that Tree Coding can efficiently deal with any communication graph if the number of rounds is sub-logarithmic. Again, we use complete tree level codes. In each round new complete tree levels are generated, where the objective is to build only a small number of trees to keep the read/write complexity small.

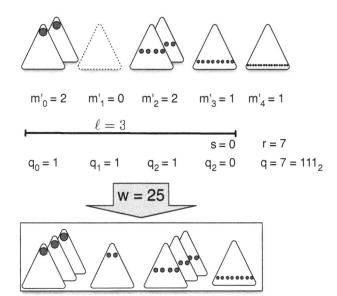

Figure 11: Dynamic generation of new tree level codes.

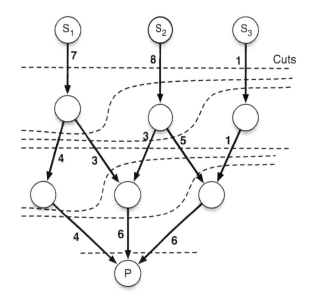

Figure 12: Series of cuts of the weight of the flow in the communication graph.

We will only sketch the lengthy and involved proof for the optimal performance, which will appear in the full paper.

THEOREM 8. *Tree Coding performs optimally for all communication graphs in the online model with $k = p(\delta + 1)^{t-1} \log^2 n$ trees where p is the number of peers in depth 1, t is the number of rounds, δ is the in-degree of the communication graph and n the number of blocks. The average read/write communication complexity is bounded by $O(pn(\delta + 1)^{t-1} \log^3 n)$.*

PROOF. The following strategy is used for each node. When a peer requests information from a seed, the node receives in each round at most $\log n$ new complete tree level codes similar to the proof of Theorem 7.

If a peer Q requests w blocks from a non-seeding peer P, we consider the following cases:

1. If the request w is larger than the amount of available independent code blocks at P, then P forwards all its block nodes to Q.

2. In all other cases P produces new complete tree level codes according to the following description.

Let m_j denote the number of complete tree level codes of depth j at P. Then, the node has $\sum_{j=0}^{\log n} m_j 2^j$ code blocks. First Q calculates the number of independent complete level trees $m'_1, \ldots, m'_{\log n}$, i.e. the minimum number of tree levels which can maximize the rank of the receiver's matrix.

Now given m'_j complete tree level codes of depth j choose the largest ℓ with $\sum_{j=0}^{\ell} m'_j 2^j \leq w$. Let $r = w - \sum_{j=0}^{\ell} m'_j 2^j$. Choose $s = \lfloor r/2^\ell \rfloor$ and let $q = r \bmod 2^\ell$ with binary representation $\sum_i q_i 2^i$. For the transmission the complete tree level codes $z_j = m'_j + q_j$ for depth $j < \ell$ and $z_\ell = m'_\ell + q_\ell + s$ for depth ℓ are constructed as linear combinations of all tree levels of smaller depth. See Figure 11 for an example.

Now each of the z_j new tree level codes is constructed by a linear combination of all $\sum_{\nu=j}^{\log n} m'_\nu 2^{\nu-j}$ code blocks in the corresponding sub-tree of P.

For the read/write complexity we count the number of trees after each round. By induction assume that the maximum number of different trees in each level $M = \max_i \{m_i\}$ in round t is bounded by $M(t) = 2(\delta + 1)^{t-1} - 1$, which is true for the first round. In round $t + 1$ each peer receives at most $\delta M(t) + \delta$ trees in each level from all sending peers. Thus the maximum entry in the next round is

$$
\begin{aligned}
M(t+1) &= M(t) + \delta M(t) + \delta \\
&= (M(t) + 1)(\delta + 1) - 1 \\
&= 2(\delta + 1)^t - 1
\end{aligned}
$$

proving the induction.

Since there are at most $\log n$ levels the maximum number of trees is $(2(\delta + 1)^{t-1} - 1) \log n$. Applying Theorem 6 proves the claimed average read/write complexity of $O(n(\delta + 1)^{t-1} \log^3 n)$.

We consider a peer P_i in a fixed round t. The maximum flow $f(P_{i,t})$ in the communication graph from the seeds to $P_{i,t}$ describes the optimal information flow. In [4] it is shown that the rank of the linear vectors equals this flow when Network Coding is used. Now, we will show that Tree Network Coding achieves the same rank as the original Network Coding.

We prove this by an induction over a series of minimum cuts of weight $f(P_{i,t})$. First we choose the cut which separates all seeds from their successors in round 1. Then, we successively move each of the peers of the next round from one side of the cut to the other until we establish the cut which separates all peers in round 2. This way we continue until we have reached the t-th round. Clearly, each of these cuts has weight of at least $f(P_{i,t})$ since the communication graph is a directed acyclic graph, see Figure 12.

Coding Method	Depth	Average R/W Complexity
BT, TC	1	$O(n)$
TC	2	$O(ptn \log^3 n)$
TC	any	$O(p(\delta+1)^{t-1} n \log^3 n)$
NC	any	$O(n^2)$

Table 1: Upper bounds

Now, we consider the series of matrices defined by all vectors which are affected by a cut and show that the rank of each of the matrices is at least $f = f(P_{i,t})$. In the first round the seeds transmit independent complete tree level codes with at least f blocks. By Lemma 1 the rank of this vector is at least f.

Assume that the rank of the matrix of all vectors on a given cut is at least f. Then, consider the vectors corresponding to the incoming edges of the node Q which will be flipped from one side to the other side of the cut. Let r be the flow which these edges contribute to the flow from the seeds to the peer $P_{i,t}$. Of course the weight of these edges must be at least r and by induction the matrix can be reduced to r code blocks on these incoming edges without decreasing the rank of the overall matrix below f. Now consider a remaining code block of the highest level. For each outgoing edge of Q with non-zero weight this code block contributes to a new encoding. So, for each possible flow to the next peer, we can find a new created code block which can replace this code block in the cut of the matrix. This argument can be repeated for the next highest code block.

Of course, the linear combinations have to be chosen with care. However, using the probabilistic method it can be shown that such rank-preserving linear combinations exist (and if the basis of the Galois field is large enough this can be guaranteed with high probability). $\square$

5. SUMMARY AND OUTLOOK

In this paper we have shown that certain restricted linear network coding schemes can provide optimal performance. For this, we have presented strategies for communication networks with a restricted depth or a very small number of rounds. If the number of rounds is bounded by $O(\log \log n)$ then the read/write complexity of these network codes is only a polylogarithmic factor slower than BitTorrent. However, it is better than Network Coding, if the number of rounds is at most $o((\log n - \log p)/\log \delta)$ for p peers, n blocks and in-degree δ.

Optimal Performance.

Table 1 summarizes the results for BitTorrent (BT), Tree Coding (TC) and Network Coding (NC). Note that the maximum average read/write complexity is in any case $O(n^2)$ since they constitute special cases of Network Coding.

The contribution in this paper is two-fold. First we have shown that Tree Coding is in fact efficient for a small number of trees using a divide-and-conquer strategy. Then, we have shown that a clever use of dynamic re-encoding allows optimal performance like full Network Coding. These observations hold for an online model where only the current round is known to the peers. Furthermore, only local knowledge is necessary for the strategies, i.e. the knowledge

of data available at the sender and receiver side. For this we have introduced a dynamic version of Tree Coding and have restricted ourselves to use only complete levels of the trees, which allows a perfect balance.

Lower bounds.

We have also shown that BitTorrent fails for some communication graphs of depth 2 even in the offline model where all future communication is known.

Outlook.

The main open question is whether there is an efficient network coding with optimal performance for all communication graphs. If it does not exist one might hope for a network coding with nearly optimal performance and good efficiency, since users would rather compromise on the data distribution than the performance.

The knowledge of the number of transmitted blocks during a round is not very realistic. BitTorrent and Network Coding already work in a stronger online setting where the bandwidth of the current round is not known. It is an open question whether efficient network coding schemes exist in this strong online model.

6. REFERENCES

[1] R. Ahlswede, Ning Cai, S. Y. R. Li, and R. W. Yeung. Network information flow. *Information Theory, IEEE Transactions on*, 46(4):1204–1216, 2000.

[2] M. Castro, P. Druschel, A. Kermarrec, A. Nandi, A. Rowstron, and A. Singh. Splitstream: High-bandwidth content distribution in cooperative environments. In *International Workshop on Peer-to-Peer Systems (IPTPS), LNCS*, volume 2, 2003.

[3] M. Castro, P. Druschel, A. Kermarrec, and A. Rowstron. SCRIBE: A large-scale and decentralized application-level multicast infrastructure. *IEEE Journal on Selected Areas in communications (JSAC)*, 20(8):1489–1499, 2002.

[4] P. Chou, Y. Wu, and K. Jain. Practical network coding. In *Proceedings of the 41st Allerton Conference on Communication, Control, and Computing*, September 2003.

[5] Bram Cohen. Incentives build robustness in BitTorrent. Technical report, bittorrent.org, 2003.

[6] D. Estrin, D. Farinacci, A. Helmy, D. Thaler, S. Deering, M. Handley, V. Jacobson, and C. Liu. Protocol independent Multicast-Sparse Mode (PIM-SM): protocol specification. RFC 2362, Internet Engineering Task Force, June 1998.

[7] Christos Gkantsidis and Pablo Rodriguez. Network coding for large scale content distribution. In *INFOCOM*, pages 2235–2245. IEEE, 2005.

[8] Kirsten Hildrum, John D. Kubiatowicz, Satish Rao, and Ben Y. Zhao. Distributed object location in a dynamic network. In *SPAA '02: Proceedings of the fourteenth annual ACM symposium on parallel algorithms and architectures*, pages 41–52, New York, NY, USA, 2002. ACM Press.

[9] Dave Levin, Katrina Lacurts, Neil Spring, and Bobby Bhattacharjee. Bittorrent is an auction: analyzing and

improving bittorrent's incentives. *SIGCOMM Comput. Commun. Rev.*, 38(4):243–254, 2008.

[10] Christian Ortolf, Christian Schindelhauer, and Arne Vater. Classifying peer-to-peer network coding schemes. In *SPAA '09: Proceedings of the twenty-first annual symposium on Parallelism in algorithms and architectures*, pages 310–318, New York, NY, USA, 2009. ACM.

[11] Christian Ortolf, Christian Schindelhauer, and Arne Vater. Paircoding: Improving File Sharing Using Sparse Network Codes. In *ICIW '09: Proceedings of the 2009 Fourth International Conference on Internet and Web Applications and Services*, pages 49–57, Washington, DC, USA, 2009. IEEE Computer Society.

[12] Michael Piatek, Tomas Isdal, Thomas Anderson, Arvind Krishnamurthy, and Arun Venkataramani. Do incentives build robustness in BitTorrent? In *NSDI'07*, Cambridge, MA, April 2007.

[13] S. Ratnasamy, P. Francis, M. Handley, R. Karp, and S. Shenker. A scalable content-addressable network. In *Computer Communication Review*, volume 31, pages 161–172. Dept. of Elec. Eng. and Comp. Sci., University of California, Berkeley, 2001.

[14] Sylvia Ratnasamy, Mark Handley, Richard M. Karp, and Scott Shenker. Application-level multicast using content-addressable networks. In Jon Crowcroft and Markus Hofmann, editors, *Networked Group Communication, Third International COST264 Workshop, NGC 2001, London, UK, November 7-9, 2001, Proceedings*, volume 2233 of *Lecture Notes in Computer Science*, pages 14–29. Springer, 2001.

[15] Antony Rowstron and Peter Druschel. Pastry: Scalable, decentralized object location, and routing for large-scale peer-to-peer systems. *Lecture Notes in Computer Science, In Proc. of the International Conference on Distributed Systems Platforms (IFIP/ACM),*, 2218:329–350, 2001.

[16] Ion Stoica, Robert Morris, David Karger, Frans Kaashoek, and Hari Balakrishnan. Chord: A scalable Peer-To-Peer lookup service for internet applications. In Roch Guerin, editor, *Proceedings of the ACM SIGCOMM 2001 Conference (SIGCOMM-01)*, volume 31, 4 of *Computer Communication Review*, pages 149–160, New York, August 27–31 2001. ACM Press.

[17] D. Waitzman, C. Partridge, and S. Deering. Distance vector multicast routing protocol. RFC 1075, Internet Engineering Task Force, November 1988.

[18] Mea Wang and Baochun Li. How practical is network coding? *Quality of Service, 2006. IWQoS 2006. 14th IEEE International Workshop on*, pages 274–278, June 2006.

[19] Shelley Q. Zhuang, Ben Y. Zhao, Anthony D. Joseph, Randy H. Katz, and John D. Kubiatowicz. Bayeux: An architecture for scalable and fault-tolerant wide-area data dissemination. In *Proceedings of NOSSDAV*, June 2001.

Optimal Gossip-Based Aggregate Computation

Jen-Yeu Chen[*]
Department of Electrical Engineering
National Dong-Hwa University
ShouFeng, Hualien 97401, Taiwan, ROC.
jenyeu@ieee.org

Gopal Pandurangan[†]
Division of Mathematical Sciences
Nanyang Technological University
Singapore 637371
gopalpandurangan@gmail.com

ABSTRACT

Motivated by applications to modern networking technologies, there has been interest in designing efficient gossip-based protocols for computing aggregate functions. While gossip-based protocols provide robustness due to their randomized nature, reducing the message and time complexity of these protocols is also of paramount importance in the context of resource-constrained networks such as sensor and peer-to-peer networks.

We present the first provably almost-optimal gossip-based algorithms for aggregate computation that are both time optimal and message-optimal. Given a n-node network, our algorithms guarantee that all the nodes can compute the common aggregates (such as Min, Max, Count, Sum, Average, Rank etc.) of their values in optimal $O(\log n)$ time and using $O(n \log \log n)$ messages. Our result improves on the algorithm of Kempe et al. [11] that is time-optimal, but uses $O(n \log n)$ messages as well as on the algorithm of Kashyap et al. [10] that uses $O(n \log \log n)$ messages, but is not time-optimal (takes $O(\log n \log \log n)$ time). Furthermore, we show that our algorithms can be used to improve gossip-based aggregate computation in sparse communication networks, such as in peer-to-peer networks.

The main technical ingredient of our algorithm is a technique called *distributed random ranking (DRR)* that can be useful in other applications as well. DRR gives an efficient distributed procedure to partition the network into a forest of (disjoint) trees of small size. Since the size of each tree is small, aggregates within each tree can be efficiently obtained at their respective roots. All the roots then perform a uniform gossip algorithm on their local aggregates to reach a distributed consensus on the global aggregates.

Our algorithms are non-address oblivious. In contrast, we show a lower bound of $\Omega(n \log n)$ on the message complexity of any address-oblivious algorithm for computing aggregates. This shows that non-address oblivious algorithms are needed to obtain significantly better message complexity. Our lower bound holds regard-

[*]Supported in part by NSC Grant NSC98-2221-E259-010.

[†]Supported in part by NSF Award CCF-0830476. Prof. Pandurangan is also with the Department of Computer Science, Brown University, Providence, RI 02912.

less of the number of rounds taken or the size of the messages used. Our lower bound is the first non-trivial lower bound for gossip-based aggregate computation and also gives the first formal proof that computing aggregates is strictly harder than rumor spreading in the address-oblivious model.

Categories and Subject Descriptors

F.2 [**ANALYSIS OF ALGORITHMS AND PROBLEM COMPLEXITY**]: Miscellaneous; C.2.4 [**COMPUTER COMMUNICATION NETWORKS**]: Distributed Systems; H.3.4 [**INFORMATION STORAGE AND RETRIEVAL**]: Systems and Software—*Distributed systems*

General Terms

Algorithms, Performance, Theory

Keywords

Gossip-based protocols, aggregate computation, distributed randomized protocols, probabilistic analysis, lower bounds

1. INTRODUCTION
1.1 Background and Previous Work

Aggregate statistics (e.g., Average, Max/Min, Sum, and, Count etc.) are significantly useful for many applications in networks [2, 4, 7, 8, 11, 13, 15, 26]. These statistics have to be computed over data stored at individual nodes. For example, in a peer-to-peer network, the average number of files stored at each node or the maximum size of files exchanged between nodes is an important statistic needed by system designers for optimizing overall performance [24, 27]. Similarly, in sensor networks, knowing the average or maximum remaining battery power among the sensor nodes is a critical statistic. Many research efforts have been dedicated to developing scalable and distributed algorithms for aggregate computation. Among them gossip-based algorithms [1, 4, 6, 10, 11, 14, 18, 19, 22, 25] have recently received significant attention because of their simplicity of implementation, scalability to large network size, and robustness to frequent network topology changes. In a gossip-based algorithm, each node exchanges information with a randomly chosen communication partner in each round. The randomness inherent in the gossip-based protocols naturally provides robustness, simplicity, and scalability [9, 10]. We refer to [9, 10, 11] for a detailed discussion on the advantages of gossip-based computation over centralized and deterministic approaches and their attractiveness to emerging networking technologies such as peer-to-peer, wireless, and sensor networks. This paper focuses on designing efficient gossip-based protocols for aggregate computation that have low message and time complexity. This is especially useful in the context of resource-constrained networks such as sensor and wireless networks, where reducing message and time complexity can yield significant benefits in terms of lowering congestion and lengthening node lifetimes.

Much of the early work on gossip focused on using randomized communication for rumor propagation [5, 9, 23]. In particular, Karp et al. [9] gave a rumor spreading algorithm (for spreading a single message throughout a network of n nodes) that takes $O(\log n)$ communication rounds and $O(n \log \log n)$ messages. It is easy to establish that $\Omega(\log n)$ rounds are needed by any gossip-based rumor spreading algorithm (this bound also holds for gossip-based aggregate computation). They also showed that any rumor spreading algorithm needs at least $\Omega(n \log \log n)$ messages for a class of randomized gossip-based algorithms referred to as *address-oblivious* algorithms [9]. Informally, an algorithm is called address-oblivious if the decision to send a message to its communication partner in a round does not depend on the partner's address. Karp et al.'s algorithm is address-oblivious. For non-address oblivious algorithms, they show a lower bound of $\omega(n)$ messages, if the algorithm is allowed only $O(\log n)$ rounds.

Kempe et al. [11] were the first to present randomized gossip-based algorithms for computing aggregates. They analyzed a gossip-based protocol for computing sums, averages, quantiles, and other aggregate functions. In their scheme for estimating average, each node selects another random node to which it sends half of its value; a node on receiving a set of values just adds them to its own halved value. Their protocol takes $O(\log n)$ rounds and uses $O(n \log n)$ messages to converge to the true average in a n-node network. Their protocol is address-oblivious. The work of Kashyap et al. [10] was the first to address the issue of reducing the message complexity of gossip-based aggregate protocols, even at the cost of increasing the time complexity. They presented an algorithm that significantly improves over the message complexity of the protocol of Kempe et al. Their algorithm uses only $O(n \log \log n)$ messages, but is not time optimal — it runs in $O(\log n \log \log n)$ time. Their algorithm achieves this $O(\log n / \log \log n)$ factor reduction in the number of messages by randomly clustering nodes into groups of size $O(\log n)$, selecting representative for each group, and then having the group representatives gossip among themselves. Their algorithm is not address-oblivious. For other related work on gossip-based protocols, we refer to [10, 4] and the references therein.

1.2 Our Contributions

We present the first provably almost-optimal gossip-based algorithms for computing various aggregate functions that improves upon previous results. Given a n-node network, our algorithms guarantee that all the nodes can compute the common aggregates (such as Min, Max, Count, Sum, Average, Rank etc.) of their values in optimal $O(\log n)$ time and using $O(n \log \log n)$ messages. Our result (cf. Table 1) improves on the algorithm of Kempe et al. [11] (called as "uniform gossip") that is time-optimal, but uses $O(n \log n)$ messages as well as on the algorithm of Kashyap et al. [10] (called as "efficient gossip") that uses $O(n \log \log n)$ messages, but is not time-optimal (takes $O(\log n \log \log n)$ time).

Our algorithms use a simple scheme called *distributed random ranking (DRR)* that gives an efficient distributed protocol to partition the network into a forest of disjoint trees of $O(\log n)$ size. Since the size of each tree is small, aggregates within each tree can be efficiently obtained at their respective roots. All the roots then perform a uniform gossip algorithm on their local (tree) aggregates to reach a distributed consensus on the global aggregates. Our idea of forming trees and then doing gossip among the roots of the trees is similar to the idea of Kashyap et al. The main novelty is that our DRR technique gives a simple and efficient distributed way of decomposing the network into disjoint trees (groups) which takes only $O(\log n)$ rounds and $O(n \log \log n)$ messages. This leads to a simpler and faster algorithm than that of [10]. The paper of [22] proposes the following heuristic: divide the network into clusters

(called the "bootstrap phase"), aggregate the data within the clusters — these are aggregated in a small subset of nodes within each cluster called clusterheads; the clusterheads then use gossip algorithm of Kempe et al to do inter-cluster aggregation; and, finally the clusterheads will disseminate the information to all the nodes in the respective clusters. It is not clear in [22] how to efficiently implement the bootstrap phase of dividing the network into clusters. Also, only numerical simulation results are presented in [22] to show that their approach gives better complexity than the algorithm of Kempe et al. It is mentioned *without proof* that their approach can take $O(n \log \log n)$ messages and $O(\log n)$ time. Hence, to the best of our knowledge, our work presents the first rigorous protocol that provably shows these bounds.

Our second contribution is analyzing gossip-based aggregate computation in sparse networks. In sparse topologies such as P2P networks, point-to-point communication between all pairs of nodes (as assumed in gossip-based protocols) may not be a reasonable assumption. On the other hand, a small number of neighbors in such networks makes it feasible to send one message simultaneously to all neighbors in one round: in fact, this is a standard assumption in the distributed message passing model [21]. We show how our DRR technique leads to improved gossip-based aggregate computation in such (arbitrary) sparse networks, e.g., P2P network topologies such as Chord [27]. The improvement relies on a key property of the DRR scheme that we prove: *height* of each tree produced by DRR in any *arbitrary* graph is bounded by $O(\log n)$ whp. In Chord, for example, we show that DRR-gossip takes $O(\log^2 n)$ time whp and $O(n \log n)$ messages. In contrast, uniform gossip gives $O(\log^2 n)$ rounds and $O(n \log^2 n)$ messages.

Our algorithm is non-address oblivious, i.e., some steps use addresses to decide which partner to communicate in a round. The time complexity of our algorithm is optimal. The message complexity is within a factor $o(\log \log n)$ of the optimal because Karp et al [9] showed a lower bound of $\omega(n)$ for any non-address oblivious rumor spreading algorithm that operates in $O(\log n)$ rounds. (Computing aggregates is at least as hard as rumor spreading.)

Our third contribution is a non-trivial lower bound of $\Omega(n \log n)$ on the message complexity of any address-oblivious algorithm for computing aggregates. This lower bound holds regardless of the number of rounds taken or the size of the messages (i.e., even assuming that nodes that can send arbitrarily long messages). Our result shows that non-address oblivious algorithms (such as ours) are needed to obtain a significant improvement in message complexity. We note that this bound is significantly larger than the $\Omega(n \log \log n)$ messages shown by Karp et al. for rumor spreading. Thus our result also gives the first formal proof that computing aggregates is strictly harder than rumor spreading in the address-oblivious model. Another implication of our result is that the algorithm of Kempe et al. [11] is asymptotically message optimal for the address-oblivious model.

Our algorithm, henceforth called *DRR-gossip*, proceeds in phases. In phase one, every node runs the DRR scheme to construct a forest of (disjoint) trees. In phase two, each tree computes its local aggregate (e.g., sum or maximum) by a convergecast process; the local aggregate is obtained at the root. Finally in phase three, all the roots utilize a suitably modified version of the uniform gossip algorithm of Kempe et al. [11] to obtain the global aggregate. Finally, if necessary, the roots forward the global aggregate to other nodes in their trees.

2. MODEL

The network $G(V)$ consists of a set V of n nodes; each node $i \in V$ has a data value denoted by v_i. All the node values form a value

Table 1: DRR-gossip vs. other gossip-based algorithms.

Algorithm	time complexity	message complexity	address oblivious?
efficient gossip [10]	$O(\log n \log \log n)$	$O(n \log \log n)$	no
uniform gossip [11]	$O(\log n)$	$O(n \log n)$	yes
DRR-gossip [this paper]	$O(\log n)$	$O(n \log \log n)$	no

vector $\mathbf{v} = [v_i]$. The goal is to compute aggregate functions such as Min, Max, Sum, Average etc., over $\mathbf{v}$ in a distributed manner.

The nodes communicate in discrete time-steps referred to as *rounds*. As in prior works on this problem [9, 10], we assume that rounds are synchronized and all nodes can communicate simultaneously in a given round. Each node can communicate with every other node. In a round, each node can choose a communication partner independently and uniformly at random. A node i is said to *call* a node j if i chooses j as a communication partner. (This is known as the *random phone call* model [9].) Once a call is established, we assume that information can be exchanged in both directions along the link. In one round, a node can call only *one* other node. We assume that nodes have unique addresses. The length of a message is limited to $O(\log n + \log s)$, where s is the range of values. It is important to limit the size of messages used in aggregate computation, as communication bandwidth is often a costly resource in distributed settings. All the above assumptions are also used in prior works [10, 11]. Similar to the algorithms of [10, 11], our algorithm can tolerate the following two types of failures: (i) some fraction of nodes may crash initially, and (ii) links are lossy and messages can get lost. Thus, while nodes cannot fail once the algorithm has started, communication can fail with a certain probability δ. Without loss of generality, $1/\log n < \delta < 1/8$: Larger values of δ, requires only $O(1/\log(1/\delta))$ repeated calls to bring down the probability below $1/8$, and smaller values only make it easier to prove our claims.

Throughout the paper, "with high probability (whp)" means "with probability at least $1 - 1/n^\alpha$, for some constant $\alpha > 0$".

3. DRR-GOSSIP ALGORITHMS

3.1 Phase I: Distributed Random Ranking

The Distributed Random Ranking (DRR) algorithm is as follows (cf. Algorithm 1). Every node $i \in V$ chooses a rank independently and uniformly at random from $[0, 1]$. (Equivalently, each node can choose a rank uniformly at random from $[1, n^3]$ which leads to the same asymptotic bounds; however, choosing from $[0, 1]$ leads to a smoother analysis, e.g., allows use of integrals.) Each node i then samples up to $\log n - 1$ random nodes sequentially (one in each round) till it finds a node of higher rank to connect to. If none of the $\log n - 1$ sampled nodes have a higher rank then node i becomes a "root". Since every node except root nodes connects to a node with higher rank, there is no cycle in the graph. Thus this process results in a collection of disjoint trees which together constitute a forest $\mathbb{F}$.

In the following two theorems, we show the upper bounds of the number of trees and the size of each tree produced by the DRR algorithm; these are critical in bounding the time complexity of DRR-gossip.

THEOREM 1 (NUMBER OF TREES). *The number of trees produced by the DRR algorithm is $O(n/\log n)$ whp.*

Proof: Assume that ranks have already been assigned to the nodes. All ranks are distinct with probability 1. Number the nodes according to the order statistic of their ranks: the ith node is the node with the ith smallest rank. Let the indicator random variable X_i take the value of 1 if the ith smallest node is a root and

---

Algorithm 1: $\mathbb{F} = \mathrm{DRR}(G)$

foreach *node* $i \in V$ **do**
    choose $rank(i)$ independently and uniformly at random from $[0, 1]$
    set $found = \mathrm{FALSE}$ // higher ranked node not yet found
    set $parent(i) = \mathrm{NULL}$ // initially every node is a root node
    set $k = 0$ // number of random nodes probed
    repeat
        sample a node u independently and uniformly at random from V and get its rank
        if $rank(u) > rank(i)$ **then**
            set $parent(i) = u$
            set $found = TRUE$
            set $k = k + 1$
        end
    until $found == TRUE$ *or* $k < \log n - 1$
    if $found == TRUE$ **then**
        send a connection message including its identifier, i, to its parent node $parent(i)$
    end
    Collect the connection messages and accordingly construct the set of its children nodes, $Child(i)$
    if $Child(i) = \emptyset$ **then**
        become a leaf node
    else
        become an intermediate node
    end
end

---

0 otherwise. Let $X = \sum_{i=1}^{n} X_i$ be the total number of roots. The ith smallest node becomes a root if all the nodes that it samples have rank smaller than or equal to itself, i.e., $\Pr(X_i = 1) = \left(\frac{i}{n}\right)^{\log n - 1}$. Hence, by linearity of expectation, the expected number of roots (and thus, trees) is:

$$E[X] = \sum_{i=1}^{n} \Pr(X_i = 1) = \sum_{i=1}^{n} \left(\frac{i}{n}\right)^{\log n - 1}$$
$$= \Theta\left(\int_1^n \left(\frac{i}{n}\right)^{\log n - 1} di\right) = \Theta\left(\frac{n}{\log n}\right).$$

Note that X_is are independent (but not identically distributed) random variables, since the probability that the ith smallest ranked node becomes the root depends only on the $\log n - 1$ random nodes that it samples and independent of the samples of the rest of the nodes. Thus, applying a Chernoff's bound [16], we have $\Pr(X > 6E[X]) \leq 2^{-E[X]} = o(1/n)$. ∎

THEOREM 2 (SIZE OF A TREE). *The number of nodes in every tree produced by the DRR algorithm is at most $O(\log n)$ whp.*

Proof: We show that the probability that a tree of size $\Omega(\log n)$ is produced by the DRR algorithm goes to zero asymptotically. Fix a set S of $k = c \log n$ nodes, for some sufficiently large positive constant c. We first compute the probability that this set of k nodes form a tree. For the sake of analysis, we will direct tree edges as follows: a tree edge (i, j) is directed from node i to node j if $rank(i) < rank(j)$, i.e. i connects to j. Without loss of generality, fix a permutation of S: $(s_1, \ldots, s_\alpha, \ldots, s_\beta, \ldots, s_k)$ where $rank(s_\alpha) > rank(s_\beta), 1 \leq \alpha < \beta \leq k$. This permutation induces a directed spanning tree on S in the following sense: s_1 is the root and any other node s_α $(1 < \alpha \leq k)$ connects to a node in the totally (strictly) ordered set $\{s_1, \ldots, s_{\alpha-1}\}$ (as fixed by the above permutation). For convenience, we denote the event that a node s connects to any node on a directed tree T as "$s \triangleright T$." Note that "$s \triangleright T$" implies that s's rank is less than that of any node on the tree T. Also, we denote the event of a directed spanning tree being induced on the totally (strictly) ordered set $\{s_1, s_2, \ldots, s_\alpha, \ldots, s_h\}$ as T_h, where a node s_α can only connect to its preceding nodes in the ordered set. As a special case, T_1 is the event of the induced directed tree containing only the root node s_1. We are interested in the event T_k, i.e., the set S of k nodes forming a directed spanning tree in the above fashion. In the following, we bound the probability of the event T_k happening:

$$
\begin{aligned}
\Pr(T_k) &= \Pr\left(T_1 \cap (s_2 \triangleright T_1) \cap (s_3 \triangleright T_2) \cap \cdots \cap (s_k \triangleright T_{k-1})\right) \\
&= \Pr(T_1)\Pr(s_2 \triangleright T_1 \mid T_1)\Pr(s_3 \triangleright T_2 \mid T_2) \ldots \\
&\quad \ldots \Pr(s_k \triangleright T_{k-1} \mid T_{k-1}).
\end{aligned} \tag{1}
$$

To bound each of the terms in the product, we use the principle of deferred decisions: when a new node is sampled (i.e., for the first time) we assign it a random rank. For simplicity, we assume that each node sampled is a new node — this does not change the asymptotic bound, since there are now only $k = O(\log n)$ nodes under consideration and each node samples at most $O(\log n)$ nodes. This assumption allows us to use the principle of deferred decisions to assign random ranks without worrying about sampling an already sampled node. Below we bound the conditional probability $\Pr(s_\alpha \triangleright T_{\alpha-1} \mid T_{\alpha-1})$, for any $2 \leq \alpha \leq k$ as follows. Let $r_q = rank(s_q)$ be the rank of node s_q, $1 \leq q \leq \alpha$; then

$$
\Pr(s_\alpha \triangleright T_{\alpha-1} \mid T_{\alpha-1})
$$
$$
\leq \int_0^1 \int_0^{r_1} \int_0^{r_2} \cdots \int_0^{r_{\alpha-1}} \sum_{h=0}^{\log n - 1} \left(\frac{\alpha-1}{n}\right) r_\alpha^h \, dr_\alpha \ldots dr_1.
$$

The explanation for the above bound is as follows: Since $T_{\alpha-1}$ is a directed spanning tree on the first $\alpha - 1$ nodes, and s_α connects to $T_{\alpha-1}$, we have $r_1 > r_2 > \cdots > r_{\alpha-1} > r_\alpha$. Hence r_1 can take any value between 0 and 1, r_2 can take any value between 0 and r_1 and so on. This is captured by the respective ranges of the integrals. The term inside the integrals is explained as follows. There are at most $\log n - 1$ attempts for node s_α to connect to any one of the first $\alpha - 1$ nodes. Suppose, it connects in the hth attempt. Then, the first $h - 1$ attempts should connect to nodes whose rank should be less than r_α, hence the term r_α^h (as mentioned earlier, we assume that we don't sample an already sampled node, this doesn't change the bound asymptotically). The term $(\alpha - 1)/n$ is the probability that s_α connects to any one of the first $\alpha - 1$ nodes in the hth attempt. Simplifying the right hand side, we have,

$$
\Pr(s_\alpha \triangleright T_{\alpha-1} \mid T_{\alpha-1})
$$
$$
\leq \frac{\alpha-1}{n} \int_0^1 \int_0^{r_1} \int_0^{r_2} \cdots \int_0^{r_{\alpha-1}} \sum_{h=0}^{\log n - 1} r_\alpha^h \, dr_\alpha \ldots dr_1
$$
$$
= \frac{\alpha-1}{n}\left(\frac{0!}{\alpha!} + \frac{1!}{(\alpha+1)!} + \frac{2!}{(\alpha+2)!} + \cdots + \frac{(\log n)!}{(\log n + \alpha)!}\right).
$$

The above expression is bounded by $\frac{b}{n}$, where $0 < b < 1$ if $\alpha > 2$ and $0 < b \leq \left(1 - \frac{1}{\log n + 2}\right)$ if $\alpha = 2$. Besides, $\Pr(T_1) \leq \frac{1}{\log n}$ (cf. Theorem 1); hence, the equation (1) is bounded by $\left(\frac{b}{n}\right)^{k-1} \frac{1}{\log n}$.

Using the above, the probability that a tree of size $k = c \log n$ is produced by the DRR algorithm is bounded by

$$
\binom{n}{k} k! \left(\frac{b}{n}\right)^{k-1} \frac{1}{\log n} \leq \frac{(ne)^k}{k^k} O(\sqrt{k}) \frac{k^k}{e^k} \left(\frac{b}{n}\right)^{k-1} \frac{1}{\log n}
$$
$$
\leq \frac{c' \cdot n}{\log^{\frac{1}{2}} n} \cdot b^{k-1} = o(1/n),
$$

if c sufficiently large. ∎

Complexity of Phase I — the DRR algorithm

THEOREM 3. *The message complexity of the DRR algorithm is $O(n \log \log n)$ whp. The time complexity is $O(\log n)$ rounds.*

Proof: Let $d = \log n - 1$. Fix a node i. Its rank is chosen uniformly at random from $[0, 1]$. The expected number of nodes sampled before a node i finds a higher ranked node (or else, all d nodes will be sampled) is computed as follows. The probability that exactly k nodes will be sampled is $\Theta\left(\frac{1}{k+1} \frac{1}{k}\right)$, since the last node sampled should be the highest ranked node and i should be the second highest ranked node (whp, all the nodes sampled will be unique). Hence the expected number of nodes probed is $\sum_{k=1}^{d} \Theta\left(k \frac{1}{k+1} \frac{1}{k}\right) = O(\log d)$. Hence the number of messages exchanged by node i is $O(\log d)$. By linearity of expectation, the total number of messages exchanged by all nodes is $O(n \log d) = O(n \log \log n)$.

To show concentration, we set up a Doob martingale [16] as follows. Let X denote the random variable that counts the total number of nodes sampled by all nodes. $E[X] = O(n \log d)$. Assume that ranks have already been assigned to the nodes. Number the nodes according to the order statistic of their ranks: the ith node is the node with the ith smallest rank. Let the indicator r.v. Z_{ik} $(1 \leq i \leq n, 1 \leq k \leq d)$ indicate whether the kth sample by the ith *smallest ranked* node succeeded or not (i.e., it found a higher ranked node). If it succeeded then $Z_{ij} = 1$ for all $j \leq k$ and $Z_{ij} = 0$ for all $j > k$. Thus $X = \sum_{i=1}^{n} \sum_{k=1}^{d} Z_{ik}$. Then the sequence $X_0 = E[X], X_1 = E[X|Z_{11}], \ldots, X_{nd} = E[X|Z_{11}, \ldots, Z_{nd}]$ is a Doob martingale. Note that $|X_\ell - X_{\ell-1}| \leq d$ $(1 \leq \ell \leq nd)$ because fixing the outcome of a sample of one node affects only the outcomes of other samples made by the same node and not the samples made by other nodes. Applying Azuma's inequality, for a positive constant ϵ we have:

$$
\Pr(|X - E[X]| \geq \epsilon n) \leq 2\exp\left(-\frac{\epsilon^2 n^2}{2n(\log n)^3}\right) = o(1/n).
$$

The time complexity is immediate since each node probes at most $O(\log n)$ nodes in as many rounds. ∎

3.2 Phase II: Convergecast and Broadcast

In the second phase of our algorithm, the local aggregate of each tree is obtained at the root by the Convergecast algorithm — an aggregation process starting from leaf nodes and proceeding upward along the tree to the root node. For example, to compute the local max/min, all leave nodes simply send their values to their parent nodes. An intermediate node collects the values from its children, compares them with its own value and sends its parent node the max/min value among all received values and its own. A root node then can obtain the local max/min value of its tree.

After the Convergecast process, each root broadcasts its address to all other nodes in its tree via the tree links. This process proceeds from the root down to the leaves via the tree links (these two-way

---

Algorithm 2: $\mathbf{cov}_{max}$ =convergecast-max($\mathbb{F}$,$\mathbf{v}$)

Input: The forest $\mathbb{F}$, and the value vector $\mathbf{v}$ over all nodes in $\mathbb{F}$

Output: The local Max aggregate vector $\mathbf{cov}_{max}$ over all the roots

foreach *leaf node* **do** send its value to its parent

foreach *intermediate node* **do**
- collect values from its children
- compare collected values with its own value
- update its value to the maximum amid all and send the maximum to its parent.

end

foreach *root node z* **do**
- collect values from its children
- compare collected values with its own value
- update its value to the local maximum value $\mathbf{cov}_{max}(z)$.

end

Algorithm 3: $\mathbf{cov}_{sum}$ =convergecast-sum($\mathbb{F}$,$\mathbf{v}$)

Input: The forest $\mathbb{F}$ and the value vector $\mathbf{v}$ over all nodes in $\mathbb{F}$

Output: The local Sum aggregate vector $\mathbf{cov}_{sum}$ over all the roots.

Initialization: every node i stores a row vector $(v_i, w_i = 1)$ including its value v_i and a size count w_i

foreach *leaf node $i \in \mathbb{F}$* **do**
- send its parent a message containing the vector $(v_i, w_i = 1)$
- reset $(v_i, w_i) = (0, 0)$.

end

foreach *intermediate node $j \in \mathbb{F}$* **do**
- collect messages (vectors) from its children
- compute and update $v_j = v_j + \sum_{k \in Child(j)} v_k$, and $w_j = w_j + \sum_{k \in Child(j)} w_k$, where $Child(j) = \{j$'s children nodes$\}$
- send computed (v_j, w_j) to its parent
- reset its vector $(v_j, w_j) = (0, 0)$ when its parent successfully receives its message.

end

foreach *root node $z \in \tilde{V}$* **do**
- collect messages (vectors) from its children
- compute the local sum aggregate $\mathbf{cov}_{sum}(z, 1) = v_z + \sum_{k \in Child(z)} v_k$, and the size count of the tree $\mathbf{cov}_{sum}(z, 2) = w_z + \sum_{k \in Child(z)} w_k$, where $Child(z) = \{z$'s children nodes$\}$.

end

---

links were already established during Phase 1.) At the end of this process, all non-root nodes know the identity (address) of their respective roots.

Complexity of Phase II

Every node except the root nodes needs to send a message to its parent in the upward aggregation process of the Convergecast algorithms. So the message complexity is $O(n)$. Since each node can communicate with at most one node in one round, the time complexity is bounded by the size of the tree. (This is the reason for bounding size and not just the height.) Since the tree size (hence, tree height also) is bounded by $O(\log n)$ (cf. Theorem 2) the time complexity of Convergecast and Broadcast is $O(\log n)$. Moreover, as the number of roots is at most $O(n/\log n)$ by Theorem 1, the message complexity for broadcast is also $O(n)$.

3.3 Phase III: Gossip

In the third phase, all roots of the trees compute the global aggregate by performing the gossip algorithm on the overlaying graph $\tilde{G} = clique(\tilde{V})$, where $\tilde{V} \subseteq V$ is the set of roots and $|\tilde{V}| = m = O(n/\log n)$ (cf. Theorem 1). Since the trees are formed randomly, roots don't know each other's address. However, the gossip procedure on the roots (i.e., the nodes of $\tilde{G}$) can be implemented as described below.

In each round of the gossip procedure, every root independently and uniformly at random selects a node in V (i.e., calls a node of the graph G) to send its message. If the selected node is another root then the task is completed. If not, the selected node will *forward* the received message to the root of the tree it belongs to. We note that all nodes in a tree know their root's address at the end of Phase II (cf. Section 3.2) — here is where we use a non-address oblivious communication. Thus, to traverse through an edge of $\tilde{G}$, a message needs at most two hops of G.

Algorithm 4, Gossip-max, and Algorithm 5, Gossip-ave (which is a modification from the Push-Sum algorithm of [11]) compute the Max and Ave aggregates respectively. (Other aggregates such as Min, Sum etc., can be calculated by a suitable modification.) Note that, in addition to the gossip procedure, the Gossip-max algorithm needs a sampling procedure in which every root inquires values from other roots. Similar to the gossip procedure, the sampling procedure requires the selected node, if it is a not a root itself, to forward the inquiry message to the root of its tree. The inquiry message contains the inquiring root's address so that the inquired root can send back its value accordingly.

Algorithm 6, Data-spread, a modification of Gossip-max, can be used by a root node to spread its value. If a root needs to spread a particular value over the network, it sets this value as its initial value and all other roots set their initial value to $-\infty$.

3.3.1 Performance of Gossip-max and Data-spread

Let m denote the number of roots. By Theorem 1, we have $m = |\tilde{V}| = O(n/\log n)$ where $n = |V|$. Karp, et al. [9] show that all m nodes of a complete graph can know a particular rumor (e.g., the Max in our application) in $O(\log m) = O(\log n)$ rounds with high probability by using their Push algorithm (a prototype of our Gossip-max algorithm) with uniform selection probability. Similar to the Push algorithm, Gossip-max needs $O(m \log m) = O(n)$ messages for all roots to obtain Max if the selection probability is uniform, i.e., $1/m$. However, in the implementation of the Gossip-max algorithm on the forest, the root of a tree is selected with a *probability proportional to its size (number of nodes in the tree)*. Hence, the selection probability is not uniform. In this case, we can only guarantee that after the gossip procedure of the Gossip-max algorithm, a portion of the roots including the root of the largest tree will possess the Max. After the gossip procedure, roots can sample a $O(\log n)$ number of other roots to confirm and update, if necessary, their values and reach consensus on the global maximum, Max.

Gossip Procedure

We show the following theorem for Gossip-Max.

THEOREM 4. *After the gossip procedure of the Gossip-max algorithm, at least $\Omega(\frac{c \cdot n}{\log n})$ roots obtain the global maximum, Max, whp, where $n = |V|$ and $0 < c < 1$ is a constant.*

Proof: As per our failure model, a message may fail to reach the selected root node with probability ρ (which is at most 2δ, since failure may occur either during the initial call to a non-root node or during the forwarding call from the non-root node to the root of

Algorithm 4: $\hat{\mathbf{x}}_{max}$ =Gossip-max(G, $\mathbb{F}$, $\tilde{V}$, $\mathbf{y}$)

Initialization: every root $i \in \tilde{V}$ is set the initial value $x_{0,i} = y(i)$ from the input $\mathbf{y}$.
/* To compute Max, $x_{0,i} = y(i) = \mathbf{cov}_{max}(i)$; To compute the largest tree size (used in computing Ave), $x_{0,i} = y(i) = \mathbf{cov}_{sum}(i, 2)$. */
Gossip procedure:
for $t=1 : O(\log n)$ *rounds* **do**

> Every root $i \in \tilde{V}$ independently and uniformly at random, selects a node in V and sends the selected node a message containing its current value $x_{t-1,i}$.
>
> Every node $j \in V - \tilde{V}$ forwards any received messages to its root.
>
> Every root $i \in \tilde{V}$
> — collects messages and compares the received values with its own value
> — updates its current value $x_{t,i}$, which is also the $\hat{\mathbf{x}}_{max,t}(i)$, node i's current estimate of Max, to the maximum among all received values and its own.

end
Sampling procedure:
for $t=1 : \frac{1}{c}\log n$ *rounds* **do**

> Every root $i \in \tilde{V}$ independently and uniformly at random selects a node in V and sends each of the selected nodes an inquiry message.
>
> Every node $j \in V - \tilde{V}$ forwards any received inquiry messages to its root.
>
> Every root $i \in \tilde{V}$, upon receiving inquiry messages, sends the inquiring roots its value.
>
> Every root $i \in \tilde{V}$, updates $x_{t,i}$, i.e. $\hat{\mathbf{x}}_{max,t}(i)$, to the maximum value it inquires.

end

Algorithm 5: $\hat{\mathbf{x}}_{ave}$ =Gossip-ave(G, $\mathbb{F}$, $\tilde{V}$, $\mathbf{cov}_{sum}$)

Initialization: Every root $i \in \tilde{V}$ sets a vector $(s_{0,i}, g_{0,i}) = \mathbf{cov}_{sum}(i)$, where $s_{0,i}$ and $g_{0,i}$ are the local sum of values and the size of the tree rooted at i, respectively.
for $t = 1 : O(\log m + \log(1/\epsilon))$ *rounds* **do**

> Every root node $i \in \tilde{V}$ independently and uniformly at random selects a node in V and sends the selected node a message containing a row vector $(s_{t-1,i}/2, g_{t-1,i}/2)$.
>
> Every node $j \in V - \tilde{V}$ forwards any received messages to the root of its tree.
>
> Let $A_{t,i} \subseteq \tilde{V}$ be the set of roots whose messages reach root node i at round t. Every root node $i \in \tilde{V}$ updates its row vector by
> $$s_{t,i} = s_{t-1,i}/2 + \sum_{j \in A_{t,i}} s_{t-1,j}/2,$$
> $$g_{t,i} = g_{t-1,i}/2 + \sum_{j \in A_{t,i}} g_{t-1,j}/2.$$
>
> Every root node $i \in \tilde{V}$ updates its estimate of the global average by $\hat{\mathbf{x}}_{ave,t}(i) = \hat{x}_{ave,t,i} = s_{t,i}/g_{t,i}$.

end

---

its tree). For convenience, we call those roots who know the Max value (the global Maximum) as the max-roots and those who do not as the non-max-roots.

Let R_t be the number of max-roots in round t. Our proof is in two steps. We first show that, whp, $R_t > 4\log n$ after $8\log n/(1-$

Algorithm 6: $\hat{\mathbf{x}}_{ru}$ =Data-spread(G, $\mathbb{F}$, $\tilde{V}$, x_{ru})

Initialization: A root node $i \in \tilde{V}$ which intends to spread its value x_{ru}, $|x_{ru}| < \infty$ sets $x_{0,i} = x_{ru}$. All the other nodes j set $x_{0,j} = -\infty$.
Run gossip-max(G, $\mathbb{F}$, $\tilde{V}$, $\mathbf{x}_0$) on the initialized values.

ρ) rounds of Gossip-max. If $R_0 > 4\log n$ then the task is completed. Consider the case when $R_0 < 4\log n$. Since the initial number of max-roots is small in this case, the chance that a max-root selects another max-root is small. Similarly, the chance that two or more max-roots select the same root is also small. So, in this step, whp a max-root will select a non-max-root to send out its gossip message. If the gossip message successfully reaches the selected non-max-root, R_t will increase by 1. Let X_i denote the indicator of the event that a gossip message i from some max-root successfully reaches the selected non-max-root. We have $Pr(X_i = 1) = (1 - \rho)$. Then $X = \sum_{i=1}^{8\log n/(1-\rho)} X_i$ is the minimal number of max-roots after $8\log n/(1-\rho)$ rounds. Clearly, $E[X] = 8\log n$. Here we conservatively assume the worst situation that initially there is only one max-root and at each round only one max-root selects a non-max-root. So X is the minimal number of max-roots after $8\log n/(1-\rho)$ rounds. For clarity, let $\tilde{n} = 8\log n/(1-\rho)$. Define a Doob martingale sequence $Z_0, Z_1, \ldots, Z_{\tilde{n}}$ by setting $Z_0 = E[X]$, and, for $1 \le i \le \tilde{n}$, $Z_i = E[X|X_1,\ldots,X_i]$. It is clear that $Z_{\tilde{n}} = X$ and, for $1 \le i \le \tilde{n}$, $|Z_i - Z_{i-1}| \le 1$.

Applying Azuma's inequality and setting $\epsilon = 1/2$:

$$Pr(|X - E[X]| \ge \epsilon E[X]) = Pr(|Z_{\tilde{n}} - Z_0| \ge \epsilon E[X])$$
$$\le 2\exp\left(-\frac{\epsilon^2 E[X]^2}{2\sum_{i=1}^{\tilde{n}} 1^2}\right) = 2\exp\left(-\frac{\epsilon^2 E[X]^2}{2(\frac{8\log n}{1-\rho})}\right)$$
$$= 2\exp\left(\log n^{-(1-\rho)}\right) = 2 \cdot n^{-(1-\rho)},$$

where ρ could be arbitrary small. W. l. o. g., let $\rho < 1/4$, then $Pr(|X - E[X]| \ge \epsilon E[X]) \le 2 \cdot n^{-\frac{3}{4}}$. Hence, whp, after $8\log n/(1-\rho) = O(\log n)$ rounds, $R_t \ge R_0 + X > R_0 + \frac{1}{2}E[X] = R_0 + 4\log n > 4\log n$.

In the second step of our proof, we lower bound *the increasing rate* of R_t when $R_t > 4\log n$. In each round, there are R_t messages sent out from max-roots. Let Y_i denote the indicator of an event that such a message i from a max-root successfully reaches a non-max-root. $Y_i = 0$ when either of the following events happen: (1) The message i fails in routing to its destination; (2) The message i is sent to another max-root, although it successfully travels over the network. The probability of this event is at most $((1 - \rho)R_t\log n)/n$ since whp the size of a tree is $O(\log n)$ (cf.Theorem 2). (3) The message i and at least one another message are destined to the same non-max-root. As the probability of three or more messages are destined to a same node is very small, we only consider the case that two messages select the same non-max-root. We also conservatively exclude both these two messages on their possible contributions to the increase of R_t. This event happens with probability at most $((1 - \rho)R_t\log n)/n$.

Applying union bound [16],

$$Pr(Y_i = 0) \le \rho + \frac{2(1-\rho)R_t\log n}{n}.$$

Since $R_t \le \frac{cn}{\log n}$ for any constant $0 < c < 1$ (otherwise, the task is completed), $Pr(Y_i = 0) \le \rho + 2c(1-\rho) = c' + (1-c')\rho$, where $c' = 2c < 1$ is a constant that is suitably fixed so that $c' + (1-$

$c')\rho < 1$. Consequently, we have $Pr(Y_i = 1) > (1-c')(1-\rho)$, and $E[Y] = \sum_{i=1}^{R_t} E[Y_i] > (1-c')(1-\rho)R_t$.

Applying Azuma's inequality as before,

$$Pr(|Y - E[Y]| > \epsilon E[Y]) < 2\exp\left(-\frac{\epsilon^2 E[Y]^2}{2R_t}\right)$$
$$< 2\exp\left(-\frac{\epsilon^2(1-c')^2(1-\rho)^2 R_t}{2}\right).$$

Since in this step, whp $R_t > 4\log n$, and $(1-c')^2(1-\rho)^2 > 0$, setting $\epsilon = \frac{1}{2}$ and $\alpha = O(1)$, we obtain

$$Pr\left(Y < \frac{1}{2}(1-c')(1-\rho)R_t\right) < 2 \cdot n^{-\alpha}.$$

Thus, whp, $R_{t+1} > R_t + \frac{1}{2}(1-c')(1-\rho)R_t = \beta R_t$, where $\beta = 1 + \frac{1}{2}(1-c')(1-\rho) > 1$. Therefore, whp, after $(8\log n/(1-\rho) + \log_\beta n) = O(\log n)$ rounds, at least $\Omega(\frac{c \cdot n}{\log n})$ roots will have the Max. ∎

Sampling Procedure

From Theorem 4, after the gossip procedure, there are $\Omega(\frac{cn}{\log n}) = \Omega(cm)$, $0 < c < 1$ roots with the Max value. For all roots to reach consensus on Max, they sample each other as in the sampling procedure. It is possible that the root of a larger tree will be sampled more frequently than the roots of smaller trees. However, this non-uniformity is an advantage, since the roots of larger trees would have obtained Max (in the gossip procedure) with higher probability due to this same non-uniformity. Hence, in the sampling procedure, a root without Max can obtain Max with higher probability by this non-uniform sampling. Thus, we have the following theorem.

THEOREM 5. *After the sampling procedure of Gossip-max algorithm, all roots know the Max value, whp.*

Proof: After the sampling procedure, the probability that none of the roots possessing the Max is sampled by a root not knowing the Max is at most $\left(\frac{m-cm}{m}\right)^{\frac{1}{c}\log n} < \frac{1}{n}$. Thus, after the sampling procedure, with probability at least $1 - \frac{1}{n}$, all the roots will know the Max. ∎

Complexity of Gossip-max and Data-spread algorithms

In this phase, the gossip procedure takes $O(\log n)$ rounds and $O(m\log n) = O(n)$ messages. The sampling procedure takes $O(\frac{1}{c}\log n) = O(\log n)$ rounds and $O(\frac{m}{c}\log n) = O(n)$ messages. To sum up, this phase totally takes $O(\log n)$ rounds and $O(n)$ messages for all the roots in the network to reach consensus on Max. The complexity of Data-spread algorithm is the same as Gossip-max algorithm.

3.3.2 Performance of Gossip-ave

When the uniformity assumption holds in gossip (i.e., in each round, nodes are selected uniformly at random), it has been shown in [11] that on an m-clique with probability at least $1 - \delta'$, Gossip-ave (uniform push-sum in [11]) needs $O(\log m + \log\frac{1}{\epsilon} + \log\frac{1}{\delta'})$ rounds and $O(m(\log m + \log\frac{1}{\epsilon} + \log\frac{1}{\delta'}))$ messages for all m nodes to reach consensus on the global average within a relative error of at most ϵ. When uniformity does not hold, the performance of uniform gossip will depend on the distribution of selection probability. In efficient gossip algorithm [10], it is shown that the node being selected with the largest probability will have the global average, Ave, in $O(\log m + \log\frac{1}{\epsilon})$ rounds. Here, we show in Theorem 6 that the same upper bound holds for our Gossip-ave algorithm, namely, the root of the largest tree will have Ave after $O(\log m + \log\frac{1}{\epsilon})$ rounds of the gossip procedure of Gossip-ave algorithm. In this bound, $m = O(n/\log n)$ is the number of roots (obtained from the DRR algorithm) and the relative error $\epsilon = n^{-\alpha}$, $\alpha > 0$.

Algorithm 7: DRR-gossip-max

Run $DRR(G)$ to obtain the forest $\mathbb{F}$ and $\tilde{V}$.
Run Convergecast-max($\mathbb{F}$,**v**) to obtain local Maximum of every tree $\mathbf{cov}_{max}$.
Run Gossip-max(G, $\mathbb{F}$, $\tilde{V}$, $\mathbf{cov}_{max}$) to obtain global Maximum Max at all the roots.
Every root node broadcasts the Max to all nodes in its tree.

Algorithm 8: DRR-gossip-ave

Run DRR(G) algorithm to obtain the forest $\mathbb{F}$ and $\tilde{V}$.
Run Convergecast-sum($\mathbb{F}$, **v**) algorithm to obtain the local Sum of values of every tree $\mathbf{cov}_{sum}(*,1)$ and the size of every tree $\mathbf{cov}_{sum}(*,2)$.
Run Gossip-max(G, $\mathbb{F}$, $\tilde{V}$, $\mathbf{cov}_{sum}(*,2)$) algorithm on the size of trees to find the root of the largest tree. At the end of this step, a root z will know that it is the one with the largest tree size.
Run Gossip-ave(G, $\mathbb{F}$, $\tilde{V}$, $\mathbf{cov}_{sum}$) algorithm for the root z of the largest tree to obtain the global average Ave.
Run Data-spread(G, $\mathbb{F}$, $\tilde{V}$, Ave) algorithm — the root z of the largest tree uses its average estimate, i.e., Ave, as the value to spread.
Every root broadcasts its value to all the nodes in its tree.

THEOREM 6. *Whp, there exists a time $T_{ave} = O(\log m + \alpha\log n) = O(\log n)$, $\alpha > 0$, such that for all time $t \geq T_{ave}$, the relative error of the estimate of average aggregate on the root of the largest tree, z, is at most $\frac{2}{n^\alpha - 1}$, where the relative error is $\frac{|\hat{x}_{ave,t,z} - x_{ave}|}{|x_{ave}|}$, and the average aggregate, Ave, is $x_{ave} = \frac{\sum_i v_i}{n}$.*

Due to space limitation, readers are referred to the full version of this paper [3] for the proof.

Complexity of Gossip-ave

Gossip-ave algorithm needs $O(\log m + \log\frac{1}{\epsilon}) = O(\log n)$ rounds and $m \cdot O(\log n) = O(n)$ messages for the root of the largest tree to have the global average aggregate, Ave, within a relative error of at most $\frac{2}{n^\alpha - 1}$, $\alpha > 0$.

3.4 DRR-gossip Algorithms

Putting together our results from the previous subsections, we present Algorithm 7, DRR-gossip-max, and Algorithm 8, DRR-gossip-ave, for computing Max and Ave, respectively.

The complexity of DRR-gossip algorithms

To conclude from the previous sections, the time complexity of the DRR-gossip algorithms is $O(\log n)$ since all the phases need $O(\log n)$ rounds. The message complexity is dominated by the DRR algorithm in the phase I which needs $O(n\log\log n)$ messages.

4. SPARSE NETWORKS: LOCAL-DRR ALGORITHM

In sparse networks, a small number of neighbors makes it feasible for each node to send messages to all of its neighbors simultaneously in one round. In fact, this is a standard assumption in the traditional message passing distributed computing model [21] (here it is assumed messages sent to different neighbors in one round can all be different). We show how DRR-gossip can be used to improve gossip-based aggregate computation in such networks.

We assume that, in a round of time, a node of an arbitrary undirected graph can communicate directly only with its immediate neighbors (i.e., nodes that are connected directly by an edge). (Note that, in previous sections, any two nodes can communicate with each other in a round under a complete graph model.) Thus, on such a communication model, we have a variant of the DRR algorithm, called the *Local-DRR algorithm*, where a node only exchange rank information with its immediate neighbors. Each node chooses a random rank in $[0, 1]$ as before. Then each node connects to its highest ranked neighbor (i.e., the neighbor which has the highest rank among all its neighbors). A node that has the highest rank among all its neighbors will become a root. Since every node, except root nodes, connects to a node with higher rank, there is no cycle in the graph. Thus this process results in a collection of disjoint trees. As shown in Theorem 7 below, the key property is that the *height* of each tree produced by the Local-DRR algorithm on an *arbitrary* graph is bounded by $O(\log n)$ whp. This enables us to bound the time complexity of the Phase II of the DRR-gossip algorithm, i.e., Convergecast and Broadcast, on an arbitrary graph by $O(\log n)$ whp.

THEOREM 7. *On an arbitrary undirected graph, all the trees produced by the Local-DRR algorithm have a height of at most $O(\log n)$ whp.*

Proof: Fix any node u_0. We first show that the path from u_0 to a root is at most $O(\log n)$ whp. Let $u_1, u_2, \ldots$ be the successive ancestors of u_0, i.e., u_1 is the parent of u_0 (i.e., u_0 connects to u_1), u_2 is the parent of u_1 and so on. (Note $u_1, u_2, \ldots$ are all null if u_0 itself is the root). Define the complement value to the rank of u_i as $C_i := 1 - rank(u_i)$, $i \geq 0$. The main thrust of the proof is to show that the sequence C_i, $i \geq 0$ decreases geometrically whp. We adapt a technique used in [17].

For $t \geq 0$, let I_t be the indicator random variable for the event that a root has not been reached after t jumps, i.e., $u_0, u_1, \ldots, u_t$ are not roots. We need the following Lemma.

LEMMA 8. $\forall t \geq 1$ *and* $\forall z \in [0, 1]$, $E[C_{t+1}I_t | C_tI_{t-1} = z] \leq z/2$.

Proof: We can assume that $z \neq 0$; since $C_{t+1} \leq C_t$ and $I_t \leq I_{t-1}$, the lemma holds trivially if $z = 0$. Therefore, we have $I_{t-1} = 1$ and $C_t = z > 0$. We focus on the node u_t. Denote the set of neighbors of node u_t by U; the size of U is at most $n - 1$. Let Y be the random variable denoting the number of "unexplored" nodes in set U, i.e., those that do not belong to the set $\{u_0, u_1, \ldots, u_{t-1}\}$. If $Y = 0$, then u_t is a root and hence $C_{t+1}I_t = 0$. We will prove that for all $d \geq 1$,

$$E[C_{t+1}I_t | ((C_tI_{t-1} = z) \wedge (Y = d))] \leq z/2. \quad (2)$$

Showing the above is enough to prove the lemma, because if the lemma holds conditional on all positive values of d, it also holds unconditionally. For convenience, we denote the l.h.s. of (2) as Φ.

Fix some $d \geq 1$. In all arguments below, we condition on the event "$(C_tI_{t-1} = z) \wedge (Y = d)$". Let $v_1, v_2, \ldots, v_d$ denote the d unexplored nodes in U. If $rank(v_i) < rank(u_t)$ for all i ($1 \leq i \leq d$), then u_t is a root and hence $C_{t+1}I_t = 0$. Therefore, conditioning on the value $y = \min_i C_i = min_i(1 - rank(v_i)) \leq z$, and considering the d possible values of i that achieve this minimum, we get,

$$\Phi = d \int_0^z y(1 - y)^{d-1} dy.$$

Evaluating the above yields

$$\Phi = \frac{1 - (1 - z)^d(1 + zd)}{(d + 1)}.$$

We can show that the r.h.s of the above is at most $z/2$ by a straightforward induction on d. ∎

Using Lemma 8, we now prove Theorem 7.

We have $E[C_1I_0] \leq E[C_1] \leq 1$. Hence by Lemma 8 and an induction on t yields that $E[C_tI_{t-1}] \leq 2^{-t}$. In particular, letting $T = 3 \log n$, where c is some suitable constant, we get $E[C_TI_{T-1}] \leq n^{-3}$.

Now, suppose $u_T = u$ and that $C_TI_{T-1} = z$. The degree of node u is at most n; for each of these nodes v, $\Pr(rank(v) > rank(u)) = \Pr(1 - rank(v) < 1 - rank(u)) = \Pr(1 - rank(v) < z) = z$. Thus the probability that u is not a root is at most nz; more formally, $\forall z, \Pr(I_T = 1 | C_TI_{T-1} = z) \leq nz$. So,

$$\Pr(I_T = 1) \leq \log n E[C_TI_{T-1}] \leq n/n^3 = 1/n^2.$$

Hence, whp, the number of hops from any fixed note to the root is $O(\log n)$. By union bound, the statement holds for all nodes whp. ∎

Similar to Theorem 1, we can bound the number of trees produced by the Local-DRR algorithm on an arbitrary graph.

THEOREM 9. *Let G be an arbitrary connected undirected graph having n nodes. Let $d_i = O(n/\log n)$ be the degree of node i, $1 \leq i \leq n$. The number of trees produced by the Local-DRR algorithm is $O(\sum_{i=1}^n \frac{1}{d_i+1})$ whp. Hence, if $d_i = d$, $\forall i$, then the number of trees is $O(n/d)$ whp.*

Proof: Let the indicator random variable X_i take the value of 1 if node i is a root and 0 otherwise. Let $X = \sum_{i=1}^n X_i$ be the total number of roots. $\Pr(X_i = 1) = 1/(d_i + 1)$ since, this is the probability its value is the highest among all of its d_i neighbors. Hence, by linearity of expectation, the expected number of roots (hence, trees) is $E[X] = \sum_{i=1}^n E[X_i] = \sum_{i=1}^n \frac{1}{d_i+1}$. To show concentration, we cannot directly use a standard Chernoff bound since X_is are not independent (connections are not independently chosen, but fixed by the underlying graph). However, one can use the following Lemma, a variant of the Chernoff bound from [20].

LEMMA 10. *([20]) Let $Z_1, Z_2, \ldots, Z_s \in \{0, 1\}$ be random variables such that for all l, and for any $S_{l-1} \subseteq \{1, \ldots, l - 1\}$, $\Pr(Z_l = 1 | \bigwedge_{j \in S_{l-1}} Z_j = 1) \leq \Pr(Z_l = 1)$. Then for any $\delta > 0$, $\Pr(\sum_{l=1}^s Z_l \geq \mu(1+\delta)) \leq (\frac{e^\delta}{(1+\delta)^{1+\delta}})^\mu$, where $\mu = \sum_{l=1}^s E[Z_l]$.*

By Lemma 10, for random variables, $X_1, \ldots, X_i, \ldots, X_n$ and for any $S_{i-1} \subseteq \{1, \ldots, i - 1\}$, $\Pr(X_i = 1 | \bigwedge_{j \in S_{i-1}} X_j = 1) \leq \Pr(X_i = 1)$. This is because if a node's neighbor is a root, then the probability that the node itself is a root is 0. Also, the assumption of $d_i = O(n/\log n)$ ensures that $E[X]$ is $\Omega(\log n)$, so the Chernoff bound yields a high probability on the concentration of X to its mean $E[X]$. ∎

We make two assumptions regarding the network communication model: (1) as mentioned earlier, a node can send a message simultaneously to all its neighbors (i.e., nodes that are connected directly by an edge) in the same round; (2) there is a routing protocol which allows any node to communicate with a *random* node in the network in $O(T)$ rounds and using $O(M)$ messages whp. Assumption (1) is standard in distributed computing literature[4, 21]. As for Assumption (2), there are well-known techniques for sampling a random node in a network, e.g., using random walks (e.g., [28]) or using special properties of the underlying topology, e.g., as in P2P topologies such as Chord [12]. Under the above assumptions, we obtain the performance of DRR-gossip using the Local-DRR algorithm on sparse graphs in the following Theorem.

THEOREM 11. *On a d-regular graph* $G(V, E)$, *where* $|V| = n$ *and* $d = O(n/\log n)$, *the time complexity of the DRR-gossip algorithms is* $O(\log n + T \log \frac{n}{d})$ *whp by using the Local-DRR algorithm and a routing protocol running in* $O(T)$ *rounds and* $O(M)$ *messages (whp) between a gossip pair; the corresponding message complexity is* $O(|E| + \frac{n}{d} M \log \frac{n}{d})$ *whp.*

Proof: Phase I (Local-DRR) takes $O(1)$ time, since each node can find its largest ranked neighbor in constant time (Assumption 1) and needs $O(|E|)$ messages in total (since at most two messages travel through an edge). Phase II (convergecast and broadcast) takes $O(\log n)$ time (by Theorem 8 and Assumption 1) and $O(n)$ messages. Phase III (uniform gossip) takes $O(T \log \frac{n}{d})$ time (Assumption 2) and needs $O(\frac{n}{d} M \log \frac{n}{d})$ messages (Assumption 2 and Theorem 9). ∎

We can apply the above theorem to Chord [27]. Each node in Chord has a degree $d = O(\log n)$. Chord admits an efficient (non-trivial) protocol (cf. [12]) which satisfies Assumption (2) with $T = O(\log n)$ and $M = O(\log n)$ (both in expectation, which is sufficient here). Hence the above theorem shows that DRR-gossip takes $O(\log^2 n)$ time and $O(n \log n)$ messages whp. In contrast, the straightforward uniform gossip [11] gives $O(T \log n) = O(\log^2 n)$ rounds and $O(M \cdot n \log n) = O(n \log^2 n)$ messages whp.

5. LOWER BOUND FOR ADDRESS OBLIVIOUS ALGORITHMS

We conclude by showing a non-trivial lower bound result on gossip-based aggregate computation: any address-oblivious algorithm for computing aggregates requires $\Omega(n \log n)$ messages, *regardless of the number of rounds or the size of the (individual) messages*. We assume the random phone call model: i.e., communication partners are chosen randomly (without depending on their addresses). The following theorem gives a lower bound for computing the Max aggregate. The argument can be adapted for other aggregates as well.

THEOREM 12. *Any address-oblivious algorithm that computes the Maximum value,* Max, *in a n-node network needs* $\Omega(n \log n)$ *messages whp (regardless of the number of rounds).*

Proof: We lower bound the number of messages exchanged between nodes before a large fraction of the nodes correctly knows the (correct) maximum value. Suppose nodes can send messages that are arbitrary long. (The bound will hold regardless of this assumption.) Without loss of generality, we will assume that a node can send a list of all node addresses and the corresponding node values learned so far (without any aggregation). For any node i to have correct knowledge of the maximum, it should somehow know the values at all other nodes. (Otherwise, an adversary —who knows the random choices made by the algorithm — can always make sure that the maximum is at a node which is not known by i.) There are two ways that i can learn about another node j's value: (1) direct way: i gets to know j's value by communicating with j directly (at the beginning, each node knows only about its own value); and (2) indirect way: i gets to know j's value by communicating with a node $w \neq j$ which has a knowledge of j's value. Note that w itself may have learned about j's value either directly or indirectly.

Let v_i be the (initial) value associated with node i, $1 \leq i \leq n$. We will assume that all values are *distinct*. By the adversary argument, the requirement is that at the end of any algorithm, on the average, at least half of the nodes should know (in the above direct or indirect way) all of the v_i, $1 \leq i \leq n$. Otherwise, the adversary can make any value that is not known to more than half of the nodes, the maximum. We want to show that the number of messages needed to satisfy the above requirement is at least $cn \log n$, for some (small) constant $c > 0$. In fact, we show something stronger: at least

$cn \log n$ (for some small $c > 0$) messages are needed if we require even $n^{\Omega(1)}$ values to be known to at least $\Omega(n)$ nodes.

We define a stage (consisting of one or more rounds) as follows. Stage 1 starts with round 1. If stage t ends in round j, then stage $t + 1$ starts in round $j + 1$. Thus, it remains to describe when a stage ends. We distinguish sparse and dense stages. A sparse stage contains at most ϵn messages (for a suitably chosen small constant $\epsilon > 0$, fixed later in the proof). The length of these stages is maximized, i.e., a sparse stage ends in a round j if adding round $j + 1$ to the stage would result in more than ϵn messages. A dense stage consists of only one round containing more than ϵn messages. Observe that the number of messages during the stages 0 to j is at least $(j - 1)\epsilon n/2$ because any pair of consecutive stages contains at least ϵn messages by construction.

Let $S_i(t)$ be the set of *nodes* that know v_i at the beginning of stage t. At the beginning of stage 1, $|S_i(1)| = 1$, for all $1 \leq i \leq n$.

At the beginning of stage t, we call a value as *typical* if it is known by at most $6^t \log n$ nodes (i.e., $|S_i(t)| \leq 6^t \log n$) *and* it was typical at the beginning of all stages prior to t. All values are typical at the beginning of stage 1. Let k_t denote the number of typical values at the beginning of stage t.

The proof of the Theorem follows from the following claim. (Constants specified will be fixed in the proof; we don't try to optimize these values).

Claim: At the beginning of stage t, at least $(1/6)^t n$ values are typical w.h.p., for all $t \leq \delta \log n$, for a fixed positive constant δ.

The above claim will imply the theorem since at the end of stage $t = \delta \log n$, $|S_i(t)| \leq o(n)$ for at least $n^{\Omega(1)}$ values, i.e., at least $n^{\Omega(1)}$ values are not yet known to $1 - o(1)$ fraction of the nodes after stage $t = \delta \log n$. (The adversary can make any of these $n^{\Omega(1)}$ values the maximum to ensure that any algorithm fails.) Hence the number of messages needed is at least $\Omega(n \log n)$.

We prove the above claim by induction: We show that if the claim holds at the beginning of a stage then it hold at the end of the stage. We show this regardless whether the stage is dense or sparse, and thus we have two cases.

Case 1: The stage is dense. A dense stage consists of only one round with at least ϵn messages. Fix a typical value v_i. Let $U_i(t) = V - S_i(t)$, i.e., the set of nodes that do not know v_i at the beginning of stage t. For $1 \leq k(i) \leq |U_i(t)|$, let $x_{k(i)}$ denote the indicator random variable that denotes whether the $k(i)$th of these nodes gets to know the value v_i in this stage. Let $X_i(t) = \sum_{k(i)=1}^{|U_i(t)|} x_{k(i)}$. Let u be a node that does not know v_i. u can get to know v_i either by calling a node that knows the value or being called by a node that knows the value. The probability it gets to know v_i by calling is at most $6^t \log n/n$ and the probability that it gets called by a node knowing the value is at most $6^t \log n/n$ (this quantity is $o(1)$, since $t \leq \delta \log n$ and δ is sufficiently small). Hence the total probability that it gets to know v_i is at most $2 \cdot 6^t \log n/n$. Thus, the expected number of nodes that get to know v_i in this stage is $E[X_i(t)] = \sum_{k(i)=1}^{|U_i(t)|} \Pr\{x_{k(i)} = 1\} \leq 2 \cdot 6^t \log n$. The variables $x_{k(i)}$ are not independent, but are negatively correlated in the sense of Lemma 10 by which we have

$$\Pr(X_i(t) > 5 \cdot 6^t \log n)$$
$$= \Pr(X_i(t) > (1 + 3/2) \cdot 2 \cdot 6^t \log n) \leq 1/n^2.$$

By union bound, w.h.p., at most $5 \cdot 6^t$ new nodes get to know each typical value. Thus w.h.p. the total number of nodes knowing a typical value (for every such value) in this stage is at most $6^t \log n + 5 \cdot 6^t \log n = 6^{t+1} \log n$, thus satisfying the induction hypothesis. It also follows that a typical value at the beginning of a dense phase remains typical at the end of the phase, i.e., $k_{t+1} = k_t$ w.h.p.

Case 2: The stage is sparse. By definition, there are at most ϵn messages in a sparse stage. Each of these messages can be a push or a pull. (A push message is one that is sent by a calling node to the called node and a pull message is the message obtained by the calling node from the called node.) A sparse stage may consist of multiple rounds.

Fix a typical value v_i. W.h.p, there are at most $6^t \log n$ nodes that know a typical value at the beginning of this stage. Using pull messages, since the origin is chosen uniformly at random, the probability that one of these nodes is contacted is at most $1/n(\epsilon n) = \epsilon$. Hence the expected number of messages sent by nodes knowing this typical value is at most $\epsilon 6^t \log n$. Thus the expected number of new nodes that get to know this typical value is at most $\epsilon 6^t \log n$. The high probability bound can be shown as earlier.

We next consider the effect of push messages. We focus on values that are typical at the beginning of this stage. We show that with high probability at least some constant fraction of the typical values remain typical at the end of this phase. As defined earlier, let k_t be the number of such typical values. In this stage, at most ϵn nodes are involved in pushing — let this set be Q. Consider a random typical value x. Since a typical value is known by at most $6^t \log n$ nodes and destinations are uniformly randomly chosen, the probability that x is known to a node in Q is $O(\frac{6^t \log n}{n})$. Hence the expected number of times that x will be pushed by set Q is at most $O(\epsilon 6^t \log n)$. Now, the number of times x has to be pushed is at least $(6 - \epsilon) \cdot 6^t \log n$ to exceed the required expansion for this value whp (as argued in the above para, pulling only results in at most $\epsilon 6^t \log n$ messages having being sent out w.h.p). By Markov's inequality, the probability that x is pushed more than $(6 - \epsilon) \cdot 6^t \log n$ times by nodes in set Q is at most $\frac{\epsilon}{6-\epsilon}$. Hence the expected number of typical values that can expand is at most $\frac{\epsilon}{6-\epsilon} k_t$. Thus, in expectation, at least $1 - \frac{\epsilon}{6-\epsilon}$ fraction of the typical values remain typical. High probability bound can be shown similar to case 1. We want $1 - \frac{\epsilon}{6-\epsilon} > 1/6$, for the induction hypothesis to hold; this can be satisfied by choosing ϵ small enough. ∎

6. CONCLUDING REMARKS

We presented an almost-optimal gossip-based protocol for computing aggregates that takes $O(n \log \log n)$ messages and $O(\log n)$ rounds. We also showed how our protocol can be applied to improve performance in networks with a fixed underlying topology. The main technical ingredient of our approach is a simple distributed randomized procedure called DRR to partition a network into trees of small size. The improved bounds come at the cost of sacrificing address-obliviousness. However, as we show in our lower bound, this is necessary if we need to break the the $\Omega(n \log n)$ message barrier. An interesting open question is to establish whether $\Omega(n \log \log n)$ messages is a lower bound for gossip-based aggregate computation in the non-address oblivious model. Another interesting direction is to see whether the DRR technique can be used to obtain improved bounds for other distributed computing problems.

7. REFERENCES

[1] S. Boyd, A. Ghosh, B. Prabhakar, and D. Shah. Randomized gossip algorithms. *IEEE Trans. on Infor. Theory*, 52(6):2508–2530, 2006.

[2] J.-Y. Chen and J. Hu. Analysis of distributed random grouping for aggregate computation on wireless sensor networks with randomly changing graphs. *IEEE Trans. on Parallel and Distributed Systems*, 19:1136–1149, 2008.

[3] J.-Y. Chen and G. Pandurangan. Optimal gossip-based aggregate computation. 2009. http://arxiv.org/pdf/1001.3242.

[4] J.-Y. Chen, G. Pandurangan, and D. Xu. Robust aggregate computation in wireless sensor network: distributed randomized algorithms and analysis. *IEEE Trans. on Parallel and Distributed Systems*, 17(9):987–1000, Sep. 2006.

[5] A. Demers, D. Greene, C. Hauser, W. Irish, J. Larson, S. Shenker, H. Sturgis, D. Swinehart, and D. Terry. Epidemic algorithms for replicated database maintenance. In *PODC*, pages 1–12, 1987.

[6] A. G. Dimakis, A. D. Sarwate, and M. J. Wainwright. Geographic gossip: efficient aggregation for sensor networks. In *IPSN*, pages 69–76, 2006.

[7] J. Gao, L. Guibas, N. Milosavljevic, and J. Hershberger. Sparse data aggregation in sensor networks. In *IPSN*, pages 430–439, 2007.

[8] M. Jelasity, A. Montresor, and O. Babaoglu. Gossip-based aggregation in large dynamic networks. *ACM Trans. Comput. Syst.*, 23(3):219–252, 2005.

[9] R. M. Karp, C. Schindelhauer, S. Shenker, and B. Vöcking. Randomized rumor spreading. In *FOCS*, pages 565–574, 2000.

[10] S. Kashyap, S. Deb, K. V. M. Naidu, R. Rastogi, and A. Srinivasan. Efficient gossip-based aggregate computation. In *PODS*, pages 308–317, 2006.

[11] D. Kempe, A. Dobra, and J. Gehrke. Gossip-based computation of aggregate information. In *FOCS*, pages 482–491, 2003.

[12] V. King, S. Lewis, J. Saia, and M. Young. Choosing a random peer in chord. *Algorithmica*, 49(2):147–169, 2007.

[13] B. Krishnamachari, D. Estrin, and S. B. Wicker. The impact of data aggregation in wireless sensor networks. In *DEBS*, pages 575–578, 2002.

[14] P. Kyasanur, R. R. Choudhury, and I. Gupta. Smart gossip: An adaptive gossip-based broadcasting service for sensor networks. In *MASS*, pages 91–100, 2006.

[15] S. Madden, M. J. Franklin, J. M. Hellerstein, and W. Hong. Tag: a tiny aggregation service for ad-hoc sensor networks. *SIGOPS Oper. Syst. Rev.*, 36(SI):131–146, 2002.

[16] M. Mitzenmacher and E. Upfal. *Probability and Computing*. Cambridge University Press, 2005.

[17] R. Morselli, B. Bhattacharjee, M. A. Marsh, and A. Srinivasan. Efficient lookup on unstructured topologies. In *PODC*, pages 77–86, 2005.

[18] D. Mosk-Aoyama and D. Shah. Computing separable functions via gossip. In *PODC*, pages 113–122, 2006.

[19] S. Nath, P. B. Gibbons, S. Seshan, and Z. R. Anderson. Synopsis diffusion for robust aggregation in sensor networks. In *SenSys*, pages 250–262, 2004.

[20] A. Panconesi and A. Srinivasan. Randomized distributed edge coloring via an extension of the Chernoff-Hoeffding bounds. *SIAM Journal on Computing*, 26:350–368, 1997.

[21] D. Peleg. *Distributed Computing: A Locality-Sensitive Approach*. SIAM, 2000.

[22] R. D. Pietro and P. Michiardi. Brief announcement: Gossip-based aggregate computation: computing faster with non address-oblivious schemes. In *PODC*, 2008, page 442. Extended version at http://www.eurecom.fr/~michiard/downloads/podc08_a_ext.pdf.

[23] B. Pittel. On spreading a rumor. *SIAM J. Appl. Math.*, 47(1):213–223, 1987.

[24] A. I. T. Rowstron and P. Druschel. Pastry: Scalable, decentralized object location, and routing for large-scale peer-to-peer systems. In *Middleware*, pages 329–350, 2001.

[25] R. Sarkar, X. Zhu, and J. Gao. Hierarchical spatial gossip for multi-resolution representation in sensor netowrk. In *IPSN*, pages 420–429, 2007.

[26] N. Shrivastava, C. Buragohain, D. Agrawal, and S. Suri. Medians and beyond: new aggregation techniques for sensor networks. In *SenSys*, pages 239–249, 2004.

[27] I. Stoica, R. Morris, D. Karger, M. F. Kaashoek, and H. Balakrishnan. Chord: A scalable peer-to-peer lookup service for internet applications. In *SIGCOMM*, pages 149–160, 2001.

[28] M. Zhong and K. Shen. Random walk based node sampling in self-organizing networks. *SIGOPS Oper. Syst. Rev.*, 40(3):49–55, 2006.

On the Bit Communication Complexity of Randomized Rumor Spreading[*]

Pierre Fraigniaud
CNRS and Univ. Paris Diderot
Paris, France
pierre.fraigniaud@liafa.jussieu.fr

George Giakkoupis
CNRS and Univ. Paris Diderot
Paris, France
ggiak@liafa.jussieu.fr

ABSTRACT

We study the communication complexity of rumor spreading in the random phone-call model. Suppose n players communicate in parallel rounds, where in each round every player calls a randomly selected communication partner. A player u is allowed to exchange messages during a round only with the player that u called, and with all the players that u received calls from, in that round. In every round, a (possibly empty) set of rumors to be distributed among all players is generated, and each of the rumors is initially placed in a subset of the players. Karp *et. al* [16] showed that no rumor-spreading algorithm that spreads a rumor to all players with constant probability can be both time-optimal, taking $O(\lg n)$ rounds, and message-optimal, using $O(n)$ messages per rumor. For address-oblivious algorithms, in particular, they showed that $\Omega(n \lg \lg n)$ messages per rumor are required, and they described an algorithm that matches this bound and takes $O(\lg n)$ rounds.

We investigate the number of communication bits required for rumor spreading. On the lower-bound side, we establish that any address-oblivious algorithm taking $O(\lg n)$ rounds requires $\Omega(n(b + \lg \lg n))$ communication bits to distribute a rumor of size b bits. On the upper-bound side, we propose an address-oblivious algorithm that takes $O(\lg n)$ rounds and uses $O(n(b + \lg n \lg b))$ bits. These results show that, unlike the case for the message complexity, optimality in terms of both the running time and the bit communication complexity is attainable, except for very small rumor sizes $b \ll \lg \lg n \lg \lg \lg n$.

Categories and Subject Descriptors

F.2.2 [**Analysis Of Algorithms And Problem Complexity**]: Nonnumerical Algorithms and Problems; E.4 [**Data**]: Coding And Information Theory—*Data compaction and compression*

[*]Research supported in part by the ANR projects ALADDIN and PROSE, and by the INRIA project GANG.

General Terms

Algorithms, Performance, Theory

Keywords

rumor spreading, random phone call, bit communication complexity

1. INTRODUCTION

We study the problem of information spreading in a distributed environment where information is exchanged using randomized communication. Suppose n players communicate in parallel rounds, where in each round every player *calls* a randomly selected communication partner. Each player u is allowed to exchange messages during a round only with the player that u called, and with all the (zero or more) players that called u, in that round. This communication model is often referred to as the *random phone-call model* [16]. In every round, zero or more pieces of information, called *rumors*, are generated, and each rumor is placed to one or more players, the *sources* of the rumor. The goal is that each rumor be distributed among all players within a small number of rounds from the round that the rumor was generated, and by using a small amount of communication between players.[1]

A motivating example for this problem is the maintenance of replicated databases, for instance, on name servers in a large corporate network [4]. In such a system, updates are injected at various nodes and at various times, and these updates must be propagated to all nodes in the network. It is desirable that all databases converge to the same content quickly, and with little communication overhead. The motivation for using a randomized communication model is that such a scheme is simple, scalable, and naturally fault tolerant [4, 11].

A simple rumor-spreading algorithm for the random phone-call model is the so-called *push* algorithm. A rumor r is spread as follows. In each round, starting from the round in which r is generated, every *informed* player u (i.e., every player who knows r) forwards r to the player v that u calls in that round; we say that u *pushes* r to v. The distribution of

[1]A variant of this problem that is often considered in the literature is when each rumor has exactly one source. As we discuss later, with one source per rumor the number of rumors generated per round is essentially bounded by n, since all rumors generated at the same round by the same source can be grouped into a single large rumor; this trick does not work when a rumor can have more than one sources.

r is terminated after $\Theta(\lg n)$ rounds, at which time all players know r with high probability [13, 17]. The runtime of the push algorithm is asymptotically optimal for the random phone-call model, as we will see later. However, the algorithm suffers from high communication overhead, performing $\Theta(n \lg n)$ transmissions of the rumor. Intuitively, the number of informed players roughly doubles in each round, until a constant fraction of the players is informed; and in each subsequent round, the number of non-informed players halves. Thus, in the last $\Theta(\lg n)$ rounds $\Theta(n)$ players push the rumor in each round.

The *push-pull* rumor-spreading algorithm, proposed in [16], has asymptotically optimal runtime as well, but it has a smaller communication overhead than the push algorithm. A rumor r is distributed as follows. In each round from the round when r is generated, every informed player u pushes r to the player that u calls in this round, as in the push algorithm, and, in addition, u forwards r to every player v that calls u in this round; we say that r is *pulled* from u to v. In the basic version of this algorithm, where a rumor is assumed to have a single source, the distribution of r is terminated after $\lg_3 n + \Theta(\lg \lg n)$ rounds. By that time, with high probability, all players know r, and r has been transmitted $\Theta(n \lg \lg n)$ times. The intuition is that the push and pull transmissions roughly triple the number of informed player in each round until a constant fraction of the players is informed, and, from this point on, the pull transmissions shrink the fraction of non-informed players from s_{t-1} to $s_t = s_{t-1}^2$, in each round t. Thus, only $\Theta(\lg \lg n)$ additional rounds are required after a constant fraction of players is informed. Note that when a rumor may have more than one sources, the message complexity per rumor can be as bad as $\Theta(n \lg n)$—e.g., when the rumor has $\Theta(n)$ sources. A variant of the basic push-pull algorithm, also proposed in [16], uses a more robust termination criterion that detects when a large fraction of players is informed. This algorithm takes $O(\lg n)$ rounds and uses $\Theta(n \lg \lg n)$ messages per rumor, regardless of the number of sources per rumor.

On the lower-bound side, it is known that no decentralized rumor-spreading algorithm for the random phone-call model taking $O(\lg n)$ rounds and using $O(n)$ messages per rumor can guarantee that a rumor is spread to all players with constant probability [16]. In other words, it is not possible to achieve simultaneously optimality both in terms of the running time and the message complexity in the random phone-call model.[2] Moreover, for the case of *address-oblivious* algorithm, such as the push and push-pull algorithms above, $\Omega(n \lg \lg n)$ messages are required, regardless of the number of rounds [16]. So, the push-pull protocol is asymptotically optimal among the address-oblivious algorithm in terms of time and message complexity.

In this paper, we investigate the communication complexity of rumor spreading in the random phone-call model, measured in terms of the number of *bits* exchanged between players. The standard approach to measuring the communication complexity has been in terms of messages, counting

one message for every quadruplet $\langle r, t, u, v \rangle$ such that information regarding rumor r is exchanged in round t between players u and v. In the rumor-spreading algorithms that have been proposed each such exchange of information typically involves the actual rumor r, plus the values of some small counters, such as the age of the rumor. Arguably, for some applications the volume of information exchanged is at least as relevant as the number of messages, and trying to minimize the number of bits exchanged, in addition to the number of messages, is desirable. This is especially true when a large number of rumors are spread simultaneously, or when rumors are large.

1.1 Our results

As we saw above, no rumor-spreading algorithm in the random phone-call model can be both time-optimal, taking $O(\lg n)$ rounds, and message-optimal, using $O(n)$ messages per rumor. We show that the situation is different when bit communication complexity is considered in place of message complexity. Specifically, we describe an address-oblivious algorithm that uses $O(\lg n)$ rounds and $O(n(b + \lg \lg n \lg b))$ bits of communication to distribute a b-bit rumor among all players with high probability. Also, $O(n \lg \lg n)$ messages per rumor are exchanged. These guarantees hold even when the rumors are generated by an adversary. On the lower-bound side, we establish that any address-oblivious algorithm taking $O(\lg n)$ rounds requires $\Omega(n(b + \lg \lg n))$ communication bits to spread a b-bits rumor to all players with constant probability. These two results imply that, unlike the case for the message complexity, optimality in terms of both the running time and the bit communication complexity is attainable, except for very small rumor sizes $b \ll \lg \lg n \lg \lg \lg n$.

Discussion

Our rumor-spreading algorithm can be described as a push-pull algorithm with "concise" feedback. Note that the original push-pull algorithms proposed in [16] require $O(nb \lg \lg n)$ communication bits per b-bit rumor.[3] So, our algorithm saves a $\lg \lg n$ factor for large b, and a $b / \lg \lg b$ factor for small b.

Informally, the algorithm works as follows. When a player learns a new rumor r, she pushes r in all subsequent rounds, until the 3rd time she pushes the rumor to some player who already knows it (when a rumor is pushed, the recipient informs the sender whether she knew the rumor). These push transmissions guarantee that a constant fraction of the players is informed within roughly $\lg n$ rounds, and that r is pushed no more than $4n$ times. Pull transmissions take place only every $\lg n / \lg \lg n$ rounds—there are $\Theta(\lg \lg n)$ pull rounds during the lifetime of r. Say u calls v in such a round. Ideally, we would like the set of rumors pulled from v to u to consist of exactly those rumors that v knows and u does not know; and this should be achieved without communicating more than roughly $nb / \lg \lg n$ additional bits per b-bit rumor, per pull round. This is a non trivial task, since players do not know the number or size of the rumors currently circulating; an unbounded number of rumors can be generated in each round, and any b-bit string can be a valid rumor, for any b. Also, the fact that a rumor may have more than one sources

---

[2] Note that if the players knew the complete communication graph and the set of informed players in each round then $\Theta(\lg n)$ rounds and $n - 1$ messages would be required to distribute a rumor started by a single source. The $\Omega(\lg n)$ time bound follows by a simple reachability argument based on the fact that node degrees in the communication graphs are sharply concentrated around their mean value 2.

[3] More precisely, for the basic version this complexity holds for one source per rumor, and for the other version the exact complexity is $O(n(b + \lg \lg \lg n) \lg \lg n)$ bits.

precludes "grouping" into a big rumor all the rumors started at the same time by the same player, which would effectively bound by n the number of rumors generated per round. For these reasons simple solutions such as the use of fingerprints to uniquely describe a rumor with fewer bits do not work. At the core of our rumor-spreading algorithm is a simple data structure for approximate set membership, used to encode the set of rumors that a player knows using roughly $\lg b$ bits per b-bit rumor. This data structure is deterministic, and allows for some false positives. When u calls v in a pull round, u sends to v this data structure of the recent rumors that u knows; and based on that, v decides which rumors to transmit to u.

For the lower bound, note that an $\Omega(n \lg \lg n)$ bound on the number of bits communicated per rumor is immediate from the same bound of [16] on the number of messages. So, we just have to show an $\Omega(nb)$ bound, which seems like a trivial information-theory result. However, a more careful look reveals that this is not the case: Information may be conveyed not just by the content of the messages exchanged, but also by the round in which they are exchanged. Even sending no messages through an established connection also conveys information. In fact, the $\Omega(nb)$ bound no longer holds if we can have more than $O(\lg n)$ rounds. The following (impractical) protocol spreads a b-bit rumor using only $O(n \lg n \lg b)$ bits, within $O(2^b \lg n)$ rounds. We modify the push algorithm such that for each rumor r, the size b of r is pushed instead of r, and also transmissions take place only in rounds t that are equal to r modulo 2^b (where r is viewed as a binary number). So, within $O(2^b \lg n)$ rounds, every player learns b and, thus, r, which is the last b bits of the round in which the player was informed.

We prove the $\Omega(nb)$ bound in two steps. We first establish the bound for large rumors, using essentially a counting argument. Then we reduce the case of smaller rumors into the previous case, by showing that given an algorithm that spreads small rumors using $o(nb)$ bits, we can devise an algorithm that spreads large rumors using $o(nb)$ bits as well. Error-correcting codes are used in this construction. We note that the $\Omega(nb)$ bound holds also for non address-oblivious algorithms.

1.2 Related work

There is a large literature on deterministic rumor spreading and related information dissemination problems in various communication models. For an overview of this volume of work see [12, 14, 15]. The problem of randomized rumor spreading was introduced in [13], where the runtime of the push algorithm in the random phone-call model was analyzed. This result was later refined in [17]. Randomized rumor spreading in the setting where players correspond to nodes in a graph (other than the complete graph), and in each round a player chooses its communication partner at random *among its graph neighbors*, was first studied in [11]. There, bounds on the runtime of the push algorithm in arbitrary graphs were derived, and the runtime of the same algorithm in the hypercube and in random graphs was analyzed. The runtime and message complexity of randomized rumor spreading in random graphs were also studied in [9, 10], where a push-pull algorithm was analyzed, as well as two variations of it where players can remember their recent connections, or they initiate multiple calls per round. Push-pull algorithms have also been proposed and analyzed

for random d-regular graphs [1], and for scale-free graphs [8]. In [5], a quasirandom analogue to the random phone-call model was introduced. In this model, each player has a cyclic list of all the players (or of all its neighbors, in case of rumor spreading in a graph). A player initially calls a player at a random position in her list, but from then on she calls her neighbors in the order of the list. It was shown that the push algorithm in the quasirandom model performs asymptotically at least as well as in the random model, for all the cases of graphs studied in [11], even when the lists are determined by an adversary. Rumor spreading in the quasirandom model was further explored in [6].

2. MODEL

In the random phone-call model [16], n players communicate in parallel rounds, in each of which every player u chooses a player v independently and uniformly at random, and u *calls* v. In a given round, u can only communicate with the player that u called, and with the players that called u, in that round. Communication inside each round is assumed to proceed in parallel, that is, any information received in a round cannot be forwarded to another player in the same round. In each call, communication between the caller and the receiver proceeds sequentially: one player sends a message, then the other sends a message back, and so on. No restrictions are imposed on the type or the size of information exchanged.

In each round, an adversary generates a (possibly empty) set of rumors, and places each rumor r to a non-empty subset of players, the *sources* of r. A rumor is just a binary string, and any binary string of any size represents a possible rumor; so, there are exactly 2^b distinct rumors of size b. No limit is imposed on the number of rumors generated in a round. However, we assume that rumors generated in two different rounds t_1, t_2 with $|t_1 - t_2| = O(\lg n)$ are distinct (this assumption is made to simplify the exposition of our algorithm, and can be relaxed). If player u calls player v and rumor r is transmitted from u to v we say that r is *pushed*, while if r is transmitted from v to u we say that r is *pulled*.

We measure the bit communication complexity of rumor spreading, that is, the total number of bits exchanged between players. Specifically, in our rumor-spreading algorithm, each message exchanged is either related to a single rumor, or to a set of rumors of the same size. In the latter case, to count the bits communicated per rumor we divide the size of the message by the size of the set of rumors. For the lower bound, we assume that a set of b-bit rumors are started by a single source at a round t, and that no other rumors are generated. To count the bits communicated per rumor, we count the total number of bits exchanged between players, from round t until the distribution of rumors finishes, and then divide by the number of rumors.

We focus on the class of *address-oblivious* algorithms, that is, when player u calls player v, u and v do not know the id of each other. Of course, they can communicate their ids, but this exchange of information is also counted in the bit communication complexity.

3. UPPER BOUND AND OUR RUMOR-SPREADING ALGORITHM

We establish the following upper bound on the performance of rumor spreading in the random phone-call model.

THEOREM 3.1. *There is some address-oblivious algorithm guaranteeing that, with high probability, any rumor is distributed to all players within* $O(\lg n)$ *rounds using* $O(nb + n \lg \lg n \lg b)$ *bits of communication, where b is the rumor's size.*

In Section 3.1, we present a rumor-spreading algorithm, and in Section 3.2, we prove that this algorithm meets the performance guarantees of Theorem 3.1.

3.1 Algorithm description

In this algorithm, the distribution of a rumor is not affected by rumors of different size. So, in our description we focus only on rumors of the same size b. Also, very small rumors are treated slightly differently, as we explain at the end of this section.

The algorithm is a push-pull algorithm with feedback. Consider a b-bit rumor r starting from a set of players S in round t_{start}. The distribution of r continues until round $t_{end} = t_{start} + 6 \lg n - 1$, after which the rumor is considered *cold*. Whenever r is pushed or pulled, its age, that is, the difference between the current round and t_{start}, is also communicated—$O(\lg \lg n)$ bits are required for that. Suppose that a player u learns r in round t; if $u \in S$ we say that u learns r in round $t = t_{start} - 1$. From the next round $t + 1$ on, u *pushes* r in every round until the 3rd time that u has pushed r to a player who already knows the rumor from a previous round, or until the round t_{end} is reached. After that time, u does not push r again. A player can tell if in some round she pushed a rumor to someone who already knew the rumor, because in every push transmission the recipient sends back a (constant-size) feedback containing that information.[4]

Pull transmissions occur only every $\lg n / \lg \lg n$ rounds, on rounds that are multiples of $\lg n / \lg \lg n$; these rounds are called *pull rounds*. (During pull rounds, push transmissions take place normally, as in regular rounds.) Suppose that player u calls player v in pull round t. Player u then sends to v a *digest* of the rumors that u has learned recently, and, based on this digest, v decides which rumors should be pulled to u. Next we describe the details of how the digest is created, and which rumors are pulled.

Digest

The digest of u in round t is built from all the non-cold rumors that u knows at the beginning of round t. Let $R_{b,i}$ be the subset of these rumors consisting of the rumors of size b that were generated during the i-th previous epoch, where an *epoch* is the time interval from the beginning of a pull round until the beginning of the next pull round. The digest of u consists of one component $D_{b,i}$ for each non-empty set $R_{b,i}$. Suppose that $R_{b,i} = \{r_1, \dots, r_\kappa\}$, for some $i, \kappa \geq 1$. The elements of $R_{b,i}$ are indexed such that if the r_k are interpreted as a binary numbers then $r_1 < \cdots < r_\kappa$. The digest $D_{b,i}$ for $R_{b,i}$ consists of two parts:

---

[4] The idea that a player stops pushing a rumor after a fixed number of unnecessary push transmissions was also suggested in [4]. An alternative stopping criterion that would also work is that a player stops pushing a rumor after a constant number of push transmissions (regardless of their outcome). The analysis for this approach is similar to that of Theorem 4.1.3 (Stage A) in [11].

1. the list $\langle b, i, p_1, p_2, \dots, p_{\kappa-1} \rangle$, where p_k, for $1 \leq k < \kappa$, is the position of the leftmost bit (most significant bit) where r_k and r_{k+1} differ; and

2. the subset $\{r_{j\ell} : j = 1, \dots, \lfloor \kappa/\ell \rfloor\}$ of $R_{b,i}$ containing every ℓ-th rumor, where $\ell = \lg n$.

Note that the size of $D_{b,i}$ is $O(\lg \lg \lg n + \kappa \lg b + \kappa b/\ell)$ bits. If $R_{b,i} = \emptyset$, i.e., if u does not know any non-cold rumor of size b generated in the i-th previous epoch, we will write $D_{b,i} = \emptyset$.

We now explain how from digest $D_{b,i} \neq \emptyset$ we obtain information about whether a given b-bit rumor r is a member of $R_{b,i}$. Let $x[j]$ denote the j-th leftmost bit of bit-string x. From the definition of the p_k and the assumption that $r_k < r_{k+1}$, we have that for $1 \leq j < p_k$, $r_k[j] = r_{k+1}[j]$, and

$$r_k[p_k] = 0 \neq 1 = r_{k+1}[p_k].$$

Based on this observation, we describe a simple algorithm that for any given r, computes an index k with $1 \leq k \leq \kappa$ such that

$$r \notin R_{b,i} \setminus \{r_k\}$$

The algorithm does not tell whether $r = r_k$. We denote this index by $\mathrm{ind}(r, D_{b,i})$, and we compute it as follows. We start with the list $1, \dots, \kappa$ of all indices, and in each step we eliminate one of the first two indices remaining, until there is only one index left; this last index is $\mathrm{ind}(r, D_{b,i})$. For each index $k < \kappa$ in the current list, we maintain the leftmost bit position at which r_k and $r_{k'}$ differ, where k' is the index following k in the current list; so, for the initial list of indices we have the positions $p_1, p_2, \dots, p_{\kappa-1}$ described in the first component of $D_{b,i}$. Maintaining these positions does not require knowledge of the actual rumors. Let k_1, k_2 be the first two of the indices remaining at the beginning of a step, and let q_1, q_2 be the bit positions currently associated with them. If $r[q_1] = 1$ then $r \neq r_{k_1}$, and, so, k_1 is removed from the list of indices in this step. The bit positions associated with the indices remaining do not change. If $r[q_1] = 0$, instead, then $r \neq r_{k_2}$, and, so, k_2 is removed from the list. Also the bit position associated with k_1 is updated to the leftmost of the positions q_1 and q_2.

Note that the second component $D_2 = \{r_{j\ell} : 1 \leq j \leq \kappa/\ell\}$ of $D_{b,i}$ is not used in computing $\mathrm{ind}(r, D_{b,i})$. The set D_2 is non-empty only when $|R_{b,i}| \geq \ell$, and it can sometimes be used together with $\mathrm{ind}(r, D_{b,i})$ to infer that $r \notin R_{b,i}$. Let $\mathrm{range}(r, D_{b,i})$ denote the set $\{k_1 + 1, \dots, k_2\}$, where r_{k_1} is the largest element of D_2 such that $r_{k_1} < r$, or $k_1 = 0$ if no such element exits; and r_{k_2} is the smallest element of D_2 such that $r \leq r_{k_2}$, or $k_2 = \kappa$ if no such element exits. Clearly, if $\mathrm{ind}(r, D_{b,i}) = k \notin \mathrm{range}(r, D_{b,i})$ then $r \neq r_k$, and, thus, $r \notin R_{b,i}$.

Based on u's digest, player v determines which rumors should be pulled from v to u as follows. Let $R'_{b,i}$ be the set of non-cold b-bit rumors that v knows, generated in the i-th previous epoch. If $D_{b,i} = \emptyset$ then all the rumors in $R'_{b,i}$ are pulled. Otherwise, for each $r \in R'_{b,i}$, v computes $\mathrm{ind}(r, D_{b,i})$ and $\mathrm{range}(r, D_{b,i})$, as described above, and r is pulled iff at least one of the following two conditions is satisfied:

(1) $\mathrm{ind}(r, D_{b,i}) \notin \mathrm{range}(r, D_{b,i})$;

(2) $\mathrm{ind}(r, D_{b,i}) = \mathrm{ind}(r', D_{b,i})$, for some $r' \in R'_{b,i} \setminus \{r\}$.

Note that if (1) holds then u does not know r; and if (2) holds then u knows at most one of r and r', thus, the bits transmitted are at most twice the bits necessary. Note, however, that the following bad scenario is possible: u does not know r, but $\mathrm{ind}(r, D_{b,i}) \in \mathrm{range}(r, D_{b,i})$ and $\mathrm{ind}(r', D_{b,i}) \neq \mathrm{ind}(r, D_{b,i})$, for all $r' \in R'_{b,i} \setminus \{r\}$; thus, r is not pulled. Nevertheless, we show that condition (2) ensures that the desired performance guarantees for the distribution of r are still met.

The digest structure employed by our algorithm can be viewed as essentially a data structure for approximate set membership. This problem is traditionally addressed using Bloom filters [2] (see also the survey [3]). Similarly to Bloom filters, our approach allows for false positives, but, unlike them, it is deterministic; and in addition to the information whether an element is a member of the set, it also gives the order of the element in that set. This feature is exploited by our algorithm to tackle the problem of false positives.

The case of very small rumors

In the algorithm above, if $b = (\lg \lg n)^{o(1)}$ then all but a $o(1)$ fraction of the bits used to distribute a single b-bit rumor are used to transmit the age information contained in the digest. We handle this issue by making the following two changes to the algorithm. For every rumor r of size $b = (\lg \lg n)^{o(1)}$, the beginning of the distribution of r is delayed until the next round that is a multiple of $6 \lg n$; i.e., if r is generated in round t, its distribution starts in round $t_{start} = \lceil t/6 \lg n \rceil \cdot 6 \lg n$. (Recall that $t_{end} = t_{start} + 6 \lg n - 1$.) Because of this modification, the epoch information for these rumors contained in the digest is no longer useful and is omitted. Apart from these two changes, the protocol remains the same. Note that these changes could also be applied to the other rumor sizes, but the resulting delays and bursty traffic may be undesirable; thus, we use these modifications only for very small rumors.

3.2 Analysis of algorithm

For the analysis, we distinguish two phases in the distribution of a rumor. Roughly speaking, in the first phase the rumor is *pushed* to at least a $\frac{1}{2} + \epsilon$ fraction of the players, and in the second phase the rumor is *pulled* to the remaining players. Below, we bound the duration of each phase, and then we bound the total number of bits communicated in the two phases. We only consider the case of rumor sizes $b = (\lg \lg n)^{\Omega(1)}$; for smaller rumors, the analysis is essentially the same.

3.2.1 Phase I: Pushing the rumor to a $\frac{1}{2} + \epsilon$ fraction of the players

For the analysis of this phase, we focus on a single rumor r of size b. To simplify notation we assume that r is generated in round $t_{start} = 1$. We prove the following lemma.

LEMMA 3.1. *With probability $1 - n^{-3+o(1)}$, at least a 3/4 fraction of the players knows r at the end of round $\tau = \lg n + 3 \lg \lg n$.*

We start by introducing some notation. S_t denotes the number of players who know r at the end of round t. A push transmission is called *bad* if the recipient already knows the rumor from a previous round. The number of bad push transmissions of r during the first t rounds is denoted B_t.

CLAIM 3.2. *Let $\tau_1 = \inf\{t : S_t \geq (\lg n)^4\}$. With probability $1 - n^{-3+o(1)}$, $B_{\tau_1} \leq 2$ and $\tau_1 \leq 4 \lg \lg n + O(1)$.*

PROOF. Fix some ordering of the set of players, and call a push transmission of r from u to v *good* if it is not bad

(i.e., v has not learn r in a previous round), and no player $u' < u$ pushes r to v in this round. The number of good push transmissions of r in the first τ_1 rounds is at most $2(\lg n)^4 - 3$ (at most $(\lg n)^4 - 2$ in the first $\tau_1 - 1$ rounds, and at most $(\lg n)^4 - 1$ in round τ_1). Also, the probability that a given push transmission of r in some of the first τ_1 rounds is good is at least $1 - \frac{2(\lg n)^4 - 3}{n}$, regardless of the other transmissions in the same round. This is because if we ignore the outcome of this transmission and of the pull transmissions in this round (if it is a pull round) then at most $2(\lg n)^4 - 3$ players know r at the end of the round. So, the probability that 3 or more of the push transmissions of r in the first τ_1 rounds are not good is at most

$$\binom{2(\lg n)^4}{3} \left(\frac{2(\lg n)^4 - 3}{n} \right)^3$$
$$\leq \frac{(2(\lg n)^4)^3}{3!} \left(\frac{2(\lg n)^4 - 1}{n} \right)^3$$
$$= n^{-3+o(1)},$$

From this, it is immediate that the probability that $B_{\tau_1} \geq 3$ is at most $n^{-3+o(1)}$. Also, if there are at most 2 non-good transmissions of r then no player stops pushing r in the first τ_1 rounds, and it is easy to verify that $\tau_1 \leq 4 \lg \lg n + O(1)$. $\square$

Let $H_t \subseteq S_t$ be the number of players who know r at the end of round t, and they have not performed more than 2 bad push transmissions of r by that time. Clearly,

$$S_t - \lfloor B_t/3 \rfloor \leq H_t \leq S_t.$$

The players in H_t are precisely the players who push r in round $t + 1$, if $t < t_{end}$.

CLAIM 3.3. *For any round $t < t_{end}$, if $H_t \geq (\lg n)^4$ and $S_t \leq \frac{3}{4} n$ then, with probability $1 - n^{-\omega(1)}$,*

$$S_{t+1} \geq S_t + H_t \left(1 - \frac{S_t}{n} \right) \left(1 - \frac{S_t}{2n} \right) \left(1 - \frac{1}{\lg n} \right), \quad (3.1)$$

and

$$B_{t+1} \leq B_t + \frac{H_t S_t}{n} \left(1 + \frac{1}{\lg n} \right) + (\lg n)^3. \quad (3.2)$$

PROOF. The expected number of players who learn r in round $t + 1$ is at least

$$(n - S_t) \left(1 - \left(1 - \frac{1}{n} \right)^{H_t} \right) \geq (n - S_t) \left(\frac{H_t}{n} - \frac{H_t^2}{2n^2} \right)$$
$$= H_t \left(1 - \frac{S_t}{n} \right) \left(1 - \frac{H_t}{2n} \right),$$

which is in $\Omega((\lg n)^4)$. Since the events: "player u learns r in round $t + 1$," for players u who do not know r at the end of round t, are negatively dependent [7], we can apply Chernoff bounds to obtain that the probability that fewer than $H_t \left(1 - \frac{S_t}{n} \right) \left(1 - \frac{H_t}{2n} \right) \left(1 - \frac{1}{\lg n} \right)$ players learn r is $e^{-\Omega((\lg n)^2)} = n^{-\Omega(\lg n)}$. For B_{t+1}, we have that the expected number of bad push transmissions in round $t + 1$ is $\frac{H_t S_t}{n}$, and, by Chernoff bounds, we can show that the probability there are more than $\frac{H_t S_t}{n} \left(1 + \frac{1}{\lg n} \right) + (\lg n)^3$ bad push transmissions is also $e^{-\Omega((\lg n)^2)}$. $\square$

138

Let $\mathcal{E}$ denote the event: "$B_{\tau_1} \leq 2$ and $\tau_1 \leq 4 \lg \lg n + O(1)$ and, for all t with $\tau_1 \leq t < t_{end}$ such that $H_t \geq (\lg n)^4$ and $S_t \leq \frac{3}{4} n$, inequalities (3.1) and (3.2) hold." By Claims 3.2 and 3.3,

$$\Pr[\mathcal{E}] = 1 - n^{-3+o(1)}. \qquad (3.3)$$

We prove Lemma 3.1 by showing that $\mathcal{E}$ implies $S_\tau \geq 3n/4$.

The claims we describe below assume that n is greater than some appropriate constant.

CLAIM 3.4. Let $\tau_2 = \inf\{t : S_t \geq n/\lg n\}$. If $\mathcal{E}$ occurs then $B_{\tau_2} \leq 4n/(\lg n)^2$ and $\tau_2 \leq \lg n + O(1)$.

PROOF. We show by induction on $t = \tau_1 + 1, \ldots, \tau_2$ that $B_t \leq 4 S_{t-1}/\lg n$ and $S_t \geq S_{t-1}(2 - \frac{4}{\lg n})$. From this, it follows that $B_{\tau_2} \leq 4 S_{\tau_2-1}/\lg n < 4n/(\lg n)^2$, and $\tau_2 \leq \frac{\lg n}{\lg(2-4/\lg n)} = \lg n + O(1)$, as desired. The induction is as follows. For the base case $t = \tau_1 + 1$, by (3.2), we have $B_{\tau_1+1} \leq 2 + \frac{S_{\tau_1}^2}{n}(1 + \frac{1}{\lg n}) + (\lg n)^3 \leq 2 + \frac{S_{\tau_1}}{\lg n}(1 + \frac{1}{\lg n}) + \frac{S_{\tau_1}}{\lg n} \leq \frac{3 S_{\tau_1}}{\lg n}$. Also, by (3.1), $S_{\tau_1+1} \geq S_{\tau_1} + S_{\tau_1}(1 - \frac{S_{\tau_1}}{n} - \frac{S_{\tau_1}}{2n} - \frac{1}{\lg n}) \geq S_{\tau_1}(2 - \frac{5}{2 \lg n})$. Similarly, for the induction step we have that if $t \geq \tau_1 + 1$ then

$$\begin{aligned}
B_{t+1} &\leq B_t + \frac{H_t S_t}{n}\left(1 + \frac{1}{\lg n}\right) + (\lg n)^3 \\
&\leq \frac{4 S_{t-1}}{\lg n} + \frac{S_t}{\lg n}\left(1 + \frac{1}{\lg n}\right) + \frac{S_{t-1}}{\lg n} \\
&\leq \frac{5 S_t}{(2 - \frac{4}{\lg n})\lg n} + \frac{S_t}{\lg n}\left(1 + \frac{1}{\lg n}\right) \\
&= (3.5 + o(1)) S_t / \lg n,
\end{aligned}$$

where the second and third inequalities were obtained using the induction hypothesis. Also,

$$\begin{aligned}
S_{t+1} &\geq S_t + \left(S_t - \frac{B_t}{3}\right)\left(1 - \frac{S_t}{n} - \frac{S_t}{2n} - \frac{1}{\lg n}\right) \\
&\geq S_t + \left(S_t - \frac{4 S_t}{3(2 - \frac{4}{\lg n})\lg n}\right)\left(1 - \frac{1}{\lg n} - \frac{1}{2\lg n} - \frac{1}{\lg n}\right) \\
&= S_t\left(2 - \frac{19 + o(1)}{6 \lg n}\right). \quad \square
\end{aligned}$$

CLAIM 3.5. Let $\tau_3 = \inf\{t : S_t \geq n/8\}$. If $\mathcal{E}$ occurs then $B_{\tau_3} \leq n/16$ and $\tau_3 \leq \tau_2 + 2 \lg \lg n$.

PROOF. It is similar to the proof of Claim 3.4. We show by induction on $t = \tau_2 + 1, \ldots, \tau_3$ that $B_t \leq S_{t-1}/2$ and $S_t \geq 3 S_{t-1}/2$. From this, it follows that $B_{\tau_3} \leq S_{\tau_3-1}/2 < n/16$, and $\tau_3 - \tau_2 \leq \frac{\lg \lg n}{\lg(3/2)} \leq 2 \lg \lg n$, as desired. For the base case $t = \tau_2 + 1$ of the induction, we have that $B_{\tau_2+1} \leq \frac{4n}{(\lg n)^2} + \frac{S_{\tau_2}}{8}(1 + \frac{1}{\lg n}) + (\lg n)^3 = S_{\tau_2}(\frac{1}{8} + o(1))$. Also, $S_{\tau_2+1} \geq S_{\tau_2} + (S_{\tau_2} - \frac{B_{\tau_2}}{3})(1 - \frac{1}{8} - \frac{1}{16} - \frac{1}{\lg n}) = S_{\tau_2}(2 - \frac{3}{16} - o(1))$. For the induction step, we have that if $t \geq \tau_2 + 1$ then $B_{t+1} \leq \frac{S_{t-1}}{2} + \frac{S_t}{8}(1 + \frac{1}{\lg n}) + (\lg n)^3 \leq \frac{S_t}{3} + \frac{S_t}{8}(1 + \frac{1}{\lg n}) + (\lg n)^3 = S_t(\frac{11}{24} + o(1))$, and $S_{t+1} \geq S_t + (S_t - \frac{S_t}{6})(1 - \frac{1}{8} - \frac{1}{16} - \frac{1}{\lg n}) \geq S_t(2 - \frac{17}{46} - o(1))$. $\square$

CLAIM 3.6. If $\mathcal{E}$ occurs then $S_{\tau_3+5} \geq 3n/4$.

PROOF. We compute S_t, for $t = \tau_3 + 1, \tau_3 + 2, \ldots$, under the worst-case assumptions that $S_{\tau_3} = n/8$ and $B_{\tau_3} = n/16$, and also that inequalities (3.1) and (3.2) hold as equalities, and $H_t = S_t - \lfloor B_t/3 \rfloor$. We obtain that $S_{\tau_3+5} \geq 3n/4$, for all n greater than a sufficiently large constant. $\square$

Combining now Equation (3.3) and Claims 3.4–3.6 yields Lemma 3.1.

3.2.2 Phase II: Pulling the rumor to the rest of the players

For this phase, we consider the distribution of all the b-bit rumors generated in the same epoch as r; we denote by R the set of these rumors. To ease comprehension we first study the case of $|R| = O(n)$, separately. In the analysis of this case, only the first component of the digests for rumors in R is used.

The case of $|R| = O(n)$

We prove the following result.

LEMMA 3.7. If at the end of round $\tau' \leq 4 \lg n$ every rumor in R is known to at least a $3/4$ fraction of the players then, with probability $1 - |R| \cdot n^{-3+o(1)}$, all players know all the rumors in R at the end of round $\tau' + 2 \lg n$.

Intuitively, the proof proceeds by lower-bounding the speed at which the slowest-spreading rumor in R is distributed. A key observation is that if a player u does not know a given rumor $r \in R$, but the digest D for the rumors in R that u knows is non-empty and $\text{ind}(r, D) = k$, then for r to be pulled to u it suffices that u call a player who knows both r and the k-th rumor described in D.

Below, r denotes an arbitrary rumor in R. For $i \geq 1$, t_i is the i-th pull round from round $\tau' + 1$, and $U_{i,r}$ is the number of players who do not know r at the end of round t_i. Also $U_{0,r}$ is the same quantity for round τ'. Finally, $U_i = \max_{r \in R} U_{i,r}$.

CLAIM 3.8. For any $i \geq 0$ such that $t_{i+1} \leq t_{end}$, if $U_i \geq (\lg n)^2 \sqrt{n}$ then, with probability $1 - n^{-\omega(1)}$,

$$U_{i+1,r} \leq \frac{2}{n} U_i^2 \left(1 + \frac{1}{\lg n}\right).$$

PROOF. Consider a player u who does not know r at the beginning of round t_{i+1}, and let D be the digest of u for this round, for the rumors in R that u knows. We distinguish two cases:

If $D = \emptyset$ then r is *not* pulled to u in round t_{i+1} iff u calls a player who does not know r, which happens with probability at most $U_{i,r}/n$.

Otherwise, if $\text{ind}(r, D) = k$ then for r to be pulled to u it suffices that u calls a player who knows both r and r_k, the k-th rumor in D; thus, the probability that r is *not* pulled to u is at most $(U_{i,r} + U_{i,r_k})/n$.

So, in both cases, the probability that r is not pulled to u in round t_{i+1} is at most $\frac{2}{n} U_i$. (This bound holds independently of pull transmissions performed by other players in this round.) Therefore, the expected number of players who do not know r at the beginning of round t_{i+1}, and r is not pulled to them in this round is at most $\frac{2}{n} U_i U_{i,r} \leq \frac{2}{n} U_i^2$. And, since $U_i \geq (\lg n)^2 \sqrt{n}$, by applying Chernoff bounds, we obtain that the number of these players is at most $\frac{2}{n} U_i^2 (1 + \frac{1}{\lg n})$ with probability $1 - e^{-\Omega(\lg^2 n)}$. Hence, the same upper bound applies also to $U_{i+1,r}$. $\square$

CLAIM 3.9. For any $i \geq 0$ such that $t_{i+7} \leq t_{end}$, if $U_i \leq (\lg n)^2 \sqrt{n}$ then, with probability $1 - n^{-3+o(1)}$, all players know r at the end of round t_{i+7}.

PROOF. If player u does not know r at the end of round t_i then u does not learn r by the end of round t_{i+7} only if r is not pushed to u in any of the 7 pull rounds following t_i, which happens with probability at most $\left(\frac{2U_i}{n}\right)^7$—by the same reasoning as in the proof of Claim 3.8. Thus, the probability that all players know r at the end of round t_{i+7} is at least $1 - U_{i,r}\left(\frac{2U_i}{n}\right)^7 = 1 - n^{-3+o(1)}$. □

Lemma 3.7 can now be obtained as follows. If for all $i \geq 0$ such that $U_i \geq (\lg n)^2\sqrt{n}$,

$$U_{i+1,r} \leq \frac{2}{n}U_i^2\left(1 + \frac{1}{\lg n}\right) = \frac{aU_i^2}{n},$$

where $a = 2(1 + \frac{1}{\lg n})$, then, for those i,

$$U_i \leq \frac{n}{a}\left(\frac{aU_0}{n}\right)^{2^i} \leq \frac{n(a/4)^{2^i}}{a}.$$

From this and Claim 3.8, it follows that $U_{\lg\lg n} < (\lg n)^2\sqrt{n}$ with probability $1 - |R| \cdot n^{-\omega(1)}$. And if $U_{\lg\lg n} < (\lg n)^2\sqrt{n}$ then, by Claim 3.9, it is $U_{\lg\lg n+7} = 0$ with probability $1 - |R| \cdot n^{-3+o(1)}$. Therefore, with probability $1 - |R| \cdot n^{-3+o(1)}$, we have $U_{\lg\lg n+7} = 0$, which implies that all players know all the rumors in R at the end of round $\tau' + \lg n + 7\lg n/\lg\lg n$.

Now, combining Lemmata 3.1 and 3.7 (the former applied for all $r \in R$, and the latter for $\tau' = \tau$) yields the desired bound on the number of rounds of our algorithm.

The case of $|R| = \omega(n)$

For large sets R the previous approach does not work—note the dependence on $|R|$ of the probabilistic bound of Lemma 3.7. We remove this dependence by utilizing the second component of the digests. This component is used to decouple the progress of the distribution of a rumor r from that of rumors that are further than $O(\ell\lg\lg n)$ from r in the ordered list of the rumors in R.

For the analysis, we consider an extra pull phase, before the pull phase we described in the previous case. During this phase every player learns sufficiently many of the rumors in R that are close to r. More specifically, suppose that $R = \{r_1, \ldots, r_\kappa\}$, where $r_1 < \cdots < r_\kappa$. Fix a rumor $r = r_\rho \in R$, and, for $i = 0, \pm 1, \ldots, \pm\lg n$, define

$$R_i = \{r_k : (i-\tfrac{1}{2})\ell\lg n < k-\rho \leq (i+\tfrac{1}{2})\ell\lg n \text{ and } 1 \leq k \leq \kappa\}.$$

The extra pull phase in the distribution of r is completed when every player knows at least a $1/3$ fraction of the rumors in each of the sets R_i. The next lemma is used to bound the length of this phase. We say that a set $R' \subseteq R$ is a *contiguous* subset of R if $R' = \{r_k : k_1 \leq k \leq k_2\}$, for some $k_1 \geq 1$ and $k_2 \leq \kappa$.

LEMMA 3.10. *Let R' be a contiguous subset of R with $|R'| = \omega(\ell\lg\lg n)$. If at the end of round $\tau' \leq 4\lg n$ every rumor in R' is known to at least a $3/4$ fraction of the players then, with probability $1 - n^{-3+o(1)}$, every player knows at least a $1/3$ fraction of the rumors in R' at the end of round $\tau' + 2\lg n$.*

PROOF. We start by showing that initially, i.e., at the end of round τ', one out of two players already knows half of the rumors in R'. Let f be the fraction of players who each knows half or more of the rumors at the end of round τ'. The average number of rumors a player knows at that

time is bounded from below by $\frac{3|R'|}{4}$, and from above by $f|R'| + (1-f)\frac{|R'|}{2}$. Combining the two yields $f \geq \frac{1}{2}$.

Next we show that if in a pull round player u calls a player v who knows $m = \omega(\ell)$ of the rumors in R' then at the end of the round u knows at least $m - O(\ell)$ of the rumors in R'. Let R'_v be the subset of R' that v knows, and let D_u be the digest of u for rumors in R. Let also $I = \bigcup_{r \in R'_v} \text{range}(r, D_u)$, and $R_{u,I}$ be the subset of $R \cap I$ that u knows. If $|R_{u,I}| < |R'_v| = m$, then it is easy to see that at least $m - |R_{u,I}|$ rumors from $R'_v \setminus R_{u,I}$ will be pulled to u. Note that $R_{u,I}$ contains at most 2ℓ rumors that are not in R', those that correspond to the leftmost and the rightmost of the intervals range(r, D_u), for $r \in R'_v$. Therefore, at the end of the round, u knows at least $m - 2\ell$ of the rumors in R'.

The lemma now follows similarly to the bound on the number of pull rounds required for the standard push-pull algorithm. The fraction of players who at the end of the i-th pull round from round τ' do not know at least $\frac{|R'|}{2} - O(i\ell)$ of the rumors in R' is roughly the square of the corresponding fraction for the $(i-1)$-th pull round; and $\lg\lg n + O(1)$ pull rounds suffice for all players to learn $\frac{|R'|}{2} - O(\ell\lg\lg n) > \frac{|R'|}{3}$ of the rumors in R', with high probability. □

The next lemma is the analogue of Lemma 3.7.

LEMMA 3.11. *If at the end of round $\tau' \leq 4\lg n$ every player knows at least a $1/3$ fraction of the rumors in each of the sets R_i, for $i = 0, \pm 1, \ldots, \pm\lg n$, then, with probability $1 - n^{-3+o(1)}$, all players know r at the end of round $\tau' + 2\lg n$.*

PROOF. It is similar to the proof of Lemma 3.7. The key difference is that now we do not focus on the progress of the distribution of all the rumors in R. Instead, in the i-th pull round from round τ', we focus on the progress of the rumors in $\bigcup_{|j| \leq \lg n - i} R_j$. We drop the two outermost R_j, i.e., $R_{\pm(\lg n-i)}$, after the i-th pull round, because, in the next pull round, the progress of rumors in these sets may be impeded by *external* rumors, i.e., rumors not in $\bigcup_{|j| \leq \lg n - i} R_j$. However, since each player knows at least $\frac{1}{3}\ell\lg n \gg \ell$ of the rumors in each R_j, rumors in the remaining R_j are not affected by external rumors in the next pull round. □

Combining Lemmata 3.1, 3.10, and 3.11 (the first lemma applied for all rumors in $\bigcup_{|j| \leq \lg n} R_j$; the second applied for $\tau' = \tau$ and $R' = R_i$, for $i = 0, \pm 1, \ldots, \lg n$; and the third applied for $\tau' = \tau + 2\lg n$) yields the desired bound on the number of rounds of our algorithm.

3.2.3 Number of bits communicated

We now establish an upper bound on the number of communication bits used to distribute rumor $r \in R$. Specifically, we show the following lemma.

LEMMA 3.12. *With probability $1 - n^{-3+o(1)}$, the total number of bits communicated for the distribution of r is at most $(6 + o(1))nb + 6n\lg\lg n\left(\lg b + \frac{\lg\lg\lg n}{|R|} + O(1)\right)$.*

First we count the overhead induced by unnecessary push transmissions. A push transmission of r from player u to player v in round t is unnecessary if one of the following two conditions applies:

- v already knows r at the beginning of round t; such a push transmission is called *bad*.

- v does not know r, but in round t, r is pulled to v from some player or r is pushed to v form a player u' such that $u' < u$, with respect to some fixed ordering of the players; such a push transmission is called *unlucky*.

Clearly, bad push transmissions of r result in a communication overhead of at most $3nb'$ bits, where

$$b' = b + \Theta(\lg \lg n)$$

is the size of the rumor plus the age counter. The next result bounds the overhead due to unlucky push transmissions.

CLAIM 3.13. *With probability $1 - n^{\omega(1)}$, unlucky push transmissions of r result in a communication overhead of at most $(1 + o(1))nb'$ bits.*

PROOF. Let $\mathbf{S}_t$ be the set of players who know r at the end of round t, and let $S_t = |\mathbf{S}_t|$; $\mathbf{S}_0$ is the set of sources of r. Fix the sequence $\{\mathbf{S}_t : t \geq 0\}$. All the probabilistic statements described below will be implicitly conditioned on this sequence. For any round t and any player $u \in \mathbf{S}_t$, let $X_{u,t}$ be the indicator random variable that is 1 iff u performs an unlucky push transmission of r in round t. The expected value of $X_{u,t}$ is at most $\frac{S_{t+1} - S_t}{S_{t+1}}$: this expected value is a non-decreasing value of u, for $u \in \mathbf{S}_t$; and if u is the largest player that pushes r in round t and this transmission is bad or unlucky then the recipient is equally likely to be any of the players in $\mathbf{S}_{t+1}$. So, the expected value of the total number $\sum_t \sum_{u \in \mathbf{S}_t} X_{u,t}$ of unlucky push transmissions of r is at most $n - S_0$. The upper bound above on the expectation of each $X_{u,t}$ holds independently of the values of the other indicator variables, so, we can apply Chernoff bounds to obtain that at most $(1 + o(1))n$ unlucky push transmissions of r occur, with probability $1 - n^{\omega(1)}$. $\square$

Next we count the overhead induced by pull transmissions. The size of the digest for the rumors in R that a player knows is at most $(\lg \lg \lg n + |R| \lg b) + \frac{|R|b}{\ell} + O(|R|)$. Since there are at most $6 \lg \lg n$ pull rounds during which the rumors in R are not cold, the total overhead per rumor because of the digests is at most $6n \lg \lg n \left(\frac{\lg \lg \lg n}{|R|} + \lg b + \frac{b}{\ell} + O(1) \right)$. Finally, there are at most $n|R|$ redundant pull transmissions of rumors in R. This is because for every redundant pull transmission of a rumor in R there is at least one useful transmission of another rumor in R (see the second-to-last paragraph in Section 3.1). Note that, because of the way unlucky push transmissions were defined, there are no "unlucky" pull transmissions.

Combining the above we obtain that, with probability $1 - n^{-3+o(1)}$, the total number of bits communicated for the distribution of r is at most $nb' + 3nb' + (1 + o(1))nb' + 6n(\lg \lg n)\left(\frac{\lg \lg \lg n}{|R|} + \lg b + O(1)\right) + nb'$, where the first term nb' accounts for the useful transmissions of r. The above expression is equal to the expression in the statement of Lemma 3.12.

4. LOWER BOUND

In this section, we prove the following lower bound on the performance of rumor-spreading algorithms in the random phone-call model.

THEOREM 4.1. *For any $b \geq 1$, no address-oblivious algorithm can guarantee that for any rumor of size b, this rumor is distributed to all players within $O(\lg n)$ rounds, with constant probability, and $o(nb + n \lg \lg n)$ bits of communication are used, in expectation.*

Karp *et. al* established a lower bound of $\Omega(n \lg \lg n)$ on the expected number of *messages*, for any address-oblivious algorithm guaranteeing that any one-bit rumor is distributed to all players with constant probability (Theorem 4.1 in [16]). From this result, it is immediate that $\Omega(n \lg \lg n)$ bits of communication are required in expectation, for any b. Hence, it remains to prove that the theorem holds for rumor sizes $b = \omega(\lg \lg n)$. We first consider the case $b = \omega(\lg n)$, in Section 4.1, and then we reduce to this case the case of smaller b, in Section 4.2.

4.1 The case of large rumors

Suppose that $b = \omega(\lg n)$. Consider the following setting, which we will refer to as the *single b-bit rumor scenario*: There is only one rumor, which is drawn uniformly at random among all the b-bit rumors. The rumor starts from player s in round 0. The size b, the source s, and the start round of the rumor are known to all players. Also, in each phone call, the two participants know the id of one another; so, the rumor-spreading algorithm can be non address oblivious. Suppose now that an algorithm guarantees that in the above scenario, the rumor is spread to all players within $\rho = O(\lg n)$ rounds, with at least some constant probability $p > 0$. We show that the algorithm uses an expected number of $\Omega(nb)$ communication bits. The theorem then follows.

We bound the expected number of bits exchanged by a single player. Consider a player $u \neq s$, and let B_u be the total number of bits u exchanges (sends or receives) in the first ρ rounds, i.e., in rounds $0, \ldots, \rho - 1$. Define the events:

- $\mathcal{E}$: all players know the rumor at the end of round $\rho - 1$;
- $\mathcal{E}_u$: u knows the rumor at the end of round $\rho - 1$;
- $\mathcal{C}$: u receives at most $2\rho + \lg n$ calls in the first ρ rounds;
- $\mathcal{B}_k$: u exchanges at most k bits with other players in the first ρ rounds, i.e., $B_u \leq k$.

We have that for any k,

$$\mathbb{E}[B_u] \geq k \Pr[B_u \geq k] \geq k \Pr[\mathcal{E}] \cdot \Pr[B_u \geq k \mid \mathcal{E}]$$
$$\geq kp(1 - \Pr[\mathcal{B}_k \mid \mathcal{E}]),$$

since $\Pr[\mathcal{E}] \geq p$. Also,

$$\Pr[\mathcal{B}_k \mid \mathcal{E}] = \Pr[\mathcal{B}_k \wedge \mathcal{E}] / \Pr[\mathcal{E}] \leq p^{-1} \Pr[\mathcal{B}_k \wedge \mathcal{E}_u]$$
$$\leq p^{-1} \left(\Pr[\mathcal{B}_k \wedge \mathcal{E}_u \mid \mathcal{C}] + \Pr[\mathcal{C}] \right).$$

Since the expected number of calls that u receives in the first ρ rounds is ρ, using Chernoff bounds we can show that

$$\Pr[\mathcal{C}] \leq e^{-(\rho + \lg n)/3} \leq e^{-\lg n/3}.$$

Also, a counting argument yields the following claim.

CLAIM 4.1. $\Pr[\mathcal{B}_k \wedge \mathcal{E}_u \mid \mathcal{C}] \leq 6^{3\rho + \lg n + k} / 2^b$.

PROOF. We start with two definitions. An *i-call-history* of u specifies the player that u calls, and the set of players that u receives calls from in each of the first i rounds. An *i-history* of u specifies an i-call-history of u, and also the sequence of messages exchanged between u and each of the players that u communicates with in the first i rounds.

For any ρ-call-history of u in which u receives no more than $2\rho + \lg n$ calls, there are at most $6^{\rho+(2\rho+\lg n)+k}$ distinct ρ-histories of u with that ρ-call-history, in which at most k bits are exchanged between u and the rest of the players. This follows from the observation that any such ρ-history can be represented by a string of length at most $\rho+(2\rho+\lg n)+k$ over the alphabet $\{end\text{-}round, begin\text{-}call, send\text{-}0, send\text{-}1, recv\text{-}0, recv\text{-}1\}$: the messages that u exchanges during round i are described by the substring between the i-th and the $(i+1)$-th $end\text{-}round$ symbols of the string; the $begin\text{-}call$ symbols separate the communication streams of u with different players in the same round; and the sending (receipt) of bit $x = 0, 1$ by u is represented by the symbol $send\text{-}x$ $(recv\text{-}x)$.

So, for any ρ-call-history of u in which u receives no more than $2\rho + \lg n$ calls, there are at most $6^{\rho+(2\rho+\lg n)+k}$ rumors that u can distinguish in ρ rounds exchanging at most k bits.[5] Therefore, conditioned on any such ρ-call-history of u, the probability that in the first ρ rounds, u learns the rumor and it exchanges no more than k bits is at most $6^{\rho+(2\rho+\lg n)+k}/2^b$. (Recall that the rumor is chosen at random among the 2^b b-bit rumors.) This implies the claim. $\square$

Combining all the above yields

$$\mathbb{E}[B_u] \geq kp\big(1 - p^{-1}6^{3\rho+\lg n+k}2^{-b} - p^{-1}e^{-\lg n/3}\big),$$

and setting $k = \lfloor (b - 1 + \lg p)/\lg 6 - 3\rho - \lg n \rfloor = \Theta(b)$, we obtain $\mathbb{E}[B_u] \geq kp\big(1/2 - p^{-1}e^{-\lg n/3}\big) = \Theta(b)$. Thus, the expected value of the total number of bits exchanged is at least $\sum_{u \neq s} \mathbb{E}[B_u]/2 = \Omega(nb)$.

4.2 The case of smaller rumors

Suppose now that $\omega(\lg\lg n) \leq b \leq O(\lg n)$. We show that given an algorithm $\mathcal{A}$ that provides the guarantees described in Theorem 4.1 for that b, we can devise an algorithm $\mathcal{A}'$ that contradicts the result of Section 4.1. That is, for some $b' = \omega(\lg n)$, $\mathcal{A}'$ guarantees that in the single b'-bit rumor scenario, the rumor is distributed to all players within $O(\lg n)$ rounds, with constant probability, and $o(nb')$ communication bits are used, in expectation. Roughly speaking, $\mathcal{A}'$ encodes the b'-bit rumor as a collection of b-bit rumors, which are then spread using $\mathcal{A}$.

Suppose that $\mathcal{A}$ ensures that with probability p any b-bit rumor is distributed to all players within ρ rounds. To ease comprehension we consider the case $p = 1$ separately, first. If $p = 1$ then $\mathcal{A}'$ is the following simple algorithm. Let $b' = 2^{b/2-1}b$ (to simplify exposition we assume that b is even). The b'-bit rumor is divided into $2^{b/2}$ substrings $w_0, \ldots, w_{2^{b/2}-1}$ of size $b/2$ each. For each w_i, a b-bit rumor is build consisting of w_i and its index i. All these $2^{b/2}$ b-bit rumors are then spread in parallel (starting at round 0) as in algorithm $\mathcal{A}$. With probability $p = 1$, every player learns all the rumors within ρ rounds, and can easily reconstruct the initial b'-bit rumor. Note that $b' = \omega(\lg n)$ and the expected total number of bits communicated is $2^{b/2} \cdot o(nb) = o(nb')$, as desired.

When $p < 1$ the above scheme does not work, because $\mathcal{A}$ does not guarantee that, with constant probability, every

player learns *all* the $2^{b/2}$ rumors. (E.g., it may be that with probability $1/2$ all players learn the first of these rumors and they do not learn the second, and with probability $1/2$ they all learn the second and not the first.) We tackle this problem by employing an error-correction scheme which facilitates reconstruction of the b' bit rumor by just a fraction of the b-bit rumors (such schemes are often called erasure codes). Recall from code theory that a q-ary (ℓ, M, d)-code is a set of M codewords, where each codeword is a string of length ℓ over an alphabet of size q, and the minimum distance between codewords is d, i.e., any two codewords differ in at least d positions. We employ a q-ary (ℓ, M, d)-code C with $q = \ell = 2^{b/2}$, $M = q^{\ell/4}$, and $d = \ell/2$. By the Gilbert–Varshamov bound (see, e.g., [18]), such a code C exists, because $M < q^{\ell}/\sum_{i=0}^{d-1}\binom{\ell}{i}(q-1)^i$. Algorithm $\mathcal{A}'$ is then as follows. The rumor size is $b' = 2^{b/2-3}b$. Each b'-bit rumor is mapped to a distinct codewords of C, and this codeword is distributed instead of the actual rumor. Similarly to the case $p = 1$, for each q-ary symbol of the codeword, a b-bit rumor is built consisting of that symbol and its order in the codeword, and the resulting ℓ rumors are spread as in algorithm $\mathcal{A}$. Now, for a player to be able to reconstruct the codeword it suffices to learn $\ell - d + 1$ different b-bit rumors, since any two codewords differ in at least d positions. We can lower-bound the probability that this happens as follows. We assume without loss of generality that $p \geq 1 - 1/e$—if this is not the case, we can achieve that by re-sending the b-bit rumors in the rounds $i\rho$, for $i = 1, \ldots, 1/p$. Let X_i be an indicator random variable that is 1 iff all players learn the i-th b-bit rumor by round ρ, and let $X = \sum_i X_i$. It is $\mathbb{E}[X_i] \geq p$, and, thus,

$$\mathbb{E}[X] \geq p\ell.$$

Also, if p' is the probability that *every* player learns at least $\ell - d + 1$ of the ℓ b-bit rumors by round ρ then

$$\mathbb{E}[X] \leq p'\ell + (1 - p')(\ell - d) \leq p'\ell + \ell - d.$$

Therefore, $p\ell \leq p'\ell + \ell - d$, which yields

$$p' \geq p - 1 + d/\ell \geq 1/2 - 1/e,$$

since $p \geq 1 - 1/e$. We have thus shown that, with constant probability, all players learn enough b-bit rumors in the first ρ rounds to reconstruct the codeword, and learn the b'-bit rumor. As in case $p = 1$, $b' = \omega(\lg n)$ and the total number of bits communicated in expectation is $\ell \cdot o(nb) = o(nb')$.

5. ACKNOWLEDGMENTS

We thank the anonymous referees of this paper for their helpful comments.

6. REFERENCES

[1] P. Berenbrink, R. Elsässer, and T. Friedetzky. Efficient randomised broadcasting in random regular networks with applications in peer-to-peer systems. In *Proc. 27th ACM Symp. on Principles of Distributed Computing (PODC)*, pages 155–164, 2008.

[2] B. Bloom. Space/time trade-offs in hash coding with allowable errors. *Communications of the ACM*, 13(7):422–426, 1970.

---

[5] Different executions of the algorithm that have the same ρ-history of u are indistinguishable to u until at least the beginning of round ρ. So, in all these executions, within the first ρ rounds, u learns the same rumor, if any.

[3] A. Broder and M. Mitzenmacher. Network applications of Bloom filters: A survey. *Internet Mathematics*, 1(4):485–509, 2005.

[4] A. Demers, D. Greene, C. Hauser, W. Irish, J. Larson, S. Shenker, H. Sturgis, D. Swinehart, and D. Terry. Epidemic algorithms for replicated database maintenance. In *Proc. 6th ACM Symp. on Principles of Distributed Computing (PODC)*, pages 1–12, 1987.

[5] B. Doerr, T. Friedrich, and T. Sauerwald. Quasirandom rumor spreading. In *Proc. 19th ACM-SIAM Symp. on Discrete Algorithms (SODA)*, pages 773–781, 2008.

[6] B. Doerr, T. Friedrich, and T. Sauerwald. Quasirandom rumor spreading: Expanders, push vs. pull, and robustness. In *Proc. 36th Int. Colloq. on Automata, Languages and Programming (ICALP)*, pages 366–377, 2009.

[7] D. Dubhashi and D. Ranjan. Balls and bins: A study in negative dependence. *Random Struct. Algorithms*, 13(2):99–124, 1998.

[8] R. Elsässer. On randomized broadcasting in power law networks. In *Proc. 20th Int. Symp. on Distributed Computing (DISC)*, pages 370–384, 2006.

[9] R. Elsässer. On the communication complexity of randomized broadcasting in random-like graphs. In *Proc. 18th ACM Symp. on Parallelism in Algorithms and Architectures (SPAA)*, pages 148–157, 2006.

[10] R. Elsässer and T. Sauerwald. The power of memory in randomized broadcasting. In *Proc. 19th ACM-SIAM Symp. on Discrete Algorithms (SODA)*, pages 218–227, 2008.

[11] U. Feige, D. Peleg, P. Raghavan, and E. Upfal. Randomized broadcast in networks. *Random Structures and Algorithms*, 1(4):447–460, 1990.

[12] P. Fraigniaud and E. Lazard. Methods and problems of communication in usual networks. *Discrete Appl. Math.*, 53(1-3):79–133, 1994.

[13] A. Frieze and G. Grimmett. The shortest-path problem for graphs with random arc-lengths. *Discrete Appl. Math.*, 10:57–77, 1985.

[14] S. Hedetniemi, T. Hedetniemi, and A. Liestman. A survey of gossiping and broadcasting in communication networks. *NETWORKS*, 18:319–349, 1988.

[15] J. Hromkovic, R. Klasing, B. Monien, and R. Piene. Dissemination of information in interconnection networks (broadcasting & gossiping). In *Combinatorial Network Theory*, pages 125–212. Springer, 1995.

[16] R. Karp, C. Schindelhauer, S. Shenker, and B. Vocking. Randomized rumor spreading. In *Proc. 41st IEEE Symp. on Foundations of Computer Science (FOCS)*, pages 565–574, 2000.

[17] B. Pittel. On spreading a rumor. *SIAM J. Appl. Math.*, 47(1):213–223, 1987.

[18] J. H. van Lint. *Introduction to Coding Theory*. Springer Verlag, 3rd edition, 1998.

Algorithms and Application for Grids and Clouds

Geoffrey C. Fox
School of Informatics and Computing and Digital Science Center
Indiana University
Bloomington IN
gcf@indiana.edu

Abstract

We discuss the impact of clouds and grid technology on scientific computing using examples from a variety of fields — especially the life sciences. We cover the impact of the growing importance of data analysis and note that it is more suitable for these modern architectures than the large simulations (particle dynamics and partial differential equation solution) that are mainstream use of large scale "massively parallel" supercomputers. The importance of grids is seen in the support of distributed data collection and archiving while clouds are and will replace grids for the large scale analysis of the data.

We discuss the structure of algorithms (and the associated applications) that will run on current clouds and use either the basic "on-demand" computing paradigm or higher level frameworks based on MapReduce and its extensions. Looking at performance of MPI (mainstay of scientific computing) and MapReduce both theoretically and experimentally shows that current MapReduce implementations run well on algorithms that are a "Map" followed by a "Reduce" but perform poorly on algorithms that iterate over many such phases. Several important algorithms including parallel linear algebra falls into latter class. One can define MapReduce extensions to accommodate iterative map and reduce but these have less fault tolerance than basic MapReduce. We discuss clustering, dimension reduction and sequence assembly and annotation as example algorithms.

Categories & Subject Descriptors: D.1.3,G.3, J.3

General Terms: Algorithms, Performance

Keywords: MPI, Grids, Clouds, Data Deluge, MapReduce, Life Sciences, Dimension Reduction, Clustering, BLAST

Bio

Fox received a Ph.D. in Theoretical Physics from Cambridge University and is now professor of Informatics and Computing, and Physics at Indiana University where he is director of the Digital Science Center and Associate Dean for Research and Graduate Studies at the School of Informatics and Computing. He previously held positions at Caltech, Syracuse University and Florida State University. He has supervised the PhD of 61 students and published over 600 papers in physics and computer science. He currently works in applying computer science to Bioinformatics, Defense, Earthquake and Ice-sheet Science, Particle Physics and Chemical Informatics. He is principal investigator of FutureGrid – a new TeraGrid facility to enable development of new approaches to computing. He is involved in several projects to enhance the capabilities of Minority Serving Institutions. His website is http://www.infomall.org.

SPAA'10, June 13–15, 2010, Thira, Santorini, Greece.
ACM 978-1-4503-0079-7/10/06.

The Cilkview Scalability Analyzer

Yuxiong He[*]　　　Charles E. Leiserson[†]　　　William M. Leiserson[‡]

Intel Corporation
Nashua, New Hampshire

ABSTRACT

The Cilkview scalability analyzer is a software tool for profiling, estimating scalability, and benchmarking multithreaded Cilk++ applications. Cilkview monitors logical parallelism during an instrumented execution of the Cilk++ application on a single processing core. As Cilkview executes, it analyzes logical dependencies within the computation to determine its work and span (critical-path length). These metrics allow Cilkview to estimate parallelism and predict how the application will scale with the number of processing cores. In addition, Cilkview analyzes scheduling overhead using the concept of a "burdened dag," which allows it to diagnose performance problems in the application due to an insufficient grain size of parallel subcomputations.

Cilkview employs the Pin dynamic-instrumentation framework to collect metrics during a serial execution of the application code. It operates directly on the optimized code rather than on a debug version. Metadata embedded by the Cilk++ compiler in the binary executable identifies the parallel control constructs in the executing application. This approach introduces little or no overhead to the program binary in normal runs.

Cilkview can perform real-time scalability benchmarking automatically, producing gnuplot-compatible output that allows developers to compare an application's performance with the tool's predictions. If the program performs beneath the range of expectation, the programmer can be confident in seeking a cause such as insufficient memory bandwidth, false sharing, or contention, rather than inadequate parallelism or insufficient grain size.

Categories and Subject Descriptors

D.2.2 [**Software Engineering**]: Design Tools and Techniques; D.1.3 [**Programming Techniques**]: Concurrent Programming—

This work was supported in part by the National Science Foundation under Grants 0615215, 0712243, and 0822896 and in part by the Defense Advanced Research Projects Agency under Contract W31P4Q-08-C-0156. Cilk, Cilk++, and Cilkview are registered trademarks of Intel Corporation.

[*]Author's current address: Microsoft Research, Redmond, Washington. Email address: yuxhe@microsoft.com.

[†]Author is Professor of Computer Science and Engineering at MIT and an Intel consultant. Email address: cel@mit.edu

[‡]Email address: william.m.leiserson@intel.com.

parallel programming; I.6.6 [**Simulation and Modeling**]: Simulation Output Analysis

General Terms

Measurement, Performance, Theory.

Keywords

Burdened parallelism, Cilk++, Cilkview, dag model, multicore programming, multithreading, parallelism, parallel programming, performance, scalability, software tools, span, speedup, work.

1. INTRODUCTION

Although the performance of serial application programs can be measured by execution time, multithreaded applications exhibit one additional dimension: *scalability*. How does execution time scale as the number of processing cores increases. Although performance tools to analyze serial applications are widely available, few tools exist that effectively address scalability issues for multithreaded programs on multicore machines. When a serial application fails to run as quickly as one expects, various tools, such as gprof [26], Intel® VTune[TM] [44], Intel® Performance Tuning Utility [1], etc., can be used to analyze the program execution and identify performance bottlenecks. Parallel-performance tools, such as Intel® Thread Profiler [30] of VTune and Intel® Parallel Amplifier [29] of Intel® Parallel Studio, can provide important data about a multithreaded application, but since the information gathered is specific to how the computation was scheduled for the particular run, these tools do not address how performance scales.

The Cilkview scalability analyzer,[1] which runs under the Pin [35] dynamic instrumentation framework, gathers statistics during a single instrumented run of a multithreaded Cilk++ [28,33] application, analyzes the logical parallelism within the computation, and estimates the application's scalability over various numbers of cores. It also provides a framework for benchmarking actual runs of the application so that the actual behavior can be compared with the scalability predictions.

To illustrate Cilkview, consider the problem of analyzing the simple quicksort program shown in Figure 1. First, it is helpful to understand the Cilk++ extensions to C++, which consist of three keywords: `cilk_spawn`, `cilk_sync`, and `cilk_for`. Parallel work is created when the keyword `cilk_spawn` precedes the invocation of a function, as in line 15 of the figure. A function cannot safely use the values returned by its spawned children until it

---
[1]The examples in this article were produced with an as-yet-unreleased version of Cilkview, but the latest released version (available at `http://software.intel.com/en-us/articles/intel-cilk/`) differs insubstantially.

```
1    // Parallel quicksort

3    #include <algorithm>
4    #include <iterator>
5    #include <functional>
6    #include <cmath>
7    #include <cilkview>

9    using namespace std;

11   template <typename T>
12   void qsort(T begin, T end) {
13     if (begin != end) {
14       T middle = partition(begin, end,
               bind2nd(less<typename
               iterator_traits<T>::value_type>()
               ,*begin));
15       cilk_spawn qsort(begin, middle);
16       qsort(max(begin + 1, middle), end);
17       cilk_sync;
18     }
19   }

21   // Simple test code:
22   int cilk_main() {
23     int n = 100;
24     double a[n];
25     cilk::cilkview cv;
26     cilk_for (int i=0; i<n; ++i) {
27       a[i] = sin((double) i);
28     }

30     cv.start();
31     qsort(a, a + n);
32     cv.stop();
33     cv.dump(``qsort'');

35     return 0;
36   }
```

Figure 1: Parallel quicksort implemented in Cilk++.

executes a `cilk_sync` statement, which acts as a local "barrier." In the quicksort example, the `cilk_sync` statement on line 17 avoids the anomaly that would occur if the recursively spawned function in line 15 did not complete before the return, thus leaving the vector to be sorted in an intermediate and inconsistent state. The keyword `cilk_for`, as in line 26, indicates a parallel for loop, which allows all iterations of the loop to operate in parallel.

The Cilkview API allows users to control which portions of their Cilk++ program are analyzed. For example, the program in Figure 1 restricts the analysis to the sorting function by designating "start" and "stop" points in the code on lines 30 and 32, respectively. Without these start and stop points, Cilkview defaults to reporting the full run of the application from beginning to end.

Figure 2 shows the scalability profile produced by Cilkview that results from running the quicksort application in Figure 1 on 10 million numbers. Included in the graphical output are curves indicating estimated upper and lower bounds of performance over different numbers of cores. The area between the upper and lower bounds indicates an estimation of the program's speedup with the given input. Cilkview produces this output from a single instrumented serial run of the application. Section 4 describes the Cilkview output in more detail.

In addition to scalability estimation, Cilkview supports a framework for automatically benchmarking an application across a range of processor core counts. For each benchmark run, Cilkview measures the total elapsed time and plots the results. If scalability analysis is enabled, the benchmark data — shown in Figure 2 as crosses — is overlaid on the scalability profile. In the figure, the benchmark runs represent the actual speedup of the quicksort program using from 1 to 8 cores of an 8-core Intel® Core™ i7 machine.

To produce the upper-bound estimate for a program's speedup, Cilkview employs the "dag" (directed acyclic graph) model of multithreading [4,5], which is founded on earlier theoretical work on

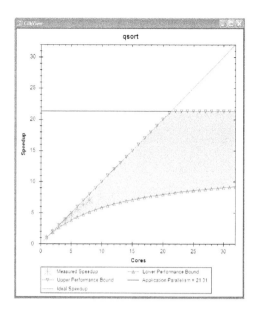

Figure 2: The scalability profile produced by Cilkview for the quicksort program from Figure 1.

dag scheduling [7,17,25]. In this model, parallelism is an intrinsic property of an application execution which depends on its logical construction but not on how it is scheduled. The dag model uses two performance measures — work and span — to gauge the theoretical parallelism of a computation and predict its scalability.

The actual performance of a multithreaded application is determined not only by its intrinsic parallelism, but also by the performance of the runtime scheduler. The Cilk++ runtime system contains a provably efficient work-stealing scheduling algorithm [5,20], which on an ideal parallel computer scales application performance linearly with processor cores, as long as the application exhibits sufficient parallelism. In practice, however, scheduler performance is also influenced by other factors, such as overheads for task migration, which is needed for load balancing, and bandwidth to memory, if the application is memory bound. We introduce the concept of a "burdened" dag, which embeds the task-migration overhead of a job into the dag model. Burdening allows Cilkview to estimate lower bounds on application speedup effectively. Cilkview does not currently analyze the impact of limited memory bandwidth on application scalability.

Cilkview employs dynamic instrumentation [8,35] to collect scalability statistics during a serial execution of the program code. Since performance analysis can suffer from perturbations due to the instrumentation, Cilkview attempts to minimize this impact in two ways. First, Cilkview operates on the optimized production binary executable, rather than on a specially compiled "debug" version of the application. Debug versions require recompilation and may differ significantly from the production executable. Second, Cilkview relies on metadata that the Cilk++ compiler embeds in the binary executable to identify the parallel control constructs (spawns and syncs), rather than placing calls to null functions or other runtime instrumentation in the execution path. By using metadata, rather than embedding instrumentation in-line in the code, the impact on the performance of the production executable is negligible.

The remainder of this paper is organized as follows. Section 2 provides a brief tutorial on the theory of parallelism, which provides the foundation for Cilkview's upper bounds on speedup. Section 3 describes the Cilk++ runtime system and introduces the concept of "burdening," the basis for Cilkview's lower-bound estimations. With this theoretical understanding of Cilk++'s performance

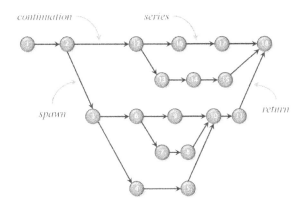

Figure 3: A dag representation of a multithreaded execution. Each vertex is a strand. Edges represent ordering dependencies between instructions.

model in hand, Section 4 describes the output of Cilkview in detail. Section 5 illustrates how Cilkview output can be used to diagnose performance problems in a "stencil" program. Section 6 presents the binary instrumentation framework that Cilkview uses and how Cilkview computes scalability metrics during a job's execution. Section 8 discusses related work. Finally, Section 9 concludes with a discussion of directions for future research.

2. THE DAG MODEL FOR MULTITHREADING

For a parallel program to obtain good performance, the program must exhibit sufficient parallelism. This section reviews the dag model of multithreading [4,5], which provides a general and precise quantification of parallelism based on the theory developed by Graham [25]; Brent [7]; Eager, Zahorjan, and Lazowska [17]; and Blumofe and Leiserson [4,5]. Tutorials on the dag model can be found in [13, Ch. 27] and [33].

The *dag model of multithreading* views the execution of a multi-threaded program as a set of vertices called *strands* — sequences of serially executed instructions containing no parallel control — with graph edges indicating ordering dependencies between strands, as illustrated in Figure 3. We say that a strand x *precedes* a strand y, denoted $x \prec y$, if x must complete before y can begin. If neither $x \prec y$ nor $y \prec x$, we say that the strands are in *parallel*, denoted by $x \parallel y$. In Figure 3, for example, we have $1 \prec 2$, $6 \prec 8$, and $4 \parallel 9$. A strand can be as small as a single instruction, or it can represent a longer chain of serially executed instructions. A *maximal strand* is one that cannot be included in a longer strand. We can dice a maximal strand into a series of smaller strands in any manner that is convenient.

The dag model of multithreading can be interpreted in the context of the Cilk++ programming model. Normal serial execution of one strand after another creates a *serial edge* from the first strand to the next. A cilk_spawn of a function creates two dependency edges emanating from the instruction immediately before the cilk_spawn: the *spawn edge* goes to the strand containing the first instruction of the spawned function, and the *continuation edge* goes to the strand containing the first instruction after the spawned function. A cilk_sync creates a *return edge* from the strand containing the final instruction of each spawned function to the strand containing the instruction immediately after the cilk_sync. A cilk_for can be viewed as parallel divide-and-conquer recursion using cilk_spawn and cilk_sync over the iteration space.

The dag model admits two natural measures that allow us to define parallelism precisely, as well as to provide important bounds on performance and speedup.

The Work Law

The first measure is *work*, which is the total time spent in all the strands. Assuming for simplicity that it takes unit time to execute a strand, the work for the example dag in Figure 3 is 18.

We can adopt a simple notation to be more precise. Let T_P be the fastest possible execution time of the application on P processors. Since the work corresponds to the execution time on 1 processor, we denote it by T_1. One reason that work is an important measure is that it provides a lower bound on P-processor execution time:

$$T_P \geq T_1/P . \qquad (1)$$

This **Work Law** holds because, in our simple theoretical model, P processors can execute at most P instructions in unit time. Thus, with P processors, to do all the work requires at least T_1/P time.

We can interpret the Work Law (1) in terms of the *speedup* on P processors, which using our notation, is just T_1/T_P. The speedup tells us how much faster the application runs on P processors than on 1 processor. Rewriting the Work Law, we obtain $T_1/T_P \leq P$, which is to say that the speedup on P processors can be at most P. If the application obtains speedup P (which is the best we can do in our model), we say that the application exhibits *linear speedup*. If the application obtains speedup greater than P (impossible in our model due to the Work Law, but possible in practice due to caching and other processor effects), we say that the application exhibits *superlinear speedup*.

The Span Law

The second measure is *span*, which is the maximum time to execute along any path of dependencies in the dag. Assuming that it takes unit time to execute a strand, the span of the dag from Figure 3 is 9, which corresponds to the path $1 \prec 2 \prec 3 \prec 6 \prec 7 \prec 8 \prec 10 \prec 11 \prec 18$. This path is sometimes called the *critical path* of the dag, and span is sometimes referred to in the literature as critical-path length. Since the span is the theoretically fastest time the dag could be executed on a computer with an infinite number of processors (assuming no overheads for communication, scheduling, etc.), we denote it by T_∞. Like work, span also provides a bound on P-processor execution time:

$$T_P \geq T_\infty . \qquad (2)$$

This **Span Law** arises for the simple reason that a finite number of processors cannot outperform an infinite number of processors, because the infinite-processor machine could just ignore all but P of its processors and mimic a P-processor machine exactly.

Parallelism

We define *parallelism* as the ratio of work to span, or T_1/T_∞. Parallelism can be viewed as the average amount of work along each step of the critical path. Moreover, perfect linear speedup cannot be obtained for any number of processors greater than the parallelism T_1/T_∞. To see why, suppose that $P > T_1/T_\infty$, in which case the Span Law (2) implies that the speedup satisfies $T_1/T_P \leq T_1/T_\infty < P$. Since the speedup is strictly less than P, it cannot be perfect linear speedup. Another way to see that the parallelism bounds the speedup is to observe that, in the best case, the work is distributed evenly along the critical path, in which case the amount of work at each step is the parallelism. But, if the parallelism is less than P, there isn't enough work to keep P processors busy at every step.

As an example, the parallelism of the dag in Figure 3 is $18/9 = 2$.

Thus, there is little point in executing it with more than 2 processors, since additional processors surely will be starved for work.

In general, one does not need to estimate parallelism particularly accurately to diagnose scalability problems. All that is necessary is that the parallelism exceed the actual number of processors by a reasonable margin. Thus, the measures of work and span need not be particularly precise. A binary order of magnitude is usually more than sufficient. Cilkview takes advantage of this looseness in measurement by performing simple instruction-counting for work and span, rather than attempting to use high-resolution timers.

Upper bounds on speedup

The Work and Span Laws engender two important upper bounds on speedup. The Work Law implies that the speedup on P processors can be at most P:

$$T_1/T_P \leq P . \tag{3}$$

The Span Law dictates that speedup cannot exceed parallelism:

$$T_1/T_p \leq T_1/T_\infty. \tag{4}$$

In Figure 2, the upper bound on speedup provided by the Work Law corresponds to the line of slope 1. The upper bound provided by the Span Law corresponds to the horizontal line at 23.07.

rinstru

3. THE BURDENED-DAG MODEL

The dag model in Section 2 provides upper bounds on the best possible speedup of a multithreaded application based on the work and span. Actual speedup is influenced not only by these intrinsic characteristics, but also by the performance of the scheduling algorithm and the cost of migrating tasks to load-balance the computation across processor cores. This section discusses prior work on scheduling bounds and proposes a new model, called "burdened dags," for incorporating migration costs.

Work-stealing scheduling

Although optimal multiprocessor scheduling is NP-complete [23], Cilk++'s runtime system employs a "work-stealing" scheduler [5,20] which achieves provably tight asymptotic bounds. In theory, an application with sufficient parallelism can rely on the Cilk++ runtime system to dynamically and automatically exploit an arbitrary number of available processor cores near optimally.

Cilk++'s work-stealing scheduler operates as follows. When the runtime system starts up, it allocates as many system threads, called **workers**, as there are processors (although the programmer can override this default decision). In the common case, each worker's stack operates just as in C++. When a subroutine is spawned, the subroutine's activation frame containing its local variables is pushed onto the bottom of the stack. The worker begins work on the child (spawned) subroutine. When the child returns to its parent, the parent's activation frame is popped off the bottom of the stack. Since Cilk++ operates just like C++ in the common case, ordinary execution imposes little overhead.

When a worker runs out of work, however, it becomes a **thief** and "steals" the top (oldest) frame from another **victim** worker's stack. Thus, the stack is in fact a double-ended queue, or **deque**, with the worker operating on the bottom and thieves stealing from the top. This strategy has the great advantage that all communication and synchronization is incurred only when a worker runs out of work. If an application exhibits sufficient parallelism, one can prove mathematically [5] that stealing is infrequent, and thus the overheads of communication and synchronization to effect a steal

```
// Snippet A
cilk_for (int i=0; i<2; ++i) {
    for (int j=0; j<n; ++j) {
        f(i,j);
    }
}

// Snippet B
for (int j=0; j<n; ++j) {
    cilk_for (int i=0; i<2; ++i) {
        f(i,j);
    }
}
```

Figure 4: An example of how migration overhead can affect performance.

is negligible. Specifically, the Cilk++ randomized work-stealing scheduler can execute an application with T_1 work and T_∞ span on P processors in expected time

$$T_P \leq T_1/P + \delta T_\infty , \tag{5}$$

where δ is a constant called the **span coefficient**. (We omit the notation for expectation for simplicity.)

Inequality (5) can be interpreted as follows. If the parallelism T_1/T_∞ exceeds the number P of processors by a sufficient margin, the bound guarantees near-perfect linear speedup. To see why, assume that $T_1/T_\infty \gg P$. Equivalently, we have $T_\infty \ll T_1/P$. Thus, in Inequality (5), the T_1/P term dominates the δT_∞ term, and thus the running time is $T_P \approx T_1/P$, leading to a speedup of $T_1/T_P \approx P$.

The key weakness in this argument stems from what is meant by "sufficient." The proof of the bound assumes that the scheduling overheads are at most a constant. The larger the constant hidden by the big-O, however, the greater the factor by which the parallelism T_1/T_∞ must exceed the number P of processors to guarantee near-perfect linear speedup. In particular, to estimate speedup accurately for all P, asymptotics are not good enough, especially when parallelism is modest. Moreover, naively using an upper bound on the constant hidden by the big-O yields poor scalability estimates.

Migration overhead

As an example of how migration overhead can affect performance, consider the two snippets in Figure 4. In this code, f(i,j) is some small function. The work of each of the two snippets involves $2n$ function calls. The span of each snippet involves n function calls, since the for loops in n run serially. Thus, the parallelism of each snippet is about 2. Nevertheless, Snippet A will generally outperform Snippet B by a wide margin. The reason is that Snippet A only requires one steal in order to realize the parallelism, whereas Snippet B requires one steal for each of the n iterations of the for loop. Thus, Snippet B incurs substantial migration overhead.

Burdened dags

The migration cost, or **burden**, for a steal includes the explicit costs of bookkeeping to set up the context to run the stolen task and the implicit costs of cache misses in order to migrate the stolen task's working set. There is also some minor bookkeeping overhead when a function returns to discover that its parent has been stolen, but this cost can be considered as an indirect part of the cost of a steal. Although the scheduling cost modeled by the burden generally depends upon what is stolen, we have found that a fixed cost suffices in practice. Cilkview assumes a burden of 15,000 instructions.

The **burdened-dag model** augments the dag model by including the burden on each continuation edge of the dag, which is akin to assuming that every continuation is stolen. Figure 5 shows the burdened dag for the computation from Figure 3. Cilkview computes the **burdened span** by finding the longest path in the burdened dag.

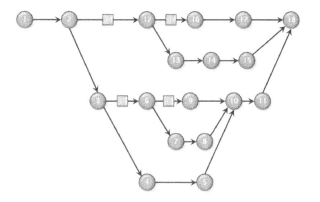

Figure 5: The burdened dag of the computation from Figure 3. Squares indicate the burdens on continuation edges and represent potential migration overhead.

The following theorem shows how migration costs can be incorporated into the bound from Inequality (5).

THEOREM 1. *Let T_1 be the work of an application program, and let $\widehat{T}_\infty$ be its burdened span. Then, a work-stealing scheduler running on P processors can execute the application in expected time*

$$T_P \leq T_1/P + 2\delta\widehat{T}_\infty \,,$$

where δ is the span coefficient.

PROOF. Let G be the ordinary dag arising from the P-processor execution, and let $\widehat{G}$ be the corresponding burdened dag. Consider the more-explicit dag G' that arises during the P-processor execution, where all migration overheads incurred explicitly by the scheduler or implicitly by the application are accounted for with additional vertices and edges. Let T_1' and T_∞' be the work and span, respectively, of G'. The accounting argument in [5] can be used to show that for any constant $\varepsilon > 0$, we have

$$T_P \leq T_1'/P + \delta T_\infty' + O(\log(1/\varepsilon))$$

with probability at least $1 - \varepsilon$. Moreover, the number of steals is at most $\delta P T_\infty' + O(P\log(1/\varepsilon))$.

Let us now look at work. Every path in G' corresponds to a path in the burdened dag $\widehat{G}$, except that G' omits overheads for continuations that are not stolen. Thus, we have $T_\infty' \leq \widehat{T}_\infty$. Since we only have a migration overhead when a continuation is stolen, the total amount of overhead in G' is at most $\delta P T_\infty' + O(P\log(1/\varepsilon))$, from which it follows that $T_1' \leq T_1 + \delta P T_\infty' + O(P\log(1/\varepsilon)) \leq T_1 + \delta P\widehat{T}_\infty + O(P\log(1/\varepsilon))$. Consequently, we have

$$
\begin{aligned}
T_p &\leq & T_1'/P + \delta T_\infty' + O(\log(1/\varepsilon)) \\
&\leq & (T_1 + \delta P\widehat{T}_\infty + O(P\log(1/\varepsilon)))/P + \delta\widehat{T}_\infty + O(\log(1/\varepsilon)) \\
&\leq & T_1/P + 2\delta\widehat{T}_\infty + O(\log(1/\varepsilon))
\end{aligned}
$$

with probability at least $1 - \varepsilon$. Therefore, the expected time is bounded by $T_P \leq T_1/P + 2\delta\widehat{T}_\infty$. □

COROLLARY 2. *Let T_1 be the work of an application program, $\widehat{T}_\infty$ its burdened span, and δ the span coefficient. Then, a work-stealing scheduler running on P processors achieves speedup at least*

$$\frac{T_1}{T_P} \geq \frac{T_1}{T_1/P + 2\delta\widehat{T}_\infty} \,. \tag{6}$$

in expectation.

1) Parallelism Profile	
Work:	5,570,609,776 instructions
Span:	261,374,874 instructions
Burdened span:	262,078,779 instructions
Parallelism:	21.31
Burdened parallelism:	21.26
Spawns:	8,518,398
Syncs:	8,518,398
Average maximal strand:	218
2) Speedup Estimate	
2 processors:	1.85 – 2.00
4 processors:	3.23 – 4.00
8 processors:	5.13 – 8.00
16 processors:	7.27 – 16.00
32 processors:	9.20 – 21.31

Figure 6: Textual output for the quicksort program from Figure 1.

Cilkview applies Corollary 2 to compute an estimated lower bound on speedup. Our experimental results show that a typical value of span coefficient δ has range $0.8 - 1.0$. Cilkview uses $\delta = 0.85$, and a corresponding estimated speedup lower bound $T_P \leq T_1/P + 1.7\widehat{T}_\infty$. An example is the lower curve in Figure 2. In addition, it computes the **burdened parallelism** as $T_1/\widehat{T}_\infty$.

4. TEXTUAL OUTPUT AND BENCHMARKING

Cilkview employs the dag and burdened dag models described in Sections 2 and 3, respectively, to analyze scalability. In addition to graphical output, which was illustrated in Figure 2 for the quicksort program, Cilkview also provides a textual report with explicit numbers, as is illustrated in Figure 6 for quicksort. The textual report is broken into two parts, the Parallelism Profile and the Speedup Estimate.

The Parallelism Profile displays the statistics collected during the run of the program. The statistics include work, span, parallelism, burdened span, and burdened parallelism, whose meaning was described in Sections 2 and 3. The other three statistics shown are the following:

- Spawns — the number of spawns encountered during the run.
- Syncs — the number of syncs encountered during the run.
- Average maximal strand — the work divided by 1 plus twice the number of spawns plus the number of syncs.

When the average maximal strand is small (less than 500), the overhead from spawning, which is generally negligible, may be noticeable. In the quicksort code, for example, the value of 218 indicates that the parallel recursion might be terminated early and replaced by ordinary function calls. Although this change might lower the parallelism slightly, it would lead to a faster serial execution due to less spawn overhead.

The Speedup Estimate section profiles the estimated speedups on varying numbers of processor cores. The estimates are displayed as ranges with lower and upper bounds. The upper bound is the minimum of number of cores and parallelism, based on Inequalities (3) and (4). The lower bound is based on Inequality (6).

Whereas Cilkview generates its textual report from an application run using the Pin instrumentation framework, it also supports direct benchmarking of the application, automatically running it across a range of processor counts. Each benchmark result represents the actual speedup of the run on the given number of processor cores. To use Cilkview for benchmarking, the following practices are recommended:

```
void stencil_kernel (int t, int x,
    int y, int z) {
  int s = z * NXY + y * NX + x;
  float *A_cur = &A[t & 1][s];
  float *A_next = &A[(t + 1) & 1][s];
  float div = c0 * A_cur[0]
    + c1 * ((A_cur[1] + A_cur[-1])
    + (A_cur[NX] + A_cur[-NX])
    + (A_cur[NXY] + A_cur[-NXY]))
    + c2 * ((A_cur[2] + A_cur[-2])
    + (A_cur[NX2] + A_cur[-NX2])
    + (A_cur[NXY2] + A_cur[-NXY2]))
    + c3 * ((A_cur[3] + A_cur[-3])
    + (A_cur[NX3] + A_cur[-NX3])
    + (A_cur[NXY3] + A_cur[-NXY3]))
    + c4 * ((A_cur[4] + A_cur[-4])
    + (A_cur[NX4] + A_cur[-NX4])
    + (A_cur[NXY4] + A_cur[-NXY4]));
  A_next[0] = 2 * A_cur[0] - A_next[0]
    + vsq[s] * div;
}

void stencil_loop (int t0, int t1,
    int x0, int x1, int y0, int y1,
    int z0, int z1){
  for(int t = t0; t < t1; ++t) {
    for(int z = z0; z < z1; ++z) {
      for(int y = y0; y < y1; ++y) {
        cilk_for(int x = x0; x < x1; ++x) {
          // stencil computation kernel
          stencil_kernel(t, x, y, z);
} } } } }

void cilk_main(int argc, char** argv) {
  ...
  // Compute wave equation for 20 time steps
  // on a 500x500x500 array
  stencil_loop(1, 20, 4, 495, 4, 495, 4, 495);
  ...
}
```

Figure 7: A naive implementation of the stencil computation using `cilk_for`.

- Make the system as quiet as possible by killing unnecessary processes so that measurements are as exact as possible.
- Turn off hyperthreading in the BIOS so that per-processor measurements are meaningful.
- Turn off power saving in the BIOS, which makes clock speeds unpredictable.
- Run trials multiple times to moderate effects due to specific cores on which the OS schedules the worker threads.
- If necessary, pin the workers to specific cores to enhance repeatability.

Programmer Interface

The Cilkview API allows users to control which portions of their Cilk++ application program are reported for both scalability analysis and benchmarking. The API provides the `start()` and `stop()` methods for a `cilkview` object to indicate the section to report. In addition, the API provides a `dump(const char *)` method that can label the reported section. Consequently, Cilkview can generate reports for multiple sections of code in an application by reusing the same `cilkview` object. In addition, multiple `cilkview` objects can be created if the sections overlap.

5. PERFORMANCE DIAGNOSIS

This section presents an example of how Cilkview can be used to diagnose the performance problems of a Cilk++ program that computes a 25-point 3D stencil. We start with an analysis of the program as written, and then we modify it step by step to improve its performance, each time using Cilkview to understand how the program can be improved.

Figure 7 shows a "stencil" program to solve the wave equation

$$\frac{\partial^2 u}{\partial t^2} = c\nabla^2 u$$

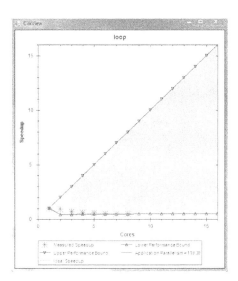

Figure 8: Cilkview's output for the code from Figure 7.

in parallel using the finite-difference method described by Courant, Friedrichs, and Lewy [14]. For a given 3D coordinate (x, y, z) at time t, the code derives the value of $A[x, y, z]$ at time t using the value of $A[x, y, z]$ and the 24 neighboring values $\{A[x, y, z'] : 1 \le |z - z'| \le 4\} \cup \{A[x, y', z] : 1 \le |y - y'| \le 4\} \cup \{A[x', y, z] : 1 \le |x - x'| \le 4\}$ at time $t - 1$, where there are 8 neighbors for each dimension. The multiplicative coefficients $\{c_i : 0 \le i \le 4\}$ and the phase velocities $vsq[x, y, z]$ are constants. Since intermediate values in the computation can be thrown away, the code uses only two 3D arrays of coordinates, one for even values of t and the other for odd values.

We benchmarked this application on an 8-core Intel® Core™ i7 machine with two Xeon® E5520 2.27-GHz quad-core chips (hyperthreading disabled), 6 GB of DRAM, a shared 8-MB L3-cache, and private L2- and L1-caches with 256 KB and 32 KB, respectively. This machine is the same as the one we used to benchmark the quicksort program from Section 1.

Performance problem — low burdened parallelism: Running the program on 2 or more processors takes longer than its serial execution time. Cilkview's scalability estimation and benchmarking results are shown in Figure 8. The parallelism of the program is 119.39, but its burdened parallelism is only 0.87. The estimated speedup lower bound is far less than the upper bound. In fact, it is less than 1.0, portending a possible slowdown in parallel execution. The trial data confirms this hypothesis.

Diagnosis: The low burdened parallelism and the large gap between the upper and lower speedup bounds indicates that the overhead of load balancing from running the code in parallel could negate any benefit obtained from parallel execution. The amount of stolen work is too small to justify the overhead of load balancing. At the source-code level, the problem is that the granularity of spawned tasks is too small. Observe that in the source code from Figure 8, `cilk_for` is used in the inner loop, and hence the amount of work per iteration is tiny, resulting in small tasks and a low burdened parallelism.

Solution: Generally, it is better to parallelize outer loops than inner loops. We move the `cilk_for` from the innermost loop to the first nested loop, as shown in Figure 9. This change significantly increases the granularity of spawned tasks.

Performance problem — subrange benchmark results: Cilkview now reports good parallelism and burdened parallelism

```
void stencil_revised_loop (int t0, int t1,
    int x0, int x1, int y0, int y1,
    int z0, int z1){
  for(int t = t0; t < t1; ++t) {
    cilk_for(int z = z0; z < z1; ++z) {
      for(int y = y0; y < y1; ++y) {
        for(int x = x0; x < x1; ++x) {
          // stencil computation kernel
          stencil_kernel(t, x, y, z);
} } } } }
```

Figure 9: A revised implementation of the stencil in which an outer loop has been parallelized using cilk_for, rather than the inner loop.

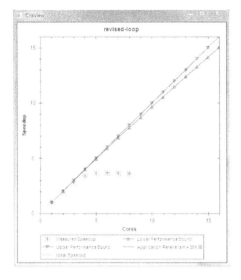

Figure 10: Cilkview's output for the code from Figure 9.

for the improved program, as shown in Figure 10. The estimated lower bound on speedup is close to the upper bound of perfect linear speedup, which indicates that this program has sufficient parallelism and good granularity for its spawned tasks. As seen in the figure, however, the benchmark data produced by Cilkview for an 8-core machine shows that the actual speedup does not scale linearly. The performance is well beneath the range of expectation.

Diagnosis: Since Cilkview accurately diagnoses problems involving inadequate parallelism and insufficient grain size, we can be confident that neither of these problems is the cause of the poor performance. The programmer can now look to other common sources of meager performance, such as insufficient memory bandwidth, false sharing, and lock contention.

The algorithm in Figure 9 applies the kernel to all space-time points at time t before computing any point at time $t + 1$. Modern computers operate with a cache-memory hierarchy. If the number of 3D points computed during a time step exceed the size of a given cache by a sufficient margin, the application incurs a number of cache misses proportional to the compute time. In this case, one time step of the computation involves 125 M 3D points, which exceeds even the L3-cache. Looking at Figure 10 more closely, we can see that the speedup levels off around 4–5 cores. At this point, the processor cores' demand for memory bandwidth saturates the memory subsystem. Because this stencil implementation is a memory-bandwidth hog, the performance falls below the predicted range.

How can one determine that a multithreaded program is limited by memory bandwidth? One indication is an unusually high value of CPI (cycles per instruction), but there can be other reasons for a high CPI. A simple test that often diagnoses memory-bandwidth problems is to run two benchmarks:

```
void co_cilk(int t0, int t1, int x0, int dx0, int
    x1, int dx1, int y0, int dy0, int y1, int dy1,
    int z0, int dz0, int z1, int dz1 ) {
  int dt = t1 - t0, dx = x1 - x0;
  int dy = y1 - y0, dz = z1 - z0;

  if (dx >= dx_threshold && dx >= dy && dx >= dz &&
      dt >= 1 && dx >= 2 * ds * dt * NPIECES) {
    //divide and conquer along x direction
    int chunk = dx / NPIECES;
    for (i = 0; i < NPIECES - 1; ++i) {
      cilk_spawn co_cilk(t0, t1, x0+i*chunk, ds, x0
          + (i+1) * chunk, -ds, y0, dy0, y1, dy1,
          z0, dz0, z1, dz1);
    }
    cilk_spawn co_cilk(t0, t1, x0+i*chunk, ds, x1,
        -ds, y0, dy0, y1, dy1, z0, dz0, z1, dz1);
    cilk_sync;

    cilk_spawn co_cilk(t0, t1, x0, dx0, x0, ds, y0,
        dy0, y1, dy1, z0, dz0, z1, dz1);
    for (i = 1; i < NPIECES; ++i) {
      cilk_spawn co_cilk(t0, t1, x0+i*chunk, -ds,
          x0 + i * chunk, ds, y0, dy0, y1, dy1, z0
          , dz0, z1, dz1);
    }
    cilk_spawn co_cilk(t0, t1, x1, -ds, x1, dx1, y0
        , dy0, y1, dy1, z0, dz0, z1, dz1);
  } else if (dy >= dyz_threshold && dy >= dz && dt
      >= 1 && dy>=2*ds*dt*NPIECES) {
    //similarly divide and conquer along y.
    ......
  } else if (dz >= dyz_threshold && dt >= 1  && dz
      >= 2 * ds * dt * NPIECES) {
    //similarly divide and conquer along z.
    ......
  }  else if (dt > dt_threshold) {
    int hdt = dt / 2;
    //decompose over time t direction
    co_cilk(t0, t0 + hdt, x0, dx0, x1, dx1, y0, dy0
        , y1, dy1, z0, dz0, z1, dz1);
    co_cilk(t0 + hdt,  t1, x0+dx0*hdt, dx0, x1+dx1*
        hdt, dx1, y0+dy0*hdt, dy0, y1+dy1*hdt, dy1
        , z0+dz0*hdt, dz0, z1+dz1*hdt, dz1);
  } else {
    //compute base case
    co_basecase_nv(t0, t1, x0, dx0, x1, dx1, y0,
        dy0, y1, dy1, z0, dz0, z1, dz1);
  }
}
```

Figure 11: Cache-oblivious code for the stencil computation.

1. On a P-core machine, run P simultaneous serial executions.
2. Run 1 serial execution of the program alone on 1 core.

If the execution time in Case 1 is significantly larger than in Case 2, it is likely that the demand for memory bandwidth is high enough to be a limiting factor on program scalability.

Solution: Divide-and-conquer recursion, properly coarsened at the leaves so as not to incur too much function-call overhead, generally taxes memory bandwidth less than iterative methods that stride through arrays multiple times. Frigo and Strumpen [21, 22] devised a so-called "cache-oblivious" [19] stencil algorithm to solve the memory-bandwidth problem and preserve parallelism. The algorithm advances time nonuniformly by strategically decomposing the space-time points recursively. On an ideal machine, when a subarray fits into a cache at a given level in the hierarchy, no cache misses are incurred except for those needed to bring the subarray into the cache.

The revised cache-oblivious implementation is shown in Figure 11. Its scalability estimation and trial results are shown in Figure 12. As the figure shows, Cilkview reports good ideal and burdened parallelism. Since access to memory is no longer a bottleneck, the program achieves linear speedup.

6. IMPLEMENTATION

Cilkview collects a program's parallelism information during a serial execution of the program code running under the Pin [35] dy-

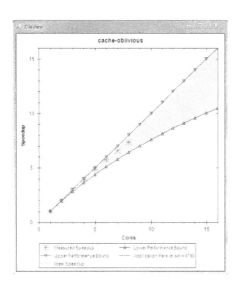

Figure 12: Cilkview's output for the code from Figure 11.

namic instrumentation framework. Since Cilkview operates on the optimized executable binary produced by the compiler, no recompilation of the code is necessary. Metadata in Cilk++ binaries allows Cilkview to identify the parallel control constructs in the executing application precisely and to collect statistics efficiently. When the application executes in a normal production environment, the metadata imposes no overhead on performance.

In our implementation of Cilkview, we decided to eschew direct timing measurements, which are generally not repeatable, and use instruction counts as a surrogate for time. Although instruction counts are a coarse measure of performance, the parallelism measurement need not be surgically precise: generally, parallelism estimates accurate to within a binary order of magnitude suffice to diagnose problems of inadequate parallelism. If an application with parallelism approximately 100 is running on 8 cores, one does not care whether the parallelism is really 95.78, 103.44, or even 1000. What matters is that the parallelism is significantly larger than the number of processors. Cilkview answers the simple question, "Does my application suffer from inadequate parallelism?" and, with the burdened analysis, "Does my application suffer from too fine-grained task creation?" Additional digits of precision rarely make a significant difference in the answers to these questions.

This section first reviews Cilkview's instrumentation strategy. Then, we present Cilkview's algorithm to compute performance measurements of a Cilk++ program according to logical dependencies of tasks. Finally, we discuss some sources of inaccuracy in Cilkview's measurements.

Instrumentation strategy

The design principle behind Cilkview's instrumentation strategy is to encode the logical parallel dependencies among tasks as part of an executable binary without compromising the performance of the production code. Cilkview relies on an enhanced version of the x86 binary executable format that provides metadata relevant to multithreaded execution. As part of the ordinary compilation process, the Cilk++ compiler embeds this metadata into the executable using a standard *multithreaded executable format* (**MEF**).

Cilkview operates directly on the optimized MEF binary executable distributed to end users, rather than on a "debug" version, thereby avoiding the problem of measuring an application that has been perturbed by instrumentation overhead. The MEF binary includes metadata to inform Cilkview of where Cilk++'s high-level

```
Function P spawns function C:
    C. work = P. work
    C. span = P. span
    C. burdened-span = P. burdened-span
    C. cwork = 0
    C. cspan = −∞
    C. cburden-span = −∞
    P. work = 0
    P. burdened-span += BURDEN

Function C returns from spawn with parent P:
    P. cwork += C. work
    P. cspan = max {P. cspan, C. span}
    P. cburden-span = max {P. cburden-span, C. burdened-span}

cilk_sync in function P:
    P. work += P. cwork
    P. cwork = 0
    P. span = max {P. span, P. cspan}
    P. cspan = −∞
    P. burdened-span = max {P. burdened-span, P. cburden-span}
    P. cburden-span = −∞
```

Figure 13: The Cilkview algorithm.

parallel control constructs appear in the executable segment. In particular, Cilkview requires metadata to mark the beginning and end of each spawned function, the beginning and end of each called function, and the location of each `cilk_sync`.

MEF metadata is stored in a platform-specific nonloadable section of the executable. Although this section resides in the disk image, it is not loaded into memory during normal execution. Thus, when an application executes normally, the metadata introduces no overhead. When the application executes under Cilkview, however, Cilkview reads the metadata and instruments the corresponding addresses in the executable segment to collect measurements. The performance of Cilkview is typically 2–10 times normal execution time on one core. Users report that this slowdown is acceptable for the insights on scalability that Cilkview provides.

Algorithm

With the support of the instrumentation framework, Cilkview computes three basic performance measures: work, span, and burdened span. As Cilkview executes the Cilk++ program serially under Pin, it associates six state variables — *work*, *span*, *burdened-span*, *cwork*, *cspan*, and *cburden-span* — with each function, whether spawned or called. The variables *work*, *span* and *burdened-span* store the accumulated work, span, and burdened span, respectively, from the beginning of the program to the current point of execution. The variables *cwork*, *cspan*, and *cburden-span* store the accumulated work and span, respectively, of child functions that run logically in parallel with the current function.

Conceptually, for each instruction, Cilkview increments the variables[2] *work*, *span*, and *burdened-span* of the current function. In addition, it executes certain actions at spawns and syncs, as shown in Figure 13. The constant BURDEN represents the task-migration overhead during a successful steal. This cost, which can be visualized as burdened nodes in Figure 5, is added to the spawning function's *burdened-span* at a `cilk_spawn`. At a `cilk_sync`, Cilkview incorporates the work and span of the parallel children into the function's own state variables.

---

[2] Actually, Cilkview counts instructions on a basic-block basis, which is more efficient.

Cilkview models the task-migration cost BURDEN as a constant. This cost could be evaluated with a more precise model that varies the estimated BURDEN value depending on the structure of the program, but since we only need rough measures of work, span, and burdened span, an upper-bound value determined by experimentation suffices to diagnose most scalability problems. Cilkview assumes a burden of 15,000 instructions.

Having gathered the three statistics: *work*, *span*, and *burdened-span*, Cilkview uses Inequalities (3), (4), and (6) to estimate the bounds of the instrumented program's speedup.

Sources of inaccuracy

When a program is deterministic, a program's work and span as determined by a serial run equal those of parallel runs, modulo scheduling overheads, caching effects, and the like. Consequently, Cilkview can collect the *work* and *span* information during a serial execution and infer that the work and span will not change substantially during a parallel run, except for these overheads, which can be shown to be minimal if the application contains sufficient parallelism [5].

When a program is nondeterministic, however, a parallel run may give different work and span from the serial one. Cilk++ allows some forms of nondeterminism to be encapsulated in *reducer hyperobjects* [18]. For a reducer hyperobject, the Cilk++ runtime manages local "views" of the hyperobject locally on the workers and combines them automatically with a *reduce* operation when subcomputations join at a sync. When and where the reduce operations occur is scheduler dependent, however, and this nondeterminism can affect the work and span. In particular, reduce operations never occur during a serial execution, and since Cilkview obtains its measurements for work and span during a serial run of the program, it never sees reducer overheads.

Reducers only occur because work was stolen, however. Since steals are infrequent for programs with sufficient parallelism [5], reduce operations seldom occur and tend to impede performance minimally. When implementing Cilkview, we therefore felt comfortable using the serial work and span without attempting to estimate reducer overheads, even though the measurements may suffer from some inaccuracies for programs with inadequate parallelism.

Another source of potential inaccuracy arises from the implementation of `cilk_for`. A `cilk_for` loop is implemented as a parallel divide-and-conquer tree over the iterations of the loop. Rather than recursing down to a single iteration, however, which would result in the overhead of one spawn per iteration, the Cilk++ runtime system automatically coarsens the recursion. That is, when the range of iterations drops below some *grain size*, it reverts to an ordinary serial `for` loop. The default grain size is computed dynamically according to the number of loop iterations and the number of cores. Different grain sizes affect the work and span of the program. Cilkview performs its measurements assuming that the default grain size is 1 unless the user specifies the grain size explicitly. Thus, it may overestimate the true work due to spawning overhead, while assuming as much parallelism as possible. As a result, Cilkview's estimate of parallelism may indicate somewhat more parallelism than actually exists, but generally not enough to influence diagnosis of performance problems.

7. BENCHMARK APPLICATIONS

This section illustrates Cilkview's scalability analysis on six benchmark applications. These applications were selected to cover a wide variety of multithreaded programs across different domains. The speedup estimation of each application was produced by the instrumented execution under Cilkview, and we used Cilkview to

benchmark runs of the application on our 8-core Intel®Core™ i7 processor using 1 to 8 workers. Figure 14 shows the graphical outputs of Cilkview on these benchmark applications. We now briefly describe each application and its Cilkview output.

Bzip2. Bzip2 [46] is a popular package for file compression. The Cilk++ implementation [10] of bzip2 was coded by John F. Carr of Intel Corporation. It compresses several blocks of data in parallel and applies a stream "reducer" [18] to ensure that the parallel compressed data is written to the output file in the correct order. As shown in Figure 14(a), this application exhibits a parallelism of 12.25 when run on a data file of 28 MB, and it obtained about 7 times speedup on the 8-core machine. The performance fits within the estimated scalability range.

Murphi. This application [16] is a finite-state machine verification tool used widely in the design of cache-coherence algorithms, link-level protocols, and executable memory-model analyses. Murphi verifies a protocol by traversing the entire state space in what is essentially a graph-traversal process. The Cilk++ implementation [27] parallelizes two of the search algorithms in the standard Murphi 3.1 package. Parallelizing the depth-first search is straightforward, and breadth-first search was parallelized using the PBFS algorithm [34]. Figure 14(b) shows the Cilkview output for the breadth-first implementation on adash, an example program included in the Murphi package.

Collision detection. This application was adapted from an industrial CAD application. The application reads two data files, each of which comprises a model of an assembly of three-dimensional parts. It then compares the models and outputs another data file listing all the parts from one assembly that collide with parts from the other assembly. Each model is stored in a ternary tree, and the collision-detection search performs recursive traversals of these ternary trees. The Cilk++ implementation searches the tree branches in parallel. It uses a list "reducer" [18] to collect the colliding parts. As shown in Figure 14(c), Cilkview predicts a good speedup on an input problem of two 9.9 MB files, and the implementation performed well.

Memcpy. This utility copies a block of memory from a source location to a destination location. The Cilk++ parallel memcpy replaces the `for` loop of the serial implementation with a `cilk_for` loop to enable parallelism. The Cilkview output in Figure 14(d) for copying a 477 MB block indicates linear speedup for the estimated lower and upper bounds. The speedups for actual runs were smaller than predicted, since memory bandwidth is a major bottleneck.

Min poset. Computing the minimal elements of a partially ordered finite set (poset) is a fundamental problem with numerous applications in combinatorics and algebraic geometry. One of them is optimizing the size of dags encoding polynomial expressions. In this case, given the terms of a polynomial, one is interested in determining the monomials that make up the set of minimal elements of a poset generated by the terms of the polynomial using the divisibility relation. The Cilk++ implementation of a parallel divide-and-conquer sieving algorithm for min poset was coded by Yuzhen Xie of the University of Western Ontario. The application was run on the poset generated by a polynomial with 14,869 terms, each with up to 28 variables, and produced 14 minimal elements. As shown in Figure 14(e), it obtained near-perfect linear speedup, as predicted by Cilkview.

Bivariate polynomial multiplication. The Basic Polynomial Algebra Subroutines (BPAS) package [36,37] provides a complete set of parallel routines in Cilk++ for FFT-based dense polynomial arithmetic over finite fields, such as polynomial multiplication and normal-form computations. Polynomial arithmetic sits at the core of every computer-algebra system, including Maple and Mathemat-

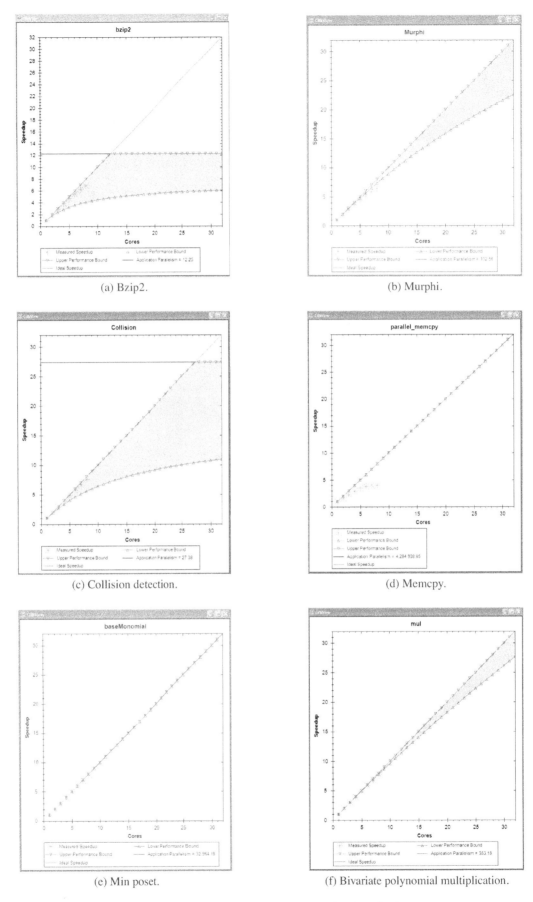

(a) Bzip2.

(b) Murphi.

(c) Collision detection.

(d) Memcpy.

(e) Min poset.

(f) Bivariate polynomial multiplication.

Figure 14: Cilkview graphical output for six benchmark applications.

ica, and the efficiency of polynomial computations greatly impacts the responsiveness of these software packages. A Cilk++ version of polynomial multiplication that uses the truncated Fourier transform was coded by Yuzhen Xie and Marc Moreno Maza of the University of Western Ontario. The application input was two bivariate polynomials all of whose partial degrees are equal to 1023. As shown in Figure 14(f), Cilkview predicts a linear speedup, which the benchmarking results confirm.

8. RELATED WORK

This section overviews tools for measuring parallel application performance. We survey the tools and discuss strategies for instrumenting performance.

Much work [49–51] has been devoted to diagnosing communication and synchronization problems in message-passing systems such as MPI. Tools for shared-memory systems [3, 24] tend to focus on an explicit threading (e.g., Pthreads, WinAPI threads, etc.). MPI and explicit-threading programs statically partition their work into threads and then map each thread to a core. Since these models do not perform dynamic load balancing, the performance tools focus on analyzing communication and synchronization, rather than on scalability *per se*.

Dynamic multithreaded concurrency platforms — e.g., Cilk-5 [20], Cilk++ [33], Fortress [2], Hood [6], Java Fork/Join Framework [31], OpenMP 3.0 [42], Task Parallel Library (TPL) [32], Intel® Threading Building Blocks (TBB) [45], and X10 [12] — have engendered their share of tools. Most, including Thread Profiler (in VTune [44]), Parallel Amplifier (in Parallel Studio [29]), and OMPtrace [11], gather low-level information specific to how the computation was scheduled and which cannot be easily adapted to forecast scalability. An exception is Cilk-5, which provided an option for computing work and span during an instrumented run. Unlike Cilkview, Cilk-5 instrumentation runs required recompilation, were based on actual time as measured by hardware cycle counters, and introduced overhead into the instrumented binary.

HPCToolkit [47, 48] is a profiling tool for multithreaded programming models ranging from explicit threading to dynamic multithreading. Its metrics are parallel idleness and overhead, which are qualitatively analogous to parallelism and burden. High idleness of a code segment means its parallelism is low and concurrency should be increased. High overhead means high burden, and concurrency should be decreased. Idleness and overhead are insufficient quantitatively to compute the logical concurrency of the program such as span and parallelism, which are critical for scalability prediction, but they are useful metrics for tuning.

Performance tools differ with respect to their strategies for instrumenting applications. Tools such as OPARI [40], Pablo [43], and Tau [41] add instrumentation to source code during the build process. Since source instrumentation can interfere with compiler optimizations, such as inlining and loop transformations, measurements may not accurately reflect the performance of fully optimized code. VTune [44] uses static binary instrumentation to augment application binaries for code profiling. Some tools use instrumented libraries [11, 39, 49]. One major problem with source instrumentation, static binary instrumentation, and instrumentation libraries is that they require source recompilation, binary rewriting, or library relinking, which can be inconvenient for analyzing large production codes.

Dynamic instrumentation supports the analysis of fully optimized binaries by inserting instrumentation in the executing application. Cilkview and various other tools [9, 15, 38] use dynamic instrumentation to collect metrics directly on the optimized binary. This strategy introduces little or no overhead to the program bi-

nary in normal runs. During performance-collection runs, however, dynamic instrumentation can dilate total execution time with overhead [48]. For Cilkview, it does not matter, however, because Cilkview counts instructions instead of measuring execution time.

9. CONCLUSION

This section discusses directions for future research concerning how Cilkview's capabilities might be extended.

Most contemporary mainstream multicore processors have limited memory bandwidth. Indeed, a single core of the Intel® Core^{TM} 2, for example, can saturate the available memory bandwidth. Thus, programs such as the standard daxpy loop[3], which are bandwidth-limited, do not run significantly faster on multiple cores than on one. The current implementation of Cilkview does not consider the influence of memory bandwidth on a program's execution time. Therefore, for a program like daxpy loop or parallel memcpy, where memory-bandwidth is the major performance bottleneck, real speedup of the program running on a multicore processor can deviate from Cilkview's estimation. Section 5 suggested one kind of test to diagnose bandwidth problems based on running concurrent copies of the serial program. It would be interesting to determine whether a tool could be built to diagnose memory-bandwidth problems by modeling caches during an instrumented run.

Some profilers, such as gprof [26], help a programmer analyze the running time of a serial program and diagnose performance bottlenecks without obligating the programmer to insert instrumentation by hand. Profilers typically provide data concerning the time spent in each called function and the function's children. For parallel programs, it would be desirable to have a profiler that produces comparable data for span. By knowing which parts of the code are bottlenecks for parallelism, the programmer can better focus her or his efforts on improving multicore performance. How to obtain and display profile data for span is a good research question. It seems difficult to employ gprof's strategy of sampling the programming counter noninvasively to obtain a good estimate of span, but binary instrumentation may be a reasonable approach. However the profile data is obtained, it remains a research question how best to lay out the data to convey parallelism bottlenecks to the programmer.

After computing a program's span, the programmer may wish to determine how much speedup might be gained by optimizing a function on the critical path. It could be that speeding up a function by just a small amount causes it to fall off the critical path, whereas speeding up another function may reduce the critical path by the full savings in time. Algorithms for this kind of sensitivity analysis are well known if the dag is given in full. Computing a sensitivity analysis as the dag unfolds on the fly seems like an interesting research problem, especially if one wishes to take into account that certain lines of code may appear multiple times on the critical path.

10. ACKNOWLEDGMENTS

Many thanks to our great team members at Cilk Arts — now at Intel Corporation since the acquisition of our little company in July 2009 — and to the many customers who helped us refine the Cilkview tool. In particular, many thanks to Barry Tannenbaum of Intel, who implemented the original graphical output application for Cilkview. Matteo Frigo, formerly of Intel and now of Axis Semiconductor, offered much valuable advice on the implementation of Cilkview. John F. Carr of Intel helped with the benchmarking of applications. We greatly appreciate the constructive comments made by the anonymous reviewers.

---

[3]The daxpy routine computes $ax + y$ for scalar a and vectors x and y.

11. REFERENCES

[1] A. Alexandrov, S. Bratanov, J. Fedorova, D. Levinthal, I. Lopatin, and D. Ryabtsev. Parallelization made easier with Intel Performance-Tuning Utility. *Intel Technology Journal*, 2007. http://www.intel.com/technology/itj/2007/v11i4//1-abstract.htm.

[2] E. Allen, D. Chase, J. Hallett, V. Luchangco, J.-W. Maessen, S. Ryu, G. L. S. Jr., and S. Tobin-Hochstadt. *The Fortress Language Specification, Version 1.0*. Sun Microsystems, Inc., 2008.

[3] T. E. Anderson and E. D. Lazowska. Quartz: a tool for tuning parallel program performance. *SIGMETRICS Perform. Eval. Rev.*, 18(1):115–125, 1990.

[4] R. D. Blumofe and C. E. Leiserson. Space-efficient scheduling of multithreaded computations. *SIAM J. Comput.*, 27(1):202–229, 1998.

[5] R. D. Blumofe and C. E. Leiserson. Scheduling multithreaded computations by work stealing. *JACM*, 46(5):720–748, 1999.

[6] R. D. Blumofe and D. Papadopoulos. Hood: A user-level threads library for multiprogrammed multiprocessors. Technical Report, University of Texas at Austin, 1999.

[7] R. P. Brent. The parallel evaluation of general arithmetic expressions. *JACM*, 21(2):201–206, 1974.

[8] D. Bruening. *Efficient, Transparent, and Comprehensive Runtime Code Manipulation*. PhD thesis, MIT EECS, 2004.

[9] B. Buck and J. K. Hollingsworth. An API for Runtime Code Patching. *Int. J. High Perf. Comput. Appl.*, 14(4):317–329, 2000.

[10] J. Carr. A parallel bzip2. Available from http://software.intel.com/en-us/articles/a-parallel-bzip2/, 2009.

[11] J. Caubet, J. Gimenez, J. Labarta, L. D. Rose, and J. S. Vetter. A dynamic tracing mechanism for performance analysis of OpenMP applications. In *WOMPAT*, pp. 53–67, 2001.

[12] P. Charles, C. Grothoff, V. Saraswat, C. Donawa, A. Kielstra, K. Ebcioglu, C. von Praun, and V. Sarkar. X10: An object-oriented approach to non-uniform cluster computing. In *OOPSLA*, pp. 519–538, 2005.

[13] T. H. Cormen, C. E. Leiserson, R. L. Rivest, and C. Stein. *Introduction to Algorithms*. The MIT Press, third edition, 2009.

[14] R. Courant, K. Friedrichs, and H. Lewy. On the partial difference equations of mathematical physics. *IBM J. R&D*, 11(2):215–234, 1967.

[15] L. DeRose, T. Hoover Jr., and J. K. Hollingsworth. The Dynamic Probe Class Library - an infrastructure for developing instrumentation for performance tools. In *IPDPS*, p. 10066b, 2001.

[16] D. L. Dill, A. J. Drexler, A. J. Hu, and C. H. Yang. Protocol verification as a hardware design aid. In *ICCD*, pp. 522–525, 1992.

[17] D. L. Eager, J. Zahorjan, and E. D. Lazowska. Speedup versus efficiency in parallel systems. *IEEE Trans. Comput.*, 38(3):408–423, 1989.

[18] M. Frigo, P. Halpern, C. E. Leiserson, and S. Lewin-Berlin. Reducers and other Cilk++ hyperobjects. In *SPAA*, pp. 79–90, 2009.

[19] M. Frigo, C. E. Leiserson, H. Prokop, and S. Ramachandran. Cache-oblivious algorithms. In *FOCS*, pp. 285–297, New York, New York, 1999.

[20] M. Frigo, C. E. Leiserson, and K. H. Randall. The implementation of the Cilk-5 multithreaded language. In *PLDI*, pp. 212–223, 1998.

[21] M. Frigo and V. Strumpen. Cache oblivious stencil computations. In *ICS*, pp. 361–366, 2005.

[22] M. Frigo and V. Strumpen. The cache complexity of multithreaded cache oblivious algorithms. In *SPAA*, pp. 271–280, 2006.

[23] M. R. Garey and D. S. Johnson. *Computers and Intractability*. W. H. Freeman, 1979.

[24] A. J. Goldberg and J. L. Hennessy. Performance debugging shared memory multiprocessor programs with MTOOL. In *SC'91*, pp. 481–490, 1991.

[25] R. L. Graham. Bounds for certain multiprocessing anomalies. *Bell System Technical Journal*, 45:1563–1581, 1966.

[26] S. Graham, P. Kessler, and M. McKusick. An execution profiler for modular programs. *Software—Practice and Experience*, 13(8):671–685, 1983.

[27] Y. He. Multicore-enabling the Murphi verification tool. Available from http://software.intel.com/en-us/articles/ multicore-enabling-the-murphi-verification-tool/, 2009.

[28] Intel Corp. *Intel Cilk++ SDK Programmer's Guide*, 2009. Available from http://software.intel.com/en-us/articles/ download-intel-cilk-sdk/. Document No. 322581-001US.

[29] Intel Corp. Intel Parallel Amplifier. Available from http://software.intel.com/sites/products/documentation/ studio/amplifier/en-us/2009/ug_docs/index.htm. Document No. 320486-003US, 2009.

[30] Intel Corp. Intel Thread Profiler. Available from http://software.intel.com/en-us/articles/intel-thread-profiler-for-windows-documentation/, 2010.

[31] D. Lea. A Java fork/join framework. In *Java Grande*, pp. 36–43, 2000.

[32] D. Leijen, W. Schulte, and S. Burckhardt. The design of a task parallel library. In *OOPSLA*, pp. 227–242, 2009.

[33] C. E. Leiserson. The Cilk++ concurrency platform. *J. Supercomput.*, 51(3):244–257, 2010.

[34] C. E. Leiserson and T. B. Schardl. A work-efficient parallel breadth-first search algorithm (or how to cope with the nondeterminism of reducers). In *SPAA*, 2010.

[35] C.-K. Luk, R. Cohn, R. Muth, H. Patil, A. Klauser, G. Lowney, S. Wallace, V. J. Reddi, and K. Hazelwood. Pin: building customized program analysis tools with dynamic instrumentation. In *PLDI*, pp. 190–200, 2005.

[36] M. M. Maza and Y. Xie. Balanced dense polynomial multiplication on multi-cores. In *PDCAT*, pp. 1–9, 2009.

[37] M. M. Maza and Y. Xie. FFT-based dense polynomial arithmetic on multi-cores. In *HPCS*, pp. 378–399, 2009.

[38] B. P. Miller, M. D. Callaghan, J. M. Cargille, J. K. Hollingsworth, R. B. Irvin, K. L. Karavanic, K. Kunchithapadam, and T. Newhall. The Paradyn parallel performance measurement tool. *IEEE Computer*, 28(11):37–46, 1995.

[39] B. Mohr, A. D. Malony, F. Schlimbach, G. Haab, J. Hoeflinger, and S. Shah. A performance monitoring interface for OpenMP. In *IWOMP*, 2002.

[40] B. Mohr, A. D. Malony, S. Shende, and F. Wolf. Design and prototype of a performance tool interface for OpenMP. *J. Supercomput.*, 23(1):105–128, 2002.

[41] S. Moore, F. Wolf, J. Dongarra, S. Shende, A. Malony, and B. Mohr. A scalable approach to MPI application performance analysis. In *EUROPVMMPI*, pp. 309–316, 2005.

[42] OpenMP Architecture Review Board. OpenMP application program interface, version 3.0. http://www.openmp.org/mp-documents/spec30.pdf, 2008.

[43] D. A. Reed, R. A. Aydt, R. J. Noe, P. C. Roth, K. A. Shields, B. W. Schwartz, and L. F. Tavera. Scalable performance analysis: The Pablo performance analysis environment. In *Scalable Parallel Lib. Conf.*, pp. 104–113, 1993.

[44] J. Reinders. *VTune Performance Analyzer Essentials*. Intel Press, 2005.

[45] J. Reinders. *Intel Threading Building Blocks*. O'Reilly, 2007.

[46] J. Seward. bzip2 and libbzip2, version 1.0.5: A program and library for data compression. Available from http://www.bzip2.org.

[47] N. R. Tallent and J. M. Mellor-Crummey. Effective performance measurement and analysis of multithreaded applications. In *PPoPP*, pp. 229–240, 2009.

[48] N. R. Tallent, J. M. Mellor-Crummey, and M. W. Fagan. Binary analysis for measurement and attribution of program performance. In *PLDI*, pp. 441–452, 2009.

[49] J. Vetter. Dynamic statistical profiling of communication activity in distributed applications. In *SIGMETRICS*, pp. 240–250, 2002.

[50] J. S. Vetter and M. O. McCracken. Statistical scalability analysis of communication operations in distributed applications. *SIGPLAN Not.*, 36(7):123–132, 2001.

[51] C. E. Wu, A. Bolmarcich, M. Snir, D. Wootton, F. Parpia, A. Chan, and E. Lusk. From trace generation to visualization: A performance framework for distributed parallel systems. In *SC'00*, p. 50, 2000.

Towards Optimizing Energy Costs of Algorithms for Shared Memory Architectures

Vijay Anand Korthikanti
Department of Computer Science
University of Illinois Urbana-Champaign
vkortho2@illinois.edu

Gul Agha
Department of Computer Science
University of Illinois Urbana-Champaign
agha@illinois.edu

ABSTRACT

Energy consumption by computer systems has emerged as an important concern. However, the energy consumed in executing an algorithm cannot be inferred from its performance alone: it must be modeled explicitly. This paper analyzes energy consumption of parallel algorithms executed on shared memory multicore processors. Specifically, we develop a methodology to evaluate how energy consumption of a given parallel algorithm changes as the number of cores and their frequency is varied. We use this analysis to establish the optimal number of cores to minimize the energy consumed by the execution of a parallel algorithm for a specific problem size while satisfying a given performance requirement. We study the sensitivity of our analysis to changes in parameters such as the ratio of the power consumed by a computation step versus the power consumed in accessing memory. The results show that the relation between the problem size and the optimal number of cores is relatively unaffected for a wide range of these parameters.

Categories and Subject Descriptors

F.2.2 [**Analysis of Algorithms and Problem Complexity**]: Nonnumerical Algorithms and Problems—*Sorting and searching*; B.2.1 [**Arithmetic and Logic Structures**]: Design Styles—*Parallel*; B.3.2 [**Memory Structures**]: Design Styles—*Cache memories*

General Terms

Theory, Measurement

Keywords

Energy, Performance, Parallel Algorithms, Shared Memory Architectures

1. INTRODUCTION

Our work is motivated by two facts. First and foremost, computers consume a significant amount of energy: in the US alone, they are estimated to already consume 13% of the total electricity [21]. Thus computer use represents a significant source of greenhouse gasses, a critical problem for sustainability in an era of climate change, and the emissions they cause have become an increasing cause for concern globally [1]. Second, the limited energy storage capacity of batteries is a critical problem for mobile devices.

As CPUs hit the power wall, multicore architectures have been proposed as a way to increase computation cycles while keeping power consumption constant. It turns out that in multicore architectures, it is possible to scale the speed of the individual cores or leave them idle, thus reducing their energy consumption. Because the relation between the power consumed by a core and the frequency at which the core operates is nonlinear, there is an interesting trade-off between the energy and performance.

We examine the relation between performance of parallel algorithms and their *energy requirements* on *shared memory multicore processors*. We believe this sort of analysis can provide programmers with intuitions about the energy required by the parallel algorithms they are using–thus guiding the choice of algorithm, architecture and the number of cores used for a particular application. Moreover, the analysis could help in the design of more energy efficient parallel algorithms. We believe that the energy efficiency of parallel algorithms should be considered just as important as their performance.

The paper focuses on the current generation of multicore architectures, specifically, multicore processors which use a hierarchical shared memory. The Parallel Random Access Machine (PRAM) provides an abstract model of shared memory architectures [11]. However, the PRAM model contains no notion of a memory hierarchy; i.e., PRAM does not model the differences in the access speeds between the private cache on a core and the shared memory that is addressable by all cores. Thus, PRAM cannot accurately model the actual execution time of the algorithms on modern multicore architectures. More recently, several models emphasizing memory hierarchies have been proposed [6, 4, 3]. In particular, the *Parallel External Memory* (PEM) model is an extension of the PRAM model which includes a single level of memory hierarchy [3]. A more general model is the *Multicore* model [6] which models multiple levels of the memory hierarchy. In our analysis, we choose to use the PEM model. Our choice is motivated by the fact that the PEM model is simpler, and we believe it is sufficient to illustrate the trade-offs that we are interested in analyzing.

Parallel algorithms are parameterized by the number of

cores on which they may be executed (usually from a single core to some large number). Problems are parameterized by the size of their input, and a *problem instance* is the problem for a fixed input value. We define the performance of a parallel algorithm as the time required for the completion of a problem instance. The problem of energy scalability under iso-performance of a parallel algorithm as follows. *Given a problem instance and a fixed performance requirement, what is the number of cores which minimizes energy consumption in executing the parallel algorithm on the problem instance* .

In order to focus on some essential aspects of the problem, and given the space limitations, we make a few simplifying assumptions. We assume that all cores are homogeneous and that cores that are idle consume no power. Moreover, we assume that shared memory access time is constant i.e., there are no memory bottle necks.

Contributions of the paper: This paper is the first one to propose a methodology to analyze energy scalability for parallel algorithms running on shared memory architectures. We illustrate our methodology by analyzing several algorithms such as parallel addition, parallel prefix sums and parallel mergesort. Not surprisingly, the energy requirements for an instruction and for memory accesses are critical factors in determining the energy required by an algorithm. For each of our examples, we analyze the sensitivity of energy scalability is to these energy parameters.

Outline of the paper. The next section discusses related work. Sec. 3 provides the background for our analysis, a justifications for our assumptions and the description of constants that are used in the analysis. Sec. 4 explains our methodology for evaluating the energy scalability of parallel algorithms through an example. Sec. 6 applies our methodology to other parallel algorithms: namely, parallel prefix sums and parallel mergesort. Finally, Sec. 7 discusses the results and future work.

2. RELATED WORK

In [15] we presented a methodology to evaluate energy scalability under iso-performance of parallel algorithms running on message passing parallel architectures.[1] In this paper, we evaluate the same metric for parallel algorithms running on shared memory based multicore architectures. Our current work extends the previous model in two ways. First, we extend the energy model to include leakage power, a significant component of the total energy consumed. Second, we use the *parallel external memory model (PEM)* [3] which extends the standard PRAM model with memory hierarchies at cores. Note that we evaluate the energy scalability metric for a different class of algorithms–viz., algorithms designed for the PEM model.

Previous research has studied software-controlled dynamic power management in multicore processors. Researchers have taken two approaches for dynamic power management. Specifically, they have used one or both of two *control knobs* for runtime power performance adaptation: namely, *dynamic concurrency throttling*, which adapts the level of concurrency at runtime, and *dynamic voltage and frequency scaling* [9, 19, 13, 23, 10]. This body of work provides runtime tools which may be used with profilers for the code. By contrast, we develop methods for theoretically analyzing parallel al-

gorithms in order to statically determine how to minimize the energy consumed under a fixed performance budget.

Li and Martinez develop an analytical model relating the power consumption and performance of a parallel application running on a multicore processors [18]. This model considers parallel efficiency, granularity of parallelism, and voltage/frequency scaling in relating power consumption and performance. However, the model does not consider total energy consumed by an entire parallel application, or even the structure of the parallel algorithm. Instead, it is assumed that the algorithmic structure (communication and computation) of a parallel algorithm can be represented by a parallel efficiency metric. A generic analysis based on this metric is then used–irrespective of the algorithmic structure.

The notion of energy scalability under iso-performance is in some ways analogous to *performance scalability under iso-efficiency* as defined by Kumar et al. [16]; The latter is a measure of an algorithm's ability to effectively utilize an increasing number of processors in a multicomputer architecture. Recall that efficiency measures the ratio of the speed-up obtained by an algorithm to the number of processes used. Kumar measures scalability by observing how large a problem size has to grow as a function of the number of processors used in order to maintain *constant efficiency*.

Wang and Ziavras have analyzed performance energy trade offs for matrix multiplication on an FPGA based mixed-mode chip multiprocessor [24]. Their analysis is based on a specific parallel application executed on a specific multiprocessor architecture. In contrast, our general methodology of evaluating energy scalability can be used for a broad range of parallel applications and multicore architectures.

Cho and Melhem studied the interaction between parallelization and energy consumption in a parallelizable application [8]. Given the ratio of serial and parallel portion in an application and the number of processors, they derive the optimal frequencies allocated to the serial and parallel regions in the application to minimize the total energy consumption, while the execution time is preserved. This analysis is less detailed compared to our energy scalability analysis in the sense that they divide the whole parallel application execution into serial and parallel regions and express total energy as a function of the length of these regions. In other words, they do not consider the structure (shared memory synchronization and computation) and problem size of the parallel application.

Bingham and Greenstreet have proposed a generic energy complexity metric, ET^α, for modeling energy-time trade-offs of CMOS technology [5]. Prior to this, various researchers have promoted the use of the ET [11] and ET^2 [20] metrics for modeling the trade-offs. These models try to abstract away the voltage/frequency scaling issues from the programmer, while reasoning about energy complexity of the computation. In contrast, we explicitly represent frequency in our model and view both concurrency throttling and voltage/frequency scaling as two orthogonal control knobs to control energy. Moreover, these models do not account for the energy required for memory accesses (or for message passing), which forms a significant proportion of the total energy consumed.

3. MODEL AND ASSUMPTIONS

We first define the parallel computation model and the energy model we use in our analysis.

---

[1]Note that the much of the description of related work in this section is similar to that given in our earlier paper [15].

3.1 Parallel Computation Model

The Parallel External Memory (PEM) model [3] is a computational model with P cores and a two-level memory hierarchy. The memory hierarchy consists of the external memory (main memory) shared by all the cores and P internal memories (caches). Each cache is of size M, is partitioned in blocks of size B and is exclusive to a core, i.e., cores cannot access other caches belonging to a different core. To perform any operation on data, a core must have the data in its cache. Data is transferred between the main memory and the cache in blocks of size B (see Fig 1).

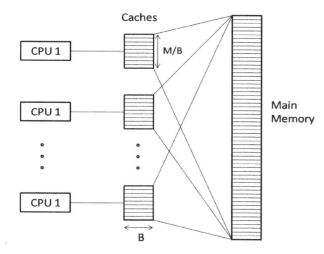

Figure 1: The PEM model

Multiple cores can access distinct blocks of the shared memory concurrently. There are three variants of the PEM model (as in the case with PRAM model); these variants determine how the same block of shared memory may be accessed by different cores.

- *Concurrent Read, Concurrent Write* (CRCW): multiple cores can read and write the same block in the main memory concurrently.

- *Concurrent Read, Exclusive Write* (CREW): multiple cores can only read the same block concurrently, but cannot write to it.

- *Exclusive Read, Exclusive Write* (EREW): there is no simultaneous access of any kind to the same block of the main memory by multiple cores.

In this paper, we consider only the CREW PEM model. We leave concurrent writes and their energy scalability under iso-performance in the PEM model for future work. To simplify the presentation, we also make the following architectural assumptions

1. All active cores operate at the same frequency and the frequency of the cores can be varied using a frequency (voltage) probe and cores switch to *idle* state if there is no computation left at them.

2. The computation and cache access time of the cores can be scaled by scaling the frequency of the cores.

3. Shared memory access (both read and write) cannot be scaled and thus takes constant time.

The computation time T_{busy} on a given core is proportional to the number of cycles, including cache accesses μ, executed on the core. Let X be the frequency of a core, then:

$$T_{busy} = \textit{(number of cycles)} \times \frac{1}{X} \qquad (1)$$

We denote the time for which a given core is active (not idle) as T_{active}.

3.2 Energy Model

The following equation approximates power consumption in a CMOS circuit:

$$P = C_L V^2 f + I_L V \qquad (2)$$

where C_L is the load capacitance, V is the supply voltage, I_L is the leakage current, and f is the operational frequency. The first term corresponds to the dynamic power-consumption component of the total power consumption, while the second term corresponds to the leakage power consumption.

Recall that a linear increase in the voltage supply leads to a linear increase in the frequency of the core. However, a linear increase in the voltage supply also leads to a nonlinear (typically cubic) increase in power consumption. Thus, for simplicity, we model the dynamic and leakage energies consumed by a core, E, to be the result of the above mentioned critical factor:

$$E_{dynamic} = E_d \cdot T_{busy} \cdot X^3 \qquad (3)$$

$$E_{leakage} = E_l \cdot T_{active} \cdot X \qquad (4)$$

where E_d and E_l are some hardware constants [7].

In order to reason about energy in the PEM model, we assume that shared memory accesses (both reads and writes) consume a constant amount of energy. Because recent processors have introduced efficient support for low power modes that can reduce the power consumption to near zero, it is reasonable to assume that the energy consumed by idle cores is zero.

The following parameters and constants are used in the rest of the paper.

- E_m : Energy consumed for single memory access (both read and write).

- F : Maximum frequency of a single core

- N : Input size of the parallel application

- P : Number of cores allocated for the parallel application.

- M_c : Number of cycles executed at maximum frequency for single shared memory access time

4. METHODOLOGY

We now present our methodology to evaluate energy scalability under iso-performance for a given parallel algorithm $\mathcal{A}$ in the PEM model:

Step 1 Find the critical path $\pi_{\mathcal{A}}$ in the execution of $\mathcal{A}$. Note that the *critical path* is the longest path through the task dependency graph (where edges represents task serialization) of parallel algorithm. The length of the critical path can be determined by measuring the execution of the longest thread. Note that the critical path length gives a lower bound on execution time of a parallel algorithm.

Step 2 Partition $\pi_\mathcal{A}$ into memory accesses (reads and writes), synchronization breaks and computation steps.

Step 3 Scale the computation steps of $\pi_\mathcal{A}$ so that the parallel performance of $\mathcal{A}$ matches the specified performance requirement. We do this by scaling the computation time of $\pi_\mathcal{A}$ to the difference between (a)the required performance and (b) the time taken for memory accesses and synchronization breaks in the critical path. We thus obtain the new reduced frequency at which all P cores should run.

Step 4 Evaluate the sum total of computation cycles at all cores.

Step 5 Evaluate the *memory complexity* (total number of memory accesses) of $\mathcal{A}$. The example algorithms we discuss later show that the message complexity of parallel algorithms may depend on both the input size and the number of cores used.

Step 6 Evaluate the total active time at all the cores assuming the frequency obtained in Step 3. Observe that, scaling $\pi_\mathcal{A}$ may lead to an increase in active time in other paths (at other cores).

Step 7 Frame an expression for energy consumption of the parallel algorithm using the energy model. The energy expression is the sum of the energy consumed by 1) computation, E_{comp}, 2) memory accesses, E_{mem} and 3) leakage, E_{leak}

$$E_{comp} = E_d \cdot (\text{Total no. of computation cycles}) \cdot X^2 \quad (5)$$
$$E_{mem} = E_m \cdot (\text{Total number of memory accesses}) \quad (6)$$
$$E_{leak} = E_l \cdot T_{active} \cdot X \quad (7)$$

Note that E_{comp} is lower if the cores run at a lower frequency, while E_{leak} may increase as the active cores take longer to finish. E_{mem} may increase as more cores are used since the computation is more distributed.

Step 8 Analyze the equation to obtain the number of cores required for minimum energy consumption as a function of input size. In particular, we compute the appropriate number of cores that are required to guarantee a required level of *performance*.

Example: Adding Numbers.

We illustrate our methodology using a simple parallel addition algorithm. Initially, all N numbers are stored contiguously in the main memory and caches of all P cores are empty. Without loss of generality, we assume that the input size N is a multiple of the number of cores P. In the first phase of the algorithm, each core transfers (N/P) numbers from memory to their own caches and computes their sum. The transfer and summation of (N/P) numbers by each core happens in a series of steps. In each step, a core transfers a block of numbers B from main memory to its cache and computes the sum of B numbers and the result

obtained in the previous step. At the end of the first phase, each of P cores possesses a partial sum. With access to a distinct additional auxiliary block of main memory by each core, in the CREW PEM model, the sum of P partial sums is efficiently computed in parallel in a tree fashion in $\log(P)$ steps (for simplicity, we assume P to be a power of 2). In the first step, half of the cores transfer their partial sums in parallel to their respective auxiliary blocks in main memory. The other half of the cores then read in parallel the elements that were stored in the auxiliary blocks of the first half, and sum it with their local partial sum. The same step is recursively performed until there is only one core left. At the end of the computation, one core will store the sum of all N numbers. Figure 2 depicts the execution of the parallel addition algorithm for the case $P = 4$.

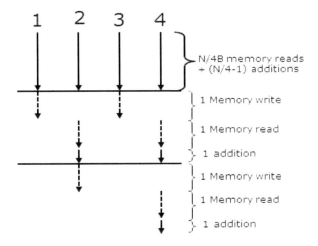

Figure 2: Example scenario: Adding N numbers using 4 cores; execution of 4th core represents the critical path

Now we describe the steps needed to evaluate the energy scalability under iso-performance. In the above algorithm, the critical path is easy to find: it is the execution path of the core that has the sum of all numbers at the end (Step 1). We can see that there are $N/(B \cdot P) + \log(P)$ memory reads, $\log(P)$ synchronization breaks and $((N/P) - 1 + \log(P))$ computation steps (step 2). Now, we obtain a reduced frequency at which all P cores should run to complete in time T (Step 3):

$$X' = F \cdot \frac{(\frac{N}{P} - 1 + log(P)) \cdot \beta}{T \cdot F - (\frac{N}{B \cdot P} + 2 \cdot \log(P)) \cdot M_c} \quad (8)$$

where β represents number of cycles required per addition. In order to achieve energy savings, we require $0 < X' < F$. Note that this restriction provides a lower bound on the input size as a function of P and M_c. The total number of computational cycles of the parallel algorithm evaluates to $((N/P - 1) \cdot P + (P - 1)) \cdot \beta$ i.e., $(N - 1) \cdot \beta$ (step 4).

We next evaluate the total number of memory accesses by the parallel algorithm (Step 5). It is trivial to see that the number of memory accesses for this parallel algorithm when running on P cores is $(N/B) + 2 \cdot (P - 1)$. Note that in this algorithm, the message complexity is both dependent on P and on the input size N. We now evaluate the total active time at all the cores, running at new frequency X' (Step 5).

Under the assumption that cores switch to idle state when there is no computation left at them, the total active time evaluates to:

$$T_{active} = \frac{M_c}{F}(\frac{N}{B} + 3 \cdot (P-1)) + \frac{\beta}{X'} \cdot (N-1) \quad (9)$$

where the first term represents the total active time spent by all the cores during memory transfers and the second term represents the total active time spent by all cores performing computations.

We derive the equation for energy consumption using Equation 5 (Step 6). The energy consumed for computation, memory accesses and leakage while the algorithm is running on P cores at reduced frequency X' is:

$$E_{comp} = E_d \cdot (N-1) \cdot \beta \cdot X'^2 \quad (10)$$

$$E_{mem} = E_m \cdot ((N/B) + 2 \cdot (P-1)) \quad (11)$$

$$E_{leak} = E_l \cdot T_{active} \cdot X' \quad (12)$$

Finally, Step 7 involves analysis of the equation obtained. We do this in the next section.

5. ANALYZING ENERGY CONSUMPTION

We now analyze the energy expression obtained above for the addition algorithm to evaluate energy scalability under iso-performance. While we could differentiate the function with respect to the number of cores to compute the minimum, this results in a rather complex expression. Instead, we analyze the graphs expressing energy scalability under iso-performance.

Note that the energy expression is dependent on many variables such as N (input Size), P (number of cores), β (number of cycles per addition), M_c (number of cycles executed at maximum frequency for single memory accesses time), E_m (energy consumed for single memory accesses), and F (maximum frequency of a core). We can simplify a couple of these parameters without loss of generality. In most architectures, the number of cycles involved per addition is just two (one cache transfer and one addition operation), so we assume $\beta = 3$. We also set leakage energy constant as $E_l = 1$. We express all energy values with respect to this normalized energy value.

In order to graph the required differential, we must make some assumptions about the other parameters. While these assumptions compromise generality, we discuss the sensitivity of the analysis to a range of values for these parameters. One such parameter is the the energy consumed for single cycle at maximum frequency as a multiple of leakage energy constant. We assume this ratio to be 10, i.e., that $E_d \cdot F^2 = 10 \cdot E_l$. It turns out that this parameter is not very significant for our analysis; in fact, large variations in the parameter do not affect the shapes of the graphs significantly. Another parameter, k, represents the ratio of the energy consumed for single memory accesses, E_m, and the energy consumed for executing a single instruction at the maximum frequency. Thus, $E_m = k \cdot E_d \cdot F^2$. We fix the required performance T to be that of the running time of the sequential algorithm at maximum frequency F and analyze the sensitivity of our results to a range of values of both k and M_c. The sequential algorithm for this problem is trivial: it takes (N/B) memory accesses and $N-1$ additions to compute the sum of N numbers. The running time of the sequential algorithm is given by $T_{seq} = \beta \cdot (N-1) \cdot (1/F) + (N/B) \cdot (M_c/F)$.

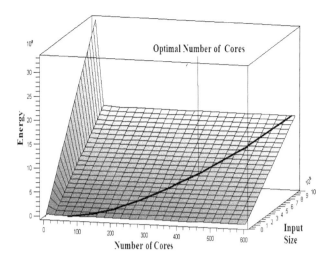

Figure 3: Addition: Energy curve with energy on Z axis, number of cores on X axis and input size on Y axis with $k = 1000$, $\beta = 2$, $M_c = 1000$. Black curve on the XY plane is the plot of optimal number of cores required for minimum energy consumption with varying input size(10^7 to 10^9).

Fig. 3 plots energy E as a function of input size and number of cores. We can see that for any input size N, initially energy decreases with increasing M and later on increases with increasing M. As explained earlier, this behavior can be understood by the fact that energy for computation decreases with an increase in number of cores running at reduced frequencies, and energy for memory accesses increases with increasing cores. Furthermore, we can see that increasing the input size leads to an increase in the optimal number of cores required for minimum energy consumption.

We now consider the sensitivity of this analysis with respect to the ratio k. Fig. 4 plots the optimal number of cores required for minimum energy consumption by varying k for an input size 10^8. The results show that for a given input size in the range considered, the optimal number of cores required for minimum energy consumption decreases with increasing k. (The curve approximates c/k, where c is some constant). We observe that this trend remains the same for whole of the input range (10^7 to 10^9).

Fig. 5 plots the optimal number of cores required for minimum energy consumption by varying M_c for an input size 10^8. The results show that for a given input size in the range considered, the optimal number of cores required for minimum energy consumption increases with increasing M_c. (The curve approximates a negative exponential curve with positive coefficient). We observe that this trend also remains the same for whole of the input range (10^7 to 10^9).

The above graph analysis depicts the exact behavior of optimal number of cores as function of input size for the given input range and appears to generalize to larger input sizes. However, we have been unable to give an analytic expression for the asymptotic behavior of the optimal number of cores as a function of input size as the energy expression is very complex.

6. CASE STUDIES

We now analyze *parallel prefix sums* and *parallel mergesort*

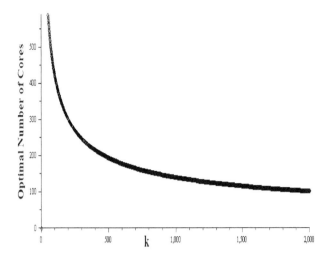

Figure 4: Sensitivity analysis: optimal number of cores on **Y** axis, and k (ratio of the energy consumed for single memory accesses and the energy consumed for executing a single instruction at the maximum frequency) on **X** axis with input size $N = 10^8$ and $M_c = 500$.

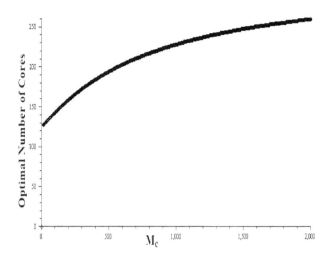

Figure 5: Sensitivity analysis: optimal number of cores on **Y** axis, and M_c (no of cycles executed at maximum frequency for single memory accesses time) on **X** axis with input size $N = 10^8$ and $k = 500$.

algorithms that have an optimal I/O complexity under the PEM model [3]. The prefix sums algorithm we consider is cache oblivious, whereas the mergesort algorithm is not cache oblivious.

6.1 Parallel Prefix Sums

Given an ordered set A of N elements, the all-prefix-sums operation returns an ordered set B of N elements, such that i^{th} element in B is the sum of all elements of A whose index is less than or equal to i. For this specific problem, a PRAM based algorithm is also an efficient PEM algorithm as it is, without any modifications [3]. Without loss of generality, we assume N to be multiple of P and P to be some power of 2. The PRAM algorithm by Ladner and Fischer [17] is as follows: First, every core sums N/P elements serially. At this stage, every core contains a partial sum (there are P partial sums). Next, every odd numbered core sends its partial sum to its adjacent (right) even numbered core using auxiliary blocks (as in the parallel addition algorithm). The even numbered cores then sum their partial sum with the obtained partial sum (from odd numbered cores) yielding $P/2$ partial sums at $P/2$ cores. The algorithm then recursively evaluates the prefix sums of the $P/2$ partial sums. Next, with the exception of the Pth core, every even numbered core sends its computed prefix sum to its adjacent (right) odd numbered core. Odd numbered cores (except for first) then sum their partial sums with the obtained prefix sums to obtain their prefix-sums. Thus all-prefix-sums of the initial P partial sums of P cores is computed. Finally, every core distributes its prefix sum across N/P elements serially to obtain the all-prefix-sums of the ordered set A.

Now we describe the steps needed to evaluate the energy scalability under iso-performance. Since P is some power of 2, the critical path of the algorithm is the execution path of the Pth core. (Step 1). We see that there are $2 \cdot N/(B \cdot P) + 2 \cdot \log(P) - 1$ memory reads, $2 \cdot \log(P) - 1$ synchronization breaks and $(2 \cdot (N/P - 1) + 2 \cdot \log(P) - 1)$ computation steps

(step 2). Now, we obtain a reduced frequency at which all P cores should run to complete in time T (Step 3):

$$X' = F \cdot \frac{(2 \cdot (\frac{N}{P} - 1) + 2 \cdot \log(P) - 1) \cdot \beta}{T \cdot F - (2 \cdot \frac{N}{B \cdot P} + 4 \cdot \log(P) - 2) \cdot M_c} \quad (13)$$

where β represents number of cycles required per addition or subtraction. In order to achieve energy savings, we require $0 < X' < F$. Note that this restriction provides a lower bound on the input size as a function of P and M_c. The total number of computational cycles of the parallel algorithm evaluates to $2 \cdot ((N/P - 1) \cdot P + (2P - \log(p) - 2)) \cdot \beta$, which is $(2N - \log(p) - 2) \cdot \beta$ (step 4).

We next evaluate the sum total of memory accesses in total required by the parallel algorithm (Step 5). It is trivial to see that number of memory accesses for this parallel algorithm when running on P cores is $2 \cdot (N/B) + 2 \cdot (2P - \log(P) - 2)$. We now evaluate the total active time at all the cores, running at the new frequency X' (Step 5). Since all the cores are active all along the critical path, the total active time evaluates to:

$$\begin{aligned} T_{active} &= \left(2 \cdot \frac{N}{B \cdot P} + 4 \cdot \log(P) - 2\right) \cdot \frac{M_c}{F} \cdot P \\ &+ \left(2 \cdot (\frac{N}{P} - 1) + 2 \cdot \log(P) - 1\right) \cdot \frac{\beta}{X'} \cdot P \end{aligned}$$

We frame an equation for energy consumption using equation 5 (Step 6). The energy consumed for computation, memory accesses and leakage while the algorithm is running on P cores at reduced frequency X' is:

$$E_{comp} = E_d \cdot (2N - \log(P) - 2) \cdot \beta \cdot X'^2 \quad (14)$$

$$E_{mem} = E_m \cdot (2 \cdot \frac{N}{B} + 2 \cdot (2P - \log(P) - 2)) \quad (15)$$

$$E_{leak} = E_l \cdot T_{active} \cdot X' \quad (16)$$

Energy Analysis We use the same assumptions that were used earlier for analyzing the energy scalability of the parallel addition algorithm. In particular, we assume the required performance to be the running time of the sequential algorithm at maximum frequency F. The sequential algorithm is very much similar to that of the addition algorithm except that we output all intermediate sums (prefix sums) along the execution. Thus, it takes (N/B) memory accesses and $N-1$ additions to compute the all-prefix-sums of N numbers. The running time of the sequential algorithm is given by $T_{seq} = \beta \cdot (N-1) \cdot (1/F) + (N/B) \cdot (M_c/F)$.

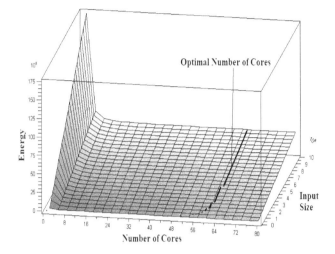

Figure 6: **Prefix-Sums: Energy curve with energy on Z axis, number of cores on X axis and input size on Y axis with $k = 1000$, $\beta = 2$, $M_c = 1000$. Black curve on the XY plane is the plot of optimal number of cores required for minimum energy consumption with varying input size.(10^7 to 10^9).**

Observation: Fig. 6 shows that for any input size N, initially energy decreases with increasing P and later on increases with increasing P. As explained earlier, this behavior can be understood by the fact that energy for computation decreases with an increase in number of cores running at reduced frequencies, and energy for memory accesses increases with increasing cores. However, for the same valuations of the constants and the input range, optimal number of cores for minimal energy consumption for parallel addition algorithms is far less compared to that of the parallel prefix sum algorithm. Furthermore, we can see that increasing the input size leads to an increase in the optimal number of cores required for minimum energy consumption.

We now consider the sensitivity of this analysis with respect to the ratio k. Fig. 7 plots the optimal number of cores required for minimum energy consumption by fixing the input size (10^8) and varying k. The plot shows that for a fixed input size, the optimal number of cores required for minimum energy consumption decreases with increasing k. Furthermore, we observe that this trend remains the same for whole of the input range (10^7 to 10^9). Note that this graph differs from the one obtained for the parallel addition algorithm.

Fig. 8 plots the optimal number of cores required for minimum energy consumption by fixing the input size (10^8) and varying M_c. The plot shows that for a fixed input size, the optimal number of cores required for minimum energy consumption initially decreases and later on increases with increasing M_c. We also observe that this trend remains the

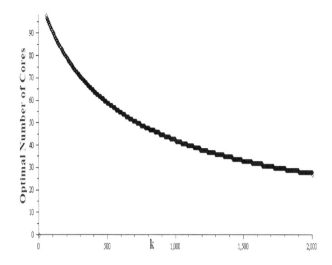

Figure 7: **Sensitivity analysis: optimal number of cores on Y axis, and k (ratio of the energy consumed for single memory accesses and the energy consumed for executing a single instruction at the maximum frequency) on X axis with input size $N = 10^8$ and $M_c = 500$.**

same for the entire range of the input values plotted (10^7 to 10^9). Note that this structure of the sensitivity curve is very different from that of the parallel addition algorithm. Looking at the energy and the sensitivity curves, we conjecture that the asymptotic nature of the required metric is quite different for both the algorithms.

6.2 Parallel Merge Sort

We consider a pipelined *d-way mergesort algorithm* developed by Lars Arge et al. for the PEM model [3]. It is similar to the sorting algorithm of Goodrich [12].

A d-way mergesort partitions the input into d subsets, sorts each subset recursively and then merges them. To achieve optimal parallel speedup, the sorted subsets are sampled and these sample sets are merged first. Each level of the recursion is performed in multiple rounds with each round producing progressively finer samples until eventually a list of samples is the whole sorted subset of the corresponding level of recursion. The samples retain information about the relative order of the other elements of the set through rankings. These rankings allow for a quick merge of future finer samples at higher levels of recursion. Each round is pipelined up the recursion tree to maximize parallelism (see [3] for details).

THEOREM 1. *(Lars Arge et al. [3]) Given a set S of N items stored contiguously in memory, one can sort S in CREW PEM model using $P \leq N/B^2$ processors each having a private cache of size $M = B^{O(1)}$ in $O(\frac{N}{P \cdot B} \log_{\frac{M}{B}} \frac{N}{B})$ parallel memory accesses, $O(\frac{N}{P} \log N)$ internal computational complexity per processor and $O(N)$ total memory.* $\square$

Recall that the best known sequential algorithm for the mergesort algorithm in the *external memory model* (EM) takes $O(\frac{N}{B} \log_{\frac{M}{B}} \frac{N}{B})$ memory accesses and $O(N \log N)$ computational steps [2]. Considering the assumptions of Theorem 1, we now evaluate energy scalability under iso-performance

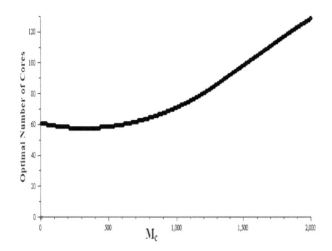

Figure 8: Sensitivity analysis: optimal number of cores on Y axis, and k (no of cycles executed at maximum frequency for single memory accesses time) on X axis with input size $N = 10^8$ and $k = 500$.

of the parallel mergesort algorithm assuming the required performance to be that of the sequential algorithm. Since all cores are active until the end of the computation, the critical path of the algorithm is the execution sequence on any one of the cores. By Theorem 1, critical path comprises of $O(\frac{N}{P \cdot B} \log_{\frac{M}{B}} \frac{N}{B})$ memory accesses and $O(\frac{N}{P} \log N)$ computation steps (step 2). Note that reduced frequency at which all P cores should run to complete in time T_{seq} decreases with P.

Since each core performs an equal amount of computation, the total number of computational cycles of the parallel algorithm is $O(N \log(N))$ (not dependent on P). Thus by Equation 3, the energy consumed for computation E_{comp} by the algorithm decreases with P. However, since the total number of memory accesses at all P cores is $O(\frac{N}{B} \log_{\frac{M}{B}} \frac{N}{B})$ (also not dependent on P), the energy consumed for memory accesses E_{mem} does not vary with increasing cores. Further, by Equation 4, the leakage energy E_{leak} dissipated at the cores running at the reduced frequency also decreases with P. Using the above three observations, we see that the energy consumed by the parallel algorithm to maintain the same performance as the sequential algorithm decreases with increasing cores under the restriction $P \leq N/B^2$. One could easily generalize the above observation to a general class of parallel algorithms which pocesses optimal computational cost and optimal I/O complexity.

7. CONCLUSIONS

Our analysis confirms that energy and performance characterisics of algorithms on shared memory multicore architectures differ considerably from each other. While the analysis we presented is limited to a few parallel algorithms, these algorithms are very different in nature. Moreover, for purposes of interpreting our results concretely, we fixed some values of parameters for values of relative computation versus memory access time and energy required. These values will vary depending on the architecture. Interestingly, the analysis is fairly robust over a wide range of parameter val-

ues. However, some of our simplifying assumptions, such as constant time and energy for a memory access, will not hold as we scale up the architecture. However, we do not believe it is necessarily useful to consider more complicated models for shared memory architectures, given that shared memory architectures are themselves not scalable [22].

We observe that the performance and energy behavior of algorithms in the shared memory model we use is significantly different from the behavior of comparable algorithms in message-passing architectures (see used our earlier analysis for message-passing architectures [15]). This is because in our current work, we model communication as well as local accesses through a hierarchical shared memory. In fact, the results in this paper would be similar if we were to replace communication through shared memory with message passing, while modeling the local memory hierarchy at each core.

Because the energy expressions are rather complicated, it is not straight-forward to obtain the asymptotic energy scalability under iso-performance for many algorithms. However, because of memory bottlenecks, as we observed earlier, shared memory multicore architectures cannot scale arbitrarily [22]. Thus an asymptotic analysis would not necessarily be very insightful.

A variant of our analysis would tell us how to maximize *energy efficiency* (i.e., performance/energy ratio), or some related utility functions, by changing the number and frequency at which the cores operate. We believe parallel applications in mobile multicore devices may benefit from this type of an analysis.

Acknowledgments

The authors would like thank Soumya Krishnamurthy (Intel) for motivating us to look at this problem. We would also like to thank George Goodman and Bob Kuhn (Intel), and MyungJoo Ham (Illinois) for helpful feedback and comments.

8. REFERENCES

[1] http://www.greenpeace.org/raw/content/ international/press/reports/make-it-green-cloud-computing.pdf. *Greenpeace International*, 2010.

[2] A. Aggarwal and S. Vitter, Jeffrey. The input/output complexity of sorting and related problems. *Communications of ACM*, 31(9):1116–1127, 1988.

[3] L. Arge, M. T. Goodrich, M. J. Nelson, and N. Sitchinava. Fundamental parallel algorithms for private-cache chip multiprocessors. In *SPAA*, pages 197–206, 2008.

[4] M. A. Bender, J. T. Fineman, S. Gilbert, and B. C. Kuszmaul. Concurrent cache-oblivious b-trees. In *SPAA*, pages 228–237, 2005.

[5] B. D. Bingham and M. R. Greenstreet. Computation with energy-time trade-offs: Models, algorithms and lower-bounds. In *ISPA*, pages 143–152, 2008.

[6] G. E. Blelloch, R. A. Chowdhury, P. B. Gibbons, V. Ramachandran, S. Chen, and M. Kozuch. Provably good multicore cache performance for divide-and-conquer algorithms. In *SODA*, pages 501–510, 2008.

[7] A. Chandrakasan, S. Sheng, and R. Brodersen. Low-power cmos digital design. *IEEE Journal of Solid-State Circuits*, 27(4):473–484, 1992.

[8] S. Cho and R. Melhem. Corollaries to Amdahl's Law for Energy. *Computer Architecture Letters*, 7(1):25–28, 2008.

[9] M. Curtis-Maury, A. Shah, F. Blagojevic, D. Nikolopoulos, B. de Supinski, and M. Schulz. Prediction Models for Multi-dimensional Power-Performance Optimization on Many Cores. In *International Conference on Parallel architectures and compilation techniques*, pages 250–259, 2008.

[10] R. Ge, X. Feng, and K. Cameron. Performance-Constrained Distributed DVS Scheduling for Scientific Applications on Power-Aware Clusters. In *International Conference on Supercomputing*. IEEE Computer Society Washington, DC, USA, 2005.

[11] R. Gonzalez and M. A. Horowitz. Energy dissipation in general purpose microprocessors. *IEEE Journal of Solid-State Circuits*, 31:1277Ű1284, 1995.

[12] M. T. Goodrich. Communication-efficient parallel sorting. *SIAM Journal of Computing*, 29(2):416–432, 1999.

[13] C. Isci, A. Buyuktosunoglu, C. Cher, P. Bose, and M. Martonosi. An Analysis of Efficient Multi-Core Global Power Management Policies: Maximizing Performance for a Given Power Budget. In *International Symposium on Microarchitecture*, volume 9, pages 347–358, 2006.

[14] R. M. Karp and V. Ramachandran. Parallel algorithms for shared-memory machines. *Handbook of Theoretical Computer Science (vol. A): Algorithms and Complexity*, pages 869–941, 1990.

[15] V. A. Korthikanti and G. Agha. Analysis of parallel algorithms for energy conservation in scalable multicore architectures. In *ICPP*, pages 212–219, 2009.

[16] V. Kumar, A. Grama, A. Gupta, and G. Karypis. *Introduction to Parallel Computing: Design and Analysis of Algorithms*. Benjamin-Cummings Publishing Co., Inc. Redwood City, CA, USA, 1994.

[17] R. E. Ladner and M. J. Fischer. Parallel prefix computation. *ACM Journal*, 27(4):831–838, 1980.

[18] J. Li and J. Martinez. Power-Performance Considerations of Parallel Computing on Chip Multiprocessors. *ACM Transactions on Architecture and Code Optimization*, 2(4):1–25, 2005.

[19] J. Li and J. Martinez. Dynamic Power-Performance Adaptation of Parallel Computation on Chip Multiprocessors. In *International Symposium on High-Performance Computer Architecture*, pages 77–87, 2006.

[20] A. J. Martin. Towards an energy complexity of computation. *Information Processing Letters*, 39:181Ű187, 2001.

[21] M. P. Mills. The internet begins with coal. *Green Earth Society, USA*, 1999.

[22] R. Murphy. On the effects of memory latency and bandwidth on supercomputer application performance. *IEEE International Symposium on Workload Characterization*, pages 35–43, Sept. 2007.

[23] S. Park, W. Jiang, Y. Zhou, and S. Adve. Managing Energy-Performance Tradeoffs for Multithreaded Applications on Multiprocessor Architectures. In *ACM SIGMETRICS International Conference on Measurement and Modeling of Computer Systems*, pages 169–180. ACM New York, NY, USA, 2007.

[24] X. Wang and S. Ziavras. Performance-Energy Tradeoffs for Matrix Multiplication on FPGA-Based Mixed-Mode Chip Multiprocessors. In *International Symposium on Quality Electronic Design*, pages 386–391, 2007.

Computing the Throughput of Probabilistic and Replicated Streaming Applications*

Anne Benoit, Fanny Dufossé,
Matthieu Gallet and Yves Robert
ENS Lyon
Lyon, France
{Anne.Benoit | Fanny.Dufosse |
Matthieu.Gallet |
Yves.Robert}@ens-lyon.fr

Bruno Gaujal
LIG, INRIA
Grenoble, France
Bruno.Gaujal@imag.fr

ABSTRACT

In this paper, we investigate how to compute the throughput of probabilistic and replicated streaming applications. We are given (i) a streaming application whose dependence graph is a linear chain; (ii) a one-to-many mapping of the application onto a fully heterogeneous target, where a processor is assigned at most one application stage, but where a stage can be replicated onto a set of processors; and (iii) a set of I.I.D. (Independent and Identically-Distributed) variables to model each computation and communication time in the mapping. How can we compute the throughput of the application, i.e., the rate at which data sets can be processed? We consider two execution models, the **Strict** model where the actions of each processor are sequentialized, and the **Overlap** model where a processor can compute and communicate in parallel. The problem is easy when application stages are not replicated, i.e., assigned to a single processor: in that case the throughput is dictated by the critical hardware resource. However, when stages are replicated, i.e., assigned to several processors, the problem becomes surprisingly complicated: even in the deterministic case, the optimal throughput may be lower than the smallest internal resource throughput. To the best of our knowledge, the problem has never been considered in the probabilistic case. The first main contribution of the paper is to provide a general method (although of exponential cost) to compute the throughput when mapping parameters follow I.I.D. exponential laws. This general method is based upon the analysis of timed Petri nets deduced from the application mapping; it turns out that these Petri nets exhibit a regular structure in the **Overlap** model, thereby enabling to reduce the cost and provide a polynomial algorithm. The second main contribution of the paper is to provide bounds for the throughput when stage parameters are arbitrary I.I.D. and N.B.U.E. (New Better than Used in Expectation) variables: the throughput is bounded from below by the exponential case and bounded from above by the deterministic case.

Categories and Subject Descriptors

F.2.0 [**Theory of Computation**]: Analysis of Algorithms and Problem Complexity—*General*

General Terms

Algorithms, Theory, Performance

Keywords

scheduling, probabilistic streaming applications, replication, throughput, timed Petri nets

1. INTRODUCTION

In this paper, we deal with streaming applications, or *workflows*, whose dependence graph is a linear chain composed of several stages. Such applications operate on a collection of data sets that are executed in a pipeline fashion [16, 15, 19]. They are a popular programming paradigm for streaming applications like video and audio encoding and decoding, DSP applications, etc [7, 18, 21]. Each data set is input to the linear chain and traverses it until its processing is complete. While the first data sets are still being processed by the last stages of the pipeline, the following ones have started their execution. In steady state, a new data set enters the system every $\mathcal{P}$ time-units, and several data sets are processed concurrently within the system. A key criterion to optimize is the *period*, or equivalently its inverse, the *throughput*. The period $\mathcal{P}$ is defined as the time interval between the completion of two consecutive data sets. The system can process data sets at a rate $\rho = 1/\mathcal{P}$, where ρ is the throughput.

The application is executed on a fully heterogeneous platform, whose processors have different speeds, and whose interconnection links have different bandwidths. We assume that the mapping of the application onto the platform is given, and that this mapping is one-to-many. In other words, when mapping application stages onto processors, we enforce the rule that any given processor will execute at most one stage. However, a given stage may well be executed by several processors. Indeed, if the computations of a given stage are independent from one data set to another, then two consecutive computations (for different data sets) of the same stage can be mapped onto distinct processors. Such a stage is said to be *replicated*, using the terminology of Subhlok and Vondran [16, 17] and of the DataCutter team [5, 15, 20]. This also corresponds to the *dealable* stages of Cole [6]. Finally, we consider two execution models, the **Strict** model where the actions of each processor are sequentialized, and the **Overlap** model where a processor can process a data set while it is simultaneously sending the previous data set to its successor and receiving the next data set.

The major novelty of the paper is to introduce randomness in the execution of the application onto the platform. Consider the computations performed by a given processor on different data-sets: we assume that the execution times of the computations are random variables that obey arbitrary I.I.D. (Independent and Identically-Distributed) probability laws. Similarly, we assume that the execution times of all the communications taking place on a given interconnection link are random variables that obey arbitrary I.I.D. probability laws. Note that the I.I.D. hypothesis apply to all events (computations or communications) that occur on the same hardware resource (either a processor or a communication link), and does not restrict the heterogeneity of the application/platform mapping. In other words, processors may well have different speeds, links may well have different bandwidths, stages may well have very different computation and data volumes; furthermore, the distribution law may well vary from one computation to another, or from one communication to another. To the best of our knowledge, this paper is the first attempt to compute the throughput of a mapping whose parameters obey probability distribution laws.

In the deterministic case, and without replication, the throughput of a given mapping is easily seen to be dictated by the critical hardware resource: the period is the largest cycle-time of any resource, be it a processor or communication link. However, when stages are replicated, the problem becomes surprisingly complicated: even in the deterministic case, the optimal throughput may be lower than the smallest internal resource throughput. This result was shown in [3], using a representation of the mapping based on timed Petri nets. In this paper we build upon the latter construction to tackle the probabilistic case.

The first main contribution is to provide a general method (although of exponential cost) to compute the throughput when mapping parameters follow I.I.D. exponential laws. This general method is based upon the detailed analysis of the timed Petri nets deduced from the application mapping for each execution model, **Strict** and **Overlap**. It turns out that the Petri nets exhibit a regular structure in the **Overlap** model, thereby enabling to reduce the cost and provide a polynomial algorithm. The second main contribution of the paper is to provide bounds for the throughput when stage parameters are arbitrary I.I.D. and N.B.U.E. (New Better than Used in Expectation) variables: the throughput is bounded from below by the exponential case and bounded from above by the deterministic case.

Our last contribution departs from the main trend of the paper and deals with the problem of determining the optimal mapping, i.e., the one-to-many mapping that optimizes the throughput. Indeed, the optimal mapping could enjoy a particular structure that renders the computation of the throughput easier than for an arbitrary given mapping. It could even be polynomial for arbitrary laws and both the **Strict** and **Overlap** models! We prove that this is in fact not the case: determining the optimal mapping is NP-complete, even in the deterministic case and without any communication cost (hence for both models).

The paper is organized as follows. First in Section 2, we formally describe the framework and the optimization problems, and we introduce the random variables that are used for the probabilistic study. Then we explain how to compute the throughput when communication and computation times follow I.I.D. exponential laws (Section 3). We give a general method which turns out to be of exponential complexity in the general case, but we provide a polynomial algorithm for the **Overlap** model. Then in Section 4, we deal with arbitrary I.I.D. and N.B.U.E. laws, and we establish the

above-mentioned bounds on the throughput. We assess the NP-completeness of the mapping optimization problem in Section 5. Finally, we present some conclusions and directions for future work in Section 6.

2. MODELS

In this section, we first describe the workflow application, the target platform, and the communication models that we consider (Section 2.1). The replication model is presented in Section 2.2.

Before moving to the probabilistic study, we recall existing results for the deterministic case in Section 2.3. Finally, we give a detailed presentation of the random variables that we consider to model processor speeds and link bandwidths (Section 2.4).

2.1 Application, platform and communication models

We deal with streaming applications, or *workflows*, whose dependence graph is a linear chain composed of N stages, called T_i ($1 \leq i \leq N$). Each stage T_i has a size w_i, expressed in flop, and needs an input file F_{i-1} of size δ_{i-1}, expressed in bytes. Finally, T_i produces an output file F_i of size δ_i, which is the input file of stage T_{i+1}. All these sizes are independent of the data set. Note that T_1 produces the initial data and does not receive any input file, while T_N gathers the final data.

The workflow is executed on a fully heterogeneous platform with M processors. The speed of processor P_p ($1 \leq p \leq M$) is denoted as s_p (in flops). We assume bidirectional links $\text{link}_{p,q} : P_p \rightarrow P_q$ between any processor pair P_p and P_q, with bandwidth $b_{p,q}$ bytes per second. These links are not necessarily physical, they can be logical. For instance, we can have a physical star-shaped platform, where all processors are linked to each other through a central switch. The time needed to transfer a file F_i from P_p to P_q is $\frac{\delta_i}{b_{p,q}}$, while the time needed to process T_i on P_p is $\frac{w_i}{s_p}$. An example of linear chain application and fully connected target platform is provided in Figure 1.

We consider two different realistic common models for communications. The **Overlap** model allows to overlap communications and computations: a processor can simultaneously receive values for the next data set, compute result for the current data set, and send output data for the previous data set. Requiring multi-threaded programs and full-duplex network interfaces, this model allows for a better use of computational resources. On the contrary, in the **Strict** model, there is no overlap of communications by computations: a processor can either receive a given set of data, compute its result or send this result. This is the typical execution of a single-threaded program, with one-port serialized communications. Although leading to a less efficient use of physical resources, this model allows for simpler programs and hardware.

2.2 Replication model

When mapping application stages onto processors, we enforce the rule that any given processor will execute at most one stage. But instead of considering *one-to-one mappings* [4], we allow stage replication, and rather consider one-to-many mappings, in which each stage can be processed by several processors. This is possible when the computations of a given stage are independent from one data set to another. In this case, two consecutive computations (different data sets) for the same stage can be mapped onto distinct processors. Such a stage is said to be *replicated* [16, 17, 5, 15, 20] or *dealable* [6].

Note that the computations of a replicated stage can be fully sequential for a given data set, what matters is that they do not depend upon results for previous data sets, hence the possibility to process different data sets in different locations. The following scheme illustrates the replication of a stage T_i onto three processors:

$$\ldots T_{i-1} \begin{array}{c} \diagup \\ -- \\ \diagdown \end{array} \begin{array}{l} T_i \text{ on } P_1: \text{ data sets } \mathbf{1,4,7,\ldots} \\ T_i \text{ on } P_2: \text{ data sets } \mathbf{2,5,8,\ldots} \\ T_i \text{ on } P_3: \text{ data sets } \mathbf{3,6,9,\ldots} \end{array} \begin{array}{c} \diagdown \\ -- \\ \diagup \end{array} T_{i+1} \ldots$$

For $1 \leq i \leq N$, let R_i denote the number of processors participating to the processing of T_i. For $1 \leq p \leq M$, if P_p participates to the work of T_i, then we write $p \in Team_i$ and define $R'_p = R_i$. As outlined in the scheme, the processors allocated to a replicated stage execute successive data sets in a round-robin fashion. This may lead to a load imbalance: more data sets could be allocated to faster processors. But this would imply out-of-order execution and would require a complicated data management if, say, a replicated stage is followed by a non-replicated one in the application pipeline. In particular, large buffers would be required to ensure the in-order execution on the non-replicated stage. This explains why round-robin execution has been enforced in all the papers referenced above, and we enforce this rule too.

Because of the round-robin rule, the execution of a replicated stage is slowed down by the slowest processor involved in the round-robin. Let P_{slow} be the slowest processor involved in the replication of T_i. Then, if $p \in Team_i$, P_p processes one data set every R_i data sets at the speed dictated by P_{slow}, and thus its computation time (per data set) is $C_{\text{comp}}(p) = \frac{w_i}{R_i \times s_{slow}}$. Note that this implies that if processors of different speeds are processing a same stage, some of them will remain partly idle during the execution.

2.3 Computing the throughput in the deterministic case

The throughput ρ is defined as the average number of data sets which can be processed within one time unit. Equivalently, we aim at minimizing the period $\mathcal{P}$, which is the inverse of the throughput and corresponds to the time-interval that separates two consecutive data sets entering the system. We can derive a lower bound for the period as follows. Let $C_{\text{exec}}(p)$ be the cycle-time of processor P_p. If we enforce the **Overlap** model, then $C_{\text{exec}}(p)$ is equal to the maximum of its reception time $C_{\text{in}}(p)$, its computation time $C_{\text{comp}}(p)$, and its transmission time $C_{\text{out}}(p)$: $C_{\text{exec}}(p) = \max \{C_{\text{in}}(p), C_{\text{comp}}(p), C_{\text{out}}(p)\}$. If we enforce the **Strict** model, then $C_{\text{exec}}(p)$ is equal to the sum of the three operations: $C_{\text{exec}}(p) = C_{\text{in}}(p) + C_{\text{comp}}(p) + C_{\text{out}}(p)$. Note that in both models, the maximum cycle-time, $\mathcal{M}_{\text{ct}} = \max_{1 \leq p \leq M} C_{\text{exec}}(p)$, is a lower bound for the period.

If no stage is replicated, then the throughput is simply determined by the critical resource (maximum cycle-time): $\rho = 1/\mathcal{M}_{\text{ct}}$. However, when stages are replicated, the previous result is no longer true, and more sophisticated techniques are required. Here are the main results that we established previously in [3]:

- Model **Overlap**: the throughput can be determined in polynomial time.
- Model **Strict**: determining the complexity of this problem remains an open question. However, the throughput can be computed in time $O\left(\text{lcm}_{1 \leq i \leq N}(R_i)^3\right)$, a possibly exponential resolution time.

In the following, we investigate how to compute the throughput when execution and communication times are subject to random variations.

2.4 Random variables

We consider in the following that the time to execute a stage, and the time to transfer data, are random variables. Thus, in the deter-

ministic case, we can denote the n-th computation time of stage T_i on processor P_p by $c_p = w_i/s_p$. Similarly, the n-th communication time of the file F_i sent by P_p to P_q is given by $d_{p,q} = \delta_i/b_{p,q}$.

Let $X_p(n)$ be the random variable giving the actual computation time of the n-th data set processed by P_p, where $p \in Team_i$ (recall that each processor deals with only one stage). In the deterministic case, we have $X_p(n) = w_i/s_p$ for all n, but in the probabilistic setting the $X_p(n)$ will be random variables obeying I.I.D. laws. Similarly, let $Y_{p,q}(n)$ be the random variable giving the actual communication time of the n-th file of type F_i transferred from P_p to P_q, where $p \in Team_i$ and $q \in Team_{i+1}$. In the deterministic case, we have $Y_{p,q}(n) = \delta_i/b_{p,q}$ for all n. Again, in the probabilistic setting, the $Y_{p,q}(n)$ will be random variables obeying I.I.D. laws. Finally, we let (X, Y) denote the mapping of an application $(T_1, \ldots, T_N)$ on a platform $(P_1, \ldots, P_M)$.

The probability that the computation time of T_i on P_p is larger than x is given by $\Pr(X_p(n) > x)$, while its expected value is given by $\mathbf{E}[X_p(n)]$. This definition is general and does not imply any special constraint on the involved random variables. However, some of our results are only valid for specific classes of random variables. Below we recall the definition of these specific classes:

Exponential variables. An important class of random variables is the one of variables with exponential distribution. The probability that an exponential random variable X with a rate λ is larger than t is given by $\Pr(X > t) = e^{-\lambda t}$.

New Better than Used in Expectation variables. A random variable X is said to have a N.B.U.E. distribution if, and only if, $\mathbf{E}[X - t | X > t] \leq \mathbf{E}[X]$, for all $t > 0$. In other words, the N.B.U.E. assumption for communication or computation times means that if a computation (or a communication) has already been processed for a duration t and it is not finished yet, then the remaining time is smaller than the processing time of a fresh operation. This assumption is often true since in most cases, a partial execution of a stage should not increase the remaining work, especially when the amount of computation and communication are bounded from above. Note that exponential variables have the N.B.U.E. property, with equality in that case ($\mathbf{E}[X - t | X > t] = \mathbf{E}[X]$, for all $t > 0$). Also, note that there exist many statistical procedures to test if a random variable is N.B.U.E. ([14]).

Independent and identically-distributed variables. A collection of random variables is said to be independent and identically-distributed (I.I.D.) if each random variable has the same probability distribution as the others and all variables are mutually independent. This assumption will hold true throughout the paper: processing times $\{X_p(n)\}_{1 \leq p \leq M, n \in \mathbb{N}}$ and communication times $\{Y_{p,q}(n)\}_{1 \leq p,q \leq M, n \in \mathbb{N}}$ always are independent I.I.D. sequences. Thus, we assume that the amount of work is independent from the amount of data. For example, this is the case when data are compressed (and dependent of the data content), while the running time of the algorithm are dependent of he original data size.

3. COMPUTING THE THROUGHPUT WITH EXPONENTIAL LAWS

In this section, we consider the case of exponential laws: all processing times and communication times are exponentially distributed. In the corresponding Petri net, all transitions (modeling processing times or modeling communication times) have exponential firing times. The probability of the firing time t_i of a transition is given by $\Pr(t_i > x) = 1 - e^{-\lambda_i x}$. The firing rate λ_i corresponds either to the processing rate of one processor or the communication rate over one link.

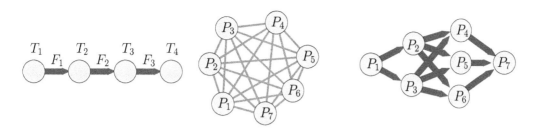

Figure 1: Example A: Four-stage pipeline, seven-processor computing platform, mapping with replication.

The study of the exponential case is motivated by two facts. First, one can get explicit formulas in this case. Second (as we will see in Section 4), exponential laws are extreme cases among all N.B.U.E. variables.

In the rest of this section, we first recall the design principles of the timed Petri net model (Section 3.1). Then in Section 3.2, we explain the general method which allows us to compute the throughput for both the **Overlap** and the **Strict** models. However, this general method has a high complexity. In the **Overlap** case, we provide a simpler method, building upon the relative simplicity of the timed Petri net (Section 3.3). Finally in Section 3.4, we derive a polynomial algorithm for the **Overlap** case when we further assume that the communication network is homogeneous.

3.1 Timed Petri nets

As in [3], we model the system formed by a given mapping (of an application onto a platform) by a timed Petri net. Here we briefly recall design principles:

- any path followed by the input data sets is fully developed into the timed Petri net (as a row); there are $\text{lcm}_{1 \leq i \leq N}(R_i)$ such rows;
- any computation or communication is represented by a transition, whose firing time is the same as the computation time (respectively communication time); it appears on a column of the timed Petri net, which has $2N - 1$ columns;
- dependencies between two successive operations are represented by places between the transitions corresponding to these operations.

The complete timed Petri nets representing Example A (Figure 1) with the **Overlap** and **Strict** models are shown in Figure 2. There are four processing stages, thus three communications and a total of seven columns. Dependences between a computation and the following communication are denoted by (A), between a communication and a computation by (B), dependences due to the round-robin distribution of computations by (C), and those due to the round-robin distribution of communications by (D). In the example, stages 1 and 4 are not replicated, while T_2 (resp. T_3) is replicated onto two (resp. three) processors, as depicted in Figure 1. There are thus $2 \times 3 = 6$ rows in both Petri nets. The dependencies depend upon the model (**Overlap** or **Strict**), and they enforce the round-robin distribution of data sets. Note that in all cases, the timed Petri net is an event graph (each place has a single input transition and a single output transition).

3.2 General method to compute the throughput

THEOREM 1. *Let us consider the system (X, Y) formed by the mapping of an application onto a platform. Then the throughput can be computed in time $O\left(\exp(\text{lcm}_{1 \leq i \leq N}(R_i))^3\right)$.*

PROOF. First, we present the main steps of the complete proof:
1. model the system by a timed Petri net;
2. transform this timed Petri net into a Markov chain;
3. compute the stationary measure of this Markov chain;
4. derive the throughput from the marginals of the stationary measure.

Model the system as a timed Petri net.

As said before, the transformation of the initial system into a timed Petri net is fully described in [3] and we do not detail it entirely here. Recall from Section 3.1 that it consists in $R = \text{lcm}_{1 \leq i \leq N}(R_i)$ rows and $2N - 1$ columns, and examples for both models are depicted in Figure 2. This step is done in time $O(RN)$, and the expectation of the delay between two successive firings of any transition gives the throughput of the system.

Transformation of the timed Petri net into a Markov chain.

To compute the expectation of the delay between two successive firings of any transition, we transform the above timed Petri net into a Markov chain $(Z_1, Z_2, \ldots)$. To each possible marking of the timed Petri net, we associate a state x_i. There are $(2N + 3(N - 1))R$ places, and each place contains either zero or one token. Thus, there are at most $2^{(2N+3(N-1))R}$ possible different markings, leading to the same number of states in the Markov chain.

Due to the exponential size of the number of states of the Markov chain, we only consider the part of the timed Petri net corresponding to communications in examples. This part is shown in Figure 3.

On Example A, places are named $(\mathcal{P}_1, \mathcal{P}_2, \mathcal{P}_3, \mathcal{P}_4, \mathcal{P}_5, \mathcal{P}_6, \mathcal{P}_7, \mathcal{P}_8, \mathcal{P}_9, \mathcal{P}_{10}, \mathcal{P}_{11}, \mathcal{P}_{12})$, while transitions are named (a, b, c, d, e, f). Thus, a state is defined by a 12-uple, each number equal to either 0 or 1 being the number of tokens in the place. In the Markov chain, moving from a state to another corresponds to the firing of a transition of the timed Petri net. Thus, arrows in the graphical representation of the Markov chain are labeled with the names of the transitions. The complete list of possible states and the corresponding transitions are given in Figure 4.

If in state x_i, transition $\mathcal{T}_j$ can be fired leading to state x_k, then the transition rate of the corresponding arrow is set to λ_j.

Computation of the throughput.

Using this new representation, we are able to compute the throughput. The throughput is the number of completed last stage T_N per time unit. In terms of Petri nets, this is also the expected number of firings per time unit of the transitions in the last column. Thus, in terms of Markov chains, the throughput is given by the probability of being in one of the states enabling these transitions. By construction of the Markov chain, all of its states are positive recurrent. Thus, it admits a stationary distribution, giving the probability

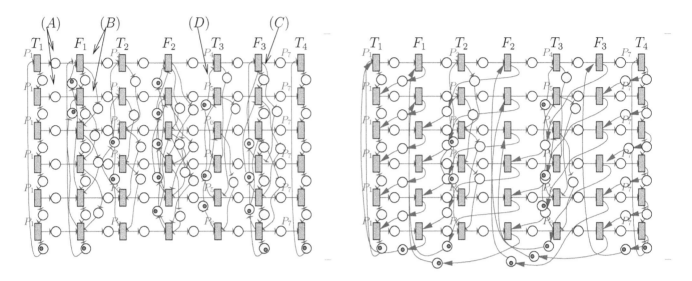

Figure 2: Timed Petri net representing Example A, Overlap and Strict model.

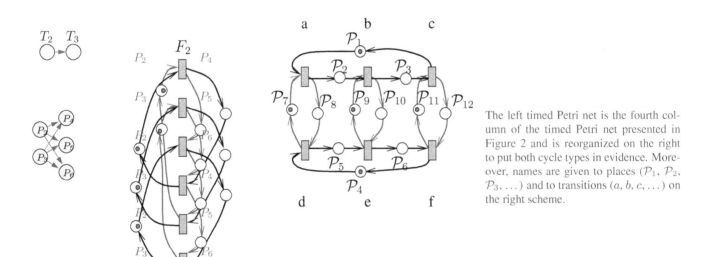

The left timed Petri net is the fourth column of the timed Petri net presented in Figure 2 and is reorganized on the right to put both cycle types in evidence. Moreover, names are given to places ($\mathcal{P}_1$, $\mathcal{P}_2$, $\mathcal{P}_3$, ...) and to transitions ($a, b, c, ...$) on the right scheme.

Figure 3: Example A: Part of the timed Petri net corresponding to communication F_2.

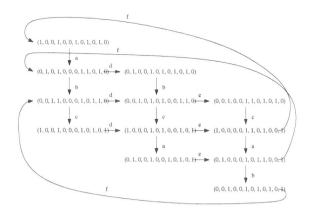

Figure 4: List of all possible states of the Markov chain corresponding to the reduced timed Petri net of Example A.

of each state. This stationary distribution can be computed in polynomial time in the size of the Markov chain by solving a linear system [10]. The sum of the probability of the valid states returns the throughput.

□

3.3 Overlap **model**

We now focus on the **Overlap** model. As in the deterministic case, constraints applying to our system form a very regular timed Petri net which is feed forward (dependencies only from column C_i to column C_{i+1}, for $1 \leq i \leq 2N - 2$), giving an easier problem than the **Strict** model.

THEOREM 2. *Let us consider the system (X, Y) formed by the mapping of an application onto a platform, following the* **Overlap** *communication model. Then the throughput can be computed in time $O\left(N \exp(\max_{1 \leq i \leq N}(R_i))\right)$.*

PROOF. First, let us give the overall structure of the proof:

1. split the timed Petri net into columns C_i, with $1 \leq i \leq 2N - 1$;
2. separately consider each column C_i;
3. separately consider each connected component D_j of C_i;
4. note that each component D_j is made of many copies of the same pattern $\mathcal{P}_j$, of size $u_j \times v_j$;
5. transform $\mathcal{P}_j$ into a Markov chain $\mathcal{M}_j$;
6. determine a stationary measure of $\mathcal{M}_j$, using a combinatorial trick based on Young diagrams [13];
7. compute the throughput of $\mathcal{P}_j$ in isolation (called hereinafter inner throughput of component D_j in the following);
8. combine the inner throughputs of all components to get the global throughput of the system.

To decrease the overall complexity, we use the same idea as in [3]: thanks to the regularity of the global timed Petri net, we split it into a polynomial number of columns, and we compute the throughput of each column independently.

Let us focus on a single column. We have two cases to consider: (i) the column corresponds to the computation of a single processor (columns C_{2i-1}, for $1 \leq i \leq N$); (ii) the column corresponds to communications between two sets of processors (columns C_{2i}, for $1 \leq i \leq N - 1$).

In case (i), cycles do not interfere: any cycle involves a single processor, and any processor belongs to exactly one cycle. Thus, the inner throughput is easily computed, this is the expectation of

the number of firings per time unit. The processing time $X_p(n)$ being exponential, this is equal to the rate λ_p of X_p.

On the contrary, case (ii) is more complex and requires a more detailed study. Let us consider the i-th communication (it corresponds to column C_{2i}): it involves R_i senders and R_{i+1} receivers. We know from its structure that the timed Petri net is made of $g = \gcd(R_i, R_{i+1})$ connected components (see [3] for further details). Let u_j be equal to R_i/g and v_j be equal to R_{i+1}/g. Then each connected component D_j in this column is made of $c = \frac{R}{\text{lcm}(R_i, R_{i+1})}$ copies of a pattern $\mathcal{P}_j$ of size $u_j \times v_j$. Since these components are independent, we can compute the throughput of each of them independently. In the case of Example B presented in Figure 5, we consider a 4-stage application, such that stages are replicated on respectively 5, 21, 27 and 11 processors. More precisely, we focus on the second communication, involving 21 senders and 27 receivers. In this case, we have $g = 3$ connected components, made of 55 copies of pattern $\mathcal{P}_j$ of size $u_j \times v_j = 9 \times 7$.

Each pattern is a timed Petri net $\mathcal{P}_j$ with a very regular structure, which can be represented as a rectangle of size (u_j, v_j), also denoted (u, v) to ease notations, as shown in Figure 5. As said before, determining the throughput of $\mathcal{P}$ is equivalent to determining a stationary measure of a Markov chain. We know that the stationary measure of a Markov chain with t states can be computed in time $O\left(t^3\right)$ [10]. Thus, we need to determine the number of states of the transformation of $\mathcal{P}_j$ into a Markov chain. Let $\mathcal{M}_j$ be this Markov chain.

The number of states of $\mathcal{M}_j$ is by definition the number of possible markings, and we can directly determine it. A valid marking of $\mathcal{P}_j$ of Figure 5 is represented in Figure 6. The regularity of the structure imposes some constraints to valid markings: a transition can be fired for the k-th time if, and only if, all the transitions above it or on its left have been fired k times. In other terms, if a processor sends a file to q receivers $P_1, \ldots, P_q$, it can send the k-th instance of the file to P_i if and only if it has sent the k first instances of the file to $P_1, \ldots, P_{i-1}$.

In our rectangular representation of the timed Petri net, the borderline between transitions that have been fired $k + 1$ times and those that have been fired k times is the union of two Young diagrams, as displayed on Figure 6. Since there is only a single token in each column and in each row, we cannot have three simultaneous Young diagrams.

Let us compute the number of states of the Markov chain $\mathcal{M}_j$. As said in the previous paragraph, the borderline can be seen as two Young diagrams, or two paths. The first one is from coordinates $(i, 0)$ to $(0, j)$, and the second one goes from (u, j) to (i, v) (see Figure 7). If i and j are given, then there are $\alpha_{i,j} = \begin{pmatrix} i + j \\ i \end{pmatrix}$ possible paths from $(i, 0)$ to $(0, j)$, where $\begin{pmatrix} n \\ k \end{pmatrix}$ is equal to $\frac{n!}{k!(n-k)!}$. Similarly, there are $\alpha_{u-1-i, v-1-j}$ possible paths from (u, j) to (i, v). Thus, if i and j are given, then there are $\alpha_{i,j} \times \alpha_{u-1-i, v-1-j}$ possible markings. If i and j are not given anymore, then the total number $S(u, v)$ of valid markings can be easily determined:

$$
\begin{aligned}
S(u, v) &= \sum_{i=0}^{u-1} \sum_{j=0}^{v-1} \alpha_{i,j} \alpha_{u-1-i, v-1-j} \\
&= \sum_{i=0}^{u-1} \sum_{j=0}^{v-1} \begin{pmatrix} i + j \\ i \end{pmatrix} \begin{pmatrix} u + v - 2 - i - j \\ u - 1 - i \end{pmatrix} \\
&= \begin{pmatrix} u + v - 1 \\ u - 1 \end{pmatrix} v = \frac{(u+v-1)!}{(u-1)! v!} v.
\end{aligned}
$$

Thus, the final Markov chain of a single connected component

3 connected components

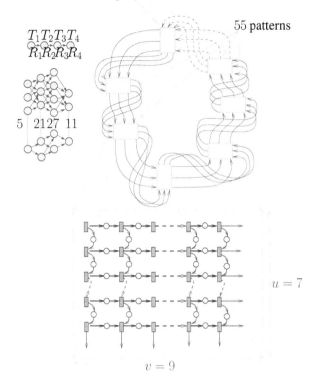

55 patterns

$u = 7$

$v = 9$

Figure 5: Example B, with stages replicated on 5, 21, 27 and 11 processors, and structure of the timed Petri net corresponding to the second communication.

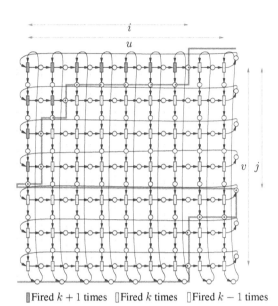

▮Fired $k + 1$ times   ▯Fired k times   ▯Fired $k - 1$ times

Figure 6: Valid marking of $\mathcal{P}_j$, the reduced timed Petri net of the second communication of Example B.

has exactly $S(u, v) = \frac{(u+v-1)!}{(u-1)!v!} v$ states, and its inner throughput can be computed in time $S(u, v)^3$.

Let us now come to the computation of the global throughput of the system. Actually, the throughput is given by the following iteration. The throughput of one strongly connected component is the minimum of its inner throughput and the throughput of all its input components, so once all inner throughputs are known, the computation of the throughput is linear in the number of components.

In column C_{2i}, we have $g = \gcd(R_i, R_{i+1})$ connected components so that the total computation time to obtain their throughput is equal to $gS(u, v)$. Since we have $S(gu, gv) \geq gS(u, v)$, $u = R_i/g$ and $v = R_{i+1}/g$, the total computation time to determine the throughput of C_{2i} is less than $S(R_i, R_{i+1})$.

Finally, the total computation time of the throughput is equal to $\sum_{i=1}^{N-1} S(R_i, R_{i+1})^3$, leading to our result of a throughput that can be computed in time $O\left(N \exp(\max_{1 \leq i \leq N}(R_i))^3\right)$.

□

3.4 Overlap model, homogeneous communication network

In the case where all the communication times in one column are all I.I.D., with the same rate in component D_j, denoted λ_j, then the inner throughput of each strongly connected component (i.e., the throughput of the component if isolated from the global timed Petri net) can be computed explicitly with a very simple formula. This reduces the overall computation of the throughput to

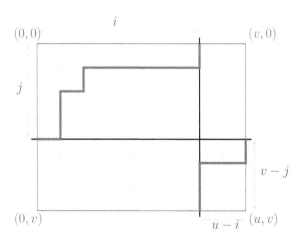

Figure 7: Representation with Young diagrams of a valid marking.

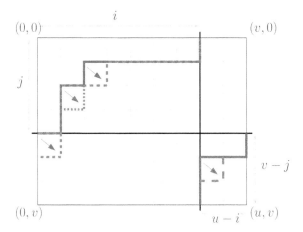

Figure 8: Reachable states from a given position.

a simple computation of minimums over the strongly connected components, which can be done in polynomial time.

THEOREM 3. *Let us consider the system (X, Y) formed by the mapping of an application onto a platform, following the **Overlap** communication model with a homogeneous communication network. Then the throughput can be computed in polynomial time.*

In the process of proving Theorem 3 (see companion research report [2]), we establish several interesting properties. First, we prove that the inner throughput of a processor component D_j is $\rho_j = \lambda_j$. Then, for a communication strongly connected component D_j, which is made of copies of a same pattern of size $u_j \times v_j$, we prove that its inner throughput is equal to $\rho_j = \frac{\lambda_j}{v_j + u_j - 1}$. This latter value, obtained in the exponential case, has to be compared with the throughput in the deterministic case where all communication times are deterministic ($1/\lambda_j$), which is equal to $\rho_j = \frac{\lambda_j}{\max(v_j, u_j)}$. The fact that the throughput in the exponential case is lower than the throughput in the deterministic case will be explained in Section 4. However, the fact that the throughput can be computed explicitly is much more unexpected, since such explicit formulas are known to be very hard to obtain, even for simple event graphs [1].

The global throughput can then be computed in polynomial time from all inner throughputs, and it is equal to:

$$\rho = \sum_{D_j \in C_{2N-1}} \min_{D_{j'} \prec D_j} \rho_{j'}, \quad (1)$$

where $D_{j'} \prec D_j$ means that there exists a path from component $D_{j'}$ to component D_j, or $D_{j'} = D_j$. Because of the structure of the timed Petri net, if $D_{j'}$ is in column $C_{i'}$ and D_j is in column C_i, then $i' < i$ or $j' = j$. The computation can thus be done column by column. For any component in the first column, its throughput must be equal to its inner throughput ρ_j. The computation for column i only depends on results from column $i - 1$ by construction of the Petri net. Moreover, the total number of components is polynomial in the number of processors M. We obtain therefore a polynomial complexity ($2N - 1$ columns in the timed Petri net, and a polynomial number of components).

The detailed proof of this theorem can be found in [2]. It starts similarly to the proof of Theorem 2, but the computation of inner throughputs is simplified, since we have explicit formulas in all cases (as explained above).

4. COMPARISON RESULTS IN CASE OF GENERAL I.I.D. VARIABLES

In the previous section, we have shown how to compute the throughput when all communication times and all processing times are exponential variables (and this even in polynomial time for the homogeneous **Overlap** case). In general, it is well known that the computation of the throughput is hard for arbitrary random communication times and processing times, even for very simple cases [12]. However, the fact that in our case, the throughput is an increasing and convex function of communication times and processing times implies that one can use stochastic comparisons to construct bounds on the throughput in the case where communication times and processing times are I.I.D. N.B.U.E. variables (see Section 4.1). Moreover, the lower and upper bounds are obtained by the deterministic and exponential cases respectively.

4.1 Theoretical comparison

DEFINITION 1. *Let $\{V(n)\}_{n \in \mathbb{N}}$ and $\{W(n)\}_{n \in \mathbb{N}}$ be two real random variable sequences:*
- *V is smaller than W for the strong order (denoted $V \leq_{\mathrm{st}} W$) if for all increasing function f,*
$\mathbf{E}[f(V(1), V(2), \cdots)] \leq \mathbf{E}[f(W(1), W(2), \cdots)]$.
- *V is smaller than W for the increasing convex order (hereinafter denoted $V \leq_{\mathrm{icx}} W$) if for all increasing convex function g, we have*
$\mathbf{E}[g(V(1), V(2), \cdots)] \leq \mathbf{E}[g(W(1), W(2), \cdots)]$.

In the following, we consider a very general system that is either **Strict** or **Overlap** and whose processing times and communication times are I.I.D..

THEOREM 4. *Consider two systems $(X^{(1)}, Y^{(1)})$ and $(X^{(2)}, Y^{(2)})$. If we have for all n, $\forall 1 \leq p \leq M$, $X_p^{(1)}(n) \leq_{\mathrm{st}} X_p^{(2)}(n)$ and $\forall 1 \leq p, q \leq M, Y_{p,q}^{(1)}(n) \leq_{\mathrm{st}} Y_{p,q}^{(2)}(n)$, then $\rho^{(1)} \geq \rho^{(2)}$.*

PROOF. Consider the Petri nets modeling both systems. They only differ by the firing times of the transitions. Then for $b = 1, 2$, let $D_k^b(n)$ be the time when transition $\mathcal{T}_k$ ends its n-th firing. The Petri net being an event graph (all places have a single input transition and all places have a single output transition), the variables $D_k^b(n)$ satisfy a (max,plus) linear equation[1]: $D^b(n) = D^b(n-1) \otimes A^b(n)$, where the matrices $A^b(n)$ are such that $A^b(n)_{ij} = \sum_k T_k^b(n)$ if a path connects transtions $\mathcal{T}_p$ and $\mathcal{T}_q$ with one token in the first place of the path and no token in any other place. Now, the firing times of the transitions $T_k^b(n)$ are either communication times or processing times so that there exists i, j (only depending on k, in a bijective way) such that $T_k^b(n) = X_p^{(b)}(n)$ or $T_k^b(n) = Y_{p,q}^{(b)}(n)$. Therefore, $T_k^1(n)$ and $T_k^2(n)$ are I.I.D. sequences such that $T_k^1(n) \leq_{\mathrm{st}} T_k^2(n)$ for all n and k, so that the same holds for the sequence of matrices $A^b(n)$. Now, the (max,plus) matrix product and the sum are increasing functions. This implies that $D^1(n) \leq_{\mathrm{st}} D^2(n)$.

Finally, the throughput $\rho^{(b)}$ is the limit of $n/\mathbf{E}[D^b(n)]$ when n goes to infinity, so that $\rho^{(1)} \geq \rho^{(2)}$, which concludes the proof. □

THEOREM 5. *Let us consider two systems with I.I.D. communication and processing times $(X^{(1)}, Y^{(1)})$ and $(X^{(2)}, Y^{(2)})$. If we have for all n, $\forall 1 \leq p \leq M, X_p^{(1)}(n) \leq_{\mathrm{icx}} X_p^{(2)}(n)$ and $\forall 1 \leq p, q \leq M$, $Y_{p,q}^{(1)}(n) \leq_{\mathrm{icx}} Y_{p,q}^{(2)}(n)$, then $\rho^{(1)} \geq \rho^{(2)}$.*

[1]The product $\otimes$ is defined as: $(V \otimes M)_k = \max_i(V_i + M_{ik})$.

PROOF. The proof is similar to the previous one, using the fact that $D_k^b(n)$ is also a convex function (a composition of maximum and sums) of the communication and processing times. □

THEOREM 6. *Let us consider any system* $(X^{(1)}, Y^{(1)})$, *such that* $X_p^{(1)}(n)$ *and* $Y_{p,q}^{(1)}(n)$ *are N.B.U.E.. Let us also consider two new systems* $(X^{(2)}, Y^{(2)})$ *and* $(X^{(3)}, Y^{(3)})$ *such that:*

- $\forall 1 \leq p \leq M, X_p^{(2)}(n)$ *has an exponential distribution, and* $\mathbf{E}[X_p^{(2)}(n)] = \mathbf{E}[X_p^{(1)}(n)]$,
- $\forall 1 \leq p, q \leq M, Y_{p,q}^{(2)}(n)$ *has an exponential distribution, and* $\mathbf{E}[Y_{p,q}^{(2)}(n)] = \mathbf{E}[Y_{p,q}^{(1)}(n)]$,
- $\forall 1 \leq p \leq M, X_p^{(3)}(n)$ *is deterministic and for all integers* n, $X_p^{(3)}(n) = \mathbf{E}[X_p^{(1)}(n)]$,
- $\forall 1 \leq p, q \leq M, Y_{p,q}^{(3)}(n)$ *is deterministic and for all* n, $Y_{p,q}^{(3)}(n) = \mathbf{E}[Y_{p,q}^{(1)}(n)]$.

Then we have $\rho^{(3)} \geq \rho^{(1)} \geq \rho^{(2)}$.

PROOF. A direct consequence of the N.B.U.E. assumption is that if V is N.B.U.E. and W is exponential with the same mean as V, then $V \leq_{icx} W$ (see [9], for example). It is also direct to show that if U is deterministic and $U = \mathbf{E}[V]$, then $U \leq_{icx} V$. Therefore, a direct application of Theorem 5 shows that $\rho^{(3)} \geq \rho^{(1)} \geq \rho^{(2)}$. □

In particular, Theorem 6 implies that in the **Overlap** case with a homogeneous communication network, as soon as communication times and processing times are N.B.U.E., then the throughput ρ can be bounded explicitly. It is comprised between the throughput of the system in which all random processing times are replaced by their mean values (given by Formula (1), where the inner throughput of processing components are the same as in the exponential case and the throughput of communication components is replaced by $\frac{\lambda_i}{\max(u_i, v_i)}$), and the throughput of the system in which all random processing times are replaced by exponential variables with the same mean value, given by Formula (1).

4.2 Numerical experiments

In this section, we compare the behavior of several random distributions of same mean for an application made of $N = 8$ stages, and a 31-processor platform. The expected throughput is numerically determined using the ERS software [11], by simulation up to convergence to the stationary behavior. Figure 9 shows that at least 100,000 samples are required to reach stable values, leading to running times close to the minute. We compare constant, exponential, uniform and Pareto distributions. As can be seen in Table 1, all throughputs are comprised between the throughput of the deterministic system and the one with exponential laws, in accordance with Theorem 6 for uniform distributions that are N.B.U.E.. Also note that the bounds still hold for the Pareto law even though it is not N.B.U.E.. Moreover, these plots are quite close, which is good news: replacing a random variable by either a constant value or by an exponential law with same mean may well lead to very good approximations.

5. FINDING THE OPTIMAL MAPPING

In this section, we depart from the main trend of the paper in that we do not consider that the mapping of the application onto the platform is given. Instead, we aim at determining the optimal mapping, i.e., the one-to-many mapping that optimizes the throughput. The rationale is that the optimal mapping could enjoy a particular structure that would facilitate renders the computation of the throughput. In other words, computing the *optimal* throughput might be

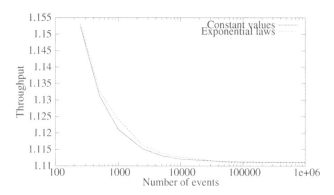

Figure 9: Evolution of the measured throughput with the number of samples.

Distribution	Throughput
Constant with mean c	2.0299
Exponential between $c/2$ and $3c/2$	2.0314
Uniform between $c/10$ and $19c/10$	2.0305
Pareto with mean c	2.0300

Table 1: Throughput obtained with several distributions of same mean.

easier than computing the throughput of an arbitrary mapping We prove that this is not the case: determining the optimal mapping is NP-complete, even in the deterministic case and without any communication cost (hence for both models). Note that the one-to-one problem, i.e., without replication, was shown to have polynomial complexity in [4].

THEOREM 7. *In the deterministic case, the problem of finding the one-to-many mapping (with replication) which minimizes the period on a heterogeneous platform without communication costs, is NP-complete.*

PROOF. Consider the associated decision problem: given a period K, does there a mapping whose period does not exceed K? The problem is obviously in NP: given a period and a mapping, it is easy to check in polynomial time whether it is valid or not.

The NP-completeness is obtained by a reduction from the problem 3-PARTITION, which is NP-complete in the strong sense [8]. Let $\mathcal{I}_1$ be an instance of 3-PARTITION: given a set of integers $A = \{a_1, ..., a_{3m}\}$ and an integer B, such that $\forall 1 \leq i \leq 3m, \frac{B}{4} < a_i < \frac{B}{2}$ and $\sum_{1 \leq i \leq 3m} a_i = mB$, does it exist m disjoint subsets $A_1, ..., A_m$ of A such that $\forall 1 \leq j \leq m, \sum_{a_i \in A_j} a_i = B$? We construct an instance $\mathcal{I}_2$ of our problem with $3m$ pipeline stages and $\frac{m(m+1)}{2} B$ processors such that:

- $\forall 1 \leq k \leq 3m, w_k = m! \times a_k$ (computation cost of stage T_k);
- $\forall 1 \leq j \leq m$, there are exactly $j \times B$ processors of speed $\frac{m!}{j}$;
- the period is fixed to $K = 1$.

Note that in this instance the sum of the speeds of all processors is equal to the sum of computation costs of all stages. This proves that in a mapping of period 1, processors cannot be idle. Therefore, all processors allocated to a same stage must have the same speed (see Section 2.2). Also, since 3-PARTITION is NP-complete in the strong sense, we can encode $\mathcal{I}_1$ in unary. Then, the values in $\mathcal{I}_2$ (stage computation costs, processor speeds, period) can be encoded in binary and thus their size is polynomial in the size of $\mathcal{I}_1$.

Now we show that $\mathcal{I}_1$ has a solution if and only if $\mathcal{I}_2$ has a solution. Suppose first that $\mathcal{I}_1$ has a solution $A_1, ..., A_m$. For all

$1 \leq j \leq m$, for all i such that $a_i \in A_j$, we associate the stage T_i of computation cost w_i to $a_i \times j$ processors of speed $\frac{m!}{j}$. Since $\sum_{a_i \in A_j} a_i \times j = B \times j$, this solution respects the number of available processors. We obtain, for all $1 \leq i \leq 3m$ such that $a_i \in A_j$, a period $\frac{a_i \times j}{a_i \times j} = 1$. This proves that this mapping is a valid solution for $\mathcal{I}_2$.

Suppose now that $\mathcal{I}_2$ has a solution. We know that all processors allocated to a given stage have same speeds, otherwise the period would be greater than 1. For $1 \leq j \leq m$, let A_j be the set of a_k such that stage T_k is mapped onto processors of speed $\frac{m!}{j}$. We obtain $\forall j, \sum_{a_k \in A_j} a_k \times m! \leq j \times B \frac{m!}{j}$, which means $\forall j, \sum_{a_k \in A_j} a_k \leq B$. Since we have $\sum_{1 \leq i \leq 3m} a_i = mB$, we derive that $\forall j, \sum_{a_k \in A_j} a_k = B$. Therefore, $A_1, ..., A_m$ is a solution for $\mathcal{I}_1$. This concludes the proof. $\square$

6. CONCLUSION

In this paper, we have investigated how to compute the throughput achieved by a given one-to-many mapping of a streaming application onto a target heterogeneous platform. The major novelty is the introduction of I.I.D. variables to model computation and communication times. In previous work [3], we have introduced methods to compute the throughput in the deterministic case, using timed Petri nets. We extended these results to the situation where computation and communication times follow I.I.D. exponential laws, providing a method whose cost may be exponential. We have refined this result and derived a polynomial-time algorithm for the **Overlap** model and a homogeneous communication network. In the general case of arbitrary I.I.D. and N.B.U.E. random variables, we have established bounds, and the lower and upper bounds are obtained by the deterministic and exponential cases respectively. Both bounds can be computed in polynomial time under the **Overlap** model with a homogeneous communication network. We also proved that determining the mapping that maximizes the throughput is an NP-complete problem, even in the simpler deterministic case with no communication costs.

Now that we have new methods to evaluate the throughput of a given mapping in a probabilistic setting, we will devote future work to designing polynomial time heuristics for the NP-complete problem mentioned above. Thanks to the methodology introduced in this paper, we will be able to compute the throughput of heuristics and compare them together. This would be a first and important step in the field of scheduling streaming applications on large-scale platforms whose load and performance are subject to dynamic variations.

7. REFERENCES

[1] F. Baccelli and D. Hong. Analyticity of iterates of random non-expansive maps. Research Report 3558, INRIA, Sophia-Antipolis, 1998.

[2] A. Benoit, F. Dufossé, M. Gallet, B. Gaujal, and Y. Robert. Computing the throughput of probabilistic and replicated streaming applications. Research Report RR-2010-03, LIP, France, 2010.

[3] A. Benoit, M. Gallet, B. Gaujal, and Y. Robert. Computing the throughput of replicated workflows on heterogeneous platforms. In *ICPP'2009, the International Conference of Parallel Processing*, 2009.

[4] A. Benoit and Y. Robert. Mapping pipeline skeletons onto heterogeneous platforms. *J. Parallel Distributed Computing*, 68(6):790–808, 2008.

[5] M. D. Beynon, T. Kurc, A. Sussman, and J. Saltz. Optimizing execution of component-based applications using group instances. *Future Generation Computer Systems*, 18(4):435–448, 2002.

[6] M. Cole. Bringing Skeletons out of the Closet: A Pragmatic Manifesto for Skeletal Parallel Programming. *Parallel Computing*, 30(3):389–406, 2004.

[7] DataCutter Project: Middleware for Filtering Large Archival Scientific Datasets in a Grid Environment. http://www.cs.umd.edu/projects/hpsl/ResearchAreas/DataCutter.htm.

[8] M. R. Garey and D. S. Johnson. *Computers and Intractability, a Guide to the Theory of NP-Completeness*. W.H. Freeman and Company, 1979.

[9] B. Gaujal and J.-M. Vincent. *Introduction to Scheduling*, chapter Comparisons of stochastic task-resource systems. CC Press, 2009.

[10] O. Häggström. *Finite Markov Chains and Algorithmic Applications*. Cambridge University Press, 2002.

[11] A. Jean-Marie. ERS: a tool set for performance evaluation of discrete event systems. http://www-sop.inria.fr/mistral/soft/ers.html.

[12] J. Kamburowski. Bounding the distribution of project duration in pert networks. *Operation Research Letters*, 12:17–22, 1992.

[13] D. E. Knuth. *The Art of Computer Programming. Volume 3, second edition*. Addison-Wesley, 1998.

[14] Y. Kumazawa. Tests for new better than used in expectation with randomly censored data. *Sequen.Anal.*, 5:85–92, 1986.

[15] M. Spencer, R. Ferreira, M. Beynon, T. Kurc, U. Catalyurek, A. Sussman, and J. Saltz. Executing multiple pipelined data analysis operations in the grid. In *Supercomputing'02*. ACM Press, 2002.

[16] J. Subhlok and G. Vondran. Optimal mapping of sequences of data parallel tasks. In *PPoPP'95*, pages 134–143. ACM Press, 1995.

[17] J. Subhlok and G. Vondran. Optimal latency-throughput tradeoffs for data parallel pipelines. In *SPAA'96*, pages 62–71. ACM Press, 1996.

[18] K. Taura and A. Chien. A heuristic algorithm for mapping communicating tasks on heterogeneous resources. In *HCW'00*, pages 102–115. IEEE Computer Society Press, 2000.

[19] N. Vydyanathan, U. Catalyurek, T. Kurc, P. Saddayappan, and J. Saltz. Toward optimizing latency under throughput constraints for application workflows on clusters. In *Euro-Par'07: Parallel Processing*, LNCS 4641, pages 173–183. Springer Verlag, 2007.

[20] N. Vydyanathan, U. Catalyurek, T. Kurc, P. Saddayappan, and J. Saltz. A duplication based algorithm for optimizing latency under throughput constraints for streaming workflows. In *ICPP'2008*, pages 254–261. IEEE Computer Society Press, 2008.

[21] Q. Wu and Y. Gu. Supporting distributed application workflows in heterogeneous computing environments. In *ICPADS'08*. IEEE Computer Society Press, 2008.

Brief Announcement:
Flashcrowding in Tiled Multiprocessors
under Thermal Constraints

Enoch Peserico[*]

Dip. Ing. Informazione, Univ. Padova, Italy

enoch@dei.unipd.it

ABSTRACT

This work argues that, in the face of growing thermal constraints, under an increasing number of scenarios the most effective tiled processor design is one that can support efficient *flashcrowding*: in a nutshell, placing on a chip far more computational power than it can sustain for extended periods of time, and concentrating computation into a few transient hotspots.

Categories and Subject Descriptors: B.8.0 [Hardware]: Performance and Reliability - General

General Terms: Design.

Keywords: multicore, tiled, energy, thermal, hot spot.

1. INTRODUCTION

We present the case for *flashcrowding*, the counterintuitive strategy of actively concentrating computation into a few transient hotspots. This introduction briefly reviews the current trends in processor design, putting our work into perspective; Section 2 argues in favour of flashcrowding based on a simple tiled multiprocessor model; finally, Section 3 summarises the essential issues in flashcrowding architectures and sketches a roadmap of future work.

Chip feature density has grown exponentially in the last decades. Initially, greater density was exploited increasing clock rate and architectural complexity (superscalarity, speculative and/or out-of-order execution etc.), improving IPC while retaining an easy sequential programming model. The price was a substantial increase in energy consumption that, in the last decade, has become unsustainable – first in mobile computers and in very large computing facilities, and finally even on small servers and desktop PCs. For the latter the issue is not so much consumption as heat dissipation: the chip would grow too hot, resulting in higher soft fault rate, decreased chip lifetime, and increased circuit resistance leading to a nasty thermal feedback loop. In fact, heat dissipation must be addressed not only at the "global", chip-wide level, but also at a local level, to avoid small *hot spots* of high energy density that cannot spread heat quickly enough to the rest of the package. This has forced architects, over the last decade, to considerably slow, or even stop, increasing clock rate, to scale down voltages, and to exploit

[*]Supported in part by Univ. Padova under Project AACSE.

greater feature density by simply "tiling" the chip with an increasing number cores (as of early 2010, 4-8 on general purpose commercial designs and dozens or hundreds on designs of an experimental nature and/or specialised for highly parallel tasks [2, 4]).

Yet chips still generally sport far fewer cores than their transistor count would allow, spaced evenly across the chip area to balance the thermal load. In part this stems from the difficulty of abandoning the sequential programming paradigm, so that software still exhibits far less parallelism than it could. But in part the cause is more fundamental. Only so much energy reduction can be achieved through aggressive voltage scaling, and static leakage (which voltage downscaling actually *exacerbates*) is close to dominating the power budget [7]. We are already past the feature size at which we can fill the chip to the brim with computational circuitry and still retain thermal sustainability. Hence cores are increasingly padded with circuitry that, although less effective in terms of computational "firepower", consumes far less energy (often simply by being turned off when not needed) and can still help the computation – e.g. by reducing chip traffic through larger caches and/or data compression engines [1], or by performing specialised computational tasks such as encryption [10].

2. FLASHCROWDING

In a(n increasing) number of scenarios the current design trajectory may not be optimal. The key consideration is that one must avoid hot spots of high temperature, not necessarily of high energy consumption; and these two issues coincide in the long term, but not in the short term. Instead of spacing apart on the die a relatively small number of "padded" cores, we propose to pack tightly a large number of more minimalistic cores – far more than thermal constraints allow to be simultaneously active for extended periods of time – and to concentrate at any given time the computation into one or a few small hot spots consisting of several adjacent cores. This obviously causes the temperature in the hot spot to grow; but before it can reach a critical threshold, the computation is migrated to a nearby area of the chip, allowing the current one to be turned off and cool down. We call this approach *flashcrowding*.

An *extremely* simplified model of a tiled multiprocessor can provide a rough understanding of the parameters affecting the performance of flashcrowding and of the operating regions where it may be most effective. We assume a rectangular die formed by a mesh of "tiles". Each tile can be either a minimalist core including a small cache, or a generic

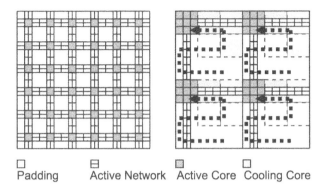

□ Padding   ⊟ Active Network   ▨ Active Core   □ Cooling Core

Figure 1: A "classic" 36 core layout (left), with each core occupying 9 tiles (8 of them "padding"); and a flashcrowding layout with 324 cores (right), sustaining 4 mobile hotspots of 9 cores each.

"padding" tile containing e.g. cache or special purpose hardware. We lump all padding tiles into a single category, simply assuming that a core tile serviced by i padding tiles boosts its performance by some *enhancement factor* $f(i)$, and ignoring whether such a boost originates from fewer cache misses, fewer pipeline stalls, dedicated arithmetic circuitry etc. Obviously $f(i)$ depends on the application; the lower it is, the greater the gains of flashcrowding. We also assume that each tile can communicate with adjacent tiles through networking circuitry consuming negligible space, but – if active – non-negligible power. In a flashcrowding architecture there is no padding: all the chip's tiles are small cores with a modicum of local memory. However, only a small fraction of them are active at any given time – roughly the same number as in a classic architecture, or perhaps a few more (those that can be "purchased" with the thermal budget of the missing padding).

The fundamental advantage of flashcrowding is that it keeps all the cores operating in a hotspot extremely close together, minimising both inter-core communication latency and inter-core communication power by a factor that, to a first approximation, is proportional to the increase in the linear density of the cores (in the example of Figure 1 this is a factor 3). This targets two significant performance bottlenecks. Modern Networks On Chip can consume over 30% of the total energy budget [9]. Similarly, increasing the locality of computation within the chip in a tiled multiprocessor can reduce execution time by $40 - 50\%$ for several applications [8], thus also leading to further energy savings.

As a secondary benefit, a flashcrowding architecture is capable of absorbing short bursts of workload. This can be extremely advantageous for large scale parallel and distributed applications – from simulation of large physical systems to backbone Internet routing – that have dishomogeneous workloads varying too quickly to allow constant rebalancing between chips, and thus tend to be slowed down at any given time by the most heavily loaded chip.

Flashcrowding does have some drawbacks. The first is the need for continuous migration. In terms of sheer performance, this is less of an issue than it might initially appear. The controlling parameter is the length of time for which a hot spot can compute before it becomes too hot. [6] provides an excellent analytical model that allows one to compute this time with fairly good precision from a small number of pa-

rameters of the chip. It turns out that, even if dissipating as much $5W/mm^2$, several dozen milliseconds must pass before the local temperature has increased by $10K$. This is the same time between two consecutive context switches on a modern OS, and much longer than necessary to power-up a core [5]; and it may be considerably improved by designing chip and package for increased thermal capacity. Less obvious is whether constantly going through such a temperature cycle would be harmless to the chip in the long term.

The second drawback of flashcrowding is wasted die space: most of the time, most cores are simply turned off. Classical architectures re-use this space with "padding" hardware, gaining minor performance benefits (the $f(i)$ factor in the model above) in exchange for a modest increase in power consumption – or not so modest: with the rise of static leakage as a major source of heat even caches can account for over 40% of the energy budget of embedded/mobile system chips [3]. In ultimate analysis the performance advantage of flashcrowding hinges on whether reduced communication costs due to increased locality can outweigh the performance increase provided by the padding (discounted by the padding's energy costs).

3. CONCLUSIONS AND FUTURE WORK

Flashcrowding – the counterintuitive strategy of overcrowding a chip with far more processing power than it can sustain and then actively concentrating computation into a few transient hotspots – not only allows a chip to absorb short bursts of computational overload, but it can improve performance by effectively trading extra processor circuitry (like larger caches, specialised computational hardware etc.) for greater locality and thus reduced intra-chip communication costs. A thorough evaluation of this tradeoff requires exploring a very large solution space spanning microarchitectural choices, software design and compiler optimisations; although current technological trends (feature size continues to shrink and thus locality becomes a scarcer, more valuable resource whereas extra circuitry becomes more readily available) seem certainly to favour flashcrowding architectures in the long run.

4. REFERENCES

[1] A. Alameldeen and D. Wood. Adaptive cache compression for high-performance processors. In *Proc. of ISCA*, 2004.

[2] S. Borkar. Thousand core chips: a technology perspective. In *Proc. of DAC*, 2007.

[3] M. Geiger, S. McKee, and G. Tyson. Beyond basic region caching: Specializing cache structures for high performance and energy conservation. In *Proc. of HiPEAC*, 2005.

[4] J. Howard et al. A 48 core IA32 message-passing processor with DVFS in 45nm cmos. In *Proc. of ISSCC*, 2010.

[5] R. Kumar, K. Farkas, N. Jouppi, P. Ranganathan, and D. Tullsen. Single-isa heterogeneous multi-core architectures: The potential for processor power reduction. In *Proc. of MICRO*, 2003.

[6] P. Michaud and Y. Sazeide. Atmi: Analytical model of temperature in microprocessors. In *Proc. of MoBS*, 2007.

[7] R. Jejurikar, C. Pereira, and R. Gupta. Leakage aware dynamic voltage scaling for real time embedded systems. In *Proc. of DAC*, 2004.

[8] K. Shaw and W. Dally. Migration in single chip multiprocessors. *Comp. Arch. Letters*, 1, 2002.

[9] V. Soteriou and L.-S. Peh. Exploring the design space of self-regulating power-aware on/off interconnection networks. *IEEE Trans. Parallel Distrib. Syst.*, 18(3), 2007.

[10] L. Spracklen. Sun's 3rd generation on-chip Ultrasparc security accelerator. In *Proc. of HOT CHIPS 21*, 2009.

Brief Announcement: On Regenerator Placement Problems in Optical Networks *

Arunabha Sen, Sujogya Banerjee, Pavel Ghosh and Sudheendra Murthy
Computer Science and Engineering Program
School of Computing, Informatics and Decision Systems Engineering
Arizona State University
{asen, sujogya, pavel.ghosh, sudhi}@asu.edu

Hung Ngo
Department of Computer Science and Engineering
University of Buffalo (SUNY)
hung.ngo@ubuffalo.edu

ABSTRACT

Optical reach is defined as the distance optical signal can traverse before its quality degrades to a level that necessitates regeneration. It typically ranges from 500 to 2000 miles, and as a consequence, regeneration of optical signal becomes essential in order to establish a *lightpath* between a source-destination node pair whose distance exceeds the limit. In a *translucent optical network*, the optical signal is regenerated at selected nodes of the network before the signal quality degrades below the acceptable threshold. Given the optical reach of the signal, to minimize the overall network design cost, the goal of the *regenerator placement problem* is to find the minimum number of regenerators necessary in the network, so that every pair of nodes is able to establish a lightpath between them. In this paper, we study the regenerator placement problem and present complexity result for that.

ACM Categories: Computer Applications
General Terms: Algorithms, Theory
Keywords: optical networks, regenerator placement

1. INTRODUCTION

In a *translucent optical network*, the optical signal is regenerated at the regeneration points (typically a subset of the network nodes with the regeneration capability) to carry the signal over long distances. *Optical reach* (the distance an optical signal can travel before its quality degrades to a level that necessitates regeneration) usually ranges from 500 to 2000 miles [4]. To transmit an optical signal beyond this distance, it is essential to *re-amplify, reshape* and *re-time* (a process often called *3R regeneration*) it. The *Regenerator Placement Problem* (RPP) problem is to find i) the minimum number of regenerators and ii) their locations, so that a communication path can be established between every pair of source-destination nodes in the network.

*This research is supported in part by the U. S. Army Research Office, the Air Force Office of Scientific Research and Defense Threat Reduction Agency.

The RPP has been studied by a number of researchers [4, 5, 2]. However most of the published methods of locating regenerators operate by iteratively improving previously computed routes until they become feasible. These methods usually generate a path between each pair of nodes and then place regenerators, as needed, along those paths to make them feasible. However, this approach usually results in placing a significantly higher number of regenerators than are needed to ensure that a path can be established between every source-destination node pair.

Although most of the studies indicated earlier focused on the technological aspects of regenerator placement in optical networks, the theoretical computer science community also has investigated these problems [2]. In a recent paper in SPAA [2], the authors claim that their study is the first that presents a theoretical framework to study the RPP and related problems. They present polynomial time algorithms, NP-complete proofs, approximation algorithms and inapproximability results for four different versions of the RPP problem.

The contribution of this paper is the following:

- We show that the RPP can be effectively solved using an approximation algorithm for the minimum connected dominated set problem.
- We point out several serious flaws of the algorithm presented for the solution of RPP in [2].

2. REGENERATOR PLACEMENT PROBLEM

In this section, we first discuss the approach taken in [2] for the solution of the RPP. After pointing out a few limitations of their approach, we present our technique in subsection 2.2.

2.1 Flammini et al. approach to RPP

An optical network is modeled as an unweighted undirected graph $G = (V, E)$ in [2]. The length of a path is measured in terms of the number of edges that constitute the path and the notion of optical reach is incorporated by putting a bound (d) on the number of edges a lightpath can traverse before requiring regeneration. A connection between a source (s) and a destination (t) comprises of a sequence of lightpaths from s to a regenerator node, or from one regenerator node to another, or from one regenerator node to t (of length at most d) whose concatenation form a path from s to t. A solution to the RPP consists of identification of the smallest subset of nodes $U \subseteq V$ to place the regenerators, such that paths can be established between source-destination node pairs.

We make a few comments on the network model and solution technique proposed in [2].

Comment 1: Given that in reality the distance between nodes are not identical and deterioration of signal strength is proportional to the distance traversed by an optical signal, we feel that an edge-weighted graph would have been a more appropriate model for the RPP, instead of the un-weighted graph used in [2]. In our model described in section 2.2, we use an edge-weighted graph model, where the weights on the edges represent the distance between the nodes.

Comment 2: The authors in [2] make a distinction between *simple path case* and *non-simple path case*. They correctly note that if only simple paths are acceptable for lightpath establishment, then the number of regenerators needed to establish connection between the nodes can be significantly higher than the number of regenerators needed when non-simple paths are also acceptable. However, we would like to point out that the distinction should not be drawn between simple and non-simple path cases as non-simple path cases are acceptable under some conditions and unacceptable under some others. We elaborate our observation with an example shown in Figure 1. In the figure, the weights assigned on the edges represent the distance between the corresponding nodes in miles. If the optical reach is 3250 miles, we can establish a non-simple path $P_1 : A - B - C - D - F - G - B - C - H$ from node A to H, with signal regeneration at node D. The two path segments that make up the path from A to H are $(P_{1,1} : A - B - C - D)$ and $(P_{1,2} : D - F - G - B - C - H)$. However, this may not be an acceptable solution when we consider free wavelengths available on each of the fiber links. Let λ_1 be the only wavelength available on the fiber links AB and CH and let wavelengths $\{\lambda_1, \lambda_2, \ldots\}$ be available on the remaining links. In this scenario both the path segments $P_{1,1}$ and $P_{1,2}$ must use wavelength λ_1 to set up the lightpath. This will not be an acceptable solution since the link BC appears in both path segments. Thus in this case, the non-simple path P_1 from A to H will be unacceptable. However, the non-simple path P_2 from A to H given by $A - B - G - F - D - F - G - B - C - H$ will be perfectly acceptable, as this path will be composed of two path segments $P_{2,1} : A - B - G - F - D$ and $P_{2,2} : D - F - G - B - C - H$. The difference between the two cases is that in the first case the two path segments $P_{1,1}$ and $P_{1,2}$ share an edge, BC, that is traversed in the same direction and in the second case the two path segments $P_{2,1}$ and $P_{2,2}$ do not share any edge that is traversed in the same direction. Since in an optical network, traffic in opposite directions are normally carried by two different optical fibers, the non-simple path P_1 is unacceptable, whereas the non-simple path P_2 is acceptable. The authors in [2] do not make a distinction between these two types of non-simple paths. If X, Y, Z represent the number of regenerators that will be needed for a RPP problem instance for the cases where (i) only simple paths are acceptable, (ii) all simple and non-simple paths are acceptable and (ii) all simple and only non-simple paths that do not

share any edge that is traversed in the same direction are acceptable, respectively, then $X \geq Z \geq Y$.

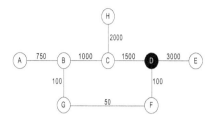

Figure 1: Example illustrates need for edge-disjointness among directed path segments

Comment 3: In proof of the Theorem 2.8 in [2], the authors describe an algorithm to find a solution to a version of RPP denoted by RPP/∞/req. RPP/∞/req problem states that given route requests between different source-destination pairs and an optical reach $d > 0$, find locations for the smallest number of regenerators. The algorithm starts by transforming the instance of RPP/∞/req problem to an instance of the set-cover problem. Unfortunately, the algorithm at times may fail to find a solution of the RPP/∞/req problem. The solution computed by this algorithm when executed on the graph $G = (V, E)$ is shown in Figure 2. For this graph the solution corresponding to the set-cover instance is the solution for the RPP/∞/req problem with $d = 2$. But it is not a solution for the RPP/∞/req problem for the graph G with $d = 2$ as the path length between the nodes v_2 and v_3 is greater than 2. Also the solution of the set-cover instance of RPP/∞/req problem does not always guarantee that a simple path can be found between every source-destination node pairs, once regenerators are placed at the locations identified by the algorithm. The Figure 3 shows another example where the solution returned by this algorithm for the RPP/∞/req problem with $d = 3$ is the solution corresponding to the set-cover instance of graph $G = (V, E)$. In Figure 3 the algorithm returns node r as the final solution for placement of a regenerator. However, if a regenerator is placed at only this node, the path between the leaf nodes v_1 and v_2 will be non-simple. In order to have at least one simple path between every pairs of nodes the correct solution has to place regenerators at nodes a and b.

2.2 Our approach to solution of the RPP

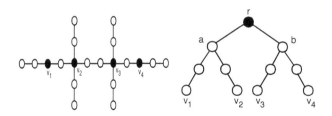

Figure 2: Solution returned by the algorithm for RPP/∞/req problem instance of graph G, where $d = 2$

Figure 3: Solution returned by the algorithm for RPP/∞/req problem instance of graph G, where $d = 3$. There is no simple path between v_1 and v_2 in the solution

In our model $G = (V, E)$ is a connected *edge-weighted* graph with edge-weights representing distances between the corresponding nodes.

Path Segment w.r.t. node set V': Given a source node s, a destination node t and a subset $V' \subseteq V$, a subpath PS of a path from s to t (henceforth called a $s-t$ path) is referred to as a *path segment*, if the end-points of PS are in $V' \cup \{s, t\}$ and no intermediate node is in V'.

Optical reach constraint: Given a path in a network between a source and a destination, the optical reach constraint ensures that the distance of any path segment between two regenerator nodes, or the distance from the source to a regenerator or the distance from a regenerator to the destination on the $s-t$ path does not exceed fiber's optical reach.

Regenerator Placement Problem (RPP): Given $G = (V, E)$, the problem is to find the smallest $V' \subseteq V$ such that there exists a path between every pair of nodes $\{s, t\} \in V$ where (i) no path segment of the $s-t$ path has a length greater than R and (ii) no two path segments of the $s-t$ path share an edge that is traversed in the same direction.

Reachability Graph: Given a network graph $G = (V, E)$ with edge weights representing the distances between the nodes, and an optical reach distance R, the *reachability graph $G' = (V', E')$* corresponding to G is constructed as follows: $V' = V$ and two nodes v_i and v_j in V' will have an edge between them if the shortest path length between those two nodes in V is at most R.

Theorem 1: The Minimum Connected Dominating Set (MCDS) of the reachability graph $G' = (V', E')$ of the network graph $G = (V, E)$ represents the solution of Regenerator Placement Problem (RPP), in non-trivial cases in which G' is not a clique.

Proof: The proof follows from the following lemmas.

Lemma 1: If there's an α-approximation algorithm for the MCDS problem, then there's an α-approximation algorithm for the RPP.

Proof: Given an instance $[G = (V, E), w : E \to \mathbb{R}^+, R]$ of the RPP problem, construct an instance $G' = (V', E')$ of the MCDS problem in the following way: Set $V' = V$, and let $(u, v) \in E'$ iff $d_G(u, v) \leq R$. Here $d_G(u, v)$ denotes the shortest distance between the nodes u and v in G in terms of the distance function w. For convenience, define a distance function $w' : E' \to \mathbb{R}^+$ by assigning $w'(uv) = d_G(u, v)$.

Let $\emptyset \neq S \subseteq V = V'$ be a MCDS of the graph G'. Consider any two vertices s and t in V. Without loss of generality, assume $st \notin E'$. (Otherwise, there's a path from s to t of length $\leq R$ and we're done.) We need to show that there's a walk from s to t in G such that no two path segments in the walk share an edge that is traversed in the same direction twice. First, let s' be the vertex in S for which $w'(ss')$ is smallest, and t' be the vertex in S for which $w'(tt')$ is smallest. If $s \in S$ then $s = s'$. If $t \in S$, then $t = t'$.

Let $s' = s_1, s_2, \ldots, s_m = t'$ be the shortest path in $G'[S]$ between s' and t'. Since S is a connected dominating set, such a path exists. Now, for each edge $s_i s_{i+1} \in E'$ on this path, there's a corresponding (s_i, s_{i+1})-path in G with length $\leq R$. Hence, putting everything together, we can find a walk from s to t in G consisting of segments $s = s_0 \rightsquigarrow s_1$, $s_1 \rightsquigarrow s_2, \ldots, s_{m-1} \rightsquigarrow s_m, s_m \rightsquigarrow t = s_{m+1}$. Each segment has length $\leq R$.

Now, suppose there's some edge $uv \in E$ which is traversed twice in the same direction (from u to v). Suppose uv was

used in the segment $s_i \rightsquigarrow s_{i+1}$ and then again in segment $s_j \rightsquigarrow s_{j+1}$. Without loss of generality, assume $i < j$. Now, on the $s_j \rightsquigarrow s_{j+1}$ segment, the length of the $s_j \rightsquigarrow u$ part has to be at least the length of the $u \rightsquigarrow s_{i+1}$ part. Otherwise, from s_i we could have gone to u, and then take the $u \rightsquigarrow s_j$ path to s_j; this "shortcut" would contradict that fact that the s', t'-path we chose was a shortest path.

Thus, the $v \rightsquigarrow s_{i+1}$ part is strictly shorter than the $s_j \rightsquigarrow u$ path. Consequently, from s_{i+1} we can go to v and then take the $v \rightsquigarrow s_{j+1}$ branch; this would be shorter than the current $s_j \rightsquigarrow s_{j+1}$ path, again contradicting the shortest path choice. This proves that a feasible solution for the MCDS instance is a feasible solution for the RPP instance.

Lemma 2: If there's an α-approximation algorithm for the RPP, then there's an α-approximation algorithm for the MCDS problem.

Proof: Consider an instance G of the MCDS problem. Construct an instance G' of the RPP by setting $G' = G$, and $R = 1$. Set the weight of each edge to be 1. It's easy to see that if a solution is feasible for RPP on G' then it is feasible for MCDS problem on G.

However, both lemma 1 and 2 holds except the trivial case when reachability graph G' is clique. If G' is a clique then solution of RPP will return 0 node while MCDS of G' will give exactly 1 node.

From recent [3], we know that MINIMUM CONNECTED DOMINATING SET (MCDS) can be approximated to within about $\ln n + O(1)$. We also know that MCDS cannot be approximated (unless $P = NP$) to within $\ln n - \Theta(\ln \ln n)$ [1].

Corollary 3: There's a $O(\ln n)$-approximation algorithm for the RPP.

Comment 4: In [2] the authors present an algorithm for the RPP/∞/req with approximation ratio of $\frac{3}{2} \log m + 1$, where the demand matrix is all-to-all. If the demand matrix is all-to-all m is $O(n^2)$, where n is the number of nodes in the network. In this case the approximation ratio becomes $3 \log n + 1$. In our MCDS based approach for the solution of RPP, we can provide better performance, as MCDS can be computed with approximation ratio $\ln \delta + 2$ where δ is the maximum degree in the input graph [3].

3. REFERENCES

[1] M. Chlebík and J. Chlebíková. Approximation hardness of dominating set problems in bounded degree graphs. *Information and Computation*, 206(11):1264–1275, 2008.

[2] M. Flammini, M. Spaccamela, et al. On the complexity of the regenerator placement problem in optical networks. In *Proceedings of the 21st SPAA*, pages 154–162. ACM, 2009.

[3] L. Ruan, H. Du, X. Jia, W. Wu, Y. Li, and K. Ko. A greedy approximation for minimum connected dominating sets. *Theoretical Computer Science*, 329(1-3):325–330, 2004.

[4] J. Simmons, M. Archit, and N. Holmdel. Network design in realistic¿ all-optical¿ backbone networks. *IEEE Communications Magazine*, 44(11):88–94, 2006.

[5] X. Yang and B. Ramamurthy. Sparse regeneration in translucent wavelength-routed optical networks: architecture, network design and wavelength routing. *Photonic network communications*, 10(1):39–53, 2005.

Brief Announcement: A Reinforcement Learning Approach for Dynamic Load-Balancing of Parallel Digital Logic Simulation

Sina Meraji
School of computer Science,
McGill University
845 Sherbrooke St. W.
Montreal, Quebec
smeraj@cs.mcgill.ca

Wei Zhang
School of computer Science,
McGill University
845 Sherbrooke St. W.
Montreal, Quebec
weizhang@cs.mcgill.ca

Carl Tropper
School of computer Science,
McGill University
845 Sherbrooke St. W.
Montreal, Quebec
carl@cs.mcgill.ca

ABSTRACT

In this paper, we present a dynamic load-balancing algorithm for parallel digital logic simulation making use of reinforcement learning. We first introduce two dynamic load-balancing algorithms oriented towards balancing the computational and communication load respectively and then utilize reinforcement learning to create an algorithm which is a combination of the first two algorithms. In addition, the algorithm determines the value of two important parameters-the number of processors which participate in the algorithm and the load which is exchanged during its execution. We investigate the algorithms on gate level simulations of several open source VLSI circuits.

Categories and Subject Descriptors

C.2.4 [**Computer Systems Organization**]: Distributed Systems—*Distributed Applications*; I.2.6 [**Computing Methodologies**]: Learning—*Parameter Learning*

General Terms

Algorithms, Verification, Performance

Keywords

Digital Logic Simulation, Dynamic load-balancing, Reinforcement Learning, Time Warp, Verilog

1. INTRODUCTION

The size growth of current digital circuits makes it difficult to fit the simulation models of these circuits into a single processors' memory. In addition to the demand for memory, the need for decreased simulation time is a major challenge for the verification process. As a result, the sequential simulation of digital circuits has become a bottleneck in the design process. At the same time, parallel discrete event simulation has emerged as a viable alternative to provide a fast, cost effective approach for the performance analysis of complex systems. We map the logical gates to logical processes (LPs) and distribute them between different processors. In order to synchronize the LPs, we utilized Jefferson's Time Warp [4] which is the most widely employed approach. Time Warp simulators for digital logic circuits were used in [2, 6, 1, 7]. In this paper we utilize Verilog XTW(VXTW) [1],

which is XTW with a front end capable of parsing all synthesizable Verilog files.

In order to achieve good performance, dynamic load balancing is applied during the simulation. The dynamic load-balancing of parallel digital simulation is examined in [3, 9] for small circuits (up to 25k gates). In this paper, we introduced two new dynamic load-balancing algorithms which balance the computational and communication load during the simulation. The algorithms utilized a combination of centralized and distributed approaches to balance the load. We also present a protocol which selects a load-balancing algorithm and its associated parameters using reinforcement learning [5]. The protocol can learn directly from experience with the system for which it is employed.

The rest of this brief announcement is organized as follows. In section 2, we briefly discuss Verilog XTW (VXTW). In Section 3 we introduce two new dynamic load-balancing algorithms for digital logic simulation. Section 4 introduces our learning algorithm. The performance analysis of the two dynamic load-balancing algorithms and the learning algorithm is addressed in section 5. Finally, the last section contains our conclusion and our thoughts for future work.

2. VERILOG XTW (VXTW)

In [7] the authors show that XTW has the best performance of the Time Warp based simulators which are employed for digital logic simulation. Unfortunately, XTW can only read bench files. In order to read Verilog design files a front end was added to XTW. This front-end changes the data format and generates the bench input data from Verilog descriptions. The Synopsys Design Compiler (DC) was used and a Verilog Parser was developed for this front-end. The result of this addition is known as Verilog XTW (VXTW) [1].

3. DYNAMIC LOAD-BALANCING

We define the load of a processor to be the number of events which are processed by its LPs since the last load-balance. During the course of our experiments we observed that the load on different processors differs a lot. As a result, we developed two new dynamic load-balancing approaches for parallel digital logic simulation. We utilize a combination of centralized and distributed approach to balance the load. In both of the algorithms, each processor sends its load and communication information to a master node. The master node creates two sets of overloaded and underloaded processors and uses computation (communication) data to match the processors of these two sets. We utilize a graph bipartite matching algorithm for this issue. Afterward, the master node informs each overloaded processor about its corresponding under-loaded match. Finally, the selected processors consider their local computation and communication data to transfer some LPs to their corresponding matches.

4. REINFORCEMENT LEARNING FOR OPTIMIZING DYNAMIC LOAD-BALANCING

Reinforcement Learning (RL) is an area of the artificial intelligence which is concerned with the interaction of an agent with its environment. The agent takes actions which cause changes in the environment and the environment, in its turn, sends numerical responses to the agent indicating the effectiveness of its actions. The agent's objective is to maximize the long term sum of the numerical responses-it wants to become more competent than its initial knowledge might allow [8] it to be. In this paper we utilize an RL approach to select the appropriate dynamic load balancing algorithm and tune its parameters for different configurations and circuits.

Our learning algorithm learns the values of three control parameters: A) The choice of dynamic load-balancing algorithm (computation or communication), P) The percentage of nodes which participate in the load-balancing algorithm, L) The number of LPs which are transferred from one node to another one in each cycle of the dynamic load-balancing algorithm. From our experimental results, the computation and communication algorithms produce different results for a different number of processors. In addition, different circuits require different algorithms. As a result, one of the control parameters that the RL decides upon is the type of load-balancing algorithm. Meanwhile, In both the computation and communication algorithms, we make use of a parameter P, the percentage of nodes which participate in the algorithm. For example, when we have a small number of processors (e.g. 2-6) and we use the computation algorithm we cannot have a large value for P. Having a large P results in more nodes participating in load-balancing algorithm and more LPs being transferred in each load-balancing cycle thereby increasing the communication overhead in a small network. If this increase is more than the speed-up that we can achieve because of load-balancing, the total simulation time will increase. Different values of L also have a significant impact on the simulation-we cannot simply make L a constant. As the reward function we used Event Commit Rate which shows the number of committed events for each cycle.

5. EXPERIMENTAL RESULTS

In this section we present performance results for the dynamic load-balancing algorithms. A=1 and 2 indicate whether the type of the load-balancing algorithm is computation or communication respectively. P is the percentage of nodes which participate in the load-balancing algorithm and L indicates the number of LPs transferred in each cycle of the algorithm. L can have the following 4 values: 50, 100, 150,and 200 and P could be either 10% or 20%. Hence, considering the two possible values of A, 1 and 2, we will have 16 actions in each execution of the learning algorithm. Each experiment result is the average of 10 simulation runs. We utilized VXTW, which can parse all synthesizable Verilog files. The Verilog source files utilized in this simulation are the OpenSparc T2 processor, the LEON processor and two Viterbi decoders designed at the Rennsalaer Polytechnic Institute (RPI). Our experimental platform consists of 32 dual core, 64 bit Intel processors.

Figure 1 shows the performance of different load-balancing algorithms and the Learning method on the OpenSparc T2 processor. We depict the best results which could be achieved by setting A (1 or 2), P and L. As can be seen, in almost all of the cases the learning method improves the simulation time more than other methods. If the learning method does not find a better result, its simulation time is at least as good as the best result of the other algorithms. An interesting point is the simulation time of the algorithms with two nodes. As can be seen, with two nodes the dynamic load-balancing algorithms not only cannot improve the simulation time but actually worsens the situation in some cases. The reason for this is that when we have two nodes, the communication overhead of transferring LPs is larger than the benefit we achieve from load-balancing. When we have more than four processors, the problem disappears in most of the cases and we can improve the simulation time. Using the learning method, we can improve the simulation time up to 88.6%, 87.1%, 84.9%

and 80.84% for OpenSparc T2, large RPI, small RPI and LEON circuits respectively.

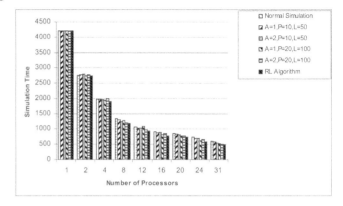

Figure 1: The average simulation time of computation and communication load-balancing algorithms and the learning method for OpenSparc T2 processor

6. CONCLUSION

In this paper, we present a dynamic load balancing algorithm for parallel digital logic simulation upon reinforcement learning. We introduce two dynamic load-balancing algorithms for balancing the computation and communication load during a Time Warp simulation of digital circuits described by Verilog. We also developed a reinforcement learning algorithm which learns to select the algorithm (communication or computation) and which adjusted the parameters of the algorithm. The simulation results indicate that simulation time is reduced up to 88.6% using this approach. As for our future work, we plan to study the effect of the multi-agent technique in which we have more than one learning agent and in which the agents communicate with each other to learn the control parameters.

7. REFERENCES

[1] Sina Meraji and Wei Zhang and Carl Tropper, *On the Scalability of Parallel Verilog Simulation*, THE 38th INTERNATIONAL CONFERENCE ON PARALLEL PROCESSING (ICPP-2009), 2009, Vienna, Austria

[2] Hervé Avril and Carl Tropper, *Clustered time warp and logic simulation*, SIGSIM Simul. Dig., volume 25, number 1, 1995, 112-119

[3] Avril, Hervé and Tropper, Carl, *The dynamic load balancing of clustered time warp for logic simulation*, SIGSIM Simul. Dig., volume 26, number 1, 1996, 20-27

[4] Jefferson, David R., *Virtual time*, ACM Trans. Program. Lang. Syst., volume 7, number 3, 1985, 404-425

[5] Leslie Pack Kaelbling and Michael L. Littman and Andrew W. Moore, *Reinforcement Learning: A Survey*, Journal of Artificial Intelligence Research, volume 4, pages 237-285 1996

[6] Lijun Li and Hai Huang and Carl Tropper, *DVS: An Object-Oriented Framework for Distributed Verilog Simulation*, PADS '03: Proceedings of the seventeenth workshop on Parallel and distributed simulation, 2003

[7] Qing XU and Carl Tropper, *XTW, a parallel and distributed logic simulator*, ASP-DAC '05: Proceedings of the 2005 conference on Asia South Pacific design automation, 2005, 1064-1069, Shanghai, China

[8] Russell, Stuart J. and Norvig, Peter, *Artificial Intelligence: A Modern Approach*, 2003

[9] Schlagenhaft, Rolf and Ruhwandl, Martin and Sporrer, Christian and Bauer, Herbert, *Dynamic load balancing of a multi-cluster simulator on a network of workstations*, SIGSIM Simul. Dig., volume 25, number 1, 1995, 175-180

Brief Announcement: Locality-aware Load Balancing for Speculatively-parallelized Irregular Applications

Youngjoon Jo and Milind Kulkarni
School of Electrical and Computer Engineering
Purdue University
{yjo, milind}@purdue.edu

ABSTRACT

Load balancing is an important consideration when running data-parallel programs. While traditional techniques trade off the cost of load imbalance with the overhead of mitigating that imbalance, when speculatively parallelizing *amorphous data-parallel* applications, we must also consider the effects of load balancing decisions on locality and speculation accuracy. We present two *data centric* load balancing strategies which account for the intricacies of amorphous data-parallel execution. We implement these strategies as schedulers in the Galois system and demonstrate that they outperform traditional load balancing schedulers, as well as a data-centric, non-load-balancing scheduler.

Categories and Subject Descriptors: D.3.4 [Processors]: Runtime Environments

General Terms: Languages

Keywords: Speculative parallelization, Irregular programs, Data partitioning, Load balancing

1. INTRODUCTION

A common source of inefficiency in data-parallel programs (where elements from an iteration space are processed in parallel) is *load imbalance*, where different threads perform different amounts of work. Load imbalance can arise because one thread is assigned more work than another, or because the work assigned to one thread takes longer (due to, *e.g.*, locality effects). A number of load balancing schedulers have been proposed to minimize the effects of load imbalance, ranging from dynamic schedulers that allocate work on-demand [11] to work-stealing schedulers that allow threads without work to "steal" work from other threads [1, 2].

In recent work, we have identified a more general form of data-parallelism that arises in many irregular programs, called *amorphous data-parallelism* [5]. An amorphous data-parallel application is organized around a worklist of *active nodes*, which represent computation over a shared data structure. To process an active node, a portion of the data structure, called the node's *neighborhood* is read or written; this execution may generate new active nodes, which are added to the worklist. Parallelism arises by processing active nodes with disjoint neighborhoods in parallel. Active nodes with overlapping neighborhoods are said to *conflict*, and cannot be processed in parallel. In general, these applications must be parallelized using speculative parallelization [8].

Amorphous data-parallel algorithms differ from traditional data-parallel programs in notable ways. First, the iteration space may not

be fixed: work may be added to the worklist during execution. Second, because the applications operate over irregular data structures, adjacent elements in the worklist may not exhibit locality. Finally, and most importantly, elements in the worklist may not be independent of each other; there may be cross-iteration dependences that must be respected.

Existing load balancing techniques, which have focused on traditional data-parallelism, do not perform well when faced with amorphous data-parallel programs. Load balancing schedulers suited for amorphous data parallel programs must address additional factors beyond run-time overhead and load balance: they must account for newly created work, how that work may be assigned to improve locality, and how load balancing decisions may impact misspeculation rates. Absent these considerations, a load balancing scheduler may deliver good load balance, but at the cost of overall performance.

In this brief announcement, we present two novel, *data centric* load balancing algorithms, *dynamic partition allocation* and *partition stealing*, as well as a data-centric version of the traditional work-stealing algorithm. These approaches account for the effects of speculatively parallelized, amorphous data-parallel programs. We implement our schedulers in the Galois system. Across three benchmarks from the Lonestar benchmark suite, we find that data-centric load balancing can improve performance by up to 66% over a non load-balancing scheduler, and by up to 25% over the best load balancing schedulers that do not account for locality effects.

2. BACKGROUND

2.1 The Galois system

The Galois system uses speculative techniques to parallelize amorphous data-parallel applications [8]. The system uses data partitioning to improve locality and reduce speculation overhead [7]. The data structure used in a program is partitioned (typically, into more partitions than threads). To minimize conflict detection overhead, two active nodes are considered to conflict if their neighborhoods lie in the same partition. It is hence critical to minimize the chance that two threads work on active nodes with neighborhoods in the same partition. To achieve this, partitions are mapped to threads and active nodes from a partition are executed by the thread that owns the partition. This minimizes misspeculation, as only neighborhoods that cross partition boundaries can trigger conflicts. This *static, partition-based* scheduler is the default scheduler used by the optimized Galois system.

2.2 Load balancing techniques

A common load balancing strategy is *guided self scheduling* [11]. All the work is placed in a centralized worklist, and work is handed out to threads in chunks that decrease in size as computation progresses. While this approach improves load balance without incurring too much overhead from accessing the central worklist, it does not address locality. Furthermore, because the chunks of work are created in a partition-agnostic manner, it is quite likely that different threads will receive active nodes from the same partition, increasing misspeculation (as their neighborhoods will necessarily conflict).

An alternate approach to load balancing is *work-stealing* [2]. A work-stealing scheduler is organized around a set of *deques*, one per thread. Each thread takes work from the front of its deque, and places any newly generated work at the front, as in a stack. If a thread runs out of work, it steals work from the *back* of a randomly chosen deque. Thus, locality is enhanced during normal operation by processing newly generated work immediately, while steals preserve locality by removing work from the back of the victim's deque.

There are a few drawbacks to workstealing in the context of amorphous data-parallelism. First, if new work is rarely created, workstealing can lead to poor locality: the initial assignment of work may either be random, or use *binary splitting* [1], which places all the work in one worklist and distributes work through steals. In either case, there is no guarantee that locality will be attained. Second, steals potentially increase misspeculation: if a thief steals work from the same partition that another thread is working on, only one of the two threads will be able to make forward progress.

3. DATA-CENTRIC LOAD BALANCING

To address the problem of load imbalance in amorphous data-parallel programs without sacrificing locality or increasing misspeculation, we must take a *data-centric* approach to load balancing. We present three schedulers that leverage partitioning information when making load-balancing decisions: a variant

Partition-aware work-stealing: A simple strategy is to add partition-awareness to the work stealing scheduler. The scheduler adopts a data-centric model, using the same initial distribution of active nodes as the default Galois scheduler. Until steals start to occur, the application will enjoy the same locality as the static scheduler. Unfortunately, because steals do not consider partitioning information, they may still suffer from the misspeculation effects discussed in the previous section.

Dynamic partition allocation: In dynamic partition allocation, active nodes are associated with partitions as in the static scheduler. However, rather than assigning every partition to a thread prior to execution, the partitions are all placed in a centralized worklist. When parallel execution begins, and any time a thread runs out of work, it retrieves a new *partition* from the central worklist. As a result, the steady state of the scheduler is for a single partition to be assigned to each thread and the remainder of the partitions to be in the central worklist. Each thread treats the set of active nodes in a single partition as a stack, with newly generated work in that partition being processed immediately.

This scheduler attempts to gain the benefits of dynamic scheduling without incurring its costs. There are fewer accesses to the centralized worklist, as work is distributed at the partition granularity. Furthermore, work is handed out in locality-preserving chunks, reducing misspeculation.

Partition stealing: The final data-centric scheduler we investigate is a variant of work-stealing. The initial distribution of work to threads is partition-based, as in the static partitioned scheduler, and in partitioned work-stealing. However, rather than stealing individual pieces of work—or larger, but still essentially random chunks—when a thread runs out of work it attempts to steal a *partition* from another, randomly selected, thread. When a thread is operating in its normal, non-stealing mode, it behaves as in the static partitioned scheduler. This scheduler attempts to mitigate the misspeculation effects of workstealing by ensuring that each thread works in separate partitions.

4. EVALUATION

Methodology: We evaluated three benchmarks from the Lonestar suite of irregular programs [6]: Delaunay triangulation (DT), Delaunay mesh refinement (DMR) and preflow push (PFP). For each benchmark, we evaluated 6 different load balancing schedulers: (i) the default static, data-centric scheduler, used as the baseline for our comparisons; (ii) *self*, a scheduler using guided self-scheduling; (iii) *steal*, a workstealing scheduler using binary splitting; (iv) *steal**, a workstealing scheduler that assigns initial work using partition information; (v) *dynamic(P)*, a dynamic partition-allocation scheduler; and (vi) *steal(P)*, a partition-stealing scheduler.

Our schedulers were implemented in the Galois system, using partition-locking [7]. The system, schedulers and applications were written in Java 6 and executed on the Sun HotSpot VM version 1.6 with a 12GB heap. To account for the effects of JIT compilation, each configuration was run 10 times, and the average of the two median run-times was recorded. All of our experiments were conducted on a Sun Niagara 2 server, consisting of two 8-core chips in an SMP configuration.

Results: Figure 1 shows the performance of the six load-balancing schedulers, relative to the static scheduler. The non-data-centric schedulers are plotted with solid lines, while the data-centric schedulers are shown with dashed lines.

DT does not suffer from significant load imbalance, as new work is not generated; on 32 threads, the average time each thread is idle when using the static scheduler is only 13%. As such, the primary goal of a load balancing scheduler should be to preserve locality and performance. Unfortunately, *self* and *steal* perform poorly, because they do not consider partitioning information. However, introducing data-centrism improves performance: *steal(P)* performs similarly to the default static scheduler, and outperforms the best non-data-centric scheduler by up to 9%.

DMR has more load imbalance, as new work is generated; the mean idleness with the static scheduler is 21% on 32 threads. Again, we see that by ignoring locality effects, the non-data-centric schedulers perform poorly, while the data-centric schedulers perform well. The best data-centric scheduler, *dynamic(P)* outperforms the best non-data-centric scheduler, *self*, by up to 24%, and outperforms the static scheduler by up to 12%.

PFP has the worst load imbalance: the static scheduler has an average mean idleness of 58% on 32 threads, and 69% on 8 threads. Because most of the work in PFP is generated during execution, the initial distribution of work has little bearing on performance, and *steal* and *steal** exhibit similar behavior. The two other data-centric schedulers outperform the work-stealing schedulers up to 16 threads, at which point overheads and abort ratios cause their performance to become comparable. All the load balancing schedulers, save *self*, substantially outperform the static scheduler. *Dynamic(P)* outperforms the static scheduler by up to 66%, and outperforms the best non-data-centric scheduler, *steal*, by up to 25%.

5. RELATED WORK

Markatos and LeBlanc identified the tension between schedulers

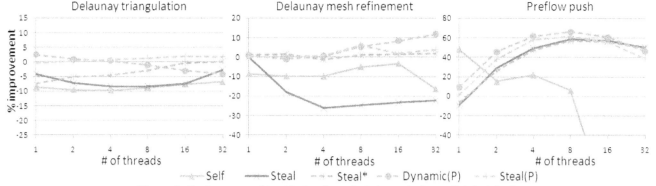

Figure 1: Performance of load balancing schedulers relative to Galois default.

that attempt to improve locality and schedulers that attempt to improve load balance, and noted that most schedulers target load balance at the expense of locality [9]. They noted that in many cases, it is more important to concentrate on locality, even if that results in poorer load balance. Our work echoes their finding in the context of amorphous data-parallelism, where locality-aware schedulers outperform schedulers that do not pay heed to data-locality concerns.

Krishnamoorthy *et al.* investigated a locality-aware load-balancing scheduler for sparse-matrix computations [4]. However, these applications do not use speculation or generate new work, unlike our target algorithms, and hence most load balancing can be accomplished through a static partitioning. Guo *et al.* studied a work-stealing scheduler for X10 [3], which preserves locality by limiting a thread's steal targets to other threads working on local data.

6. CONCLUSIONS

While load balancing has been an active area of research for decades, the emerging paradigm of amorphous data-parallel applications introduces new challenges. In addition to the usual issues surrounding load balance, worklist overheads and unequal distribution of work, amorphous data-parallel applications demand that extra attention be paid to locality and speculation effects. The increased importance of locality degrades the performance of traditional load balancing schedulers; in fact, a locality-aware, non-load-balancing scheduler provides better performance than many load-balancing, locality-oblivious schedulers.

We introduced three *data-centric* schedulers: a partition-aware variant of work stealing, a data-centric dynamic scheduler and a data-centric work stealing scheduler. Across three benchmarks, we find that our load balancing schedulers outperform the default, locality-ware scheduler by up to 2% on Delaunay triangulation, 12% on Delaunay mesh refinement and 66% on preflow push. Furthermore, on each benchmark, our data-centric schedulers outperformed the best non-data-centric schedulers by up to 9% on Delaunay triangulation, 24% on Delaunay mesh refinement and 25% on preflow push. Clearly, making load balancing decisions with an eye toward data-centrism is critical to achieving high performance on amorphous data-parallel programs.

References

[1] *Intel Threading Building Blocks Reference Manual, Rev 1.9.* 2008.

[2] Robert D. Blumofe and Charles E. Leiserson. Scheduling multi-threaded computations by work stealing. *J. ACM*, 46(5):720–748, 1999.

[3] Yi Guo, Jisheng Zhao, Vincent Cave, and Vivek Sarkar. SLAW: A scalable locality-aware adaptive work-stealing scheduler for multi-core systems. In *PPoPP '10: Proceedings of the 15th ACM SIGPLAN symposium on Principles and practice of parallel programming*, pages 341–342, 2010.

[4] S. Krishnamoorthy, U. Catalyurek, J. Nieplocha, and P Sadayappan. An approach to locality-conscious load balancing and transparent memory hierarchy management with a global-address-space parallel programming model. In *IEEE International Parallel and Distributed Processing Symposium (IPDPS)*, 2006.

[5] Milind Kulkarni, Martin Burtscher, Rajasekhar Inkulu, Keshav Pingali, and Calin Cascaval. How much parallelism is there in irregular applications? In *PPoPP '09: Proceedings of the 14th ACM SIGPLAN symposium on Principles and practice of parallel programming*, pages 3–14, New York, NY, USA, 2009. ACM.

[6] Milind Kulkarni, Martin Burtscher, Keshav Pingali, and Calin Cascaval. Lonestar: A suite of parallel irregular programs. In *2009 IEEE International Symposium on Performance Analysis of Systems and Software (ISPASS)*, pages 65–76, April 2009.

[7] Milind Kulkarni, Keshav Pingali, Ganesh Ramanarayanan, Bruce Walter, Kavita Bala, and L. Paul Chew. Optimistic parallelism benefits from data partitioning. In *ASPLOS XIII: Proceedings of the 13th international conference on Architectural support for programming languages and operating systems*, pages 233–243, New York, NY, USA, 2008. ACM.

[8] Milind Kulkarni, Keshav Pingali, Bruce Walter, Ganesh Ramanarayanan, Kavita Bala, and L. Paul Chew. Optimistic parallelism requires abstractions. In *PLDI '07: Proceedings of the 2007 ACM SIGPLAN conference on Programming language design and implementation*, pages 211–222, New York, NY, USA, 2007. ACM.

[9] E. P. Markatos and T. J. LeBlanc. Load balancing vs. locality management in shared-memory multiprocessors. Technical report, Rochester, NY, USA, 1991.

[10] OpenMP. http://www.openmp.org.

[11] Constantine D. Polychronopoulos and David J. Kuck. Guided self-scheduling: A practical scheduling scheme for parallel supercomputers. *IEEE Transactions on Computers*, C-36(12), 1987.

[12] Alexandros Tzannes, George C. Caragea, Rajeev Barua, and Uzi Vishkin. Lazy binary-splitting: a run-time adaptive work-stealing scheduler. In *PPoPP '10: Proceedings of the 15th ACM SIGPLAN symposium on Principles and practice of parallel programming*, pages 179–190, New York, NY, USA, 2010. ACM.

Brief Announcement: Serial-Parallel Reciprocity in Dynamic Multithreaded Languages

Kunal Agrawal
Washington University in St.
Louis
kunal@cse.wustl.edu

I-Ting Angelina Lee
MIT Computer Science and
Artificial Intelligence
Laboratory
angelee@mit.edu

Jim Sukha
MIT Computer Science and
Artificial Intelligence
Laboratory
sukhaj@mit.edu

ABSTRACT

In dynamically multithreaded platforms that employ work stealing, there appears to be a fundamental tradeoff between providing provably good time and space bounds and supporting *SP-reciprocity*, the property of allowing arbitrary calling between parallel and serial code, including legacy serial binaries. Many known dynamically multithreaded platforms either fail to support SP-reciprocity or sacrifice on the provable time and space bounds that an efficient work-stealing scheduler could otherwise guarantee.

We describe PR-Cilk, a design of a runtime system that supports SP-reciprocity in Cilk and provides provable bounds on time and space. In order to maintain the space bound, PR-Cilk uses *subtree-restricted work stealing*. We show that with subtree-restricted work stealing, PR-Cilk provides the same guarantee on stack space usage as ordinary Cilk. The completion time guaranteed by PR-Cilk is slightly worse than ordinary Cilk. Nevertheless, if the number of times a C function calls a Cilk function is small, or if each Cilk function called by a C function is sufficiently parallel, PR-Cilk still guarantees linear speedup.

Categories and Subject Descriptors: D.1.3 [Programming Techniques]: Concurrent Programming

General Terms: Algorithms, Design, Languages, Performance, Theory

Keywords: Cilk, dynamic multithreading, Intel Threading Building Blocks, scheduling, work stealing, serial-parallel reciprocity

1. INTRODUCTION

Work stealing [3, 5, 6, 4, 7, 9, 10, 11, 14, 19, 23] is fast becoming a standard way to load-balance dynamically multithreaded computations on multicore hardware. Concurrency platforms that support work stealing include Cilk-1 [4], Cilk-5 [10], Cilk++ [18], Fortress [2], Hood [6], Java Fork/Join Framework [15], Task Parallel Library (TPL) [17], Threading Building Blocks (TBB) [20], and X10 [8]. Work stealing admits an efficient implementation that guarantees bounds on both completion time and stack space usage [5, 10], but many existing implementations that achieve these bounds — including Cilk-1, Cilk-5, and Cilk++ — do not exhibit *series-parallel reciprocity*, or *SP-reciprocity*[16] for short, *i.e.*, the property of allowing arbitrary calling between parallel and serial code, including legacy (and third-party) serial binaries. Without SP-reciprocity, it can be difficult to integrate a parallel library into an existing legacy code base.

Unfortunately, supporting SP-reciprocity in a concurrency plat-

form that employs work stealing often weakens the bounds on program completion time or stack space consumption that the platform could otherwise guarantee.[1] For instance, TBB supports SP-reciprocity by employing a heuristic referred to as "depth-restricted work stealing" [22] to limit stack space usage, but it does not guarantee a provably good time bound. In [16], the authors propose a modification to the Cilk-5 runtime that provides provable time and space bounds and supports SP-reciprocity, but their system requires additional operating system support. In addition, the space bound of [16] is slightly weaker than Cilk-5.

In this work, we present another point in the design space for work-stealing concurrency platforms, referred to as *PR-Cilk*, which employs the heuristic of "subtree-restricted work stealing". PR-Cilk supports SP-reciprocity, preserves the same space bound as Cilk-5, and provides a provable but slightly weaker time bound as compared to Cilk-5. To be more precise, let T_1 be the *work* of a deterministic computation (its serial running time), and let T_∞ be the *span* of the computation (its theoretical running time on an infinite number of processors). Let V be the number of Cilk function instances which are called from some C function, and let $\widetilde{T}_\infty$ be the "aggregate span" of the computation, where $\widetilde{T}_\infty$ is bounded by the sum over all the spans for each of the V Cilk function instances. We prove that PR-Cilk executes the computation on P processors in expected time $\mathrm{E}[T] = O(T_1/P + \widetilde{T}_\infty + V \lg P)$. We do not present the proof due to space constraints, but to summarize, this bound achieves linear speedup when V is small, or when each of the V Cilk function instances has sufficient parallelism. As for space, PR-Cilk achieves the same space bound as Cilk; if S_1 is the stack space usage of the serial execution, then the stack space S_P consumed during a P-processor execution satisfies $S_P \leq PS_1$.

2. DIFFICULTIES OF SP-RECIPROCITY

This section outlines some of the challenges in supporting SP-reciprocity in a language such as Cilk [10]. In particular, the design of Cilk's work-stealing scheduler and its support of the "cactus stack" abstraction prevent Cilk from efficiently supporting SP-reciprocity. We also outline some of the difficulties associated with other approaches for supporting SP-reciprocity.

Cilk's work-stealing scheduler

In Cilk, the programmer specifies the logical parallelism of a program using the keywords **spawn** and **sync**. When a function A *spawns* a function B (by preceding the invocation of B with the keyword **spawn**), the *parent* function A invokes the *child* function

---

[1] Although Fortress, Java Fork/Join Framework, TPL, and X10 employ work stealing, they do not suffer from the same problems, because they are byte-code interpreted by a virtual-machine environment.

B without suspending the parent, thereby exposing potential parallelism. The keyword **sync** acts as a local barrier, indicating that the control cannot pass the **sync** statement until all previously spawned functions have returned.

Cilk's work-stealing scheduler load-balances parallel execution across the available *worker* threads while respecting the program's logical parallelism. Cilk follows the "lazy task creation" strategy described in [14], where the worker suspends the parent function when a child function is spawned and begins working on the child. Operationally, when a worker encounters a **spawn**, it invokes the child function and suspends the parent, just as with an ordinary subroutine call, but it also places the parent frame on the bottom of its *deque* (double-ended queue). When the child returns, the worker tries to pops the parent frame off the bottom of its deque and resume the parent frame. Pushing and popping frames from the bottom of the deque is the common case, and mirrors precisely the behavior of C or other Algol-like languages in their use of a stack.

A worker exhibits behavior that differs from ordinary serial stack execution if it runs out of work. This condition can happen due to two cases. First, the worker may stall at a **sync** in a function because some of the function's spawned children have not yet returned. Second, the worker may return from a **spawn** and find that its deque is empty (*i.e.*, all its ancestor frames have been stolen).[2] When the worker has no work, the worker becomes a *thief*, and attempts to steal the topmost frame from a randomly chosen *victim* worker. If a frame exists, the steal is *successful* and the worker resumes the stolen frame; otherwise, the worker continues trying to work-steal.

Cilk's support for the cactus-stack abstraction

An execution of a serial Algol-like language, such as C [13] or C++ [21], can be viewed as a "walk" of an *invocation tree*, which dynamically unfolds during execution and relates function instances by the "calls" relation: if function instance A calls function instance B, then A is a *parent* of the *child* B in the invocation tree. Such serial languages use a *linear-stack representation*: the stack pointer is advanced as a function is invoked and restored as the function returns. With a linear stack, frames for caller and callee are allocated in contiguous space. This representation is space-efficient, because all the children of a given function can use and reuse the same region of the stack.

The notion of the invocation tree can be extended to include spawns, as well as calls, but unlike the serial walk of an invocation tree, a parallel execution unfolds the tree more haphazardly and in parallel. Since multiple children of a function may be extant simultaneously due to spawns, a linear-stack data structure no longer suffices for storing activation frames. Instead, the tree of extant activation frames forms a *cactus stack* [12].

Cilk supports the cactus stack abstraction by allocating frames for Cilk functions in noncontiguous space, where each frame is linked to its parent frame. These frames in the noncontiguous memory are referred as *shadow frames* to differentiate from the *activation frames* in the linear stacks. As a result, the call / return linkage for a Cilk function (henceforth referred to as the *Cilk linkage*) differs from the ordinary C linkage: a Cilk function passes parameters and returns value via its shadow frame. That means, if a parent passes a pointer of its local variable to its child, the pointer refers to the location in the shadow frame. Thus, when a worker's deque is empty, its corresponding linear stack can be emptied as well; the

worker can freely pop off the suspended activation frames in its linear stack. Since a worker only steals when its deque is empty, each worker uses no more stack space than the space used by the serial execution of the program. Moreover, with this strategy, multiple extant children can share a single view of their parent frame, as required by the cactus stack abstraction.

This implementation allows Cilk to provide a provable space bound, but does not allow for SP-reciprocity because it uses the Cilk linkage to spawn, which is incompatible with the ordinary C linkage. A sharp delineation exists between C and Cilk: while a Cilk function may call a C function, a C function may not call back to a Cilk function, unless the C function is also recompiled to use the special Cilk linkage.

Other alternatives

Alternatively, one may conceivably implement the memory abstraction of a cactus stack using ordinary linear stacks, and thus eliminate the special linkage to allow SP-reciprocity. For example, if a Cilk function A executing on worker p has multiple extant children, other workers executing these extant children may share a single view of A's frame sitting in p's stack space. This strategy compromises either the completion time or stack space bound, however. A key obstacle is the fact that once a frame has been allocated, its location in virtual memory cannot be changed, because there may be a pointer to a variable in the frame elsewhere in the system. Thus, if A's frame is shared among workers, p cannot pop A off its stack until all A's extant children return. If p runs out of work before A can be resumed, in general p has two options. First, p can block and wait for A's children to complete. This option causes workers to block and therefore invalidates Cilk's completion time bound. Second, p can go steal work from some other worker. In this case, p has no choice but to push the stolen work, say B, onto its stack below A.[3] If A is already deep in the stack, and B is close to the top of the invocation tree, p's stack can grow twice as deep as what it would be in a serial execution. Furthermore, even when A is done executing and can return, the stack space where A resides cannot be reused until B also returns. This scenario could occur recursively, consuming impractically large stack space.

A combination of the two options is also possible. TBB operates on linear stacks with ordinary linkage and thus provides SP-reciprocity. TBB allows work-stealing as in the second option, but to limit space consumption, TBB employs *depth-restricted work stealing*, where a worker is restricted to steal only tasks which are deeper than the worker's deepest blocked task. The fact that a thief can steal from arbitrary part of the invocation tree (provided the depth restriction is not violated) makes it difficult to prove a nontrivial upper bound on the completion time, however. For a lower bound, [22] describes a computation for which TBB with depth-restricted work stealing runs asymptotically serially, but for which Cilk can achieve linear speedup.

3. PR-Cilk DESIGN

PR-Cilk supports SP-reciprocity and guarantees provable time and space bounds by using a strategy called *subtree-restricted work stealing*. In addition, PR-Cilk uses shadow frames of Cilk functions and the ordinary activation frames for C functions. Some modifications to the runtime system and the compiler are required in order to support transitioning between two different types of frames and linkages. Due to space limit, however, we focus our attention on how PR-Cilk supports subtree-restricted work stealing using "parallel regions", a mechanism adapted from HELPER [1].

---

[2]In this second case, the worker first checks whether the parent is stalled on a **sync** statement and whether this child is the last child to return. If so, it resumes the parent function after the **sync**.

[3]We assume the stack grows downward.

To remind ourselves of the problem, suppose a worker p executes a C function *foo* which calls a Cilk function A. Since *foo* uses the activation frame, the stack space associated with *foo* can not be removed from p's stack until all the descendants of A in the invocation tree are completed. If p runs out of the work before all children of A finish, as we mentioned earlier, p must either block and wait for A's extant children to complete (thus sacrificing the time bound) or steal (and potentially consume excessive space). PR-Cilk addresses this problem by using *subtree-restricted work stealing*, which forces p to steal from only within A's subtree in the invocation tree. Notice that, in any serial execution, the stack depth of any frame within A's subtree is greater than the stack depth of A, where p is stalled. Therefore, no processor can use more stack space than the serial execution, and we maintain the Cilk stack space bound. Furthermore, any work p steals is work that must be completed in order for A to return, and p is (in some sense) helping to complete its own work. At a glance, it may seem that PR-Cilk's subtree-restricted work stealing is similar to TBB's depth-restricted work-stealing; in fact, subtree-restricted work stealing is more restrictive than depth-restricted work-stealing. In this case, however, the stronger restriction implies a better provable completion time bound, because a stronger restriction eliminates certain undesirable schedules that the weaker restriction allows.

By default in Cilk, a worker is only allowed to steal from the top of a deque; Cilk has no mechanism for limiting work stealing to some subtree of the invocation tree. To support subtree-restricted work stealing, PR-Cilk augments the Cilk-5 runtime system with *parallel regions*. A parallel region construct for Cilk was originally described in HELPER [1] as a way of supporting nested parallelism in locked critical sections. Here, we use the term *parallel region* to refer to a subcomputation with nested parallelism whose root represents a Cilk function called by a C function, but the mechanism for supporting parallel regions is almost identical.

Conceptually, each parallel region R_A is an instance of a Cilk function that uses its own *deque pool* — a set of deques — for self-contained scheduling. When a worker p starts a parallel region R_A, the runtime system creates a new deque pool for R_A, denoted by $\texttt{dqpool}(R_A)$. The runtime system allocates a deque $q \in \texttt{dqpool}(R_A)$ to a worker p when p is *assigned* to R_A. In order to support nested parallel regions, each worker p maintains a chain of deques, each for a different region, with the bottom deque in the chain being p's active deque. Whenever a worker p tries to steal, it only steals from deques in the same pool as p's active deque.

We can directly use the design of parallel regions to support subtree-restricted work stealing in PR-Cilk. When worker p calls a Cilk function A from a C function *foo*, it implicitly invokes a function called $\texttt{start\_region}$. The $\texttt{start\_region}$ call causes p to start a new region, which involves p creating a new deque pool $\texttt{dqpool}(R_A)$ and creating a new deque q for itself in $\texttt{dqpool}(R_A)$. After creating the region, p continues to execute A, which may spawn more functions under region R_A, and the frames associated with these functions are added to q. Other workers may later be assigned to this region by randomly stealing into the region. Any additional work created by these workers within R_A is added to some deque in $\texttt{dqpool}(R_A)$ as well. If p later stalls on a **sync** in A, it can now steal work from any deque in the pool $\texttt{dqpool}(R_A)$, since such work belongs to the subtree rooted at A.

Since PR-Cilk uses the same policy for workers entering and leaving parallel regions as described in [1], the completion time and stack space bounds in [1] can be simplified and applied directly to PR-Cilk. PR-Cilk computations have more structure than HELPER, however. Specifically in PR-Cilk, regions are not associated with locks, so a worker is assigned to a region only by either starting the region or stealing into the region, whereas in HELPER, a worker can also be assigned to a region via acquiring a lock associated with the region. Given this property, we believe that one can potentially improve the time bound. As future work, we hope to improve the time bound and explore the implications of having different entering and leaving policies for parallel regions, as the completion time may be affected depending on the policy used.

Acknowledgments

We like to thanks Matteo Frigo of Axis Semiconductor, and members of the Supertech Research Group at MIT CSAIL for helpful discussions. This research was supported in part by NSF Grant CNS-0615215.

4. REFERENCES

[1] K. Agrawal, C. E. Leiserson, and J. Sukha. Helper locks for fork-join parallel programming. In *PPoPP '10*, Jan. 2010.

[2] E. Allen, D. Chase, J. Hallett, V. Luchangco, J.-W. Maessen, S. Ryu, G. L. S. Jr., and S. Tobin-Hochstadt. *The Fortress Language Specification Version 1.0*. Sun Microsystems, Inc., Mar. 2008.

[3] N. S. Arora, R. D. Blumofe, and C. G. Plaxton. Thread scheduling for multiprogrammed multiprocessors. In *SPAA '98*, pages 119–129, June 1998.

[4] R. D. Blumofe, C. F. Joerg, B. C. Kuszmaul, C. E. Leiserson, K. H. Randall, and Y. Zhou. Cilk: An efficient multithreaded runtime system. *Journal of Parallel and Distributed Computing*, 37(1):55–69, August 1996.

[5] R. D. Blumofe and C. E. Leiserson. Scheduling multithreaded computations by work stealing. *Journal of the ACM*, 46(5):720–748, Sept. 1999.

[6] R. D. Blumofe and D. Papadopoulos. Hood: A user-level threads library for multiprogrammed multiprocessors. Technical Report, University of Texas at Austin, 1999.

[7] F. W. Burton and M. R. Sleep. Executing functional programs on a virtual tree of processors. In *FPCA '81*, pages 187–194, Oct. 1981.

[8] P. Charles, C. Grothoff, V. Saraswat, C. Donawa, A. Kielstra, K. Ebcioglu, C. von Praun, and V. Sarkar. X10: An object-oriented approach to non-uniform cluster computing. In *OOPSLA '05*, pages 519–538. ACM, 2005.

[9] V. W. Freeh, D. K. Lowenthal, and G. R. Andrews. Distributed Filaments: Efficient fine-grain parallelism on a cluster of workstations. In *OSDI '94*, pages 201–213, Nov. 1994.

[10] M. Frigo, C. E. Leiserson, and K. H. Randall. The implementation of the Cilk-5 multithreaded language. In *PLDI '98*, pages 212–223, 1998.

[11] R. H. Halstead, Jr. Multilisp: A language for concurrent symbolic computation. *ACM TOPLAS*, 7(4):501–538, Oct. 1985.

[12] E. A. Hauck and B. A. Dent. Burroughs' B6500/B7500 stack mechanism. *Proceedings of the AFIPS Spring Joint Computer Conference*, pages 245–251, 1968.

[13] B. W. Kernighan and D. M. Ritchie. *The C Programming Language*. Prentice Hall, Inc., second edition, 1988.

[14] D. A. Kranz, R. H. Halstead, Jr., and E. Mohr. Mul-T: A high-performance parallel Lisp. In *PLDI '89*, pages 81–90, June 1989.

[15] D. Lea. A Java fork/join framework. In *Java Grande Conference*, pages 36–43, 2000.

[16] I.-T. A. Lee, S. Boyd-Wickizer, Z. Huang, and C. E. Leiserson. Using thread-local memory mapping to support cactus stacks in work-stealing runtime systems. Submitted for publication.

[17] D. Leijen, W. Schulte, and S. Burckhardt. The design of a task parallel library. In *OOPSLA '09*, pages 227–242, 2009.

[18] C. E. Leiserson. The Cilk++ concurrency platform. In *46th Design Automation Conference*. ACM, July 2009.

[19] R. S. Nikhil. Cid: A parallel, shared-memory C for distributed-memory machines. In *LCPC '94*, Aug. 1994.

[20] J. Reinders. *Intel Threading Building Blocks: Outfitting C++ for Multi-core Processor Parallelism*. O'Reilly Media, Inc., 2007.

[21] B. Stroustrup. *The C++ Programming Language*. Addison-Wesley, Boston, MA, third edition, 2000.

[22] J. Sukha. Brief announcement: A lower bound for depth-restricted work stealing. In *SPAA '09*, Aug. 2009.

[23] M. T. Vandevoorde and E. S. Roberts. WorkCrews: An abstraction for controlling parallelism. *International Journal of Parallel Programming*, 17(4):347–366, Aug. 1988.

Low Depth Cache-Oblivious Algorithms

Guy E. Blelloch
Carnegie Mellon University
Pittsburgh, PA USA
guyb@cs.cmu.edu

Phillip B. Gibbons
Intel Labs Pittsburgh
Pittsburgh, PA USA
phillip.b.gibbons@intel.com

Harsha Vardhan Simhadri
Carnegie Mellon University
Pittsburgh, PA USA
harshas@cs.cmu.edu

ABSTRACT

In this paper we explore a simple and general approach for developing parallel algorithms that lead to good cache complexity on parallel machines with private or shared caches. The approach is to design nested-parallel algorithms that have low depth (span, critical path length) and for which the natural sequential evaluation order has low cache complexity in the cache-oblivious model. We describe several cache-oblivious algorithms with optimal work, polylogarithmic depth, and sequential cache complexities that match the best sequential algorithms, including the first such algorithms for sorting and for sparse-matrix vector multiply on matrices with good vertex separators.

Using known mappings, our results lead to low cache complexities on shared-memory multiprocessors with a single level of private caches or a single shared cache. We generalize these mappings to multi-level cache hierarchies of private or shared caches, implying that our algorithms also have low cache complexities on such hierarchies. The key factor in obtaining these low parallel cache complexities is the low depth of the algorithms we propose.

Categories and Subject Descriptors

F.2 [**Theory of Computation**]: Analysis of Algorithms and Problem Complexity; D.1.3 [**Programming Techniques**]: Concurrent Programming—*Parallel programming*; D.2.8 [**Software Engineering**]: Metrics—*complexity measures, performance measures*

General Terms

Algorithms, Theory

Keywords

Cache-oblivious algorithms, sorting, sparse-matrix vector multiply, graph algorithms, parallel algorithms, multiprocessors, schedulers.

1. INTRODUCTION

Due to the physical realities of building machines it seems likely that locality will always play a role in designing efficient algorithms for parallel machines. Indeed many parallel models have been designed to take account of locality on both shared [4, 48,

7] and distributed memory machines [48, 33, 12]. These models, however, assume a fixed number of processors for which the algorithm designer or programmer have to map their algorithms onto. What seems to be emerging instead as the dominant programming paradigm for shared memory parallel machines is one based on dynamic parallelism. In such models the programmer expresses the full parallelism without concern of how it maps onto processors. The runtime system then supplies a scheduler that maps this dynamic parallelism onto the processors of the machine. A common form of programming in this model is based on nested parallelism—consisting of nested parallel loops and/or fork-join constructs [13, 26, 20, 35, 44]. If locality is not of concern, performance costs in such models can be calculated in terms of *work* (number of operations) and *depth* (also known as the span or the critical path length) and can be mapped onto runtime on a fixed number of processors. This can greatly simplify how programmers think about parallelism. It is not clear, however, how to capture locality in these models in a high-level way.

In this paper we are interested in analyzing the locality of algorithms written with dynamic nested parallelism. We consider a paradigm based on analyzing the cost of an algorithm using in addition to work and depth the cache complexity in the sequential cache-oblivious model. The *cache-oblivious model* (*ideal-cache model*) [38] is a two-level model of computation comprised of an unbounded memory and a cache of size M. Data are transferred between the two levels using cache lines of size B; all computation occurs on data in the cache. Both M and B are unknown to the algorithm, and the goal is to minimize an algorithm's *cache complexity* (number of cache lines transferred). Sequential algorithms designed for this model have the advantage of achieving good sequential cache complexity across *all* levels of a (single processor) multi-level cache hierarchy, regardless of the values of M_i and B_i at each level i [38]. Researchers have developed cache-oblivious algorithms for a many problems [6, 22, 34].

The cache complexity $Q(n; M, B)$ for a natural sequential execution of a parallel program (on input of size n) can be used to bound the cache complexity $Q_p(n; M, B)$ for the same program on certain p-processor parallel machines with a single level of cache(s) [1, 15]. In particular, for a shared-memory parallel machine with private caches (each processor has its own cache) using a work-stealing scheduler, $Q_p(n; M, B) < Q(n; M, B) + O(pMD/B)$ with probability $1 - \delta$ [1],[1] and for a shared cache using a parallel-depth-first (PDF) scheduler, $Q_p(n; M + pBD, B) \leq Q(n; M, B)$ [15], where D is the depth of the computation. These results apply to nested-parallel computations—computations starting with a single thread and using nested fork-join parallelism—that use binary forking (spawning) of threads. (When viewed as a computation dag where the nodes are constant-work tasks and the edges are dependences between tasks, the dags for such compu-

---

[1]In this paper, δ is an arbitrarily small positive constant.

tations are series-parallel.) The "natural" sequential execution is simply one that runs each call in a fork to completion before starting the next.

These results for a single level of cache(s) suggest a simple approach for developing cache-efficient parallel algorithms: Develop a nested-parallel algorithm with (1) low cache-oblivious complexity for the sequential ordering, and (2) low depth; then use the results to bound the cache complexity on a parallel machine. Low depth is important because D shows up in the term for additional misses for private caches, and additional cache size for a shared cache. Moreover, we show that algorithms designed with this approach can also achieve good parallel cache complexity on *multi-level* private or shared caches. For example, we show that for a work-stealing scheduler on a multi-level private cache hierarchy $Q_p(n; M_i, B_i) < Q(n; M_i, B_i) + O(pM_iD/B_i)$ with probability $1 - \delta$ for each level i, and that this bound is tight.

As an example of the approach consider Strassen's matrix multiply. It is nested-parallel because the seven recursive calls can be made in parallel and the matrix addition can be implemented by forking off a tree of parallel calls. For $n \times n$ matrices the total depth is $O(\log^2 n)$—$O(\log n)$ levels of recursion, each with $O(\log n)$ depth for the additions. As shown in [38], the sequential cache complexity is $Q(n; M, B) = O(n^{\lg 7}/(B\sqrt{M}))$. Thus, we have that $Q_p(n; M, B) < Q(n; M, B) + O(pM \log^2(n)/B)$ for a single level of private caches and $Q_p(n; M + pB \log^2 n, B) \leq Q(n; M, B) = O(n^{\lg 7}/(B\sqrt{M}))$ for a shared cache. For practical parameters these bounds indicate either only marginally more total misses than the sequential version for private caches or only a marginally larger cache size for shared caches. Similarly good bounds are obtained for multi-level hierarchies of private or shared caches, using our results for such hierarchies.

Although matrix multiply and some other known cache-oblivious algorithms are naturally parallel with low depth (*e.g.*, matrix transpose and FFT [38]), many are not. Importantly, prior cache-oblivious sorting algorithms with optimal sequential cache complexity [23, 24, 25, 36, 38] are not parallel. This paper presents the first low (*i.e.*, polylogarithmic) depth cache-oblivious sorting algorithm with optimal cache complexity. Under the standard "tall cache" assumption $M = \Omega(B^2)$ [38], our (deterministic) sorting algorithm has cache complexity $Q(n; M, B) = O(\frac{n}{B} \log_M n)$ and work $W = O(n \log n)$, which are optimal, and depth $D = O(\log^2 n)$. We improve the depth for a randomized version. In contrast, parallelizing the prior algorithms using known techniques would result in depth at least $\Omega(\sqrt{n})$. We illustrate how our sorting algorithm can be used to construct the first polylogarithmic depth, cache-oblivious, optimal cache complexity algorithms for other important problems such as list ranking and tree contraction. Finally, we present the first cache-oblivious, low cache complexity algorithm for sparse-matrix vector (SpMV) multiply on matrices with good vertex separators (roughly speaking a sparse matrix has good separators if the corresponding graph can be partitioned by removing a reasonably small set of vertices and their incident edges so no partition is too large). All planar graphs have good separators. The SpMV algorithm is optimal work, $O(\log^2 n)$ depth, and its sequential cache complexity improves upon the previous best sequential algorithm and is optimal for planar graphs.

Other work on parallel cache-oblivious algorithms has concentrated on bounding cache misses for particular classes of algorithms. This includes results by Frigo *et al.* [39] for a class of algorithms with a regularity condition, by Blelloch *et al.* [14] for a class of binary divide-and-conquer algorithms, and by Chowdhury and Ramachandran [28, 29] for a class of dynamic programming and Gaussian elimination-style problems. Recent work by Chowdhury et.

Algorithm 1 MERGE$((A, s_A, l_A), (B, s_B, l_B), (C, s_C))$

Merges $A[s_A : s_A + l_A)$ and $B[s_B : s_B + l_B)$
into array $C[s_C : s_C + l_A + l_B)$

1: **if** $l_B = 0$ **then**
2:      Copy $A[s_A : s_A + l_A)$ to $C[s_C : s_C + l_A)$
3: **else if** $l_A = 0$ **then**
4:      Copy $B[s_B : s_B + l_B)$ to $C[s_C : s_C + l_B)$
5: **else**
6:      $\forall k \in [1 : \lfloor n^{1/3} \rfloor]$, find pivots (a_k, b_k) such that $a_k + b_k = k\lceil n^{2/3} \rceil$ and $A[s_A + a_k] \leq B[s_B + b_k + 1]$ and $B[s_B + b_k] \leq A[s_A + a_k + 1]$.
7:      $\forall k \in [1 : \lfloor n^{1/3} \rfloor]$. MERGE$((A, s_A + a_k, a_{k+1} - a_k), (B, s_B + b_k, b_{k+1} - b_k), (C, s_C + a_k + b_k))$
8: **end if**

---

al. [31] has studied cache oblivious algorithms for a parallel model with a tree of caches. Our design motive is to have a generic approach that enables one to analyze an algorithm independently of the model in a simple way and then map onto different machines; we study SpMV-multiply, sorting and related algorithms as specific instances of our general approach. Our work may also be contrasted with that of [7], which presents cache-efficient algorithms for private caches but the algorithms are not cache oblivious and are based on a fixed number of processors p.

A preliminary version of this paper appeared as a three page brief announcement in SPAA'09 [17].

2. SORTING

In this section, we present the first cache-oblivious sorting algorithm that achieves optimal work, polylogarithmic depth, and good sequential cache complexity. Prior cache-oblivious algorithms with optimal cache complexity [23, 24, 25, 36, 38] have $\Omega(\sqrt{n})$ depth.

2.1 Algorithm Preliminaries

Our sorting algorithm uses known algorithms for matrix transpose, prefix sum and merging as subroutines. We first describe the exact variants of these algorithms that the sorting algorithm uses. The costs are summarized in Figure 1. The standard divide-and-conquer matrix-transpose algorithm [38] is work optimal, has logarithmic depth and has optimal cache complexity when $M = \Omega(B^2)$. A simple variant of the tree-based parallel prefix-sums algorithm has logarithmic depth and cache complexity $O(n/B)$. As usual the algorithm works in two phases generating partial sums in a tree in one phase and propagating results down in the next. Each phase is implemented using divide-and-conquer over the tree. For cache efficiency, the tree of partial sums is laid out in the infix order. This gives an algorithm that runs with cache complexity $O(n/b)$ and depth $O(\log n)$ even if the cache only has a single cache line.

Algorithm 1 merges two arrays A and B of sizes l_A and l_B ($l_A + l_B = n$). The pivots ranked $\{n^{2/3}, 2n^{2/3}, \dots\}$ can be found using a dual binary search on the arrays. This takes $O(n^{1/3} \cdot \log n)$ work, $O(\log n)$ depth and at most $O(n^{1/3} \log (n/B))$ cache misses. Once the locations of pivots have been identified, the subarrays which are of output size $n^{2/3}$ each can be recursively merged and appended. The recursive relation for the cache complexity is

$$Q(n; M, B) \leq \begin{cases} k_1 n^{1/3}(\log (n/B) + Q(n^{2/3}; M, B)) & n > cM \\ k_2 n/B + 1 & \text{otherwise} \end{cases}$$

for some positive constants c, k_1 and k_2. When $n > cM$, this

Problem	Depth	Cache Complexity	Section
Matrix Transpose ($n \times m$ matrix)	$O(\log{(n+m)})$	$O(\lceil nm/B \rceil)$	[38]
Prefix Sums	$O(\log n)$	$O(\lceil n/B \rceil)$	2.1
Merge	$O(\log n)$	$O(\lceil n/B \rceil)$	2.1
Sort (deterministic)*	$O(\log^2 n)$	$O(\lceil n/B \rceil \lceil \log_M n \rceil)$	2.2
Sort (randomized; bounds are w.h.p.)*	$O(\log^{1.5} n)$	$O(\lceil n/B \rceil \lceil \log_M n \rceil)$	2.3
Sparse-Matrix Vector Multiply (m nonzeros, n^ϵ separators)*	$O(\log^2 n)$	$O(\lceil m/B + n/M^{1-\epsilon} \rceil)$	4

Figure 1: Low-depth cache-oblivious algorithms. New algorithms are marked (*). All algorithms are work optimal and their cache complexities match the best sequential algorithms. The bounds assume $M = \Omega(B^2)$.

recursion satisfies

$$Q(n; M, B) = O(n/B + n^{1/3} \log{(n/B)}).$$

If $M = \Omega(B^2)$ and $n > cM$, then the first term in the expression for cache complexity $O(n/B)$ is asymptotically larger than $n^{1/3} \log{(n/B)}$, making the second term redundant. Therefore, in all cases, $Q(n; M, B) = O(\lceil n/B \rceil)$. The recurrence relation for depth is:

$$D(n) \leq \log n + D(n^{2/3}),$$

which solves to $D(n) = O(\log n)$. It is easy to see that the work involved is linear.

Using this merge algorithm in a mergesort in which the two recursive calls are parallel gives an algorithm with depth $O(\log^2 n)$ and cache complexity $O((n/B) \log_2{(n/M)})$, which is not optimal. Blelloch et al. [14] analyze similar merge and mergesort algorithms with the same (suboptimal) cache complexities but with larger depth.

2.2 Deterministic Sorting

Our parallel sorting algorithm is based on a version of sample sort [37, 45], and has optimal cache complexity. Sample sorts first use a sample to select a set of pivots that partition the keys into buckets, then route all the keys to their appropriate buckets, and finally sort within the buckets. Compared to prior cache-friendly (sequential) sample sort algorithms [2, 41], which with slight modification can be improved to $\Omega(\sqrt{n})$ depth, our cache-oblivious algorithm uses (and analyzes) a new parallel bucket-transpose algorithm for the key distribution phase, in order to achieve $O(\log^2 n)$ depth.

The algorithm (Algorithm COSORT in Figure 2) first splits the set of elements into $\sqrt{n}$ subarrays of size $\sqrt{n}$ and recursively sorts each of the subarrays. Then, samples are chosen to determine pivots. This step can be done either deterministically or randomly. We first describe a deterministic version of the algorithm for which the **repeat** and **until** statements are not needed; Section 2.3 will describe a randomized version that uses these statements. For the deterministic version, we choose every $(\log n)$-th element from each of the subarrays as a sample. The sample set, which is smaller than the given data set by a factor of $\log n$, is then sorted using the mergesort algorithm outlined above. Because mergesort is reasonably cache-efficient, using it on a set slightly smaller than the input set is not too costly in terms of cache complexity. More precisely, this mergesort does not incur more than $O(\lceil n/B \rceil)$ cache misses. We can then pick $\sqrt{n}$ evenly spaced keys from the sample set $\mathcal{P}$ as pivots to determine bucket boundaries. To determine the bucket boundaries, the pivots are used to split each subarray using the cache-oblivious merge procedure. This procedure also takes no more than $O(\lceil n/B \rceil)$ cache misses.

Once the subarrays have been split, prefix sums and matrix transpose operations can be used to determine the precise location in the buckets where each segment of the subarray is to be sent. This mapping information is stored in a matrix T of size $\sqrt{n} \times \sqrt{n}$. Note that none of the buckets will be loaded with more than $2\sqrt{n} \log n$ keys because of the way we select pivots.

Once the bucket boundaries have been determined, the keys need to be transferred to the buckets. Although a naive algorithm to do this is not cache-efficient, we show that the bucket transpose algorithm (Algorithm B-TRANSPOSE in Figure 2) is. The bucket transpose is a four way divide-and-conquer procedure on the (almost) square matrix T which indicates a set of segments of subarrays (segments are contiguous in each subarray) and their target locations in the bucket. The matrix T is cut in half vertically and horizontally and separate recursive calls are assigned the responsibility of transferring the keys specified in each of the four parts. Note that ordinary matrix transpose is the special case of $T_{i,j} = \langle j, i, 1 \rangle$ for all i, j.

LEMMA 2.1. *Algorithm B-TRANSPOSE transfers a matrix of $\sqrt{n} \times \sqrt{n}$ keys into bucket matrix B of $\sqrt{n}$ buckets according to offset matrix T in $O(n)$ work, $O(\log n)$ depth, and $O(\lceil n/B \rceil)$ sequential cache complexity.*

PROOF. (sketch) For each node v in the recursion tree of bucket transpose, we define the node's size $s(v)$ to be n^2, the size of its submatrix T, and the node's weight $w(v)$ to be the number of keys that T is responsible for transferring. We identify three classes of nodes in the recursion tree:

1. Light-1 nodes: A node v is light-1 if $s(v) < M/100$, $w(v) < M/10$, and its parent node is of size $\geq M/100$.

2. Light-2 nodes: A node v is light-2 if $s(v) < M/100$, $w(v) < M/10$, and its parent node is of weight $\geq M/10$.

3. Heavy leaves: A leaf v is heavy if $w(v) \geq M/10$.

The union of these three sets covers the responsibility for transferring all the keys, i.e., all leaves are accounted for in the subtrees of these nodes.

From the definition of a light-1 node, it can be argued that all the keys that a light-1 node is responsible for fit inside a cache, implying that the subtree rooted at a light-1 node cannot incur more than M/B cache misses. It can also be seen that light-1 nodes can not be greater than $4n/(M/100)$ in number leading to the fact that the sum of cache complexities of all the light-1 nodes is no more than $O(\lceil n/B \rceil)$.

Light-2 nodes are similar to light-1 nodes in that their target data fits into a cache of size M. If we assume that they have combined weight of $n - W$, then there are no more than $4(n-W)/(M/10)$ of them, putting the aggregate cache complexity for their subtrees at $40(n-W)/B$.

A heavy leaf of weight w incurs $\lceil w/B \rceil$ cache misses. There are no more than $W/(M/10)$ of them, implying that their aggregate cache complexity is $W/B + 10W/M < 11W/B$. Therefore, the cache complexities of light-2 nodes and heavy leaves adds up to

Algorithm COSORT(A, n)
_____
if $n < 10$ **then**
    return Sort A sequentially
end if
$h \leftarrow \lceil \sqrt{n} \rceil$
$\forall i \in [1:h]$, Let $A_i \leftarrow A[h(i-1)+1:hi]$
$\forall i \in [1:h]$, $S_i \leftarrow$ COSORT(A_i, h)
repeat
    Pick an appropriate sorted pivot set $\mathcal{P}$ of size h
    $\forall i \in [1:h]$, $M_i \leftarrow$ SPLIT($S_i, \mathcal{P}$)
    {Each array M_i contains for each bucket j a start location in S_i for bucket
    j and a length of how many entries are in that bucket, possibly 0.}
    $L \leftarrow h \times h$ matrix formed by rows M_i with just the lengths
    $L^T \leftarrow$ TRANSPOSE(L)
    $\forall i \in [1:h]$, $O_i \leftarrow$ PREFIX-SUM(L_i^T)
    $O^T \leftarrow$ TRANSPOSE(O)   {O_i is the ith row of O}
    $\forall i, j \in [1:h]$, $T_{i,j} \leftarrow \langle M_{i,j}\langle 1\rangle, O_{i,j}^T, M_{i,j}\langle 2\rangle \rangle$
    {Each triple corresponds to an offset in row i for bucket j, an offset in
    bucket j for row i and the length to copy.}
until No bucket is too big
Let $B_1, B_2, \ldots, B_h$ be arrays (buckets) of sizes dictated by T
B-TRANSPOSE($S, B, T, 1, 1, h$)
$\forall i, B_i' \leftarrow$ COSORT(B_i, length(B_i))
return $B_1' \| B_2' \| \ldots \| B_h'$

Algorithm B-TRANSPOSE(S, B, T, i_s, i_b, n)
_____
if ($n = 1$) **then**
    Copy $S_{i_s}[T_{i_s, i_b}\langle 1\rangle : T_{i_s, i_b}\langle 1\rangle + T_{i_s, i_b}\langle 3\rangle]$
    to $B_{i_b}[T_{i_s, i_b}\langle 2\rangle : T_{i_s, i_b}\langle 2\rangle + T_{i_s, i_b}\langle 3\rangle]$
else
    B-TRANSPOSE($S, B, T, i_s, i_b, n/2$)
    B-TRANSPOSE($S, B, T, i_s, i_b + n/2, n/2$)
    B-TRANSPOSE($S, B, T, i_s + n/2, i_b, n/2$)
    B-TRANSPOSE($S, B, T, i_s + n/2, i_b + n/2, n/2$)
end if

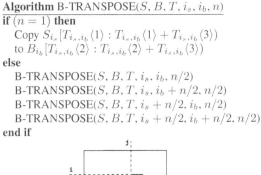
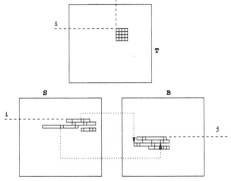

Bucket transpose diagram: The 4x4 entries shown for T dictate the mapping from the 16 depicted segments of S to the 16 depicted segments of B. Arrows highlight the mapping for two of the segments.

Figure 2: Cache-Oblivious Sorting and Bucket-Transpose Algorithms

another $O(\lceil n/B \rceil)$. We also note that the validity of this proof does not depend on the size of the individual buckets. The statement of the lemma holds even for the case where each of the buckets is as large as $O(\sqrt{n}\log n)$. $\square$

THEOREM 2.2. _On an input of size n, the deterministic COSORT has $Q(n; M, B) = O(\lceil n/B \rceil \lceil \log_M n \rceil)$ sequential cache complexity, $O(n \log n)$ work, and $O(\log^2 n)$ depth._

PROOF. All the subroutines other than recursive calls to COSORT have linear work and cache complexity $O(\lceil n/B \rceil)$. Also, the subroutine with the maximum depth is the mergesort used to find pivots; its depth is $O(\log^2 n)$. Therefore, the recurrence relations for the work, depth, and cache complexity are as follows:

$$W(n) = O(n) + \sqrt{n}W(\sqrt{n}) + \sum_{i=1}^{\sqrt{n}} W(n_i)$$

$$D(n) = O(\log^2 n) + \max_{i=1}^{\sqrt{n}} \{D(n_i)\}$$

$$Q(n; M, B) = O\left(\left\lceil \frac{n}{B} \right\rceil\right) + \sqrt{n}Q(\sqrt{n}; M, B) + \sum_{i=1}^{\sqrt{n}} Q(n_i; M, B),$$

where the n_is are such that their sum is n and none individually exceed $2\sqrt{n}\log n$. The base case for the recursion for cache complexity is $Q(n; M, B) = O(\lceil n/B \rceil)$ for $n < cM$ for some constant c. Solving these recurrences proves the theorem. $\square$

2.3 Randomized Sorting

A simple randomized version of the sorting algorithm is to randomly pick $\sqrt{n}$ elements for pivots, sort them using brute force (compare every pair) and using the sorted set as the pivot set $\mathcal{P}$. This step takes $O(n)$ work, $O(\log n)$ depth (let c_n be a constant

such that depth is at most $c_n \log(n)$) and has cache complexity $O(n/B)$ and the probability that the largest of the resultant buckets are larger than $3\sqrt{n}\log n$ is not more $1 - 1/n$. When one of the buckets is too large ($> 3\sqrt{n}\log n$), the process of selecting pivots and recomputing bucket boundaries is repeated. Because the probability of this happening repeatedly is low, the overall depth of the algorithm is small. Further, the recursion is stopped when the problem size reduces to 2^{40}.

THEOREM 2.3. _On an input of size n, the randomized version of COSORT has, with probability greater than $1 - 1/n$, $Q(n; M, B) = O(\lceil n/B \rceil \lceil \log_M n \rceil)$ sequential cache complexity, $O(n \log n)$ work, and $O(\log^{1.5} n)$ depth._

PROOF. (sketch) In a call to randomized COSORT with input size n, the loop terminates with probability $1 - 1/n$ in each round and takes less than 2 iterations on average to terminate. Each iteration of the while loop, including the brute force sort requires $O(n)$ work and incurs at most $O(\lceil n/B \rceil)$ cache misses with high probability. Therefore,

$$\mathbb{E}[W(n)] = O(n) + \sqrt{n}\,\mathbb{E}[W(\sqrt{n})] + \sum_{i=1}^{\sqrt{n}} \mathbb{E}[W(n_i)],$$

where each $n_i < 3\sqrt{n}\log n$ and $\sum_{i=1}^{\sqrt{n}} n_i = n$. This implies that $\mathbb{E}[W(n)] = O(n\log n)$. Similarly for cache complexity we have

$$\mathbb{E}[Q(n; M, B)]$$
$$= O\left(\frac{n}{B}\right) + \sqrt{n}\,\mathbb{E}[Q(\sqrt{n}; M, B)] + \sum_{i=1}^{\sqrt{n}} \mathbb{E}[Q(n_i; M, B)],$$

which implies $\mathbb{E}[Q(n; M, B)] = O\left(\frac{n}{B}\log_{\sqrt{M}} n\right) = O\left(\frac{n}{B}\log_M n\right)$. To show the high probability bounds for work and cache complexity, we can use Chernoff bounds since the fan out at each level of recursion is high.

To analyze the depth of the dag, we obtain high probability bounds on the depth of each level of recursion tree (we assume that the levels are numbered starting with the root at level 0). To get sufficient confidence bounds at each level we might have to execute the outer loop more times toward the leaves where the problem size is small. Each iteration of the outer loop at node N of input size m at level k in the recursion tree has depth $\log m$ and the termination probability of the loop is $1 - 1/m$.

We first show probability bounds on the depth of a maximal path in the computation dag. We represent the path as a recursion tree and show that the sum of depths of all nodes at level d in the recursion tree is at most $c_d \log^{3/2} n / \log_2 \log_2 n$ with probability at least $1 - 1/n^{(\log_2 \log_2 n)^2}$ (for some constant c_d to be defined shortly) and that the recursion tree is at most $1.5 \log_2 \log_2 n$ levels deep. This will prove that the depth of the recursion tree (*i.e.*the path) is $1.5 c_d \log^{3/2} n$ with probability at least

$$1 - (1.5 \log_2 \log_2 n)/n^{\log_2^2 \log_2 n}.$$

Since each of the paths is a candidate for the critical path, the actual depth is a maximum over all such paths. We will argue that there are not more than $C(n) = n^{1.5 \log_2 \log_2 n}$ such paths. Then, by the union bound, it follows that the probability that any single path is longer than $1.5 c_d \log^{3/2} n$ is less than

$$1.5 \log \log n / n^{(\log_2 \log_2 n)^2 - 1.5 \log_2 \log_2 n}$$

(high probability bound).

The maximum number of levels in the recursion tree can be bounded using the recurrence relation $X(n) \geq 1 + X(3\sqrt{n} \log n)$ and $X(2^{40}) = 1$. Using induction, it is straightforward to show that this solves to $X(n) < 1.5 \log_2 \log_2 n$. Similarly the number of paths $C(n)$ can be bounded using the relation $C(n) > (\sqrt{n} C(\sqrt{n}))(\sqrt{n} C(2\sqrt{n} \log n))$. Again, using induction, this relation can be used to show that $C(n) = n^{1.5 \log_2 \log_2 n}$.

To compute the sum of the depth of nodes at level d in the recursion tree, we consider two cases: (1) when $d > 80 \log_2 \log_2 \log_2 n$ and (2) otherwise.

Case 1: The size of a node one level deep in the recursion tree is at most $3\sqrt{n} \log n \leq n^{1/2+r}$ for $r = 1/6$. Also, the size of a node which is d levels deep is at most $n^{(1/2+r)^d}$, each costing $c_n (1/2 + r)^d \log n$ depth per trial. Since there are at most 2^d nodes at level d in the recursion tree, and the failure probability of a loop in any node is no more than $1/2$, we show that the probability of having to execute more than $(2^d \cdot \log^{1/2} n)/((1 + 2r)^d \cdot \log_2 \log_2 n)$ loops is small. Since we are estimating the sum of 2^d independent variables, we use Chernoff bounds of the form:

$$Pr[X > (1+\delta)\mu] \leq e^{-\delta^2 \mu}, \qquad (1)$$

with $\mu = (2 \cdot 2^d)$, $\delta = (1/2)(\log^{1/2} n/((1+2r)^d \cdot \log_2 \log_2 n)) - 1$. The resulting probability bound is less than $1/n^{\log_2^2 \log_2 n}$ for $d > 80 \log_2 \log_2 \log_2 n$. Therefore, the contribution of nodes at level d in the recursion tree to the depth of recursion tree is at most $2^d \cdot (1/2 + r)^d c_n \log n \cdot \log^{1/2} n/((1 + 2r)^d \cdot \log_2 \log_2 n) = c_n \log^{3/2} n / \log_2 \log_2 n$ with probability at least $1 - 1/n^{\log_2^2 \log_2 n}$.

Case 2: We classify all nodes at level d in to two kinds, the large ones with size greater than $\log^2 n$ and the smaller ones with size at most $\log^2 n$. The total number of nodes is at most $2^d < (\log_2 \log_2 n)^{80}$. Consider the small nodes. Each small node can contribute a depth of at most $2c_n \log_2 \log_2 n$ to the recursion tree and there are at most $(\log_2 \log_2 n)^{80}$ of them. If we set c_d to be the

minimum number such that $c_d \log^{3/2} n > c_n \log_2 \log_2^{82} n$, then the contribution of small nodes to depth of the recursion tree at level d is lesser than $c_d \log^{3/2} n / \log_2 \log_2 n$.

We use Chernoff bounds to bound the contribution of large nodes to the depth of the recursion tree. Suppose that there are j large nodes. We show that with probability not more than $1/n^{\log^2 \log n}$, it takes more than $10 \cdot j$ loop iterations at depth d for j of them to succeed. For this, consider $10 \cdot j$ random independent trials with success probability at least $1 - 1/\log^2 n$ each. The expected number of failures is no more than $\mu = 10 \cdot j/\log^2 n$. We want to show that the probability that there are greater than $9 \cdot j$ failures in this experiment is tiny. Using Chernoff bounds with the above μ, and $\delta = (0.9 \cdot \log^2 n - 1)$, we infer that this probability is less than $1/n^{\log_2^2 \log_2 n}$. Since $j < 2^d$, the depth contributed by the larger nodes is at most $2^d (1/2 + 1/6)^d \log n < c_d \log^{3/2} n / \log_2 \log_2 n$.

We have shown that each level in the recursion tree adds at most $c_d \log^{3/2} n / \log_2 \log_2 n$ depth to a path with probability at least $1 - 1/n^{\log_2^2 \log n}$. The proof follows from the union bound described earlier. $\square$

3. APPLICATIONS OF SORTING: GRAPH ALGORITHMS

In this section, we make use of the fact that the PRAM algorithms for many problems can be decomposed into primitive operations such as scans and sorts. Our approach is similar to that of [7] except that we use the cache-oblivious model instead of the parallel external memory model. Arge et al. [5] demonstrate a cache-oblivious algorithm for list ranking using priority queues and use it to construct other graph algorithms. But their algorithms have $\Omega(n)$ depth because list ranking uses a serially-dependent sequence of priority queue operations to compute independent sets. Our parallel algorithms derived from sorting are the same as in [27] except that we use different algorithms for the primitive operations scan and sort, which suit our cache-oblivious framework. Moreover, a careful analysis (using standard techniques) is required to prove our sequential cache complexity and depth bounds under this framework.

List Ranking. A basic strategy for list ranking [40] is the following: (i) shrink the list to size $O(n/\log n)$, and (ii) apply pointer jumping on this shorter list. Stage (i) is achieved through finding independent sets in the list of size $\Theta(n)$ and removing them to yield a smaller problem. This can be done randomly using the random mate technique in which case, $O(\log \log n)$ rounds of such reduction would suffice. Alternately, we could use the deterministic technique described in section 3.1 of [40]: use two rounds of Cole and Vishkin's deterministic coin tossing [32] to find a $O(\log \log n)$-ruling set and then convert the ruling set to an independent set of size at least $n/3$ in $O(\log \log n)$ rounds. Arge et al. [8] show how this conversion can be made cache-efficient, and it is straightforward to change this algorithm to a cache-oblivious one. Stage (ii) uses $O(\log n)$ rounds of pointer jumping, each round essentially involving a sort operation to figure out the next level of pointer jumping. Thus, the cache complexity of this stage is asymptotically the same as sorting and its depth is $O(\log n)$ times the depth of sorting:

THEOREM 3.1. *The deterministic list ranking outlined above has* $Q(n; M, B) = O(\lceil n/B \rceil \lceil \log_M n \rceil)$ *sequential cache complexity,* $O(n \log n)$ *work, and* $O(D_{sort}(n) \log n)$ *depth.*

Graph Algorithms. We tabulate the complexity measures of basic graph algorithms on bounded degree graphs (Figure 3). The al-

Problem	Depth	Cache Complexity
List Ranking	$D_{LR}(n) = O(D_{sort}(n)\log n)$	$O(Q_{sort}(n))$
Euler Tour on Trees	$O(D_{LR}(n))$	$O(Q_{sort}(n))$
Tree Contraction	$O(D_{LR}(n)\log n)$	$O(Q_{sort}(n))$
Least Common Ancestors (k queries)	$O(D_{LR}(n))$	$O(\lceil k/n \rceil Q_{sort}(n))$
Connected Components	$O(D_{LR}(n)\log n)$	$O(Q_{sort}(|E|)\log(|V|/\sqrt{M}))$
Minimum Spanning Forest	$O(D_{LR}(n)\log n)$	$O(Q_{sort}(|E|)\log(|V|/\sqrt{M}))$

Figure 3: Low-depth cache-oblivious graph algorithms. All algorithms are deterministic. The bounds assume $M = \Omega(B^2)$. D_{sort} and Q_{sort} are the depth and cache complexity of cache-oblivious sorting.

gorithms that lead to these complexities are straightforward cache-oblivious adaptations of known PRAM algorithms (as described for the external memory model in [27]) using primitives from earlier sections. For instance, finding an Euler Tour involves scanning the input to compute the successor function for each edge and running a list ranking. Tree contraction involves constructing an Euler tour of the tree, finding an independent set on it and contracting the tour to recursively solve a smaller problem. Finding Least Common Ancestors of a set of vertex pairs in a tree involves computing the Euler tour and reducing the problem to a range minima query problem (which is solved with search trees). Deterministic algorithms for Connected Components and Minimum Spanning Forest are similar and use tree contraction as their basic idea; the cache bounds are slightly worse than those in [27]: $\log(|V|/\sqrt{M})$ versus $\log(|V|/M)$. While [27] uses knowledge of M to transition to a different approach once the *vertices* in the contracted graph fit within the cache, cache-obliviously we need for the *edges* to fit before we stop incurring misses.

4. SPARSE-MATRIX VECTOR MULTIPLY

We consider the problem of multiplying a sparse $n \times n$ matrix with m non-zeros by a dense vector. For general sparse matrices Bender *et al.* [10] show a lower bound on cache complexity, which for $m = O(n)$ matches the sorting lower bound. However, for certain matrices common in practice the cache complexity can be improved. For example, for matrices with non-zero structure corresponding to a well-shaped d-dimensional mesh, a multiply can be performed with cache complexity $O(m/B + n/M^{1/d})$ [11]. This requires pre-processing to lay out the matrix in the right form. However, for applications that run many multiplies over the same matrix, as with many iterative solvers, the cost of the pre-processing can be amortized. Note that for $M \geq B^d$ (e.g., the tall-cache assumption in 2 dimension), the cache complexity reduces to $O(m/B)$ which is asymptotically the same as scanning memory.

The cache-efficient layout and bounds for well-shaped meshes can easily be extended to graphs with good edge separators [14]. The layout and algorithm, however, is not efficient for graphs such as planar graphs or graphs with constant genus that have good vertex separators but not necessarily any good edge separators. In this paper we generalize the results to graphs with good vertex separators and present the first cache-oblivious, low cache complexity algorithm for the sparse-matrix multiplication problem on such graphs. We do not analyze the cost of finding the layout, which involves the recursive application of finding vertex separators, as it can be amortized across many solver iterations. Our algorithm for matrices with n^ϵ separators has linear work, $O(\log^2 n)$ depth, and $O(m/B + n/M^{1-\epsilon})$ sequential cache complexity.

Let S be a class of graphs that is closed under the subgraph relation. We say that S satisfies a $f(n)$-*vertex separator theorem* if there are constants $\alpha < 1$ and $\beta > 0$ such that every graph

Algorithm BuildTree(V, E)
if $|E| = 1$ **then**
   return V
end if
$(V_a, V_{sep}, V_b) \leftarrow$ FindSeparator(V, E)
$E_a \leftarrow \{(u, v) \in E \mid u \in V_a \vee v \in V_a\}$
$E_b \leftarrow E - E_a$
$V_{a,sep} \leftarrow V_a \cup V_{sep}$
$V_{b,sep} \leftarrow V_b \cup V_{sep}$
$T_a \leftarrow$ BuildTree$(V_{a,sep}, E_a)$
$T_b \leftarrow$ BuildTree$(V_{b,sep}, E_b)$
return SeparatorTree(T_a, V_{sep}, T_b)

Algorithm SparseMxV(x, T)
if isLeaf(T) **then**
   $T.u.$value $\leftarrow x[T.v.$index$] \otimes T.w_{vu}$
   $T.v.$value $\leftarrow x[T.u.$index$] \otimes T.w_{uv}$
   {Two statements for the two edge directions}
else
   SparseMxV$(T.$left$)$ and SparseMxV$(T.$right$)$
   for all $v \in T.$vertices **do**
      $v.$value $\leftarrow (v.$left$\rightarrow$value $\oplus$ $v.$right$\rightarrow$value$)$
   end for
end if

Figure 4: Cache-Oblivious Algorithms for Building a Separator Tree and for Sparse-Matrix Vector Multiply

$G = (V, E)$ in S with n vertices can be partitioned into three sets of vertices V_a, V_s, V_b such that $|V_s| \leq \beta f(n)$, $|V_a|, |V_b| \leq \alpha n$, and $\{(u, v) \in E \mid (u \in V_a \wedge v \in V_b) \vee (u \in V_b \wedge v \in V_a)\} = \emptyset$ [43]. In our presentation we assume the matrix has symmetric non-zero structure (if it is asymmetric we can always add zero weight reverse edges while at most doubling the number of edges).

We now describe how to build a separator tree assuming we have a good algorithm FindSeparator for finding separators. For planar graphs this can be done in linear time [43]. The algorithm for building the tree is defined by Algorithm BuildTree in Figure 4. At each recursive call it partitions the edges into two subsets that are passed to the left and right children. All the vertices in the separator are passed to both children. Each leaf corresponds to a single edge. We assume that FindSeparator only puts a vertex in the separator if it has an edge to each side and always returns a separator with at least one vertex on each side unless the graph is a clique. If the graph is a clique, we assume the separator contains all but one of the vertices, and that the remaining vertex is on the left side (V_a) of the partition. By convention we place any edges between vertices in the separator in E_b.

Every vertex of degree Δ in our original graph corresponds to a binary tree embedded in the separator tree with Δ leaves, one for each of its incident edges. To see this consider a single vertex. Every time it appears in a separator, its edges are partitioned into two sets, and the vertex is copied to both recursive calls. Because the vertex will appear in Δ leaves, it must appear in $\Delta - 1$ separators, so it will appear in $\Delta - 1$ internal nodes of the separator tree. We refer to the tree for a vertex as the *vertex tree*, each appearance of a vertex in the tree as a *vertex copy*, and the root of each tree as the *vertex root*. The tree is used to sum the values for matrix vector multiply.

We reorder the rows/columns of the matrix based on a preorder traversal of their root locations in the separator tree (*i.e.*, all vertices in the top separator will appear first). This is the order we will use for the input vector x and output vector y when calculating $y = Ax$. We keep a vector R in this order that points to each of the corresponding roots of the tree. The separator tree is maintained as a tree T in which each node keeps its copies of the vertices in its separator. Each of these vertex copies will point to its two children in the vertex tree. Each leaf of T is an edge and includes the indices of its two endpoints and its weight. In all internal vertex copies we keep an extra value field to store a temporary variable, and in the leaves we keep two value fields, one for each direction. Finally we note that all data for each node of the separator tree is stored adjacently (*i.e.*, all its vertex copies are stored one after the other), and the nodes are stored in preorder. This is important for cache efficiency.

Our algorithm for sparse-matrix vector multiplication is described in Algorithm SparseMxV in Figure 4. This algorithm will take the input vector x and leave the results of the matrix multiplication in the root of every vertex. To gather the results up into a result vector y we simply use the root pointers R to fetch each root. The algorithm does not do any work beyond the recursive calls on the way down the recursion, but when it gets to a leaf the edge multiplies its two endpoints by its weight putting the result in its temporary value. If the matrix is symmetric then only one weight is needed. Then on the way back up the recursion the algorithms sums these values. In particular whenever it gets to an internal node of a vertex tree it adds the two children. Since the algorithm works bottom up the values of the children are always ready when the parent reads them.

THEOREM 4.1. *Let $\mathcal{M}$ be a class of matrices for which the adjacency graphs satisfy an n^ϵ-vertex separator theorem. Algorithm SparseMxV on an $n \times n$ matrix $A \in \mathcal{M}$ with $m \geq n$ non-zeros has $O(m)$ work, $O(\log^2 n)$ depth and $O(\lceil m/B + n/M^{1-\epsilon} \rceil)$ sequential cache complexity.*

PROOF. For a constant k we say a vertex copy is heavy if it appears in a separator node with size (memory usage) larger than M/k. We say a vertex is heavy if it has any heavy vertex copies. We first show that the number of heavy vertex copies for any constant k is bounded by $O(n/M^{1-\epsilon})$ and then bound the number of cache misses based on the number of heavy copies.

For a node of n vertices, the size $X(n)$ of the tree rooted at the node is bounded by the separator condition giving the recurrence relation:

$$X(n) \quad \leq \quad \max_{1/2 \geq \alpha' \geq \alpha} \{X(\alpha' n) + X((1-\alpha')n) + \beta n^\epsilon\}$$

This recurrence is satisfied by $X(n) = k(n - n^\epsilon)$, $k = \beta/(\alpha^\epsilon + (1-\alpha)^\epsilon - 1)$. Therefore, there exists a constant c such that for $n < cM$, the subtree rooted at node of n vertices fits into the cache. We use this to count the number of heavy vertex copies $H(n)$. The recurrence relation for $H(n)$ is:

$$H(n) \leq \max_{\alpha \leq \alpha' \leq \frac{1}{2}} \{H(\alpha' n) + H((1-\alpha')n) + \beta n^\epsilon\},$$

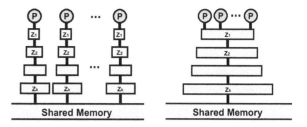

Figure 5: *Left:* **Parallel Multi-level Distributed Hierarchy (PMDH).** *Right:* **Parallel Multi-level Shared Hierarchy (PMSH).**

for $n > cM$ and 0 otherwise. This recurrence relation is satisfied by $H(n) = k(n/(cM)^{1-\epsilon} - \beta n^\epsilon) = O(n/M^{1-\epsilon})$.

Now we note that if a vertex is not heavy (*i.e.*, light) it is only used by a single subtree that fits in cache. Furthermore because of the ordering of the vertices based on where the roots appear, all light vertices that appear in the same subtree are adjacent. Therefore the total cost of cache misses for light vertices is $O(n/B)$. We note that the edges are traversed in order so they only incur $O(m/B)$ misses. Now each of the heavy vertex copies can be responsible for at most $O(1)$ cache misses. In particular reading each child can cause a miss. Furthermore reading the value from a heavy vertex (at the leaf of the recursion) could cause a miss since it is not stored in the subtree that fits into cache. But the number of subtrees that just fit into cache (*i.e.*, their parents don't) and read a vertex u is bounded by one more than the number of heavy copies of u. Therefore we can count each of those misses against a heavy copy. We therefore have a total of $O(m/B + n/M^{1-\epsilon})$ misses.

The work is simply proportional to the number of vertex copies, which is less than twice m and hence is bounded by $O(m)$. For the depth we note that the two recursive calls can be made in parallel and furthermore the **for all** statement can be made in parallel. Furthermore the tree is depth $O(\log n)$ because of the balance condition on separators. Since the branching of the **for all** takes $O(\log n)$ depth, the total depth is bounded by $O(\log^2 n)$. $\square$

5. MAPPING TO PARALLEL MULTI-LEVEL HIERARCHIES

In this section, we discuss how (low-depth) algorithms designed for the cache-oblivious model can be scheduled on natural multi-level generalizations of one-level private or shared cache machines, such that we can upper bound the parallel cache complexity and the parallel run time. We begin by defining the two models we consider.

5.1 PMDH and PMSH Models

We consider a *Parallel Multi-level Distributed Hierarchy (PMDH)* (Figure 5(left)), where each of the p processors has a multi-level private hierarchy and a *Parallel Multi-level Shared Hierarchy (PMSH)* (Figure 5(right)), where all the processors share a multi-level cache hierarchy. All computation by a processor p occurs on data in p's (private or shared) level-one cache. One or more cache lines of a given cache at level $i < k$ fit precisely in a cache line of its "parent" cache at level $i + 1$. We assume the cache hierarchy is inclusive: each cached word at level $i < k$ is also cached in its parent cache at level $i + 1$. A processor requesting a memory word *fetches* the cache line containing the word from the lowest-level ancestor cache containing the line (and populates all intervening caches). If the processor writes to the memory word, only the level-one cache line is updated and the line becomes *dirty*. Whenever a dirty line is evicted from a cache, its contents are written back to the corresponding line in its parent cache. Each cache is fully associative and uses an optimal replacement policy (within the constraints of being inclusive).

Cache Consistency in PDMH. In private cache models, the same memory word can be in the caches of multiple processors and these copies must be kept consistent. As in the two-level private cache model studied by Frigo *et al.* [39], the multi-level PMDH assumes a variant of the *dag consistency* cache consistency model [19] that uses an optimal replacement policy instead of LRU replacement. (We revisit LRU replacement in Section 6.) Caches are *non-interfering* in that the cache misses of one processor can be analyzed independent of other processors. To maintain this property, Frigo *et al.* use the BACKER protocol [19]. This protocol manages caches so that if an instruction j is a descendant of instruction i, then values written to memory words by i are reflected in j's memory accesses. However, concurrent writes to objects by instructions that do not have a path between them in the dag will not be communicated between processors executing these instructions. Such writes are *reconciled* to shared memory and reflected in other cache copies only when a descendant of the instruction that performed these writes tries to access them. Reconciliation of a memory block involves updating all written words within the block; the protocol must track all such writes. In case of multiple writes to the same word, an arbitrary write succeeds. Concurrent reads are permitted. We likewise assume the same non-interfering property, with the same reconciliation process.

5.2 Extending Private Cache Results to Multiple Levels

Because each processor in the PMDH model has its own private memory hierarchy, it is better to have each processor work on parts of computations that are as far apart as possible. The work stealing scheduler [21, 9, 1] is an ideal choice for such a system. In its simpler form, a work stealing scheduler maintains a task dequeue for each processor. When a processor spawns a new job, the new job is queued at the tail of its dequeue. When a processor runs out of work, it pulls out the job at the head of its task queue. If its own task queue is empty, the processors randomly picks another task queue to steal from. This version of the work stealing is referred to as *randomized work stealing*. Another (perhaps less practical) version of work stealing uses a single shared task dequeue for all processors; we refer to this as *centralized work stealing*.

We derive run time bound for algorithms under randomized work stealing for the PMDH such that the only algorithm-specific metrics in the bound are W, D and the sequential cache complexity Q. (To simplify notation, we will use $Q(M, B)$ instead of $Q(n; M, B)$ in the remainder of this section.) Given a particular execution X of a computation A on some parallel machine P, let $c(x)$ be the cost of instruction x. This cost includes the time for accessing the data used by x; if the access needs to fetch the data from level i cache, the cost is C_i (we view the shared memory as level $k + 1$). The latency added work under execution X is $W^{lat}_{A,P}(X) = \sum_{x \in A} c(x)$. The *latency-added work*, $W^{lat}_{A,P}$, of a computation is the maximum of $W^{lat}_{A,P}(X)$ over all executions X. This can be bounded by $W + \sum_{i=2}^{k+1}(Q(M_{i-1}, B_{i-1}) - Q(M_i, B_i)) \cdot C_i + (\#S)(M_k/B_k)C_k$, where $\#S$ is the number of steals. The *latency added depth* $D^{lat}_{A,P}$ can be defined using $c(x)$ similarly: it is the maximum of $\sum_{x \in P} c(x)$ over all paths P in A. We note that $D \cdot C_{k+1}$ is a pessimistic upper bound on the latency-added depth for any machine.

THEOREM 5.1. (**Upper Bounds**) *For any $\delta > 0$, when a cache-oblivious nested-parallel computation A with binary forking, sequential cache complexity $Q(M, B)$, work W, and depth D is scheduled on a PMDH P of p processors using randomized work stealing:*

- *The number of steals is $O(p(D^{lat}_{A,P} + \log 1/\delta))$ with probability at least $1 - \delta$.*

- *All the caches at level i incur a total of less than $Q(M_i, B_i) + O(p(D^{lat}_{A,P} + \log 1/\delta)M_i/B_i)$ cache misses with probability at least $1 - \delta$.*

- *The computation completes in time not more than $W^{lat}_{A,P}/p + D^{lat}_{A,P} < W/p + O(p(DC_{k+1} + \log 1/\delta)C_{k+1}M_k/B_k) + \sum_{i=1}^{k} C_i(Q(M_{i-1}, B_{i-1}) - Q(M_i, B_i)))/p + DC_{k+1}$ with probability at least $1 - \delta$.*

PROOF. We use Lemma 12 from [21] to bound the number of steals. Since that result uses a simpler model for the computation that does not charge cache miss costs towards run time, we reduce our dag to a simpler form on which the lemma can be applied directly. For each instruction in A, we replace the instruction by a chain of $c(x)$ (according to some execution) sequential instructions. Each of these replaced instructions take unit time. If x is a fork (join) point, the last (first) node in this chain does the equivalent fork (join). Since we assume a dag-consistent memory model, the run time of this modified computation A' is the same as that of A. Since the depth of A' under any execution does not exceed $D^{lat}_{A,P}$, the schedule involves not more than $O(p(D^{lat}_{A,P} + \log 1/\delta))$ steals with probability at least $1 - \delta$, all the caches at level i incur a total of at most $Q(M_i, B_i) + O(p(D^{lat}_{A,P} + \log 1/\delta)M_i/B_i)$ cache misses with probability at least $1 - \delta$. To bound the running time of the computation A' which has at most $W^{lat}_{A,P}$ instructions and $D^{lat}_{A,P}$ depth, we use Theorem 13 from [21]. Since $W^{lat}_{A,P} \le W + \sum_i C_i \cdot (Q(M_{i-1}, B_{i-1}) - Q(M_i, B_i))$, the run time is at most $W + O(p(D^{lat}_{A,P} + \log 1/\delta)C_k M_k/B_k + \sum_i C_i(Q(M_{i-1}, B_{i-1}) - Q(M_i, B_i)))$ with probability at least $1 - \delta$, the claim about the running time follows. □

Thus, for constant δ, the parallel cache complexity at level i exceeds the sequential cache complexity by $O(pD^{lat}_{A,P}M_i/B_i)$ with probability $1 - \delta$. The bounds in Theorem 5.1 carry over to centralized work stealing without the δ terms, *e.g.*, the parallel cache complexity exceeds the sequential cache complexity by $O(pD^{lat}_{A,P}M_i/B_i)$. Throughout this section, the runtime bounds do not include scheduler overheads (which would increase the runtime by at most a small constant factor).

THEOREM 5.2. (**Lower Bound**) *For a PMDH P with any given number of processors $p = \Omega(\log D)$, cache sizes $M_1 < \cdots < M_k \le M/3$ for some a priori upper bound M, cache line sizes $B_1 \le \cdots \le B_k$, and cache latencies $C_1 < \cdots < C_{k+1}$, and for any given depth $D' \ge 3(\log p + \log M) + C_{k+1} + c_0$ (for some constant c_0), we can construct a nested-parallel computation DAG with binary forking and depth D', whose (expected) parallel cache complexity on P, for all levels i, exceeds the sequential cache complexity $Q(M_i, B_i)$ by $\Omega(pD^{lat}_{A,P}M_i/B_i)$ when scheduled using randomized or centralized work stealing.*

PROOF. **Randomized work stealing:** Such a construction is shown in Figure 6(a). Based on the earlier lemma, we know that there exist a constant K such that the number of steals is at most KpD with probability at least $1 - (1/pD)$. We construct the DAG such that it consists of a binary fanout to $p/3$ spines of length $D = $

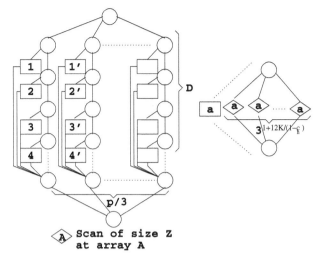

(a) Randomized work stealing

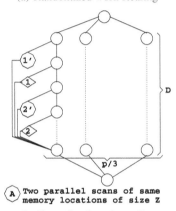

(b) Centralized work stealing

Figure 6: DAGs used in the proof of Theorem 5.2.

$D' - 2(12K/(1-c_h) + \log(p/3) + \log M)$ each ($c_h \in (0,1)$ is a constant that we will define shortly). Each of the first $D/2$ nodes on the spine forks off a "superscan" that consists of $3^{1+12K/(1-c_h)}$ identical parallel scans of length M each. A scan over an array A of size M is a binary tree forking out in to M parallel leaves, each leaf scanning one of the consecutive words in the array A. The remaining $D/2$ nodes on the spine are the joins corresponding to superscans forked up the spine. Note that $D_{A,P}^{lat} = D' + C_{k+1}$ because each path in the DAG contains at most one memory request.

In a sequential execution, a processor executes the superscans one by one and can reuse a subsequence of length M_i/B_i (at level i) for all the identical scans with in a superscan. In other words, sequential execution gets $(pD/6)(3^{1+12K/(1-c_h)}-1)\lceil(M_i-B_i)/B_i\rceil$ cache hits at level i cache, and the sequential cache complexity $Q(M_i, B_i)$ is $(pD/6)(\lceil M_i/B_i\rceil+3^{1+12K/(1-c_h)}\lceil(M-M_i)/B_i\rceil)$.

We argue that in the case of randomized work stealing, there are a large number of superscans such that the probability that at least two scans from such superscans are executed by different processors is greater than some positive constant. This implies that the cache complexity is $\Theta(pDM_i/B_i)$ higher that the sequential cache complexity (claim A).

1. Once the $p/3$ spines have been forked, each spine is occupied by at least one processor till the stage where work along a spine has been exhausted. This property follows directly from the nature of the work stealing protocol.

2. In the early stages of computation after spines have been forked, but before the computation enters the join phase on the spines, exactly $p/3$ processors have a spine node on the head of their work queue. Therefore, the probability that a random steal will get a spine node and hence a fresh super-scan is $1/3$.

3. At any moment during the computation, the probability that more than $p/2$ of the latest steals of the p processors found fresh spine nodes is exponentially small in terms of p and therefore less than $1/2$.

4. If processor p stole a fresh superscan A and started the scans in it, the probability that the work from the superscan A is not stolen by some other processor before p executes the first $2/3$-rd of the scan is at most a constant $c_h \in (0,1)$. This is because the probability that p currently got a fresh superscan does not depend on events in the history, and therefore, with probability at least $1/2$, more than $p/2$ processors did not steal a fresh superscan in the latest steal. This means that these processors which stole a stale superscan got less than $2/3$-rd fraction of the superscan to work on before they need to steal again. Therefore, by the time p finishes $2/3$-rd of the work, there would have been at least $p/2$ steal attempts and there is a probability of at least $1/16$ that two of these steals stole from p. Two steals from p would cause p to lose work from it's fresh superscan. In this scenario, p does not execute more than $5/6$-th of the scan even if it comes back to steal work from the higher instance of scan A.

5. Since there are at most KpD steals with high probability, there are no more than $(1-c_h)pD/12$ superscans which incur more than $12K/(1-c_h)$ steals. On an average, about $(1-c_h)pD/6$ superscans are stolen from before the first processor that touched the superscan executes $2/3$-rd of it. Therefore, on an average, there are no less than $(1-c_h)pD/12$ superscans which get fewer than $12K/1-c_h$ steals and are stolen from before one processor executes $2/3$-rd of it. Such superscans, by construction have at least two different processors execute a complete scan. This proves claim A.

Centralized work stealing: The construction for centralized work stealing is shown in Figure 6(b). The DAG ensures each steal causes a scan of a completely different set of memory locations. The bound follows from the fact that unlike the case in sequential computation, cache access overlap in the pairs of parallel scans are never exploited. $\square$

Clearly this lower bound also applies to more general multi-level cache models such as studied in [3, 4, 30, 42, 46, 49].

5.3 Extending Shared Cache Results to Multiple Levels

Finally, we consider the PMSH model. For the case of a single level of shared cache, our previous work [15] showed that the parallel depth-first (PDF) scheduler was a good choice for mapping good sequential cache complexity to provably good parallel cache complexity. In the PDF scheduler [16, 15] tasks are prioritized according to their ordering in the natural sequential execution, *i.e.*, according to the ordering used to analyze the sequential cache complexity Q; the ith task in the sequential execution is given priority rank i. A processor completing a task is assigned the lowest ranked task among all the available tasks that are ready to execute. The relative ranking of available tasks can be efficiently determined on-the-fly without having to perform a sequential execution [16].

The results from [15] stated in Section 1 for a single level of shared cache can be generalized to the PMSH:

THEOREM 5.3. *When a cache-oblivious nested-parallel computation A with sequential cache complexity $Q(M, B)$, work W, and depth D is scheduled on a PMSH P of p processors using a PDF scheduler, then the cache at each level i incurs fewer than $Q(p(M_i - B_i D_{A,P}^{lat}), B_i)$ cache misses. Moreover, the computation completes in time not more than $W_{A,P}^{lat}/p + D_{A,P}^{lat}$.*

PROOF. (sketch) The cache bound follows because (1) inclusion implies that hits/misses/evictions at levels $< i$ do not alter the number of misses at level i, (2) caches sized for inclusion imply that all words in a line evicted at level $> i$ will have already been evicted at level i, and hence (3) the key property of PDF schedulers, $Q_p(M + pBD_{A,P}^{lat}, B) \leq Q(M, B)$, holds at each level i of a PMSH. The time bound follows because the schedule is greedy (and we are not accounting for scheduler overheads). □

Thus, our approach for developing cache-efficient parallel algorithms via (i) low cache-oblivious sequential cache complexity and (ii) low depth is validated for shared-cache hierarchies (and PDF schedulers) as well.

6. DISCUSSION

A goal of the work described in this paper is to develop a simple model for accounting for locality with dynamic parallelism—cleanly separating the cost-model from any particular machine model while still being useful in bounding costs on various machines. We believe the approach of analyzing cache complexity in the cache-oblivious model, and work and depth with dynamic nested parallelism as described in the paper achieves this goal. The approach, however, does have some limitations and ignores some details. We briefly describe these here. Firstly the general bounds on the parallel cache misses rely on low-depth (as the title of the paper implies). It seems that avoiding this would require a modified model for cache complexity, or taking into account particular properties of programs as studied in some previous work [39, 14, 29]. A more general approach to handle algorithms with higher depth would be useful.

Secondly, our scheduler results assume DAG consistency using the BACKER protocol, which at present is not implemented on real machines. The backer protocol avoids cache protocol misses due false sharing (multiple threads writing to different locations of a shared cache line) by resolving cache line conflict when writing back to memory. Strong consistency is not guaranteed and not needed by our DAG consistent algorithms. Maintaining strong consistency per cache line could create problems on the algorithms and scheduling techniques we described by forcing cache lines to "ping-pong" among processors. It would be interesting to develop a model and algorithms that avoid these problems, but ultimately if this makes the process of designing or analyzing algorithms more complicated, or breaks the abstraction between a high-level model and the machines below, this would be a argument to modify cache consistency protocols.

Thirdly, our scheduler results assume an optimal cache replacement policy. Note that for practical purposes, each level of cache could instead use a multi-level inclusive LRU replacement policy. Unlike in the case of optimal replacement, where a complete memory access profile may be needed a priori at all levels in order to compute what to replace, implementing a multi-level LRU replacement policy does not require that all levels of the cache hierarchy see the memory access profile. Assuming that a cache line evicted at level i is sent to level $i + 1$ and that any access

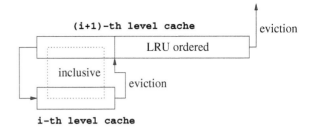

Figure 7: Multi-level LRU

to a memory location not at level i is serviced by passing it from higher levels in the memory hierarchy through cache level $i + 1$, it is possible for cache level $i + 1$ to know exactly what memory words are contained in the lower level cache. From the order in which cache lines were evicted by level i, cache level $i + 1$ can fill up the rest of its slots and order them in LRU order (see Figure 7). It follows from [47] that the number of cache misses at each level under the multi-level LRU policy is within a factor of two of the number of misses for a cache half the size running the optimal replacement policy. For example, under multi-level LRU, the upper bound on the cache misses in Theorem 5.1 becomes $2Q(M_i/2, B_i) + O(p(D_{A,P}^{lat} + \log 1/\delta)M_i/B_i)$.

Finally, our scheduler results are for multi-level hierarchies of private or shared caches. It would be interesting to extend these results to more general multi-level models [3, 4, 18, 30, 42, 46, 49], while preserving the goal of supporting a simple model for algorithm design and analysis.

Acknowledgements. We thank Vijaya Ramachandran for discussions on this work. This work was funded in part by IBM, Intel, and the Microsoft-sponsored Center for Computational Thinking.

7. REFERENCES

[1] U. A. Acar, G. E. Blelloch, and R. D. Blumofe. The data locality of work stealing. *Theory of Computing Systems*, 35(3), 2002.

[2] A. Aggarwal, B. Alpern, A. Chandra, and M. Snir. A model for hierarchical memory. In *ACM STOC '87*, 1987.

[3] B. Alpern, L. Carter, E. Feig, and T. Selker. The uniform memory hierarchy model of computation. *Algorithmica*, 12, 1994.

[4] B. Alpern, L. Carter, and J. Ferrante. Modeling parallel computers as memory hierarchies. In *Proc. 1993 Conf. on Programming Models for Massively Parallel Computers*, 1993.

[5] L. Arge, M. A. Bender, E. D. Demaine, B. Holland-Minkley, and J. I. Munro. Cache-oblivious priority queue and graph algorithm applications. In *ACM STOC '02*, 2002.

[6] L. Arge, G. S. Brodal, and R. Fagerberg. Cache-oblivous data structures. In D. Mehta and S. Sahni, editors, *Handbook of Data Structures and Applications*. CRC Press, 2005.

[7] L. Arge, M. T. Goodrich, M. Nelson, and N. Sitchinava. Fundamental parallel algorithms for private-cache chip multiprocessors. In *ACM SPAA '08*, 2008.

[8] L. Arge, M. T. Goodrich, and N. Sitchinava. Parallel external memory graph algorithms. Manuscript, 2009.

[9] N. S. Arora, R. D. Blumofe, and C. G. Plaxton. Thread scheduling for multiprogrammed multiprocessors. In *ACM SPAA '98*, 1998.

[10] M. A. Bender, G. S. Brodal, R. Fagerberg, R. Jacob, and

E. Vicari. Optimal sparse matrix dense vector multiplication in the I/O-model. In *ACM SPAA '07*, 2007.

[11] M. A. Bender, B. C. Kuszmaul, S.-H. Teng, and K. Wang. Optimal cache-oblivious mesh layout. Computing Research Repository (CoRR) abs/0705.1033, 2007.

[12] G. Bilardi. Models for parallel and hierarchical computation. In *Proc. 4th ACM International Conf. on Computing Frontiers*, 2007.

[13] G. E. Blelloch. Programming parallel algorithms. *Commun. ACM*, 39(3), 1996.

[14] G. E. Blelloch, R. A. Chowdhury, P. B. Gibbons, V. Ramachandran, S. Chen, and M. Kozuch. Provably good multicore cache performance for divide-and-conquer algorithms. In *ACM-SIAM SODA '08*, 2008.

[15] G. E. Blelloch and P. B. Gibbons. Effectively sharing a cache among threads. In *ACM SPAA '04*, 2004.

[16] G. E. Blelloch, P. B. Gibbons, and Y. Matias. Provably efficient scheduling for languages with fine-grained parallelism. *Journal of the ACM*, 46(2), 1999.

[17] G. E. Blelloch, P. B. Gibbons, and H. V. Simhadri. Brief announcement: Low-depth cache oblivious sorting. In *ACM SPAA '09*, 2009.

[18] G. E. Blelloch, P. B. Gibbons, and H. V. Simhadri. Low-depth cache oblivious algorithms. Technical Report CMU-CS-TR-134, Computer Science Department, Carnegie Mellon University, 2009 http://reports-archive.adm.cs.cmu.edu/anon/2009/CMU-CS-09-134.pdf.

[19] R. D. Blumofe, M. Frigo, C. F. Joerg, C. E. Leiserson, and K. H. Randall. Dag-consistent distributed shared memory. In *IPPS '96*, 1996.

[20] R. D. Blumofe, C. F. Joerg, B. C. Kuszmaul, C. E. Leiserson, K. H. Randall, and Y. Zhou. Cilk: An efficient multithreaded runtime system. *J. Parallel Distrib. Comput.*, 37(1), 1996.

[21] R. D. Blumofe and C. E. Leiserson. Scheduling multithreaded computations by work stealing. *Journal of the ACM*, 46(5), 1999.

[22] G. S. Brodal. Cache-oblivious algorithms and data structures. In *Proc. 9th Scandinavian Workshop on Algorithm Theory*, 2004. LNCS, vol. 3111. Springer.

[23] G. S. Brodal and R. Fagerberg. Cache oblivious distribution sweeping. In *ICALP '02*, 2002. LNCS, vol. 2380. Springer.

[24] G. S. Brodal, R. Fagerberg, and G. Moruz. Cache-aware and cache-oblivious adaptive sorting. In *ICALP '05*, 2005. LNCS, vol. 3580. Springer.

[25] G. S. Brodal, R. Fagerberg, and K. Vinther. Engineering a cache-oblivious sorting algorithm. *ACM Journal of Experimental Algorithmics*, 12, 2008.

[26] P. Charles, C. Donawa, K. Ebcioglu, C. Grothoff, A. Kielstra, C. von Praun, V. Saraswat, and V. Sarkar. X10: An object-oriented approach to non-uniform clustered computing. In *Proc. ACM SIGPLAN Conf. on Object-Oriented Programming Languages and Applications*, 2005.

[27] Y.-J. Chiang, M. T. Goodrich, E. F. Grove, R. Tamassia, D. E. Vengroff, and J. S. Vitter. External-memory graph algorithms. In *ACM-SIAM SODA '95*, 1995.

[28] R. A. Chowdhury and V. Ramachandran. The cache-oblivious gaussian elimination paradigm: theoretical framework, parallelization and experimental evaluation. In *ACM SPAA '07*, 2007.

[29] R. A. Chowdhury and V. Ramachandran. Cache-efficient dynamic programming algorithms for multicores. In *ACM SPAA '08*, 2008.

[30] R. A. Chowdhury, V. Ramachandran, and F. Silvestri. Oblivious algorithms for multicore, network, and petascale computing. Manuscript, 2009.

[31] R. A. Chowdhury, F. Silvestri, B. Blakeley, and V. Ramachandran. Oblivious algorithms for multicores and network of processors. In *IEEE IPDPS '10*, 2010.

[32] R. Cole and U. Vishkin. Deterministic coin tossing and accelerating cascades: micro and macro techniques for designing parallel algorithms. In *ACM STOC '86*, 1986.

[33] D. E. Culler, R. M. Karp, D. A. Patterson, A. Sahay, K. E. Schauser, E. E. Santos, R. Subramonian, and T. von Eicken. Logp: Towards a realistic model of parallel computation. In *ACM PPOPP '93*, 1993.

[34] E. D. Demaine. Cache-oblivious algorithms and data structures. In *Lecture Notes from the EEF Summer School on Massive Data Sets*, LNCS. Springer-Verlag, 2002.

[35] K. Fatahalian, T. J. Knight, M. Houston, M. Erez, D. R. Horn, L. Leem, J. Y. Park, M. Ren, A. Aiken, W. J. Dally, and P. Hanrahan. Sequoia: Programming the memory hierarchy. In *Supercomputing '06*, 2006.

[36] G. Franceschini. Proximity mergesort: Optimal in-place sorting in the cache-oblivious model. In *ACM-SIAM SODA '04*, 2004.

[37] W. D. Frazer and A. C. McKellar. Samplesort: A sampling approach to minimal storage tree sorting. *Journal of the ACM*, 17(3), 1970.

[38] M. Frigo, C. E. Leiserson, H. Prokop, and S. Ramachandran. Cache-oblivious algorithms. In *IEEE FOCS '99*, 1999.

[39] M. Frigo and V. Strumpen. The cache complexity of multithreaded cache oblivious algorithms. In *ACM SPAA '06*, 2006.

[40] J. Jaja. *An Introduction to Parallel Algorithms*. Addison-Wesley, 1992.

[41] P. Kumar. Cache oblivious algorithms. In U. Meyer, P. Sanders, and J. Sibeyn, editors, *Algorithms for Memory Hierarchies*. Springer, 2003.

[42] E. Ladan-Mozes and C. E. Leiserson. A consistency architecture for hierarchical shared caches. In *ACM SPAA '08*, 2008.

[43] R. J. Lipton and R. E. Tarjan. A separator theorem for planar graphs. *SIAM Journal on Applied Mathematics*, 36, 1979.

[44] OpenMP Architecture Review Board. OpenMP application program interface. Technical Report Version 3.0, 2008.

[45] S. Rajasekaran and J. H. Reif. Optimal and sublogarithmic time randomized parallel sorting algorithms. *SIAM J. Comput.*, 18(3), 1989.

[46] J. E. Savage and M. Zubair. A unified model for multicore architectures. In *Proc. 1st International Forum on Next-Generation Multicore/Manycore Technologies*, 2008.

[47] D. D. Sleator and R. E. Tarjan. Amortized efficiency of list update and paging rules. *Commun. ACM*, 28(2), 1985.

[48] L. G. Valiant. A bridging model for parallel computation. *Commun. ACM*, 33(8), 1990.

[49] L. G. Valiant. A bridging model for multicore computing. In *ESA*, 2008.

Managing the Complexity of Lookahead for LU Factorization with Pivoting

Ernie Chan and Robert van de Geijn
Department of Computer Sciences
The University of Texas at Austin
Austin, Texas 78712
{echan,rvdg}@cs.utexas.edu

Andrew Chapman
Microsoft Corporation
One Microsoft Way
Redmond, Washington 98052
andrew.chapman@microsoft.com

ABSTRACT

We describe parallel implementations of LU factorization with pivoting for multicore architectures. Implementations that differ in two different dimensions are discussed: (1) using classical partial pivoting versus recently proposed incremental pivoting and (2) extracting parallelism only within the Basic Linear Algebra Subprograms versus building and scheduling a directed acyclic graph of tasks. Performance comparisons are given on two different systems.

Categories and Subject Descriptors

D.1.3 [**Software**]: Concurrent Programming

General Terms

Algorithms, Performance

Keywords

LU factorization with partial pivoting, algorithm-by-blocks, directed acyclic graph, lookahead

1. INTRODUCTION

LU factorization with partial pivoting is simultaneously perhaps the most important operation for solving linear systems and often the most difficult one to parallelize due to the pivoting step. In this paper, we compare different strategies for exploiting shared-memory parallelism when implementing this operation. A simple approach is to link to multithreaded Basic Linear Algebra Subprograms (BLAS) [11] libraries. A strategy that requires nontrivial changes to libraries like Linear Algebra PACKage (LAPACK) [2] is to add *lookahead* to classical LU factorization with partial pivoting. A recently proposed *algorithm-by-blocks* with *incremental pivoting* [5, 26] changes the pivoting strategy to increase opportunities for parallelism, at some expense to the numerical stability of the algorithm. To manage the resulting complexity, we introduced the SuperMatrix runtime system [8] as a general solution for parallelizing LU factorization with pivoting, which maps an

algorithm-by-blocks to a directed acyclic graph (DAG) and schedules the tasks from the DAG in parallel. This approach solves the programmability issue that faces us with the introduction of multicore architectures by separating the generation of a DAG to be executed from the scheduling of tasks.

The contributions of the present paper include:

- An implementation of classical LU factorization with partial pivoting within a framework that separates programmability issues from the runtime scheduling of a DAG of tasks.

- A comparison of different pivoting strategies for LU factorization.

Together these contributions provide further evidence that the SuperMatrix runtime system solves the problem of programmability while providing impressive performance.

In our previous SPAA paper [7], we first introduced this concept of using out-of-order scheduling to parallelize matrix computation using the Cholesky factorization as a motivating example, an operation which directly maps to an algorithm-by-blocks. On the other hand, LU factorization with partial pivoting does not easily map well to an algorithm-by-blocks. Our solution addresses programmability since we can use the same methodology to parallelize this more complex operation without adding any extra complexity to the code that implements LU factorization with partial pivoting.

The rest of the paper is organized as follows. In Section 2, we present LU factorization with partial pivoting and several traditional methods for parallelizing the operation. We describe the SuperMatrix runtime system in Section 3. In Section 4, we describe LU factorization with incremental pivoting and its counterpart for QR factorization. Section 5 provides performance results, and we conclude the paper in Section 6.

2. LU FACTORIZATION WITH PARTIAL PIVOTING

We present the right-looking unblocked and blocked algorithms for computing the LU factorization with partial pivoting using standard Formal Linear Algebra Method Environment (FLAME) notation [16] in Figure 1. The thick and thin lines have semantic meaning and capture how the algorithms move through the matrix where the symbolic partitions reference different submatrices on which computation occurs within each iteration of the loop.

We first describe the updates performed within the loop of the unblocked algorithm. The SWAP routine takes the vector $\left(\begin{array}{c} \alpha_{11} \\ a_{21} \end{array} \right)$, finds the index of the element with the largest magnitude in that vector, which is stored in π_1, and exchanges that element with α_{11}. Next, the pivot is applied (PIV) where the rest of the π_1-th row is

Algorithm: $[A, p] := \text{LUPIV_UNB}(A)$

Partition

$A \rightarrow \left(\begin{array}{c|c} A_{TL} & A_{TR} \\ \hline A_{BL} & A_{BR} \end{array}\right), p \rightarrow \left(\begin{array}{c} p_T \\ \hline p_B \end{array}\right)$

where A_{TL} is 0×0, p_T has 0 elements

while $n(A_{TL}) < n(A)$ **do**

Repartition

$\left(\begin{array}{c|c} A_{TL} & A_{TR} \\ \hline A_{BL} & A_{BR} \end{array}\right) \rightarrow \left(\begin{array}{c|c|c} A_{00} & a_{01} & A_{02} \\ \hline a_{10}^T & \alpha_{11} & a_{12}^T \\ \hline A_{20} & a_{21} & A_{22} \end{array}\right),$

$\left(\begin{array}{c} p_T \\ \hline p_B \end{array}\right) \rightarrow \left(\begin{array}{c} p_0 \\ \hline \pi_1 \\ \hline p_2 \end{array}\right)$

where α_{11} and π_1 are scalars

$\left[\left(\begin{array}{c} \alpha_{11} \\ \hline a_{21} \end{array}\right), \pi_1\right] := \text{SWAP}\left(\begin{array}{c} \alpha_{11} \\ \hline a_{21} \end{array}\right)$

$\left(\begin{array}{c|c} a_{10}^T & a_{12}^T \\ \hline A_{20} & A_{22} \end{array}\right) := \text{PIV}\left(\pi_1, \left(\begin{array}{c|c} a_{10}^T & a_{12}^T \\ \hline A_{20} & A_{22} \end{array}\right)\right)$

$a_{21} := a_{21}/\alpha_{11}$

$A_{22} := A_{22} - a_{21}a_{12}^T$

Continue with

$\left(\begin{array}{c|c} A_{TL} & A_{TR} \\ \hline A_{BL} & A_{BR} \end{array}\right) \leftarrow \left(\begin{array}{c|c|c} A_{00} & a_{01} & A_{02} \\ \hline a_{10}^T & \alpha_{11} & a_{12}^T \\ \hline A_{20} & a_{21} & A_{22} \end{array}\right),$

$\left(\begin{array}{c} p_T \\ \hline p_B \end{array}\right) \leftarrow \left(\begin{array}{c} p_0 \\ \hline \pi_1 \\ \hline p_2 \end{array}\right)$

endwhile

Algorithm: $[A, p] := \text{LUPIV_BLK}(A)$

Partition

$A \rightarrow \left(\begin{array}{c|c} A_{TL} & A_{TR} \\ \hline A_{BL} & A_{BR} \end{array}\right), p \rightarrow \left(\begin{array}{c} p_T \\ \hline p_B \end{array}\right)$

where A_{TL} is 0×0, p_T has 0 elements

while $n(A_{TL}) < n(A)$ **do**

Determine block size b

Repartition

$\left(\begin{array}{c|c} A_{TL} & A_{TR} \\ \hline A_{BL} & A_{BR} \end{array}\right) \rightarrow \left(\begin{array}{c|c|c} A_{00} & A_{01} & A_{02} \\ \hline A_{10} & A_{11} & A_{12} \\ \hline A_{20} & A_{21} & A_{22} \end{array}\right),$

$\left(\begin{array}{c} p_T \\ \hline p_B \end{array}\right) \rightarrow \left(\begin{array}{c} p_0 \\ \hline p_1 \\ \hline p_2 \end{array}\right)$

where A_{11} **is** $b \times b$ **,** p_1 **is** $b \times 1$

$\left[\left(\begin{array}{c} A_{11} \\ \hline A_{21} \end{array}\right), p_1\right] := \text{LUPIV_UNB}\left(\begin{array}{c} A_{11} \\ \hline A_{21} \end{array}\right)$

$\left(\begin{array}{c|c} A_{10} & A_{12} \\ \hline A_{20} & A_{22} \end{array}\right) := \text{PIV}\left(p_1, \left(\begin{array}{c|c} A_{10} & A_{12} \\ \hline A_{20} & A_{22} \end{array}\right)\right)$

$A_{12} := L_{11}^{-1}A_{12}$

$A_{22} := A_{22} - A_{21}A_{12}$

Continue with

$\left(\begin{array}{c|c} A_{TL} & A_{TR} \\ \hline A_{BL} & A_{BR} \end{array}\right) \leftarrow \left(\begin{array}{c|c|c} A_{00} & A_{01} & A_{02} \\ \hline A_{10} & A_{11} & A_{12} \\ \hline A_{20} & A_{21} & A_{22} \end{array}\right),$

$\left(\begin{array}{c} p_T \\ \hline p_B \end{array}\right) \leftarrow \left(\begin{array}{c} p_0 \\ \hline p_1 \\ \hline p_2 \end{array}\right)$

endwhile

Figure 1: The right-looking unblocked and blocked algorithms (left and right, respectively) for computing the LU factorization with partial pivoting. Here the matrix is pivoted like LAPACK does so that $\text{PIV}(p, A) = LU$ upon completion. In this figure, L_{ii} denotes the unit lower triangular matrix stored over A_{ii}, and $n(A)$ stands for the number of columns of A.

interchanged with $\left(\begin{array}{c|c} a_{10}^T & a_{12}^T \end{array}\right)$. Finally, a_{21} is scaled by $\frac{1}{\alpha_{11}}$, and a rank-one update is performed over A_{22}.

In the blocked algorithm, the LU factorization (LUPIV) subproblem calls the unblocked algorithm, which updates the column panel $\left(\begin{array}{c} A_{11} \\ \hline A_{21} \end{array}\right)$ and stores all the pivot indices in p_1. We then apply all of those pivots to the left and right of the current column panel. Next, a triangular solve with multiple right-hand sides (TRSM) is performed over A_{12} with L_{11}, which is the unit lower triangular matrix of A_{11}. Finally, A_{22} is updated with general matrix-matrix multiplication (GEMM). Both TRSM and GEMM are examples of level-3 BLAS operations [11].

The problem instances of TRSM and GEMM incurred within this right-looking blocked algorithm are quite easily parallelized. The bulk of the computation in each iteration lies in the GEMM call so that straight forward implementations (e.g., LAPACK's blocked implementation `dgetrf`) can exploit parallelism by only linking to multithreaded BLAS libraries and thus attain high performance. As such, many opportunities for parallelism are lost since implicit synchronization points exist between each call to a parallelized BLAS routine.

2.1 Algorithm-by-blocks

By storing matrices hierarchically [12] and viewing submatrix blocks as the unit of data and operations with blocks (tasks) as the unit of computation, we reintroduced the concept of algorithms-by-blocks [19]. We reformulate the blocked algorithm presented in Figure 1 (right) as an algorithm-by-blocks in Figure 2 (left) using the FLASH [21] extension to the FLAME application programming interface (API) for the C programming language [3] for creating and accessing hierarchical matrices. Notice that the FLAME/C and FLASH application programming interfaces were typeset to closely resemble the FLAME notation and thus easily facilitate the translation from algorithm to implementation. We assume that the matrix A and the vector p are both stored hierarchically with one level of blocking. This storage scheme has an additional benefit in that spatial locality is maintained when accessing the contiguously stored submatrices.

The matrix object A Figure 2 (left) is itself encoded as a matrix of matrices in FLASH where the top-level object consists of references to the submatrix blocks. We stride through the matrix using a unit block size while decomposing the subproblems into operations on individual blocks. The algorithmic block size b in Figure 1 (right) now manifests itself as the storage block size of each contiguously stored submatrix block.

In Figure 2 (right), we illustrate the tasks that overwrite each block in a 3×3 matrix of blocks within each iteration of the loop in Figure 2 (left). We will use the notation $A_{i,j}$ to denote the i, j-th block within the matrix of blocks.

In the first iteration, we perform the task LUPIV_0 on the entire left column panel of the matrix where the symbolic partition A_{11} references $A_{0,0}$, and A_{21} references $A_{1,0}$ and $A_{2,0}$. For convenience, we choose to make each LUPIV task updating a column panel of blocks an atomic operation because it cannot be easily partitioned into finer-grained tasks operating on individual blocks. For example, if we call the unblocked algorithm to perform LUPIV_0, a

```
1   FLA_Error FLASH_LU_piv_blk( FLA_Obj A, FLA_Obj p )
2   {
3     FLA_Obj ATL, ATR,      A00, A01, A02,       pT,    p0,
4             ABL, ABR,      A10, A11, A12,       pB,    p1,
5                            A20, A21, A22               p2,
6                            AB0, AB1, AB2;
7
8     FLA_Part_2x2( A,    &ATL, &ATR,
9                         &ABL, &ABR,      0, 0, FLA_TL );
10    FLA_Part_2x1( p,    &pT,
11                        &pB,       0, FLA_TOP );
12
13    while ( FLA_Obj_width( ATL ) < FLA_Obj_width( A ) )
14    {
15      FLA_Repart_2x2_to_3x3(
16          ATL, /**/ ATR,       &A00, /**/ &A01, &A02,
17        /* ************* */   /* ******************* */
18                               &A10, /**/ &A11, &A12,
19          ABL, /**/ ABR,       &A20, /**/ &A21, &A22,
20          1, 1, FLA_BR );
21      FLA_Repart_2x1_to_3x1( pT,       &p0,
22                                      /* ** */   /* ** */
23                                       &p1,
24                             pB,       &p2,
25                             1, FLA_BOTTOM );
26      /*------------------------------------------------*/
27      FLA_Merge_2x1( A11,
28                     A21,       &AB1 );
29      FLASH_LU_piv( AB1, p1 );
30      FLA_Merge_2x1( A10,
31                     A20,       &AB0 );
32      FLASH_Apply_pivots( FLA_LEFT, FLA_NO_TRANSPOSE,
33                          p1, AB0 );
34      FLA_Merge_2x1( A12,
35                     A22,       &AB2 );
36      FLASH_Apply_pivots( FLA_LEFT, FLA_NO_TRANSPOSE,
37                          p1, AB2 );
38      FLASH_Trsm( FLA_LEFT, FLA_LOWER_TRIANGULAR,
39                  FLA_NO_TRANSPOSE, FLA_UNIT_DIAG,
40                  FLA_ONE, A11, A12 );
41      FLASH_Gemm( FLA_NO_TRANSPOSE, FLA_NO_TRANSPOSE,
42                  FLA_MINUS_ONE, A21, A12, FLA_ONE, A22 );
43      /*------------------------------------------------*/
44      FLA_Cont_with_3x3_to_2x2(
45          &ATL, /**/ &ATR,       A00, A01, /**/ A02,
46                                 A10, A11, /**/ A12,
47        /* ************* */     /* ****************** */
48          &ABL, /**/ &ABR,       A20, A21, /**/ A22,
49          FLA_TL );
50      FLA_Cont_with_3x1_to_2x1( &pT,       p0,
51                                           p1,
52                                          /* ** */   /* ** */
53                                &pB,       p2,
54                                FLA_TOP );
55    }
56    return FLA_SUCCESS;
57  }
```

Iteration 1

Iteration 2

Iteration 3

Figure 2: Left: The FLASH implementation of LU factorization with partial pivoting. Right: The tasks that overwrite each block in every iteration within LU factorization with partial pivoting on a 3×3 matrix of blocks. The subscripts denote the order in which the tasks can be sequentially executed within the algorithm-by-blocks. Certain blocks have two tasks overwriting it where the task pictured on top must be executed first.

pivot may occur within $A_{2,0}$ in one iteration and then within $A_{1,0}$ within the next iteration.

The application of the pivots is partitioned into separate tasks updating each of the two column panels to the right of the current one with the tasks PIV_1 and PIV_2. Just like the LU factorization subproblem, the application of the pivots to a column panel is done atomically.

The TRSM update of A_{12} is partitioned into two independent tasks. TRSM_3 overwrites $A_{0,1}$, which was previously updated by PIV_1, so PIV_1 must complete execution before TRSM_3 can begin. This situation is an example of a flow dependency (read-after-write) between these two tasks where one task reads the output of another task, which also occurs for PIV_2 and TRSM_4 on $A_{0,2}$. The update of $A_{2,2}$ is decomposed into four independent tasks overwriting $A_{1,1}$, $A_{1,2}$, $A_{2,1}$, and $A_{2,2}$. The same flow dependencies occur between the GEMM and PIV tasks.

Clearly, this approach generalizes to matrices partitioned with a large number of blocks.

2.2 Lookahead

The difficulty in exploiting a coarser granularity of parallelism from LU factorization with partial pivoting lies with each LUPIV task and the resulting pivoting across the entire matrix, which become bottlenecks within each iteration. In order to alleviate this problem, lookahead is used, which is also called compute-ahead in the literature [1, 27]. An early study of look-ahead for distributed-memory parallelization of LU factorization can already be found in [13]. For this operation, the update of A_{22} is subdivided and partially computed so that the LUPIV from the next iteration can be performed ahead of the current iteration in parallel with the rest of the update to A_{22}.

For example in Figure 2 (right), PIV_1 and PIV_2 are independent and thus can be executed in parallel along with TRSM_3 and TRSM_4. GEMM_5, GEMM_6, GEMM_7, and GEMM_8 are also all independent of each other. In order to apply lookahead, we first schedule PIV_1, TRSM_3, and then GEMM_5 and GEMM_6 to execute first. Once those tasks are complete, we can then schedule LUPIV_9 to execute alongside PIV_2, TRSM_5, and then GEMM_7 and GEMM_8.

The difficulty with traditional approaches for implementing lookahead is that the code becomes obfuscated and quite complex. Applying this technique to a wide range of different linear algebra algorithms has not been done because this solution does not inherently address programmability. First, finding the inherent bottleneck to computation is nontrivial. Second, partitioning the rest of the computation in order to allow the next iteration to start is often quite difficult. Moreover, lookahead can be applied to more than one iteration, which further complicates the code.

3. SUPERMATRIX RUNTIME SYSTEM

Instead of exposing the details of parallelization, like lookahead, within the code that implements the linear algebra operation, we developed the SuperMatrix runtime system through a clear separation of concerns where we divide the process of exploiting parallelism into two phases: *analyzer* and *dispatcher*. During the analyzer phase, the execution of tasks is delayed, and instead the DAG is constructed dynamically for which only the input and output matrix operands of each task are needed to perform the dependence analysis. Tasks represent the nodes of the graph and data dependencies between tasks represent the edges [7, 8]. Once the analyzer is done, the dispatcher phase is invoked which dispatches and schedules tasks to threads.

3.1 Analyzer

The FLASH code in Figure 2 (left) invokes the analyzer phase that generates the DAG of tasks. Only flow dependencies occur between tasks from LU factorization with partial pivoting. For example, the analyzer stores tasks as depicted in Figure 2 (right) given a 3×3 matrix of blocks and constructs the resulting DAG shown in Figure 3 (left).

In nearly all the linear algebra operation we have studied thus far [26], each operation is decomposed into tasks where each matrix operand consists of a single block, such as TRSM and GEMM. By contrast, LUPIV and PIV require that a matrix operand be a column panel of blocks, which was not previously supported by the SuperMatrix runtime system. We introduce the concept of *macroblocks*, which is a matrix partition representing several blocks, so a task's matrix operand can either be a single block or a macroblock. For instance, LUPIV_0 updates the macroblock consisting of $A_{0,0}$, $A_{1,0}$, and $A_{2,0}$. This macroblock mechanism is needed in order to properly detect data dependencies between tasks and thus correctly construct the DAG. Once the DAG is built, the dispatcher does not need knowledge of a task updating a single block or macroblock and hence a further separation of concerns.

3.2 Dispatcher

Once the DAG is constructed, the dispatcher is invoked in order to dynamically schedule the tasks in parallel. In [6], we discussed several different scheduling algorithms and heuristics. In this paper we will only use a single queue implementation from which all threads enqueue and dequeue ready tasks. We define ready tasks as ones where all of its dependent tasks have been executed, so every task residing on the queue can be executed in parallel.

LUPIV_0 is the only initial ready task within the DAG in Figure 3 (left) and thus is enqueued. Once a thread dequeues that task from the single queue and executes it, then PIV_1 and PIV_2, both of which are the dependent tasks of LUPIV_0, become ready and get enqueued. The dispatcher continues this process until all tasks have been executed.

A typical scheduling of tasks is to use a simple first-in first-out (FIFO) queue ordering. Since a thread can choose any task on the queue to dequeue instead of strictly the one at the head of the queue, we can apply different heuristics to either improve the load balance or data locality of tasks executed by each thread.

One particular heuristic is sorting the queue according to the heights of each task within the DAG. The height of a task is the distance between itself and its farthest leaf where a leaf is a task in the DAG without any dependent tasks. Conversely, a root is a task that does not depend upon any other tasks. In Figure 3 (left), LUPIV_0 is the only root, and PIV_{15} and PIV_{16} are leaves. The height of a root in the DAG represents the critical path of execution. By sorting the queue with this heuristic and having each thread dequeue from the head of queue, we attempt to schedule tasks on the critical path of execution and thus reduce the time to execute all tasks.

This height sorting heuristic mimics the concept of lookahead. In Figure 3 (left), GEMM_5 and GEMM_6 both have a height of six while GEMM_7 and GEMM_8 have a height of five. By sorting the tasks, threads will execute GEMM_5 and GEMM_6 first and then potentially execute LUPIV_9 in parallel with GEMM_7 and GEMM_8 since all three of those tasks have the same height.

An algorithm-by-tiles similar to our algorithm-by-blocks had already been proposed for a parallel out-of-core LU factorization in [28]. In that implementation, parallelism is extracted within operations with tiles that are brought in from disk rather than across operations with tiles, and a DAG of tasks is neither built nor scheduled. Their approach is also similar to ours in that it also implements classical LU factorization with partial pivoting.

4. ALTERNATIVES

We present two alternatives to using LU factorization with partial pivoting as a solution for solving linear systems.

4.1 LU factorization with incremental pivoting

We now review an approach, incremental pivoting, that avoids many of the dependencies exhibited in the classical LU factorization with partial pivoting [23, 24, 26].

While we refer the reader to the aforementioned papers for details, we very briefly give a flavor of how incremental pivoting works. Recall that Gaussian elimination is one formulation of LU factorization. As elements below the diagonal are eliminated in Gaussian elimination, we can choose to swap the current row where a zero is to be introduced with the row being used to eliminate that row. Thus, at each step, the row among such a pair of rows that has the largest magnitude pivot element could be swapped to be used to introduce a zero in the other row after swapping. Incremental pivoting works similarly but with blocks.

In Figure 3 (right), we present the DAG for LU factorization with incremental pivoting on a 3×3 matrix of blocks. Here, each LUPIV task updates the symbolic partition A_{11} which only consists of a single block as opposed to a macroblock. The TRSM tasks update the blocks composing A_{12}, which is similar to TRSM within LU factorization with partial pivoting, but these tasks are prepended with the application of the pivots. LUSA and FSSA are "structurally-aware" kernels that update A_{21} and A_{22}, respectively, which update the matrix according to the LUPIV task performed within each iteration. Notice that the DAG produced from incremental has a shorter critical path of execution and more opportunities for exploiting parallelism within the DAG.

Strictly speaking, LU factorization with partial pivoting is numerically unstable due to the potential for 2^n in element growth where n is the matrix dimension. In practice, it is considered to be stable based on decades of experience. Incremental pivoting is inherently less stable than partial pivoting [23] and has not been used for decades, so it is not known if it is stable in practice.

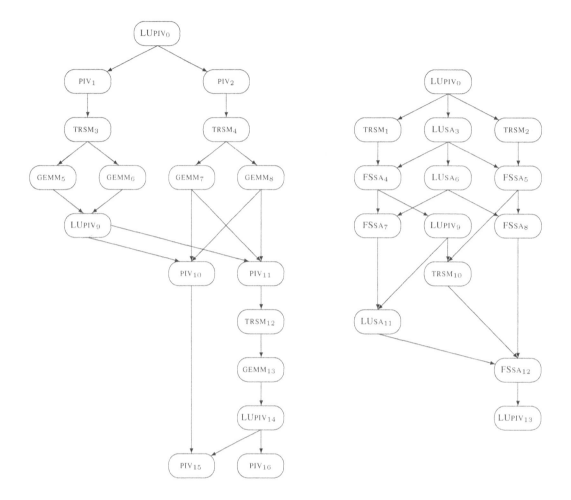

Figure 3: The directed acyclic graphs for LU factorization with partial (left) and incremental (right) pivoting on a 3×3 matrix of blocks.

4.2 QR factorization

QR factorization based on orthogonal transformations, such as Householder transformations, is a numerically stable alternative but requires twice the number of floating point operations than LU factorization.

In [25], two Householder-based algorithms-by-blocks for QR factorization were studied. One was implemented using a classical high-performance QR factorization while the other implemented an incremental scheme, first proposed for out-of-core computation [17], not unlike LU with incremental pivoting. As with LU factorization, the incremental scheme was shown to exhibit more parallelism. What is different is that this incremental QR factorization approach is guaranteed to be stable. Thus, if stability is a concern, this alternative solution method can be employed despite the extra computational cost.

5. PERFORMANCE

We compare the performance of LU factorization with partial and incremental pivoting within the SuperMatrix runtime system with other high-performance libraries and show their performance on two different platforms.

5.1 Target architectures

We performed experiments on a single SMP node of a large distributed-memory cluster `ranger.tacc.utexas.edu` containing 3,936 nodes for which it uses a 2.6.18.8 Linux kernel. Each node consists of four sockets with 2.3 GHz AMD Opteron Quad-Core 64-bit processors with a total of 16 cores providing a theoretical peak performance of 147.2 GFLOPS. Each node contains 32 GB of memory, and each socket has a 2 MB L3 cache, which is shared between the four cores. The OpenMP implementation provided by the Intel C Compiler 10.1 served as the underlying threading mechanism used by SuperMatrix. We linked to GotoBLAS2 1.00 and Intel MKL 10.0.

We also gathered results on a 16 core UMA machine running Windows Server 2008 R2 Enterprise which consists of four sockets with 2.4 GHz Intel Xeon E7330 Quad-Core processors providing a theoretical peak performance of 153.6 GFLOPS. This machine contains 8 GB of memory, and each socket has two 3 MB L2 caches shared between each pair of cores. We compiled using Microsoft Visual C++ 2010 and Intel Visual Fortran 11.1. We linked to GotoBLAS2 1.00 and Intel MKL 10.2.

5.2 Implementations

We report the performance (in GFLOPS, one billion floating point operations per second) for several implementations of LU factorization using double precision floating point arithmetic. We used an operation count of $\frac{2}{3}n^3$ of useful computation for each implementation presented to calculate the rate of execution. We tuned the storage and algorithmic block size for each problem size when possible, yet we mapped 16 threads to each of the 16 cores on both machines for all experiments.

SuperMatrix:.

We used the SuperMatrix runtime system embedded within the open source library libflame [29]. Both LU factorization with partial and incremental pivoting are implemented using SuperMatrix. For the partial pivoting implementation, we used the scheduling heuristic for sorting tasks according to their heights within the DAG as described in Section 3. For the incremental pivoting implementation, we used the cache affinity scheduling algorithm described in [6] which attempts to balance between both data locality and load balance simultaneously. SuperMatrix requires that the matrices are stored hierarchically. We call a serial BLAS library for the execution of tasks on a single thread.

LAPACK + Multithreaded BLAS:.

We linked the sequential implementation of dgetrf provided by LAPACK 3.0 to multithreaded BLAS routines from GotoBLAS and MKL. Parallelism is only exploited within each call to a multithreaded BLAS routine. dgetrf assumes that the matrices are stored in the traditional "flat" column-major order storage.

Multithreaded GotoBLAS/MKL:.

We linked to the highly optimized multithreaded implementations of dgetrf within GotoBLAS and MKL. These implementations exploit parallelism internally.

5.3 Results

Performance results are reported in Figure 4. Several comments are in order:

- For smaller problem sizes with SuperMatrix, LU factorization with incremental pivoting ramps up in performance more quickly than partial pivoting because there are more opportunities for parallelism within the DAG as shown in Figure 3.

  Despite having many more bottlenecks to parallelism, the SuperMatrix implementation of LU factorization with partial pivoting achieves much better performance for asymptotically large problem sizes because the kernels invoked by partial pivoting are much more efficient than the ones for incremental pivoting. The bulk of the computation in partial pivoting lies with calls to GEMM which is a highly-tuned kernel whereas incremental pivoting predominantly calls the structurally-aware tasks LUSA and FSSA, which we have hand coded. In order to implement these tasks, we use an inner algorithmic block size to stride through each matrix operand. For instance the storage block size is typically 192×192, yet we use an inner block size of around 48. As we stride through the matrix operands of each task, we perform computation on submatrix partitions as in a typical FLAME algorithm. BLAS operations are highly tuned for larger problem sizes, such as GEMM performed with 192×192 blocks, as opposed to multiple calls to GEMM and TRSM on much smaller submatrices [14].

  Another difference in asymptotic performance of LU with partial pivoting versus incremental pivoting is due to the fact that the former amortizes $O(n^2)$ operations related to pivoting over $O(n^3)$ operations while the latter amortizes $O(b^2)$

operations related to pivoting over $O(b^3)$ operations where n is the total matrix size and b is the storage block size. Since b is typically fixed as n increases, asymptotically the performance of the algorithm that uses incremental pivoting is slower than that of partial pivoting.

As the problem sizes grow asymptotically large, the use of sorting to provide lookahead achieves good load balance between threads. Since all the computational kernels invoked by partial pivoting are significantly faster than incremental pivoting, partial pivoting outperforms incremental pivoting despite incremental pivoting having better parallel efficiency. Unfortunately, partial pivoting does not scale as well as incremental pivoting when using more threads because of the inherent bottlenecks within LU factorization with partial pivoting.

- In order to perform the subproblem for LU factorization with partial pivoting, we copy the macroblock from storage-by-blocks to a flat matrix, execute the subproblem using a serial implementation of dgetrf, and then copy theresult back into the original macroblock. We made a small optimization not to copy the matrix for the LU subproblem if there is only one block within the macroblock. To apply the pivots to a macroblock, we hand coded a kernel that is structurally-aware of the storage-by-blocks instead of copying into a flat matrix and calling the optimized LAPACK implementation dlaswp.

  Performing the copy for the LU subproblem does not incur a significant performance penalty because that task performs $O(n^2b)$ operations on $O(nb)$ data, so the copying is essentially amortized across the computational cost of the task. Also, the LU subproblem is only invoked once per iteration of the loop on a single column panel in the hierarchically stored matrix A. The application of the pivots is performed on every other column panel within every iteration of the loop. The relative cost of copying a column panel into a flat matrix would be too high due to the small amount of operations done by the application of the pivots.

  This hand coded implementation for applying the pivots is not as highly optimized as the implementation of dlaswp provided by both GotoBLAS and MKL, so a performance penalty is incurred when compared to the multithreaded implementations of dgetrf provided by both. The SuperMatrix implementations can attain better performance if we develop optimized structurally-aware kernels.

- The sequential implementation of dgetrf linked to multithreaded BLAS implementations does not perform as well as the others because of the many lost opportunities for parallelism.

If numerical stability is not an issue, then we can employ incremental pivoting for smaller problem sizes and then switch to partial pivoting for large problem sizes to provide the best performance with SuperMatrix.

In Figure 4 (top left), we also compare the performance of the SuperMatrix implementation of LU factorization with partial pivoting where use a simple FIFO ordering of tasks as opposed to sorting the tasks according to their heights within the DAG. As we can clearly see, sorting tasks, which mimics lookahead, nearly doubles the performance for SuperMatrix. This scheduling heuristic is completely subsumed within the runtime system and is not exposed within the code that implements this operation.

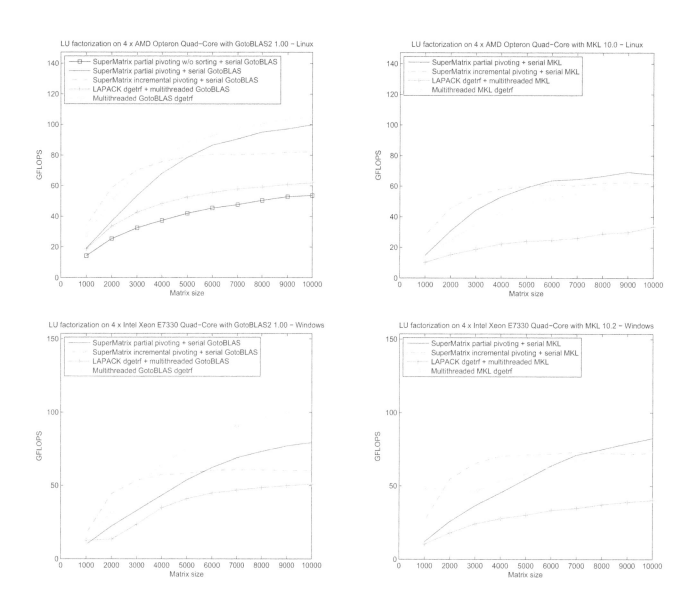

Figure 4: Performance of different implementations of LU factorization on two different platforms.

6. CONCLUSION

In this paper, we have shown a solution for parallelizing LU factorization with partial pivoting that also addresses programmability by separating the runtime system from the code that implements the operation. By using this separation of concerns, we are able to subsume the idea of lookahead seamlessly. As such, this strategy is highly competitive with finely tuned, high-performance implementations provided by commercial libraries.

We believe the SuperMatrix runtime system is the only solution for parallelizing matrix computations that addresses programmability. Hierarchically Tiled Arrays (HTA) [18] and Unified Parallel C (UPC) [20] both provide programming language support for blocked computation, but those two do not perform dependence analysis in order to exploit parallelism between operations within algorithms from which UPC uses lookahead embedded within its code to parallelize LU factorization with partial pivoting. SMP Superscalar (SMPSs) [22] is a general-purpose runtime system that also constructs a DAG using the input and output operands of tasks, but they do not focus on developing algorithms-by-blocks in or-

der to parallelize matrix computations. Parallel Linear Algebra for Scalable Multi-core Architectures (PLASMA) [4, 5] uses a similar DAG scheduling methodology to parallelize matrix computations, but the details of parallelization are not separated from the code from whom LU factorization with incremental pivoting has been implemented thus far and not partial pivoting. SuperLU [9] and High-Performance LINPACK (HPL) [10] both use lookahead in order to parallelize LU factorization with partial pivoting for distributed-memory computer architectures, yet neither addresses programmability since the lookahead strategy is embedded directly within the code that implements this operation. Communication avoiding LU factorization [15] is a fundamentally different pivoting strategy from partial and incremental pivoting since it was designed to limit communication between nodes of distributed-memory architectures.

Additional information

For additional information on FLAME visit
http://www.cs.utexas.edu/users/flame/.

7. ACKNOWLEDGMENTS

This research is sponsored by Microsoft Corporation and NSF grants CCF–0540926 and CCF–0702714. *Any opinions, findings and conclusions or recommendations expressed in this material are those of the author(s) and do not necessarily reflect the views of the National Science Foundation (NSF).* We thank the Texas Advanced Computing Center (TACC) for access to their equipment.

8. REFERENCES

[1] C. Addison, Y. Ren, and M. van Waveren. OpenMP issues arising in the development of parallel BLAS and LAPACK libraries. *Scientific Programming*, 11(2):95–104, April 2003.

[2] E. Anderson, Z. Bai, C. Bischof, L. S. Blackford, J. Demmel, J. J. Dongarra, J. D. Croz, S. Hammarling, A. Greenbaum, A. McKenney, and D. Sorensen. *LAPACK Users' Guide (Third ed.)*. SIAM, Philadelphia, 1999.

[3] P. Bientinesi, E. S. Quintana-Ortí, and R. A. van de Geijn. Representing linear algebra algorithms in code: The FLAME application programming interfaces. *ACM Transactions on Mathematical Software*, 31(1):27–59, March 2005.

[4] A. Buttari, J. Langou, J. Kurzak, and J. Dongarra. Parallel tiled QR factorization for multicore architectures. *Concurrency and Computation: Practice and Experience*, 20(13):1573–1590, September 2008.

[5] A. Buttari, J. Langou, J. Kurzak, and J. Dongarra. A class of parallel tiled linear algebra algorithms for multicore architectures. *Parallel Computing*, 35(1):38–53, January 2009.

[6] E. Chan. Runtime data flow scheduling of matrix computations. Technical Report TR-09-27, The University of Texas at Austin, Department of Computer Sciences, August 2009.

[7] E. Chan, E. S. Quintana-Ortí, G. Quintana-Ortí, and R. van de Geijn. SuperMatrix out-of-order scheduling of matrix operations for SMP and multi-core architectures. In *SPAA '07: Proceedings of the Nineteenth ACM Symposium on Parallelism in Algorithms and Architectures*, pages 116–125, San Diego, CA, USA, June 2007.

[8] E. Chan, F. G. Van Zee, P. Bientinesi, E. S. Quintana-Ortí, G. Quintana-Ortí, and R. van de Geijn. SuperMatrix: A multithreaded runtime scheduling system for algorithms-by-blocks. In *PPoPP '08: Proceedings of the Thirteenth ACM SIGPLAN Symposium on Principles and Practice of Parallel Programming*, pages 123–132, Salt Lake City, UT, USA, February 2008.

[9] J. W. Demmel, J. R. Gilbert, and X. S. Li. An asynchronous parallel supernodal algorithm for sparse Gaussian elimination. *SIAM Journal on Matrix Analysis and Applications*, 20(4):915–952, October 1999.

[10] J. J. Dongarra, J. R. Bunch, C. B. Moler, and G. W. Stewart. *LINPACK Users' Guide*. SIAM, Philadelphia, 1979.

[11] J. J. Dongarra, J. Du Croz, S. Hammarling, and I. Duff. A set of level 3 basic linear algebra subprograms. *ACM Transactions on Mathematical Software*, 16(1):1–17, March 1990.

[12] E. Elmroth, F. Gustavson, I. Jonsson, and B. Kagstrom. Recursive blocked algorithms and hybrid data structures for dense matrix library software. *SIAM Review*, 46(1):3–45, 2004.

[13] A. Gerasoulis and I. Nelken. Scheduling linear algebra parallel algorithms on MIMD architectures. In *Proceedings of the Fourth SIAM Conference on Parallel Processing for Scientific Computing*, pages 68–95, Philadelphia, PA, USA, 1990.

[14] K. Goto and R A. van de Geijn. Anatomy of a high-performance matrix multiplication. *ACM Transactions on Mathematical Software*, 34(3):12:1–12:25, May 2008.

[15] L. Grigori, J. W. Demmel, and H. Xiang. Communication avoiding Gaussian elimination. In *SC '08: Proceedings of the 2008 ACM/IEEE Conference on Supercomputing*, pages 1–12, Austin, TX, USA, November 2008.

[16] J. A. Gunnels, F. G. Gustavson, G. M. Henry, and R. A. van de Geijn. FLAME: Formal linear algebra methods environment. *ACM Transactions on Mathematical Software*, 27(4):422–455, December 2001.

[17] B. C. Gunter and R. A. van de Geijn. Parallel out-of-core computation and updating the QR factorization. *ACM Transactions on Mathematical Software*, 31(1):60–78, March 2005.

[18] J. Guo, G. Bikshandi, B. B. Fraguela, M. J. Garzaran, and D. Padua. Programming with tiles. In *PPoPP '08: Proceedings of the Thirteenth ACM SIGPLAN Symposium on Principles and Practice of Parallel Programming*, pages 111–122, Salt Lake City, UT, USA, February 2008.

[19] F. G. Gustavson. New generalized matrix data structures lead to a variety of high-performance algorithms. In *Proceedings of the IFIP TC2/WG2.5 Working Conference on Software Architectures for Scientific Computing Applications*, pages 211–234, Ottawa, ON, Canada, October 2000.

[20] P. Husbands and K. Yelick. Multi-threading and one-sided communication in parallel LU factorization. In *SC '07: Proceedings of the 2007 ACM/IEEE Conference on Supercomputing*, pages 1–10, Reno, NV, USA, November 2007.

[21] T. Meng Low and R. van de Geijn. An API for manipulating matrices stored by blocks. FLAME Working Note #12 TR-04-15, The University of Texas at Austin, Department of Computer Sciences, May 2004.

[22] J. M. Perez, R. M. Badia, and J. Labarta. A dependency-aware task-based programming environment for multi-core architectures. In *Cluster '08: Proceedings of the 2008 IEEE International Conference on Cluster Computing*, pages 142–151, Tsukuba, Japan, September 2008.

[23] E. S. Quintana-Ortí and R. A. van de Geijn. Updating an LU factorization with pivoting. *ACM Transactions on Mathematical Software*, 35(2):11:1–11:16, July 2008.

[24] G. Quintana-Ortí, E. S. Quintana-Ortí, E. Chan, R. van de Geijn, and F. G. Van Zee. Design of scalable dense linear algebra libraries for multithreaded architectures: The LU factorization. In *MTAAP '08: Proceedings of the 2008 Workshop on Multithreaded Architectures and Applications*, pages 1–8, Miami, FL, USA, April 2008.

[25] G. Quintana-Ortí, E. S. Quintana-Ortí, E. Chan, R. A. van de Geijn, and F. G. Van Zee. Scheduling of QR factorization algorithms on SMP and multi-core architectures. In *PDP '08: Proceedings of the Sixteenth Euromicro International Conference on Parallel, Distributed and Network-Based Processing*, pages 301–310, Toulouse, France, February 2008.

[26] G. Quintana-Orti, E. S. Quintana-Orti, R. A. van de Geijn, F. G. Van Zee, and E. Chan. Programming matrix algorithms-by-blocks for thread-level parallelism. *ACM Transactions on Mathematical Software*, 36(3):14:1–14:26, July 2009.

[27] P. Strazdins. A comparison of lookahead and algorithmic blocking techniques for parallel matrix factorization. *International Journal of Parallel and Distributed Systems and Networks*, 4(1):26–35, June 2001.

[28] S. Toledo. Locality of reference in LU decomposition with partial pivoting. *SIAM Journal on Matrix Analysis and Applications*, 18(4):1065–1081, October 1997.

[29] F. G. Van Zee. `libflame`: *The Complete Reference*. `http://www.lulu.com/content/5915632/`, 2009.

New Algorithms for Efficient Parallel String Comparison

Peter Krusche
Department of Computer Science
University of Warwick
Coventry, CV4 7AL, UK
peter@dcs.warwick.ac.uk

Alexander Tiskin
Department of Computer Science and Centre for
Discrete Mathematics and Its Applications
(DIMAP)
University of Warwick
Coventry, CV4 7AL, UK
tiskin@dcs.warwick.ac.uk

ABSTRACT

In this paper, we show new parallel algorithms for a set of classical string comparison problems: computation of string alignments, longest common subsequences (LCS) or edit distances, and longest increasing subsequence computation. These problems have a wide range of applications, in particular in computational biology and signal processing. We discuss the scalability of our new parallel algorithms in computation time, in memory, and in communication. Our new algorithms are based on an efficient parallel method for $(\min, +)$-multiplication of distance matrices. The core result of this paper is a scalable parallel algorithm for multiplying implicit simple unit-Monge matrices of size $n \times n$ on p processors using time $O(\frac{n \log n}{p})$, communication $O(\frac{n \log p}{p})$ and $O(\log p)$ supersteps. This algorithm allows us to implement scalable LCS computation for two strings of length n using time $O(\frac{n^2}{p})$ and communication $O(\frac{n}{\sqrt{p}})$, requiring local memory of size $O(\frac{n}{\sqrt{p}})$ on each processor. Furthermore, our algorithm can be used to obtain the first generally work-scalable algorithm for computing the longest increasing subsequence (LIS). Our algorithm for LIS computation requires computation $O(\frac{n \log^2 n}{p})$, communication $O(\frac{n \log p}{p})$, and $O(\log^2 p)$ supersteps for computing the LIS of a sequence of length n. This is within a $\log n$ factor of work-optimality for the LIS problem, which can be solved sequentially in time $O(n \log n)$ in the comparison-based model. Our LIS algorithm is also within a $\log p$-factor of achieving perfectly scalable communication and furthermore has perfectly scalable memory size requirements of $O(\frac{n}{p})$ per processor.

Categories and Subject Descriptors

F.2.m [**Nonnumerical Algorithms and Problems**]: Miscellaneous

General Terms

Algorithms, Theory

Keywords

BSP algorithms, longest common subsequences, longest increasing subsequences

1. INTRODUCTION

In this paper, we show new parallel algorithms for a set of classical string comparison problems: computation of string alignments, longest common subsequences (LCS) or edit distances, and longest increasing subsequence computation. These problems have a wide range of applications, in particular in signal processing and computational biology (see e.g. [10]). Our new algorithms are based on computing matrix distance products for a specific type of monotonic matrices called simple unit-Monge matrices. Simple unit-Monge matrices in particular arise when computing the longest common subsequence (LCS), or equivalently the edit distance, or gapped alignments for two strings. We also consider a special case of this problem, which consists in computing the longest increasing subsequence (LIS) of a sequence of data items (see e.g. [5] and references therein). A few parallel algorithms have been proposed for the problem, however, no generally work-scalable algorithm for computing the LIS is known. On the EREW PRAM model with p processors, Nakashima and Fujiwara [17] showed that the problem can be solved using parallel time $O(\frac{n \log n}{p})$, but only if $p < \frac{n}{m^2}$ where m is the length of the LIS. This algorithm becomes asymptotically sequential once $m > \sqrt{n}$. Any sequence of n numbers must have either a monotonically increasing or a monotonically decreasing subsequence of minimum length $\sqrt{n}$ (see [9, 11]). Therefore, for any sequence of numbers, the condition $p < \frac{n}{m^2}$ definitely inhibits parallelism either for running the algorithm on the sequence itself, or on its reversal. Semé [19] gives a BSP-style algorithm which uses time $O(n \log(\frac{n}{p}))$. Since $1 \le p \le n$, we have $O(n \log(\frac{n}{p})) = O(n \log n)$, which is asymptotically the same as for the sequential algorithm. In [14], we gave a scalable parallel algorithm for the LIS problem which runs in time $O(\frac{n^{1.5}}{p})$. While this is not work-optimal for LIS computation either, our algorithm was the first to achieve general scalability not only in the running time, but also in memory and communication.

The LIS problem is equivalent to computing the longest common subsequence (LCS) of two permutation strings. This problem can be solved in time $O(n \log n)$ (see [12]) in the comparison-based model, which only allows for less-than or equal comparison between sequence elements. While multiple work-optimal and scalable algorithms for the general LCS problem exist, it has so far remained open to obtain a similar result for the LIS problem. Further examples for algorithmic applications of Monge matrices in string comparison are shown in [18, 15, 2, 22], applications to other areas are discussed in [7, 20].

We discuss the scalability of our new parallel algorithms in computation time, in memory, and in communication. Scalable memory and communication allow efficient implementation of parallel algorithms on large-scale systems that use distributed memory, since algorithms achieving these properties allow to share not only the work of the sequential computation between processors, but also the communication overhead.

The core result of this paper is a parallel algorithm for multiplying implicit simple unit-Monge matrices of size $n \times n$ on p processors using time $O(\frac{n \log n}{p})$, communication $O(\frac{n \log p}{p})$ and $O(\log p)$ supersteps. This algorithm allows to implement scalable LCS computation for two strings of length n using time $O(\frac{n^2}{p})$ and communication $O(\frac{n}{\sqrt{p}})$, requiring local memory of size $O(\frac{n}{\sqrt{p}})$ on each processor. Furthermore, our algorithm can be used to obtain the first generally work-scalable algorithm for computing the longest increasing subsequence (LIS) of a sequence of numbers. Our algorithm uses computation $O(\frac{n \log^2 n}{p})$, communication $O(\frac{n \log p}{p})$, and $O(\log^2 p)$ supersteps to obtain the LIS of a sequence, which is within a $\log n$-factor of work-optimality. Our LIS algorithm is also within a $\log p$-factor of achieving perfectly scalable communication, and furthermore has perfectly scalable memory size requirements of $O(\frac{n}{p})$ per processor.

The remainder of this paper is structured as follows. In Section 2, we introduce the cost model for parallel algorithms and a few notions of scalability. After this, we give formal definitions for our problems in Section 3. In Section 4, we recall an algorithm for $(\min, +)$ multiplication of simple unit-Monge matrices from [23], and show how it can be efficiently parallelized. Section 5 describes the application of our algorithm to two problems in string comparison: LCS and LIS computation.

2. SCALABILITY IN THE BSP MODEL

The bulk-synchronous parallel (BSP) model was introduced by Valiant [24] and was the first widely-used model to recognise the impact of data locality on the practical performance of parallel algorithms. We now define different notions of scalability based on the BSP model which give a good indication of whether a theoretical algorithm can be practically scalable. A BSP computation runs on a computer that has p independent, identical processors, which each have a fixed amount of local memory. BSP algorithms proceed in *supersteps*. Each superstep has a phase of local computations, in which each processor works on the data it holds in its local memory. After this computation phase, processors exchange data over a communication network. In this work, we use the same separation of communication and computation cost as in the BSP model. We analyze the asymptotic time required for executing the computation and communication in all supersteps, as well as the number of required supersteps, and the minimum size of the local memory. Based on these properties of parallel algorithms, we define our concepts of asymptotic scalability. To characterize the costs of a parallel computation, we denote the total work $\mathcal{W}(n)$ as a function of the problem size n. We assume that a particular sequential algorithm achieving running time $\mathcal{W}(n)$ requires $\mathcal{M}(n)$ memory. Further, let $\mathcal{I}(n)$ be the maximum of the input and the output size of the problem. E.g. for standard (non-Strassen) $n \times n$ matrix multiplication, we have problem size n, total work $\mathcal{W}(n) = O(n^3)$, $\mathcal{I}(n) = O(n^2)$, and further $\mathcal{M}(n) = O(n^2)$. For a given problem of size n, we take a sequential algorithm running in time $\mathcal{W}(n)$ as our reference algorithm if a lower bound of $\Omega(\mathcal{W}(n))$ on the total work exists. However, lower bounds, if known, are usually tied to a specific theoretical model of computation which might not correspond completely to the model used for specifying the paral-

lel algorithm. Therefore, we can also consider work optimality in relation to the best known (or most practical), but not necessarily optimal algorithm. We study the following desirable properties in parallel algorithms.

DEFINITION 2.1 (WORK-OPTIMALITY). *The overall computation time $W(n, p)$ on p processors is the sum of the maximum local computation times over all supersteps. If a sequential algorithm takes time $\mathcal{W}(n)$, we say that a parallel algorithm is asymptotically work-optimal w.r.t. this sequential algorithm if $W(n, p) = O(\frac{\mathcal{W}(n)}{p})$.*

For example, a parallel matrix multiplication algorithm with running time $W(n, p) = O(\frac{n^3}{p})$ is work-optimal w.r.t. the standard $O(n^3)$ sequential method.

DEFINITION 2.2 (SCALABLE COMMUNICATION). *The overall communication cost $H(n, p)$ is the sum over the communication in all supersteps. An algorithm achieves asymptotically scalable communication if*

$$H(n, p) = O\left(\frac{\mathcal{I}(n)}{p^c}\right), \quad \text{where } c > 0 \text{ is a constant.}$$

In the context of multi-core CPUs, scalable communication is a simple model for sharing memory bus bandwidth.

DEFINITION 2.3 (SCALABLE MEMORY). *The memory cost $M(n, p)$ is the maximum amount of local storage required by a processor across all supersteps. Assume that the sequential reference algorithm requires memory $\mathcal{M}(n)$. An algorithm achieves asymptotically scalable memory if*

$$M(n, p) = O\left(\frac{\mathcal{M}(n)}{p^c}\right), \quad \text{where } c > 0 \text{ is a constant.}$$

Achieving scalable memory is important for algorithms running on hierarchical distributed memory systems: it allows to choose subproblem sizes to fit subproblems into different levels of local memory that are accessed independently (e.g. CPU caches or different memory banks) by recursive partitioning.

DEFINITION 2.4 (SYNCHRONIZATION EFFICIENCY). *An algorithm is synchronization efficient if the total number of supersteps $S(p)$ is not a function of the problem size n.*

Finally, a parallel algorithm can have *slackness conditions*, which are requirements on the relation between n and p to achieve the scalability criteria shown above. A simple example for such a slackness condition is given by BSP parallel prefix computation (see [6]). Given n values $x_1, x_2, \ldots, x_n$ and an associative operator $\oplus$, we would like to compute the values $x_1, x_1 \oplus x_2, x_1 \oplus x_2 \oplus x_3, \ldots, \bigoplus_{i=1,2,\ldots,n} x_i$. There is a BSP algorithm for this problem which uses $W(n, p) = O(\frac{n}{p})$, $H(n, p) = O(p)$, $M(n, p) = O(\frac{n}{p})$ and $S = O(1)$ if $n \geq p^2$. The slackness condition of requiring $n \geq p^2$ is necessary for the algorithm to be asymptotically work-optimal.

3. MONGE MATRICES

We denote the set of integers $\{i, i+1, \ldots, j\}$ by $[i : j]$. We further denote the set of odd half-integers $\{i + \frac{1}{2}, i + \frac{3}{2}, \ldots, j - \frac{1}{2}\}$ by $\langle i : j \rangle$. We use odd half-integers as a convenient notation for looking at exactly one point between two adjacent integers.[1] We mark odd half-integer variables by a hat (ˆ) symbol. We also allow indexing matrices by odd half-integers. When indexing a matrix M by odd half-integer values $\hat{\imath}$ and $\hat{\jmath}$, we define that $M(\hat{\imath}, \hat{\jmath}) = M(i, j)$ with $i = \hat{\imath} + \frac{1}{2}$ and $j = \hat{\jmath} + \frac{1}{2}$. Therefore, if a matrix has integer indices $[1:m] \times [1:n]$, it has odd half-integer indices $\langle 0:m \rangle \times \langle 0:n \rangle$. We will work with implicit representations of certain types of matrices, which store the differences between matrix elements rather than the elements themselves. We define *distribution matrices* and *density matrices* as follows.

DEFINITION 3.1. *The elements of the distribution matrix M^Σ of matrix M with indices from $\langle 0:m \rangle \times \langle 0:j \rangle$ are defined as*

$$M^\Sigma(i, j) = \sum_{(\hat{\imath}, \hat{\jmath}) \in \langle i:m \rangle \times \langle 0:j \rangle} M(\hat{\imath}, \hat{\jmath}),$$

where $(i, j) \in [0:m] \times [0:n]$.

DEFINITION 3.2. *The density matrix $M^\square$ of a matrix M with indices (i, j) from $[0:m] \times [0:n]$ is defined as*

$$
\begin{aligned}
M^\square(\hat{\imath}, \hat{\jmath}) = {} & M\left(\hat{\imath} + \tfrac{1}{2}, \hat{\jmath} - \tfrac{1}{2}\right) - M\left(\hat{\imath} - \tfrac{1}{2}, \hat{\jmath} - \tfrac{1}{2}\right) - \\
& M\left(\hat{\imath} + \tfrac{1}{2}, \hat{\jmath} + \tfrac{1}{2}\right) + M\left(\hat{\imath} - \tfrac{1}{2}, \hat{\jmath} + \tfrac{1}{2}\right),
\end{aligned}
$$

having $(\hat{\imath}, \hat{\jmath}) \in \langle 0:m \rangle \times \langle 0:n \rangle$.

A distribution matrix has exactly one more row and one more column than its density matrix. For matrices M for which $(M^\Sigma)^\square = M$, this row and column will contain only zeros. Matrices M for which $(M^\Sigma)^\square = M$ are called *simple*. All Monge matrices we work with in this paper are simple.

DEFINITION 3.3. *A matrix M is called a Monge matrix, if*

$$M(i, j) + M(i', j') \le M(i, j') + M(i', j)$$

for all $i \le i'$, and $j \le j'$ (see [7] for a survey on Monge matrices and their applications).

DEFINITION 3.4. *A permutation matrix P contains only elements that are either 0 or 1, and has*

$$\sum_i P(i, j) = 1 \text{ for all fixed } j, \text{ and } \sum_j P(i, j) = 1 \text{ for all fixed } i.$$

We notice that a matrix M is Monge if and only if its density matrix $M^\square$ is nonnegative (see [20, 7]). Therefore, distribution matrices of permutation matrices are Monge.

DEFINITION 3.5. *The distribution matrix P^Σ of a permutation matrix P is called a simple unit-Monge matrix.*

Elements of a simple unit-Monge matrix can be queried efficiently using its density matrix as an implicit representation (see [21]). Random access to elements of P^Σ can be implemented by looking at the nonzeros of P as points in the two-dimensional plane. Querying matrix elements then reduces to *orthogonal range counting*, which is a well studied problem in computational geometry (see e.g. [8]). Our algorithms in this paper do not require random access to P^Σ. Instead, we use the following observation from [20] to compute values of distribution matrices incrementally.

---

[1] The notation of half-integer variables stems from the application of Monge matrices to computing longest paths in grid graphs (see [18] and Section 3.2 of [20]), where integers are used to label the nodes of the primal graph, and half-integers to label the nodes of the dual graph. We do not define or use these concepts here, but keep the notation for consistency with that work.

THEOREM 3.6 ([20], P. 11, THEOREM 2). *Let P be an $n \times n$ permutation matrix. If we are given a value $P^\Sigma(i, j)$ for fixed i and j, and the locations of the nonzeros in P, we can compute all four values $P^\Sigma(i \pm 1, j \pm 1)$ in time $O(s(n))$ if $s(n)$ is the time needed to retrieve the location of the nonzero in a specific row or column.*

An important problem for simple unit-Monge matrices is their multiplication in the $(\min, +)$ semiring. Tiskin [21, 20] gave an efficient method to multiply such matrices. We will define the problem here and discuss in Section 5 how it can be applied to string comparison.

Consider the product $M_C = M_A \odot M_B$ of two matrices over $[0:n] \times [0:n]$, which is defined as

$$M_C(i, k) = \min_j(M_A(i, j) + M_B(j, k)), \tag{1}$$

where $i, j, k \in [0:n]$. Computing the product by evaluation of all elementary products $M_A(i, j) + M_B(j, k)$ runs in time $O(n^3)$. If M_A and M_B are Monge matrices, we can achieve running time $O(n^2)$ using the efficient algorithm for computing row-maxima in Monge matrices from [1]. For implicit simple unit-Monge matrices, we can improve further on $O(n^2)$ by using their density matrices as an implicit representation.

LEMMA 3.7 (SEE [20] FOR PROOF.). *The $(\min, +)$ product of two simple unit-Monge matrices is also a simple unit-Monge matrix.*

We would like to compute the product $P_C^\Sigma = P_A^\Sigma \odot P_B^\Sigma$ of two simple unit-Monge matrices P_A^Σ and P_B^Σ with

$$P_C^\Sigma(i, k) = \min_j(P_A^\Sigma(i, j) + P_B^\Sigma(j, k)), \tag{2}$$

where $i, j, k \in [0:n]$. Our algorithms work on the implicit representation of simple unit-Monge matrices, i.e. we are given P_A and P_B as inputs. Since these are permutation matrices, it is possible to store them using $O(n)$ space by storing only the locations of their nonzeros. Therefore, we compute an $n \times n$ permutation matrix P_C, such that the permutation distribution matrix P_C^Σ is the $(\min, +)$ product of permutation distribution matrices P_A^Σ and P_B^Σ. Matrices P_A, P_B and P_C have half-integer indices ranging over $\langle 0:n \rangle$.

4. PARALLEL MONGE MATRIX MULTIPLICATION

In [14], a parallel algorithm for simple unit-Monge matrix multiplication running in $W(n, p) = O(\frac{n^{1.5}}{p})$, $H(n, p) = M(n, p) = \left(\frac{n}{p}\right)^{0.5}$, and $S = O(1)$ was shown. In this paper, we give a new parallel algorithm for simple unit-Monge matrix multiplication, based on a newer and faster sequential multiplication method (see [20]). It runs in $W(n, p) = O(\frac{n \log n}{p})$, $H(n, p) = O(\frac{n \log p}{p})$, $M(n, p) = O(\frac{n}{p})$, and $S = O(\log p)$.

We start with the recent algorithm from [23] (see also [20]) as the basis for our parallel algorithm. This algorithm works by partitioning the input permutation matrices into two half-sized parts each. Assume for simplicity of presentation that without loss of generality n is a power of 2. We define $P_{A,lo}$ as the $\frac{n}{2} \times \frac{n}{2}$ sized permutation matrix which is induced by the nonzeros in $P_A(\langle 0: n \rangle, \langle 0:\frac{n}{2} \rangle)$. Analogously, we obtain $P_{A,hi}$ from $P_A(\langle 0:n \rangle, \langle \frac{n}{2}: n \rangle)$, $P_{B,lo}$ from $P_B(\langle 0:\frac{n}{2} \rangle, \langle 0:n \rangle)$, and $P_{B,hi}$ from $P_B(\langle \frac{n}{2}: n \rangle, \langle 0:n \rangle)$. We then have

$$P'^\Sigma_{C,lo} = P_{A,lo}^\Sigma \odot P_{B,lo}^\Sigma \quad \text{and} \quad P'^\Sigma_{C,hi} = P_{A,hi}^\Sigma \odot P_{B,hi}^\Sigma, \tag{3}$$

Matrices $P'_{C,lo}$ and $P'_{C,hi}$ can be obtained by recursively calling our multiplication algorithm for matrices of size $\frac{n}{2} \times \frac{n}{2}$ to compute the result of Equation (3). We can preserve the indices of the rows and columns in P_A and P_B which were deleted obtaining $P_{A,lo}$, $P_{A,hi}$, $P_{B,lo}$, and $P_{B,hi}$, and use them to convert the resulting matrices $P'_{C,lo}$ and $P'_{C,hi}$ to matrices $P_{C,lo}$ and $P_{C,hi}$ of size $n \times n$ by adding rows or columns of zeros. Notice that since P_A and P_B are permutation matrices, the sum $P_{C,lo} + P_{C,hi}$ of the resulting matrices will form a permutation matrix as well. We get (see [23] for details)

$$P_C^\Sigma(i,k) = \min(P_{C,lo}^\Sigma(i,k) + P_{C,hi}^\Sigma(0,k),$$
$$P_{C,hi}^\Sigma(i,k) + P_{C,lo}^\Sigma(i,n)). \qquad (4)$$

The full procedure for this divide step of the computation is shown in Algorithm 1. The function ImplicitMult carries out the highest-score matrix multiplication recursively on the two subproblems and will be defined in Algorithm 3.

It now remains to merge the partial results $P_{C,lo}$ and $P_{C,hi}$ to obtain P_C according to (4). By analysing the difference

$$\delta(i,k) = (P_{C,lo}^\Sigma(i,k) + P_{C,hi}^\Sigma(0,k))$$
$$-(P_{C,hi}^\Sigma(i,k) + P_{C,lo}^\Sigma(i,n)), \qquad (5)$$

we get

$$\delta(i,k) = \sum_{\hat{\imath}\in\langle 0:i\rangle, \hat{k}\in\langle 0:k\rangle} P_{C,hi}(\hat{\imath},\hat{k})$$
$$-\sum_{\hat{\imath}\in\langle i:n\rangle, \hat{k}\in\langle k:n\rangle} P_{C,lo}(\hat{\imath},\hat{k}). \qquad (6)$$

Based on the sign of δ, we can determine the nonzeros of P_C as follows:

1. If $\delta(\hat{\imath}+\frac{1}{2}, \hat{k}+\frac{1}{2}) \leq 0$, we have $P_C(\hat{\imath},\hat{k}) = P_{C,lo}(\hat{\imath},\hat{k})$.

2. If $\delta(\hat{\imath}-\frac{1}{2}, \hat{k}-\frac{1}{2}) \geq 0$, we have $P_C(\hat{\imath},\hat{k}) = P_{C,hi}(\hat{\imath},\hat{k})$.

3. If $\delta(\hat{\imath}+\frac{1}{2}, \hat{k}+\frac{1}{2}) > 0$ and $\delta(\hat{\imath}-\frac{1}{2}, \hat{k}-\frac{1}{2}) < 0$, we have $P_C(\hat{\imath},\hat{k}) = 1$.

Consider two coordinates (i,k) on the two-dimensional plane. We assign different colours to areas in the plane based on the sign of $\delta(i,k)$ as follows. Let $\mathtt{Colour}(i,k) = \mathtt{red}$ if $\delta(i,k) < 0$, $\mathtt{Colour}(i,k) = \mathtt{green}$ if $\delta(i,k) = 0$, and $\mathtt{Colour}(i,k) = \mathtt{blue}$ if $\delta(i,k) > 0$. Furthermore, we can define a set of colours for each half-integer point on the plane as the set of the colours of all four adjacent integer pairs. We have $\mathtt{ColourSet}(\hat{\imath},\hat{k}) = \{\mathtt{Colour}(\hat{\imath} \pm \frac{1}{2}, \hat{k} \pm \frac{1}{2})\}$. Using this colouring, we can determine the nonzeros of P_C by using Algorithm 2 to separate its areas. Since δ is monotonic in both its parameters, we can find the nonzeros in P_C by tracing the upper or lower boundary of the set $\delta^{-1}(\{0\})$, which corresponds to the green area in Figure 1. This can be done in linear time by computing values of δ incrementally along a path on the upper or lower boundary of $\delta^{-1}(\{0\})$ (see also [23]). Algorithm 2 shows how to trace the upper boundary of the area where $\delta(i,k) = 0$. The colours correspond to the three cases shown above: in the red area, we have $P_C(\hat{\imath},\hat{k}) = P_{C,lo}(\hat{\imath},\hat{k})$, and in the blue area, $P_C(\hat{\imath},\hat{k}) = P_{C,hi}(\hat{\imath},\hat{k})$. In the green area, we find nonzeros that correspond to case 3 from above. Since we only advance the values $\hat{\imath}$ and $\hat{k}$ in steps of one, we can use Theorem 3.6 to compute all required values of the difference function δ in constant time starting with $\delta(n,0) = 0$. When we have isolated a nonzero that corresponds to case 3, we store its location in list L. Array T contains for each column $\hat{k}$ the respective row $\hat{\imath}$ of the top boundary of the green area.

Once we have separated the green area from the red and the blue areas, we can locate the nonzeros in P_C according to the three

Algorithm 1 Recursive simple unit-Monge matrix multiplication, divide step

```
procedure ImplicitMult_Split_Recurse( P_A, P_B )
input: Two implicit unit-Monge matrices P_A and P_B
       of sizes n × n
output: A pair of matrices (P_{C,lo}, P_{C,hi})
        of sizes n × n

if n = 1 return ((1),(1))
{ 1. Compute the index transformation to obtain
  the half-sized matrices P_{A,lo}, P_{A,hi}, P_{B,lo}, P_{B,hi}}

{ Split P_A into P_{A,lo} and P_{A,hi} }
i_lo = 1/2
i_hi = 1/2
for î = 1/2 to n − 1/2
  let ĵ s.t. P_A(î,ĵ) = 1
  if ĵ > n/2
    I_hi(i_hi) = î
    i_hi ← i_hi + 1
  else
    I_lo(i_lo) = î
    i_lo ← i_lo + 1
for all (î,ĵ) ∈ ⟨0 : n⟩² with P_A(î,ĵ) = 1
  if ĵ > n/2
    let î' s.t. I_hi(î') = î
    P_{A,hi}(î',ĵ − n/2) = 1
  else
    let î' s.t. I_lo(î') = î
    P_{A,lo}(î',ĵ) = 1
{ Split P_B into P_{B,lo} and P_{B,hi} }
k_lo = 1
k_hi = 1
for k̂ = 1/2 to n − 1/2
  let ĵ s.t. P_B(ĵ,k̂) = 1
  if ĵ > n/2
    K_hi(k_hi) = k̂
    k_hi ← k_hi + 1
  else
    K_lo(k_lo) = k̂
    k_lo ← k_lo + 1
for all (ĵ,k̂) ∈ ⟨0 : n⟩² with P_B(ĵ,k̂) = 1
  if ĵ > n/2
    let k̂' s.t. K_hi(k̂') = k̂
    P_{B,hi}(ĵ − n/2,k̂) = 1
  else
    let k̂' s.t. K_lo(k̂') = k̂
    P_{B,lo}(ĵ,k̂) = 1

{ 2. Recursive calls }

P'_{C,lo} = ImplicitMult(P_{A,lo}, P_{B,lo})
P'_{C,hi} = ImplicitMult(P_{A,hi}, P_{B,hi})
for all (î,k̂) ∈ ⟨0 : n/2⟩² with P'_{C,lo}(î,k̂) = 1
  P_{C,lo}(I_lo(î), K_lo(k̂)) = 1
for all (î,k̂) ∈ ⟨0 : n/2⟩² with P'_{C,hi}(î,k̂) = 1
  P_{C,hi}(I_hi(î), K_hi(k̂)) = 1
return (P_{C,lo}, P_{C,hi})
```

conditions shown above. The full sequential method as described in [23] is shown in Algorithm 3. The running time of this algorithm is $O(n \log n)$, since in each recursive step, we take linear time to partition into two half-sized subproblems using Algorithm 1, and

Algorithm 2 Tracing the top boundary of $\delta^{-1}(\{0\})$

```
procedure Trace_Top (P_{C,lo}, P_{C,hi})
input: A pair of n × n matrices (P_{C,lo}, P_{C,hi})
output: Array T containing the top boundary,
        and a list L of nonzeros from case 3
```

$\hat{\imath} = n - \frac{1}{2}$
$\hat{k} = \frac{1}{2}$
```
while î > 0
  if ColourSet(î, k̂) = { red, green, blue }
    { We have discovered a nonzero in P_C. }
    L ← L ∪ {(î, k̂)}
    { we move up, see case (a) in Figure 1 }
    î ← î - 1
  else if ColourSet(î, k̂) = { red, green }
  { if the half-integer point above is
    monochromatic red, we have reached the
    top boundary. }
    if ColourSet(î - 1, k̂) = { red }
    { store top boundary in column k
      as an integer in T[k̂] }
      T[k̂] = î
    { top boundary, go right, see case (b) in
      Figure 1 }
      k̂ ← k̂ + 1
    else { otherwise, we are tracing the left
      boundary and need to move up.
      See case (c) in Figure 1 }
      î ← î - 1
return (T, L)
```

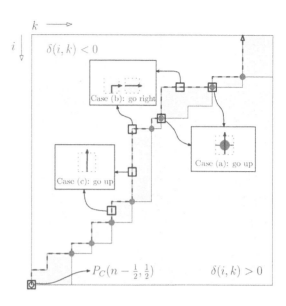

Figure 1: Illustration of Algorithm 2

we also take linear time to merge the results of these subproblems using Algorithms 2 and 3.

For the parallel version of this algorithm, we assume that the nonzeros of the input matrices are initially distributed arbitrarily, but in equal fractions across p processors. Obtaining a parallel version of Algorithm 1 is straightforward. We execute each step on p processors in parallel, each processor can work independently on the set of nonzeros it holds for splitting the input matrices. In the recursive call, we partition the processors into two subsets of size $\frac{p}{2}$, to execute the recursive calls in parallel. After $\log p$ such recursive steps, each processor works on an independent subproblem of multiplying two implicit matrices with $\frac{n}{p}$ nonzeros each. Each processor can solve this subproblem in time $O(\frac{n}{p} \log \frac{n}{p}) = O(\frac{n \log n}{p})$. It remains to merge the resulting $P_{C,lo}$ and $P_{C,hi}$ matrices. We now describe a parallel version of Algorithm 2.

In order to achieve scalable communication, we partition the output matrix P_C into a grid of blocks sized $\frac{n}{p} \times \frac{n}{p}$ (assuming w.l.o.g. that n is a multiple of p). For each such block, we find the colour of its four corners in order to determine the types of the nonzeros contained in it. We compute $\texttt{Colour}(r \cdot \frac{n}{p}, s \cdot \frac{n}{p})$ for all pairs $(r, s) \in [0 : p] \times [0 : p]$. This results in p^2 values that give the value of $\texttt{Colour}$ at all intersections of the $p \times p$ grid (see Figure 2, left). We call a block for which all the corners have the same colour *monochromatic*. According to these values, we can determine where the nonzeros in each block come from:

- If the block is monochromatic red, all nonzeros within the block are taken from $P_{C,lo}$ since the value of δ is negative throughout the block and therefore case 1 from above applies to all values of P_C inside this block.

Algorithm 3 Recursive simple unit-Monge Matrix Multiplication

```
procedure ImplicitMult( P_A, P_B )
input: Implicit n × n unit-Monge matrices P_A, P_B
output: An n × n matrix P_C, with P_C^Σ = P_A^Σ ⊙ P_B^Σ
```

$(P_{C,lo}, P_{C,hi}) \leftarrow \texttt{ImplicitMult\_Split\_Recurse}(P_A, P_B)$
$(T, L) \leftarrow \texttt{Trace\_Top}(P_{C,lo}, P_{C,hi})$

```
for k̂ ∈ ⟨0 : n⟩
  { Nonzeros from case 3 were stored in list L.
    When we do not have such a nonzero, we use
    the nonzeros from P_{C,lo} and P_{C,hi}
    according to cases 1 and 2. }
  if there is any î with (î, k̂) ∈ L
    P_C(î, k̂) = 1
  else { ... distinguish cases 1 and 2 using
    the top boundary of the green area }
  if there is any î with P_{C,lo}(î, k̂) = 1
      and î ≤ T[k̂]
    { nonzeros from case 1 are copied from P_{C,lo} }
      P_C(î, k̂) = 1
  else if there is any î with P_{C,hi}(î, k̂) = 1
      and î ≥ T[k̂]
    { nonzeros from case 2 are copied from P_{C,hi} }
      P_C(î, k̂) = 1
return P_C
```

213

- If the block is monochromatic blue, all nonzeros within the block are taken from $P_{C,hi}$ since the value of δ is positive throughout the block and therefore case 2 from above applies to all values of P_C inside this block.

- If the block is monochromatic green, the block cannot contain any nonzeros since it does not contain areas in which δ becomes positive or negative. Therefore, none of the three cases shown above can apply to any value of P_C contained in this block.

- If the block is non-monochromatic, it must have an intersection with $\delta^{-1}(\{0\})$, and we need to trace the boundary of $\delta^{-1}(\{0\})$ through the block to locate nonzeros corresponding to case 3. Furthermore, knowing the intersection of the boundary with the block, we can distinguish the nonzeros from cases 1 and 2 within the block.

OBSERVATION 4.1. *We can have at most $O(p)$ blocks which are non-monochromatic.*

PROOF. The upper boundary of $\delta^{-1}(\{0\})$ intersects at most $2p$ blocks in our grid, the same is true for the lower boundary. Therefore, the maximum number of non-monochromatic blocks is $4p$ (see also Figure 2, right). $\square$

LEMMA 4.2. *If P_C is of size $n \times n$ and $n > p^3$, we can compute* Colour$(r \cdot \frac{n}{p}, s \cdot \frac{n}{p})$ *for all pairs $(r, s) \in [0 : p] \times [0 : p]$ using $W(n,p) = O(\frac{n}{p})$, $H(n,p) = O(\frac{n}{p})$, $S = O(1)$ and $M(n,p) = O(\frac{n}{p})$.*

PROOF. The value of $\delta(i, j)$ can be split into the two sums

$$
\begin{aligned}
\delta_{lo}(i,k) &= \sum_{i \in \langle i:n \rangle, \hat{k} \in \langle k:n \rangle} P_{C,lo}(\hat{i}, \hat{k}), \text{ and} \\
\delta_{hi}(i,k) &= \sum_{i \in \langle 0:i \rangle, \hat{k} \in \langle 0:k \rangle} P_{C,hi}(\hat{i}, \hat{k}).
\end{aligned}
\tag{7}
$$

We can compute the values δ_{lo} and δ_{hi} on a $p \times p$ grid using parallel prefix in BSP time $W(n,p) = O(\frac{n}{p})$ and communication $O(p^2)$ in a constant number of supersteps. This can be implemented by distributing the nonzeros of $P_{C,lo}$ and $P_{C,hi}$ in "strips" of size $\frac{n}{p} \times n$. Processor $q, q \in [1 : p]$ receives all nonzeros $(\hat{i}, \hat{k})$ with $(q-1) \cdot \frac{n}{p} < \hat{i} \leq q \cdot \frac{n}{p}$ in a single superstep using communication $O(\frac{n}{p})$. Then, each processor q can compute p values

$$
\begin{aligned}
\delta'_{q,lo}(r) &= \sum_{\hat{i},\hat{k}} P_{C,lo}(\hat{i}, \hat{k}), \text{ and} \\
\delta'_{q,hi}(r) &= \sum_{\hat{i},\hat{k}} P_{C,hi}(\hat{i}, \hat{k}), \text{ with } r \in [1:p], \\
&\qquad \hat{i} \in \langle (q-1) \cdot \tfrac{n}{p} : q \cdot \tfrac{n}{p} \rangle, \text{ and} \\
&\qquad \hat{k} \in \langle (r-1) \cdot \tfrac{n}{p} : r \cdot \tfrac{n}{p} \rangle.
\end{aligned}
\tag{8}
$$

We have p^2 values each for $\delta'_{q,lo}$ and $\delta'_{q,hi}$, one value for each grid intersection, which we broadcast to all processors. After the broadcast, each processor can evaluate Colour$(r \cdot \frac{n}{p}, s \cdot \frac{n}{p})$ for all grid points $(r, s) \in [0 : p] \times [0 : p]$ in time $O(p^2)$. If $n > p^3$, we have $O(\frac{n}{p} + p^2) = O(\frac{n}{p})$, therefore, we get the claimed bounds on computation and communication. $\square$

LEMMA 4.3. *Given the nonzeros of two $n \times n$ permutation matrices P_A and P_B, distributed equally across $p < \sqrt[3]{n}$ processors, we can compute the nonzeros of a matrix P_C with $P_C^\Sigma = P_A^\Sigma \odot P_B^\Sigma$ using $W(n,p) = O(\frac{n \log n}{p})$, $H(n,p) = O(\frac{n}{p} \log p)$, $M(n,p) = O(\frac{n}{p})$, and $S = O(\log p)$.*

PROOF. We have $W(n,p) = O(\frac{n \log n}{p})$ due to the last recursive step in the parallel version of Algorithm 1. Afterwards, we combine the resulting $P_{C,lo}$ and $P_{C,hi}$ matrices in $\log p$ supersteps until we have obtained a distributed version of P_C. At level l of this merging tree, we have $r = p/2^l$ processors merging matrices of size $(\frac{n}{2})^l \times (\frac{n}{2})^l$. This can be done in a constant number of supersteps using $W(n,p) = O(\frac{n}{p})$, $M(n,p) = H(n,p) = O(\frac{n}{p})$ due to Lemma 4.2. We have $\log p$ such levels, which gives the claimed bounds. $\square$

This new parallel algorithm is work-optimal w.r.t. the sequential method shown in [23], and has scalable communication within a log-factor of the optimum. Our algorithm has cubic slackness, requiring $n > p^3$ since otherwise, the work for computing the values of Colour in the proof of Lemma 4.2 becomes dominant. However, this poses no realistic restriction on the problem sizes even on hundreds of thousands of processors – the expected problem size to justify use of a parallel system of that scale should easily be large enough. The only criterion by which the algorithm from [14] is superior to our new method is the number of required supersteps: in [14], only a constant number of supersteps is required. Our new algorithm could be adapted to run in a constant number of supersteps, however, this would introduce an exponential slackness condition which would render the method impractical. The new algorithm is also much simpler than the previous algorithm shown in [14], and is very likely to be practical. In the next section, we will introduce two applications of this algorithm.

5. APPLICATIONS IN STRING COMPARISON

A common application of unit-Monge matrices is longest common subsequence (LCS) computation. We study a generalisation of this problem called *semi-local string comparison*, which can be used to obtain efficient parallel LCS algorithms. In this problem, we are interested in computing LCS lengths for one string and all substrings of the other string. Schmidt [18] proposed an algorithm for computing all longest paths in grid dags, which was applied to string-substring LCS computation by Alves et al. [3], who gave an $O(n^2)$ algorithm for semi-local comparison of two strings of length n. Tiskin (see [21, 20]) developed further understanding of the algorithm and its data structures, obtaining a subquadratic time algorithm for semi-local string comparison including string-substring and prefix-suffix LCS computation. Semi-local string comparison is a traditional tool for obtaining efficient parallel algorithms for LCS computation (see [4, 2, 13]). A summary of other algorithmic applications is given in [20].

We first describe the semi-local string comparison problem. Let $x = x_1 x_2 \ldots x_m$ and $y = y_1 y_2 \ldots y_n$ be two strings over an alphabet Σ of size σ. We distinguish between contiguous *substrings*

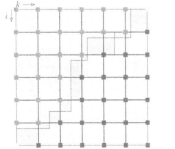
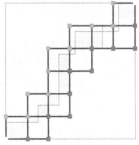

Figure 2: Partitioning into a grid of $p \times p$ blocks

Table 1: BSP running times of different parallel algorithms for LCS computation.

References	$W(n,p)$	$H(n,p)$	$M(n,p)$	S	global/semi-local
[16] + [25]		$O(n)$	$O(\frac{n}{p})$	$O(p)$	● / –
[16] + [2, 21]	$O(\frac{n^2}{p})$	$O(n)$	$O(\frac{n}{p})$	$O(p)$	● / ●
[13]		$O\left(\frac{n \log p}{\sqrt{p}}\right)$	$O(\frac{n}{\sqrt{p}})$	$O(\log p)$	● / ●
Shown here		$O\left(\frac{n}{\sqrt{p}}\right)$	$O(\frac{n}{\sqrt{p}})$	$O(\log^2 p)$	● / ●

of a string x, which can be obtained by removing zero or more characters from the beginning and/or the end of x, and *subsequences*, which can be obtained by deleting zero or more characters in any position. The *longest common subsequence* (LCS) of two strings is the longest string that is a subsequence of both input strings; its length (the LLCS) is a measure for the similarity of the two strings. In *global string comparison*, we are only interested in the LLCS of the two inputs. Solutions to the semi-local LCS problem are given by a *highest-score matrix*. In a highest-score matrix $A_{x,y}$, each entry $A_{x,y}(i,j)$ is related to the length of the LCS of two substrings of x and y. Each entry $A_{x,y}(i,j)$ with $0 < i < j < n$ gives the LLCS of x and substring $y_i \ldots y_j$. In a similar way, matrix A contains the LLCS of all *prefixes* $x_1 x_2 \ldots x_i$ and y, as well as all *suffixes* $y_j \ldots y_n$ and x, or also the LLCS of all suffixes $x_i \ldots x_m$ and all prefixes $y_1 \ldots y_j$ from $A_{x,y}$.

THEOREM 5.1 (SEE [21]). *For every highest-score matrix A, there exists a permutation matrix P_A with $A(i,j) = j - i - P_A^\Sigma(i,j)$ (i.e. P_A^Σ is simple unit-Monge). We call P_A the implicit highest-score matrix for A.*

The process of assembling a highest-score matrix $A_{x,yz}$ from $A_{x,y}$ and $A_{x,z}$ is called highest-score matrix composition (see [13, 20]). Highest-score composition is a method for parallel string alignment since it allows to create independent subproblems by computing highest-score matrices for parts of the input strings. The dominant part of the work in highest-score matrix composition is the $(\min, +)$ multiplication of $P_{A_{x,y}}^\Sigma$ and $P_{A_{x,z}}^\Sigma$. Our algorithm from Section 4 can therefore be used to improve the scalability of parallel string alignment as follows.

THEOREM 5.2. *Given two strings x and y of length n which are distributed in equal fractions between $p < \sqrt[3]{n}$ processors, we can compute a distributed version of their implicit highest-score matrix $A_{x,y}$ using $W(n,p) = O(\frac{n^2}{p})$, $H(n,p) = O(\frac{n}{\sqrt{p}} + \frac{n \log^2 p}{p}) = O(\frac{n}{\sqrt{p}})$, $M(n,p) = O(\frac{n}{\sqrt{p}})$, and $S = O(\log^2 p)$.*

PROOF. As the first step, each processor compares a single pair of substrings from $x_{(q-1) \cdot \frac{n}{\sqrt{p}}} \ldots x_{q \cdot \frac{n}{\sqrt{p}}}$ and $y_{(r-1) \cdot \frac{n}{\sqrt{p}}} \ldots y_{r \cdot \frac{n}{\sqrt{p}}}$ with $q, r \in [1 : \sqrt{p}]$. This requires computation time $O(\frac{n^2}{p})$.

After that, our unit-Monge matrix multiplication algorithm is used at every level of a quadtree-like merging step to compute distributed implicit highest-score matrices for longer pairs of substrings. At the bottom level, the matrices are merged sequentially, requiring time $O(\frac{n}{\sqrt{p}} \log \frac{n}{\sqrt{p}}) = O(\frac{n \log n}{\sqrt{p}})$.

At higher levels of the quadtree, blocks are merged in parallel. In particular at level $\log r$, $1 \leq r \leq p$, the block size is $\frac{n}{\sqrt{r}}$, and each merge is performed by a group of p/r processors using computation time $O(\frac{\frac{n}{\sqrt{r}} \log \frac{n}{\sqrt{r}}}{p/r})$. The sum of the computation time over all

$\log p$ levels of the merging phase is equal to $O(\frac{n \log n}{\sqrt{p}})$. Therefore, we get the overall running time

$$W(n,p) = O\left(\frac{n^2}{p} + \frac{n \log n}{\sqrt{p}} \cdot \log p\right) = O\left(\frac{n^2}{p}\right).$$

The communication and memory requirements are dominated by each processor having to read and store the data for the two substrings of length $\frac{n}{\sqrt{p}}$ it needs to compare, which gives $H(n,p) = M(n,p) = O(\frac{n}{\sqrt{p}})$. Overall, we need $S = O(\log^2 p)$ supersteps since each level $\log r$ in the merging tree requires $\log p/r$ supersteps to execute. □

Table 1 shows a selection of work-optimal parallel algorithms for LCS computation. Our new algorithm allows to improve the communication to $H(n,p) = O(\frac{n}{\sqrt{p}})$. The communication cost is dominated by the amount of communication necessary to read the input strings, i.e. the communication necessary for highest-score matrix composition is not the asymptotically predominant part of the algorithm's communication. The only other algorithm to achieve scalable communication was shown in [13]. This algorithm is based on a parallel highest-score matrix multiplication method based on the Algorithm from [21], which runs in time $W(n,p) = O(\frac{n^{1.5}}{p^{0.75}})$, $H(n,p) = O(\frac{n}{\sqrt{p}})$, and $S = O(1)$. Its asymptotic running time is inferior to our method, but this does not affect the upper bound for LCS computation since the dominant part of the work is computing the highest-score matrices for comparing pairs of substrings in the beginning. Since the highest-score matrix multiplication method from [13] runs in $S = O(1)$, we can get $S = O(\log p)$ for LCS computation. However, this is at the expense of higher overhead due to the slower multiplication algorithm, and another $\log p$-factor in the communication cost. Furthermore, our new method is much simpler and therefore more likely to be useful in practice.

Another application of our algorithm is parallel computation of longest increasing subsequences. Using our new algorithm for simple unit-Monge matrix multiplication shown here, we can get within a $\log n$-factor of work-optimality for this problem. In [14], it is shown that we can solve the LIS problem by iterated application of highest-score matrix composition to solve the problem of semi-local *permutation string comparison*. In permutation string comparison, we have $|x| = |y| = |\Sigma| = n$, and x and y each contain exactly one instance of every character. The LIS problem for a string x can be solved by observing that any LCS of x and the sequence of all characters from Σ in ascending order is a LIS of x.

THEOREM 5.3. *The semi-local LCS problem for permutation strings of length n can be solved on a BSP computer with $p < \sqrt[3]{n}$ processors using $W(n,p) = O(\frac{n \log^2 n}{p})$, $H(n,p) = O(\frac{n \log p}{p})$, $S = O(\log^2 p)$ and $M(n,p) = O(\frac{n}{p})$.*

PROOF. We partition one of the input strings into substrings of length n/p, and compute the highest-score matrix for each of these substrings compared to the other input string in parallel in time $O(\frac{n \log^2 n}{p})$ (see [23]), which is the computationally dominant part of this algorithm. This is possible because the inputs are permutation strings, and therefore only $\frac{n}{p}$ character matches exist for each substring. In [14], we also show how to achieve scalable memory of $M(n,p) = \frac{n}{p}$ for this operation using parallel sorting. We then start merging the highest-score matrices in parallel using our new parallel highest-score matrix multiplication algorithm. Consider level $l \in [0 : \log p]$ of the merging process, and let $r = 2^l$. We again use the fact that the resulting highest score matrix for comparing a permutation string and a permutation-substring of length $2rn/p$ can be stored in $O(2rn/p)$ space. Furthermore, each merge is performed by a group of $2r$ processors. By taking the sum over all values r corresponding to the $\log p$ levels of the merging process, we get computation time $O(\sum_r (\frac{2rn \log(2rn/p)}{p})/(2r)) = O(\frac{n \log n}{p})$, and communication cost $O(\sum_r \frac{2rn}{p}/(2r)) = O(\frac{n \log p}{p})$ for the merging phase. This analysis includes the top level of the merging tree where $r = p$. The number of supersteps $S = O(\log^2 p)$, as the merging tree contains $O(\log p)$ levels which require $O(\log p)$ supersteps each. $\quad\square$

6. CONCLUSIONS AND OUTLOOK

In this paper, we have shown new parallel algorithms for string comparison which achieve scalable memory and computation. In particular, we have improved upon the best known parallel scalability for computing longest increasing subsequences, reaching within a log-factor of optimality. Furthermore, we have improved the bounds for scalable communication for the classical string comparison problem of LCS or edit distance computation. It remains an open problem whether fully scalable communication for LCS computation can be achieved. Our algorithm can be regarded as a step towards obtaining a first generally work-optimal parallel algorithm for computing the longest increasing subsequence (LIS) of a sequence of data items. To our knowledge, no such algorithm has been found yet.

7. ACKNOWLEDGEMENTS

We would like to thank the anonymous reviewers for their helpful comments and suggestions. Alexander Tiskin is supported by a Royal Society Leverhulme Trust Senior Research Fellowship, and by the Centre for Discrete Mathematics and its Applications (DIMAP), University of Warwick, EPSRC award EP/D063191/1.

8. REFERENCES

[1] A. Aggarwal, M. Klawe, S. Moran, P. Shor, and R. Wilber. Geometric applications of a matrix-searching algorithm. *Algorithmica*, 2(1):195–208, Nov. 1987.

[2] C. E. R. Alves, E. N. Cáceres, and S. W. Song. A coarse-grained parallel algorithm for the all-substrings longest common subsequence problem. *Algorithmica*, 45(3):301–335, 2006.

[3] C. E. R. Alves, E. N. Cáceres, and S. W. Song. An all-substrings common subsequence algorithm. *Discrete Applied Mathematics*, 156(7):1025–1035, April 2008.

[4] A. Apostolico, M. J. Atallah, L. L. Larmore, and S. McFaddin. Efficient parallel algorithms for string editing and related problems. *SIAM J. Comput.*, 19(5):968–988, 1990.

[5] S. Bespamyatnikh and M. Segal. Enumerating longest increasing subsequences and patience sorting. *Information Processing Letters*, 76:7–11, 2000.

[6] R. Bisseling. *Parallel Scientific Computation: A Structured Approach Using BSP and MPI.* Oxford University Press, 2004.

[7] R. E. Burkard, B. Klinz, and R. Rudolf. Perspectives of Monge properties in optimization. *Discrete Applied Mathematics*, 70(2):95–161, 1996.

[8] M. de Berg, O. Cheong, M. van Kreveld, and M. Overmars. *Computational Geometry: Algorithms and Applications.* Springer, 2008.

[9] P. Erdős and G. Szekeres. A combinatorial problem in geometry. *Compositio Math.*, 2:463–470, 1935.

[10] D. Gusfield. *Algorithms on Strings, Trees, and Sequences.* Cambridge University Press, 1997.

[11] J. Hammersley. A few seedlings of research. In *Proc. of 6th Berkeley Symp. Math. Stat. Prob.*, 1972.

[12] J. W. Hunt and T. G. Szymanski. A fast algorithm for computing longest common subsequences. *Communications of the ACM*, 20(5):350–353, May 1977.

[13] P. Krusche and A. Tiskin. Efficient parallel string comparison. In *ParCo*, volume 38 of *NIC Series*, pages 193–200. John von Neumann Institute for Computing, 2007.

[14] P. Krusche and A. Tiskin. Parallel longest increasing subsequences in scalable time and memory. In *Proceedings of PPAM 2009, to appear.*, 2010.

[15] G. M. Landau, E. W. Myers, and J. P. Schmidt. Incremental string comparison. *SIAM Journal on Computing*, 27(2):557–582, 1998.

[16] W. F. McColl. Scalable Computing. In J. van Leeuwen, editor, *Computer Science Today: Recent Trends and Developments*, volume 1000, pages 46–61. Springer-Verlag, 1995.

[17] T. Nakashima and A. Fujiwara. A cost optimal parallel algorithm for patience sorting. *Parallel Processing Letters*, 16(1):39–52, 2006.

[18] J. P. Schmidt. All highest scoring paths in weighted grid graphs and their application to finding all approximate repeats in strings. *SIAM Journal on Computing*, 27(4):972–992, 1998.

[19] D. Semé. A CGM algorithm solving the longest increasing subsequence problem. In *Proc. of ICCSA 2006*, volume 3984 of *LNCS*, pages 10–21. Springer, 2006.

[20] A. Tiskin. Semi-local string comparison: Algorithmic techniques and applications. Extended version of [21, 23], arXiv: 0707.3619.

[21] A. Tiskin. Semi-local longest common subsequences in subquadratic time. *Journal of Discrete Algorithms*, 6(4):570–581, 2008.

[22] A. Tiskin. Periodic string comparison. In *Proc of Combinatorial Pattern Matching (CPM) 2009*, volume 5577 of *Lecture Notes in Computer Science*, pages 193–206, 2009.

[23] A. Tiskin. Fast distance multiplication of unit-Monge matrices. In *Proceedings of ACM-SIAM SODA*, pages 1287–1296, 2010.

[24] L. G. Valiant. A bridging model for parallel computation. *Communications of the ACM*, 33(8):103–111, 1990.

[25] R. A. Wagner and M. J. Fischer. The string-to-string correction problem. *Journal of the ACM*, 21(1):168–173, 1974.

A Local O(n²) Gathering Algorithm*

Bastian Degener
Heinz Nixdorf Institute
Computer Science
Department
University of Paderborn
Germany
degener@upb.de

Barbara Kempkes
Heinz Nixdorf Institute
Computer Science
Department
University of Paderborn
Germany
barbaras@upb.de

Friedhelm Meyer auf der Heide
Heinz Nixdorf Institute
Computer Science
Department
University of Paderborn
Germany
fmadh@upb.de

ABSTRACT

The gathering problem, where n autonomous robots with restricted capabilities are required to meet in a single point of the plane, is widely studied. We consider the case that robots are limited to see only robots within a bounded vicinity and present an algorithm achieving gathering in $\mathcal{O}(n^2)$ rounds in expectation. A round consists of a movement of all robots, in random order. All previous algorithms with a proven time bound assume global view on the configuration of all robots.

General Terms

Algorithms, Performance, Theory

Categories and Subject Descriptors

F.1.2 [**Theory of Computation**]: Modes of Computation; F2.2 [**Theory of Computation**]: Nonnumerical Algorithms and Problems

Keywords

swarm robotics, local algorithms, distributed algorithms, gathering, geometric networks

1. INTRODUCTION

Over the last decade, there was a trend to consider large scale systems of autonomous robots with limited capabilities instead of systems with few but powerful computing entities. Such systems often are resilient against transient failures, scale well and behave well under dynamics. Yet it is not obvious which kinds of tasks robots with limited capabilities are able to solve. One challenge that gained great interest in recent years due to its simplicity is to gather a group of n robots in a common point. Most research focused on

the question of which robot capabilities are crucial in which time model to solve the gathering problem in finite time, often assuming the robots to have a global view on the current situation. Some work also exists about robots with a local view [10, 3, 2]. Here, the robots normally have a circular visibility range with a constant radius. However, apart from few exceptions, no runtime bounds are given. Considering locality is reasonable in large robotic systems to guarantee scalability. Moreover, in many practical applications global knowledge is not accessible to the robots. The main contribution of this paper is an algorithm that terminates in expected $\mathcal{O}(n^2)$ rounds, while our robots only have knowledge about their local environment from a constant visibility range.

Related work.

In the literature, several robot abilities are distinguished. When considering the gathering problem, robots are normally assumed to be *oblivious*, which means that the robots do not remember anything from the past. When taking a decision, they therefore rely only on the information which is available in the environment. Another common robot constraint is *anonymity*. In this case, robots do not know ID numbers and they cannot distinguish their neighbors from each other. Another type of constraint is the *compass-model*. If all robots use the same coordinate system, some tasks are easier to solve than if the robots' local coordinate systems can be arbitrarily distorted and scaled (the robots are called *disoriented*). There also exist some compass models in between. For example, the robots can share the directions of the coordinate system, but the axis-scales can be different.

Several time models were proposed. If no runtime bounds but convergence or termination is considered, asynchronous models are often used. In such models, robots may become active at any time, their algorithm executions may be split over several activation periods. In the most general case, the only restriction is that, on an infinite time scale, every robot is activated infinitely often. Time in such a setting is typically defined in terms of rounds. A round finishes as soon as every robot was active at least once. Such asynchronous models typically exclude the problem of concurrency, and therefore maybe interfering activations. This problem is crucial for many synchronous time models.

For the gathering problem, it was shown recently in [8] that robots which are anonymous, disoriented, oblivious and cannot communicate are able to gather in a so called semi-synchronous time model if and only if n is odd. In [18] and [12], the effect of compass models is studied under various aspects. Another focus are negative results, showing under which circumstances robots cannot gather (e.g. [17]). If at least one robot behaves maliciously, gathering is only possible if there are at least three robots in total [1]. In

---
*Partially supported by the EU within FP7-ICT-2007-1 under contract no. 215270 (FRONTS) and DFG-project "Smart Teams" within the SPP 1183 "Organic Computing" and International Graduate School "Dynamic Intelligent Systems"

[5], the authors not only restrict the robots by prohibiting communication, memory and a common coordinate system, but they also use robots which have an extent. The challenge here is that the view of a robot can be blocked by another robot. Again, the results are stated without runtime bounds. In [4], upper bounds of $\mathcal{O}(n^2)$ for the easier convergence problem in several time models are shown, but with robots having a global view. There are algorithms with local view and runtime statements for similar problems, such as transforming a long winding chain of robots into a short one [14, 9, 6]. There is also work for gathering on graphs instead of Euclidean spaces [7, 13, 15]. The authors in [11] point out that having no further assumptions on the robots leads to an exponential lower bound for randomized algorithms for gathering and propose a linear time gathering algorithm, on the base of multiplicity detection. However, in contrast to our work, their algorithm is not local and randomization is inherently needed. The results in [16], [3] and [2] are the closest to ours. In [16], robots converge to the convex hull of some stationary devices, [3] solves the robot convergence and [2] the robot gathering problem locally. All three algorithms basically let a robot move to the center of the smallest enclosing circle around its neighbors. It is shown that the algorithms solve the respective problems in finite time, but no runtime bounds are given.

Problem description and notation.

We are given a set N of n robots in the plane. We assume a discrete time model. A *configuration* at time t is described by the robot positions $p_1(t), ..., p_n(t)$ at time t. The configuration at time 0 is called *start configuration*. If clear from the context, we will sometimes also refer to a robot r_i's position by r_i. G_t denotes the unit disk graph on the positions. $d(r_i, r_j)$ describes the (Euclidean) distance between the two robots r_i and r_j ($d(r_i, r_j)$ varies over time, but it will always be clear from the context). Two robots are connected, if they are within distance 1 of each other. We call this distance the *connection range*. We assume G_0 to be connected. To make sure that the robots do not split into several groups, our algorithm will keep G_t connected at all times. In contrast, the *viewing range* defines the locality: Robots can see all robots within distance 2 and therefore twice as far as the connection range. (For our algorithm it would suffice if every robot knew the positions of all robots within its 2-hop neighborhood, but using the Euclidean distance for the viewing range simplifies the description.)

The goal is to gather the robots in one point, using the restricted robots as described in the robot model. In order to measure the quality of the algorithm, we count the number of rounds (see Round model) until they have gathered.

When a robot executes the algorithm, it computes *target positions* for itself and neighboring robots. These positions are reached before the next time step starts.

Our analysis is based on the convex hull of the robots. We distinguish the *global convex hull* $CH(t)$ at time t, which describes the convex hull of all robot positions at time t, and the *local convex hull* $C_r(t)$ of a robot r at time t. The local convex hull is the convex hull of all robots which are within viewing range of r at time t.

Round model.

One of the most common round models for robot formation problems is the asynchronous round model. Time is modeled as a sequence of discrete points of time (*time steps*). In each time step at most one robot is active. A *round* ends as soon as each robot has been active at least once. This model assumes that robots are never active concurrently, so no conflicts among these actions of active robots have to be handled. Usually, the analysis of robotic strate-

gies in this model is done assuming activation of robots in worst case order in each round.

In this paper we assume weaker models for activation: In the *random order model*, we assume that, in each step, a randomly, uniformly chosen robot becomes active. The choices in different steps are independent. Note that the expected number of steps per round is $\mathcal{O}(n \log n)$ in this model.

In the *random permutation model*, we assume a fixed random permutation of the robots to be initially chosen. This permutation then prescribes the order of activation in each round. Note that each round takes exactly n steps in this model.

These time models are used for the analysis of our algorithm. Implementations should be distributed and should allow parallel activations of robots. For example, a slight variant of the random order model can be implemented as follows: We assume synchronized time steps. In each step, each robot wakes up with some given probability p. An awaken robot becomes active, if no other robot in its connection range is awaken. Note that several robots may now be active concurrently. But as their connection ranges are disjoint, no interference between the actions initiated by the active robots will appear. Choosing $p = 1/n$ leads to a round model which is very close to the random activation model (up to a slightly non-uniform probability distribution, because a robot with few neighbors has a slightly larger probability for becoming active than one with many neighbors).

In Section 4, we will present a variant of this model which uses a probability for wake-up which is dependent on the number of neighbors in G_t. It employs a distributed protocol for handling interferences which is tailored to our gathering algorithm. We will prove a $\mathcal{O}(n^2)$ bound for the expected number of time steps instead of rounds in this model.

Robot model.

We use robots with limited capabilities, trying to understand which capabilities are necessary to prove runtime bounds for the gathering problem with local view. Our robots

- have a limited viewing range
- are oblivious (they do not have memory)
- do not have a common coordinate system
- can assign target positions to robots connected with them (the robots thus need to be able to communicate)
- can measure positions of robots within viewing distance relative to their own position accurately
- can compute complex geometric properties (straight lines through given points, angles, ...)
- can share a position with another robot.

The possibility to assign target positions to neighbors makes the robot model more powerful than the ones studied in the literature. On the other hand, we use the strong restriction of a local viewing range. Note further that communication cannot be used to perform complex tasks, since when using oblivious robots, all gathered information is lost after one step. Consequently, when active, a robot can

- see all positions of robots within its viewing range relative to its own position
- compute target positions for all robots within its connection range.

- tell robots within its connection range their target positions

- move to its own target position (In our strategy, the maximum travelled distance in one step is 2)

When inactive, a robot can

- be told a target position

- move to this target position (In our strategy, the maximum travelled distance in one step is 3)

As soon as two robots share the same position, our algorithm will keep the robots together. So we say that two robots fuse when they share the same position for the first time. Concerning the round model, they now act as one robot, that is, their probability to be activated in a time step t is equal to the probability of non-fused robots.

2. DESCRIPTION OF THE ALGORITHM

The main idea of the algorithm is as follows. Each robot that is a vertex of the convex hull of the robot positions within its local viewing range tries to decrease the area that is covered by the robots as much as possible under the constraint that the unit disk graph of the robots remains connected. In addition, if there are too many robots in a given area, the complexity of the problem will be reduced by fusing single robots into one. As soon as all robots are close together, they can gather in one final step. Note that robots assuming to be a vertex of the global convex hull of robots but which are only a vertex of their local convex hull do not do any harm, because they never leave the global convex hull of robots. Note further that since the robots have a limited viewing range, we must guarantee that the robots do not split into several groups which will never find each other again.

We can now formally describe the algorithm LOCALGATHERING. It is executed by robot r at the time t in which it is active.

See Figure 1 for an illustration of Step 3b of the algorithm. Note that the algorithm is deterministic. We will bound the expected value for the number of rounds until all robots have gathered in one point in the next section; the only randomness used is the stochastic round model. In particular, the algorithm can also be executed in an asynchronous worst case round model, the only difference is that we cannot guarantee the runtime in this case.

3. ANALYSIS OF THE ALGORITHM

This section is dedicated to the analysis of the correctness and runtime of the algorithm LOCALGATHERING. We will first show some preliminaries and then analyze the runtime, measured in the number of rounds needed until the robots have gathered. This number will be shown to be $\mathcal{O}(n^2)$ in expectation, where the randomness comes only from the stochastic round model, while the algorithm itself is deterministic.

Preliminaries.

In order to prove that the robots gather in one point, we first show that G_t stays connected at all times and thus that the robots do not split into several groups. We prove this in the following lemma.

LEMMA 3.1. *If the network is connected before a robot r executes the algorithm, it is still connected afterwards.*

LOCALGATHERING: The algorithm for robot r at time t:

1. Compute the sets A_r and B_r of the robots within the viewing resp. connection range of r. Let C_r denote the convex hull of A_r.

2. (Termination) If $A_r = B_r$ (i.e. no robots from A_r have distance between 1 and 2 to r), then move all robots from A_r to the position $p_t(r)$ of r.

3. Else (B_r is a proper subset of A_r)

3.a (Fusion) If the positions in B_r can be rearranged such that the resulting new set A_r' is still contained in C_r, is still connected, and at least two robots share the same position (are fused), perform this rearrangement. Fused robots will alway have the same position from now on.

3.b (Reduction) If fusion is not possible and r lies on the boundary of C_r, they do the following:

   (a) Compute the two first intersections of the boundary of C_r with the boundary of r's connection range if started from $p_r(t)$ in clockwise/ counterclockwise direction. (Note that these are the intersections which are in maximum distance to each other.)

   (b) Compute the line segment l between these intersections.

   (c) Move all robots on r's side of l to their respective closest point on l.

PROOF. If the action in step 2 of the algorithm is executed, no robot was in the viewing, but not the connection range of r. Therefore, the robots which are moved to $p_r(t)$ were only connected to robots which are moved to the same point, keeping the connection. If r executes the action in step 3a of the algorithm, the robots in r's viewing range stay connected by definition. Moreover, since only robots within r's connection range are moved, edges of the unit disk graph G_t ending outside r's viewing range are not affected.

Now let r be a robot executing the action in step 3b of the algorithm in time step t. Since again only robots within r's connection range are moved, we only need to prove that all robots in the local convex hull $C_r(t)$ stay connected. For these robots (we now denote them by R), the straight line s which contains l separates R in two disjoint subsets R_1 and R_2 (let R_1 contain the robots on l). See Figure 1 for an illustration. Let R_1 be the subset which contains r, and let v be an arbitrary robot from R_1. According to the algorithm, all robots from R_1 are moved to their projection on l, if it exists, and otherwise to their closest point on l (which is the closer end of l). It follows that the distance of v to its neighbors in R_1 can only decrease. If v is moved to its projection on l, by the definition of a projection its distance to the robots in R_2 can also not increase. If no projection of v on l exists, the movement of v can be split in two: If v was moved to its projection v' on s, the distance to its neighbors in R_2 would also not grow. From v', v can be moved to its target position by projecting it to another straight line s': s' is orthogonal to l and intersects l in v's target position (and thus in the end of l which is closer to v). Again, all robots from R_2 are positioned on the other side of s' from v's point of view, and thus its distance to the robots from R_2 can again not increase. □

COROLLARY 3.2. *If Step 2 of the algorithm (termination) is executed, the algorithm has gathered all robots in one position.*

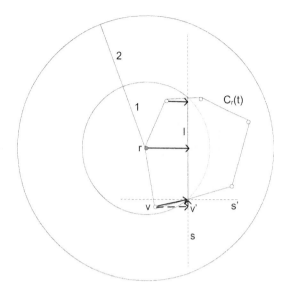

Figure 1: Illustration of step 3b of the algorithm and its correctness

Note that in rounds without fusions, if two robots were in each others connection range before the round, they still are afterwards.

In order to compute the number of rounds until the robots have gathered, we use two progress measures. Since fused robots never part again, fusing robots is progress. The other measure is the area of the convex hull which is truncated in one round. We will prove that we have progress concerning at least one of the two measures in each round: Either two robots are fused or the area decreases in expectation by a constant. Since fused robots never part again, the first measure is monotonically decreasing. We now show that this also holds for the second one.

LEMMA 3.3. *For all t and t' with $t' > t$ it holds: $CH(t') \subseteq CH(t)$.*

PROOF. If robots are rearranged while two robots fuse, a robot leaves neither the local convex hull nor the global convex hull of robots. If a vertex r of the convex hull moves itself and neighboring robots to the line segment l, l is completely inside the local convex hull of r and therefore again no robot leaves the global convex hull. □

The next Lemma states another helpful fact and shows that a simple implementation of Step 3a of the algorithm is sufficient.

LEMMA 3.4. *If $|B_r| > 16$, then Step 3a of the algorithm (Fusion) is always possible.*

PROOF. Insert a grid with step width 1 into the intersection of r's viewing range and $C_r(t)$. It is always possible to insert such a grid which has at most 16 points. If there are more robots in r's connection range than points on the grid, moving the robots to the grid points guarantees that the unit disk graph of the robots in r's viewing range stays connected and that no robot leaves $C_r(t)$. □

Progress in rounds without fusions.

Since we start with n robots, there can be at most $n-1$ rounds in which robots fuse. It remains to bound the number of rounds without fusions. In order to achieve this, we will prove that the area of the convex hull is decreased in expectation by a constant in

such rounds (Lemma 3.8). The idea of the proof is to bound the area which is truncated by a single robot which is a vertex of the global convex hull of robots (Proposition 3.6). This area directly depends on the internal angle of the global convex hull at the robot position at the moment the robot turns active. We show a relation between the internal angle at this moment and at the beginning of the round, so that we are able to sum up the progress of all robots by using the sum of the internal angles of the global convex hull at the beginning of the round.

Before we start with the proofs, we need to introduce some notation. In this subsection we will always consider a fixed round without a fusion. Moreover,

- m denotes the number of *vertex robots*, that is robots which are a vertex of the global convex hull CH at the beginning of the round. For ease of description, we renumber the vertex robots to $r_1, ..., r_m$.

- β_i^* is the internal angle of the global convex hull at vertex robot r_i at the beginning of the round.

Now consider a vertex robot r_i which is still a vertex of the global convex hull $CH(t)$ in the first time step t in which it is active in this round.

- Let p_1 and p_2 denote the first intersections of the *global* convex hull $CH(t)$ with the boundary of r_i's connection range if started from $p_{r_i}(t)$ in clockwise/ counterclockwise direction (the intersections which are in maximal distance to each other). Let T denote the triangle with the vertices $p_{r_i}(t)$, p_1 and p_2. Then β_i is the internal angle of T in vertex $p_{r_i}(t)$.

- Let p_1' and p_2' denote the intersections of the *local* convex hull C_{r_i} and the boundary of r_i's connection range if started from $p_{r_i}(t)$ in clockwise/ counterclockwise direction (the intersections which are in maximal distance to each other). Let T^* denote the triangle with the vertices $p_{r_i}(t)$, p_1' and p_2'. Then α_i is the internal angle of T^* in vertex $p_{r_i}(t)$.

Figure 2 illustrates the described angles. Note that $\alpha_i \leq \beta_i$, since the global convex hull contains the local convex hull at the beginning of time step t.

In order to bound the area which is truncated by a single robot, we start by showing that the internal angle of the local convex hull of this robot cannot be small, since otherwise robots can be fused.

PROPOSITION 3.5. *Consider a fixed round in which no robots are fused. Then α_i is greater than $\frac{\pi}{3}$ for all robots r_i which are a vertex of the global convex hull in the moment they turn active.*

PROOF. If $\alpha_i \leq \frac{\pi}{3}$ for a robot r_i, there exists one position p from which all robots are in distance at most 1 which were within viewing, but not connection range of $p_{r_i}(t)$. See Figure 3 for an illustration. r_i can be moved to the point of the local convex hull closest to the point shown as p in Figure 3. Moreover, because G_t is always connected, there must have been at least one robot in the connection range of r_i. All these robots can now fuse with r_i. Afterwards, no robots remain in the old connection range of r_i and thus the robots from $C_{r_i}(t)$ are connected. □

PROPOSITION 3.6. *Consider a fixed round in which no robots are fused, and a robot r_i which is a vertex of the global convex hull in the time step t in which it turns active. The area of the global convex hull is reduced by at least $\frac{1}{2}\cos(\frac{\beta_i}{2})$ in this time step.*

PROOF. Consider the triangle T as defined above. Since the global convex hull $CH(t)$ contains the local convex hull $C_r(t)$, no

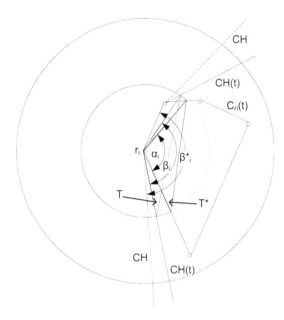

Figure 2: **Angles used in this subsection.** *CH* indicates the global convex hull at the beginning of the round. β_i and α_i are internal angles of the triangles T and T^* at the first time step in which r_i turns active in the round, β_i^* is the internal angle of the global convex hull at the beginning of the round.

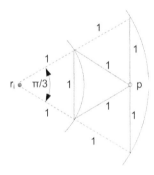

Figure 3: **Illustration of a position from which all neighbors are in connection range. The indicated sector of the circle must contain the local convex hull, if $\alpha_i \leq \frac{\pi}{3}$.**

point of l or the circular segment defined by l and the connection range of r_i can lie strictly inside of T (see Figure 4 for an illustration). As robot r_i moves all robots in its viewing range to this segment, the triangle T cannot contain any robots at the end of time step t. Since T is completely contained in the global convex hull, the area of the global convex hull is reduced by at least the area of T, which is $\sin(\frac{\beta_i}{2}) \cdot \cos(\frac{\beta_i}{2}) \geq \sin(\frac{\alpha_i}{2}) \cdot \cos(\frac{\beta_i}{2}) \geq \frac{1}{2} \cdot \cos(\frac{\beta_i}{2})$, where the first inequality follows from $\beta_i \geq \alpha_i$ and the second follows from Proposition 3.5: According to this proposition, α_i is at least $\frac{\pi}{3}$, giving that $\sin(\frac{\alpha_i}{2}) \geq \frac{1}{2}$. □

The next lemma will be helpful when showing that the convex hull is reduced in expectation by a constant $\frac{1}{c}$. The constant c is the maximum number of robots that can be within the viewing range of a robot without fusing at least two of them. Lemma 3.4 states an upper bound for c of 16.

LEMMA 3.7. *A vertex robot r_i is never moved by the activation of another robot prior to its own activation with probability at least*

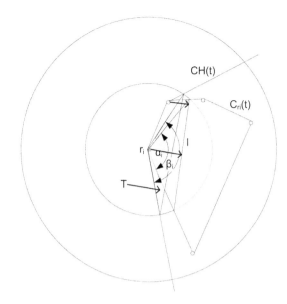

Figure 4: **Illustration of the proof of Proposition 3.6**

a) $\frac{1}{c}$, *in the random order model*

b) $\frac{1}{4c}$, *in the random permutation model.*

PROOF. At the moment t in which it is active, a robot can only have c neighbors (in its connection range), since otherwise robots could be fused. This also holds for all time steps of the current round before t, because once neighbors, robots stay connected at least until the next fusion. Therefore, the probability that a vertex robot r_i is active before any of its neighbors in the random order model is at least

$$\sum_{t=0}^{\infty} \frac{1}{n}(1-\frac{c}{n})^t = \frac{1}{n}\frac{1}{1-(1-\frac{c}{n})} = \frac{1}{c}$$

In the random permutation model, the probability is at least

$$\frac{1}{n} + \left(\sum_{t=1}^{n-1} \frac{1}{n-t} \left(\prod_{j=0}^{t-1} 1 - \frac{c}{n-t} \right) \right)$$

Easy computations show that this is $\geq \frac{1}{4c}$. □

LEMMA 3.8. *Consider a fixed round in which no robots are fused. The expected value for the area by which the global convex hull is reduced in this round is at least $\frac{1}{c}$ in the random order model resp. $\frac{1}{4c}$ in the random permutation model.*

PROOF. Let r_i denote a robot which is a vertex of the global convex hull CH at the beginning of the round. Remember that β_i^* is the internal angle of CH of robot r_i. Since CH is a convex polygon, the sum of its internal angles is $\sum_{i=1}^{m} \beta_i^* = \pi \cdot (m-2)$. We want to use this sum of internal angles to determine the area by which the global convex hull is truncated in this round. Since robot r_i truncates the global convex hull by $\frac{1}{2}\cos(\frac{\beta_i}{2})$ (Proposition 3.6), we need a relation between the internal angle of CH in robot r_i in the beginning of the round (β_i^*) and β_i, the internal angle in robot r_i of the triangle T at the beginning of the first time step t in which r_i is active.

Note that r_i may have neighbors which were moved by other robots before. Consider the case that r_i is active before any other robot in its connection range. This means that r_i's position cannot have changed in this round before time step t. If other robots have

221

moved before time step t in this round, they have not left the global convex hull and thus it can only have shrunk. This means that the internal angle of the global convex hull in robot r_i can only have decreased: At the beginning of time step t it is smaller than or equal to β_i^*. Finally, the triangle T is completely contained in the global convex hull at time step t. It follows that β_i is not larger than the internal angle of the global convex hull at r_i at the beginning of time step t, and thus $\beta_i^* \geq \beta_i$, if r_i is the first vertex of the convex hull which becomes active in its neighborhood.

Now we compute a lower bound for the expected area by which r_i truncates the global convex hull in the time step t in which it is first active, depending only on its internal angle of the global convex hull at the *beginning* of the round. For this, let a_i denote the random variable which describes the area truncated by robot r_i in the round. The following computations are for the random order model, they can be computed analogously for the random permutation model.

$$
\begin{aligned}
E[a_i] &\geq \; Pr[r_i \text{ is the first activated robot in its connection} \\
&\qquad \text{range}] \cdot (\text{area truncated in this case}) \\
&= \; \frac{1}{c} \cdot \frac{1}{2} \cos\left(\frac{\beta_i}{2}\right) \\
&\geq \; \frac{1}{2c} \cos\left(\frac{\beta_i^*}{2}\right)
\end{aligned}
$$

The equality follows from Lemma 3.7. Finally, lower bounding the cosine in the interval $[0; \frac{\pi}{2}]$ by the straight line g with $g(x) = 1 - \frac{2}{\pi} x$, we can use the sum of all internal angles of the global convex hull ($\sum_{i=1}^{m} \beta_i^* = \pi \cdot (m-2)$) to estimate the expected truncated area in the round:

$$
\begin{aligned}
E\left[\sum_{i=1}^{m} a_i\right] &= \sum_{i=1}^{m} E[a_i] \\
&\geq \sum_{i=1}^{m} \frac{1}{2c} \cos\left(\frac{\beta_i^*}{2}\right) \\
&\geq \frac{1}{2c}\left(\sum_{i=1}^{m} -\frac{2}{\pi} \cdot \frac{\beta_i^*}{2} + 1\right) \\
&= \frac{1}{2c}\left(m - \frac{1}{\pi} \sum_{i=1}^{m} \beta_i^*\right) \\
&= \frac{1}{2c}\left(m - \frac{1}{\pi} \cdot \pi \cdot (m-2)\right) = \frac{1}{2c}(m - m + 2) \\
&= \frac{1}{c}
\end{aligned}
$$

$\square$

Note that we only use the first time a robot turns active in a round. If it turns active again, it may reduce the size of the convex hull further, but it will never increase the convex hull (Lemma 3.3). It follows that activating robots more than once in a round can only improve our result.

Runtime of the algorithm.

We can now put together the results to bound the number of rounds until the robots have gathered.

THEOREM 3.9. *Our local gathering algorithm needs expected $O(n^2)$ rounds in the random order and the random permutation model.*

PROOF. In each round, each robot r performs exactly one of the following three operations:

1. it moves all robots in its viewing range to its own position

2. it fuses two robots

3. if it is a vertex of the convex hull of its neighboring robots, it truncates a part of this local convex hull, otherwise it does nothing.

Since the unit disk graph of the robots always stays connected (Lemma 3.1), the first operation is only executed by a robot r if all robots are within connection range of r. It follows that after executing the first operation, the gathering has been achieved. Consequently, there is only one round in which this operation is performed.

The second operation can be performed at most $n-1$ times, since fused robots never part again and after at most $n-1$ fusions, all robots have fused to one robot.

The global convex hull of the start configuration can have an area of at most n^2, because we assume the G_t to be connected. Since according to Lemma 3.8 the area of the convex hull is truncated in expectation by a constant in a round without fusions and since the area of the global convex hull never increases (Lemma 3.3), there can be at most $\mathcal{O}(n^2)$ rounds in expectation without fusions. Summing up the number of rounds for each operation leads to the desired bound. $\square$

4. VARIANT OF THE ROUND MODEL

So far, we have formulated our round models in a global fashion. Now we show that a variant also exists which can be implemented in a distributed synchronous setting.

Consider the following local activation protocol: In a time step, each robot r first computes the size b_r of B_r, the set of robots within its connection range. Then it wakes up with probability $\frac{1}{\max(c, b_r)}$, where c is the maximum number of neighbors a robot can have without fusing robots. It becomes active if no other robot r_1 in B_r with a smaller b_{r_1} woke up. If r is active, it performs our local gathering algorithm.

Note that the parallel executions never interfere. Note further that such a time step needs a computation of B_r, followed by just one step for parallel executions of our local gathering algorithm.

THEOREM 4.1. *Our local gathering algorithm needs expected $O(n^2)$ time steps in the local activation model.*

PROOF. Consider a time step.

If no fusion is possible, each robot r wakes up with probability $\frac{1}{c}$, and becomes active with probability $p \geq \frac{1}{c}(1 - \frac{1}{c})^{c-1}$. As p is constant, Lemma 3.8 yields that, in such a time step, an expected constant size part of the convex hull is truncated. Thus, expected $O(n^2)$ time steps without fusion suffice.

If a fusion is possible, $b_r > c$ holds for some robot r. r wakes up with probability $\frac{1}{b_r}(1 - \frac{1}{b_r})^{b_r} \geq \frac{1}{e \cdot n}$. Thus expected $O(n^2)$ time steps in which a fusion is possible suffice to perform all at most $n-1$ many fusions. $\square$

5. CONCLUSION AND FUTURE WORK

We presented a local gathering algorithm with expected runtime $\mathcal{O}(n^2)$. This is the first algorithm that solves the gathering problem with local view only and provides a runtime guarantee. We use a randomized round model in order to guarantee in our analysis the relation between inner angles of the convex hull at the beginning of a round and at the time in which a robot moves. This is a rather technical assumption and it would be worthwhile to study whether it can be dropped in favor of an asynchronous worst case round model.

Furthermore, the runtime guarantee comes at the price of robots being able to move other robots within their vicinity. From an algorithmic point of view, the robots still act locally, for example in the sense that they do not know the global convex hull but rely only on the convex hull of robots in their vicinity. Still, this approach makes it difficult to apply the algorithm in a deterministic synchronous round model, or even in an asynchronous model where a robot can start to move while other robots have not reached their target position yet. It remains open if a similar runtime bound can be reached without this robot ability. In particular, having runtime bounds on the natural local algorithms considered in [16, 2, 3] that do not have this property would be nice. Our algorithm furthermore relies on the fact that the robots may look twice as far as needed for the connection of the network, which is not needed in [16, 2, 3]. Another open question is whether there are local gathering algorithms with runtime $o(n^2)$.

Note further that in order not to increase the convex hull globally, robots must not increase the convex hull locally. It would be nice to have lower bounds for any algorithm that obeys this constraint or at least for our algorithm.

6. REFERENCES

[1] Noa Agmon and David Peleg. Fault-tolerant gathering algorithms for autonomous mobile robots. In *SODA '04: Proceedings of the fifteenth annual ACM-SIAM symposium on Discrete algorithms*, pages 1070–1078, Philadelphia, PA, USA, 2004. Society for Industrial and Applied Mathematics.

[2] Hideki Ando, Yoshinobu Oasa, Ichiro Suzuki, and Masafumi Yamashita. Distributed memoryless point convergence algorithm for mobile robots with limited visibility. *Robotics and Automation, IEEE Transactions on*, 15(5):818–828, Oct 1999.

[3] Hideki Ando, Yoshinobu Suzuki, and Masafumi Yamashita. Formation agreement problems for synchronous mobile robotswith limited visibility. In *Proc. IEEE Syp. of Intelligent Control*, pages 453–460, 1995.

[4] Reuven Cohen and David Peleg. Convergence properties of the gravitational algorithm in asynchronous robot systems. *SIAM Journal on Computing*, 34(6):1516–1528, 2005.

[5] Jurek Czyzowicz, Leszek Gasieniec, and Andrzej Pelc. Gathering few fat mobile robots in the plane. *Theoretical Computer Science*, 410(6-7):481 – 499, 2009. Principles of Distributed Systems.

[6] Bastian Degener, Barbara Kempkes, Peter Kling, and Friedhelm Meyer auf der Heide. A continuous, local strategy for constructing a short chain of mobile robots. In *17th International Colloquium on Structural Information and Communication Complexity*, 2010.

[7] Anders Dessmark, Pierre Fraigniaud, Dariusz R. Kowalski, and Andrzej Pelc. Deterministic rendezvous in graphs. *Algorithmica*, 46(1):69 – 96, 2006.

[8] Yoann Dieudonné and Franck Petit. Self-stabilizing deterministic gathering. In *Algorithmic Aspects of Wireless Sensor Networks*, pages 230–241, 2009.

[9] Miroslaw Dynia, Jaroslaw Kutylowski, Pawel Lorek, and Friedhelm Meyer auf der Heide. Maintaining communication between an explorer and a base station. In *IFIP 19th World Computer Congress, TC10: 1st IFIP International Conference on Biologically Inspired Computing*, pages 137–146, 1 January 2006.

[10] Paola Flocchini, Giuseppe Prencipe, Nicola Santoro, and Peter Widmayer. Gathering of asynchronous robots with limited visibility. *Theoretical Computer Science*, 337(1-3):147 – 168, 2005.

[11] Taisuke Izumi, Tomoko Izumi, Sayaka Kamei, and Fukuhito Ooshita. Randomized gathering of mobile robots with local-multiplicity detection. In *Stabilization, Safety, and Security of Distributed Systems*, pages 384–398, 2009.

[12] Taisuke Izumi, Yoshiaki Katayama, Nobuhiro Inuzuka, and Koichi Wada. Gathering autonomous mobile robots with dynamic compasses: An optimal result. In *Distributed Computing*, pages 298–312, 2007.

[13] Ralf Klasing, Euripides Markou, and Andrzej Pelc. Gathering asynchronous oblivious mobile robots in a ring. *Theoretical Computer Science*, 390(1):27 – 39, 2008.

[14] Jaroslaw Kutylowski and Friedhelm Meyer auf der Heide. Optimal strategies for maintaining a chain of relays between an explorer and a base camp. *Theoretical Computer Science*, 410(36):3391–3405, 2009.

[15] Sonia Martínez. Practical multiagent rendezvous through modified circumcenter algorithms. *Automatica*, 45(9):2010 – 2017, 2009.

[16] Friedhelm Meyer auf der Heide and Barbara Schneider. Local strategies for connecting stations by small robotic networks. In *IFIP International Federation for Information Processing, Volume 268; Biologically- Inspired Collaborative Computing*, pages 95–104. Springer Boston, September 2008.

[17] Giuseppe Prencipe. Impossibility of gathering by a set of autonomous mobile robots. *Theoretical Computer Science*, 384(2-3):222 – 231, 2007. Structural Information and Communication Complexity (SIROCCO 2005).

[18] Samia Souissi, Xavier Défago, and Masafumi Yamashita. Gathering asynchronous mobile robots with inaccurate compasses. In *Principles of Distributed Systems*, pages 333–349, 2006.

Delays Induce an Exponential Memory Gap for Rendezvous in Trees*

Pierre Fraigniaud
CNRS and University Paris Diderot
France
pierre.fraigniaud@liafa.jussieu.fr

Andrzej Pelc
Université du Québec en Outaouais
Canada
andrzej.pelc@uqo.ca

ABSTRACT

The aim of rendezvous in a graph is meeting of two mobile agents at some node of an unknown anonymous connected graph. The two identical agents start from arbitrary nodes in the graph and move from node to node with the goal of meeting. In this paper, we focus on rendezvous in trees, and, analogously to the efforts that have been made for solving the exploration problem with compact automata, we study the size of memory of mobile agents that permits to solve the rendezvous problem deterministically.

We first show that if the delay between the starting times of the agents is *arbitrary*, then the lower bound on memory required for rendezvous is $\Omega(\log n)$ bits, even for the line of length n. This lower bound meets a previously known upper bound of $O(\log n)$ bits for rendezvous in arbitrary trees of size at most n. Our main result is a proof that the amount of memory needed for rendezvous *with simultaneous start* depends essentially on the number ℓ of leaves of the tree, and is exponentially less impacted by the number n of nodes. Indeed, we present two identical agents with $O(\log \ell + \log \log n)$ bits of memory that solve the rendezvous problem in all trees with at most n nodes and at most ℓ leaves. Hence, for the class of trees with polylogarithmically many leaves, there is an exponential gap in minimum memory size needed for rendezvous between the scenario with arbitrary delay and the scenario with delay zero. Moreover, we show that our upper bound is optimal by proving that $\Omega(\log \ell + \log \log n)$ bits of memory is required for rendezvous, even in the class of trees with degrees bounded by 3.

Categories and Subject Descriptors

G.2.2 [**Discrete Mathematics**]: Graph Theory—*Network problems*; F.1.0 [**Theory of Computation**]: Computation by Abstract Devices—*General*

General Terms

Algorithms, Theory.

Keywords

rendezvous, exploration, robots, mobile entities, abstract state machine.

1. INTRODUCTION

The rendezvous in a network [1, 4] is the following task. Two identical mobile agents, initially located in two nodes of the network, move along links from node to node, and eventually have to get to the same node at the same time. The network is modeled as an undirected connected graph, and agents traverse links in synchronous rounds. In this paper we consider deterministic rendezvous, and seek rendezvous protocols that do not rely on the knowledge of node labels, and can work in anonymous graphs as well (cf. [3]). This assumption is motivated by the fact that, even when nodes are equipped with distinct labels, agents may be unable to perceive them or nodes may refuse to reveal their labels, e.g., due to security reasons. (Note also that if nodes of the graph are labeled using distinct names, then agents can meet at some a priori agreed node, and rendezvous reduces to graph exploration).

Obviously, deterministic rendezvous is not possible if the initial positions of the two agents are symmetric, i.e., if there is an automorphism of the graph that carries one node on the other. Hence, lots of efforts have been dedicated to the study of the feasibility of rendezvous, and to the time required to achieve this task, when feasible. For instance, deterministic rendezvous with agents equipped with tokens used to mark nodes was considered, e.g., in [26]. Deterministic rendezvous of agents equipped with unique labels was discussed in [12, 13, 24]. (In this latter scenario, symmetry is broken by the use of the different labels of agents, and thus rendezvous is sometimes possible even for symmetric initial positions of the agents). Recently, rendezvous using variants of Universal Traversal Sequences was investigated in [30]. Surprisingly though, as opposed to what was done for the graph exploration problem (see, e.g., [10, 18, 23, 28]), or for other tasks such as routing (see, e.g., [16, 17]), very little is known on the amount of memory required by

*Part of this work was done during this author's visit at the Research Chair in Distributed Computing of the Université du Québec en Outaouais. The first author is supported by the ANR projects ALADDIN and PROSE, and by the INRIA project GANG. The second author is supported in part by NSERC discovery grant and by the Research Chair in Distributed Computing of the Université du Québec en Outaouais.

the agents for achieving rendezvous. Up to our knowledge, the only existing results prior to this work are dedicated to rendezvous in rings and trees. Memory needed for randomized rendezvous in the ring is discussed, e.g., in [25]. Memory needed for deterministic rendezvous in trees is discussed in [19] where it is proved that the minimum memory size guaranteeing rendezvous in all trees of size at most n is $\Theta(\log n)$ bits, even if the two agents start at different times, and at least $\Omega(\log \log n)$ bits, even if the two agents start at the same time.

The aim of this paper is to determine the space complexity of rendezvous in trees.

1.1 Our results

We first show that if the delay between the starting times of the agents is arbitrary, then the lower bound on memory required for rendezvous is $\Omega(\log n)$ bits, even for the line of length n. This lower bound matches the upper bound from [19] in the case of arbitrary trees.

Our main result is a proof that the amount of memory needed for rendezvous *with simultaneous start* in trees depends essentially on the number ℓ of leaves of the tree, and is exponentially less impacted by the number n of nodes. Indeed, we show two identical agents with $O(\log \ell + \log \log n)$ bits of memory that solve the rendezvous problem in all trees with n nodes and ℓ leaves. Hence, for the class of trees with polylogarithmically many leaves, there is an exponential gap in minimum memory size needed for rendezvous between the scenario with arbitrary delay and the scenario with delay zero.

Moreover, we show that the size $O(\log \ell + \log \log n)$ of memory is optimal, even in the class of trees with degrees bounded by 3. More precisely, for infinitely many integers ℓ, we show a class of arbitrarily large trees with maximum degree 3 and with ℓ leaves, for which rendezvous requires $\Omega(\log \ell)$ bits of memory. This lower bound, together with a result from [19] showing that $\Omega(\log \log n)$ bits of memory are required for rendezvous with simultaneous start in the line of length n, implies that our upper bound $O(\log \ell + \log \log n)$ cannot be improved, even for trees with maximum degree 3.

1.2 Other related work

The rendezvous problem was first mentioned in [29]. Authors investigating rendezvous (cf. [3] for an extensive survey) considered either the geometric scenario (rendezvous in an interval of the real line, see, e.g., [8, 9, 20], or in the plane, see, e.g., [6, 7]). Many papers, e.g., [1, 2, 5, 8, 22] study the probabilistic setting: inputs and/or rendezvous strategies are random.

A natural extension of the rendezvous problem is that of gathering [15, 22, 27, 31], when more than 2 agents have to meet in one location. In [32] the authors considered rendezvous of many agents with unique labels. The impact of memory size on the feasibility of the related task of tree exploration, for trees with unlabeled nodes, has been studied in [14, 21]. In [14] the authors showed that no agent can explore with termination all trees of bounded degree and that memory of size $O(\log^2 n)$ bits is enough to explore all trees of size n and return to the starting node. In [21] it was shown that the latter task can be accomplished by an agent with memory of size $O(\log n)$ bits.

2. FRAMEWORK AND PRELIMINARIES

We consider trees whose nodes are unlabeled, and edges incident to a node v have distinct labels in $\{0, \ldots, d-1\}$, where d is the degree of v. Thus every undirected edge $\{u, v\}$ has two labels, which are called its *port numbers*[1] at u and at v. Port numbering is *local*, i.e., there is no relation between port numbers at u and at v (we do not assume any sense of direction, of any kind). A pair of distinct nodes u, v of a tree is called *symmetric* if there exists an automorphism of the tree preserving port numbering, that carries one node on the other. Recall that an automorphism of the tree is a bijection $f : V \to V$, where V is the set of nodes of the tree, such that for any $w, w' \in V$, w is adjacent to w' if and only if $f(w)$ is adjacent to $f(w')$. It preserves port numbering if for any $w, w' \in V$, the port number corresponding to edge $\{w, w'\}$ at node w is equal to the port number corresponding to edge $\{f(w), f(w')\}$ at node $f(w)$. So u and v are symmetric if there exists an automorphism f preserving port numbering, and such that $f(u) = v$.

We consider mobile agents traveling in trees with locally labeled ports. The tree and its size are a priori unknown to the agents. We first define precisely an individual agent. An agent is an abstract state machine $\mathcal{A} = (S, \pi, \lambda, s_0)$, where S is a set of states among which there is a specified state s_0 called the *initial* state, $\pi : S \times \mathbb{Z}^2 \to S$, and $\lambda : S \to \mathbb{Z}$. Initially the agent is at some node u_0 in the initial state $s_0 \in S$. The agent performs actions in rounds measured by its internal clock. Each action can be either a move to an adjacent node or a null move resulting in remaining in the currently occupied node. State s_0 determines a natural number $\lambda(s_0)$. If $\lambda(s_0) = -1$ then the agent makes a null move (i.e., remains at u_0). If $\lambda(s_0) \geq 0$ then the agent leaves u_0 by port $\lambda(s_0)$ modulo the degree of u_0. When incoming to a node v in state $s \in S$, the behavior of the agent is as follows. It reads the number i of the port through which it entered v and the degree d of v. The pair $(i, d) \in \mathbb{Z}^2$ is an input symbol that causes the transition from state s to state $s' = \pi(s, (i, d))$. If the previous move of the agent was null, (i.e., the agent stayed at node v in state s) then the pair $(-1, d) \in \mathbb{Z}^2$ is the input symbol read by the agent, that causes the transition from state s to state $s' = \pi(s, (-1, d))$. In both cases s' determines an integer $\lambda(s')$, which is either -1, in which case the agent makes a null move, or a non negative integer indicating a port number by which the agent leaves v (this port is $\lambda(s') \mod d$). The agent continues moving in this way, possibly infinitely.

Since we consider the rendezvous problem for identical agents, we assume that agents are copies A and A' of the same abstract state machine $\mathcal{A}$, starting at two distinct nodes v_A and $v_{A'}$, called the *initial positions*. We will refer to such identical machines as a *pair of agents*. It is assumed that the internal clocks of a pair of agents tick at the same rate. The clock of each agent starts when the agent starts executing its actions. Agents start from their initial position with *delay* $\theta \geq 0$, controlled by an adversary. This means that the later agent starts executing its actions θ rounds after the first agent. Agents do not know which of them is first and what is the value of θ. We seek agents with small memory, measured by the number of states of the corre-

---

[1]In the absence of port numbers, rendezvous is usually impossible, as the adversary may prevent an agent from taking some edge incident to the current node.

sponding automaton, or equivalently by the number of bits on which these states are encoded. An automaton with K states requires $\Theta(\log K)$ bits of memory.

Initial positions forming a symmetric pair of nodes are crucial for our considerations. Indeed, if the initial positions are not a symmetric pair, then there exists a pair of agents that can meet in a given tree, for any delay θ, and, if the initial position is symmetric, then meeting is impossible for any pair of agents, for $\theta = 0$. We say that a pair of agents solve the rendezvous problem *with arbitrary delay* (resp. *with simultaneous start*) in a class of trees, if, for any tree in this class and for any initial positions that are not symmetric, both agents are eventually in the same node of the tree in the same round, regardless of the starting rounds of the agents (resp. provided that they start in the same round). Hence, in particular, solving the rendezvous problem with simultaneous start means achieving rendezvous whenever it is possible.

Consider any tree T and the following sequence of trees constructed recursively: $T_0 = T$, and T_{i+1} is the tree obtained from T_i by removing all its leaves. $T' = T_j$ for the smallest j for which T_j has at most two nodes. If T' has one node, then this node is called the *central node* of T. If T' has two nodes, then the edge joining them is called the *central edge* of T. A tree T with port labels is called *symmetric*, if there exists a non-trivial automorphism f of the tree (i.e., an automorphism f such that $f(u) \neq u$, for some $u \in V$) preserving port numbering. If a tree with port labels has a central node, then it cannot be symmetric. In a non-symmetric tree, every pair of nodes is non-symmetric, hence rendezvous is feasible for all initial positions of agents.

The following statement is an easy consequence of the techniques and results from [21].

FACT 2.1. *There exists an agent accomplishing the following task in an arbitrary tree, using $O(\log m)$ bits of memory in trees with at most m nodes: it finds the number m of nodes in the tree, and*

- *if the tree has a central node, then the agent goes to this node, and stops;*

- *if the tree has a central edge but is not symmetric, then, for any initial position, the agent goes to the same extremity of the central edge, and stops; moreover, it knows which port of this extremity corresponds to the central edge;*

- *if the tree is symmetric, then the agent goes to one of the extremities of the central edge; moreover, to whichever extremity it goes, the agent knows which port of this extremity corresponds to the central edge; finally, the number of rounds used to go to this extremity of the central edge differs by at most m, for any two initial positions of the agent in an m-node tree.*

In the sequel, the procedure accomplishing the above task will be called Procedure `recognize`.

3. RENDEZVOUS WITH ARBITRARY DELAY

It was proved in [19] that rendezvous with arbitrary delay can be accomplished in n-node trees using $O(\log n)$ bits of memory. It was also observed that rendezvous requires

$\Omega(\log n)$ bits of memory in arbitrarily large trees with $2n+1$ nodes and maximum degree n. The lower bound examples were trees T_n consisting of two nodes u and v of degree n, both linked to a common node w, and to $n-1$ leaves. However, these trees have linear degree and the reason for the logarithmic memory requirement is simply that agents with smaller memory are incapable of having an output function λ with range of linear size, and thus the adversary can place agents in nodes u and v and distribute ports in such a way that none of the agents can ever get to node w, which makes rendezvous infeasible.

This example leaves open the question if rendezvous with sub-logarithmic memory is possible, e.g., in all trees with constant maximum degree. It turns out that if the delay is arbitrary, this is not the case: rendezvous requires logarithmic memory even for the class of lines.

THEOREM 3.1. *Rendezvous with arbitrary delay in the n-node line requires agents with memory $\Omega(\log n)$.*

PROOF. Let k be the number of memory bits of the agent and $K = 2^k$ be its number of states. Place one agent at some node u of the infinite line where each edge has the same port number at its two extremities. In any interval of length $K + 1$ there exist two nodes at which the agent is in the same state. Let x_1 be the first node of the trajectory of the agent in which this happens and let s be the state of the agent at x_1. Let x_2 be the second node of the trajectory of the agent at which the agent is in state s. Let δ be the distance between u and x_1 and let d be the distance between x_1 and x_2.

We construct the following instance of the rendezvous problem (see Fig. 1). The line is of length $8(K + 1) + 1$. Let e be the central edge of this line. Assign number 0 to ports leading to edge e from both its extremities, and assign other port labels so that ports leading to any edge at both its extremities get the same number 0 or 1. (This is equivalent to 2-edge-coloring of the line.) Let z be the endpoint of the line, for which x_1 is between z and x_2. Let y_1 and y_2 be symmetric images of x_1 and x_2, respectively, according to the axis of symmetry of the line. Let y_0 be the node distinct from y_2, at distance d from y_1. Let v be the node at distance δ from y_0, such that the vectors $[x_1, u]$ and $[y_0, v]$ have opposite directions. The other agent is placed at node v.

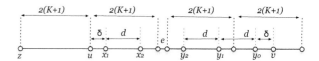

Figure 1: Construction in the proof of Theorem 3.1.

Let t_1 be the number of rounds that the agent starting at u takes to reach[2] x_1 in state s. Let t_2 be the number of rounds that the agent starting at v takes to reach y_1 in state s. Let $\theta = t_2 - t_1$. The adversary delays the agent starting at u by θ rounds. Hence the agent starting at u reaches x_1 at the

---

[2]Here we say that the agent *reaches* node w in state s, if s is the state of the agent in w after the application of the transition function; Hence, once the agent has reached w is state s, it leaves w by port $\lambda(s)$.

same time t and in the same state as the agent starting at v reaches y_1. The points x_1 and y_1 are symmetric positions, hence rendezvous is impossible after time t. Before time t the two agents were on different sides of edge e, in view of $\delta + d \leq 2(K + 1)$, hence rendezvous did not occur, although the initial positions of the agents are not a symmetric pair. The size of the line is $O(K) = O(2^k)$, which concludes the proof. □

Together with the logarithmic upper bound from [19], the result above completely solves the problem of determining the minimum memory of the agents permitting rendezvous with arbitrary delay. Hence in the rest of the paper we concentrate on rendezvous with simultaneous start, thus assuming that the delay $\theta = 0$.

4. RENDEZVOUS WITH SIMULTANEOUS START

4.1 Upper bound

It turns out that the size of memory needed for rendezvous with simultaneous start depends on two parameters of the tree: the number n of nodes and the number ℓ of leaves. In fact we show that rendezvous in trees with n nodes and ℓ leaves can be done using only $O(\log \ell + \log \log n)$ bits of memory. Thus, for trees with polylogarithmically many leaves, $O(\log \log n)$ bits of memory are enough. In view of Theorem 3.1, this shows an exponential gap in the minimum memory size needed for rendezvous between the scenarios with arbitrary delay and with delay zero.

THEOREM 4.1. *There is a pair of identical agents solving rendezvous with simultaneous start in all trees, and using, for any integers n and ℓ, $O(\log \ell + \log \log n)$ bits of memory in trees with at most n nodes and at most ℓ leaves.*

The rest of the subsection is dedicated to the proof of Theorem 4.1. Let T be any tree. Let T' be the *contraction* of T, that is the tree obtained from T by replacing every path[3] in T joining two nodes of degree different from 2 by an edge (the ports of this edge correspond to the ports at both extremities of the contracted path). Notice that if T has ℓ leaves, then its contraction T' has at most $2\ell - 1$ nodes. Our rendezvous algorithm uses Procedure recognize, mentioned in Section 2, as a subroutine for solving the problem in the simple case where the contraction tree T' is non symmetric, i.e., either there is a central node, or there is a central edge and the two edge-labeled trees obtained by removing the central edge in T' are not isomorphic. (The isomorphism must preserve both the structure of the trees, and the labeling of the edges). Indeed, in a non symmetric case, Fact 2.1 states that two agents performing Procedure recognize will eventually identify a single node of T', and hence a single node of T as well, at which they will rendezvous. The difficult and more challenging case is when the contraction tree T' has a central edge with two non distinguishable extremities, in which case the ability to solve the rendezvous problem depends on the large tree T, and the initial positions of the two agents. Identifying whether these two positions are symmetric or not in T, and, in the latter

case, achieving rendezvous, is complicated by the constraint that the agents must use sub-logarithmic memory when ℓ is small. The main part of the proof will be dedicated to describing how this task can actually be achieved in a memory efficient manner.

Rendezvous proceeds in two phases. During the first phase, each of the two agents starts by executing procedure recognize in T, ignoring the degree-2 nodes. That is, protocol recognize is modified so that whenever an agent enters a degree-2 node through port $i \in \{0, 1\}$ in some state s, it will leave that node at the next round by port $(i + 1) \mod 2$, in the same state s. More precisely, let s_0 be the initial state of an agent executing recognize. Our modified agent starts in a state s_0^*, and leaves the initial node through port 0. The agent proceeds in states s_0^* until it enters a node of degree different from 2. At such a node, independently of the incoming port number, the agent enters state s_0. From that point on, the agent performs recognize by ignoring degree-2 nodes. We call recognize-bis the protocol recognize modified in this way. Observe that, in trees with no nodes of degree 2, the two protocols recognize and recognize-bis perform similarly (only the beginnings of the two protocols slightly differ). Hence, protocols recognize and recognize-bis perform similarly in T'. Formally, the following holds.

CLAIM 4.1. *The states at nodes of degrees different from 2 of an agent performing recognize-bis in T starting from some node u are identical to the states of an agent performing recognize in T' starting from node v, where v is the first node of degree different from 2 reached when leaving u through port 0.*

Using this claim, rendezvous in T is achieved as follows.

- If there is a central node in T', then that node is identified by protocol recognize (cf. Fact 2.1). Hence, from Claim 4.1, the corresponding node in T is identified by recognize-bis. Rendezvous is achieved by waiting for the other agent at that node.

- Similarly, if there is a central edge in T', and the tree T' is not symmetric, then one extremity of that edge is identified by protocol recognize (cf. Fact 2.1). Hence, from Claim 4.1, the corresponding node in T is identified by recognize-bis. Rendezvous is achieved by waiting for the other agent at that node.

We are left with the case in which the contraction tree T' is symmetric. In this case, according to Fact 2.1, the two agents may end up in two different nodes of T after having performed recognize-bis. These two nodes correspond to the two extremities of the central edge of the symmetric tree T'. For instance, in the n-node path with an odd number of edges, the two agents may end up in the two symmetric extremities of the path after having performed recognize-bis. Also, in the binomial tree with n-nodes (cf.[11]), the two agents may end up in the two symmetric roots of the two binomial subtrees of T with $n/2$ nodes. Still, we prove that rendezvous is possible with little memory assuming that the two initial positions of the agents were not symmetric in T. Actually, the first of the two key ingredients in our proof is showing how rendezvous can be achieved in the path using agents with $O(\log \log n)$ bits of memory.

More precisely, in the lemma below, we consider *blind* agents in paths, that is agents that ignore port labels. More

---

[3]Here, by *path* we mean a sequence of adjacent nodes of degree 2, all pairwise distinct.

precisely, when entering a node, such an agent can just distinguish between the incoming edge and the other edge (if any). We use blind agents for an explicit reason: the NSC for rendezvous in path by blind agents can easily be characterized. Specifically, let $P = (v_1, \ldots, v_m)$ be an m-node path, and consider two identical blind agents initially located at nodes v_a and v_b, $a < b$. Rendezvous using blind agents is possible if and only if m odd, or m even and $a - 1 \neq m - b$.

Of course, a standard agent can simulate the behavior of a blind agent. When applying the lemma below with standard agents, we will make sure that the starting positions v_a and v_b are such that rendezvous is achievable even with blind agents.

LEMMA 4.1. *There exists a pair of identical blind agents accomplishing rendezvous with simultaneous start in all paths, whenever it is possible, and using $O(\log \log m)$ bits of memory in paths with at most m nodes.*

PROOF. Let $P = (v_1, \ldots, v_m)$ be an m-node path, and consider two identical blind agents initially located at nodes v_a and v_b, $a < b$. To achieve rendezvous, the two agents perform a sequence of traversals of P, executed at lower and lower speeds, aiming at eventually meeting each other at some node. More precisely, for an integer $s \geq 1$, a traversal of the path is performed at *speed* $1/s$, if the agent remains idle $s - 1$ rounds before traversing any edge. For instance, traversing P from v_1 to v_m at speed $1/s$ requires $(m - 1)s$ rounds. Our rendezvous algorithm for the line, called $\texttt{prime}$, performs as follows.

Begin
    start in arbitrary direction;
    move at speed 1 until reaching one extremity
       of the path;
    $p \leftarrow 2$;
    While no rendezvous **do**
       traverse the entire path twice, at speed $1/p$;
       $p \leftarrow$ smallest prime larger than p;
End

We now prove that, whenever rendezvous is possible for blind agents (i.e., when m odd, or m even and $a - 1 \neq m - b$), the two agents meet before the pth iteration of the loop, for $p = O(\log n)$. Let p_j be the jth prime number ($p_1 = 2$). Hence the speed of each agent at the jth execution of the loop is $1/p_j$. If rendezvous has not occurred during the jth execution of the loop, then the two agents have crossed the same edge, say $e = \{v_c, v_{c+1}\}$, at the same time t, in opposite directions. This can occur if, for instance, the agent initially at v_a moves to node v_1, traverses twice the path at successive speeds $p_1, \ldots, p_{j-1}$, and, $c\, p_j$ rounds after having eventually started walking at speed p_j, traverses the edge e at time t, while the other agent initially at v_b moves to v_m, traverses twice the path at successive speeds $p_1, \ldots, p_{j-1}$, and, $(m - c)p_j$ rounds after having eventually started walking at speed p_j, traverses the same edge e in the other direction at the same time t. In fact, there are four cases to consider, depending on the two starting directions of the two agents: towards v_1 or towards v_m. From these four cases, we get that one of the following four equalities must hold (the first one corresponds to the previously described scenario: v_a moves towards v_1 while v_b moves towards v_m):

$$
\begin{aligned}
t &= (a - 1) + 2(m - 1)\sum_{i=1}^{j-1} p_i + c\, p_j \\
  &= (m - b) + 2(m - 1)\sum_{i=1}^{j-1} p_i + (m - c)p_j
\end{aligned}
$$

or

$$
\begin{aligned}
t &= (a - 1) + 2(m - 1)\sum_{i=1}^{j-1} p_i + (m - 1)p_j + (m - c)p_j \\
  &= (b - 1) + 2(m - 1)\sum_{i=1}^{j-1} p_i + c\, p_j
\end{aligned}
$$

or

$$
\begin{aligned}
t &= (m - a) + 2(m - 1)\sum_{i=1}^{j-1} p_i + (m - c)p_j \\
  &= (m - b) + 2(m - 1)\sum_{i=1}^{j-1} p_i + (m - 1)p_j + c\, p_j
\end{aligned}
$$

or

$$
\begin{aligned}
t &= (m - a) + 2(m - 1)\sum_{i=1}^{j-1} p_i + (m - c)p_j \\
  &= (b - 1) + 2(m - 1)\sum_{i=1}^{j-1} p_i + c\, p_j
\end{aligned}
$$

Therefore we get that

$$p_j \text{ divides } |a - b|, \text{ or } p_j \text{ divides } |m - (a + b) + 1|.$$

As a consequence, since the p_i's are primes, we get that if the two agents have not met after the jth execution of the loop, then

$$\prod_{i \in \mathcal{I}} p_i \text{ divides } |a - b| \quad \text{and} \quad \prod_{i \in \mathcal{J}} p_i \text{ divides } |m - (a + b) + 1|$$

where $\mathcal{I} \cup \mathcal{J} = \{1, \ldots, j\}$. Therefore, since the p_i's are primes, $\prod_{i=1}^{j} p_i$ divides $|a - b| \cdot |m - (a + b) + 1|$. Hence, if rendezvous is feasible, it must occur at or before the jth execution of the loop, where j is the largest index such that $\prod_{i=1}^{j} p_i$ divides $|a - b| \cdot |m - (a + b) + 1|$. Thus it must occur at or before the jth execution of the loop, where j is the largest index such that $\prod_{i=1}^{j} p_i \leq m^2$.

Let $\pi(x)$ be the number of prime numbers smaller than or equal to x. On the one hand, we have $\prod_{i=1}^{j} p_i \geq 2^{\pi(p_j)}$. Hence, rendezvous must occur at or before the jth execution of the loop, where j is the largest index such that $2^{\pi(p_j)} \leq m^2$, i.e., $\pi(p_j) \leq 2 \log m$. On the other hand, from the Prime Number Theorem we get that $\pi(x) \sim x/\ln(x)$, i.e.,

$$\lim_{x \to \infty} \frac{\pi(x)}{x/\ln(x)} = 1.$$

Hence, for m large enough, $\pi(x) \geq x/(2\ln(x))$. Thus rendezvous must occur at or before the jth execution of the loop, where j is the largest index such that $p_j/\ln p_j \leq 4 \log m$.

From the above, we get that (1) rendezvous must occur whenever it is feasible, and (2) it occurs at or before the jth execution of the loop, where $\log p_j \leq O(\log \log m)$. Since the next prime p can be found using $O(\log p)$ bits, e.g., by exhaustive search, we get that $\texttt{prime}$ performs rendezvous using agents with $O(\log \log m)$ bits of memory. $\square$

The (blind) agents described in Lemma 4.1 perform a protocol called $\texttt{prime}$. This protocol uses the infinite sequence of prime numbers. We denote by $\texttt{prime}(i)$ the protocol $\texttt{prime}$ modified so that it stops after having considered the ith prime number.

We now come back to our general rendezvous protocol in trees (with port numbers). If the agents detect symmetry of the contraction tree, a second phase begins. Let $\nu = 2x$ be the number of nodes in the contraction tree T'. (We have ν even since T' is symmetric with respect to its central edge). We define a (non-simple) path called the *rendezvous path*, denoted by P, that will be used by the agents to rendezvous using protocol $\texttt{prime}$. To define P, let u and v be the two extremities of the path in T corresponding to the central edge in T'. This path is called the *central path*, and is denoted by C. Abusing notation, C will also be used as a shortcut for the instruction: "traverse C".

Let BW (for "basic walk") be the instruction of performing the following actions: leave by port 0, and, perpetually, whenever entering a degree-d node by port $i \in \{0, \ldots, d-1\}$, leave that node by port $(i+1) \bmod d$. Similarly, let CBW (for "counter basic walk"), be the instruction of performing the following: leave by the port used to enter the current node at the previous step, and, perpetually, whenever entering a degree-d node by port i, leave that node by port $(i-1) \bmod d$. For $j \geq 1$, let BW(j) (resp., CBW(j)) be the instruction to execute BW (resp., CBW) until j nodes of degree different from 2 have been visited. Let B_u (resp., B_v) be the path corresponding to the execution of BW$\big(2(\nu - 1)\big)$ from u (resp., from v). Note that a node can be visited several times by the walk, and thus neither B_u nor B_v are simple. Note also that since T' has ν nodes, it has $\nu - 1$ edges, and thus both B_u and B_v are closed paths, i.e., their extremities are u and v, respectively. Let $\overline{B}_u$ (resp., $\overline{B}_v$) be the path corresponding to the execution of CBW$\big(2(\nu - 1)\big)$ from u (resp., from v). We define

$$P = \big(B_u \mid C_{u \to v} \mid \overline{B}_v \mid C_{v \to u}\big)^{5\ell} \mid \big(B_u \mid C_{u \to v} \mid \overline{B}_v\big)$$

where "$\mid$" denotes the concatenation of paths, $C_{u \to v}$ (resp., $C_{v \to u}$) denotes the path C traversed from u to v (resp., from v to u), and, for a closed path Q, Q^α denotes Q concatenated with itself α times.

The path P is well defined. Indeed, the sequence

$$B_u \mid C_{u \to v} \mid \overline{B}_v \mid C_{v \to u}$$

leads back to node u. Also, the two extremities of the path are u and v. Now, the agents have no clue whether they are standing at u or at v. Nevertheless, we have the following.

CLAIM 4.2. *Starting from an extremity u or v of the central path C, an agent performing the sequence of instructions*

$$\Big(\text{BW}\big(2(\nu - 1)\big), C, \text{CBW}\big(2(\nu - 1)\big), C\Big)^{5\ell}$$

followed by

$$\text{BW}\big(2(\nu - 1)\big), C, \text{CBW}\big(2(\nu - 1)\big)$$

traverses the path P from one of its extremities to the other.

Before establishing the claim, note that instructions BW$\big(2(\nu-1)\big)$ and CBW$\big(2(\nu-1)\big)$ are meaningful, since agents can have counters of size $O(\log \ell)$ bits, and they know ν in view of Fact 2.1. To establish the claim, it suffices to notice that the path $\overline{P}$ reverse to P is given by

$$\begin{aligned}
\overline{P} &= \big(B_v \mid C_{v \to u} \mid \overline{B}_u\big) \mid \big(C_{u \to v} \mid B_v \mid C_{v \to u} \mid \overline{B}_u\big)^{5\ell} \\
&= \big(B_v \mid C_{v \to u} \mid \overline{B}_u \mid C_{u \to v}\big)^{5\ell} \mid \big(B_v \mid C_{v \to u} \mid \overline{B}_u\big).
\end{aligned}$$

The two agents will use protocol prime along the path P to achieve rendezvous. However, to make sure that rendezvous succeeds, the two agents must not start prime simultaneously at the two extremities of P, in order to break symmetry. Unfortunately, this requirement is not trivial to satisfy. Indeed, Fact 2.1 guaranties that the delay between the times the two agents reach the two extremities of C (and thus of P as well) does not exceed n, but no guarantee can be given for the minimum delay, which could be zero. This is because the delay does not depend on the tree T', but on the tree T. Hence two agents starting simultaneously in T

```
Begin
    for consecutive values i ≥ 1 do
        /* try rendezvous */
        for j = 0, 1, . . . , 2(ν − 1) do
            perform BW(j);
            perform CBW(j); /* back to init. position */
        perform prime(i) on the rendezvous path P;
        /* reset */
        go to the other extremity of the central path C;
        for j = 0, 1, . . . , 2(ν − 1) do
            perform BW(j);
            perform CBW(j); /* back to init. position */
        return to the original extremity of the
            central path C;
End
```

Figure 2: Second phase of the rendezvous (performed when the contraction tree is symmetric).

may actually finish the first phase of our protocol (i.e., the execution of recognize-bis) at the same time, even if T is not symmetric, and even if T is symmetric but the starting positions were not symmetric. The second key ingredient in our proof is a technique guaranteeing eventual desynchronization of the two agents. A high level description of this technique is summarized in Figure 2. We describe this technique in detail below.

The outer loop of the protocol in Figure 2 states how many consecutive prime numbers the protocol will test while performing prime along the path P. Performing prime(i) for successive values of i, instead of just prime, is for avoiding a perpetual execution of prime in the case when the two agents started the execution of phase 2 at the same time from the two extremities of P. For every number $i \geq 1$ of primes to be used in prime, the protocol performs two inner loops. The first one is an attempt to achieve rendezvous along P, while the second one is used to upper bound the delay between the two agents at the end of the outer loop, in order to guarantee that the next execution of the outer loop will start with a delay between the two agents that does not exceed n.

During the first inner loop, an agent executing the protocol performs a series of basic walks, of different lengths. For $j = 0$, the agent performs nothing. In this case, prime(i) is performed on P directly. For $j > 0$, the agent performs a basic walk in T to the jth node of degree different from 2 that it encounters along its walk. When $j = 2(\nu - 1)$, the basic walk is a complete one, traversing each edge of T twice. Each BW(j) is followed by a CBW(j), so as to come back to the original position at the same extremity of the path P. Once this is done, the agent performs prime(i) on P.

The second inner loop aims at resetting the two agents. For this purpose, each agent goes to the other extremity of C, performs the same sequence of actions as the other agent had performed during its execution of the first inner loop, and returns to its original extremity of C. This enables resetting the two agents in the following sense.

CLAIM 4.3. *Let t and t' be the times of arrival of the two agents at the two extremities of C after the execution of recognize-bis. Then the difference between the times the two agents enter each execution of the outer loop of the protocol in Figure 2 is at most $|t - t'|$.*

To establish the claim, just notice that, during every execution of the outer loop, the sets of actions performed by the two agents inside the loop are identical, differing only by their orders.

A consequence of Claim 4.3 is the following lemma.

LEMMA 4.2. *Let t and t' be the times of arrival of the two agents at the two extremities of C after the execution of* recognize-bis. *For every i, the delay between the two agents at the beginning of each execution of* prime(i) *cannot exceed $|t - t'| + 18n\ell$. On the other hand, for every i, if at the beginning of each execution of* prime(i) *the delay between the two agents is zero, then their initial positions were symmetric in T.*

PROOF. For $j \geq 1$, let l_j and l'_j be the lengths (i.e., numbers of edges) of the paths in T between the jth and the $(j + 1)$th node of degree different from 2 that is met by the two agents, respectively, during their basic walk from their positions at the two extremities of C. At the jth iteration of the first inner loop, one agent has traversed $2\sum_{a=1}^{j}\sum_{b=1}^{a} l_b$ edges during BW(a) and CBW(a) for all $a = 1, \ldots, j$. The other agent has traversed $2\sum_{a=1}^{j}\sum_{b=1}^{a} l'_b$ edges during the same BW(a) and CBW(a). Since the number of rounds of prime(i) is the same for both agents, we get that their "desynchronization" is at most:

$$
\begin{aligned}
|t - t'| + 2\sum_{a=1}^{j}\sum_{b=1}^{a} |l_b - l'_b| &\leq n + 4(\nu - 1)\sum_{b=1}^{2(\nu-1)} |l_b - l'_b| \\
&\leq n + 4(\nu - 1)\sum_{b=1}^{2(\nu-1)} \max\{l_b, l'_b\} \\
&\leq n + 8(\nu - 1)n \\
&\leq 9\nu n \\
&\leq 18n\ell.
\end{aligned}
$$

This completes the proof of the first statement in the lemma. Assume now that, at the beginning of each of the $2\nu - 1$ executions of prime(i) in the outer loop, the delay between the two agents is zero. This implies that, for every $j = 0, \ldots, 2(\nu - 1)$ we have

$$
t + 2\sum_{a=1}^{j}\sum_{b=1}^{a} l_b = t' + 2\sum_{a=1}^{j}\sum_{b=1}^{a} l'_b .
$$

Therefore, $t = t'$ and $l_j = l'_j$ for every $j = 1, \ldots, 2(\nu - 1)$. In other words, the two agents started at the same time, and all segments of degree-2 nodes encountered by the agents were of the same length. Since the contraction tree T' is symmetric, it follows that the initial positions of the two agents were symmetric in T. □

In view of the lemma, at each execution i of the outer loop, there is an execution j of prime(i) for which the two agents do not start the second phase at the same time from their respective extremities of P. Moreover, during this jth execution of prime(i), the delay between the two agents is at most $|t - t'| + 18n\ell$. Hence, from Fact 2.1, this delay δ is at most $19n\ell$. The length of the rendezvous path P is at least $20n\ell$ because B_u and B_v are each of length at least $2n$. Therefore, at the first time when both agents are simultaneously in the jth execution of prime(i), they occupy two non symmetric positions in P: one is at one extremity of P, and the other is at some node of P at distance $\delta > 0$

along P from the other extremity of P. Moreover, since the delay δ between the two agents is smaller than the length of the path P, the agent first executing prime(i) has not yet completed the first traversal of P when the other agent starts prime(i). As a consequence, the two agents act as if prime(i) were executed with both agents starting simultaneously at non symmetric positions in the path. Now, for small values of i, prime(i) may not achieve rendezvous in P. However, in view of Lemma 4.1, for some $i = O(\log n)$, rendezvous will be completed whenever the initial positions of the agents were not symmetric in T.

We complete the proof by checking that each agent uses $O(\log \ell + \log \log n)$ bits of memory. Protocol recognize-bis executed in T consumes the same amount of memory as Protocol recognize executed in T'. Since T' has at most $2\ell - 1$ nodes, recognize-bis uses $O(\log \ell)$ bits of memory. During the second phase of the rendezvous, a counter is used for identifying the index j of the inner loop. Since $j \leq 2\nu \leq 4\ell$, this counter uses $O(\log \ell)$ bits of memory. All executions of prime are independent, and performed one after the other. Thus, in view of Lemma 4.1, a total of $O(\log \log n)$ bits suffice to implement these executions. The index i of the outer loop grows until it is large enough so that prime(i) achieves rendezvous in a path of length $O(n\ell)$. Thus, $i \leq \log(n\ell)$, and thus $O(\log \log(n\ell)) = O(\log \log n)$ bits suffice to encode this index. This completes the proof of Theorem 4.1.

4.2 The lower bound $\Omega(\log \ell)$

In this section we prove that rendezvous with simultaneous start in trees with ℓ leaves requires $\Omega(\log \ell)$ bits of memory even in the class of trees with maximum degree 3. Together with the lower bound of $\Omega(\log \log n)$ on memory size needed for rendezvous on the n-node line[1], established in [19], this result proves that our upper bound $O(\log \ell + \log \log n)$ from Section 4.1 cannot be improved even for trees of maximum degree 3.

THEOREM 4.2. *For infinitely many integers ℓ, there exists an infinite family of trees with ℓ leaves, for which rendezvous with simultaneous start requires $\Omega(\log \ell)$ bits of memory.*

PROOF. Let $\ell = 2^i$. Consider a complete binary tree of depth $i - 1$ (thus with 2^{i-1} leaves). Label ports in this tree by assigning, at each node, label 0 to the port leading to the parent, and labels 1 and 2 to the ports leading to children. This labeling determines a fixed order of all nodes (e.g., using the lexicographic order of the sequences of ports leading from the root to nodes). For any binary vector of length 2^{i-1} modify the tree by attaching to each leaf corresponding to 1 an additional leaf and adding nothing at leaves corresponding to 0. Assign numbers 1 and 0 to ports corresponding to newly created edges (1 at the old leaf which becomes a node of degree 2, and 0 at the new leaf). Clearly there are $2^{2^{i-1}} = 2^{\ell/2}$ resulting labeled trees. Call them *side trees*.

For any pair of side trees T' and T'' and for any positive even integer m, consider the tree T consisting of side trees T' and T'' whose roots are joined by a path of length $m + 1$ (i.e., there are m added nodes of degree two). Ports at the added nodes of degree two are labeled as follows: both ports

---

[1] Notice that the lower bound $\Omega(\log \log n)$ holds for n-node trees with many leaves as well: it suffices to attach $\ell/2$ leaves on each extremity of the line and the argument from [19] goes through.

at the central edge have label 0, and ports at both ends of any other edge of the line have the same label 0 or 1. (This corresponds to a 2-edge-coloring of the line). Call any tree resulting from this construction a *two-sided tree*. For any two-sided tree consider initial positions of the agents at nodes u and v of the line adjacent to roots of its side trees.

Consider agents with k bits of memory (thus with $K = 2^k$ states). A *tour* of a side tree associated with an initial position (u or v) is the part of the trajectory of the agent in this side tree between consecutive visits of the associated initial position. Observe that the maximum duration D of a tour is smaller than $K \cdot (3 \cdot 2^{i-1})$. Indeed, the number of nodes in a side tree is at most $3 \cdot 2^{i-1} - 1$, hence the number of possible pairs (state, node of the side tree) is at most $K \cdot (3 \cdot 2^{i-1} - 1)$. A tour of longer duration than this value would cause the agent to leave the same node twice in the same state, implying an infinite loop. Such a tour could not come back to the initial position.

For a fixed agent with the set S of states and a fixed side tree, we define the function $p : S \to S$ as follows. Let s be the state in which the agent starts a tour. Then $p(s)$ is the state in which the agent finishes the tour. Now we define the function $q : S \to S \times \{1, \ldots, D\}$, called the *behavior function*, by the formula $q(s) = (p(s), t)$, where t is the number of rounds to complete the tour when starting in state s. The number of possible behavior functions is at most $F = (KD)^K$. A behavior function depends on the side tree for which it is constructed.

Suppose that $k \leq \frac{1}{3} \log \ell$. We have $D < 3K2^{i-1} = \frac{3}{2}K\ell$, hence $KD < \frac{3}{2}K^2\ell$. Hence we have $\log K + \log \log(KD) \leq k + \log \log(\frac{3}{2}K^2\ell) \leq k + 2 + \log k + \log \log \ell$, which is smaller than $\frac{2}{3} \log \ell$ for sufficiently large k. It follows that $K \log(KD) < \ell^{2/3} < \ell/2$, which implies $F = (KD)^K < 2^{\ell/2}$. Thus the number of possible behavior functions is strictly smaller than the total number of side trees. It follows that there are two side trees T_1 and T_2 for which the corresponding behavior functions are equal.

Consider two instances of the rendezvous problem for any length $m + 1$ of the joining line, where m is a positive even integer: one in which both side trees are equal to T_1, and the other for which one side tree is T_1 and the other is T_2. Rendezvous is impossible in the first instance because in this instance initial positions of the agents form a symmetric pair of nodes. Consider the second instance, in which the initial positions of the agents do not form a symmetric pair. Because of the symmetry of labeling of the joining line, agents cannot meet inside any of the side trees. Indeed, when one of them is in one tree, the other one is in the other tree. Since the behavior function associated with side trees T_1 and T_2 is the same, the agents leave these trees always at the same time and in the same state. Hence they cannot meet on the line, in view of its odd length. This implies that they never meet, in spite of asymmetric initial positions. Hence rendezvous in the second instance requires $\Omega(\log \ell)$ bits of memory. $\square$

5. REFERENCES

[1] S. Alpern, The rendezvous search problem, SIAM J. on Control and Optimization 33 (1995), 673-683.

[2] S. Alpern, Rendezvous search on labelled networks, Naval Reasearch Logistics 49 (2002), 256-274.

[3] S. Alpern and S. Gal, The theory of search games and rendezvous. Int. Series in Operations research and Management Science, Kluwer Academic Publisher, 2002.

[4] J. Alpern, V. Baston, and S. Essegaier, Rendezvous search on a graph, Journal of Applied Probability 36 (1999), 223-231.

[5] E. Anderson and R. Weber, The rendezvous problem on discrete locations, Journal of Applied Probability 28 (1990), 839-851.

[6] E. Anderson and S. Fekete, Asymmetric rendezvous on the plane, Proc. 14th Annual ACM Symp. on Computational Geometry (1998), 365-373.

[7] E. Anderson and S. Fekete, Two-dimensional rendezvous search, Operations Research 49 (2001), 107-118.

[8] V. Baston and S. Gal, Rendezvous on the line when the players' initial distance is given by an unknown probability distribution, SIAM J. on Control and Opt. 36 (1998), 1880-1889.

[9] V. Baston and S. Gal, Rendezvous search when marks are left at the starting points, Naval Reasearch Logistics 48 (2001), 722-731.

[10] S. A. Cook and C. Rackoff. Space Lower Bounds for Maze Threadability on Restricted Machines. SIAM J. Comput. 9 (1980), 636-652.

[11] T.H. Cormen, C.E. Leiserson, R.L. Rivest, Introduction to Algorithms, McGraw-Hill 1990.

[12] G. De Marco, L. Gargano, E. Kranakis, D. Krizanc, A. Pelc, U. Vaccaro, Asynchronous deterministic rendezvous in graphs, Theoretical Computer Science 355 (2006), 315-326.

[13] A. Dessmark, P. Fraigniaud, D. Kowalski, A. Pelc. Deterministic rendezvous in graphs. Algorithmica 46 (2006), 69-96.

[14] K. Diks, P. Fraigniaud, E. Kranakis, A. Pelc, Tree exploration with little memory, Journal of Algorithms 51 (2004), 38-63.

[15] P. Flocchini, G. Prencipe, N. Santoro, P. Widmayer, Gathering of asynchronous oblivious robots with limited visibility, Proc. 18th Annual Symposium on Theoretical Aspects of Computer Science (STACS 2001), LNCS 2010, 247-258.

[16] P. Fraigniaud and C. Gavoille. A Space Lower Bound for Routing in Trees. In 19th Annual Symp. on Theoretical Aspects of Computer Science (STACS 2002), Springer LNCS 2285, 65-75.

[17] P. Fraigniaud and C. Gavoille. Routing in Trees. In 28th Int. Colloquium on Automata, Languages and Programming (ICALP 2001), Springer LNCS 2076, 757-772.

[18] P. Fraigniaud and D. Ilcinkas. Digraphs Exploration with Little Memory. 21st Symp. on Theoretical Aspects of Comp. Science (STACS 2004), Springer LNCS 2996, 246-257.

[19] P. Fraigniaud, A. Pelc, Deterministic rendezvous in trees with little memory, Proc. 22nd International Symposium on Distributed Computing (DISC 2008), Springer LNCS 5218, 242-256.

[20] S. Gal, Rendezvous search on the line, Operations Research 47 (1999), 974-976.

[21] L. Gasieniec, A. Pelc, T. Radzik, X. Zhang, Tree

exploration with logarithmic memory, Proc. 18th Annual ACM-SIAM Symposium on Discrete Algorithms (SODA 2007), 585-594.

[22] A. Israeli and M. Jalfon, Token management schemes and random walks yield self stabilizing mutual exclusion, Proc. 9th Annual ACM Symposium on Principles of Distributed Computing (PODC 1990), 119-131.

[23] M. Koucký, Universal Traversal Sequences with Backtracking, Proc. 16th IEEE Conference on Computational Complexity (2001), 21-26.

[24] D. Kowalski, A. Malinowski, How to meet in anonymous network, in 13th Int. Colloquium on Structural Information and Comm. Complexity, (SIROCCO 2006), Springer LNCS 4056, 44-58.

[25] E. Kranakis, D. Krizanc, and P. Morin, Randomized Rendez-Vous with Limited Memory, Proc. 8th Latin American Theoretical Informatics (LATIN 2008), Springer LNCS 4957, 605-616.

[26] E. Kranakis, D. Krizanc, N. Santoro and C. Sawchuk, Mobile agent rendezvous in a ring, Proc. 23rd Int. Conference on Distributed Computing Systems (ICDCS 2003), IEEE, 592-599.

[27] W. Lim and S. Alpern, Minimax rendezvous on the line, SIAM J. on Control and Optimization 34 (1996), 1650-1665.

[28] O. Reingold. Undirected connectivity in log-space. Journal of the ACM 55(2008), 1-24.

[29] T. Schelling, The strategy of conflict, Oxford University Press, Oxford, 1960.

[30] A. Ta-Shma and U. Zwick. Deterministic rendezvous, treasure hunts and strongly universal exploration sequences. Proc. 18th ACM-SIAM Symposium on Discrete Algorithms (SODA 2007), 599-608.

[31] L. Thomas, Finding your kids when they are lost, Journal on Operational Res. Soc. 43 (1992), 637-639.

[32] X. Yu and M. Yung, Agent rendezvous: a dynamic symmetry-breaking problem, Proc. International Colloquium on Automata, Languages, and Programming (ICALP 1996), LNCS 1099, 610-621.

Best-effort Group Service in Dynamic Networks[*]

Bertrand Ducourthial
Université de Technologie de
Compiègne
CNRS Heudiasyc UMR6599
Compiègne, France
Bertrand.Ducourthial@utc.fr

Sofiane Khalfallah
Université de Technologie de
Compiègne
CNRS Heudiasyc UMR6599
Compiègne, France
Sofiane.Khalfallah@utc.fr

Franck Petit
Université Pierre et Marie
Curie
CNRS LiP6 UMR7606—INRIA
REGAL
Paris, France
Franck.Petit@lip6.fr

ABSTRACT

We propose a group membership service for dynamic ad hoc networks. It maintains as long as possible the existing groups and ensures that each group diameter is always smaller than a constant, fixed according to the application using the groups. The proposed protocol is self-stabilizing and works in dynamic distributed systems. Moreover, it ensures a kind of *continuity* in the service offer to the application while the system is converging, except if too strong topology changes happen. Such a *best effort* behavior allows applications to rely on the groups while the stabilization has not been reached, which is very useful in dynamic ad hoc networks.

Categories and Subject Descriptors

C.4 [**Performance of Systems**]: [Fault tolerance, Reliability, availability, and serviceability]; C.2.1 [**Computer-communication networks**]: Network Architecture and Design—*Wireless communication*

General Terms

Algorithms

Keywords

Group maintenance, Best effort, Stabilization, Dynamic network, Vehicular network

1. INTRODUCTION

Self-stabilization in dynamic networks.

A *dynamic* network can be seen as an (*a priori* infinite) sequence of networks over time. In this paper, we focus on dynamic *mobile* networks. Examples of such networks are *Mobile Ad hoc* networks (MANETs) or *Vehicular Ad hoc* networks (VANETs).

[*]Supported by Région Picardie, proj. APREDY.

Designing applications on top of such networks require dealing with the lack of infrastructure [22, 15]. One idea consists in building virtual structures such as clusters, backbones, or spanning trees. However, when the nodes are moving, the maintenance of such structures may require more control. The dynamic of the network increases the control overhead. Thus, distributed algorithms should require less overall organization of the system in order to remain useful in dynamic networks.

Another paradigm for building distributed protocols in mobile ad hoc networks consists in designing self-stabilizing algorithms [4]. These algorithms have the ability to recover by themselves (*i.e.*, automatically) from an inconsistent state caused by transient failures that may affect a memory or a message. In this context, the topology changes can be considered as transient failures because they lead to an inconsistency in some memories. Indeed, when a node appears or disappears in the network, all its neighbors should update their neighborhood knowledge.

Self-stabilizing algorithms have been intensively studied the two last decades for their ability to tolerate transient faults [9]. However, it is important to notice that such algorithms do not ensure all the time the desirable behavior of the distributed system, especially when faults occur and during a certain period of time following them. In dynamic systems, it becomes illusory to expect an application that continuously ensures the service for which it has been designed. In other words, what we can only expect from the distributed algorithms is to behave as "the best" as possible, the result depending on the dynamic of the network.

In this paper, we propose a new approach in the design of distributed solutions for dynamic environments. We borrow the term *"best-effort"* from the networking community to qualify the algorithms resulting of our approach. Roughly speaking, a best-effort algorithm is a self-stabilizing algorithm that also maintains an extra property, called *continuity*, conditioned by the topology changes.

Continuity aims to improve the output of the distributed protocol during the convergence phase of the algorithm, provided that a topological property is preserved. This means that there is a progression in the successive outputs of the distributed protocols, except if the network dynamic is too high. This is important in a distributed system where the dynamic (that is, the frequent topology changes) can prevent the system to converge to the desirable behavior. Since the output of the protocol will certainly be used before the stabilization, the continuity ensures that third party applications can rely on it instead of waiting. The output will certainly be modified in the future, but without challenging previous ones.

In some aspects, our approach is close to the ones introduced in [17] and in [10]. In [17], the authors introduce the notion of *safe-convergence* which guarantees that the system quickly converges to a safe configuration, and then, it gracefully moves to an optimal configuration without breaking safety. However, the solution in [17] works on a static network. In [10], the authors use the notion of *passage predicate* to define a *superstabilizing* system, *i.e.*, a system which is stabilizing and when it is started from a legitimate state and a single topology change occurs, the passage predicate holds and continues to hold until the protocol reaches a legitimate state. By contrast, the continuity property is intended to be satisfied *before* a legitimate configuration has been reached. It must be satisfied during the stabilization phase, and between two consecutive stabilization phases (convergence phase followed by stability phase).

We illustrate our approach by specifying a new problem, called *Dynamic Group Service* inspired from vehicular ad hoc networks (VANET), an emblematic case of dynamic ad hoc networks. We then design a best effort distributed protocol called GRP for solving this problem: we prove that it is self-stabilizing and fulfills a continuity property, allowing applications to use the groups while the convergence may be delayed because of the dynamic of the network.

Dynamic group service.

Vehicular ad hoc networks currently attract a lot of attention [3]. Many VANET applications require cooperation among close vehicles during a given period: collaborative driving, distributed perception, chats and other infotainment applications. Vehicles that collaborate form a *group*. A group is intended to grow until a limit depending on the application. For instance, the distributed perception should not involve too far vehicles, a chat should be responsive enough, that limits the number of hops, etc. When the group diameter is larger than the bound given by the application, it should be split into several smaller groups. However, a group should not be split if this is not mandatory by the diameter constraint in order to ensure the best duration of service to the application relying on it. Even if another partitioning of the network would have been better (*e.g.*, less groups, no isolated vehicle), it is preferable to maintain the composition of existing groups. It is expected that, thanks to the mobility of the nodes, small groups will eventually succeed in merging. It is thus more important to maintain existing groups as long as possible.

Best-effort GRP algorithm.

To solve the *Dynamic Group Service*, we propose a best-effort distributed algorithm called GRP (for GRouP) designed for unreliable message passing systems. This algorithm stabilizes the views (the local knowledge of the group to which belongs the node) in such a way that all the members of a group will eventually share the same view (in which only the members appear). The groups' diameters are smaller than a fixed applicative constant Dmax and neighbor groups merge while the diameter constraint is fulfilled. Moreover, our algorithm admits the following continuity property: no node disappears from a group except if a topology change leads to the violation of the diameter constraint. This allows to the applications requiring the groups (*e.g.*, chat) to run before

the convergence of GRP, that may be delayed because of the dynamic of the network.

To the best of our knowledge, only a few number of papers address the problem of group membership maintenance in the context of self-stabilization. Recently, in [6], the authors propose a self-stabilizing *k*-clustering algorithm for static networks. In [11], the authors propose a self-stabilizing group communication protocol. It relies on a mobile agent that collects and distributes information during a random walk. This protocol does not allow building groups that strech over at most *k* hops.

Group communication structures have been proposed in the literature to achieve fault-tolerance in distributed systems [2], by providing for instance replication, virtual synchrony, reliable broadcast, or atomic broadcast (*e.g.*, [21, 14]). Other works deal with the *k*-clustering or *k*-dominating set problem, *e.g.*, [1, 5, 8, 16, 17, 18, 20], where nodes in a group are at most at distance *k* from a *cluster-head* or *dominant node*. The aim of these algorithms is to optimize the partitioning of the network. The group service we propose in this paper is different in the sense that its aim is neither to optimize any partitioning nor to build group centered to some nodes. Instead, it tries to maintain existing groups as long as possible while satisfying a constraint on the diameter, without relying on a specific node (that may move or leave).

Organization.

In Section 2, we describe the distributed system we consider in this paper. We also state what it means for a protocol to be self-stabilizing and best effort regarding a continuity property conditioned by topology changes. Next, in Section 3, we specify the Dynamic Group Service problem and in Section 4, we describe our GRP algorithm solving it[1]. The proofs are given in Section 5. Finally, we make some concluding remarks in Section 6.

2. MODEL

We define the distributed system $\mathcal{S}$ as follows.

System.

Let V be the set of nodes, spread out in an Euclidean space. The total number of nodes in V is finite but unknown. Each node is equipped with a processor unit (including local memory) and a communication device. A node can move in the Euclidean space. It is either *active* or *inactive*. When it is active, it can compute, send and receive messages by executing a local algorithm. The *distributed protocol* $\mathcal{P}$ is composed of all the local algorithms.

We define the *vicinity* of a node v as the part of the Euclidean space from where a node u can send a message that can be received by v (the vicinity depends on the communication devices, the obstacles, etc.).

At any time instant t, there is a *communication link* from

---

[1] Note that the algorithm has been successfully implemented using the Airplug software suite. The detailed algorithm used for the implementation is available on our website (as long as the software):
http://www.hds.utc.fr/~ducourth/airplug/
doku.php?id=en:dwl:grp:accueil
Some screenshot movies are also available here:
http://www.hds.utc.fr/~ducourth/airplug/
doku.php?id=en:doc

u to v if (i) both u and v have the state active (at t), and (ii) u is into the vicinity of v (at t). A communication link is oriented because u could be in the vicinity of v while the converse is false. A node v can receive a message from u if there is a communication link from u to v and (iii) u is sending a message, (iv) no other node in the vicinity of v is currently sending a message, and (v) v is not sending a message itself (any active node that is not sending is able to receive).

By the way, a communication over a link may fail. We assume that on each node the message sending is driven by a *timer*. We admit the following *fair channel* hypothesis: there exists two time constants τ_1 and τ_2 with $\tau_1 \geq \tau_2$ such that, starting from a date t, any node v is able to receive before the date $t + \tau_1$ a message from a node u, providing that there is a communication link from u to v between t and $t + \tau_1$ and u attempts to send a message every τ_2 units of time.

A *configuration* c of $\mathcal{S}$ is the union of states of memories of all the processors and the contents of all the communication links. An empty communication link is denoted in the configuration by a link that contains an empty set of messages. By the way, there is a single topology per configuration. Let $\mathcal{C}$ be the set of configurations. An *execution* of a distributed protocol $\mathcal{P}$ over $\mathcal{S}$ is a sequence of configurations $c_0, c_1, \ldots$ of $\mathcal{S}$ so that $\forall i \geq 0$, c_i moves to c_{i+1} by changing a link, the content of a link or the memory of at least one process including its message buffers (*i.e.*, by sending or receiving messages).

We denote by G^{c_i} the topology of $\mathcal{S}$ during the configuration c_i. In a *static* system $\mathcal{S}$, we have $G^{c_i} = G^{c_0}$ in every execution $c_0, c_1, c_2, \ldots$. Otherwise, the system $\mathcal{S}$ is said to be *dynamic*.

Self-Stabilization.

Let $\mathcal{X}$ be a set. Then $x \vdash \Pi$ means that an element $x \in \mathcal{X}$ satisfies the predicate Π defined on the set $\mathcal{X}$ and $X \vdash \Pi$ with $X \subset \mathcal{X}$ means that any $x \in X$ satisfies $x \vdash \Pi$. We define a special predicate true as follows: $\forall x \in \mathcal{X}$, $x \vdash$ true. Let Π_1 and Π_2 be two predicates defined on the set of configurations $\mathcal{C}$ of the system $\mathcal{S}$. Π_2 is an *attractor* for Π_1 if and only if the following condition is true: for any configuration $c_1 \vdash \Pi_1$ and for any execution $e = c_1, c_2, \ldots$, there exists $i \geq 1$ such that for any $j \geq i$, $c_j \vdash \Pi_2$.

Define a *specification* of a task as the predicate Π on the set $\mathcal{C}$ of configurations of system $\mathcal{S}$. A protocol $\mathcal{P}$ is self-stabilizing for Π if and only if there exists a predicate $\mathcal{L}_\mathcal{P}$ (called the legitimacy predicate) defined on $\mathcal{C}$ such that the following conditions hold:
1. For any configuration $c_1 \vdash \mathcal{L}_\mathcal{P}$, and for any execution $e = c_1, c_2, \ldots$, we have $e \vdash \Pi$ (correctness).
2. Π is an attractor for true (closure and convergence).

Best effort requirement.

We denote by Π_T a *topological* predicate defined on the pairs of successive configurations in an execution. Such a predicate is intended to be false when an "important topology" change happens. We denote by Π_C a *continuity* predicate defined on the pairs of successive configurations in an execution. Such a predicate is intended to be false when the quality of the outputs produced by protocol $\mathcal{P}$ in the two successive configurations decreases.

The protocol $\mathcal{P}$ offers a best effort continuity of services if $\Pi_T \Rightarrow \Pi_C$.

3. DYNAMIC GROUP SERVICE PROBLEM

The Dynamic Group Service protocol is inspired from applications requirements in Vehicular Ad hoc networks (VANET), such as collaborative perception or infotainment applications.

Informal specification.

On each node v, a variable view$_v$ gives the composition of the group to which v belongs. This will be used by the applications. The agreement property says that all nodes in group of v agree on the composition of the group. The safety property says that the diameter of each group is smaller than a constant Dmax. The maximality property says that small groups merge to form larger groups.

To deal with the dynamic of the network, the algorithm should be able to satisfy these three properties in finite time after the last failure or topology change (self-stabilization). To allow the applications to run while the convergence has not been reached, the algorithm should ensure a best effort requirement: if the distance between the members of a group remains smaller than Dmax (topological property), then no node will leave the group (continuity property). This is important because the convergence may be delayed due to the dynamic of the network.

Formal specification.

Let $G(V, E)$ be a graph. Let $d(u, v)$ be the *distance* between u and v (length of the shortest path from u to v in G). A *subgraph* $H(V_H, E_H)$ is defined as follows:

$$V_H \subseteq V \text{ and}$$
$$\forall (u, v) \in E, (u \in V_H \text{ and } v \in V_H) \Rightarrow (u, v) \in E_H$$

Two subgraphs $H_1(V_1, E_1)$ and $H_2(V_2, E_2)$ of a graph G are said *distinct* if $V_1 \cap V_2 = \emptyset$. Let $X \subseteq V$ be a set of nodes. We denote by $d_X(u, v)$ the distance between u and v in the subgraph $H(X, E_H)$, that is, the length of the shortest path from u to v with only edges of E_H. If such a path does not exists, then $d_X(u, v) = +\infty$.

Given a graph G, the problem considered in this paper consists in designing a distributed protocol that provides a partition of G into disjoint subgraphs called *groups* that satisfies constraints described below. Denote by view$_v^c$ the knowledge of v about its group in configuration c (output of the local algorithm on node v).

Let Π_A be the predicate called *agreement property*, defined on the configurations as follows. For $c \in \mathcal{C}$, $\Pi_A(c)$ holds if and only if there exists a partition of disjoint subgraphs $H_1(V_1, E_1), H_2(V_2, E_2), \ldots, H_i(V_i, E_i), \ldots$ of $G(V, E)$ such that for every nodes $u, v \in V$, we have:

$$(u \in V_i \text{ and } v \in V_i) \Leftrightarrow \text{view}_u^c = \text{view}_v^c = V_i$$

When the agreement property is fulfilled, the output of the local algorithms (variables view) denotes group of nodes. We will denote such a group by Ω:

$$\Omega_v^c = \text{view}_v^c \text{ if } \Pi_A(c) \text{ holds} \quad ; \quad \Omega_v^c = \emptyset \text{ else}$$

When they are non null (Π_A holds), the groups Ω_v ($v \in V$) define a partition of G into disjoint subgraphs. However these groups may be disconnected, too large or too small. Other properties are then required.

Let `Dmax` be an integer representing the maximal admissible distance between two nodes belonging to the same group (this constant is given by the distributed application that need the groups, and that required the GRP algorithm to build them).

Let Π_S be the predicate called *safety property*, defined on the configurations as follows. For $c \in \mathcal{C}$ satisfying Π_A, $\Pi_S(c)$ holds if each group is connected and its diameter is smaller than `Dmax`:

$$\forall v \in V, \max_{x,y \in \Omega_v^c} d_{\Omega_v^c}(x,y) \leq \texttt{Dmax}$$

In others words, when the safety property is fulfilled, the groups are connected (inter-node distance is finite) and they are not too large. However they could be too small.

Let Π_M be the predicate called *maximality property*, defined on the configurations as follows. For $c \in \mathcal{C}$ satisfying Π_A, $\Pi_M(c)$ holds if, by merging two existing groups, we cannot obtain a partition satisfying the safety property:

$$\forall u,v \in V \text{ with } \Omega_u^c \neq \Omega_v^c,$$
$$\exists x,y \in \Omega_u^c \cup \Omega_v^c \text{ such that } d_{\Omega_u^c \cup \Omega_v^c}(x,y) > \texttt{Dmax}$$

The problem considered in this paper is to design a self-stabilizing protocol regarding predicates $\Pi_A \wedge \Pi_S \wedge \Pi_M$: after the last failure or topology change, the algorithm converges in finite time to a behavior where Π_A, Π_S, and Π_M are fulfilled. Note that this requirement is suitable for fixed topologies only. We then complete the specifications for dynamic systems, that is for topological changes.

Let $G^c(V^c, E^c)$ be the graph modeling the topology of the system at configuration c. We introduce the following notation: d^c refers to the distance in the graph G^c, and $d_X^c(u,v)$ denotes the distance between u and v in G^c by considering only edges of the subgraph $H(X, E_H)$ of G^c.

Let Π_T be the predicate called *topological property*, defined on any couple of two successive configurations c_i, c_{i+1} of an execution e as follows. For $c_i, c_{i+1} \in e$ that both satisfy Π_A, $\Pi_T(c_i, c_{i+1})$ holds if, for any pair of nodes belonging to the same group in c_i, the distance between them will still be smaller than `Dmax` in c_{i+1}:

$$\forall v \in V, \max_{x,y \in \Omega_v^{c_i}} d_{\Omega_v^{c_i}}^{c_{i+1}}(x,y) \leq \texttt{Dmax}$$

In other words, if a topology change occurred between c_i and c_{i+1}, it has preserved the maximal distance condition. Finally, we are looking for protocols attempting to preserve a group partition when a topology change occurs.

Let Π_C be the predicate called *continuity property*, defined on the couples of successive configurations as follows. For $c_i, c_{i+1} \in e$ that both satisfy Π_A, $\Pi_C(c_i, c_{i+1})$ holds if, in any group, no node disappears:

$$\forall v \in V, \Omega_v^{c_i} \subset \Omega_v^{c_{i+1}}$$

In other words, when the continuity property is fulfilled, an application can work with the given views because they define groups from which no node will disappear. Obviously, if the dynamic of the network is too large, such a property cannot be satisfied. We then introduce the best effort requirement:

$$\Pi_T \Rightarrow \Pi_C$$

4. GRP DISTRIBUTED PROTOCOL

The GRP distributed protocol is designed for solving the Distributed Group Service problem in an unreliable message passing system.

4.1 Principle of the GRP distributed protocol

For each node v, the candidates to form a group are neighbors up to distance `Dmax`. Each node v periodically exchanges messages with its neighbors and maintains a list of nodes being at distance at most `Dmax`. Each message sent by v contains the list of v. The list of v contains nodes at distance at most `Dmax` that are in the group or candidates to join the group.

Our mechanism needs to take into account symmetric links only, *i.e.*, links between pairs of nodes u and v so that if v is considered by u as a neighbor, then u (resp. v) is considered as a neighbor by v. In order to implement this, we use marks. Each node proceeds as follows: if v receives a list from u that does not contain itself, then it adds $\underline{u}$ in its list (which will be sent to the neighbors at the next timer expiration). To the converse, when v receives a list from u that contains either v or $\underline{v}$, then it adds u in its list. Marked nodes are not propagated farther than the neighborhood.

Malformed lists are rejected (such as lists larger than `Dmax`). Moreover, when a node v receives a list from u which is too long compared to its current list, it rejects it to avoid any split of its current group. In this case, v adds $\underline{\underline{u}}$ in its list, meaning that u and v cannot belong to the same group. To the converse, if the received list is not too long, it is merged with the current list, meaning that u enters to the group of v. Symmetrically, u will accept v in its group.

Several nodes may be accepted concurrently by distant members of a given group. In some cases, a too large group may be obtained. Then one of the new members must leave the group (instead of splitting the existing group). To avoid any inopportune change in the views (which are used by the applications), a new member enters in the view of a node only after the end of its *quarantine* period. This allows guaranteeing that its arrival has been approved by all the members (no conflicts). A node arrival is propagated to the group's members in $O(\texttt{Dmax})$; this defines the quarantine period duration.

When it is necessary to chose which node has to leave the group (to fulfill the diameter constraint), the choice is done using a *priority* computed by Function `pr`. Priorities are totally ordered; if $\texttt{pr}(u) < \texttt{pr}(v)$, then u has the priority. A powerful implementation of priorities is the oldness of nodes in the groups: the priority of a node is incremented by a logical clock [19], except if it belongs to a group (of more than one node) in which case the priority remains stable. The last entered nodes in a group have then less priority than the nodes entered before them.

Priorities on the nodes allow to easily define priorities on the groups by taking the smallest priority of the members. Priorities on the groups allows to ensure the merging of neighbor groups (and the maximality property Π_M) in particular cases (loop of groups willing to merge).

4.2 Building the lists

In the sequel, a node v is an *ancestor* of node u if a path exists from u to v. The messages sent to the neighbors contain *ordered list of ancestors' sets*. The *ordered list of ancestors' sets* of a node v is defined by: $(a_v^0, a_v^1, \ldots, a_v^p)$

where any node $x \in a_v^i$ satisfies $d(x,v) = i$ ($a_v^0 = \{v\}$) and p is the distance of the farthest ancestor of v.

Computations are done using the r-operator ant [7, 13, 12]. Let $\mathbb{S}$ be the set of lists of vertices' sets. For instance, if a,b,c,d,e are vertices, $(\{d\}, \{b\}, \{a,c\})$ and $(\{c\}, \{a,e\}, \{b\})$ belong to $\mathbb{S}$. Let $\oplus$ be the operator defined on $\mathbb{S}$ that merges two lists while deleting needless or repetitive information (a node appears only one time in a list of ancestors' sets). For instance:
$(\{d\}, \{b\}, \{a,c\}) \oplus (\{c\}, \{a,e\}, \{b\}) =$
$(\{d,c\}, \{b,a,e\}, \{a,c,b\}) = (\{d,c\}, \{b,a,e\})$.

Finally, let r be the endomorphism of $\mathbb{S}$ that inserts an empty set at the beginning of a list. For instance:
$r(\{d\}, \{b\}, \{a,c\}) = (\emptyset, \{d\}, \{b\}, \{a,c\})$.

We then define the operator ant by: $\mathrm{ant}(l_1, l_2) = l_1 \oplus r(l_2)$, where l_1 and l_2 are lists belonging to $\mathbb{S}$. This is a strictly idempotent r-operator [12] inducing a partial order relation. It leads to self-stabilizing static tasks (building the complete ordered lists of ancestor sets) in the register model [13]. Since our wireless communication model admits bounded links, these results can be extended to this model. (Refer to the discussion related to r-operators in wireless networks in [7].)

4.3 GRP algorithm

The GRP algorithm works as follows (see Figure 1). Each node v computes its output ($\mathtt{list}_v$, $\mathtt{view}_v$ and the priorities) when its timer T_c expires. It broadcasts its output in the neighborhood when the timer T_s expires. Timers T_c and T_s are chosen according to the *fair channel hypothesis*: T_c expires every τ_1 unit of time while T_s expires every τ_2 units of times ($\tau_2 \leq \tau_1$). All messages received from the neighborhood are collected on v in $\mathtt{msgSet}_v$. If a neighbor sends more than one message before the timer expiration, only the last received is kept. After computation, the variable $\mathtt{msgSet}_v$ is reset in order to detect when a neighbor leaves.

A computation consists in building the ordered list of ancestor' sets as well as the view (see Figure 2). The list is sent to the neighbors to be used in their ant computation. The view is the output of the protocol used by the applications (*e.g.*, chat, collaborative perception...) which requested the GRP algorithm, and which determined the diameter constraint $\mathtt{Dmax}$ (fixed during all the execution).

First, the incoming lists are checked. Line 3, when the list sent by u and received by v does not contain v, is malformed or is too long[2] with respect to $\mathtt{Dmax}$, it is replaced by $(\underline{u})$. When u receives the list of v containing $\underline{u}$, it accepts the list of v and sends a list containing v. Thanks to this triple handshake, the link has been detected as symmetric (by the way, asymmetric link information are not propagated).

Line 6, if the received list is too long with respect to the current list of v, the sender u is marked as incompatible ($\underline{u}$). Roughly speaking, a list received by a node u from another node v is compatible if, by combining its list with the one of v, u does not increase the diameter of its group beyond $\mathtt{Dmax}$. In order to reach this goal, it is enough to test if the sum of the lengths of both lists is less than or equal to $\mathtt{Dmax} + 1$. But, such simple test would avoid merging two groups by taking advantage of short cuts between both groups. In other words, this would ignore the knowledge that nodes of a group have on nodes belonging to the

other group. The technical condition used in Function $\mathtt{compatibleList()}$ deals with such an optimization (Figure 4).

Then a first computation is performed using the ant operator. Thanks to the $\mathtt{goodList}$ test, the sizes of the incoming lists are smaller than $\mathtt{Dmax} + 1$ (function $\mathtt{goodList}$ is given in Figure 3). However, the computed list could reach the size of $\mathtt{Dmax} + 2$ while the maximum is $\mathtt{Dmax} + 1$ (the ant operation increases by one the list sizes). In this case, a choice has to be done between either the local node v or the farthest nodes in the received lists. This choice is done by using priorities, Line 16. If nodes belong to the same group, node priorities are compared. If nodes are not in the same group, this is a group merging and group priorities are compared (to avoid loops of groups willing to merge). If the local node v has not the priority on the too far node w the lists in which w appears are ignored (Line 19). At the opposite side of the group, node w keeps the list containing v but the end of its ordered list of ancestor's sets will be truncated (meaning that v and w will not belong to the same group). Indeed, after the too far nodes have been all examined, the list of ancestors is computed again (Lines 24-27) and is truncated (Line 28) in order to delete the too far nodes (these remaining too fare nodes have less priority than v).

In order to not include a node in a view while it could be rejected later, a *quarantine mechanism* is used. The quarantine period of a node willing to enter in a group is equal to $\mathtt{Dmax}$ timers. Each time a computation is done (and then the new node progresses in the group), its quarantine period decreases. Since the group diameter is less than or equal to $\mathtt{Dmax}$, any conflict would have been detected before the new node enters into a view. Moreover, if a member of the group accepts the new node, then all the members will accept it.

Finally, the priority is updated. This depends on the implementation of function $\mathtt{pr}$. When using oldness in the group, the priority increases as for logical clocks if the node is not in a group and it remains stable if the node belongs to a group (by the way, the priority of a node refers to the value of the logical clock when it joined its group). Priority must be totally ordered; if $\mathtt{pr}(u) < \mathtt{pr}(v)$, then u has the priority.

5. PROOFS

We first focus on the self-stabilizing property of our algorithm. We show that assuming a fixed topology, the system converges in finite time to an execution satisfying the statements in Section 3, *i.e.*, $\Pi_S \wedge \Pi_A \wedge \Pi_M$ is an attractor. Next, we prove that, assuming topological changes preserving the maximal distance condition over the groups, then continuity is preserved, *i.e.*, $\Pi_T \Rightarrow \Pi_C$.

5.1 Stabilization

In this section, we prove that our protocol is self-stabilizing by showing that Π_S and Π_A and Π_M are attractors—Propositions 8, 7 and 12, respectively.

We begin by showing that eventually lists will become correct (Propositions 1 and 2). We first prove that any execution cannot remain infinitely with configurations having lists larger than $\mathtt{Dmax}$. We denote by $e_{\mathtt{Dmax}}$ the suffix of an execution e such that, for any configuration $c \in e_{\mathtt{Dmax}}$, for any node $v \in V$, the size of $\mathtt{list}_v$ is smaller than or equal to $\mathtt{Dmax} + 1$.

---

[2]$s(\mathtt{list})$ returns the number of elements in $\mathtt{list}$; $\mathtt{list}.i$ returns the ith element of $\mathtt{list}$, starting from 0.

Algorithm GRP, node v

1   Upon reception of a message `msg` sent by a node `u`:
2   update message of u in $\mathtt{msgSet}_v$

3   Upon T_c timer expiration:
4   compute()
5   reset $\mathtt{msgSet}_v$
6   restart timer T_c with duration τ_1

7   Upon T_s timer expiration:
8   **send**($\mathtt{list}_v$ with priorities) to the neighbors
9   restart timer T_s with duration τ_2

Figure 1: Algorithm GRP

PROPOSITION 1 (DMAX). *On a fixed topology, any execution e reaches in finite time a suffix e_{Dmax}.*

PROOF. Starting from configuration c_1, the system will reach in finite time a configuration in which every node has computed its list after expiration of its timer. After such a computation, the size of the lists is bounded by `Dmax`+1 (because it is truncated at the `Dmax` + 1 position, Line 28). $\square$

Starting from this proposition, we now prove that any execution cannot remain infinitely with configurations having a non existing node in a list. We denote by e_{exist} the suffix of an execution e such that, for any configuration $c \in e_{\text{exist}}$, for any node $v \in V$, every node $u \in \mathtt{list}_v^c$ satisfies $u \in V$.

PROPOSITION 2 (EXIST). *On a fixed topology, any execution e reaches in finite time a suffix e_{exist}.*

PROOF. Let $c \in e_{\text{Dmax}}$ be a configuration (Proposition 1). Let u be a node label such that $u \notin V$ and denote by U_k^c the set of nodes having u in their list at position k in configuration c. Consider the function $\phi(c)$ defined by $\phi(c) = \min\{k \in \mathbb{N}, U_k^c \neq \emptyset\}$ and $\phi(c) = \infty$ if $\forall k \in \mathbb{N}, U_k^c = \emptyset$. We prove that ϕ is continuously growing along the execution to be eventually equal to infinity forever.

Consider a node v in $U_{\phi(c)}^c$: v contains u at position $\phi(c)$ in its computed list and no node in configuration c contains u at a smaller position in its computed list. Until the next expiration of its timer, v cannot receive a list containing u in a smaller position than $\phi(c)$. Hence, the system will reach in finite time a configuration in which the node v has computed a new list that does not contain u at a position smaller than $\phi(c)+1$. After a timer (fair channel Hypothesis), the system reaches in finite time a configuration in which the neighbors of v have received this list.

After finite time, any node $v \in U_{\phi(c)}^c$ will do the same. The system then reaches in finite time after configuration c a configuration c' in which $U_{\phi(c)}^{c'}$ is empty, meaning that $\phi(c) < \phi(c')$.

By iteration, ϕ is growing along the execution. Since the size of the lists is bounded by `Dmax` + 1 (Proposition 1), there exists a configuration c'' reached in finite time after c in which $\phi(c'') = \infty$, meaning that u does not appear anymore in the computed lists of the nodes forever. $\square$

Next, we establish the connection between marked nodes in the algorithms and subgraphs (Propositions 3, 4, 5 and 6). We call *double-marked edge* an edge (u, v) such that either u double-marks v or v double-marks u (denoted by $\underline{\underline{u}}$ in the algorithm). The following proposition is a consequence of the double-marked edge technique. A node v double-marks its neighbor u only if the list sent by u cannot be accepted by v (Lines 7 and 19). In this case, node v will ignore the list sent by u. Reciprocally, if u has been double-marked by v, u will detect an asymmetric link (u does not appear in the list it received after Line 2) and only the identity of v will be kept by u, the rest of the list of v will be ignored (Line 4).

PROPOSITION 3 (NO PROPAGATION). *Let u and v be two vertices of G and suppose that, in any execution e, there exists a configuration c_e from which any path from u to v in G contains a double-marked edge. Then u will eventually disappear from $\mathtt{list}_v^c$ and v will eventually disappear from $\mathtt{list}_u^c$.*

The following proposition is a consequence of the *ant* computation (see Section 4.2). It propagates nodes identities (providing there is no edge-marking technique for limiting it) [13, 7].

PROPOSITION 4 (PROPAGATION). *Let u and v be two vertices of G and suppose that, in any execution e, there exists a configuration c_e from which there exists a path from u to v in G without double-marked edge. Then $\mathtt{list}_v^c$ will eventually contain u and $\mathtt{list}_u^c$ will eventually contain v.*

PROPOSITION 5 (DOUBLE-MARKED EDGE). *Suppose that $d(u, v) > $ `Dmax`. Then any execution admits a suffix e_{edge} such that, for any configuration $c \in e_{edge}$, there is a double-marked edge on any path from u to v.*

PROOF. Let v and w two nodes of G such that $d(v, w) = $ `Dmax`+1. Without loss of generality, we suppose that $pr(w) < pr(v)$. Suppose that there exists a path from v to w that does not contain any double-marked edge. By Proposition 4, there exists a neighbor u of v such that u sends to v a list containing w. The size of this list is larger than `Dmax`. There are two cases:
(i) $u \notin \mathtt{view}_v$. In this case, $\mathtt{list}_u$ is replaced by $(\underline{\underline{u}})$.
(ii) $u \in \mathtt{view}_v$. In this case, v computes a list using the one sent by u. Since $d(u, v) > $ `Dmax`, the resulting list is too long. Since $pr(w) < pr(v)$, the computation will be done again without the list provided by u, which will be replaced by $(\underline{\underline{u}})$.

Procedure compute() on node v

    ▷ *Checking the received lists*

1   **for all** list_u in msgSet **do**
2   delete marked nodes except $\underline{v}$ in list_u ▷ *Marked nodes are only useful between neighbors.*
3   **if** $\neg$ goodList(list_u) **then**   ▷ *List of u cannot be used;*
4   replace list_u by $(\underline{u})$ in msgSet   ▷ *this list is ignored but the sender is kept.*
5   **end if**   ▷ *Now, incoming lists cannot be larger than Dmax.*
6   **if** $u \notin \text{view}_v$ **and** $\neg$ compatibleList(list_u) **then**   ▷ *u is new, but its list cannot be accepted;*
7   replace list_u by $(\underline{u})$ in msgSet   ▷ *u is denoted as an incompatible neighbor*
8   **end if**
9   **end for**

    ▷ *Computing the list of ancestors' sets of v.*

10    $\text{list}_v \leftarrow (v)$
11   **for all** $\text{list}_u \in$ msgSet **do**
12        $\text{list}_v \leftarrow \text{ant}(\text{list}_v, \text{list}_u)$ ▷ *Computation using the* ant *r-operator.*
13   **end for**

    ▷ *Removal of incoming lists containing too far nodes (after* ant *computation,* list_v *cannot be larger than* Dmax $+ 1$*)*

14   **if** $s(\text{list}_v) = \text{Dmax} + 2$ **then**   ▷ *The list is too long.*
15   **for all** w at position $\text{Dmax} + 1$ in list_v **do**   ▷ *Scanning too far nodes.*
16   **if** $\text{pr}(w) < \text{pr}(v)$ **then**   ▷ *Far node w has the priority.*
17   **for all** $\text{list}_u \in$ msgSet **do**   ▷ *Looking for lists that provided w;*
18   **if** w is at position Dmax **then**   ▷ *they contain w in their last place.*
19   replace list_u by $(\underline{u})$ in msgSet   ▷ *The neighbor that provided w is ignored.*
20   **end if**
21   **end for**
22   **end if**
23   **end for**

    ▷ *Computing* list_v *again, without the incoming lists that contained too far nodes with priority.*

24        $\text{list}_v \leftarrow (v)$
25   **for all** list_u in msgSet **do**
26            $\text{list}_v \leftarrow \text{ant}(\text{list}_v, \text{list}_u)$
27   **end for**
28   keeping up to $\text{Dmax} + 1$ first elements in list_v ▷ *Deleted too far nodes have not the priority.*
29   **end if**
30   Update quarantines: quarantine of new nodes is Dmax, non null quarantine of others decreases by 1
31    $\text{view}_v \leftarrow$ non marked nodes in list_v with null quarantine
32   Update priorities: priority of nodes increase only when they are not in a group

Figure 2: Procedure compute

In the two cases, u is double-marked by v. Hence, any path from u to v will eventually contains a double-marked edge. $\square$

Let denote by $H_v^c(V_{H_v}, E_{H_v})$ the subgraph of $G(V, E)$ defined in the configuration c by: for any node u in V_{H_v}, $v \in \text{list}_u^c$. Such a subgraph is composed of vertices containing v in their list. We prove that eventually H_u and H_v are distinct when $d(u, v) > \text{Dmax}$.

PROPOSITION 6 (SUBGRAPHS). *Suppose that $d(u, v) > $ Dmax. Then any execution admits a suffix $e_{subgraph}$ such that, for any configuration $c \in e_{subgraph}$, H_u and H_v are distinct subgraphs.*

PROOF. By Proposition 5, there exists a suffix s_1 such that any path from u to v contains a double-marked edge. By Proposition 3, there exists a suffix s_2 included in s_1 such that for any configuration c in this suffix, $u \notin \text{list}_v^c$ and $v \notin \text{list}_u^c$. Then $u \notin H_v$ and $v \notin H_u$. Let consider a node w such that $w \in H_v$ and $w \in H_u$. Then there exists at least one path from u to v containing

w. The length of such a path is larger than Dmax. Then, by Proposition 5, it admits a double-marked edge, either on the subpath from u to w or from the subpath from w to v.

Now, let consider all the paths from u to v containing w; they all contain a double-marked edge. Suppose that for one path P_1, this double-marked edge is between w and v and for a second path P_2, it is between u and w. Then, by considering edges of P_1 from u to w and edges of P_2 from w to v, we obtain a path from u to v without any double-marked edge, which is a contradiction. Then, all paths from u to v containing w admit a double-marked edge, and this edge is always between u and w or always between w and v. Thus, w cannot belong to both H_u and H_v, meaning that there is no node w such that $w \in H_u$ and $w \in H_v$.

Hence, any execution reaches a suffix such that, for any configuration c in this suffix, H_u^c and H_v^c are distinct. $\square$

The preceding propositions give the Agreement. Consider any execution $e_{subgraphs}$. Denote by e_{agree} the suffix of an execution e such that $\Pi_A(c)$ holds for any configuration $c \in e_{agree}$, that is $V_{H_v} = \text{view}_w^c$ for any $w \in H_v$. The following proposition is given by Propositions 6, 4 and 3.

239

Function goodList(list)

1   **if** v or $\underline{v}$ are in $\text{list}.1$ **and** $s(\text{list}) \le \text{Dmax} + 1$ **and** $\emptyset \notin \text{list}$ **then**
2   **return** true
3   **else**
4   **return** false

Figure 3: Function goodList

Function compatibleList(list)

1   **if** $s(\text{list}_v) + s(\text{list}) \le \text{Dmax} + 1$ **or**
        $\exists i \in \{0, \dots, s(\text{list}_v)\}, \text{list}_v.i \subseteq \text{list}.1 \wedge \min(s(\text{list}_v) + s(\text{list}) + 1 - i, s(\text{list}) + 1 + i/2) \le \text{Dmax}$
2   **return** true   ▷ *Refer to Proposition 13.*
3   **else**
4   **return** false

Figure 4: Function compatibleList

PROPOSITION 7 (AGREEMENT). *On a fixed topology, any execution e reaches in finite time a suffix e_{agree}.*

PROOF. By Proposition 6, for any execution, there exists a suffix such that, for any nodes u and v in G, if $d(u,v) > \text{Dmax}$, then the subgraphs H_u and H_v are distinct. Consider now two nodes w and v such that w belongs to H_v

By Proposition 4, for any execution, there exists a suffix such that, for any configuration c in this suffix, the identities of H_v will be in list_w^c.

By Proposition 3, for any execution, there exists a suffix such that, for any configuration c in this suffix, the list_w^c contains only vertices of H_v.

After the end of the quarantine period, all the nodes in list_w belong to view_w. Then the system reaches a suffix in which all the nodes of H_v and only these nodes appear in view_w, for any vertex $w \in H_v$. Hence, $\text{view}_v^c = \text{view}_w^c = \Omega_v^c$. This gives Π_A. □

Now we have the agreement, there is a connection between subgraphs and groups. We then prove the Safety. Consider any execution e_{agree}. Denote by e_{safe} the suffix of an execution e such that $\Pi_S(c)$ holds for any configuration $c \in e_{safe}$. The following proposition is a consequence of Prop. 6.

PROPOSITION 8 (SAFETY). *On a fixed topology, any execution e reaches in finite time a suffix e_{safe}.*

PROOF. By Proposition 6, for any execution and any nodes u and v in G satisfying $d(u,v) > \text{Dmax}$, the subgraphs H_u and H_v will eventually be distinct. Hence, for any execution, there exists a suffix e_{safe} such that, for any configuration $c \in e_{safe}$, for any vertex v in G, $\text{Diam}(H_v^c) \le \text{Dmax}$.

Then, by Proposition 7, we have $\max_{x,y \in \Omega_v^c} d_{\Omega_v^c}(x,y) \le \text{Dmax}$. This gives Π_S. □

We consider any execution e_{agree}. In order to prove the maximality property, we introduce the following definitions. An edge (u,v) is *internal* in a given configuration c if $\Omega_u^c = \Omega_v^c$. In the converse case ($\Omega_u^c \neq \Omega_v^c$), it is *external*. An external edge involves double-marked nodes and it is then not propagated by the algorithm (marked nodes are deleted, see line 2 in Procedure compute()). We denote by *nee* (resp. *ndg*) the function defined on $\mathcal{C}$ that returns the number of

external edges in a given configuration (resp. the number of distinct groups in configuration c: $ndg(c) = |\{\Omega_v^c, v \in V\}|$.

PROPOSITION 9 (NEE). *If nee is decreasing along a suffix e_s of an execution e, ndg is also decreasing along e_s.*

PROOF. Let (u,v) be an external edge in a configuration c_i and assume that it is an internal edge in configuration c_{i+1}. This means that $\Omega_u^{c_i} \neq \Omega_v^{c_i}$ and $\Omega_u^{c_{i+1}} = \Omega_v^{c_{i+1}}$. Hence $nee(c_i) > nee(c_{i+1}) \Rightarrow ndg(c_i) > ndg(c_{i+1})$. □

We prove that any execution reaches in finite time a suffix in which the function *nee* does not increase. We denote by e_{notincr} such a suffix: $\forall c_i, c_{i+1} \in e_{\text{notincr}}, nee(c_{i+1}) \le nee(c_i)$.

PROPOSITION 10 (NOT INCR.). *On a fixed topology, any execution e reaches in finite time a suffix e_{notincr}.*

PROOF. Let $c \in e_{agree}$ be a configuration (Proposition 7). Let (u,v) be an internal edge in configuration c. Then we have $\Omega_u^c = \Omega_v^c$ and u is in list_v^c. In order (u,v) becomes an external edge, one of its extremity (say v) would have double-marked the other (in Procedure compute()). But this cannot happen after the goodList test (line 3) because $c \in e_{\text{subgraphs}}$. This cannot happen after the compatibleList test (line 6) because u is in already in view_v^c. □

Now, we prove that any execution reaches in finite time a suffix in which the function *nee* is decreasing while Π_M is not true. We denote by e_{decr} such a suffix: $\forall c_i \in e_{\text{decr}}$, $\Pi_M(c_i) \vee \exists c_j \in e_{\text{decr}}, i < j$ and $nee(c_i) > nee(c_j)$.

PROPOSITION 11 (DECREASING). *On a fixed topology, any execution e reaches in finite time a suffix e_{decr}.*

PROOF. Let $c \in e_{\text{notincr}}$ be a configuration (Proposition 10). Starting from such a configuration, the *nee* function cannot increase. Suppose that Π_M is not true in c. Then, by definition of Π_M, there exists two neighbors nodes x and y with different views that could merge their groups without breaking Π_S. By fair channel hypothesis, a timer later the system reaches a configuration c' in which x (resp. y) has received the list sent by y (resp. x).

Without loss of generality, suppose that Ω_x has the smallest priority among all the subgraphs that can merge, and

240

Ω_y has the smallest priority among all the groups that can merge with Ω_x.

During the `compute()` Procedure on x and y, the `goodList` tests are true because $c' \in e_{\text{notincr}}$ and then $c' \in e_{\text{safe}}$. The `compatibleList` test is true on both x and y because they cannot have change their list since configuration c. Hence we obtain: $x \in \text{list}_y$ and $y \in \text{list}_x$.

Since Ω_y has the smallest priority among the neighbors of Ω_x, no member of Ω_x can receive a message from a group with a smallest priority. Therefore x will never receive and then will never send to y a list with a too far node with a smallest priority than y one's. Hence y will never double-mark x and x will remain in the list of y.

Similarly, since Ω_x has the smallest priority among the groups that can merge, no member of Ω_y can receive a message from a group with a smallest priority. Therefore y will never receive and then will never send to x a list with a too far node with a smallest priority than x one's. Hence x will never double-mark y and y will remain in the list of x.

After `Dmax` timer, the list of y (resp. x) has reached any $u \in \Omega_x$ (resp. Ω_y) thanks to the fair channel Hypothesis. Moreover the quarantine of these new members reaches 0 and they are now included in view_u. Thus, the edge (x, y) becomes an internal edge.

Hence, starting from configuration c with $\neg \Pi_M(c)$, the system reaches in finite time a configuration c'' with $nee(c) > nee(c'')$. $\square$

The following proposition is given by Propositions 9, 10 and 11; it shows that any execution reaches in finite time a suffix in which Π_M is true. We denote by e_{max} such a suffix.

PROPOSITION 12 (MAXIMALITY). *On a fixed topology, any execution e reaches in finite time a suffix e_{max}.*

PROOF. By Prop. 10, the execution reaches a suffix e_{notincr} such that the *nee* function will no more increase. By Prop. 11, the execution reaches a suffix e_{decr} such that the *nee* function decreases while Π_M is not true. Hence, while Π_M is false, the number of external edges will eventually decrease. By Prop. 9, this means that the number of subgraphs will eventually decrease while Π_M is false. Since the graph is finite, the number of subgraphs cannot decrease infinitely and Π_M will eventually become true. $\square$

5.2 Best-effort requirement

We now consider the dynamic of the network. We show that if the continuity property is violated into a group, then there exists a pair of nodes belonging to that group such that the distance between them is larger that `Dmax`. The following technical proposition justifies the compatibleList test.

PROPOSITION 13 (COMPATIBLE LISTS). *Let v be a node having the list $(a_v^0, a_v^1, \ldots, a_v^p)$, $(p \geq 0)$ and assume that its neighbor w sends the list $(a_w^0, a_w^1, \ldots, a_w^q)$, $(q \geq 0)$. Then, the diameter of the group of v after v accepts w remains smaller than or equal to `Dmax` if and only if there exists $i \in \{0, \ldots, p\}$ such that w is neighbor of all the nodes belonging to a_v^i and either $p - i + 1 + q \leq$ `Dmax` or $i/2 + q + 1 \leq$ `Dmax`.*

PROOF. Let $c \in e_{\text{safe}}$ be a configuration (Proposition 8). Let w be the first node of Ω_w^c for which the list of ancestor's sets is received by v. Then, the only external edges between Ω_v^c and Ω_w^c known by v are those joining w (external

edges are not propagated). Hence, without loss of generality, assume that only these external edges exist between the groups.

($\Rightarrow$) Assume that the conditions are fulfilled. Let $u \in a_v^k$ and $u' \in a_w^l$ be two nodes in the lists of v and w respectively. There exists at most two families of shortest paths from u to u', depending on the external edge used to reach w. Let P_1 be a path that includes the edge (v, w). It starts from u and joins v by k edges in the group of v, joins w by the edge (u, v) and then reaches u' by l edges in the group of u. Let P_2 be a path from the second family. It starts from u and joins a node $v' \in a_v^i$ by $|k - i|$ internal edges in the group of v, then joins w by the edge (v', w) and then reaches u' by l internal edges in the group of u.

The length of P_1 is bounded by $k + 1 + q$. But since P_1 is a shortest path, it is shorter to reach u' from u by joining a node of a_v^0 (*i.e.*, v) than by joining a node of a_v^i (such as v'). Hence we have $k \leq i/2$ and the length of P_1 is bounded by $i/2 + 1 + q$, which is smaller than `Dmax` by hypothesis. The length of P_2 is bounded by $p - i + 1 + q$, which is also smaller than `Dmax` by assumption.

Hence, for any node u and u' belonging to the group of v and w respectively, there exists a path from u to u' with less than `Dmax` edges. The list of w is then compatible with the list of v, and can then be accepted by v.

($\Leftarrow$) Assume by contradiction that the conditions are not fulfilled and that v accepts the list of w, *i.e.*, v includes the list of w by computing its new list with `ant`—refer to Lines $14 - 16$ of Procedure `compute()`. That means that the list of w is compatible—refer to Lines $6 - 8$—, which contradicts the assumption. Then the nodes of list_v^c will be propagated in the lists of nodes of list_v^c and reciprocally. But at least one node $u \in \text{list}_v^c$ will see that a node $u' \in \text{list}_w^c$ is too far from it and reciprocally. Either u or u' will reject the lists of its neighbors that contain the too far node (depending on the priority between u and u') and either the group of v or the group of w splits (when a neighbor is rejected by u, it disappears from list_u, and then from view_u; it is then no more in H_v). $\square$

PROPOSITION 14. *For any execution e, for any configuration c_i in e, $\Pi_T(c_i, c_{i+1}) \Rightarrow \Pi_C(c_i, c_{i+1})$.*

PROOF. Suppose that there exists a configuration c_i and a node v such that $\text{view}_v^{c_i} \not\subseteq \text{view}_v^{c_{i+1}}$. Then there exists a node u such that $u \in \text{view}_v^{c_i}$ and $u \notin \text{view}_v^{c_{i+1}}$. This cannot happen after u or v has added a new node in its view, thanks to the quarantine mechanism. This can only happen because either u or v removed a node from their views.

Without loss of generality, suppose that v removed a node x: $x \in \text{view}_v^{c_i}$ and $x \notin \text{view}_v^{c_{i+1}}$. If $x \notin \text{view}_v^{c_{i+1}}$, then (i) the quarantine of x is not null or (ii) x is not in $\text{list}_v^{c_{i+1}}$ or (iii) x is marked in $\text{list}_v^{c_{i+1}}$ (Line 31 in Procedure `compute()`).
(i) The first case is exclude because x was already in $\text{view}_v^{c_i}$.
(ii) In the second case, if v has not received the message of x while it received it before, then x left the neighborhood of v. Then, in configuration c_{i+1}, there is not path from x to v with only nodes of $\Omega_v^{c_i}$ and $d_{\Omega_v^{c_i}}^{c_{i+1}}(x, v) = +\infty$. Thus $\neg \Pi_T(c_i, c_{i+1})$ (*a neighbor left*).
(iii) In the third case, if x is simple marked, its list is not good while it was in configuration c_i, which is exclude (Line 3). If x is double-marked, this cannot happen after the compatibleList test (Line 7) because x was in $\text{view}_v^{c_i}$. If this happened after Line 19, then x sent a list with a too far

241

node y having priority on v. If $y \notin \Omega_v^{c_i}$, then $y \notin \mathtt{view}_v^{c_i}$. Then the quarantine of y is not null and no node of $\Omega_v^{c_i}$ has admitted y in its view. Therefore, thanks to Prop. 13, y would have never been propagated inside $\Omega_v^{c_i}$ until v, because of the compatibleList test (Line 6). Finally, if $y \in \Omega_v^{c_i}$, then the distance from y to v in configuration c_{i+1} is larger than $\mathtt{Dmax}$: $d_{\Omega_v^{c_i}}^{c_{i+1}}(x,v) > \mathtt{Dmax}$ and $\neg \Pi_T(c_i, c_{i+1})$. $\square$

6. CONCLUSION

This paper introduces the best effort requirement to complete the self-stabilization for designing algorithm in dynamic networks. To illustrate this approach, a new problem inspired from VANET has been specified: the *Dynamic Group Service*. A best effort distributed protocol called GRP has been designed and proved for solving this problem in message passing. The algorithm is self-stabilizing and fulfills a continuity property whenever the dynamic allows it. The protocol has been implemented and its performances studied by simulation. We believe that the best effort requirement is promising for building useful services in dynamic networks.

7. REFERENCES

[1] A.D. Amis, R. Prakash, and D.H.T. Vuaong. Max-min *d*-cluster formation in wireless ad hoc networks. In *IEEE INFOCOM*, pages 32–41, 2000.

[2] Kenneth P. Birman. The process group approach to reliable distributed computing. *Commun. ACM*, 36(12):37–53, 1993.

[3] J. Blum, A. Eskandarian, and L. Hoffman. Challenges of intervehicle ad hoc networks. *IEEE Transaction on Intelligent Transportation Systems,*, 5:347–351, 2004.

[4] O. Brukman, S. Dolev, Y. Haviv, and R. Yagel. Self-stabilization as a foundation for autonomic computing. In *The Second International Conference on Availability, Reliability and Security (ARES)*, pages 991–998, Vienna, April 2007.

[5] G.V. Chockler, I. Keidar, and R. Vitenberg. Group communication specifications: a comprehensive study. *ACM Computing Surveys*, 4(33):1–43, 2001.

[6] A. K. Datta, L. L. Larmore, and P. Venula. A self-stabilizing O(k)-time k-clustering algorithm. *Computer Journal*, 2009.

[7] S. Delaët, B. Ducourthial, and S. Tixeuil. Self-stabilization with r-operators revisited. In *Journal of Aerospace Computing, Information, and Communication*, 2006.

[8] Murat Demirbas, Anish Arora, Vineet Mittal, and Vinodkrishnan Kulathumani. A fault-local self-stabilizing clustering service for wireless ad hoc networks. *IEEE Trans. Parallel Distrib. Syst.*, 17(9):912–922, 2006.

[9] S. Dolev. *Self-Stabilization*. The MIT Press, 2000.

[10] S. Dolev and T. Herman. Superstabilizing protocols for dynamic distributed systems. In *Proceedings of the fourteenth annual ACM symposium on Principles of distributed computing (PODC)*, page 255, New York, NY, USA, 1995. ACM.

[11] S. Dolev, E. Schiller, and J.L. Welch. Random walk for self-stabilizing group communication in ad hoc networks. *IEEE Transactions on Mobile Computing*, 5(7):893–905, 2006.

[12] B. Ducourthial. r-semi-groups: A generic approach for designing stabilizing silent tasks. In 9th *Stabilization, Safety, and Security of Distributed Systems (SSS'2007)*, pages 281–295, Paris, novembre 2007.

[13] B. Ducourthial and S. Tixeuil. Self-stabilization with path algebra. *Theor. Comput. Sci.*, 293(1):219–236, 2003.

[14] R. Guerraoui and A. Schiper. Software-based replication for fault-tolerance. *IEEE Transaction on Computers*, 30(4):68–74, 1997.

[15] Arshad Jhunka and Sandeep S. Kulkarni. On the design of mobility-tolerant TDMA-based media access control (MAC) protocol for mobile sensor networks. In Tomasz Janowski and Hrushikesha Mohanty, editors, *ICDCIT*, volume 4882 of *Lecture Notes in Computer Science*, pages 42–53. Springer, 2007.

[16] Colette Johnen and Le Huy Nguyen. Robust self-stabilizing weight-based clustering algorithm. *Theor. Comput. Sci.*, 410(6-7):581–594, 2009.

[17] Hirotsugu Kakugawa and Toshimitsu Masuzawa. A self-stabilizing minimal dominating set algorithm with safe convergence. In *20th International Parallel and Distributed Processing Symposium (IPDPS 2006)*, 2006.

[18] S. Kutten and D. Peleg. Fast distributed construction of small-dominating sets and applications. *Journal of Algorithms*, 28(1):40–66, 1998.

[19] L. Lamport. Time, clocks and the ordering of events in a distributed system. *Communications of the ACM*, 21(7):558–565, 1978.

[20] L. D. Penso and V. C Barbosa. A distributed algorithm to find k-dominating sets. *Discrete Applied Mathematics*, 141(1-3):243–253, 2004.

[21] F.B. Schneider. Impliementing fault tolerant services using the state machine approach: a tutorial. *Computing Surveys*, 22(4):299–319, 2990.

[22] I. Stojmenovic. *Handbook of Wireless Networks and Mobile Computings*. John Wiley & Sons, 2002.

Deadlock Avoidance for Streaming Computations with Filtering

Peng Li   Kunal Agrawal   Jeremy Buhler   Roger D. Chamberlain

Dept. of Computer Science and Engineering
Washington University in St. Louis
St. Louis, MO 63130, USA
{pengli, kunal, jbuhler, roger}@@wustl.edu

ABSTRACT

The paradigm of computation on streaming data has received considerable recent attention. Streaming computations can be efficiently parallelized using systems of computing nodes organized in dataflow-like architectures. However, when these nodes have the ability to *filter*, or discard, some of their inputs, a system with finite buffering is vulnerable to deadlock. In this paper, we formalize a model of streaming computation systems with filtering, describe precisely the conditions under which such systems may deadlock, and propose provably correct mechanisms to avoid deadlock. Our approach relies on adding extra "dummy" tokens to the data streams and does not require global run-time coordination among nodes or dynamic resizing of buffers. This approach is particularly well-suited to preventing deadlock in distributed systems of diverse computing architectures, where global coordination or modification of buffer sizes may be difficult or impossible in practice.

Categories and Subject Descriptors

C.2.4 [**Computer-Communication Networks**]: Distributed Systems—*Distributed applications*; D.1.3 [**Programming Techniques**]: Concurrent Programming—*Distributed programming*; F.1.2 [**Computation by Abstract Devices**]: Modes of Computation—*Parallelism and concurrency*

General Terms

Algorithms, Design, Theory

Keywords

Data Filtering, Dataflow, Architecturally Diverse Platforms

1. INTRODUCTION

Streaming computation, a classic and still-popular computing paradigm, provides a convenient way to express high throughput-oriented parallel and pipelined computations. Application areas that use the streaming model include signal

processing [25], molecular modeling [7], computational biology [13], and multimedia [15]. A streaming application is typically implemented as a network of *computing nodes* connected by unidirectional communication *channels*; we refer to such an implementation hereafter as a *system*. Abstractly, a system is a directed dataflow multigraph, with the node at the tail of each edge (channel) able to transmit data, in the form of one or more discrete *tokens*, to the node at its head.

Figure 1a shows the dataflow graph of a small system. Compute node u, having no inputs, is a data *source* that can spontaneously generate tokens; v and w are intermediate nodes that operate on their single input streams; x, with no outputs, is a *sink* that computes some final result stream from two input streams. A realization of this system would map each node onto a physical computing resource in any way that permits the required topology of communication and has satisfactory performance.

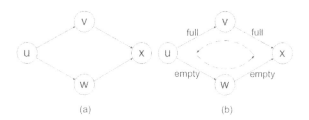

Figure 1: A streaming application example and a possible deadlock.

This paper is largely motivated by our previous work on Auto-Pipe [4, 8], a compiler and infrastructure for mapping abstract systems of compute nodes onto diverse computing resources such as chip multiprocessors, reconfigurable logic, and graphics engines. Auto-Pipe does not support feedback loops in a system, so *we will assume hereafter that the dataflow graphs of systems are directed acyclic multigraphs (DAMGs)*, which are most common in streaming applications.

We study a streaming computation model in which tokens are *indexed* with non-negative integer timestamps. A data stream emitted by a node is a sequence of tokens with strictly increasing but not necessarily consecutive indices. For example, a source node might be a sensor that is occasionally triggered by some interesting event to emit a token containing data on that event along with the time at which it occurred. Streams have finite length; the last token in a stream is always an *End-Of-Stream (EOS)* token with index ∞.

Communication channels in our model are reliable and ordered, so that tokens emitted in index order can never be received out of order. However, a system provides no timing guarantees, so there may be an arbitrary finite delay before a token emitted onto a channel is received. Each channel uv can hold some fixed number of sent but not-yet-received tokens; this number is uv's *buffer size* or *capacity*, denoted $|uv|$.

Algorithm 1 describes how a node with an arbitrary number of input and output channels processes the streams of tokens on its inputs. *A single computation can consume only input tokens with the same index*; at any time, a node's current *computation index* is the index of the last set of inputs that it consumed. Computation on data with index i does not require that all input channels contain tokens with that index; it is well-defined even if only a subset of input channels ever receive tokens with index i. However, a node may not proceed to compute for index i unless it knows that no further tokens with this index will ever arrive at its inputs. A computation may output tokens with the same index as the inputs on any subset of a node's outputs, including the empty set. We say that a computation *filters* an input on a channel q if it does not result in an output token on q. Filtering is a data-dependent behavior, performed independently by each node, that cannot be predicted at the time that a system is instantiated.

Algorithm 1: Single-node behavior in a system.

ComputeIndex $\leftarrow$ 0 ;
while *ComputeIndex* $\neq$ *Index of EOS* **do**
    if *not source node* **then**
        wait until every input channel has a pending token ;
        let T be minimum index of any pending token ;
        remove pending tokens with index T from input channels ;
    else
        $T \leftarrow$ ComputeIndex $+$ 1 ;
    ComputeIndex $\leftarrow T$;
    perform computation on data tokens with index T ;
    if *not sink node* **then**
        emit output tokens with index T ;

Computation on indexed token streams with filtering models applications that search their input streams for interesting events. For example, the popular bioinformatics search tool BLAST [2] may be viewed as a pipeline of compute nodes over a stream of DNA or protein sequence, in which each node identifies a progressively smaller subset of the stream as significant and filters away the rest. BLAST can be implemented as a linear pipeline, albeit with multiple channels between each successive pair of nodes. However, this paper generalizes to more complex computations with multiple data sources, such as an application to fuse data from an array of different environmental sensors.

The filtering model is challenging in that dynamically determined stream rates make it hard to compute a feasible and efficient execution schedule at system compilation time. Moreover, filtering can cause some nodes in a system to block due to empty input channels. For example, in Fig-

ure 1a, if node u generates inputs to both nodes v and w, v may emit output on channel vx, while w filters its inputs and emits nothing on wx. In this situation, node x is not able to consume the next token from vx because it does not know whether w will ever emit a corresponding token on wx. Because the system has bounded channel buffers, such blocking situations can lead to *deadlock*. For example, if channels uw and wx remain empty due to filtering while uv and vx fill, the system may reach the situation shown in Figure 1b. Node x is unable to consume data since it is waiting to receive data that must be sent from u, but u is unable to generate any more output because it is blocked trying to emit onto the full path from u to x. Hence, the system cannot make progress. Avoiding or remedying such deadlocks is an important consideration in system design.

In this work, we describe how to prevent deadlock in streaming applications where some or all nodes may filter tokens. Because Auto-Pipe can map systems to a diverse, physically distributed array of computing devices, we have devised approaches that do not require global coordination among nodes, addition of new channels for control, or modification of channel buffer sizes. Instead, our approach augments data streams with extra *dummy* tokens — tokens that contain just an index but no data. These dummy tokens serve to inform downstream nodes that certain data items have been filtered and therefore the downstream node is allowed to proceed with its computation without waiting for these data items to appear.

We present three algorithms for generating these dummy messages. The first algorithm is a rather naive and potentially inefficient algorithm based on the observation that a streaming application that has no filtering is not susceptible to deadlocks. Therefore, if a node sends a dummy message on a channel every time it filters a data item on that channel, then there is no possibility of deadlock. This approach may be good enough for some applications and has the advantage of being simple and not requiring any information about the buffer sizes on various channels. However, this algorithm may increase the channel traffic and it negates the advantage of filtering nodes. Our other two algorithms are more efficient in that they try to send fewer dummy messages than this naive algorithm by using information about buffer sizes. For both of these approaches, at compile time a dummy message interval is computed for each channel based on buffer sizes of downstream channels and dummy messages are sent at this interval. Since the buffer sizes (or at least a lower bound on them) are known at compile time and buffer sizes do not change during execution, this interval computation is a static overhead before the application starts running.

2. CONDITIONS FOR DEADLOCK

During a computing process, one node may be temporarily blocked by another due to an empty input or full output channel. However, not every blocking situation is a deadlock. In this section, we derive the conditions under which blocking can lead to deadlock.

Definition 1. (**Liveness**) If a node can increase its compute index in finite time, we say the node is *live*, or equivalently that it *makes progress*.

Definition 2. (**Blocking Relation**) If a node v is waiting for input from an upstream neighbor u, or if v is waiting to send output to a downstream neighbor u because the channel buffer between them is full, we say that u *blocks* v, denoted $u \dashv v$. If there exists a sequence of nodes $v_1 \ldots v_n$ such that $v_i \dashv v_{i+1}$ for $1 \leq i < n$, we write $v_1 \dashv^+ v_n$.

Definition 3. (**Deadlock**) A system is said to *deadlock* if no node in the system is live but some channel in the system still retains unprocessed tokens (so that the computation is incomplete).

We do not distinguish between local deadlock and global deadlock, as proposed in [10], because both of them will cause the computation not to complete. Now we prove that blocking cycle is a sufficient and necessary condition of deadlock.

THEOREM 2.1 (**Deadlock Theorem**). *A system eventually deadlocks if and only if, at some point in the computation, there exists a node u s.t. $u \dashv^+ u$.*

PROOF. ($\leftarrow$) Suppose that at some point in the computation, there is a node u such that $u \dashv^+ u$. Because a blocked node cannot make progress, no node on the cycle involving u can make progress. Hence, once the blocking cycle occurs, it will remain indefinitely. Moreover, not every pair of successive nodes in the cycle can be linked by an empty channel; otherwise, we would have that u is waiting for input from u, which is impossible because the graph of computing nodes is a DAMG. Hence, the blocking cycle contains at least one full channel, which means there are unprocessed tokens, and so the system is deadlocked.

($\rightarrow$) Suppose that $u \dashv^+ u$ does not hold for any node u at any point in the computation. We show that, as long as there is any data in the system, *some* node is able to make progress; hence, the computation will never halt with unprocessed data on a channel.

At any point in the computation, either every node with input data can make progress, or some such node u is blocked. Let H be the directed graph obtained by tracing all blocking relationships outward from u, such that there is an edge from v to w iff $v \dashv w$. (H is also called a "waiting-for graph." [6, 19]) By assumption, H has no cycles and is therefore a DAG. Let v_0 be a topologically minimal node in H, which is not blocked by any node. If v_0 has tokens on its input channels, it is able to consume them and so make progress. Otherwise, v_0's input channels are all empty, so that it cannot block any upstream neighbors. Moreover, since v_0 itself is not blocked, either it is a source node that can advance its computation index by spontaneously producing tokens, or it must have received the EOS marker and so cannot block any downstream neighbors (which contradicts v_0's presence in H). Conclude that v_0 is able to make progress, as desired. □

Definition 4. (**Blockwise** (*not* clockwise) and **Counterblockwise**) Let C be a cycle of blocked nodes $v_1 \ldots v_n$, such that $v_1 \dashv^+ v_n$ and $v_n \dashv v_1$. The direction of increasing index on C is called *blockwise*, while the opposite direction is *counterblockwise*.

A channel on C between v_i and v_{i+1} may be oriented either blockwise from v_i to v_{i+1} or counterblockwise from v_{i+1} to v_i. Because $v_i \dashv v_{i+1}$, *a blockwise channel on a blocking cycle is always empty, while a counterblockwise channel is always full*. For example, in Figure 1b, uw and wx are

blockwise channels while uv and vx are counterblockwise channels.

We notice that not all systems have deadlocks. For example, a system with just two nodes connected by one channel will never deadlock, even with filtering; the sender can block the receiver because the channel is empty, or the receiver can block the sender because the channel is full, but they cannot block each other at the same time. However, even quite simple systems, such as one with just two nodes connected by two parallel data channels, can deadlock.

Definition 5. (**Potential Deadlock**) A system with finite buffer sizes on all channels has a *potential deadlock* if, given the node topology and channel buffer sizes, there exist input streams and histories of filtering at each node such that a deadlock is possible.

Definition 6. (**Undirected Cycle**) Given a system abstracted as a DAMG G, an undirected cycle of G is a cycle in the undirected graph G' that is the same as G except that all edge directions have been removed.

For example, in the graph of Figure 1a, $uvxw$ is an undirected cycle that can become blocking. We now show that in a general DAMG, *every* undirected cycle can become blocking.

THEOREM 2.2 (**Potential Deadlock Theorem**). *Given a system S abstracted as a DAMG G, S has potential deadlocks if and only if G has an undirected cycle.*

PROOF. ($\rightarrow$) By definition, if S has a potential deadlock, then a deadlock can happen given the right pattern of inputs and filtering. By the Deadlock Theorem, such a deadlock implies the presence of a blocking cycle of nodes, which implies an undirected cycle of channels in G.

($\leftarrow$) Suppose that there is an undirected cycle C of channels in G. We will construct a set of tokens and a filtering history that causes C to become a blocking cycle, implying a deadlock.

First, we arbitrarily choose a direction on C to be the blockwise direction. We then topologically sort the nodes of the DAMG. We mark each channel and node with values calculated as follows. For each node u, if u is a sink node, $M_u = 0$; otherwise, $M_u = \max_{uv} M_{uv}$, where uv is any outbound channel from u. For each outbound channel uv, if uv is a counterblockwise channel in C, $M_{uv} = M_v + |uv| + 1$; otherwise, $M_{uv} = M_v$.

The filtering history for each channel out of each node is as follows. Each input consumed by a node u results in output tokens (i.e. no filtering) on any output channel of u that is not on cycle C or is oriented counterblockwise on C. For an output channel uv that is oriented blockwise on C, u emits tokens on uv until its computation index reaches M_{uv}, then filters (i.e. emits no output on uv) for any larger index.

The above construction ensures that:

- For a blockwise channel uv in C, $u \dashv v$ because v will consume all M_{uv} inputs sent to it by u, leaving the channel empty.

- For a counterblockwise channel uv in C, $v \dashv u$ because u tries to send $|uv| + 1$ tokens to v after v becomes unable to consume tokens, and so uv becomes full and blocks further output by u.

Since each node in C now blocks its blockwise neighbor, it follows that for any node u in C, $u \dashv^+ u$, which implies a deadlock. $\square$

The above proof shows that given enough input tokens and arbitrary filtering rules, any undirected cycle of G could cause a deadlock. In order to avoid deadlocks, we will enumerate these undirected cycles and schedule extra tokens for their channels so as to avoid the possibility of creating a blocking cycle.

3. DEADLOCK AVOIDANCE ALGORITHMS

In our design of deadlock avoidance algorithms, we assume that at runtime, the nodes have no access to any *dynamic global information*. For example, a node u does not know whether any of the other nodes in the system are blocked. Our designs are based on the following objectives. First, we wish deadlock avoidance to be minimally intrusive on the nodes. That is, we do not want nodes to have to perform massive computations during runtime in order to prevent deadlocks. Second, we wish to make no modifications to the system's communication topology. In particular, we do not want to add extra data or control channels; rather, we will avoid deadlock using only tokens sent on the existing data channels. Third, we do not wish to size channel buffers at runtime, since such reconfiguration is expensive and may not be possible if some channel buffer sizes are, e.g., determined by ASIC or FPGA hardware.

In order to achieve these goals, we focus on designs that use *static* computations that can be performed at system construction time to configure the system such that no deadlocks will occur at runtime. In general, we cannot statically choose "large enough" channel capacities to avoid any possible deadlock; Buck [3] showed that it is undecidable whether an arbitrary dynamic dataflow computation remains within any particular channel capacity bound. We therefore augment the data streams between nodes by inserting additional tokens, called *dummies*, to limit the number of tokens that can remain unprocessed on any channel.

A *dummy* is a distinguished class of token with an index but no content of its own. A dummy may be emitted as a standalone token, or it may be combined with a regular data token with the same index (such a data token may be said to have a "dummy flag" set). All compute nodes can recognize dummies, and a subset of nodes (to be specified) can generate them. The purpose of dummy tokens is to communicate a node's current computation index to its descendants in the system, even if that node has not recently sent any data tokens.

3.1 Using Dummies to Simulate Non-Filtering Computation

The simplest use of dummy tokens is as direct one-for-one replacement of missing data: if a node u has an output channel q, and it performs a computation for index i that does not result in a data token being emitted on q, then it instead emits a dummy token on q with index i. Receiving a dummy token with index i on all inputs causes a node to perform a "null computation" and so to emit dummy tokens with index i on all outputs. This use of dummies, hereafter called the **Naive Algorithm**, simulates a computation in which no node ever filters its inputs. We claim that such a computation is immune from deadlocks.

THEOREM 3.1 (**Filtering Theorem**). *If no node ever filters any input, then the system cannot deadlock.*

PROOF. The proof is by contradiction. Suppose there is a deadlock; then by the Deadlock Theorem, the computation reaches a state in which some node $y \dashv^+ y$. Let C be the cycle of blocked nodes that includes y. Each node z on cycle C may be labeled with one of four types, depending on the directions of the channels that link z to its two neighbors in C:

1. Both channels are oriented blockwise, as for node w in Figure 1b;

2. Both channels are oriented counterblockwise, as for node v in Figure 1b;

3. The channel located to blockwise of z is oriented blockwise, while that to counterblockwise of z is oriented counterblockwise, as for node u in Figure 1b;

4. The channel located to blockwise of z is oriented counterblockwise, while that to counterblockwise of z is oriented blockwise, as for node x in Figure 1b.

The rest of proof introduces the important concepts of *minval* and *maxval*, which will also be used in later proofs.

Definition 7. (**minval** and **maxval**) For any full channel q, minval(q) is defined to be *lowest* index of any token queued on q, while maxval(q) is defined to be the *highest* such index. For an empty channel q', minval(q') is defined to be the index of the token that has most recently traversed q'.

We now argue that, in the absence of filtering, the minval of a channel on C is always $\geq$ that of its counterblockwise neighbor. Let z be a node between two channels on the cycle.

- If z has type 1, both channels are empty, with one pointing into z and one pointing out. Because z does not filter, every token input to z causes a token to be emitted; hence, the two channels have the same minval.

- If z has type 2, both channels are full, with the blockwise channel pointing into z and other pointing out. Any value output by z has a strictly smaller index than a value waiting to be input to it, so the blockwise channel has the larger minval.

- If z has type 3, then both channels are outputs from z, and the blockwise channel is empty while the other is full. Because z does not filter, it always emits tokens with a given index on both channels at once. Hence, the minval of the blockwise channel is at least the index of the most recently emitted value on the other channel, which is $\geq$ the latter's minval.

- If z has type 4, then both channels are inputs to z, and the blockwise channel is full while the other is empty. The minval of the full channel must be strictly greater than that of the empty channel; otherwise, z could consume a value from the full channel.

Hence, the minvals of the channels in C increase monotonically to blockwise. Moreover, because there are no directed cycles in the original network, there is always a node of type 4 in C, and so the minvals of all channels in C cannot be identical. But this is impossible, because traversing the entire cycle implies that the minval of some channel is strictly greater than itself. Conclude that no blocking cycle can exist in the absence of filtering. $\square$

We extend the definitions of minval and maxval straightforwardly from a single channel to a directed path p composed of channels, provided that p is either completely full or completely empty. Hence, the minval of a full path p is the lowest index of any token queued on p, and so forth.

The Naive Algorithm is straightforward but costly in terms of wasted channel bandwidth: the total number of tokens sent by the computation always equals the number of distinct computation indices times the number of channels. Real distributed computing systems have limited channel bandwidths, so that communication costs can become a bottleneck. In fact, for many applications, such as the BLAST application mentioned above, the primary purpose of most nodes is to filter the data stream. Using the Naive Algorithm for such applications would negate the communication bandwidth savings achieved by their natural filtering. Hence, we next give algorithms that reduce the number of dummy tokens sent while still ensuring that the resulting system is free from deadlock.

3.2 Limiting the Frequency of Dummy Tokens

We now consider how to avoid emitting dummies for every data token filtered by a node. Our approach includes two parts. We first extend the behavior of each compute node u to include *propagation* of received dummy tokens, as well as *generation* of dummies on each output channel q of u at a statically defined *dummy interval* $[q]$. If $[q] = \infty$, then u never generates new dummies on output q; otherwise, it is guaranteed to emit a dummy each time its computation index advances by at least $[q]$, which is computed by Algorithm 3. Using this extended behavior with the specified dummy intervals, we obtain a system that is deadlock-free yet sends many fewer dummies than the Naive Algorithm when some nodes filter their inputs.

Algorithm 2 describes how we extend the behavior of a computation node to include generation and propagation of dummy tokens. Generator nodes are guaranteed to emit a dummy on channel q whenever the computation index has advanced by least $[q]$ since the last dummy, regardless of whether any real output has been sent. *All nodes propagate any incoming dummy token to all their output channels, combining it if needed with any data token with the same index to be emitted on each channel. Hence, even with dummies, no node ever emits two tokens with the same index on the same channel.* This approach is referred as the "Propagation Algorithm" later.

In the algorithm description and subsequently, $|p|$ denotes the sum of all channel buffer sizes on a directed path p. A *maximal* directed path is one that is not a proper prefix of a longer directed path.

Algorithm 3 iterates over all undirected cycles of the system, which may in general require time exponential in the system size; however, the algorithm is only run at system construction time and so does not impact runtime performance. For each node with two output channels on the same

---

Algorithm 2: Single-node behavior with dummy propagation.

ComputeIndex $\leftarrow 0$;
foreach *output port q* **do**
  $\text{LastOutputIndex}_q \leftarrow 0$;
while *ComputeIndex $\neq$ Index of EOS* **do**
  if *not source node* **then**
    wait until every input channel has a pending token ;
    let T be minimum index of any pending token ;
    consume pending tokens with index T from input channels ;
  else
    $T \leftarrow$ ComputeIndex $+ 1$;
  foreach *output channel q* **do**
    if *$T - \text{LastOutputIndex}_q \geq [q]$ **OR** some pending token with index T is a dummy* **then**
      schedule a dummy token with index T for output q ;
      $\text{LastOutputIndex}_q \leftarrow T$;
  ComputeIndex $\leftarrow T$;
  perform computation on data tokens with index T ;
  if *not sink node* **then**
    emit output tokens with index T, combined with any scheduled dummies ;

Algorithm 3: Dummy interval calculation with dummy propagation.

Input: A system abstracted as graph $G = \{V, E\}$
Output: Dummy intervals for each channel
foreach *edge $uv \in E$* **do** $[uv] \leftarrow \infty$;
foreach *undirected cycle C of G* **do**
  foreach *node u with two output channels uv_1, uw_1 on C* **do**
    let $p_1 = uv_1 \ldots v_m$ be maximal directed path on C starting with uv_1 ;
    let $p_2 = uw_1 \ldots w_n$ be maximal directed path on C starting with uw_1 ;
    $[uv_1] \leftarrow \min([uv_1], |p_2|)$;
    $[uw_1] \leftarrow \min([uw_1], |p_1|)$;

---

undirected cycle, the algorithm calculates a dummy interval for each channel that (as we will prove) is small enough to guarantee that the cycle can never become blocking. Channels that are not the *first channel on a directed path on some undirected cycle*, including those not on a cycle at all, receive intervals of ∞.

THEOREM 3.2. *If all nodes behave according to Algorithm 2, using the intervals calculated by Algorithm 3, then the system is deadlock-free.*

PROOF. Suppose not; that is, suppose that the system as constructed above experiences a deadlock. According to the Deadlock Theorem, the system must at some point contain a blocking cycle C. We will show by contradiction that C cannot exist.

Let C be given. Divide C into alternating maximal directed paths of blockwise and counterblockwise edges, as shown in Figure 2. Choose an arbitrary node with two output channels on C (as s_1 in Figure 2) and, proceeding to blockwise from this node, label these *paths* in blockwise order as $p_{e1}, p_{f1}, \ldots p_{ek}, p_{fk}$ ("e" means "empty" while "f" means "full" here). By the Deadlock Theorem, each path p_{ei} consists entirely of empty channels, while each path p_{fi} consists entirely of full channels.

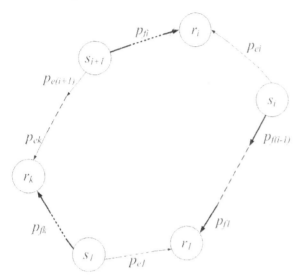

Figure 2: The division of a blocking cycle for Theorem 3.2.

For convenience, let $p_{f0} = p_{fk}$. Label each node between p_{ei} and p_{fi} as the *receiver* r_i, and label each node between $p_{f(i-1)}$ and p_{ei} as the *sender* s_i. Each sender node has two output channels on C, both of which receive finite dummy intervals according to Algorithm 3.

The key observation is that, given the rules for assigning dummy intervals, *node s_i cannot emit more than $|p_{f(i-1)}|$ tokens along path $p_{f(i-1)}$ without also sending a dummy token τ along path p_{ei}.* Because path $p_{f(i-1)}$ is entirely full, while path p_{ei} is entirely empty, the dummy τ must have already been emitted by s_i and been propagated to receiver r_i by the time the blocking cycle C formed.

Recall the definitions of minval and maxval for paths as given in Section 3.1. Algorithm 2 and Algorithm 3 above imply that

$$\text{minval}(p_{ei}) \geq \text{maxval}(p_{f(i-1)}) - |p_{f(i-1)}|. \quad (1)$$

Because each channel receives at most one token with a given index, we have that, since p_{fi} is full,

$$\text{maxval}(p_{f(i-1)}) - |p_{f(i-1)}| \geq \text{minval}(p_{f(i-1)}). \quad (2)$$

Finally, because the cycle C is a blocking cycle, r_i remains blocked by its counterblockwise neighbor even after receiving dummy token τ. Hence, we have that

$$\text{minval}(p_{fi}) > \text{minval}(p_{ei}). \quad (3)$$

Combining these three inequalities for a given i yields $\text{minval}(p_{fi}) > \text{minval}(p_{f(i-1)})$. But this inequality holds for every i, and so we have transitively that $\text{minval}(p_{fk}) > \text{minval}(p_{f0})$, which is impossible because these two paths are the same. Hence, blocking cycle C cannot exist, and so deadlock is impossible. $\square$

We note that in Algorithm 2, one cannot suppress a dummy on a channel q even if a data token has been sent within the last $[q]$ indices. Suppose that a data token was sent along p_{ei} from node s_i in the proof above; it could be filtered by any node on p_{ei} before reaching r_i, thereby invalidating Inequality 3. Similarly, one cannot permit both a data token and a dummy token with a given index T to be sent separately, as doing so would invalidate Inequality 2.

This scheme for deadlock avoidance can greatly reduce the frequency of dummy tokens on some channels in a system. In particular, a source node with two output channels q_1 and q_2 that emits a series of n tokens only on q_1 would have to emit n dummy tokens under the Naive Algorithm but only about $n/[q_2]$ tokens with the revised approach. Unfortunately, propagation of dummy tokens ensures that a node receives all tokens (with distinct indices) emitted by any of its ancestors, even if the node is not on any of the cycles that required emitting the dummies in the first place! Hence, nodes with many ancestors that participate in undirected cycles may be flooded with useless dummy tokens.

We can somewhat limit dummy propagation by noticing that, if we consider the communication links in our computing system as an undirected graph and segment this graph into its *biconnected components*, then every potentially blocking cycle is confined to a single biconnected component. Hence, it is not necessary to propagate dummies beyond the component in which they originate. We may compute biconnected components in time linear in the number of nodes and channels using Hopcroft and Tarjan's algorithm [12], then label each channel with its biconnected component. A dummy arriving on some input channel q is then propagated only on output channels labeled with the same component as q.

3.2.1 Calculating Dummy Intervals Without Enumeration of the Cycles

Algorithm 3 for calculating dummy intervals requires enumerating every undirected cycle in G. While the algorithm could be carried out as written using a method for cycle enumeration [24, 17], this approach may do more work than necessary. In particular, suppose that for some node u with output channels uv_1 and uw_1, the maximal directed path on a given cycle C starting with v_1 is p_1. This path may also be maximal with respect to a large number of other cycles in G, whether through w_1 or through another child of u. Enumerating all such cycles will not change the eventual dummy interval $[uv_1]$.

We can modify Algorithm 3 to interchange the order of its doubly-nested **foreach** loop: for each node u with two output channels, consider all undirected cycles involving just these two channels. In fact, we need not actually enumerate all such cycles. Rather, for each channel uv_1 out of u, it is sufficient to enumerate directed paths p_1 beginning with uv_1, then test whether each such p_1 is maximal with respect to *some* (simple) undirected cycle involving node u. If so, then we must set $[uv_1] \leftarrow \min([uv_1], |p_1|)$.

The following connectivity test verifies whether a given p_1 is maximal with respect to some undirected simple cycle involving u. Suppose p_1 ends with some vertex x. Delete from G every vertex on p_1 other than x, as well as all outgoing edges from x. Let G^* be the undirected copy of the resulting graph. If there exists a simple path in G^* connecting x to any other child w of u, then G has an undirected simple cycle containing p_1 that reaches u through edge uw. Moreover, the path p_1 is maximal with respect to this cycle because the path includes an edge that is into x in G. Conversely, if p_1 is maximal for any simple cycle involving uv_1 and some other uw, that cycle induces a path from x to w that is disjoint from the other vertices of p_1.

The connectivity test for p_1 can be implemented in time linear in $|G|$ with any graph traversal algorithm. To avoid exploring paths that cannot lead back to another child of u in G, we may restrict the test to use only edges in the same biconnected component of G (properly, of its undirected copy) as the edge uv_1.

Algorithm 4 shows the revised, non-cycle-enumerating algorithm for computing dummy intervals. Note that, for efficiency, the paths p_1 should be enumerated in increasing order by length, so that the algorithm is finished with edge uv_1 as soon as it discovers a cycle. Note also that each induced path from x to some other child w of u ends with some maximal directed path p_2 starting with uw. As a further optimization, if the **foreach** loop over edges has not yet processed uw, we may set $[uw] \leftarrow \min([uw], |p_2|)$ to set an upper bound on the lengths of paths to explore for uw when its turn comes.

Algorithm 4: Dummy interval calculation with propagation, no cycle enum.

Input: A system abstracted as graph $G = \{V, E\}$
Output: Dummy intervals for each channel
foreach *edge* $uv \in E$ **do** $[uv] \leftarrow \infty$;
foreach *node* u *with two output channels in the same biconnected component* **do**
    foreach *edge* uv_1 *out of* u **do**
        let G_0 be the biconnected component of G containing uv_1 ;
        foreach *directed path* p_1 *in* G_0 *starting with edge* uv_1 **do**
            let x be the end vertex of path p_1 ;
            $G^* \leftarrow G_0$;
            delete from G^* all vertices on p_1 except x ;
            delete from G^* all outgoing edges from x ;
            if G^* *contains a simple undirected path from x to any child of* u **then**
                $[uv_1] \leftarrow \min([uv_1], |p_1|)$;

3.3 Eliminating Dummy Propagation

In this section, we propose yet another deadlock avoidance scheme that uses a method similar to Algorithm 3 to assign dummy intervals to output channels. The key difference between the new scheme and that of the previous section is that dummy tokens no longer propagate. Since propagation is not required, we no longer need to send a dummy if we can send a data token with the same index; rather, the behavior at each node ensures only that *some* token is sent on channel q at least once each time the computation index increases by at least $[q]$. By increasing the frequency of dummy generation on some channels, we can guarantee freedom from deadlock without the need for dummy propagation. Hence this approach is referred as the "Non-Propagation Algorithm" later.

Algorithm 5 describes node behavior in which dummies are *never* propagated beyond the channel on which they first appear, while Algorithm 6 gives a revised procedure to assign dummy intervals to channels. To avoid propagation,

the new dummy interval computation assigns finite dummy intervals to *all* channels on the directed paths found by the previous algorithm, rather than just the first node. The assigned intervals are smaller than before for paths with two or more channels. As in the previous section, this algorithm may take exponential time, but it executes at configuration time and has no effect on the runtime of a computation. Also as in the previous section, we may replace the cycle enumeration of Algorithm 6 with the more efficient path enumeration and connectivity testing of Algorithm 4.

Algorithm 5: Single-node behavior without dummy propagation.

ComputeIndex $\leftarrow 0$;
foreach *output port* q **do**
    LastOutputIndex$_q \leftarrow 0$;
while *ComputeIndex* $\neq$ *Index of EOS* **do**
    if *not source node* **then**
        wait until every input channel has a pending token ;
        let T be minimum index of any pending token ;
        consume pending tokens with index T from input channels ;
    else
        $T \leftarrow$ ComputeIndex $+ 1$;
    ComputeIndex $\leftarrow T$;
    perform computation on data tokens with index T ;
    foreach *output channel* q **do**
        if *a data token with index T will be emitted on q* **then**
            schedule a token with index T for output q ;
            LastOutputIndex$_q \leftarrow T$;
        else if $T -$ *LastOutputIndex*$_q \geq [q]$ **then**
            schedule a dummy token with index T for output q ;
            LastOutputIndex$_q \leftarrow T$;
    if *not sink node* **then**
        emit output tokens with index T, including any dummies;

THEOREM 3.3. *If all nodes behave according to Algorithm 5, using the intervals calculated by Algorithm 6, then the system cannot deadlock.*

PROOF. As before, suppose that a blocking cycle C occurs in a system using this deadlock avoidance scheme. Divide cycle C into paths, senders, and receivers as before. Label the nodes on path p_{ei} $v_0, \ldots v_n$, with $v_0 = s_i$ and $v_n = r_i$.

Let $\gamma = \lceil |p_{f(i-1)}|/n \rceil$, the dummy interval defined for the channels on p_{ei} by Algorithm 6.

We first prove that if r_i has received no token with index minval($p_{f(i-1)}$), then the last token received by node v_j of p_{ei} must have index at most minval($p_{f(i-1)}$) $+ (\gamma - 1) \cdot (n-j)$. The proof is by induction on i in decreasing order. In the base case, when $j = n$, the lemma is trivially true, since $v_n = r_i$.

For the inductive step, by the inductive hypothesis, the last token received by v_{j+1} had index at most $M_{j+1} =$ minval($p_{f(i-1)}$) $+ (\gamma - 1) \cdot (n - j - 1)$, and so v_j's last token sent to v_{j+1} had index at most M_{j+1}. Now suppose that v_j has received a token with an index, say M', greater than

$$M_j = \text{minval}(p_{f(i-1)}) + (\gamma - 1) \cdot (n - j).$$

Algorithm 6: Dummy interval calculation without dummy propagation.

Input: A system abstracted as graph $G = \{V, E\}$
Output: Dummy intervals for each channel
foreach *edge* $uv \in E$ **do** $[uv] \leftarrow \infty$;
foreach *undirected cycle* C *of* G **do**
    foreach *node* u *with two output channels* uv_1, uw_1 *on* C **do**
        let $p_1 = uv_1 \ldots v_m$ be maximal directed path on C starting with uv_1 ;
        let $p_2 = uw_1 \ldots w_n$ be maximal directed path on C starting with uw_1 ;
        $[uv_1] \leftarrow \min([uv_1], \lceil |p_2|/m \rceil)$;
        for i *in* $2 \ldots m$ **do**
            $[v_{i-1}v_i] \leftarrow \min([v_{i-1}v_i], \lceil |p_2|/m \rceil)$;
        $[uw_1] \leftarrow \min([uw_1], \lceil |p_1|/n \rceil)$;
        for i *in* $2 \ldots n$ **do**
            $[w_{i-1}w_i] \leftarrow \min([w_{i-1}w_i], \lceil |p_1|/m \rceil)$;

We have that $M_j - M_{j+1} = \gamma - 1$, and so $M' - M_{j+1} \geq \gamma$, which means the interval between v_j's last received and last sent tokens is at least γ. Algorithms 5 and 6 therefore ensure that v_j must have sent a token, either real or dummy, to v_{j+1} with index $> M_{j+1}$. But this contradicts our IH. Thus, we conclude that the last token received by v_j has index at most M_j, as desired.

Next, we observe a special case of the fact proved above: if r_i has not received a token with index at least $\mathrm{minval}(p_{f(i-1)})$, then s_i's most recently received token has some index T, where

$$
\begin{aligned}
T \quad &\leq \quad \mathrm{minval}(p_{f(i-1)}) + (\gamma - 1) \cdot n \\
&< \quad \mathrm{minval}(p_{f(i-1)}) + |p_{f(i-1)}| \\
&\leq \quad \mathrm{maxval}(p_{f(i-1)}).
\end{aligned}
$$

But this is impossible because s_i has already emitted a token with index $\mathrm{maxval}(p_{f(i-1)})$, so it must have received such a token.

Conclude that $\mathrm{minval}(p_{ei}) \geq \mathrm{minval}(p_{f(i-1)})$. As in Theorem 3.2, we also have $\mathrm{minval}(p_{fi}) > \mathrm{minval}(p_{ei})$ because cycle C is blocking, and so a contradiction follows using the cycle-following argument of that theorem. Hence, blocking cycle C cannot exist, and no deadlock occurs. $\square$

3.4 A Comparison of Algorithms

In this section, we discuss the relative efficiency of the proposed algorithms in terms of the total number of dummy messages sent on all channels during the computation. Since the Naive Algorithm does not take advantage of channel buffers, it always sends more dummy messages than the other two algorithms. However, the Propagation and the Non-Propagation algorithms are incomparable; each may outperform the other based on the graph topology and buffer sizes.

In most cases, we expect the Non-Propagation algorithm to perform better. Propagation algorithm has two inherent disadvantages over the Non-Propagation algorithm. First, it sends dummy messages at specific intervals regardless of whether the node is actually filtering any inputs. (Here we assume that the nodes are capable of filtering data, they just happen not to for that particular set of inputs.) Therefore, if no node ever filters any data, the Propagation algorithm will still send dummy messages while the Non-Propagation algorithm will never send any dummy messages. Second, all downstream nodes propagate the dummy messages they receive. Therefore, in some cases, the dummy messages will be sent downstream even if they are no longer required. Due to these reasons, in most cases, we expect the Non-Propagation algorithm to be more efficient in terms of the number of dummy messages sent. Out preliminary empirical analysis confirms this intuition and we find that in our Mercury BLAST application, during one sequence search which had a filtering ratio greater than 95% and $q = 1024$, 72000 dummies were sent as a result of the Non-Propagation algorithm while this number would be 4×10^8 if the Propagation algorithm was used.

However, in theory, there are circumstances for which the Propagation algorithm will generate fewer dummy messages. Generally, this situation arises when the nodes filter a very large number of messages, sending virtually no real messages on some channels. Consider the following case. Let $u_1 u_2 \ldots u_{k+1}$ be some maximal path on an undirected cycle and the dummy interval for $u_1 u_2$ is q in the Propagation Algorithm. When the computation index increases from 0 to m at node u_1, in case of the Propagation Algorithm, u_1 will send $\lfloor m/q \rfloor$ dummies, which are then propagated by u_i ($1 < i \leq k$), so the total number of dummies is $k * \lfloor m/q \rfloor$. According to Algorithm 6, in the Non-Propagation algorithm, the dummy interval for every channel on this path is at most $\lceil q/k \rceil$. If all tokens are filtered by u_1, the total number of dummy messages sent by the Non-Propagation algorithm is about $k * \lfloor m/\lceil q/k \rceil \rfloor$, which is about k times larger than the number of messages sent by the Propagation algorithm.

4. RELATED WORK

The streaming computation paradigm can be seen as an example of coarse-grained dataflow computing, which has two distinct domains: synchronous dataflow (SDF) [16] and dynamic dataflow (DDF) [3]. In SDF, data consumption and production rates are known at compile time, so we can compute a valid schedule statically to avoid deadlocks. In DDF, data rates are dynamic and cannot be known at compile time. Another issue of DDF is how to decide which data is consumed during one firing. Buck [3] used control switches to select the ports to read from and/or send to, which is called "Boolean Dataflow." Prior to that, *tagged-tokens*, similar to the ones we use, were proposed and implemented in the MIT Tagged-Token Dataflow Machine [22] and the Manchester Dataflow Computer [11].

Our computation model is similar to Kahn's process networks (KPNs) [14]. A KPN consists of processes (we call them nodes) and unidirectional channels. The original KPN model has infinite channel buffers, which is impractical, so Parks et al. [23] introduced bounded memory models similar to the one we use. They also recognized that these networks have potential for deadlocks like the ones we study, which they call *artificial deadlocks* to distinguish them from deadlocks due to a directed cycle of empty channels.

Deadlock treatment in distributed systems has been well studied. Chandy et al. developed algorithms to detect distributed deadlocks based on probes [6, 5]. Mitchell and Merritt designed a deadlock detection algorithm using public and private labels [19], which are similar to the notion of Chandy's probe. After raising the issue of artificial deadlock in bounded KPNs, Parks tried to avoid such deadlocks by dynamically increasing channel capacity. Geilen and Basten improved Parks' idea and proposed a new scheduling algorithm which guarantees fairness and behaves correctly for bounded and effective KPNs [10]. Here "effective" means all tokens produced are ultimately consumed. This algorithm also requires dynamic changes to channel capacity. Nandy and Bussa claimed that runtime mechanisms could detect artificial deadlocks in bounded KPNs early [20], but deadlocks with multiple sources on blocking cycle were not identified in their work. Olson and Evans improved Mitchell's algorithm to detect local deadlocks in bounded KPNs [21]. Later, Allen et al. from the same group proposed algorithms using private and public set to detect all deadlocks in bounded KPNs and to resolve them if possible [1]. However, not all detected deadlocks can be resolved. We note that all these deadlock avoidance and resolution algorithms require runtime change to channel capacities, while our algorithms do not.

In our algorithms, we use dummy tokens to avoid deadlocks, inspired by null messages [9, 18] in parallel discrete-event simulation (PDES). In PDES, each message has a timestamp. To avoid deadlock, processes periodically send null messages, which contain only timestamps. These null messages let receivers advance their local clock values safely so that deadlocks are avoided.

5. CONCLUSIONS AND FUTURE WORK

We have characterized deadlocks in our model of streaming computation with filtering nodes and have presented three deadlock avoidance algorithms under this model. Our techniques are provably effective, in that a system that uses them can never deadlock, and are *lightweight* in the sense that they do not require global control or extra communication channels and do not depend on dynamic buffer resizing. These are important considerations because we wish to apply our solutions to systems built with Auto-Pipe, which may utilize distributed, diverse computing resources that cannot easily be coordinated or modified at runtime. Our techniques require minimal infrastructural support, since dummy tokens use the existing communication channels, and our modifications to the behavior of nodes are minimal.

There are several directions for future work. First, our algorithms for computing the dummy token intervals take exponential time. This drawback is not significant now since the computation occurs at configuration time and not at runtime, and the size of most graphs is relatively small. However, the size of graphs may increase in the future, and it would be useful to come up with polynomial time algorithms for computing or lower-bounding the dummy intervals. Second, we provide techniques for computing dummy intervals given buffer sizes. We would like to address the inverse problem where we statically size the buffers given that the system is willing to tolerate a certain dummy frequency. (Note that we are not talking about dynamic buffer resizing.) Third, we plan to implement our algorithms in Auto-Pipe and evaluate the performance impact of sending dummy tokens.

6. ACKNOWLEDGMENTS

This work was supported by NSF awards CNS-0751212 and CNS-0905368 and by NIH award R42 HG003225 (through BECS Technology, Inc.). R.D. Chamberlain is a principal in BECS Technology, Inc.

7. REFERENCES

[1] G.E. Allen, P.E. Zucknick, and B.L. Evans. A distributed deadlock detection and resolution algorithm for process networks. In *Proc. of IEEE Int'l Conf. Acoustics, Speech, Signal Processing (ICASSP)*, volume 2, pages 33–36, April 2007.

[2] S. F. Altschul, T. L. Madden, A. A. Schäffer, J. Zhang, Z. Zhang, W. Miller, and D. J. Lipman. Gapped BLAST and PSI-BLAST: a new generation of protein database search programs. *Nucleic Acids Res*, 25(17):3389–3402, 1997.

[3] Joseph T. Buck. *Scheduling Dynamic Dataflow Graphs with Bounded Memory Using the Token Flow Model*. PhD thesis, University of California, Berkeley, 1993.

[4] Roger D. Chamberlain, Mark A. Franklin, Eric J. Tyson, James H. Buckley, Jeremy Buhler, Greg Galloway, Saurabh Gayen, Michael Hall, E.F. Berkley Shands, and Naveen Singla. Auto-Pipe: Streaming applications on architecturally diverse systems. *IEEE Computer*, 43(3):42–49, March 2010.

[5] K. Mani Chandy, Jayadev Misra, and Laura M. Haas. Distributed deadlock detection. *ACM Trans. Comput. Syst.*, 1(2):144–156, 1983.

[6] K. Many Chandy and Jayadev Misra. A distributed algorithm for detecting resource deadlocks in distributed systems. In *PODC '82: Proceedings of the First ACM SIGACT-SIGOPS Symposium on Principles of Distributed Computing*, pages 157–164, New York, NY, USA, 1982. ACM.

[7] Mattan Erez, Jung Ho Ahn, Ankit Garg, William J. Dally, and Eric Darve. Analysis and performance results of a molecular modeling application on Merrimac. In *Proc. of ACM/IEEE Supercomputing Conference*, Nov. 2004.

[8] Mark A. Franklin, Eric J. Tyson, J. Buckley, Patrick Crowley, and John Maschmeyer. Auto-pipe and the X language: A pipeline design tool and description language. In *Proc. of Int'l Parallel and Distributed Processing Symp.*, 2006.

[9] Richard Fujimoto. Parallel discrete event simulation. *Commun. ACM*, 33(10):30–53, 1990.

[10] Marc Geilen and Twan Basten. Requirements on the execution of Kahn process networks. In *Proc. of the 12th European Symposium on Programming, ESOP 2003*, pages 319–334. Springer Verlag, 2003.

[11] J. R Gurd, C. C Kirkham, and I. Watson. The Manchester prototype dataflow computer. *Commun. ACM*, 28(1):34–52, 1985.

[12] John Hopcroft and Robert Tarjan. Efficient algorithms for graph manipulation. *Journal of the ACM*, 16:372–378, 1973.

[13] Arpith C. Jacob, Joseph M. Lancaster, Jeremy Buhler, Brandon Harris, and Roger D. Chamberlain. Mercury BLASTP: Accelerating protein sequence alignment. *ACM Transactions on Reconfigurable Technology and Systems*, 1(2), 2008.

[14] Gilles Kahn. The semantics of simple language for parallel programming. In *Proc. of IFIP Congress*, pages 471–475, 1974.

[15] Brucek Khailany, William J. Dally, Ujval J. Kapasi, Peter Mattson, Jinyung Namkoong, John D. Owens, Brian Towles, Andrew Chang, and Scott Rixner.

Imagine: Media processing with streams. *IEEE Micro*, 21(2):35–46, March/April 2001.

[16] Edward A. Lee and David G. Messerschmitt. Synchronous data flow. *Proceedings of the IEEE*, 75(9):1235–1245, September 1987.

[17] Hongbo Liu and Jiaxin Wang. A new way to enumerate cycles in graph. In *AICT-ICIW '06: Proceedings of the Advanced Int'l Conference on Telecommunications and Int'l Conference on Internet and Web Applications and Services*, pages 57–59, Washington, DC, USA, 2006. IEEE Computer Society.

[18] Jayadev Misra. Distributed discrete-event simulation. *ACM Comput. Surv.*, 18(1):39–65, 1986.

[19] Don P. Mitchell and Michael J. Merritt. A distributed algorithm for deadlock detection and resolution. In *PODC '84: Proceedings of the Third Annual ACM Symposium on Principles of Distributed Computing*, pages 282–284, New York, NY, USA, 1984. ACM.

[20] Bharath Nandy and Nagaraju Bussa. Artificial deadlock detection in process networks for eclipse. In *Proc. of IEEE International Conference on Application-specific Systems, Architectures and Processors*, pages 22–27, Washington, DC, USA, 2005. IEEE Computer Society.

[21] Alex G. Olson and Brian L. Evans. Deadlock detection for distributed process networks. In *Proc. of IEEE Int'l Conf. Acoustics, Speech, Signal Processing (ICASSP)*, volume 5, pages v/73–v/76 Vol. 5, March 2005.

[22] Gregory M. Papadopoulos and David E. Culler. Monsoon: an explicit token-store architecture. In *Proc. of 17th Annual Int'l Symp. on Comp. Arch.*, pages 82–91, 1990.

[23] Thomas M. Parks. *Bounded Scheduling of Process Networks*. PhD thesis, University of California, Berkeley, Dec 1995.

[24] R. C. Read and R. E. Tarjan. Bounds on backtrack algorithms for listing cycles, paths, and spanning trees. *Networks*, 5:237–252, 1975.

[25] Eric J. Tyson, James Buckley, Mark A. Franklin, and Roger D. Chamberlain. Acceleration of atmospheric Cherenkov telescope signal processing to real-time speed with the Auto-Pipe design system. *Nuclear Instruments and Methods in Physics Research A*, 585(2):474–479, October 2008.

Implementing and Evaluating Nested Parallel Transactions in Software Transactional Memory

Woongki Baek, Nathan Bronson, Christos Kozyrakis, Kunle Olukotun
Computer Systems Laboratory
Stanford University
Stanford, CA 94305
{wkbaek,nbronson,kozyraki,kunle}@stanford.edu

ABSTRACT

Transactional Memory (TM) is a promising technique that simplifies parallel programming for shared-memory applications. To date, most TM systems have been designed to efficiently support single-level parallelism. To achieve widespread use and maximize performance gains, TM must support nested parallelism available in many applications and supported by several programming models.

We present NesTM, a software TM (STM) system that supports closed-nested parallel transactions. NesTM is based on a high-performance, blocking STM that uses eager version management and word-granularity conflict detection. Its algorithm targets the state and runtime overheads of nested parallel transactions. We also describe several subtle correctness issues in supporting nested parallel transactions in NesTM and discuss their performance impact.

Through our evaluation, we quantitatively analyze the performance of NesTM using STAMP applications and microbenchmarks based on concurrent data structures. First, we show that the performance overhead of NesTM is reasonable when single-level parallelism is used. Second, we quantify the incremental overhead of NesTM when the parallelism is exploited in deeper nesting levels and draw conclusions that can be useful in designing a nesting-aware TM runtime environment. Finally, we demonstrate a use-case where nested parallelism improves the performance of a transactional microbenchmark.

Categories and Subject Descriptors

D.1.3 [**Programming Techniques**]: Concurrent Programming – parallel programming

General Terms

Algorithms, Design, Performance

Keywords

Transactional Memory, Nested Parallelism, Parallel Programming

1. INTRODUCTION

Transactional Memory (TM) [13] has surfaced as a promising technique to simplify parallel programming. TM addresses the difficulty of lock-based synchronization by allowing programmers to simply declare certain code segments as *transactions* that execute in an *atomic* and *isolated* way with respect to other code. TM takes responsibility for all concurrency control. The potential of TM has motivated extensive research on hardware, software, and hybrid implementations. We focus on software TM (STM) [8,11,19], because it is the only approach compatible with existing and upcoming multicore chips.

Most TM systems, thus far, have assumed that the code within a transaction executes sequentially. However, real world applications often include the potential for *nested parallelism* in various forms such as nested parallel loops, recursive function calls, and calls to parallel libraries [21]. As the number of cores scales, it is important to fully exploit the parallelism available at all levels to achieve the best possible performance. In this spirit, several parallel programming models that support nested parallelism have been proposed [1, 20]. Hence, to maximize performance gain and integrate well with popular programming models, TM must support nested parallelism.

However, efficiently exploiting nested parallelism in TM is not trivial. The general challenge of nested parallelism is amortizing the overhead for initiating, synchronizing, and balancing inner-level, fine-grained parallelism [5]. Nested parallelism within transactions exacerbates this challenge due to the extra overheads for initiating, versioning, and committing nested transactions. The design of a TM system that supports nested parallel transactions is also challenging. First, the conflict detection scheme must be able to correctly track dependencies in a hierarchical manner instead of a flat way. Nested parallel transactions may conflict and restart without necessarily aborting their parent transaction. Second, apart from the runtime overhead, we must ensure that the memory overhead necessary for tracking the state of nested transactions is small. Third, since some applications may not use nested parallelism, we must ensure that its overhead is reasonable when only a single level of parallelism is used.

A few recent works on nested parallelism in STM have discussed the semantics of nested parallel transactions and provided prototype implementations [2, 4, 18, 22]. However, the following questions still require further investigations. First, what is a cost-effective algorithm for nested parallelism in high-performance STMs? Second, using a detailed performance analysis, what are the practical tradeoffs and issues when using nested parallelism in STM? Answering these questions is also important to guide future work on nesting-aware TM runtime environments.

This paper presents *NesTM*, an STM that supports closed-nested parallel transactions. NesTM is based on a high-performance, blocking STM that uses eager versioning and word-granularity conflict detection. NesTM extends the baseline STM to support nested parallel transactions in a manner that keeps state and runtime overheads small.

The specific contributions of this work are:

- We propose an STM system that supports nested parallelism with transactions and parallel regions nested in arbitrary manners.

- We present several complications of concurrent nesting, describe solutions for correct execution, and discuss their impact on performance.

- We provide a quantitative performance analysis of NesTM across multiple use scenarios. First, we show that the performance overhead of NesTM is reasonable when using only a single level of parallelism. Second, we quantify the overhead of NesTM when we exploit the parallelism in deeper nesting levels. Finally, we demonstrate that NesTM improves the performance of a transactional microbenchmark that uses nested parallelism.

The rest of the paper is organized as follows. Section 2 reviews the baseline STM and the semantics of nested parallel transactions. Section 3 describes NesTM and Section 4 discusses subtle correctness issues. Section 5 presents the quantitative evaluation. Section 6 reviews related work. Finally, Section 7 concludes the paper.

2. BACKGROUND

2.1 Baseline STM

Our starting point is a blocking STM algorithm that uses eager versioning [11, 19]. This approach has been shown to have performance advantages over non-blocking or lazy versioning STMs and is used by the Intel STM compiler [19] and the Microsoft Bartok environment [11]. While we focus on an STM with word-granularity conflict detection, our findings can apply to STMs that perform object-granularity conflict detection.

The exact code we start with is an eager variant of TL2 STM [6, 9]. It maintains an undo log for data written within a transaction. The STM uses a global version clock to establish serializability. Using a hashing function, each memory word is associated with a variable (voLock) that either acts as a lock or stores a version number (i.e., the clock value when the word was written by a committing transaction). When a transaction reads data, it inserts them in its read-set. When a transaction writes data, it acquires the associated locks. The code for the read and write barriers is carefully optimized to keep the overhead per call (some parts are in assembly) small. Conflicts are detected by checking the associated voLocks when read, write, and commit barriers are executed. A randomized exponential backoff scheme is used for contention management.

2.2 Semantics of Concurrent Nesting

We describe a few concepts for nested parallel transactions. Additional discussion is available in [2, 16].

Definitions and concepts: At runtime, each transaction is assigned with a *transaction ID (TID)*, a unique positive integer. *Root* transaction (TID 0) is reserved to represent the globally committed state of the system. Every non-root transaction has a unique *parent* transaction. *Top-level* transactions are the ones whose parent is the root transaction. Following the assumption in [16], a transaction is only allowed to execute when it does not have any active children.

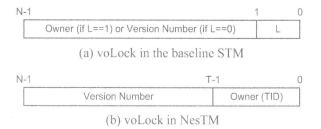

(a) voLock in the baseline STM

(b) voLock in NesTM

Figure 1: Comparison of voLocks.

Transactional semantics: We describe the definition of conflict discussed in [2] for TM systems with closed nesting. For a memory object l, let readers(l) be a set of active transactions that have l in their read-sets. writers(l) is defined similarly. When a transaction T accesses l, the following two cases are conflicts:

- T reads from l: if there exists a transaction T' such that $T' \in$ writers(l), $T' \neq T$ and $T' \notin$ ancestors(T).
- T writes to l: if there exists a transaction T' such that $T' \in$ readers(l) $\cup$ writers(l), $T' \neq T$ and $T' \notin$ ancestors(T).

As for the commit semantics, if T is not a top-level transaction, its read- and write-sets are merely merged into its parent's read- and write-sets. Otherwise, all the values written by T become visible to other transactions and its read- and write-sets are reset. If T aborts, all the changes made by T are discarded and previous states are restored [16].

3. DESIGN AND IMPLEMENTATION OF NESTM

This section describes the NesTM algorithm, an execution example, and the main issues related to performance.

3.1 NesTM Algorithm

The key design goal of NesTM is to keep state and runtime overheads small in supporting nested parallel transactions. For instance, we do not want to significantly increase memory footprint by using multiple sets of locks and global version clocks to support multiple nested parallel regions. The blocking, eager versioning STM used as our baseline has a useful property that helps us meet our goal: once a transaction writes (i.e., acquires a lock) to a memory object, it is guaranteed to have an exclusive ownership for the object until it commits or aborts.

Before discussing the NesTM algorithm, we describe the changes in the version-owner locks (voLock) compared to the baseline STM. As shown in Figure 1, voLock in the baseline STM is a word-sized data structure (i.e., N=32 and 64 on 32-bit and 64-bit machines) that encodes the version or owner information on the associated memory object. If L=1 (locked), the remaining N-1 bits store the owner information. If L=0 (unlocked), the remaining N-1 bits store the version number. This encoding is sufficient to support only top-level transactions because once a transaction locks a memory object, no other transactions are allowed to access the object until the transaction commits or aborts. In NesTM, however, other transactions can correctly access the locked object as long as they are descendants of the owner. To allow this, the ownership information should always be available in voLock to consult the ancestor relationship at any time. Similarly, the version number in voLock should also be always available to serialize the conflicting transactions.

```
1:  procedure IsInReadSet(Self, addr)
2:    acquireLock(Self.commitLock)
3:    result ← addr ∈ Self.RS
4:    releaseLock(Self.commitLock)
5:    return result
6:  procedure DoomHighestConflictTx(Self, Owner)
7:    ptr ← Self
8:    while ptr.Parent ∉ {Root, Owner, Ances(Owner)} do
9:      ptr.doomed ← true
10:     ptr ← ptr.Parent
11: procedure ValidateReaders(Self, Owner, addr)
12:   ptr ← Self
13:   hcr ← NIL
14:   while ptr ∉ {Root, Owner, Ances(Owner)} do
15:     if getTS(addr) > ptr.rv and isInReadSet(ptr, addr) then
16:       ptr.doomed ← true
17:       hcr ← ptr
18:     ptr ← ptr.Parent
19:   return hcr
20: procedure TxStart(Self)
21:   Self.aborts ← 0
22:   checkpoint()
23:   if isAnyDoomedAnces(Self) then
24:     return fail
25:   Self.doomed ← false
26:   Self.rv ← GlobalClock
27:   return success
28: procedure TxLoad(Self, addr)
29:   if Self.doomed = true or isAnyDoomedAnces(Self) then
30:     TxAbort(Self)
31:   retry_load:
32:   rb ← RollbackCounter
33:   cv ← getVoVal(addr)
34:   Owner ← extractOwn(cv)
35:   value ← Memory[addr]
36:   if Owner = Self then
37:     Self.RS.insert(addr)
38:     return value
39:   else if Owner ∈ Ances(Self) and cv = getVoVal(addr) then
40:     if rb ≠ RollbackCounter then
41:       goto retry_load
42:     if extractTS(cv) > Self.rv then
43:       TxAbort(Self)
44:     else
45:       Self.RS.insert(addr)
46:       return value
47:   else
48:     if Owner ∉ Ances(Self) and Self.aborts%p = p − 1 then
49:       DoomHighestConflictTx(Self, Owner)
50:     TxAbort(Self)
51: procedure TxAbort(Self)
52:   Self.doomed ← false
53:   Self.aborts ← Self.aborts + 1
54:   Self.RS.reset()
55:   atomicIncrementRollbackCounter()
56:   for all e in Self.WS do          ▷ Traversing direction: backward
57:     Memory[e.addr] ← Self.WS.lookup(e.addr)
58:   for all e in Self.WS do          ▷ Traversing direction: forward
59:     Owner ← getOwner(e.addr)
60:     if Owner = Self then
61:       setVoVal(e.addr, e.prevVoLock)
62:   Self.WS.reset()
63:   doContentionManagement()
64:   restoreCheckpoint()
```

Algorithm 1: Pseudocode for the basic functions in NesTM.

```
1:  procedure TxStore(Self, addr, data)
2:    if Self.doomed = true or isAnyDoomedAnces(Self) then
3:      TxAbort(Self)
4:    Owner ← getOwner(addr)
5:    if Owner = Self then
6:      cv ← getVoVal(addr)
7:      Self.WS.insert(addr, Memory[addr], cv)
8:      Memory[addr] ← data
9:    else
10:     cnt ← 1
11:     repeat
12:       cv ← getVoVal(addr)
13:       ov ← cv
14:       nv ← extractTS(cv) | Self.TID
15:       if extractOwner(cv) ∈ Ances(Self) then
16:         ov ← atomicCAS(getVoAddr(addr), cv, nv)
17:         if ov = cv then
18:           hcr ← ValidateReaders(Self, extractOwner(cv), addr)
19:           if hcr ≠ NIL then
20:             setVoVal(addr, cv)
21:             TxAbort(Self)
22:           Self.WS.insert(addr, Memory[addr], cv)
23:           Memory[addr] ← data
24:           return
25:       cnt ← cnt + 1
26:     until cnt = C
27:     if Self.aborts % p = p − 1 then
28:       DoomHighestConflictTx(Self, extractOwner(ov))
29:     TxAbort(Self)

30: procedure TxCommit(Self)
31:   if Self.doomed = true or isAnyDoomedAnces(Self) then
32:     TxAbort(Self)
33:   wv ← Fetch&Increment(GlobalClock)
34:   acquireLock(Self.Parent.commitLock)
35:   for all e in Self.RS do
36:     cv ← getVoVal(e.addr)
37:     Owner ← extractOwner(cv)
38:     if Owner = Self then
39:       continue
40:     else if Owner ∈ Ances(Self) then
41:       if extractTS(cv) > Self.rv then
42:         releaseLock(Self.Parent.commitLock)
43:         TxAbort(Self)
44:     else
45:       releaseLock(Self.Parent.commitLock)
46:       if Self.aborts % p = p − 1 then
47:         DoomHighestConflictTx(Self, Owner)
48:       TxAbort(Self)
49:   mergeRWSetsToParent(Self)
50:   releaseLock(Self.Parent.commitLock)
51:   for all e in Self.WS do
52:     Owner ← getOwner(e.addr)
53:     if Owner = Self then
54:       nv ← wv | Self.Parent.TID
55:       setVoVal(e.addr, nv)
56:   Self.RS.reset()
57:   Self.WS.reset()
```

Algorithm 2: Pseudocode for the basic functions in NesTM.

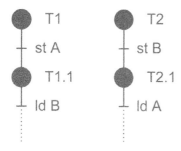

Figure 2: A livelock scenario avoided by eventual rollback of the outer transaction.

To enable this, we modify the voLock as shown in Figure 1. T least significant bits (LSBs) are used to encode the owner of the associated object. Since TID 0 is reserved for the root transaction, NesTM can support up to $2^T - 1$ concurrent transactions. While we use T=10 (i.e., 1023 transactions) in this paper, it is tunable. The remaining N-T bits store the version number. Since the global version clock increases by 2^T at the commit of each transaction, it can saturate faster than the baseline STM. Recent work discusses how to handle the version clock overflow [10].

Algorithms 1 and 2 provide the pseudocode for NesTM algorithm. We summarize the key functions below.

TxStart: This barrier is almost identical to the one in the baseline STM except that it returns "fail" when there are any doomed ancestors of the transaction we attempt to initiate. The return value can be used to restart the doomed ancestor in order to guarantee forward progress.

TxLoad: Following the conflict definition of nested parallel transactions in Section 2.2, a transaction can read a memory object only if the owner of the object is itself or its ancestor. When it is the owner, it can safely read the memory object without checking the version number (the reason will be explained in the discussion of TxStore). When the owner is its ancestor, it relies on the version number to ensure serializability. If the owner is neither itself nor its ancestor, the transaction conflicts with the owner. In lines 48–49 in Algorithm 1, it periodically calls DoomHighestConflictTx. This is to avoid potential livelock cases. Figure 2 illustrates an example. If only nested transactions (i.e., T1.1 and T2.1) abort and restart, none of them can make forward progress because the memory objects are still (crosswise) locked by ancestors. To avoid the livelock, at least one of the ancestors should abort and release the acquired memory objects. For this purpose, NesTM periodically checks and dooms ancestors. Note that we could use a more precise livelock detection mechanism, but it would also incur a large runtime overhead. Also note that similar livelock cases exist even in the baseline STM. Finally, note that *RollbackCounter* is used to avoid the *invalid-read* problem discussed in Section 4.1.

TxStore: When a transaction attempts to write to a memory object, it can safely do so if it is the owner of the memory object. Otherwise, it attempts to acquire the lock for the memory object, if the owner is an ancestor. If it fails, the transaction conflicts and DoomHighestConflictTx is also periodically called to avoid any potential livelock (lines 27–28 in Algorithm 2). If it successfully acquires the lock, it calls ValidateReaders with parameters consisting of Self, Owner (the previous owner for the object), and addr. In ValidateReaders, the transaction itself and all its ancestors that are also not an ancestor of Owner are validated for the object (lines 11–19 in Algorithm 1). The key insight of this is that once a transaction T or any of its descendants writes (i.e., acquires

the lock) to a memory object, T is guaranteed to have an exclusive ownership for the object until it commits or aborts. Therefore, if we ensure that there were no conflicting writes to an object for T and all of its ancestors at the time when T first attempts to write to the object, the object is guaranteed to be valid throughout T and its ancestors' execution. If there is any invalid reader, it transfers the ownership to the previous owner and triggers rollback (lines 19–21 in Algorithm 2). Note that validating each transaction is protected by the *commit-lock* of that validated transaction to avoid the problem with non-atomic commit discussed in Section 4.2. Also, note that TxStore can be expensive when a transaction executes in a deep nesting level due to read-set search for itself and its ancestors. We will discuss this performance issue in Section 3.3.

TxCommit: If a transaction or any of its ancestors is doomed, it aborts (lines 31–32 in Algorithm 2). Otherwise, it validates all the entries in its read-set (lines 35–48 in Algorithm 2). Once the read-set is validated, it merges its read- and write-sets to its parent's (line 49 in Algorithm 2). Note that to avoid the problem with the non-atomic commit discussed in Section 4.2, the process of read-set validation and merging is protected by the commit-lock of the parent. To reduce the execution time in the critical section, merging is done by linking (instead of copying) the pointers in read- and write-sets implemented using linked-lists. Then, the version number and ownership for each object in the write-set are incremented and transferred to the parent.

TxAbort: After updating transactional metadata and incrementing RollbackCounter, the write-set is traversed backward (i.e., from the newest to oldest) to roll back the speculatively-written memory values. Then, the write-set is traversed forward (i.e., from the oldest to newest) to restore the value of voLock to the first observed value. Note that the voLock is released only when the owner of the memory location is the transaction itself (lines 60 in Algorithm 1) to avoid the double-release problem [22]. Finally, the checkpoint is restored to restart the transaction.

Note that by calling DoomHighestConflictTx in TxLoad, Tx-Store, and TxCommit, possible livelock scenarios similar to Figure 2 can be avoided. In addition, a randomized exponential backoff scheme is used for the contention management to probabilistically provide liveness.

3.2 Example

Figure 3 illustrates an example of how a simple application using nested parallel transactions executes on NesTM. Initially, GC=0 and TS(A)=TS(B)=0. Note that GC is incremented by 2^{10} in the real implementation. For simplicity, we assume GC is incremented by 1 in this and subsequent examples.

At (wall clock) time 0, T1 starts (RV(T1)=0). At time 2, T1 reads B. At time 3 and 4, T2 starts (RV(T2)=0) and writes to A. At time 5, T2 commits and GC=1 and TS(A)=1. At time 6, threads executing T1.1 and T1.2 (children of T1) are forked and T1.1 and T1.2 start (RV(T1.1)=RV(T1.2)=1). At time 7, both T1.1 and T1.2 successfully read A because RV(T1.1)=RV(T1.2)≥TS(A). At time 8, T1.2 attempts to write to A. T1.2 validates itself and its ancestors (T1) by calling ValidateReaders. T1.2 is valid because A is in its read-set and RV(T1.2)≥TS(A). T1 is not doomed because A is not in its read-set (read-sets of T1.1 and T1.2 have not been merged yet). Therefore, T1.2 can successfully write to A. At time 9, T1.2 successfully commits and GC=2 and TS(A)=2. Also, the read- and write-sets of T1.2 are merged into the ones of T1. At time 10, T1.1 attempts to commit but fails because A is in the read-set of T1.1 and RV(T1.1)<TS(A). GC is incremented to 3 due to this unsuccessful commit.

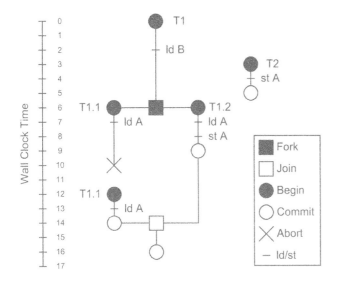

Figure 3: An example of a TM application running on NesTM.

At time 12, T1.1 restarts (RV(T1.1)=3). At time 13, T1.1 successfully reads A because the owner of A is T1 (an ancestor of T1.1) and RV(T1.1)≥TS(A). At time 14, T1.1 successfully commits, GC is incremented to 4 (but still TS(A)=2), and T1 resumes its execution after child threads join. At time 16, T1 successfully commits because it has an ownership for A (transferred from T1.2) and RV(T1)≥TS(B). GC and TS(A) are incremented to 5.

3.3 Qualitative Performance Analysis

Table 1 provides a symbolic comparison of the common- and worst-case time complexity of TM barriers in baseline STM and NesTM. NesTM has two different implementations: (1) NesTM-L: linked-lists are used to implement read- and write-sets; ancestor relationship is checked by pointer chasing and (2) NesTM-H: hash tables are used to implement read- and write-sets; ancestor bit vector (ABV) is used for fast ancestor relationship check. We assume the common case is a case in which the nesting depth is small and there is strong temporal locality between reads and writes (i.e., a transaction writes to a recently-read memory object). On the other hand, we assume the worst case is a case in which the nesting depth is large and there is weak temporal locality between reads and writes.

In the common case, the time complexity of NesTM-L TM barriers can be almost similar to the ones in the baseline STM because the nesting depth is small (i.e., $d \simeq 1$) and only a few entries in the read-set need to be looked up at each write to check the validity due to the strong temporal locality between reads and writes. However, in the worst case, the time complexity of NesTM-L TM barriers is significantly higher than the baseline STM. In contrast, NesTM-H still shows a comparable time complexity as the baseline STM due to the use of hash tables and ABV. Our current NesTM implementation follows NesTM-L; the implementation of NesTM-H is part of our future work.

In addition to the differences in the time complexity of TM barriers, there are three performance issues to note. First, temporal locality is lost when accessing transactional metadata of nested transactions. Since, when a child transaction commits, its read- and write-set entries are merged to its parent, there is no temporal locality for these entries when a new transaction begins on the same core. Second, the same memory objects in the read-set are repeatedly validated across different nesting levels. Finally, when a

large number of child transactions simultaneously attempt to commit, contention on the commit-lock of the parent can become the critical performance bottleneck. We quantify these performance issues in Section 5.

4. COMPLICATIONS OF CONCURRENT NESTING

We now discuss subtle correctness issues we have encountered while developing NesTM. We also describe our on-going efforts on the correctness and liveness of NesTM.

4.1 Invalid Read

Problem: In the read barrier, reading a voLock and the corresponding memory value does not occur atomically. Because of this, eager STMs are potentially vulnerable to the *invalid-read* problem. A transaction may incorrectly read an invalid memory value speculatively written by an aborting transaction. If the aborting transaction restores the original voLock value, the validation process at the end of the reading transaction will miss the problem. In flat STMs, this problem can be simply avoided by always incrementing the timestamp values of voLocks even when an aborting transaction releases them. In NesTM, however, this technique cannot be used due to the *self-livelock* problem. If an aborting descendant increments the timestamp value of the voLock for a memory object, its ancestor that has the memory object in its read-set can be aborted due to that incremented timestamp value. Eventually, the subtree rooted by the ancestor cannot make any forward progress.

Solution: To correctly address both invalid-read and self-livelock problems at the same time, we propose the *RollbackCounter* scheme. On abort, a transaction atomically increases the global Rollback-Counter in addition to restoring the values of voLocks in its write-set to the first observed values. When a transaction attempts to read a memory object, it first samples the value of RollbackCounter before reading the value of the associated voLock (line 32 in Algorithm 1). After ensuring the voLock value remains unchanged (line 39), the previously sampled value of RollbackCounter is compared with the current value. If the two values match, it is guaranteed that there has been no aborting transaction since the voLock value was read, thus no possibility of invalid read. If the two values differ, it conservatively avoids the invalid-read problem by retrying the whole process (line 41).

Performance impact: Since only a single, global RollbackCounter is used, false positives can degrade the performance by making transactions repeat the process several times even when they did not actually read invalid memory values. Furthermore, the extra code added to access the RollbackCounter in the read barrier can degrade the performance.

Possible alternatives: Instead of using the eager version management (VM) scheme, a lazy VM scheme can be used (while still using the encounter-lock scheme) to avoid the invalid-read problem. However, it can cause significant performance issues because the write-set of a transaction is frequently accessed by the transaction itself and its descendants.

4.2 Non-atomic Commit

Problem: Figure 4 illustrates a potential serializability violation scenario due to the non-atomic commit. Initially, GC and TS(A) are set to 0. After reading A at time 3, T1.1 initiates its commit at time 4. At time 5, A is validated. At time 6, T2 writes to A. At time 7, T2 commits and GC=1 and TS(A)=1. At time 8, T1.2 starts (RV(T1.2)=1). At time 10, T1.2 attempts to write to A. By calling **ValidateReaders** in Algorithm 1, T1.2 validates itself and

	Baseline	NesTM-L (Linked list)		NesTM-H (Hash + ABV)	
		Common Case	Worst Case	Common Case	Worst Case
Read	$O(1)$	$\sim O(1)$	$O(d)$	$\sim O(1)$	$O(d)$
Write	$O(1)$	$\sim O(1)$	$O(d \cdot (R + d))$	$\sim O(1)$	$O(d)$
Commit	$O(R + W)$	$\sim O(R + W)$	$O(d \cdot R + W)$	$\sim O(R + W)$	$O(d + R + W)$

Table 1: A symbolic comparison of the common- and worst-case time complexity of TM barriers in baseline STM and NesTM. R, W, and d denote read-set size, write-set size, and nesting depth, respectively.

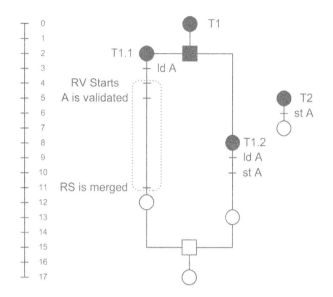

Figure 4: A potential serializability violation scenario due to the non-atomic commit.

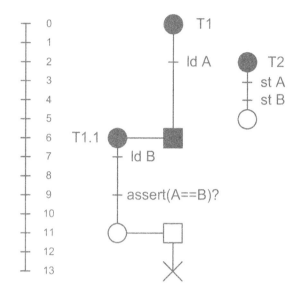

Figure 5: A problematic scenario due to a zombie transaction.

its ancestors (i.e., T1). T1.2 is valid because RV(T1.2)≥TS(A). T1 is not doomed because A is not yet in its read-set (i.e., T1.1's read-set has not been merged yet). Therefore, T1.2 can successfully write to A. At time 11, T1.1 merges its read-set to its parent's. At time 17, T1 successfully commits because it has an ownership for A (transferred from T1.2). However, this violates serializability because T1 eventually commits even when the two reads by T1.1 and T1.2 observe different versions of A.

Solution: The cause of this problem is that the commit process of T1.1 does not appear atomic to T1's descendants that validate T1 by calling ValidateReaders. To address this problem, we propose the *commit-lock* scheme. With this scheme, when a nested transaction attempts to commit, it must acquire the commit-lock of its parent. In addition, when a descendant validates its ancestor by calling ValidateReaders, it must also acquire the commit-lock of the validated ancestor. This ensures that the commit process of a transaction's child appears atomic to a validating descendant of the transaction. In the previous example, with the commit-lock scheme, T1.1's commit either happens *before* or *after* the validation by T1.2. In the first case, T1 will be doomed because RV(T1)<TS(A) and eventually aborted. In the second case, T1.1 will be aborted because A is owned by T1.2 when T1.1 attempts to commit. Therefore, no serializability violation occurs in both cases.

Performance impact: The commit-lock scheme essentially serializes the commits of child transactions. When a large number of child transactions simultaneously attempt to commit, performance can be hugely degraded due to the serialized commit.

Possible alternatives: We could also address this problem by introducing a *ValidationCounter* to each transaction. The Validation-

Counter increments every time when a transaction is validated by its descendant. When a child transaction attempts to commit, it samples the value of ValidationCounter of the parent. It then validates its read-set *without* acquiring the commit-lock of the parent. After the read-set validation, it acquires the commit-lock of the parent. It then compares the previously sampled value of ValidationCounter with the current value. If the two values match, it can safely merge its read-set to its parent's because it is guaranteed that there has been no validation by any descendant of the parent. If the two values differ, it releases the commit-lock of the parent and conservatively repeats the whole process. An evaluation of this alternative is left as future work.

4.3 Zombie Transactions

Problem: Figure 5 illustrates a problematic scenario due to a zombie transaction. Initially, GC=0 and TS(A)=TS(B)=0. At time 0, T1 starts (RV(T1)=0). At time 2, T2 starts (RV(T2)=0). Then, T2 writes to A and B at times 3 and 4. At time 5, T2 commits and GC=1 and TS(A)=TS(B)=1. At time 6, T1.1 starts (RV(T1.1)=1). At time 7, T1.1 can successfully read B because B's owner is the root and RV(T1.1)≥TS(B). However, if a programmer assumes that A is always equal to B within transactions and inserts an assertion check, the program will be unexpectedly terminated by failing the assertion check. Note that if T1 could reach to its commit, it would eventually abort, thus no serializability violation. Other well-known anomalies such as infinite loops can also occur. Currently, NesTM admits zombie transactions because we have not been able to find an efficient solution to avoid them in an unmanaged environment.

Feature	Description
Processors	In-order, single-issue, x86 cores
L1 Cache	64-KB, 64-byte line, private 4-way associative, 1 cycle latency
Network	256-bit bus, split transactions pipelined, MESI protocol
L2 Cache	8-MB, 64-byte line, shared 8-way associative, 10 cycle latency
Main Memory	100 cycles latency up to 8 outstanding transfers

Table 2: Parameters for the simulated CMP system.

# Threads	G	I	K	L	S	V	Y
1	13.9	13.9	3.7	0.1	7.2	22.2	4.7
2	11.5	17.4	3.6	0.1	6.5	21.6	3.4
4	15.6	14.6	3.9	0.1	5.6	21.9	-0.5
8	11.1	17.3	5.6	0.0	3.4	20.9	3.0
16	4.8	16.4	16.1	3.7	0.1	20.9	5.5

Table 3: Normalized performance difference (%) of NesTM relative to the baseline STM for STAMP applications. G, I, K, L, S, V, and Y indicate genome, intruder, kmeans, labyrinth, ssca2, vacation, and yada, respectively.

4.4 Correctness Status

At this point, we do not have a hand proof of the correctness (serializability) and liveness of the NesTM algorithm. Therefore, the correctness and liveness of the NesTM algorithm still remain *unchecked*. However, we hope that our paper will generate in-depth discussions on formally proving and verifying correctness and liveness guarantees of timestamp-based, concurrently-nested STM.

To establish some evidence of correctness, we have subjected the NesTM algorithm to exhaustive tests using our model checker (ChkTM) [3] and simulator. ChkTM verifies every possible execution of a small TM program running on the NesTM model. We configured ChkTM to generate every possible program with four threads (i.e., [1, 2, 1.1, 1.2]), each running only one transaction that performs at most two transactional memory operations (i.e., read or write), each accessing one of the two shared-memory words. ChkTM then explored every possible interleaving of every possible program. ChkTM, thus far, has not reported any serializability violation. Currently, ChkTM fails to verify NesTM with larger configurations (e.g., more threads or memory operations) due to the state space explosion.

To check the correctness and liveness of NesTM for a larger configuration, we performed extensive random tests by running a small microbenchmark on the implemented NesTM algorithm and simulator. The microbenchmark runs 14 concurrent threads (i.e., [1, 2, 1.1, 1.2, 2.1, 2.2, 1.1.1, 1.1.2, 1.2.1, 1.2.2, 2.1.1, 2.1.2, 2.2.1, 2.2.2]), each running one transaction that performs at most four transactional reads or writes to two shared-memory words. To better expose any potential bugs, we injected random delays at various points in the NesTM code (e.g., between lines 33 and 35 in Algorithm 1). The serializability checker compares the values observed by each transactional read and the final memory state of a concurrent run of the test program with the ones produced in a serial schedule. If this check fails, the checker reports a serializability violation. The liveness checker checks whether the test program successfully terminates or not. So far, NesTM has passed more than one million consecutive random tests without reporting any serializability or liveness violation.

5. EVALUATION

5.1 Methodology

We use an execution-driven simulator for x86 multi-core systems. Table 2 summarizes architectural parameters. All operations, except for loads and stores, have a CPI of 1.0, however all the details in the memory hierarchy timings are modeled, including contention and queueing events. We use the simulation results as our main results because they allow us to report results for larger CMP configurations and provide detailed performance breakdowns without perturbing the results.

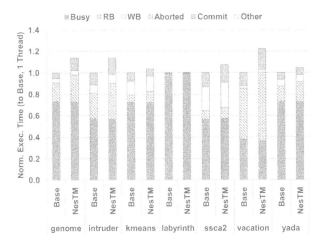

Figure 6: Execution time breakdowns of STAMP applications with 1 thread.

Our evaluation aims to answer the following three questions: **Q1:** What is the runtime overhead due to NesTM when we do not need nested parallelism (i.e., running only top-level transactions)? **Q2:** What is the incremental overhead if we push down the available parallelism to a deeper nesting level (NL)? **Q3:** How does nested parallelism improve application performance? Q1 and Q3 address the practicality of NesTM, while Q2 provides insights into the overheads and the issues that a nesting-aware runtime system should address.

For Q1, we use seven of the eight STAMP applications with the simulation datasets [6][1]. For Q2, we use two microbenchmarks that implement concurrent hash table (hashtable) and red-black tree (rbtree). Finally, for Q3, we use a microbenchmark, c-hashtable that uses composed hash tables. Further details on the benchmarks are provided later in this section.

5.2 Q1: Overhead for Top-Level Parallelism

Table 3 compares the baseline STM and NesTM running the STAMP benchmarks using only top-level transactions. It lists the normalized performance difference (NPD)[2] calculated using the following equation:

$$NPD(\%) = \frac{T_{NesTM} - T_{Base}}{T_{Base}} \times 100$$

Overall, Table 3 shows that the maximum NPD is about 20% across all benchmarks and thread counts. While NesTM barri-

---

[1]We exclude bayes because its non-deterministic behavior makes it difficult to compare results across STMs.
[2]A positive NPD means that NesTM is slower.

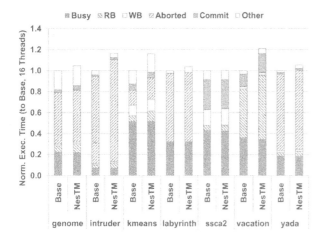

Figure 7: Execution time breakdowns of STAMP applications with 16 threads.

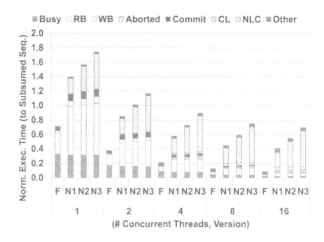

Figure 8: Execution time breakdowns of **hashtable**.

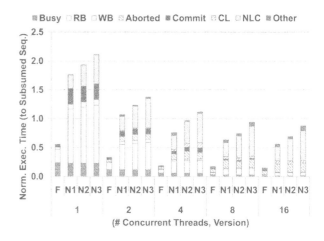

Figure 9: Execution time breakdowns of **rbtree**.

ers have additional code, some of it can be conditionally skipped when top-level transactions are used. To investigate the exact overheads further, we show the execution time breakdowns of STAMP applications in Figures 6 and 7. The execution time of each application is normalized to the execution time on the baseline STM with 1 (Figure 6) and 16 (Figure 7) threads, respectively. Execution time is broken into "busy" (useful instructions and cache misses), "RB" (read barriers), "WB" (write barriers), "aborted" (time spent on aborted transactions), "commit" (commit overhead), and "other" (work imbalance, etc.).

With 1 thread (Figure 6), NPD is relatively high (i.e., NesTM is slower) when transactions include a large number of TM barriers (e.g., intruder, vacation) [6]. This is mainly due to the extra overhead in NesTM barriers that cannot be amortized in this case. On the other hand, the overhead is negligible when very large transactions with few TM barriers are used (e.g., labyrinth). With more threads (Figure 7), more time is spent on aborted transactions with several applications (e.g., intruder, kmeans, yada). This is due to the validation that NesTM performs at the first write to each variable. This extra validation often detects conflicts more aggressively than the baseline STM, leading to more time spent on aborted transactions.

5.3 Q2: Incremental Overhead of Deeper Nesting

To study the incremental overhead of pushing down the available parallelism to deeper nesting levels (NLs), we use two microbenchmarks. hashtable and rbtree perform concurrent accesses to a hash table with 4K buckets and a red-black tree. Among 4K operations, 12.5% are inserts (writes) and 87.5% are look-ups (reads). Each benchmark has 4 versions. flat uses only top-level transactions, each performing 16 operations (hashtable) and 4 operations (rbtree). N1 pushes down the parallelism to NL=1, using the same code enclosed with one big outermost transaction[3]. N2 and N3 are implemented by adding more outer transactions in a repeated manner.

In Figures 8 and 9, we show the execution time breakdowns of hashtable and rbtree. The execution time of each microbenchmark is normalized to the execution time on an STM that flat-

---

[3]While flat and nested versions have different transactional semantics (i.e., whether to perform 4K operations atomically or not), we compare them to investigate performance issues.

tens and serializes nested transactions (i.e., performs all 4K operations sequentially in a top-level transaction). In addition to the segments explained in Section 5.2, each bar contains newly added segments: "CL" (time spent acquiring the commit locks of parents), and "NLC" (time spent committing non-leaf transactions).

We observe that NesTM continues to scale up to 16 threads. For example, N1 versions of hashtable and rbtree are faster than the subsumed version by 2.4× and 1.8× with 16 threads. Due to the larger number of conflicts, rbtree does not scale as well as hashtable. Figures 8 and 9 also reveal the three major performance challenges in NesTM. First, the runtime overhead of the read and write barriers of nested transactions is more expensive than those of top-level transactions. This is mainly due to more cache misses when accessing each entry in read- and write-sets. Since previously used entries in read- and write-sets of a transaction are merged to its parent, NesTM cannot exploit temporal locality on accessing transactional metadata when it runs nested transactions. In contrast, when top-level transactions are used, there is significant locality in metadata accesses. This performance issue might be mitigated using prefetching techniques.

Second, commit time increases linearly with the nesting level mainly due to the repeated read-set validation across different nesting levels. Alternatively, a runtime may choose different policies

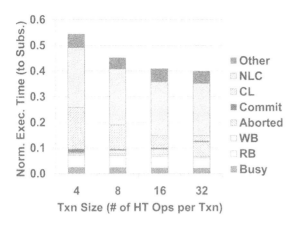

Figure 10: Execution time breakdowns of **hashtable** with various transaction sizes.

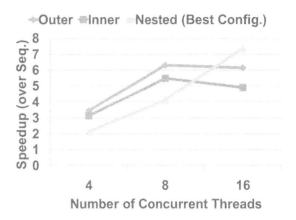

Figure 11: Scalability of the three versions of **c-hashtable**.

(e.g., serialization, reader-lock) depending on the nesting depth to achieve better performance. Finally, contention on the commit-locks of parents can become a performance bottleneck when a large number of nested transactions simultaneously commit. Since conflicts are infrequent in hashtable even with 16 threads, many child transactions can simultaneously commit and trigger this lock contention. In contrast, due to frequent conflicts in rbtree with 16 threads, this commit-lock contention is not a critical issue.

To understand the performance impact of transaction sizes, we measure the performance of hashtable by varying the transaction size from 4 to 32 operations per transaction. Figure 10 presents the normalized execution time with 16 threads. With smaller transactions (e.g., 4), a significant portion of the time is spent on the commit-lock contention because more (small) transactions simultaneously attempt to commit. With larger transactions (e.g., 32), the performance overhead due to the commit-lock contention is mitigated, while more time is spent on aborted (large) transactions.

To study how much work is required to amortize the overhead of nested transactions, we compare the performance of nested versions of hashtable with flat by varying the amount of computational workload in transactions. The amount of workload is proportional to the number of loop iterations. With little work, NPD is high due to the unamortized overhead of repeated read-set validation. One possible optimization is to use lightweight hardware support for validation [7]. With sufficient work, the overhead is amortized and nested versions comparably perform (e.g., N1: 39.7% with 1K iterations, N3: 9.9% with 10K iterations) to flat.

5.4 Q3: Improving Performance using Nested Parallelism

c-hashtable operates on a two-level structure with customer data with a single, first-level (L1) hash table and multiple, second-level (L2) hash tables. The L1 hash table stores customer information, and the L2 hash tables store customer orders. Each customer operation must be atomic including the updates to both levels. There are three ways in exploiting the parallelism in c-hashtable: (1) outer: parallelism in the L1 hash table across customers, (2) inner: parallelism in the L2 hash tables (multiple transactions from a single customer), and (3) nested: parallelism in both levels. Nested parallelism can be advantageous if each level alone (outer or inner) does not have sufficient parallelism to saturate a large-scale system.

In the experiment in Figure 11, the L1 hash table has 20 buckets and the L2 hash tables have 15 buckets. There are 256 randomly

generated customers and each customer places 32 orders. The three lines in Figure 11 show the speedup of outer, inner, and nested over the sequential run without TM barriers. At lower thread counts (e.g., 4), outer performs best due to rare conflicts and low overhead (e.g., thread synchronization, coarse-grain transactions). With 16 concurrent threads, however, nested performs best by efficiently exploiting the parallelism at both levels. Scalability of the other versions is limited mainly due to frequent conflicts at higher thread counts.

6. RELATED WORK

Moss and Hosking discussed the reference model for closed and open nesting in transactional memory and described preliminary architectural sketches [16]. In addition, they proposed a simpler model called linear nesting in which nested transactions run sequentially. There has been previous work on supporting linear nesting in HTM [14, 15] and STM [12, 17]. Our work differs since NesTM targets concurrent nesting.

Recently, there has been research on supporting nested parallelism in STM [2, 4, 18, 22]. Agrawal et al. proposed CWSTM, a theoretical STM algorithm that supports nested parallel transactions with the lowest upper bound of time complexity [2]. In [4], Barreto et al. proposed a practical implementation of the CWSTM algorithm. While achieving depth-independent time complexity of TM barriers, their work builds upon rather complex data structures such as concurrent stacks that could introduce additional runtime (especially to top-level transactions) and state overheads [4]. In contrast, NesTM extends a timestamp-based STM. Ramadan and Witchel proposed SSTM, a lazy STM-based design that supports nested parallel transactions [18]. However, their work extends a lazy STM and does not provide a detailed performance analysis. Our algorithm differs by extending an eager STM that has lower baseline overheads. Finally, Volos et al. proposed NePaLTM that supports nested parallelism inside transactions [22]. While efficiently supporting nested parallelism when no or low transactional synchronization is used, NePaLTM serially executes nested parallel transactions using mutual exclusion locks. In contrast, NesTM implements concurrent execution of nested transactions.

7. CONCLUSION AND FUTURE WORK

This paper presented NesTM, an STM system that extends a state-of-the-art eager STM with closed-nested parallel transactions. NesTM is designed to keep state and runtime overheads small. We also discussed the subtle corner cases of concurrent nesting. Finally, we evaluated the performance of NesTM across multiple scenarios. Our future work will focus on a more rigorous correctness argument. We will also investigate how to improve the performance of NesTM by exploring alternative implementations, nesting-aware contention management, and lightweight hardware support.

Acknowledgements

We would like to thank Richard Yoo and the anonymous reviewers for their feedback. We also want to thank Sun Microsystems for making the TL2 code available. Woongki Baek was supported by a Samsung Scholarship and an STMicroelectronics Stanford Graduate Fellowship. This work was supported by NSF Awards number 0546060, the Stanford Pervasive Parallelism Lab, and the Gigascale Systems Research Center (GSRC).

8. REFERENCES

[1] The OpenMP Application Program Interface Specification, version 3.0. http://www.openmp.org, May 2008.

[2] K. Agrawal, J. T. Fineman, and J. Sukha. Nested parallelism in transactional memory. In *PPoPP '08: Proceedings of the 13th ACM SIGPLAN Symposium on Principles and practice of parallel programming*, pages 163–174, New York, NY, USA, 2008. ACM.

[3] W. Baek, N. Bronson, C. Kozyrakis, and K. Olukotun. Implementing and Evaluating a Model Checker for Transactional Memory Systems. In *ICECCS '10: Proceedings of the 15th IEEE International Conference on Engineering of Complex Computing Systems*, March 2010.

[4] J. Barreto, A. Dragojević, P. Ferreira, R. Guerraoui, and M. Kapalka. Leveraging parallel nesting in transactional memory. In *PPoPP '10: Proceedings of the 15th ACM SIGPLAN symposium on Principles and practice of parallel programming*, pages 91–100, New York, NY, USA, 2010. ACM.

[5] R. Blikberg and T. Sorevik. Load balancing and OpenMP implementation of nested parallelism. *Parallel Comput.*, 31(10-12):984–998, 2005.

[6] C. Cao Minh, J. Chung, C. Kozyrakis, and K. Olukotun. STAMP: Stanford transactional applications for multi-processing. In *IISWC '08: Proceedings of The IEEE International Symposium on Workload Characterization*, September 2008.

[7] C. Cao Minh, M. Trautmann, J. Chung, A. McDonald, N. Bronson, J. Casper, C. Kozyrakis, and K. Olukotun. An effective hybrid transactional memory system with strong isolation guarantees. In *Proceedings of the 34th Annual International Symposium on Computer Architecture*. June 2007.

[8] D. Dice, O. Shalev, and N. Shavit. Transactional locking II. In *DISC'06: Proceedings of the 20th International Symposium on Distributed Computing*, March 2006.

[9] D. Dice and N. Shavit. Understanding tradeoffs in software transactional memory. In *CGO '07: Proceedings of the International Symposium on Code Generation and Optimization*, March 2007.

[10] P. Felber, C. Fetzer, and T. Riegel. Dynamic performance tuning of word-based software transactional memory. In *PPoPP '08: Proceedings of the 13th ACM SIGPLAN Symposium on Principles and practice of parallel programming*, pages 237–246, New York, NY, USA, 2008. ACM.

[11] T. Harris, M. Plesko, A. Shinnar, and D. Tarditi. Optimizing memory transactions. In *PLDI '06: Proceedings of the 2006 ACM SIGPLAN Conference on Programming Language Design and Implementation*, New York, NY, USA, 2006. ACM Press.

[12] T. Harris and S. Stipic. Abstract nested transactions. In *Second ACM SIGPLAN Workshop on Transactional Computing*, 2007.

[13] M. Herlihy and J. E. B. Moss. Transactional memory: Architectural support for lock-free data structures. In *Proceedings of the 20th International Symposium on Computer Architecture*, pages 289–300, 1993.

[14] A. McDonald, J. Chung, B. D. Carlstrom, C. Cao Minh, H. Chafi, C. Kozyrakis, and K. Olukotun. Architectural Semantics for Practical Transactional Memory. In *ISCA '06: Proceedings of the 33rd annual international symposium on Computer Architecture*, pages 53–65, Washington, DC, USA, June 2006. IEEE Computer Society.

[15] M. J. Moravan, J. Bobba, K. E. Moore, L. Yen, M. D. Hill, B. Liblit, M. M. Swift, and D. A. Wood. Supporting nested transactional memory in LogTM. In *Proceedings of the 12th international conference on Architectural support for programming languages and operating systems*, pages 359–370, New York, NY, USA, 2006. ACM Press.

[16] J. E. B. Moss and T. Hosking. Nested Transactional Memory: Model and Preliminary Architecture Sketches. In *OOPSLA 2005 Workshop on Synchronization and Concurrency in Object-Oriented Languages (SCOOL)*. University of Rochester, October 2005.

[17] Y. Ni, V. S. Menon, A.-R. Adl-Tabatabai, A. L. Hosking, R. L. Hudson, J. E. B. Moss, B. Saha, and T. Shpeisman. Open nesting in software transactional memory. In *PPoPP '07: Proceedings of the 12th ACM SIGPLAN symposium on Principles and Practice of Parallel Programming*, pages 68–78, New York, NY, USA, 2007. ACM Press.

[18] H. E. Ramadan and E. Witchel. The Xfork in the Road to Coordinated Sibling Transactions. In *The Fourth ACM SIGPLAN Workshop on Transactional Computing (TRANSACT 09)*, February 2009.

[19] B. Saha, A.-R. Adl-Tabatabai, R. L. Hudson, C. Cao Minh, and B. Hertzberg. McRT-STM: A high performance software transactional memory system for a multi-core runtime. In *PPoPP '06: Proceedings of the 11th ACM SIGPLAN symposium on Principles and practice of parallel programming*, New York, NY, USA, March 2006. ACM Press.

[20] Supercomputing Technologies Group, Massachusetts Institute of Technology Laboratory for Computer Science. *Cilk 5.4.6 Reference Manual*, Nov. 2001.

[21] Y. Tanaka, K. Taura, M. Sato, and A. Yonezawa. Performance Evaluation of OpenMP Applications with Nested Parallelism. In *LCR '00: Languages, Compilers, and Run-Time Systems for Scalable Computers*, pages 100–112, London, UK, 2000. Springer-Verlag.

[22] H. Volos, A. Welc, A.-R. Adl-Tabatabai, T. Shpeisman, X. Tian, and R. Narayanaswamy. NePaLTM: Design and Implementation of Nested Parallelism for Transactional Memory Systems. In *ECOOP*, 2009.

Transactions in the Jungle*

Rachid Guerraoui
EPFL Switzerland
rachid.guerraoui@epfl.ch

Thomas A. Henzinger
IST Austria
tah@ist.ac.at

Michał Kapałka
EPFL Switzerland
michal.kapalka@epfl.ch

Vasu Singh
IST Austria
vasu.singh@ist.ac.at

ABSTRACT

Transactional memory (TM) has shown potential to simplify the task of writing concurrent programs. Inspired by classical work on databases, formal definitions of the semantics of TM executions have been proposed. Many of these definitions assumed that accesses to shared data are solely performed through transactions. In practice, due to legacy code and concurrency libraries, transactions in a TM have to share data with non-transactional operations. The semantics of such interaction, while widely discussed by practitioners, lacks a clear formal specification. Those interactions can vary, sometimes in subtle ways, between TM implementations and underlying memory models.

We propose a correctness condition for TMs, *parametrized opacity*, to formally capture the now folklore notion of strong atomicity by stipulating the two following intuitive requirements: first, every transaction appears as if it is executed instantaneously with respect to other transactions and non-transactional operations, and second, non-transactional operations conform to the given underlying memory model. We investigate the inherent cost of implementing parametrized opacity. We first prove that parametrized opacity requires either instrumenting non-transactional operations (for most memory models) or writing to memory by transactions using potentially expensive read-modify-write instructions (such as compare-and-swap). Then, we show that for a class of practical relaxed memory models, parametrized opacity can indeed be implemented with constant-time instrumentation of non-transactional writes and no instrumentation of non-transactional reads. We show that, in practice, parametrizing the notion of correctness allows developing more efficient TM implementations.

Categories and Subject Descriptors

D.1.3 [**Programming Techniques**]: Concurrent Programming; D.2.4 [**Software Engineering**]: Software/Program Verification

*This research was supported by the Swiss National Science Foundation and by the Velox FP7 European project.

General Terms

Theory, Verification

Keywords

Transactional memory, memory models, correctness

1. INTRODUCTION

Transactional memory (TM) [15, 25] offers a promising paradigm for concurrent programming in the multi-core era. A TM allows a programmer to think in terms of coarse-grained code blocks—transactions—that appear to be executed atomically; and at the same time, a TM yields a high level of parallelism. The mutual interaction between transactions is formalized by the notion of *serializability* [22] or *opacity* [13]. Serializability, a common correctness notion in database transactions, requires that committed transactions look as if they executed sequentially. But, it was observed [8, 14] that serializability is not sufficient for memory transactions, where it is important that even aborted transactions do not observe an inconsistent state of the memory. This gave rise to a new correctness criterion called opacity. The idea of opacity is to give programmers an illusion that there is no concurrency between transactions, whether committed or aborted. That is, opacity requires that all transactions "look like" they executed in some sequential order, consistent with their real-time order. Most of the TM implementations [8, 14] satisfy opacity. The formal definition of opacity has allowed for a clear understanding of transactions [13] and also for development of model checking techniques for TM algorithms [10, 11, 12].

Ideally, a program could execute all operations on shared data within transactions, and have non-transactional operations on thread-local data. In practice, however, due to the presence of legacy code and concurrency libraries, and due to programming idioms like privatization and publication, transactions have to interact with non-transactional operations [1, 7, 9, 29, 19, 21, 26, 20]. Moreover, demanding segregation of transactional data from non-transactional data poses an additional burden on the programmer. The interaction between transactions and non-transactional operations has been expressed using a notion of *strong atomicity* [19, 17] in the literature. The intuition behind strong atomicity is that transactions execute atomically with respect to other transactions and non-transactional operations. Unfortunately, strong atomicity has not been formally defined, which has thus led to multiple interpretations [28]. Consider, for example, the execution depicted in Figure 1 (adapted from [9]). The transaction executed by thread 1 updates variables x and y. Thread 2 reads the variables x and y non-transactionally. Is it possible that thread 2 reads x as 1 and y as 0? According to the definition by Martin et al. [19], strong atom-

Thread 1	Thread 2
atomic {	
$\quad x := 1$	
$\quad y := 1$	$r_1 := x$
}	$r_2 := y$

Figure 1: Can $r_1 = 1$ and $r_2 = 0$? It depends on the memory model (initially $x = y = 0$).

icity allows this result. But, according to the definition of strong atomicity by Larus et al. [17], this result is not allowed. The ambiguity in this definition can be attributed to an implicit assumption on the interaction between non-transactional operations, which in turn, depends upon the underlying memory model [2]. A *memory model* specifies the set of allowed behaviors of memory accesses in a shared memory program. A relaxed memory model allows the underlying system to reorder memory instructions, while a stringent memory model like sequential consistency enforces instructions to execute in program order. While Martin et al. [19] assume a relaxed memory model which allows reordering independent reads (for example, RMO [30]), Larus et al. [17] assume a sequentially consistent memory model.

We provide a general formal framework for describing the interactions between transactions and non-transactional operations. We consider opacity as a correctness condition for transactions, and parametrize it by a memory model. We claim that while a TM can be implemented in a way to ensure opacity for transactions, there is little one can do (on a given platform or run-time environment) to change the underlying memory model. Hence, it is desirable to define opacity *parametrized* by a memory model. Moreover, we want the definition of parametrized opacity to be implementation-agnostic (like opacity), so that it allows for transactional objects with semantics richer than that of simple read-write variables.

We present a definition of a memory model which is general enough to capture a variety of memory models. Intuitively, we formalize a memory model as a function which, depending upon the sequence of operations, gives the set of possible orders of operations. Our formalism can capture common memory models like TSO, PSO, RMO [30], and Alpha [27]. Moreover, we allow different processes to observe different orders of operations, which allows us to capture memory models with non-atomic stores, like IA-32 [6]. We classify memory models on the basis of the possible reorderings of operations they allow.

Our formalization of parametrized opacity is guided by the following intuition:

Opacity for transactions. Whatever the memory model is, executions that are purely transactional must ensure opacity. Indeed, the semantics of transactions should be intuitive and strong—in the end, we want TMs to be as easy to use as coarse-grained locking. Consider Figure 2(a). Thread 2 should observe x as 0 or 2, because the intermediate state of a transaction ($x = 1$) is not visible to other transactions. Also, y can be observed as 0 or 2. Moreover, y can be observed as 2 only if x is observed as 2, because the effect of transactions is visible in real-time order. Thus, the possible values of z are 0 and 2. Note that even if thread 2 aborts, opacity requires that z is 0 or 2.

Efficiency of non-transactional operations. Executions that are purely non-transactional have to adhere to the given memory model. In particular, parametrized opacity should not strengthen the semantics of non-transactional operations. The motivation here is to avoid a framework that would inherently require non-transactional operations to be instrumented with additional memory fences or software barriers, even for very weak memory mod-

els. This supports the ideology of software memory models like Java which inherently provide weak guarantees, and require special synchronization for stronger guarantees. In Figure 2(b), a memory model may relax the order of write operations in Thread 1 or the read operations in Thread 2, resulting in $r_1 = 1$ and $r_2 = 0$.

Isolation of transactions from non-transactional operations. Transactions should appear, both to other transactions and non-transactional operations, as if they were executed instantaneously. In particular, isolation of transactions should be respected, regardless of the memory model. The intermediate computations of transactions, or updates by aborted transactions, should never be visible to non-transactional operations. Moreover, the non-transactional operations concurrent to a transaction should appear as if they happened before or after this transaction. In Figure 2(c), Thread 2 cannot observe an intermediate state of a transaction, and thus $z \neq 1$. Moreover, the effect of a non-transactional operation cannot show up in the middle of a transaction. Thus, $r_1 = r_2$.

Note that opacity parametrized by sequential consistency gives the notion of strong atomicity as proposed by Larus et al. [17]. On the other hand, parametrized opacity for a relaxed memory model like RMO matches the notion of strong atomicity given by Martin et al. [19].

In practice, TM implementations that guarantee strong atomicity require that non-transactional operations, instead of accessing memory directly, adhere to an access protocol as defined by the TM implementation. This modification of the semantics of non-transactional operations is known as *instrumentation*. For example, Tabatabai et al. [26] propose a TM implementation, where the non-transactional read and write operations follow the locking discipline as required by the transactions. The formal definition of opacity parametrized by a memory model allows us to theoretically analyze the cost of creating TM implementations that guarantee parametrized opacity. While parametrized opacity is the intuitive correctness property for transactional programs with non-transactional operations, we show that, without instrumentation, it cannot be achieved on most memory models. Even for the small class of idealized memory models, where parametrized opacity can be achieved without instrumentation, we show that a TM implementation *must* use expensive read-modify-write operations for each object read and modified by a transaction.

Next, we focus on TM implementations that instrument non-transactional write operations, without any instrumentation for non-transactional read operations. We start with a basic result that shows that for memory models that allow reordering independent reads, it is possible to achieve parametrized opacity without instrumenting the read operations, and treating every non-transactional write as a transaction in itself. Note that this might not provide a practical solution, as we do not want a non-transactional operation to carry the overhead associated with a transaction. Moreover, we want non-transactional operations to finish in bounded time, while a transaction, in general, may take arbitrarily long to finish. The next question we ask is whether we can obtain parametrized opacity for a class of memory models with constant-time instrumentation on the writes? We show that for a class of memory models that allows reordering a read of a variable following a read or write of another variable (like Alpha [27] and Java [18]), it is indeed possible to achieve parametrized opacity with constant-time instrumentation for non-transactional write operations. We also discuss how to adapt the constant-time write instrumentation solution for memory models that do not allow to reorder data-dependent reads (like RMO [30]).

Using our theoretical framework, we examine existing TM implementations that guarantee parametrized opacity. TM implemen-

Thread 1	Thread 2
$atomic$ {	
$\quad x := 1$	
$\quad x := 2$	$atomic$ {
}	$\quad z := x - y$
$atomic$ {	}
$\quad y := 2$	
}	

(a) Can $z < 0$?

Thread 1	Thread 2
$x := 1$	$r_1 := y$
$y := 1$	$r_2 := x$

(b) Can $r_1 = 1$ and $r_2 = 0$?

Thread 1	Thread 2
$atomic$ {	$z := x$
$\quad x := 1$	
$\quad x := 2$	
}	
$atomic$ {	
$\quad r_1 := z$	
$\quad r_2 := z$	
}	

(c) Can $z = 1$ or $r_1 \neq r_2$?

Figure 2: Motivating examples for the definition of parametrized opacity (initially $x = y = z = 0$ in every case)

tations in the literature that satisfy strong atomicity [26], in fact, are implemented with sequential consistency of non-transactional operations in mind. We observe that a TM implementation can be designed to be more efficient, if it is to satisfy opacity parametrized by a weaker memory model. We extract the key practical ideas from our proofs which shall help to design more efficient TM implementations that guarantee opacity parametrized by relaxed memory models.

2. PRELIMINARIES

We first describe a framework of a shared memory system consisting of shared objects and operations on those objects.

Operations. We consider a shared-memory system consisting of a set P of processes that communicate by executing commands on a set Obj of shared objects. Let C be a set of commands on shared objects, where arguments and return values are treated as part of a command. For example, in a system that supports only reading and writing of shared (natural number) variables, we have $C = \{\text{rd}, \text{wr}\} \times \mathbb{N}$. We define *operations* $O \subseteq C \times Obj$ as the set of all allowed command-object pairs. For ease of readability, we write (rd, v, x) and (wr, v, x) instead of, respectively, $((\text{rd}, v), x)$ and $((\text{wr}, v), x)$.

Besides commands on shared objects, every process $p \in P$ can execute the following special operations: start to start a new transaction, commit to commit the current transaction, and abort to abort the transaction. Let $\hat{O} = O \cup \{\text{start}, \text{commit}, \text{abort}\}$.

Object semantics. We use the concept of a *sequential specification* [16] to describe the semantics of objects. Given an object $x \in Obj$, we define the semantics $[\![x]\!] \subseteq C^*$ as the set of all sequences of commands on x that could be generated by a single process accessing x.

Example. Let x be a shared variable (with initial value 0) that supports only the commands to read and write its value. Then, $[\![x]\!]$ is a subset of $(\{\text{rd}, \text{wr}\} \times \mathbb{N})^*$, such that, for every sequence $c_1 \ldots c_n$ in $[\![x]\!]$, and for all $i, v \in \mathbb{N}$, if $c_i = (\text{rd}, v)$, then either (a) the latest write operation preceding c_i in $c_1 \ldots c_n$ is (wr, v), or (b) $v = 0$ and no write operation precedes c_i in $c_1 \ldots c_n$.

Histories. We define an *operation instance* as (o, p, k), where $o \in \hat{O}$ is an operation, $p \in P$ is a process that issues the operation, and $k \in \mathbb{N}$ is a natural number representing the identifier of the operation instance. A *history* $h \in (\hat{O} \times P \times \mathbb{N})^*$ is a sequence of operation instances such that, for every pair (o, p, i), (o', p', j) of operation instances in h, we have $i \neq j$. Intuitively, we want each operation instance in a history to have a unique identifier. For a natural number k, when we say "operation k", we mean "operation instance with identifier k", i.e., the element of h of the form (o, p, k), where $o \in \hat{O}$ and $p \in P$. A *transaction* of a process p is a subsequence $(o_1, p, i_1) \ldots (o_n, p, i_n)$ of a history h, such that (i) o_1 is a start operation, (ii) either operation i_n is the last oper-

ation instance of p in h, or $o_n \in \{\text{commit}, \text{abort}\}$, and (iii) all operations $o_2, \ldots, o_{n-1}$ belong to set O. A transaction T is *committed* (resp. *aborted*) in a history h if the last operation instance of T has a commit operation (resp. an abort operation). A transaction T is *completed* if T is committed or aborted. Given a history h and a natural number k, we say that operation k is *transactional* in h if operation k is part of a transaction in h. Otherwise, operation k is said to be *non-transactional*. We assume that every history h is *well-formed*: that is, every non-transactional operation in h belongs to set O. Intuitively, well-formedness of a history requires that every commit and abort of a transaction matches a corresponding start, and that there are no nested transactions. We denote by H the set of all histories.

Given a history h, we define the *real-time* partial order relation $\prec_h \subset \mathbb{N} \times \mathbb{N}$ of the operation identifiers in h, such that, for two natural numbers i and j, we have $i \prec_h j$, if:
(i) operations i and j belong to transactions T and T', respectively, where T is completed in h and the last operation instance of T precedes the first operation instance of T' in h, or
(ii) operation i precedes operation j in h, both operations are executed by the same process, and at least one of those operation instances is transactional.

Sequential histories. We say that a history h is *sequential* if, for every transaction T in h, every operation instance between the start operation instance of T and the last operation instance of T in h is a part of T. That is, intuitively, no transaction overlaps with another transaction or with any non-transactional operation in h. We say that a sequential history s *respects* a partial or a total order $\prec \subseteq \mathbb{N} \times \mathbb{N}$ if, for every pair (i, j), if $i \prec j$ then operation i precedes operation j in s.

Let s be a sequential history. We denote by $s|_x$ the subsequence of all commands invoked on object x in s. We say that s is *legal* if, for every object x, we have $s|_x \in [\![x]\!]$. We denote by *visible*(s) the longest subsequence of s that does not contain any operation instance of a non-committed transaction T, except if T is not followed in s by any other transaction or non-transactional operation instance. We say that an operation k in s is *legal* in s if history *visible*(s') is legal, where s' is the prefix of s that ends with operation k.

Example. Consider the history h depicted in Figure 3(a). The transaction of process p_1 finishes before the transaction of process p_3 starts. The precedence relation $\prec_h$ consists of elements $(1, 2)$, $(5, 7)$, $(1, 9)$, and many more. On the other hand, $(1, 6)$ and $(6, 9)$ are not in $\prec_h$. An example of a sequential history is given in Figure 3(b). Note that s respects $\prec_h$. History s is legal if $v = 0$ and $v' = 1$.

3. DEFINING PARAMETRIZED OPACITY

In this section, we first formalize the notion of a memory model. Then, we define parametrized opacity, i.e., opacity parametrized by

id	p_1	p_2	p_3
1	wr, 1, x		
2	start		
3		rd, 1, y	
4	wr, 1, y		
5	commit		
6		rd, v, x	
7			start
8			commit
9			rd, v', x

(a) History h

id	p_1	p_2	p_3
6		rd, v, x	
1	wr, 1, x		
2	start		
4	wr, 1, y		
5	commit		
3			rd, 1, y
7			start
8			commit
9			rd, v', x

(b) Sequential history s

Figure 3: An example of a history and a sequential history. Every history is read top to bottom. Notation: wr, 1, x in the column marked with process p and in the row marked with id k stands for the operation instance $(((wr, 1), x), p, k)$.

a given memory model. Finally, we give a classification of memory models based on the reorderings of operations they allow.

3.1 A Memory Model

A memory model describes the semantics of memory accesses in a shared memory system. We formalize a memory model as a per-process reordering of the history. The memory model is defined in such a way that it allows different processes to have different views of the history, similar to the formalism by Sarkar et al. [24].

We define a *process view* as a function $view : P \to 2^{\mathbb{N} \times \mathbb{N}}$ such that $view(p)$ is a partial order on the set of natural numbers for every process $p \in P$. Let V be the set of all process views. A *memory model* is given by the function $M : H \to 2^V$ that maps a history to a set of process views. Intuitively, a process view allows different processes to observe different orders of operations in a given history. This helps capturing memory models that allow non-atomic stores, e.g., IA-32 [6].

Well-formed memory models. A memory model M is *well-formed* if, for every history $h \in H$, every view $view \in M(h)$, every process $p \in P$, and every pair $(i, j) \in view(p)$: (i) operations i and j are non-transactional in h, (ii) i precedes j in h, and (iii) $(j, i) \notin view(p')$ for every process $p' \in P$. Intuitively, condition (i) requires that a memory model imposes an order only on non-transactional operations, condition (ii) requires that a view does not force a process to observe some operations out of program order, and condition (iii) requires that a view does not force two processes to observe operations in different orders.[1] All memory models we know of are indeed well-formed.

Capturing dependence of operations. Often, memory models disallow reordering two operations if the latter one is control- or data-dependent on the former one [18, 30]. To capture those memory models, we distinguish between dependent and independent operation instances. We do so by using additional commands: $\{cdrd, ddrd, cdwr, ddwr\} \times \mathbb{N} \times 2^{\mathbb{N}}$. For example, an operation instance (o, p, k) in h with $o = ((cdrd, v, \{k_1, \ldots, k_n\}), x)$ denotes a read operation which reads value v from variable x, and is control-dependent on operations $k_1 \ldots k_n$ in h.

Examples. We consider histories with only read and write operations on shared variables. We say that a view $view$ is identical across processes, if $view(p) = view(p')$ for all processes $p, p' \in P$.

Sequential consistency M_{SC} requires that the order of opera-

tions of a process in a history is preserved in every view, and all processes view an identical order of operations of different processes. Formally, for all histories h, we have $view \in M_{SC}(h)$ if (a) $view$ is identical across processes, and (b) for every process $p \in P$, and every pair (o_1, p, i), (o_2, p, j) of non-transactional operations such that operation i precedes operation j in h, we have $(i, j) \in view(p)$.

Total store order M_{tso} allows a write operation to forward the value of a variable to a following read operation, and allows reordering of a write operation followed by a read operation to a different variable. Formally, for every history h, we have $view \in M_{tso}(h)$ if (a) $view$ is identical across processes, and (b) for every process p, and for every pair (o_1, p, i), (o_2, p, j) of non-transactional operations such that operation i precedes operation j in h, we have $(i, j) \in view(p)$ if one of following conditions holds:

(i) o_2 is a write operation,

(ii) o_1 and o_2 are to the same object x, or

(iii) o_1 is a read operation of the form (rd, v, x) such that (wr, v, x) is not the last preceding write operation to x by process p in h.

The intuition for the last case is to allow two read operations to different variables to be reordered if the first read obtains the value from a store buffer.

Relaxed memory order allows reordering of reads to the same variable. It also allows reordering of read and write operations to different variables, unless the first operation is a read, and the second operation is either a write control/data-dependent on the first operation, or a read data-dependent on the first operation. RMO is specified by the memory model M_{rmo} such that, for every history h, we have $view \in M_{rmo}(h)$ if (a) $view$ is identical across processes, and (b) for every process p, and for every pair (o_1, p, i), (o_2, p, j) of non-transactional operations such that operation i precedes operation j in h, we have $(i, j) \in view(p)$ if one of the following conditions holds:

(i) o_1 and o_2 are to the same object x, and one of them is a write,

(ii) o_1 is a read of a variable x and $o_2 = ((cdwr, v, K), y)$ or $o_2 = ((ddwr, v, K), y)$ for some $v \in \mathbb{N}$ and $K \subseteq \mathbb{N}$ such that $i \in K$, or

(iii) o_1 is a read of a variable x and $o_2 = ((ddrd, v, K), y)$ for some $v \in \mathbb{N}$ and $K \subseteq \mathbb{N}$ such that $i \in K$.

3.2 Parametrized Opacity

We now define the notion of parametrized opacity, i.e., opacity parametrized by a given memory model. Recall that, intuitively, parametrized opacity requires that (1) every transaction appears as if it took place instantaneously between its first and last operation, and (2) non-transactional operations ensure the requirements specified by the given memory model.

We say that a history h ensures *opacity parametrized by a memory model* M, if there exists a total order $\ll$ on the set of transactional operations in h and a process view $view \in M(h)$, such that, for every process $p \in P$, there exists a sequential history s that satisfies the following conditions: (i) s is a permutation of h, (ii) s respects relation $\ll \cup \prec_h \cup view(p)$, and (iii) every operation is legal in s.

Example. The history h depicted in Figure 3(a) is parametrized opaque with respect to memory model M_{SC} if $v = 1$ and $v' = 1$. This is because: (a) operation 3 reads the value of y as 1 which is written by the transaction of process p_1, (b) operation 1 writes x as 1 before the transaction, and (c) SC requires that p_2 reads x after y. Moreover, h is parametrized opaque with respect to memory model M_{rmo} if v is either 0 or 1, and $v' = 1$. This is because RMO allows reordering of reads of different variables.

---

[1]Note that condition (iii) does not disallow non-atomic stores, where different processes *may* observe stores in different orders. The condition disallows memory models that *force* processes to observe different orders.

3.3 Classes of Memory Models

We now present a classification of memory models on the basis of reorderings they allow. We build the following four classes depending upon the restrictions posed by the memory model.

We define the class *read-read restrictive memory models*, denoted by M_{rr}, as the set of memory models M such that for all histories h, for all $i, j \in \mathbb{N}$, if operation i is a read operation to x and operation j is a read operation to y such that $x \neq y$, and both operations i, j are by process p, then for all process views $view \in M(h)$, for all $p' \in P$, we have $(i, j) \in view(p')$. Intuitively, M_{rr} restricts the order of read operations to different variables.

We define the class *read-write restrictive memory models*, denoted by M_{rw}, as the set of memory models M such that for all histories h, for all $i, j \in \mathbb{N}$, if operation i is a read operation to x and operation j is a write operation to y such that $x \neq y$, and both operations i, j are by process p, then for all process views $view \in M(h)$, for all $p' \in P$, we have $(i, j) \in view(p')$.

Analogously, we define the class *write-read restrictive memory models* M_{wr} and the class *write-write restrictive memory models* M_{ww}.

Examples. The SC memory model M_{SC} is in $M_{rr} \cap M_{rw} \cap M_{wr} \cap M_{ww}$. The TSO memory model M_{tso} is in $M_{rr} \cap M_{rw} \cap M_{ww}$ and $M_{tso} \notin M_{wr}$. The partial store order (PSO) memory model M_{pso} is in $M_{rr} \cap M_{rw}$ and $M_{pso} \notin M_{ww} \cup M_{wr}$. Note that these classes do not impose any restrictions on views of different processes, and thus memory models which allow non-atomic stores (like IA-32 [6]) can also be classified under these classes. For example, the IA-32 memory model has a similar classification as TSO.

4. TM IMPLEMENTATIONS

We now define a TM implementation $\mathcal{I}$, and when a given TM implementation ensures opacity parametrized by a given memory model M. Intuitively, $\mathcal{I}$ ensures opacity parametrized by M if every history *generated* by $\mathcal{I}$ ensures opacity parametrized by M. We thus need to define what a TM implementation is, and precisely which histories are generated by a given TM implementation.

Instructions. We start by defining hardware primitives that a TM implementation is allowed to use. Let *Addr* be a set of memory addresses. We define the set *In* of *instructions* as follows, where $a \in Addr$ and $v, v' \in \mathbb{N}$:

$$In ::= \langle \text{load } a, v \rangle \mid \langle \text{store } a, v \rangle \mid \langle \text{cas } a, v, v' \rangle$$

We call the store and CAS instructions update instructions. An operation of a history corresponds to a sequence of instructions. To know the begin and end points of an operation at the level of hardware, we use two special instructions $\triangleright, \triangleleft$ for each operation. For every operation $o \in \hat{O}$, we denote the *invocation* (instruction) of o as $(\triangleright, o)$, and the *response* (instruction) of o as $(\triangleleft, o)$. Let $\hat{In} = In \cup (\{\triangleright, \triangleleft\} \times O)$.

Traces. We define an *instruction instance* as (in, p, k), where $in \in \hat{In}$ is an instruction, $p \in P$ is the process that issues the instance, and $k \in \mathbb{N}$ is an operation identifier. A *trace* $r \in (\hat{In} \times P \times \mathbb{N})^*$ is a sequence of instruction instances. Let $k \in \mathbb{N}$ be an operation identifier. A *complete operation trace* of operation k is a sequence of the form $((\triangleright, o), p, k) (in_1, p, k) \ldots (in_m, p, k) ((\triangleleft, o), p, k)$, where $p \in P$ is a process, $o \in \hat{O}$ is an operation, and $in_1 \ldots in_m \in In$ are instructions. An *incomplete operation trace* of operation k is a sequence of the form $((\triangleright, o), p, k) (in_1, p, k) \ldots (in_m, p, k)$, where $p \in P$, $o \in \hat{O}$, and $in_1 \ldots in_m \in In$.

Let r be a trace. Given a process $p \in P$, we denote by $r|_p$ the longest subsequence of instruction instances in r issued by pro-

id	p_1	p_2
1	$(\triangleright, \text{start})$	
1	$\langle \text{cas } g, 0, 1 \rangle$	
2		$(\triangleright, (\text{rd}, 1, x))$
1	$(\triangleleft, \text{start})$	
2		$\langle \text{load } x, 1 \rangle$
3	$(\triangleright, (\text{wr}, 1, x))$	
2		$(\triangleleft, (\text{rd}, 1, x))$
3	$\langle \text{store } a_x, 1 \rangle$	
3	$(\triangleleft, (\text{wr}, 1, x))$	
4	$(\triangleright, \text{commit})$	
4	$\langle \text{store } g, 0 \rangle$	
4	$(\triangleleft, \text{commit}))$	

(a) Trace r

id	p_1	p_2
1	start	
2		rd, 1, x
3	wr, 1, x	
4	commit	

(b) History h_1

id	p_1	p_2
2		rd, 1, x
1	start	
3	wr, 1, x	
4	commit	

(c) History h_2

Figure 4: A trace and corresponding histories. Notation for trace: in **in column** p **and row marked with id** k **represents the instruction instance** (in, p, k)

cess p. We assume that every trace r satisfies the following property: for every process $p \in P$, the sequence $r|_p$ is a sequence of complete operation traces, possibly ending with an incomplete operation trace. We say that a history h *corresponds* to a trace r if:

(i) given any natural number k, an operation (o, p, k) is in h if and only if there is an instruction instance $((\triangleright, o), p, k)$ in r, and
(ii) operation k occurs before operation j if some instruction instance with identifier k occurs in r before some instruction instance with identifier j.

Intuitively, a history h that corresponds to a trace r represents the logical order of operations in r. If we assign a point in time to every instruction in r, and every operation in h, then every operation (o, p, k) in h must be somewhere in between the corresponding invocation instruction $((\triangleright, o), p, k)$ and response instruction $((\triangleleft, o), p, k)$ in r.

Example. Consider the trace r shown in Figure 4(a). In r, the start operation issues a CAS instruction to address g to change the value from 0 to 1, and the commit instruction stores value 0 to g. Histories h_1 and h_2 are two examples of histories that correspond to r. In the trace given in Figure 4(a), the (single) invocation instance of process p_2 is non-transactional, while all invocation instances of process p_1 are transactional in r.

A trace r is *well-formed* if every history h corresponding to r is well-formed. We assume that every trace is well-formed. Let r be a trace, and p be a process. A *transaction* T of p in r is a sequence in $r|_p$ of the form $((\triangleright, \text{start}), p, k) (in_1, p, k_1) \ldots (in_m, p, k_m)$, where the following conditions are satisfied:

- $in_m \in \{(\triangleleft, \text{commit}), (\triangleleft, \text{abort})\}$, or (in_m, p, k_m) is the last instruction instance of r_p, and

- for all j s.t. $1 \leq j < m$, we have $in_j \notin \{(\triangleright, \text{start}), (\triangleleft, \text{commit}), (\triangleleft, \text{abort})\}$

Moreover, T is committed (resp. aborted) if the last instruction instance in T is a response of a commit (resp. abort) operation. An instance $((\triangleright, o), p, k)$ of an invocation is said to be *transactional* in a trace r if it belongs to some transaction in r. Otherwise, the instance is said to be *non-transactional*.

TM implementations. A *TM implementation* $\mathcal{I} = \langle \mathcal{I}_T, \mathcal{I}_N \rangle$ is a pair, where $\mathcal{I}_T : \hat{O} \to 2^{In^*}$ is the implementation for transactional operations, and $\mathcal{I}_N : O \to 2^{In^*}$ is the implementation for non-transactional operations.

Let $\mathcal{I} = \langle \mathcal{I}_T, \mathcal{I}_N \rangle$ be a TM implementation. We say that a complete operation trace $((\triangleright, o), p, k) (in_1, p, k) \ldots (in_m, p, k)$

$((\triangleleft, o), p, k)$ is *transactionally* (resp. *non-transactionally*) generated by $\mathcal{I}$, if sequence $in_1 \dots in_m$ is in $\mathcal{I}_T(o)$ (resp. in $\mathcal{I}_N(o)$). We say that an incomplete operation trace $((\triangleright, o), p, k)$ (in_1, p, k) $\dots (in_m, p, k)$ is *transactionally* (resp. *non-transactionally*) generated by $\mathcal{I}$, if sequence $in_1 \dots in_m$ is a prefix of some element in $\mathcal{I}_T(o)$ (resp. in $\mathcal{I}_N(o)$).

Given a trace r and a TM implementation $\mathcal{I}$, we say that r is *generated* by $\mathcal{I}$ if for every transactional (resp. non-transactional) operation k in r, the complete or incomplete operation trace of operation k in r is transactionally (resp. non-transactionally) generated by $\mathcal{I}$.

Instrumentation. We say that a TM implementation $\mathcal{I} = \langle \mathcal{I}_T, \mathcal{I}_N \rangle$ is *uninstrumented* if for every variable x, we have $\mathcal{I}_N(\mathsf{rd}, v, x) = \{\langle \mathsf{load}\ a_x, v \rangle\}$ and $\mathcal{I}_N(\mathsf{wr}, v, x) = \{\langle \mathsf{store}\ a_x, v \rangle\}$, where a_x is the address of the global copy of variable x. Otherwise, the TM implementation is *instrumented*. Note that these terms refer only to the implementation of non-transactional operations.

Languages. We define the *language $L(\mathcal{I})$* of a TM implementation as the set of all traces generated by a TM implementation. We define that a TM implementation $\mathcal{I}$ *guarantees* opacity parametrized by a memory model M if, for every trace $r \in L(\mathcal{I})$, there is a history h that corresponds to r such that h ensures opacity parametrized by M.

Note that our definition of a trace does not require that after an instruction of the form $\langle \mathsf{store}\ a_x, v \rangle$, the subsequent load of a_x is of the form $\langle \mathsf{load}\ a_x, v \rangle$. Indeed, the underlying hardware may execute a relaxed memory model (which, in principle, may be different from the programmer's memory model at the level of operations). For example, a programmer may wish to guarantee opacity parametrized by sequential consistency on a hardware with memory model RMO. But for the sake of simplicity, in the following sections, we assume that the underlying hardware guarantees a strong memory model equivalent to linearizability, that is, every instruction is executed to completion when it is issued. Note that our impossibility results hold even when the underlying hardware executes a weaker memory model.

5. ACHIEVING PARAMETRIZED OPACITY

We use our theoretical framework to investigate the inherent cost of achieving opacity parametrized by a memory model.

5.1 Uninstrumented TM Implementations

We first study uninstrumented TM implementations, as those ones do not pose any overhead on non-transactional operations. We show that for most of the practical memory models, uninstrumented TM implementations cannot achieve parametrized opacity (Theorem 1). Moreover, we show that even to achieve opacity parametrized by very relaxed memory models, it is required that transactional write operations for variables read and modified are implemented as expensive compare-and-swap instructions (Theorem 2). Finally, we establish a complementary result to Theorem 1. We show that with an idealized memory model that relaxes the order of all operations to different variables, it is possible to obtain parametrized opacity with an uninstrumented TM implementation (Theorem 3).

We first prove an auxiliary lemma, which states that if a solo running committed transaction consists of a write operation, then the transaction must consist of a store or a compare-and-swap instruction.

Lemma 1. For every memory model M, an uninstrumented TM

implementation $\mathcal{I}$ guarantees parametrized opacity only if, for all traces $r \in L(\mathcal{I})$, and for every committing transaction T in r such that there is no instruction instance of another transaction between the first and last instruction instances of T in r, if there is an operation (wr, v, x) in T, then the transaction T in r contains an update instruction to a_x with value v.

PROOF. Let the value of a_x be initially 0. Consider the trace r depicted in Figure 5(a). Let T be the committed transaction of process p in r. We observe that T consists of an operation $o_1 = (\mathsf{wr}, v, x)$. Note that the invocation of the non-transactional operation $o_2 = (\mathsf{rd}, v', x)$ occurs after the last instruction of T, that is, the response of the commit operation. As the TM implementation $\mathcal{I}$ is uninstrumented, we have $\mathcal{I}_N(\mathsf{rd}, v', x) = \{\langle \mathsf{load}\ a_x, v' \rangle\}$. Note that as r has a single process, there is only one history h corresponding to r. By definition of $\prec_h$, we know that $o_1 \prec_h o_2$. Thus, to guarantee parametrized opacity, we must have $v = v'$. Thus, T must issue an update instruction to a_x with value v. □

Theorem 1. Given a memory model M such that $M \in (M_{rr} \cup M_{rw} \cup M_{wr} \cup M_{ww})$, there does not exist any uninstrumented TM implementation that guarantees opacity parametrized by M.

PROOF. By contradiction, we assume that there exists an uninstrumented TM implementation $\mathcal{I}$ that ensures opacity parametrized by a memory model $M \in (M_{rr} \cup M_{rw} \cup M_{wr} \cup M_{ww})$. We consider four cases, each corresponding to a different class of memory models, in each case showing a trace r of $\mathcal{I}$, involving two processes p_1 and p_2, that violates opacity parametrized by M. In the following, we assume that a_x and a_y are initialized to 0.

Case 1. Let $M \in M_{rr}$. That is, M does not allow reordering two read operations to different variables. Trace r is depicted in Figure 5(b). Let T consist of operations (wr, v_1, x) and (wr, v_2, y). Let $v_1 \neq 0$ and $v_2 \neq 0$. From Lemma 1, we know that T updates addresses a_x and a_y with values v_1 and v_2, respectively. Without loss of generality, we assume that a_x is updated before a_y.[2] Let the trace r consist of two non-transactional operations (rd, v_3, x) and (rd, v_4, y) issued by process p_2 (with identifiers j and k respectively). As $\mathcal{I}$ is uninstrumented, the non-transactional read operations are implemented as load instructions. Let the two load instructions $\langle \mathsf{load}\ a_x, v_3 \rangle$ and $\langle \mathsf{load}\ a_y, v_4 \rangle$ of process p_2 execute between the updates of a_x and a_y. Thus, we have $v_3 = v_1$ and $v_4 = 0$. Note that if T is an aborted transaction in r, then there is no history h corresponding to r such that h satisfies opacity parametrized by M. This is because operation j observes the update to a_x. Thus, T is a committed transaction in r. Consider an arbitrary history h corresponding to r. By definition of M_{rr}, every process view $view \in M(h)$ requires that $(j, k) \in view(p)$ for all $p \in P$. On the other hand, legality requires operation j to appear after T, and operation k to appear before T. Thus, there does not exist a sequential history which satisfies conditions (ii) and (iii) of parametrized opacity at the same time.

Case 2. Let $M \in M_{wr}$. That is, M does not allow reordering a write followed by a read operation to a different variable. The trace r is shown in Figure 5(c). Let T consist of operations $o_1 = (\mathsf{rd}, v_1, x)$ and $o_2 = (\mathsf{wr}, v_2, y)$. Let $v_2 \neq 0$. From Lemma 1, we know that T updates address a_y with value v_2. Let r consist of two non-transactional operations of p_2 in the order

---

[2]Figure 5(b) shows the updates as part of the commit operation. In general, the updates can happen anywhere during the transaction, but always as two separate instructions.

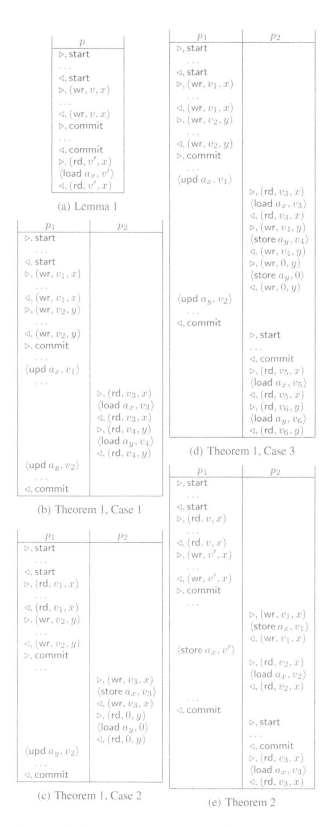

(a) Lemma 1

(b) Theorem 1, Case 1

(c) Theorem 1, Case 2

(d) Theorem 1, Case 3

(e) Theorem 2

Figure 5: Different traces r constructed in Lemma 1, Theorem 1, and Theorem 2. An $\langle \text{upd } a, v \rangle$ instruction denotes a store or a successful cas instruction to address a with value v. We omit the instruction identifiers. We use ... as a shorthand for a sequence of instructions.

(wr, v_3, x) (with identifier j) followed by $(\text{rd}, 0, y)$ (with identifier k), such that $v_3 \neq v_1$. As $\mathcal{I}$ is uninstrumented, p_2 executes $\langle \text{store } a_x, v_3 \rangle$ followed by $\langle \text{load } a_y, 0 \rangle$. Let these two instructions execute after the response of o_1 and immediately before the update of a_y by process p_1.[3] Note that as p_2 does not change the value of a_y, the use of CAS instruction by p_1 to update a_y will be successful. The key point to note here is that once p_1 updates a_y with value v_2, transaction T cannot abort. This is because r can be extended to trace r', where a non-transactional read by process p_2 executes $\langle \text{load } a_y, v_2 \rangle$. If T is an aborted transaction, then no history corresponding to r' is parametrized opaque with respect to M. Thus, T is a committed transaction. Consider an arbitrary history h corresponding to r. Legality requires that operation k occurs before T and operation j occurs after T. By definition of M_{wr}, every view $view \in M(h)$ requires that $(j, k) \in view(p)$ for all $p \in P$. Thus, h does not ensure opacity parametrized by M.

Case 3. Let $M \in M_{rw}$. That is, M does not allow reordering a read followed by a write operation to a different variable. The trace r is depicted in Figure 5(d). Let T consist of operations $o_1 = (\text{wr}, v_1, x)$ and $o_2 = (\text{wr}, v_2, y)$. Let $v_1 \neq 0$ and $v_2 \neq 0$. From Lemma 1, we know that T updates addresses a_x and a_y with values v_1 and v_2. Without loss of generality, we assume that a_x is updated before a_y. Process p_2 issues the following operations non-transactionally in the order: (rd, v_3, x), (wr, v_4, y), $(\text{wr}, 0, y)$. Since $\mathcal{I}$ is uninstrumented, those three operations are executed as: $\langle \text{load } a_x, v_3 \rangle$, $\langle \text{store } a_y, v_4 \rangle$, and $\langle \text{store } a_y, 0 \rangle$. Let r be such that those three instructions occur immediately before the update of a_y with value v_2. As p_2 changes and restores the value of a_y to 0, process p_1 does not observe the change, and thus, the update of a_y with value v_2 is successful. As in case 2, T cannot be an aborting transaction, once T updates a_y. We now extend r as follows: after the response of the commit operation of T, let p_2 execute a transaction T' followed by two non-transactional operations: (rd, v_5, x), (rd, v_6, y).

We show now that the value of a_y must remain equal to v_2 after T commits. Assume otherwise: that T stores value $v' \neq v_2$ to a_y just before committing. Consider a trace r' in which p_1 performs the same actions as in r and then reads y non-transactionally, and in which p_2 does not perform any actions. Since p_1 cannot distinguish r' from r, p_1 returns value v' in the non-transactional read after T, thus violating opacity parametrized by M—a contradiction.

Therefore, $v_6 = v_2$. Note also that $v_5 = v_1$. Consider an arbitrary history h corresponding to r. Legality requires that the first non-transactional read by process p_2 occurs after T, and the two non-transactional writes of p_2 occur before T. This contradicts the expected process view for a memory model $M \in M_{rw}$. Thus, the history h does not ensure opacity parametrized by M.

Case 4. Let $M \in M_{ww}$. That is, M does not allow reordering two write operations to different variables. The trace r is similar to the one for case 3, except that (1) T consists of four operations: (rd, v_1', x), (rd, v_2', y), (wr, v_1, x) and (wr, v_2, y), and (2) p_2 executes operation (wr, v_3, x) instead of (rd, v_3, x). Let $v_1 \neq 0$ and $v_2 \neq 0$ and $v_3 \neq 0$. As in case 3, we know that T updates addresses a_x and a_y with values v_1 and v_2, and we assume that a_x is updated before a_y. Since $\mathcal{I}$ is uninstrumented, the non-transactional write operations are implemented as store instructions. Let the three store instructions: $\langle \text{store } a_x, v_3 \rangle$, $\langle \text{store } a_y, v_4 \rangle$, and $\langle \text{store } a_y, 0 \rangle$ by process p_2 occur immediately before the update of a_y with value v_2 by process p_1 in trace r. As in case 2, T cannot be an aborting transaction, after it updates a_y. Now, note that after updating

---

[3]For simplicity, we assume that the transaction loads the value of a_x before the response of o_1. The argument holds in general, as the value of a_x is loaded before the update of a_y.

On transaction start:
$lg := g$
while $(lg \neq p)$ **do**
   if $lg = 0$
      $\langle \text{cas } g, lg, p \rangle$
   endif
   $lg := g$
endwhile
return

On transaction read of x:
if $\exists v \cdot (x, v) \in readset(p)$
   return v
endif
$\langle \text{load } a_x, v \rangle$
add (x, v) to $readset(p)$
return v

On transaction write of x with value v':
issue a transactional read of x
if $\exists v \cdot (x, v) \in writeset(p)$
   update (x, v) to (x, v') in $writeset(p)$
   return
endif
add (x, v) to $writeset(p)$
return

On transaction abort:
empty $readset(p)$
empty $writeset(p)$
$\langle \text{store } g, 0 \rangle$
return

On transaction commit:
while $writeset(p)$ is not empty
   pick and remove (x, v') from $writeset(p)$
   pick and remove (x, v) from $readset(p)$
   $\langle \text{cas } x, v, v' \rangle$
endwhile
empty $readset(p)$
$\langle \text{store } g, 0 \rangle$
return

Figure 6: A global lock based TM implementation

a_y, even if T observes the non-transactional write to a_x, T cannot overwrite a_x with v_2: this requires the non-transactional write to x to appear before the transaction, but T observes x as 0, and not as v_1'. We can extend the trace r exactly as in case 3 now, and show a contradiction between the legality and the process view required by a memory model $M \in M_{ww}$. Thus, for every history h corresponding to r, we know that h does not ensure opacity parametrized by M. $\square$

We saw in the classification of memory models (Section 3.3) that most of the practical memory models do restrict some order of operations. Thus, Theorem 1 gives an intuition that without instrumentation, it is not possible to achieve opacity parametrized by practical memory models. We now show that for an idealized memory model, which allows reordering all operations to different variables, achieving parametrized opacity is still expensive: a TM implementation must use a cas instruction within a transaction to update every variable which is read and written by the transaction.

Theorem 2. For every memory model M, an uninstrumented TM implementation $\mathcal{I}$ guarantees parametrized opacity with respect to M only if, for all traces $r \in L(\mathcal{I})$, and for every variable x, if a committed transaction T consists of operations (rd, v, x) and (wr, v', x), then T contains a $\langle \text{cas } x, v, v' \rangle$ instruction.

PROOF. Consider a trace r with two processes p_1 and p_2 as shown in Figure 5(e). Let T be a transaction of process p_1 in r, such that T consists of operations (rd, v, x) and (wr, v', x). By Lemma 1, we know that T updates a_x with value v' using either a store or a compare-and-swap instruction. Suppose T changes the value of a_x using a store instruction. Let r consist of two non-transactional operations (wr, v_1, x) followed by (rd, v_2, x) of process p_2. As $\mathcal{I}$ is uninstrumented, we know that a read operation is implemented as a load, and a write as a store. Consider the trace r where $\langle \text{store } a_x, v_1 \rangle$ instruction of process p_2 occurs immediately before $\langle \text{store } a_x, v' \rangle$ instruction of process p_1 and the instruction $\langle \text{load } a_x, v_2 \rangle$ occurs immediately after $\langle \text{store } a_x, v' \rangle$, such that we get $v_2 = v'$. For a corresponding history of r to be parametrized

opaque with respect to M, the transaction T has to be a committed transaction. After the response of the commit of T, let there be an empty transaction T' of process p_2 in r followed by a non-transactional read of x, with a load instruction $\langle \text{load } x, v_3 \rangle$. Note that we have $v_3 = v'$. We argue that irrespective of the memory model M, there does not exist a history h corresponding to r such that h ensures opacity parametrized by M. This is because the operation (wr, v_1, x) of process p_2 can appear neither before T (as the read of v in T returns 0), nor after T (as the read after T' returns v'). Thus, an uninstrumented TM implementation has to use a cas instruction to update a variable x in a transaction T, if T consists of both read and write operations to x. $\square$

Theorem 3. Given a memory model $M \notin (M_{rr} \cup M_{rw} \cup M_{wr} \cup M_{ww})$, there exists an uninstrumented TM implementation that guarantees opacity parametrized by M.

PROOF. Consider an uninstrumented global lock based TM implementation $\mathcal{I}$ described in pseudo code in Figure 6. $\mathcal{I}$ acquires a global lock g during the start of each transaction, and releases the lock (using $\langle \text{store } g, 0 \rangle$) immediately before the response of the commit or abort of the transaction. Moreover, for every variable x, every transaction T loads the value of a_x only at the first read or write operation to x within T (if such an operation exists in T), and if T writes to x, then $\mathcal{I}$ uses a CAS instruction to update a_x in T. Consider an arbitrary trace $r \in L(\mathcal{I})$. Consider a history h corresponding to the trace r obtained by choosing the following logical points of execution of an operation within an operation trace: start operation at the successful cas instruction, commit and abort operations at $\langle \text{store } g, 0 \rangle$ instruction, every non-transactional read at the load instruction, every non-transactional write at the store instruction, and every transactional read or write at its invocation. First, we note that the history h obtained is such that for every pair T, T' of transactions in h, either $T \prec_h T'$ or $T' \prec_h T$. Now, consider a variable x and a transaction T in h. Let $k_1 \ldots k_n$ be a sequence of non-transactional operation instances to x in h, which occur between the first and last operations of the transaction T. We create a sequential history s from h by repeating the following two steps for all variables:

Step 1. Consider a non-transactional write operation k_i for some $1 \leq i \leq n$. If there is a load of x in T before the store instruction, or there is no load or cas of x in T after the store instruction with identifier k_i in r, we place all operations $k_i \ldots k_n$ after the transaction T in s. For all other non-transactional write operations k_i, we place all operations $k_1 \ldots k_i$ before the transaction T in s. We now have no non-transactional write operation to x between the first and last operations of T.

Step 2. For all remaining non-transactional read operations o, we place o before T in s if the load instruction corresponding to o precedes the update to x by T in r, and after T otherwise.

Note that as the memory model freely allows reordering instructions to independent variables, we can move operations of different variables freely with respect to each other. Moreover, the two steps do not change the order of non-transactional operations of a process to a variable. $\square$

5.2 Instrumented TM Implementations

In practice, TM implementations use instrumentation of non-transactional operations to achieve parametrized opacity. We now investigate instrumented TM implementations. Typically, a history contains more read operations than write operations. So, it is worthwhile to study whether we can achieve parametrized opacity by just instrumenting the non-transactional write operations and leaving the non-transactional read operations uninstrumented.

We first show that it is indeed possible to achieve parametrized opacity with uninstrumented reads for a class of memory models that allow to reorder read operations (Theorem 4). The construction implements non-transactional write operations as single operation transactions. Then, we show that for memory models that do not belong to set $M_{rr} \cup M_{wr}$, it is possible to implement parametrized opacity with uninstrumented reads and with constant-time instrumentation of writes (Theorem 5).

Theorem 4. There exists a TM implementation with uninstrumented reads that guarantees parametrized opacity for memory models $M \notin M_{rr}$.

PROOF. Consider a global lock based TM implementation $\mathcal{I}$ that treats transactional operations as in the proof of Theorem 3, and shown in Figure 6. Moreover, $\mathcal{I}$ implements a non-transactional write operation (wr, x, v) as: acquire the global lock g using cas (as in transaction start), followed by the instruction $\langle \mathsf{store}\ x, v \rangle$, followed by $\langle \mathsf{store}\ g, 0 \rangle$. Intuitively, $\mathcal{I}$ treats every non-transactional write operation as a transaction in itself. $\mathcal{I}$ implements non-transactional read operations as load instructions (no instrumentation).

Consider an arbitrary trace $r \in L(\mathcal{I})$. Note that there exists a history h corresponding to r (obtained using the logical points as in Theorem 3) such that no non-transactional write occurs between the first and last operation of a transaction, and for every pair T, T' of transactions, either $T \prec_h T'$ or $T' \prec_h T$. Consider a variable x. Given a transaction T in h, let $k_1 \ldots k_n$ be the identifiers of non-transactional read operation instances in h, which occur between the first and last operation of the transaction T. We create a sequential history s from h as in Theorem 3: for all non-transactional read operations o to x, we place o before T in s if the load instruction corresponding to o precedes the cas instruction to x by T in r, and after T otherwise. Note that as the memory model freely allows reordering read operations to different variables, we can move reads of different variables freely with respect to each other. $\square$

Theorem 5. There exists a TM implementation $\mathcal{I}$ with constant-time instrumentation of writes and no instrumentation of reads, such that $\mathcal{I}$ guarantees opacity parametrized by any memory model $M \notin M_{rr} \cup M_{wr}$.

PROOF. We build a TM implementation $\mathcal{I}$ which uses a global lock to execute transactions (as in Theorem 3 and 4). Moreover, $\mathcal{I}$ uses a version number per process. When a process p issues a non-transactional write operation, p increments its version number, and writes the value, the process id, and the version number using a store instruction. $\mathcal{I}$ does not use instrumentation for non-transactional read operations. Now, we prove that $\mathcal{I}$ guarantees opacity parametrized by M, where $M \notin M_{rr} \cup M_{wr}$.

Consider an arbitrary trace $r \in L(\mathcal{I})$. Consider a history h corresponding to the trace r obtained by choosing the logical points as in Theorem 3. We know that for every two transactions T, T' in h, we have $T \prec_h T'$ or $T' \prec_h T$. Consider an arbitrary transaction T in h and a variable x. Let $k_1 \ldots k_m$ be the identifiers of the non-transactional operations to x that occur between the first and last operation of T in h. Note that as $\mathcal{I}$ uses cas instruction for variables which are written in a transaction, no non-transactional write to x stores to a_x between a load and a successful update of a_x in T. We thus can obtain a sequential history from h by repeating the following for all variables x and for all transactions in h: for a non-transactional write operation k_i to x such that operation k_i occurs between the start and end of transaction T, if the corresponding store to a_x occurs after a load of a_x in T, then we place

operation k_i after T in s. Otherwise we place k_i before T in s. If the load corresponding to a non-transactional read occurs after the update of a_x in T, then we place the operation after T, otherwise before T.

If a process issues non-transactional reads of x and y, such that their corresponding loads occur between the updates by a transaction, we need to reorder the non-transactional reads for legality. Thus, we want $M \notin M_{rr}$. Similarly, note that if a process issues a non-transactional write of x followed by a read of y, such that the corresponding store to a_x and load of a_y occur between the updates to a_x and a_y, we need to reorder the non-transactional accesses for legality. Thus, we want $M \notin M_{wr}$. But interestingly, we built $\mathcal{I}$ in such a way that it first adds all variables to be updated in the writeset. Only then, $\mathcal{I}$ starts updating the variables using cas instruction. Hence, if a process issues a non-transactional read which loads a value updated by T, we know that every following non-transactional write can also occur after T. Thus, we do not require that $M \notin M_{rw}$. Similarly, if a process issues two non-transactional writes, then we know that either both the writes occur before T or after T. This implies that $\mathcal{I}$ guarantees parametrized opacity even for memory models which restrict the order of a read/write followed by a write to a different variable, but allow reordering read/write followed by a read to a different variable. $\square$

6. CONCLUDING REMARKS

Discussion. Given that a programmer expects behavior of non-transactional operations within the scope of behaviors under the given memory model, one can build a more efficient implementation which guarantees opacity with respect to the programmer's memory model. Relaxed memory models like Alpha [27] and Java [18] are neither in M_{rr}, nor in M_{wr}. So, our construction provides an inexpensive way to guarantee opacity parametrized by memory models like Alpha. Moreover, memory models like RMO [30] relax the order of reads as long as they are not data dependent. This implies that if we use special synchronization for data-dependent reads, we can use the construction of Theorem 5 for a vast class of memory models.

We now discuss the construction we used in Theorems 3 and 5. We use global locks for transactions in the construction for the sake of simplicity. But the central idea of the construction, given below, can be extended to practical lazy-versioning TM implementations which rely on some form of two-phased locking. The idea is that for many memory models, it is not necessary for a transaction to successfully update all variables it writes, if there is a concurrent non-transactional write. For example, in Theorem 5, if a transaction observes that a non-transactional operation has written a new value, then the transaction's cas operation fails, but the transaction can still commit. This sounds counterintuitive to the general belief that transactions must be atomic, and thus, appear to perform their updates completely. We suggest that the non-transactional operations, although isolated from transactions from a programmer's point of view, can be used to mask updates of transactions.

Using our theoretical framework, we also observe that no matter what the given memory model M is, if a TM implementation allows a transaction to update the value of an address a_x more than once, then the TM implementation needs to instrument read operations in order of guarantee opacity parametrized by M. This is because a load of a_x (corresponding to a non-transactional operation), if sandwiched between the two updates of a_x, can observe the intermediate state of a transaction. This is also known as *dirty reads* in the literature.

Related work. Various formalisms for memory models have been proposed in the literature [3, 4, 5, 12, 23, 24]. Most of these formalisms are tailored to capture the intricacies of specific memory models. Our reason for building a formalism for memory models was to obtain a general framework, with the focus on classification of memory models on the basis of reordering of instructions they allow. The interaction of transactions with non-transactional operations has been widely studied. The study was pioneered by Grossman et al. [9], where the authors raised several issues that need to be tackled in order to create TM implementations that handle non-transactional operations properly. The authors express the correctness property using sample executions, and thus it lacks a formal specification. Work by Scott et al. [28] focuses on providing a set of rules that should hold irrespective of the memory model. Menon et al. [20] define correctness by mapping transactions to critical sections, thus providing an intuitive definition of single global lock atomicity. Type systems and operational semantics for transactional programs with non-transactional accesses have been proposed by Abadi et al. [1] and Grossman et al. [21].

Conclusion. We formalized the correctness property of opacity parametrized by a memory model. Intuitively, parametrized opacity requires two things. Firstly, transactions are isolated from other transactions and non-transactional operations. Secondly, the behavior of non-transactional operations is governed by the underlying memory model. We used our formalism to prove several results on achieving parametrized opacity with instrumented or uninstrumented TM implementations under different memory models. In particular, we show that for most memory models, parametrized opacity cannot be achieved without instrumenting non-transactional operations. On the positive side, we show that with constant-time instrumentation for writes, and no instrumentation for reads, it is indeed possible to achieve opacity parametrized by a significant class of memory models. The practical relevance of our work lies in the fact that while creating TM implementations, one may use the relaxations provided by the memory model to create more efficient TM implementations.

7. REFERENCES

[1] Martín Abadi, Andrew Birrell, Tim Harris, and Michael Isard. Semantics of transactional memory and automatic mutual exclusion. In *POPL*, pages 63–74, 2008.

[2] Sarita V. Adve and Kourosh Gharachorloo. Shared memory consistency models: A tutorial. *IEEE Computer*, 29(12):66–76, 1996.

[3] Arvind and Jan-Willem Maessen. Memory Model = Instruction Reordering + Store Atomicity. In *ISCA*, pages 29–40, 2006.

[4] Gérard Boudol and Gustavo Petri. Relaxed memory models: An operational approach. In *POPL*, pages 392–403, 2009.

[5] Sebastian Burckhardt, Madanlal Musuvathi, and Vasu Singh. Verifying local transformations on relaxed memory models. In *CC*, pages 104–123, 2010.

[6] Intel Corporation. *Intel 64 and IA-32 Architectures Software Developer's Manual Volume 3A*. 2008.

[7] Luke Dalessandro and Michael Scott. Strong isolation is a weak idea. In *TRANSACT*, 2009.

[8] D. Dice, O. Shalev, and N. Shavit. Transactional locking II. In *DISC*, pages 194–208. Springer, 2006.

[9] Dan Grossman, Jeremy Manson, and William Pugh. What do high-level memory models mean for transactions? In *MSPC*, pages 62–69, 2006.

[10] Rachid Guerraoui, Thomas A. Henzinger, Barbara

[11] Jobstmann, and Vasu Singh. Model checking transactional memories. In *PLDI*, pages 372–382. ACM, 2008.

[11] Rachid Guerraoui, Thomas A. Henzinger, and Vasu Singh. Nondeterminism and completeness in transactional memories. In *CONCUR*, pages 21–35. Springer, 2008.

[12] Rachid Guerraoui, Thomas A. Henzinger, and Vasu Singh. Software transactional memory on relaxed memory models. In *CAV*, pages 321–336, 2009.

[13] Rachid Guerraoui and Michał Kapałka. On the correctness of transactional memory. In *PPoPP*, 2008.

[14] M. Herlihy, V. Luchangco, M. Moir, and W. N. Scherer. Software transactional memory for dynamic-sized data structures. In *PODC*, pages 92–101, 2003.

[15] M. Herlihy and J. E. B. Moss. Transactional memory: Architectural support for lock-free data structures. In *ISCA*, pages 289–300. ACM Press, 1993.

[16] Maurice Herlihy and Jeannette M. Wing. Linearizability: A correctness condition for concurrent objects. *ACM Transactions on Programming Languages and Systems*, 12(3):463–492, 1990.

[17] J. R. Larus and R. Rajwar. *Transactional Memory*. Synthesis Lectures on Computer Architecture. Morgan & Claypool, 2007.

[18] Jeremy Manson, William Pugh, and Sarita V. Adve. The Java memory model. In *POPL*, pages 378–391. ACM, 2005.

[19] Milo M. K. Martin, Colin Blundell, and E. Lewis. Subtleties of transactional memory atomicity semantics. *Computer Architecture Letters*, 5(2), 2006.

[20] Vijay Menon, Steven Balensiefer, Tatiana Shpeisman, Ali-Reza Adl-Tabatabai, Richard L. Hudson, Bratin Saha, and Adam Welc. Practical weak-atomicity semantics for Java STM. In *SPAA*, pages 314–325, 2008.

[21] Katherine F. Moore and Dan Grossman. High-level small-step operational semantics for transactions. In *POPL*, pages 51–62. ACM, 2008.

[22] C. H. Papadimitriou. The serializability of concurrent database updates. *Journal of the ACM*, pages 631–653, 1979.

[23] Vijay A. Saraswat, Radha Jagadeesan, Maged Michael, and Christoph von Praun. A theory of memory models. In *PPoPP*, pages 161–172, New York, NY, USA, 2007. ACM.

[24] Susmit Sarkar, Peter Sewell, Francesco Zappa Nardelli, Scott Owens, Tom Ridge, Thomas Braibant, Magnus O. Myreen, and Jade Alglave. The semantics of x86-CC multiprocessor machine code. In *POPL*, pages 379–391, 2009.

[25] N. Shavit and D. Touitou. Software transactional memory. In *PODC*, pages 204–213, 1995.

[26] Tatiana Shpeisman, Vijay Menon, Ali-Reza Adl-Tabatabai, Steven Balensiefer, Dan Grossman, Richard L. Hudson, Katherine F. Moore, and Bratin Saha. Enforcing isolation and ordering in STM. In *PLDI*, pages 78–88. ACM, 2007.

[27] Richard L. Sites, editor. *Alpha Architecture Reference Manual*. Digital Press, 2002.

[28] Michael F. Spear, Luke Dalessandro, Virendra J. Marathe, and Michael L. Scott. Ordering-based semantics for software transactional memory. In *OPODIS*, pages 275–294, 2008.

[29] Michael F. Spear, Virendra J. Marathe, Luke Dalessandro, and Michael L. Scott. Privatization techniques for software transactional memory. In *PODC*, pages 338–339, 2007.

[30] D. Weaver and T. Germond, editors. *The SPARC Architecture Manual (version 9)*. Prentice-Hall, Inc., 1994.

Lightweight, Robust Adaptivity for Software Transactional Memory

Michael F. Spear
Department of Computer Science and Engineering
Lehigh University
spear@cse.lehigh.edu

ABSTRACT

When a program uses Software Transactional Memory (STM) to synchronize accesses to shared memory, the performance often depends on which STM implementation is used. Implementations vary greatly in their underlying mechanisms, in the features they provide, and in the assumptions they make about the common case. Consequently, the best choice of algorithm is workload-dependent. Worse yet, for workloads composed of multiple phases of execution, the "best" choice of implementation may change during execution.

We present a low-overhead system for adapting between STM implementations. Like previous work, our system enables adaptivity between different parameterizations of a given algorithm, and it allows adapting between the use of transactions and coarse-grained locks. In addition, we support dynamic switching between fundamentally different STM implementations. We also explicitly support irrevocability, retry-based condition synchronization, and privatization. Through a series of experiments, we show that our system introduces negligible overhead. We also present a candidate use of dynamic adaptivity, as a replacement for contention management. When using adaptivity in this manner, STM implementations can be simplified to a great degree without lowering throughput or introducing a risk of pathological slowdown, even for challenging workloads.

Categories and Subject Descriptors

D.1.3 [**Programming Techniques**]: Concurrent Programming—*Parallel Programming*; D.3.3 [**Programming Languages**]: Language Constructs and Features—*Concurrent Programming Structures*

General Terms

Algorithms, Design, Performance

Keywords

Atomicity, Serializability, Synchronization, Adaptivity

1. INTRODUCTION

Software Transactional Memory (STM) promises to simplify parallel programming by replacing critical sections with "atomic" sections. The widely-repeated belief is that with STM, programmers need not worry about how atomic sections are implemented; rather, they can rely on a run-time system to maximize concurrency by executing atomic sections in parallel.

In the last decade, dozens of STM algorithms have been published, each of which appears well suited to some workloads [1,5,7,8,11,13,18,20,27,28,36,38,41,42,44]. The emergence of new algorithms has not ebbed in recent years, and the imminent arrival of commercial hardware support for transactional memory [6,9,31] is likely to increase the number of available STM implementations. Furthermore, there is no consensus about how to support I/O and condition synchronization within transactions, or even about how transactions relate to a given language's memory model. Different STM implementations address these properties with varying degrees of efficiency, if at all. As a result, the most widely held conclusion from STM research so far may be that the best choice of algorithm depends critically on the workload. A mechanism to select the best STM algorithm during execution is clearly needed.

Some research into adaptivity explored selection between between using STM or using a single lock. Other work considered choosing between parameterizations of a single STM implementation. We outline some of the key results below:

Acquisition Time: Marathe et al. were the first to study adaptivity, and showed in their nonblocking Adaptive STM [21] that the time at which to-be-written locations are acquired (locked) has a drastic impact on scalability. While eager acquisition (encounter-time locking) has lower single-thread overhead, Marathe showed that lazy acquisition (commit-time locking) provided better throughput for some multithreaded workloads. In later work, Marathe et al. presented a pathological case in which eager acquisition livelocks, while lazy acquisition scales slightly [22].

Granularity of Conflict Detection: Felber et al. similarly showed that for a given implementation of transactions, adaptivity within the library can have a profound impact on scalability [11]. In their work, varying the granularity of conflict detection along two dimensions for a fixed choice of STM algorithm could vary performance dramatically, with a bad parameterization leading to performance 3× worse than the best parameterization. This mechanism could also effectively transition the runtime to a single-lock mode, albeit one with higher overhead than is strictly necessary.

Pathology Avoidance: To avoid pathologically bad behavior, some systems [26, 34] provide a pessimistic mode of operation, where some transactions (or even accesses to some variables) are performed in a manner that is visible to all concurrent transactions. With this support, some transactions are guaranteed to win conflicts and make progress.

Locks or Transactions: Usui et al. showed [43] that the overhead of STM may favor the use of a single lock over transactions even for scalable workloads. The best choice depends on the number of threads, the amount of instrumentation, and the amount of parallelism available in the workload. For example, if STM scales well up to 8 threads, but transactions run at 25% of the speed of lock-based code, then locks should be preferred for ≤ 4 threads, and transactions preferred for ≥ 5 threads.

The common characteristics of these research efforts include (a) similarities in the underlying STM algorithm (all use "ownership records" or "orecs" to mediate concurrent access); (b) adaptivity between a fixed set of alternatives, using fixed policies; and (c) limited attention to language-level semantics [23, 25], irrevocability [3, 39, 45], and self-abort [15]. In this paper, we present a lightweight mechanism for supporting adaptivity that addresses these areas: we enable adaptivity among fundamentally different STM implementations; we support the creation of arbitrarily complex adaptivity policies; and we support irrevocability, self-abort, and strong semantics.

Our mechanism allows adaptivity in two dimensions. At a coarse granularity, we allow a system-wide policy to select an STM implementation; such switching requires expensive inter-thread synchronization. Within each STM implementation, we also allow fine-grained adaptivity, to optimize the chosen STM implementation for an active transaction. At this level, adaptivity is an inexpensive, thread-local operation that can be performed frequently.

The remainder of this paper is organized as follows: in Section 2 we describe our implementation framework, discussing both how it enables safe transitioning between modes and how it avoids additional overhead. Sections 3 and 4 discuss the STM algorithms we currently support, and describe how adaptivity enables simplifications and optimizations to STM implementations. In Section 5 we present a set of transition policies that can be used in place of contention management [14, 32] without introducing overhead. We experimentally evaluate our system in Section 6, and conclude with a discussion of future directions in Section 7.

2. COARSE-GRAINED ADAPTIVITY

Our adaptivity mechanism allows the library to choose among any set of STM algorithms dynamically. While we do consider such issues as the use of self-abort, irrevocability [3, 39, 45], and retry-based condition synchronization [15], our discussion in this section uses the basic four-function STM API from Figure 1, and assumes subsumption nesting.

In most implementations, these functions are statically linked to the executable, or else inlined directly into program code [10, 44]. Adaptivity then requires each API function to begin with a branch that selects instrumentation corresponding to the current STM algorithm [19, 29, 30]. To avoid this per-access overhead, Ni et al. proposed that the API be reached through indirect calls [26]. In their system, each transaction has local pointers to the API functions, and adaptivity is achieved by changing the values of these

TMBegin	create a checkpoint; read global metadata and set per-thread metadata as required by the STM algorithm; may block; implemented as a macro that calls `setjmp`, then makes an STM library call.
TMCommit	attempts to commit a transaction; on failure, restart via `longjmp`; may contain a fast-path for read-only transactions.
TMRead	instrumented read of shared memory; may cause the transaction to restart.
TMWrite	instrumented write to shared memory; may cause the transaction to restart.

Figure 1: A simple four-function STM API.

pointers. This optimization enabled fine-grained switching between parameterizations of a single STM algorithm.

Our approach resembles that used by Ni et al.: we also reach `TMCommit`, `TMRead`, and `TMWrite` through per-thread pointers. However, we use a single global pointer to specify `TMBegin`. This enables inexpensive coordination when switching among different STM algorithms.

2.1 Low-Overhead Coordination

We prohibit coarse-grained switching when there are in-flight transactions. To initiate a switch, a thread first blocks new transactions from starting, then waits until all in-flight transactions commit or abort, then changes the mode, and finally allows transactions to resume. The pseudocode in Figure 2 describes the general behavior we require.

To reduce overhead, we employ several simplifications. Since `TMBegin` starts with a `setjmp`, we use the transaction's pointer to the checkpoint buffer in place of the `flag` variable. On the x86, we also eliminate the memory fence by using a locked instruction to set this pointer (on SPARC, using a memory fence is less expensive).[1] Lastly, we eliminate the test and branch (and the need for a SWITCHING flag) through the use of the global `TMBegin` function pointer.

To initiate a switch, thread T atomically sets the `TMBegin` pointer to a dummy function (`Block`) that (a) unsets the caller's `flag`, (b) spins while `TMBegin` equals `Block`, and then (c) calls `longjmp`. Using `Block` removes `TMBegin` lines 4–8 from the critical path of all transactions.

To complete a mode switch, thread T waits for all transactions to abort or commit (aborted transactions will call `Block` when they restart). T then updates each thread's `TMRead`, `TMWrite`, and `TMCommit` pointers to indicate the new algorithm, and finally updates the global `TMBegin` pointer. If the selection of a new algorithm is computationally intensive, it can be determined before waiting for threads to unset their flags. To reduce waiting times, threads' local read, write, and commit pointers can optionally be set to a special function that immediately aborts.

Apart from the cost of an indirect function call, STM implementations incur no penalty with this rendezvous mechanism. The ordering (and hence the memory fence or locked instruction) is required in the begin function of any STM system that supports irrevocability [26, 39], for roughly the same purpose. As we discuss in Section 4, we implement irrevocability via a mode switch; given the ordering in `TMBegin`,

---

[1] A locked instruction is required on the x86 since its memory model is slightly weaker than SPARC TSO.

```
TMBegin:                  to change modes:
1  call setjmp            atomically set SWITCHING
2  set flag               for each thread
3  memory fence             spin while flag is set
4  if SWITCHING           ... // change the mode
5    unset flag           unset SWITCHING
6    while SWITCHING
7      spin
8    call longjmp
   ... // STM-specific code

TMCommit:
   ... // STM-specific code
   flag = false
```

Figure 2: Mode Switching Support (Unoptimized)

irrevocable mode switches require no further ordering. The most significant noticeable cost of our mechanism occurs when the underlying implementation uses a single coarse-grained lock for all concurrency control. In this situation, the setjmp is unnecessary, since transactions never roll back.

2.2 Optimizing Instrumentation

While it is correct to reach the instrumentation for any STM algorithm through indirect function calls, such a mechanism unfairly penalizes algorithms whose instrumentation is sufficiently small. At the extreme limit, if transactions are implemented via a single global lock, and the programmer is not permitted to explicitly abort transactions, then no instrumentation of loads and stores is required.

We use the technique proposed by Ni et al. [26] to address this situation. We provide two versions of any code that can be executed transactionally: the first version has no instrumentation, and can be called from nontransactional contexts as well as from transactional contexts that require no instrumentation. The second version is instrumented so that accesses to shared variables are performed via indirect function calls through the STM API. For function pointers, we also recommend the methods proposed by Ni et al.

We produce an additional version of code called from transactional contexts. This version is specialized for the TML algorithm [42], and all instrumentation of loads and stores is inlined. We provide this code because (a) TML instrumentation is extremely lightweight and (b) TML's benefits are much lower if its instrumentation is not inlined. If a TML-instrumented version of a function is unavailable, then the standard STM-instrumented version can be used, with TML instrumentation reached via function pointers.

3. STM SYSTEMS IMPLEMENTED

We currently support 10 STM implementations. These implementations differ in the following dimensions:

- Parallelism: The runtime may forbid any concurrency, may only allow parallelism among read-only transactions, or may allow any nonconflicting transactions to progress in parallel.
- Self-abort: Some runtimes allow transactions to explicitly abort themselves (e.g., to wait on a condition [15]).
- Metadata: Conflicts may be detected using a single lock, Bloom filters [2], orecs, or by logging values.

- Writes: Speculative writes may be performed immediately, or buffered until commit time.
- Semantics:[2] The implementation may support implicit privatization and publication, through which data can be accessed both nontransactionally and with transactional instrumentation (though not at the same time).

In this context, we have implemented the following algorithms. A summary appears in Table 1:

Mutex: All transactions are protected by a single mutex lock. There is no concurrency, self-abort is not supported, writes are performed in-place with no read or write instrumentation, and the semantics are at least as strong as ELA.

TML: The Transactional Mutex Lock algorithm [42] is essentially a highly optimized, eager, in-place update STM with a single orec. Only read-read concurrency is permitted, self-abort is not supported, writes are performed in-place with lightweight, inlined instrumentation, and the semantics are at least as strong as ELA.

TMLLazy: This algorithm extends TML by buffering all writes until commit time. This modification enables TML to support self-abort, but requires more expensive instrumentation, to include a hashtable-based write set. After CGL and TML, TMLLazy usually offers the lowest single-thread overhead. As with TML, TMLLazy does not allow read-write or write-write concurrency.

NOrec: NOrec extends TMLLazy with value-based conflict detection [5,27]. NOrec provides strong semantics, supports self-abort, and allows write-write concurrency.

Ring: We provide an optimized variant of RingSTM [41] based on the FastPath speculative parallelization system [37]. Ring uses an array of Bloom filters [2] for concurrency control, and supports self-abort, ELA semantics, and write-write concurrency. We use the serialized writeback variant of RingSTM, which tends to offer the lowest latency [40].

NOrecPrio: The original RingSTM proposal included a simple priority scheme, in which consecutive aborts increase a transaction's priority (in a manner akin to Scherer and Scott's "Karma" [32]), and the existence of high-priority transactions causes all lower-priority writers to block at their commit point. We provide an extension to NOrec that includes this support. This mechanism has a significant impact on throughput when conflicts are common. NOrecPrio should only be chosen when (a) strong semantics are required and (b) transactions appear to be starving.

Orec-Eager: This system uses the write-through variant of TinySTM [11]. An array of 1M orecs are used for concurrency control, and updates are made directly to memory. As in TinySTM, we hard-coded the abort-on-conflict contention management policy. Our orecs differ from previously published works in that they use the most significant bit as the lock bit, rather than the least significant bit. This change admits simpler read and validation instrumentation. Orec-Eager supports self-abort, but not ELA semantics.

---

[2]In our study, we only consider "ELA" semantics, in which privatization is always supported but publication cannot be performed through a potentially racy operation [25]. ELA prohibits compiler reordering of memory accesses, whereas stronger semantics do not. However, ELA is the strongest semantics that still allows a transaction to become irrevocable without first aborting and restarting. Supporting stronger semantics also introduces overhead for workloads that may use either self-abort or irrevocability from within the same instance of a transaction.

	Parallelism Allowed	Self-Abort	Type of Metadata	Writes	Semantics
Mutex	none	no	lock	in-place	ELA+
TML	read-only	no	counter	in-place	ELA+
TMLLazy	read-only	yes	counter	buffered	ELA+
NOrec	full	yes	value-based	buffered	ELA+
Ring	full	yes	Bloom Filters	buffered	ELA
NOrecPrio	full	yes	value-based	buffered	ELA+
Orec-Eager	full	yes	orecs	in-place	none
Orec-Lazy	full	yes	orecs	buffered	none
Orec-ELA	full	yes	orecs	buffered	ELA
Fair	full	yes	orecs	buffered	none

Table 1: Summary of STM systems provided

Orec-Lazy: This orec-based STM with commit-time locking differs from previous systems [7, 20, 36] in that global time uses the mechanism of Wang et al. [44]. This mechanism requires committing writer transactions to validate before incrementing the global timestamp, which eliminates a common optimization for skipping commit-time validation [7, 28, 38], but avoids the need to check an orec before accessing a location (the check after accessing the location is still needed). This use of global time provides the best scalability.[3] Orec-Lazy does not provide ELA semantics.

Orec-ELA: This extension adds ELA semantics to Orec-Lazy through the use of a "cleanup counter" [23, 35].

Fair: The Fair algorithm extends Orec-Lazy with starvation avoidance [36]. After repeated aborts, transactions switch to a mode in which all read operations are made visible, thereby enabling better conflict detection and resolution. Like Orec-Lazy, Fair does not provide ELA semantics.

4. FINE-GRAINED ADAPTIVITY

Our indirection-based interface to the STM runtime system enables us to simplify each implementation and reduce overhead. We discuss two interesting mechanisms below.

4.1 Read-Only Optimizations

Many transactional workloads include read-only transactions. Furthermore, it almost always holds that a transaction performs at least one instrumented read before performing any writes, and in many workloads the first write does not appear until near the end of the transaction. These properties admit optimizations for the part of a transaction body that precedes its first write.

Read-Only Commit Overhead: The commit routine of most STM implementations begins with a branch to determine if the transaction is read-only or not, since read-only transactions can commit with much less overhead than writer transactions (typically, such transactions neither validate nor modify global metadata at commit time [5, 7, 41]). This small constant overhead can be avoided if read-only transactions always call a read-only commit function.

Per-Read Overhead: In buffered-update STM systems, read instrumentation begins with a lookup in the write set, to detect reads to locations for which the transaction has a buffered write. In each transaction, this lookup results in every read before the first write including a never-taken branch, and every read after the first write including an always taken branch. In systems with in-place update, a fast-path exists for reads to locations that are locked by the reading transaction. This fast-path results in a never-taken branch until the transaction performs its first write.

Static optimization often cannot remove the branches discussed above. In addition to meet-over-all-paths analysis constraints, complications arise due to transaction nesting. Suppose transaction W performs a write before calling nested transaction R; R begins by executing K reads; and R is sometimes called from a non-nested context. Optimizing R for the read-only case would require the compiler to produce two versions of R, since the optimized version could not be called from W.

Our adaptive system provides a mechanism for dynamically detecting when a write has occurred in a transaction, and optimizing the remainder of the transaction's implementation accordingly. Recall that the read, write, and commit instrumentation for transactions are reached through thread-local pointers. At begin time, a transaction's read pointer indicates instrumentation optimized for transactions that have not yet performed a write, the commit pointer indicates the read-only commit function, and the write pointer indicates instrumentation for performing *the first write*.[4] When called, this write function changes the thread's read, write, and commit pointers to indicate instrumentation for a writing transaction. The rollback and non-read-only commit functions reset the read, write, and commit pointers to the read-only optimized instrumentation.

This mechanism is precise, and handles nesting without requiring code cloning. In terms of the impact on instruction count, consider a buffered-update STM and a transaction performing r_1 reads before the first write, and r_2 reads after the first write. Our mechanism will save r_1 tests and not-taken branches, r_2 tests and always-taken branches, and one test and branch at commit time. The cost is three writes of constants to thread-local fields during the first write, and three writes of constants to thread-local data after committing a writing transaction.

4.2 Irrevocability

Our current system provides irrevocability [3, 39, 45] by shutting off all concurrency. There are two novel aspects: first, since we only offer ELA semantics and weaker, we can safely become irrevocable in-flight, without an abort. Secondly, we achieve irrevocability through adaptivity.

To become irrevocable, a transaction attempts to atomically change the begin function pointer to the `Block` function, which prevents new transactions from starting. The transaction then waits for all active transactions to commit or abort, and then validates its read set. If the validation succeeds, the thread releases any orecs it holds, commits any pending writes from its write buffer, sets its read and write function pointers to functions that perform uninstrumented reads and writes, and sets its commit function pointer to the "irrevocable commit" function.

At this point, the transaction continues to run instrumented code; thus each load and store incurs minor overhead (the transaction calls functions that simply perform a load or store). At commit time, the transaction resets its read, write, and commit pointers, and restores the global begin pointer to its previous state.

Thus an irrevocable transaction runs more slowly than if it was in Mutex mode, since loads and stores are not inlined. However, it is much faster than without our mode switch-

---

[3]We use "check-twice" timestamps for Orec-Eager, since abort-on-conflict favors incarnation numbers [11].

[4]This code may or may not include optimizations for the dynamic property of executing the first write (e.g., in-place orec systems can skip a write-after-write test).

ing mechanism, as it would otherwise require a branch on every read and write even after becoming irrevocable. Furthermore, when irrevocability is not used, there is no per-memory-access branch, and there is no branch at commit time. We also observe that as in the case of read-only optimizations, this technique seamlessly handles composition.

As an optimization, there is no mode switch in the case of a transaction running in Mutex mode, since the transaction is already trivially running in serial irrevocable mode. Similarly, in TML mode we achieve irrevocability by simply performing the TML write instrumentation.

5. PROGRESS VIA ADAPTIVITY

To demonstrate how adaptivity can be used, we present a set of policies that can be used in place of contention management (CM). For many workloads, CM is barely needed, but for other workloads, complex CM instrumentation is necessary. By choosing the simplest CM policy for most of our implementations (usually abort-on-conflict), we can avoid the overheads of per-access CM bookkeeping, remote abort, and globally-visible CM metadata. If CM appears necessary, the system can switch to either NOrecPrio or Fair, both of which are designed to handle contention.

For this use of adaptivity, we employ a simple state machine that takes seven parameters. These parameters can be reset at any program phase boundary [17,33], that is, at any point where the programmer suspects that sharing patterns are likely to change significantly. For example, they could be reset whenever threads reach a barrier.

- Feature Requirements – Phases must declare their STM feature requirements. Currently, we consider semantics (ELA or None) and self-abort/retry (yes or no). Since there is no cost, we always provide support for adaptivity-based irrevocability.
- Current STM Algorithm – We must, of course, always know what STM algorithm is in use, in order to determine which algorithm to try next.
- Consecutive Aborts – We increment a thread-local variable when a transaction aborts, and zero it upon commit. Large values suggest that a transaction is starving, and also indicate livelock.
- Abort Threshold – We use a per-phase constant as a threshold to trigger adaptivity. This enables threads to make completely local decisions about when to adapt. When the current STM algorithm supports priority, we multiply the abort threshold by the Karma threshold of the priority mechanism (so that the runtime has time to increase priority many times before deciding that it would be better to perform a mode switch).
- Begin Delay – When Mutex is the underlying STM implementation, we count the backoff delay experienced by a thread attempting to acquire the mutex lock. This statistic approximates the loss in parallelism from choosing Mutex.
- Delay Threshold – When the begin delay exceeds this threshold, a switch occurs.
- Disable Adaptivity – A phase may explicitly shut off adaptivity, in the event that it is known that a particular algorithm is best.

5.1 Adaptivity Strategy and Implementation

We consider two criteria when changing the STM algorithm to improve throughput. First, one can select sys-

tems with progressively stronger progress guarantees (that is, transition from eager to lazy to livelock-free to starvation-avoiding). Second, one can make the granularity of conflict detection finer at each transition (moving from the single sequence lock of TML to the thousands of bits in Ring's filters to a million orecs to NOrec's word-level conflict detection). The set of candidate systems is limited by the phase's feature needs: some STM implementations do not support ELA semantics, and others do not support self-abort. We consider four policies, corresponding to the four possible combinations of semantics and rollback.

The "X" Policy: This policy is suitable when neither ELA semantics nor explicit rollback are required. The policy transitions from Mutex to Orec-Eager to Orec-Lazy to Fair to NOrec to NOrecPrio. Single-threaded code always chooses Mutex, and multithreaded code only moves from Mutex when transactions are long enough that the slowdown incurred by STM can be offset by an increase in parallelism. Transitions from Orec-Eager and Orec-Lazy strengthen progress guarantees. Transitioning from Fair occurs when priority does not suffice to stop a pathology. In this unlikely case, the only possibilities are that a corner-case is being exploited to cause livelock, or that the granularity of conflict detection is too coarse. Livelock-free NOrec solves both of these problems, and NOrecPrio adds starvation avoidance.

The "R" Policy: This policy mimics the "X" policy, except that it replaces Mutex with TMLLazy as the initial mode, and is thus suitable for workloads requiring self-abort. With its low instrumentation overhead, TMLLazy is our fastest implementation that supports self-abort. However, once there is a significant incidence of aborts (corresponding to a workload with multiple threads and a reasonable frequency of writing transactions), the mode switches to Orec-Eager, which admits write-write parallelism.

The "E" Policy: When ELA semantics (privatization safety) are required, the Orec-Eager, Orec-Lazy, and Fair policies cannot be used. In this situation, our transitions attempt to increase the granularity of conflict detection. We begin with Mutex, and then transition to TML (in the hopes of many read-only transactions), and then TMLLazy (for the same reason). Should consecutive aborts remain too high, the system transitions to Ring, then Orec-ELA, and then to NOrec. As with the "X" policy, we switch to NOrecPrio only to address pathological starvation concerns.

The "ER" Policy: The "ER" policy mirrors the "E" policy, but adds the requirement that self-abort be supported. Thus the system starts in TMLLazy mode, and otherwise follows the "E" transitions.

Our systems all treat NOrecPrio as a terminal state. While it would be trivial to add departure from it after some interval (say, after each thread performs 1000 commits), we prefer to continue using NOrecPrio until the next program phase. The cost of this choice is highest for the "X" and "R" policies, whose relaxed semantics requirements admit more scalable algorithms when there is a high ratio of writer transactions.

5.2 When Transitions Happen

Transitions occur in three ways. First, we provide an API call to transition the program at any point where there are no active threads. One such call is made automatically at the beginning of every program, during STM initialization.

Second, when a Mutex transaction commits, it may initiate a transition if it determines that it was blocked for too long before acquiring the lock. Placing the transition after the commit maximizes throughput: the thread knows that there are other active transactions, and that (with high likelihood) one of them holds the lock and is in-flight. The mode switch immediately blocks future transactions from starting. However, many threads may be attempting to acquire the lock. They will all complete before the mode switch, since they are already inside the Mutex version of `TMBegin`.

Third, we use transaction aborts as a hook for making switches. In this manner, again, all computation of mode switches occurs off the critical path: there must be multiple transactional threads, and at least one of them is either active (in the case of TML and Orec-Eager, where conflicts can be detected before commit time), or has just committed and is probably about to start a new transaction.

For transitions from all systems other than TML and Mutex, we could cause immediate aborts in all concurrent active transactions by setting threads' commit, read, and write function pointers to methods that abort the caller. Unlike the transition from Mutex, we do not need to wait for all such transactions to commit, but rather for them to commit *or* abort and clean up. Should they all commit, and commit in parallel, the decision to abort early causes wasted work. In the worst case, where they all abort, the manner in which we implemented our STMs ensures that none spend time in fruitless spin-waiting before doing so.

5.3 STM Metadata Considerations

When switching to a new STM system, all of its invariants must be restored. Since we reuse STM metadata (for example, the four orec-based systems use the same table of orecs), some care must be taken to ensure that a prior mode does not invalidate the new mode's invariants. For example, if Orec-Eager and Orec-Lazy use different variables as the global clock, the orec table must be zeroed during a mode switch. We avoid such problems by providing a per-STM function, called during a mode switch, to restore invariants.

Not all metadata requires management at mode switches. For example, our epoch-based allocator [12, 16, 22] does not need any manipulation during mode switches, because the same allocator metadata is used by a thread regardless of STM algorithm. We expect the same to be true of any quiescence tables added to support strong semantics [25].

6. EVALUATION

We measure the overhead of our adaptive mechanism by comparing the performance of our STM implementations to the performance of highly optimized versions of RSTM [30]. We also assess how adaptivity performs as a replacement for contention management, using STAMP benchmarks [4].

All experiments were performed on a Sun Ultra27 with 6GB RAM and a 2.93GHz Intel Xeon W3540 (Nehalem) processor with four cores (8 hardware threads). All executables were compiled with gcc version 4.4.1 with –O3 optimizations. Microbenchmarks were run for five seconds. All data points are the average of five trials.

6.1 Overhead Analysis

Since our main focus is on creating a mechanism for low-overhead adaptivity, we begin by showing that the combination of indirect function calls, read-only optimizations, and adaptivity-based irrevocability results in a system no slower than existing implementations. We use a red-black tree mi-

	Threads				
	1	2	4	6	8
Mutex	87%	81%	82%	83%	85%
Orec-ELA	123%	120%	116%	111%	109%
Orec-Eager	109%	101%	97%	99%	100%
Orec-Lazy	118%	92%	103%	108%	106%
Fair	111%	106%	102%	104%	104%
NOrec	98%	96%	94%	94%	93%
NOrecPrio	98%	89%	88%	90%	89%
Ring	99%	110%	111%	106%	110%
TML	105%	104%	106%	105%	103%
TMLLazy	105%	98%	93%	93%	93%

Table 2: Relative Speed Versus RSTM Implementations

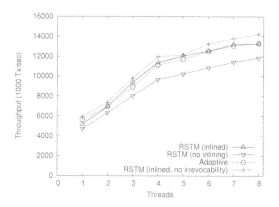

Figure 3: Overhead of adaptivity, using the Orec-Eager runtime.

crobenchmark with 8-bit keys; threads repeatedly execute insert, lookup, and delete operations with equal probability.

We compare against implementations of our algorithms within the RSTM framework [30]. We back-ported our optimizations into RSTM so that any differences in performance between an algorithm running in our system and an algorithm running in RSTM can be attributed to differences in mechanism. Specifically, RSTM inlines much instrumentation, but places branches on the critical path of this instrumentation to support irrevocability. Our system reaches instrumentation through indirect function calls, but instrumentation does not have branches for irrevocability, and employs the read-only optimizations described in Section 4. Table 2 summarizes the results of this experiment, with additional results appearing in an appendix. Note that RSTM was configured with irrevocability support.

Six of the ten systems consistently outperformed their inlined counterparts. To understand why, especially when RSTM inlines instrumentation, tested RSTM with (a) inlining and irrevocability, (b) inlining and no irrevocability, and (c) no inlining and no irrevocability. For Orec-Eager (Figure 3), removing irrevocability support from the inlined RSTM runtime gives a 15% single-thread improvement and 6% improvement on average. Inspecting the compiler output, we found that inlining did not enable more static optimization of the code; in particular, inlining did not enable the compiler to remove the branches that our techniques from Section 4 target. Removing these branches, and branches related to read-only optimizations, compensates for the cost of an indirect function call.

Of the remaining systems, we expect lower performance in two cases. Mutex incurs extra overhead at begin time (due to a `setjmp` call); this results in a significant constant overhead. In NOrecPrio, we removed optimizations for transac-

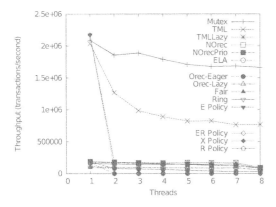

Figure 4: Pathological "Collision" Microbenchmark

tions with zero priority, to since NOrecPrio should only be used when priority is needed. This leaves two unexpected results: NOrec and TMLLazy both perform slightly worse under our mechanism. For TMLLazy this is not a concern, since it should only be used at low thread counts. For NOrec, our mechanism causes a slowdown of up to 8%.

6.2 Pathology Avoidance

We next consider the role that adaptivity can play in preventing livelock and starvation. While we fully expect that better policies can be discovered, our hope is that the simple policies proposed in Section 5 suffice to prevent pathological behavior, while also resulting in good overall performance.

To this end, we assess a microbenchmark designed to force starvation [36]: half of the threads attempt to forward-traverse a doubly linked list and modify every element, while the other half of the threads backward-traverse the same list while modifying every element. In this workload, eager STM algorithms livelock, and lazy algorithms admit starvation. We configured the runtime to transition from Mutex after a spin delay of 2048 cycles, and to transition among STM algorithms after 32 consecutive aborts. Figure 4 depicts throughput, and Table 3 lists the peak and minimum per-thread commit rates for an 8-threaded run. The "Ratio" column shows the relative difference between the commit count of the "Worst" and "Best" threads.

Surprisingly, Mutex provides excellent fairness. Unfortunately, our X and E policies do not converge upon Mutex for multithreaded workloads. This is a case in which Usui's mechanism would be desirable [43]. Once Mutex is abandoned, the system quickly settles upon the "most fair" system for a given semantics. Thus with no semantics specified, the expensive but extremely even-handed "Fair" runtime is chosen, whereas when ELA semantics are needed, "NOrecPrio" is selected. While these choices satisfy our first goal of preventing livelock and starvation, they incur too much latency, suggesting that more work is needed to develop high-performance STM algorithms that ensure fairness and also provide strong semantics. Alternatively, pathological workloads may be best served by a fair mutex [24].

6.3 Maximizing Throughput

We next assess the ability of our simple policies to maximize throughput. We consider seven STAMP benchmarks [4].[5]

---
[5] The released version of "yada" is known to have bugs.

	Total Transactions	Worst	Best	Ratio
Mutex	8322233	849533	1220701	1.43×
Orec-ELA	282025	1525	136304	89.37×
Orec-Eager	0	0	0	N/A
Orec-Lazy	274131	2279	109604	48.09×
Fair	137066	15600	19285	1.23×
NOrec	447261	3228	271977	84.25×
NOrecPrio	409127	24832	88559	3.56×
Ring	397629	101	288094	2852.41×
TML	3519083	343459	727618	2.11×
TMLLazy	471460	47	282923	6019.63×
E Policy	408445	24877	85129	3.42×
ER Policy	408337	24972	95931	3.84×
X Policy	136156	15267	19119	1.25×
R Policy	135313	15366	19285	1.25×

Table 3: Commit behavior for collision microbenchmark at 8 threads.

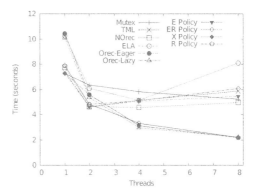

Figure 5: STAMP SSCA2

Since we are evaluating the use of adaptivity to avoid conflicts, we chose the "high contention" STAMP parameters, when available. Otherwise, the default parameters were used. While we tested all ten STM implementations, we omit curves that are not relevant to the discussion; specifically, if a curve never offers peak performance, and is never selected by one of our policies, we do not include it. We also omit Mutex in workloads where its performance is equal to the STM systems at one thread, since Mutex does not scale.

SSCA2: SSCA2 (Figure 5) shows two groupings: Orec-Eager and Orec-Lazy offer peak throughput; the X and R policies match this throughput at high thread counts, while offering the lower latency of Mutex and TML at low thread counts. The second grouping corresponds to ELA semantics: here NOrec performs best at high thread counts. Since true conflicts are rare (at 8 threads, NOrec aborts only 10 times per thread, while committing more than 2.8M transactions, Orec-ELA aborts 600 times per thread, and Ring aborts 33K times per thread), there are never enough consecutive aborts to force the E and ER policies to transition away from Orec-ELA. As a result, our mechanism transitions to Orec-ELA at 4 threads, but not to the higher-performing NOrec runtime. At 8 threads, increased aborts lead the policies to choose NOrec.

Vacation: Vacation emphasizes the cost of transactional instrumentation at one thread (Figure 6). Fortunately, our adaptive policies are able to avoid this cost, for the most part. The large gap between TMLLazy and Mutex (and hence between the E/X policies and the ER/R policies) suggests that an additional runtime, based on Mutex but offering undo logging, may be desirable to avoid overhead when self-abort is needed. With multiple threads, our STM implementations perform roughly equivalently, despite substantially different abort rates, and it is easy for our adaptive

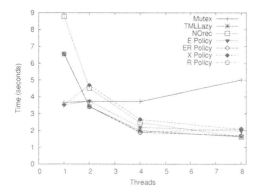

Figure 6: STAMP Vacation (High Contention)

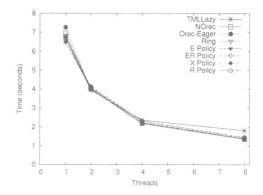

Figure 8: STAMP Genome

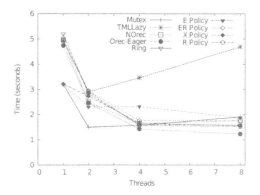

Figure 7: STAMP KMeans (High Contention)

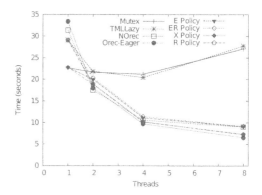

Figure 9: STAMP Intruder

policies to perform well. At 8 threads, NOrec outperforms its orec-based counterparts, but the X and R policies do not transition to it, resulting in slightly slower run times.

KMeans: KMeans (Figure 7) executes a clustering algorithm. There are many read-only transactions, and much nontransactional work. Mutex scales up to two threads, after which point Orec-Eager is fastest. The true conflict rate is high (about 25% at 8 threads), and thus our adaptivity policy quickly moves away from Orec-Eager to the slightly lower-performing Orec-Lazy. When ELA semantics are required, the system chooses NOrec, which performs best.

Genome: There is little of interest in the Genome workload (Figure 8), as all STM implementations scale at roughly the same rate. We note that the adaptive policies succeed in remaining tightly grouped with the best algorithms, rather than experiencing a performance degradation at 8 threads.

Intruder: Intruder shows the same behavior as SSCA2 (Figure 9). When ELA semantics are not requested, performance matches the best orec-based system, and when ELA semantics are required, performance tracks with NOrec, the best ELA implementation.

Bayes: The Bayes benchmark (Figure 10) exhibits nondeterminism, as the order in which transactions commit dictates the total number of transactions performed. There are very few transactions, despite the long running time, and very few aborts. Consequently, our heuristic does not effectively move the STM out of TML modes, and thus our performance is far from best except with the X policy, which moves directly from Mutex to Orec-Eager, bypassing TML.

Labyrinth: In the labyrinth workload (Figure 11), Orec-based and NOrec-based STMs never experience any aborts,

but TML and TMLLazy transactions may starve; Ring transactions also experience aborts. As a result, our consecutive-abort-based adaptivity policy is able to steer the workload toward the STM implementations that give the best performance. Unfortunately, there are only about 1000 total transactions in the workload, despite the long running time. As a result, the performance of the adaptive systems does not match the Orec/NOrec systems, as it takes several seconds to trigger transitions.

Taken as a whole, these experiments demonstrate that adaptivity can prevent worst-case behavior, even when using only a simple heuristic such as consecutive aborts. Across all workloads, we observe single-thread performance that competes favorably, while respecting both the semantics and self-abort requirements of the application. We also see the system adapt to select a good STM implementation at each thread count. While an exploration of more powerful adaptivity policies is clearly needed, these initial results already demonstrate the effectiveness of our low-cost mechanism.

7. CONCLUSIONS AND FUTURE WORK

In this paper we present a low-overhead mechanism to enable adaptivity in software transactional memory. Unlike previous work, our system is aware of advanced transactional features, such as self-abort, irrevocability, and language-level semantics; it also supports both coarse-grained adaptivity among fundamentally different STM algorithms, and fine-grained adaptivity within an STM implementation.

Our experiments confirm that the cost of adaptivity is low. Often the adaptive system is faster than its non-adaptive

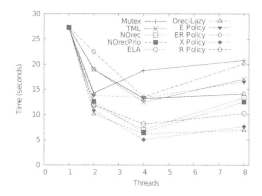

Figure 10: STAMP Bayes

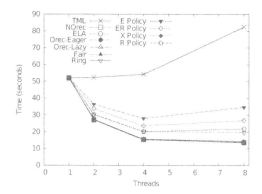

Figure 11: STAMP Labyrinth

counterpart, since the cost of adaptivity is offset by simplifications to the STM implementations. We also evaluate the use of adaptivity in place of contention management, and show that adaptivity enables our simpler STM implementations to achieve good performance and resilience to pathologies.

There are many exciting directions for future work. First, we are adding more STM implementations, such as ones that use visible readers [8,18] or ELA semantics with fine-grained starvation avoidance, since these systems may offer better performance in some cases. Secondly, we intend to integrate fine-grained irrevocability and retry support [36,39,45], as well as support for ALA semantics [25]. We are also adding a system that can use best-effort hardware TM, as well as systems that coordinate via adaptivity (e.g., by overwriting another transaction's function pointers to direct it to abort).

We are also exploring new adaptivity policies. We have implementing a "profiling" mode, which can be used at the beginning of a phase to estimate the duration of transactions and their frequency of reads and writes. By measuring these statistics once per change of algorithm, we hope to incur minimal cost while providing adaptivity policies with detailed information. Coupling this with automatic phase detection [33] could produce very robust systems.

Our system is available as open-source software, to enable more widespread research into STM adaptivity.

Acknowledgments

We thank Luke Dalessandro, Dave Dice, Torvald Riegel, and Sean White for numerous helpful discussions during the conduct of this research. Kyle Liddell developed the software interface between RSTM and STAMP, and Kostas Menychtas produced the version of RingSW upon which our implementation is based. We would also like to thank Adam Welc and our reviewers for their insights and suggestions.

8. REFERENCES

[1] M. Abadi, T. Harris, and M. Mehrara. Transactional Memory with Strong Atomicity Using Off-the-Shelf Memory Protection Hardware. In *Proceedings of the 14th ACM SIGPLAN Symposium on Principles and Practice of Parallel Programming*, Raleigh, NC, Feb. 2009.

[2] B. H. Bloom. Space/Time Trade-offs in Hash Coding with Allowable Errors. *Communications of the ACM*, 13(7):422–426, 1970.

[3] C. Blundell, J. Devietti, E. C. Lewis, and M. Martin. Making the Fast Case Common and the Uncommon Case Simple in Unbounded Transactional Memory. In *Proceedings of the 34th International Symposium on Computer Architecture*, San Diego, CA, June 2007.

[4] C. Cao Minh, J. Chung, C. Kozyrakis, and K. Olukotun. STAMP: Stanford Transactional Applications for Multi-processing. In *Proceedings of the IEEE International Symposium on Workload Characterization*, Seattle, WA, Sept. 2008.

[5] L. Dalessandro, M. F. Spear, and M. L. Scott. NOrec: Streamlining STM by Abolishing Ownership Records. In *Proceedings of the 15th ACM SIGPLAN Symposium on Principles and Practice of Parallel Programming*, Bangalore, India, Jan. 2010.

[6] D. Dice, Y. Lev, M. Moir, and D. Nussbaum. Early Experience with a Commercial Hardware Transactional Memory Implementation. In *Proceedings of the 14th International Conference on Architectural Support for Programming Languages and Operating Systems*, Washington, DC, Mar. 2009.

[7] D. Dice, O. Shalev, and N. Shavit. Transactional Locking II. In *Proceedings of the 20th International Symposium on Distributed Computing*, Stockholm, Sweden, Sept. 2006.

[8] D. Dice and N. Shavit. TLRW: Return of the Read-Write Lock. In *Proceedings of the 4th ACM SIGPLAN Workshop on Transactional Computing*, Raleigh, NC, Feb. 2009.

[9] S. Diestelhorst and M. Hohmuth. Hardware Acceleration for Lock-Free Data Structures and Software-Transactional Memory. In *Proceedings of the Workshop on Exploiting Parallelism with Transactional Memory and other Hardware Assisted Methods*, Boston, MA, Apr. 2008.

[10] P. Felber, C. Fetzer, U. Müller, T. Riegel, M. Süßkraut, and H. Sturzrehm. Transactifying Applications using an Open Compiler Framework. In *Proceedings of the 2nd ACM SIGPLAN Workshop on Transactional Computing*, Portland, OR, Aug. 2007.

[11] P. Felber, C. Fetzer, and T. Riegel. Dynamic Performance Tuning of Word-Based Software Transactional Memory. In *Proceedings of the 13th ACM SIGPLAN Symposium on Principles and Practice of Parallel Programming*, Salt Lake City, UT, Feb. 2008.

[12] K. Fraser. *Practical Lock-Freedom*. PhD thesis, King's College, University of Cambridge, Sept. 2003.

[13] J. Gottschlich and D. Connors. Extending Contention Managers for User-Defined Priority-Based Transactions. In *Proceedings of the Workshop on Exploiting Parallelism with Transactional Memory and other Hardware Assisted Methods*, Boston, MA, Apr. 2008.

[14] R. Guerraoui, M. Herlihy, and B. Pochon. Toward a Theory of Transactional Contention Managers. In *Proceedings of the 24th ACM Symposium on Principles of Distributed Computing*, Las Vegas, NV, July 2005.

[15] T. Harris, S. Marlow, S. Peyton Jones, and M. Herlihy. Composable Memory Transactions. In *Proceedings of the 10th ACM SIGPLAN Symposium on Principles and Practice of Parallel Programming*, Chicago, IL, June 2005.

[16] R. L. Hudson, B. Saha, A.-R. Adl-Tabatabai, and B. Hertzberg. A Scalable Transactional Memory Allocator. In *Proceedings of the 2006 International Symposium on Memory Management*, Ottawa, ON, Canada, June 2006.

[17] J. Lau, E. Perelman, and B. Calder. Selecting Software Phase Markers with Code Structure Analysis. In *Proceedings of the 2006 International Symposium on Code Generation and Optimization*, New York, NY, Mar. 2006.

[18] Y. Lev, V. Luchangco, V. Marathe, M. Moir, D. Nussbaum, and M. Olszewski. Anatomy of a Scalable Software Transactional Memory. In *Proceedings of the 4th ACM SIGPLAN Workshop on Transactional Computing*, Raleigh, NC, Feb. 2009.

[19] Y. Lev, M. Moir, and D. Nussbaum. PhTM: Phased Transactional Memory. In *Proceedings of the 2nd ACM SIGPLAN Workshop on Transactional Computing*, Portland, OR, Aug. 2007.

[20] V. Marathe and M. Moir. Toward High Performance Nonblocking Software Transactional Memory . In *Proceedings of the 13th ACM SIGPLAN Symposium on Principles and Practice of Parallel Programming*, Salt Lake City, UT, Feb. 2008.

[21] V. J. Marathe, W. N. Scherer III, and M. L. Scott. Adaptive Software Transactional Memory. In *Proceedings of the 19th International Symposium on Distributed Computing*, Cracow, Poland, Sept. 2005.

[22] V. J. Marathe, M. F. Spear, C. Heriot, A. Acharya, D. Eisenstat, W. N. Scherer III, and M. L. Scott. Lowering the Overhead of Nonblocking Software Transactional Memory. In *Proceedings of the 1st ACM SIGPLAN Workshop on Languages, Compilers, and Hardware Support for Transactional Computing*, Ottawa, ON, Canada, June 2006.

[23] V. J. Marathe, M. F. Spear, and M. L. Scott. Scalable Techniques for Transparent Privatization in Software Transactional Memory. In *Proceedings of the 37th International Conference on Parallel Processing*, Portland, OR, Sept. 2008.

[24] J. M. Mellor-Crummey and M. L. Scott. Algorithms for Scalable Synchronization on Shared-Memory Multiprocessors. *ACM Transactions on Computer Systems*, 9(1), 1991.

[25] V. Menon, S. Balensiefer, T. Shpeisman, A.-R. Adl-Tabatabai, R. Hudson, B. Saha, and A. Welc. Practical Weak-Atomicity Semantics for Java STM. In *Proceedings of the 20th ACM Symposium on Parallelism in Algorithms and Architectures*, Munich, Germany, June 2008.

[26] Y. Ni, A. Welc, A.-R. Adl-Tabatabai, M. Bach, S. Berkowits, J. Cownie, R. Geva, S. Kozhukow, R. Narayanaswamy, J. Olivier, S. Preis, B. Saha, A. Tal, and X. Tian. Design and Implementation of Transactional Constructs for C/C++. In *Proceedings of the 23rd ACM SIGPLAN Conference on Object Oriented Programming Systems Languages and Applications*, Nashville, TN, USA, Oct. 2008.

[27] M. Olszewski, J. Cutler, and J. G. Steffan. JudoSTM: A Dynamic Binary-Rewriting Approach to Software Transactional Memory. In *Proceedings of the 16th International Conference on Parallel Architecture and Compilation Techniques*, Brasov, Romania, Sept. 2007.

[28] T. Riegel, P. Felber, and C. Fetzer. A Lazy Snapshot Algorithm with Eager Validation. In *Proceedings of the 20th International Symposium on Distributed Computing*, Stockholm, Sweden, Sept. 2006.

[29] T. Riegel, C. Fetzer, and P. Felber. Automatic Data Partitioning in Software Transactional Memories. In *Proceedings of the 20th ACM Symposium on Parallelism in Algorithms and Architectures*, Munich, Germany, June 2008.

[30] Rochester Synchronization Group. Rochester STM, 2006–2010. http://www.cs.rochester.edu/research/synchronization/rstm/.

[31] B. Saha, A.-R. Adl-Tabatabai, and Q. Jacobson. Architectural Support for Software Transactional Memory. In *Proceedings of the 39th IEEE/ACM International Symposium on Microarchitecture*, Orlando, FL, Dec. 2006.

[32] W. N. Scherer III and M. L. Scott. Advanced Contention Management for Dynamic Software Transactional Memory. In *Proceedings of the 24th ACM Symposium on Principles of Distributed Computing*, Las Vegas, NV, July 2005.

[33] X. Shen, Y. Zhong, and C. Ding. Locality Phase Prediction. In *Proceedings of the 11th International Conference on Architectural Support for Programming Languages and Operating Systems*, Boston, MA, Oct. 2004.

[34] N. Sonmez, T. Harris, A. Cristal, O. S. Unsal, and M. Valero. Taking the Heat Off Transactions: Dynamic Selection of Pessimistic Concurrency Control. In *Proceedings of the 23rd International Parallel and Distributed Processing Symposium*, Rome, Italy, May 2009.

[35] M. F. Spear, L. Dalessandro, V. J. Marathe, and M. L. Scott. Ordering-Based Semantics for Software Transactional Memory. In *Proceedings of the 12th International Conference On Principles Of DIstributed Systems*, Luxor, Egypt, Dec. 2008.

[36] M. F. Spear, L. Dalessandro, V. J. Marathe, and M. L. Scott. A Comprehensive Strategy for Contention Management in Software Transactional Memory. In *Proceedings of the 14th ACM SIGPLAN Symposium on Principles and Practice of Parallel Programming*, Raleigh, NC, Feb. 2009.

[37] M. F. Spear, K. Kelsey, T. Bai, L. Dalessandro, M. L. Scott, C. Ding, and P. Wu. Fastpath Speculative Parallelism. In *Proceedings of the 22nd International Workshop on Languages and Compilers for Parallel Computing*, Newark, DE, Oct. 2009.

[38] M. F. Spear, V. J. Marathe, W. N. Scherer III, and M. L. Scott. Conflict Detection and Validation Strategies for Software Transactional Memory. In *Proceedings of the 20th International Symposium on Distributed Computing*, Stockholm, Sweden, Sept. 2006.

[39] M. F. Spear, M. M. Michael, and M. L. Scott. Inevitability Mechanisms for Software Transactional Memory. In *Proceedings of the 3rd ACM SIGPLAN Workshop on Transactional Computing*, Salt Lake City, UT, Feb. 2008.

[40] M. F. Spear, M. M. Michael, M. L. Scott, and P. Wu. Reducing Memory Ordering Overheads in Software Transactional Memory. In *Proceedings of the 2009 International Symposium on Code Generation and Optimization*, Seattle, WA, Mar. 2009.

[41] M. F. Spear, M. M. Michael, and C. von Praun. RingSTM: Scalable Transactions with a Single Atomic Instruction. In *Proceedings of the 20th ACM Symposium on Parallelism in Algorithms and Architectures*, Munich, Germany, June 2008.

[42] M. F. Spear, A. Shriraman, L. Dalessandro, and M. Scott. Transactional Mutex Locks. In *Proceedings of the 4th ACM SIGPLAN Workshop on Transactional Computing*, Raleigh, NC, Feb. 2009.

[43] T. Usui, Y. Smaragdakis, R. Behrends, and J. Evans. Adaptive Locks: Combining Transactions and Locks for Efficient Concurrency. In *Proceedings of the 18th International Conference on Parallel Architecture and Compilation Techniques*, Raleigh, NC, Sept. 2009.

[44] C. Wang, W.-Y. Chen, Y. Wu, B. Saha, and A.-R. Adl-Tabatabai. Code Generation and Optimization for Transactional Memory Constructs in an Unmanaged Language. In *Proceedings of the 2007 International Symposium on Code Generation and Optimization*, San Jose, CA, Mar. 2007.

[45] A. Welc, B. Saha, and A.-R. Adl-Tabatabai. Irrevocable Transactions and their Applications. In *Proceedings of the 20th ACM Symposium on Parallelism in Algorithms and Architectures*, Munich, Germany, June 2008.

Appendix 1: Additional Microbenchmark Results

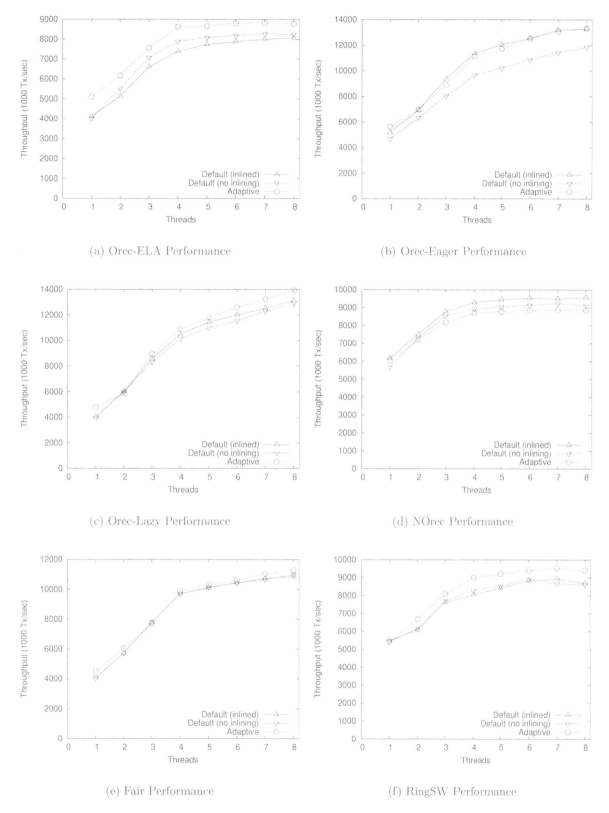

(a) Orec-ELA Performance

(b) Orec-Eager Performance

(c) Orec-Lazy Performance

(d) NOrec Performance

(e) Fair Performance

(f) RingSW Performance

Figure 12: Microbenchmark performance for STM runtimes, using the RSTM RBTree-256 Benchmark.

TLRW: Return of the Read-Write Lock

Dave Dice
Sun Labs at Oracle
One Network Drive
Burlington, MA 01803-0903, USA
dave.dice@oracle.com

Nir Shavit
Tel-Aviv University & Sun Labs at Oracle
Tel-Aviv 69978, Israel
shanir@cs.tau.ac.il

ABSTRACT

TL2 and similar STM algorithms deliver high scalability based on write-locking and invisible readers. In fact, no modern STM design locks to read along its common execution path because doing so would require a memory synchronization operation that would greatly hamper performance.

In this paper we introduce TLRW, a new STM algorithm intended for the single-chip multicore systems that are quickly taking over a large fraction of the computing landscape. We make the claim that the cost of coherence in such single chip systems is down to a level that allows one to design a scalable STM based on read-write locks. TLRW is based on byte-locks, a novel read-write lock design with a low read-lock acquisition overhead and the ability to take advantage of the locality of reference within transactions. As we show, TLRW has a painfully simple design, one that naturally provides coherent state without validation, implicit privatization, and irrevocable transactions. Providing similar properties in STMs based on invisible-readers (such as TL2) has typically resulted in a major loss of performance.

In a series of benchmarks we show that when running on a 64-way single-chip multicore machine, TLRW delivers surprisingly good performance (competitive with and sometimes outperforming TL2). However, on a 128-way 2-chip system that has higher coherence costs across the interconnect, performance deteriorates rapidly. We believe our work raises the question of whether on single-chip multicore machines, read-write lock-based STMs are the way to go.

Categories and Subject Descriptors

D.2.8 [Software Engineering]: Algorithms

General Terms

Algorithms, Performance

Keywords

Multiprocessors, Transactional Memory, Read-Write Locks

1. INTRODUCTION

STM design has come a long way since the first STM algorithm by Shavit and Touitou [27], which provided a non-blocking implementation of static transactions (see [4, 7, 10, 15, 19, 21, 22, 24, 26, 27, 28]). A fundamental paper by Ennals [7] suggested that on modern operating systems, deadlock avoidance is the only compelling reason for making transactions non-blocking, and that there is no reason to provide it for transactions at the user level. Lock-based STMs typically outperform the fastest lock-free ones, even those that avoid indirection in accessing shared transactional metadata [10, 29, 18]. Deadlocks and livelocks are dealt with using timeouts and the ability of transactions to request other transactions to abort. Ennals's view was quickly seconded by Dice and Shavit [5] and by Saha et al [26]. The final barrier to the acceptance of such lock-based algorithms was removed with the introduction of global clock based consistency by Dice, Shalev, and Shavit [4] (the idea of using a global clock for internal consistency was independently proposed by Reigel, Felber, and Fetzer in the context of their non-blocking Snapshot Isolation STM and LSA algorithms[24, 25]).

Today, most, if not all new lock-based STMs use a variation of the TL2/LSA style global-clock algorithm using invisible reads. When we say invisible reads, we mean that the STM does not know how many readers might be accessing a given memory location. The drawback of invisible read based STMs are the overheads associated with maintaining and validating a read-set of locations [4], and the unacceptably high cost of providing *implicit privatization* [21] and *proxy privatization*[1] [15, 17]. One should note that STMs that use centralized data structures, such as RingSTM [28] or compiler assisted coarse grained locking schemes [21], can provide implicit privatization without the need for explicit visible readers.

Despite these drawbacks, using invisible reads is compelling since visible reads require that the number of readers, or at the very least, the existence of readers, be recorded per memory location. This is a task that on the face of it requires a relatively expensive synchronization per read operation. There are novel mechanisms such as the scalable non-zero indicators (SNZI) of Ellen et al [6], that greatly reduce the synchronization overhead of detecting readers.

---

[1]Proxy privatization is the case of implicit privatization where one thread's transaction privatizes an object that is then used privately by another thread. This might, in some cases, turn out to be harder than privatizing for a thread's own use.

Unfortunately, SNZI at the very least requires a CAS per increment or decrement operation. Moreover, when contended it requires a distributed tree of cache-line independent nodes leading to the "indicator" location. This is an unacceptable space complexity in practice.

1.1 Our New Approach

In this paper, we examine STM design in the context of multicore systems-on-a-chip, a class of architectures that is already common in the server space and is rapidly taking over the desktop computing space. For such systems, we claim that the cost of coherence is down to a level that suggests another way to approach the problem: designing visible-reader based STMs using *read-write* locks.[2]. We call our new read-write lock based STM design *TLRW*, and its key algorithmic technique, the *byte-lock*.

Why design an STM based on read-write locking? Because the overall design is significantly simpler and more streamlined than invisible read based STMs like TL2, TinySTM [8], or McRT [26], in which one locks only written locations and validates coherence of the ones being read. In contrast, in a read-write lock-based STM, a transaction locks every location before either reading or writing. Then, upon completion, it releases all the locks. This simple design confers amazing benefits:

- No costly validation of the read and write set (what you lock is what you get).

- Stronger progress properties (especially for long transactions) than invisible read based STMs such as TL2.

- Implicit privatization including implicit proxy privatization.

- Support for irrevocable transactions [30].

The TLRW design provides the latter two properties naturally and with virtually no overhead.

Read-write lock based STMs like TLRW have been suggested in the past [23, 26], but dismissed because of the overhead of performing a costly synchronization operations per read access (empirically measured to slowdown STMs by several orders of magnitude on some benchmarks [26]). Even on multicore chips, existing read-write lock designs that count readers simply do not scale because of these synchronization overheads. To overcome this problem, we introduce *byte-locks*, a new class of high performance read-write locks designed to deliver scalable performance in the face of high levels of read-lock acquisition.

The idea behind byte-locks is in itself very simple, and we ourselves were surprised at the scalable performance they deliver in the context of TLRW transactions. In a nutshell, in a byte-lock, we split the lock record into an array of bytes, one per thread. On modern AMD, Intel, and Sun processors, these bytes can be written individually and read in batches. Each thread is assigned a byte, which it uses as a flag indicating it is reading the location. The byte is set using a simple store followed by a store-load memory barrier. This has the advantage of avoiding CAS operations that typically have excessive local latency, can be interfered with and require a retry, and on systems such as Niagara, may incur

a cache invalidation [3]. As we show, the benefit of this design is scalable performance in the common case. The lock-word also contains a 32 bit counter that is incremented or decremented using CAS by all reader threads that were not assigned a byte in the byte-array. On current architectures one can use 48 bytes that align on a single cache line (or 112 that align on two cache lines with little performance loss).

We support our thesis, that read-write lock-based STMs are a viable approach on state-of-the-art single chip multicore systems, through a series of benchmarks. These are, unfortunately, standard micro benchmarks and not real applications, but we hope they will suffice to convince the reader of the benefits and drawbacks of our design. We tested TLRW on single chip UltraSPARC® T2 (Niagara II) and Core® i7 (Nehalem) multicore machines. Our results indicate that TLRW, which always provides implicit privatization, often matches and sometimes outperforms TL2, and always outperforms a version of TL2 with implicit privatization. In some cases, such as for long transactions, TLRW has stronger progress properties than TL2 because the only source of aborts are time-outs, so chances are better that a transaction does not abort after much of it has already completed.

We also tested TLRW on a 128-way Enterprise T5140® server (Maramba) machine, a 2-chip Niagara system, which has relatively high inter-chip coherence costs. Here, as expected, the performance of TLRW was consistently inferior to that of TL2, though in some cases it matched that of TL2 with privatization. Our conclusion, as we hope the reader will agree, is that TLRW suggests a new design direction for lock-based STMs. We believe this direction will become increasingly viable as the cost of coherence on multicore systems drops.

The next section describes our new TLRW algorithm in detail. We then provide a performance section that analyzes its behavior.

2. READ-WRITE LOCK BASED TRANSACTIONAL LOCKING

The TLRW algorithm we describe here is a simple one phase commit style algorithm using read-write locks. This means that threads acquire locks for reading as well as for writing. This approach, by its very nature, guarantees internal consistency [4] and implicit privatization [21]. As we will show, it also allows for a simple implementation of irrevocable transactions [30]. Finally, it avoids some of the performance overheads of invisible-read based STMs such as TL2 [4] and TinySTM [8], since read sets do not record values and there is no need for read-set validation.

Unfortunately, STMs using naive read-write locks have abominable scalability since reading a location requires an update of a "read counter," which requires a CAS operation. Thus, locations that are shared by multiple readers (such as the root of a red-black tree) become hotspots and cause a deterioration in performance.

The claim we wish to make in this paper is that on new multicore machines, as long as one remains on chip (i.e. low coherence costs), using read-write locks is a viable approach if one can get low overhead read-write locks.

---

[2]The trend with new multicore processors by all main manufacturers seems to be towards lower synchronization and coherence costs.

2.1 Read-write Byte-locks

The key idea in our new TLRW algorithm is the use of a new class of read-write lock which we call a *byte-lock*. The byte-lock is directed at minimizing read-lock acquisition overheads. The basic lock structure consists of 64 bytes aligned across a single cache line and logically split into three distinct zones: an *owner* field, a *byte-array*, and a *read-counter*. The *owner* field is set to the thread id of the writer owning the lock and is set to 0 if no writer holds the lock. In the most basic implementation the *byte array* consists of $k = 48$ bytes, one per reader thread with the lower k ids. We will call these k threads the *slotted* threads and the remaining $n - k$ (where n is the total number of threads in the system) the *unslotted* threads. The algorithm will be highly effective for slotted threads and have standard read-write lock performance for the unslotted ones. The third field is a 32-bit *reader-count* of the number of current reader threads used by unslotted reader threads.

Here is how the byte-lock is used to implement a read-write lock by a thread i.

- *To acquire a lock for writing*: thread i uses a CAS to set the owner field from 0 to i. If the field is non-0 there is another owner, so i spins, re-reading the owner field until it is 0. Once the owner field is set to i, it spins until all readers have drained out. To do so, if i is slotted, it sets its reader byte to 0 (just in case it was already a reader). If i is unslotted, it checks a local indicator (such as a transaction's read-set) to determine if it is a reader and decrements its reader-count if it is. In both cases, slotted and unslotted, i then spins until all of the locations of the byte array and the reader-count are 0. Spinning is efficient since one can read 8 bytes of the lock word at a time (on SPARC, more on Intel). To release the write-lock simply store a 0 into the owner field.

- *To acquire a lock for reading*: We implement the lock following the flag principle [12]. Readers store their own byte and then fetch and check the owner, while writers CAS the owner field (we CAS to resolve writer vs. writer conflicts) and then fetch all the reader bytes. In detail:

  - If the thread i is slotted then: if i is the owner or the ith byte in the byte array is set, proceed. Otherwise, store a non-zero value into the ith byte and execute a memory write barrier (no use of CAS). Sparc, Intel, and AMD architectures allow byte-wise stores. If the owner field is non-0, store 0 into the ith byte and spin until the owner becomes 0. In other words, writers get precedence. Repeat until the ith byte is set and no owner is detected. To release, store a 0 to the ith byte field. There is no need for a memory barrier instruction.

  - If thread i is unslotted then: if i is the owner or a local indicator (such as a transaction's read-set) indicates it is a reader, then proceed. Otherwise, increment the reader-count by 1 using a CAS. Check the owner, and if it is non-0 use a CAS to decrement the read-counter by 1. Repeat until after the reader-count is incremented, no owner is

detected. To release, decrement the reader count field using a CAS.

Finally, we note that we allow read-write locks to time-out while attempting to acquire the lock. If lock acquisition times out the thread aborts the transaction and returns an appropriate indication.

The size of the byte-array is based on 64 byte AMD, Sun, or Intel architectures. One can extend k to 112 threads by allowing the lock to extend into a second cache line at the cost of an additional cache access upon read (to be explained later).

The important feature of the new byte-lock is that unlike standard read-write locks, for all slotted threads, reading a location protected by a byte-lock requires a store followed by a memory barrier instruction. It thus avoids a *CAS on the same location* for any of the k slotted threads. CAS has typically high local latency. More importantly perhaps, it is optimistic and can be interfered with and require a retry (one thread's success is bound to cause the next thread to fail), and on systems such as Niagara, may incur a cache invalidation [3]. For unslotted readers, the byte-lock behaves like a normal read-write lock, with threads CASing the same read-counter.

Notice that for slotted threads, there are additional performance benefits. There is no need for a writer to separately track if it is a reader, which means that when used in an STM, it will not have to traverse the read set except to release locks at the end of a transaction. There is also no need for second memory barrier instruction to set the read byte to 0, a thread can simply wait for the processor's pipeline flush. This saves a CAS in many cases relative to standard read/write locks.

2.2 CAS-less Byte-locks

While slotted readers avoid using a CAS, all writer threads, slotted or not, still execute a CAS operation per access. We can actually remove the use of a CAS for any of the slotted threads, both for reading and for writing.

The changes in order to do so are as follows. The lock data structure will have, in addition to the owner field indicating which thread owns the lock for writing, an atomically accessible owner lock field for slotted threads. Each byte will now contain one bit that indicates a read state, and one that indicates a write state. So for example, a byte may be in a state in which both the read and write states are 1, both 0, or only one of them is 0.

Slotted readers behave as in the algorithm above, with the small change of releasing the lock by storing a 0 into the read-bit of their slot's byte. Unslotted readers are unchanged.

To acquire write permission, a slotted writer will first use the slots and owner lock field to acquire the lock for writing as follows:

- Store a non-zero value into the write bit in the assigned slot in the lock's array (leave the read bit unchanged); Execute a memory write barrier instruction to make sure the store is globally visible before the following read or write.

- Scan through the array and owner lock field to check if there is another slot with the write bit set to 1 or if the owner lock field is set to 1. If true, lower the write bit (no need for a memory write barrier) and retry from Step 1 (One can add a backoff scheme to this retry).

- Otherwise, there is no other slot with its write bit set and the owner lock is free. Set the owner field to your thread ID (to let readers know there is a writer and cause them to drain out) and store 0 into the read bit of your slot. Execute a memory write barrier instruction to make sure the write of the owner field is visible to all readers. You now have acquired write permission.

- Wait for all currently active readers to depart and relinquish reader access. That is, wait until the read indicator field is 0 and the read bits have been observed as 0 and for all slots of the array (you already lowered your own).

- Enter the critical section and start writing.

- To release the lock, set the owner field to null and then set the write-bit in the associated slot to 0. No need for a store-load memory barrier.

One can add tests if the owner field is null as optimizations before the first and third steps.

We next describe how unslotted threads acquire the lock for writing.

Unslotted writes perform an algorithm similar to the above use a CAS to acquire the write-lock. They then scan through the array in a manner similar to the slotted writers. If there is no other slot with its write bit set, set the owner field to your thread ID (notifying readers that they must drain out). Execute a memory write barrier instruction to make sure the write of the owner field is visible to all readers. You now have acquired write permission.. If you are also a reader use a CAS to decrement the read-indicator counter.

Now, as with a slotted write, wait for all currently active readers to depart and relinquish reader access, then enter the critical section and start writing. To release the lock set the owner field to null and then release the owner-lock (store 0 into it). No need for a memory write barrier.

2.3 The Basic TLRW byte-lock Algorithm

In our TLRW design, we associate a byte-lock with every transacted memory location (one could alternately use a byte-lock per object). We stripe the locks across the memory, so that multiple locations share the same lock. This saves space but can lead to false write conflicts in a manner similar to [4, 31]. We maintain thread local read- and write-sets as linked lists. These sets track locations on which locks are held. The write set contains undo values since our algorithm will store new values in-place, but it should be noted that our algorithm could support a redo log as well, in which case read-locks would be acquired during the speculative execution phase and write-lock acquisition would be deferred until commit-time.

We now describe the basic TLRW algorithm. Unlike TL2, TLRW does not require safe loads. The following sequence of operations is performed by a *transaction*, one that performs both reads and writes to the shared memory.

1. **Run through an execution:** Execute the transaction code. Locally maintain a *read-set* of addresses loaded and an *undo write set* of address/value pairs

stored. This logging functionality is implemented simply by augmenting loads with instructions that record the read address and replacing stores with code recording the address and value to-be-written in case the transaction must abort.[3]

The transactional read attempts to acquire a location's read-lock. (As an optimization it can delay waiting for a bus lock to be released). If the acquisition is successful, it reads the location, records the location in the read-set and returns the location's value. Similarly, a transactional write acquires the location's write lock, records the current value in the undo set, and writes the value to the location.

2. **Time out abort:** The only source of *aborts* is a time out by some thread while attempting to acquire a lock. In such a case, threads use the undo write log to return all locations to their pre-transaction values. It then releases all the read and write locks it holds.

3. **Commit** release the write locks and then the read locks.

The beauty of this algorithm in comparison to most STM algorithms in the literature, is its simplicity. The only reason to abort transactions is deadlock avoidance, which makes for a very strong progress property. Other more elaborate schemes, such as detecting cycles in a 'waits for' graph are also possible and may be worthwhile in some contexts.

The following safety properties follow almost immediately from the fact that a transaction holds locks on all locations it reads or writes. TLRW Transactions are internally consistent (i.e. operate on consistent states [4, 9]), are externally consistent (i.e. are serializable [13]), and provide implicit privatization and implicit proxy privatization. In terms of liveness, from the fact that byte-locks are deadlock-free and eventually transactions time out, it follows that TLRW Transactions never deadlock.

In terms of lockout-freedom, guarantees are similar to those of the TL2 algorithm in the sense that livelocks can happen only if transactions time-out again and again. However, notice that here transactions do not cause each other to repeatedly abort by invalidating each other's read set. Livelocks can happen only if some threads are slow to release locks. To lower the chances of such livelocks, we use an exponential backoff scheme on the completion time, the delay before a transaction is timed-out. Notice that we add spinning to byte-lock acquisition attempts only as an optimization, while exponentially backing off on the completion time is crucial.

2.4 Irrevocable Transactions

A further benefit of TLRW is that one can readily implement irrevocable transactions. Irrevocable transactions, introduced by [30], are transactions that never abort, and can be used in case the transaction contains an I/O operation or is long and will never complete in an optimistic fashion (a hash table resize or an iterator call on a search structure). We use the "irrevocable transaction" approach best outlined

---

[3]Notice that there is no need for non-faulting loads or trap handlers. In TL2 one had to use a non-faulting load as a transaction fetch may have loaded from a just privatized region that had been made unreachable.

in a paper by Welc et al [30, 23], albeit in a much simpler fashion, and with a stronger progress guarantee.

The idea outlined by Welc et al is simple. We will guarantee that there is always no more than one active irrevocable transaction, allowing some active irrevocable transaction to complete. This is done by maintaining a global *irrevocable-bit* or, to guarantee stronger progress, an *irrevocable-lock* consisting of a CLH queue-lock [2, 16]. Any irrevocable transaction sets the bit (alternately attempts to acquire the CLH lock) using a CAS. Once the bit is set (alternately the CLH lock is acquired), the transaction proceeds without ever timing out. If a deadlock situation arises, the *revocable* transactions involved in it will eventually time out and free the locations that will allow the single irrevocable transaction to proceed. Notice that by using a CLH lock, we can guarantee FCFS order on the irrevocable transactions so they are guaranteed to never starve. While such transactions are in progress, all revocable transactions that do not overlap in memory can proceed as usual.

The overhead of the irrevocable bit mechanism is minimal since transactions are spinning locally, and if one deals with long transactions, the CLH lock can be replaced by a monitor style lock that allow transactions to sleep while they are queued (the overhead of such a lock will be mitigated by the transactions cost, say, the cost of an I/O operation or its being long.

3. EMPIRICAL PERFORMANCE EVALUATION

This section presents a comparison of our TLRW algorithm using byte-locks to algorithms representing state-of-the-art lock-based [7] STMs on a set of microbenchmarks that include the now standard concurrent red-black tree structure [11] and a randomized work-distribution benchmark in the style of [27].

The red-black tree was derived from the `java.util.TreeMap` implementation found in the Java 6.0 JDK. That implementation was written by Doug Lea and Josh Bloch. In turn, parts of the Java TreeMap were derived from the Cormen et al [1]. We would have preferred to use the exact Fraser-Harris red-black tree but that code was written to to their specific transactional interface and could not readily be converted to a simple form.

The red-black tree implementation exposes a key-value pair interface of *put*, *delete*, and *get* operations. The put operation installs a key-value pair or the value if it already exists. The get operation returns an indication if the key was present in the data structure. Finally, delete removes a key from the data structure, returning an indication if the key was found to be present in the data structure. The key range of 2K elements generates a small size tree while the range of 20K elements creates a large tree, implying a larger transaction size for the set operations. We report the aggregate number of successful transactions completed in the measurement interval, which in our case is 10 seconds.

In the random-array benchmark each worker thread loops, generating a random index into the array and then executes a transaction having R reads, W writes, and RW read-modify-write operations. (The order of the read, write, and read-write accesses within a transaction is also randomized). The index is selected with replacement via a uniform random number generator. While overly simplistic we believe

our model still captures critical locality of reference properties found in actual programs. We report the aggregate number of successful transactions completed in the measurement interval, which in our case is 10 seconds.

For our experiments we used 64-way Sun UltraSPARC® T2 multicore machine running Solaris™ 10. This is a machine with 8 cores that multiplex 8 hardware threads each and share an on chip L2 cache. We also used a 128-way Enterprise T5140® server (Maramba) machine, a 2-chip Niagara system. Finally, we used an Intel Core2® i7-920 (Nehalem) processor with 4 cores that each multiplex 2 hardware threads.

In our benchmarks we "transactified" the data structures by hand: explicitly adding transactional load and store operators, but ultimately we believe that compilers should perform this transformation. We did so since our goal is to explore the mechanisms and performance of the underlying transactional infrastructure and not the language-level expression of "atomic." Our benchmarked algorithms included:

Mutex We respectively used the Solaris and Linux POSIX threads library mutex as a coarse-grained locking mechanism.

TL2 The transactional locking algorithm of [4] using the GV4 global clock algorithm that attempts to update the shared clock in every transaction, but only once: even if the CAS fails, it continues on to validate and commit. We use the latest version of TL2 which (through several code optimizations, as opposed to algorithmic changes) has about 25% better single threaded latency than the version used in in [4]. This algorithm is representative of a class of high performance lock-based algorithms such as [26, 30, 8].

TL2-IP A version of TL2 with an added mechanism to provide implicit privatization. Our scheme, which we discovered independently in 2007, was also discovered by Marathe et al. [20] who in turn attribute the idea to Detlefs et al. It works by using a simplistic GV1 global clock advanced with CAS [4] before the validation of the read-set. We also add a new *egress* global variable, whose value "chases" the clock in the manner of a ticket lock. We opted to use GV1 so we could leverage the global clock as the incoming side of a ticket lock. In the transactional load operator each thread keeps track of the most recent GV (global clock) value that it observed, and if it changed since the last load, we refresh the thread local value and revalidate the read-set. That introduces a validation cost that is in the worst case quadratic. These two changes – serializing egress from the commit – and revalidation are sufficient to give TL2 implicit privatization. These changes solve both halves of the implicit privatization problem, the 1st half being the window in commit where a thread has acquired write locks, validated its read-set, but some other transaction races past and writes to a location in the 1st thread's read-set, privatizing a region to which the 1st thread is about to write into. Serializing egress solves that problem. The 2nd half of the serialization problem is that one can end up with zombie reader transactions if a thread reads some variable and then accesses a region contingent or dependent on that variable, but some other thread stores into that variable, privatizing the region. Revalidating the read-set avoids that problem by forcing the 1st thread to discover the update and causing it to self-abort.

TLRW-IOMux A version of our read-write lock-based STM with the byte-locks replaced by a pair of counters to track read-lock acquisition. One counter is incremented upon read lock access, and the other is decremented once the read lock is released. We found this splitting of the reader-count performed better than using a single reader-count that is both incremented and decremented.

TLRW-bytelock A version of our new byte-lock based TLRW algorithm that has a lock spanning a single line with $k = 48$. We used the simplest byte-lock form (in which writers always perform a CAS). We also tried a lock spanning two 64 byte cache lines with $k = 112$ which we will call *TLRW-bytelock-128*. We plan to, but did not, devise a dynamic switching mechanism between the two forms though as the reader will see, the data indicates such a mechanism would be beneficial.

Our algorithm uses early (encounter order) lock acquisition and an undo write set.

TLRW-BitLock It is precisely the same as TLRW-ByteLock except that we replace the a 48-byte reader array with a 64-bit reader mask field. To keep things as similar and comparable as possible we constrained the mask field to supporting only 48 "slots," with the unslotted threads using the reader counter. Similarly, we padded the lock records so they are the same length in both TLRW-ByteLock and TLRW-BitLock. Stores of 0 or 1 into the reader array in TLRW-ByteLock code become CAS-based loops that load and set or clear the bit associated with a slotted thread. What were previously loads of a slot in the reader array now become loads of the reader bitmask and a mask/test of the thread's bit.

We begin by noting that we implemented a version of TLRW-ByteLock with lazy acquisition (instead of early acquisition and an undo write set) but do not include the results as they were not better than those yielded by TLRW-ByteLock with early acquisition.

Another issue we needed to resolve was to understand which fraction of the performance benefit shown by TLRW-ByteLock arises from CAS-avoidance and which fraction from the fact that we have a very efficient test to determine if a thread is already a member of the read-set for a given stripe. Not surprisingly given spatial and temporal locality it's common to find a thread read a given stripe multiple times within the same transaction. That is, read-after-read is common. Without a fast thread-has-already-read-this-stripe test we'd need to revert to Bloom filters, hash tables, or simple scanning of the read-set to determine if thread was already a member of the read-set for the stripe. (If the thread was not already a reader of that stripe then we need to atomically bump the read counter and add the stripe to the thread's local read set list). Similarly, such a fast read-set membership test is also useful when upgrading a stripe from read to write status (write-after-read is also very common).

Our benchmarking showed that TLRW-bitlock exhibits awful performance when compared to TLRW-ByteLock, in particular it melted down at a concurrency level beyond 30 threads, suggesting that CAS-avoidance is the key to TLRW-bytelock performance.

Having ruled out possible benefits of these two variations of TLRW, let us move on to compare its performance with that of other the remaining algorithms listed above.

Consider the two benchmarks of Figure 1 of a Red-Black Tree with 25% puts and 25% deletes when tree size is 2K and 20K respectively, and the left side of Figure 2 when the level of modifications is down to 10%. As can be seen, the performance of TL2 and TLRW-bytelock, and TLRW-bytelock-128 are about the same, with similar scalability curves in both cases. This is encouraging since the red-black tree is a particularly trying data structure for TLRW because the transactions read sets tend to overlap at the top of the tree: in effect, the root must be locked by all transactions. As can be seen, the TLRW-bytelock slightly outperfroms the TLRW-bytelock-128 up to about 50 threads, after which the TLRW-bytelock-128 wins. This suggests that one should dynamically switch between the two, which we hope to investigate in the future.

Next, in Figure 2, we show what happens when we consider transactions with smaller overlaps. If we compare TLRW-bytelock with TL2-IP, the form of TL2 that provides implicit privatization, we can see that TLRW-bytelock has a significant performance advantage. To convince ourselves that the scalability of TLRW is due to the use of byte-locks, consider the throughput of the TLRW-IOMux algorithm. Here the same TLRW algorithm runs, with locks implemented using the best reader counters we could invent. As can be seen TLRW-IOMux performs poorly, essentially collapsing as the level of concurrency increases beyond 32 threads.

The left side of Figure 2 shows that TLRW and TL2 continue to scale about the same on a smaller tree when the level of modifications goes down, but for deferent reasons. TL2 does well, as has been explained in other papers [4] despite the high abort rate, because it locks the nodes at the head of the tree only rarely and because the cost of a retry is very low. To understand why TLRW-bytelock performs well, consider that it has significantly lower abort rates than TL2, as seen in Figure 2. This helps mitigate the cost of locking the head of the tree.

Next, consider Figure 4, which contains a chart that describes the common execution path (fast-path) instruction counts (assuming no concurrent activity) for transactional load and store operations in the speculative phase. In the table, *Read-after-read*, for instance, is a subsequent read to a data stripe that's already been read in the same transaction. The number V is the variable-length look-aside time where TL2 checks for a match in the write-set, and the number L is the cost of scanning the read-set for a match in TLRW-ByteLock.

We note that the low costs of coherence on Sun's Niagara architecture is not unique. The new Intel Core $i7^{TM}$ Nehalem class X86 machines also have very low store-load memory barrier and CAS costs (about 2 and 8 cycles respectively). On the other hand, the computational overheads of the TL2 algorithm are handled better by the Nehalem's deep pipeline. As an example, Figure 3 shows the results for the same benchmark as in Figure 1 on the Nehalem.

As noted earlier, the read sharing at the top of the red-black tree impacts TLRW performance. In Figure 5, we

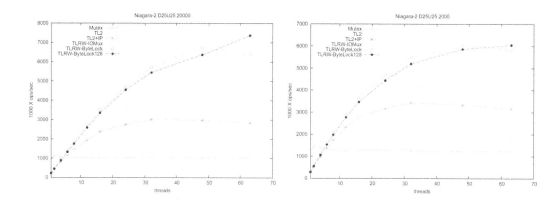

Figure 1: Throughput of Red-Black Tree with 25% puts and 25% deletes when tree size is 2K and 20K respectively on a 64 thread Niagara II.

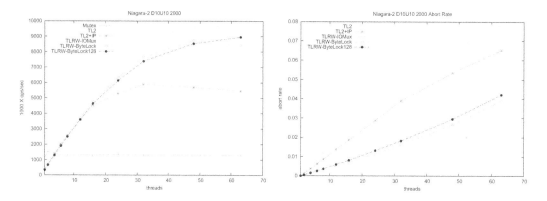

Figure 2: Throughput of Red-Black Tree with 10% puts and 10% deletes and its related abort rates (lower abort rate is better.).

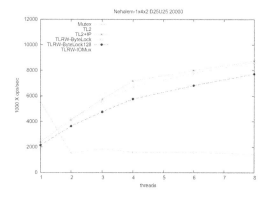

Figure 3: Throughput of Red-Black Tree with 25% puts and 25% deletes when tree size is 20K on an 8 thread Nehalem processor.

show what happens when we consider transactions with less read sharing. Our artificial random array benchmark, tries to capture the behavior of data structures such as hash tables that are highly distributed. In the benchmark, there is no inter-transaction locality, but within a given transaction the benchmark on the left hand side exhibits strong spatial locality (all accesses are at small offsets from the original randomly selected index) and the one on the right exhibits moderate spatial locality.

In the random array benchmark, all the TLRW algorithms outperform TL2. The TLRW-IOMux is the best performer since the cost of using CAS operations on the reader counters is low given that the sets of locations accessed are mostly disjoint and there are therefore few invalidations. Here one can also see that TLRW-bytelock which aligns along one cache line performs as well as TLRW-IOMux and outperforms TLRW-bytelock-128 that incurs an extra cache invalidation given that most locations are not shared by transactions.

Next we present the results of benchmarking a real application, the MSF (Minimum Spanning Forest) benchmark introduced by Kang and Bader [14]. The MSF program takes a graph file (we used the US Western roads system as input, just as in [14]) and computes a minimum spanning forest. The algorithm is concurrent and the implementation by Kang and Bader uses transactional memory. A purely sequential thread-unsafe version of the program with no transactional overhead completes in 15.9 secs.

In Figure 6 we see the results of running the MSF application (The application performs a fixed amount of work and reports the duration it took). Bader and Kang reported that TL2 scaled well but the absolute performance was poor.

Operation	Under TL2	Under TLRW-ByteLock
1st read	39 + V	24 + 1Membar
1st write	18	31 + 1CAS
Read-after-read	39 + V	12
Read-after-write	39 + V	13
write-after-read	18	39 + 1CAS + L
write-after-write	18	13

Figure 4: A chart that describes the fast-path instruction counts for loads and stores in TL2 and TLRW-bytelock transactions. Notice that we are not counting the commit time costs which are negligible for TLRW-bytelock yet involve a CAS per written location in TL2. As can be seen, TLRW-ByteLock can leverage intra-transaction spatial and temporal locality, that is, the fact that transactions re-access the same locations one after the other in the same short intervals.

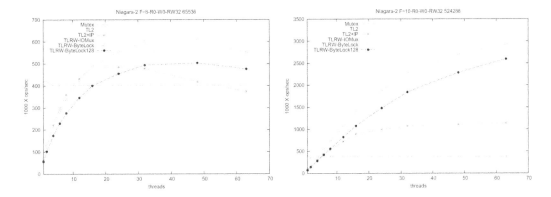

Figure 5: Throughput of the randomized work distribution benchmark on a 64 thread Niagara II. On the left a small array of 60K locations and a pattern of strong intra-transaction spatial locality and on the right 500K locations with moderate intra-transaction spatial locality. Sets of 32 locations are read and then written in these arrays.

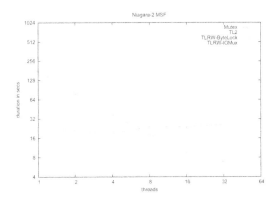

Figure 6: Latency (lower is better) of the transactified MSF application of Kang and Bader.

Our results recapitulate their findings with TL2, but also show that TLRW-ByteLock both scales well and shows a significant improvement over TL2 in terms of absolute performance.

We now consider the case of irrevocable transactions. We ran a benchmark in which in addition to put and remove, we ran an iteration operator over the nodes of the tree (a classical Java library operation).

For reference, the baseline score for TLRW-byteLock without the iterator, as seen in Figure 1, is 5.5 million operations per second. In a typical run, when 31 threads executed 25% put and 25% removes, and there was one iterator thread that did not execute in irrevocable mode (i.e., it is just a normal thread) the throughput for the 31 threads dropped to 0.61 million and yet the iterator had 7718 successes and 3990 failures. In a typical TL2 run the iterator never succeeds. This seems to support our claim that TLRW in general may have better progress properties than TL2. But those properties come at a cost because the iterator (even though it is revocable) badly degraded the performance of the other 31 threads. If we use 31 threads and the iterator thread operates in irrevocable mode, then throughput for the 31 threads drops to 0.44 million operations, and the iterator thread improves slightly to 8408 successes. However, now there are 0 failures. From our benchmarking of the irrevocable mode, we conclude that it is a good tool for guaranteeing progress (necessary in the case of I/O) but seems to have a negligible benefit for throughput.

Finally, we demonstrate how badly the TLRW algorithms perform on systems where write-sharing (coherency traffic) is expensive, which is the basis of our we claim that TLRW-bytelock should be viewed as an algorithm for single chip systems. In Figure 7 we show the throughput of a red-black tree with threads spread evenly across a 2-chip Maramba machine. The threads are not bound to cores and the oper-

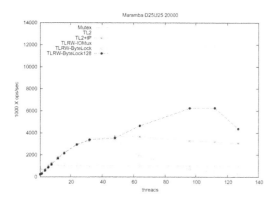

Figure 7: Throughput of Red-Black Tree on a 128 thread Maramba machine with 25% puts and 25% deletes when the tree size is 20K.

ating system spreads them out so that half the threads on one chip communicate with threads on the other through an interconnect that is typically twice as slow as an on chip memory access. This proves to be an intolerable coherence cost for the TLRW algorithms. Note that if threads are restricted to one chip TLRW performs well.

4. CONCLUSIONS

This paper introduced TLRW, a new form of transactional locking that is in an algorithmic sense orthogonal to the invisible-readers based approach at the basis of all Ennals-style lock-based algorithms [7]. It overcomes many of the drawbacks of invisible-read based STMs, providing implicit privatization without a performance loss. The key to the new algorithm is the byte-lock, a new type of read-write lock that supports high read acquisition levels with little overhead. As our benchmarks show, TLRW using *byte-locks* suggest a new direction in STM design for the case of single chip multicore systems. Our hope is that others will find new ways to carry this approach further. Examples of possible directions are dynamically switching among the 64 and 128 array sizes, and perhaps scaling further to 3 and 4 cache lines. Also, one can think of more elaborate deadlock detection and resolution schemes, partial rollbacks of locks in a transaction, more aggressive irrevocable transaction schemes, multiplexed bytes in the byte-lock instead of the reader count and so on.

Readers interested in TLRW code can email: `tlrw-feedback@oracle.com`.

5. REFERENCES

[1] CORMEN, T., LEISERSON, C., RIVEST, R., AND STEIN, C. *Introduction to Algorithms*, second edition ed. MIT Press. Cambridge, MA, 2001.

[2] CRAIG, T. Building FIFO and priority-queueing spin locks from atomic swap. Technical Report TR 93-02-02, University of Washington, Department of Computer Science, February 1993.

[3] DICE, D. Weblog: http://blogs.sun.com/dave/entry/ cas_and_cache_trivia_invalidate, 2008.

[4] DICE, D., SHALEV, O., AND SHAVIT, N. Transactional locking II. In *Proc. of the 20th International Symposium on Distributed Computing (DISC 2006)* (2006), pp. 194–208.

[5] DICE, D., AND SHAVIT, N. Understanding tradeoffs in software transactional memory. In *CGO '07: Proceedings of the International Symposium on Code Generation and Optimization* (Washington, DC, USA, 2007), IEEE Computer Society, pp. 21–33.

[6] ELLEN, F., LEV, Y., LUCHANGCO, V., AND MOIR, M. Snzi: scalable nonzero indicators. In *PODC '07: Proceedings of the twenty-sixth annual ACM symposium on Principles of distributed computing* (New York, NY, USA, 2007), ACM, pp. 13–22.

[7] ENNALS, R. Software transactional memory should not be obstruction-free. www.cambridge.intel-research.net/ rennals/notlockfree.pdf.

[8] FELBER, P., FETZER, C., AND RIEGEL, T. Dynamic performance tuning of word-based software transactional memory. In *PPoPP '08: Proceedings of the 13th ACM SIGPLAN Symposium on Principles and practice of parallel programming* (New York, NY, USA, 2008), ACM, pp. 237–246.

[9] GUERRAOUI, R., AND KAPALKA, M. On the correctness of transactional memory. In *PPoPP '08: Proceedings of the 13th ACM SIGPLAN Symposium on Principles and practice of parallel programming* (New York, NY, USA, 2008), ACM, pp. 175–184.

[10] HARRIS, T., AND FRASER, K. Concurrent programming without locks.

[11] HERLIHY, M., LUCHANGCO, V., MOIR, M., AND SCHERER, III, W. N. Software transactional memory for dynamic-sized data structures. In *Proceedings of the twenty-second annual symposium on Principles of distributed computing* (2003), ACM Press, pp. 92–101.

[12] HERLIHY, M., AND SHAVIT, N. *The Art of Multiprocessor Programming*. Morgan Kaufmann Publishers, San Mateo, CA, 2008.

[13] HERLIHY, M. P., AND WING, J. M. Linearizability: a correctness condition for concurrent objects. *ACM Trans. Program. Lang. Syst. 12*, 3 (1990), 463–492.

[14] KANG, S., AND BADER. D. A. An efficient transactional memory algorithm for computing minimum spanning forest of sparse graphs. In *PPoPP '09: Proceedings of the 14th ACM SIGPLAN Symposium on Principles and practice of parallel programming* (New York, NY, USA, 2009), ACM. To appear.

[15] LEV, Y., LUCHANGCO, V., MARATHE, V., MOIR, M., AND OLSZEWSKI, D. N. M. Anatomy of a scalable software transactional memory. In *Transact 2009 Workshop Submission* (2008).

[16] MAGNUSSEN, P., LANDIN, A., AND HAGERSTEN, E. Queue locks on cache coherent multiprocessors. In *Proceedings of the 8th International Symposium on Parallel Processing (IPPS)* (April 1994), IEEE Computer Society, pp. 165–171.

[17] MARATHE, V. Personal communication.

[18] MARATHE, V. J., AND MOIR, M. Toward high performance nonblocking software transactional memory. In *PPoPP '08: Proceedings of the 13th ACM SIGPLAN Symposium on Principles and practice of parallel programming* (New York, NY, USA, 2008), ACM, pp. 227–236.

[19] MARATHE, V. J., SPEAR, M. F., HERIOT, C., ACHARYA, A., EISENSTAT, D., SCHERER III, W. N., AND SCOTT, M. L. Lowering the overhead of software transactional memory. Tech. Rep. TR 893, Computer Science Department, University of Rochester, Mar 2006. Condensed version submitted for publication.

[20] MARATHE, V. J., SPEAR, M. F., AND SCOTT, M. L. Scalable techniques for transparent privatization in software transactional memory. *Parallel Processing, International Conference on 0* (2008), 67–74.

[21] MENON, V., BALENSIEFER, S., SHPEISMAN, T., ADL-TABATABAI, A.-R., HUDSON, R. L., SAHA, B., AND WELC, A. Single global lock semantics in a weakly atomic stm. In *Transact 2008 Workshop* (2008).

[22] MOIR, M. HybridTM: Integrating hardware and software transactional memory. Tech. Rep. Archivist 2004-0661, Sun Microsystems Research, August 2004.

[23] NI, Y., WELC, A., ADL-TABATABAI, A.-R., BACH, M., BERKOWITS, S., COWNIE, J., GEVA, R., KOZHUKOW, S., NARAYANASWAMY, R., OLIVIER, J., PREIS, S., SAHA, B., TAL, A., AND TIAN, X. Design and implementation of transactional constructs for c/c++. In *OOPSLA 08: Proceedings of the Conference on Object-Oriented Programming, Systems, Languages and Applications* (2008).

[24] RIEGEL, T., FELBER, P., AND FETZER, C. A lazy snapshot algorithm with eager validation. In *20th International Symposium on Distributed Computing (DISC)* (September 2006).

[25] RIEGEL, T., FETZER, C., AND FELBER, P. Snapshot isolation for software transactional memory. In *TRANSACT06* (Jun 2006).

[26] SAHA, B., ADL-TABATABAI, A.-R., HUDSON, R. L., MINH, C. C., AND HERTZBERG, B. Mcrt-stm: a high performance software transactional memory system for a multi-core runtime. In *PPoPP '06: Proceedings of the eleventh ACM SIGPLAN symposium on Principles and practice of parallel programming* (New York, NY, USA, 2006), ACM, pp. 187–197.

[27] SHAVIT, N., AND TOUITOU, D. Software transactional memory. *Distributed Computing 10*, 2 (February 1997), 99–116.

[28] SPEAR, M. F., MICHAEL, M. M., AND VON PRAUN, C. Ringstm: scalable transactions with a single atomic instruction. In *SPAA '08: Proceedings of the twentieth annual symposium on Parallelism in algorithms and architectures* (New York, NY, USA, 2008), ACM, pp. 275–284.

[29] TABBA, F., MOIR, M., GOODMAN, J. R., HAY, A. W., AND WANG, C. Nztm: nonblocking zero-indirection transactional memory. In *SPAA '09: Proceedings of the twenty-first annual symposium on Parallelism in algorithms and architectures* (New York, NY, USA, 2009), ACM, pp. 204–213.

[30] WELC, A., SAHA, B., AND ADL-TABATABAI, A.-R. Irrevocable transactions and their applications. In *SPAA '08: Proceedings of the twentieth annual symposium on Parallelism in algorithms and architectures* (New York, NY, USA, 2008), ACM, pp. 285–296.

[31] ZILLES, C., AND RAJWAR, R. Transactional memory and the birthday paradox. In *SPAA '07: Proceedings of the nineteenth annual ACM symposium on Parallel algorithms and architectures* (New York, NY, USA, 2007), ACM, pp. 303–304.

Fast Distributed Approximation Algorithms for Vertex Cover and Set Cover in Anonymous Networks

Matti Åstrand
matti.astrand@helsinki.fi

Jukka Suomela
jukka.suomela@cs.helsinki.fi

Helsinki Institute for Information Technology HIIT, University of Helsinki
P.O. Box 68, FI-00014 University of Helsinki

ABSTRACT

We present a distributed algorithm that finds a maximal edge packing in $O(\Delta + \log^* W)$ synchronous communication rounds in a weighted graph, independent of the number of nodes in the network; here Δ is the maximum degree of the graph and W is the maximum weight. As a direct application, we have a distributed 2-approximation algorithm for minimum-weight vertex cover, with the same running time. We also show how to find an f-approximation of minimum-weight set cover in $O(f^2 k^2 + fk \log^* W)$ rounds; here k is the maximum size of a subset in the set cover instance, f is the maximum frequency of an element, and W is the maximum weight of a subset. The algorithms are deterministic, and they can be applied in anonymous networks.

Categories and Subject Descriptors

C.2.4 [**Computer-Communication Networks**]: Distributed Systems; F.2.2 [**Analysis of Algorithms and Problem Complexity**]: Nonnumerical Algorithms and Problems—*computations on discrete structures*

General Terms

Algorithms, Theory

1. INTRODUCTION

In this work, we present deterministic distributed approximation algorithms for two classical problems: minimum-weight vertex cover and minimum-weight set cover.

1.1 Edge Packings and Vertex Covers

Let $\mathcal{G} = (V, E)$ be a simple, undirected, node-weighted graph; each node $v \in V$ is associated with a positive weight w_v. A set $C \subseteq V$ is a *vertex cover* if each edge has at least one endpoint in C, and it is a *minimum-weight vertex cover* if it also minimises its total weight

$$w(C) = \sum_{v \in C} w_v.$$

While vertex cover is a classical NP-hard optimisation problem, there is a simple technique for obtaining efficient approximation algorithms: find a maximal edge packing (a maximal dual solution) and output all saturated nodes. For a nonnegative function $y \colon E \to [0, +\infty)$, let us define the shorthand notation

$$y[v] = \sum_{e \in E \colon v \in e} y(e)$$

for each $v \in V$. We say that y is an *edge packing* if $y[v] \leq w_v$ for all $v \in V$. A node $v \in V$ is *saturated* in the edge packing y if $y[v] = w_v$. An edge $e = \{u, v\} \in E$ is saturated if u or v or both are saturated, i.e., $y(e)$ cannot be increased without violating the constraint $y[u] \leq w_u$ or $y[v] \leq w_v$. An edge packing y is *maximal* if all edges are saturated.

Let $C(y)$ be the set of nodes saturated in y. The classical result by Bar-Yehuda and Even [6] shows that if y is a maximal edge packing then $C(y)$ is a 2-approximation of a minimum-weight vertex cover; for the sake of completeness, we give a short proof here. First, observe that $C(y)$ is a vertex cover by definition: if an edge is not covered by $C(y)$, then y is not maximal. To show the approximation ratio, let C^* be a minimum-weight vertex cover. As $C(y)$ contains at most two endpoints of each edge and C^* contains at least one endpoint of each edge, we have

$$w(C(y)) = \sum_{v \in C(y)} y[v] = \sum_{e \in E} y(e) \, |e \cap C(y)|$$
$$\leq 2 \sum_{e \in E} y(e) \, |e \cap C^*| = 2 \sum_{v \in C^*} y[v] \leq 2w(C^*).$$

In a centralised setting, a maximal edge packing y is easy to find: for each $e \in E$, in an arbitrary order, increase the value $y(e)$ until one of the endpoints of e becomes saturated. In this work, we give an efficient *distributed* algorithm that finds a maximal edge packing, and hence also a 2-approximation of a minimum-weight vertex cover.

1.2 Fractional Packings and Set Covers

To deal with the set cover problem in a distributed setting, it is convenient to restate the problem by using a bipartite graph $\mathcal{H} = (S \cup U, A)$. Each node $s \in S$ represents a *subset*, each node $u \in U$ represents an *element* of the universe, and an edge $\{s, u\} \in A$ denotes that the element $u \in U$ is a member of the subset $s \in S$. Each subset node $s \in S$ is associated with a positive weight w_s. A collection $C \subseteq S$ is a *set cover* if each element $u \in U$ has at least one neighbour in C, and it is a *minimum-weight set cover* if it also minimises its total weight $w(C) = \sum_{s \in C} w_s$.

Let $y: U \to [0, +\infty)$ be a nonnegative function. Define the shorthand notation

$$y[s] = \sum_{u \in N(s)} y(u)$$

for each $s \in S$; here $N(s) \subseteq U$ is the set of elements adjacent to the subset node s. We say that y is a *fractional packing* if $y[s] \leq w_s$ for all subset nodes $s \in S$. A subset node $s \in S$ is *saturated* in the fractional packing y if $y[s] = w_s$. An element $u \in U$ is saturated if at least one adjacent subset node s with $\{s, u\} \in A$ is saturated, i.e., $y(u)$ cannot be increased. A fractional packing y is *maximal* if all elements $u \in U$ are saturated.

The classical result mentioned in Section 1.1 has a straightforward generalisation to the set cover problem [6]. Let $C(y)$ be the set of subset nodes $s \in S$ saturated in y. Let f be the maximum degree of the elements $u \in U$, that is, an element occurs in at most f subsets. Now if y is a maximal fractional packing, then $C(y)$ is an f-approximation of a minimum-weight set cover. The proof in the previous section holds almost verbatim, replacing the constant 2 with f.

1.3 Model of Distributed Computing

In our vertex cover algorithm, the graph $\mathcal{G} = (V, E)$ represents a distributed system: each node $v \in V$ is a computational entity and each edge $\{u, v\} \in E$ denotes a communication link between the nodes u and v. Similarly, in our set cover algorithm, the graph $\mathcal{H} = (S \cup U, A)$ represents a distributed system, and each node $x \in S \cup U$ is a computational entity. (Naturally, we do not assume that the physical structure of a real-world distributed system is exactly equal to $\mathcal{H}$; it is sufficient that we can efficiently simulate computation in $\mathcal{H}$ by using the physical computers and communication links between them. Section 5 gives an example of such a simulation.)

We use the model of synchronous distributed algorithms. All nodes execute the same algorithm. During each *synchronous communication round*, each node in parallel (i) performs local computation, (ii) sends one message to each of its neighbours, (iii) waits while the messages are propagated along the edges of the communication graph, and (iv) receives one message from each of its neighbours. As usual, the running time of a synchronous distributed algorithm is the total number of synchronous communication rounds.

In the case of the vertex cover problem, each node $v \in V$ gets its own weight w_v as input. When the algorithm terminates, each node must produce one bit of output: whether it is part of the vertex cover or not. In the set cover problem, each subset node $s \in S$ gets its own weight w_s as input; the elements $u \in U$ have no input. When the algorithm terminates, each $s \in S$ must output one bit indicating whether it is in the set cover or not.

Our algorithms are designed for *anonymous networks*; we do not assume that the nodes have any unique identifiers. Hence we have to specify carefully how the nodes can address their neighbours when they send and receive messages. We consider two models:

Port-Numbering Model. A node v with degree $\deg(v)$ can refer to its neighbours by integers $1, 2, \ldots, \deg(v)$; these integers are called *port numbers*. A node can send a different message to each neighbour, and it knows which message was received from which neighbour.

Broadcast Model. There are no port numbers. A node has to send the same message to each neighbour, and it does not know which message was received from which neighbour.

Put otherwise, in the port-numbering model, a node v produces a *vector* with $\deg(v)$ outgoing messages and it receives a *vector* with $\deg(v)$ incoming messages; the ith outgoing message corresponds to the same neighbour as the ith incoming message. In the broadcast model, a node v produces only *one* outgoing message and it receives a *multiset* with $\deg(v)$ incoming messages. We discuss the properties of the broadcast model in more detail in Section 7.

1.4 Notation

We focus on the case of bounded degrees and bounded weights. In the vertex cover algorithm, we assume that there are global parameters Δ and W such that $\deg(v) \leq \Delta$ and $w_v \in \{1, 2, \ldots, W\}$ for all $v \in V$. We assume that all nodes know these two parameters, which may represent, e.g., intrinsic hardware constraints such as the number of physical communication ports in a device and the precision of the registers used to store the weights; note that the algorithms are fast even if one chooses a very large value of W such as $W = 2^{64}$.

Similarly, in the case of the set cover algorithm, we assume that there are global parameters f, k, and W such that $\deg(u) \leq f$, $\deg(s) \leq k$, and $w_s \in \{1, 2, \ldots, W\}$ for all $u \in U$ and $s \in S$.

Throughout this work, logarithms are to base 2. The function $\log^* n$ denotes the iterated logarithm of n, that is, $\log^* n = 0$ if $n \leq 1$, and otherwise $\log^* n = 1 + \log^*(\log n)$.

1.5 Contributions

In Section 3, we present a distributed algorithm that finds a maximal edge packing in $O(\Delta + \log^* W)$ synchronous communication rounds. As a direct application, we have a distributed 2-approximation algorithm for minimum-weight vertex cover with the same running time. For unweighted graphs ($W = 1$), the running time is simply $O(\Delta)$. This algorithm assumes the port-numbering model.

In Section 4, we present a distributed algorithm that finds a maximal fractional packing in $O(f^2 k^2 + fk \log^* W)$ rounds. Again, as a direct application, we have a distributed f-approximation algorithm for minimum-weight set cover with the same running time. This algorithm does not require port numbering; we show how to implement the algorithm in the broadcast model.

In Section 5, we show how to apply the algorithm of Section 4 to find a maximal edge packing and 2-approximation of vertex cover in $O(\Delta^2 + \Delta \log^* W)$ rounds in the broadcast model.

Our algorithms are strictly *local* in the sense that that running time of the algorithm does not depend on the number of nodes in the network [27, 31]. Moreover, our algorithms are deterministic. Among others, this means that standard techniques [4, 5, 23] can be used to convert our algorithms into efficient *self-stabilising algorithms* [10].

2. RELATED WORK

In an unweighted graph, a maximal matching provides a maximal edge packing and therefore a 2-approximation of a minimum vertex cover. Hańćkowiak et al.'s [13] distributed

deterministic	weighted	approximation	time ($W = 1$)	algorithm
no	yes	2	$O(\log n)$	[12]
no	yes	2	$O(\log n)$	[17]
yes	no	3	$O(\Delta)$	[30]
yes	no	2	$O(\log^4 n)$	[13] (matching)
yes	no	2	$O(\Delta + \log^* n)$	[28] (matching)
yes	no	2	$O(\Delta^2)$	[2]
yes	yes	$2 + \varepsilon$	$O(\log(\varepsilon^{-1}) \log n)$	[16]
yes	yes	$2 + \varepsilon$	$O(\varepsilon^{-4} \log \Delta)$	[21] + [14]
yes	yes	2	$O(\Delta + \log^* n)$	[28] (edge colouring)
yes	yes	2	$O(1)$ if $\Delta \le 3$	[2]
yes	yes	2	$O(\Delta)$	this work

In the table, $n = |V|$ and $\varepsilon > 0$. The running times are stated for the case of unweighted graphs. For randomised algorithms the running times hold in expectation or with high probability.

algorithm finds a maximal matching in $O(\log^4 n)$ rounds, and Panconesi and Rizzi's [28] algorithm finds a maximal matching in $O(\Delta + \log^* n)$ rounds.

In a weighted graph, we can use an edge colouring to find a maximal edge packing. Given an edge colouring with k colours, we can find a maximal edge packing in $O(k)$ rounds: first saturate all edges of colour 1 in parallel, then saturate all edges of colour 2 in parallel, etc. For example, Panconesi and Rizzi's [28] algorithm finds an $O(\Delta)$-edge colouring in $O(\Delta + \log^* n)$ rounds, and hence provides an $O(\Delta + \log^* n)$-time algorithm for finding a maximal edge packing.

However, any deterministic algorithm that uses maximal matchings or edge colourings has two drawbacks. First, such algorithms assume that each node has a unique identifier – indeed, finding a maximal matching or an edge colouring is impossible in anonymous networks. Second, the running time of any such algorithm must depend on the number of nodes in the network, even in the case $\Delta = 2$ – this is the seminal result by Linial [25].

Other vertex cover algorithms are summarised in Table 1. To our knowledge, none of the algorithms from prior work has the same combination of features as our algorithm: (i) deterministic, (ii) 2-approximation, (iii) for weighted vertex cover, and (iv) running time independent of n.

Many vertex cover algorithms have also a generalisation to set covering. For example, LP approximation schemes [18, 21] and deterministic rounding [14] provide a $(2 + \varepsilon)$-approximation for vertex cover, and the same technique gives an $(f + \varepsilon)$-approximation for set cover. However, there are also algorithms that are relevant specifically in the case of the set cover problem. A trivial constant-time algorithm provides a k-approximation: each element $u \in U$ chooses an adjacent subset $s \in S$ of minimum weight; all such subsets are added to the cover. Randomised LP rounding [18, 20, 21, 22] gives the expected approximation factor of $O(\log k)$.

Several lower bounds are known for local algorithms (distributed algorithms with running time independent of the number of nodes in the network). Czygrinow et al. [9] and Lenzen and Wattenhofer [24] have shown that finding a constant-factor approximation of maximum independent set in a directed cycle is not possible in $O(1)$ rounds using a deterministic algorithm. As a direct consequence, even if $W = 1$ and $\Delta = 2$, there is no deterministic local $(2 - \varepsilon)$-

approximation algorithm for vertex cover. A straightforward local reduction shows that there is no deterministic local $(\min\{f, k\} - \varepsilon)$-approximation algorithm for set cover, either (see Section 6 for details). This lower bound is tight, as our local algorithm achieves the approximation factor f and the trivial algorithm achieves the approximation factor k.

The running time of our edge packing algorithm depends on both Δ and W, and both of these are unavoidable. First, even if $W = 1$, there is no $O(1)$-approximation algorithm for vertex cover with running time $o(\log \Delta / \log \log \Delta)$ [19]. Second, even if $\Delta = 2$, there is no deterministic algorithm for maximal edge packing with running time $O(1)$ [2].

3. VERTEX COVER IN THE PORT-NUMBERING MODEL

In this section we present an algorithm that finds a maximal edge packing (and hence a 2-approximation of vertex cover) in $O(\Delta + \log^* W)$ rounds. The algorithm uses the port-numbering model.

3.1 Overview

Our algorithm works in two phases. Phase I constructs a (possibly non-maximal) edge packing y, and a (possibly improper) node colouring c in the graph $\mathcal{G}$. We say that an edge is *multicoloured* if its endpoints have different colours in c. The key observation is that if an edge is not saturated in y, then it is multicoloured in c. Phase II uses the colouring c to saturate all multicoloured edges.

Phase I uses the degrees and the weights of the nodes in $\mathcal{G}$ to derive both the edge packing y and the colouring c. It turns out that in those cases in which finding multicoloured edges is impossible – regular graphs with equal node weights – we can saturate the edges already during Phase I.

Phase I uses steps that are similar to, e.g., Khuller et al.'s [16] algorithm or Papadimitriou and Yannakakis's [29] "safe algorithm": each node $v \in V$ offers $w_v / \deg(v)$ units to each incident edge, and each edge accepts the minimum of the offers that it receives. Phase II is similar to the graph colouring algorithm by Goldberg et al. [11] and the edge colouring algorithm by Panconesi et al. [28]: we partition the multicoloured edges into Δ forests of rooted trees, and we use Cole and Vishkin's [8] colour reduction techniques to 3-colour each tree.

3.2 Phase I

For an edge packing y and an improper colouring c, let $r_y(v) = w_v - y[v]$ be the *residual weight* of $v \in V$, and let

$$E_{yc} = \big\{ \{u,v\} \in E : r_y(v) > 0,\, r_y(u) > 0,\, c(u) = c(v) \big\}$$

be the set of edges that are not saturated in y and not multicoloured in c. Let $\mathcal{G}_{yc} = (V_{yc}, E_{yc})$ be the subgraph of $\mathcal{G}$ induced by E_{yc}, and let $\deg_{yc}(v)$ be the degree of $v \in V_{yc}$ in the subgraph $\mathcal{G}_{yc}$.

In the distributed algorithm, the colour $c(v)$ is stored in the local memory of the node $v \in V$, and identical copies of the value $y(e)$ are stored in both endpoints of the edge $e \in E$. During Phase I, the colours will be sequences of rational numbers. Initially, we set $y(e) \leftarrow 0$ for each $e \in E$, and $c(v)$ is an empty sequence for each node $v \in V$. At this point, no edge is saturated or multicoloured, and hence $\mathcal{G}_{yc} = \mathcal{G}$.

During the algorithm, we will increment the values $y(e)$ and add more elements to the sequences $c(v)$ until $E_{yc} = \emptyset$. It turns out that it is sufficient to repeat the following steps for Δ times:

(i) Set $x(v) \leftarrow r_y(v) / \deg_{yc}(v)$ for each node $v \in V_{yc}$.

(ii) Set $y(e) \leftarrow y(c) + \min\{x(u), x(v)\}$ for each edge $e = \{u,v\} \in E_{yc}$.

(iii) Add the element $x(v)$ to the sequence $c(v)$ for each node $v \in V_{yc}$, and add the element 1 for each node $v \in V \setminus V_{yc}$.

The following lemma shows the correctness of the algorithm.

LEMMA 1. *In each iteration of steps (i)-(iii), the maximum degree of $\mathcal{G}_{yc}$ decreases by at least one.*

PROOF. Let $v \in V_{yc}$ before step (i). If we have $x(u) \geq x(v)$ for each neighbour u of v in $\mathcal{G}_{yc}$, then we will saturate v during the step (ii). Otherwise there is a neighbour u of v with $x(u) < x(v)$. If the edge $\{u,v\}$ is not saturated after step (ii), it is multicoloured after step (iii). In summary, each node is removed from $\mathcal{G}_{yc}$ or loses at least one edge. Moreover, edges which were saturated remain saturated and edges which were multicoloured remain multicoloured. $\square$

It follows that after Δ iterations, $\mathcal{G}_{yc}$ is empty and all edges are saturated or multicoloured. At this point, the colours $c(v)$ are – somewhat inconveniently – sequences of Δ rational numbers. However, the rational numbers in $c(v)$ are not arbitrary, as shown by the following lemma.

LEMMA 2. *For each $v \in V$ and for each element q of $c(v)$, we have $0 < q \leq W$ and $q(\Delta!)^{\Delta} \in \mathbb{N}$.*

PROOF. A simple induction shows that if we multiply each weight w_v by $(\Delta!)^k$ before running the algorithm, then $x(v)$, $y(e)$, and $r_y(v)$ will be integral during the first k iterations of steps (i)-(iii). $\square$

Hence an injection can be defined from the possible values of $c(v)$ to the set $\{1, 2, \ldots, \chi\}$ for $\chi = (W(\Delta!)^{\Delta})^{\Delta}$. In what follows, we re-interpret the colouring c as a mapping $c : V \to \{1, 2, \ldots, \chi\}$.

3.3 Phase II

Let

$$A = \big\{ (u,v) : \{u,v\} \in E,$$
$$r_y(v) > 0,\, r_y(u) > 0,\, c(u) < c(v) \big\}$$

be the set of unsaturated edges, oriented from a lower to higher colour. Note that the directed graph $\mathcal{G}' = (V, A)$ is acyclic, and c is a proper χ-colouring in $\mathcal{G}'$.

We partition A in Δ forests, $F_1, F_2, \ldots, F_{\Delta}$: using the port numbering, each node u adds the first outgoing edge to F_1, the second outgoing edge to F_2, etc. The outdegree of each node in $\mathcal{F}_i = (V, F_i)$ is at most one, and hence it is a forest of rooted trees, with edges oriented towards the root nodes.

For each forest $\mathcal{F}_i$ in parallel, we can find a 3-colouring in $O(\log^* \chi)$ rounds by using a Cole-Vishkin style colour reduction algorithm [8, 11]. For each $j \in \{1, 2, 3\}$, let F_{ij} consist of the edges $(u,v) \in F_i$ such that u has colour j in the forest $\mathcal{F}_i$.

We consider each $i \in \{1, 2, \ldots, \Delta\}$ and $j \in \{1, 2, 3\}$ in sequence, and saturate all edges in F_{ij}. Since the graph induced by F_{ij} consists of rooted stars (i.e., rooted trees of height 1), it is easy to saturate all edges of F_{ij} in parallel. Consider a star, with the root node $v \in V$ and with the leaf nodes $L \subset V$. In one communication round, the root node can gather the residual weights $r_y(u)$ for all leaves $u \in L$ and compute the ratio

$$\alpha = \sum_{u \in L} \frac{r_y(u)}{r_y(v)}.$$

If $\alpha < 1$, we increase $y(\{u,v\})$ for each $u \in L$ by $r_y(u)$, and we saturate all leaf nodes. Otherwise we increase $y(\{u,v\})$ for each $u \in L$ by $r_y(u)/\alpha$, and we saturate the root node.

The sets F_{ij} form a partition of A. In summary, we have saturated all edges of A in $O(\Delta + \log^* \chi)$ communication rounds.

THEOREM 1. *There is a deterministic algorithm that finds a maximal edge packing in $O(\Delta + \log^* W)$ synchronous communication rounds.*

PROOF. Phase II saturates all edges that were not saturated in Phase I. Since Phase I takes $O(\Delta)$ rounds and Phase II takes $O(\Delta + \log^* \chi)$ rounds, it is sufficient to show that $\log^* \chi = O(\log^* \Delta + \log^* W)$. To this end, let $M = \max\{W, \Delta, 4\}$ and observe that $\log \log \chi \leq 4 \log M$. $\square$

4. SET COVER IN THE BROADCAST MODEL

In this section we present an algorithm that finds a maximal fractional packing (and hence an f-approximation of set cover) in $O(f^2 k^2 + fk \log^* W)$ rounds in the broadcast model.

Our fractional packing algorithm builds on the same basic idea as the edge packing algorithm in Section 3: we construct a (non-maximal) packing and an (improper) colouring hand in hand, and if a step does not improve the packing, we can show that it will improve the colouring. However, there are also many differences between the two algorithms. For example, while the edge packing algorithm runs the Cole-Vishkin colour reduction step only once, in the case of fractional packing we will have to run the colour reduction step repeatedly.

4.1 Preliminaries

Recall that we represent a set cover instance as a bipartite graph $\mathcal{H} = (S \cup U, A)$ with subset nodes $s \in S$ and elements $u \in U$. We use $N(s) \subseteq U$ to denote the set of elements adjacent to $s \in S$, and conversely $N(u) \subseteq S$ to denote the set of subset nodes adjacent to $u \in U$. Let

$$K = \big\{(u, s, v) : s \in S,\, u \in N(s),\, v \in N(s),\, u \neq v\big\}$$

consist of all length-2 simple paths in $\mathcal{H}$ that start and end in U. If we interpret $(u, s, v) \in K$ as a directed edge from u to v, we can construct the directed multigraph $\mathcal{K} = (U, K)$. In $\mathcal{K}$ there are $|N(u) \cap N(v)|$ directed edges from u to v. The outdegree, indegree, and number of distinct neighbours of any node $u \in U$ in $\mathcal{K}$ is at most $D = (k-1)f$. The graph $\mathcal{K}$ is used only in the analysis of the algorithm; we do not maintain it explicitly.

During the execution of the algorithm, each element $u \in U$ is associated with two values: $y(u) \in [0, +\infty)$ and $c(u) \in \{1, 2, \ldots, D+1\}$. Here y is a fractional packing, and c is an improper colouring of $\mathcal{K}$. We say that an edge $(u, s, v) \in K$ is *multicoloured* if $c(u) \neq c(v)$. Recall that an element $u \in U$ is *saturated* if it is adjacent to a saturated subset node $s \in S$.

Let $r_y(s) = w_s - y[s]$ be the residual weight of the subset node $s \in S$. Let $U_y \subseteq U$ be the set of elements $u \in U$ that are *not* saturated in y, let

$$U_{yi} = \big\{ u \in U_y : c(y) = i \big\}$$

consist of unsaturated elements of colour i, and let $U_{yi}(s) = U_{yi} \cap N(s)$ be the set of unsaturated elements of colour i adjacent to s. Let

$$K_{yc} = \big\{ (u, s, v) \in K : u \in U_y,\, v \in U_y,\, c(u) = c(v) \big\}$$

be the set of edges of $\mathcal{K}$ that are not multicoloured in c and join unsaturated elements. We define the subgraph $\mathcal{K}_{yc}$ of $\mathcal{K}$ by setting $\mathcal{K}_{yc} = (U_y, K_{yc})$.

Remark 1. Even thought the definitions resemble those of the edge packing algorithm, they are not completely analogous. In Section 3, we associate a colour $c(v)$ with each *node* of $\mathcal{G}$ and a value $y(e)$ with each *edge* of $\mathcal{G}$. In this section, we associate a colour $c(u)$ with each *node* of $\mathcal{K}$ and also a value $y(u)$ with each *node* of $\mathcal{K}$.

4.2 Algorithm

Initially, we set $y(u) \leftarrow 0$ and $c(u) \leftarrow 1$ for each element $u \in U$. None of the nodes of $\mathcal{K}$ is saturated and none of the edges is multicoloured, and hence $\mathcal{K}_{yc} = \mathcal{K}$; see Figure 1 for an example.

The algorithm consists of $D + 1$ *iterations*. Each iteration $j \in \{1, 2, \ldots, D+1\}$ proceeds as follows:

(a) For each colour $i \in \{1, 2, \ldots, D+1\}$, perform the *saturation phase* for colour i; see Section 4.3.

(b) Perform the *colouring phase*; see Section 4.4.

Eventually, after the last iteration, U_y will be empty and hence y is a maximal edge packing.

4.3 Saturation Phases

The saturation phase for colour i consists of the following steps; see Figure 1a for an example. In the following, we use the shorthand notation $S' = \{s \in S : U_{yi}(s) \neq \emptyset\}$.

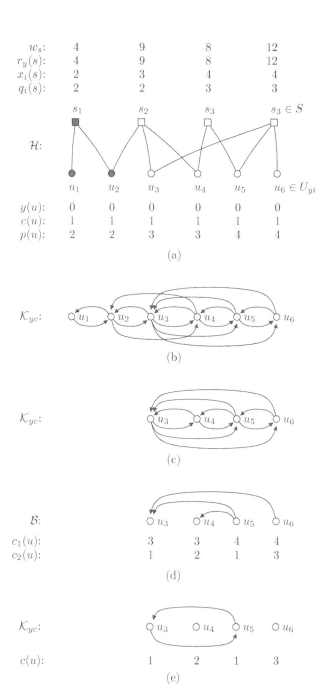

w_s:	4	9	8	12
$r_y(s)$:	4	9	8	12
$x_i(s)$:	2	3	4	4
$q_i(s)$:	2	2	3	3
	s_1	s_2	s_3	$s_3 \in S$

$\mathcal{H}$:

	u_1	u_2	u_3	u_4	u_5	$u_6 \in U_{yi}$
$y(u)$:	0	0	0	0	0	0
$c(u)$:	1	1	1	1	1	1
$p(u)$:	2	2	3	3	4	4

(a)

$\mathcal{K}_{yc}$: u_1 u_2 u_3 u_4 u_5 u_6

(b)

$\mathcal{K}_{yc}$: u_3 u_4 u_5 u_6

(c)

$\mathcal{B}$: u_3 u_4 u_5 u_6

$c_1(u)$:	3	3	4	4
$c_2(u)$:	1	2	1	3

(d)

$\mathcal{K}_{yc}$: u_3 u_4 u_5 u_6

$c(u)$:	1	2	1	3

(e)

Figure 1: Fractional packing algorithm, the first iteration. Initially, all elements are in U_{y1}. **(a)** The saturation phase for colour $i = 1$; black nodes are newly saturated. **(b)** Directed multigraph $\mathcal{K}_{yc}$ before the saturation phase. **(c)** Graph $\mathcal{K}_{yc}$ after the saturation phase. Nodes u_1 and u_2 are saturated and hence removed from the graph. Nodes u_3 and u_4 were adjacent to the saturated node u_2, and hence their outdegree has decreased. **(d)** Subgraph $\mathcal{B} = \mathcal{B}_1$. Nodes u_5 and u_6 were not adjacent to any saturated node; hence they have a positive outdegree in $\mathcal{B}$. A χ-colouring c_1 of $\mathcal{B}$ and a weak 3-colouring c_2 of $\mathcal{B}$; for each node, at least one of the successors has a different colour in c_2. **(e)** Graph $\mathcal{K}_{yc}$ after the colouring phase. In comparison with figure (b), the outdegree of each node has decreased by at least one.

(i) Each $u \in U$ broadcasts $y(u)$. Each $s \in S$ computes $y[s]$ and $r_y(s)$.

(ii) Each $s \in S$ broadcasts $r_y(s)$. Each $u \in U$ determines whether it is saturated and whether it is in U_{yi}.

(iii) Each $u \in U$ broadcasts a bit indicating whether $u \in U_{yi}$. Each $s \in S$ computes the size of $U_{yi}(s)$. Each $s \in S'$ sets $x_i(s) \leftarrow r_y(s)/|U_{yi}(s)|$.

(iv) Each $s \in S'$ broadcasts $x_i(s)$. Each $u \in U_{yi}$ sets $p(u) \leftarrow \min \{x_i(s) : s \in N(u)\}$.

(v) Each $u \in U_{yi}$ broadcasts $p(u)$. Each $s \in S'$ sets $q_i(s) \leftarrow \min \{p(v) : v \in U_{yi}(s)\}$.

(vi) Each $u \in U_{yi}$ sets $y(u) \leftarrow y(u) + p(u)$.

These steps require $O(1)$ rounds per colour, in total $O(D)$ rounds. Clearly the edge packing y remains feasible after the saturation phase.

We will use the following observation in the colouring phase.

LEMMA 3. *Consider a node $u \in U_{yi}$ that was not saturated in step (vi). Let s be a neighbour of u with $p(u) = x_i(s)$, and let v be a neighbour of s with $q_i(s) = p(v)$. Then s is not saturated, $v \neq u$, and $p(u) > p(v)$.*

PROOF. If u is not saturated, the subset node s is not saturated either. Hence there was a neighbour $t \in U_{yi}(s)$ that increased $y(t)$ by less than $x_i(s)$, that is, $p(t) < x_i(s)$. This means that $p(v) = q_i(s) \leq p(t) < x_i(s) = p(u)$, and the claim follows. $\square$

4.4 Colouring Phase

We begin by introducing some notation that facilitates the analysis of the colouring phase. For each colour i, let us define the set

$$B_i = \big\{(u, s, v) \in K : p(u) = x_i(s),$$
$$q_i(s) = p(v),\ u, v \in U_{yi}\big\}$$

and the subgraph $\mathcal{B}_i = (U_{yi}, B_i)$ of the graph $\mathcal{K}_{yc}$. Each node $u \in U_{yi}$ is associated with a value $p(u)$, and Lemma 3 shows that these values are strictly decreasing in the direction of the edges. It follows that the subgraphs $\mathcal{B}_i$ are directed acyclic graphs. The subgraphs are by construction node-disjoint; let $\mathcal{B}$ be the union of these graphs.

Now consider a colour i and an element $u \in U_{yi}$ that was not saturated in any of the saturation phases. Then we can choose two nodes s and v as in Lemma 3; in particular, $v \neq u$. Note that before this iteration, both u and v were unsaturated and they had the same colour i; therefore (u, s, v) was an edge in $\mathcal{K}_{yc}$. If v became saturated during the saturation phases, the edge (u, s, v) is no longer part of $\mathcal{K}_{yc}$. Otherwise the edge (u, s, v) is in the set B_i. In summary, each element that was not saturated either loses at least one outgoing edge during the saturation phases, or has at least one outgoing edge in the subgraph $\mathcal{B}$.

Now we are ready to describe the distributed algorithm that implements the colouring phase. First, we use the rational numbers $p(u)$ and a reasoning similar to Lemma 2 to construct a χ-colouring c_1 of the subgraph $\mathcal{B}$, with

$$\chi = W(k!)^{(D+1)^2}.$$

Second, we use the algorithm that we describe in Section 4.5 to construct a *weak 3-colouring* c_2 of $\mathcal{B}$ in $O(\log^* \chi)$ rounds: each element $u \in U_{yi}$ with a positive outdegree in $\mathcal{B}$ has at least one successor v with a different colour. Put otherwise, there is a subgraph $\mathcal{B}'$ of $\mathcal{B}$ such that c_2 is a proper 3-colouring of $\mathcal{B}'$, and each node with a positive outdegree in $\mathcal{B}$ has a positive outdegree in $\mathcal{B}'$ as well.

Then we set $c_3(u) \leftarrow 3c(u) + c_2(u)$ for each node $u \in U_{yi}$ to construct an improper $3(D+1)$-colouring c_3 of $\mathcal{K}_{yc}$, with the following properties:

(a) If (u, s, v) is an edge of $\mathcal{B}'$ then $c_3(u) \neq c_3(v)$.

(b) If $(u, s, v) \in K$ and $c(u) \neq c(v)$ then $c_3(u) \neq c_3(v)$.

In other words, edges in $\mathcal{B}'$ become multicoloured, and multicoloured edges in $\mathcal{K}$ remain multicoloured. Finally, we use a trivial $O(D)$-time colour reduction algorithm to construct an improper $(D+1)$-colouring c_4 of $\mathcal{K}_{yc}$ with the same properties.

We set $c \leftarrow c_4$; after that, we have $e \notin K_{yc}$ for each edge e of $\mathcal{B}'$. Hence the outdegree of each node $u \in U_y$ in K_{yc} has decreased by at least one during the iteration: either we saturated a neighbour of u in one of the saturation phases, or we have at least one outgoing edge in $\mathcal{B}$. In the latter case, we also have at least one outgoing edge in $\mathcal{B}'$, which we multicoloured in the colouring phase. In the worst case, a node $u \in U$ loses only one outgoing edge during each iteration $j = 1, 2, \dots, D$ and finally becomes saturated and removed from U_y during the last iteration $j = D + 1$.

THEOREM 2. *There is a deterministic algorithm that finds a maximal fractional packing in $O(f^2 k^2 + f k \log^* W)$ synchronous communication rounds.*

PROOF. Each iteration takes $O(D + \log^* \chi)$ communication rounds and there are $O(D)$ iterations. The claim follows from $\log^* \chi = O(\log^* D + \log^* W)$ and $D = O(fk)$. $\square$

4.5 Weak Colour Reduction

In the colour reduction algorithm, each node $u \in U_y$ maintains a value $c'(u)$. Let $\mathcal{B}(u) \subseteq U_y$ be the set of successors of u in $\mathcal{B}$ and let $L(u) = \{c'(v) : v \in \mathcal{B}(u), c'(v) \neq c'(u)\}$. If $L(u) \neq \emptyset$, we define $\ell(u) = \min L(u)$. The graph $\mathcal{B}'$ is defined to consist of all edges (u, s, v) of $\mathcal{B}$ such that $L(u) \neq \emptyset$ and $\ell(u) = c'(v)$; see Figure 2 for an example. Let $\mathcal{B}'(u) \subseteq \mathcal{B}(u)$ be the set of successors of u in $\mathcal{B}'$.

We do not maintain $\mathcal{B}$ or $\mathcal{B}'$ explicitly. Nevertheless, each node $u \in U_y$ can compute the current values of $L(u)$ and $\ell(u)$ by using the following algorithm:

(i) Each $v \in U_y$ broadcasts the triplet

$$(c'(v), c(v), p(v)).$$

Let $M(s)$ be the set of messages received by $s \in S$.

(ii) Each $s \in S$ broadcasts the triplets

$$\big\{(c'(v), i, x_i(s)) : (c'(v), i, p(v)) \in M(s),$$
$$p(v) = q_i(s)\big\}.$$

Let $M'(u)$ be the set of triplets received by $u \in U_y$.

(iii) Each $u \in U_y$ constructs

$$L(u) = \big\{c'(v) : (c'(v), i, x_i(s)) \in M'(u),$$
$$c(u) = i,\ p(u) = x_i(s)\big\}.$$

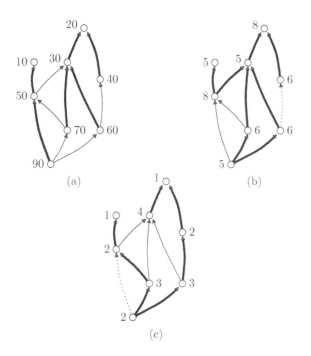

(a)   (b)

(c)

Figure 2: Weak colour reduction, two iterations. Arrows illustrate the directed acyclic graph $\mathcal{B}$, the numbers are the current values of $c'(u)$, and thick lines highlight the subgraph $\mathcal{B}'$. Dotted edges are not properly coloured; nevertheless, each node with a positive outdegree has at least one successor with a different colour.

Now we are ready to describe how the algorithm manipulates the colours c'. Initially, we set $c' \leftarrow c_1$. At this point, if $\mathcal{B}(u) \neq \emptyset$, we also have $L(u) \neq \emptyset$ and hence $\mathcal{B}'(u) \neq \emptyset$.

Then we apply repeatedly the Cole–Vishkin colour reduction technique for trees [8, 11]. In the Cole–Vishkin algorithm, each node is assumed to have at most one successor. Each node in parallel inspects the current colour of its successor and chooses a new colour; it is guaranteed that the successor chooses a different colour. In our case, each node $u \in U_y$ with $L(u) \neq \emptyset$ may have several successors in $\mathcal{B}'$, but all successors of u have the same colour $\ell(u)$. Hence we can simply proceed as if u had only one successor of colour $\ell(u)$; the Cole–Vishkin algorithm then guarantees that the new colour of u is different from the new colour of each $v \in \mathcal{B}'(u)$. In particular, if $L(u)$ was nonempty, it will be nonempty also after each colour reduction step. Hence we maintain the invariant that $\mathcal{B}(u) \neq \emptyset$ implies $\mathcal{B}'(u) \neq \emptyset$. After $O(\log^* \chi)$ iterations, we have reduced the number of colours in c' to 3.

5. VERTEX COVER IN THE BROADCAST MODEL

The edge packing algorithm from Section 3 assumed that we have a port numbering in the graph $\mathcal{G}$. Now we proceed to show how to find a maximal edge packing in the broadcast model. Naturally, we can represent an edge packing instance $(\mathcal{G}, w)$ as a fractional packing instance $(\mathcal{H}, w)$. We have $f = 2$ and $k = \Delta$; each node $v \in V$ is associated with a subset node $s(v) \in S$, and each edge $e \in E$ is associated

with an element $u(e) \in U$. The algorithm $\mathcal{A}$ of Section 4 finds a maximal fractional packing in $\mathcal{H}$; hence it is sufficient to design an algorithm that simulates the execution of $\mathcal{A}$ in $\mathcal{H}$, using the broadcast model and the communication network $\mathcal{G}$. It should be noted that while the elements $u \in U$ are computational entities in $\mathcal{H}$, we do not have any internal state associated with an edge $e \in E$ in $\mathcal{G}$. Nevertheless, the simulation is possible (without increasing the number of communication rounds, but at the cost of increasing message complexity).

For each $v \in V$ and i, let $h(v, i)$ be the full history of all messages that the subset node $s(v)$ has sent during the communication rounds $1, 2, \ldots, i$ in $\mathcal{A}$; similarly, for each $e \in E$, let $h(e, i)$ be the full history of the element $u(e)$. We maintain the following invariant: after the communication round i, each node $v \in V$ knows $h(v, i)$. The base case $i = 1$ is trivial. For the general $i > 1$, we use an algorithm in which each $v \in V$ broadcasts $h(v, i-1)$. Hence for each edge $e = \{v, u\} \in E$ incident to v, the node v knows both $h(v, i-1)$ and $h(u, i-1)$, which constitute the full history of messages received by $u(e)$ before the round i. In particular, v can simulate $u(e)$ in $\mathcal{A}$ for i rounds to determine $h(e, i)$ for each incident $e \in E$, and then v can simulate $s(v)$ in $\mathcal{A}$ for 1 round to determine $h(v, i)$. Eventually, v can determine the multiset of the values $f(s(e))$ for incident edges e; in particular, v knows whether $\mathcal{A}$ saturates the subset node $s(v)$.

6. LOWER BOUNDS

In this section, we focus on the unweighted set cover problem. Let us fix the constants $k \geq 1$ and $f \geq 1$, and let $p = \min\{f, k\}$. We have already seen how to find a p-approximation of a minimum-size set cover: if $f < k$, we can apply the f-approximation algorithm from Section 4, and if $f \geq k$, we can apply the trivial k-approximation algorithm. Neither of the algorithms needs unique identifiers – port numbering is sufficient – and the running time is independent of the number of nodes.

If we assume the port-numbering model, no deterministic algorithm can achieve a better approximation ratio than p, regardless of the running time. To see this, consider the complete bipartite graph $K_{p,p}$, and choose the port numbers in a symmetric manner (see Figure 3 for an example in the case $p = 3$). Any deterministic distributed algorithm has to make the same decision for each subset node as their local views are identical. Hence the solution computed by the algorithm has size p, while there is an optimal solution of size 1.

If we had unique node identifiers, we could use them to break symmetry. However, if we focus on strictly local algorithms (with running time independent of the number of nodes), it turns out that we have the same lower bound p for the best possible approximation factor.

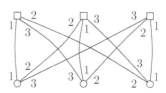

Figure 3: A symmetric set cover instance, $f = k = 3$.

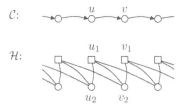

Figure 4: A local reduction from the problem of finding an independent set in a numbered directed cycle $\mathcal{C}$ to the problem of finding a set cover in the graph $\mathcal{H}$. In this example, $p = 3$.

In a *directed cycle*, each node has one incoming edge and one outgoing edge. A *numbered directed n-cycle* is a directed n-cycle in which each node is assigned a unique identifier from the set $\{1, 2, \ldots, n\}$. Czygrinow et al. [9] and Lenzen and Wattenhofer [24] show that a constant-time deterministic algorithm cannot find a large independent set in a numbered directed n-cycle; the following lemma is an adaptation of their results:

LEMMA 4 ([9, 24]). *Let $\mathcal{A}$ be a deterministic distributed algorithm that finds an independent set in any numbered directed cycle in $O(1)$ communication rounds. For any $\alpha > 1$ there exists an integer n_0 with the following property: for every $n \geq n_0$ there is a numbered directed n-cycle $\mathcal{C}$ in which $\mathcal{A}$ outputs an independent set with fewer than n/α nodes.*

We use this result and a simple local reduction to establish the lower bound. To reach a contradiction, let ε be a positive constant, and assume that there exists a deterministic local algorithm $\mathcal{A}'$ that computes a $(p - \varepsilon)$-approximation of a minimum set cover, provided that each subset node and each element is associated with a unique node identifier. The running time of $\mathcal{A}'$ must be independent of the number of nodes in the network; however, the algorithm $\mathcal{A}'$ and its running time may depend on the value of p.

We show that $\mathcal{A}'$ can be used to find a large independent set in a numbered directed cycle. Given a numbered directed n-cycle $\mathcal{C} = (V, E)$, with n divisible by p, construct a set cover instance $\mathcal{H} = (S \cup U, A)$ as follows. For each node $v \in V$ there is a subset node $v_1 \in S$ and an element $v_2 \in U$. There is an edge $\{u_1, v_2\} \in A$ iff the unique directed path from $u \in V$ to $v \in V$ in $\mathcal{C}$ has length at most $p - 1$. See Figure 4 for an illustration.

The unique node identifiers in $\mathcal{H}$ are inherited from $\mathcal{C}$ (e.g., if the identifier of $v \in V$ is i then the identifier of $v_1 \in S$ is $2i - 1$ and the identifier of $v_2 \in U$ is $2i$). Clearly, any computation in $\mathcal{H}$ can be simulated by a distributed algorithm in $\mathcal{C}$; the running time increases by a constant factor $O(p)$.

Now let us simulate the algorithm $\mathcal{A}'$ in $\mathcal{H}$, and let $C \subseteq S$ be the set cover computed by $\mathcal{A}'$. An optimal set cover C^* in $\mathcal{H}$ would take every pth subset node from S; hence $|C^*| = n/p$. By assumption, $|C| \leq (p - \varepsilon)|C^*| = (1 - \varepsilon/p)n$. This implies that the complement $S \setminus C$ has size at least $n\varepsilon/p$.

Let $X = \{v \in V : v_1 \in S \setminus C\}$; again, $|X| \geq n\varepsilon/p$. Let $\mathcal{C}'$ be the subgraph of $\mathcal{C}$ induced by the set X. The subgraph $\mathcal{C}'$ consists of paths (and isolated nodes which we consider as paths of length 0). Since C is a set cover in $\mathcal{H}$, there cannot be a path with p or more nodes in $\mathcal{C}'$. Thus there

are at least $n\varepsilon/p^2$ connected components in the subgraph $\mathcal{C}'$. Let I consist of the nodes in $\mathcal{C}'$ with indegree 0 (i.e., the first node of each path). By construction, I is an independent set for $\mathcal{C}$, with $|I| \geq n\varepsilon/p^2$. Choosing $\alpha = p^2/\varepsilon$ and a sufficiently large n contradicts Lemma 4.

7. DISCUSSION

Usually, in the study of deterministic distributed algorithms, one takes for granted that each node has a unique identifier. There are only a few positive results related to anonymous networks. Mayer et al. [26] study local algorithms for weak colouring in anonymous networks with odd degrees; however, they have to assume not only a port numbering but also an orientation in order to break symmetry. Angluin [1], Attiya et al. [3], and Yamashita and Kameda [32] have studied computation in the port-numbering model, but many of their theorems are impossibility results, and the positive results focus on computability instead of time complexity. Boldi and Vigna [7] is a rare example of a work that explicitly considers the broadcast model, which is strictly weaker than the port-numbering model.

Our work shows that there are non-trivial graph problems that can be solved very efficiently in the broadcast model. Indeed, if we consider the approximability of the vertex cover problem, the broadcast model is surprisingly capable: our algorithm finds a 2-approximation in the broadcast model, and it is known that a deterministic local algorithm cannot find a better approximation even if we had unique node identifiers. Incidentally, finding a better constant factor approximation has been conjectured to be computationally hard even from the perspective of centralised algorithms [15].

While challenging to design, deterministic distributed algorithms in the broadcast model have many curious properties. If a deterministic distributed algorithm $\mathcal{A}$ uses the broadcast model, the output of $\mathcal{A}$ (together with the input) must have the same automorphisms as the graph $\mathcal{G}$ (and local inputs, if any): in a symmetric graph, the output must be symmetric. Moreover, we can apply the same reasoning to any covering graph of $\mathcal{G}$ [31, §5]. Consider, e.g., the case that $\mathcal{G}$ is the Frucht graph, which is 3-regular but has only the trivial automorphism. The universal covering graph of $\mathcal{G}$ is the infinite 3-regular tree $\mathcal{T}$. If we apply $\mathcal{A}$ to $\mathcal{T}$, then each node must produce the same output, as this is the only solution with the same automorphisms as $\mathcal{T}$. Because $\mathcal{A}$ cannot distinguish between $\mathcal{G}$ and $\mathcal{T}$, we conclude that if we apply $\mathcal{A}$ to $\mathcal{G}$, each node must produce the same output. In particular, if $\mathcal{A}$ finds a maximal edge packing, it must produce the solution $y(e) = 1/3$ for each edge e. None of this holds in the port-numbering model, as the port numbers may be used to break symmetry – for example, a prior algorithm [2] never sets $y(e) = 1/3$ in any graph.

In summary, distributed algorithms that use the broadcast model are able to produce highly symmetric solutions without explicitly identifying the symmetries in the input. This property may make such algorithms attractive also in a non-distributed setting.

8. ACKNOWLEDGEMENTS

Thanks to Christos Koufogiannakis, Valentin Polishchuk, and Joel Rybicki for discussions and comments. This work was supported in part by the Academy of Finland, Grants 116547 and 132380, by Helsinki Graduate School in Computer Science and Engineering (Hecse), and by the Foundation of Nokia Corporation.

9. REFERENCES

[1] D. Angluin. Local and global properties in networks of processors. In *Proc. 12th Symposium on Theory of Computing (STOC 1980)*, pages 82–93. ACM Press, 1980.

[2] M. Åstrand, P. Floréen, V. Polishchuk, J. Rybicki, J. Suomela, and J. Uitto. A local 2-approximation algorithm for the vertex cover problem. In *Proc. 23rd Symposium on Distributed Computing (DISC 2009)*, volume 5805 of *LNCS*, pages 191–205. Springer, 2009.

[3] H. Attiya, M. Snir, and M. K. Warmuth. Computing on an anonymous ring. *Journal of the ACM*, 35(4):845–875, 1988.

[4] B. Awerbuch and M. Sipser. Dynamic networks are as fast as static networks. In *Proc. 29th Symposium on Foundations of Computer Science (FOCS 1988)*, pages 206–219. IEEE, 1988.

[5] B. Awerbuch and G. Varghese. Distributed program checking: a paradigm for building self-stabilizing distributed protocols. In *Proc. 32nd Symposium on Foundations of Computer Science (FOCS 1991)*, pages 258–267. IEEE, 1991.

[6] R. Bar-Yehuda and S. Even. A linear-time approximation algorithm for the weighted vertex cover problem. *Journal of Algorithms*, 2(2):198–203, 1981.

[7] P. Boldi and S. Vigna. An effective characterization of computability in anonymous networks. In *Proc. 15th Symposium on Distributed Computing (DISC 2001)*, volume 2180 of *LNCS*, pages 33–47. Springer, 2001.

[8] R. Cole and U. Vishkin. Deterministic coin tossing with applications to optimal parallel list ranking. *Information and Control*, 70(1):32–53. 1986.

[9] A. Czygrinow, M. Hańćkowiak, and W. Wawrzyniak. Fast distributed approximations in planar graphs. In *Proc. 22nd Symposium on Distributed Computing (DISC 2008)*, volume 5218 of *LNCS*, pages 78–92. Springer, 2008.

[10] S. Dolev. *Self-Stabilization*. The MIT Press, Cambridge, MA, 2000.

[11] A. V. Goldberg, S. A. Plotkin, and G. E. Shannon. Parallel symmetry-breaking in sparse graphs. *SIAM Journal on Discrete Mathematics*, 1(4):434–446, 1988.

[12] F. Grandoni, J. Könemann, and A. Panconesi. Distributed weighted vertex cover via maximal matchings. *ACM Transactions on Algorithms*, 5(1):1–12, 2008.

[13] M. Hańćkowiak, M. Karoński, and A. Panconesi. On the distributed complexity of computing maximal matchings. *SIAM Journal on Discrete Mathematics*, 15(1):41–57, 2001.

[14] D. S. Hochbaum. Approximation algorithms for the set covering and vertex cover problems. *SIAM Journal on Computing*, 11(3):555–556, 1982.

[15] S. Khot and O. Regev. Vertex cover might be hard to approximate to within $2 - \epsilon$. *Journal of Computer and System Sciences*, 74(3):335–349, 2008.

[16] S. Khuller, U. Vishkin, and N. Young. A primal-dual parallel approximation technique applied to weighted set and vertex covers. *Journal of Algorithms*, 17(2):280–289, 1994.

[17] C. Koufogiannakis and N. E. Young. Distributed and parallel algorithms for weighted vertex cover and other covering problems. In *Proc. 28th Symposium on Principles of Distributed Computing (PODC 2009)*, pages 171–179. ACM Press, 2009.

[18] F. Kuhn. *The Price of Locality: Exploring the Complexity of Distributed Coordination Primitives*. PhD thesis, ETH Zürich, 2005.

[19] F. Kuhn, T. Moscibroda, and R. Wattenhofer. What cannot be computed locally! In *Proc. 23rd Symposium on Principles of Distributed Computing (PODC 2004)*, pages 300–309. ACM Press, 2004.

[20] F. Kuhn, T. Moscibroda, and R. Wattenhofer. Fault-tolerant clustering in ad hoc and sensor networks. In *Proc. 26th International Conference on Distributed Computing Systems (ICDCS 2006)*. IEEE Computer Society Press, 2006.

[21] F. Kuhn, T. Moscibroda, and R. Wattenhofer. The price of being near-sighted. In *Proc. 17th Symposium on Discrete Algorithms (SODA 2006)*, pages 980–989. ACM Press, 2006.

[22] F. Kuhn and R. Wattenhofer. Constant-time distributed dominating set approximation. *Distributed Computing*, 17(4):303–310, 2005.

[23] C. Lenzen, J. Suomela, and R. Wattenhofer. Local algorithms: Self-stabilization on speed. In *Proc. 11th Symposium on Stabilization, Safety, and Security of Distributed Systems (SSS 2009)*, volume 5873 of *LNCS*, pages 17–34. Springer, 2009.

[24] C. Lenzen and R. Wattenhofer. Leveraging Linial's locality limit. In *Proc. 22nd Symposium on Distributed Computing (DISC 2008)*, volume 5218 of *LNCS*, pages 394–407. Springer, 2008.

[25] N. Linial. Locality in distributed graph algorithms. *SIAM Journal on Computing*, 21(1):193–201, 1992.

[26] A. Mayer, M. Naor, and L. Stockmeyer. Local computations on static and dynamic graphs. In *Proc. 3rd Israel Symposium on the Theory of Computing and Systems (ISTCS 1995)*, pages 268–278. IEEE, 1995.

[27] M. Naor and L. Stockmeyer. What can be computed locally? *SIAM Journal on Computing*, 24(6):1259–1277, 1995.

[28] A. Panconesi and R. Rizzi. Some simple distributed algorithms for sparse networks. *Distributed Computing*, 14(2):97–100, 2001.

[29] C. H. Papadimitriou and M. Yannakakis. Linear programming without the matrix. In *Proc. 25th Symposium on Theory of Computing (STOC 1993)*, pages 121–129. ACM Press, 1993.

[30] V. Polishchuk and J. Suomela. A simple local 3-approximation algorithm for vertex cover. *Information Processing Letters*, 109(12):642–645, 2009.

[31] J. Suomela. Survey of local algorithms, 2010. Manuscript submitted for publication.

[32] M. Yamashita and T. Kameda. Computing on anonymous networks: Part I – characterizing the solvable cases. *IEEE Transactions on Parallel and Distributed Systems*, 7(1):69–89, 1996.

A Work-Efficient Parallel Breadth-First Search Algorithm (or How to Cope with the Nondeterminism of Reducers)

Charles E. Leiserson
Tao B. Schardl

MIT Computer Science and Artificial Intelligence Laboratory
32 Vassar Street
Cambridge, MA 02139

ABSTRACT

We have developed a multithreaded implementation of breadth-first search (BFS) of a sparse graph using the Cilk++ extensions to C++. Our PBFS program on a single processor runs as quickly as a standard C++ breadth-first search implementation. PBFS achieves high work-efficiency by using a novel implementation of a multiset data structure, called a "bag," in place of the FIFO queue usually employed in serial breadth-first search algorithms. For a variety of benchmark input graphs whose diameters are significantly smaller than the number of vertices — a condition met by many real-world graphs — PBFS demonstrates good speedup with the number of processing cores.

Since PBFS employs a nonconstant-time "reducer" — a "hyperobject" feature of Cilk++ — the work inherent in a PBFS execution depends nondeterministically on how the underlying work-stealing scheduler load-balances the computation. We provide a general method for analyzing nondeterministic programs that use reducers. PBFS also is nondeterministic in that it contains benign races which affect its performance but not its correctness. Fixing these races with mutual-exclusion locks slows down PBFS empirically, but it makes the algorithm amenable to analysis. In particular, we show that for a graph $G = (V, E)$ with diameter D and bounded outdegree, this data-race-free version of PBFS algorithm runs in time $O((V + E)/P + D \lg^3(V/D))$ on P processors, which means that it attains near-perfect linear speedup if $P \ll (V + E)/D \lg^3(V/D)$.

Categories and Subject Descriptors

F.2.2 [**Theory of Computation**]: Nonnumerical Algorithms and Problems—*Computations on discrete structures*; D.1.3 [**Software**]: Programming Techniques—*Concurrent programming*; G.2.2 [**Mathematics of Computing**]: Graph Theory—*Graph Algorithms*.

General Terms

Algorithms, Performance, Theory

This research was supported in part by the National Science Foundation under Grant CNS-0615215. TB Schardl is an MIT Siebel Scholar.

Keywords

Breadth-first search, Cilk, graph algorithms, hyperobjects, multithreading, nondeterminism, parallel algorithms, reducers, work-stealing.

1. INTRODUCTION

Algorithms to search a graph in a breadth-first manner have been studied for over 50 years. The first breadth-first search (BFS) algorithm was discovered by Moore [26] while studying the problem of finding paths through mazes. Lee [22] independently discovered the same algorithm in the context of routing wires on circuit boards. A variety of parallel BFS algorithms have since been explored [3, 9, 21, 25, 31, 32]. Some of these parallel algorithms are *work efficient*, meaning that the total number of operations performed is the same as to within a constant factor as that of a comparable serial algorithm. That constant factor, which we call the *work efficiency*, can be important in practice, but few if any papers actually measure work efficiency. In this paper, we present a parallel BFS algorithm, called PBFS, whose performance scales linearly with the number of processors and for which the work efficiency is nearly 1, as measured by comparing its performance on benchmark graphs to the classical FIFO-queue algorithm [10, Section 22.2].

Given a graph $G = (V, E)$ with vertex set $V = V(G)$ and edge set $E = E(G)$, the BFS problem is to compute for each vertex $v \in V$ the distance $v.dist$ that v lies from a distinguished *source* vertex $v_0 \in V$. We measure distance as the minimum number of edges on a path from v_0 to v in G. For simplicity in the statement of results, we shall assume that G is connected and undirected, although the algorithms we shall explore apply equally as well to unconnected graphs, digraphs, and multigraphs.

Figure 1 gives a variant of the classical serial algorithm [10, Section 22.2] for computing BFS, which uses a FIFO queue as an auxiliary data structure. The FIFO can be implemented as a simple array with two pointers to the head and tail of the items in the queue. Enqueueing an item consists of incrementing the tail pointer and storing the item into the array at the pointer location. Dequeueing consists of removing the item referenced by the head pointer and incrementing the head pointer. Since these two operations take only $\Theta(1)$ time, the running time of SERIAL-BFS is $\Theta(V + E)$. Moreover, the constants hidden by the asymptotic notation are small due to the extreme simplicity of the FIFO operations.

Although efficient, the FIFO queue Q is a major hindrance to parallelization of BFS. Parallelizing BFS while leaving the FIFO queue intact yields minimal parallelism for *sparse* graphs — those for which $|E| \approx |V|$. The reason is that if each ENQUEUE operation must be serialized, the *span*[1] of the computation — the longest

---

[1]Sometimes called *critical-path length* or *computational depth*.

```
SERIAL-BFS(G, v_0)
1   for each vertex u ∈ V(G) − {v_0}
2       u.dist = ∞
3   v_0.dist = 0
4   Q = {v_0}
5   while Q ≠ ∅
6       u = DEQUEUE(Q)
7       for each v ∈ V such that (u, v) ∈ E(G)
8           if v.dist == ∞
9               v.dist = u.dist + 1
10              ENQUEUE(Q.v)
```

Figure 1: A standard serial breadth-first search algorithm operating on a graph G with source vertex $v_0 \in V(G)$. The algorithm employs a FIFO queue Q as an auxiliary data structure to compute for each $v \in V(G)$ its distance $v.dist$ from v_0.

serial chain of executed instructions in the computation — must have length $\Omega(V)$. Thus, a *work-efficient* algorithm — one that uses no more work than a comparable serial algorithm — can have *parallelism* — the ratio of work to span — at most $O((V+E)/V) = O(1)$ if $|E| = O(V)$.[2]

Replacing the FIFO queue with another data structure in order to parallelize BFS may compromise work efficiency, however, because FIFO's are so simple and fast. We have devised a multiset data structure called a *bag*, however, which supports insertion essentially as fast as a FIFO, even when constant factors are considered. In addition, bags can be split and unioned efficiently.

We have implemented a parallel BFS algorithm in Cilk++ [20, 23]. Our *PBFS* algorithm, which employs bags instead of a FIFO, uses the "reducer hyperobject" [14] feature of Cilk++. Our implementation of PBFS runs comparably on a single processor to a good serial implementation of BFS. For a variety of benchmark graphs whose diameters are significantly smaller than the number of vertices — a common occurrence in practice — PBFS demonstrates high levels of parallelism and generally good speedup with the number of processing cores.

Figure 2 shows the typical speedup obtained for PBFS on a large benchmark graph, in this case, for a sparse matrix called Cage15 arising from DNA electrophoresis [30]. This graph has $|V| = 5,154,859$ vertices, $|E| = 99,199,551$ edges, and a diameter of $D = 50$. The code was run on an Intel Core i7 machine with eight $2.53\,$GHz processing cores, $12\,$GB of RAM, and two $8\,$MB L3-caches, each shared among 4 cores. As can be seen from the figure, although PBFS scales well initially, it attains a speedup of only about 5 on 8 cores, even though the parallelism in this graph is nearly 700. The figure graphs the impact of artificially increasing the *computational intensity* — the ratio of the number of CPU operations to the number of memory operations, suggesting that this low speedup is due to limitations of the memory system, rather than to the inherent parallelism in the algorithm.

PBFS is a nondeterministic program for two reasons. First, because the program employs a bag reducer which operates in non-constant time, the asymptotic amount of work can vary from run to run depending upon how Cilk++'s work-stealing scheduler load-balances the computation. Second, for efficient implementation, PBFS contains a benign race condition, which can cause additional work to be generated nondeterministically. Our theoretical analysis of PBFS bounds the additional work due to the bag reducer when the race condition is resolved using mutual-exclusion locks. Theoretically, on a graph G with vertex set $V = V(G)$, edge set

---
[2]For convenience, we omit the notation for set cardinality within asymptotic notation.

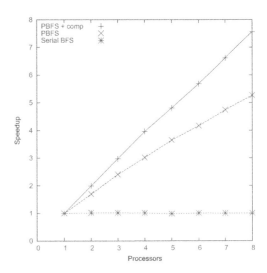

Figure 2: The performance of PBFS for the Cage15 graph showing speedup curves for serial BFS, PBFS, and a variant of PBFS where the computational intensity has been artificially enhanced and the speedup normalized.

$E = E(G)$, diameter D, and bounded out-degree, this "locking" version of PBFS performs BFS in $O((V+E)/P + D\lg^3(V/D))$ time on P processors and exhibits effective parallelism $\Omega((V+E)/D\lg^3(V/D))$, which is considerable when $D \ll V$, even if the graph is sparse. Our method of analysis is general and can be applied to other programs that employ reducers. We leave it as an open question how to analyze the extra work when the race condition is left unresolved.

The remainder of this paper is divided into two parts. Part I consists of Sections 2 through 5 and describes PBFS and its empirical performance. Part II consists of Sections 6 through 9 and describes how to cope with the nondeterminism of reducers in the theoretical analysis of PBFS. Section 10 concludes by discussing thread-local storage as an alternative to reducers.

Part I — Parallel Breadth-First Search

The first half of this paper consists of Sections 2 through 5 and describes PBFS and its empirical performance. Section 2 provides background on dynamic multithreading. Section 3 describes the basic PBFS algorithm, and Section 4 describes the implementation of the bag data structure. Section 5 presents our empirical studies.

2. BACKGROUND ON DYNAMIC MULTITHREADING

This section overviews the key attributes of dynamic multithreading. The PBFS software is implemented in Cilk++ [14, 20, 23], which is a linguistic extension to C++ [28], but most of the vagaries of C++ are unnecessary for understanding the issues. Thus, we describe Cilk-like pseudocode, as is exemplified in [10, Ch. 27], which the reader should find more straightforward than real code to understand and which can be translated easily to Cilk++.

Multithreaded pseudocode

The linguistic model for multithreaded pseudocode in [10, Ch. 27] follows MIT Cilk [15, 29] and Cilk++ [20, 23]. It augments ordinary serial pseudocode with three keywords — **spawn**, **sync**, and **parallel** — of which **spawn** and **sync** are the more basic.

Parallel work is created when the keyword **spawn** precedes the invocation of a function. The semantics of spawning differ from a

```
 1  x = 10          1  x = 10          1  x = 10
 2  x++             2  x++             2  x++
 3  x += 3          3  x += 3          3  x += 3
 4  x += -2         4  x += -2            x' = 0
 5  x += 6          5  x += 6          4  x' += -2
 6  x--                x' = 0          5  x' += 6
 7  x += 4          6  x'--            6  x'--
 8  x += 3          7  x' += 4            x'' = 0
 9  x++             8  x' += 3          7  x'' += 4
10  x += -9         9  x'++             8  x'' += 3
                   10  x' += -9         9  x''++
                       x += x'         10  x'' += -9
                                           x += x'
                                           x += x''

        (a)                (b)                (c)
```

Figure 3: The intuition behind reducers. (a) A series of additive updates performed on a variable x. (b) The same series of additive updates split between two "views" x and x'. The two update sequences can execute in parallel and are combined at the end. (c) Another valid splitting of these updates among the views x, x', and x''.

C or C++ function call only in that the parent ***continuation*** — the code that immediately follows the spawn — may execute in parallel with the child, instead of waiting for the child to complete, as is normally done for a function call. A function cannot safely use the values returned by its children until it executes a **sync** statement, which suspends the function until all of its spawned children return. Every function syncs implicitly before it returns, precluding orphaning. Together, **spawn** and **sync** allow programs containing fork-join parallelism to be expressed succinctly. The scheduler in the runtime system takes the responsibility of scheduling the spawned functions on the individual processor cores of the multicore computer and synchronizing their returns according to the fork-join logic provided by the **spawn** and **sync** keywords.

Loops can be parallelized by preceding an ordinary **for** with the keyword **parallel**, which indicates that all iterations of the loop may operate in parallel. Parallel loops do not require additional runtime support, but can be implemented by parallel divide-and-conquer recursion using **spawn** and **sync**.

Cilk++ provides a novel linguistic construct, called a ***reducer hyperobject*** [14], which allows concurrent updates to a shared variable or data structure to occur simultaneously without contention. A reducer is defined in terms of a binary associative **REDUCE** operator, such as sum, list concatenation, logical AND, etc. Updates to the hyperobject are accumulated in local ***views***, which the Cilk++ runtime system combines automatically with "up-calls" to REDUCE when subcomputations join. As we shall see in Section 3, PBFS uses a reducer called a "bag," which implements an unordered set and supports fast unioning as its REDUCE operator.

Figure 3 illustrates the basic idea of a reducer. The example involves a series of additive updates to a variable x. When the code in Figure 3(a) is executed serially, the resulting value is $x = 16$. Figure 3(b) shows the same series of updates split between two "views" x and x' of the variable. These two views may be evaluated independently in parallel with an additional step to ***reduce*** the results at the end, as shown in Figure 3(b). As long as the values for the views x and x' are not inspected in the middle of the computation, the associativity of addition guarantees that the final result is deterministically $x = 16$. This series of updates could be split anywhere else along the way and yield the same final result, as demonstrated in Figure 3(c), where the computation is split across three views x, x', and x''. To encapsulate nondeterminism in this way, each of the views must be reduced with an associative RE-

```
PBFS(G, v_0)
 1   parallel for each vertex v ∈ V(G) − {v_0}
 2       v.dist = ∞
 3   v_0.dist = 0
 4   d = 0
 5   V_0 = BAG-CREATE()
 6   BAG-INSERT(V_0, v_0)
 7   while ¬BAG-IS-EMPTY(V_d)
 8       V_{d+1} = new reducer BAG-CREATE()
 9       PROCESS-LAYER(revert V_d, V_{d+1}, d)
10       d = d + 1

PROCESS-LAYER(in-bag, out-bag, d)
11   if BAG-SIZE(in-bag) < GRAINSIZE
12       for each u ∈ in-bag
13           parallel for each v ∈ Adj[u]
14               if v.dist == ∞
15                   v.dist = d + 1          // benign race
16                   BAG-INSERT(out-bag, v)
17       return
18   new-bag = BAG-SPLIT(in-bag)
19   spawn PROCESS-LAYER(new-bag, out-bag, d)
20   PROCESS-LAYER(in-bag, out-bag, d)
21   sync
```

Figure 4: The PBFS algorithm operating on a graph G with source vertex $v_0 \in V(G)$. PBFS uses the recursive parallel subroutine PROCESS-LAYER to process each layer. It contains a benign race in line 15.

DUCE operator (addition for this example) and intermediate views must be initialized to the identity for REDUCE (0 for this example).

Cilk++'s reducer mechanism supports this kind of decomposition of update sequences automatically without requiring the programmer to manually create various views. When a function spawns, the spawned child inherits the parent's view of the hyperobject. If the child returns before the continuation executes, the child can return the view and the chain of updates can continue. If the continuation begins executing before the child returns, however, the continuation receives a new view initialized to the identity for the associative REDUCE operator. Sometime at or before the **sync** that joins the spawned child with its parent, the two views are combined with REDUCE. If REDUCE is indeed associative, the result is the same as if all the updates had occurred serially. Indeed, if the program is run on one processor, the entire computation updates only a single view without ever invoking the REDUCE operator, in which case the behavior is virtually identical to a serial execution that uses an ordinary object instead of a hyperobject. We shall formalize reducers in Section 7.

3. THE PBFS ALGORITHM

PBFS uses ***layer synchronization*** [3, 32] to parallelize breadth-first search of an input graph G. Let $v_0 \in V(G)$ be the source vertex, and define ***layer*** d to be the set $V_d \subseteq V(G)$ of vertices at distance d from v_0. Thus, we have $V_0 = \{v_0\}$. Each iteration processes layer d by checking all the neighbors of vertices in V_d for those that should be added to V_{d+1}.

PBFS implements layers using an unordered-set data structure, called a ***bag***, which provides the following operations:

- bag = BAG-CREATE(): Create a new empty bag.
- BAG-INSERT(bag, x): Insert element x into bag.
- BAG-UNION(bag_1, bag_2): Move all the elements from bag_2 to bag_1, and destroy bag_2.
- bag_2 = BAG-SPLIT(bag_1): Remove half (to within some

```
15.1    set = FALSE
15.2    if TRY-LOCK(v)
15.3        if v.dist == ∞
15.4            v.dist = d + 1
15.5            set = TRUE
15.6        RELEASE-LOCK(v)
15.7    if set
15.8        BAG-INSERT(out-bag, v)
```

Figure 5: Modification to the PBFS algorithm to resolve the benign race.

constant amount GRAINSIZE of granularity) of the elements from bag_1, and put them into a new bag bag_2.

As Section 4 shows, BAG-CREATE operates in $O(1)$ time, and BAG-INSERT operates in $O(1)$ amortized time. Both BAG-UNION and BAG-SPLIT operate in $O(\lg n)$ time on bags with n elements.

Let us walk through the pseudocode for PBFS, which is shown in Figure 4. For the moment, ignore the **revert** and **reducer** keywords in lines 8 and 9.

After initialization, PBFS begins the **while** loop in line 7 which iteratively calls the auxiliary function PROCESS-LAYER to process layer $d = 0, 1, \ldots, D$, where D is the diameter of the input graph G. To process $V_d = in\text{-}bag$, PROCESS-LAYER uses parallel divide-and-conquer, producing $V_{d+1} = out\text{-}bag$. For the recursive case, line 18 splits $in\text{-}bag$, removing half its elements and placing them in $new\text{-}bag$. The two halves are processed recursively in parallel in lines 19–20.

This recursive decomposition continues until $in\text{-}bag$ has fewer than GRAINSIZE elements, as tested for in line 11. Each vertex u in $in\text{-}bag$ is extracted in line 12, and line 13 examines each of its edges (u, v) in parallel. If v has not yet been visited — $v.dist$ is infinite (line 14) — then line 15 sets $v.dist = d + 1$ and line 16 inserts v into the level-$(d+1)$ bag. As an implementation detail, the destructive nature of the BAG-SPLIT routine makes it particularly convenient to maintain only two bags at a time, ignoring additional views set up by the runtime system.

This description skirts over two subtleties that require discussion, both involving races.

First, the update of $v.dist$ in line 15 creates a race, since two vertices u and u' may both be examining vertex v at the same time. They both check whether $v.dist$ is infinite in line 14, discover that it is, and both proceed to update $v.dist$. Fortunately, this race is benign, meaning that it does not affect the correctness of the algorithm. Both u and u' set $v.dist$ to the same value, and hence no inconsistency arises from both updating the location at the same time. They both go on to insert v into bag $V_{d+1} = out\text{-}bag$ in line 16, which could induce another race. Putting that issue aside for the moment, notice that inserting multiple copies of v into V_{d+1} does not affect correctness, only performance for the extra work it will take when processing layer $d + 1$, because v will be encountered multiple times. As we shall see in Section 5, the amount of extra work is small, because the race is rarely actualized.

Second, a race in line 16 occurs due to parallel insertions of vertices into $V_{d+1} = out\text{-}bag$. We employ the reducer functionality to avoid the race by making V_{d+1} a bag reducer, where BAG-UNION is the associative operation required by the reducer mechanism. The identity for BAG-UNION — an empty bag — is created by BAG-CREATE. In the common case, line 16 simply inserts v into the local view, which, as we shall see in Section 4, is as efficient as pushing v onto a FIFO, as is done by serial BFS.

Unfortunately, we are not able to analyze PBFS due to unstructured nondeterminism created by the benign race, but we can ana-

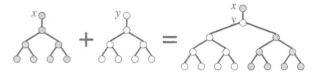

Figure 6: Two pennants, each of size 2^k, can be unioned in constant time to form a pennant of size 2^{k+1}.

lyze a version where the race is resolved using a mutual-exclusion lock. The locking version involves replacing lines 15 and 16 with the code in Figure 5. In the code, the call TRY-LOCK(v) in line 15.2 attempts to acquire a lock on the vertex v. If it is successful, we proceed to execute lines 15.3–15.6. Otherwise, we can abandon the attempt, because we know that some other processor has succeeded, which then sets $v.dist = d + 1$ regardless. Thus, there is no contention on v's lock, because no processor ever waits for another, and processing an edge (u, v) always takes constant time. The apparently redundant lines 14 and 15.3 avoid the overhead of lock acquisition when $v.dist$ has already been set.

4. THE BAG DATA STRUCTURE

This section describes the bag data structure for implementing a dynamic unordered set. We first describe an auxiliary data structure called a "pennant." We then show how bags can be implemented using pennants, and we provide algorithms for BAG-CREATE, BAG-INSERT, BAG-UNION, and BAG-SPLIT. Finally, we discuss some optimizations of this structure that PBFS employs.

Pennants

A **pennant** is a tree of 2^k nodes, where k is a nonnegative integer. Each node x in this tree contains two pointers $x.left$ and $x.right$ to its children. The root of the tree has only a left child, which is a complete binary tree of the remaining elements.

Two pennants x and y of size 2^k can be combined to form a pennant of size 2^{k+1} in $O(1)$ time using the following PENNANT-UNION function, which is illustrated in Figure 6.

```
PENNANT-UNION(x, y)
1   y.right = x.left
2   x.left = y
3   return x
```

The function PENNANT-SPLIT performs the inverse operation of PENNANT-UNION in $O(1)$ time. We assume that the input pennant contains at least 2 elements.

```
PENNANT-SPLIT(x)
1   y = x.left
2   x.left = y.right
3   y.right = NULL
4   return y
```

Each of the pennants x and y now contains half the elements.

Bags

A **bag** is a collection of pennants, no two of which have the same size. PBFS represents a bag S using a fixed-size array $S[0..r]$, called the **backbone**, where 2^{r+1} exceeds the maximum number of elements ever stored in a bag. Each entry $S[k]$ in the backbone contains either a null pointer or a pointer to a pennant of size 2^k. Figure 7 illustrates a bag containing 23 elements. The function BAG-CREATE allocates space for a fixed-size backbone of null pointers, which takes $\Theta(r)$ time. This bound can be improved to $O(1)$ by keeping track of the largest nonempty index in the backbone.

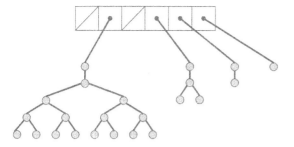

Figure 7: A bag with $23 = 010111_2$ elements.

The BAG-INSERT function employs an algorithm similar to that of incrementing a binary counter. To implement BAG-INSERT, we first package the given element as a pennant x of size 1. We then insert x into bag S using the following method.

BAG-INSERT(S,x)
```
1  k = 0
2  while S[k] ≠ NULL
3      x = PENNANT-UNION(S[k].x)
4      S[k++] = NULL
5  S[k] = x
```

The analysis of BAG-INSERT mirrors the analysis for incrementing a binary counter [10, Ch. 17]. Since every PENNANT-UNION operation takes constant time, BAG-INSERT takes $O(1)$ amortized time and $O(\lg n)$ worst-case time to insert into a bag of n elements.

The BAG-UNION function uses an algorithm similar to ripple-carry addition of two binary counters. To implement BAG-UNION, we first examine the process of unioning three pennants into two pennants, which operates like a full adder. Given three pennants x, y, and z, where each either has size 2^k or is empty, we can merge them to produce a pair of pennants (s,c), where s has size 2^k or is empty, and c has size 2^{k+1} or is empty. The following table details the function $FA(x,y,z)$ in which (s,c) is computed from (x,y,z), where 0 means that the designated pennant is empty, and 1 means that it has size 2^k:

x	y	z	s	c
0	0	0	NULL	NULL
1	0	0	x	NULL
0	1	0	y	NULL
0	0	1	z	NULL
1	1	0	NULL	PENNANT-UNION(x,y)
1	0	1	NULL	PENNANT-UNION(x,z)
0	1	1	NULL	PENNANT-UNION(y,z)
1	1	1	x	PENNANT-UNION(y,z)

With this full-adder function in hand, BAG-UNION can be implemented as follows:

BAG-UNION(S_1,S_2)
```
1  y = NULL    // The "carry" bit.
2  for k = 0 to r
3      (S_1[k],y) = FA(S_1[k],S_2[k],y)
```

Because every PENNANT-UNION operation takes constant time, computing the value of $FA(x,y,z)$ also takes constant time. To compute all entries in the backbone of the resulting bag takes $\Theta(r)$ time. This algorithm can be improved to $\Theta(\lg n)$, where n is the number of elements in the smaller of the two bags, by maintaining the largest nonempty index of the backbone of each bag and unioning the bag with the smaller such index into the one with the larger.

The BAG-SPLIT function operates like an arithmetic right shift:

BAG-SPLIT(S_1)
```
1   S_2 = BAG-CREATE()
2   y = S_1[0]
3   S_1[0] = NULL
4   for k = 1 to r
5       if S_1[k] ≠ NULL
6           S_2[k-1] = PENNANT-SPLIT(S_1[k])
7           S_1[k-1] = S_1[k]
8           S_1[k] = NULL
9   if y ≠ NULL
10      BAG-INSERT(S_1,y)
11  return S_2
```

Because PENNANT-SPLIT takes constant time, each loop iteration in BAG-SPLIT takes constant time. Consequently, the asymptotic runtime of BAG-SPLIT is $O(r)$. This algorithm can be improved to $\Theta(\lg n)$, where n is the number of elements in the input bag, by maintaining the largest nonempty index of the backbone of each bag and iterating only up to this index.

Optimization

To improve the constant in the performance of BAG-INSERT, we made some simple but important modifications to pennants and bags, which do not affect the asymptotic behavior of the algorithm. First, in addition to its two pointers, every pennant node in the bag stores a constant-size array of GRAINSIZE elements, all of which are guaranteed to be valid, rather than just a single element. Our PBFS software uses the value GRAINSIZE = 128. Second, in addition to the backbone, the bag itself maintains an additional pennant node of size GRAINSIZE called the **hopper**, which it fills gradually. The impact of these modifications on the bag operations is as follows.

First, BAG-CREATE must allocate additional space for the hopper. This overhead is small and is done only once per bag.

Second, BAG-INSERT first attempts to insert the element into the hopper. If the hopper is full, then it inserts the hopper into the backbone of the data structure and allocates a new hopper into which it inserts the element. This optimization does not change the asymptotic runtime analysis of BAG-INSERT, but the code runs much faster. In the common case, BAG-INSERT simply inserts the element into the hopper with code nearly identical to inserting an element into a FIFO. Only once in every GRAINSIZE insertions does a BAG-INSERT trigger the insertion of the now full hopper into the backbone of the data structure.

Third, when unioning two bags S_1 and S_2, BAG-UNION first determines which bag has the less full hopper. Assuming that it is S_1, the modified implementation copies the elements of S_1's hopper into S_2's hopper until it is full or S_1's hopper runs out of elements. If it runs out of elements in S_1 to copy, BAG-UNION proceeds to merge the two bags as usual and uses S_2's hopper as the hopper for the resulting bag. If it fills S_2's hopper, however, line 1 of BAG-UNION sets y to S_2's hopper, and S_1's hopper, now containing fewer elements, forms the hopper for the resulting bag. Afterward, BAG-UNION proceeds as usual.

Finally, rather than storing $S_1[0]$ into y in line 2 of BAG-SPLIT for later insertion, BAG-SPLIT sets the hopper of S_2 to be the pennant node in $S_1[0]$ before proceeding as usual.

5. EXPERIMENTAL RESULTS

We implemented optimized versions of both the PBFS algorithm in Cilk++ and a FIFO-based serial BFS algorithm in C++. This section compares their performance on a suite of benchmark graphs. Figure 8 summarizes the results.

Implementation and Testing

Our implementation of PBFS differs from the abstract algorithm in some notable ways. First, our implementation of PBFS does not use locks to resolve the benign races described in Section 3. Second, our implementation of PBFS does not use the BAG-SPLIT routine described in Section 4. Instead, our implementation uses a "lop" operation to traverse the bag. It repeatedly divides the bag into two approximately equal halves by lopping off the most significant pennant from the bag. After each lop, the removed pennant is traversed using a standard parallel tree walk. Third, our implementation assumes that all vertices have bounded out-degree, and indeed most of the vertices in our benchmark graphs have relatively small degree. Finally, our implementation of PBFS sets GRAINSIZE $= 128$, which seems to perform well in practice. The FIFO-based serial BFS uses an array and two pointers to implement the FIFO queue in the simplest way possible. This array was sized to the number of vertices in the input graph.

These implementations were tested on eight benchmark graphs, as shown in Figure 8. Kkt_power, Cage14, Cage15, Freescale1, Wikipedia (as of February 6, 2007), and Nlpkkt160 are all from the University of Florida sparse-matrix collection [11]. Grid3D200 is a 7-point finite difference mesh generated using the Matlab Mesh Partitioning and Graph Separator Toolbox [16]. The RMat23 matrix [24], which models scale-free graphs, was generated by using repeated Kronecker products [2]. Parameters $A = 0.7$, $B = C = D = 0.1$ for RMat23 were chosen in order to generate skewed matrices. We stored these graphs in a compressed-sparse-rows (CSR) format in main memory for our empirical tests.

Results

We ran our tests on an Intel Core i7 quad-core machine with a total of eight 2.53-GHz processing cores (hyperthreading disabled), 12 GB of DRAM, two 8-MB L3-caches each shared between 4 cores, and private L2- and L1-caches with 256 KB and 32 KB, respectively. Figure 8 presents the performance of PBFS on eight different benchmark graphs. (The parallelism was computed using the Cilkview [19] tool and does not take into account effects from reducers.) As can be seen in Figure 8, PBFS performs well on these benchmark graphs. For five of the eight benchmark graphs, PBFS is as fast or faster than serial BFS. Moreover, on the remaining three benchmarks, PBFS is at most 15% slower than serial BFS.

Figure 8 shows that PBFS runs faster than a FIFO-based serial BFS on several benchmark graphs. This performance advantage may be due to how PBFS uses memory. Whereas the serial BFS performs a single linear scan through an array as it processes its queue, PBFS is constantly allocating and deallocating fixed-size chunks of memory for the bag. Because these chunks do not change in size from allocation to allocation, the memory manager incurs little work to perform these allocations. Perhaps more importantly, PBFS can reuse previously allocated chunks frequently, making it more cache-friendly. This improvement due to memory reuse is also apparent in some serial BFS implementations that use two queues instead of one.

Although PBFS generally performs well on these benchmarks, we explored why it was only attaining a speedup of 5 or 6 on 8 processor cores. Inadequate parallelism is not the answer, as most of the benchmarks have parallelism over 100. Our studies indicate that the multicore processor's memory system may be hurting performance in two ways.

First, the memory bandwidth of the system seems to limit performance for several of these graphs. For Wikipedia and Cage14, when we run 8 independent instances of PBFS serially on the 8 processing cores of our machine simultaneously, the total runtime is at

Name Description	Spy Plot	$\|V\|$ $\|E\|$ D	Work Span Parallelism	SERIAL-BFS T_1 PBFS T_1 PBFS T_1/T_8
Kkt_power Optimal power flow, nonlinear opt.		2.05M 12.76M 31	241M 2.3M 103.85	0.504 0.359 5.983
Freescale1 Circuit simulation		3.43M 17.1M 128	349M 2.3M 152.72	0.285 0.327 5.190
Cage14 DNA electrophoresis		1.51M 27.1M 43	390M 1.6M 245.70	0.262 0.283 5.340
Wikipedia Links between Wikipedia pages		2.4M 41.9M 460	606M 3.4M 178.73	0.914 0.721 6.381
Grid3D200 3D 7-point finite-diff mesh		8M 55.8M 598	1,009M 12.7M 79.27	1.544 1.094 4.862
RMat23 Scale-free graph model		2.3M 77.9M 8	1.050M 11.3M 93.22	1.100 0.936 6.500
Cage15 DNA electrophoresis		5.15M 99.2M 50	1.410M 2.1M 674.65	1.065 1.142 5.263
Nlpkkt160 Nonlinear optimization		8.35M 225.4M 163	3.060M 9.2M 331.45	1.269 1.448 5.983

Figure 8: Performance results for breadth-first search. The vertex and edge counts listed correspond to the number of vertices and edges evaluated by SERIAL-BFS. The work and span are measured in instructions. All runtimes are measured in seconds.

least 20% worse than the expected $8T_1$. This experiment suggests that the system's available memory bandwidth limits the performance of the parallel execution of PBFS.

Second, for several of these graphs, it appears that contention from true and false sharing on the distance array constrains the speedups. Placing each location in the distance array on a different cache line tends to increase the speedups somewhat, although it slows down overall performance due to the loss of spatial locality. We attempted to modify PBFS to mitigate contention by randomly permuting or rotating each adjacency list. Although these approaches improve speedups, they slow down overall performance due to loss of locality. Thus, despite its somewhat lower relative speedup numbers, the unadulterated PBFS seems to yield the best overall performance.

PBFS obtains good performance despite the benign race which induces redundant work. On none of these benchmarks does PBFS examine more than 1% of the vertices and edges redundantly. Using a mutex lock on each vertex to resolve the benign race costs a substantial overhead in performance, typically slowing down PBFS by more than a factor of 2.

Yuxiong He [18], formerly of Cilk Arts and Intel Corporation, used PBFS to parallelize the Murphi model-checking tool [12]. Murphi is a popular tool for verifying finite-state machines and is widely used in cache-coherence algorithms and protocol design, link-level protocol design, executable memory-model analysis, and analysis of cryptographic and security-related protocols. As can be seen in Figure 9, a parallel Murphi using PBFS scales well, even

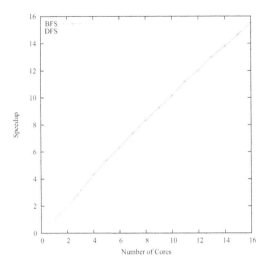

Figure 9: Multicore Murphi application speedup on a 16-core AMD processor [18]. Even though the DFS implementation uses a parallel depth-first search for which Cilk++ is particularly well suited, the BFS implementation, which uses the PBFS library, outperforms it.

outperforming a version based on parallel depth-first search and attaining the relatively large speedup of 15.5 times on 16 cores.

Part II — Nondeterminism of Reducers

The second half of this paper consists of Sections 6 through 9 and describes how to cope with the nondeterminism of reducers in the theoretical analysis of PBFS. Section 6 provides background on the theory of dynamic multithreading. Section 7 gives a formal model for reducer behavior, Section 8 develops a theory for analyzing programs that use reducers, and Section 9 employs this theory to analyze the performance of PBFS.

6. BACKGROUND ON THE DAG MODEL

This section overviews the theoretical model of Cilk-like parallel computation. We explain how a multithreaded program execution can be modeled theoretically as a dag using the framework of Blumofe and Leiserson [7], and we overview assumptions about the runtime environment. We define deterministic and nondeterministic computations. Section 7 will describe how reducer hyperobjects fit into this theoretical framework.

The dag model

We shall adopt the dag model for multithreading similar to the one introduced by Blumofe and Leiserson [7]. This model was designed to model the execution of spawns and syncs. We shall extend it in Section 7 to deal with reducers.

The dag model views the executed computation resulting from the running of a multithreaded program[3] as a *dag (directed acyclic graph)* A, where the vertex set consists of *strands* — sequences of serially executed instructions containing no parallel control — and the edge set represents parallel-control dependencies between strands. We shall use A to denote both the dag and the set of strands in the dag. Figure 10 illustrates such a dag, which can be viewed as a parallel program "trace," in that it involves executed instructions, as opposed to source instructions. A strand can be as small as a single instruction, or it can represent a longer computation. We shall assume that strands respect function boundaries, meaning

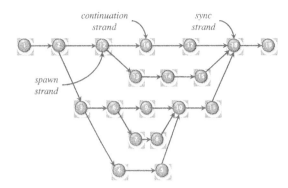

Figure 10: A dag representation of a multithreaded execution. Each vertex represents a strand, and edges represent parallel-control dependencies between strands.

that calling or spawning a function terminates a strand, as does returning from a function. Thus, each strand belongs to exactly one function instantiation. A strand that has out-degree 2 is a *spawn strand*, and a strand that resumes the caller after a spawn is called a *continuation strand*. A strand that has in-degree at least 2 is a *sync strand*.

Generally, we shall dice a chain of serially executed instructions into strands in a manner that is convenient for the computation we are modeling. The *length* of a strand is the time it takes for a processor to execute all its instructions. For simplicity, we shall assume that programs execute on an *ideal parallel computer*, where each instruction takes unit time to execute, there is ample memory bandwidth, there are no cache effects, etc.

Determinacy

We say that a dynamic multithreaded program is *deterministic* (on a given input) if every memory location is updated with the same sequence of values in every execution. Otherwise, the program is *nondeterministic*. A deterministic program always behaves the same, no matter how the program is scheduled. Two different memory locations may be updated in different orders, but each location always sees the same sequence of updates. Whereas a nondeterministic program may produce different dags, i.e., behave differently, a deterministic program always produces the same dag.

Work and span

The dag model admits two natural measures of performance which can be used to provide important bounds [6, 8, 13, 17] on performance and speedup. The *work* of a dag A, denoted by $\mathrm{Work}(A)$, is the sum of the lengths of all the strands in the dag. Assuming for simplicity that it takes unit time to execute a strand, the work for the example dag in Figure 10 is 19. The *span*[4] of A, denoted by $\mathrm{Span}(A)$, is the length of the longest path in the dag. Assuming unit-time strands, the span of the dag in Figure 10 is 10, which is realized by the path $\langle 1, 2, 3, 6, 7, 8, 10, 11, 18, 19 \rangle$. Work/span analysis is outlined in tutorial fashion in [10, Ch. 27] and [23].

Suppose that a program produces a dag A in time T_P when run on P processors of an ideal parallel computer. We have the following two lower bounds on the execution time T_P:

$$T_P \geq \mathrm{Work}(A)/P ,\qquad (1)$$
$$T_P \geq \mathrm{Span}(A) .\qquad (2)$$

Inequality (2), which is called the *Work Law*, holds in this simple performance model, because each processor executes at most 1 instruction per unit time, and hence P processors can execute at most

---

[3]When we refer to the running of a program, we shall generally assume that we mean "on a given input."

[4]The literature also uses the terms *depth* [4] and *critical-path length* [5].

P instructions per unit time. Inequality (2), called the **Span Law**, holds because no execution that respects the partial order of the dag can execute faster than the longest serial chain of instructions.

We define the **speedup** of a program as T_1/T_P — how much faster the P-processor execution is than the serial execution. Since for deterministic programs, all executions produce the same dag A, we have that $T_1 = \text{Work}(A)$, and $T_\infty = \text{Span}(A)$ (assuming no overhead for scheduling). Rewriting the Work Law, we obtain $T_1/T_P \leq P$, which is to say that the speedup on P processors can be at most P. If the application obtains speedup P, which is the best we can do in our model, we say that the application exhibits **linear speedup**. If the application obtains speedup greater than P (which cannot happen in our model due to the Work Law, but can happen in models that incorporate caching and other processor effects), we say that the application exhibits **superlinear speedup**.

The **parallelism** of the dag is defined as $\text{Work}(A)/\text{Span}(A)$. For a deterministic computation, the parallelism is therefore T_1/T_∞. The parallelism represents the maximum possible speedup on any number of processors, which follows from the Span Law, because $T_1/T_P \leq T_1/\text{Span}(A) = \text{Work}(A)/\text{Span}(A)$. For example, the parallelism of the dag in Figure 10 is $19/10 = 1.9$, which means that any advantage gained by executing it with more than 2 processors is marginal, since the additional processors will surely be starved for work.

Scheduling

A randomized "work-stealing" scheduler [1, 7], such as is provided by MIT Cilk and Cilk++, operates as follows. When the runtime system starts up, it allocates as many operating-system threads, called **workers**, as there are processors (although the programmer can override this default decision). Each worker's stack operates like a **deque**, or double-ended queue. When a subroutine is spawned, the subroutine's activation frame containing its local variables is pushed onto the bottom of the deque. When it returns, the frame is popped off the bottom. Thus, in the common case, the parallel code operates just like serial code and imposes little overhead. When a worker runs out of work, however, it becomes a **thief** and "steals" the top frame from another **victim** worker's deque. In general, the worker operates on the bottom of the deque, and thieves steal from the top. This strategy has the great advantage that all communication and synchronization is incurred only when a worker runs out of work. If an application exhibits sufficient parallelism, stealing is infrequent, and thus the cost of bookkeeping, communication, and synchronization to effect a steal is negligible.

Work-stealing achieves good expected running time based on the work and span. In particular, if A is the executed dag on P processors, the expected execution time T_P can be bounded as

$$T_P \leq \text{Work}(A)/P + O(\text{Span}(A)) , \qquad (3)$$

where we omit the notation for expectation for simplicity. This bound, which is proved in [7], assumes an ideal computer, but it includes scheduling overhead. For a deterministic computation, if the parallelism exceeds the number P of processors sufficiently, Inequality (3) guarantees near-linear speedup. Specifically, if $P \ll \text{Work}(A)/\text{Span}(A)$, then $\text{Span}(A) \ll \text{Work}(A)/P$, and hence Inequality (3) yields $T_P \approx \text{Work}(A)/P$, and the speedup is $T_1/T_P \approx P$.

For a nondeterministic computation such as PBFS, however, the work of a P-processor execution may not readily be related to the serial running time. Thus, obtaining bounds on speedup can be more challenging. As Section 9 shows, however, PBFS achieves

$$T_P(A) \leq \text{Work}(A_\upsilon)/P + O(\tau^2 \cdot \text{Span}(A_\upsilon)) , \qquad (4)$$

where A_υ is the "user dag" of A — the dag from the programmer's perspective — and τ is an upper bound on the time it takes to perform a REDUCE, which may be a function of the input size. (We shall formalize these concepts in Sections 7 and 8.) For nondeterministic computations satisfying Inequality (4), we can define the **effective parallelism** as $\text{Work}(A_\upsilon)/(\tau^2 \cdot \text{Span}(A_\upsilon))$. Just as with parallelism for deterministic computations, if the effective parallelism exceeds the number P of processors by a sufficient margin, the P-processor execution is guaranteed to attain near-linear speedup over the serial execution.

Another relevant measure is the number of steals that occur during a computation. As is shown in [7], the expected number of steals incurred for a dag A produced by a P-processor execution is $O(P \cdot \text{Span}(A))$. This bound is important, since the number of REDUCE operations needed to combine reducer views is bounded by the number of steals.

7. MODELING REDUCERS

This section reviews the definition of reducer hyperobjects from [14] and extends the dag model to incorporate them. We define the notion of a "user dag" for a computation, which represents the strands that are visible to the programmer. We also define the notion of a "performance dag," which includes the strands that the runtime system implicitly invokes.

A reducer is defined in terms of an algebraic **monoid**: a triple $(T, \otimes, e)$, where T is a set and $\otimes$ is an associative binary operation over T with identity e. From an object-oriented programming perspective, the set T is a base type which provides a member function REDUCE implementing the binary operator $\otimes$ and a member function CREATE-IDENTITY that constructs an identity element of type T. The base type T also provides one or more UPDATE functions, which modify an object of type T. In the case of bags, the REDUCE function is BAG-UNION, the CREATE-IDENTITY function is BAG-CREATE, and the UPDATE function is BAG-INSERT. As a practical matter, the REDUCE function need not actually be associative, although in that case, the programmer typically has some idea of "logical" associativity. Such is the case, for example, with bags. If we have three bags B_1, B_2, and B_3, we do not care whether the bag data structures for $(B_1 \cup B_2) \cup B_3$ and $B_1 \cup (B_2 \cup B_3)$ are identical, only that they contain the same elements.

To specify the nondeterministic behavior encapsulated by reducers precisely, consider a computation A of a multithreaded program, and let $V(A)$ be the set of executed strands. We assume that the implicitly invoked functions for a reducer — REDUCE and CREATE-IDENTITY — execute only serial code. We model each execution of one of these functions as a single strand containing the instructions of the function. If an UPDATE causes the runtime system to invoke CREATE-IDENTITY implicitly, the serial code arising from UPDATE is broken into two strands sandwiching the point where CREATE-IDENTITY is invoked.

We partition $V(A)$ into three classes of strands:

- V_ι: **Init strands** arising from the execution of CREATE-IDENTITY when invoked implicitly by the runtime system, which occur when the user program attempts to update a reducer, but a local view has not yet been created.

- V_ρ: **Reducer strands** arising from the execution of REDUCE, which occur implicitly when the runtime system combines views.

- V_υ: **User strands** arising from the execution of code explicitly invoked by the programmer, including calls to UPDATE.

We call $V_\iota \cup V_\rho$ the set of **runtime strands**.

Since, from the programmer's perspective, the runtime strands are invoked "invisibly" by the runtime system, his or her understanding of the program generally relies only on the user strands. We capture the control dependencies among the user strands by defining the **user dag** $A_\upsilon = (V_\upsilon, E_\upsilon)$ for a computation A in the same manner as we defined an ordinary multithreaded dag. For example, a spawn strand e_1 has out-degree 2 in A_υ with an edge (v_1, v_2) going to the first strand v_2 of the spawned child and the other edge (v_2, v_3) going to the continuation v_3; if v_1 is the final strand of a spawned subroutine and v_2 is the sync strand with which v_1 syncs, then we have $(v_1, v_2) \in E_\upsilon$; etc.

To track the views of a reducer h in the user dag, let $h(v)$ denote the view of h seen by a strand $v \in V_\upsilon$. The runtime system maintains the following invariants:

1. If $u \in V_\upsilon$ has out-degree 1 and $(u, v) \in E_\upsilon$, then $h(v) = h(u)$.

2. Suppose that $u \in V_\upsilon$ is a spawn strand with outgoing edges $(u, v), (u, w) \in E_\upsilon$, where $v \in V_\upsilon$ is the first strand of the spawned subroutine and $w \in V_\upsilon$ is the continuation in the parent. Then, we have $h(v) = h(u)$ and

$$h(w) = \begin{cases} h(u) & \text{if } u \text{ was not stolen;} \\ \text{new view} & \text{otherwise.} \end{cases}$$

3. If $v \in V_\upsilon$ is a sync strand, then $h(v) = h(u)$, where u is the first strand of v's function.

When a new view $h(w)$ is created, as is inferred by Invariant 2, we say that the old view $h(u)$ **dominates** $h(w)$, which we denote by $h(u) \succ h(w)$. For a set H of views, we say that two views $h_1, h_2 \in H$, where $h_1 \succ h_2$, are **adjacent** if there does not exist $h_3 \in H$ such that $h_1 \succ h_3 \succ h_2$.

A useful property of sync strands is that the views of strands entering a sync strand $v \in V_\upsilon$ are totally ordered by the "dominates" relation. That is, if k strands each have an edge in E_υ to the same sync strand $v \in V_\upsilon$, then the strands can be numbered $u_1, u_2, \ldots, u_k \in V_\upsilon$ such that $h(u_1) \succeq h(u_2) \succeq \cdots \succeq u_k$. Moreover, $h(u_1) = h(v) = h(u)$, where u is the first strand of v's function. These properties can be proved inductively, noting that the views of the first and last strands of a function must be identical, because a function implicitly syncs before it returns. The runtime system always reduces adjacent pairs of views in this ordering, destroying the dominated view in the pair.

If a computation A does not involve any runtime strands, the "delay-sequence" argument in [7] can be applied to A_υ to bound the P-processor execution time: $T_P(A) \leq \text{Work}(A_\upsilon)/P + O(\text{Span}(A_\upsilon))$. Our goal is to apply this same analytical technique to computations containing runtime strands. To do so, we augment the A_υ with the runtime strands to produce a **performance dag** $A_\pi = (V_\pi, E_\pi)$ for the computation A, where

- $V_\pi = V(A) = V_\upsilon \cup V_\iota \cup V_\rho$,
- $E_\pi = E_\upsilon \cup E_\iota \cup E_\rho$,

where the edge sets E_ι and E_ρ are constructed as follows.

The edges in E_ι are created in pairs. For each init strand $v \in V_\iota$, we include (u, v) and (v, w) in E_ι, where $u, w \in V_\upsilon$ are the two strands comprising the instructions of the UPDATE whose execution caused the invocation of the CREATE-IDENTITY corresponding to v.

The edges in E_ρ are created in groups corresponding to the set of REDUCE functions that must execute before a given sync. Suppose that $v \in V_\upsilon$ is a sync strand, that k strands $u_1, u_2, \ldots, u_k \in A_\upsilon$ join at v, and that $k' < k$ reduce strands $r_1, r_2, \ldots, r_{k'} \in A_\rho$ execute before the sync. Consider the set $U = \{u_1, u_2, \ldots, u_k\}$, and let $h(U) = \{h(u_1), h(u_2), \ldots, h(u_k)\}$ be the set of $k' + 1$ views that must be reduced. We construct a **reduce tree** as follows:

```
1   while |h(U)| ≥ 2
2       Let r ∈ {r₁, r₂, ..., r_k'} be the reduce strand that reduces a "min-
            imal" pair h_j, h_{j+1} ∈ h(U) of adjacent strands, meaning that if
            a distinct r' ∈ {r₁, r₂, ..., r_k'} reduces adjacent strands h_i, h_{i+1} ∈
            h(U), we have h_i ≻ h_j
3       Let U_r = {u ∈ U : h(u) = h_j or h(u) = h_{j+1}}
4       Include in E_ρ the edges in the set {(u, r) : u ∈ U_r}
5       U = U − U_r ∪ {r}
6   Include in E_ρ the edges in the set {(r, v) : r ∈ U}
```

Since the reduce trees and init strands only add more dependencies between strands in the user A_υ that are already in series, the performance dag A_π is indeed a dag.

Since the runtime system performs REDUCE operations opportunistically, the reduce strands in the performance dag may execute before their predecessors have completed. The purpose of performance dags, as Section 8 shows, is to account for the cost of the runtime strands, not to describe how computations are scheduled.

8. ANALYSIS OF PROGRAMS WITH NONCONSTANT-TIME REDUCERS

This section provides a framework for analyzing programs that contain reducers whose REDUCE functions execute in more than constant time.

We begin with a lemma that bounds the running time of a computation in terms of the work and span of its performance dag.

LEMMA 1. *Consider the execution of a computation A on a parallel computer with P processors using a work-stealing scheduler. The expected running time of A is $T_P(A) \leq \text{Work}(A_\pi)/P + O(\text{Span}(A_\pi))$.*

PROOF. The proof follows those of [7] and [14], with some salient differences. As in [7], we use a delay-sequence argument, but we base it on the performance dag.

The normal delay-sequence argument involves only a user dag. This dag is augmented with "deque" edges, each running from a continuation on the deque to the next in sequence from top to bottom. These deque edges increase the span of the dag by at most a constant factor. The argument then considers a path in the dag, and it defines an instruction as being **critical** if all its predecessors in the augmented dag have been executed. The key property of the work-stealing algorithm is that every critical instruction sits atop of some deque (or is being executed by a worker). Thus, whenever a worker steals, it has a $1/P$ chance of executing a critical instruction. With constant probability, P steals suffice to reduce the span of the dag of the computation that remains to be executed by 1. Consequently, the expected number of steals is $O(P \cdot \text{Span}(A_\pi))$. A similar but slightly more complex bound holds with high probability.

This argument can be modified to work with performance dags containing reducers that operate in nonconstant-time. As instructions in the computation are executed, we can mark them off in the performance dag. Since we have placed reduce strands after strands in the performance dag before which they may have actually executed, some reduce strands may execute before all of their predecessors in the performance dag complete. That is okay. The main property is that if an instruction is critical, it has a $1/P$ chance of being executed upon a steal, and that P steals have a constant expectation of reducing the span of the dag that remains to execute by 1. The crucial observation is that if an instruction in a reduce strand is critical, then its sync node has been reached, and thus a worker must be executing the critical instruction, since reduces are performed eagerly when nothing impedes their execution. It follows that the expected running time of A is $T_P(A) \leq \text{Work}(A_\pi)/P + O(\text{Span}(A_\pi))$. $\square$

We want to ensure that the runtime system joins strands quickly when reducers are involved. Providing a guarantee requires that we examine the specifics of how the runtime system handles reducers.

First, we review how the runtime system handles spawns and steals, as described by Frigo et al. [14]. Every time a Cilk function is stolen, the runtime system creates a new **frame**.[5] Although frames are created and destroyed dynamically during a program execution, the ones that exist always form a rooted **spawn tree**. Each frame F provides storage for temporary values and local variables, as well as metadata for the function, including the following:

- a pointer $F.lp$ to F's left sibling, or if F is the first child, to F's parent;
- a pointer $F.c$ to F's first child;
- a pointer $F.r$ to F's right sibling.

These pointers form a left-child right-sibling representation of the part of the spawn tree that is distributed among processors, which is known as the **steal tree**.

To handle reducers, each worker in the runtime system uses a hash table called a **hypermap** to map reducers into its local views. To allow for lock-free access to the hypermap of a frame F while siblings and children of the frame are terminating, F stores three hypermaps, denoted $F.hu$, $F.hr$, and $F.hc$. The $F.hu$ hypermap is used to look up reducers for the user's program, while the $F.hr$ and $F.hc$ hypermaps store the accumulated values of F's terminated right siblings and terminated children, respectively.

When a frame is initially created, its hypermaps are empty. If a worker using a frame F executes an UPDATE operation on a reducer h, the worker tries to get h's current view from the $F.hu$ hypermap. If h's view is empty, the worker performs a CREATE-IDENTITY operation to create an identity view of h in $F.hu$.

When a worker returns from a spawn, first it must perform up to two REDUCE operations to reduce its hypermaps into its neighboring frames, and then it must **eliminate** its current frame. To perform these REDUCE operations and elimination without races, the worker grabs locks on its neighboring frames. The algorithm by Frigo et al. [14] uses an intricate protocol to avoid long waits on locks, but the analysis of its performance assumes that each REDUCE takes only constant time.

To support nonconstant-time REDUCE functions, we modify the locking protocol. To eliminate a frame F, the worker first reduces $F.hu \otimes= F.hr$. Second, the worker reduces $F.lp.hc \otimes= F.hu$ or $F.lp.hr \otimes= F.hu$, depending on whether F is a first child.

Workers eliminating $F.lp$ and $F.r$ might race with the elimination of F. To resolve these races, Frigo et al. describe how to acquire an abstract lock between F and these neighbors, where an abstract lock is a pair of locks that correspond to an edge in the steal tree. We shall use these abstract locks to eliminate a frame F according to the locking protocol shown in Figure 11.

The next lemma analyzes the work required to perform all eliminations using this locking protocol.

LEMMA 2. *Consider the execution of a computation A on a parallel computer with P processors using a work-stealing scheduler. The total work involved in joining strands is $O(\tau P \cdot \mathrm{Span}(A_\pi))$, where τ is the worst-case cost of any* REDUCE *or* CREATE-IDENTITY *for the given input.*

PROOF. Since lines 3–15 in the new locking protocol all require $O(1)$ work, each abstract lock is held for a constant amount of time.

The analysis of the time spent waiting to acquire an abstract lock in the new locking protocol follows the analysis of the locking protocol in [14]. The key issue in the proof is to show that

---

[5]When we refer to frames in this paper, we specifically mean the "full" frames described in [14].

```
1  while TRUE
2      Acquire the abstract locks for edges (F, F.lp) and (F.F.r) in an
           order chosen uniformly at random
3      if F is a first child
4          L = F.lp.hc
5      else L = F.lp.hr
6      R = F.hr
7      if L == ∅ and R == ∅
8          if F is a first child
9              F.lp.hc = F.hu
10         else F.lp.hr = F.hu
11         Eliminate F
12         break
13     R' = R; L' = L
14     R = ∅; L = ∅
15     Release the abstract locks
16     for each reducer h ∈ R
17         if h ∈ F.hu
18             F.hu(h) ⊗= R(h)
19         else F.hu(h) = R(h)
20     for each reducer h ∈ L
21         if h ∈ F.hu
22             F.hu(h) = L(h) ⊗ F.hu(h)
23         else F.hu(h) = L(h)
24
```

Figure 11: A modified locking protocol for managing reducers, which holds locks for $O(1)$ time.

the time for the ith abstract lock acquisition by some worker w is independent of the time for w's jth lock acquisition for all $j > i$. To prove this independence result, we shall argue that for two workers w and v, we have $\Pr\{v \text{ delays } w_j | v \text{ delays } w_i\} = \Pr\{v \text{ delays } w_j | v \text{ does not delay } w_i\} = \Pr\{v \text{ delays } w_j\}$, where w_i and w_j are w's ith and jth lock acquisitions, respectively.

We shall consider each of these cases separately. First, suppose that v delays w_i. After w_i, v has succeeded in acquiring and releasing its abstract locks, and all lock acquisitions in the directed path from w's lock acquisition to v's have also succeeded. For v to delay w_j, a new directed path of dependencies from w to v must occur. Each edge in that path is oriented correctly with a $1/2$ probability, regardless of any previous interaction between v and w. Similarly, suppose that v does not delay w_i. For v to delay w_j, a chain of dependencies must form from one of w's abstract locks to one of v's abstract locks after w_i completes. Forming such a dependency chain requires every edge in the chain to be correctly oriented, which occurs with a $1/2$ probability per edge regardless of the fact that v did not delay w_i. Therefore, we have $\Pr\{v \text{ delays } w_j | v \text{ delays } w_i\} = \Pr\{v \text{ delays } w_j | v \text{ does not delay } w_i\} = \Pr\{v \text{ delays } w_j\}$.

For all workers $v \neq w$, the probability that v delays w_j is independent of whether v delays w_i. Consequently, every lock acquisition by some worker is independent of all previous acquisitions, and by the analysis in [14], the total time a worker spends in abstract lock acquisitions is $O(m)$ in expectation, where m is the number of abstract lock acquisitions that worker performs. Moreover, the total time spent in abstract lock acquisitions is proportional to the number of elimination attempts.

Next, we bound the total number of elimination attempts performed in this protocol. Since each successful steal creates a frame in the steal tree that must be eliminated, the number of elimination attempts is at least as large as the number M of successful steals. Each elimination of a frame may force two other frames to repeat this protocol. Therefore, each elimination increases the number of elimination attempts by at most 2. Thus, the total number of elimination attempts is no more than $3M$.

Finally, we bound the total work spent joining strands using this protocol. The total time spent acquiring abstract locks and performing the necessary operations while the lock is held is $O(M)$. Each failed elimination attempt triggers at most two REDUCE operations, each of which takes τ work in the worst case. Therefore, the total expected work spent joining strands is $O(\tau M)$. Using the analysis of steals from [7], the total work spent joining strands is $O(\tau P \cdot \text{Span}(A_\pi))$. □

The following two lemmas bound the work and span of the performance dag in terms of the span of the user dag. For simplicity, assume that A makes use of a single reducer. (These proofs can be extended to handle many reducers within a computation.)

LEMMA 3. *Consider a computation A with user dag A_υ and performance dag A_π, and let τ be the worst-case cost of any* CREATE-IDENTITY *or* REDUCE *operation for the given input. Then, we have* $\text{Span}(A_\pi) = O(\tau \cdot \text{Span}(A_\upsilon))$.

PROOF. Each successful steal in the execution of A may force one CREATE-IDENTITY. Each CREATE-IDENTITY creates a nonempty view that must later be reduced using a REDUCE operation. Therefore, at most one REDUCE operation may occur per successful steal, and at most one reduce strand may occur in the performance dag for each steal. Each spawn in A_υ provides an opportunity for a steal to occur. Consequently, each spawn operation in A may increase the size of the dag by 2τ in the worst case.

Consider a critical path in A_π, and let p_υ be the corresponding path in A_υ. Suppose that k steals occur along p_υ. The length of that corresponding path in A_π is at most $2k\tau + |p_\upsilon| \leq 2\tau \cdot \text{Span}(A_\upsilon) + |p_\upsilon| \leq 3\tau \cdot \text{Span}(A_\upsilon)$. Therefore, we have $\text{Span}(A_\pi) = O(\tau \cdot \text{Span}(A_\upsilon))$. □

LEMMA 4. *Consider a computation A with user dag A_υ, and let τ be the worst-case cost of any* CREATE-IDENTITY *or* REDUCE *operation for the given input. Then, we have* $\text{Work}(A_\pi) = \text{Work}(A_\upsilon) + O(\tau^2 P \cdot \text{Span}(A_\upsilon))$.

PROOF. The work in A_π is the work in A_υ plus the work represented in the runtime strands. The total work in reduce strands equals the total work to join stolen strands, which is $O(\tau P \cdot \text{Span}(A))$ by Lemma 2. Similarly, each steal may create one init strand, and by the analysis of steals from [7], the total work in init strands is $O(\tau P \cdot \text{Span}(A))$. Thus, we have $\text{Work}(A_\pi) = \text{Work}(A_\upsilon) + O(\tau P \cdot \text{Span}(A_\pi))$. Applying Lemma 3 yields the lemma. □

We now prove Inequality (4), which bounds the runtime of a computation whose nondeterminism arises from reducers.

THEOREM 5. *Consider the execution of a computation A on a parallel computer with P processors using a work-stealing scheduler. Let A_υ be the user dag of A. The total running time of A is* $T_P(A) \leq \text{Work}(A_\upsilon)/P + O(\tau^2 \cdot \text{Span}(A_\upsilon))$.

PROOF. The proof follows from Lemmas 1, 3, and 4. □

9. ANALYZING PBFS

This section applies the results of Section 8 to bound the expected running time of the locking version of PBFS.

First, we bound the work and span of the user dag for PBFS.

LEMMA 6. *Suppose that the locking version of PBFS is run on a connected graph $G = (V, E)$ with diameter D. The total work in PBFS's user dag is $O(V + E)$, and the total span of PBFS's user dag is $O(D \lg(V/D) + D \lg \Delta)$, where Δ is the maximum out-degree of any vertex in V.*

PROOF. In each layer, PBFS evaluates every vertex v in that layer exactly once, and PBFS checks every vertex u in v's adjacency list exactly once. In the locking version of PBFS, each u is assigned its distance exactly once and added to the bag for the next layer exactly once. Since this holds for all layers of G, the total work for this portion of PBFS is $O(V + E)$.

PBFS performs additional work to create a bag for each layer and to repeatedly split the layer into GRAINSIZE pieces. If D is the number of layers in G, then the total work PBFS spends in calls to BAG-CREATE is $O(D \lg V)$. The analysis for the work PBFS performs to subdivide a layer follows the analysis for building a binary heap [10, Ch. 6]. Therefore, the total time PBFS spends in calls to BAG-SPLIT is $O(V)$.

The total time PBFS spends executing BAG-INSERT depends on the parallel execution of PBFS. Since a steal resets the contents of a bag for subsequent update operations, the maximum running time of BAG-INSERT depends on the steals that occur. Each steal can only decrease the work of a subsequent BAG-INSERT, and therefore the amortized running time of $O(1)$ for each BAG-INSERT still applies. Because BAG-INSERT is called once per vertex, PBFS spends $O(V)$ work total executing BAG-INSERT, and the total work of PBFS is $O(V + E)$.

The sequence of splits performed in each layer cause the vertices of the layer to be processed at the leaves of a balanced binary tree of height $O(\lg V_d)$, where V_d is the set of vertices in the dth layer. Since the series of syncs that PBFS performs mirror this split tree, the divide-and-conquer computation to visit the vertices in a layer and then combine the results has span $O(\lg V_d)$. Each leaf of this tree processes at most a constant number of vertices and looks at the outgoing edges of those vertices in a similar divide-and-conquer fashion. This divide-and-conquer evaluation results in a computation at each leaf with span $O(\lg \Delta)$. Each edge evaluated performs some constant-time work and may trigger a call to BAG-INSERT, whose worst-case running time would be $O(\lg V_{d+1})$. Consequently, the span of PBFS for processing the dth layer is $O(\lg V_d + \lg V_{d+1} + \lg \Delta)$. Summing this quantity over all layers in G, the maximum span for PBFS is $O(D \lg(V/D) + D \lg \Delta)$. □

We now bound the expected running time of PBFS.

THEOREM 7. *Consider the parallel execution of PBFS on a connected graph $G = (V, E)$ with diameter D running on a parallel computer with P processors using a work-stealing scheduler. The expected running time of the locking version of PBFS is* $T_P(\text{PBFS}) \leq O(V + E)/P + O(D \lg^2(V/D)(\lg(V/D) + \lg \Delta))$, *where Δ is the maximum out-degree of any vertex in V. If we have $\Delta = O(1)$, then the expected running time of PBFS is* $T_P(\text{PBFS}) \leq O(V + E)/P + O(D \lg^3(V/D))$.

PROOF. To maximize the cost of all CREATE-IDENTITY and REDUCE operations in PBFS, the worst-case cost of each of these operations must be $O(\lg(V/D))$. Applying Theorem 5 with $\tau = O(\lg(V/D))$, $\text{Work}(\text{PBFS}) = O(V + E)$, and $\text{Span}(\text{PBFS}) = O(D \lg(V/D) + D \lg \Delta)$, we get $T_P(\text{PBFS}) \leq O(V + E)/P + O(D \lg^2(V/D)(\lg(V/D) + \lg \Delta))$. If we have $\Delta = O(1)$, this formula simplifies to $T_P(\text{PBFS}) \leq O(V + E)/P + O(D \lg^3(V/D))$. □

10. CONCLUSION

Thread-local storage [27], or ***TLS***, presents an alternative to bag reducers for implementing the layer sets in a parallel breadth-first search. The bag reducer allows PBFS to write the vertices of a layer in a single data structure in parallel and later efficiently traverse them in parallel. As an alternative to bags, each of the P workers could store the vertices it encounters into a vector within its own TLS, thereby avoiding races. The set of elements in the P vectors could then be walked in parallel using divide-and-conquer. Such a structure appears simple to implement and practically efficient, since it avoids merging sets.

Despite the simplicity of the TLS solution, reducer-based solutions exhibit some advantages over TLS solutions. First, reducers provide a processor-oblivious alternative to TLS, enhancing portability and simplifying reasoning of how performance scales. Second, reducers allow a function to be instantiated multiple times in parallel without interference. To support simultaneous running of functions that use TLS, the programmer must manually ensure that the TLS regions used by the functions are disjoint. Third, reducers require only a monoid — associativity and an identity — to ensure correctness, whereas TLS also requires commutativity. The correctness of some applications, including BFS, is not compromised by allowing commutative updates to its shared data structure. Without commutativity, an application cannot easily use TLS, whereas reducers seem to be good whether commutativity is allowed or not. Finally, whereas TLS makes the nondeterminism visible to the programmer, reducers encapsulate nondeterminism. In particular, reducers hide the particular nondeterministic manner in which associativity is resolved, thereby allowing the programmer to assume specific semantic guarantees at well-defined points in the computation. This encapsulation of nondeterminism simplifies the task of reasoning about the program's correctness compared to a TLS solution.

Nondeterminism can wreak havoc on the ability to reason about programs, to test their correctness, and to ascertain their performance, but it also can provide opportunities for additional parallelism. Well-structured linguistic support for encapsulating nondeterminism may allow parallel programmers to enjoy the benefits of nondeterminism without suffering unduly from the inevitable complications that nondeterminism engenders. Reducers provide an effective way to encapsulate nondeterminism. We view it as an open question whether a semantics exists for TLS that would encapsulate nondeterminism while providing a potentially more efficient implementation in situations where commutativity is allowed.

11. ACKNOWLEDGMENTS

Thanks to Aydın Buluç of University of California, Santa Barbara, who helped us obtain many of our benchmark tests. Pablo G. Halpern of Intel Corporation and Kevin M. Kelley of MIT CSAIL helped us debug PBFS's performance bugs. Matteo Frigo of Axis Semiconductor helped us weigh the pros and cons of reducers versus TLS. We thank the referees for their excellent comments. Thanks to the Cilk team at Intel and the Supertech Research Group at MIT CSAIL for their support.

12. REFERENCES

[1] N. S. Arora, R. D. Blumofe, and C. G. Plaxton. Thread scheduling for multiprogrammed multiprocessors. In *SPAA*, pp. 119–129, 1998.

[2] D. Bader, J. Feo, J. Gilbert, J. Kepner, D. Koester, E. Loh, K. Madduri, B. Mann, and T. Meuse. HPCS scalable synthetic compact applications #2, 2007. Available at http://www.graphanalysis.org/benchmark/HPCS-SSCA2_Graph-Theory_v2.2.doc.

[3] D. A. Bader and K. Madduri. Designing multithreaded algorithms for breadth-first search and *st*-connectivity on the Cray MTA-2. In *ICPP*, pp. 523–530, 2006.

[4] G. E. Blelloch. Programming parallel algorithms. *CACM*, 39(3), 1996.

[5] R. D. Blumofe, C. F. Joerg, B. C. Kuszmaul, C. E. Leiserson, K. H. Randall, and Y. Zhou. Cilk: An efficient multithreaded runtime system. *JPDC*, 37(1):55–69, 1996.

[6] R. D. Blumofe and C. E. Leiserson. Space-efficient scheduling of multithreaded computations. *SIAM J. on Comput.*, 27(1):202–229, 1998.

[7] R. D. Blumofe and C. E. Leiserson. Scheduling multithreaded computations by work stealing. *JACM*, 46(5):720–748, 1999.

[8] R. P. Brent. The parallel evaluation of general arithmetic expressions. *JACM*, 21(2):201–206, 1974.

[9] G. Cong, S. Kodali, S. Krishnamoorthy, D. Lea, V. Saraswat, and T. Wen. Solving large, irregular graph problems using adaptive work-stealing. In *ICPP*, pp. 536–545, 2008.

[10] T. H. Cormen, C. E. Leiserson, R. L. Rivest, and C. Stein. *Introduction to Algorithms*. The MIT Press, third edition, 2009.

[11] T. A. Davis. University of Florida sparse matrix collection, 2010. Available at http://www.cise.ufl.edu/research/sparse/matrices/.

[12] D. L. Dill, A. J. Drexler, A. J. Hu, and C. H. Yang. Protocol verification as a hardware design aid. In *ICCD*, pp. 522–525, 1992.

[13] D. L. Eager, J. Zahorjan, and E. D. Lazowska. Speedup versus efficiency in parallel systems. *IEEE Trans. Comput.*, 38(3):408–423, 1989.

[14] M. Frigo, P. Halpern, C. E. Leiserson, and S. Lewin-Berlin. Reducers and other Cilk++ hyperobjects. In *SPAA*, pp. 79–90, 2009.

[15] M. Frigo, C. E. Leiserson, and K. H. Randall. The implementation of the Cilk-5 multithreaded language. In *PLDI*, pp. 212–223, 1998.

[16] J. R. Gilbert, G. L. Miller, and S.-H. Teng. Geometric mesh partitioning: Implementation and experiments. *SIAM J. on Sci. Comput.*, 19(6):2091–2110, 1998.

[17] R. L. Graham. Bounds for certain multiprocessing anomalies. *Bell Sys. Tech. J.*, 45:1563–1581, 1966.

[18] Y. He. Multicore-enabling the Murphi verification tool. Available from http://software.intel.com/en-us/articles/multicore-enabling-the-murphi-verification-tool/, 2009.

[19] Y. He, C. E. Leiserson, and W. M. Leiserson. The Cilkview scalability analyzer. In *SPAA*, 2010.

[20] Intel Corporation. *Intel Cilk++ SDK Programmer's Guide*, 2009. Document Number: 322581-001US.

[21] R. E. Korf and P. Schultze. Large-scale parallel breadth-first search. In *AAAI*, pp. 1380–1385, 2005.

[22] C. Y. Lee. An algorithm for path connection and its applications. *IRE Trans. on Elec. Comput.*, EC-10(3):346–365, 1961.

[23] C. E. Leiserson. The Cilk++ concurrency platform. *J. Supercomput.*, 51(3):244–257, 2010.

[24] J. Leskovec, D. Chakrabarti, J. M. Kleinberg, and C. Faloutsos. Realistic, mathematically tractable graph generation and evolution, using Kronecker multiplication. In *PKDD*, pp. 133–145, 2005.

[25] J. B. Lubos, L. Brim, and J. Chaloupka. Parallel breadth-first search LTL model-checking. In *ASE*, pp. 106–115, 2003.

[26] E. F. Moore. The shortest path through a maze. In *Int. Symp. on Th. of Switching*, pp. 285–292, 1959.

[27] D. Stein and D. Shah. Implementing lightweight threads. In *USENIX*, pp. 1–9, 1992.

[28] B. Stroustrup. *The C++ Programming Language*. Addison-Wesley, third edition, 2000.

[29] Supertech Research Group, MIT/LCS. *Cilk 5.4.6 Reference Manual*, 1998. Available from http://supertech.csail.mit.edu/cilk/.

[30] A. van Heukelum, G. T. Barkema, and R. H. Bisseling. Dna electrophoresis studied with the cage model. *J. Comput. Phys.*, 180(1):313–326, 2002.

[31] A. Yoo, E. Chow, K. Henderson, W. McLendon, B. Hendrickson, and U. Catalyurek. A scalable distributed parallel breadth-first search algorithm on BlueGene/L. In *SC '05*, p. 25, 2005.

[32] Y. Zhang and E. A. Hansen. Parallel breadth-first heuristic search on a shared-memory architecture. In *AAAI Workshop on Heuristic Search, Memory-Based Heuristics and Their Applications*, 2006.

Parallel Approximation Algorithms for Facility-Location Problems

Guy E. Blelloch   Kanat Tangwongsan

Carnegie Mellon University

{guyb, ktangwon}@cs.cmu.edu

ABSTRACT

This paper presents the design and analysis of parallel approximation algorithms for facility-location problems, including NC and RNC algorithms for (metric) facility location, k-center, k-median, and k-means. These problems have received considerable attention during the past decades from the approximation algorithms community, which primarily concentrates on improving the approximation guarantees. In this paper, we ask: *Is it possible to parallelize some of the beautiful results from the sequential setting?*

Our starting point is a small, but diverse, subset of results in approximation algorithms for facility-location problems, with a primary goal of developing techniques for devising their efficient parallel counterparts. We focus on giving algorithms with low depth, near work efficiency (compared to the sequential versions), and low cache complexity.

Categories and Subject Descriptors

F.2 [**Theory of Computation**]: Analysis of Algorithms and Problem Complexity

General Terms

Algorithms, Theory

Keywords

Parallel algorithms, approximation algorithms, facility location problems

1. INTRODUCTION

Facility location is an important and well-studied class of problems in approximation algorithms, with far-reaching implications in areas as diverse as machine learning, operations research, and networking: the popular k-means clustering and many network-design problems are all examples of problems in this class. Not only are these problems important because of their practical value, but they appeal to study

because of their special stature as "testbeds" for techniques in approximation algorithms. Recent research has focused primarily on improving the approximation guarantee, producing a series of beautiful results, some of which are highly efficient—often, with the sequential running time within constant or polylogarithmic factors of the input size.

Despite significant progress on these fronts, work on developing parallel approximation algorithms for these problems remains virtually non-existent. Although variants of these problems have been considered in the the distributed computing setting [, ,], to the best our of knowledge, almost no prior work has looked directly in the parallel setting where the total work and parallel time (depth) are the parameters of concern. The only prior work on these problems is due to Wang and Cheng, who gave a 2-approximation algorithm for k-center that runs in $O(n \log^2 n)$ depth and $O(n^3)$ work [ ], a result which we improve in this paper.

Deriving parallel algorithms for facility location problems is a non-trivial task and will be a valuable step in understanding how common techniques in approximation algorithms can be parallelized efficiently. Previous work on facility location commonly relies on techniques such as linear-program (LP) rounding, local search, primal dual, and greedy. Unfortunately, LP rounding relies on solving a class of linear programs not known to be solvable efficiently in polylogarithmic time. Neither do known techniques allow for parallelizing local-search algorithms. Despite some success in parallelizing primal-dual and greedy algorithms for set-covering, vertex-covering, and related problems, these algorithm are obtained using problem-specific techniques, which are not readily applicable to other problems.

Summary of Results. In this paper, we design and analyze several algorithms for (metric) facility location, k-median, k-means and k-center problems, focusing on parallelizing a diverse set of techniques in approximation algorithms. We study the algorithms on the EREW PRAM and the Parallel Cache Oblivious model [ ]. The latter model captures memory locality. We are primarily concerned with minimizing the work (or cache complexity) while achieving polylogarithmic depth in these models. We are less concerned with polylogarithmic factors in the depth since such measures are not robust across models. By work, we mean the total operation count. All algorithms we develop are in NC or RNC, so they have polylogarithmic depth.

We first present a parallel RNC algorithm mimicking the greedy algorithm of Jain et al. [ ]. This is the most challenging algorithm to parallelize because the greedy algorithm is inherently sequential. We show the algorithm gives a

$(6 + \varepsilon)$-approximation and does $O(m \log_{1+\varepsilon}^2 m)$ work, which is within a logarithmic factor of the serial algorithm. Then, we present a simple RNC algorithm using the primal-dual approach of Jain and Vazirani [ ] which leads to a $(3 + \varepsilon)$-approximation and for input of size m runs in $O(m \log_{1+\varepsilon} m)$ work, which is the same as the sequential work. The sequential algorithm is a 3-approximation. Following that, we present a local-search algorithm for k-median and k-means, with approximation factors of $5 + \varepsilon$ and $81 + \varepsilon$, matching the guarantees of the sequential algorithms. For constant k, the algorithm does $O(n^2 \log n)$ work, which is the same as the sequential counterpart. Furthermore, we present a 2-approximation algorithm for k-center with $O((n \log n)^2)$ work, based on the algorithm of Hochbaum and Shmoys [ ]. Finally, we show a $O(m \log_{1+\varepsilon}^2 (m))$-work randomized rounding algorithm, which yields a $(4 + \varepsilon)$-approximation, given an optimal linear-program solution as input. The last two algorithms run in work within a logarithmic factor of the serial algorithm counterparts.

Related Work. Facility-location problems have had a long history. Because of space consideration, we mention only some of the results here, focusing on those concerning metric instances. For the (uncapacitated) metric facility location, the first constant factor approximation was given by Shmoys et al. [ ], using an LP-rounding technique, which has subsequently been improved [,]. A different approach, based on local-search techniques, has been used to obtain a 3-approximation [, ,]. Combinatorial algorithms based on primal-dual and greedy approaches with constant approximation factors are also known [, ,]. Other approximation algorithms and hardness results have also been given by [, , , , , , ,]. An open problem is to close the gap between the best known approximation factor of 1.5 [ ] and the hardness result of 1.463 [ ].

The first constant factor approximation for k-median problem was given by Charikar et al. [ ], which was subsequently improved by [ ] and [ ] to the current best factor of $3 + \varepsilon$. For k-means, constant-factor approximations are known for this problem [,]; a special case when the metric space is the Euclidean space has also been studied [ ]. For k-center, tight bounds are known: there is a 2-approximation algorithm due to [,], and this is tight unless $\mathsf{P} = \mathsf{NP}$.

The study of parallel approximation algorithms has been slow since the early 1990s. There are RNC and NC parallel approximation algorithms for set cover [,], vertex cover [,], special cases of linear programs (e.g., positive LPs and cover-packing LPs) [, ,], and k-center [ ]. These algorithms are typically based on parallelizing their sequential counterparts, which usually contain an inherently sequential component (e.g., a greedy step which requires picking and processing the minimum-cost element before proceeding to the next). A common idea in these parallel algorithms is that instead of picking only the most cost-effective element, they make room for parallelism by allowing a small slack (e.g., a $(1 + \varepsilon)$ factor) in what can be selected. This idea often results in a slightly worse approximation factor than the sequential version. For instance, the parallel set-cover algorithm of Rajagopalan and Vazirani is a $(2(1 + \varepsilon) \ln n)$-approximation, compared to a $(\ln n)$-approximation produced by the standard greedy set cover. Likewise, the parallel vertex-cover algorithm of Khuller et al. is a $2/(1 - \varepsilon)$-approximation as opposed to the optimal 2-approximation given by various known sequential algorithms. Only recently has the approx-

imation factor for vertex cover been improved to 2 in the parallel case [ ].

Several approximation algorithms have been proposed for distributed computing; see, e.g. [ ], for a survey. For facility location, recent research has proposed a number of algorithms, both for the metric and non-metric cases [, ,]. The work of Pandit and Pemmaraju [ ] is closely related our primal-dual algorithm; their algorithm is a 7-approximation in the CONGEST model for distributed computing. Both their algorithm and ours have a similar preprocessing step and rely on the $(1 + \varepsilon)$-slack idea although their algorithm uses a fixed $\varepsilon = 1$. The model and the efficiency metrics studied are different, however.

2. PRELIMINARIES AND NOTATION

Let F denote a set of *facilities* and C denote a set of *clients*. For convenience, let $n_c = |C|$, $n_f = |F|$, and $m = n_c \times n_f$. Each facility $i \in F$ has a cost of f_i, and each client $j \in C$ incurs a cost ("distance") $d(j, i)$ to use the facility i. We assume throughout that there is a metric space (X, d) with $F \cup C \subseteq X$ that underlies our problem instances. Thus, the distance d is symmetric and satisfies the triangle inequality. As a shorthand, denote the cost of the optimal solution by opt, the facility set of the optimal solution by F^*, and the facility set produced by our algorithm by F_A. Furthermore, we write $d(u, S)$ to mean the minimum distance from u to a member of S, i.e., $d(u, S) = \min\{d(u, w) : w \in S\}$.

Let G be a graph. We denote by $\deg_G(v)$ the degree of the node v in G and use $\Gamma_G(v)$ to denote the neighbor set of the node v. We drop the subscript (i.e., writing $\deg(v)$ and $\Gamma(v)$) when the context is clear. Let $V(G)$ and $E(G)$ denote respectively the set of nodes and the set of edges.

Parallel Models. All the parallel algorithms in this paper can be expressed in terms of a set of simple operations on vectors and dense matrices, making it easy to analyze costs on a variety of parallel models. In particular, the distances $d(\cdot, \cdot)$ can be represented as a dense $n \times n$ matrix, where $n = n_c + n_f$, and any data at clients or facilities can be represented as vectors. The only operations we need are parallel loops over the elements of the vector or matrix, transposing the matrix, sorting the rows of a matrix, and summation, prefix sums and distribution across the rows or columns of a matrix or vector. A prefix sum returns to each element of a sequence the sum of previous elements. The summation or prefix sum needs to be applied using a variety of associative operators, including min, max, and addition.

We refer to all the operations other than sorting as the *basic matrix operation*. The basic matrix operations on m elements can all be implemented with $O(m)$ work and $O(\log m)$ time on the EREW PRAM [ ], and with $O(m/B)$ cache complexity and $O(\log m)$ depth in the parallel cache oblivious model. For the parallel cache oblivious model, we assume a tall cache $M > B^2$, where M is the size of the cache and B is the block size. Sorting m elements takes $O(m \log m)$ work and $O(\log m)$ time on an EREW PRAM [ ], and $O(\frac{m}{B} \log_{M/B} m)$ cache complexity and $O(\log^2 m)$ depth on the parallel cache oblivious model [ ]. All algorithms described in this paper are *cache efficient* in the sense that the cache complexity in the cache oblivious model is bounded by $O(w/B)$ where w is the work in the EREW model. All algorithms use a polylogarithmic number of calls to the basic matrix operations and sorting and are thus in RNC—do polynomial work with polylogarithmic depth and possibly use randomization.

Given this set up, the problems considered in this paper can be defined as follows:

Facility Location. The goal of this problem is to find a set of facilities $F_S \subseteq F$ that minimizes the objective function

$$\text{FacLoc}(F_S) = \sum_{i \in F_S} f_i + \sum_{j \in C} d(j, F_S) \qquad (1)$$

Note that we do not need an explicit client-to-facility assignment because given a set of facilities F_S, the cost is minimized by assigning each client to the closest open facility.

Non-trivial upper- and lower-bounds for the cost of the optimal solution are useful objects in approximation algorithms. For each client $j \in C$, let $\gamma_j = \min_{i \in F}(f_i + d(j, i))$ and $\gamma = \max_{j \in C} \gamma_j$. The following bounds can be easily established:

$$\gamma \leq \text{opt} \leq \sum_{j \in C} \gamma_j \leq \gamma n_c. \qquad (2)$$

Furthermore, metric facility location has a natural integer-program formulation for which the relaxation yields the pair of primal and dual programs shown in Figure 1.

k-Median and k-Means. Unlike facility location, the k-median objective does not take into consideration facility costs, instead limiting the number of opened centers (facilities) to k. Moreover, in these problems, we typically do not distinguish between facilities and clients; every node is a client, and every node can be a facility. Formally, let $V \subseteq X$ be the set of nodes, and the goal is to find a set of at most k centers $F_S \subseteq V$ that minimizes the objective $\text{kMed}(F_S) = \sum_{j \in V} d(j, F_S)$. Almost identical to k-median is the k-means problem with the objective $\text{kMeans}(F_S) = \sum_{j \in C} d^2(j, F_S)$.

k-Center. Another type of facility-location problem which has a hard limit on the number of facilities to open is k-center. The k-center problem is to find a set of at most k centers $F_S \subseteq V$ that minimizes the objective $\text{kCenter}(F_S) = \max_{j \in V} d(j, F_S)$. In these problems, we will use n to denote the size of V.

3. DOMINATOR SET

We introduce and study two variants of the maximal independent set (MIS) problem, which will prove to be useful in nearly all algorithms described in this work. The first variant, called the *dominator set* problem, concerns finding a maximal set $I \subseteq V$ of nodes from a simple graph $G = (V, E)$ such that none of these nodes share a common neighbor (neighboring nodes of G cannot both be selected). The second variant, called the *U-dominator set* problem, involves finding a maximal set $I \subseteq U$ of the U-side nodes of a bipartite graph $H = (U, V, E)$ such that none of the nodes have a common V-side neighbor. We denote by $\text{MaxDom}(G)$ and $\text{MaxUDom}(H)$ the solutions to these problems, resp.

Both variants can be equivalently formulated in terms of maximal independent set. The first variant amounts to finding a maximal independent set on

$$G^2 = (V, \{uw : uw \in E \text{ or } \exists z \text{ s.t. } uz, zw \in E\}),$$

and the second variant a maximal independent set on

$$H' = (U, \{uw : \exists z \in V \text{ s.t. } uz, zw \in E\}).$$

Because of this relationship, on the surface, it may seem that one could simply compute G^2 or H' and run an existing MIS algorithm. Unfortunately, computing graphs such as G^2 and H' appears to need $O(n^\omega)$ work, where ω is the matrix-multiply constant, whereas the naïve greedy-like sequential algorithms for the same problems run in $O(|E|) = O(n^2)$. This difference makes it unlikely to obtain work efficient algorithms via this route.

In this section, we develop near work-efficient algorithms for these problems, bypassing the construction of the intermediate graphs. The key idea is to compute a maximal independent set in-place. Numerous parallel algorithms are known for maximal independent set, but the most relevant to us is an algorithm of Luby [ ], which we now sketch.

The input to the algorithm is a graph $G = (V, E)$. Luby's algorithm constructs a maximal independent set $I \subseteq V$ by proceeding in multiple rounds, with each round performing the following computation:

Algorithm 3.1 The select step of Luby's algorithm for maximal independent set.

---

1. For each $i \in V$, **in parallel**, $\pi(i) = $ a number chosen u.a.r. from $\{1, 2, \ldots, 2n^4\}$.

2. Include a node i in the maximal independent set I if $\pi(i) < \min\{\pi(j) : j \in \Gamma(i)\}$, where $\Gamma(i)$ is the neighborhood of i in G.

This process is termed the *select step* in Luby's work. Following the select step, the newly selected nodes, together with their neighbors, are removed from the graph before moving on to the next round.

Implementing the select step: We describe how the select step can be performed in-place for the first variant; the technique applies to the other variant. We will be simulating running Luby's algorithm on G^2, without generating G^2. Since G^2 has the same node set as G, step 1 of Algorithm 3.1 remains unchanged. Thus, the crucial computation for the select step is to determine efficiently, for each node i, whether $\pi(i)$ holds the smallest number among its neighbors in G^2, i.e., computing efficiently the test in step 2. To accomplish this, we simply pass the $\pi(i)$ to their neighbors taking a minimum, and then to the neighbors again taking a minimum. These can be implemented with a constant number of basic matrix operations, in particular distribution and summation using minimum over the rows and columns of the $|V|^2$ matrix.

Lemma 3.1 *Given a graph $G = (V, E)$, a maximal dominator set $I \subseteq V$ can be found in expected $O(\log^2 |V|)$ depth and $O(|V|^2 \log |V|)$ work. Furthermore, given a bipartite graph $G = (U, V, E)$, a maximal U-dominator set $I \subseteq U$ can be found in expected $O((\log |U|) \cdot \max\{\log |U|, \log |V|\})$ depth and $O(|V||U| \max\{\log |U|, \log |V|\})$ work.*

For sparse matrices, which we do not use in this paper, this can easily be improved to $O(|E| \log |V|)$ work.

4. FACILITY LOCATION: GREEDY

The greedy scheme underlies an exceptionally simple algorithm for facility location, due to Jain et al. [ ]. Despite the simplicity, the algorithm offers one of the best known

Minimize	$\sum_{i\in F, j\in C} d(j,i)x_{ij} + \sum_{i\in F} f_i y_i$	Maximize	$\sum_{j\in C} \alpha_j$

$$\textbf{Subj. to:} \begin{cases} \sum_{i\in F} x_{ij} \geq 1 & \text{for } j \in C \\ y_i - x_{ij} \geq 0 & \text{for } i \in F, j \in C \\ x_{ij} \geq 0,\ y_i \geq 0 \end{cases} \qquad \textbf{Subj. to:} \begin{cases} \sum_{j\in C} \beta_{ij} \leq f_i & \text{for } i \in F \\ \alpha_j - \beta_{ij} \leq d(j,i) & \text{for } i \in F, j \in C \\ \beta_{ij} \geq 0,\ \alpha_j \geq 0 \end{cases}$$

Figure 1: The primal (left) and dual (right) programs for metric (uncapacitated) facility location.

approximation guarantees for the problem. To describe the algorithm, we will need some definitions.

Definition 4.1 (Star, Price, and Maximal Star) *A star* $\mathcal{S} = (i, C')$ *consists of a facility* i *and a subset* $C' \subseteq C$. *The price of* $\mathcal{S}$ *is* $\mathsf{price}(\mathcal{S}) = (f_i + \sum_{j\in C'} d(j,i))/|C'|$. *A star* $\mathcal{S}$ *is said to be* maximal *if all strict super sets of* C' *have a larger price, i.e., for all* $C'' \supsetneq C'$, $\mathsf{price}((i, C'')) > \mathsf{price}((i, C'))$.

The greedy algorithm of Jain et al. proceeds as follows:

> Until no client remains, pick the cheapest star (i, C'), open the facility i, set $f_i = 0$, remove all clients in C' from the instance, and repeat.

This algorithm has a sequential running time of $O(m \log m)$, and using techniques known as factor-revealing LP, Jain et al. show that the algorithm has an approximation factor of 1.861 [ ]. From a parallelization point of view, the algorithm is highly sequential—at each step, only the minimum-cost option is chosen, and every subsequent step depends on the preceding one. In this section, we describe how to overcome this sequential nature and obtain an RNC algorithm inspired by the greedy algorithm of Jain et al. We show that the parallel algorithm is a $(6 + \varepsilon)$-approximation using elementary techniques. It remains an open problem whether factor-revealing LP techniques can be used to show a better approximation bound for the parallel algorithm.

The key idea to parallelization is that much faster progress will be made if we allow a small slack in what can be selected in each round; however, a subselection step is necessary to ensure that facility and connection costs are properly accounted for.

We present the parallel algorithm in Algorithm 1.1 and now describe step 1 in greater detail; steps 2 – 3 can be implemented using standard techniques [,]. As observed in Jain et al. [ ], for each facility i, the lowest-priced star centered at i consists of the κ_i closest clients to i, for some κ_i. Following this observation, we can presort the distance between facilities and clients for each facility. Let i be a facility and assume without loss of generality that $d(i,1) \leq d(i,2) \leq \cdots \leq d(i,n_c)$. Then, the cheapest maximal star for this facility can be found as follows. Use a prefix-sum computation to compute the sequence $p^{(i)} = \{(f_i + \sum_{j\leq k} d(i,k))/k\}_{k=1}^{n_c}$. Then, find the smallest index k such that $p_k^{(i)} < p_{k+1}^{(i)}$ or use $k = n_c$ if no such index exists. It is easy to see that the maximal lowest-priced star centered at i is the facility i together with the client set $\{1, \ldots, k\}$.

Crucial to this algorithm is a subselection step, which ensures that every facility and the clients that connect to it are adequately accounted for in the dual-fitting analysis. This subselection process can be seen as scaling back on the aggressiveness of opening up the facilities, mimicking the greedy algorithm's behavior more closely.

4.1 Analysis

We present a dual-fitting analysis of the above algorithm. The analysis relies on the client-to-facility assignment π, defined in the description of the algorithm. The following easy-to-check facts will be useful in the analysis.

Fact 4.2 *For each iteration of the execution, the following holds: (1) If* $\mathcal{S}_i$ *is the cheapest maximal star centered at* i, *then* j *appears in* $\mathcal{S}_i$ *if and only if* $d(j,i) \leq \mathsf{price}(\mathcal{S}_i)$. *(2) If* $t = \mathsf{price}(\mathcal{S}_i)$, *then* $\sum_{j\in C} \max(0, t - d(j,i)) = f_i$.

Now consider the dual program in Figure 1. For each client j, set α_j to be the τ setting in the iteration that the client was removed. For convenience, assume without loss of generality that $\alpha_1 \leq \alpha_2 \leq \cdots \leq \alpha_{n_c}$, and define $W_i = \{j \in C : \alpha_j \geq (3 + \varepsilon)d(j,i)\}$ for all $i \in F$. We begin the analysis by relating the cost of the solution that the algorithm outputs to the cost of the dual program.

Lemma 4.3 *The cost of the algorithm's solution* $\sum_{i\in F_A} f_i + \sum_{j\in C} d(j, F_A)$ *is upper-bounded by* $2(1 + \varepsilon)^2 \sum_{j\in C} \alpha_j$.

PROOF. Consider that in step 4(c), a facility i is opened if at least a $\frac{1}{2(1+\varepsilon)}$ fraction of the neighbors "chose" i. Furthermore, we know from the definition of H that, in that round, $f_i + \sum_{j\in \Gamma_H(i)} d(j,i) \leq \tau(1 + \varepsilon) \deg(i)$. By noting that we can partition C by which facility the client is assigned to in the assignment π, we establish

$$\sum_{j\in C} \alpha_j \cdot 2(1 + \varepsilon)^2 \geq \sum_{i\in F_A} \left(f_i + \sum_{j:\pi_j = i} d(j,i) \right)$$
$$\geq \sum_{i\in F_A} f_i + \sum_{j\in C} d(j, F_A),$$

as desired. □

In the series of claims that follows, we show that when scaled down by a factor of $3 + \varepsilon$, the α setting determined above is a dual feasible solution.

Claim 4.4 *Let* $i \in F$. *Assuming* W_i *is non-empty, if* j' *is the lowest-numbered client that connects to* i *(i.e.,* $j' = \min\{j : \pi_j = i\}$, *so it is* ∞ *if* i *is never opened), and* $j_0 = \min\left(j', \arg\min_{j\in W_i} \alpha_j\right)$, *then*

$$\sum_{j\in W_i} \max(0, \alpha_{j_0} - d(j,i)) \leq f_i.$$

PROOF. Let R be the set of clients which remain at the beginning of the iteration that τ was set to α_{j_0}. First, note that if $j_0 < j'$, then i must be opened after this iteration. As a consequence of Fact 4.2, we have $\sum_{j\in W_i} \max(0, \alpha_{j_0} - d(j,i)) \leq \sum_{j\in R} \max(0, (1 + \varepsilon)\alpha_{j_0} - d(j,i)) < f_i$. Therefore,

---

Algorithm 4.1 Parallel greedy algorithm for metric facility location.

In rounds, the algorithm performs the following steps until no client remains:

1. For each facility i, **in parallel**, compute $\mathcal{S}_i = (i, C^{(i)})$, the lowest-priced maximal star centered at i.

2. Let $\tau = \min_{i \in F} \text{price}(\mathcal{S}_i)$, and let $I = \{i \in F : \text{price}(\mathcal{S}_i) \leq \tau(1 + \varepsilon)\}$.

3. Construct a bipartite graph $H = (I, C', \{ij : d(i, j) \leq \tau(1 + \varepsilon)\})$, where $C' = \{j \in C : \exists i \in I \text{ s.t. } d(i, j) \leq \tau(1 + \varepsilon)\}$.

4. **Facility Subselection:** while $(I \neq \emptyset)$:

   (a) Let $\Pi : I \to \{1, \ldots, |I|\}$ be a random permutation of I.

   (b) For each $j \in C'$, let $\varphi_j = \arg\min_{i \in \Gamma_H(j)} \Pi(i)$.

   (c) For each $i \in I$, if $|\{j : \varphi_j = i\}| \geq \frac{1}{2(1+\varepsilon)} \deg(i)$, add i to F_A (open i), set $f_i = 0$, remove i from I, and remove $\Gamma_H(i)$ from both C and C'.

   Note: In the analysis, the clients removed in this step have π_j set as follows. If the facility φ_j is opened, let $\pi_j = \varphi_j$; otherwise, π_j is set to any facility i we open in this step such that $ij \in E(H)$. Note that any facility that is opened is at least $1/(2(1 + \varepsilon))$ paid for by the clients that select it, and that since every client is assigned to at most one facility, they only pay for one edge.

   (d) Remove $i \in I$ (and the incident edges) from the graph H if on the remaining graph, $\frac{f_i + \sum_{j \in \Gamma_H(i)} d(j,i)}{\deg(i)} > \tau(1 + \varepsilon)$. These facilities will show up in the next round (outer-loop).

   Note: After f_i is set to 0, facility i will still show up in the next round.

---

in the rest of the proof, we will assume that $j_0 = j'$ and that i was actually opened.

Now suppose for a contradiction that $\sum_{j \in W_i} \max(0, \alpha_{j_0} - d(j, i)) > f_i$, so then because $j_0 = j'$, we know that R is in fact the set of clients that remain at the beginning of the iteration in which i was first opened (i.e., i was a center of some star and $f_i > 0$ at that point). Furthermore, we know that if the cost the star centered at i in this iteration is t_i, then $f_i = \sum_{j \in R} \max(0, t_i - d(j, i))$. Therefore, since $W_i \subseteq R$ and $t_i \geq \alpha_{j_0}$, we have $f_i = \sum_{j \in R} \max(0, t_i - d(j, i)) \geq \sum_{j \in R} \max(0, \alpha_{j_0} - d(j, i)) \geq \sum_{j \in W_i} \max(0, \alpha_{j_0} - d(j, i)) > f_i$, which gives a contradiction. $\square$

Claim 4.5 *Let $i \in F$, and j, j' be clients such that $j' \leq j$. Then, $\alpha_j \leq \alpha_{j'} + d(i, j') + d(i, j)$.*

The proof of this claim closely parallels that of Jain et al. [ ] and is omitted due to space considerations. Combining Claims and , we have the following lemma:

Lemma 4.6 *Let $i \in F$. Then,*

$$\sum_{j \in W_i} \left[\alpha_j - (3 + \varepsilon)d(j, i) \right] \leq (3 + \varepsilon)f_i.$$

PROOF. We first note that if W_i is empty, the lemma is trivially true. Thus, we assume W_i is non-empty and define j_0 as follows: let j' be the lowest-numbered client that connects to i or ∞ if i is never opened. Then, $j_0 = \min(j', \arg\min_{j \in W_i} \alpha_j)$. Now if $j_0 = j'$, then $d(j_0, i) \leq (1 + \varepsilon)\alpha_{j_0}$. Otherwise, we have $j_0 \in W_i$, in which case $d(j_0, i) \leq \alpha_j$ by the definition of W_i. Therefore, in either case, $d(j_0, i) \leq (1 + \varepsilon)\alpha_{j_0}$.

Next we let $T = \{j \in W_i : \alpha_{j_0} \geq d(j, i)\}$. Applying

Claims and , we have

$$\sum_{j \in W_i} (\alpha_j - d(j, i))$$
$$\leq \sum_{j \in W_i} (\alpha_{j_0} + d(j_0, i)) \leq \sum_{j \in W_i} (2 + \varepsilon)\alpha_{j_0}$$
$$\leq (2 + \varepsilon)f_i + \sum_{j \in T} (2 + \varepsilon)d(j, i) + \sum_{j \in W_i \setminus T} (2 + \varepsilon)d(j, i)$$
$$\leq (2 + \varepsilon)f_i + \sum_{j \in W_i} (2 + \varepsilon)d(j, i),$$

which completes the proof. $\square$

Using this lemma, we argue that the setting $\alpha'_j = \alpha_j / (3 + \varepsilon)$ and $\beta'_{ij} = \max(0, \alpha'_j - d(j, i))$ yields a dual feasible solution. First, our choice of β'_{ij}'s ensures that all constraints of the form $\alpha_j - \beta_{ij} \leq d(j, i)$ are satisfied. Then, by the lemma above, we have $\sum_{j \in C} \max(0, \alpha_j - (3 + \varepsilon)d(j, i)) = \sum_{j \in W_i} [\alpha_j - (3 + \varepsilon)d(j, i)] \leq (3 + \varepsilon)f_i$, which implies that $\sum_{j \in C} \max(0, \alpha_j - (3 + \varepsilon)d(j, i)) \leq (3 + \varepsilon)f_i$. Hence, we conclude that for all facility $i \in F$, $\sum_{j \in C} \beta'_{ij} \leq f_i$, proving the following corollary:

Corollary 4.7 *The setting $\alpha'_j = \frac{\alpha_j}{3+\varepsilon}$ and $\beta'_{ij} = \max(0, \alpha'_j - d(j, i))$ is a dual feasible solution.*

Running time analysis.

Consider the algorithm's description in Algorithm . The rows can be presorted to give each client its distances from facilities in order. In the original order, each element can be marked with its rank. Step 1 then involves a prefix sum on the sorted order to determine how far down the order to go and then selection of all facilities at or below that rank. Steps 2–3 require reductions and distributions across the rows or columns of the matrix. The subset $I \subset F$ can be represented as a bit mask over F. Step 4 is more interesting to analyze; the following lemma bounds the number of rounds facility subselection is executed, the proof of which is analogous to Lemma 4.1.2 of Rajagopalan and Vazirani [ ]; we present here for completeness a simplified version of their proof, which suffices for our lemma.

Lemma 4.8 *With probability* $1 - o(1)$, *the subselection step terminates within* $O(\log_{1+\varepsilon} m)$ *rounds.*

PROOF. Let $\Phi = |E|$. We will show that if Φ' is the potential value after an iteration of the subselection step, then $\mathbf{E}[\Phi - \Phi'] \geq c\Phi$, for some constant $c > 0$. The lemma then follows from standard results in probability theory. To proceed, define $\mathsf{chosen}_i = |\{j \in C' : \varphi_j = i\}|$. Furthermore, we say that an edge ij is *good* if at most $\theta = \frac{1}{2}(1 - \frac{1}{1+\varepsilon})$ fraction of neighbors of i have degree higher than j.

Consider a good edge ij. We will estimate $\mathbf{E}[\mathsf{chosen}_i | \varphi_j = i]$. Since ij is good, we know that

$$\sum_{j' \in \Gamma_H(i)} \mathbf{1}_{\{\deg(j') \leq \deg(j)\}} \geq (1 - \theta) \deg(i).$$

Therefore, $\mathbf{E}[\mathsf{chosen}_i | \varphi_j = i] \geq \frac{1}{2}(1 - \theta) \deg(i)$, as it can be shown that $\mathbf{Pr}[\varphi_{j'} = i | \varphi_j = i] \geq \frac{1}{2}$ for all $j' \in \Gamma_H(i)$ and $\deg(j') \leq \deg(j)$. By Markov's inequality and realizing that $\mathsf{chosen}_i \leq \deg(i)$, we have

$$\mathbf{Pr}\left[\mathsf{chosen}_i \geq \frac{1}{2(1 + \varepsilon)} \deg(i) \;\middle|\; \varphi_j = i\right] = p_0 > 0.$$

Finally, we note that $\mathbf{E}[\Phi - \Phi']$ is at least

$$\sum_{ij \in E} \mathbf{Pr}\left[\varphi_j = i \text{ and } \mathsf{chosen}_i \geq \frac{1}{2(1 + \varepsilon)} \deg(i)\right] \cdot \deg(j)$$

$$\geq \sum_{\text{good } ij \in E} \frac{1}{\deg(j)} p_0 \deg(j)$$

$$\geq p_0 \sum_{ij \in E} \mathbf{1}_{\{ij \text{ is good}\}}.$$

Since at least θ fraction of the edges are good, $\mathbf{E}[\Phi - \Phi'] \geq p_0 \theta \Phi$. Since $\ln(1/(1 - p_0\theta)) = \Omega(\log(1 + \varepsilon))$, the lemma follows from standard results in probability [ ]. $\square$

It is easy to see that each subselection step can be performed with a constant number of basic matrix operations over the D matrix. Therefore, if the number of rounds the main body is executed is r, the algorithm makes $O(r \log_{1+\varepsilon} m)$ calls to the basic matrix operations described in Section with probability exceeding $1 - o(1)$. It also requires a single sort in the preprocessing. This means $O(r \log_{1+\varepsilon} m \log m)$ time implies a total of $O(rm \log_{1+\varepsilon} m)$ work (with probability exceeding $1 - o(1)$) on the EREW PRAM. Furthermore, it is cache efficient (cache complexity is $O(w/B)$) since the sort is only applied once and does not dominate the cache bounds.

Bounding the number of rounds.

Before describing a less restrictive alternative, we point out that the simplest way to bound the number of rounds by a polylogarithm factor is to rely on the common assumption that the facility cost, as well as the ratio between the minimum (non-zero) and the maximum client-facility distance, is polynomially bounded in the input size. As a result of this assumption, the number of rounds is upper-bounded by $\log_{1+\varepsilon}(m^c) = O(\log_{1+\varepsilon} m)$, for some $c \geq 1$.

Alternatively, we can apply a preprocessing step to ensure that the number of rounds is polylogarithm in m. The basic idea of the preprocessing step is that if a star is "relatively cheap," opening it right away will harm the approximation factor only slightly. Using the bounds in Equation ( ), if $\mathcal{S}_i$ is the lowest-priced maximal star centered at i, we know we can afford to open i and discard all clients attached to it if $\mathsf{price}(\mathcal{S}_i) \leq \frac{\gamma}{m^2}$. Therefore, the preprocessing step involves: (1) computing $\mathcal{S}_i$, the lowest-priced maximal star centered at i, for all $i \in F$, (2) opening all i such that $\mathsf{price}(\mathcal{S}_i) \leq \frac{\gamma}{m^2}$, (3) setting f_i of these facilities to 0 and removing all clients attached to these facilities.

Computing γ takes $O(\log n_c + \log n_f)$ depth and $O(m)$ work. The rest of the preprocessing step is at most as costly as a step in the main body. Thus, the whole preprocessing step can be accomplished in $O(\log m)$ depth and $O(m)$ work. With this preprocessing step, three things are clear: First, τ in the first iteration of the main algorithm will be at least $\frac{\gamma}{m^2}$, because cheaper stars have already been processed in preprocessing. Second, the cost of our final solution is increased by at most $n_c \times \frac{\gamma}{m^2} \leq \frac{\gamma}{m} \leq \mathsf{opt}/m$, because the facilities and clients handled in preprocessing can be accounted for by the cost of their corresponding stars—specifically, there can be most n_c stars handled in preprocessing, each of which has price $\leq \gamma/m^2$; and the price for a star includes both the facility cost and the connection cost of the relevant clients and facilities. Finally, in the final iteration, $\tau \leq n_c \gamma$. As a direct consequence of these observations, the number of rounds is upper-bounded by $\log_{1+\varepsilon}(\frac{n_c \gamma}{\gamma/m^2}) \leq \log_{1+\varepsilon}(m^3) = O(\log_{1+\varepsilon} m)$, culminating in the following theorem:

Theorem 4.9 *Let* $0 < \varepsilon \leq 1$ *be fixed. For sufficiently large input, there is a greedy-style* RNC $O(m \log^2_{1+\varepsilon}(m))$-*work algorithm that yields a factor-$(6 + \varepsilon)$ approximation for the metric facility-location problem.*

5. FACILITY LOCATION: PRIMAL-DUAL

The primal-dual scheme is a versatile paradigm for combinatorial algorithms design. In the context of facility location, this scheme underlies the Lagrangian-multiplier preserving (LMP) 3-approximation algorithm of Jain and Vazirani, enabling them to use the algorithm as a subroutine in their 6-approximation algorithm for k-median [ ].

The algorithm of Jain and Vazirani consists of two phases, a primal-dual phase and a postprocessing phase. To summarize this algorithm, consider the primal and dual programs in Figure . In the primal-dual phase, starting with all dual variables set to 0, we raise the dual variables α_j's uniformly until a constraint of the form $\alpha_j - \beta_{ij} \leq d(j, i)$ becomes tight, at which point β_{ij} will also be raised, again, uniformly to prevent these constraints from becoming overtight. When a constraint $\sum_j \beta_{ij} \leq f_i$ is tight, facility i is tentatively opened and clients with $\alpha_j \geq d(j, i)$ are "frozen," i.e., we stop raising their α_j values from this point on. The first phase ends when all clients are frozen. In the postprocessing phase, we compute and output a maximal independent set on a graph G of tentatively open facilities; in this graph, there is an edge between a pair of facilities i and i' if there is a client j such that $\alpha_j > d(j, i)$ and $\alpha_j > d(j, i')$. Thus, the maximal

[1]This means $\alpha \sum_{i \in F_A} f_i + \sum_{j \in C} d(j, F_A) \leq \alpha \cdot \mathsf{opt}$, where α is the approximation ratio.

independent set ensures proper accounting of the facility cost (i.e., each client "contributes" to at most one open facility, and every open facility has enough contribution). Informally, we say that a client j "pays" for or "contributes" to a facility i if $\beta_{ij} = \alpha_j - d(j,i) > 0$.

Remarks. We note that in the parallel setting, the description of the postprocessing step above does not directly lead to an efficient algorithm, because constructing G in polylogarithmic depth seems to need $O(mn_f)$ work, which is much more than one needs sequentially.

In this section, we show how to obtain a work-efficient RNC $(3+\varepsilon)$-approximation algorithm for facility location, based on the primal-dual algorithm of Jain and Vazirani. Critical to bounding the number of iterations in the main algorithm by $O(\log m)$ is a preprocessing step, which is similar to that used by Pandit and Pemmaraju in their distributed algorithm [ ].

Preprocessing: Assuming γ as defined in Equation ( ), we will open every facility i that satisfies

$$\sum_{j \in C} \max\left(0, \frac{\gamma}{m^2} - d(j,i)\right) \geq f_i.$$

Furthermore, for all clients j such that there exists an opened i and $d(j,i) \leq \gamma/m^2$, we declare them connected and set $\alpha_j = 0$. The facilities opened in this step will be called *free* facilities and denoted by the set F_0.

Main Algorithm: The main body of the algorithm is described in Algorithm 5.1. The algorithm outputs a bipartite graph $H = (F_T, C, E)$, constructed as the algorithm executes. Here F_T is the set of facilities declared open during the iterations of the main algorithm and E is given by $E = \{ij : i \in F, j \in C, \text{ and } (1+\varepsilon)\alpha_j > d(j,i)\}$.

Post-processing. As a post-processing step, we compute $I = \text{MAXUDOM}(H)$. Thus, the set of facilities $I \subseteq F_T$ has the property that each client contributes to the cost of at most one facility in I. Finally, we report $F_A = I \cup F_0$ as the set of facilities in the final solution.

5.1 Analysis

To analyze approximation guarantee of this algorithm, we start by establishing that the α_j setting produced by the algorithm leads to a dual feasible solution.

Claim 5.1 *For any facility i,*

$$\sum_{j \in \Gamma_H(i)} \max(0, \alpha_j - d(j,i)) \leq f_i.$$

The proof of this claim is omitted in the interest of space. It follows from this claim that setting $\beta_{ij} = \max(0, \alpha_j - d(j,i))$ provides a dual feasible solution. Next we relate the cost of our solution to the cost of the dual solution. To ease the following analyses, we use a client-to-facility assignment $\pi : C \to F$, defined as follows: For all $j \in C$, let $\varphi(j) = \{i : (1+\varepsilon)\alpha_j \geq d(j,i)\}$. Now for each client j, **(1)** if there exists $i \in F_0$ such that $d(j,i) \leq \gamma/m^2$, set π_j to *any* such i; **(2)** if there exists $i \in I$ such that ij is an edge in H, then $\pi_j = i$ (i is unique because of properties of I) ; **(3)** if there exists $i \in I$ such that $i \in \varphi(j)$, then $\pi_j = i$; **(4)** otherwise, pick $i' \in \varphi(j)$ and set π_j to $i \in I$ which is a neighbor of a neighbor of i'.

Clients of the first case, denoted by C_0, are called *freely connected*; clients of the cases (2) and (3), denoted by C_1,

are called *directly connected*. Otherwise, a client is *indirectly connected*.

The following lemmas bound the facility costs and the connection costs of indirectly connected clients.

Lemma 5.2

$$\sum_{i \in F_A} f_i \leq \frac{\gamma}{m} + \sum_{j \in C_1} (1+\varepsilon)\alpha_j - \sum_{j \in C_0 \cup C_1} d(j, \pi_j)$$

PROOF. When facility $i \in F_T$ was opened, it must satisfy $f_i \leq \sum_{j:ij \in E(G)}(1+\varepsilon)\alpha_j - d(j,i)$. If client j has contributed to i (i.e., $(1+\varepsilon)\alpha_j - d(j,i) > 0$) and $i \in I$, then j is directly connected to it. Furthermore, for each client j, there is at most one facility in I that it contributes to (because $I = \text{MAXUDOM}(H)$). Therefore, $\sum_{i \in I} f_i \leq \sum_{j \in C_1}(1+\varepsilon)\alpha_j - d(j, \pi_j)$. Furthermore, for each "free" facility, we know that $f_i \leq \sum_{j \in C} \max(0, \gamma^2/m^2 - d(j,i))$, so by our choice of π, $f_i \leq \frac{\gamma}{m^2} \times n_c - \sum_{j \in C_0 : \pi_j = i} d(j,i)$. Thus, $\sum_{i \in F_0} f_i \leq \gamma/m - \sum_{j \in C_0} d(j,i)$. Combining these results and observing that F_A is the disjoint union of I and F_0, we have the lemma. $\square$

Lemma 5.3 *For each indirectly connected client j (i.e., $j \notin C_0 \cup C_1$), we have $d(j, \pi_j) \leq 3(1+\varepsilon)\alpha_j$.*

PROOF. Because $j \notin C_0 \cup C_1$ and $I = \text{MAXUDOM}(H)$, there must exist a facility $i' \in \varphi(j)$ and a client j' such that j' contributed to both i and i', and $(1+\varepsilon)\alpha_j \geq d(j,i')$. We claim that both $d(j',i')$ and $d(j',i)$ are upper-bounded by $(1+\varepsilon)\alpha_j$. To see this, we note that because j' contributed to both i and i', $d(j',i') \leq (1+\varepsilon)\alpha_{j'}$ and $d(j',i) \leq (1+\varepsilon)\alpha_{j'}$. Let ℓ be the iteration in which j was declared frozen, so $\alpha_j = t_\ell$. Since $i' \in \varphi(j)$, i' must be declared open in iteration $\leq \ell$. Furthermore, because $(1+\varepsilon)\alpha_{j'} > d(j',i')$, $\alpha_{j'}$ must be frozen in or prior to iteration ℓ. Consequently, we have $\alpha_{j'} \leq t_\ell = \alpha_j$. Combining these facts and applying the triangle inequality, we get $d(j,i) \leq d(j,i') + d(i',j') + d(j',i) \leq (1+\varepsilon)\alpha_j + 2(1+\varepsilon)\alpha_{j'} \leq 3(1+\varepsilon)\alpha_j$. $\square$

By Lemmas 5.2 and 5.3, we establish

$$3\sum_{i \in F_A} f_i + \sum_{j \in C} d(j, \pi_j) \leq \frac{3\gamma}{m} + 3(1+\varepsilon)\sum_{j \in C} \alpha_j. \quad (3)$$

Now since $\{\alpha_j, \beta_{ij}\}$ is dual feasible, its value can be at most that of the primal optimal solution; that is, $\sum_j \alpha_j \leq \text{opt}$. Therefore, combining with Equation ( ), we know that the cost of the solution returned by parallel primal-dual algorithm in this section is at most $3\sum_{i \in F_A} f_i + \sum_{j \in C} d(j, C) \leq (3 + \varepsilon')\text{opt}$ for some $\varepsilon' > 0$ when the problem instance is large enough.

Running Time Analysis.

We analyze the running of the algorithm presented, starting with the main body of the algorithm. Since $\sum_j \alpha_j \leq \text{opt}$ and $\text{opt} \leq n_c\gamma$, no α_j can be bigger than $n_c\gamma \leq m\gamma$. Hence, the main algorithm must terminate before $\ell > 3\log_{1+\varepsilon} m$, which upper-bounds the number of iterations to $O(\log_{1+\varepsilon} m)$. In each iteration, steps 1, 3, and 4 perform trivial work. Step 2 can be broken down into (1) computing the max for all $i \in F, j \in C$, and (2) computing the sum for each $i \in F$. These can all be implemented with the basic matrix operations, giving a total of $O(\log_{1+\varepsilon} m)$ of basic matrix operations over a matrix of size m.

321

Algorithm 5.1 Parallel primal-dual algorithm for metric facility location

For iteration $\ell = 0, 1, \ldots$, the algorithm performs the following steps until all facilities are opened or all clients are frozen, whichever happens first.

1. For each unfrozen client j, **in parallel**, set α_j to $\frac{\gamma}{m^2}(1+\varepsilon)^\ell$.

2. For each unopened facility i, **in parallel**, declare it open if

$$\sum_{j \in C} \max(0, (1+\varepsilon)\alpha_j - d(j,i)) \geq f_i.$$

3. For each unfrozen client j, **in parallel**, freeze this client if there exists an opened facility i such that $(1+\varepsilon)\alpha_j \geq d(j,i)$.

4. Update the graph H by adding edges between pairs of nodes ij such that $(1+\varepsilon)\alpha_j > d(j,i)$.

After the last iteration, if all facilities are opened but some clients are *not* yet frozen, we determine in parallel the α_j settings of these clients that will make them reach an open facility (i.e., $\alpha_j = \min_i d(j,i)$). Finally, update the graph H as necessary.

The preprocessing step, again, involves some reductions over the rows and columns of the matrix. This includes the calculations of γ_j's and the composite γ. The post-processing step relies on computing the U-dominating set, as described in Section 2 which runs in $O(\log m)$ matrix operations.

The whole algorithm therefore runs in $O(\log_{1+\varepsilon} m)$ basic matrix operations and is hence work efficient compared to the $O(m \log m)$ sequential algorithm of Jain and Vazirani. Putting these altogether, we have the following theorem:

Theorem 5.4 *Let $\varepsilon > 0$ be fixed. For sufficiently large m, there is a primal-dual RNC $O(m \log_{1+\varepsilon} m)$-work algorithm that yields a factor-$(3+\varepsilon)$ approximation for the metric facility-location problem.*

6. OTHER RESULTS

In this section, we consider other applications of dominator set in facility-location problems.

6.1 k-Center

Hochbaum and Shmoys [ ] show a simple factor-2 approximation for k-center. The algorithm performs a binary search on the range of distances. We show how to combine the dominator-set algorithm from Section 3 with standard techniques to parallelize the algorithm of Hochbaum and Shmoys, resulting in an RNC algorithm with the same approximation guarantee. Consider the set of distances $\mathcal{D} = \{d(i,j) : i \in C \text{ and } j \in V\}$ and order them so that $d_1 < d_2 < \cdots < d_p$ and $\{d_1, \ldots, d_p\} = \mathcal{D}$, where $p = |\mathcal{D}|$. The sequence $\{d_i\}_{i=1}^p$ can be computed in $O(\log |V|)$ depth and $O(|V|^2 \log |V|)$ work. Let H_α be a graph defined as follows: the nodes of H_α is the set of nodes V, but there is an edge connecting i and j if and only if $d(i,j) \leq \alpha$.

The main idea of the algorithm is simple: find the smallest index $t \in \{1, 2, \ldots, p\}$ such that $\mathrm{MAXDOM}(H_{d_t}) \leq k$. Hochbaum and Shmoys observe that the value t can be found using binary search in $O(\log p) = O(\log |V|)$ probes. We parallelize the probe step, consisting of constructing $H_{d_{t'}}$ for a given $t' \in \{1, \ldots, p\}$ and checking whether $|\mathrm{MAXDOM}(H_{d_{t'}})|$ is bigger than k. Constructing $H_{d_{t'}}$ takes $O(1)$ depth and $O(|V|^2)$ work, and using the maximal-dominator-set algorithm from Section 3, the test can be performed in expected $O(\log^2 |V|)$ depth and expected $O(|V|^2 \log |V|)$ work. The approximation factor is identical to the original algorithm, hence proving the following theorem:

Theorem 6.1 *There is an RNC 2-approximation algorithm with $O((|V| \log |V|)^2)$ work for k-center.*

6.2 Facility Location: LP Rounding

LP rounding was among the very first techniques that yield non-trivial approximation guarantees for metric facility location. The first constant-approximation algorithm was given by Shmoys et al. [ ]. Although we do not know how to solve the linear program for facility location in polylogarithmic depth, we demonstrate another application of the dominator-set algorithm and the slack idea by parallelizing the randomized-rounding step of Shmoys et al. The algorithm yields a $(4+\varepsilon)$-approximation, and the randomized rounding is an RNC algorithm.

The randomized rounding algorithm of Shmoys et al. consists of two phases: a filtering phase and a rounding phase. In the following, we show how to parallelize these phases and prove that the parallel version has a similar guarantee. Our presentation differs slightly from the original work but works in the same spirit.

Filtering: The filtering phase is naturally parallelizable. Fix α to be a value between 0 and 1. Given an optimal primal solution (x, y), the goal of this step is to produce a new solution (x', y') with properties as detailed in Lemma 6.2. Let $\delta_j = \sum_{i \in F} d(i,j) \cdot x_{ij}$, $B_j = \{i \in F : d(i,j) \leq (1+\alpha)\delta_j\}$, and $\mathsf{mass}(B_j) = \sum_{i \in B_j} x_{ij}$. We compute x'_{ij} and y'_i as follows: (1) let $x'_{ij} = x_{ij}/\mathsf{mass}(B_j)$ if $i \in B_j$ or 0 otherwise, and (2) let $y'_i = \min(1, (1+1/\alpha)y_i)$.

Lemma 6.2 *Given an optimal primal solution (x, y), there is a primal feasible solution (x', y') such that (1) $\sum_i x'_{ij} = 1$, (2) if $x'_{ij} > 0$, then $d(j,i) \leq (1+\alpha)\delta_j$, and (3) $\sum_i f_i y_i \leq (1+\frac{1}{\alpha})\sum_i f_i y'_i$.*

PROOF. By construction, (1) clearly holds. Furthermore, we know that if $x'_{ij} > 0$, it must be the case that $i \in B_j$, so $d(j,i) \leq (1+\alpha)\delta_j$, proving (2). By definition of y'_i, $\sum_i f_i y_i \leq (1+\frac{1}{\alpha})\sum_i f_i y'_i$, proving (3). Finally, since in an optimal LP solution, $\sum_i x_{ij} = 1$, we know that $\mathsf{mass}(B_j) \geq \frac{\alpha}{1+\alpha}$, by an averaging argument. Therefore, $x'_{ij} \leq (1+\frac{1}{\alpha})x_{ij} \leq \min(1, (1+\frac{1}{\alpha})y_i) = y'_i$, showing that (x', y') is primal feasible. $\square$

Rounding: The rounding phase is more challenging to parallelize because it is inherently sequential—a greedy algorithm which considers the clients in an increasing order of δ_j and appears to need $\Omega(n_c)$ steps. We show, however, that we can achieve parallelism by eagerly processing the clients $S = \{j : \delta_j \leq (1+\varepsilon)\tau\}$. This is followed by a clean-up step, which uses the dominator-set algorithm to rectify the excess facilities. We precompute the following information: (1) for each j, let i_j be the least costly facility in B_j, and (2) construct $H = (C, F, ij \in E$ iff. $i \in B_j)$.

There is a preprocessing step to ensure that the number of rounds is polylogarithmic in m. Let θ be the value of the optimal LP solution. By an argument similar to that of Section 4, we can afford to process all clients with $\delta_j \leq \theta/m^2$ in the first round, increasing the final cost by at most $\theta/m \leq \mathsf{opt}/m$. The algorithm then proceeds in rounds, each performing the following steps:

---

1. Let $\tau = \min_j \delta_j$.
2. Let $S = \{j : \delta_j \leq (1+\varepsilon)\tau\}$ and
3. Let $J = \textsc{MaxUDom}(H)$, add $I = \{i_j : j \in J\}$ to F_A; finally, remove all of S and $\cup_{j \in S} B_j$ from $V(H)$.

Since J is U-dominator of H, we know that for all distinct $j, j' \in J$, $B_j \cap B_{j'} = \emptyset$; therefore, $\sum_{i \in I} f_i = \sum_{j \in J} f_{i_j} \leq \sum_{j \in J} \left(\sum_{i \in B_j} x'_{ij} f_{i_j} \right) \leq \sum_{j \in J} y'_i f_{i_j} \leq \sum_{j \in J} y'_i f_i$, proving the following claim:

Claim 6.3 *In each round,* $\sum_{i \in I} f_i \leq \sum_{i \in \cup_j B_j} y'_i f_i$.

Like our previous analyses, we will define a client-to-facility assignment π convenient for the proof. For each $j \in C$, if $i_j \in F_A$, let $\pi_j = i_j$; otherwise, set $\pi_j = i_{j'}$, where j' is the client that causes i_j to be shut down (i.e., either $i_j \in B_{j'}$ and j' was process in a previous iteration, or both j and j' are processed in the same iteration but there exists $i \in B_j \cap B_{j'}$).

Claim 6.4 *Let j be a client. If $i_j \in F_A$, then $d(j, \pi_j) \leq (1+\alpha)\delta_j$; otherwise,* $d(j, \pi_j) \leq 3(1+\alpha)(1+\varepsilon)\delta_j$.

PROOF. If $i_j \in F_A$, then by Lemma 6.2, $d(j, \pi_j) \leq (1+\alpha)\delta_j$. If $i_j \notin F_A$, we know that there must exist $i \in B_j$ and j' such that $i \in B_{j'}$ and $\delta_{j'} \leq (1+\varepsilon)\delta_j$. Thus, applying Lemma 6.2 and the triangle inequality, we have $d(j, \pi_j) \leq d(j, i) + d(i, j') + d(j', i_{j'}) \leq 3(1+\alpha)(1+\varepsilon)\delta_j$. $\square$

Running Time Analysis: The above algorithm will terminate in at most $O(\log_{1+\varepsilon} m)$ rounds because the preprocessing step ensures the ratio between the maximum and the minimum δ_j values are polynomially bounded. Like previous analyses, steps 1 – 2 can be accomplished in $O(1)$ basic matrix operations, and step 3 in $O(\log m)$ basic matrix operations on matrices of size m. This yields a total of $O(\log_{1+\varepsilon} m \log m)$ basic matrix operations, proving the following theorem:

Theorem 6.5 *Given an optimal LP solution for the primal LP in Figure 4, there is an RNC rounding algorithm yielding a $(4+\varepsilon)$-approximation with $O(m \log m \log_{1+\varepsilon} m)$ work. It is cache efficient.*

7. k-MEDIAN: LOCAL SEARCH

Local search, LP rounding, and Lagrangian relaxation are among the main techniques for approximation algorithms for k-median. In this section, building on the algorithms from previous sections, we present an algorithm for the k-median problem, based on local-search techniques. The natural local-search algorithm for k-median is very simple: starting with any set F_A of k facilities, find some $i \in F_A$ and $i' \in F \setminus F_A$ such that swapping them decreases the k-median cost, and repeat until no such moves can be found. Finding an improving swap or identifying that none exists takes $O(k(n-k)n)$ time sequentially, where n is the number of nodes in the instance. This algorithm is known to be a 5-approximation [,].

The key ideas in this section are that we can find a good initial solution S_0 quickly and perform each local-search step fast. Together, this means that only a small number of local-search steps is needed, and each step can be performed fast. To find a good initial solution, we observe that any optimal k-center solution is an n-approximation for k-median. Therefore, we will use the 2-approximation from Section 6.1 as a factor-$(2n)$ solution for the k-median problem. At the beginning of the algorithm, for each $j \in V$, we order the facilities by their distance from j, taking $O(n^2 \log n)$ work and $O(\log n)$ depth.

Let $0 < \varepsilon < 1$ be fixed. We say that a swap (i, i') such that $i \in F_A$ and $i' \in F \setminus F_A$ is *improving* if $\textsc{kMed}(F_S - i + i') < (1 - \beta/k)\textsc{kMed}(F_S)$, where $\beta = \varepsilon/(1+\varepsilon)$. The parallel algorithm proceeds as follows. In each round, find and apply an improving swap as long as there is one. We now describe how to perform each local-search step fast. During the execution, the algorithm keeps track of φ_j, the facility client j is assigned to, for all $j \in V$. We will consider all possible test swaps $i \in F_A$ and $i' \in V \setminus F_A$ simultaneously in parallel. For each potential swap (i, i'), every client can independently compute $\Delta_j = d(j, F_A - i + i') - d(j, F_A)$; this computation trivially takes $O(n_c)$ work and $O(1)$ depth, since we know φ_j and the distances are presorted. From here, we know that $\textsc{kMed}(F_A - i + i') - \textsc{kMed}(F_A) = \sum_j \Delta_j$, which can be computed in $O(n)$ work and $O(\log n)$ depth. Therefore, in $O(k(n-k)n)$ work and $O(\log n)$ depth, we can find an improving swap or detect that none exists. Finally, a round concludes by applying an improving swap to F_A and updating the φ_j values.

Arya et al. [ ] show that the number of rounds is bounded by

$$O\left(\log_{1/(1-\beta/k)}\left(\textsc{kMed}(S_0)/\mathsf{opt}\right)\right) = O\left(\log_{1/(1-\beta/k)}(n)\right)$$

Since for $0 < \varepsilon < 1$, $\ln\left(1/(1-\beta/k)\right) \leq \frac{2}{k}\ln\left(1/(1-\beta)\right)$, we have the following theorem, assuming constant k, which is often the case in many applications:

Theorem 7.1 *For constant k, there is an NC $O(k^2(n-k)n \log_{1+\varepsilon}(n))$-work algorithm which gives a factor-$(5+\varepsilon)$ approximation for k-median.*

Remarks. Relative to the sequential algorithm, this algorithm is work efficient—regardless of the range of k. In addition to k-median, this approach is applicable to k-means, yielding an $(81+\varepsilon)$-approximation [ ] in general metric spaces and a $(25+\varepsilon)$-approximation for the Euclidean space [ ], and the same parallelization techniques can be used to achieve the same running time. Furthermore, there is a factor-3 approximation local-search algorithm for facility location, in which a similar idea can be used to perform each local-search step efficiently; however, we do not know how to bound the number of rounds.

8. CONCLUSION

This paper studies the design and analysis of parallel approximation algorithms for facility-location problems, including facility location, k-center, k-median, and k-means. We presented several efficient algorithms, based on a diverse set of approximation algorithms techniques.

Acknowledgments. We thank IBM, Intel, and Microsoft for generous gifts that helped support this work. We thank Anupam Gupta for valuable suggestions and conversations.

References

[1] V. Arya, N. Garg, R. Khandekar, A. Meyerson, K. Munagala, and V. Pandit. Local search heuristics for k-median and facility location problems. *SIAM J. Comput.*, 33(3):544–562, 2004.

[2] B. Berger, J. Rompel, and P. W. Shor. Efficient *NC* algorithms for set cover with applications to learning and geometry. In *FOCS'89*, pages 54–59, 1989.

[3] G. E. Blelloch, P. B. Gibbons, and H. V. Simhadri. Low depth cache-oblivious sorting. In *SPAA'10*, 2010.

[4] J. Byrka. An optimal bifactor approximation algorithm for the metric uncapacitated facility location problem. In *AP-PROX'07*, 2007. 29–43.

[5] M. Charikar and S. Guha. Improved combinatorial algorithms for facility location problems. *SIAM J. Comput.*, 34(4):803–824, 2005. ISSN 0097-5397.

[6] M. Charikar, S. Guha, É. Tardos, and D. B. Shmoys. A constant-factor approximation algorithm for the k-median problem. *J. Comput. System Sci.*, 65(1):129–149, 2002. ISSN 0022-0000. Special issue on STOC, 1999 (Atlanta, GA).

[7] F. A. Chudak. Improved approximation algorithms for uncapacitated facility location. In *Integer programming and combinatorial optimization (IPCO)*, volume 1412 of *Lecture Notes in Comput. Sci.*, pages 180–194. Springer, Berlin, 1998.

[8] F. A. Chudak and D. B. Shmoys. Improved approximation algorithms for the uncapacitated facility location problem. *SIAM J. Comput.*, 33(1):1–25, 2003. ISSN 0097-5397.

[9] R. Cole. Parallel merge sort. *SIAM J. Comput.*, 17(4):770–785, 1988.

[10] M. Elkin. Distributed approximation: a survey. *SIGACT News*, 35(4):40–57, 2004.

[11] J. Gehweiler, C. Lammersen, and C. Sohler. A distributed $O(1)$-approximation algorithm for the uniform facility location problem. In *SPAA'06*, pages 237–243, 2006.

[12] T. F. Gonzalez. Clustering to minimize the maximum intercluster distance. *Theoret. Comput. Sci.*, 38(2-3):293–306, 1985. ISSN 0304-3975.

[13] S. Guha and S. Khuller. Greedy strikes back: improved facility location algorithms. *J. Algorithms*, 31(1):228–248, 1999. ISSN 0196-6774.

[14] A. Gupta and K. Tangwongsan. Simpler analyses of local search algorithms for facility location. *CoRR*, abs/0809.2554, 2008.

[15] D. S. Hochbaum and D. B. Shmoys. A unified approach to approximation algorithms for bottleneck problems. *J. Assoc. Comput. Mach.*, 33(3):533–550, 1986. ISSN 0004-5411.

[16] D. S. Hochbaum and D. B. Shmoys. A best possible heuristic for the k-center problem. *Mathematics of Operations Research*, 10(2):180–184, 1985. ISSN 0364765X. URL http://www.jstor.org/stable/3689371.

[17] K. Jain and V. V. Vazirani. Approximation algorithms for metric facility location and k-median problems using the primal-dual schema and Lagrangian relaxation. *Journal of the ACM*, 48(2):274–296, 2001.

[18] K. Jain, M. Mahdian, E. Markakis, A. Saberi, and V. V. Vazirani. Greedy facility location algorithms analyzed using dual fitting with factor-revealing LP. *Journal of the ACM*, 50(6):795–824, 2003.

[19] J. JáJá. *An Introduction to Parallel Algorithms.* Addison-Wesley, 1992. ISBN 0-201-54856-9.

[20] T. Kanungo, D. M. Mount, N. S. Netanyahu, C. D. Piatko, R. Silverman, and A. Y. Wu. A local search approximation algorithm for k-means clustering. *Comput. Geom.*, 28(2-3):89–112, 2004. ISSN 0925-7721.

[21] S. Khuller, U. Vishkin, and N. E. Young. A primal-dual parallel approximation technique applied to weighted set and vertex covers. *J. Algorithms*, 17(2):280–289, 1994.

[22] M. R. Korupolu, C. G. Plaxton, and R. Rajaraman. Analysis of a local search heuristic for facility location problems. *J. Algorithms*, 37(1):146–188, 2000. ISSN 0196-6774. (Preliminary version in 9th SODA, 1998).

[23] C. Koufogiannakis and N. E. Young. Distributed and parallel algorithms for weighted vertex cover and other covering problems. In *PODC*, pages 171–179, 2009.

[24] F. T. Leighton. *Introduction to Parallel Algorithms and Architectures: Array, Trees, Hypercubes.* Morgan Kaufmann Publishers Inc., San Francisco, CA, USA, 1992. ISBN 1-55860-117-1.

[25] M. Luby. A simple parallel algorithm for the maximal independent set problem. *SIAM J. Comput.*, 15(4):1036–1053, 1986.

[26] M. Luby and N. Nisan. A parallel approximation algorithm for positive linear programming. In *STOC'93*, pages 448–457, 1993.

[27] M. Mahdian, E. Markakis, A. Saberi, and V. Vazirani. A greedy facility location algorithm analyzed using dual fitting. In *Approximation, randomization, and combinatorial optimization (Berkeley, CA, 2001)*, volume 2129 of *Lecture Notes in Comput. Sci.*, pages 127–137. Springer, Berlin, 2001.

[28] M. Mahdian, Y. Ye, and J. Zhang. Improved approximation algorithms for metric facility location problems. In *Approximation algorithms for combinatorial optimization*, volume 2462 of *Lecture Notes in Comput. Sci.*, pages 229–242. Springer, Berlin, 2002.

[29] T. Moscibroda and R. Wattenhofer. Facility location: distributed approximation. In *PODC'05*, pages 108–117, 2005.

[30] R. Motwani and P. Raghavan. *Randomized algorithms.* Cambridge University Press, New York, NY, USA, 1995. ISBN 0-521-47465-5.

[31] M. Pál and E. Tardos. Group strategyproof mechanisms via primal-dual algorithms. In *FOCS'03*, pages 584–593, 2003.

[32] S. Pandit and S. V. Pemmaraju. Return of the primal-dual: distributed metric facility location. In *PODC'09*, pages 180–189, 2009.

[33] S. Rajagopalan and V. V. Vazirani. Primal-dual *RNC* approximation algorithms for set cover and covering integer programs. *SIAM J. Comput.*, 28(2):525–540, 1998.

[34] D. B. Shmoys, É. Tardos, and K. Aardal. Approximation algorithms for facility location problems (extended abstract). In *STOC*, pages 265–274, 1997.

[35] A. Srinivasan. New approaches to covering and packing problems. In *SODA*, pages 567–576, 2001.

[36] M. Sviridenko. An improved approximation algorithm for the metric uncapacitated facility location problem. In *Integer programming and combinatorial optimization*, volume 2337 of *Lecture Notes in Comput. Sci.*, pages 240–257. Springer, Berlin, 2002.

[37] Q. Wang and K. H. Cheng. Parallel time complexity of a heuristic algorithm for the k-center problem with usage weights. In *Proc. IEEE Symposium on Parallel and Distributed Processing*, pages 254–257, Dec. 1990.

[38] N. E. Young. Sequential and parallel algorithms for mixed packing and covering. In *FOCS*, pages 538–546, 2001.

Simplifying Concurrent Algorithms by Exploiting Hardware Transactional Memory

Dave Dice
Sun Labs
dave.dice@oracle.com

Yossi Lev
Sun Labs, Brown Univ.
levyossi@cs.brown.edu

Virendra J. Marathe
Sun Labs
virendra.marathe@oracle.com

Mark Moir
Sun Labs
mark.moir@oracle.com

Dan Nussbaum
Sun Labs
dan.nussbaum@oracle.com

Marek Olszewski
Sun Labs, MIT
mareko@csail.mit.edu

ABSTRACT

We explore the potential of hardware transactional memory (HTM) to improve concurrent algorithms. We illustrate a number of use cases in which HTM enables significantly simpler code to achieve similar or better performance than existing algorithms for conventional architectures. We use Sun's prototype multicore chip, code-named Rock, to experiment with these algorithms, and discuss ways in which its limitations prevent better results, or would prevent production use of algorithms even if they are successful. Our use cases include concurrent data structures such as double ended queues, work stealing queues and scalable non-zero indicators, as well as a scalable malloc implementation and a simulated annealing application. We believe that our paper makes a compelling case that HTM has substantial potential to make effective concurrent programming easier, and that we have made valuable contributions in guiding designers of future HTM features to exploit this potential.

Categories and Subject Descriptors

D.1.3 [**Programming Techniques**]: Concurrent Programming

General Terms

Algorithms, Design, Performance

Keywords

Transactional Memory, Synchronization, Hardware

1. INTRODUCTION

This paper explores the potential of hardware transactional memory (HTM) to simplify concurrent algorithms, data structures, and applications. To this end, we present a number of relatively simple algorithms that use HTM to solve problems that are substantially more difficult to solve in conventional systems.

At the risk of stating the obvious, simplifying concurrent algorithms has many potential benefits, including improving the readability, maintainability, and flexibility of code, making concurrent programming tractable for more programmers, and adding to the array of techniques for programmers to use to exploit concurrency. Furthermore, simplifying code by separating program semantics from implementation details enables applications to benefit from platform-specific implementations and future improvements thereto.

Our experiments use the HTM feature of a prototype multicore processor developed at Sun, code named Rock. Our aim is to demonstrate the potential of HTM *in general* to simplify concurrent algorithms, not to evaluate Rock's HTM feature (this is reported elsewhere [11, 12]). In some cases we use Rock's HTM feature in a way that may not be suitable for production use. Throughout the paper, we attempt to illuminate the properties of an HTM feature required for a particular technique to be successful and acceptable to use. We hope that our observations in this regard are helpful to designers of future HTM features.

The examples we present merely scratch the surface of the potential ways HTM can be used to simplify and improve concurrent programs. Nonetheless, we believe that they yield valuable contributions to understanding of the potential of HTM, and important observations about what must be done in order to exploit it.

In Section 2, we review a number of techniques that employ HTM. Section 3 presents our first use of HTM, implementing a concurrent double-ended queue (deque), which is straightforward with transactions, and surprisingly difficult in conventional architectures. Next, in Section 4, we examine an important restricted form of deque called a *work stealing queue* (ws-queue), which is at the heart of a number of parallel programming patterns. In Section 5, we use HTM to simplify the implementation of Scalable Non-Zero Indicators (SNZIs), which have been shown to be useful in improving the scalability of software TM (STM) algorithms and readers-writer locks. Next, in Section 6, we show how HTM can be used to obviate the need for special kernel drivers to support a scalable malloc implementation that significantly outperforms other implementations in widespread use. Finally, in Section 7, we explore the use of HTM to simplify a simulated annealing application from the PARSEC benchmark suite [4], while simultaneously improving its performance. We summarize our observations and guidance for designers of future HTM features in Section 8, and conclude in Section 9.

2. TECHNIQUES FOR EXPLOITING HTM

Given hardware support for transactions, simple wrappers can be used to execute a block of code in a transaction. Such wrappers can diagnose reasons for transaction failures and decide whether to back off before retrying, for example. A *best-effort* HTM feature such as Rock's [11, 12] does not guarantee to be able to commit a given transaction, even if it is retried repeatedly. In this case, an alternative software technique is needed in case a transaction cannot be committed. The use of such alternatives can be made transparent with compiler and runtime support. This is the approach taken by Hybrid TM (HyTM) [7] and Phased TM (PhTM) [27], which support transactional programs in such a way that transactions can use HTM, but can also transparently revert to software alternatives when the HTM transactions do not succeed.

Transactional Lock Elision (TLE) [10, 36] aims to improve the performance of lock-based critical sections by using hardware transactions to execute nonconflicting critical sections in parallel, without acquiring the lock. When such use of HTM to elide a lock acquisition is not successful, the lock is acquired and the critical section executed normally. TLE is similar to Speculative Lock Elision as proposed by Rajwar and Goodman [34], but is more flexible because software rather than hardware determines when to use a hardware transaction and when to acquire the lock. Compared to HyTM and PhTM, TLE imposes less overhead on single-threaded code, and requires less infrastructure, but puts the burden back on the programmer to determine and enforce locking conventions, avoid deadlocks, etc., and furthermore, does not compose well.

3. DOUBLE-ENDED QUEUES

In this section, we consider a concurrent double-ended queue (*deque*). The LinkedBlockingDeque implementation included in java.util.concurrent [23] synchronizes all accesses to a deque using a single lock, and therefore is blocking and does not exploit parallelism between concurrent operations, even if they are at opposite ends of the deque and do not conflict.

Improving on such algorithms to allow nonconflicting operations to execute in parallel is surprisingly difficult. The first obstruction-free deque algorithms, due to Herlihy *et al.* [20] are complex and subtle, and require careful correctness proofs.

Achieving a stronger nonblocking progress property, such as lock-freedom [17], is more difficult still. Even lock-free deques that do not allow concurrent operations to execute in parallel are publishable results [30], and even using sophisticated multi-location synchronization primitives such as DCAS, the task is difficult enough that incorrect solutions have been published [8], fixes for which entailed additional overhead and substantial verification efforts [14].

Even if we do not require a nonblocking implementation, until recently, constructing a deque algorithm that allows concurrent opposite-end operations without deadlocking has generally been regarded to be difficult [22]. In fact, the authors only became aware of such an algorithm *after* the initial version of this paper was submitted. Paul McKenney presents two such algorithms in [29]. While the simpler of the two (which uses two separate single-lock deques for head and tail operations) is relatively straightforward in hindsight, it was not immediately obvious even to some noted concurrency experts [18, 28]. In fact, McKenney invented the more complex algorithm first. This algorithm, which hashes requests into multiple single-lock dequeues, is not at all straightforward, and yields significantly lower throughput than the simpler one does.

In contrast, the transactional implementation is no more complex than sequential code that could be written by any competent programmer, regardless of experience with concurrency. We believe such implementations are generally straightforward given adequate support for transactions. Essentially, we just write simple, sequential code and wrap it in a transaction. The details of exploiting parallelism and avoiding deadlock are thus shifted from the programmer to the system. In addition to significantly simplifying the task of the programmer, this also establishes an abstraction layer that allows for portability to different architectures and improvements over time, without modifying the application code.

Our experimental harness creates a deque object initially containing five elements, and spawns a specified number of threads, dividing them evenly between the two ends of the deque. Each thread repeatedly and randomly pushes or pops an element on its end of the deque, performing 100,000 such operations. We measure the interval between when the first thread begins its operations and when the last thread completes its operations. Each data point presented is the geometric mean of three values obtained by omitting the maximum and minimum of five measured throughputs.

We test a variety of implementations, varying synchronization mechanisms and the algorithm that implements the deque itself. A simple unsynchronized version (labeled *none* in Figure 1) gives a sense of the cost of achieving correct concurrent execution. We test several non-HTM versions, including a compiler-supported STM-only implementation using the TL2 STM [13], two direct-coded single-lock implementations (pthreads lock, hand-coded spinlock) and the simpler of McKenney's lock-based algorithms [29]. Using HTM, we test direct-coded and compiler-supported HTM-only implementations, a compiler-supported PhTM [27] implementation (using TL2 when in the software phase) and a compiler-supported HyTM [7] implementation (using the SkySTM STM [25]). Finally, we test a TLE [10, 36] implementation combining HTM and our hand-coded spinlock.

Our deque implementations do not admit much parallelism between same-end operations, and threads perform deque operations as fast as they can, with relatively little "non critical" work between deque operations. We therefore do not expect much more than a 2x improvement over single-threaded throughput.

Figure 1 presents the results of our deque experiments. First, note that the single-thread overhead for the various synchronization mechanisms ranges between factors of 2.5 and 4 (except for STM-only synchronization, for which the slowdown is much worse).

STM-only synchronization (labeled *C-STL2* in Figure 1) uses compiler support built on a TL2-based [13] runtime system. Overheads for STM-only execution are significant, with a single-thread run achieving only 12% of the pthread-lock version's throughput.

Next we consider lock-based implementations. The pthreads lock implementation that comes with Solaris™ (*D-PTL*) yields a 77% decrease in throughput going from one thread to two, with a continuing decrease (to 83%) as we go out to sixteen threads. To factor out possible effects of using a general-purpose lock that parks and unparks waiting threads, and the Solaris™ implementation thereof in particular, we also test a simple hand-coded spinlock.

The hand-coded spinlock (*D-SpLB*) yields essentially the same single-thread throughput as the pthreads lock, and a 34% *speedup* on two threads, dropping off a bit at higher thread counts. It may seem counterintuitive that *any* speedup is achieved with a single-lock implementation, but this is possible because there is some code that executes between the end of one critical section and the beginning of the next, which can be overlapped by multiple threads.

McKenney's two-queue algorithm [29] (*ldeque*) performs well. Its single-thread performance is only 13% lower than that of the pthreads lock, and it achieves nearly a 2x speedup at two threads, most of which it maintains out to sixteen threads. This algorithm is nearly the best across the board, only being outperformed (slightly) by the direct-coded HTM-only implementation.

The direct-coded HTM-based implementation without backoff (not shown) generally fails to complete within an acceptable period of time at larger thread counts, due to excessive conflicts. This is consistent with our previous experience [11, 12]: due to Rock's simple "requester-wins" conflict resolution mechanism, transactions can repeatedly abort each other if they are re-executed immediately; this problem can be addressed with a simple backoff mechanism.

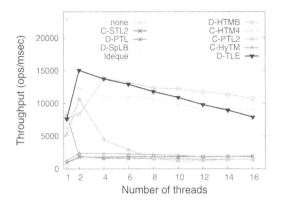

Figure 1: Deque benchmark. Key: *none*: **unsynchronized.**
C-STL2: **Compiled STM-only (TL2).** *D-PTL*: **Direct-coded
single-lock (pthreads).** *D-SpLB*: **Direct-coded single-lock (spinlock with backoff).** *ldeque*: **McKenney's two-lock deque implementation.** *D-HTMB*: **Direct-coded HTM-only (with backoff).**
C-HTM4: **Compiled HTM-only.** *C-PTL2*: **Compiled PhTM
(TL2 STM).** *C-HyTM*: **Hybrid TM.** *D-TLE*: **Direct-coded TLE.**

The direct-coded HTM-only implementation (*D-HTMB*) employs
such a backoff mechanism, implemented in software. This version
yields 94% of the single-thread throughput yielded by the pthreads-
lock version, achieving nearly a factor of two speedup when run on
four or more threads and maintaining most of that speedup out to
sixteen threads. (We have not investigated in detail why the expected performance increase is not realized at two threads.)

The compiler-supported HTM-only implementation (*C-HTM4*)
performs similarly to the direct-coded implementation but associated compiler and runtime infrastructure reduces throughput by
about 20% over most of the range.

PhTM (*C-PTL2*) incurs significant overhead, yielding 63% of the
pthreads-lock's single-thread throughput, but increasing throughput by a factor of 1.9 going from one thread to two. However, this
throughput degrades severely at higher threading levels because a
large fraction of transactions are executed in software.

Two factors contribute to this poor performance. First, it can
be difficult to diagnose the reason for hardware transaction failure on Rock and to construct a general and effective policy about
how to react [11, 12]. Given our results with the HTM-only implementations, it seems that PhTM should not need to resort to using software transactions for this workload, but our statistics show
that this happens reasonably frequently, especially at higher concurrency levels. Coherence conflicts are the dominant reason for
hardware transaction failure, so we believe our PhTM implementation could achieve better results by trying harder to complete the
transaction using HTM before failing over to software mode.

Second, in our current PhTM implementation, when one transaction resorts to using STM, all other concurrent (HTM) transaction
attempts are aborted; when they retry, they use STM as well. Subsequently, to ensure forward progress, we do not attempt to switch
back to using HTM (system-wide) until the thread that initiated
the switch to software mode completes. Furthermore, we do not attempt to prioritize the transaction being run by that thread, or to aggressively switch back to hardware mode when it is done—instead,
when that transaction finishes, all other concurrently-running software transactions are allowed to finish before the switch back to
hardware mode is made. All of these observations point to significant opportunities to improve the performance of PhTM for

this workload, which we have not yet attempted. Nevertheless,
we should not underestimate the difficulty of constructing efficient
policies that are effective across a wide range of workloads.

HyTM (*C-HyTM*) has even more overhead than PhTM, yielding only 15% of the pthreads-lock's throughput on a single thread.
HyTM's instrumentation of the hardware path is responsible for
most of the slowdown. HyTM does achieve about a factor of two
speedup on two threads, maintaining most of that advantage out to
sixteen threads, outperforming PhTM on eight or more threads.

While the HTM-only results reported above indicate strong potential for hardware transactions to make some concurrent programming problems significantly easier, we emphasize that there is no
guarantee that Rock's HTM will not repeatedly abort transactions
used by deque operations. Without such a guarantee, we could
not recommend using the HTM-only implementations in production code, even though it works reliably in these experiments. Furthermore, our PhTM and HyTM results illustrate the overhead and
complexity of attempting to transparently execute transactions in
software when the HTM is not effective.

Transactional Lock Elision (TLE) [10] (*D-TLE*) yields good performance over the entire range; in fact, on two threads, it is best of
any of the variants tested. While this is encouraging for the use of
best-effort HTM features, we note that TLE gives up several advantages of the transactional programming approach, such as compos-
ability of data structures implemented using it and the ability to use
it to implement nonblocking data structures. Whether a TM system
is useful for building nonblocking data structures depends on properties of the HTM, as well as properties of the software alternative
used in case hardware transactions fail. The original motivation for
TM was to make it easier to implement nonblocking data structures,
so designers of future HTM features should consider the ability of
a proposed implementation to do so, in addition to the following
conclusions we draw from our experience:

- If guarantees are made for small transactions, such that there
  is no need for a software alternative, TM-based implementations of concurrent data structures that use such transactions
  are easier to use and are more widely applicable.

- Better conflict resolution policies than Rock's simple requester-wins can reduce the need for aggressive backoff, which
  may be difficult to tune in a way that is generally effective.

- Avoiding transaction failures for relatively obscure reasons,
  such as sibling interference [11, 12], and providing better
  support for diagnosing the reasons for transaction failures,
  significantly improves the usefulness of an HTM feature.

4. WORK STEALING QUEUES

In this section, we discuss the use of HTM in implementing
work stealing queues (ws-queues) [1, 6], which are used to support
a number of popular parallel programming frameworks. In these
frameworks, a runtime system manages a set of *tasks* using a technique called *work stealing* [1, 6, 16]. Briefly, each thread in such a
system repeatedly removes a task from its ws-queue and executes
it. Additional tasks produced during this execution are pushed onto
the thread's ws-queue for later execution. For load balancing purposes, if a thread finds its queue empty, it can *steal* one or more
tasks from another thread's ws-queue.

The efficiency of the ws-queues, especially for the common case
of accessing the local ws-queue, can be critical for performance.
As a result, a number of clever and intricate ws-queue algorithms
have been developed [1, 6, 16]. In most cases, a thread pushes and
pops tasks to and from one end of its ws-queue, and stealers steal

from the other end. Thus, only the owner accesses one end, and only pop operations are executed on the other.

Existing ws-queue implementations [1, 6, 16] exploit these restrictions to achieve simpler and more efficient implementations than are known for general double-ended queues. Nonetheless, these algorithms are quite complex, and reasoning about their correctness can be a daunting task. As an illustration of the complexity of such algorithms, querying a Sun internal bug database for "work stealing" yields 21 hits, all of which are related to the work stealing algorithm used by the HotSpot Java VM's garbage collector, and a search for bugs tagged with the names of the files in which the work stealing algorithm is implemented yields 360 hits, many of which are directly related to tricky concurrency-related bugs.

In this section, we present several transactional work stealing algorithms, which demonstrate tradeoffs between simplicity, performance, and requirements of the HTM feature used. We have evaluated these algorithms on Rock using the benchmark used in [6]. Briefly, this benchmark simulates the parallel execution of a program represented by a randomly generated DAG, each node of which represents a single task. A node's children represent the tasks spawned by that node's task. The parameters D and B control the depth of the tree and the maximum branching factor of each node, respectively; see [6] for details. For this paper, we concentrate on medium sized trees generated using D=16 and B=6; our experiments with other values yield similar conclusions. The ws-queue array's size is initialized to 128 entries. We measure the time to "execute" the whole DAG, and we report the result as throughput in terms of tasks processed per millisecond. For each point, we discard the best and the worst of five runs, and report the geometric mean of the remaining three. We observed occasional variability for all algorithms, which we believe is related to architecture and system factors rather than the algorithms themselves.

The results of our experiments are presented in Figure 3. All of the algorithms scale well, which is not surprising given that concurrent accesses to ws-queues happen only as a result of stealing, which is rare. The Chase-Lev (CL) [6] algorithm provides the highest throughput, and the algorithm due to Arora *et al.* (ABP) [1] provides about 96% of the throughput of CL.

We begin with a trivial algorithm that stores the elements of the ws-queue in an array, and implements all operations by enclosing simple sequential code in a transaction. When a pushTail operation finds the array full, it "grows" the array by replacing it with a larger array and copying the relevant entries from the old array to the new one. Similarly, when a popTail operation finds a drop in the size of the ws-queue, with respect to the size of the array, below a particular threshold (one-third, only if the array size is greater than 128, in our experiments), it "shrinks" the array by replacing it with a smaller array. (Note that although the array did not grow or shrink in our experiments reported here, it did grow and shrink a few times in some other experiments, with no noticeable performance impact.) This algorithm, executed using PhTM (see Section 2), scales as well as ABP and CL (see curve labeled "PhTM (all)"), but provides only about 68% of the throughput of CL.

In our experiments, nearly all transactions succeeded using HTM, so the performance gap between PhTM and CL is mainly due to the overhead of the system infrastructure for supporting transactions (including the latency of hardware transactions). Nonetheless, unless the HTM can commit transactions of *any* size, the trivial algorithm requires a software alternative such as PhTM provides—and associated system software complexity and overhead—due to the occasional need to grow or shrink the size of the ws-queue.

We therefore modified the algorithm to avoid large transactions altogether, in order to explore what could be achieved by directly

```
1   WSQueue {
2     volatile int head;
3     volatile int tail;
4     int size;
5     Value[] array;
6   }
7
8   void WSQueue::pushTail(Value new_value)
9   {
10    while (true) {
11      BEGIN_TXN;              // delete for nontxl
12      if (tail - head != size) {
13        array[tail % size].set(new_value);
14        tail++;
15        return;               // commits, see caption
16      }
17      COMMIT_TXN;             // delete for nontxl
18      grow();
19    }
20  }
21
22  void WSQueue::grow()
23  {
24    int new_size = size * 2;
25    copyArray(new_size);
26  }
27
28  void WSQueue::shrink()
29  {
30    int new_size = size / 2;
31    copyArray(new_size);
32  }
33
34  void WSQueue::copyArray(int new_size)
35  {
36    Value[] old_array = array;
37    Value[] new_array = new Value[new_size];
38    for (int i=head; i<tail; i++) {
39      new_array[i % new_size].set
40              (array[i % size].get());
41    }
42    BEGIN_TXN;
43    array = new_array;
44    size = new_size;
45    COMMIT_TXN;
46    delete old_array;
47  }
48
49  Value WSQueue::stealHead()
50  {
51    BEGIN_TXN;
52    return (head < tail) ?
53          array[head++ % size].get() : Empty;
54    COMMIT_TXN;
55  }
56
57  Value WSQueue::popTail()   // Txl version
58  {
59    Value tailValue;
60    BEGIN_TXN;
61    tailValue = (tail == head) ?
62            Empty : array[--tail].get();
63    COMMIT_TXN;
64    if (sizeBelowThreshold()) shrink();
65    return tailValue;
66  }
67
68  Value WSQueue::popTail()   // Nontxl version
69  {
70    tail--;
71    MEMBAR_STORE_LOAD;        // see text
72    int h = head;
73    // head = h;              // see text
74    if (tail < h) {
75      tail++;          // failed; undo increment
76      return Empty;
77    }
78    if (sizeBelowThreshold()) shrink();
79    return array[tail % size].get();
80  }
```

Figure 2: Work stealing pseudocode. Returning from within a transaction commits the transaction.

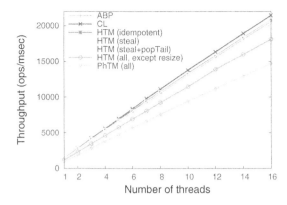

Figure 3: Work stealing benchmark. $D = 16$, $B = 6$.

using an HTM that makes guarantees only for small transactions. The first such algorithm is presented in Figure 2. To avoid using large transactions for operations that grow the ws-queue, we modified the pushTail operation so that it commits without attempting to increase the size of the ws-queue if it observes that the ws-queue is full (see line 12). In this case, the thread executing the operation then calls `grow` (line 18) *outside* the transaction.

The `grow` procedure calls `copyArray`, which does array allocation and copying nontransactionally (lines 37–41), and uses a transaction to make the new array current, and record its size (lines 42–45). Like the Chase-Lev algorithm [6], `grow` does not need to modify the head and tail variables.

Similarly, to avoid large transactions for operations that shrink the ws-queue, we modified the popTail operation so that the transaction contains only the code that pops an item from the ws-queue (see lines 61 and 62). Like the `grow` procedure, the `shrink` procedure does its array allocation and copying nontransactionally, and uses a transaction to make the new array current.

The algorithm with this modification is slightly more difficult to reason about because of the possibility of stealHead operations being executed concurrently with growing or shrinking the array. However, much of the simplicity of the trivial algorithm is retained: All of the operations that modify the state of the ws-queue are still executed entirely within transactions, and we only need to consider complete executions of the stealHead operation between steps of the `grow` and `shrink` procedures, rather than considering arbitrary interleavings. Concurrent stealHead operations can only reduce the relevant portion of the array for copying, but no harm is done if stolen elements are unnecessarily copied, as they are outside the range specified by head and tail.

Previous ws-queue algorithms [1, 6] have been carefully optimized to avoid expensive synchronization primitives (such as CAS) in common-case pushTail and popTail operations. As a result, these more complex algorithms are likely to outperform our simple HTM-based algorithm. Our results confirm that this is the case on Rock. Specifically, the modified algorithm—labeled "HTM (all, except resize)" in Figure 3—improves on the trivial PhTM algorithm by roughly 23%, but still provides only about 84% of the throughput of CL. Therefore, we explored whether we could eliminate transactions from the common-case operations, while still using them in less common operations to keep the algorithm simple.

First, we modified pushTail to not use a hardware transaction in the common case (it still uses one in `copyArray`). The resulting algorithm—labeled "HTM (steal+popTail)" in Figure 3—performs

about 10% better than the modified algorithm described above, and comes very close to matching the hand-crafted ABP algorithm.

However, reasoning that the algorithm remains correct with this change becomes somewhat more difficult for several reasons. The order of the store to tail and to the array element is now important, whereas in the transactional version, they could have been written in either order. This affects not only the difficulty of reasoning about the algorithm, but also how it is expressed: We are prevented from using the compact post-increment notation to increment tail, as in the transactional stealHead and popTail operations.

Furthermore, head may change during the pushTail operation. As a result, the pushTail operation may grow the array unnecessarily if a concurrent stealHead operation has made a slot available in the array. This behavior is benign in terms of correctness, but the algorithm is at least somewhat more complex because of the need to reason about it. Even so, this algorithm is still considerably simpler and easier to reason about than the previous work stealing algorithms, and its performance is very close to theirs.

We next modified the algorithm so that popTail also does not use transactions. We must now reason about concurrent interleavings of popTail and stealHead operations, whereas this was not necessary when both were executed as transactions. As before, the fact that the only operations that can execute during the popTail operation are stealHead operations executed using transactions makes this reasoning fairly manageable.

However, now a more subtle issue arises. Since the transactional version of popTail is executed atomically, the order of its accesses to head and tail is unimportant. In the nontransactional version, it is critical that popTail updates tail and *then* reads head to determine whether the ws-queue was empty when tail was modified (in which case we need to undo this modification, and return Empty). In many memory consistency models, including TSO [37] (which is supported by Rock), the load of head may be reordered before the store to tail. To avoid this, a `membar #storeload` instruction is required (line 71). Identifying the problem and reasoning that the memory barrier solves it is considerably more complex than thinking about the less aggressively optimized versions. Furthermore, the memory barrier makes the popTail code less compact and less readable than the transactional version.

Nonetheless, using a transactional stealHead operation still makes it considerably easier to reason about this algorithm than existing nontransactional algorithms [1, 6], in which popTail uses CAS to remove the last element, to avoid a race with a concurrent stealHead operation that cannot occur if stealHead is transactional. This algorithm—labeled "HTM (steal)" in Figure 3—performs comparably with ABP, and delivers about 96% of the throughput of CL.

Researchers have recently observed [24, 33] that in some contexts, *idempotent work stealing*, in which an element may be returned from a ws-queue multiple times, suffices for some applications. They show that, given this weaker semantics, the memory barrier discussed above can be elided. However, their algorithms are not much less complex than the existing algorithms, and are considerably more complex than our algorithms that use HTM.

Interestingly, given the weaker semantics required by idempotent work stealing, we too can eliminate the memory barrier from the popTail operation. However, this change alone results in an algorithm in which a popTail operation and a concurrent stealHead operation can each think the other took the last element from the ws-queue, which results in an element being lost. We overcome this problem by performing an additional store in popTail in order to "undo" the effect of potential concurrent stealHead operations (see line 73). The resulting algorithm is significantly simpler than others [24, 33], again due to the use of hardware transactions for the stealHead operation. Whether this algorithm yields any performance benefit over the version with the memory barrier depends on details of the architecture; for Rock, where memory barriers are inexpensive, we observed little significant improvement.

Although our first modification eliminated the large transactions associated with growing and shrinking the ws-queue, it may seem that implementations that use HTM directly for other operations require guarantees for at least small transactions. Interestingly, however, with a little care, successful stealing is not necessary to ensure forward progress of the overall application. In particular, even if *all* stealHead operations are unsuccessful, eventually every thread will complete the work in its own ws-queue and the application will complete. Thus, we can use a purely best-effort HTM feature with the algorithm that uses hardware transactions only for stealHead operations, but not for the simpler algorithms that use transactions for pushTail and/or popTail.

Finally, we note that our HTM-based algorithms can deallocate the old array immediately after replacing it with a new one (see line 46 in Figure 2) because the owner is guaranteed not to access the old array again, and any concurrent stealHead operations accessing the old array fail when the new array is installed. This behavior of the stealer depends on the assumption that the hardware transaction is effectively "sandboxed" – a transaction either aborts immediately when something it has read changes, or its inconsistent state is not observable to the external world. This avoids the need for complex and expensive memory management techniques such as hazard pointers [31] or Repeat Offender mechanisms [19], or simpler but wasteful techniques such as not deallocating the old array, which are often used in practice.

5. SCALABLE NON-ZERO INDICATORS

Next we explore using HTM to simplify and improve the performance of Scalable Non-Zero Indicators (or SNZI, which is pronounced "snazzy") [15]. SNZI objects have been used in scalable STM implementations [25] and readers-writer locks [26]. SNZI supports Arrive, Depart and Query operations, with Query indicating whether there is a *surplus* of arrivals (i.e., there have been more Arrive than Depart operations).

A SNZI implementation based on a single counter is trivial but not scalable. Previous scalable SNZI algorithms use a tree of SNZI nodes: Arrive and Depart operations on a child may invoke Arrive and/or Depart on its parent, but only when the surplus at the child might change from zero to nonzero, or vice versa. These algorithms maintain the following SNZI invariant: *every SNZI node has a surplus iff it has a descendant that has a surplus or the number of Arrive operations that started at the node is greater than the number of Depart operations that started at the node.* This way, threads may arrive at any node (the corresponding depart should start at the same node), and propagate upward only as necessary to maintain the invariant. Queries are made directly at the root. Note that an arrival at a node must propagate up the tree only if the node's surplus is zero, and a departure must propagate only if it will make the surplus zero. This way, SNZI nodes act as "filters" for nodes higher in the tree, thus reducing contention and improving scalability.

A key difficulty in previous CAS-based SNZI algorithms arises when multiple threads concurrently arrive at a node with zero surplus. Ensuring that exactly one of them propagates a surplus up the tree in a nonblocking manner involves first attempting to do the propagation, then detecting whether multiple threads have performed such a propagation, and if so, performing compensating depart operations to ensure the invariant is maintained. These algorithms are subtle and require careful correctness proofs.

As in Section 4, by using hardware transactions we can avoid

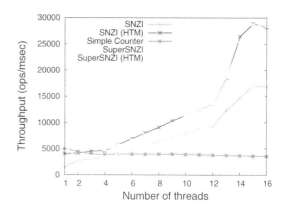

Figure 4: Throughput results for SNZI algorithm.

the "mistakes" due to concurrency, and thus avoid the need for complicated code to detect and compensate for them. In particular, if two threads concurrently attempt to propagate a surplus to the same parent node using hardware transactions, these transactions will conflict and will not be able to both commit successfully. If one succeeds, the other will retry and find that it no longer needs to propagate its contribution to the surplus up the tree, allowing it to complete its operation fairly quickly.

Interestingly, because the writes performed by a hardware transaction are not visible to others until it commits, our HTM-based SNZI algorithm can update each node's counter *before* propagating its surplus to the node's parent (if needed). This allows a simple iterative description of the algorithm, whereas previous algorithms are expressed recursively, requiring careful reasoning about the order of recursive execution.

We compare the performance of our HTM-based SNZI algorithms to the previous CAS-based implementations, as well as to a simple counter-based implementation. For both the HTM and CAS-based SNZI algorithms, we include *SuperSNZI* [15] versions that adapt to the level of contention by switching between direct arrivals at the root node (when there is little contention) and tree arrivals that start at the tree leaves (when contention on the root node grows). To test scalability, each of a number of threads repeatedly arrives at and departs from a single SNZI object without doing any work in between the operations. An additional thread repeatedly queries the SNZI once per microsecond. Each data point is the geometric mean of the throughputs of 10 runs.

Figure 4 presents the performance results for each of the algorithms. At low thread counts, the HTM-based SuperSNZI version performs slightly better than the non-SuperSNZI HTM-based variant, both of which perform comparably to the simple counter-based and non-HTM SuperSNZI algorithms at one thread. At higher thread counts, the HTM-based algorithms perform comparably to one another, outperforming the non-HTM-based algorithms by a wide margin—at 16 threads, they nearly double the throughput of the non-HTM SNZI algorithms and achieve nearly eight times the throughput of the simple counter-based algorithm.

Interestingly, the non-SuperSNZI HTM variant remains competitive at low thread counts—performing better than the simple counter-based solution at two threads and higher—despite the fact that the HTM transactions often have to update multiple SNZI nodes at low contention levels. This is in contrast to the non-HTM SNZI versions, where the more complex SuperSNZI algorithm is required in order to remain competitive with the simple counter at low thread counts. Without it, the basic CAS-based SNZI algorithm performs

Implementation	T=1		T=2		T=4		T=8		T=16		T=256	
libc	1019	1920K	723	1928K	624	1944K	619	2040K	624	2104K	622	5560K
libumem	1153	2336K	2289	2408K	4705	2616K	9026	2712K	15381	3416K	12433	13080K
Hoard	1154	3048K	2285	3504K	4419	4416K	8914	6240K	16319	9952K	10520	63648K
CLFMalloc	1980	3080K	4178	3016K	8490	3032K	16736	11256K	31948	19528K	31134	69576K
LFMalloc/RCS	9767	2344K	19221	2352K	36767	2432K	72667	2656K	128660	3040K	126191	7904K
LFMalloc/HTM	3988	2360K	8020	2368K	16167	2448K	32147	2736K	63055	3056K	59881	7280K
LFMalloc/TLE	4177	2360K	8438	2368K	16775	2512K	33445	2736K	66178	3056K	65253	7920K
LFMalloc/mutex	1502	2360K	2961	2368K	5927	2448K	11641	2736K	20847	3056K	20709	7856K
LFMalloc/spin	4582	2360K	9112	2368K	18152	2448K	36154	2672K	69527	3056K	29749	7920K

Table 1: Malloc results, showing throughput in malloc-free pairs per millisecond and memory footprint in KB.

more than three times worse than the simple counter-based algorithm when run with one thread, largely due to the multiple CAS operations required to make changes to multiple nodes in the tree.

Note that, with 16 timed threads, one shares a core with the query thread, impeding scalability. Also, the improvement for all algorithms at 12 threads is because, after 12 threads, the nodes in middle layer of the tree have non-zero surpluses most of the time. Thus, more Arrive operations can complete without modifying the root node, resulting in shorter Arrive operations *and* less contention.

We have also implemented the *resettable* SNZI-R variant [15, 25] using HTM, with similar conclusions.

The HTM implementations used in these experiments include a software backup that can be used if transactions fail repeatedly, and thus these algorithms can be used with purely best-effort HTM that makes no guarantees about committing small transactions. For the Arrive operation, the software backup arrives directly at the root with a CAS operation (this is correct without changes to the HTM transactions thanks to Rock's strong atomicity guarantee). In the case of a Depart operation that fails to complete using a hardware transaction, the software backup uses the same Depart code used by the CAS-based SNZI algorithm, starting from the node at which the previous Arrive operation started.

This algorithm is still considerably simpler than the CAS-based SNZI algorithm as compensating undo operations are not needed, as discussed above. Moreover, the transactions used are small enough that the software backup was never used during our experiments (our SNZI trees are three levels deep, which has been sufficient to achieve scalable results on some of the largest multicore systems available [25, 26]). Thus, given an HTM with guarantees for such transactions, similar results could be achieved with an even simpler algorithm that does not include the software backup.

6. MEMORY ALLOCATION

In this section, we use HTM to simplify LFMalloc, a fast and scalable memory allocator due to Dice and Garthwaite [9]. The key idea behind LFMalloc is to maintain per-processor data structures to alleviate the poor scalability of central data structures such as those used by libc's allocator, while avoiding the excessive memory use of per-thread data structures. Per-processor data structures ensure that synchronization conflicts occur only due to scheduling events such as preemption and migration. LFMalloc exploits this observation using lightweight Restartable Critical Section (RCS) synchronization implemented using special Solaris™ scheduling hooks. The result is excellent performance and a reasonable memory footprint. It has the significant disadvantage, however, of requiring a special kernel driver to implement RCS.

Using HTM to synchronize the per-processor data structures eliminates the need for a special kernel driver. (Interestingly, for convenience, Dice and Garthwaite built a transactional interface imple-

mented using RCS.) LFMalloc is described in detail in [9]; here we describe changes we made, and compare the performance of various implementations.

We use the mmicro benchmark [9] to compare malloc implementations. Each thread repeatedly allocates 64 200-byte blocks and then frees them in the same order. In Table 1, we report throughput in malloc/free pairs per millisecond and total memory footprint in KB. As expected, libc's malloc consistently has the smallest memory footprint, but provides low single-thread throughput, becoming even worse as the number of threads increases. libumem and Hoard [2] improve on its single-thread performance and have much better scalability, but also have significantly larger memory footprints. Consistent with previous results [9], unmodified LFMalloc consistently provides dramatically better throughput than any of the previous implementations, and its memory footprint is much lower than that of libumem or Hoard, though somewhat higher than that of the libc allocator. For comparison we also include Michael's Lock-free CLFMalloc [32] allocator, which consistently provides higher throughput than other previous allocators.

The high single-thread performance of LFMalloc is due to the lack of any synchronization on local heaps, except when a thread is preempted or migrated during an allocation. LFMalloc also scales better than any of the previous implementations due to its use of per-processor data structures. We have also rerun other benchmarks described in [9], and overall the performance and scalability of LFMalloc is substantially better than previous allocators. However, its use of a special kernel driver is a barrier to adoption.

By replacing the RCS blocks in LFMalloc with hardware transactions, we obviate the need to implement and install a special kernel driver. As shown in Table 1, the resulting implementation has significantly higher overhead than the RCS-based LFMalloc (due to the latency of hardware transactions), but it still performs significantly better than the previous implementations, and maintains LFMalloc's competitive memory footprint. Even so, without a guarantee that the HTM feature can always (eventually) commit the small and simple transactions used in this implementation, it would not be usable in practice (see [12] for a detailed discussion).

We achieved a more robust implementation that is usable even without guarantees for such transactions using a per-processor lock to protect the per-processor data structures, and then using TLE to elide the lock. As shown in Table 1, TLE performs slightly worse than HTM for one thread due to the additional overhead to examine the lock. However, TLE outperforms HTM slightly at higher threading levels because when a transaction fails, there is a quick way to make progress (namely acquiring the lock), whereas the HTM-only version may retry repeatedly. Furthermore, there is virtually no lock contention because conflicts occur only due to relatively rare events such as preemption and migration.

We also tried implementations that use *only* a lock, without TLE. As in Section 3, we tried both pthreads mutex locks and hand-coded spinlocks. As before, the hand-coded spinlock provides significantly better performance than the more general pthreads lock.

It is tempting to conclude that the spinlock implementation should be used. However, all of the lock-based implementations can suffer when a thread is preempted while holding the lock, as evidenced by their poor performance with 256 threads. We note that, even though this *can* happen with the TLE variant, it is much less likely because the lock is held much less frequently. In contrast, if a hardware transaction is aborted when the thread executing it is preempted, no thread ever has to wait for another that is not running.

While preemption while holding a lock can be avoided by using the Solaris `schedctl` library call, our results show that HTM has the potential to provide an effective alternative approach. A robust HTM with low latency and guarantees for small simple transactions could deliver significantly better performance than the previous allocators tested, perhaps approaching the performance of the RCS-based `LFMalloc` implementations, while avoiding long waiting periods due to locking, and not requiring a special kernel driver.

7. THE CANNEAL BENCHMARK

Next we discuss how HTM can be used to simplify the `canneal` benchmark of the PARSEC suite [4], which uses a simulated annealing algorithm to optimize the routing cost of a chip design. In each iteration, each thread examines two randomly chosen elements on the chip, and evaluates how swapping their locations would affect the routing cost. The locations are swapped if the cost would decrease, and with some probability even if it would increase, to allow escaping from local optima; this probability is inversely proportional to the increase in the routing cost, but is also decreased during runtime to allow convergence.

The original implementation [4] uses an aggressive synchronization scheme that performs swaps atomically, but accesses location information without holding locks when deciding whether to swap. As a result, the locations of the elements examined when the gain or loss from a potential swap is evaluated may change during the evaluation. Such "races" can cause an inaccurate evaluation of the swap gain/loss value. However, the simulated annealing algorithm should naturally recover over time from any resulting mistakes [4].

While the benchmark is mostly straightforward, the code to swap two elements atomically is more complex. To avoid deadlock, locations are first ordered. Then:

1. The location of the first element is "locked" by atomically replacing the pointer to its location with a special value using a CAS instruction. While the location is locked, it cannot be changed by any other swap operation; moreover, attempts to read the location spin until it is unlocked.

2. A second CAS atomically fetches the location of the second element, and replaces it with the original location of the first.

3. The location of the first element is unlocked and replaced with the original location of the second using a regular store instruction, as the location does not change once locked.

This approach also complicates read accesses, which must first check whether a location is locked.

7.1 Simplifying the Atomic Swap Operation

We replaced the above-described code for swapping two elements with a hardware transaction that simply executes the swap. This change allowed us to replace all read accesses to location information with simple loads. This is possible because Rock's HTM feature provides *strong atomicity* [5], so that ordinary loads and stores can be used together with transactions.

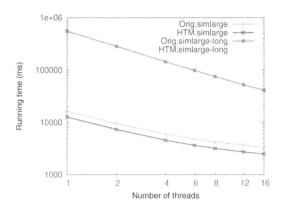

Figure 5: Execution time for the `canneal` benchmark.

Our modified implementation simply retries hardware transactions without backoff until they succeed; we expect very little contention between swap operations for any reasonable input. If the HTM feature does not make guarantees for the small transactions used by this algorithm, a software alternative would be necessary. Given that conflicts are rare, it seems that a simple TLE scheme should be effective. However, using TLE would again require additional overhead and at least some additional complexity for reading locations. This again illustrates the benefit of being able to rely on hardware transactions without providing a software alternative.

To evaluate our modified implementation on Rock, we initially used the PARSEC suite's [4] `simlarge` configuration. We first observed that the original implementation did not scale very well. Bhadauria *et al.* [3] made similar observations, blaming workload imbalance and a large serial portion that caused one thread to execute more operations than all others. Investigating further, however, we found that by increasing the number of iterations executed, a routing with significantly lower cost is achieved, and the scalability of the algorithm improves substantially.

Figure 5 shows results for the original implementation vs. the simplified variant of `canneal`, denoted as Orig and HTM respectively, for two configurations: the first uses the original `simlarge` configuration, which evaluates $1,920,000$ potential swaps, and the second (labeled with "simlarge-long" in Figure 5) uses the same input file, but evaluates $75,000,000$ potential swaps. We measure the execution time for varying thread counts, using the configurations described above. The results are plotted on a log-log scale.

In a single-thread run, the simplified HTM-based implementation completes about 21% faster than the original for the short run, and about 25% faster for the long run. This gain is mostly due to reading locations using regular load instructions, which is enabled by the use of a hardware transactions to swap elements.

Both implementations achieved a speedup of about 5x using 16 threads on the short run, and over 12x on the long one. All runs of the same configuration achieved about the same routing cost, with the long configuration achieving a 28% cheaper routing.

These results show that the ability to execute a simple hardware transaction that swaps the value of two memory locations enables significant performance improvements *and* simpler code. We reiterate, however, that the simpler code is acceptable in practice only given sufficient guarantees that a software alternative for the transactions is not needed.

7.2 Further simplifications and improvements

Depending on the HTM feature used, additional simplifications and performance improvements are possible.

First, if *all* accesses to location information were performed inside hardware transactions, we could eliminate the level of indirection for location information by storing and accessing it "in place". (This level of indirection could possibly be eliminated anyway by encoding location information in a single word, but such constraints do not apply if the data is accessed in hardware transactions.) Whether this would result in a performance benefit depends crucially on the latency of a small transaction that is read-only, or at least does not modify any shared data or encounter any conflicts. This points out the potential benefit of optimizing certain classes of small and simple transactions.

Second, if we could use a single hardware transaction to decide whether to perform a swap and perform it if so, this would eliminate the races discussed above, obviating the need to reason about whether they affect correctness and convergence.

However, this more ambitious simplification places significantly stronger requirements on the HTM feature. In particular, the computation to decide whether to swap two elements examines their neighbors; thus the number of locations accessed is not bounded by a constant in the algorithm. Furthermore, the transaction would make nested function calls (e.g., for the `exp()` library function). On Rock, it is not reasonable to rely on hardware transactions alone for such transactions (see [11, 12]). Making this reasonable would require that the HTM guarantee to (eventually) commit transactions that perform a number of data-dependent loads that is not bounded by any constant in the algorithm (the number of neighbors depends on the input data), and that make nested function calls.

8. DISCUSSION

The examples we have presented—and others we have omitted due to time and space constraints—make a compelling case that HTM has strong potential to simplify the development of concurrent algorithms that are scalable, efficient, and correct. However, in many cases this potential depends critically on certain properties of the HTM feature used.

An important property required by many of our examples is the ability to rely on a small and simple hardware transaction to eventually commit. Without such a guarantee, most of our examples require a software alternative to hardware transactions. Apart from adding significant complexity in most cases, the need to work correctly with such software alternatives can add significant overhead to common-case code, regardless of how infrequently the alternative is actually needed. For example, using TLE to provide a software alternative for swap transactions in `canneal` requires reads to check the lock, adding significant overhead.

An important question is how such guarantees can be stated, and how programmers can determine whether their code meets the criteria for the guarantee. This can be difficult, given the range of possible scenarios, however unlikely they may be. The requirement to provide such guarantees can stifle important innovation and optimizations. This tension may be alleviated by a last-resort fallback mechanism, such as parking all other threads, aborting their transactions, and executing a transaction alone if it fails to complete. While this can make designs more flexible and criteria for guarantees easier to state, dependence on such mechanisms in any but rare circumstances may have disastrous performance consequences.

We also note that some of our algorithms depend on strong atomicity [5]. Examples include the simple load for read accesses in `canneal`, and the optimized local operations in our work stealing algorithms. If strong atomicity were not provided, correct algorithms could be achieved in many cases by replacing simple load and store instructions with very small transactions. However, the performance benefit of using the nontransactional instructions

would be lost unless transaction latency were very low, at least for such simple transactions. We have observed several examples in which HTM could be used profitably if common-case latency for certain classes of transactions were very low. Classes to consider include: read-only transactions, transactions that do not write shared data, or do not conflict on shared data, transactions that access only a single (shared) memory location, etc.

Rock's simple "requester-wins" conflict resolution policy requires the use of backoff in situations of heavy contention. While backoff is simple and can be hidden in library code, it has the disadvantage that it may waste time by backing off too much or not enough if not properly tuned to the workload. Designers should therefore consider more sophisticated conflict resolution policies to reduce the number of aborts and the reliance on backoff mechanisms.

The original motivation for HTM [21] was to make it easier to build nonblocking data structures. The question arises, therefore, of whether a given HTM feature is actually useful for this purpose. Nonblocking progress guarantees typically forbid waiting only *in software*. For example, waiting for a response to a request for a cache line is not usually considered to violate nonblocking progress conditions. However, if an HTM implementation allows a running transaction to wait for a preempted one, it cannot claim to support nonblocking data structures. For example, it would not enable sharing between an interrupt handler and the interrupted thread [35].

It seems easy to avoid such problems by aborting any transaction being executed by a thread when it is preempted or suffers another long-latency event such as a page fault. However, there is a tension between such approaches and the desire to provide guarantees that certain classes of transactions can eventually be completed. Such guarantees may need to be stated in terms of the length of transactions relative to the frequency of disruptive events such as interrupts. Balancing these concerns is a challenge for designers who hope to achieve all of the potential benefits of HTM.

We have also noted the value of Rock's "sandboxing" property, namely that it is not possible to cause bad events such as program crashes inside a transaction. This property allows simpler and faster code to be used in many cases, for example because consistency checks that are normally required for correctness can be elided in the common case. However, we must emphasize the importance of good feedback about the reasons for transaction failure, both to allow appropriate responses and to facilitate debugging and analysis. As reported previously [11, 12], Rock's feedback about aborted transactions can be difficult to interpret in some cases, and its support for debugging of code inside hardware transactions is very limited. Future HTM features should improve on both aspects.

9. CONCLUDING REMARKS

We have presented several examples demonstrating the potential power of hardware transactional memory (HTM) to enable the development of concurrent algorithms that are simpler than nontransactional counterparts, perform better than them, or both. We have also highlighted the properties required of an HTM feature to enable these uses, and summarized these observations with the hope of assisting designers of future HTM features to enable maximal benefit from HTM.

References

[1] N. S. Arora, R. D. Blumofe, and C. G. Plaxton. Thread Scheduling for Multiprogrammed Multiprocessors. In *Proc. 10th annual ACM Symposium on Parallel Algorithms and Architectures*, pages 119–129, 1998.

[2] E. D. Berger, K. S. McKinley, R. D. Blumofe, and P. R. Wilson. Hoard: a scalable memory allocator for multithreaded applications. In

Proc. ninth international conference on Architectural Support for Programming Languages and Operating Systems, pages 117–128, New York, NY, USA, 2000. ACM.

[3] M. Bhadauria, V. M. Weaver, and S. A. McKee. Understanding PARSEC performance on contemporary CMPs. In *Proc. International Symposium on Workload Characterization*, October 2009.

[4] C. Bienia, S. Kumar, J. P. Singh, and K. Li. The PARSEC benchmark suite: Characterization and architectural implications. In *Proc. 17th International Conference on Parallel Architectures and Compilation Techniques*, October 2008.

[5] C. Blundell, E. C. Lewis, and M. Martin. Deconstructing Transactions: The Subtleties of Atomicity. In *the 4th Annual Workshop on Duplicating, Deconstructing, and Debunking*, 2005.

[6] D. Chase and Y. Lev. Dynamic Circular Work-Stealing Deque. In *Proc. 17th Annual ACM Symposium on Parallelism in Algorithms and Architectures*, pages 21–28, 2005.

[7] P. Damron, A. Fedorova, Y. Lev, V. Luchangco, M. Moir, and D. Nussbaum. Hybrid transactional memory. In *Proc. 12th Symposium on Architectural Support for Programming Languages and Operating Systems*, Oct. 2006.

[8] D. Detlefs, C. H. Flood, A. Garthwaite, P. Martin, N. N. Shavit, and G. L. Steele Jr. Even better DCAS-based concurrent deques. In *Proc. 14th International Conference on Distributed Computing*, pages 59–73. IEEE, 2000. http://citeseer.nj.nec.com/detlefs00even.html.

[9] D. Dice and A. Garthwaite. Mostly lock-free malloc. In *Proc. 3rd International Symposium on Memory Management*, pages 163–174, New York, NY, USA, 2002. ACM.

[10] D. Dice, M. Herlihy, D. Lea, Y. Lev, V. Luchangco, W. Mesard, M. Moir, K. Moore, and D. Nussbaum. Applications of the adaptive transactional memory test platform. Transact 2008 workshop. http://research.sun.com/scalable/pubs/TRANSACT2008-ATMTP-Apps.pdf.

[11] D. Dice, Y. Lev, M. Moir, and D. Nussbaum. Early experience with a commercial hardware transactional memory implementation. In *Proc. 14th international conference on Architectural Support for Programming Llanguages and Operating Systems*, pages 157–168, New York, NY, USA, 2009. ACM.

[12] D. Dice, Y. Lev, M. Moir, D. Nussbaum, and M. Olszewski. Early experience with a commercial hardware transactional memory implementation. Technical Report TR-2009-180, Sun Microsystems Laboratories, 2009.

[13] D. Dice, O. Shalev, and N. Shavit. Transactional locking II. In *Proc. International Symposium on Distributed Computing*, 2006.

[14] S. Doherty and M. Moir. Nonblocking algorithms and backwards simulation. In *Proc. 21st International Conference on Distributed Computing*, 2009.

[15] F. Ellen, Y. Lev, V. Luchangco, and M. Moir. SNZI: Scalable NonZero Indicators. In *Proc. 26th Annual ACM Symposium on Principles of Distributed Computing*, pages 13–22, 2007.

[16] M. Frigo, C. E. Leiserson, and K. H. Randall. The Implementation of the Cilk-5 Multithreaded Language. In *Proc. ACM SIGPLAN 1998 Conference on Programming Language Design and Implementation*, pages 212–223, 1998.

[17] M. Herlihy. Wait-Free Synchronization. *ACM Transactions on Programming Languages and Systems*, 13(1):124–149, 1991.

[18] M. Herlihy. Personal communication, 2010. See "Sadistic homework problem" in various presentations.

[19] M. Herlihy, V. Luchangco, P. Martin, and M. Moir. Nonblocking memory management support for dynamic-sized data structures. *ACM Trans. Comput. Syst.*, 23(2):146–196, 2005.

[20] M. Herlihy, V. Luchangco, and M. Moir. Obstruction-free synchronization: Double-ended queues as an example. In *Proc. 23rd International Conference on Distributed Computing Systems*, 2003.

[21] M. Herlihy and J. E. B. Moss. Transactional memory: Architectural support for lock-free data structures. In *Proc. 20th Annual International Symposium on Computer Architecture*, pages 289–300, 1993.

[22] M. Herlihy and N. Shavit. *The Art of Multiprocessor Programming*. Morgan Kaufmann, 2008.

[23] JSR166: Concurrency Utilities. http://gee.cs.oswego.edu/dl/concurrency-interest/.

[24] D. Leijen, W. Schulte, and S. Burckhardt. The Design of a Task Parallel Library. In *Proc. 24th ACM SIGPLAN Conference on Object Oriented Programming Systems Languages and Applications*, pages 227–242, New York, NY, USA, 2009. ACM.

[25] Y. Lev, V. Luchangco, V. J. Marathe, M. Moir, D. Nussbaum, and M. Olszewski. Anatomy of a Scalable Software Transactional Memory. In *Proc. 4th ACM SIGPLAN Workshop on Transactional Computing*, 2009. http://research.sun.com/scalable/pubs/TRANSACT2009-ScalableSTMAnatomy.pdf.

[26] Y. Lev, V. Luchangco, and M. Olszewski. Scalable Reader-Writer Locks. In *Proc. 21st Annual Symposium on Parallelism in Algorithms and Architectures*, pages 101–110, 2009.

[27] Y. Lev, M. Moir, and D. Nussbaum. PhTM: Phased Transactional Memory. The Workshop on Transactional Computing, Aug. 2007. http://research.sun.com/scalable/pubs/TRANSACT2007-PhTM.pdf.

[28] P. McKenney. Personal communication, 2010.

[29] P. E. McKenney. *Is Parallel Programming Hard, And, If So, What Can You Do About It?* kernel.org, Corvallis, OR, USA, 2010. http://www.rdrop.com/users/paulmck/perfbook/perfbook.2010.01.23a.pdf [Viewed January 24, 2010].

[30] M. Michael. Cas-based lock-free algorithm for shared deques. In *Proc. Ninth Euro-Par Conference on Parallel Processing*, pages 651–660, 2003.

[31] M. M. Michael. Hazard Pointers: Safe Memory Reclamation for Lock-Free Objects. *IEEE Transactions on Parallel and Distributed Systems*, 15(6):491–504, 2004.

[32] M. M. Michael. Scalable Lock-free Dynamic Memory Allocation. In *Proc. ACM SIGPLAN 2004 Conference on Programming Language Design and Implementation*, pages 35–46, 2004.

[33] M. M. Michael, M. T. Vechev, and V. A. Saraswat. Idempotent work stealing. In *Proc. 14th ACM SIGPLAN Symposium on Principles and Practice of Parallel Programming*, pages 45–54, New York, NY, USA, 2009. ACM.

[34] R. Rajwar and J. R. Goodman. Speculative lock elision: Enabling highly concurrent multithreaded execution. In *Proc. 34th International Symposium on Microarchitecture*, pages 294–305, Dec. 2001.

[35] H. E. Ramadan, C. J. Rossbach, D. E. Porter, O. S. Hofmann, A. Bhandari, and E. Witchel. MetaTM/txLinux: Transactional memory for an operating system. In *Proc. 34th Annual International Symposium on Computer Architecture*, 2007.

[36] C. J. Rossbach, O. S. Hofmann, D. E. Porter, H. E. Ramadan, A. Bhandari, and E. Witchel. TxLinux: Using and managing hardware transactional memory in the operating system. In *Proc. 21st ACM SIGOPS Symposium on Operating Systems Principles*, pages 87–102, 2007.

[37] The SPARC Architecture Manual Version 8, 1991. http://www.sparc.org/standards/V8.pdf.

334

A Universal Construction for Wait-Free Transaction Friendly Data Structures

Phong Chuong
Dept. of Computer Science
University of Toronto
Toronto, ON, Canada
chuongph@cs.utoronto.ca

Faith Ellen
Dept. of Computer Science
University of Toronto
Toronto, ON, Canada
faith@cs.utoronto.ca

Vijaya Ramachandran
Computer Science Dept.
University of Texas at Austin
Austin, TX, USA
vlr@cs.utexas.edu

ABSTRACT

Given the sequential implementation of any data structure, we show how to obtain an efficient, wait-free implementation of that data structure shared by any fixed number of processes using only shared registers and CAS objects. Our universal construction is transaction friendly, allowing a process to gracefully exit from an operation that it wanted to perform, and it is cache-efficient in a multicore setting where the processes run on cores that share a single cache. We also present an optimized shared queue based on this method.

Categories and Subject Descriptors

E.1 [**Data Structures**]: Distributed data structures; Lists, stacks, and queues

General Terms

Algorithms, Theory

Keywords

Universal construction, wait-free, abortable data structure, transaction friendly, cache-efficiency

1. INTRODUCTION

In a recent CACM article, Maurice Herlihy [12] said, "For the foreseeable future, concurrent data structures will lie at the heart of multicore applications, and the larger our library of scalable concurrent data structures, the better we can exploit the promise of multicore architectures". One way to obtain a large variety of provably correct concurrent data structures is to have methods for automatically constructing them from sequential implementations. These are called universal constructions.

A universal construction is *wait-free* if every process can complete its operation on the shared data structure within a finite number of its own steps, no matter how other processes are scheduled. It is *non-blocking*, a less stringent condition, if the operation of some process is completed within

a finite number of steps. Non-blocking and wait-free universal constructions were first introduced by Herlihy [10], who proved that p-consensus objects and registers are sufficient to implement any sequentially specified data structure in a shared-memory system with p or fewer processes. Since then, a variety of other non-blocking and wait-free universal constructions have been proposed. (See Section 2.)

A transaction is a collection of shared memory operations, that either all fail (without changing the shared memory) or all succeed, as an atomic operation. Failure may occur as a result of a conflict between transactions, or because a process that is performing the transaction decides not to complete it. We call a universal construction *transaction friendly* if a process can exit from (or 'abort') an uncompleted operation on the shared data structure that it no longer wishes to perform. This might happen, for example, if a process decides not to complete an operation on the shared data structure because it observes too much contention.

If each process is responsible for performing its own operation, it is often easy for a process to exit from an operation that it has not yet completed. In wait-free universal constructions, where processes may help one another complete their operations, difficulties can arise. In particular, it is necessary to ensure that there is no other process that is still trying to help perform that operation and might eventually succeed in doing so.

In this paper, we present the first wait-free universal construction that is transaction friendly. It only performs read, write, and compare&swap (CAS) on relatively small single records, and hence can be implemented on existing machines. We represent the sequential data structure directly and apply operations to it in-place. A feature of our implementation is that queries (i.e. operations that do not change the sequential data structure) do not change our representation of the shared data structure. If a sequential data structure has size s and is shared by p processes, we use a total of $\Theta(s + p)$ words of shared memory. If t is the worst case time complexity to perform an operation on the sequential data structure and w is the maximum number of different words of memory accessed by an operation on the sequential data structure, then the worst case number of steps a process takes to perform an operation on the shared data structure is $\Theta(pt \log w)$, of which $\Theta(pw)$ are shared memory accesses.

When implemented on a multicore with p cores and a shared cache, the cache complexity of our algorithm matches the sequential cache bound Q for any sequence S of data structure operations in the following sense. Suppose the memory is organized into blocks and f is the worst-case number of blocks read when performing a single operation. If the shared cache can hold at least $4pf$ blocks, then the cache complexity of our universal construction when executing S remains $O(Q)$. Here, each operation in S can be invoked by an arbitrary process.

Like previous wait-free universal constructions, our universal method applies operations to the data structure one at a time. For the special case of a wait-free queue, we have an optimized implementation that allows a process to perform an enqueue concurrently with a process performing a dequeue. It also allows multiple processes to perform dequeue simultaneously if the queue is empty. Care is needed to ensure no bad interactions arise between concurrent operations.

The remainder of the paper begins with a description of previous non-blocking and wait-free universal constructions. Next, we present our universal construction and a sketch of its correctness proof. A full proof of correctness appears in [5, 6]. This is followed by an analysis of the caching performance of our universal construction on a multicore machine. Finally, we give a brief overview of our optimized implementation of a shared queue. We conclude with a discussion of future directions.

2. RELATED WORK

A classical approach to construct concurrent data structures is to use mutual exclusion to ensure that only one process accesses the data structure at a time. The problem here is that if a process crashes while it is in the critical section, further accesses to the data structure are blocked.

A more recent approach is to use software transactional memory [8, 14, 15], which provides support for implementing transactions. Each operation on a shared data structure can be treated as a separate transaction. A transactional memory system ensures that successful transactions do not interfere with one another, and hence are correct, even if they are performed simultaneously. A process whose transaction has failed may decide to continue to retry the transaction; however, it is possible that it never succeeds. Moreover, because of their generality, transactional memory systems may incur a lot of overhead as compared to a universal construction.

Herlihy's original approach [10] was to represent the data structure by a shared linked list of its states, as a sequence of operations are performed. To perform an operation, a process appends a record, containing the operation and its inputs, to the end of the shared list. Processes use a p-consensus, CAS, or LL/SC object stored in each record to agree on the record that will follow it in the list. When a record has been appended to the shared list, the sequence number of the operation (i.e., the distance of the record from the beginning of the list), the state of the data structure after the operation has been applied, and the output of the operation, are also stored in the record. For nondeterministic operations, processes must also agree on the new state and the output of the operation. To achieve wait-freedom, each process i begins an operation by creating a record containing the operation and announces it by storing a pointer to it in location i of an announce array. This record is given priority to be the m'th record of the list whenever $i = m \bmod p$. All processes help apply the operation in the last record of the list before they try to append a new record to the list. The paper also describes how a counter in each record and

pointers to the last record each process has accessed can enable a process to determine when the record will no longer be accessed, and hence can be reused. This is important to prevent the space used by the shared data structure from becoming unbounded, but increases the time overhead. In this implementation, the worst case number of steps a process takes to perform its operation on the shared data structure is $\Theta(p^2 + ps + pt)$, of which $\Theta(p^2 + ps)$ are shared memory accesses. The number of records used by this implementation is $\Theta(p^3)$, each of which contains a copy of the entire data structure (of size at most s), an $O(\log p)$-bit counter, and an unbounded sequence number.

Another wait-free universal construction [9, 11], also by Herlihy, uses a CAS (or LL/SC) object $root$ that points to a record containing the current state of the data structure. To apply an operation to the data structure, the process makes a private copy, L, of the record, applies the operation to L, and then tries to change $root$ to point to L. Each process has a finite collection of at most p records. When it needs a new record into which to copy the data structure, it selects one that is not being used by any other process. To facilitate this, each record stores the number of processes currently using it. Before using the current record, a process must increment this count and then check that the record is still current. After a process finishes using a record, it must decrement its counter. In [11], wait-freedom is achieved by operation combining: After announcing its operation, a process looks through the announce array for uncompleted operations and applies all of them to L, before trying to change $root$ to point to L. If it is unsuccessful, it does this entire procedure again. Whether or not it is successful the second time, its operation is guaranteed to have been applied to the share data structure. Wait-freedom can also be achieved by having a mod p counter in $root$ [9]. The value of the counter is the index of the process whose announced operation is to be given priority. It is incremented whenever the pointer in $root$ is changed. Both variants use $\Theta(p^2)$ records, each of size $s + \Theta(\log p)$ and, in the worst case, a process does $\Theta(p^2 + ps + pt)$ shared memory accesses to perform its operation. For large linked data structures, when performing an operation, it suffices to copy only those parts of the data structure that are changed (plus, recursively, any parts that point to them). However, because storage that a process allocates may need to remain in the data structure, the memory management is more complicated.

To improve efficiency for large objects, Anderson and Moir [2] use an additional level of indirection. The data structure is viewed as being stored in a large array, which is divided into a fixed number of blocks and the LL/SC object $root$ points to an array of pointers, which point to these blocks. When a process wants to write to a block, it makes a private copy of that block, and writes to its copy. Subsequent reads and writes of that block by the process are performed on its private copy. When the operation is complete, the process tries to change $root$ to point to a new array containing pointers to these private blocks and all of the unmodified blocks, so that the private blocks become part of the array. If there are b blocks and each operation in the sequential implementation updates at most w' blocks, then their construction uses $\Theta(s + p^2 + pb + pw's/b)$ space and a process performs $\Theta(pb + p^2t + pw's/b)$ shared memory accesses in the worst case to perform its operation.

Barnes [4] describes a non-blocking universal construction

based on LL/SC that does not require copying large parts of the shared data structure. Moreover, it allows different processes to perform operations on different parts of the data structure simultaneously. When a process wants to perform an operation on the shared data structure, it copies the variables it needs to access into local memory, to create a cached copy of the relevant parts of the data structure, and applies the operation on its cached copy. Then the process tries to lock all the variables in the shared data structure that it has cached and, if successful, changes all of the variables in the shared data structure that it changed locally. Finally, whether it is successful or not, the process releases all of its locks. If it was unsuccessful, it starts its operation over again. To ensure that *some* process will be successful, all processes try to lock variables in the same order. To prevent a process that has crashed from locking out all other processes, a process that encounters a locked variable will help the process j that locked it, by trying to lock the rest of the variables that j cached and, if successful, updating those variables that have changed values. This requires each process to write a list of the at most w variables in its cache, together with their original and final values, into shared memory. The total space used by this construction is $\Theta(s + pw)$. In the worst case, a process requires $\Theta(t)$ steps for each attempt it makes to perform its operation, including $\Theta(w)$ shared memory accesses. However, because this implementation is not wait-free, the number of attempts a process makes to perform its operation is unbounded.

Afek, Dauber, and Touitou [1] present two wait-free universal constructions that are more efficient than Herlihy's. In their Group Update algorithm, active processes (i.e. those that have operations they wish to perform) maintain a dynamic list of their identifiers stored at the root of a full binary tree of height $\log p$. Like [9, 11], there is a CAS or LL/SC object that points to the shared data structure. To perform an operation, a process announces it in an announce array and then tries to add itself into the list, while also helping other processes. This takes $\Theta(\min\{p, k \log k\})$ shared memory accesses, where k is the contention. After its identifier has been inserted into the list, a process copies the data structure to a new region of shared memory and does operation combining, applying all of the uncompleted operations of the processes on the dynamic list to the shared data structure. Then it attempts to update the pointer to the shared data structure to point to its updated version. If it was unsuccessful and its operation was not applied, the process repeats this set of steps a second time, after which its operation is guaranteed to have been performed. Finally a process removes itself from the dynamic list. The total space used is $\Theta(ps + p^2 \log p)$ and the worst case number of shared memory accesses performed by a process to perform its operation is $\Theta(\min\{p, k \log k\} + kt + s)$. Jayanti [13] observed that the step complexity of inserting a process into the list and removing a process from the list can be improved to $\Theta(\log p)$, but under the unrealistic assumption that a word of memory can store p identifiers and be accessed in a single step.

In Afek Dauber and Touitou's Individual Update algorithm, processes maintain a queue of active processes represented by a tree. After announcing an operation, a process enters the queue and moves towards the root. When a process reaches the root, its operation is applied to the data structure. While moving to the root, a process helps at

most $k - 1$ other processes along the way to reach the root and apply their operations to the shared data structure. Depending on how operations are applied to the data structure, the worst-case step complexity of performing an operation is either $\Theta(ks + kt)$ or $\Theta(kt \log t)$ and requires either $\Theta(ps)$ or $\Theta(s + pt)$ words of shared memory.

More recently, Fatourou and Kallimanis [7] improved the Group Update algorithm, using two trees in a clever way, instead of one, to obtain space complexity $\Theta(ps + p^2)$ and worst-case step complexity $\Theta(\min\{k, \log p\} + kt + s)$, including $\Theta(k + s)$ shared memory operations. For large objects, they combined this universal construction with Anderson and Moir's construction, to improve the time complexity of Anderson and Moir's construction, without increasing its space complexity.

3. A UNIVERSAL CONSTRUCTION

In this section, we present a universal construction that creates a wait-free, linearizable implementation of an object from a deterministic sequential implementation.

We consider a system of p processes that communicate through a shared memory containing registers (which support read and write) and CAS objects (which support CAS, also known as compare&swap, and read), each of which is large enough to hold a small amount of information, for example pointers, names of operations, words from the sequential implementation, or arguments of operations, plus a sequence number. In addition, each process has a private local memory.

Section 3.1 describes algorithm Perform($op_i, input_i$), which is executed by process i when it needs to perform an operation on the given data structure. This execution includes a macro Help in which process i accesses the shared data structure to perform either its own operation or the operation of another process. The details of Help are deferred to section 3.2. Together, Perform and Help constitute our universal construction.

3.1 Procedure Perform

A process i begins an operation by reading *gate* on line P1 and announcing the operation in the CAS object $A[i]$, its element of the *announce array* A, on line P3.

The CAS object *gate* controls access to the stored representation of the shared data structure. It has two fields, *proc* and *seq*, which are initially $-$ and 1, respectively. When *gate.proc* $= i$, all processes help process i perform its announced operation on the shared representation. When this operation has been completed, *gate.proc* is reset to $-$ and *gate.seq* is incremented, on line P21 or F3. Thus the operation performed when *gate.seq* $= k$ is the kth operation applied to the shared data structure.

The announce array A is an array of CAS objects indexed by process id, in which a process announces an operation it wants to perform on the shared data structure. Each component, $A[i]$, has four fields: *op*, *seq*, *flag* and *arg*. The type of the operation is stored in $A[i].op$. The value of *gate.seq* read by process i immediately before announcing an operation is stored in $A[i].seq$. We show that each time process i announces a new operation, *seq* is larger, so we can use $(i, A[i].seq)$ to identify this operation. The status of process i's current operation is stored in *flag*: *done* indicates that process i has not yet announced an operation or the current operation has been applied to the data structure;

active indicates that the current operation has not yet been applied; and *exit* indicates that process i has requested that the current operation not be performed, if it has not already been assigned a position in the linearization. The input arguments of the current operation are stored in $A[i].arg$, if $A[i].flag$ contains *active* or *exit*, and the output arguments are stored there if $A[i].flag = done$. If there are a lot of input or output arguments, $A[i].arg$ can, instead, contain a pointer to a list of arguments.

After announcing its operation, if process i sees, on line P11, that $gate = (-, k)$, then it helps to choose the process whose operation will be performed next. It gives priority to process $k \bmod p$ as in [10], to ensure wait-freedom. In macro ChooseNextOp, process i sees whether process $k \bmod p$ has an announced operation to be performed, by checking whether $A[k \bmod p].flag = active$ on line C3. If so, process i will decide to nominate process $k \bmod p$. Otherwise, it will check that its own operation has not been completed, on lines C4–C5, and decide to nominate itself, on line C6. Process i nominates process m_i by performing a CAS on line P13 that tries to change $gate$ from $(-, k)$ to (m_i, k). It will read $gate$ on line P14 to find out which process was chosen.

To help perform process $g_i.proc$'s announced operation, process i begins by reading $A[g_i.proc]$ into a_i, on line P16. It first checks if $a_i.flag = done$, on line P17, and, if so, does not need to help this operation, since it has been completed. To avoid an announced operation from being performed more than once, process i checks whether $a_i.seq \leq g_i.seq$ on line P17. If not, then g_i contains an old value of $gate$. In this case, the $g_i.seq^{th}$ operation in the linearization has been completed and process i will not perform Help. If $a_i.seq \leq g_i.seq$ and $a_i.flag \neq done$, then process i will execute Help on behalf of operation $(g_i.proc, a_i.seq)$. Afterwards, on line P19 or P20, process i writes the outputs of the operation into $A[g_i.proc].arg$ and changes $A[g_i.proc].flag$ to *done* using a single CAS. Finally, process i tries to update $gate$ to $(-, g_i.seq + 1)$ on line P21, so that the next operation can be performed.

Whenever a process i wants to exit its announced operation, it changes $A[i].flag$ to *exit* on line P6, so that other processes do not choose this operation, even if i has priority to be chosen. However, process i does not return with *exited* immediately after setting $A[i].flag$ to *exit*. The reason for this is that some other processes may already be in the midst of helping to perform this operation. Instead, after changing $A[i].flag$ to *exit*, process i executes the rest of the iteration. We show that, by the time process i finishes the iteration, $gate.seq$ will have been incremented. Thus, when any process tries to help perform a subsequent operation, it reads $A[i]$ after $A[i].flag$ was set to *exit*. Since $A[i].flag$ does not become *active* until process i announces another operation on line P3, the exited operation will not be performed.

3.2 Procedure Help

When a process i performs Help, it tries to apply the operation $(g_i.proc, a_i.seq)$ as the $g_i.seq^{th}$ operation in the linearization. Help uses the caching mechanism in [4]: When a process first accesses a variable from the shared data structure during an invocation of Help, it caches it. Subsequent reads and writes of a cached variable are performed locally. After the operation has been completed locally, the process updates those records in the shared data structure whose values should be changed.

Perform(op_i, $input_i$) by process i:

P1. $g_i \leftarrow$ read $gate$
P2. $a_i \leftarrow (op_i, g_i.seq, active, input_i)$
P3. $A[i] \leftarrow$ write a_i
P4.   while $a_i.flag = active$ do
P5.   if process i should exit its operation then
P6. $CAS(A[i], a_i, (a_i.op, a_i.seq, exit, input_i))$
P7. $a_i \leftarrow$ read $A[i]$
P8.   if $a_i.flag = done$ then
P9.   Finish()
        end if
      end if
P10. $g_i \leftarrow$ read $gate$
P11.   if $g_i.proc = -$ then
P12.   ChooseNextOp()
P13. $CAS(gate, g_i, (m_i, g_i.seq))$
P14. $g_i \leftarrow$ read $gate$
      end if
P15.   if $g_i.proc \neq -$ then
P16. $a_i \leftarrow$ read $A[g_i.proc]$
P17.   if $a_i.flag \neq done$ and $a_i.seq \leq g_i.seq$ then
P18.   Help()
P19. $CAS(A[g_i.proc], (a_i.op, a_i.seq, active, a_i.arg),$
           $(a_i.op, a_i.seq, done, output_i))$
P20. $CAS(A[g_i.proc], (a_i.op, a_i.seq, exit, a_i.arg),$
           $(a_i.op, a_i.seq, done, output_i))$
      end if
P21. $CAS(gate, g_i, (-, g_i.seq + 1))$
      end if
P22. $a_i \leftarrow$ read $A[i]$
    end while
P23. if $a_i.flag = exit$ then return(*exited*) end if
P24. Finish()

Finish() by process i:

F1. $g_i \leftarrow$ read $gate$
F2. if $g_i.proc = i$ then
F3. $CAS(gate, g_i, (-, g_i.seq + 1))$ end if
F4. return($a_i.arg$)

ChooseNextOp() by process i:

C1. $m_i \leftarrow g_i.seq \bmod p \in \{0, \ldots, p-1\}$
C2. $a_i \leftarrow$ read $A[m_i]$
C3. if $a_i.flag \neq active$ then
C4. $a_i \leftarrow$ read $A[i]$
C5.   if $a_i.flag = done$ then Finish() end if
C6. $m_i \leftarrow i$
    end if

We represent each variable x in the sequential representation by a record, R_x, in the shared representation. A record is a CAS object with four fields: $val[0]$, $val[1]$, $toggle$ and seq. The fields $val[0]$ and $val[1]$ have the same type as x and the field $toggle$ is a single bit which indicates whether $val[0]$ or $val[1]$ is the current value of x. Whenever process i writes to the shared record, R_x, representing variable x, it stores the new value in $R_x.val[1 - R_x.toggle]$, complements $R_x.toggle$, and sets $R_x.seq$ to $g_i.seq$. When a process i reads R_x, it compares $R_x.seq$ with $g_i.seq$ to determine which of $R_x.val[0]$ and $R_x.val[1]$ to use. If $R_x.seq < g_i.seq$, then it uses $R_x.val[R_x.toggle]$ to get the current value of x, since no other process that is performing the operation has changed R_x. If $R_x.seq = g_i.seq$, then R_x has already been updated for the operation, so process i uses $R_x.val[1 - R_x.toggle]$ to get the previous value of x. If $R_x.seq > g_i.seq$, then the operation has already been completed. In this case, process i can stop performing the operation.

Process i begins Help by resetting its local dictionary D_i on line H1. Each entry in this dictionary is a triple containing the name of the variable (which serves as the key), the contents of the corresponding record in the shared representation of the data structure, and the current value of this variable. The second field is used to perform a CAS on the record if the value of the variable is changed by the operation. When process i accesses a variable x in the simulation of the sequential implementation, it checks, on line H20, to see if x is in the local dictionary. If x is not in the local dictionary, then, on line H21, process i reads the corresponding record, R_x, from the shared representation of the data structure and, on line H24 or H25, adds an entry to the dictionary for x. If the access is a read from x, then, on line H27, process i uses the local value of x that is stored in the dictionary. If the access is a write to x, then, on line H28, process i updates the local value of x to the new value. When process i uses an input in the simulation of the sequential implementation, then, on line H29, process i uses the corresponding value in $a_i.arg$. When process i produces an output value, then, on line H30, it writes the value to the corresponding location in $output_i$.

Help() by process i:

H1. $R_i \leftarrow \phi$

H2. $nl_i \leftarrow$ read nl

H3. if $nl_i.seq > g_i.seq$ then exit Help end if

H4. if $nl.seq < g_i.seq$

H5. then $next_i \leftarrow nl_i.ptr[nl_i.toggle]$

H6. else $next_i \leftarrow nl_i.ptr[1 - nl_i.toggle]$
    end if
    % Locally perform all the steps of operation $a_i.op$
    % with inputs $a_i.arg$, reading the record associated
    % with each variable from the shared object prior to
    % its first access by that operation.

H7. for each access of a variable with name x in the code for operation $a_i.op$ do

H8. if x is the name for a new variable in the code for $a_i.op$ then

H9. $r_i \leftarrow$ read record pointed to by $next_i$
    % if $next_i$ points to the last record in $newlist$,
    % try to append a new record to $newlist$.

H10. if $r_i = (-, -, 0, 0)$ then

H11. CAS(record pointed to by $next_i$, r_i, $(new_i, -, 0, 0)$)

H12. $r_i \leftarrow$ read record pointed to by $next_i$

H13. if $r_i = (new_i, -, 0, 0)$ then
     % the record pointed to by new_i was
     % successfully appended to $newlist$

H14. get a new record from the memory manager

H15. let new_i point to this record

H16. initialize this record to $(-, -, 0, 0)$
     end if
     end if

H17. if $r_i.seq > g_i.seq$ then exit Help end if

H18. add $(x, r_i, 0)$ to D_i

H19. $next_i \leftarrow r_i.val[0]$
     end if

H20. if there is no item with key x in D_i do

H21. $r_i \leftarrow$ read record, R_x, associated with variable x

H22. if $r_i.seq > g_i.seq$ then exit Help end if

H23. if $r_i.seq < g_i.seq$

H24. then add $(x, r_i, r_i.val[r_i.toggle])$ to D_i

H25. else add $(x, r_i, r_i.val[1 - r_i.toggle])$ to D_i
     end if
     end if

H26. let (x, r, v) be the (unique) item with key x in D_i

H27. to read from x, use the value v

H28. to write v' to x, replace (x, r, v) by (x, r, v') in D_i

H29. for inputs, use $a_i.arg$

H30. place outputs in $output_i$
     end for
     % write changed records to the shared object:

H31. for each $(x, r, v) \in D_i$ do

H32. if $r.seq < g_i.seq$ and $r.val[r.toggle] \neq v$ then

H33. if $r.toggle = 0$

H34. then $r' \leftarrow (r.val[0], v, 1, g_i.seq)$

H35. else $r' \leftarrow (v, r.val[1], 0, g_i.seq)$
     end if

H36. $CAS(R_x, r, r')$
     end if
     end for
     % update nl

H37. if $nl_i.seq < g_i.seq$ then

H38. if $nl_i.toggle = 0$

H39. then $nl_i' \leftarrow (nl_i'.ptr[0], next_i, 1, g_i.seq)$

H40. else $nl_i' \leftarrow (next_i, nl_i'.ptr[1], 0, g_i.seq)$
     end if

H41. $CAS(nl, nl_i, nl_i')$
     end if

After process i complete its simulation of the operation, on line H31, it considers each entry (x, r, v) in the dictionary. If the record has not already been updated by another process performing the same operation (i.e., if $r.seq < g_i.seq$) and the value of x was changed during the simulation of the operation (i.e., $r.val[r.toggle] \neq v$), on line H32, then process i performs the CAS on line H36 to update R_x in the shared data structure. Lines H33–H35 ensure that the value of $toggle$ is changed and the new value of v is put in the correct field.

It remains to describe what happens during the simulation of an operation when the sequential implementation allocates a new variable, x. It would be problematic to have each process that tries to perform this operation allocate a different record for x in the shared data structure. To avoid this, we maintain a nonempty shared list, *newlist*, of records that can be allocated when the operation is applied. The first field of each record in *newlist*, *val*[0], points to the next record in the list. If $r.val[0] = -$, then r is the last record in *newlist*. The shared variable in *nl* contains a pointer to the first record in *newlist*. The first time a value is written to a newly allocated record, it is written into *val*[1]. This allows other processes performing the operation to find the next element in *newlist* by following the pointer stored in *val*[0] when that the test on line H17 is unsuccessful. If the test is successful, then process i can infer that the operation has already been completed and it can stop performing the operation. When a process uses the last record in *newlist* (i.e., if line H10 is successful), it immediately tries, on line H11, to append a new record to follow it. Each process i has one unallocated record, pointed to by *new_i*, that it can use for this purpose. If it successfully appends this record to the end of *newlist* (i.e., if line H13 is successful), then it gets a new record from the shared memory manager to replace it, on line H14–H16.

All processes performing an operation use the jth record in *newlist* for the jth new variable that is allocated during that operation. Process i keeps a pointer, *next_i*, which points to the record it should use for the next variable that needs to be allocated during the simulation of the operation. On lines H4–H6, *next_i* is initialized to the beginning of *newlist*. To use the record for a newly allocated variable x, process i associates the name x with this record by adding a new entry with key x, a copy of the contents of the record to its local dictionary and the initial value 0, on line H18. Then, on line H19, it assigns *next_i* to the next element in *newlist*. Subsequent accesses to x are performed on the local copy in D_i. At the end of the operation, *nl* is updated to point to the first unused record in *newlist*, on lines H37–H41. If the sequential implementation releases variables, the corresponding records could be added to *newlist*, so it serves as a free list.

A problem could arise if another process tries to perform the operation after *nl* has been updated, because it would use different records for the newly allocated variables. In this case, although the operation has been completely applied to the shared data structure, it is possible that the output of the operation has not been stored in its announcement. To avoid this problem, *nl* consists of four fields, *ptr*[0], *ptr*[1], *toggle* and *seq*. The fields *ptr*[0] and *ptr*[1] are pointers to records, *toggle* is a bit which indicates whether *ptr*[0] or *ptr*[1] points to the beginning of *newlist* and *seq* contains the value of *gate.seq* when *nl* was last updated on line H41. Before performing the operation, process i checks whether $nl_i.seq > g_i.seq$ on line H3. If so, then the operation has been completed and process i can stop performing the operation. If not, process i checks, on line H4, whether $nl_i.seq = g_i.seq$ to determine whether *nl* has been updated for this operation and hence, which of *ptr*[0] or *ptr*[1] to use.

3.3 Correctness

We say that the shared data structure at a particular configuration *correctly represents* a state of the sequential data structure if for all variables x in the sequential data structure, $R_x.val[R_x.toggle]$ is the value of x in that state.

For every execution, we linearize each operation announced by process i if and when $A[i].flag$ is changed to *done* between its announcement and when process i announces its next operation. Suppose we apply each linearized operation up to and including this one to the sequential data structure. We prove that the output of this operation is the same in both the shared implementation and the sequential implementation, and the shared data structure at the linearization point of this operation correctly represents the state of the sequential data structure after these operations have been performed.

We also prove that if process i invokes Perform(op_i, $input_i$), it will return after executing at most $p + 1$ iterations of the while loop and either:
process i returns on line F4 after $A[i].flag$ is set to *done*, or
process i returns on line P23 after setting $A[i].flag$ to *exit* on line P6, and $A[i].flag$ is not set to *done* between when the operation was announced and process i announces its next operation.

We first establish some basic properties of the shared variables that follow from observation of the code.

- When $gate = (-, k)$, it can only change to (i, k) for some $i \in \{0, \ldots, p - 1\}$.

- When $gate = (i, k)$, it can only change to $(-, k + 1)$.

- When $A[i].flag = active$, it can only change to *done* or *exit*.

- When $A[i].flag = done$, it can only change to *active*.

- $A[i].flag$ can change to *done* only when $gate.proc = i$.

- $A[i].flag$ can change to *active* only when process i performs P3.

- $A[i].seq \le gate.seq$.

- $R_x.seq \le gate.seq$, for every variable x in the sequential implementation.

- $nl.seq \le gate.seq$.

Then the following lemma establishes key invariants needed to prove correctness.

LEMMA 1.

1. *Whenever gate.proc changes from i to $-$, $A[i].flag = done$.*

2. *After process i performs line P3:*
   (a) if it next returns on line P23, then gate.proc does not change to i
   (b) if it next returns on line F4, then gate.proc changes to i exactly once, and
   (c) between when process i next returns and when it performs line P3 after that, gate.proc $\ne i$.

3. *Between when $A[i].flag$ changes to done and when process i last performed line P3 prior to that, gate.proc changes to i exactly once.*

Consider any execution of our algorithm that ends in a configuration in which $gate.seq = k + 1$. Then at least k operations have been linearized. For any variable x, let v be its value in the sequential implementation immediately

340

after the first k operations in this linearization have been performed. Then $R_x.val[R_x.toggle] = v$, if $R_x.seq < k + 1$, and $R_x.val[1 - R_x.toggle] = v$, if $R_x.seq = k + 1$. Similarly, either $nl.ptr[nl.toggle]$ or $nl.ptr[1 - nl.toggle]$ points to the first element in $newlist$, if $nl.seq < k + 1$ or $nl.seq = k + 1$, respectively.

We prove that, after i's operation has been announced in $A[i]$, $gate.proc$ changes to $i \bmod p$ within $p + 1$ iterations of the while loop by process i. When that occurs, every process executing the while loop will help process i to complete its operation (if it has not yet been completed) by performing Help and then will try to update $A[i]$ so that $A[i].flag$ will be set to $done$ and arg will contain the output of the operation.

We also show that if process i attempts to set $A[i].flag$ to exit on line P6, then it exits Perform within one iteration of the loop on lines P4–P22: If the CAS on line P6 is unsuccessful, then we prove that $A[i].flag$ has been changed to $done$ and process i's operation has been linearized. If the CAS on line P6 is successful, then $A[i].flag$ is changed to $exit$ and we prove that it does not change back to $active$ until process i next announces another operation. Hence, when process i next performs line P22 at the end of the iteration, $A[i].flag \neq active$ and the test on line P4 is unsuccessful.

We prove that, immediately after process i performs Help for an operation that has not yet been linearized, then $output_i$ contains the output of that operation applied to the sequential data structure. For every variable x, we show that:

–if x is allocated, then there is a unique record, R_x, that corresponds to x in the shared data structure,

–if it is not changed during the sequential implementation of the operation, then R_x remains unchanged, and

–if it is changed to v, then $R_x.val[r_x.toggle] = v$.

In addition, we prove that $nl.ptr[nl.toggle]$ points to an unallocated record.

3.4 Complexity

During each iteration, process i executes $O(1)$ steps in addition to executing Help at most once. If every sequential operation accesses at most w variables and the local dictionary of each process is implemented using, for example, a red-black tree, it takes $O(\log w)$ steps, in the worst case, to cache a variable or access a cached variable. (This takes $O(1)$ expected time using a hash table with chaining.) If every sequential operation takes time at most t, the worst case number of steps a process takes to perform Help is $O(t \log w)$, of which $\Theta(w)$ are shared memory accesses.

If process i does not want to exit its operation, then it executes at most $p + 1$ iteration of the loop on lines P4–P22. Hence a process takes $O(pt \log w)$ steps during Perform. If process i wants to exit its operation, then after it performs line P5, it does not perform another complete iteration of the loop and, hence, takes $O(t \log w)$ more steps before it returns.

For each variable x in the sequential implementation, there is exactly one record, R_x, that corresponds to x in the shared representation. In addition, each process, i, has a location $A[i]$ in the announce array and has one unallocated record, pointed to by new_i. It follows that the resulting shared implementation of the data structure uses $s + O(p)$ shared objects, where s is the size of the sequential data structure.

4. CACHING PERFORMANCE

Consider the execution of Perform on a sequence of r operations of the shared data structure on a multicore with p cores (each corresponding to a process), which share a cache of size M arranged in blocks of size B. We assume LRU. We will say that a caching complexity $R(r, M, B)$ is *well-behaved* if $R(r, M, B) = \Theta(R(r, \Theta(M), B))$. (All commonly known cache complexities are well-behaved.)

LEMMA 2. *Let the shared data structure bring in at most $Q(r, M, B)$ blocks into cache and incur at most $f(r, M, B)$ cache misses for any single operation in its sequential execution of a sequence S of r operations.*

If $M \geq 4 \cdot p \cdot B \cdot f(r, M, B)$, and Q and f are well-behaved cache complexities, then the number of cache misses incurred by any execution of Perform on the sequence S is $O(Q(r, M, B))$.

As an example, a stack or queue implemented as a standard semi-infinite array has $Q(r, M, B) = r/B$, $f(r, M, B) = 1$, hence by the above lemma, the number of cache misses remains $O(r/B)$ when executed with Perform if $M \geq 4pB$. (Typically, we will have $M \gg p \cdot B$). Note that $Q(r, M, B) = \Omega(r/B)$ for any queue or stack — consider a queue (the stack is similar) with a sequence of r operations which alternate between $2M$ enqueues and $2M$ dequeues. Thus this result is optimal for stacks and queues in a strong sense.

Lemma 2 can be proved as follows. The announce array $A[1..p]$, the most recent value of $gate$, and the data read for the last operation, which together require no more than $3f(r, M, B)$ blocks in cache (assuming seq and $toggle$ are in one word) will be in cache, as will data read for other recent operations. Additionally, the cache may contain data used in older operations, which are being accessed by slow processes that have not yet read the more recent value of $gate$. Even if all but one process is executing slowly, there is at least $M' = M - p - 3pBf(r, M, B)$ space available in the cache for the shared records accessed by recent operations. We have $M' = \Theta(M)$ since $M \geq 4pBf(r, M, B)$.

The main additional source for cache misses occurs with a process that slows down considerably. Consider a slow process i. It may incur additional $O(f(r, M', B))$ cache misses for its current operation op_i if the data is so old that it has been evicted from the cache. But if the data is this old, then at least M'/B blocks of data were brought into cache since the time when op_i was executed by the fast processes. Further, process i will complete its execution of op_i with at most $3f(r, M', B)$ cache misses, and then will read the current value of $gate$. Hence, process i will incur this penalty of $3f(r, M', B)$ cache misses at most $Q(r, M', B)/(M'/B)$ times. Hence the total number of additional blocks that could be read because of slow processes (across all p processes) is $O\left(p \cdot f(r, M', B) \cdot \frac{B \cdot Q(r, M', B)}{M'}\right)$. Since $p = O(\frac{M}{Bf(r, M, B)})$ by assumption, this is $O(Q(r, M, B))$.

The caching performance looks less promising at the private cache at each core: If process i performs n_i operations, it could incur $\Theta(p \cdot n_i)$ cache misses in the worst case, in addition to the cost of reading in its private copy of the data structure values. This could occur if for each operation, process i needs to cycle through $p - 1$ iterations of helping, and needs to read in an updated value from array A each time. It is unclear how one can improve the caching performance of private caches, and determining if this is possible is left as an open question.

5. TRANSACTION FRIENDLY QUEUE

We have adapted Perform to obtain a refined version of a wait-free transaction friendly queue, implemented in the standard way as a semi-infinite array. In a queue, enqueues and dequeues have no interaction, except possibly when the queue is empty. Our queue allows an enqueue ($op = E$) and a dequeue ($op = D$) to occur concurrently, and while the queue is empty, all dequeues return within a constant number of steps with $\perp$ (to denote an empty queue).

We use Perform-Enq for enqueues and Perform-Deq for dequeues, with separate gates *egate* and *dgate*. At quiescence (i.e. when there are no enqueues or dequeues in progress), their sequence numbers give the locations of the tail and head of the queue respectively. EHelp is the Help routine for Perform-Enq and and DHelp for Perform-Deq. At each location of the queue $Q[1..]$ is a pair $(val[0], val[1])$, which starts with value $(-, -)$. When a value v is enqueued at $Q[i]$, its entry is updated to $(v, -)$, and when this value is dequeued from $Q[i]$, it is updated to (v, v). No further updates to this location can occur, hence we do not need the toggle bit. Since position i in the queue is also the current sequence number being used for gate (*dgate* or *egate*), we do not need the sequence number field either.

The pseudocode is in the appendix, where lines numbers with prefix P refer to the lines in our universal construction. We change ChooseNextOp slightly since, in addition to needing $a_i.flag$ to be *active* in order to determine if the operation should be performed, we also need to check if the operation is E when executing Perform-Enq, and D when executing Perform-Deq. Perform-Enq is the same as Perform except that *gate* is now *egate*, and Help is replaced by the two-line EHelp. Perform-Deq has a few changes from Perform, most notably to handle the case of dequeue when an empty queue is detected. As seen in the pseudocode in the appendix, this is handled using a mechanism similar to that used to handle an exit in the universal construction. We use a flag X_i to denote that an empty queue has been detected by process i, and then we use the method used earlier to handle exit to now handle both of these cases, and use the flag X_i to return the correct value (*exit* or $\perp$). The other main difference from Perform is that when the queue is empty, no dequeue can occur and hence there is no call to DHelp, nor should there be a change to *dgate* during this time (in contrast to the handling of exit). The correctness follows from the fact that if process i returns with $\perp$, then after X_i is set to *True* and $A[i].flag$ is set to *exit*, either the queue is verified to be empty, or *dgate.seq* has been incremented from the value it had when $A[i].flag$ was set to *exit*. Hence, if $A[i].flag$ has not yet been set to *done*, any process that tries to help with this dequeue request of process i will find $A[i].flag$ to be *exit*, and hence will not assign process i to *dgate.proc* in ChooseNextOp.

The linearization point for an enqueue operation is when line X2 is executed, and for a dequeue when line Y2 is executed. This is in contrast to the universal construction, where the linearization point is when $A[i].flag$ is set to *done*. It is readily verified that the corresponding statement to lines X2 and Y2 in the universal construction (namely the last statement in Help) is a valid linearization point there. For our queue, it is important to linearize at these two points rather than when $A[i].flag$ is set to *done*, due to our support of concurrent execution of enqueues and dequeues.

6. DISCUSSION

In this paper, we have described a universal construction that implements any given deterministic sequential data structure as a transaction friendly, wait-free data structure shared by any fixed number of processes. The method is efficient and uses the shared cache efficiently in a multicore implementation. We have also briefly described a shared queue based on this universal construction that appears to be quite practical. In the interests of presenting a construction that is easier to understand, we did not include some natural refinements. Instead, we discuss them briefly here.

Our universal construction uses CAS objects that contain a small, constant number of fields. For example, a record R_x in the shared data structure is a CAS object that contains two values from the sequential data structure, a toggle bit, and a sequence number. This can be avoided using indirection: Instead, each CAS object could contain a single pointer that points to a record of registers. The resulting implementation would be slower and a mechanism for managing the allocation and deallocation of these records, such as a separate free list for each process, is needed.

Randomized operations can be supported in our universal construction by using a shared array, S, of CAS objects that allow the processes to agree on all of the random choices made while applying the operation: Each of these CAS objects holds a random choice, together with the current value of *gate*. When process i wants to make its k'th random choice during the operation, it reads $S[k]$. If the sequence number stored there is greater than g_i, then the operation has already been completed and the process can stop helping it. If it is equal to g_i, process i uses the random choice recorded in $S[k]$. If it is less than g_i, process i makes a local random choice, which it tries to record, together with g_i, by performing a CAS on $S[k]$. Then it reads $S[k]$ again and uses the random choice recorded there. Note that the array S is reused for each subsequent operation.

It is necessary to assume a weak adversary, which is not aware of the local random choice of a process until it next performs a shared memory operation. A strong adversary could bias the outcome of a random choice by seeing the local random choices of a number of processes and then scheduling the process whose choice it likes best. In fact, it is impossible to have a wait-free implementation of a fair coin against a strong adversary [3].

As presented, our universal construction will not perform an operation announced by process i if process i sets $A[i].flag$ to *exit* before it is chosen or given priority to be the next operation. This is useful when process i has waiting too long to perform its operation, because the operation will be terminated, either successfully or unsuccessfully, without undue delay. For more general situations, such as when a process detects a problem during the execution or detects a conflict with a concurrent operation, it would be better if the operation exits even after it has been partially applied to the shared data structure. This can be accomplished by having a process undo all the changes the operation has made to the shared data structure if it sees that the operation is supposed to exit. Specifically, P20 is replaced by lines U1 to U15.

U1. $a_i' \leftarrow$ read $A[g_i.proc]$
U2. if $a_i'.flag = exit$ and $a_i'.seq = a_i.seq$
U3. then for each $(x, r, v) \in D_i$ do
U4. $r' \leftarrow$ read R_x
U5.   if $r'.seq = g_i.seq$ then
U6.   if $r.seq < g_i.seq$
U7.   then $old \leftarrow r.val[r.toggle]$
U8.   else $old \leftarrow r.val[1 - r.toggle]$
        end if
U9. $CAS(R_x, r', (old, old, 0, g_i.seq))$
        end for
U10. $nl_i' \leftarrow$ read nl
U11. if $nl_i'.seq = g_i.seq$ then
U12.   if $nl_i.seq < g_i.seq$
U13.   then $old \leftarrow nl_i.val[nl_i.toggle]$
U14.   else $old \leftarrow nl_i.val[1 - nl_i.toggle]$
    end if
U15. $CAS(nl, nl_i', (old, old, 0, g_i.seq))$
    end if
    end if

When process i performs this code, it first check whether the operation it just helped is supposed to exit on lines U1–U2. For each variable x whose record, R_x, was changed by the operation and has not been changed by a later operation (i.e., the test on line U5 was successful), the value of x prior to the operation is computed on lines U6–U8 and put into both $R_x.val[0]$ and $R_x.val[1]$ on line U9. $R_x.seq$ is also set to $g_i.seq$, so that a slow process still performing the operation will not modify this location. Note that process i's local dictionary D_i still contains all the records that are accessed during the operation. Correctness follows from the observation that any record R_x can change at most twice while $gate.seq$ has the same value. Similarly, nl is restored to its old value on lines U10–U15.

Currently, in Perform, a process executes lines P10–P22 after announcing that its operation should exit. We should remove line P23 and add return($exited$) after lines P8–P9, so that process i returns immediately after successfully setting $A[i].flag = exit$. Furthermore, instead of allowing a process to exit an operation only on lines P5–P9 at the beginning of an iteration of the while loop on lines P4–P22, lines P5–P9 could be put anywhere or lines P6–P9 could be executed in response to an interrupt indicating that the announced operation of process i should exit.

There are other refinements that can improve efficiency of Perform. For instance, in our current method, a process i that wants to exit and finds that its operation has not yet completed, executes one further iteration of ChooseNextOp and Help before returning. It is possible to avoid this additional iteration except when the values read for $gate.seq$ in lines P10 and P14 are congruent to $i \bmod p$; otherwise the process can exit immediately. Also, at the end of Help, we could have a pointer as a field in nl to the output needed by the operation being executed so that other (later) processes helping with the same operation do not need to execute the operation in order to determine the output.

It should be possible to avoid using sequence numbers, perhaps with standard techniques such as bounded timestamps, handshaking, or using LL/SC instead of CAS.

Currently our universal construction executes operations one at a time. We are currently trying to find ways generalize it to allow different operations to be performed concurrently on disjoint parts of the shared structure, without sacrificing correctness or wait-freedom. One approach we are considering is to have a lock, owned by an operation, associated with each record in the shared data structure, as in [4], but to give priority to operations in a way that ensures wait-freedom.

Acknowledgments. This work was supported by the Natural Science and Engineering Research Council of Canada and NSF grants CCF-0850775 and CCF-0830737.

7. REFERENCES

[1] Y. Afek, D. Dauber, and D. Touitou. Wait-free made fast. In *Proc. ACM SPAA*, pages 538–547, 1995.

[2] J. Anderson and M. Moir. Universal constructions for large objects. *IEEE Trans. Parallel Dist. Syst.*, 10(12):1317–1332, 1999.

[3] J. Aspnes and M. Herlihy. Fast randomized consensus using shared memory. *J. Algorithms*, 11(3):441–461, 1990.

[4] G. Barnes. A method for implementing lock-free shared-data structures. In *Proc. ACM SPAA*, pages 261–270, 1993.

[5] P. Chuong. A wait-free abortable universal construction. Master's thesis, University of Toronto, 2010.

[6] P. Chuong, F. Ellen, and V. Ramachandran. A universal construction for wait-free transaction friendly data structures. Manuscript, 2010.

[7] P. Fatourou and N. Kallimanis. The redblue adaptive universal construction. In *Proc. DISC*, volume 5805 of *LNCS*, pages 127–141, 2009.

[8] K. Fraser and T. L. Harris. Concurrent programming without locks. *ACM Trans. Comput. Syst.*, 25(2), 2007.

[9] M. Herlihy. A methodology for implementing highly concurrent data structures. In *Proc ACM PPoPP*, pages 197–206, 1990.

[10] M. Herlihy. Wait-free synchronization. *ACM Trans. Program. Lang. Syst.*, 13(1):124–149, 1991.

[11] M. Herlihy. A methodology for implementing highly concurrent data objects. *ACM Trans. Program. Lang. Syst.*, 15(5):745–770, November 1993.

[12] M. Herlihy. Technical perspective - highly concurrent data structures. *Commun. ACM*, 52(5):99, 2009.

[13] P. Jayanti. A time complexity lower bound for randomized implementations of some shared objects. In *Proc. ACM PODC*, pages 201–210, 1998.

[14] V. J. Marathe and M. Moir. Toward high performance nonblocking software transactional memory. In *Proc. ACM PPoPP*, pages 227–236, 2008.

[15] N. Shavit and D. Touitou. Software transactional memory. *Distributed Computing*, 10(2):99–116, 1997.

Perform-Enq(E, v_i) by process i:

P1. $g_i \leftarrow$ read $egate$
P2. $a_i \leftarrow (E, g_i.seq, active, v_i)$
P3. $A[i] \leftarrow$ write a_i
P4. while $a_i.flag = active$ do
P5.   if process i should exit its operation then
P6. $CAS(A[i], a_i, (a_i.op, a_i.seq, exit, v_i))$
P7. $a_i \leftarrow$ read $A[i]$
P8.   if $a_i.flag = done$ then
P9.   Finish()
       end if
     end if
P10. $g_i \leftarrow$ read $egate$
P11.   if $g_i.proc = -$ then
P12.   ChooseNextOp()
P13. $CAS(egate, g_i, (m_i, g_i.seq))$
P14. $g_i \leftarrow$ read $egate$
    end if
P15.   if $g_i.proc \neq -$ then
P16. $a_i \leftarrow$ read $A[g_i.proc]$
P17.   if $a_i.flag \neq done$ and $a_i.seq \leq g_i.seq$ then
P18.   EHelp()
P19. $CAS(A[g_i.proc], (a_i.op, a_i.seq, active, a_i.arg),$
          $(a_i.op, a_i.seq, done, output_i))$
P20. $CAS(A[g_i.proc], (a_i.op, a_i.seq, exit, a_i.arg),$
          $(a_i.op, a_i.seq, done, output_i))$
     end if
P21. $CAS(egate, g_i, (-, g_i.seq + 1))$
   end if
P22. $a_i \leftarrow$ read $A[i]$
  end while
P23. if $a_i.flag = exit$ then return($exited$) end if
P24. Finish()

Finish() by process i:

Lines F1 to F4 as in the universal construction with:
$gate = egate$ when called from Perform-Enq, and
$gate = dgate$ when called from Perform-Deq.

ChooseNextOp() by process i:

Lines C1 to C6 as in the universal construction with line
C3 replaced by:
In Perform-Enq: 'if $a_i.flag \neq active$ or $a_i.op \neq E$'
In Perform-Deq: 'if $a_i.flag \neq active$ or $a_i.op \neq D$'

EHelp() by process i:

X1. $output_i \leftarrow -$
X2. $\mathbf{CAS}(Q[g_i.seq], (-, -), (a_i.arg, -))$

Perform-Deq(D, $-$) by process i:

P1. $g_i \leftarrow$ read $dgate$
D1. $X_i \leftarrow False$
P2. $a_i \leftarrow (D, g_i.seq, active, -)$
P3. $A[i] \leftarrow$ write a_i
P4. while $a_i.flag = active$ do
D2. $g_i \leftarrow$ **read** $dgate$
D3. $q_i \leftarrow$ **read** $Q[g_i.seq]$
D4.   **if** $q_i = (-, -)$ **then** $X_i \leftarrow True$
D5. [**P5**]
      if (process i should exit) **or** (X_i) then
P6. $CAS(A[i], a_i, (a_i.op, a_i.seq, exit, -))$
P7. $a_i \leftarrow$ read $A[i]$
P8.   if $a_i.flag = done$ then
P9.   Finish()
       end if
     end if
P10. $g_i \leftarrow$ read $dgate$
D6. $q_i \leftarrow$ **read** $Q[g_i.seq]$
D7.   **if** $q_i \neq (-, -)$ **then**
P11.   if $g_i.proc = -$ then
P12.   ChooseNextOp()
P13. $CAS(dgate, g_i, (m_i, g_i.seq))$
P14. $g_i \leftarrow$ read $dgate$
    end if
P15.   if $g_i.proc \neq -$ then
P16. $a_i \leftarrow$ read $A[g_i.proc]$
P17.   if $a_i.flag \neq done$ and $a_i.seq \leq g_i.seq$ then
P18.   DHelp()
P19. $CAS(A[g_i.proc], (a_i.op, a_i.seq, active, a_i.arg),$
           $(D, a_i.seq, done, output_i))$
P20. $CAS(A[g_i.proc], (a_i.op, a_i.seq, exit, a_i.arg),$
           $(a_i.op, a_i.seq, done, output_i))$
     end if
P21. $CAS(dgate, g_i, (-, g_i.seq + 1))$
    end if
   end if
P22. $a_i \leftarrow$ read $A[i]$
  end while
D8. [**P23a**] if $a_i.flag = exit$ **and** $X_i = True$ **then**
         return($\bot$) end if
D9. [**P23b**] if $a_i.flag = exit$ **and** $X_i = False$ **then**
         return($exited$) end if
P24. Finish()

DHelp() by process i:

Y1. $q_i \leftarrow Q[g_i.seq]$
Y2. $output_i \leftarrow q_i.val[0]$
Y3. $\mathbf{CAS}(Q[g_i.seq], q_i, (output_i, output_i))$

Low-Contention Data Structures

[Extended Abstract]

James Aspnes[*]
Department of Computer
Science
Yale University
New Haven, CT 06511
aspnes@cs.yale.edu

David Eisenstat[†]
eisenstatdavid@gmail.com

Yitong Yin[‡]
State Key Laboratory for Novel
Software Technology
Nanjing University
Nanjing, China
yinyt@nju.edu.cn

ABSTRACT

We consider the problem of minimizing contention in static dictionary data structures, where the contention on each cell is measured by the expected number of probes to that cell given an input that is chosen from a distribution that is not known to the query algorithm (but that may be known when the data structure is built). When all positive queries are equally probable, and similarly all negative queries are equally probable, we show that it is possible to construct a data structure using linear space s, a constant number of queries, and with contention $O(1/s)$ on each cell, corresponding to a nearly-flat load distribution. All of these quantities are asymptotically optimal. For *arbitrary* query distributions, the lack of knowledge of the query distribution by the query algorithm prevents perfect load leveling in this case: we present a lower bound, based on VC-dimension, that shows that for a wide range of data structure problems, achieving contention even within a polylogarithmic factor of optimal requires a cell-probe complexity of $\Omega(\log \log n)$.

Categories and Subject Descriptors

E.1 [**Data Sstructures**]; F.1.2 [**Computation by Abstract Devices**]: Modes of Computation—*Parallelism and concurrency*

General Terms

Algorithms, Performance, Theory

---

[*]Supported in part by NSF grant CNS-0435201.

[†]Part of the work was done while David Eisenstat was a graduate student at Brown University.

[‡]Supported by the National Science Foundation of China under Grant No. 60721002. Part of the work was done while Yitong Yin was a graduate student at Yale University.

Keywords

Memory contention, data structure, cell-probe model

1. INTRODUCTION

For shared-memory multiprocessors, memory contention measures the extent to which processors might access the same memory location at the same time, and is one of the main issues for realistic systems [9,13] and theoretical models [2,7]. In [6], a theoretical model is introduced by Dwork *et al.* to formally address the contention costs of algorithmic problems. In this paper, we propose to study the contention cost of a data structure, which measures how many queries to the data structure might simultaneously access the same memory cell. To avoid the question of how many queries to the data structure are running at the same time, we measure contention indirectly, by counting the expected number of probes to a given cell for each individual query. The expected number of probes to the cell for some fixed number m of simultaneous queries can then be bounded using linearity of expectation.

With binary search, for example, the entry in the middle of the table is accessed on every query, as is the cell storing the hash function or root-level index with perfect hashing and similar index-based data structures. Depending on the query distribution, the remaining load may be balanced almost as badly over the other cells.

We consider how to avoid this problem in case of *static* data structures, where the data structure is built in advance by a construction algorithm that may know the query distribution, but queries are performed by a uniform algorithm that does not (although it may use randomization itself to spread the query load more evenly).

The assumption that the query algorithm does not know the query distribution is natural. Often the query distribution will be highly correlated with the contents of the data structure, as in our simplest case where we consider a uniform distribution on successful queries to a static dictionary. Providing the query distribution to the query algorithm in such a case would, in effect, give it significant information about the contents of the data structure.

1.1 Model

Formally, a data structure problem is a function $f : Q \times \mathcal{D} \to \{0, 1\}$, such that for every query $x \in Q$ and every data set $S \in \mathcal{D}$, $f(x, S)$ specifies the answer to the query x to data set S. A classic problem is the **membership**

problem, where $Q = [N]$ and $\mathcal{D} = \binom{[N]}{n}$ for some $N \gg n$, and $f(x, S) = 1$ if and only if $x \in S$.

We assume that the query $x \in Q$ follows some probability distribution q over Q.

For any data set $S \in \mathcal{D}$ and any query distribution q over Q, a table $T_{S,q} : [s] \to \{0, 1\}^b$ of s cells, each of which contains b bits, is prepared. Given a query x, a probabilistic cell-probing algorithm $\mathcal{A}$ computes the value of $f(x, S)$ by making t randomized adaptive cell-probes $I_x^{(1)}, I_x^{(2)}, \ldots, I_x^{(t)} \in [s]$. The algorithm $\mathcal{A}$ may depend on f, but not on S or q (except to the extent that later probes may depend on the outcome of earlier probes, whose results might encode information about S and q).

The **contention** of a cell is the expected number of probes to the cell during one execution of $\mathcal{A}$. This will be equal to the probability that the cell is probed at all, provided $\mathcal{A}$ is sensible enough not to probe the same cell twice, but it is easier to work with expectations. In more detail:

DEFINITION 1. *For a fixed table $T_{S,q}$, for a query X chosen randomly from Q according to the distribution q, the sequence of cell-probes is $I_X^{(1)}, I_X^{(2)}, \ldots, I_X^{(t)}$. Let $Y^{(t)}(x, j)$ be the 0-1 valued random variable indicating whether $I_x^{(t)} = j$. The contention of cell j at step t is defined by*

$$\Phi_t(j) := \mathrm{E}\left[Y^{(t)}(X, j)\right],$$

where the expectation is taken over both X and the random $I_x^{(t)}$. The total contention of cell j is $\Phi(j) := \sum_t \Phi_t(j)$.

It is obvious that $\sum_j \Phi_t(j) = 1$, therefore $\frac{1}{s} \le \max_j \Phi_t(j) \le 1$. Ideally, we want $\max_j \Phi_t(j)$ to approach $\frac{1}{s}$.

A **balanced cell-probing scheme** is defined as follows:

DEFINITION 2. *An (s, b, t, ϕ)-balanced-cell-probing scheme for problem $f : Q \times \mathcal{D} \to \{0, 1\}$ is a cell-probing scheme such that for any $S \in \mathcal{D}$ and any probability distribution q over Q, a table $T_{S,q} : [s] \to \{0, 1\}^b$ is constructed, such that for any query $x \in Q$, the algorithm returns $f(x, S)$ by probing at most t cells, and for a query $x \in Q$ generated according to the distribution q, the contention $\Phi_k(j)$ is bounded by ϕ for any $1 \le k \le t$ and any $j \in [s]$.*

Such schemes have the very strong property that not only is contention bounded across an execution of the query algorithm, but each individual step gives low contention.

Given a fixed table $T_{S,q}$, we can summarize the contention succinctly using linear algebra. Let P_t be a $|Q| \times s$ matrix with $P_t(x, j) := \Pr[I_X^{(t)} = j] = \mathrm{E}[Y^{(t)}(X, j)]$. The contention on all cells can be computed by $\Phi_t = qP_t$, specifically,

$$
\begin{aligned}
\Phi_t(j) &= \mathrm{E}\left[Y^{(t)}(X, j)\right] \\
&= \sum_{x \in Q} \Pr[X = x] \cdot \mathrm{E}\left[Y^{(t)}(x, j)\right] \\
&= \sum_{x \in Q} q_x \cdot P_t(x, j).
\end{aligned}
$$

Finally, for our lower bound, it will be helpful to consider data structure problems from the perspective of communication complexity. In this view, a data structure is a communication protocol between an adaptive player Alice for the cell-probing algorithm and an oblivious player Bob for

the table. The input to Bob is a pair (S, q), and the input to Alice is a query $x \in Q$, which is generated according to the distribution q. Together they compute $f(x, S)$ via communication. The contention then counts the probability of each type of message sent by Alice.

1.2 Our contributions

This paper makes following contributions:

- We formalize a natural and interesting problem: memory contention caused by concurrent data structure queries. We introduce contention to the classic cell-probe model. In our model, contention is measured by the chance that a memory cell is probed during the execution of the cell-probe algorithm. This level of abstraction allows us to study the trade-off between the contention and the complexity of data structures without regard to specific contention resolution schemes.

- We note an especially interesting class of query distributions: distributions that are uniform over both the set of positive queries and the set of negative queries (but not necessarily uniform over all queries). We introduce a linear-size, constant-time cell-probing scheme for the membership problem, with maximum contention $O(1/n)$. It is easy to see that this data structure is asymptotically optimal in all three parameters.

- We study data structures with arbitrary query distribution. For this general case, we prove a lower bound on any balanced cell-probing scheme satisfying a certain natural technical restriction. The lower bound is a time-contention trade-off: for any problem which has a non-degenerate subproblem of size n, if the contention is within a Polylog(n) factor of optimal, the time complexity is $\Omega(\log \log n)$. This directly implies the same lower bound for the membership problem.

1.3 Related work

Our first upper bound is based on the well-known FKS construction of Fredman *et al.* [8] and subsequent work by Dietzfelbinger and Meyer auf der Heyde extending these results to the dynamic case [3–5]; we will refer to this latter construction, as described in [4], by DM.

The FKS construction is a static data structure for the membership problem, based on a two-level tree of hash tables, with linear space and constant lookup time.

In DM, the hash functions used in FKS are replaced with a new family that gives a more even distribution of load across the second layer of the tree, which is used to get bounded worst-case update costs for the dynamic case. In [3] and [5], DM is implemented in the PRAM model and the model of a complete synchronized network of processors respectively. Both implementations optimize the contention on individual processors, but do not consider the contention on individual memory locations.

Membership can also be solved with optimal time and space complexity using cuckoo hashing [12]; as with FKS and DM, the contention of the standard implementation is high, mostly because all queries read the hash function parameters from the same locations.

For FKS, DM, and cuckoo hashing, contention can be decreased by storing the hash function redundantly. Under the assumption that the query is distributed uniformly within both the positive set and the negative set, this gives a maximum contention of $\Theta(\sqrt{n})$ times optimal for FKS, and $\Theta(\ln n / \ln \ln n)$ times optimal for DM and cuckoo hashing; while for arbitrary query distributions, the contentions can be arbitrarily bad. This is not surprising, given that none of these data structures are designed with memory contention in mind; nonetheless, we show that it is possible to do substantially better.

2. LOW-CONTENTION UNIFORM MEMBERSHIP QUERIES

Let $N = |U|$ be the size of the universe. We assume that $N \geq n^2$, and each cell in the table contains a b-bit word, where $b = \log_2 N$.

THEOREM 3. *For the membership problem of n elements, with the assumption that the query is uniformly distributed within both positive queries and negative queries, there exists an $(O(n), b, O(1), O(1/n))$-balanced-cell-probing scheme.*

Given a data set $S \in \binom{U}{n}$, the data structure can be constructed in expected $O(n)$ time on a unit-cost RAM.

To see how our data structure works, it may help to start by considering the query procedure for FKS hashing. FKS hashing works by taking a standard hash table and using a secondary perfect hashing scheme within each of $O(n)$ "buckets" to resolve collisions between elements hashed to the same bucket. Even though the largest bucket may contain $O(\sqrt{n})$ elements, and the size of the i-th bucket is proportional to the *square* n_i^2 of the number of items n_i in that bucket, because most buckets are small, the sum of these squares is likely to be linear in n.

FKS guarantees that all queries finish in exactly three probes: the first probe reads the parameters of the hash function; the second reads a pointer to the "bucket" in which the target item will be found, as well as information about the size of the bucket and the perfect hash function used within the bucket; and the third reads the actual element. This produces contention 1 on the cell for the first probe and contention $\Theta(n_i/n)$ on the cell for the second probe: both are much worse than our goal of $O(1/n)$.

We can reduce the contention for the first probe by replication; instead of probing a single cell, we probe one of n identical copies. The second probe is trickier; we would like to replicate the information for large buckets, but the query algorithm does not know which buckets are large.

Our approach is to organize the buckets into $\Theta(n/\log n)$ groups of $\Theta(\log n)$ buckets each. While individual buckets may vary significantly in size, we can show that when using the hash functions of DM [4], the total size of each group will be $O(\log n)$ with reasonably high probability. A bitvector encoding allows us to indicate the size of all buckets in a group in a single $O(\log n)$-bit cell, which is replicated $O(\log n)$ times to reduce contention to $O(1/n)$. Knowing the size of each bucket in the group, the query algorithm can deduce the storage range for the replicated headers of the target bucket, read the relevant header information (including both a pointer to the actual location of the bucket and the parameters of its secondary hash function) from a randomly-distributed probe, and finally use the bucket's perfect hash function to find the target element. This four-phase procedure requires a constant number of probes and still uses only $O(n)$ space with $O(1/n)$ contention, for either uniform positive or uniform negative queries.

2.1 Hash families

In [1], **universal hash classes** were introduced. For $d \geq 2$, a family of functions from U to $[m]$ is d-wise independent (or d-**universal**) if for any d distinct elements $x_1, x_2, \ldots, x_d$ from U, the hash values $h(x_1), h(x_2), \ldots, h(x_d)$ are uniformly and independently distributed over $[m]$.

Let $\mathcal{H}_m^d$ denote a d-wise independent hash family of hash functions from U to $[m]$. It is well known that if $d \geq 2$ and $m \geq n^2$, for any $S \in \binom{U}{n}$, with at least $\frac{1}{2}$ probability a uniformly random $h \in \mathcal{H}_m^d$ maps each element in S to a distinct value; i.e., it is a *perfect hash function*.

We use the following hash family, first introduced in [4].

DEFINITION 4 (DM [4]). *For $f \in \mathcal{H}_m^d$, $g \in \mathcal{H}_r^d$, and $z \in [m]^r$ the hash function $h_{f,g,z} : U \to [m]$ is defined by*

$$h_{f,g,z}(x) := (f(x) + z_{g(x)}) \bmod m.$$

The hash family $\mathcal{R}_{r,m}^d$ is

$$\mathcal{R}_{r,m}^d := \{ h_{f,g,z} \mid f \in \mathcal{H}_m^d, g \in \mathcal{H}_r^d, z \in [m]^r \}.$$

Given a hash function and a set of elements, we define the buckets and loads as follows.

DEFINITION 5. *For $h : U \to [m]$, $S \subseteq U$, and $i \in [m]$, the i-th bucket $B(S, h, i) := \{ x \in S \mid h(x) = i \}$, and the load of the i-th bucket is $\ell(S, h, i) := |B(S, h, i)|$.*

The following theorem is from [11]. It bounds the deviation of the sum of a 0-1 valued d-wise independent sequence.

THEOREM 6 (COROLLARY 4.20, [11]). *Let $X_1, \ldots, X_n$ be 0-1 valued, d-wise independent, equidistributed random variables. Let $X = \sum_i^n X_i$. If $d \leq 2E[X]$, then*

$$\Pr[X - E[X] > t] \leq O\left(\frac{(E[X])^{d/2}}{t^d} \right).$$

The following is a special case of the Hoeffding's theorem [10].

THEOREM 7 (HOEFFDING). *Let $Y_1, \ldots, Y_r$ be independent random variables with range of values in $[0, d]$. Let $Y = \sum_i^r Y_i$, and $c > e$ be some constant. If $cE[Y] \leq rd$, then*

$$\Pr[Y \geq cE[Y]] \leq \left(\frac{e}{c} \right)^{\frac{c}{d} E[Y]}.$$

For d-universal hash families, the following theorem holds.

THEOREM 8 (FACT 2.2, [4]). *Let S be a fixed set of n elements. Let f be chosen from $\mathcal{H}_m^d$ uniformly at random, where $d > 2$ is a constant and $m \leq 2n/d$. Then*

$$\Pr[\forall i \in [m], \ell(S, f, i) \leq d] \geq 1 - n \cdot (2n/m)^d.$$

The following lemma characterizes the load distribution of functions from various families.

LEMMA 9 (EXTENDED FROM [4, 8, 11]). *Fix an $S \in \binom{U}{n}$. Let $c > e$ and $d > 2$ be constants. The following holds:*

1. *For $r = n^{1-\delta}$ where $\frac{2}{d+2} < \delta < 1 - \frac{1}{d}$, and g from $\mathcal{H}_r^d$, $\Pr[\forall i \in [r], \ell(S, g, i) \leq cn/r] \geq 1 - o(1)$.*

2. *For $m = \frac{n}{\alpha \ln n}$ where $\alpha > \frac{d}{c(\ln c - 1)}$, and h' from $\mathcal{R}_{r,m}^d$, $\Pr[\forall i \in [m], \ell(S, h', i) \leq cn/m] \geq 1 - o(1)$*

3. *(FKS condition) For $s = \beta n$ where $\beta \geq 2$, and h from $\mathcal{R}_{r,s}^d$, $\Pr\left[\sum_{i \in [s]} (\ell(S, h, i))^2 \leq s\right] \geq \frac{1}{2}$.*

PROOF. Let $S = \{x_1, x_2, \ldots, x_n\}$.

1. For a fixed $j \in [r]$, let X_i be a 0-1 valued random variable that indicates whether $g(x_i) = j$, and let $X = \sum_i^n X_i$. It is obvious that $E[X] = \frac{n}{r} = n^\delta$. Due to Theorem 6,

$$\Pr\left[X - n^\delta \geq (c-1)n^\delta\right] \leq O\left(n^{\delta d/2}/n^{\delta d}\right)$$
$$= O\left(n^{-\delta d/2}\right).$$

Therefore,

$$\Pr\left[\exists j \in [r], \ell(S, g, j) > \frac{cn}{r}\right]$$
$$\leq r \cdot \Pr\left[\ell(S, g, j) > cn^\delta\right]$$
$$\leq n^{1-\delta} \cdot \Pr\left[X - n^\delta > (c-1)n^\delta\right]$$
$$\leq O\left(n^{1-\delta-\delta d/2}\right) = o(1).$$

2. We assume that h' is defined by (f, g, z) where f and g are randomly drawn from $\mathcal{H}_m^d$ and $\mathcal{H}_r^d$ respectively, and z is chosen uniformly from $[m]^r$. We define the following two events

$\mathcal{E}_1 : \forall i \in [r], \ell(S, g, i) \leq cn/r$;
$\mathcal{E}_2 : \forall i \in [r], \forall j \in [m], \ell(B(S, g, i), f, j) \leq d$.

Due to the first part, $\mathcal{E}_1$ holds with probability $1 - o(1)$. Conditioning on $\mathcal{E}_1$, according to Theorem 8, with probability $1 - O(n^{\delta(d+1)}/m^d)$, it holds that

$$\forall j \in [m], \ell(B(S, g, i), f, j) \leq d.$$

By union bound, event $\mathcal{E}_2$ holds with probability

$$1 - O(n^{1-\delta} \cdot n^{\delta(d+1)}/m^d) = 1 - O(n^{1-d(1-\delta)}(\ln n)^d)$$
$$= 1 - o(1).$$

Therefore,

$$\Pr[\mathcal{E}_1 \wedge \mathcal{E}_2] = \Pr[\mathcal{E}_1] \cdot \Pr[\mathcal{E}_2 \mid \mathcal{E}_1]$$
$$= (1 - o(1))(1 - o(1))$$
$$= 1 - o(1).$$

Conditioning on $\mathcal{E}_1 \wedge \mathcal{E}_2$, for any fixed $j \in [m]$, for $i = 1, 2, \ldots, r$, define random variable Y_i as

$$Y_i := |\{x \in S \mid g(x) = i \text{ and}$$
$$f(x) + z_{g(x)} \equiv j \pmod{m}\}|.$$

Let $Y = \sum_i^r Y_i$. Note that

$$Y_i = \ell(B(S, g, i), h', j)$$
$$= \ell(B(S, g, i), f, (j - z_i + m) \bmod m),$$

and $Y = \ell(S, h', j)$.

Because $\mathcal{E}_2$ holds, $Y_i \leq d$ for all $i \in [r]$, and Y_i are independent because z_i are independent. We can compute the expectation of Y_i conditioning on the choices of f and g as follows.

$E[Y_i \mid f, g]$
$$= \sum_{z_i \in [m]} \frac{1}{m} \ell(B(S, g, i), f, (j - z_i + m) \bmod m)$$
$$= \frac{1}{m} \sum_{k \in [m]} \ell(B(S, g, i), f, k)$$
$$= \frac{1}{m} \ell(S, g, i).$$

Therefore

$$E[Y] = E[E[Y \mid f, g]]$$
$$= \frac{1}{m} E\left[\sum_{i \in [r]} \ell(S, g, i)\right]$$
$$= \frac{|S|}{m} = \frac{n}{m}.$$

According to Theorem 7, it holds that

$$\Pr[Y \geq cn/m] \leq (e/c)^{c\alpha \ln n/d} = o(n^{-1}).$$

By union bound,

$$\Pr[\forall j \in [m], \ell(S, h', j) \leq cn/m]$$
$$= 1 - m \cdot \Pr[Y \leq cn/m]$$
$$= 1 - o(1).$$

Recall that the above holds when conditioning on $\mathcal{E}_1 \wedge \mathcal{E}_2$. Since $\Pr[\mathcal{E}_1 \wedge \mathcal{E}_2] = 1 - o(1)$, the event

$$\forall j \in [m], \ell(S, h', j) \leq cn/m$$

holds unconditionally with probability at least $(1 - o(1))(1 - o(1)) = 1 - o(1)$.

3. For every $i, j \in [n]$ where $i \neq j$, let X_{ij} be 0-1 valued random variable that indicates whether $h(x_i) = h(x_j)$. Let $X = \sum_{i \neq j} X_{ij}$ be the total number of ordered collision pairs. It is easy to see that

$$X = 2 \sum_{i \in [s]} \binom{\ell(S, h, i)}{2} = \sum_{i \in [s]} (\ell(S, h, i))^2 - n.$$

Note that h is at least 2-wise independent, thus for any $i \neq j$, $E[X_{ij}] = \Pr[h(x_i) = h(x_j)] = 1/s$, thus $E[X] = n(n-1)/s$. Due to Markov's inequality,

$$\Pr\left[\sum_{i \in [s]} (\ell(S, h, i))^2 > s\right] = \Pr[X > s - n] \leq \frac{E[X]}{(s - n)}$$
$$\leq \frac{1}{\beta(\beta - 1)}$$
$$\leq 1/2.$$

$\square$

2.2 Data structure construction

Let $c = 2e$. For $d > 2$, choose appropriate constants α and β as stated in Lemma 9, and let $r = n^{1-\delta}$ and $m = \frac{n}{\alpha \ln n}$. In addition, choose an appropriate constant $\beta \geq 2$ to make $s = \beta n$ divisible by m.

Given any data set $S \in \binom{U}{n}$, uniformly choose $f \in \mathcal{H}_s^d$, $g \in \mathcal{H}_r^d$, and $z \in [s]^r$, and construct a uniformly random $h \in \mathcal{R}_{r,s}^d$ by letting $h(x) := (f(x) + z_{g(x)}) \bmod s$. Define a new hash function $h' : U \to [m]$ by $h'(x) = h(x) \bmod m$. Note that h' is a uniformly random function from the family $\mathcal{R}_{r,m}^d$ because m divides s. Specifically,

$$h'(x) = \big(f(x) + z_{g(x)}\big) \bmod s \bmod m$$
$$= \big(f(x) \bmod m + z_{g(x)} \bmod m\big) \bmod m.$$

For uniform $f \in \mathcal{H}_s^d$ and uniform $z \in [s]^r$, $(f \bmod m)$ and $(z \bmod m)$ are uniform over $\mathcal{H}_m^d$ and $[m]^r$ respectively. Therefore, h' is uniform over $\mathcal{R}_{r,m}^d$.

We would like our hash function to satisfy the property:

$$\mathcal{P}(S) := \left\{ (g, h', h) \in \mathcal{H}_r^d \times \mathcal{R}_{r,m}^d \times \mathcal{R}_{r,s}^d \;\middle|\; \right.$$
$$\forall i \in [r], \ell(S, g, i) \le cn/r,$$
$$\text{and } \forall i \in [m], \ell(S, h', i) \le cn/m,$$
$$\left. \text{and } \sum_{i \in [s]} \ell^2(S, h, i) \le s \right\}$$

Due to Lemma 9, and by applying the union bound to all unwanted events, for the above g, h' and h, it holds that $(g, h', h) \in \mathcal{P}(S)$ with probability at least $1/2 - o(1)$. Therefore by repeatedly generating (g, h', h), we satisfy $\mathcal{P}(S)$ within expected $O(1)$ trials. Note that $\mathcal{P}(S)$ can be verified in $O(n)$ time in a unit-cost machine, thus a good hash function can be found within expected $O(n)$ time.

The data structure is organized in rows of cells where each row contains s cells. Let $T(i, j)$ represent the j-th cell in the i-th row in the data structure. T is constructed as follows:

- Let $a_0, a_1, \ldots, a_{2d-1}$ denote the $2d$ words that represent the two d-universal functions f and g. Let $T(i, j) = a_i$ for every $i \in [2d]$ and every $j \in [s]$. Let $T(2d, j) = z[j \bmod r]$ for every $j \in [s]$.

- We say that h assigns the n elements in S into s buckets, and h' arranges the buckets into m groups according to the congruence classes of h modulo m. For group $i \in [m]$, we define the *group-base-address* $GBA_S(i)$ as $GBA_S(0) = 0$ and

$$GBA_S(i) = GBA_S(i-1) + \sum_{k \in [s/m]} \ell^2(S, h, km + i - 1).$$

  The vector GBA_S can be computed in $O(n)$ time in a unit-cost machine. Due to the property $\mathcal{P}(S)$, $GBA_S(i) \le s$ for any $i \in [m]$. Let $T(2d+1, j) = GBA_S(j \bmod m)$, i.e. each bucket stores the group-base-address of the group that the bucket belongs to.

- Let a *group-histogram* be a binary string where the load of each bucket in the group is represented consecutively in unary code separated by zeros. Each group contains $s/m = \alpha\beta \ln n$ buckets, and due to property $\mathcal{P}(S)$, each group contains at most $cn/m = c\alpha \ln n$ elements from S. Therefore the group-histogram uses at most $\alpha(\beta + c) \ln n$ bits. Let $\rho := \lceil \frac{\alpha(\beta+c)\ln n}{b} \rceil$. Observe that because $b = \Theta(\log n)$, $\rho = O(1)$. Let $a'_{0j}, a'_{1j} \ldots, a'_{\rho-1,j}$ denote the ρ words that store the group-histogram of group j.

Let $T(2d+2+i, j) = a'_{i,(j \bmod m)}$, for $i = 0, 1, \ldots, \rho - 1$, and for all $j \in [s]$.

- The last two rows are used to perfectly hash each bucket. Each bucket $i \in [s]$ owns $\ell^2(S, h, i)$ cells in each row. Due to $\mathcal{P}(S)$, the total space is at most s. The spaces owned by the buckets are organized in groups. If bucket i is the k-th bucket in group j, then the spaces owned by the buckets are sorted lexicographically. This can be done in a total $O(n)$ time in a unit-cost machine.

  In the $(2d+\rho+1)$th row, for each individual bucket i, the perfect hash function h_i^* is stored repeatedly in the space owned by the bucket. In the $(2d+\rho+2)$th row, the actual data in each bucket i is stored according to the hash function h_i^*.

The table T has $(2d + \rho + 2) = O(1)$ rows, each of which contains $s = O(n)$ words, for a total of $O(n)$ words. Each step of the construction costs $O(n)$ time, for a total of $O(n)$ time.

2.3 Queries and contention

We query whether x is in S with the following algorithm. Each random choice is assumed to be independent and uniform within its range.

1. For each $i \in [2d]$, choose $j \in [s]$, and read $T(i, j)$; this gives f and g. Next choose $k \in [s/r]$ and read $T(2d, kr + g(x))$, which stores $z_{g(x)}$. We can now compute $h = (f + z_g) \bmod s$ and $h' = h \bmod m$.

2. Choose k in $[s/m]$, and read $T(2d, km + h'(x))$, which stores $GBA_S(h'(x))$. For each $i \in [\rho]$ where $\rho = \lceil \frac{\alpha(\beta+c)\ln n}{b} \rceil$, choose some $j \in [s/m]$, and read $T(2d + 1 + i, jm + h'(x))$; we thus obtain the group-histogram group $h'(x)$. With the group-base-address and the group-histogram, the exact range of the address owned by bucket $h(x)$ can be determined: it runs from $i_{h(x)}$ to $i'_{h(x)}$ inclusively, where

$$i_{h(x)} := GBA_S(h'(x))$$
$$+ \sum_{k=0}^{\lceil h(x)/m \rceil - 1} \ell^2\big(S, h, km + h'(x)\big),$$
$$i'_{h(x)} := i_{h(x)} + \ell^2(S, h, h(x)) - 1.$$

   All the values $\ell^2(S, h, km + h'(x))$ for $k \in [s/m]$ are stored in the group-histogram of group $h'(x)$.

3. If $i'_{h(x)} < i_{h(x)}$, the bucket $h(x)$ is empty: return 0. Otherwise, choose $j \in [i_{h(x)}, i'_{h(x)}]$ and read $T(2d + \rho + 1, j)$ to get the perfect hash function h^*. If $T(2d + \rho + 2, i_{h(x)} + h^*(x)) = x$, return 1, else return 0.

The correctness of the algorithm is guaranteed by the existence of hash functions with property $\mathcal{P}(S)$ and the existence of the perfect hashing scheme for each bucket, which is guaranteed. The query algorithm makes at most one probe to each row of T, thus the cell-probe complexity is $O(1)$.

For contention, we first consider the contribution of the positive queries. All events below are conditioned on the target element being in S. At each step before the last probe, an expected 1, $\frac{1}{n}\ell(S, g, i_1)$, $\frac{1}{n}\ell(S, h', i_2)$, or $\frac{1}{n}\ell(S, h, i_3)$ probes are balanced over a range of size s, s/r, s/m, or $\ell^2(S, h, i_3)$ respectively, therefore due to property $\mathcal{P}(S)$, the maximum contention is $O(1/n)$. For the last probe, the perfect hash function sends each query to a distinct cell so the contention is obviously $O(1/n)$. Therefore, the total contention contributed by positive queries is at most $O(1/n)$.

LEMMA 10. *Let $\bar{S}$ denote $U \setminus S$, and $N = |U| = \omega(n)$. For any hash function $h : U \to [k]$ which is uniform over the domain, for sufficiently large n, $\forall i \in [k], \ell(\bar{S}, h, i) \leq 2(N - n)/k$.*

PROOF. Because h is uniform over the domain, $\ell(U, h, i) = N/k$ for any $i \in [k]$. For $N = \omega(n)$, it holds that $\ell(\bar{S}, h, i) = \ell(U, h, i) - \ell(S, h, i) \leq N/k \leq 2(N - n)/k$. □

Note that g, h', and h are all uniform over the domain. This is because any d-universal function must be 1-universal. Due to Lemma 10, the loads of negative queries to all types of buckets are asymptotically even. The same argument as above can be applied to bound the contention caused by negative queries to $O(1/n)$.

3. A LOWER BOUND FOR ARBITRARY QUERY DISTRIBUTIONS

In this section, we prove a cell-probe lower bound for low-contention data structures with arbitrary query distribution. The lower bound is on the cost of queries by an algorithm that does not know the distribution; however, the algorithm that constructs the data structure may known the distribution, and may optimize the data structure to minimize contention by encoding the information of query distribution in the data structure to guide the query algorithm.

The lower bound itself is proved based on the following intuition: the more uniform a random probe is, the less specific information it retrieves; but non-uniform probes will only result in low contention if the query algorithm already has some knowledge about the query distribution. So to obtain information about a specific query, the query algorithm must steadily increase its knowledge of the query distribution through increasingly non-uniform probes. By tracking how much information the query algorithm has about the query distribution (and thus how evenly spread out it must keep its probes), we can bound the query time subject to bounds on the contention.

We formalize this argument using VC-dimension [14], a measure of complexity of classification problems, by treating a data structure problem $f : Q \times \mathcal{D} \to \{0, 1\}$ as a class of $|\mathcal{D}|$ many classifications of Q.

DEFINITION 11. *The **VC-dimension** of a data structure problem $f : Q \times \mathcal{D} \to \{0, 1\}$, denoted by VC-dim$(f)$, is the maximum n such that there exists a set $\{x_1, x_2, \dots, x_n\} \in \binom{Q}{n}$ such that for any assignment $y \in \{0, 1\}^n$, there exists some $S \in \mathcal{D}$, with $f(x_i, S) = y_i$ for all i.*

It is easy to see that the VC-dimension of the membership problem is n, where n is the cardinality of the data set. This allows us to translate our results for problems of arbitrary VC-dimension into specific results for membership.

We consider a special class of cell-probing schemes $(T, \mathcal{A})$ whose cell-probing algorithm $\mathcal{A}$ satisfies a natural restriction described as follows.

DEFINITION 12. *A **table structure** is a mapping T which for any data set $S \in \mathcal{D}$ and any query distribution q over Q, specifies a table $T_{S,q} : [s] \to \{0, 1\}^b$ of s cells, each of which contains b bits.*

*Given any query $x \in Q$, a **cell-probing algorithm** $\mathcal{A}$ returns $f(x, S)$ by making at most t^* randomized adaptive probes $I_x^{(1)}, I_x^{(2)}, \dots, I_x^{(t^*)} \in [s]$ to the table $T_{S,q}$, such that the maximum contention satisfies $\Phi_t \leq \phi^*$ for any $t \leq t^*$, and for any fixed query x and any fixed table $T_{S,q}$, the random variables $I_x^{(t)}$ for all $t \leq t^*$ are jointly independent.*

The independence of cell-probes of $\mathcal{A}$ does not make $\mathcal{A}$ non-adaptive, because the independence holds only when the query and the table are both fixed. Note that in this sense all deterministic cell-probing algorithms (both adaptive or non-adaptive) satisfy this property, because once the table and the query are both fixed, the sequence of the cell-probes of a deterministic cell-probing algorithm are fixed, hence they are jointly independent. Informally speaking, for $\mathcal{A}$, the randomness is used only for balancing the cell-probes, but is not involved in the process of decision making. The upper bound presented in the previous section and any upper bounds constructed by the technique of distributing probes across multiple copies of critical cells are all included in this definition.

We prove the following lower bound theorem.

THEOREM 13. *For any data structure problem f with a VC-dimension VC-dim$(f) = n$, if there exists a cell-probing scheme $(T, \mathcal{A})$ as defined in Definition 12, with size of cell $b \leq \text{Polylog}(n)$ and contention $\phi^* \leq \frac{\text{Polylog}(n)}{s}$, then the cell-probe complexity $t^* = \Omega(\log \log n)$.*

The theorem is proved by first running n different instances of queries in parallel and then bounding the speed with which these parallel instances of the cell-probing algorithm gather information.

LEMMA 14. *If there exists a cell-probing scheme $(T, \mathcal{A})$ for the data structure problem f where $(T, \mathcal{A})$ and f are as in Theorem 13, then there exists a communication protocol between an algorithm $\mathcal{A}''$ and a black-box $\mathcal{B}$ which is specified as follows. The input to $\mathcal{B}$ is an arbitrary **stochastic vector** $q \in [0, 1]^n$ that $\sum_{i=1}^n q_i \leq 1$, which is initially unknown to $\mathcal{A}''$. The communication between $\mathcal{A}''$ and $\mathcal{B}$ occurs in rounds.*

1. *At round t, $\mathcal{A}''$ specifies an $n \times s$ matrix P_t, called a **probe specification**, and sends it to $\mathcal{B}$, where P_t is adaptive to the information received previously by $\mathcal{A}''$, and for any $1 \leq i \leq n$, it holds that*

$$\sum_{j=1}^s P_t(i, j) \leq 1; \tag{1}$$

$$\max_{1 \leq j \leq s} P_t(i, j) \leq \frac{\phi^*}{q_i}. \tag{2}$$

2. *Upon receiving a P_t, $\mathcal{B}$ sends C_t bits to $\mathcal{A}''$, where C_t is a random variable satisfying*

$$\mathrm{E}[C_t] \leq b \cdot \sum_{j=1}^s \max_{1 \leq i \leq n} P_t(i, j), \tag{3}$$

where the expectation is conditioned on P_t, thus conditioned on all previous communication between $\mathcal{A}''$ and $\mathcal{B}$.

3. *After t^* rounds, the expected number of bits received by $\mathcal{A}''$ is at least $n \cdot 2^{-2t^*}$ bits from $\mathcal{B}$.*

PROOF. The idea of the proof is to run n instances of the cell-probing algorithm in parallel; together these instances form $\mathcal{A}''$. We observe that the cell-probes of each individual cell-probing algorithm can be specified by a probability distribution of probes over the table, and the joint distribution of the cell-probes of all n instances can be arbitrarily chosen by us as long as the marginal distribution of the cell-probe of each individual instance is the same as before, therefore (by our choice of the joint distribution) the total information obtained by $\mathcal{A}''$ in each round is bounded.

The details of the proof are given in Appendix A. □

The following two combinatorial lemmas are needed for the proof of Theorem 13.

LEMMA 15. *Let M be an $N \times n$ nonnegative matrix. Let $r = \sqrt{5\epsilon^{-1}\delta n \ln N}$. Assume that for every row $1 \leq u \leq N$, there exists a set $R_u \in \binom{\{1,2,\ldots,n\}}{r}$ of r entries such that $\sum_{i \in R_u} M(u,i) \leq \delta$. Then there exists $q \in [0,1]^n$ that $\sum_i q_i = \epsilon$, such that for all $1 \leq u \leq N$, there exists $1 \leq i \leq n$, such that $M(u,i) < q_i$.*

PROOF. For each $1 \leq u \leq N$, sort $\{M(u,i) \mid i \in R_u\}$ by non-decreasing order and let $R'_u \subseteq \{1,2,\ldots,n\}$ be the indices of the smallest $\frac{r}{2}$ entries. It holds that $\forall i \in R'_u$, $M(u,i) \leq \frac{2\delta}{r}$, as otherwise it contradicts the assumption that $\sum_{i \in R_u} M(u,i) \leq \delta$.

It holds that for any choice of such $\{R'_u\}_{1 \leq u \leq N}$, there exists a $T \subseteq \{1,2,\ldots,n\}$, such that $|T| = \frac{2n \ln N}{r}$ and T intersects all R'_u. We prove this by the probabilistic method: let T be a uniformly random subset of $\{1,2,\ldots,n\}$ of size $\frac{2n \ln N}{r}$, thus each R'_u is missed by T with probability less than $(1-r/2n)^{2n \ln N/r} < 1/N$, thus by the union bound, T intersects all R'_u with positive probability.

Fix such a T, define $q \in [0,1]^n$ as $q_i = \epsilon|T|^{-1} = \frac{r\epsilon}{2n \ln N}$ if $i \in T$, and $q_i = 0$ if otherwise. Therefore, $\sum_i q_i = \epsilon$, and for any $1 \leq u \leq N$, for such $i \in R'_u \cap T$, it holds that $M(u,i) \leq \frac{2\delta}{r} < \frac{r\epsilon}{2n \ln N} = q_i$. □

LEMMA 16. *For any nonnegative $n \times s$ matrix P that $\sum_j P(i,j) \leq 1$ for every i, let R be the largest subset of $\{1,2,\ldots,n\}$ that $\sum_{i \in R} \frac{1}{\max_j P(i,j)} \leq s$. Then it holds that*

$$|R| \geq \sum_{j=1}^{s} \max_{1 \leq i \leq n} P(i,j).$$

PROOF. The sum $\sum_j \max_i P(i,j)$ chooses exactly s entries to sum up. Let A_i be the set of chosen columns in row i. Let $x_i := \sum_{j \in A_i} P(i,j)$. Note that $x_i \leq \sum_j P(i,j) \leq 1$. By the pigeonhole principle, for any $1 \leq i \leq n$,

$$|A_i| \geq \frac{\sum_{j \in A_i} P(i,j)}{\max_j P(i,j)} = \frac{x_i}{\max_j P(i,j)}.$$

Note that $\sum_i |A_i| = s$, thus $\sum_i \frac{x_i}{\max_j P(i,j)} \leq \sum_i |A_i| = s$.

Therefore the sum $\sum_j \max_i P(i,j)$ can be written as

$$\sum_j \max_i P(i,j) = \sum_i \sum_{j \in A_i} P(i,j) = \sum_i x_i,$$

subject to the constraints that $\sum_i \frac{x_i}{\max_j P(i,j)} \leq s$ and $x_i \leq 1$. It is easy to see that the value of $\sum_i x_i$ is maximized when letting $x_i = 1$ for $i \in R$ and $x_i = 0$ for $i \notin R$, therefore $\sum_j \max_i P(i,j) = \sum_i x_i \leq |R|$. □

Proof of Theorem 13:

Given the algorithm $\mathcal{A}''$ as described in Lemma 14, we will bound the speed that $\mathcal{A}''$ gathers information. Due to Lemma 14, $\mathcal{A}''$ is a decision tree in which the current node of depth $(t-1)$ has $N_t := 2^{C_{t-1}}$ children, each of which corresponds to a next probe specification P_t. We number these P_t by $u \in [N_t]$ and denote each as $P_t^{(u)}$, where u can be interpreted as the bit string received by $\mathcal{A}''$ at round $t-1$. We then inductively bound the next C_t.

Let $M^{(t)}$ be an $N_t \times n$ matrix defined as follows:

$$M^{(t)}(u,i) := \frac{\phi^*}{\max_j P_t^{(u)}(i,j)}.$$

Each row of the matrix $M^{(t)}$ corresponds to a possible next probe specification. We say that the stochastic vector q **violates** row u of $M^{(t)}$ if there exists $1 \leq i \leq n$, such that $M^{(t)}(u,i) < q_i$. Note that if row u of $M^{(t)}$ is violated by q, then according to (2), the next probe specification cannot be $P_t^{(u)}$.

Let $r_t := \sqrt{5t^*\phi^*sn \ln N_t}$. We say that a row u of $M^{(t)}$ is **good** if there exists $R \subseteq \{1,2,\ldots,n\}$ such that $|R| = r_t$ and $\sum_{i \in R} M^{(t)}(u,i) \leq \phi^*s$.

We claim that if a row u is not good, then for the corresponding $P^{(u)}$, it holds that

$$\sum_{j=1}^{s} \max_{1 \leq i \leq n} P_t^{(u)}(i,j) \leq r_t. \tag{4}$$

The proof is as follows: If a row u of $M^{(t)}$ is not good, then by definition, for any R of size r_t, $\sum_{i \in R} M^{(t)}(u,i) > \phi^*s$, thus for any R' that $\sum_{i \in R'} \frac{1}{\max_j P_t^{(u)}(i,j)} \leq s$, it must hold that $|R'| < r_t$, therefore due to Lemma 16, it holds that $\sum_{j=1}^{s} \max_{1 \leq i \leq n} P_t^{(u)}(x_i,j) \leq r_t$.

Due to (4) and (3), the amount of information brought by a set of probes $P_t^{(u)}$ where u is a bad row in $M^{(t)}$, is bounded by br_t bits. We show by an adversary argument that there exists a q that $\mathcal{A}''$ always choose probes corresponding to bad rows. At each round t, the adversary always chooses some q that violates all the good rows in $M^{(t)}$. According to Lemma 15, the adversary can do so as long as $t \leq t^*$. Setting $\epsilon = \frac{1}{t^*}$ and $\delta = \phi^*s$ in Lemma 15, in each round, the adversary can increase the value of some q_i so that $\sum_{i=1}^{n} q_i$ is increased by at most $\frac{1}{t^*}$, thereby violating all good rows in the current $M^{(t)}$. Thus before round t^*, the vector q is always stochastic. Note that increasing the value of q_i will never make a violated row non-violated, so it will not make the adversary inconsistent.

Against such an adversary, at each round t, $\mathcal{A}''$ can only choose a probe specification $P_t^{(u)}$ where u is a bad row in $M^{(t)}$, according to Claim (4), which implies that

$$\sum_{j=1}^{s} \max_{1 \leq i \leq n} P_t(i,j) \leq r_t = \sqrt{5t^*\phi^*sn \ln N_t}$$

$$= \sqrt{5t^*\phi^*snC_{t-1} \ln 2}.$$

Due to (3), it holds that

$$\mathrm{E}[C_t] \leq b \cdot \sum_j \max_i P_t(i,j) \leq \sqrt{(5\ln 2)b^2t^*\phi^*snC_{t-1}},$$

where the expectation is conditioned on all previous rounds of communication. Therefore the following recursion holds

351

for the sequence of random variables $C_1, C_2, \ldots, C_t$:

$$\mathrm{E}[C_t \mid C_{t-1}] \leq \sqrt{(5\ln 2)b^2 t^* \phi^* sn C_{t-1}}\,.$$

The square root function is concave, thus by Jensen's inequality, it holds for the unconditional expectation that

$$\begin{aligned}
\mathrm{E}[C_t] &= \mathrm{E}[\mathrm{E}[C_t \mid C_{t-1}]] \\
&\leq \mathrm{E}\left[\sqrt{(5\ln 2)b^2 t^* \phi^* sn C_{t-1}}\right] \\
&\leq \sqrt{(5\ln 2)b^2 t^* \phi^* sn \cdot \mathrm{E}[C_{t-1}]}\,.
\end{aligned}$$

Before the first probe, q is unknown to $\mathcal{A}''$, thus due to (2), for any i, j, $P_1(x_i, j) \leq \phi^*$, therefore

$$\mathrm{E}[C_1] \leq b \cdot \sum_j \max_i P_1(x_i, j) \leq b\phi^* s.$$

Let $a_1 := b\phi^* s$ and $a := (5\ln 2)b^2 t^* \phi^* sn$. The following recursion holds for $\mathrm{E}[C_t]$ that

$$\begin{aligned}
\mathrm{E}[C_1] &\leq a_1; \\
\mathrm{E}[C_t] &\leq (a \cdot \mathrm{E}[C_{t-1}])^{\frac{1}{2}}.
\end{aligned}$$

By induction, $\mathrm{E}[C_t] \leq a_1^{2^{1-t}} a^{1-2^{1-t}}$.

After t^* rounds, the expected total number of bits received by $\mathcal{A}''$ is at least $n \cdot 2^{-2t^*}$, therefore

$$n \cdot 2^{-2t^*} \leq \sum_{t \leq t^*} \mathrm{E}[C_t] \leq \sum_{t \leq t^*} a_1^{2^{1-t}} a^{1-2^{1-t}} \leq a_1 a^{1-2^{-t^*}}.$$

With the assumption that $b \leq \mathrm{Polylog}(n)$ and $\phi^* \leq \frac{\mathrm{Polylog}(n)}{s}$, it holds that $a_1 \leq \mathrm{Polylog}(n)$ and $a \leq n \cdot \mathrm{Polylog}(n)$. Solving the above inequality, we have that $t^* \geq \log\log n - o(\log\log n) = \Omega(\log\log n)$. Theorem 13 is proved. ∎

4. CONCLUSION

In this paper, we propose to study the memory contention caused by concurrent data structure queries. To study the problem, we introduce a measure of contention to the classic cell-probe model of static data structures. We show that if all positive queries are equally probable and similarly all negatively are equally probable, then there exists a static dictionary which answers membership queries with asymptotically optimal performance of time, space and contention. For the general case that the query distribution is arbitrary, we show that for all data structure problems with non-degenerating VC-dimensions, if the randomness is used only for balancing the probes, then even with unbounded space, the time and contention cannot be both optimal.

A possible future direction is to remove the assumption of independent cell-probes in the lower bound. Note that we only rely on this assumption to make sure that the contention constraint of (2) holds conditioning on any particular sequence of previous cell-probes, which is required by the adversary argument. We suspect that with a more careful analysis, this assumption can be removed, which would imply that the lower bound holds not only for the randomized data structures that use the randomness only for balancing probes, but also for the true randomized data structures where the randomness is also involved in the computation of queries.

Another interesting and perhaps more realistic future direction is to study the contention caused by the *updates* in dynamic data structures.

5. REFERENCES

[1] J. Carter and M. Wegman. Universal classes of hash functions. *Journal of Computer and System Sciences (JCSS)*, 18(2):143–154, 1979.

[2] D. Culler, R. Karp, D. Patterson, A. Sahay, K. Schauser, E. Santos, R. Subramonian, and T. Von Eicken. LogP: Towards a realistic model of parallel computation. *ACM SIGPLAN Notices*, 28(7):1–12, 1993.

[3] M. Dietzfelbinger and F. Meyer auf der Heide. An optimal parallel dictionary. In *Proceedings of the first annual ACM Symposium on Parallel Algorithms and Architectures (SPAA)*, pages 360–368. ACM New York, NY, USA, 1989.

[4] M. Dietzfelbinger and F. Meyer auf der Heide. A new universal class of hash functions and dynamic hashing in real time. In *Proceedings of the 17th International Colloquium on Automata, Languages and Programming (ICALP)*, volume 443, pages 6–19. Springer, 1990.

[5] M. Dietzfelbinger and F. Meyer auf der Heide. How to distribute a dictionary in a complete network. In *Proceedings of the twenty-second annual ACM Symposium on Theory of Computing (STOC)*, pages 117–127. ACM New York, NY, USA, 1990.

[6] C. Dwork, M. Herlihy, and O. Waarts. Contention in shared memory algorithms. *Journal of the ACM (JACM)*, 44(6):779–805, 1997.

[7] S. Fortune and J. Wyllie. Parallelism in random access machines. In *Proceedings of the tenth annual ACM Symposium on Theory of Computing (STOC)*, pages 114–118. ACM New York, NY, USA, 1978.

[8] M. Fredman, J. Komlós, and E. Szemerédi. Storing a Sparse Table with O(1) Worst Case Access Time. *Journal of the ACM (JACM)*, 31(3):538–544, 1984.

[9] M. Herlihy, B. Lim, and N. Shavit. Low contention load balancing on large-scale multiprocessors. In *Proceedings of the fourth annual ACM Symposium on Parallel Algorithms and Architectures (SPAA)*, pages 219–227. ACM New York, NY, USA, 1992.

[10] W. Hoeffding. Probability inequalities for sums of bounded random variables. *Journal of the American Statistical Association*, 58(301):13–30, 1963.

[11] C. P. Kruskal, L. Rudolph, and M. Snir. A complexity theory of efficient parallel algorithms. *Theor. Comput. Sci.*, 71(1):95–132, 1990.

[12] R. Pagh and F. Rodler. Cuckoo hashing. *Journal of Algorithms*, 51(2):122–144, 2004.

[13] P. Tzeng and D. Lawrie. Distributing hot-spot addressing in large-scale multiprocessors. *IEEE Transactions on Computers*, 100(36):388–395, 1987.

[14] V. Vapnik and A. Y. Chervonenkis. On the uniform convergence of relative frequencies of events to their probabilities. *Theory of Probability and its Applications*, 16(2):264–280, 1971.

APPENDIX

A. PROOF OF LEMMA 14

The lemma is proved by first simulating the cell-probing algorithm $\mathcal{A}$ by a modified cell-probing algorithm $\mathcal{A}'$ which independently probes all cells in the table in every step, and then running n instances of $\mathcal{A}'$ in parallel as a new cell-probing algorithm $\mathcal{A}''$.

First, we observe that a randomized cell-probe can be simulated with bounded error by independently probing all cells.

DEFINITION 17. *A product-space cell-probe to a table of s cells is a random set $J \in 2^{[s]}$ such that the probability space of J is a product probability space.*

For the rest of the proof, we assume the assumption of Theorem 13.

ASSUMPTION 18. *Let f be a data structure problem with $VC\text{-}dim(f) = n$. There exists a cell-probing scheme $(T, \mathcal{A})$ as described in Definition 12, such that $(T, \mathcal{A})$ solves f with performance parameters (s, b, t^*, ϕ^*), where the size of cell $b \leq \mathrm{Polylog}(n)$ and the maximum contention $\phi^* \leq \frac{\mathrm{Polylog}(n)}{s}$.*

LEMMA 19. *If Assumption 18 is true, then there exists a product-space cell-probing algorithm $\mathcal{A}'$, such that on any valid table $T_{S,q}$, for any query $x \in Q$, the following properties hold for the sequence of product-space cell-probes*

$$J_x^{(1)}, J_x^{(2)}, \ldots, J_x^{(t^*)}.$$

1. *At any step $t \leq t^*$, $\mathcal{A}'$ fails (returns a special symbol $\perp$) independently with probability at most $\frac{3}{4}$. Conditioned on that there is no failure after t^* steps, which is an event with probability at least 2^{-2t^*}, it holds that $J_x^{(1)}, J_x^{(2)}, \ldots, J_x^{(t^*)}$ are jointly independent and $\mathcal{A}'$ returns what $\mathcal{A}$ returns.*

2. *For any $t \leq t^*$, the total probability of each product-space cell-probe of $\mathcal{A}'$*

$$\sum_{j \in [s]} \Pr\left[j \in J_x^{(t)}\right] \leq 1; \tag{5}$$

3. *For any $t \leq t^*$, the contention of any cell $j \in [s]$*

$$q(x_i) \cdot \Pr\left[j \in J_x^{(t)}\right] \leq \phi^*. \tag{6}$$

PROOF. A cell-probe of $\mathcal{A}$ can be represented as a random variable $I \in [s]$, where I denotes the probed cell. Let $p_i := \Pr[I = i]$. Let $J \in 2^{[s]}$ represent a product-space cell-probe. Given a probability vector p, a cell-probe I is simulated by a product-space cell-probe as follows: Independently probe each cell $i \in [s]$ with probability $p_i' := \min\{p_i, \frac{1}{2}\}$. The resulting set is J. If $|J| \neq 1$, then fails; if $J = \{i\}$, then fails with a probability $\epsilon_i := \min\{p_i, 1 - p_i\}$. Let $I = i$ if not fail.

Case 1: $p_i \leq \frac{1}{2}$ for all $i \in [s]$. Then for all $i \in [s]$, $p_i' = p_i$ and $\epsilon_i = p_i$. Let $\rho = \prod_{j \in [s]}(1 - p_j)$. Since $p_i \leq \frac{1}{2}$ for all $i \in [s]$, it holds that $\rho \geq \frac{1}{4}$.
The probability

$$\Pr[I = i] = (1 - \epsilon_i) \cdot \Pr[J = \{i\}]$$
$$= (1 - p_i) \cdot p_i \prod_{j \neq i}(1 - p_j)$$
$$= p_i \rho,$$

which is proportional to p_i. The procedure succeeds with probability $\rho \geq \frac{1}{4}$.

Case 2: Let $p_0 > \frac{1}{2}$ and all other $p_i < \frac{1}{2}$. Then $p_0' = \frac{1}{2}$ and $\epsilon_0' = 1 - p_0$, and for all $i > 0$, it holds that $p_i' = p_i$ and $\epsilon_i' = p_i$. Let $\rho' = \prod_{j>0}(1 - p_j)$. It holds that $\rho' > \frac{1}{2}$ since $\sum_{j>0} p_j = 1 - p_0 < \frac{1}{2}$.
For $i \neq 0$,

$$\Pr[I = i] = (1 - p_i) \cdot \Pr[J = \{i\}] = \frac{1}{2}\rho' p_i;$$

and for cell 0,

$$\Pr[I = 0] = p_0 \cdot \Pr[J = \{i\}] = \frac{1}{2}\rho' p_0.$$

The procedure succeeds with probability $\frac{1}{2}\rho' > \frac{1}{4}$.

For both cases, a cell-probe of $\mathcal{A}$ is simulated by a product-space cell-probe with a probability at least $\frac{1}{4}$. The event of a failure occurs independently with probability at most $\frac{3}{4}$. With a probability at least 2^{-2t^*}, no failure occurs at all, conditioned on which its is obvious that $\mathcal{A}'$ can simulate $\mathcal{A}$, and the product-space cell-probes are jointly independent since the cell-probes of $\mathcal{A}$ are jointly independent.

The total probability of a product-space cell-probe is

$$\sum_i \Pr[i \in J] = \sum_i p_i' \leq 1.$$

The probability of a probe to each cell is no greater than before, therefore the maximum contention ϕ^* not increased. $\square$

We observe that by running n instances of the product-space cell-probing algorithm in parallel, the behavior of each individual instance depend only on the marginal distribution of cell-probes of the instance, but does not depend on the joint distribution of cell-probes of all n instances. Thus, the joint distribution of cell-probes can be arbitrarily chosen by us as long as the marginal distribution of cell-probes of each individual instance is the same as before.

LEMMA 20. *Let $\mathcal{A}''$ be an algorithm that on a valid table $T_{S,q}$, for a set of n queries $\{x_1, x_2, \ldots, x_n\} \in \binom{Q}{n}$, at step t, $\mathcal{A}''$ randomly probes n sets of cells $(L_{x_1}^{(t)}, L_{x_2}^{(t)}, \ldots, L_{x_n}^{(t)})$. If for every x_i where $1 \leq i \leq n$ and every $t \leq t^*$, the marginal distribution of $L_{x_i}^{(t)}$ is identical to the distribution of $J_{x_i}^{(t)}$, where $J_{x_i}^{(t)}$ is the t's product-space cell-probe of the algorithm $\mathcal{A}'$ on the same table $T_{S,q}$, then $\mathcal{A}''$ returns $f(x_i, S)$ for expected $n \cdot 2^{-2t^*}$ number of x_i.*

PROOF. Let $\mathcal{A}''$ run an instance of $\mathcal{A}'$ with input x_i in parallel for every x_i, denoted as $\mathcal{A}'_{x_i}$. Let the set of cells probed by each individual $\mathcal{A}'_{x_i}$ at time t be $L_{x_i}^{(t)}$. On a fixed table $T_{S,q}$ and for a fixed x_i, since $L_{x_i}^{(t)}$ is identically distributed as $J_{x_i}^{(t)}$, every individual instance of $\mathcal{A}'_{x_i}$ simulates a running instance of $\mathcal{A}'$ with input query x_i. By Lemma 19, each $\mathcal{A}'_{x_i}$ terminates in t^* steps without failure with probability at least 2^{-2t^*}, thus by the linearity of expectation, after t^* time, the expected total number of terminated instances is at least $n \cdot 2^{-2t^*}$. $\square$

In the next lemma, we construct a joint distribution of cell-probes which minimizes the expected total number of probed cells.

353

LEMMA 21. *For any probability distribution of $J_i \subseteq [s]$ where $1 \leq i \leq n$ and each J_i is chosen from a product probability space, there exists a joint distribution $(L_1, L_2, \ldots, L_n)$, such that for every $1 \leq i \leq n$, L_i is identically distributed as J_i, and it holds that*

$$\mathrm{E}\left[\left|\bigcup_{1 \leq i \leq n} L_i\right|\right] \leq \sum_{j \in [s]} \max_{1 \leq i \leq n} \mathrm{Pr}\left[j \in J_i\right].$$

PROOF. We construct the joint distribution of $(L_i)_i \in (2^{[s]})^n$ as follow.

- Let $\tilde{p}_j = \max_{1 \leq i \leq n} \mathrm{Pr}[j \in J_i]$. Choose each $j \in [s]$ independently with probability $\tilde{p}_j$. Let B denote the set of chosen elements of $[s]$.

- For every $1 \leq i \leq n$, let each $j \in B$ join L_i independently with probability $\frac{\mathrm{Pr}[j \in J_i]}{\tilde{p}_j}$. Note that $\tilde{p}_j \geq \mathrm{Pr}[j \in J_i]$, therefore the probability is well-defined.

For each $1 \leq i \leq n$, and for every $j \in [s]$, j joins L_i independently with probability $\tilde{p}_j \cdot \mathrm{Pr}[j$ is chosen to $L_i \mid j \in B] = \mathrm{Pr}[j \in J_i]$, thus each L_i is identically distributed as J_i.

Note that for every L_i, all of its elements are chosen from set B. It holds that

$$\mathrm{E}\left[\left|\bigcup_{1 \leq i \leq n} L_i\right|\right] \leq \mathrm{E}\left[|B|\right] = \sum_{j \in [s]} \tilde{p}_j = \sum_{j \in [s]} \max_{1 \leq i \leq n} \mathrm{Pr}[j \in J_i].$$

□

Proof of Lemma 14: Let $\{x_1, x_2, \ldots, x_n\} \in \binom{Q}{n}$ be a set of queries which achieves the VC-dimension VC-dim$(f) = n$, i.e. any Boolean assignment of $f(x_i, S)$ is possible. Let such $\{x_1, x_2, \ldots, x_n\}$ be the input query set to $\mathcal{A}''$, where $\mathcal{A}''$ is as described in Lemma 20. By an information theoretical argument, in the worst case, $\mathcal{A}''$ has to collect expected $n \cdot 2^{-2t^*}$ bits information after t^* steps. Let the joint distribution of $(L_{x_1}^{(t)}, L_{x_2}^{(t)}, \ldots, L_{x_n}^{(t)})$ of $\mathcal{A}''$ be constructed as in Lemma 21, the total number of cells probed by $\mathcal{A}''$ in step t with $(L_{x_1}^{(t)}, L_{x_2}^{(t)}, \ldots, L_{x_n}^{(t)})$ is bounded. Let the $n \times s$ matrix P_t defined as $P_t(i, j) := \mathrm{Pr}[j \in L_{x_i}^{(t)}]$, and let $q_i := q(x_i)$. Since each $L_{x_i}^{(t)}$ is identically distributed as $J_{x_i}^{(t)}$ of $\mathcal{A}'$ which is described in Lemma 19, due to (2) and (3), it holds for the P_t that $\sum_{j \in [s]} P_t(i, j) \leq 1$ and $\max_{j \in [s]} P_t(i, j) \leq \frac{\phi^*}{q_i}$. Due to Lemma 21, the expected number of bits collected by $\mathcal{A}''$ in step t is bounded by $b \cdot \sum_{j \in [s]} \max_{1 \leq i \leq n} P_t(i, j)$. By seeing the running instance of the algorithm $\mathcal{A}''$ with the input $\{x_1, x_2, \ldots, x_n\}$ as the player $\mathcal{A}''$ of the communication game, and the table $T_{S,q}$ as the black-box $\mathcal{B}$ with private input q, Lemma 14 is proved. ∎

Flat Combining and the Synchronization-Parallelism Tradeoff

Danny Hendler
Ben-Gurion University
hendlerd@cs.bgu.ac.il

Itai Incze
Tel-Aviv University
itai.in@gmail.com

Nir Shavit
Tel-Aviv University
shanir@cs.tau.ac.il

Moran Tzafrir
Tel-Aviv University
moran.tzafrir@cs.tau.ac.il

ABSTRACT

Traditional data structure designs, whether lock-based or lock-free, provide parallelism via fine grained synchronization among threads.

We introduce a new synchronization paradigm based on coarse locking, which we call *flat combining*. The cost of synchronization in flat combining is so low, that having a single thread holding a lock perform the combined access requests of all others, delivers, up to a certain non-negligible concurrency level, better performance than the most effective parallel finely synchronized implementations. We use flat-combining to devise, among other structures, new linearizable stack, queue, and priority queue algorithms that greatly outperform all prior algorithms.

Categories and Subject Descriptors

D.1.3 [**Concurrent Programming**]: Algorithms

General Terms

Algorithms, Performance

Keywords

Multiprocessors, Concurrent Data-Structures, Synchronization

1. INTRODUCTION

In the near future we will see processors with multiple computing cores on anything from phones to laptops, desktops, and servers. The scalability of applications on these machines is governed by *Amdahl's Law*, capturing the idea that the extent to which we can speed up any complex computation is limited by how much of the computation cannot be parallelized and must be executed sequentially. In many applications, the parts of the computation that are difficult to parallelize are those involving inter-thread communication via shared data structures. The design of effective concurrent data structures is thus key to the scalability of applications on multicore machines.

But how does one devise effective concurrent data structures? The traditional approach to concurrent data structure design, whether lock-based or lock-free, is to provide parallelism via fine grained synchronization among threads (see for example the Java concurrency library in the Java 6.0 JDK). From the empirical literature, to date, we get a confirmation of this approach: letting threads add parallelism via hand crafted finely synchronized data structure design allows, even at reasonably low levels of concurrency, to overtake the performance of structures protected by a single global lock [4, 14, 10, 12, 7, 16].

The premise of this paper is that the above assertion is wrong. That for a large class of data structures, the cut-off point (in terms of machine concurrency) at which finely synchronized concurrent implementations outperform ones in which access to the structure is controlled by a coarse lock, is farther out than we ever anticipated. The reason, as one can imagine, is the cost of synchronization.

This paper introduces a new synchronization paradigm which we call *flat combining* (FC). At the core of flat combining is a surprisingly low cost way to allow a thread to acquire a global lock on a structure, learn about all concurrent access requests, and then perform the combined requests of all others on it. As we show, this technique has the dual benefit of reducing the synchronization overhead on "hot" shared locations, and at the same time reducing the overall cache invalidation traffic on the structure. The effect of these reductions is so dramatic, that in a kind of "anti-Amdahl" effect, up to high levels of concurrency, it outweighs the loss of parallelism caused by allowing only one thread at a time to manipulate the structure.

This paper will discuss the fundamentals of the flat combining approach and show a collection of basic data structures to which it can be applied. For lack of space we will not be able to show all the ways in which the approach can be further extended to support higher levels of concurrency and additional classes of structures.

1.1 Flat Combining in a nutshell

In its simplest form, the idea behind flat combining is to have a given sequential data structure D be protected by a lock and have an associated dynamic publication list of a size proportional to the number of threads that are concurrently accessing it (see Figure 1). Each thread accessing D for the first time adds a thread-local publication record to the list, and publishes all its successive access/modification requests using a simple write to the request field of its publication record (there is no need for a store-load memory barrier). In each access, after writing its request, it checks if the shared lock is free, and if so attempts to acquire it using a *compare-and-set* (CAS) operation. A thread that successfully acquires the lock becomes a *combiner*: it scans the list, collects pending requests, applies the *combined requests* to D, writes the results back to the threads' request fields in the associated publication records, and releases the lock. A thread that detects that some other thread already owns the lock, spins on its record, waiting for the owner to return a response in the request field, at which point it knows the published request has been applied to D. Once in a while, a combining thread will perform a cleanup operation on the publication list. During this cleanup it will remove records not recently used (we will later explain in more detail the mechanism for determining use times), so as to shorten the length of the combining traversals. Thus, in each repeated access request, if a thread has an active publication record, it will use it, and if not, it will create a new record and insert it into the list.

Our implementation of the flat combining mechanism allows us to provide, for any data structure, the same clean concurrent object oriented interface as used in the Java concurrency package [14] and similar C++ libraries [24]. As we show in Section 5, for any sequential object parallelized using flat combining, the resulting implementation will be *linearizable* [9] and given some simple real world assumptions also *starvation-free*. On an intuitive level, even though some method calls could be missed in the publication list by a concurrent scanning combiner, the fact that every method waits until its request is applied by the combiner, means that a later thread cannot get a response unless the missed earlier requests are still pending. These calls are therefore overlapping and can be linearized. Finally, note that flat combining is as robust as any global lock based data structure: in both cases a thread holding the lock could be preempted, causing all others to wait.[1]

As a concrete example of an application of flat combining, consider the implementation of a concurrent linearizable FIFO queue, one of the most widely used inter-thread communication structures. The applied operations on a queue are enq() and deq(). The most effective known implementations are the lock-free Michael-Scott queue [17] used in the Java concurrency package, and the basket queue of Hoffman et. al [10]. Both suffer from a complete loss of scalability beyond a rather low concurrency level, because all threads must successfully apply a CAS operation to the shared head or tail of the queue in order to complete their operation.

In contrast, in flat combining, given a sequential FIFO queue D, the combining thread can collect all pending operations, then apply the combined requests to the queue. As our empirical comparison shows, unlike the fastest known concurrent implementations, in flat combining there is vir-

tually no synchronization overhead, and the overall cache coherence traffic is significantly reduced.

The result, as seen in Figure 2, is a highly-scalable implementation of a linearizable FIFO queue that outperforms known implementations in almost all concurrency levels, and by a factor of more than 4 in high concurrency levels.

How broadly applicable is the flat combining paradigm? We claim that any data structure such that k operations on it, each taking time δ, can be combined and then applied in time *less than* $k\delta$, is a valid candidate to benefit from flat combining.[2] This applies to counters, queues, stacks etc, but also to linked lists, priority queues and so on. For example, in a linked list, all k collected modifications can be combined and applied in a single pass over the list, as opposed to k uncombined passes. In a skip-list-based priority queue, k remove-min operations can be combined and applied in $\Theta(k + \log n)$ as opposed to $\Theta(k \log n)$ uncombined ones, which as can be seen in Figure 5, outperforms prior art priority queue implementations considerably.

A further benefit of the flat combining approach is the fact that access to the core data structure being used remains sequential. This has implications on cache performance, but perhaps more importantly, on flat combining as a programming approach. As an example, considering again priority queues, we notice that one could build in a straightforward way a linearizable concurrent implementation of a state-of-the-art structure such as a pairing heap [3] by having all requests access it using flat combining. The proof of correctness of this flat combining pairing heap would be straightforward because it is only ever accessed sequentially. In contrast, based on our experience, devising a provably correct and scalable linearizable implementation of a concurrent pairing heap using fine-grained synchronization, would in itself constitute a publishable result. As seen in Figure 5, the flat-combining pairing-heap delivers impressive performance.

On the negative side, flat combining, at least in its simplest form, is not always applicable. For example, most search trees do not fit the above flat combining formula, since the cost of applying k search operations to a tree remains $\Theta(k \log n)$, while a fine grained concurrent implementation allows multiple non-blocking parallel search traversals to proceed in parallel in $\Theta(\log n)$ time. Furthermore, even in beneficially combinable structures, ones that have high levels of mutation on the data structure, there is a point on the concurrency scale in which the level of concurrency is such that a finely synchronized parallel implementation will beat the flat combining implementation. To make headway in these cases, advanced forms of flat combining are necessary, ones that involve multiple concurrent instances of flat combining. Such structures are the subject of future research.

1.2 Related Work

The idea of having a single thread perform the announced modifications of others on a concurrent data structure is not new. However, till now, the overheads of the suggested implementations have overshadowed their benefits.

The first attempt at combining operations dates back to the original software combining tree paper of Yew et. al [25]. In combining trees, requests to modify the structure

---

[1] On modern operating systems such as Solaris^{TM}, one can use mechanisms such as the *schetdl* command to control the quantum allocated to a combining thread, significantly reducing the chances of it being preempted.

[2] There are also cases of structures in which the combined cost is $k\delta$ which can to a certain extent benefit from flat combining.

are combined from the leaves of the tree upwards. The tree outputs $\frac{n}{\log n}$ requests per time unit. The resulting data structure is linearizable. However, each thread performs $\Theta(\log n)$ CAS based synchronization operations per access. This overhead was improved by Shavit and Zemach in their work on combining funnels [22], where trees of combined operations are built dynamically and are thus shallower. Nevertheless, as our empirical evidence shows, the synchronization overhead makes combining trees non-starters as a basis for concurrent data structure design.

A slightly different approach was taken by Oyama et. al [26]. They protect the data structure with a single lock and have threads form a list of requests on the lock. The thread acquiring the lock services the pending requests of others in LIFO order, and afterwards removes them from the list. The advantage of this approach is a lower cache miss rate on the accessed data structure because only a single thread accesses it repeatedly. Its main drawback is that all threads still need to perform CAS operations on the head of the list of requests, so scalability is mostly negative, but better than a naked lock. Since Oyama et. al were looking for a general compiler based transformation, they did not consider improved combining semantics for the data structures being implemented.

The next attempt to have a single thread perform the work of all others was the predictive log-synchronization approach of Shalev and Shavit [21]. They turned the Oyama et. al LIFO list into a FIFO queue, and added a prediction mechanism: threads do not wait for a response. Instead, they traverse the list of requests, predicting the outcome of their operation using the list as a log of the future modifications to be applied to the structure. To preserve the log structure, they allow no combining of operations.

The log-synchronization technique, however, is only sequentially consistent [13], not linearizable, and is limited to data structures to which effective prediction can be applied. As with Oyama et. al, the multiple CAS operations on the head of the queue limit scalability (the bottleneck on the log is similar to that the Michael and Scott queue [17]), and must be offset by a very high fraction of successfully predicting operations.

Unlike the above prior techniques, flat combining offers two key advantages:

- Threads do not need to succeed in a CAS on a shared location in order to have their request completed. In the common case, they only need to write and spin on a thread-local publication record, and read a single shared cached location (the lock).

- Cache invalidation traffic is reduced not only because the structure is accessed by a single thread while others spin locally, but also because the combiner thread can reduce the number of accesses due to the improved semantics of the combined operations.

In Section 6 we provide empirical evidence as to how the above two advantages lead to flat combining's superior performance.

2. FLAT COMBINING

Given a sequential data structure D, we design a *flat combining* (henceforth FC) concurrent implementation of the structure as follows.

As depicted in Figure 1, a few structures are added to the sequential implementation: a *global lock*, a *count* of the number of combining passes, and a pointer to the *head* of a *publication list*. The publication list is a list of thread-local records of a size proportional to the number of threads that are concurrently accessing the shared object.

Each thread t accessing the structure to perform an invocation of some method m on the shared object executes the following sequence of steps:

1. Write the invocation opcode and parameters (if any) of the method m to be applied sequentially to the shared object in the *request* field of your thread local publication record (there is no need to use a load-store memory barrier). The *request* field will later be used to receive the response. If your thread local publication record is marked as active continue to step 2, otherwise continue to step 5.

2. Check if the global lock is taken. If so (another thread is an active combiner), spin on the *request* field waiting for a response to the invocation (one can add a yield at this point to allow other threads on the same core to run). Once in a while while spinning check if the lock is still taken and that your record is active. If your record is inactive proceed to step 5. Once the response is available, reset the request field to null and return the response.

3. If the lock is not taken, attempt to acquire it and become a combiner. If you fail, return to spinning in step 2.

4. Otherwise, you hold the lock and are a combiner.

    - Increment the combining pass *count* by one.

    - Execute a *scanCombineApply()* by traversing the publication list from the head, combining all non-null method call invocations, setting the *age* of each of these records to the current *count*, applying the combined method calls to the structure D, and returning responses to all the invocations. As we explain later, this traversal is guaranteed to be wait-free.

    - If the *count* is such that a cleanup needs to be performed, traverse the publication list from the *head*. Starting from the second item (as we explain below, we always leave the item pointed to by the *head* in the list), remove from the publication list all records whose *age* is much smaller than the current *count*. This is done by removing the node and marking it as inactive.

    - Release the *lock*.

5. If you have no thread local publication record allocate one, marked as active. If you already have one marked as inactive, mark it as active. Execute a store-load memory barrier. Proceed to insert the record into the list with a successful CAS to the *head*. Then proceed to step 1.

We provide the particulars of the combining function and its application to a particular structure D in *scanCombineApply()* when we describe individual structures in later sections.

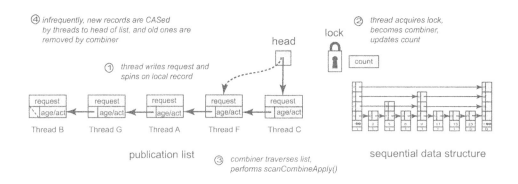

④ infrequently, new records are CASed
by threads to head of list, and old ones are
removed by combiner

head

② thread acquires lock,
becomes combiner,
updates count

lock

① thread writes request and
spins on local record

| request | request | request | request | request |
| age/act | age/act | age/act | age/act | age/act |

Thread B   Thread G   Thread A   Thread F   Thread C

publication list ③ combiner traverses list,
performs scanCombineApply()

sequential data structure

Figure 1: The flat combining structure. Each record in the publication list is local to a given thread. The thread writes and spins on the request field in its record. Records not recently used are once in a while removed by a combiner, forcing such threads to re-insert a record into the publication list when they next access the structure.

There are a few points to notice about the above algorithm. The common case for a thread is that its record is active and some other thread is the combiner, so it completes in step 2 after having only performed a store and a sequence of loads ending with a single cache miss.

In our implementation above we use a simple aging process completely controlled by combining threads. In general we expect nodes to be added and removed from the publication list infrequently. To assure this, one can implement a more sophisticated detection mechanism to control the decision process of when to remove a node from the list.

Nodes are added using a CAS only to the head of the list, and so a simple wait free traversal by the combiner is trivial to implement [8]. Thus, removal will not require any synchronization as long as it is not performed on the record pointed to from the head: the continuation of the list past this first node is only ever changed by the thread holding the global lock. Note that the first item is not an anchor or dummy node, we are simply not removing it. Once new records are inserted, if it is unused it will be removed, and even if no new nodes are added, leaving it in the list will not affect performance.

The removal of a node is done by writing a special mark bit that indicates that the node is inactive after it is removed from the list. In order to avoid the use of memory barriers in the common case, we must take care of the case in which a late arriving thread writes its invocation after the record has been removed from the list. To this end, we make sure to mark a removed record as inactive, and make this mark visible using a memory barrier, so that the late arriving thread will eventually see it and add its record back into the publication list.

We now proceed to show how FC is applied to the design of several popular concurrent data structures.

3. FLAT COMBINING QUEUES AND STACKS

Shared queues lend themselves nicely to flat combining, since on the one hand they have inherent sequential bottlenecks that are difficult to overcome by using fine-grained

synchronization, and on the other allow one to effectively apply combined sequences of operations.

We provide a linearizable FC FIFO queue implementations where the queue D is a linked list with *head* and *tail* pointers, and "fat" nodes that can contain multiple items in an indexed array (We can do this effectively because only a single combiner thread at a time will access this list. Using this approach in a concurrent setting would make the counter controlling traversal of the fat node entries a hot spot). To access the queue, a thread t posts the respective pair <ENQ,v> or <DEQ,0> to its publication record and follows the FC algorithm.

The combiner executing *scanCombineApply()* scans the publication list. For each non-null request, if it is an <ENQ,v> of value v, the item is added to the fat node at the tail of the queue, and if the queue is full a new one is allocated. An *OK* response is written back to the request field. If the request is a <DEQ,0>, an item is removed from the fat node at the head of the queue and written back to the request field. If the reader wonders why this is linearizable, notice that at the core of FC is the idea that if a posted request by some thread was missed by the combiner, then even if a request that started later was seen and successfully applied to the queue, the method call of the missed request is still pending, and so can be linearized after the one that succeeded.

Our concurrent linearizable LIFO stack implementation is similar to the FC queue algorithm described above. The data-structure is a linked list of fat nodes with a single *top* pointer. To push value v, a thread t writes the values-pair <PUSH,v> to its entry of the *combine* array. In the *scanCombineApply()*, the combiner services all requests from the fat node pointed to from the top.

As we show in Section 6, the low FC synchronization overhead and the locality of having a single thread at a time access a cached array of items in a fat node allow our FC stack and queue implementations to greatly outperform all prior-art algorithms.

4. FLAT COMBINING PRIORITY QUEUES

A *priority queue* is a multiset of items, where each item has an associated priority – a score that indicates its importance (by convention, the smaller the score, the higher the priority). A priority queue supports two methods: *add*, for adding an item to the multiset, and *removeMin*, for removing and returning an item with minimal score (highest importance). For presentation simplicity, in the descriptions that follow we assume that each item only stores a *key*, rather than storing both a key and priority value.

The prior art in this area includes a linearizable heap algorithm by Hunt et. al [11] and a skiplist-based priority queue due to Shavit and Lotan [15].

We present two FC based linearizable concurrent priority queue implementations, one based on a skiplist [19] and another based on a pairing heap [3].

4.1 A Flat Combining Skiplist Based Priority Queue

A *skiplist* [19] is a probabilistic data-structure, representing a multiset of nodes, ordered by their keys. A skiplist appears in the righthand side of Figure 1. The skiplist is composed of a collection of sorted linked lists. Each node consists of a key and an array of pointers that link it to a subset of the lists. Each list has a *level*, ranging from 0 to some maximum. The bottom-level list contains all the nodes, and each higher-level list is a sublist of the lower-level lists. The higher-level lists can be viewed as *shortcuts* into the lower-level lists. The skiplist has two sentinel nodes of maximal height with minimal and maximal keys. Skiplists support *add*, *remove*, and *find* methods.

One could readily implement a priority queue that supports *add* and *removeMin* using a skiplist by having *add* methods add an item to the skiplist, and have the *removeMin* method use the bottom (lowest level) pointer in the sentinel with the minimal key, then removing the node it points to from the skiplist, as this is the minimal key at any given point. The cost of both *add* and *removeMin* are $\Theta(\log n)$, as one needs to traverse the skiplist from the highest level to add or remove an item.

For our use, we implement *removeSmallestK* and *combinedAdd* methods. The *removeSmallestK* method receives as its parameter a number k and returns a list consisting of the k smallest items in the skiplist. It does so as follows:

- Traverse the lowest level of the skiplist from the minimal sentinel until k items (or fewer if the skiplist contains less than k items) have been traversed. Collect these items, they are the k minimal items to be returned.

- Perform a *find* traversal of the skiplist, searching for the key of the $k + 1$-th minimal item found. The *find* operation is called for locating the predecessors and successors of *newMin* in all the linked lists.[3] In all the lists which do not contain *newMin*, the *head* node is set to point to the first node greater than *newMin*.

We observe that the combined removal performed by the *removeSmallestK* method searches only once in each linked list. It thus removes the k minimal items while performing

work corresponding to *a single removal*. The overall complexity of *removeSmallestK* is thus $\Theta(k + \log n)$ as opposed to $\Theta(k \log n)$ for k uncombined removals from a skiplist.

The *combinedAdd* method will also reduce the overall cost of adding k nodes by making only a single pass through the skiplist. It receives a list of items $<i_1, i_2, \ldots, i_k>$, sorted in increasing order of their keys, and inserts them to the skiplist. This is done as follows. First, a highest level is selected at random for each of the k items. Then, the appropriate location of i_1 in the skiplist is searched, starting from the topmost list. The key idea is that, once the search arrives at a list and location where the predecessor and successor of i_1 and i_2 differ, that location is recorded before the search of i_1 proceeds. Once the search of i_1 terminates, the search of i_2 is resumed starting from the recorded location instead of starting from the top list again. This optimization is applied recursively for all subsequent items, resulting in significant time saving in comparison with regular addition of these k items.

The implementation of our *scanCombineApply* is immediate: when scanning the publication list, collect two respective lists, of the requests to *add* and of those to *removeMin*. Count the number of requests and apply the *removeSmallestK*, and sort the linked list of *add* requests[4], then apply the *combinedAdd* method, returning the appropriate results to the requesting threads.

4.2 A Flat Combining Pairing Heap Based Priority Queue

But this is not the end of the story for priority queues. The power of FC as a programming paradigm is that the data structure D at the core of the implementation is sequential. This means we can actually use the most advanced priority queue algorithm available, without a need to actually think about how to parallelize it. We thus choose to use a *pairing heap* [3] structure, a state-of-the-art heap structure with $O(1)$ amortized *add* complexity and $O(\log n))$ amortized *removeMin* complexity with very low constants, as the basis for the FC algorithm. We will not explain here why pairing heaps have impressive performance in practice and readers interested in analytic upper bounds on their complexity are referred to [18]. We simply took the sequential algorithm's code and plopped it as-is into the FC framework. The result: a fast concurrent priority queue algorithm that by Lemma 1 is provably linearizable. As we noted earlier, based on our experience, devising a provably correct and scalable linearizable implementation of a concurrent pairing heap using fine-grained synchronization would in itself constitute a publishable result. We hope a similar approach can be taken towards creating linearizable concurrent versions of other complex data structures.

5. FLAT COMBINING CORRECTNESS AND PROGRESS

In this section we outline correctness and progress arguments for the flat combining technique. For lack of space, we do not cover the details of the management of the publication list, and choose to focus on outlining the linearizable and starvation-free behavior of threads with active publication records. We also confine the discussion in this section

---

[3]This is the regular semantics of the *find* operation on skiplists.

[4]Our current implementation uses bubble sort.

to FC implementations that protect the publication list by a single lock.

Linearizability [9] is widely accepted as a correctness condition of shared object implementations. Informally, it states that, in every execution of the object implementation, each operation on the implemented object appears to take effect instantaneously at some *(linearization) point* between the operation's invocation and response (or possibly not at all if the operation is pending at the end of the execution).

To prove that an implementation is linearizable, one must show that a *linearization* can be found for each of the implementation's executions. An execution linearization is defined by specifying linearization points for all complete operations (and possibly also for some pending operations), such that the operations' total order defined by the linearization is a legal sequential history of the implemented object.

We say that an implementation of the *scanCombineApply* method is *correct* if it satisfies all the following requirements: (1) it operates as described in Section 2, (2) it does not access the FC lock protecting the publication list, and (3) it returns operation responses in the order in which it applies the operations to the data structure.

LEMMA 1. *An FC implementation using a correct scanCombineApply method is linearizable.*

Proof outline. The use of a single FC lock protecting the publication list and the correctness of the *scanCombineApply* method guarantee that executions of the *scanCombineApply* method are sequential, since there is at most a single combiner thread at any given time. A combiner thread t sequentially applies a set of combined operations to the data-structure representing the implemented object in the course of performing the *scanCombineApply* method. We linearize each applied operation just before the combiner writes its response to the respective publication record.

The total order specified by the resulting linearization is clearly a legal sequential history of the implemented object, since, from the correctness of the *scanCombineApply* method, the operations are sequentially applied to the implemented object in exactly this order.

To conclude the proof, we show that each linearization point lies between the invocation and response of the corresponding operation. This holds trivially for the operation of the combiner. As for operations of non-combiner threads, it follows from the FC algorithm and the correctness of the *scanCombineApply* method that each such thread starts spinning on its record before its linearization point and can only return a response after the combiner has written to its publication record, which happens after its linearization point.

LEMMA 2. *An FC implementation using a correct scanCombineApply method is starvation-free.*

Proof outline. Since nodes can only be inserted to the publication list immediately after its head node, *scanCombineApply* is wait-free. Let t be a thread whose publication record is constantly active. If t becomes a combiner, the claim is obvious. If t fails to acquire the lock, then there is another active combiner t'. From the correctness and wait-freedom of the *scanCombineApply* method, either t' or the subsequent combiner thread (possibly t itself) will apply t's operation and write the response to t's publication record.

6. PERFORMANCE EVALUATION

For our experiments we used two machines. The first is a 128-way Enterprise T5140® server (Maramba) machine running Solaris™ 10. This is a 2-chip Niagara system in which each chip has 8 cores that multiplex 8 hardware threads each and share an on chip L2 cache. We also used an Intel Core2® i7 (Nehalem) processor with 4 cores that each multiplex 2 hardware threads. We ran benchmarks in C++ using the same compiler on both machines, and using the scalable *Hoard* memory allocator [1] to ensure that malloc calls are not a sequential bottleneck.

6.1 Flat combining versus prior techniques

We begin our empirical evaluation by examining the relative performance of FC with respect to prior known parallelization techniques. We start by presenting data for implementations of a concurrent FIFO queue. The presented graphs are the average of 3 executions, each taking 10 seconds.

We evaluated a flat combining based queue (denoted as *fc*) as described in Section 3. We compared it to the most effective known queue implementations: the lock-free queue by Michael and Scott [20] (henceforth the MS-queue) used in the Java concurrency package and the basket queue of Hoffman et. al [10]. Michael and Scott's lock-free queue algorithm represents a queue as a singly-linked list with *head* and *tail* pointers, which are modified by CAS operations. The basket queue algorithm permits higher concurrency levels by allowing enqueue operations to operate on multiple *baskets* of mixed-order items instead of a single central location. We also compared them to implementations of queues using prior global lock based techniques: Oyama et. al's algorithm [26], combining trees [25], and Shalev and Shavit's predictive log-synchronization [21], as described in Section 1.2.

As the reader may recall, the Oyama et. al technique created a list of requests, each added using a CAS operation, and then operated on these requests one after the other. It does not combine requests. In order to understand which fraction of the FC advantage comes from the publication list mechanism itself, and which from the gain in locality by having a single combiner access the structure, we added a version of Oyama et. al in which we add the same combining feature FC uses. In the case of a queue, this is the use of "fat nodes" that hold multiple items to collect requests, and add these many requests in one pointer swing of the fat node into the structure.

In the throughput graph in Figure 2, one can clearly see that from about 4 threads and on the flat combining implementation starts to increasingly outperform all others and is from 4 to 7 times faster than the MS queue, the fastest of the prior techniques. Moreover, one can see that Oyama et. al, combining trees, and log-synchronization do not scale. In fact, Oyama scales only a bit better when we add the combining feature. This leads us to the conclusion that, at least for queues, the main advantage of FC is in the low overheads of the publication mechanism itself.

The explanation for the significantly better FC behavior is provided in the other three graphs in Figure 2. As can be seen, the MS queue requires on average 1.5 successful CASes per operations (this is consistent with the MS queue code), but suffers increasing levels of CAS failures, as does the basket queue. The combining tree requires increasing numbers of successful CASes as the tree grows to accommo-

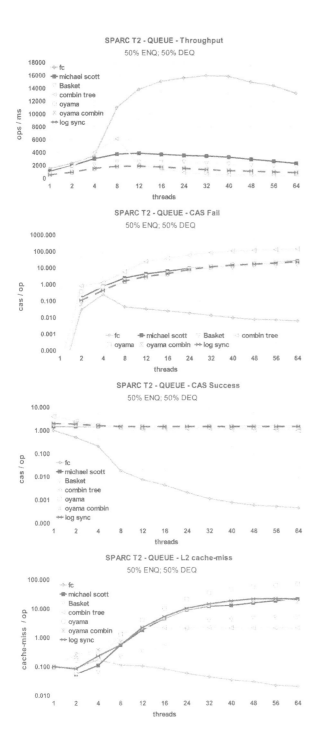

Figure 2: Concurrent FIFO Queue implementations: throughput (number of operations), average CAS failures (per operation), average CAS successes (per operation), and L2 cache misses (per operation).

date more threads. The number of failed CASes increases significantly as concurrency grows, explaining the tree's poor behavior. Similar failed CAS overheads hurt Oyama et. al. Log-synchronization requires only 3 successful CASes on average, and because of prediction threads do not compete for the lock, avoiding high CAS failure rates, and eventually overtaking the performance of the MS and basket queue algorithms.

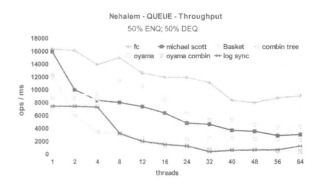

Figure 3: FIFO Queue throughput on the Nehalem architecture.

The most telling graph though is that of the L2 cache miss rates on the Niagara architecture, a dominant performance factor in multicore machines. Notice that the graph uses a logarithmic scale. As we can see, Oyama et. al and combining trees have two or more orders of magnitude more cache misses than the FC algorithm. Even the best non-FC technique, the MS-queue, has at some concurrency levels about two orders of magnitude more cache misses than the FC algorithm.

Unlike other general techniques, the flat combining implementation requires on average almost no CAS successes to complete, and has a negligible CAS failure rate. Its cache miss rate is very low. It is therefore not by chance that the FC queue outperforms the best hand crafted solution on the Niagara architecture by a wide margin.

Figure 3 shows similar behavior on the Nehalem architecture. Here we see that all the algorithms exhibit negative scalability, and yet the FC algorithm is again superior to all others. The cache miss and CAS rate graphs we do not present provide a similar picture to that on the Niagara.

6.2 Stacks

We now consider linearizable concurrent LIFO Stacks. We compare our flat-combining queue with Treiber's lock-free stack implementation [23] (denoted as 'lock free' in the graphs). Treiber's algorithm represents the stack as a singly-linked list pointed at by a top pointer which is manipulated by CAS operations. We also compare to Hendler et. al's [6] linearizable elimination-backoff stack.

Figure 4 shows the throughput of the flat combining stack, the elimination-backoff stack, and Treiber stack on the two platforms. On the Maramba (Sparc) machine flat combining clearly outperforms Treiber's algorithm by a wide margin (a factor of 9) because Treiber's algorithm *top* is a CAS synchronization bottleneck. The performance of the elimination-backoff stack algorithm improves to reach that

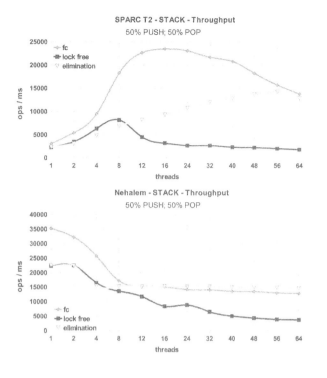

Figure 4: The throughput of LIFO stack implementations.

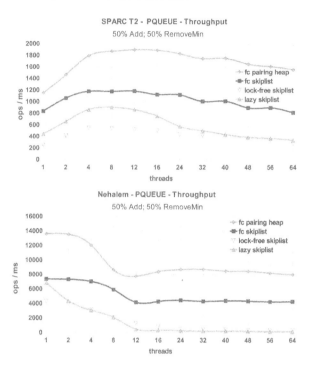

Figure 5: The throughput of Priority Queue implementations.

for details). These priority queue algorithms are quiescently consistent but *not* linearizable [8], which gives them an advantage since making them linearizable would require to add an access to a global clock variable per insert which would cause a performance deterioration.

Figure 5 shows the throughput of the priority queue algorithms on the two platforms. The lazy lock-based skiplist outperforms the lock-free one since it requires fewer CAS synchronization operations per add and remove. This reduces its overhead and allows it to be competitive at low concurrency levels since it has a certain degree of parallelism and a reasonable overhead. However, as concurrency increases the competition for marking nodes as logically deleted, together with the fact that most remove-min operations occur on the same nodes at the head of the list, causes a deterioration. As concurrency increases, the algorithm is increasingly outperformed by the FC skiplist algorithm. The surprising element here is that that best performance comes from the pairing heap based algorithm. The use of flat combining allows us to make direct use of this sequential algorithm's great efficiency, $O(1)$ for an insert, and an amortized $O(\log n)$ per remove, without paying a ridiculously high synchronization price in a fine grained implementation (assuming a scalable and provably linearizable fine grained pairing heap implementation is attainable at all).

6.4 Performance as Arrival Rates Change

In earlier benchmarks, the data structures were tested at very high arrival rates. These rates are common to some uses of concurrent data structures, but not to all. In Figure 6, we return to our queue benchmark to show the change in throughput of the various algorithms as the method call

of flat combining, since the benchmark supplies increasing equal amounts of concurrent pushes and pops that can be eliminated. Note that with a different ratio of pushes and pops the elimination queue will not perform as well. However, as can be seen, at lower concurrency rates the flat combining stack delivers more than twice the throughput of elimination-backoff stack. On the Nehalem machine, flat combining is the clear winner until there are more software threads than hardware threads, at which point its performance becomes about the same as that of the elimination-backoff stack.

6.3 Priority Queues

We compare our two flat combining priority queue implementations from Section 4: the skiplist based one (denoted as *fc skiplist*) and the pairing-heap based one (denoted as *fc pairing heap*) with the best performing concurrent priority queue in the literature, the skiplist-based concurrent priority queue due to Lotan and Shavit [15] (its performance has been shown to be significantly better than that of the linearizable concurrent heap algorithm due to Hunt et. al [11]). The Lotan and Shavit algorithm has threads add items based on their priorities to the skiplist. Each item occupies a node, and the node has a special "logically deleted" bit. To remove the minimal items, threads compete in performing a series of CAS operations along the bottom level of the skiplist. Each thread does that until it encounters the first non-deleted node it manages to CAS to a deleted state. It then performs a call to the regular skiplist remove method to remove the node from the list. We compare to two versions of the [15] algorithm, one in which the skiplist is lock-free and another in which it is a lazy lock-based skiplist (see [8]

arrival rates change when running on 32 threads. In this benchmark, we inject a "work" period between calls a thread makes to the queue. The work consists of an equal number of reads and writes to random locations. As can be seen, as the request arrival rate decreases (the total number of reads and writes depicted along the x-axis increases), the relative performance advantage of the FC algorithm decreases, while all other methods mostly remain unchanged (apart from log-synchronization, which, as it seems, benefits from the reduced arrival rate as there is less contention on the queue and less cache invalidation behavior while threads traverse the log during prediction). Nevertheless, the FC queue algorithm remains superior or equal to all other methods throughout.

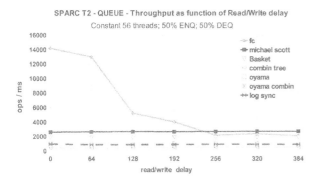

Figure 6: Performance as Arrival Rates Change. Work along the X-axis is the number of reads and writes between accesses to the shared queue.

7. DISCUSSION

We presented *flat combining*, a new synchronization paradigm based on the idea that having a single thread holding a lock perform the combined access requests of all others, delivers better performance through a reduction of synchronization overheads and cache invalidations. There are many ways in which our work can be extended, and we encourage others to continue this work.

Obviously there are many data structures that could benefit from the FC approach, we have only presented a few representative ones.

An interesting aspect is that FC will be a natural fit with the heterogenous multicore architectures of the future: the more powerful cores can get a preference in acquiring the global lock, or in some cases be assigned as combiners in a static way.

The flat combining process itself could benefit from a dynamic/reactive ability to set its various parameters: the number of combining rounds a combiner performs consecutively, the level of polling each thread performs on the combining lock, which threads get higher priority in becoming combiners, and so on. One way to do so is to perhaps use the machine learning-based approach of *smartlocks* [2].

Another interesting line of research is the use of multiple parallel instances of flat combining to speed up concurrent structures such as search trees and hash tables. Here the idea would be an extension of the style of our queue implementation: have a shared data structure but reduce overhead in bottleneck spots using flat combining. We have recently been able to show how this parallel flat-combining approach can benefit the design of unfair synchronous queues [5].

Finally, it would be interesting to build a theoretical model of why flat combining is a win, and what its limitations are.

8. ACKNOWLEDGEMENTS

This paper was supported by the European Union grant FP7-ICT-2007-1 (project VELOX), as well as grants from Sun Microsystems, Intel Corporation, and a grant 06/1344 from the Israeli Science Foundation.

9. REFERENCES

[1] BERGER, E. D., MCKINLEY, K. S., BLUMOFE, R. D., AND WILSON, P. R. Hoard: a scalable memory allocator for multithreaded applications. *SIGPLAN Not. 35*, 11 (2000), 117–128.

[2] EASTEP, J., WINGATE, D., SANTAMBROGIO, M., AND AGARWAL, A. Smartlocks: Self-aware synchronization through lock acquisition scheduling. In *4th Workshop on Statistical and Machine learning approaches to ARchitecture and compilaTion (SMARTS'10)* (2009).

[3] FREDMAN, M. L., SEDGEWICK, R., SLEATOR, D. D., AND TARJAN, R. E. The pairing heap: A new form of self-adjusting heap. *Algorithmica 1*, 1 (1986), 111–129.

[4] HANKE, S. The performance of concurrent red-black tree algorithms. *Lecture Notes in Computer Science 1668* (1999), 286–300.

[5] HENDLER, D., INCZE, I., SHAVIT, N., AND TZAFRIR, M. Scalable flat-combining based synchronous queues, 2010.

[6] HENDLER, D., SHAVIT, N., AND YERUSHALMI, L. A scalable lock-free stack algorithm. In *SPAA '04: Proceedings of the sixteenth annual ACM symposium on Parallelism in algorithms and architectures* (New York, NY, USA, 2004), ACM, pp. 206–215.

[7] HERLIHY, M., LEV, Y., AND SHAVIT, N. A lock-free concurrent skiplist with wait-free search, 2007.

[8] HERLIHY, M., AND SHAVIT, N. *The Art of Multiprocessor Programming*. Morgan Kaufmann, NY, USA, 2008.

[9] HERLIHY, M., AND WING, J. Linearizability: A correctness condition for concurrent objects. *ACM Transactions on Programming Languages and Systems 12*, 3 (July 1990), 463–492.

[10] HOFFMAN, M., SHALEV, O., AND SHAVIT, N. The baskets queue. In *OPODIS* (2007), pp. 401–414.

[11] HUNT, G. C., MICHAEL, M. M., PARTHASARATHY, S., AND SCOTT, M. L. An efficient algorithm for concurrent priority queue heaps. *Inf. Process. Lett. 60*, 3 (1996), 151–157.

[12] KUNG, H., AND ROBINSON, J. On optimistic methods for concurrency control. *ACM Transactions on Database Systems 6*, 2 (1981), 213–226.

[13] LAMPORT, L. How to make a multiprocessor computer that correctly executes multiprocess programs. *IEEE Transactions on Computers C-28*, 9 (September 1979), 690.

[14] LEA, D. util.concurrent.ConcurrentHashMap in *java.util.concurrent* the Java Concurrency Package.

http://gee.cs.oswego.edu/cgi-bin/viewcvs.cgi/jsr166/-src/main/java/util/concurrent/.

[15] LOTAN, I., AND SHAVIT., N. Skiplist-based concurrent priority queues. In *Proc. of the 14th International Parallel and Distributed Processing Symposium (IPDPS)* (2000), pp. 263–268.

[16] MELLOR-CRUMMEY, J., AND SCOTT, M. Algorithms for scalable synchronization on shared-memory multiprocessors. *ACM Transactions on Computer Systems 9*, 1 (1991), 21–65.

[17] MICHAEL, M. M., AND SCOTT, M. L. Simple, fast, and practical non-blocking and blocking concurrent queue algorithms. In *Proc. 15th ACM Symp. on Principles of Distributed Computing* (1996), pp. 267–275.

[18] PETTIE, S. Towards a final analysis of pairing heaps. In *Data Structures* (Dagstuhl, Germany, 2006), L. Arge, R. Sedgewick, and D. Wagner, Eds., no. 06091 in Dagstuhl Seminar Proceedings, Internationales Begegnungs- und Forschungszentrum für Informatik (IBFI), Schloss Dagstuhl, Germany.

[19] PUGH, W. Skip lists: a probabilistic alternative to balanced trees. *ACM Transactions on Database Systems 33*, 6 (1990), 668–676.

[20] SCOTT, M. L., AND SCHERER, W. N. Scalable queue-based spin locks with timeout. *ACM SIGPLAN Notices 36*, 7 (2001), 44–52.

[21] SHALEV, O., AND SHAVIT, N. Predictive log synchronization. In *Proc. of the EuroSys 2006 Conference* (2006), pp. 305–315.

[22] SHAVIT, N., AND ZEMACH, A. Combining funnels: a dynamic approach to software combining. *J. Parallel Distrib. Comput. 60*, 11 (2000), 1355–1387.

[23] TREIBER, R. K. Systems programming: Coping with parallelism. Tech. Rep. RJ 5118, IBM Almaden Research Center, April 1986.

[24] TZAFRIR, M. C++ multi-platform memory-model solution with java orientation. http://groups.google.com/group/cpp-framework.

[25] YEW, P.-C., TZENG, N.-F., AND LAWRIE, D. H. Distributing hot-spot addressing in large-scale multiprocessors. *IEEE Trans. Comput. 36*, 4 (1987), 388–395.

[26] YONEZAWA, O. T., OYAMA, Y., TAURA, K., AND YONEZAWA, A. Executing parallel programs with synchronization bottlenecks efficiently. In *in Proceedings of International Workshop on Parallel and Distributed Computing for Symbolic and Irregular Applications (PDSIA '99). Sendai, Japan: World Scientific* (1999), World Scientific, pp. 182–204.

Corrigendum: Weakest Failure Detector for Wait-Free Dining under Eventual Weak Exclusion*

Srikanth Sastry
Computer Science and Engr
Texas A&M University
College Station, TX, USA
sastry@cse.tamu.edu

Scott M. Pike
Computer Science and Engr
Texas A&M University
College Station, TX, USA
pike@cse.tamu.edu

Jennifer L. Welch
Computer Science and Engr
Texas A&M University
College Station, TX, USA
welch@cse.tamu.edu

ABSTRACT

This corrigendum corrects and clarifies our remarks in [2] from SPAA 2009 about the related work in [1] regarding the status of $\Diamond\mathcal{P}$ as the weakest failure detector for boosting obstruction-freedom to wait-freedom.

Categories and Subject Descriptors

C.2.4 [**Computer-Communication Networks**]: Distributed Systems—*distributed applications; network operating systems* ; F.1.1 [**Computation by Abstract Devices**]: Models of Computation—*relations between models*

General Terms

Algorithms, Reliability, Theory

Keywords

Obstruction-Freedom, Wait-Freedom, Contention Managers.

Previous work [1] defined an abstraction called a *wait-free contention manager* and proved that it is sufficient to convert any (suitably well-formed) obstruction-free algorithm into an equivalent wait-free algorithm. The same paper claimed the following result:

- "The eventually perfect failure detector $\Diamond\mathcal{P}$ is the weakest to implement a wait-free contention manager."

Our SPAA 2009 paper [2] incorrectly characterized what we believed to be a flaw in this result. We claimed therein that "although the equivalence relation between $\Diamond\mathcal{P}$ and wait-free contention management happens to be true, the reduction used to establish the equivalence is actually flawed, as is the related proof of correctness."

We wish to correct our error by the following affirmation: the result above is formally established in [1] by proving that $\Diamond\mathcal{P}$ is mutually reducible with the particular wait-free contention manager as specified in the same paper.

Within the purview of definitions in [1], $\Diamond\mathcal{P}$ is the weakest failure detector for *boosting* an obstruction-free algorithm to a wait-free one. However, this result does not imply that $\Diamond\mathcal{P}$ must also be necessary for all other reductions, contention-manager based or otherwise, that transform any obstruction-free algorithm into an equivalent wait-free algorithm.

By way of counter-example, consider a modified contention manager C that is identical to the wait-free contention manager defined in [1], except that the well-formedness condition makes one additional assumption: no active obstruction-free client p can invoke $C.Try$ so long as p has run in isolation since its most recent invocation of $C.Try$ returned.

Full analysis of contention manager C is beyond the scope of this corrigendum, but a separate paper will establish the following results. Every obstruction-free algorithm can be automatically transformed to satisfy the additional well-formedness condition (without loss of generality) such that C is sufficient to convert any obstruction-free algorithm into an equivalent wait-free algorithm. Nonetheless, the necessity proof in [1] for extracting $\Diamond\mathcal{P}$ from the wait-free contention manager in [1] fails to extract $\Diamond\mathcal{P}$ from C. Although $\Diamond\mathcal{P}$ *might* still be necessary to implement C, this result is not a consequence of the work presented in [1]. Accordingly, the weakest failure detector to transform any obstruction-free algorithm into a wait-free algorithm using other transformations remains open.

1. REFERENCES

[1] Rachid Guerraoui, Michal Kapalka, and Petr Kouznetsov. The weakest failure detectors to boost obstruction-freedom. *Distributed Computing*, 20(6):415–433, April 2008.

[2] Srikanth Sastry, Scott M. Pike, and Jennifer L. Welch. The weakest failure detector for wait-free dining under eventual weak exclusion. In *21st ACM Symposium on Parallelism in Algorithms and Architectures (SPAA)*, pp. 111–120, 2009. DOI: http://doi.acm.org/10.1145/1583991.1584021

*This work was supported in part by NSF grant 0500265 and by the Texas Higher Education Coordinating Board under grants ARP 000512-0007-2006 and ARP 000512-0130-2007.

Author Index

www.ingramcontent.com/pod-product-compliance
Lightning Source LLC
Chambersburg PA
CBHW080149060326
40689CB00018B/3904